NIGERIA AND THE POLITICS OF EVERYBODY

Recent Titles in the

CAROLINA ACADEMIC PRESS

AFRICAN WORLD SERIES

Toyin Falola, Series Editor

Africa, Empire and Globalization: Essays in Honor of A. G. Hopkins
Edited by Toyin Falola and Emily Brownell

The African Civil Service Fifty Years after Independence
Edited by Emmanuel M. Mbah and Augustine E. Ayuk

African Humanity: Creativity, Identity and Personhood
Edited by Abimbola Asojo and Toyin Falola

Against the Predators' Republic: Political and Cultural Journalism, 2007–2013
Biodun Jeyifo

Authority Stealing: Anti-Corruption War and Democratic Politics in Post-Military Nigeria
Wale Adebanwi

Conflict Resolution in Africa: Language, Law, and Politeness in Ghanaian (Akan) Jurisprudences
Samuel Gyasi Obeng

Contentious Politics in Africa: Identity, Conflict, and Social Change
Toyin Falola and Wanjala S. Nasong'o

Creative Incursions: Cultural Representations of Human Rights in Africa and the Black Diaspora
Edited by Abikal Borah, Bisola Falola, and Toyin Falola

Decolonizing the University, Knowledge Systems and Disciplines in Africa
Edited by Sabelo J. Ndlovu-Gatsheni and Siphamandla Zondi

Democracy in Africa: Political Changes and Challenges
Edited by Saliba Sarsar and Julius O. Adekunle

Democradura: *Essays on Nigeria's Limited Democracy*
Femi Mimiko

Diaspora and Imagined Nationality:
USA-Africa Dialogue and Cyberframing Nigerian Nationhood
Koleade Odutola

Èṣù: Yoruba God, Power, and the Imaginative Frontiers
Edited by Toyin Falola

Ethnicities, Nationalities, and Cross-Cultural Representations in Africa and the Diaspora
Edited by Gloria Chuku

Falolaism: The Epistemologies and Methodologies of Africana Knowledge
Abdul Karim Bangura

Gendering African Social Spaces: Women, Power, and Cultural Expressions
Edited by Toyin Falola and Wanjala S. Nasong'o

Horror in Paradise
Edited by Christopher LaMonica and J. Shola Omotola

Ifá *in Yorùbá Thought System*
Omotade Adegbindin

The Indigenous African Criminal Justice System for the Modern World
Olusina Akeredolu

Intercourse and Crosscurrents in the Atlantic World: Calabar-British Experience
David Lishilinimle Imbua

Issues in African Political Economies
Edited by Toyin Falola and Jamaine Abidogun

Julius Nyerere, Africa's Titan on a Global Stage: Perspectives from Arusha to Obama
Edited by Ali A. Mazrui and Lindah L. Mhando

The Muse of Anomy: Essays on Literature and the Humanities in Nigeria
Femi Osofisan

Narratives of Struggle: The Philosophy and Politics of Development
John Ayotunde Bewaji

Nigeria and the Politics of Everybody: Social Media, Idealism, and Activism
Toyin Falola

Nollywood: Popular Culture and Narratives of Youth Struggles in Nigeria
Paul Ugor

Pan-Africanism in Ghana: African Socialism, Neoliberalism, and Globalization
Justin Williams

Perspectives on the Religious Landscape in Africa
Edited by Lady Jane Acquah and Toyin Falola

The Philosophy of Nimi Wariboko: Social Ethics, Economy, and Religion
Edited by Toyin Falola

Political Economy of Development: Public Policy Alternatives and Progressive Ideas in Nigeria
Tayo Oke

Satires of Power in Yoruba Visual Culture
Yomi Ola

The United States' Foreign Policy in Africa in the 21st Century
Edited by Adebayo Oyebade

Urban Challenges and Survival Strategies in Africa
Edited by Adeshina Afolayan and Toyin Falola

The Vile Trade: Slavery and the Slave Trade in Africa
Edited by Abi Alabo Derefaka, Wole Ogundele, Akin Alao, and Augustus Babajide Ajibola

Women, Gender, and Sexualities in Africa
Edited by Toyin Falola and Nana Akua Amponsah

Yoruba Creativity: Cultural Practices of the Modern World
by Bessie House-Soremekun

The Yoruba in Brazil, Brazilians in Yorubaland: Cultural Encounter, Resilience, and Hybridity in the Atlantic World
Edited by Niyi Afolabi and Toyin Falola

NIGERIA AND THE POLITICS OF EVERYBODY

Social Media, Idealism, and Activism

TOYIN FALOLA

Jacob & Frances Sanger Mossiker Chair in the Humanities
University Distinguished Teaching Professor
University of Texas at Austin

CAROLINA ACADEMIC PRESS
Durham, North Carolina

Library of Congress Cataloging-in-Publication Data
Names: Falola, Toyin, author.
Title: Nigeria and the politics of everybody : social media, idealism, and activism / Toyin Falola.
Description: Durham, North Carolina : Carolina Academic Press, LLC, 2023. | Series: African world series | Includes bibliographical references and index.
Identifiers: LCCN 2023024021 | ISBN 9781531026547 (hardback) | ISBN 9781531026554 (ebook)
Subjects: LCSH: Political culture—Nigeria. | Political participation—Nigeria. | Social media—Political aspects—Nigeria. | Social change—Political aspects—Nigeria. | Internet and activism—Nigeria.
Classification: LCC JQ3096 .F35 2023 | DDC 306.209669—dc23/eng/20230609
LC record available at https://lccn.loc.gov/2023024021

Carolina Academic Press
700 Kent Street
Durham, NC 27701
(919) 489-7486
www.cap-press.com

Printed in the United States of America

To Gozie and

Ada Ifesinachukwu,

in friendship.

CONTENTS

LIST OF FIGURES

SERIES EDITOR'S PREFACE

The *Carolina Academic Press African World Series*, inaugurated in 2010, offers significant new works in the field of African and Black World studies. The series provides scholarly and educational texts that can serve both as reference works and as readers in college classes.

Studies in the series are anchored in the existing humanistic and the social scientific traditions. Their goal, however, is the identification and elaboration of the strategic place of Africa and its Diaspora in a shifting global world. More specifically, the studies will address gaps and larger needs in the developing scholarship on Africa and the Black World.

The series intends to fill gaps in areas such as African politics, history, law, religion, culture, sociology, literature, philosophy, visual arts, art history, geography, language, health, and social welfare. Given the complex nature of Africa and its Diaspora, and the constantly shifting perspectives prompted by globalization, the series also meets a vital need for scholarship connecting knowledge with events and practices. Reflecting the fact that life in Africa continues to change, especially in the political arena, the series explores issues emanating from racial and ethnic identities, particularly those connected with the ongoing mobilization of ethnic minorities for inclusion and representation.

Toyin Falola
The University of Texas at Austin

PREFACE

Let me start with a confession. I avoid social media as much as possible. I am not on Facebook. I don't use Twitter or Instagram. I was drawn to mine them for the main purpose of writing this book. I am critical of the abuses they have produced, the lives destroyed by fake news, the destructions by distractions, the abusive language, and the gross disrespect for boundaries. Evidently, several aspects of social media have not helped convince me to be a committed user or even a keen observer; it is becoming a no man's land of chaos and lawlessness, bombarded with uncensored information, fake news, misleading propositions and unnecessary frivolities. Presently, the flexible exploitation of these platforms has raised matters of concern and reaction. In Nigeria, one of the major pit-holes for social media use is that most citizens are not on social media, and only a reasonable number of users have access to the platforms. All these might have contributed to my passive conviction of the necessity of using social media.

My reservations about the use of social media and subscription to its antecedence do not mean that I am oblivious to its emerging necessities and the relevance it has maintained in contemporary societies. Let me insist that I understand the trajectories of technological innovations over the centuries and how small and big inventions have transformed the world. Hence, to say less of social media's prominent role in societal transformation would be a misplaced judgment capable of letting one lose touch with societal realities.

I appreciate the "new world" of rapid communications that has made information pass through borders without delay and in no time. Aside from the rapid spread of information and communication, it adds convenient participation in the communication system, making it a viable tool to garner feedback and create avenues for communication. Global conditions and occurrences, most especially the COVID-19 pandemic, have contributed necessity to the dynamics of social media. The world was shocked at the pandemic outbreak as no initial known vaccine or treatment could adequately cure the virus. This led to the observance of distance and the practice of remote communication systems. This pushed the essence of social media further, and the world relied partly on it to get their daily activities done. The world started wearing more virtual robes with transactions and communications happening offsite. The post-pandemic global society has not been able to wear off the effects of social media and remote approaches to activities, as it sustains its operation after seeing their benefits.

The combination of my skepticism, the dangers and opportunities driven by social media, and the possibilities of its various uses to transform Africa constitutes the driving force of this book. The idiosyncratic construct of social media and its exploitation has positioned it as a double-edged sword capable of cutting forth and back. This attribute, alongside its instrumentality in the Nigerian space and issues, has necessitated my muse for this book. Social media has been a platform for projecting social identities and personal convictions that have taken global dimensions. With access to information and rapid projection of national debacles, social media has raised nationalistic consciousness, no matter the limitation of the possibilities of impacting change. These experimental subjects of engagements on social media forged several notable personalities who see virtue in activism and resolve to demand transformation, development and salvaging of relevant issues. It has touched on core subjects in the discussion trajectories in Nigeria; therefore, one needs to examine its essence and weigh it into social benefits. The book would engage the volatility and viability of these emerging dynamics.

The book is divided into four themes. The first is the context to understand social media in the landscape of Nigeria. What does social media represent for Nigeria? It is important to understand that local contexts and factors provide multiple twists to concepts to acclimatize specific societal peculiarities. Social media is not an exemption; thus, this book tries to put it under such social peculiarities to expose the operationality of social media. The book's first part drives us through these contextual roads that herald particular understandings.

The first chapter of this book raises the major issues of the relevance of social media in Nigeria and its interaction with global, social and political engagements and issues. Undoubtedly, social media has opened space for global interactions, political engagement, and participation. Political criticism, opinions, and analyses have be-

come some of the subjects of critical discussion that have a concerning effect on the state of the nation. Policies and social trends engagements gain momentum in Nigeria, attracting public and governmental reactions that might not be necessarily satisfying. In 2020, the #EndSARS protest and other demonstrations emerged from incitements from social media influencers based on national conditions. The protest took both physical and online demonstrations that gained international attention. Further inquiries would be channeled toward cultural and social interactions and their societal implications. Chapter one aim to establish how the nation fares in what can be considered a global village and its effect on the country in contemporary time.

We have seen how the new media has been relevant in society and how it affects the situations of the state. The frivolous vulnerabilities and negative undermines of some social principles can also not be forgotten. While the citizens of Nigeria, especially the youth, could use it to express themselves, it also contributed to the violence and destruction that followed the #EndSARS protests. Whether the destructions were made worse by the citizens or the government is not the context, but the fact that there was glorified jungle justice with no basis, puts the social media heralded them on trial. It has also undermined sensitive issues and unnecessarily aggravated national conditions threatening the state. If it threatens the state, how does the state respond to it? This is the core of chapter two, which discusses the government's reactions to the threats emanating from the platforms and regulations put in place to check them.

Buhari's administration became hard on social media, increasing its wish to censor and exhibiting some hostility, using its volatility and vulnerability as justifications. On the 5th of June 2021, Buhari's government banned Twitter, following the post #EndSARS realization of social media tendencies and ability to promote decadence. The ban lasted over seven months and was called off in January 2022 after the government stated that the company had complied with its conditions. The government's reactions to social media did not start in 2021; the chapter intends to examine the government's riposte and the legislative attempts to control social media. Different bills, including the Hate Speech Bill and their implications, reactions and justifications, were examined to see how they were intended to keep social media in context and control. Chapter two also examines the instrumentality of social media to both citizens and the government, especially how the Nigerian government has deployed it toward national issues, including the COVID-19 pandemic outbreak. This instrumentality also projects the future of government exploration of the platforms in policy formation and feedback.

In chapter three, I interjected myself into the contents of social media by concentrating on the USA-Africa Dialogue which I created decades ago. Back then, one thing that social media did not have enough space for is intellectualism and a platform for cerebral engagements. I will accept that there are intellectuals who have used

these platforms for analytical discussions, but the generality of these platforms are more socially inclined than intellectual. I took this as an opportunity to create a space for intellectual discussions and conversations within the complexity of social media. This informed the projection of the USA-Africa Dialogue Series for scholars of several specialties to discuss and suggest solutions to issues that revolve around Africa and the rest of the world. I would not say that the conversations are perfect, but there has been considerable progress in the projection of knowledge and identification of recommendable solutions by the participants. Chapter three analyzes the trajectories of these discussions, their positions on African matters, Nigerian situations, the conditions of Nigerian higher education, conversation on democratic practices and how they affect Nigeria.

In the second segment, I discuss some of the major issues that have garnered attention globally and locally and their contextualization in Nigerian societies. The world evolves, and Nigeria evolves around it, immersing itself into the core of those issues heralded by local occurrences and imported incitement of similar issues. I discuss the issues that have emerged on social media and gained users' attention. This is also done online with the effect of these discussions on society and how people react to them both online and offline.

The fourth chapter tries to project how social media interacts with the subject of corruption, which has proven difficult to find solutions to and its effect on the citizens. Corruption in Nigeria has become one of the many roots of Nigerian societal problems, and chapter four engages the effect of this root on society, including the people's general reactions. Transparency International ranks Nigeria as the 26th most corrupt country out of 180 countries. With corruption embroiled in the country's many problems, the citizens are tortured, making them express themselves with rage and anger. Citizens have used social media to criticize and express their concerns. The fourth chapter further questions the structure of these conversations and how their trajectories have progressed. It asks whether these expressions of their agonies have had any effect.

Chapter five of this book is a way of engaging a historical problem the country has faced. Secession and agitations against marginalization have been problems that constantly threaten Nigerian unity. The country was thrown into chaos when it witnessed outright secession confrontations that led to the 1967 Nigerian Civil War that claimed lives and properties. These problems have not left the consciousness of Nigerians, and with emerging problems in the society, agitators and secession apologists have found more justifications for their claims. Top of these secessionist demands has been the agitations for Biafra and Yoruba Nation. Social media has indeed participated in advancing these arguments by creating explorable options to extend these sentiments across the country. I discuss suggested solutions by looking into the applicability of restructuring and the secession campaigns.

I am fascinated by how Nigerian society evolves and how cultural diffusions have changed the country's social constructs. One such idea is the change in women's societal identification and roles. Culturally, women were expected not to take very socially engaging roles, positions and interactions and to be submissive to their husbands and men. Although these limitations may vary depending on society and convictions, there is a higher tendency to generally position males above the female gender. The global community has witnessed the heralding of expressive feminist campaigns, sensitizations and consciousness. These movements have been attracting considerable achievements, with social changes occurring in several societies, especially in Europe. In a country with relatively sentimental cultures that do not provide too willing environments for female potential and enjoyment of full freedom, there is concerning resistance pulled up by the society and its agencies. Chapter six of this book discusses feminist campaigns and consciousness in Nigeria and the societal reactions to these phenomena.

Chapter seven explores further injections of these global phenomena into society, some of which are the country's redefinitions of sexual identities and sexuality. Homosexuality and other forms of sexuality have gained the attention of contemporary global societies with cultures adjusting to them. African societies have historical convictions on sexuality that might not easily conform to new social dynamics. Hence, the public expression of new forms of sexuality might meet hostile public reactions. Without going into justifications around the acceptability of these identities, I discuss what public reactions and sentiments to these issues look like in line with the social exploration of social media.

The issue of sexuality in Nigeria is still a subject of public discussion with the impact of international influence and persuasion toward acceptance. This discussion extends toward queer people and how society appreciates them. I discuss the development of queer literature and social interactions with them, especially through social media. "GraceLand" by Chris Abani and other literature have introduced queer personalities and non-conventional sexual identities into mainstream Nigerian literature. The effect of these pieces, societal reactions and acceptability of queer-themed literature formed the core ideas of chapter eight.

Today, the vast majority of social media users in Nigeria are the youth who, by their nature, are inclined to opportunities offered by it. Youth participation in social and political matters has formed the core of social media usage in Nigeria. It is a way to express opinions, talents, and conversations around any subject of interest and criticism. The youth population has become an integral part of social media, as the group seems to form the sustaining forces of many platforms. Exploring the relationship between youth participation and social media constitutes the messages outlined in chapter nine of this book.

Youth participation on social media has allowed the growth of momentum to herald pressure on the government and persuade them to submit to the people's wide opinions and feedback. It has been a form to commence and incite actions that include demonstrations. An evidential height of these expressions was the 2020 #EndSARS protest against police brutality. Social media allows the youth to find their voice and pass information about their experience with the police and other problems militating against the peaceful existence of the citizens. It has been a pseudo-meeting point where the youth aggregate their voices to resist unfavorable policies and conditions of the nation. Seeing the need to explore these resistances, the impact of #EndSARS and the future possibility, I dedicated chapter ten to discussing messages the society needs to learn from these phenomena as reasonable expectations.

The third part of this book is based on some of the major contributors. My intention is not to exclude some major individuals but to pick some with aggregative perspectives, which explains the omission of several major names. Those represented as individual contributors speak on many of the issues discussed in the book's second part. The individuals examined in this part have been able to critically examine policies, and social issues, alongside emerging points of discussion in society. They are appropriate because of their continuous reasonable maximization of social media dynamics.

Chapter eleven is dedicated to discussions on the pursuit and expression of knowledge by the late Pius Adesanmi and contextualizing his prompt reactions to issues affecting Nigeria and Nigerians. He has been able to pass his messages and analyses through publications and social media handles; he was revered for his understanding of issues and insightful comments and recommendations. He connected the past and present generations in propelling Pan-Africanism by tearing down the neo-colonial and ineffective features of the government and its parastatals through publications and comments on social media. He was a familiar face for the youth in their engagements with the government and did well to connect intellectualism to discussions. The death of Adesanmi is an occurrence that saddens me at the mention of his name, but his contributions will never let his name be forgotten. Hence, the wisdom and body of knowledge of Adesanmi, in line with society and social media, is discussed in chapter eleven.

Aside from Pius Adesanmi, I added another brilliant mind, Ayo Olukotun, who has been remarkable in his analytical skills and projections of his opinions about the country. Chapters Twelve and Thirteen examine the projections of Ayo Olukotun's ideas on national dimensions and the threatening conditions of the country. His opinions became important subjects as they were formed from his understanding of democracy and certain threats to its practice in the country. His ideologies about Nigerian democratic practices engage political occurrences since 1993 and the country's current conditions in line with governmental reactions. As a person inclined to

freedom of the press and media, the impacts of his contributions, especially within the phase of social media dynamics, became important, and I consider it an appropriate point of discussion.

Chapter fourteen points out the scholarly instincts of Abimbola Adelakun in her assessment of Nigerian situations using the instrumentalities of columns, blogs, publications and social media by which she establishes her positions on how the nation can be remade and rebuilt. Her unique approach to issues in line with contexts filled with societal incidences is worthy of intellectual discussion. The chapter tries to find an answer to understanding what she has been saying about Nigeria, the context in which she says it, and her understanding of the remaking of Nigerian society, helping us relate to her stance better. Adelakun is fascinated by the exploitation of religious practices, the contemporary issues in society and conversations around the media, which makes her fit into a discussion of social media trajectories.

While conceptualizing this book, I realized that understanding different narratives about Nigeria and its projected future opens one's worldview about the situations and makes one see them from different perspectives. In this sense, I decided to plug into Bamidele Ademola-Olateju's narrations of the nation's state and her projections of the Nigerian future without being oblivious to present predicaments. She has been providing these narrations, analyses and contextualizing Nigerian situations for years with a notable medium of contributions through the Premium Times since 2003. She relates Nigeria to its economic travails and social and political incidents in line with their effects on the Nigerian population. Her narrations of the Nigerian situations as ordinary citizens and her progression into active politics make her narratives important for discussion for the sake of perspectives. Thus, chapter fifteen of this book is dedicated to analyzing those narratives.

Chapter sixteen examines Gloria Emeagwali's approaches to issues that cut across African indigenous societies and how they relate to other diversities. Her conversations circle the exploration of indigenous and African knowledge in line with societal concerns. She has been able to plug African epistemology into diverse areas of endeavors, including scientific inquiries. She is particular about the interconnectedness of African societies, histories and cultures, and as a result, her thoughts are crucial for scholarly examinations.

While many scholars might not be very disposed to the use of social media for societal discussions and intellectual engagements because of its limitations and vulnerabilities, Farooq Kperogi seems to be one that intentionally exploits social media with an impressive engagement of the public. My interest in helping understand and analyze his political criticism and opinions made me dedicate Chapters Seventeen and Eighteen to lay a foundation for further engagements of his opinions on Nigerian politics and elections. Kperogi has been particular about the current Nigerian government and situations, and his opinions on recent policies have generated interest.

His recent publication, Digital Dissidence and Social Media Censorship in Africa, manifests his convictions about social media, its instrumentality and its interaction with the government. Chapter seventeen is specifically channeled toward his particular views on two Nigerian Presidents, while chapter eighteen gives insight into his understanding and expectations of the 2023 elections.

The nineteenth chapter depicts my interest in engaging the opinions of Moses Ochonu under scrutiny in the view of the University system and how Nigerian peculiarities and problems affect it. Ochonu, inclined toward modern African history, has been able to relate contemporary matters with the African systems, including the educational sectors. His ability to relate the contemporary African and Nigerian occurrence and their historical events and developments have given him insight into understanding the current situations. This helped me develop the conviction to put his discussions into perspective and juxtapose them with the Nigerian state, the university system, and corruption.

Furthermore, Anthony Akinola became another person of interest whose lines of thought along the lines of unity and objectivity formed the basis of my discussion in chapter twenty. Akinola has been making his opinions about the nation's state known for years, and his views have always been relevant to social issues with a touch of detribalized stance.

Victor Asemota's positions on the relevance and applicability of technology and modern social requirements are discussed in chapter twenty-one. The trajectories of his opinions and subscription to the importance of technology have been relevant to social media as a subject matter that affects society and thus makes them worthy of intellectual scrutiny. To end the second part of the book and analysis of the thoughts of some individuals whose opinions have been relevant on subjects affecting the country and Africa vis-à-vis the peculiarities of social media, I placed the contributions of Jibrin Ibrahim on Nigerian politics and how he projects its influence on the society in chapter twenty-two.

The fourth part is a three-part conclusion; the first, chapter twenty-three, is a critique of the Nigerian situation, how social media has impacted a failing Nigeria, and the possibility of a renewed country. I provide a link between current situations and a possible imagined future, in addition to the factors that might threaten national expectations. I also put certain contributors, especially those already mentioned, on a scale of influence to see whether all their opinions could change much of Nigerian political and democratic practices. The endeavor in chapter twenty-three suggests the possible negative and positive images of Nigeria's future with factors that could lead to individual results. The second part of the conclusion, chapter twenty-four, is an overall assessment of the possibilities and limits of the power of social media warriors. The chapter examines their roles along the line of political participation hierarchies and the limitation of their influence. Chapter twenty-five, the last

chapter, tries to balance the arguments by introducing perspectives from the angle of those criticized by the above contributors, examining the strength of previous arguments and positions and creating balance to allow objectivity and varieties of vantage points.

Social media is a contemporary reality that we all must adjust to. It is one of the contemporary commuters of globalization that defines recent social constructions. The realities of social media, whether positive or negative, cannot be ignored without negative consequences. This reality informed the discussions this book raises about its influence on identity, motivation for nationalism, and platform for active engagements. I also discuss the consequential possibilities and disguised limitations of social media and those that utilize it.

This manuscript was completed in 2022 when President Buhari was in power. While all the main themes and issues remain, personalities in power have changed in many instances. Many people in power had either lost their re-election bids or were replaced by others. Thus, the present tense applies as of the time of writing.

ACKNOWLEDGMENTS

The title of this book is based on the assumption that people have become the media in their own right. They control the news! They dwell on the most important issues in their society: misinformation, democracy, injustice, corruption, "tribalism," disunity, poverty, education, religion, insecurity, politics, and major events. Social media provides freedom to say anything at any time and from anywhere, including verifiable and unverifiable information turning everyone into their own journalists and audience simultaneously. The emerging issues from social media paraphernalia often spread like wildfire with the government's limited capacity to censor them. It has become a reality and a factor instrumental to social and ideological formation. If one dedicates time to following these trends and conversations, one will realize the large ocean of themes that affect the national and global state.

This book is about how social media has impacted the democratic space, allowing everybody with access to become a voice, create their agency, and promote them as they wish. There is a diversity of ownership on small and big platforms, creating a community of various interests. One cannot deny that issues relating to identity, diversity, politics, cultural diffusion, and equality are themes often attributable to the practice of democracy in the world. The preponderance of globalization processes has propagated these themes. As the contemporary chief tool of globalization, social me-

dia has also not withdrawn from creating engagements and conversations around them. Seeing the importance of these themes to democratic practice and their reenactment by social media, one cannot help but inquire to understand the relationship between them.

The themes, engagements, and how social issues are affected by this new reality cannot be possible without those, including Vinton Cerf and Bob Kahn, that contributed to the creation of the internet communication protocols upon which the logic and details of the social media are created today. They have shown the unimaginable level of exploration of the human mind and remind us that there is certainly space for new inventions that would change the face of the world. While they have created these possibilities, one must also appreciate those who have created social media communities with them, bringing the world closer to global citizenship. Mark Zuckerberg, Jack Dorsey, Mimi Kalinda, Zhang Yiming, Alexis Ohanian, the Durovs and their colleagues, and other creators of social media platforms must be appreciated for creating spaces to engage the world.

Africa and Nigeria must be encouraged to continue their paths to technological advancement and innovation that will continue to show the potential of the continents. The world has witnessed brilliant African minds that have established themselves in the technology industry, and as a result, the continent and Nigeria must learn to understand that if there will be a desired future where African countries can compete technologically with established non-African countries, deliberate investments and creating an appropriate trajectory will make the youth, institutions, and universities become leaders in the tech industry.

It would be sheer ignorance to ask if anything good can come from social media platforms, seeing their volatility and vulnerability. Social media platforms are two-edged swords capable of contributing valuably and worsening societal issues. Within these flexibilities, some individuals have found it worth putting the platforms to good use, engaging Nigerian citizens and creating needed sensitization. When the usual expectation of social media usage in many places is frivolity, it is important to appreciate those that do otherwise. This has made it possible to gather sources for this work and create the right understanding of themes as they affect the nation. The past activities and opinions of certain individuals through news and social media platforms have become sources of reformation for social media conversations. These people and their thousands of followers have been able to use the platforms to engage the citizens on issues affecting Nigerian democracy and the nation-state. It is through the lenses of their opinions that this writer has examined relevant themes to contemporary Nigerian society. These people and others that have resolved to utilize the platform for societal transformation are contributing to the contemporary positive history of social media, and they must be appreciated.

The individuals spotlighted in this book have come to be because of their years of social and political contributions and advancement of development and progressive discussions in the country. This book would not be possible without their deliberate attention to and for social issues. The late Pius Adesanmi must be appreciated for wise analyses and forecasts of the Nigerian future. If Nigerians and their leaders apply some of his recommendations and heed some of his warnings, it is sure that the country's conditions would be better than this. Ayo Olukotun's views have allowed society to see the political makeup of the nation. Abimbola Adelakun must be appreciated for her commitment to the hope of a better Nigeria and how the nation can be remade. Bamidele Ademola-Olateju's analyses of national issues and occurrences have allowed this book to stretch to many fronts in Nigerian political atmospheres. Farooq Kperogi's insistence on addressing issues related to freedom of the media and political equities and Victor Asemota's technological understandings added flesh to the social media context intended in this book. Jibrin Ibrahim, Gloria Emeagwali, and Moses Ochonu's critical evaluation of historical and political developments and the university system in the country opened remarkable lines of thought for great discussions. All of the above individuals have unknowingly been writing their legacies.

I appreciate every individual who has assisted in one way or another in writing this book. Those that I interviewed on the streets, streams of WhatsApp messages from known and unknown people, forwarded messages from Facebook, Twitter posts and commentaries, the USA-Africa Dialogue, those who unknowingly broadened my ideas, etc. These contributions formed important parts of this book.

I must also laud the commitments of my readers, critics, and those who often anticipate releasing my thoughts and anticipations. What you learn, your reactions to new knowledge, and the criticisms you take, make you members of the "wisdom of crowds," as James Surowiecki put it in *The Wisdom of Crowds: Why the Many Are Smarter than the Few and How Collective Wisdom Shapes Business, Economies, Societies, and Nations*. The "wisdom of crowds" from Bola Dauda, Michael Oladejo Afolayan, Olusegun Akeju, Peter M. J. Gross, Simi Hassam, Kareem Shamusudeen, Adebukola Bassey, Theophilus Alawonde, Oluwafunminiyi Raheem, Wale Ghazal, Segun Olopade, Pankthi Dhagia, Medinat Malefakis, Tayo Keyede and many more shows, among other things, that truth is not neutral: facts can be manipulated; the context of facts may be wrong or right; ideas can come from multiple sources; the old and the youth can combine for productive work. In proofreading the manuscript, I owe a debt of gratitude to many people: Adebukola Bassey, Sati Fwatshak, Samuel Oloruntoba, Olajumoke Jacob-Haliso, Samson Ijaola, Olushola Richards, Yahaya Halidu, Victor Angba, Raheem Oluwafunminiyi, Damilare Bello, Yombo Raji-Oyelade, Daniel

Eworo, Pelumi Folajimi, Knowledge Grey Moyo, Alabi Oritoke, Adanna Ogbonna, Temitope Fagunwa, Raji Lateef, and Ndidi Akahara.

I thank you all—whether you are an idea generator, an idea discussant, an idea critic, or an idea user—many have traveled with me on a long journey for a book based on reading over a million pages and items and one that took three years to complete. I would be the first to admit that it is ready for a revised edition!

Toyin Falola
The University of Texas at Austin
October 2022

PART A

CONTEXTS

1

NIGERIA IN THE WORLD OF SOCIAL MEDIA

INTRODUCTION

"Social media" is an umbrella term for the emerging digital communication channels used to create user-generated and oriented information, which may subsequently be shared among an unlimited number of connected fellow users within a particular platform's network. The concept of social media rests on four main pillars: enablement, time, participation, and partnership,[1] establishing digitally connected links between individuals to interact, converse, and exchange information. The major reason for the increasing embrace of social media worldwide is that it creates an avenue for people to share ideas, information, experiences, and common interests across regions with little or no external controls.

The projection of globalization through advancements in production, transportation and communication technology has undoubtedly been impacted by the evolutionary aspects of communications technology, especially 'social media,' which has guided the world further to unprecedented levels of interconnectedness, interrelation, and interdependency. Social media has revolutionized human interaction and added a global dimension to the potential consequence of every human action.

1. J. C. Bertot, P. T. Jaeger and J. M. Grimes, "Using ICTs to Create a Culture of Transparency: E-government and Social Media as Openness and Anti-Corruption Tools for Societies," *Government Information Quarterly* 27, no. 3 (2010): 264–271.

Figure 1.1. "Heavy Load" by Michael Efionayi. A heavy load with a positive and negative impact of social media. A shell, protective covering, the voice of the masses.

In the evolution of communication technology, computers transformed what is now known as the 'traditional media,' i.e., television and radio broadcasting. As computer technology improved and the internet came along (after a series of advancements said to have begun in 1969 with a United States Department of Defense project known as the Advanced Research Projects Agency Network—ARPANET),[2] dynamic internet-based digital communication platforms such as America Online, CompuServe and Prodigy emerged in the 1980s and '90s. But these were relatively unpopular outside America. Further technological improvements provided the platform for other, more sophisticated networking sites, popular among which are: (from earliest) Six Degrees (1997), LinkedIn (2002), Myspace (2003), Facebook (2004), YouTube (2005), Twitter (2006), WhatsApp (2009) and Instagram (2011).

The term 'social media' might imply mass media, the various mediums through which information is communicated within society—mostly on a large scale—which, before the advent of computers and the internet, meant letters, the printing press, telegraph and the telephone. But 'social' in the context of social media points to the highly interactive and inclusive phenomenon being qualified, different from the one-direction communication flow of traditional (mass) media. Hence, 'social media' is a term reserved for these specific internet/web-based interactive applications (apps)

2. Maryville University, "The Evolution of Social Media: How did it Begin and where Could it go Next?" https://online.maryville.edu/blog/evolution-social-media/.

which are operated on electronic devices like computers (desktops and laptops), smartphones and tablets that enable individuals around the globe to communicate, exchange information, and air their views instantaneously to wider audiences without the usual encumbrances of traditional media.

Today, social media is known and used all over the world. As of 2014, Counterpart International, in partnership with the United States Agency for International Development (USAID), put the number of social media users at about 1.75 billion;[3] that number has since risen to an estimated 3.6 billion in 2020,[4] about half the world's population. Its ability to serve as a virtual substitute for physical communication—which is restricted by distance, time, privacy, and coverage—has changed the way people interact and socialize; further, economic transactions, political entities, and social organizations have continually shifted to online mediums since their inception in 1997.

Social media has seen an exponential increase in the volume and ease of global interaction. As an interactive medium—aided by the proliferation of smart mobile devices—it has equipped users with access to a greater volume of information (sometimes shared in real-time), a conducive atmosphere for expression, increased economic opportunities, and increased participation in political activism. Social media's role extends beyond providing connectivity, creating awareness, ensuring more people have a voice, and empowering them to organize. It allows people to form transnational alliances and take their messages to the international stage. Consequently, it has also created wealth for service providers while sparking demands for greater transparency and accountability from individual governments and corporations around the world.

This chapter will examine how Nigeria has fared in a world with greater interconnectedness and information flow; and how this has impacted Nigeria's economy, politics, and social interaction.

NIGERIA BEFORE SOCIAL MEDIA

Social interaction and participation in Nigeria before the advent of social media were constrained. At this time, that is, before the introduction of the Global System of Mobile Communication (GSM) in September 2001, socio-political and infrastructural impediments to traditional media operations (Newspapers, Radio, Television and Telephone) saw a good proportion of Nigerians either living in nescience or relying largely on second-hand information which had its implications. Hence, to examine the impact of these newer technologies, the availability and performance of traditional media in this era must first be understood.

3. Counterpart International, "Social Media Networking: A Guide to Strengthening Civil Society through Social Media, 2014," https://usaid.gov/sites/default/files/documents/1866/SMGuide4CSO.pdf.

4. Jessica Clement, "Social Networks Ranked by Number of Users 2020," *Statista*, https://www.satista.com/statistics/272014/global-social-netwroks-ranked-by-number-of-users/.

Print Media (Newspapers and Magazines)

The presence of print media in Nigeria dates back to 1859, when the first newspaper *Iwe Irohin Fun Awon Ara Egba Ati Yoruba* (shortened as *Iwe Irohin*), was established in Abeokuta by the British missionary, the Reverend Henry Townsend. The advent of this paper has been tied to "the primary aim of missionary journalists...to indicate western values through the spread of education, campaign reading culture and propagate Christianity."[5] However, the paper adopted a 'pro-native stance' and came to antagonize the colonial authorities.

In the 1880s, other sets of newspapers began to emerge in the southern part of the British colony. Some of these are "*The Lagos Observer* (1982), *The Eagle and Lagos Critic* (1883), *The Mirror* (1887), *Lagos Echo* (1890), *Lagos Weekly Record* (1890), *The Chronicles* (1908), *The Pioneer* (1914), *Lagos Daily News* (1925), *The Nigerian Daily Times* (1926)."[6] Soon there were over fifty newspapers of the sort in this space.[7] The *Lagos Weekly Record,* operated by John Payne Jackson and his son Thomas Horatio Jackson stood dominant in the area for about forty years before the coming of the *West African Pilot* operated by Nnamdi Azikiwe. The *West African Pilot,* known for its "'combative style about its commitment to campaigns against racial superiority and domination...became the voice then of the movement against colonialism."[8] It was said to have "brought a more militant form of nationalism or rather anti-colonial agitation for those wanting a departure from the accommodating politics of Lagos."[9] These were later to be joined by other newspapers and magazines like *The Tribune, The Punch, The National Concord, The Guardian, Vanguard, The New Nigerian, Daily Mail Sentinel, Newswatch, TELL, The NEWS and Hotline.*

Unlike telecommunications in Nigeria, where challenges in infrastructural availability and coverage restricted the proliferation of telephones and their potential as a tool for social awareness, organization, and mobilization/participation, the print media has had a longer (about sixteen decades) and more productive experience in the area. The Nigerian print media is highly recognized for its dogged interventions, either in calling for an end to colonialism or in defense of civil rights and democracy in the face of military dictatorship, especially in the 1990s. Ayo Olutokun provides some insight into the media's history of a counter-hegemonic position regarding military dictatorships in Nigeria:

---

5. Olujimi Kayode, "Media, Mood and Movement: Media Impact on Social Movement in Nigeria," academia, 2011, www.cacdemia.edu/4102433/Media_Mood_and_Movement_Media_Impact_on_Social_Movements_in_Nigeria.

6. Lai Oso and Umaru Pate, eds. *Mass Media and Society in Nigeria* (Lagos: Malthouse Press Limited, 2011), 5.

7. Kayode, "Media, Mood and Movement."

8. Kayode, "Media, Mood and Movement."

9. Kayode, "Media, Mood and Movement."

> The Abacha years between 1993 and 1998 offer a peculiar illustration of the phenomenon of the criminalized state...which is marked by the use for private purposes the legitimate organs of state violence by those in authority and the function of such violence as an instrument in the service of their strategies of accumulation of wealth. It was in this context that a section of the media located mainly in the south-west area of the country drawing on a tradition of activism, even militancy dating back to the colonial days, invented a guerrilla strategy to oppose the military. Older than the Nigerian state by a century, many media perceive themselves as human rights activists, as demonstrated in the crusading names of such press titles as *The Champion*, *The Tribune*, *The Vanguard*, and *The Punch*.[10]

The print media has done relatively well as a vehicle for social mobilization against injustice and hegemonic and undemocratic forces in Nigeria. Collaboratively, the media— i.e., both print and broadcast media— has engaged with state operators and policymakers on several grounds, including traversing policy making, politics and human rights, culture, and economy. In doing so, they have achieved significant improvements in legislation and policy delivery as well as in the reversal of anti-people policies, prompting some to state that "there is no social movement that has evolved in Nigeria without the active collaboration of the media and the leading cadre of such movements."[11]

Notwithstanding these remarkable achievements, it is pertinent to mention that the print media was limited in its capacity as an interactive and mobilizing medium. Not all print media outfits in the country adopted a progressive attitude in their business of journalism:

- some media outfits were known to be pro-establishment entities;
- some represented the political interests of their proprietors;
- some adopted regional outlooks and promoted regional agendas;
- some were more interested in the economic aspects of the business.[12]

Also, the print media was neither equipped with the facilities for the direct interpersonal exchange of information nor the capacity to reach and command global reactions in the same manner as social media.

---

10. Ayo Olutokun, "Authoritarian State, Crisis of Democracy and the Underground Media in Nigeria," *African Affairs* 101, no. 404 (2002): 317–247.
11. Kayode, "Media, Mood and Movement in Nigeria."
12. Oso and Pate, *Mass Media and Society*, 7–8.

Broadcast Media (Radio and Television)

Broadcasting in Nigeria was introduced as a 'humble' BBC (British Broadcasting Corporation) outpost in 1932 by the British colonial establishment to serve imperialist interests—as a propaganda tool—especially during the Second World War.[13] Threatened by the capacity of Russian (USSR) external broadcast, the British government set up the Plymouth Committee assigned to:

> ...consider and recommend what steps could be taken to accelerate the provision of broadcasting services in the colonial empire, to coordinate such services with the work of the BBC and to make them a more effective instrument for promoting both local and imperial interests.[14]

From 1932 to 1959, when the Western Nigerian Regional Government established the Western Nigeria Broadcasting Corporation, owner of the Western Nigeria Television (WNBC-WNTV), broadcasting was centralized in the hands of the colonial authority. The establishment of this regional broadcasting service was a by-product of the 1954 constitution, which granted larger autonomy to the three Nigerian regions. Following the Western Region's footsteps, the other two regions established their broadcasting services. These regional broadcasting stations of the post-independence period ultimately "deviated from their original purpose of improving the lots of their people through provision of informal education for the adult populace and provision of information that could improve their social cum cultural status, and regressed to serving partisan purpose."[15]

The Murtala/Obasanjo regime of 1977 took-over state-owned television stations by the promulgation of Decree No. 24 of 1977, effectively centralizing television broadcasting in the country under the National Television Authority established by the same decree. The reason for this decree was 'national unity' in the face of the regional undertones disseminated by these stations as described below:

> Although all the Nigerian Regional Television Stations in the First Republic (post-independence period) proclaimed national goals in their operational statements, yet the dominant tone was very much sectional and essentially partisan in federal politics. The accent was on regionalism and strengthening the power base accordingly to the needs of the government in power. In short,

13. Oso and Pate, *Mass Media and Society*, 13.

14. Olu Ladele, V. Olufẹmi Adefẹla and Olu Laṣekan, *History of Nigerian Broadcasting Corporation* (Ibadan: Ibadan University Press, 1979), 12–13; quoted in Oso and Pate, *Mass Media and Society*, 13.

15. Kayode, "Media, Mood and Movement."

> programming was simply divisive and propagandistic, as the coverage traced a sectional pattern-reflective of the nation's political ideologies and diversities.[16]

The basis for the centralization of television broadcasting, though accepted as a reality, has been argued to have served as the perfect excuse for the Obasanjo regime to "stifle opposition voices and [block] out opinions and ideologies that did not flow from its notion of social relations. There was apparent attempt too at ensuring that the most potent wing of the media serving as agent of diffusion was incapacitated through coercion."[17] Reinforcing this idea, Lai Oso et al. posit that television was considered a national resource that must be deployed in promoting 'national ideals and interests.' However, "The national security doctrine behind the policy, especially coming from a military regime should be apparent to any close observer."[18]

The hold of the federal government on the National Television Authority (NTA) endured even after Section 36 of the 1979 constitution (under civilian rule) restored the rights of individuals and states to "own, establish and operate any medium for the dissemination of information, idea and opinion... provided that no person other than the Government of the Federation of the State or any person or body authorized by the president, shall own, establish or operate a television or wireless broadcasting for any purpose whatsoever."[19] Even with the emergence of state-owned broadcasting organizations—beginning with Lagos in 1980—in protest of what was considered biased reporting and unbalanced airtime, it was not until 1992 when the Babangida regime broke the federal government's broadcasting monopoly by establishing the National Broadcasting Commission (NBC) as the industry's regulatory body.

NBC, empowered to license private broadcasting organizations, issued its first set of private licenses for privately operated television and radio services in June of 1993. This action heralded the beginning of a gradual take-over of the broadcast business from the Federal and State Government owned broadcast stations; they still dominated the airwaves through FRCN and NTA radio and television stations scattered all over the thirty-six (36) states of the federation, including Abuja. Nevertheless, the last decade has brought about a very different picture as the Nigerian broadcast airwaves are now dominated by privately owned television and radio stations such as the Africa Independent Television (AIT), Channels Television, Television Continental (TVC), Arise Television, and Ray-power among others.

---

16. M. I. Egbon, "Origins and Development of Television Broadcasting in Nigeria: An Inquiry into Television Development in a Non-industrialized Nation," Ph.D. *diss.*, University of Wisconsin, Madison, 1977; quoted by Kayode, "Media, Mood and Movement."

17. Kayode, "Media, Mood and Movement."

18. Oso and Pate, *Mass Media and Society*, 14.

19. Oso and Pate, *Mass Media and Society*, 14.

Telephony

Historically, telecommunications facilities in Nigeria were first set up by the colonial administration in 1886. These facilities mainly directed the discharge of colonial administrative functions. Hence, links to Ghana, Sierra Leone, Gambia, and some other places along the West African coast to England were also established upon introducing a public telegraph service in Lagos.[20] By 1893, the colonial offices in Lagos, Ilorin, and Jebba were equipped with telephone lines, marking the gradual emergence of a national telecommunication network.

At independence in 1960, the need to expand the network of a young nation with fledgling commercial and industrial sectors saw the number of telephone lines rise to around eighteen thousand (18,000) for a population of about forty million (40 million). Nigeria External Telecommunication (NET) Limited was also established to handle external communication services, while the Department of Posts and Telecommunications handled the internal network.

The post-independence era witnessed the implementation of some expansion and modernization plans. Nigerian Telecommunication Limited was established in 1985 to administer external and internal telecommunications, while telephone lines increased to two hundred thousand (200,000). However, this advancement was bedeviled by poor and unreliable service quality and expensive customer charges. This meant only the rich members of the diplomatic corps and top government officials could afford telephone lines. The trend remained as Nigeria struggled with excessive telephone charges and limited network provision. In 1998, there were an estimated ten million (10 million) people awaiting "action and installation by Nigerian Telecommunication Ltd."[21] Within the same year, Private Telecommunication Operators (PTOs) began commercial operations to better serve their communities.

These PTOs allowed for the introduction of internet services from a fraction of the ninety-six (96) licensed operators. Twenty of these providers were focused on core telecommunications, and the remaining seventy-six delivered other telecommunications-related services like prepaid internet services and Voice Over Internet Protocol (VOIP). This, however, did not do much in aiding the proliferation of telephones, vis-à-vis improving communication, among the generality of the Nigerian populace because it still did not address the matter of cost and service sufficiency. It was not until 2001 when the GSM technology and service were introduced that phone prices gradually fell to accommodate the larger portion of the populace. Through its (text) messaging facility, communications levels gradually began to increase until social media revolutionized the process, providing more facilities and speed, further reducing costs.

---

20. Esharenana Adomi, "Mobile Telephony in Nigeria," *Library Hi Tech News* 22, no. 4 (2005): 18–20.
21. Adomi, "Mobile Telephony in Nigeria."

Nigeria, before social media, had a remarkable history of 'traditional media' presence which had critical roles in its colonial and postcolonial development phases. As an agency of information sourcing and dissemination, it enabled a relatively active civil participation in the socio-political and economic spheres. Through the crusading social activities of some of its outstanding practitioners, the traditional media has set itself apart as the single most important contributor to the survival of democracy in Nigeria. Some of the notable areas of contributions by the 'mass media' to the Nigerian entity/Nigerians by way of education, enlightenment, publicity, and critical analysis have been listed to include:

> change of decimal currency in 1971; change from left to right hand drive; President Shagari's Green Revolution; General Buhari's War Against Indiscipline; General Babangida's Social Development Programmes such as: MAMSER and DFFRI; the Problems of Advance Fraud (419); Nigeria's controversial membership to the Organization of Islamic Countries (OIC); the June 12 Presidential Election Imbroglio; the reportage of the level of destruction of Odi town in Bayelsa State by soldiers; the gruesome murder of Pa Alfred Rewane, Kudirat Abiola, Baguda Kalto, Dele Giwa and Chief Bola Ige; the killing of 19 soldiers in Benue State and the retaliation by soldiers 2001; the coverage of the Odua People's Congress and Bakassi Boy's activities.[22]

However, the traditional media has not been without its contradictions, sometimes counteracting its role as an instrument of social cohesion and accountability. This contradiction, which might be attributed to natural human fallibility or 'constraints of economic marketing and regulatory pressure,' has another dimension explored by an observer of the conduct of traditional media in post-independence Nigeria. It reads:

> Quite apparent was the subjectivity of news coverage where political adversaries were either not given mention or, in some cases, even refused commercial time...Newspapers, radio, and television stations were split along partisan lines, adhering to the political interests of the government and individuals that owned them. On many occasions, broadcasters were obliged to participate in smear campaigns in order to keep their jobs.[23]

The political and economic motive to control traditional media in its capacity as a "means of shaping popular consciousness and social reality"[24] has tampered with its performance as a mechanism for social mobility and accountability. However, traditional media was limited by its nature as it does not allow for large-scale interperson-

22. Oso and Pate, *Mass Media and Society*, 71.

23. O. Lasode, *Television Broadcasting: The Nigerian Experience (1959–1992)* (Ibadan: Caltop Publications (Nig.) Ltd., 1994), 102; quoted by Oso and Pate, *Mass Media and Society*, 71.

24. Oso and Pate, *Mass Media and Society*, 19.

al interactions between individuals. Not without its dangers, the internet has permitted some level of freedom and communication expansion.

NIGERIA AND SOCIAL MEDIA

Social media in Nigeria is a fairly recent phenomenon, especially when juxtaposed with traditional media, which has been around for over a hundred and fifty years. Social media is also referred to as the "new media,"[25] in contrast to the old, but especially of its internet use. Therefore, discussing Nigeria in the era of social media means Nigeria after the introduction of the internet,[26] and subsequently smartphones, among other new technological devices that have aided the social media revolution.

The Nigerian Communications Commission (NCC), established following the promulgation of Decree 75 of 1992, saddled with the task of restructuring and regulating the telecommunications and postal sector, transformed the telecommunications landscape in Nigeria through its issuance of "large numbers of telecommunication licenses ranging from small community licenses for local operators, to regional and national operators."[27] This action, which technically broke the monopoly of the incumbent operator (NITEL), paved the way for the introduction of internet services in the country and the explosion of telecommunications activity. This transformation was completed with the introduction of GSM services in 2001, which increased the number of telephone users and expanded connectivity and communication, especially through texting and email.

Social media has undoubtedly brought about a remarkable shift in global economic activities by tying countries' economic fortunes closer together through international transactive mediums. The advances, in conjunction with the huge opportunities inherent in the online and or information economy, have led many politically conservative countries around the world (military dictatorship in the case of Nigeria) to adjust their view of telecommunication (including social media) as a threat to national security, to treating it as a matter of grave national interest and economic development. This change in perception informed earlier deregulation and commercialization witnessed in Nigeria in the 1990s.

There are two major schools of thought on the connection between telecommunications (including social media) and economic growth; technophilia and technophobia. These schools of thought guide the discussion around the nature of the impact of

25. Ugochukwu and Ekwugha, "New Media and Youth's Online," 203–221.

26. The advent of social media (New Media) is predominantly tied to telephones (with phreaking) and the email; technologies that have been available in the West since the 1950s and 60s. In Nigeria, however, these technologies where they were available, were restricted to a privileged few. Two factors therefore were responsible for the proliferation of social media in Nigeria, the internet and affordable GSM technology.

27. Adomi, "Mobile Telephony in Nigeria," 18.

Information and Communication Technology (ICT) on the social economy. The former (technophilia) holds that telecommunications would positively affect the economy. It argues that ICT will increase productivity, create employment, and enhance both the quality of performance and the work speed in areas of economic endeavor. The latter (technophobia) views telecommunication as being detrimental to economic growth. It holds that even though ICT will result in some societal changes, its economically transformative nature is exaggerated. It is understood within this perspective that ICT will not only fail to produce as much employment as it would destroy but also widen the information gap between the illiterate and literate and between the rich and the poor.[28]

These contradictory schools of thought mostly highlight what can be termed as the advantages and disadvantages of telecommunications (social media) on economic activities/growth. Despite the valid concerns raised by technophobes, experience has shown that the economic advantages inherent in the efficient flow of information pick up the slag in economic activity and drive better productivity. Furthermore, no country can afford to turn its back on the next phase in global development, where information is both a valuable exchange commodity and critical to economic success.

Social media is a massive, profit-earning business. In the first quarter of 2019 (April), Facebook (which also owns WhatsApp, Messenger, and Instagram) raked in $67.37 billion in advert revenues, while Twitter did $2.7 billion and Snapchat $1.3 billion.[29] In the third quarter of 2020 (October), Facebook generated around $3.71 billion in revenue, with 3.21 billion users across its apps, at $6.76 per user.[30] What sets social media apart from traditional (mass) media is its capacity for a "greater scope of interactivity... using highly accessible and scalable publishing techniques."[31] Social media allows individuals to carry out tasks formerly restricted to mass media outlets and reach a wider audience through its multiple interactive mediums: cheap application calls, emailing and texting facilities, audio and video messaging, blogging, and podcasts.

---

28. Fedrick O. Asogwa, Kennedy Kelechi Ohaleme and Romanus O Ugwuanyi, "The Impact of Telecommunication Expenditure on Economic Growth in Nigeria," *Journal of Economics and Sustainable Development* 4, no. 13 (2013): 40–44.

29. Jasmine Enberg, "Q2 2019 Social Trends," *eMarketer*, July 23, 2019, http://www.emarketer.com/content/q2-2019-social-trends.

30. Andrew Hutchinson, Facebook Continues to Add Users, Posts Strong Revenue Result in Q3, *Social Media Today*, October 29, 2020, https://www.socialmediatoday.com/news/facebook-continues-to-add-users-posts-revenue-result-in-q3/588090/.

31. Robert Madu and Shedrack C. Moguluwa, "Will the Social Media Lenses be the Framework for Sustainable Development in Rural Nigeria?" *Journal of African Studies* 5, no.2 (2013): 237–254.

AREAS OF SOCIAL MEDIA IMPACT

Job Creation

Social media has expanded the opportunities available to an average (literate) Nigerian, including advertising, trading, content creation, teaching, counseling, and more. In practice, social media has created job opportunities for the unemployed population directly and indirectly. In the immediate sense, apart from bloggers who get advertising commissions and social media inventors,[32] average social media users (especially on Twitter) who have gained substantial followership to generate and direct conversations are called "influencers." They are approached by both corporate entities and private businesses to generate/direct conversations around particular products, after which they get paid for meeting agreed targets. Social media has created openings in corporate entities for professional social media managers who handle their publicity across various platforms. Additionally, opportunities for tourism promotion through sites like Instagram, a social media platform that allows users to post (publish) photos, are exponentially increased. Though this has not been harnessed to its full potential in Nigeria,[33] partly due to the security challenges the country struggles with, social media enhances productivity and wealth distribution by providing such employment opportunities.

Skill Acquisition

This is another manner through which social media boosts economic performance. In this case, social media sites like YouTube, Facebook, and Instagram that have video-sharing facilities are deployed as avenues for sharing educational content like tutorial videos to a global audience. Here, the content creator and the viewer benefit from the interaction; the platform remunerates the (registered) content creator for generating traffic, and the viewer gains a new skill. There are also blog sites where professionals (e.g., lawyers, health practitioners, writers, teachers, etc.) connect with other professionals to interact, learn new skills, and explore new opportunities. These kinds of forums have the potential to boost the Nigerian economy by providing it with a more competent workforce.

Enhancing Small Capital Investment

Social media provides artisans and other small business owners the avenue to showcase their skills and products to a wide/diverse audience with minimal costs. Its interactive nature also enables the development of customer relationships and ease of referral. Onyejelem et al. describe this more elaborately while explaining that the

---

32. Jude Egbas, "Meet the Young Nigerians who just sold their Company for N76 Billion," *pulse*, October 17, 2020, https://www.pulse.ng/business/paystack-for-n76-billion-ezra-olubi-shola-akinlade-sell-their-company-live-the-dream/3zj00kr.

33. Okonkwo E. Emeka, Afamefuna Eyisi and Nneoma G. Ololo, "Social Media Platforms and their Contributions to Tourism Development and Promotion in Nigeria," *Nsukka Journal of Humanities* 23, no.2 (2015): 104.

"suitability of social media marketing for small businesses lies in its fewer capital demands, as social media platforms can disseminate messages across an unlimited geographical space at very manageable costs."[34] In other words, small capital start-ups have better chances of success when they do not have to pay the steep charges for advertising—a critical element for ensuring patronage—via traditional media mediums.

Marketing/Business Partnerships

This is yet another area where the distinctive interactive features of social media have created avenues for Nigerians to earn. In this case, social media sites, like Facebook, not only harness their extensive coverage for marketing purposes but are also fitted with transaction facilities to complete economic transactions. Jiji is popular in Nigeria, it allows individuals to showcase their goods, interact with potential buyers and complete transactions. Myspace and LinkedIn are other social media platforms that encourage business partnerships. The former is an avenue for career musicians to connect with other musicians around the globe and to promote their music, while the latter enables people to build and maintain contacts with other professionals in their field. Many Nigerians have been able to sell their vocation and expertise through this medium to people in locations they might not be able to afford to visit. Notwithstanding the economic gains social media has afforded Nigeria/Nigerians, factors such as penetration, illiteracy, infrastructural deficiency, and cost of operation continue to hinder an expression of its full economic potential for the country's benefit.

Politics

Social media, as a point of convergence for diverse political viewpoints, is a hotbed for political discussions. The value of social media in increasing political awareness and participation has been demonstrated by several local and international incidents which originated from discussions that started or gathered momentum through one or more of these platforms. The successful organization of some of these incidences: the Arab Spring in parts of Africa and the Middle East; the Occupy movements in Africa, Asia and Eastern Europe; the Rhodes Must Fall movement in South Africa; the Black Lives Matter movement in America; the Bring Back Our Girls and EndSARS movements in Nigeria, are symbolic of a greater change than mere "enhanced communication aiding political mobilization." These rallying points have effectively marked a shift in political ontology and a change in the nature of global political engagement methods.[35] Fenton has provided the following description in analyzing the

34. Timothy E. Onyejelem, Chinelo E. Ude-Akpeh, Ngozi E. Uduma, "The Economic Potentials of Social Media and the Nigerian Developing Society: An Appraisal," *International Journal of African and Asian Studies* 15 (2015): 108–116. www.iiste.org.

35. Natalie Fenton, "Left Out? Digital Media, Radical Politics and Social Change," *Information, Community, and Society* 19, no. 3 (2016): 346–361.

nature and extent of political transformation attributed to digital internet media (which mostly describes social media):

> ...some of the key characteristics of digital media and of the internet in particular have been claimed to mark out such technology as conducive to contemporary transnational political activism. These characteristics are described as *Speed and Space*—the internet is claimed to facilitate international non-governmental organizations (NGOs) allowing protesters to respond rapidly on an international level to local events while requiring minimal resources and bureaucracy; *connectivity and participation*—the internet is described as a mediated activity that seeks to raise people's awareness, give voice to those who do not have one, offer social empowerment through participation, allow disparate people and causes to organize themselves and form alliances on a transnational level and ultimately be used as a tool for social change... [36]

Fenton argues that most times, in critiquing these movements, too much emphasis is placed on the technological aspects to neglect the historical context from whence these sorts of political actions emerged. In this manner, their true meanings and objectives are lost to momentary excitement. In our analysis of the impacts of social media on political organizations in Nigeria, we will avoid this error by digging deeper to reveal what type of political culture was enhanced by social media in Nigeria.

NIGERIAN POLITICAL CULTURE OF PARTICIPATION

Unfortunately, the culture of political participation among the masses in Nigeria does not derive from any singularity of purpose or national interest but from regional considerations/interests/sentiments, which in most cases, overrule other (noble) considerations. This tradition of disunity of purpose is first recognizable in the organized postcolonial agitation, as even then, the country or "mere geographical expression" was not united in its demand for self-determination, delaying independence by at least three years. Specifically, two post-independent incidences drove a deeper wedge between two major regions of the country—the 1960s coups and the Civil War. These factors combined with the fact that most post-independence Nigerian attempts at popular action against unfavorable government policies have either been met with brutal government crackdowns or have been defeated by counter positions stemming from myopic sentiments. With this historical influence, Nigeria cannot boast of a culture of unified and sustained civic resistance to undemocratic, anti-people government positions.

It is instructive to note that the few (post-independence) instances of sustained resistance to government excesses came from some practitioners of the traditional

36. Fenton, "Left Out?"

Figure 1.2. "Conversations on Social Media Information" by Dr. Kazeem Ekeolu. It portrays the dynamics social media brought to information dissemination and the problem of credibility attached to it.

media—radio and newspaper. Also, the few other occasions of mass action in protest against specific social grievances (BBOG and EndSARS) originated from an evolved communication medium (social media). This demonstrates the role of social media in giving voice to the otherwise obscured and the importance of safety in anonymity

and distance from physical attacks, which is critical to the Nigerian protest culture, given state tendencies for extreme repression.

Social Media Political Trends

Social media has provided a medium for citizen-state interaction in the public domain, promoting increased participation in political activity by creating awareness and providing an avenue for the masses to demand better governance, transparency, and accountability. This raises questions—how has the government responded to these demands for accountability? How has the government reacted to the instrument of social media, and how has social media affected the "social norms associated with political participation?"[37] Before addressing the above questions, it is pertinent to mention an underlying disillusionment with the government fueled by the continuous scandals and allegations of corruption labeled against its functionaries.

Social Media, Social Norms and Political Participation

Besides the increased level of interest and participation, individuals can have direct conversations with elected representatives. This may be direct or indirect as social media carries information—from independent reporters free from government control—on the inappropriate conduct of government officials, making it an effective tool for mobilizing civic engagements on scales never witnessed before. Onyechi, in her analysis of social media and youth participation in the 2015 general elections, offers an edifying description:

> In recent years, social media are said to have an impact on the public discourse and communication in the society. In particular, social media are increasingly used in political contexts. More recently, microblogging services (e.g., Twitter) and social network sites (e.g., Facebook) are believed to have the potential for increasing political participation. While Twitter is an ideal platform for users to spread not only information in general but also political opinions publicly through their networks, political institutions (e.g., politicians, political parties, political foundations, etc.) have also begun to use Facebook pages or groups for the purpose of entering into direct dialogs with citizens and encouraging more political discussions.[38]

With its large user base, social media has transformed into a *de facto* court of public opinion where political grievances are aired and debated, with an accused's personal

---

37. Usman Jimada, "Social Media in the Public Sphere of Accountability in Nigeria," *Global Media Journal* 17, no. 32 (2019): 178.

38. Ngozi J. Onyiyechi, "Taking their Destiny into their Hands: Social Media, Youth Participation and the 2015 Political Campaigns in Nigeria," *African Journalism Studies* 39, no. 1 (2018): 69–89.

and political image as collateral. This has led to dishonest politicians using social media as a tool in smear campaigns to influence elections. Furthermore, the growing recognition of social media as an effective tool for political indoctrination has shifted a bulk of politicking activities to online media platforms,[39] especially targeting the literate class that can access the facilities.

Social Demands, Accountability and Transparency

The government has been compelled to investigate when allegations have been brought against public officeholders, especially where video evidence is provided to support such claims. However, some—if not most—of such government action has been disregarded as the government of the day worries more about its international image given the international dimension that social media gives such developments. In other instances, depending on how sensitive the allegation is perceived to be, sources may be threatened, harmed, or harassed. Jimada recounts one such occasion where the accused, a top government (military) official, deemed it necessary to "take action":

> In Nigeria, two Premium Times journalists were arrested by the Nigerian Police following their reports of corruption allegations against the Nigerian Chief of Army Staff. General Tukur Buratai. Security officials sent plain clothed officers to arrest the publisher Dapo Olorunyomi and one of its correspondents that covers the judiciary, Evelyn Okakwu. This raid by the police had Amnesty International to condemn the action. While, CPI had called on the Nigerian authorities to drop charges against the journalist and desist from further attempts to intimidate the media. Lawyers of the Nigerian Chief of Army Staff had filled charges against the social media and the arrest of the journalists came a few weeks after the publication of the websites.[40]

There are many cases of extrajudicial actions taken by "powerful" government officials against their accusers, including instances where vocal social media critics have disappeared. A case in point here is Abubakar Idris Dadiyata, a Katsina State University lecturer and fierce critic of Kano State Governor Umar Ganduje, who was kidnapped at his home in Barnawa on 1 August 2019.[41] He has not been found at the time of writing in August 2022. Others, like Omoyele Sowore of Sahara Reporters, arrested in 2016 and 2019; Tonye Okio, former aid to the Governor of Bayelsa State, spent eighty-six days in prison without trial for comments he made on Facebook; and Ba-

---

39. Chinwe E. Ugochukwu and Uche P. Ekwugha, "New Media and Youth's Online Civic Engagement in Nigerian Politics: Potentials and Challenges," *European Scientific Journal* 10, no. 19 (2014): 204.

40. Jimada, "Social Media in the Public Sphere," 7.

41. Samuel Ogundipe, "Police Begin Search for Kidnapped Ganduje Critic Dadiyata," *Premium Times*, August 3, 2019, https://www.premiumtimesng.com/news/top-news/344614-police-begin-search-for-kidnapped-ganduje-critic-dadiyata.html.

ture, arrested in 2017 by the Masari Government of Katsina State over allegations he made online against the governor, accusing him of indebting the state with unnecessary loans.[42]

There also have been some instances of positive responses to demands for accountability by the government. The government has established both personal and official social media 'handles' for the timely disclosure of governance activities to keep the people informed and check the spread of misleading narratives. In yet another attempt to ensure transparency in governance activity,

> the Nigerian Vice-President on the 22nd September 2017, launched the public—private partnership Web Portal. The web portal which was built with the aid of the World Bank is to ensure public accountability and open access to good governance. All information about government and private sector partnership in the execution and awards of contracts will be in the public domain.[43]

However noble these attempts appear, the masses have not seemed to be able to overcome their distrust of government and the system enough to utilize these facilities, thereby rendering them dormant and the purpose defeated.

Government and the Instrument of Social Media

The reaction of the government toward social media has been fluctuating. Government entities have struggled between deploying it to serve their political agenda and trying to censor, muzzle or 'ban' it. In any case, a provision in the 1999 Constitution of the Federal Republic of Nigeria guarantees the rights of Nigerians to Freedom of Expression and the Press. Section 39 subsection (1) states: "Every person shall be entitled to freedom of expression including freedom to hold opinions and to receive and impart ideas and information without interference."[44]

There have been challenges in ensuring this freedom of expression guaranteed by the constitution concerning social media. However, inherent practices and usage have prompted the enactment of laws to guide its use with delineated penalties. Specifically, the National Assembly passed the Cyber Crime Act of 2015 in response to public concerns over using social media to promote hate and bigotry. Sections 24 and 26 of this Act prescribe fines and other penalties to individuals who:

> knowingly or intentionally sends a message other matter by means of computer systems or network that: is grossly offensive, pornographic or of an indecent, obscene or menacing character or causes any such message or matter to be so

42. Jimada, "Social Media in the Public Sphere."
43. Jimada, "Social Media in the Public Sphere," 6.
44. Federal Republic of Nigeria, *The Constitution of the Federal Republic of Nigeria*, Federal Government Press Lagos, 1999.

Figure 1.3. "Nigeria in the World of Social Media" by Michael Efionayi. A description of the interaction of Nigerians with social media platforms and contemporary conversations that arise with it.

> sent; or He knows to be false, for the purpose of causing annoyance, inconvenience danger, obstruction, insult, injury, criminal intimidation, enmity, hatred, ill will or needless anxiety to another or causes such a message to be sent: commits an offence under this Act and shall be liable on conviction to a fine of not more than N7, 000,000.00 or imprisonment for a term of not more than 3 years or to both such fine and imprisonment.[45]

These provisions are welcome given some disturbing usage of these tools (e.g., Boko Haram, ISIL beheading footages, cybercrime, etc.). Other attempts to subvert internet use and stifle social media through ill-conceived "copied" social media bills have been met with stiff resistance. The most recent attempt attached a $10,000 fine with a two-year jail sentence to anyone posting "abusive statements." This incident points to the recurring attempts by several Nigerian governments to clamp down on mediums that threaten the information hegemony of the government.

SOCIAL INTERACTIONS

Engaging with social media is the norm in Nigeria across all demographics—the rich, poor, educated, illiterate, old, young, Christians, Muslims, and African religion practitioners. The number of people with internet access in Nigeria as of January 2020

45. Jimada, "Social Media in the Public Sphere," 3.

was 85.4 million, having increased by 2.6 percent (2.2million) from the previous year.[46] Social media users in Nigeria in January 2020 totaled 27 million, a 14 percent (3.4million) increase from 2019. Other demographical data places the male-female ratio at fifty-one (51) percent to forty-nine (49), youths: 18–35 years at forty-nine (49) percent and those at 60 plus years at six (6) percent.[47]

As a medium of social exchange, social media has transformed the way members of society interact. In analyzing social media's "social" expressions, key aspects of socialization like education/indoctrination, cultural exchange, local and international fraternization, and entertainment are examined in the following sections to determine how these programs have influenced/changed Nigerian social habits.

Education/Indoctrination

Attendance is key in information dissemination. The large patronage of social media has made it a choice medium for people who determinedly aim to communicate ideas and messages to an extensive and varied population. Hence social media has been usurped by various groups for reasons that range from noble to unethical and outrightly nefarious. This analysis has classified social media propagation as productive and destructive. Many parents are worried about what they see as the negative impact of social media on their children. Acknowledging that social media as a very efficient means of social interaction has come to stay, certain measures must be put in place to reduce its negative implications. It is key to understand that social media is almost like every other tool available, dangerous in inexperienced hands and the choice of usage.[48]

---

46. Simon Kemp, "Digital 2020: Nigeria," *data reportal*, February 18, 2020, https://datareportal.com/reports/digital-2020-Nigeria.

47. NOI Polls, "Social Media Polls Reports," *NOI Polls*, November 2019, 7, www.noi-polls.com.

48. There are many campaigns in church and educational institutions warning young men and women as to the use of social media. Some of what they say is knowing that, here are a few recommendations to prevent its abuse:

- Parents and guardians must ensure that their wards adhere to age and time limits placed on social media usage.
- Parents should monitor their ward's social media usage to ensure they are not exposed to explicit content or are victims of cyberbullying.
- Parents and stakeholders should sensitize their wards (even through traditional mass media) on the dangers of using (wrongful) social media.
- Social media users must endeavor to frown at and call out people involved in cyberbullying, hate speech, and internet crime. As a matter of civic duty, they should report such cases to social media handlers through the avenues already provided.
- Outside social media, citizens should strive to promote the right values and instill them in the hope that wherever and whenever untoward displays are observed, they will be collectively frowned upon; these practices should then overflow into social media to curb the effects of these behaviors.

Productive Interactions

This category includes academic/educational, vocational, professional, and other creative/talented individuals who use social media to teach, inform, and empower their audiences. For these purposes, websites and videos are created on various topics—creative writing, cooking, health, economy, and faith-based messages—offering tips and other services to their subscribers/adherents. Regarding academics, apps like Zoom, Google Meet, YouTube, and Facebook, are used for educational conferences, seminars and class lectures. These facilities have been especially useful during the COVID-19 pandemic as they were used extensively by several private Universities in Nigeria.

Destructive Interactions

This covers the negative use of social media to promote anti-social behavior. Apart from governments overtly pushing ideas to influence social behavior,[49] terrorist cells and other radicalized groups deploy persuasive narratives to lure, indoctrinate, and recruit young and malleable users. Some of these sites' privacy and liberal policies allow them to be used for propaganda purposes. In Nigeria, for example, Boko Haram is a regular feature on YouTube; such terrorist groups have been known to recruit Nigerians successfully via social media.

Cultural Exchanges

Social media represents a very active and effective tool for cultural exchange. Generic terms such as "trend" and "influencer" are direct symbols of this capability. Regarding social media, trends are topics generating the most conversations, which are highlighted visually to call attention to them. These "trends" might be related to the latest political issues, though they often refer to cultural practices, observed holidays, carnivals, and other social rituals. 'Influencers' may often set these trends or promote them by pushing ideas around fashion, food/cuisine, alcohol, music, etc., thereby transferring particular social behaviors.

Another area of social media cultural transfusion is language. Until recently, English was the common language used on social media, despite linguistic provisions, particularly in a multi-lingual entity with a British colonial antecedent such as Nigeria. This is mostly because, as English speakers who share other (inherited) cultural similarities with the West, given our colonial heritage, Nigerians tend to interact more with English-speaking cultures on social media. This trend is believed to further uphold/promote the English language above other Nigerian languages, especially as "recent reports indicate that Nigeria's new generation, especially the youths, are lacking in indigenous language while fluently speaking [the] English language. So, the

49. Noam Chomsky, *Media Control: The Spectacular Achievements of Propaganda* (United States: Seven Stories Press, 1991).

English language is an appropriate medium for this class, and thus Nigerian youth seem to blend well with American/European culture and lifestyle."[50] Similarly, Nigerian social media users are exposed to other aspects of Western culture, cuisine, dress, fashion, and sexuality.

These cultural exchanges admittedly go both ways. However, technologically advanced and economically developed countries often assume superiority; their apparent socio-economic "success" serves as the basis for their role model status. Hence the emphasis is on the unbalanced nature of the said cultural exchange, as Madu and Mogoluwa point out:

> the merging cultures are usually of different degrees of synthesis and therefore, they are concerned, to different extents, by the deletion of cultural elements caused by the transfer of elements from the respective other culture. One culture loses more of its own elements than it receives others. The inferior has nothing to oppose the superior, and consequently in the course of synthesis, their inventory of cultural elements with its respective information is deleted more or less completely and replaced by the externally induced equivalences. Cultural dominance that one culture exerts over another is a function of the relation of both overall efficiencies, in the sense that a flood of cultural elements pours from the dominant culture on the dominated.[51]

Socializing /Fraternization

Through social media, Nigerians have connected and developed friendships with people in faraway places and locally. There are also increasing marriages and job opportunities arising from social media meetings. Social media's anonymous and distanced nature has also allowed users to improve their social skills.

Entertainment

Equipped with multimedia facilities and pay-per-view opportunities, social media has transformed into a hub of entertainment. Although other social media platforms like Facebook, Instagram, and WhatsApp are equipped with multimedia capabilities, YouTube, Snapchat, Netflix, and TikTok are a few dedicated to video content. Hence there is a growing trend of social media users in Nigeria seeking entertainment from the variety of content available on these apps.

50. Robert Madu and Shedrack C. Moguluwa, "Will the Social Media Lenses be the Framework for Sustainable Development in Rural Nigeria?" *Journal of African Studies* 5, no. 2 (2013): 240.

51. Madu and Moguluwa, "Will the Social Media Lenses be the Framework."

CONTEMPORARY NIGERIA AND SOCIAL MEDIA

Social media is a characteristic of contemporary society, and the nation has blended it with its paraphernalia.[52] The injection of social media into contemporary Nigeria is evident in all sectors of society and, as such, becomes relevant in academic and common discussions. One of social media's most important evidential impacts is the dynamics it introduces to information and knowledge dissemination.[53] Society has been growing more curious after much exposure to new ideologies and inventions and, as such, is in constant need of information and engagement. Information is the currency of modern Nigeria, and it has become a factor that defines the people.

Social media has remained relevant because it provides access to real-time information that cuts across the nation much faster than traditional media.[54] This factor has become the basis of both the advantages and disadvantages of social media and the structures around which many societal developments are discussed. In modern Nigerian society, activism, new ideologies, social and personal orientations, political discussions, and intellectual engagements have all gained dynamics on social media.[55] These dynamics are strengthened by the access to real-time information and how much it provides cognitive elaboration and collaboration. Cognitive elaboration is the string that ties up the participation of people in the information process and how they affect the above subjects.[56]

However, the problem with the role of social media and information is the question of credibility.[57] The same way it explains the development of the above subjects is the same way it could incite or be the basis of the above subjects, the consequences of which may not be favorable. That it can either propel the tendencies of the above subjects or misrepresent their intentions has raised the question of whether Nigeria has fared well with social media usage.

The contemporary problems in Nigeria have not gotten spectacularly better due to the emergence of social media, but there has been a swinging pendulum between how it has improved or made worse the contemporary situations of the people. One major problem affecting contemporary Nigeria is the constant security challenges that rock

---

52. Christian Fuchs, *Social Media: A Critical Introduction* (California: Sage, 2021).

53. Muhammad Naeem Khan, Muhammad Azeem Ashraf, Donald Seinen, Kashif Ullah Khan and Rizwan Ahmed Laar, "Social Media for Knowledge Acquisition and Dissemination: The Impact of the COVID-19 Pandemic on Collaborative Learning Driven Social Media Adoption," *Frontiers in Psychology* 12 (2021): 1–13.

54. David Westerman, Patric R. Spence and Brandon Van Der Heide, "Social Media as Information Source: Recency of Updates and Credibility of Information," *Journal of Computer-mediated Communication* 19, no. 2 (2014): 171–183.

55. Abiola Fashina, *Politics in Nigeria and Social Media: The Importance for Elections & Good Governance* Book 2 (Washington: Amazon Digital Services LLC—Kdp, 2022).

56. Melvin Lawrence DeFleur and Sandra Ball-Rokeach, *Theories of Mass Communication* Vol. 5 (New York: Longman, 1989).

57. Westerman, Spence and Van Der Heide, "Social Media as Information Source."

the nation's boat.[58] There is a stretch of insecurity and insurgency from the North East, the East, and almost all parts of the country. The nation struggles with insurgency, banditry, kidnapping, terrorism, vandalism, and other unspeakable crimes.[59] The role of social media in all of these is twofold: it further increases the ease of carrying out some of these nebulous acts and provides access and ways to track and control them.[60]

Social media as a platform for social networking has been a viable way to increase the crime rate in the country.[61] Miscreants and those with ill intentions use social media platforms as avenues to propagate ideologies, coordinate their acts, and implement plans. They also communicate with the public and government on demands and other engagements through their dedicated and secured websites and servers. In the same way that social media has been globalizing norms across different places and cultures, it has also been globalizing terrorism, increasing cross-border cybercrimes and motivating local criminals who become susceptible to propaganda propelled by larger groups of terrorists.[62] This is similar to the growing sentiments around secessionist agitations that have become a time bomb that could blow the country without expectation.[63] Whether true, untrue, or distorted, propaganda and information have been spread or misrepresented to create a conviction about the government, society, and the nation's unity.

People construct society, and the accumulated social values are those bits summed up from the personal convictions of those people. And both personal and societal values influence themselves with time, as can be seen from gradual cultural migrations and diffusion.[64] Social media is one of the primary drivers of this cultural migration in contemporary Nigeria. It explains the importation of several values and convictions capable of bringing about changes. These changes are capable of national transformation as well as change in national identity.[65] The question then becomes

58. Leon Usigbe, "Present Insecurity Nigeria's Greatest Threat Since Civil War—FG," *Nigerian Tribune*, September 6, 2022.

59. Bashiru Liman, *The Crisis of Insecurity in Nigeria* (Abuja: Caltop Publications (Nigeria) Limited, 2021).

60. Joshua Ebere Chukwuere and Chijioke Francis Onyebukwa, "The Impacts of Social Media on National Security: A View from the Northern and South-Eastern Region of Nigeria," *International Review of Management and Marketing* 8, no. 5 (2018): 50.

61. Simplice Asongu, Jacinta C. Nwachukwu, Stella-Maris I. Orim and Chris Pyke, "Crime and Social Media," AGDI Working Paper, No. WP/19/003, African Governance and Development Institute (AGDI), Yaoundé, 2019.

62. I. Nsudu and E.C. Onwe, "Social Media and Security Challenges in Nigeria: The Way Forward," *World Applied Sciences Journal* 35, no. 6 (2017): 993–999.

63. Chukwuere and Onyebukwa, "The Impacts of Social Media on National Security."

64. Olusegun Folorunso, Rebecca O. Vincent, Adebayo Felix Adekoya and Adewale Opeoluwa Ogunde, "Diffusion of Innovation in Social Networking Sites among University Students," *International Journal of Computer Science and security* 4, no. 3 (2010): 361–372.

65. Okafor Godson Okwuchukwu, Emmanuel Ngozi and Uzuegbunam Chikezie Emmanuel, "The Media and Challenges of National Identity in Nigeria," *American Journal of Social Sciences* 2, no. 3 (2014): 49–55.

whether there will be Nigerianism among Nigerians at the extreme of these changes, whether there will be a hybrid national identity or whether the consequences of neo-colonialism will mystify the nation if one can refer to it as one. Whichever way, it is certain that social media changes society and people, and its flexibility may not make it easy to control.

Another way Nigeria has gotten immersed in the paraphernalia of social media dynamics is through the new variables and changes it brings to political concepts in contemporary Nigeria. Undoubtedly, social media has brought about positive development in the country's politics. One much-discussed influence is its role in political participation and demands for accountability.[66] Political opinions, criticisms, and the demand for good governance have preoccupied the Nigerian social media spaces.[67] More protests and demonstrations exist to lay demands before the government and ask for social change.[68] It has been an avenue for political consciousness and sensitization across the country, and the government, politicians, and individuals are using these opportunities.

The 2012 Occupy Nigeria demonstrations and protests emerged from increasing political sensitization, part of which has been traced to social media engagements.[69] One way it has influenced this is the real-time access to information, especially about the Occupy Wall Street Protests and other movements worldwide that inspired Occupy Nigeria.[70] It became easier to mobilize citizens and get demands across to the government. The EndSARS protest of 2020 is another result of political and social media sensitization and mobilization.[71] In addition, toward the 2023 elections, there were notable social media movements toward electoral sensitization, political awareness, and electoral process intimation.[72] This was a similar development during the

66. Usman Jimada, "Social Media in the Public Sphere of Accountability in Nigeria," *Global Media Journal* 17, no. 32 (2019): 1–9.

67. Nnanyelugo Okoro and Kenneth Adibe Nwafor, "Social Media and Political Participation in Nigeria during the 2011 General Elections: The Lapses and the Lessons," *Global Journal of Arts Humanities and Social Sciences* 1, no. 3 (2013): 29–46.

68. Oluwafunminiyi Raheem and Mosunmola Adeojo, "'Not Your Colour, Not Your Size, Not Your Spec': Marching against Market Harassment and Molestation in Nigeria." In *African Women in Digital Spaces: Redefining Social Movements on the Continent and in the Diaspora*, eds. Msia Kibona and Wunpini Mohammed (Dar es Salaam: Mkuki na Nyota Publishers, 2022).

69. Temple Uwalaka and Jerry Watkins, "Social Media as the Fifth Estate in Nigeria: An Analysis of the 2012 Occupy Nigeria Protest," *African Journalism Studies* 39, no. 4 (2018): 22–41.

70. Uwalaka and Watkins, "Social Media as the Fifth Estate in Nigeria."

71. Oluwadara Abimbade, Philip Olayoku and Danielle Herro, "Millennial Activism within Nigerian Twitterscape: From Mobilization to Social Action of #ENDSARS Protest," *Social Sciences & Humanities Open* 6, no. 1 (2022): 1–9.

72. Fredrick Friday John, "Tweet and Talk: Stance of Twitter Discussants on the Candidacy of Presidential Candidates that Declared for the 2023 Election," *African Journal for the Psychological Studies of Social Issues* 25, no. 2 (2022): 42–57.

Figure 1.4. "Learning from the Sage" by Dr. Kazeem Ekeolu. Informal learning from a Nigerian elder, showing the traditional Nigerian distribution of knowledge. Will social media kill traditional ways of knowing?

2015 and 2019 elections in Nigeria.[73] Politicians and individuals have taken advantage of this and taken political campaigns and contests to social media platforms.

In the subsequent chapters, many of these contemporary subjects will be thoroughly discussed in light of the new dynamics of social media in Nigeria. Seeing the influence, vulnerability, and flexibility of social media platforms, one must ask if social media has a definitive impact on the above subjects and contemporary Nigeria and whether other considerable societal factors would override these dynamics.[74]

EMERGING REACTIONS

Social media in Nigeria has done a lot to ease communication, breaking down the barriers of time, distance, and to some extent, economic costs. With smart mobile phones, Nigerians can keep abreast with local and international occurrences at a minute's notice; keep in constant touch with friends and relatives; carry out transactions

73. Oladapo Oyebode and Rita Orji. "Social Media and Sentiment Analysis: the Nigeria Presidential Election 2019," 2019 IEEE 10th Annual Information Technology, Electronics and Mobile Communication Conference (IEMCON), 2019, 0140-0146.

74. Zizi Papacharissi, "The Virtual Sphere: The Internet as a Public Sphere," *New Media and Society* 4, no. 1 (2002): 9–27.

anywhere, anytime, and gather and disseminate information to thousands of people. On the other hand, amidst all these sociological benefits, social media is believed to have contributed to moral degeneration among Nigerian youths.[75]

In the study of social media user/audience behavior, the proposition is that it is driven by gratification needs the user seeks to fulfill. This reasoning aligns with the idea that "the media does not do things to people: rather, people do things with the media."[76] The more the new media presents the masses with viewing choices, the more motivation and gratification become important components of user analysis. And if gratification informs motivation, what types of gratification are derived from new media? Study findings suggest that gratification is derived from escape, diversion, instrumentality, reassurance, companionship, sociability, and arousal.[77]

The observations among social media users in Nigeria include the limited capacity to self-regulate its usage, increased vulnerability to peer pressure, attempts to measure up to social media peddled lifestyles and offline behaviors like clique formation and sexual experimentation. There also is an observed need by users to be the first to report events/incidences. This has resulted in scenarios where users rush to take photos or make videos of victims instead of attempting rescue; this trend perpetuates insensitivity among predominantly youthful users.

In addition to socializing, advantages of social media for communication include enhancing learning opportunities as students in both secondary schools and tertiary institutions are known to exchange ideas and work materials, engage other students from different educational backgrounds, jointly carry out assigned tasks, and glean educative information from online academic blogs. Social media has also enhanced work performance by providing speed and efficiency. Through connectivity and task-performing sites like LinkedIn, DoMyStuff, and Companyloop, critical information can be found, and information and documents can be safely exchanged.

Platforms also succeed at the communal level by allowing for increased civic engagement and economic opportunities. Social media serves as an instrument for social awareness, mobilization, and political participation. It creates a platform for people without voices to speak and be heard, fosters debates on nation-building, and helps in protesting political illegalities on international stages without bureaucratic encumbrances and at little cost. It is also an excellent avenue for keeping watch on the activities of public officeholders through the instrument of citizen journalism. Within the economic sphere, social media is a known avenue for earning, employer of labor, and contributor to national income, with social media countries of origin raking

75. Nkechi G. Onah and Nche G. Christian, "The Moral Implication of Social Media Phenomenon in Nigeria," *Mediterranean Journal of Sciences* 5, no. 20 (2014): 22–31.

76. E. Akani Olasinde, "An Analysis of the Influence of Social Media Sites on Nigerian Undergraduates," *International Policy Brief Series—Education & Science Journal* 4, no. 1 (2014): 53–65.

77. Olasinde, "An Analysis of the Influence."

in billions of dollars in revenue each year. It also provides efficient advertising opportunities for small capital ventures, helping them generate awareness and maximize capital and profit margins.

Countering these benefits, social media has the potential to be used as a weapon against individuals, interest groups, corporations, and governments. One of the most common disadvantages of increased internet usage is the vulnerability to cybercrime. Cybercrime mostly takes the form of people with computer expertise successfully breaking into otherwise secure online media or bank accounts and sometimes impersonating others to extort unsuspecting friends and family. With social media, the incidence of cyber impersonation and duping in Nigeria has increased. Even if social media is not the root cause of criminality in Nigeria, it has exacerbated it by providing an avenue for such criminals to meet their unsuspecting victims.

The internet has also impacted human nature by affecting people's patience and immediacy demands. Studies have shown that the evolution of the computer and the internet's attendant automation, speed, and prompt operation has influenced human patience. The phenomenon of social media has expanded this effect. The feeling of getting tasks that would traditionally take days and weeks to complete done in a couple of seconds or minutes has disturbed the value of patience. Specifically, this can be observed in the get-rich-quick syndrome. Economic opportunity and widespread internet access have also influenced the abundance of sexually-driven content people are exposed to online. Growing cases of sexual promiscuity are believed to be driven by certain "immoral" social media practices. In attempts to earn via social media, some social media handles and rooms thrive on displaying and exchanging obscene materials. Some platforms have even been converted into meeting places for (sexual) solicitation. While this aspect impacts interpersonal relations, these practices influence the understanding of online etiquette. Cyberbullying due to overexposure on the internet is not uncommon; it is often driven by the information posted online and/or the fast, cheap, and easy publicity available on the platform. This is a common risk among young (teenage) social media users who have been known to physically harm themselves because they are falsely accused on social media. Cyberbullying can also take the form of the threat of physical harm over spats on social media. The effects of such cyberbullying can also be psychological, resulting in anxiety, isolation, depression and even suicide.

Few developments have had the impact that mass media has on social organization, cohesion, and civic engagement, and none has had the level of impact that social media has brought to human interaction. Looking back on the history of Nigeria, we can nod our heads in appreciation of the contributions of traditional media to our existence as a country, especially at the valiance of those who have sacrificed. Now we are presented with another opportunity with social media to change ailing issues economically, politically, and culturally.

Society is constantly evolving, and new and better tools for social interaction are emerging. It is in the best interest of Nigerians to do all they can to take advantage of such life-advancing innovations or, better yet, be part of the creation process. In any case, the opportunities inherent in social media are numerous. The leadership might be correct in establishing and enforcing certain guidelines for social media usage, but it must abandon every attempt to stifle or muzzle this profitable medium. Instead, efforts should be directed at sensitization, education, and providing a conducive environment for young and creative minds to strive for excellence, especially in such a lucrative field as social media. And the first way to ensure this becomes a reality is to provide extensive, efficient, and affordable internet service to all members of society.

2

STATE REGULATIONS AND SOCIAL MEDIA

INTRODUCTION

Social media has reshaped the mechanics through which emerging democracies, particularly the Nigerian state, function. With the advent of the internet and various worldwide connectivity technologies, African countries saw an opportunity to partake in the next evolution of societies, which promises economic, social, and political incentives to both the ruling class and the citizens. However, it is imperative to point out early on that the nature of the Nigerian political structure makes it uniquely poised to have experiences that greatly contrast those of its Western counterparts.[1] This assertion is most evident in that since its inception in 1960, the Nigerian state has undergone four attempts at democratic governance, each cut abruptly by military regimes characterized by draconian laws and a disregard for civil liberties. Since the start of the fourth attempt at democratic rule, often called the Fourth Republic (1999–present), the Nigerian people have experienced relative freedom of speech and expression, enshrined in the 1999 Constitution.[2] However, despite the change from military to civilian rule, the country's po-

1. Taye Babaleye, P. Ibitoye and Akpobo Emokiniovo Odorume, "Influence of Social Media on Democratic Governance in Nigeria," *International Journal of Media Journalism and Mass Communications* 69, no. 1 (2020): 13-20.

2. Joseph Wilson and Nuhu Gapsiso, "Social Media and the Freedom of Expression in Nigeria: Posting the Mind of a Nation." In *Perspectives on the Information Society*, edited by Jonathan Bishop (Wales: The Crocels Press Limited, 2019), 301.

litical ideology remains much under the influence of the old military-indoctrinated elite. More so, two military leaders during the military regimes had rebranded, contested, and won elections as presidents since the return to democratic rule.

It should be noted that, in some cases, the incursion of former military leaders into a democratic society is difficult to prevent. The issue here, in a bid to tame what would otherwise be regarded as naive optimism, is the problematic clash of ideologies inherited from a lifetime in military service with the new democratic principles of transparency, accountability, and civil liberty. Perhaps in this regard, the Nigerian state, led by the presidents mentioned above, has undergone quite different trajectories concerning an actionable framework for controlling social media activities.

Contrary to popular belief that social media came to Nigeria as a consequence of the Obasanjo administration's attempt to open the country to the rest of the world, research shows that the seed for social media was sown in 1996 when the Nigerian Communications Commission (NCC) gave licenses to 38 internet service providers to create telecommunications infrastructure throughout the country. Since then, various private companies (foreign and otherwise) have bet on the future of Nigerian internet usage.[3] During this period, social media as a sub-category of internet communications began. Online communities, forums, blogs and chat rooms were the new places for internet users to engage anonymously in trendy political and social issues. Facebook, YouTube and African-based social networking platforms such as 2go and Eskimo were the leading internet outlets for meeting people and sharing opinions.[4]

The government did not consider these platforms as hostile tools against political establishments. And this is evident in the kinds of policies enacted by the Obasanjo administration. The first detailed attempt to provide a legal framework for regulating internet usage in Nigeria came through the Nigeria Communications Commissions Act (NCA) of 2003,[5] which empowered the Nigerian Communications Commission (NCC) to create and regulate a legal framework for the emerging telecommunications industry. But at this stage, Nigeria's emerging telecommunications industry largely focused on communication infrastructure, processing systems and products, phone carrier services, frequency spectrum, numbers, electronic addresses, and internet service providers. The NCA 2003 was therefore signed into law by President Olusegun Obasanjo to cater to the evolving state of the telecommunications industry in Nigeria with a particular focus on developing a government decision-making body to oversee the industry. The NCA 2003 was more focused on establishing a useful foundation upon which future attempts to build specific legal constraints on compa-

---

3. Isaac Echezonam Anyira, "Internet Services in Nigerian Private Universities: A Case Study," *Library Philosophy and Practice* 2 (2011): 1.

4. Elizabeth Ogunbamowojun, "Fact-Check: Is Adamu Garba's Crowwe First Social Networking Platform Built in Africa as Claimed?" *Sahara Reporters*, June 21, 2021, https://saharareporters.com/2021/06/21/fact-check-adamu-garbas-crowwe-first-social-networking-platform-built-africa-claimed.

5. Nigeria Communications Commissions Act 2003. CAP N97. L.F.N. 2004.

Figure 2.1. "The Nation in the Shackles of Social Media" by Michael Efionayi. Fake news, propaganda, over-dependency, loss of national identity and other disadvantages of social media have become chained to the nation's neck.

nies engaged in telecommunications agencies, together with how to deal with cases in which law enforcement requires details of a user during a criminal investigation.

SOCIAL MEDIA BILLS AND THEIR METAMORPHOSIS (2015–2021)

While the National Communications Commissions Act (2003) set a precedent for the government's early attempt to regulate the telecommunications industry, it was not the only bill enacted before 2015. Two Acts of the National Assembly specifically targeted internet users and what they could or could not do within the confines of the law. These are the Terrorism Prevention (Amendment) Act in 2013 and the Nigeria Cybercrime Act of 2015. In 2013, the NCC also released the Mobile Number Portability Regulation, which stated how telecommunications companies could be forced to give up details about Nigerian citizens when requested or face the potential withdrawal of their license from the Commission.

It is imperative to emphasize that the activities Nigerian citizens undertake on social media reflect the internet populace's general mood. This suggests that various social groups use the internet to reinforce their values and help expedite information gathering and management processes. Consequently, as was evident in the early 2000s, terrorism, criminal offenses, and other economic and social ills on the rise

quickly employed the internet and social media to ensure the efficiency of such bad practices. To mitigate these social ills, the Nigerian government revised the 2011 terrorism bill into the Terrorism Prevention (Amendment) Act 2013 Section 5, Subsection 2(a), which, for the first time, emphasizes internet-enabled acts of terror when it included "incitement to commit a terrorist act through the internet, or any electronic means. . .through the dissemination of terrorist information" as offenses punishable under the law. Coincidentally, the same period also saw the rise of cybercrime globally, with Nigerians becoming infamous on the global scene as major perpetrators of these criminal activities. To curtail the use of social media (such as spamming and phishing) to commit internet fraud, the Goodluck Jonathan administration introduced the Nigeria Cybercrime Act 2015. The Cybercrime Act continued the general attitude of social media and the internet as a public service that needs minimal government interference, and as such, the 2015 Act focuses only on potential cases of financial fraud carried out electronically. The Act was lauded for including socially relevant issues like child pornography, racist and xenophobic offenses, identity theft and cyber-stalking as punishable under the law.

FRIVOLOUS PETITIONS (PROHIBITION) BILL 2015

In December 2015, Bala Ibn Na'Allah, a Senator representing Kebbi South Senatorial District and Deputy Majority leader of the Nigerian 8th Senate, presented on the floor of the House a bill titled "An Act to Prohibit Frivolous Petitions, and other Matters Connected therewith" which has since being dubbed the "Frivolous Petitions (Prohibitions Etc) Bill.[6] The Frivolous Bill was the first of a series of proposed bills geared at controlling the influence of social media in Nigeria's democratic practices and society; these bills are collectively known as anti-social media bills. Frivolous Petition (Prohibition) Bill's content agitated media houses, reporters, social commenters, and internet users, which led to calls from various quarters to abandon the proposed bill. Notable among critics of this bill was the Nigerian Guild of Editors (NGE), which called any attempt to pass such a bill indistinguishable from "outlaw[ing] the freedom of expression of all Nigerian citizens and freedom of speech of all media organizations operating in print, electronic and online platforms in Nigeria and beyond." Against his critics, Senator Bala Ibn Na'Allah believed the need for such a bill would help curb the rising trend of political "blackmailers and intimidators on social media,"[7] which are usually employed, Na'Allah believes, by opposition parties and candidates to spoil the goodwill of an elected official.

6. Oladapo Adekunle Oyewole and Babatunde Raphael Ojebuyi, "Nature and Outcome of Nigeria's #NoToSocialMediaBill Twitter Protest against the Frivolous Petitions Bill 2015." In *Impacts of the Media on African Socio-Economic Development*, edited by Nelson Okorie, Babatunde Raphael Ojebuyi, Abiodun Salawu (USA: IGI Global, 2017), 106-124.

7. Henry Umoru and Joseph Erunke, "NGE Asks Senate to Suspend Frivolous Petitions Bill," *Vanguard Newspaper*, December 7, 2015.

Public outcry against the bill's content is perhaps due to draconian tendencies contained in Sections 1, 2, 3, 4 and 37 of the proposed bill. For instance, Section 1 of the bill makes it illegal to submit any statement or petition electronically to investigate an alleged breach of law by any person without a written affidavit from a State or Federal High Court.[8] Section 2 takes it further by rendering any unsworn petition or public statements for criminal or civil persecution untenable. The bill's Section 3 laid down the intended punishment for people who violate Section 1 of its decree: first, a mandatory 6 months jail time was proposed for anyone that publishes any unsworn petition or statements. Section 3 of the law contained a series of punishments that challenged Freedom of Speech and Expression with punishments that included 2 years imprisonment or ₦200,000 and ₦4 million, based on the gravity of the offense.

Also, Section 4 of the Bill penalizes anyone "for posting knowingly false statements by text message, tweets, WhatsApp or through any social media with punishment to the tune of two million Naira and/or two years imprisonment." This section stated in clear terms that attempts to instigate the public against government institutions or persons are a punishable offense with a prison sentence. In reaction to its content, critics of the Frivolous Prohibition Bill argue against the proposed bill's usefulness and necessity. Legal experts and lawmakers maintain that there are already legal frameworks that protect, persecute, and monitor misuse of the internet, especially social media. Senator David Umaru, for instance, asserts that enacting the provisions of the bill into law would be equivalent to duplication of legal provisions of the country, stating that "some of our extant Acts, such as the Penal Code, the Criminal Code, the Cybercrime Act, etc., have sufficient provisions to address the issues that the Frivolous Petitions (Prohibition, etc.) Bill 2015 seeks to address."[9] Sen. Umaru also adjudged the Bill to contradict provisions of the 1999 Constitution, especially the right to freedom of speech and the protection of privacy as regards electronic communications. In all practical sense, enacting the Frivolous Prohibition Bill would jeopardize news reportage since anonymous news sources would be treated as criminals for sharing information to expose the actions of public figures, political leaders and institutions. News publishers are at risk of sanction and persecution, provided they publish reports based on intel from anonymous sources online. The Bill would also provide a pretext to persecute whistleblowers, as contained in Sections 1, 2 and 3 of the proposed bill. It is noteworthy that the proposed bill directly contradicts Section 37 of the 1999 Constitution, which ensures that the "privacy of citizens, their homes, correspondence, telephone conversations and telegraphic communications"[10] is protected and guaranteed.

8. Oyewole and Ojebuyi, "Nature and Outcome."

9. B.A. Omodunbi, P. O. Odiase, O. M. Olaniyan and A.O. Esan, "Cybercrimes in Nigeria: Analysis, Detection and Prevention," *FUOYE Journal of Engineering and Technology* 1, no. 1 (2016): 37-42.

10. Constitution of the Federal Republic of Nigeria 1999, CAP C23, L.F.N 2004.

DIGITAL RIGHTS AND FREEDOM BILL OF 2019

The Digital Rights and Freedom Bill (officially titled: *HB 490: Digital Rights and Freedom Bill, 2016*) was originally sponsored by Hon. Chukwuemeka Ujam, representing Nkanu East/West Federal Constituency of Enugu State. It was presented to the House on April 20, 2016, and had its second reading two months later, on June 22, 2016.[11] The Bill enjoyed widespread support from media practitioners, internet users and international observers, culminating in its adoption by both Houses of the National Assembly. However, President Muhammadu Buhari refused to sign the Bill into law on March 21, 2019, almost three years after its introduction, citing that it "covers too many technical subjects and fails to address any of them extensively."[12] In a letter to the Senate President, the President maintained that some of the issues raised by the Bill deserved unambiguous clarity of terms and scope, some of which included surveillance, digital privacy and protection, and lawful interception of user data and electronic communications.[13] Despite this setback, a revised version, known officially as *HB 98: Digital Rights and Freedom Bill, 2019,* was sponsored by another member of the House of Representatives, Honorable Mohammed Tahir Monguno representing Marte-Monguno-Nganzai Federal Constituency of Borno State, on July 16, 2019. According to Hon. Monguno, the Bill has become necessary to ensure the "protection of human rights online… from infringement of citizens' fundamental freedoms."[14] The Bill passed its second reading and was handed over to the telecommunication and human rights oversight committees.

Unlike the Frivolous Prohibition Bill, which sought to control and regulate free speech on social media, the Digital Rights and Freedom Bill gave positive indicators that its content aims to protect citizens' freedom of speech. More ambitiously, the Bill under review was set up to serve as an extension of laws already protected by the Nigerian Constitution. When analyzed, digital rights activists and policymakers hold that the Bill's provisions would allow Nigeria to join the ranks of countries with a robust, forward-thinking legal framework that protects citizens' privacy and data from criminally-minded individuals, corporations, and also from government interference. Rightly so, the Bill emphasizes surveillance and electronic communication interception. It backs statutory confidentiality and recognizes digital assets and users' rights to protect such; sections of the Bill also focus on protecting victims' rights and advocating for the right to e-learning and Information Communication Technology

---

11. Kinfe Micheal Yilma, "Digital Privacy and Virtues of Multilateral Digital Constitutionalism—Preliminary Thoughts," *International Journal of Law and Information Technology* 25, no. 2 (2017): 115-138.

12. Jonathan Odumeru, "Freedom of Misinformation: Balancing Fundamental Freedoms whilst Curbing Misinformation in Nigeria," *The Public Sphere: Journal of Public Policy* 10, no. 1 (2022): 89-108.

13. Adeboye Adegoke, *Digital Rights and Privacy in Nigeria* (Abuja: Paradigm Initiative, 2020).

14. *The Digital Rights and Freedom Bill, 2019*. National Assembly Archive.

(ICT) education.[15] As regards its legal significance, the proposed Bill echoes the freedom of expression and right to privacy contained in both Section 37 and Section 39(1) of the 1999 Constitution, which maintained that "every person shall be entitled to freedom of expression, including the freedom to hold opinions and to receive and impart ideas and information without interference."[16] Coincidentally, this negates the proposed control of user data and electronic communication contained in the previously rejected Frivolous Petition (Prohibition) Bill. One of the strengths of the *HB 98* Bill is that, unlike the Frivolous Petition, it recognizes that all electronic communications cannot be treated the same way. Tweets and Facebook posts, for example, are meant to serve as public means of disseminating information, whereas WhatsApp communications and other end-to-end types of communication are regarded as private; hence, these two forms of communication are equally articulated and protected by the proposed Bill.

It is worthy of note that before the introduction of the Digital Rights Bill, the Cybercrime Act 2015 had been distorted in such a way that allowed private citizens and journalists to get detained and charged to court for violating the law.[17] A popular example of this was the unlawful arrest of a bank official for posting critical opinions about Governor Udom Gabriel Emmanuel of Akwa Ibom State on Facebook. In 2014, his predecessor, former Governor Godswill Akpabio, also arrested an editor of a newspaper for publishing articles that criticized his administration. Obinna D. Norman, founder and editor of Realm News, an online publication, was also arrested in March 2019 using the provision of the Cybercrime Act. In most of these scenarios, Section 24(1) of the Cybercrime Act criminalizes actions involving "any person who knowingly or intentionally sends a message or other matter by means of a computer system or network that is grossly offensive, pornographic or of an indecent, obscene or menacing character or causes any such message or matter to be so sent," has been interpreted and applied to cover cases of the aforementioned individual cases.

The Digital Rights and Freedom Bill protects and defines a legal framework for collecting citizens' data and private communication to remedy this constitutional conundrum. Contained in Section 2(8), the Bill proposes that "requests for private data shall follow legally stipulated procedures and court warrants shall be necessary in order for an intermediary to honor a request for private data, which request shall be reported to the concerned individual." To reinforce its stance on due diligence and legal procedures for data collection, Section 3(5) charges internet service providers to "strictly protect the privacy rights of owners against violations by third parties and by the service providers themselves or their agents whatsoever." Therefore, service providers, since they are required by various regulations of the Nigerian Communica-

---

15. Ridwan Oloyede and Douglas Onah, "A Comparative Analysis between the Digital Rights and Freedom Bill and other Legislation in Nigeria," *Paradigm Initiative Report*, December 2020.

16. Constitution of the Federal Republic of Nigeria 1999, CAP C23, L.F.N 2004.

17. Odumeru, "Freedom of Misinformation."

tions Commission to gather user information and ensure such information are available for third-party usage, the Digital Rights and Freedom Bill seeks to ensure such is adequately safeguarded by restricting access to citizens digital imprints and communications except by court order, and ensuring the citizen in question is made aware that relevant authorities have gathered her data and communications.

Although it fundamentally serves as a mechanism through which the human rights of Nigerians on the internet are protected, it does not deny the dichotomy between legal rights and responsibilities.[18] This is evident in Section 6(13 & 14) of the Bill, which demands responsibility from internet users that need their rights protected. In particular, it maintains that as much as the right to opinion, association and expression are protected, they must not contain "any speech, gesture or conduct, writing, display capable of inciting violence or prejudicial actions against or by a protected individual or groups" or any other actions that violates known civil or criminal laws of the Federal Republic.

PROTECTION FROM INTERNET FALSEHOODS AND MANIPULATIONS AND OTHER RELATED MATTERS BILL 2019

Another important Bill that needs to be studied in the context of the subject matter is SB 132: Protection from Internet Falsehoods and Manipulations and other Related Matters Bill. This Social Media Bill was sponsored by the Senator representing the Niger East Senatorial District at the 9th National Assembly, Mohammad Sani Musa.[19] According to Senator Musa, the need for a Social Media Bill specifically for online conduct came against the backdrop of a lack of legal structure that actively combats the spread, usage, and creation of fake news. The Senator opines that due to the lack of such legal structure, particular instances where social media has been used to spread falsehood, such as the alleged death of President Muhammadu Buhari and his replacement therefore with a "Jubril" from Sudan,[20] represent an extreme case of misinformation and the kind of fake news that must not be allowed to stand. Hence, his solution to this problem is the introduction of the Protection from Internet Falsehoods and Manipulations and other Related Matters Bill.[21] The proposed Bill is divided into six parts; the first part contains the aims and objectives of the Bill, which are "to prevent the transmission of false statements/declaration of facts in Nigeria and to

18. Adegoke, *Digital Rights and Privacy*.

19. Esther Iroanusi, "Updated: Bill to regulate Social Media Passes Second Reading at Senate," *Premium Times*, November 20, 2019, https://www.premiumtimesng.com/news/headlines/364236-just-in-bill-to-regulate-social-media-passes-second-reading-at-senate.html.

20. John Nwachukwu, "Jubril of Sudan: How Aisha, Yusuf Exposed 'Cloned Buhari'—Nnamdi Kanu," *Daily Post*, December 9, 2018, https://dailypost.ng/2018/12/09/2019-election-shehu-sani-reacts-freezing-peter-obis-accounts-efcc-okupes-home/.

21. Kelvein Inobemhe, "Social Media Regulation in a Democratic Nigeria: Challenges and Implication," *Media & Communication Currents* 5, no 1 (2022): 71-88.

enable measures to be taken to counter the effects of such transmission." The Bill also aims to suppress the economics of political blackmail conducted by individuals and corporate bodies operating fake social media accounts to conduct nefarious actions.

Part 2, which consists of Sections 3, 4 and 5, focuses on the "prohibition of transmission of false statements of fact." Section 5(5) of the Bill, for instance, seeks to use the argument of "burden of proof" to determine who should verify the truth or falsity of a statement shared on social media. According to 5(6), "the proof of evidence of falsehood might include that the defendant was reckless as to the truth or falsity of the statements when publishing them."[22] This suggests that while lies and fake news with intent to cause personal damage to an individual, institution, or corporate body are clear evidence of fake news for which the proposed Bill was made, cases in which statements were published without informed understanding and/or malicious intent to cause personal damages will also be treated as a breach of this Bill if passed into law.[23] Part 3 of the Bill defines regulations that shall deal with the transmission of false declaration of facts in Nigeria, clearly expressed from Section 6 through Section 15. This part of the Bill emphasizes the legal procedure through which those culpable of violating the provisions of this Bill shall be prosecuted. Section 6 (1) a-c maintains, for instance, that individuals would only be charged or arrested for spreading internet falsehood if the Court of Law orders relevant law enforcement agencies to do so, provided that an overwhelming body of evidence has been shown to the court in this effect and/or that a false declaration of facts that is of public interest is being disseminated.[24] This part also explained cited punishment of two hundred thousand Naira (₦200,000) and/or a maximum prison sentence of twelve months in the event of non-compliance from the defendant of a case wherein false statements of facts are produced.

Part 3 of the Bill expresses how regulations for internet intermediaries and providers of mass media services shall be adjudged. The part consists of ten sections that build on the regulation parameters by the proceeding part. It empowers aggrieved individuals to charge mass media outlets, internet service providers and telecommunication-system operators to the Court of Law in cases of provable social media and/or electronically sent a false statement, even in situations wherein such statements have been deleted and do not exist anymore in the public space as shown in Section 26(2) of the Bill.[25] Failure to comply with this can result in a three hundred thousand Naira (₦300,000) fine and/or twelve months in prison. Conversely, the next part of the Bill dictates the declaration of online locations of relevant parties in a case wherein social media falsehood has been alleged. By "declaration of location," this part de-

---

22. Protection from Internet Falsehoods and Manipulations and other Related Matters Bill 2019.

23. Tomiwa Ilori, "A Socio-legal Analysis of Nigeria's Protection from Internet Falsehoods, Manipulations and Other Related Matters Bill," *AfricLaw*, 2019, https://africlaw.com/2019/12/05/a-socio-legal-analysis-of-nigerias-protection-from-internet-falsehoods-manipulations-and-other-related-matters-bill/.

24. Ilori, "A Socio-legal Analysis," 8.

25. Joseph Onele, "Social Media Bill and Madness in the Hallowed Chambers: A Call for Sanity," *SSRN Electronic Journal* (2015): 1-10.

notes how an online source of information can be identified, verified, and linked to a legal entity. Hence, the Bill requires the submission of a Uniform Resource Locator (URL), domain name, and IP address, among other ways a digital profile can be established. Failure to comply with this is illegal under this Bill with up to 3 years imprisonment and/or a fine of five hundred thousand Naira (₦500,000) for individuals or up to N10 million for internet service providers and other corporate entities.[26]

Despite its good intention to curb the spread of fake news and falsehood on the internet, the Bill has been largely criticized as irrelevant, unconstitutional, pirated, and quite similar to the draconian spirit of the deposed Frivolous Prohibition (Prevention) Bill. Critics argue that the Bill is unnecessary because most of what is contained in it are already covered by extant laws in the Cybercrime Act and various provisions of the NCC.[27] It was also adjudged as irrelevant on the merit (or lack of) of its goal to execute social media regulation since most of the popular social media companies and outlets for internet communications are neither owned by Nigerians nor operate physically in the country.

HATE SPEECH (PROHIBITION) BILL 2019

Social media thrives on the provisions of freedom of expression by local and international legislations as a platform for social engagement and interaction. However, to all freedoms, there are other rights, either in the interests of other individuals or incidental to the performance of governmental functions, that always weigh whenever the issues of expression come to bare. Hate Speech is one of those exceptions to individual rights that are expressible on social media because they either offend public or private individuals. Generally, hate speech constitutes an expression through written, verbal or symbolic utterances that tend to insult people along political, religious, gender or racial divisions by derogatory implications of inferiority, hostility and de trop.[28] Although the intention of regulating freedom of speech and expression might be justifiably reasonable, the tendency of misapplication and prejudice have always been of concern to implementing legislation such as the Hate Speech Bill in Nigeria.

With the seeming conviction to restrict the right to freedom of expression from its clash with other rights, Senator Aliyu Sabi Abdullahi representing Niger State, introduced the Hate Speech Bill to the Senate in 2018. The bill has thrown the country into conversations on its justification, and it seems to create a caveat to the position of the Constitution, especially section 39, which expressly states that:

---

26. Internet Falsehoods and Manipulations Bill 2019. Section 26 (4).

27. Seun Durojaiye, "Social Media Bill Threatens Freedom of Expression in Nigeria —Amnesty International," *International Center for Investigative Reporting (ICIR)*, March 9, 2020, https://www.icirnigeria.org/social-media-bill-threatens-freedom-of-expression-in-nigeria-amnesty-international/.

28. António Guterres, *United Nations Strategy and Plan of Action on Hate Speech, Technical Report May*, 2019, 1-5.

a) Every person shall be entitled to freedom of expression, including freedom to hold opinions and to receive and impart ideas and information without interference.[29]

Seeing the broadness of the above position of the Constitution, many Bills and legislations have been enacted to control the expression of these rights and ensure that they do not affect the right of others.

The Bill was supposed to protect peaceful co-existence in Nigeria, looking at the diversity that is a particular feature of the country. Nigeria's ethnic groups and languages are not less than 250, with their respective established societies. Nigeria is also largely divided between Christianity, Islam, traditional religion and other religious minorities. However, society has been gradually affected by ethnic and religious conflicts that affect peaceful co-existence and tolerance. It was felt that if certain utterances and expressions are not contained and controlled, they might incite intolerance and hatred, which have a higher tendency to affect the security status of the State and infringe on people's lives.

Hence, the Bill was to dissuade people or groups of people from discrimination and discriminatory actions which are capable of affecting others. It ensured and promoted respect for diverse cultures, religions and political convictions by regulating what people say and building the consciousness to respect others. Hence, the prosecution of inciters and those that default the provisions of the Bill was believed by the sponsor to be an approach to protect minorities in the society who are likely to be bullied through other expressions. The Hate Speech Bill, also known as the National Commission for the Prohibition of Hate Speech Bill, aims to provide a commission to execute its functions.

The Bill provides that no expression, through publication, production, distribution, or other forms of expression and circulation, should incite hatred toward any ethnic group. Default in this respect would make the defaulter liable to being sentenced to life imprisonment, and where such default leads to the loss of life, he or she might be liable for a punitive measure of death by hanging. An act that leads to ethnic or racial harassment was punishable by 10 years imprisonment or a fine of 10 million Naira. Other related offenses of lesser magnitudes are provided to be punishable with not less than five years imprisonment. The Bill also empowers the proposed Commission to investigate, invite and receive complaints upon which the process of prosecution would be commenced.

Controversial reactions have hit the Bill since the inception of its promulgation processes. It has since been a subject of conversation among scholars, analysts, experts, and Nigerians, with different theories deployed in its examination. Research on

29. Section 39, *Constitution of the Federal Republic of Nigeria*, 1999.

the people's reaction posited that about 73.7% of respondents believed that the bill would be an affront to the people's freedom of expression, and 52.1% believed that the government tended to benefit more from the bill than it was intended to protect the citizens.[30] Other criticisms have been raised toward the tendencies of the Bill to be used with prejudice,[31] and its position against the Constitution and other laws has been the subject of discussion by legal experts.[32]

The Bill has been viewed to potentially threaten the practice of democracy in Nigeria. This is because freedom of expression and speech is fundamental to the tenets of democracy. With a Bill with too many subjective interpretations and discretions, democracy might be imprisoned and windows opened for dictatorship.[33] Amnesty International had also raised concerns about the tendencies of the speech to sabotage freedom of expression and urged the Nigerian government to drop its enactment process.[34] Hence, many believed that the bill tends to make sycophants more than it would influence society and that the punishment attributed to these offenses is not proportional to the intent of the Bill.[35]

Social media has been a platform for expression that allows more people to do so at their convenience.[36] Social media in Nigeria has been a source of uncensored statements, derogatory expressions and hate speech seeing how much freedom its dynamics have rendered.[37] Globally, the issue of hate speech has been of international concern touching on different areas of society. There have been reports that show

---

30. G.A. Esimokha, K.B. Bobmanuel and O. Asaolu, "Perception of Nigerians on Hate Speech Bill (A Study of Akungba-Okoko Residents, Ondo State)," *Journals of Humanities and Social Sciences* 24, no. 11 (2019): 59-67.

31. Joseph Onyekwere, "Hate Speech Bill is Unlawful, Illegal, Unconstitutional and Undemocratic," *The Guardian,* December 3, 2019.

32. Uzoka Ngozi Chisom, "Hate Speech and Freedom of Expression: Legal Boundaries in Nigeria," *Library Research Journal* 4, no. 1 (2019): 111-118.

33. E. Nwachukwu and N. Ihebuzor, "Online Ethnocentric Hate Speech and Nigerian Youth," In *New Media and African Society; Essays, Reviews and Research,* edited by Muiru Ngugi and Kate Omenugha (Nairobi: Nairobi Academic Press, 2020).

34. Amnesty International, "Nigeria: Bills on Hate Speech and Social Media are Dangerous Attacks on Freedom of Expression," *Amnesty International,* December 4, 2019, https://www.amnesty.org/en/latest/press-release/2019/12/nigeria-bills-on-hate-speech-and-social-media-are-dangerous-attacks-on-freedom-of-expression/.

35. Ebun-Olu Adegboruwa, "If Passed, Hate Speech Bill could Transform Nigeria into Haven for Sycophants: Adegboruwa," *The Punch,* November 20, 2019.

36. Victor Ojakorotu, Ebere Florence Nnanwube and Kelechi Johnmary Ani, "An Evaluation of the Concepts of Dangerous and Hate Speeches, and their Security Implications in the Social Media Era Nigeria," *Gender and Behaviour* 17, no. 1 (2019): 12417-12428.

37. Joseph Wilson and Rahila Jibrin, "Mitigating Hate Speech in Nigeria: The Possibilities of Artificial Intelligence," *Anàlisi* 61 (2019): 17-30. See also Nicholas Asogwa and Christian Ezeibe, "The State, Hate Speech Regulation and Sustainable Democracy in Africa: a Study of Nigeria and Kenya," *African Identities* (2020): 2-16.

individuals and institutions being victims of extreme abuse and harassment.[38] These complaints are valid, and taking necessary actions to put such a situation under control is reasonable and appropriate for any government. Hence, saying that the rationale behind the Bill is totally out of place might be an attempt to throw out the baby with the bath water.

The tentative implications of the Hate Speech Bill are bare to see. It could be agreed that social media users tend to make concerning posts out of emotions and impulses or posts that are laced with misunderstood grounds. The subjectivity of the Hate Speech Bill increases the probability of it being used as an instrument for witch-hunting and unfair prosecution. It is reasonable that unchecked discretion could attract abuse, and as a result, the arguments of the critics of the Bill, including those from social media, might not be unfounded. Hence, drawing the line around the severity of the punishments might be worth an endeavor. Would a death penalty or other proposed punishment not be too grave for the prescribed offenses? This is a more appropriate approach than any attempt to discredit or amend the positions of the Bill.

PRESS FREEDOM, SOCIAL MEDIA AND GLOBAL PERCEPTION OF NIGERIA

The world is in a constant state of struggle between democratic and authoritarian value systems. Sometimes these struggles are expressed in violent cases, as can be seen in the rise of domestic and international terrorism, like Boko Haram and Al Qaeda; general public unrest, like the January 6 Capitol Hill Riot and recent Hong Kong protests; the wave of coup d'etat in African countries; and wars within and between countries, like the Russian-Ukrainian war. Other times, these struggles are expressed in less violent ways, one of which is the state of press freedom, especially in the age of social media, where access to information and the opportunity to express opinions is unprecedented. Press freedom is, therefore, an important indicator of a country's commitment to abide by democratic values and principles irrespective of media criticism. According to Lucas Powe Jnr, a Professor of Law at the University of Texas at Austin and Supreme Court Historian for the United States, freedom of the press is "the fundamental principle of communication and expression through various media, including printed and electronic media... shall be considered a right to be exercised freely."[39] Similarly, another legal scholar maintains that press freedom is best understood as those elements shaped by socio-political realities of a people with the

---

38. Ursula Kristin Schmid, Anna Sophie Kümpel and Diana Rieger, "How Social Media Users Perceive Different Forms of Online Hate Speech: A Qualitative Multi-Method Study," *New Media & Society* 00, no. 0 (2022): 1-19.

39. Lucas Powe, *The Fourth Estate and the Constitution: Freedom of the Press in America* (California, University of California Press, 1992), 200.

view to benefit all (or the most possible) members of the society, irrespective of their socio-political class or other defining characteristics.[40]

In Nigeria, the freedom of the press is enshrined in the 1999 Constitution as contained in Section 22, which states that "the press, radio, television, and other agencies of the mass media shall at all times be free to uphold the fundamental objectives in this Chapter and uphold the responsibility and accountability of the Government to the people."[41] As noted earlier, Section 39(1) which protects the freedom of expression such that a "person shall be entitled to freedom of expression, including the freedom to hold opinions and to receive and impart ideas and information without interference."[42] The subsequent clause also gives an average Nigerian the right to share opinions and news with the public: every person shall be entitled to own, establish and operate any medium for disseminating information, ideas and opinions.[43] Besides these laws, there are also Acts of Parliament and Bills that have been introduced to consolidate freedom of the media, such as the National Broadcasting Act (2010) and the Nigeria Press Council Act of 1992. Nigerian press members have also joined local and international pressure groups to ensure continued support of their right to cover and provide news without fear of intimidation or threat to their life.

Despite all the measures mentioned above, freedom of the press has come under constant pressure from political leaders, law enforcement officials and other affluent individuals within the Nigerian society. Social media has taken a significant role in Nigeria's process of political participation.[44] This is evident in the reach and strengths of the most recent protests in the country. The #EndSARS protest started on Twitter with hashtags, retweets and public interactions before it ultimately snowballed into a full-fledged youth-powered and internationally-funded protest against unlawful detention, harassment and killing of young Nigerians by the infamous Special Anti-Robbery Squad (SARS). Prior protests and movements such as #OccupyNigeria, #NotTooYoungToRun, and #SayNoToSocialMediaBill, among others, have started from social media while effecting change in society. Perhaps, it is due to this new-found, uncontrolled mechanism of social change that the government at all levels and Nigerians themselves feel strongly about attempts to regulate social media.[45] Hence, it is not surprising that both sides of the aisle would devise means to protect what each side considers the best way to ensure that the laws that bind social media usage benefit them.

---

40. I. Bayo Oloyede, "Press Freedom: A Conceptual Analysis," *Journal of Social Sciences* 11, no. 2 (2015): 101-109.

41. Section 22, *1999 Constitution of Federal Republic of Nigeria.*

42. Section 39 (1), *1999 Constitution of Federal Republic of Nigeria.*

43. Section 39 (2), *1999 Constitution of Federal Republic of Nigeria.*

44. Apuke Oberiri, "Exploring the Extent of Press Freedom in Nigeria," *International Journal of International Relations, Media and Mass Communication Studies* 3, no.2 (2017): 28-31.

45. BBC News, "Letter from Africa: Why Nigerians Fear Social Media Sanctions," *BBC News,* November 7, 2020, https://www.bbc.com/news/world-africa-54840436.

GROWING CULTURE OF INTERNET BLACKOUTS

Internet censorship is one of the ways through which authoritarian governments around the world control the flow of information in their country. In the past couple of years (2020 to 2022), internet blackouts have greatly increased as a tool to control information and/or confuse public protests. Some of the earliest known cases can be traced to the Iranian "Green Movement" uprising in 2009, the Malaysian blackout of 2012, and the Arab Spring of 2011, whence the Egyptian government shut down the internet for a week. The rise of internet blackouts as a tool for governments to assert digital sovereignty over their citizens unsuspectingly coincides with the rise of social media as a powerful tool for gathering people, organizing protests, and sharing critical opinions on public issues.[46] More recently, many African countries have also cut off internet access during elections to ensure that social media does not affect the result; as some have suggested, this may have been done to ensure that there is no public backlash or evidence of election malpractice.[47] While the Nigerian government has never engaged in a full-blown internet blackout, the Buhari administration banned Twitter from June 5, 2021, to January 13, 2022, due to the platform's decision to delete a tweet posted by the President reported by several users as violating Twitter terms and conditions. Government representatives claimed that although the social media's decision to delete and suspend the President's account played a part, it was not the only reason the social media giant was sacked. Minister for Information and Culture, Lai Mohammed, claimed that activities on social media platforms like Twitter are targeted at undermining the democracy, stability and existence of the Nigerian state.[48] Besides actions against social media platforms, popular media outlets have also been targeted, sanctioned and arrested for publishing news regarded as "sensitive" to the Nigerian populace.

FAKE NEWS AS A TOOL FOR SOCIAL MEDIA CENSORSHIP

Fake news has existed in various forms since humanity started society. It essentially connotes information designed to manipulate, confuse or pass untrue propositions about an individual or entity to undermine or boost their public image. There exists a form of fake news for almost all stages of social development or political predicament. In wartime, for instance, propaganda is one example of fake news used to boost

46. Charlotte Mitchell, "Internet Blackouts: The Rise of Government-Imposed Shutdowns," *Al Jazeera*, June 16, 2019, https://www.aljazeera.com/features/2019/6/16/internet-blackouts-the-rise-of-government-imposed-shutdowns.

47. Hilary Matfess, "More African Countries are Blocking Internet Access During Election," *Quartz Africa*, June 1, 2016, https://qz.com/africa/696552/more-african-countries-are-blocking-internet-access-during-elections/.

48. Nimi Princewill and Stephanie Busari, "Nigeria Bans Twitter after Company Deletes President Buhari's Tweet," *CNN*, June 5, 2021, https://edition.cnn.com/2021/06/04/africa/nigeria-suspends-twitter-operations-intl/index.html.

soldier morale and undercut foreign incursion into one's country. And during peacetime, political figures have often been caught exaggerating and/or misrepresenting data about issues to favor their political leanings. However, more recently, social media has increased the rise of fake news across the board. A notorious case of this involved Cambridge Analytica, a British political consulting firm that used stolen personal data of millions of citizens to circulate targeted fake news to change their political leaning. Through data obtained from Facebook, the company has been linked to democratic interference, such as the Brexit movement in the United Kingdom, the United States Presidential election of 2016, the Nigerian general election of 2015, and more than 60 other countries.[49] Like most countries, the Nigerian state, against the backdrop of the rise of fake news, decided to regulate social media. The result of these regulations is the series of Bills discussed so far in this chapter. However, the question of the effectiveness, necessity and constitutionality of these new regulations is a different set of probes, a discourse that has been adequately explored in the preceding paragraphs.

ANTI-SOCIAL MEDIA BILL MOVEMENTS IN NIGERIA

Since the Nigerian government decided to push forward narratives and Bills to gag freedom of expression on social media in the name of protecting national security and people's sensitivity, there has been considerable pushback from relevant stakeholders. Anti-social media bill movements are a series of protests, online petitions, public dialogues and caution from international bodies geared toward free internet in Nigeria. Since the early 2010s, social media has become an effective tool to equip average Nigerians to engage in political discourse and express their views on public matters.[50] Therefore, attempts to curb their rights to free expression without state-sponsored surveillance and data breach are important to almost 30 million Nigerians who make up her social media population.[51] For instance, all Nigerian dailies had the same cover story image on July 12, 2021, wherein "Information Blackout" was boldly written to protest against a Bill that criminalizes hate speech with the death penalty as punishment.[52] The coordinated solidarity from all press organizations brought the issue into the public domain, which led to the eventual dismissal of the death penalty clause. Press groups and Non-Governmental Organizations (NGOs) such as SERAP,

---

49. Brian Ekdale and Melissa Tully, "Cambridge Analytica in Africa—What do we Know?" *Democracy in Africa*, January 10, 2020, https://democracyinafrica.org/cambridge-analytica-africa-know/.

50. John Maikomo Moses, Tordue Simon Targema and Jesse Ishaku, "Tale of an Ill-fated Scapegoat: National Security and the Struggle for State Regulation of Social Media in Nigeria," *Journal of Digital Media & Policy* (2022): 1-19.

51. Victoria Ibezim-Ohaeri, "Confronting Closing Civic Spaces in Nigeria," *SUR-International Journal on Human Rights* 26 (2017): 129.

52. Peter Eshioke Egielewa, "An Analysis of Media Coverage of the New Nigeria's Social Media Bill in Selected Nigerian Newspaper," *SAU Journal of Management and Social Sciences* 3, (2022): 151-162.

Paradigm Initiatives, Feminist Coalition, Take It Back Movement and Concerned Nigerians are among the most vocal local groups that have led successful protests against the government's attempt to enact undemocratic bills.

Besides social gatherings and physical protests, social media itself has become an effective tool for leading anti-social-media-bill movements. The most popular and consequential protests in Nigeria in recent times either started first on social media or had a strong social media arm that pushed the aggrieved's agenda to a larger audience. During the #EndSARS protest, protesters lobbied on social media for international awareness with some of the most popular and influential people in the world, such as Beyonce, Rihanna, Jack Dorsey (CEO of Twitter at the time), Anthony Joshua, Kanye West, among others, contributing to the citizens' fight for an end to police brutality.[53] International rights groups such as Human Rights Watch and Amnesty International have also, in several instances, spoken against the government's attempts to muzzle free speech and opinion in the country.

INSTRUMENTALITY AND THE FUTURE OF GOVERNMENT POLICY IN SOCIAL MEDIA

Social media has been adopted in almost all sectors of society, and the connectivity has allowed it to retain relevance in all discussions, communication and general public engagement. It is easy to access people at their convenient zones and time without the necessity of cost and physical effort. The government has employed this possibility in many instances. The government, its agencies and almost all parastatals have established official accounts on many social media platforms for information, communication, policy assessment and engagement.

The role of social media in public spaces and governmental issues cannot be underestimated, as it offers continuous and comfortable communication. Previously, research has been done on how social media affects the economy, resources governance,[54] the fight against corruption, democratic practices,[55] public policies and public administration.[56] Access to the public through social media helps the government construct and execute public policies relating to issues that affect the citizens directly.[57]

53. BBC News, "End Sars Protests: Growing List of Celebrities Pledge Support for Demonstrators," *BBC News,* October 21, 2020, https://www.bbc.com/news/world-africa-54629449.

54. Oasis Kodila-Tedika, "Natural Resource Governance: Does Social Media Matter?" *Mineral Economics* 34, no. 1 (2021): 127-140.

55. Chandan Kumar Jha and Oasis Kodila-Tedika, "Does Social Media Promote Democracy? Some Empirical Evidence, *Journal of Policy Modeling* 42, no. 2 (2020): 271-290.

56. Simplice A. Asongu and Nicholas M. Odhiambo, "Governance and Social Media in African Countries: an Empirical Investigation," *Telecommunications Policy* 43, no. 5 (2019): 411-425.

57. Asongu and Nicholas M. Odhiambo, "Governance and Social Media in African Countries: an Empirical Investigation," *Telecommunications Policy 43, no. 5* (2019): 411-425.

Figure 2.2. "Selfie over Service" by Dr. Kazeem Ekeolu. Social media frivolities and public aggrandizement over national matters.

One of Nigeria's major problems is insecurity, which has claimed thousands, especially in the country's North-Eastern region. Recently, terrorism and social vices activities have been gaining prominence through social media to recruit and communicate with themselves and members of the public. Its vulnerability made it difficult to control or censor activities on several platforms. International organizations like Al Qaeda and local terrorist groups like Boko Haram have used social media to strategize and organize crimes.[58] The government and its authorities have also been deploying means to censor posts and conversations on social media to control insecurity.

In addition, government parastatals have found social media to be one of the most effective means of public engagement. The Nigeria Centre for Disease Control (NCDC) is a perfect example of a Nigerian agency employing social media dynamics, especially during the Corona Virus outbreak in 2020.[59] The NCDC was able to engage the public through the provision of daily updates on people that contracted the disease and the fatality rate on daily bases. Individuals were prone to checking the NCDC social media platforms for updates and tracking of the disease. In addition, the NCDC sensitized the public and persuaded people to abide by COVID-19 prevention rules.[60] Similarly, other governmental agencies have taken advantage of these measures and evaluated feedback and reactions through the platforms.

Social media has emerged as one of the most effective ways of aggregating public opinion.[61] It has been a direct way to understand how the public would react to policies, actions and the inaction of the government.[62] Although these opinions might not represent the generality of how the people feel, a substantial amount of reaction suggests possibilities of the conviction of the general public. The flexibility of the credibility of social media has also suggested the risk of disseminating fake and unsubstantiated information that could dissuade the majority of the public from the right state of things.[63] However, the people's subscription to social media in Nigeria has more often than not allowed people to express their positions and opinions with less fear. The government understands this position and has been exploiting the possibilities in weighing decisions and the acceptability of their actions.

---

58. I. Nsudu and E.C. Onwe, "Social Media and Security Challenges in Nigeria: The Way Forward," *World Applied Sciences Journal* 35, no. 6 (2017): 993-999.

59. Ngozika A. Obi-Ani, Chinenye Anikwenze and Mathias Chukwudi Isiani, "Social Media and the Covid-19 Pandemic: Observations from Nigeria," *Cogent Arts & Humanities* 7, no. 1 (2020): 1-15.

60. Samuel Ayodele Dada and Ebenezer Deji Ogunrinde, "A Stylistic Analysis of Nigeria Centre for Disease Control (NCDC) COVID-19 Sensitization Advertisements on Social Media," *Journal of African Studies and Sustainable Development* 3, no. 6 (2020): 153-176.

61. Shannon C. McGregor, "Social Media as Public Opinion: How Journalists Use Social Media to Represent Public Opinion," *Journalism* 20, no. 8 (2019): 1070-1086.

62. Matthew A. Baum and Philip BK Potter, "Media, Public Opinion and Foreign Policy in the Age of Social Media," *The Journal of Politics* 81, no. 2 (2019): 747-756.

63. Oberiri Destiny Apuke and Bahiyah Omar, "Fake News and COVID-19: Modelling the Predictors of Fake News Sharing among Social Media Users," *Telematics and Informatics* 56 (2021): 1-16.

In addition, social media has been material in political participation and canvassing political support.[64] It allows citizens to evaluate government performance and participate in political conversations. Political parties and organizations have realized the need to explore social media to popularize their political ideologies and candidates.[65] It is, therefore, not out of place to discuss social media in line with the sustenance of the country's tenets of democracy. Therefore, the government understands the impact of social media on the citizens, political participation and democracy.

Social media is an ever-evolving technological space. In its infancy, platforms like Facebook and Twitter merely used "newsfeed" algorithms to allow people to view contents from friends or people they follow, usually in text-heavy communications. The next evolution of social media has expanded on this sort of information bubble methodology to content sharing such that today's newsfeed pays less attention to people that share a history (followers or friends). Instead, the information interest of each user, determined by the kind of content they previously enjoyed, determines the content they would be allowed to see in the future. This evolution of information is also moving from text-heavy content moderation to short videos with heavy filters and sound, as seen on TikTok and Instagram. This depiction of the evolution of social media highlights the growing power that social media would continue to have in the public space. Since more users would be interested in video-based content and have a less intellectual burden in processing information, it would help citizens have a better understanding of social and political issues in real-time, from the most likely person that has such information, even if they do not have any digital relation with an individual. Due to the previous gains of social media-backed protests, the citizens would continue to rely on the technology for future attempts to curb the government's excesses and raise awareness against perceived threats to their freedom and democratic values.

Consequently, there is a need to explore the future of government policy on social media. First, I propose that the most likely way to solve the problem of legal frameworks for social media that would, on the one hand, champion democratic values and, on the other hand, endure national stability can be achieved on a twofold approach. The first approach is having internationally agreed-upon digital rights conventions that mimic what is obtainable in professional fields of medicine (for example, the Geneva Convention) and laws such as the World Intellectual Property Organization (WIPO) treaties on intellectual property rights, among others. The second approach builds on the first by allowing individual countries to formulate their legal framework for digital rights and responsible usage based on the provisions

64. Z.K. Dagona, Haruna Karick and F. M. Abubakar, "Youth Participation in Social Media and Political Attitudes in Nigeria," *Journal of Sociology, Psychology and Anthropology in Practice* 5, no. 1 (2013): 1-7.

65. Leo O.N. Edegoh and Ogonna W. Anunike, "Voters' Assessment of Social Media Use for 2015 Electioneering Campaigns by the Two Leading Political Parties in Nigeria," *African Research Review* 10, no. 4 (2016): 18-40.

of the internationally agreed-upon tenets. Nigeria can champion national-conscious regulations and people-driven privileges for internet usage, especially as they affect social media by being a member of a continent-wide regulatory body. Secondly, I argue that policies on social media in Nigeria were greatly influenced by the actions of the Buhari administration, especially the government's insistence that Big Tech social media companies must open local offices in Nigeria for them to operate within Nigeria and ensure adherence to local laws, including tax remittance. As of July 2022, Twitter and Meta (formerly Facebook) had opened offices in Nigeria, with TikTok expected to follow suit. Whether or not this was done to avoid government sanction or purely from a business perspective is currently unknown.

3

THE USA-AFRICA DIALOGUE

Visions and Provisions

INTRODUCTION

Scholarly discourses and contributions have improved significantly since the advent of the internet, influencing the innovations of social messaging platforms that facilitate these discourses.[1] From the comfort of their homes or workplaces in Africa, the United States, Europe, or elsewhere, academics can now share intellectual tokens on emerging issues and argue for or against theories through social messaging platforms. Originally, these discussions may involve the conglomeration of scholars at a meeting point where specific themes are foregrounded for discussions and possibly end as soon as these conferences are over. But for the internet, intellectual conversations do not end within the four walls of conference halls. It has helped in the provision of significant changes in academia as scholars are leveraging the positives to continue spreading the gospel of intellectualism.[2] Nowadays, it is not uncommon to see scholarly groups on Facebook, Telegram, Emails, and the like where heated conversations are essential for advancing knowledge. It is thus safe to describe the internet as a hub of knowledge.

1. Carole L. Palmer, Lauren C. Teffeau and Carrie M. Pirmann, "Scholarly information practices in the online environment," *Report commissioned by OCLC Research. Published online at: www. oclc. org/programs/publications/reports/2009-02. Pdf* (2009).

2. Sheila Jasanoff, "The vanishing square: Civic learning in the Internet Age," *Hastings Center Report* 51, (2021): S5-S9.

With these social messaging platforms, scholars can think together more than before through academic dialogues to create knowledge.[3] For instance, with forums on email platforms, scholars can pool ideas together, formulate and advance theories, create meanings, and solve problems together, achieving collaborative learning. This kind of discussion usually takes the form of sharing information where academics become encouraged to open discussions on them, disseminating ideas, opinions, and suggestions. According to Louise Pendry and Jessica Salvadore, online discussion forums help to catalyze participants into working together to create solutions to problems.[4] When different scholars constantly interact over the internet to discuss particular issues or general problems, it usually triggers collective action to resolve these identified problems. Although heated exchanges of ideas and opinions on online discussion platforms may breed resentment, personal vendettas are often shelved for collective progress.

Against this backdrop, there is a need to explore the initiative behind the online discussion forum, the USA-Africa Dialogue Series[5] initiated by me, where different scholars of different academic specialties meet to pool ideas together and create solutions. Conversations on these forums revolve around Africa, the African Project—the theme of Africa rediscovering itself, including suggestions on how this could be achieved. When a topic is highlighted for discussion, scholars issue their views on them, ultimately creating viable solutions that are important but not necessarily preventing such problems from recurring. As the aphorism goes, two heads are better than one, which is the practical aspect of discussions in this Dialogue series.

The USA-Africa Dialogue Series is an online forum where scholarly discourses and contributions are foregrounded. This forum pools scholars from around the world in discussions concerning Africa. There is no doubt that Africa needs special attention to attain its peak. Africa is home to myriads of problems, including failed leadership, class stratification, poor educational system, and exploitation of scarce resources, among others, and the more conversations have not been made to create possible ways forward, the more it will continue to suffer belittlement in world affairs. Dialogues around Africa are usually from the perspectives of failing nations, questionable policies, grotesque leaders, poor educational systems, and failed governance systems.

By creating dialogue around this framework, scholars identify these problems and share the knowledge to find lasting solutions. Most of the scholars on the USA-Africa Dialogue forums are Africans; thus, it becomes imperative that they develop homegrown solutions to the problems. With these discussions, there is the creation of African knowledge for African people. This is essential because no one understands a

3. Zizi Papacharissi, "The virtual sphere: The internet as a public sphere," *New Media & Society* 4, no. 1 (2002): 9-27.

4. Louise F. Pendry and Jessica Salvatore, "Individual and Social Benefits of Online Discussion Forums," *Computers in Human Behavior* 50 (2015): 211-220.

5. https://groups.google.com/g/usaafricadialogue/.

problem more than whoever suffers from it. Most global interventions in African states do not often achieve remarkable results. Africans understand their problems and, with collaborative action, will create a new set of solutions.

I was the brain behind the USA-Africa Dialogue Series, which has continued to amass prominence as a forum where ideas are formed, and solutions are created. I do not hide my enthusiastic commitment to Africa. In various ways, I have tried to advance the dire need of Africa to attain overall civilization and progress in my various works, including books, research papers, journals, keynote speeches, and more. Out of my burning interest in Africa, I identify the need for constant dialogues on many things relating to African affairs as a viable weapon to drive the continent to progress. This has been successful, as suggestions made through this Dialogue Series have helped address issues in African countries. I created this dialogue forum with the intention that numerous scholars can discuss specific African and African American issues, as these discussions would help create new knowledge and reconstruct new identities.

The civic learning prominent in these dialogues, in turn, facilitates the social agenda as discussions become more inclusive and communal. Discussants in this Dialogue series are seen as well-informed citizens (of Africa) whose contributions need to be heard as they disseminate ideas on African problems; after all, the vision behind this dialogue series is to facilitate essential knowledge production among a coterie of African intellectuals for the benefits of all. As the moderator of this dialogue series, I believe that knowledge specific to Africa would be identified with the participation of the best minds during discourses. This forum has strengthened African voices through discussions on Africa and has helped redefine Africa's position in global affairs.

The moderator's task is identifying Africa-specific issues and leaving the forum open for active discussions.[6] By attempting not to impose ideas and ideals over the participants, the forum has witnessed an unhindered exchange of ideas: academics have the freedom to present or advance any arguments insofar as they do not contain visibly snarky remarks on descriptions of other academics. It is noteworthy to add that scholars herein have leveraged the discussions on this forum to pursue scholarly interests in African matters since the development of Africa is usually at the forefront of these discussions, with responses providing the framework for which Africa can experience an upward trajectory. One of the scholars investigating the forum notes that:

> Professor Falola's Forum could be likened to a flowing sea of knowledge that everyone can come to drink from. In these times where Africa shares gory statistics of the world, it is pertinent discussions are made on possible ways forum. Silence should not describe the state of Africa's affairs. In addition, there should be a continuous production of knowledge that would move Africa to progress: this is the apt description of the USA Africa Dialogue series. Concerned stake-

6. https://www.laits.utexas.edu/africa/ads/1.html.

Figure 3.1. "Scholarship and Social Media" by Michael Efionayi. Taking scholarship and academic conversations and activities to social media and the internet and adapting it to the peculiarities of research despite its disadvantages.

holders have adopted the suggestions made by these African scholars regarding policy implementation and execution. The Dialogue series has thus become an important reference point for suggestions on African issues. The conversations on the forum also provide "a naturalistic research method" for any serious scholar advancing interests in Africa.[7]

THE USA-AFRICA DIALOGUE AND CONVERSATIONS ON AFRICAN MATTERS

Unsurprisingly, discussions on Africa take center stage in this Dialogue series. After all, the forum had been created by an African for matters specific to Africa. The fact remains that many wrongs with the continent have rendered it a mere asterisk in international affairs. Africa has been seen as a second-rate continent with second-rate humans. Some African countries' disorderly state has not helped change these narratives. Many African territories are incapable of an independent governance system, with leaders acquiring huge debts they cannot pay, while some are known to want to perpetuate the imposition of themselves or family members on the people under

7. Koleade Odutola, "Diaspora and imagined nationality: USA-Africa Dialogue and Cyberframing Nigerian Nationhood," Ph.D. *diss.*, Rutgers University-Graduate School-New Brunswick, 2010.

them. Global institutions have intervened in African states, in some cases more than any other countries around the globe, and it appears that these institutions are created to solve African problems. This has perhaps accounted for the plethora of pessimistic views on Africa, an obtrusive anomaly that the Dialogue aims at challenging.

Africa has been described with racist slurs by westerners that need them as a pillar system. This has led to the belittlement of the African repertoire of knowledge. There is limited knowledge in Africa for the western world, and the presumed little available is unmatchable against western knowledge and civilization. African academics countered these narratives and have published exciting research on the African factory of knowledge production.[8] The fact that pan-Africanist scholars are foremost in their fields of interest rendered the views of Africans as unintelligent folks insensitive. Africans are achieving outstanding excellence and significance in their endeavors, even overtaking western scholars.

Discussions trace the need for Africans to express their love for Africa and reconstruct their identities. It is not untrue that some Africans are identified by terminology only and have no burning passion for Africanism, which has, in turn, created narratives denigrating Africans. Some African academics in the diaspora are also at fault here. On getting to other foreign countries, they tend to detach themselves from their identities, cladding themselves in borrowed robes of westernization. Such academics who are aware of the hydra-headed problems of the continent remain unconcerned and, if they eventually intervene through epistolary letters, sometimes portray themselves with a savior-complex mentality as if without them, Africa will go into extinction.

African academics suggest the need to identify as Africans as well as the need to represent African ideals and values. There has been numerous research on knowledge production in Africa; thus, it becomes imperative for Africa to portray African knowledge.[9] African philosophy of knowledge underscores the spirit of brotherhood and unity, that is, Ubuntu, the age-long Zulu philosophical slogan meaning, "I am because we are," which is a prerequisite for fostering humanity as a contradistinction to the western notion of René Descartes' "Cogito ergo sum"—"I think therefore I am," a doctrine that underscores the importance of individualism.

Out of their burning love for Africa, discussions center mostly on complex African issues. There is a problem with African states' political systems, which has hindered the development and overall civilization of the continent.[10] Many academics blame colonization and its associated negatives as the major cause of the challenges of Afri-

---

8. Toyin Falola, *Yoruba Gurus: Indigenous Production of Knowledge in Africa* (Trenton: Africa World Press, 1999).

9. Falola, *Yoruba Gurus.*

10. Kenneth Ingham, *Politics in Modern Africa: The Uneven Tribal Dimension* (New York: Taylor & Francis, 1990).

can states. If this was to be accepted, it is pertinent to highlight that African leaders have not fared better than their colonial predecessors. Undoubtedly, African states have witnessed the worst postcolonial experiences, which militate against their development as most of these states are characterized by the breakdown of law and order due to a failed governance system.[11] It is noteworthy that until now, some African states have not achieved true independence, as they still depend on their colonial rulers for policy formulation and implementation. This factor and many more contribute to the numerous problems bedeviling African countries. It is paradoxical to note that despite the abundant natural resources in African states, economies have not improved significantly as the citizens become poorer. African scholars identify the restructuring of African states to ensure progress and prosperity. Discussions suggest that African leaders should highlight development as the core of their plans and programs and eliminate colonial vestiges that keep states in the shackles of pseudo-independence.

Furthermore, discussions revolve around the issues of brain drain in Africa. Brain drain involves migrating African professionals to countries outside the continent.[12] It is an acclaimed fact that the best African minds are scattered across countries in Europe and North America. Thus African knowledge is being adopted in developing other nations, whereas Africa suffers.[13] There were discourses addressing this subject which has hindered the progress of Africa. Ironically, academics passionate about this discourse are Africans in the diaspora. The influx of African scholars to foreign countries is alarming, but no blame can be placed on them. It would be inconsistent to advocate for the compulsory live-in-Africa approach when no resources are available for fleeing academics to achieve their full potential. In Africa, intellectualism is hardly respected, including the fact that there are not enough institutions for African intellectuals to work. It thus seems attractive for them to seek greener pastures overseas, and as it is said, knowledge cannot be produced by a hungry mind, which explains why the Yoruba say, "Ebi kìì wọ'nú kọ̀rọ̀` mí̀ì wọ` ọ´" (As long as there is hunger in the inside, nothing else can inhabit the mind). Even when these academics, out of their commitment to their fatherland, contribute their quota to the development of Africa from their respective places, it has not replaced the knowledge lost. The challenge of brain drain has long-lasting effects on Africa's overall development as there are no required skills to pursue economic prosperity.[14]

11. Ingham, *Politics in Modern Africa.*

12. S.O.H. Benedict and Wilfred Isioma Ukpere, "Brain Drain and African Development: Any Possible Gain from the Drain?" *African Journal of Business Management* 6, no. 7 (2012): 2421-2428.

13. William Easterly and Yaw Nyarko, "Is the Brain Drain Good for Africa?" *Brookings Global Economy and Development Working Paper* 19, March 2008.

14. Ainalem Tebeje, "Brain Drain and Capacity Building in Africa," *IDRC Reports,* February 22, 2005.

Researchers have linked the issue of brain drain to three factors, namely: economic, socio-political, and personal factors.[15] The economic factor describes the sense that African scholars need to secure better living standards for themselves and their families. The pittance they receive in African institutions is insufficient for themselves, not to mention fulfilling their other financial responsibilities. The socio-political factor describes the sense that some African scholars found themselves in a political climate that affects their productivity and knowledge production. This propelled the urge to relocate to terrains where their academic ingenuity would be appreciated. It is not a matter of the clichéd "seeking a greener pasture" but a matter of survival away from the home environment that does not provide the opportunity for minimal survival. In light of the migration of African professionals, African states resort to dependence on foreigners to compensate for the absence of skilled labor, thus expending a huge amount of resources in return. Proffering solutions to the challenge of brain drain sometimes strike a chord among scholars with postulations that academics need to return home to produce knowledge. However, the potential return of African intellectuals in the diaspora may not alleviate the predicament because a brain drain cannot be regained. Thus, African leaders have been advised to create the best environment for knowledge to thrive.

Conversations also center on humanitarian crises in Africa. It is a fact that a cause of stability in African states can be linked to many humanitarian crises. Africa suffers the most humanitarian crises in the world, from food insecurity to health insecurity, terrorism to genocide, and a host of others. Countries cannot achieve progress where there is no internal security. With these humanitarian crises, Africa has plunged down the pedestal of progress. Countries like Rwanda, Nigeria, Somalia, and Kenya, among others, have suffered significantly from humanitarian crises. For instance, the genocide in Rwanda was a constant worry not only in African states but the world in general. The ethnic murders neutralized the country's development. The major cause of this unfortunate scenario in Rwanda was perceived ethnic marginalization. The level of insurgency in Kenya and Nigeria[16] also is a source of worry for academics. The security architecture of both countries has been rendered ineffective in the spate of attacks. Boko Haram and Al-Shabab are rapidly gaining ground in the two countries. Scholarly discussions posited that the security porosity of these two nations has left Sub-Saharan Africa unprotected from insurgents' attacks. The peace and progress of these nations are continually challenged by daring attacks, leaving the citizens and the government helpless and hopeless. During this discourse, academics identify the need for the government to cultivate a serious approach to curbing insecurity, foregrounding the notion that an insecure territory is synonymous with an extinct territory.

---

15. Sibry Tapsoba, Sabiou Kassoum, P.V. Houenou, B. Oni and M. Sethi, "Brain Drain and Capacity Building in Africa," ECA, IDRC, IOM, 2000.

16. Allswell Osini Muzan, "Insurgency in Nigeria: Addressing the Causes as Part of the Solution," *African Human Rights Law Journal* 14, no. 1 (2014): 217-243.

Coup cultures in Africa contribute to the instability in the continent.[17] Coups and counter-coups destabilize African states and plunge them into anarchy they struggle to recover from. Coup plotters usually give bad governance as an excuse for military intervention. The governance structure of most African states fails the citizens, but even with military leaders, the situation has been far worse. The major challenge against the development of African states is bad governance. Most African leaders are inept and inactive and, despite their clamor for homegrown solutions, have not been able to steer the ship of their country to sail. On getting the mantle of leadership, an average African leader becomes excessively corrupt and embezzles funds in safe accounts in European countries, now known as the retirement home of African political leaders. Without good governance, growth and development will remain an illusion to African states. Knowledge production and good governance complement each other. None can exist without the other. The plethora of African knowledge repositories will be ineffective due to bad governance. According to the popular saying, "good governance is the bulwark for any development."

With bad governance comes the citizens' loss of faith in the credibility of the states and, worse still, a loss of hope and confidence in the individual's ability to survive from one day to another. Some of these citizens wished for military intervention in the state's politics to eradicate the menace of bad leadership. Coup plotters identify with the frustrations of the masses before hijacking powers from civilian rules. They are conscious that without the citizens' majority support for political authority, the coups, no matter how well-planned, are as good as a failure. Most citizens accept the military administration with the hope that it will change the tide of things. This has proved to be false. There is an unwritten rule in global affairs on accepting democracy as the only recognized system of government.[18] Democracy has many benefits, and despite its adoption by African states, citizens have not enjoyed the dividends of democracy. Nigeria is a perfect example here. Discourses posited that military interventions hinder the development of Africa. The reason is that the world abandons states that operate forced leadership. Even when military leaders promise rapid growth and development and penalize corrupt leaders, they cannot do much when the world turns a blind eye to their challenges and fails to give them the necessary backup.

Furthermore, some military rulers are not different from the corrupt regimes they overtook, thus contributing to the challenges of such states. There is also the problem of coups succeeding coups associated with violence. Academics argue that coups guarantee dictatorship and lead to the breakdown of order. A counter-coup is hard without bloodshed, as military successions do not follow the same process as government transition in democratic dispensations.

---

17. Jonathan Powell, Abigail Reynolds and Mwita Chacha, "A New Coup Era for Africa?" *Conflict Trends* 4 (2021): 3-12.

18. Harry Collins, Robert Evans, Darrin Durant and Martin Weinel, *Experts and the Will of the People* (Cham: Palgrave Macmillan, 2020).

USA-AFRICA DIALOGUE AND CONVERSATIONS ON NIGERIAN AFFAIRS

Nigeria occupies an important status in Africa but has failed to live up to expectations, for other African countries to follow. Like the continent, Nigeria similarly suffers myriad problems that have continued to derail its path to progress. With Nigerian independence came many optimisms of progress[19] which were immediately watered down as soon as it came after the civil war (1967-1970), where millions of lives were lost. Nigeria is home to numerous opportunities that remain untapped and untappable, given that much of nothing works. It is indisputable that the country has been used as a reference point for an ailing nation and a failing economy. Nigeria has become a nation that, despite its complexities and numerous natural resources, has failed to get on track. Undoubtedly, Nigeria is a mockery of global affairs; if this continues, Africa will remain affected. All things being equal, Nigeria should be the country to drive the progress of Africa, but sadly, it has not. It is thus imperative that discussions are centered on the state of the nation's affairs to create suggestions on how the country can live up to her description as the giant of Africa.

In the USA-Africa Dialogue series, there are a plethora of discussions on the country's affairs from the perspectives of failed leadership, corruption, religious tensions, violent elections and transition of government, poor educational structure, and intimidation and oppression of the citizens. An analysis of the sorry state of Nigerian affairs shows that the country's problem is among those above. There were a series of conversations on the policies and strategies the country needs to adopt to become a force to reckon with. A blind eye cannot be turned to the country. Is there still a need to ask why Nigeria matters even when things have fallen apart?

Massive corruption by the political leaders has been a cog in the wheel of Nigeria's progress. Selfish demagogues have identified the nation's abundant resources as their personal properties. Yearly, Nigeria is listed as one of the most corrupt countries in the world as the national treasury continuously undergoes massive exploitation.[20] The country's corruption status has degenerated from the top to the bottom, with the citizens scavenging to take over the country's leftover ruins. It can be confidently posited that the nation's leaders are in a blood covenant with corruption. During electioneering, candidates often posit that their emergence would spell progress for the nation but, on getting there, become harbingers of corruption, giving credence to discussions that leaders aiming for full political powers only do so on the mandate of corruption under the garb of servant-leadership. It now seems that God created Nigeria with the complete absence of a unique characteristic: transparency. The corrup-

19. Max Siollun, *Oil, Politics and Violence: Nigeria's Military Coup Culture (1966-1976)* (NewYork: Algora Publishing, 2009).

20. Chinenye Leo Ochulor, "Failure of Leadership in Nigeria," *American Journal of Social and Management Sciences* 2, no. 3 (2011): 265-271.

tion problem in Nigeria is seen as divine and requires a *Deus ex Machina* to be resolved. The truth, however, is that the leaders manufacture corruption.

Chidi Opara, a prominent discussant on the USA-Africa, contends that corruption is the only relationship among Nigerian politicians. Nigerian politicians seem united in their struggles to exploit the country's wealth. Corruption is commonplace in Nigeria because political leaders do not see long-term plans; they are only concerned with short-term plans for their selfish interests. By alluding to the Sovereign Wealth Fund, a brainwave of the former minister of finance, Ngozi Okonjo-Iweala, during the Jonathan-led administration, Opara posits that the reason the initiative could not see the light of day was that the Nigeria Governors' Forum (NGF) were united in their mission to "shortchange the masses." If the Sovereign Wealth Fund had been implemented, it would have helped the country wriggle out of the economic crisis because it would have saved more money from crude oil sales. The absence of this is evident in the country's struggles to improve its economy. Corruption is a weapon used by Nigerian politicians to hinder national development. Thus, the problem of corruption is the problem of bad leadership.

Conversations highlighted the nation's major problem as the personality traits of corruption among the nation's leaders. There is no contention that the average Nigerian leader is corrupt, and whichever political leader advances the anti-corruption crusade is a comic character. Ex-president Muhammadu Buhari is a perfect paradigm. Before his first and second elections, President Buhari swore to cleanse the country of corruption, sometimes alluding to his time as a military head of state as proof of his transparency and ability to run a transparent government. The reality dawned on Nigerians soon enough; they did not need any world institution to confirm that corruption skyrocketed astronomically under Buhari's watch. Talks calling for President Buhari's impeachment and resignation due to ineptitude and corruption were futile. In Nigeria, it is taboo-like for the president to agree to his failings and resign or get impeached.

During the exchange of discourses, scholars linked the corruption problem in Nigeria to the unfortunate succession of bad leaders. The kind of leaders reflects the state of affairs in any country. Not many discussions are made on Nigeria's leadership as it is a well-known subject; the summary is that it is unenviable. Corruption is predominant in Nigeria because there are bad leaders. The continuous plundering of the nation's resources has caused the drastic decline of the economy. The effects are a high cost of living and low living standards among the citizens. Almost daily, the prices of goods and services experience spikes, the country's currency devalues, and purchasing power drops drastically. It is thus unsurprising for the citizens to acknowledge that the country is a hell on earth. The proposed solutions by academics to these long-lasting problems are crystal clear: the country needs to be restructured and revolutionized, and leaders need to be resolute in their struggles against corruption. But as the country's former Minister of Finance, Ngozi Okonjo-Iweala, postulat-

ed, fighting corruption in Nigeria is a dangerous game for the singular fact that aside from the leaders, the citizens are also accomplices in the country's rotten system.[21]

Conversations also center on elections in Nigeria. The electoral process in the country does not come without casualties. The violence attached to elections in Nigeria is a source of worry among African intellectuals as this has generated political apathy among the citizens. The Nigerian citizens have lost faith in the electoral process as it has now become an institution to keep the serving government in power. Simply put, elections in Nigeria are neither free nor fair. If there is anything certain in Nigerian elections, it is the violence to come. In every democratic dispensation, the election is crucial to the growth and development of such nations.[22] Without elections, there would be no transition of government. Electoral rigging has made Nigerians nurture the wrong notion that their votes would never count; thus, most become mere on-lookers in a democracy. Under this discussion, scholars attribute the negative dimension of the Nigerian political system to the system of government it operates. The American-styled presidential system of government that the nation practices gives too much power to the president, which is eventually pooled together to ensure a continuous stay in power, and it becomes easy for the president to influence the electoral process or disrupt it to stay in power. As Salawu and Hassan similarly pontificate, the failure of a transparent electoral process is detrimental to the survival of democracy in Nigeria.[23] They note that the electoral process often clashes with ethnic and cultural differences, resulting in hostility in the struggle for power and authority. As solutions, academics clamor for the impartiality of the Independent National Electoral Commission (INEC), the only institution charged with conducting free, fair, and credible elections in Nigeria. The commission is charged to stand its ground against any government's interference and execute its duties without fear or favor. However, the commission has struggled to keep up with its mandate due to excessive politicking. It seems paradoxical for an institution created and funded by the government to be completely free of its interference. This is the case with other African countries struggling to conduct a decent election.

Nigeria is a country with two dominant religions, Christianity and Islam, as the traditional religion is often not acknowledged. The doctrines of these two religions direct their members to promote peace and prosperity. However, the ideologies of these religions may be slightly different though their ultimate goal is to promote peace. However, this is not the case among the religious faithful, as both are mostly caught in needless strife to express dominance over one another, igniting communal

21. Ngozi Okonjo-Iweala, *Fighting Corruption is Dangerous: The Story Behind the Headlines* (Boston: MIT Press, 2018).

22. Jacques Thomassen, ed., *Elections and Democracy: Representation and Accountability* (Oxford: Oxford University Press, 2014).

23. Bashiru Salawu and A.O. Hassan, "Ethnic Politics and its Implications for the Survival of Democracy in Nigeria," *Journal of Public Administration and Policy Research* 3, no. 2 (2011): 28-33.

clashes and disturbances that lead to the loss of lives and properties.[24] There are scholarly discussions on the dire need to curb religious differences in the country. Over the years, faithful from both religions have found it difficult to co-exist such that to start a holy war in Nigeria only takes an expressed disapproval of one of the religions—and calamity would follow. Despite the thought that since the country has some of the most religious people in the world, its state of affairs would be spiritual-like, the reality is different. Religious clashes have been unavoidable from Kano to Katsina to Plateau to Sokoto and the rest of Nigeria. Even when the leaders are from these religions, they have been hindered in the face of these clashes. Some of them have leveraged these differences to pursue their selfish interests, hence the commonplaceness of these clashes, which continue to jeopardize the country's existence. Nigeria's peace and stability are hinged on avoiding religious clashes. In the case of Deborah Samuel,[25] it becomes evident how religious tensions led to the gruesome murder of the undergraduate student at the Shehu Shagari College of Education in Sokoto. Religious identities or affiliations are a delicate subject that must be discussed sensitively, as even academics cannot be excused from clashes of religious identities. However, there are propositions that the end to the problem of religious differences in the country is for both religions' faithful to learn to be accommodating of each other and live in harmony despite their differences. Engaging one another in discourses over the superiority of one religion over the other fuels mistrust and ignites incendiary at the slightest opportunity. The Nigerian government is also encouraged to take appropriate measures against religious fanaticism, which often results in a violent confrontation. Nigeria is an established secular state, and no religion supersedes the other.

Conversations do not turn a blind eye to the porosity of Nigeria's security architecture. Daily news reports reel out the number of lives lost and properties destroyed through insurgent attacks. Not a day passes in Nigeria without the gory details of citizens caught in the melee of terrorist attacks and some becoming kidnapping victims. Nigeria no longer has a haven, even in the corridor of power—Aso Rock. Nigerians live in fear of who the next victims are. Despite its huge budget for defense, the nation's security forces are completely neutralized by insurgents who possess superior firearms. The country's leaders have failed to take effective actions, and even when taken, the apparent dilly-dally approach makes a mockery of the sensitive situation. Academics are concerned about the spate of insecurity in the nation and proffered possible solutions. Insecurity is now a thread that has been woven around the fabric of Nigerian society.

---

24. Kamal-deen Olawale Sulaiman, "Religious Violence in Contemporary Nigeria: Implications and Options for Peace and Stability Order," *Journal for the Study of Religion* 29, no. 1 (2016): 85-103.

25. Chude Anika, "The Killing of Deborah Samuel," *Guardian*, May 23, 2022.

Furthermore, the Owo church attack[26] foregrounded that adequate security is now a thing of the past in Nigeria, as religious places are not immune from desecration by gruesome murders. The National Security Council linked the attack to the ISWAP,[27] prefiguring a disaster as the country may be in the firm grips of cabalistic humans. The country has battled Boko Haram and bandits' attacks in the North-Western region for over a decade. It has not won the war against terrorism, as terrorists have continued to launch coordinated attacks in all geo-political zones in the country. A prominent discussant on the USA-Africa Dialogue series, Oluwatoyin Adepoju, often expresses the belief that the Buhari-led government worked in tandem with militants who continue to wreak havoc and spread their tentacles. This assumption seems sensible to him if the Nigerian government's tactless approaches to the insurgency problem are to be considered. Buhari had contested the mandate to end insecurity, but this damning predicament increased under his watch. There are reports that Nigeria's government has lost the battle against terrorism. This is based on the multiple shreds of evidence that the government bribes the militants with huge sums of money to release abducted personalities, portraying how dilapidated the security architecture is. Nigeria's armed forces are grossly underfunded and heavily politicized—the Buhari-led administration did not see the need to address these issues but thought bribing militants would guarantee maximum security.

In one of my discussions on this matter, I criticized the Nigerian government for failing to live up to its expectations of curbing insecurity.[28] I questioned the government's stance on the issue of insecurity which is genuine considering the president's soft approach to the terrorists. Other academics similarly lamented the government's unconcern about terrorist attacks, lending credence to the notion that these attacks are state-sponsored and political. With all puns intended, the Nigerian security intelligence has been rendered unintelligent by these attacks. The question has always been: "Who are the terrorists?" Security experts tried to explain where the problem originated from. The answer to this question is crystal clear in the government's attitude to acts of terrorism. In Nigeria, unrehabilitated terrorists are rebranded and reintegrated into society or recruited into its armed forces. How, then, would the country be absolved of insecurity? The military is ill-equipped, so facing the insurgents is equivalent to a suicide drive or deliberately volunteering to go to the slaughter. Conversations around this topic suggest that the country must take proactive measures to find a longstanding end to insecurity and unleash brutal force on the perpetrators of these dastardly acts. The country cannot afford to be silent in the face of these attacks as it denotes their

26. Olasunkanmi Akinlotan and Abdulqudus Ogundapo, "Owo Attack: How Gunmen Attacked Owo Church, Fled—Witnesses," *Premium Times*, June 12, 2022.

27. Seye Olumide, Terhemba Daka and Oluwaseun Akingboye, "ISWAP behind Owo Church Attack, says FG," *The Guardian*, June 10, 2022.

28. Toyin Falola, "Ọ̀wọ̀: Soaring Insecurity and the Cconspiracy of State Silence," *Premium Times*, June 9, 2022.

compliance. The military should be well-equipped to render helpless the insurgents, and the National Security Council be active in forestalling any attacks.

THE USA-AFRICA DIALOGUE AND DISCUSSIONS ON NIGERIAN HIGHER EDUCATION SYSTEM

Education is an integral aspect of society, as any country serious about attaining greatness will not joke with it.[29] There are many discussions on the sorry state of the Nigerian higher education system. It appears that no one, especially in the Nigerian government, cares about the state of education in the country. Nigeria had been known to have a highly-functional education system that was the envy of other countries, but as years passed, it experienced a decline. The reality of the country's current educational system is that it does not emphasize knowledge production. This is evident in the failure of a lot of Nigerian graduates to measure up intellectually with their peers at the international level.

There are conversations that the current educational practices in Nigeria are not functional to the society. That is, society has not found the knowledge produced by universities useful. Postulations included that the Nigerian higher educational system is designed to fail comprehensively. If there were initial reservations about this, the current predicament conveys the reality. Nigerian higher education or tertiary education system is no longer characterized by academic integrity, as it had been known. Policy formulation and implementation that would move the university system forward have been heavily politicized. In saner climes, education helps solve the nations' challenges; the university produces knowledge that would benefit society—a major reason advanced countries continue to lead innovations and inventions.

An analysis of Nigerian society shows an obvious disconnect due to numerous social vices.[30] The tasks of the university system are expressed in the production of knowledge that would end these social vices and other national problems, helping to affect the overall growth and development the citizens crave. Education is the most viable instrument that can bring a nation to problems. However, with the sorry state of Nigeria's tertiary education system, the nation's pessimistic narratives have not taken a different turn. Academics linked the failure of Nigeria's university system to neglect by the government, perhaps because the university students become immediately vocal in the wake of failed leadership. Nowadays, the learning and training activities in the university system are in complete disarray, and many scholars wonder if the country holds value, which is Nelson Mandela's postulations on the importance of education. Various research has shown that Nigeria's higher education is the

29. Ajay Bhardwaj, "Importance of Education in Human Life: A Holistic Approach," *International Journal of Science and Consciousness* 2, no. 2 (2016): 23-28.

30. O.O. Ismaila and A. Jekayinfa, "Cultural Pluralism, Reconstructive Education and Nation Building in Nigeria," *International Journal of Sociology and Anthropology* 5, no. 5 (2013): 140-146.

largest in Africa, comprising millions of students.[31] It begs the question that Nigeria has not been able to lead other African countries in science and technology and good governance. Every country serious about development designs its university education to achieve a great system performance. Nigeria's higher education is a copycat of the British education system during colonialism, and concerned government agencies have tried to redesign the university system from the approach conceived at inception.

Among the numerous problems challenging the Nigerian higher education system, academics highlight insufficient funding and excessive government negligence as top factors. It is a fact that Nigeria does not suffer from a lack of universities; the problem rather lies in the funds to run these universities' administration. The poor state of universities in Nigeria is due to a lack of adequate funds. The university system is barely autonomous of the Nigerian government and, as such, cannot determine how to be self-sufficient without the government's input. There are arguments that there are more government-owned universities in the country than available funds. The cost of running a university is very high, not to mention running forty-nine varsities. And the Nigerian government keeps taking over universities and building them without a sensitive consideration of funding issues. In a country where university students pay little or nothing, universities cannot thrive on Internally Generated Revenues (IGR) because a huge chunk of these revenues does not create the needed changes. This issue of inadequate funding led to the lack of manpower witnessed in universities and the sorry state of infrastructural development.

An overview of the Nigerian higher education system points to a fact: many universities but few lecturers. Academics cite the lack of adequate manpower in Nigerian universities. An average Nigerian university lecturer hardly finds time for themselves. Most have no choice but to teach students in overcrowded and dilapidated lecture rooms. They are also drafted to juggle administrative duties with academic positions to make up for a shortage of personnel. They then receive pittance as salaries. The students, in turn, are not provided with conducive environments to thrive. There are no good libraries, and those available comprise irrelevant old books. There are no well-equipped laboratories for practical courses, and there are no comfortable office spaces with decent furniture and modern computers for the lecturer's use. Due to the aforementioned, universities have no choice but to disseminate theorized knowledge that many students struggle to cope with. Applying the concept of quality in the Nigerian higher education system foregrounds an obvious gap. Both Asiyai and Oghuvbu related the concept of quality as the measurement of the intellectual sagacity of the products of Nigeria's higher educational institutions.[32] If this definition is to be

31. Niyi Jacob Ogunode and Abubakar Musa, "Higher Education in Nigeria: Challenges and the ways Forward," *Electronic Research Journal of Behavioural Sciences* 3 (2020): 84-98.

32. R.I. Asiyai and E.P. Oghuvbu, "An Empirical Analysis of the Causes and Challenges of Quality in Higher Education in Nigeria in the 21st Century," *Journal of Sociology and Education in Africa* 8, no. 2

followed, it needs no further interpretation other than the poor-quality culture of Nigeria's higher education system.

The Nigerian higher educational system is punctured by endless industrial actions, predominantly by the Academic Staff Union of Universities (ASUU). Academic calendars in Nigerian federal universities are severely interrupted by what is popularly known in Nigerian English parlance as the "ASUU Strike." The ASUU strike can go on for many months. During this strike action, federal and state universities are shut down, and knowledge production, if there is any, is halted. Affected students are sentenced to the fate of sitting at home, cultivating hope that the strike action will be called off one day. The Union's main argument for embarking on the strike action is to pursue better welfare packages for its members to produce adequate knowledge for the students. It also shifted focus to clamoring for adequate funding and the overall revitalization of the university system. Most of their demands fall on the government's deaf ears. Therefore, the strike actions are cyclical, and the students remain affected. The fact that the Union's main weapon of ensuring the government sees the relevance of the educational system and looks into their demands is strike action only did not sit well with many Nigerian academics, especially those in the diaspora.

Discourses on Nigerian tertiary education where "ASUU Strike" is the main theme struck a chord among Nigerian academics: those at home and those abroad. While those at home—most of whom are members of the Union—argue for the necessity of the strike action, harping that there are no better ways to get the government to remain conscious of their demands other than the language of a strike, diasporan academics have questioned the effectiveness of these strike actions, especially because in the end, it is almost always a lose-lose situation for every party involved as the Union never really gains —the process of which the students are grossly affected. In one of his discussions, professor of History at Vanderbilt University, Moses Ochonu, criticized the Union for its rigidity in driving home their demands.[33] ASUU insists on strike actions as it is the only weapon the Nigerian government understands, but Ochonu believes the strike model is ineffective and outdated. His main argument for condemning the strike action was that during this process, the students are most affected, and when the strike action is eventually called off, it would be difficult for the university lecturers to cover the syllabus. He blames the Union members for their lack of sensitivity in their demands, which are too big to be met considering the country's huge debt and the fact that education is not a priority for the Nigerian government.

Moses Ochonu thinks that the ASUU strike contributes to the rot of tertiary education in Nigeria. He argues that Union members should reflect and analyze how they

---

(2009): 1-13.

33. Moses Ochonu, "For the Record: My Three Recent Facebook Reflections on the Current ASUU-FG Faceoff and My Proposals for a Holistic, Sustainable Solutions," *US-Africa Dialogue*, February 19 2022, https://groups.google.com/g/usaafricadialogue/c/cr0u8DXZLhc.

became part of Nigeria's dwindling standard of university education, which they solely attribute to the government. Reports of academic corruption dominate the tertiary education landscape, and the perpetrators are members of the revered Union. Professor Ochonu's intervention vilified the Union members, who accused most diaspora academics of insensitivity to the Union's struggles. The Union has been seen as the custodian of tertiary education in Nigeria, without whose presence, the doors of university education would be closed to most students, especially the poor. Issues revolving around the higher education system in Nigeria are critical to the national interest, and ASUU has an unwritten rule to protect this interest. The Union members—Nigerian academics—argue that it would be incongruous to think all political climates are similar. In Nigeria, the government would not call parties to a roundtable conversation if there is no strike action. The discussion also points out that the students are at the receiving end of these strike actions called struggles. Nigerian academics at home insist that their demands are for the betterment of the students.

The challenge of ASUU's struggles is that the government hardly listens to them. There is a certainty that another ASUU strike will begin after one ends. Some Nigerian academics also question the sole weapon of ASUU. To use Jibrin Ibrahim's exact words, "ASUU's strike has become part of Nigeria's national strife and trauma."[34] In his discussion, Jibrin Ibrahim accuses the Union of contributing to the decline of university education in the country. The syllabi are never completed on resumption when the Union embarks on nationwide industrial actions for many months. In the process, half-knowledge is taught to the students. That, in turn, produces half-baked graduates. Despite its clamors for restructuring tertiary education, the Union members—university lecturers and professors—are accused of being involved in academic corruption the Union fails to address. This perhaps accounted for why university lecturers are promoted despite not contributing any significance to their scholarly fields. In the same mechanism, Professor Tunji Olaopa posits that during the Union's struggles with the government, it never wins, for the end of one strike action is a prerequisite to another.[35]

Nigerian academics—at home and abroad—proffer suggestions for improving the tertiary education system in Nigeria, most of which are subsumed under one fact: the need for ASUU members and the Nigerian government to rethink their strategies and approaches. Shutting down the universities in the process of advancing the need for improving university education seemed counterproductive. Suggestions trail the path that federal universities need to be self-sufficient and autonomous. They need to be effectively weaned from the hands of the Nigerian government as it short-funds uni-

34. Jibrin Asiyai, "Options on the Titanic ASUU/Government Battle," *Premium Times*, February 25, 2022, https://www.premiumtimesng.com/opinion/513780-options-on-the-titanic-asuu-government-battle-by-jibrin-ibrahim.html.

35. Tunji Olaopa, "ASUU's Unwinnable Battles: The Need to Change Tactics," *Daily Trust*, March 16, 2022.

versities that are too many. The sole task of funding universities in Nigeria should not be the exclusive reserve of the government. Solutions included the need for Nigerian universities to reinstate charging tuition fees as revenue would tilt the universities toward self-sufficiency. The policy of no tuition fees is not sustainable in a country where most people do not pay taxes. Student loans could be added source of funding for public universities.

In an economy characterized by poor living conditions and a low standard of living, it is yet to be seen whether the latter would be adopted.

Suggestions also pointed out the need for a renewed commitment to the Union's struggles to achieve the interest pursued. This foregrounded the need for ASUU and the Nigerian government to resolve the issues and other crises bedeviling Nigeria's tertiary education system without shutting down universities.[36] It would be a welcome development if there were other ways the long-lasting feud between the Union and the government could be resolved without resorting to strike. Arguments were also made for an independent body to regulate the affairs of both ASUU and the Nigerian government in matters relating to tertiary education. It is a known fact that Nigeria's tertiary education is grossly underfunded, with a peasant budgetary allocation of not more than 3%! Recommendations were given on the need for the Nigerian government to implement the United Nation's stipulations of 26% educational budgetary allocation, which would curb the perennial curse of underfunding the universities. It was also recommended that there is the need to eradicate the challenge of academic corruption that is now commonplace in Nigeria's tertiary system. University tertiary system. University lecturers must be held accountable for their actions and inactions as this would further ensure that the proposed high standards of universities are met.

USA-AFRICA DIALOGUE AND CONVERSATIONS ON DEMOCRACY

Democracy in Africa is on a shaky foundation. It is expected that African countries practicing democracy would experience an upward trajectory, but this has not been the case. These countries struggle with development, and their citizens do not often enjoy the dividends of democracy. Furthermore, some African countries practicing democracy only do so in name only. Their state of affairs does not have any identity with democracy.[37] In other saner climes where democracy is practiced, the citizens enjoy good governance, the Constitution is upheld by both the ruler and the ruled, and the countries experience overall growth and development. But the reality is different with African countries practicing democracy. An overview of these countries

36. Toyin Falola, "Urgent Steps Towards Resolving the ASUU Strike," *Premium Times*, August 31 2020, https://opinion.premiumtimesng.com/2020/08/31/urgent-practical-steps-towards-resolving-the-asuu-strike-by-toyin-falola/.

37. Richard L. Sklar, "Democracy in Africa," *African Studies Review* 26, no. 3-4 (1983): 11-24.

informs that democracy is practiced under the guise of autocracy. The indicators of "real" democracy are ostensibly absent. The fact that the citizens enjoy some of their fundamental human rights does not translate into a good democracy. There is a need to come to terms with the fact that democratic dispensations in these countries are marred with violence and humanitarian crises.

The discussions on the USA-Africa Dialogue series reveal the problem of democracy in Africa. In theory, democracy breeds good leaders and good governance, while in practice, specifically in African countries, it has bred bad leaders and government. There have been many back-and-forth discussions to pinpoint why the citizens do not fully enjoy the dividends of democracy. African leaders often ride on the mandate of democracy to unleash autocracy in leadership positions. The tenets of democracy allow for a change in government, that is, government transition. This ensures that the government in power is legitimate and fully supported by the masses that brought it to power. In a democratic country like Nigeria, for example, the maximum tenure for the president is eight years. This is similar to other democratic African countries, albeit with slight modifications. On getting to power, however, the maximum number of years to rule becomes short in the view of African leaders who execute policies that are not in tandem with the citizens' welfare. In leadership positions, they blatantly disregard their promises to the people, amassing wealth exploited by the state and refusing to let go of power when their tenures expire.

The major threat to the survival of democracy is the autocratic nature of the leaders. For instance, the late president of Zimbabwe, Robert Mugabe, refused to let go of power when he was defeated in an election with excessive government interference.[38] To many, Robert Mugabe might represent the ideals and values of pan-Africanism but did not exhibit the ideals and values of democracy. Mugabe unleashed brutal force on his dissidents to consolidate power to pursue personal vendettas. An election brought him into power, but he would not allow that same electoral process to keep him out of power. The failure of democracy to bring the emergence of good leadership made academics wonder if western democracy is congruous to African societies. There are cultural and ethnic complexities in most African societies that determine the kind of leadership that the existence of democracy has not addressed. Western democracy is not seen as functional to the African system of leadership. Academics posited that it would take a change in African leaders' mindsets to see why democracy is essential for the growth and development of their states.

Scholars note the dwindling democratic practices in most African countries. Democracy allows the presence of opposition to keep the ruling parties on their toes and provide choices for the citizens. However, opposing forces in countries that supposedly practice democracy are greeted with intimidation and oppression. The ruling

38. Renee Montagne and Charlayne Hunter-Gault, "Zimbabwe's Mugabe Hangs on to Power," *NPR*, February 23, 2007, https://www.npr.org/templates/story/story.php?storyId=7565571.

party hardly tolerated any opposition in a bid to strengthen their grip on governance, clearing the path for autocracy and anarchy. Also, the citizens' fundamental human rights have sometimes been violated and severely restricted by the government of democratic countries. Whenever the citizens express their grievances about the anti-populist policies, the government harasses them and keeps them out of the government structure.

The dominant presence of social media in African countries leads to retaliation from the government, especially when the citizens use them as platforms to pursue their desire for good governance. In that regard, some African countries have begun to restrict their citizens' use of social media in desperate attempts to curtail their freedom of expression.[39] In Nigeria, the government once banned the use of *Twitter*, a micro-blogging platform, by the citizens, under the pretext that its activities threaten the existence and security of the nation. The Nigerian government denied them freedom of expression by unconstitutionally shutting over five million Nigerians out of this social media platform. Nigerians had begun to use *Twitter* for cyber-activism in their pursuit of good governance. Other African countries are also pandering toward dictatorship by limiting the citizens' freedom of expression.

Furthermore, democracy in African countries is threatened by the violence associated with elections. There is hardly a peaceful transition of government in most African countries. If elections are held, it occurs basically to keep the current government in power and hardly represent the people's choices. African leaders often tamper with their constitutions to enable them to stay in power for long and are not concerned with the citizens' choices. Reports confirm that the Rwandan president is set to contest elections for a fifth term. [40] He tampered with the constitution to make this possible.

Academics attempted to identify the traits behind the African thirst for perennial leadership. Conclusions are based on the suspicion that most African leaders do not fully understand the tenets of democracy. To many of them, democracy remains elusive in African societies, as evident in the kind of governance it brings.

In many African countries, the culture of democracy is declining.[41] Many years after proclaiming democracy, these countries are still experimenting with democracy as a means to an end. The breakdown of law and order characterizes African democratic states. Democracy hardly brings the benefits associated with it. The culture of

---

39. Farooq A. Kperogi, ed. *Digital Dissidence and Social Media Censorship in Africa* (New York: Routledge, 2022).

40. Chiamakar Okafor, "Rwanda President, Paul Kagame to seek Re-election in 2024," *Premium Times*, July 11, 2021, https://www.premiumtimesng.com/news/more-news/542040-rwanda-president-paul-kagame-to-seek-re-election-in-2024.html.

41. Christof Hartmann, "Leverage and Linkage: How Regionalism Shapes Regime Dynamics in Africa," In *Democratization and Competitive Authoritarianism in Africa*, edited by Matthijs Bogaards and Sebastian Elischer (Cham: Springer Wiesbaden, 2016), 79-98.

Figure 3.2. "Political Activism" by Dr. Kazeem Ekeolu. Two scholars are projecting conversations and arguments on the country's political developments.

democracy is failing in many African countries because of the poor leadership culture. Academics argue about the importance of democracy to the masses. This argument is valid because the citizens have yet to enjoy true democratic principles and ideas for years after years. Democracy allows the people to comprise an integral part of governance, but the reality in most African states differs from this. In these African

countries, democracy is not for the people but for leaders bent on keeping the seat of power for a long time. An overview of democratic practices in some countries tells that they are failing. The security architecture is continually made porous due to internal struggles, of which many casualties are recorded. Democratic leaders rule with iron fists, thus crediting the arguments that African leaders are democratic dictators. Their actions undermine and ridicule the true definition of democracy.

When democratic leaders stay longer than necessary in power, it begets citizens' mistrust and often leads them to revolution and rebellion. In most cases, these are usually met with a crackdown by the state forces, with many deaths. Scholars posit that most African leaders fail to identify with the tenets and principles of democracy. Also, the principle of popular choices for leadership is a flawed one. Populism does not equal meritocracy or accountability. This is why the citizens keep electing unpopular leaders who are neither transparent nor accountable. There is a dire need to fall back on the African educational system to promote a good culture of democracy. The traditional African system is built on the principle of communalism, which foregrounds collective efforts from the society to ensure that all members, irrespective of their class, are not left out in welfare programs. The African educational system also comprises a repertoire of knowledge in tandem with the principles and practices of democracy. This educational system must be an integral aspect of the emergence of leadership. There are other postulations that the concept of democracy, as it applies to Africa, needs to encompass the notion of social justice, as this would prove consequential in ensuring an egalitarian society that would eradicate social inequality and class stratification.

USA-AFRICA DIALOGUE AND CONVERSATIONS ON CULTURE OF LEADERSHIP

African countries are used as reference points for bad leadership. An overview of the leadership structure in most African countries leaves no room for desirability.[42] It could be posited that the challenges Africa faces today are due to the sorry state of leadership. Despite having indigenous leaders, countries in Africa have not moved forward—both economically and politically. They are fixed on a point. The problem of bad leadership is evident in the crumbling economies of some African countries and the disarray in their state affairs. Studies have revealed the worst form of leadership in African countries after independence. There are arguments that the colonial rulers fared better than the current African leaders. The leadership crisis in Africa has become a bane to development. Africans have long not enjoyed the benefits of good leadership so much that one crisis succeeds another in the quest for good governance. A good leader is sensitive to the people. Most African countries' leadership structures

42. Kola Muheeb Bakare and Micheal Avosetinyen, "Race in a Maze: The Relentless Search for and Challenges of Leadership in Africa," *Afro Asian Journal of Social Sciences* 10, no. 10 (2019): 1-25.

do not consider the welfare of the masses. Policy formulation and implementation are not considered with the interests of the citizens in mind. Thus, due to failed leadership, countries cannot forge ahead with growth and development.

Discussions highlight the problems of leadership in Africa. This is necessary to proffer solutions. A good leadership structure represents the totality of the people. Representation is key for good leaders. However, the reality is that African leaders do not represent the people's wishes to assume the leadership mantle. It seems as if many African leaders are unaware that good leadership is key to the plans and programs any government has for development. When there is a clamor that Africa is relegated to the background in global affairs, leadership struggles in Africa may contribute to this.

The citizens are looking for ways to take over governance because the leaders do not represent their wishes, hijacking governance and bringing power to the hands of the people. The implications of citizens' revolting against the government of the day are in addition to national problems. The worst crisis any nation can suffer is that of leadership. When no great leadership exists, the nation suffers from the endless cycle of bad government.

In the Dialogue series, there are responses on the kinds of leaders Africa has had to contend with. A good leader is a visionary who transforms the citizens' expectations into realities and conceives plans and programs to drive the nation into progress. However, there is a disconnect between the leaders and the state, that is, the people. The relationship between them is antagonistic. The people often have to contend with state forces because their leaders marginalize them. The expectations of the masses from the government are high. There are arguments that African leaders, in their bid to emulate the governance structure of the western nations, lost track in the process. It is pertinent for African leaders to understand that political climates are different and that what is good for the goose may not be good for the gander. African leaders must understand that they must cultivate leadership values consistent with the masses' wishes. The major development a country can have is that of positive leadership. The rest of the body is fine when the head is fine. It is difficult to separate the overall civilization of Africa from a good leadership structure. There are first-rate countries today because the state politics therein is enviable. Good leaders can take a country from the dark to light; Nelson Mandela comes to mind. African leaders can tread this road too.

Scholars point out the need for responsible leadership to curb the menace of bad leadership. Responsible leadership is conscious of the people's yearnings and aspirations and sees them as an integral part of the government. To achieve responsible leadership, there is a need for the reorientation of the thinking approach of most African leaders. In reality, some African leaders are excessively dependent on foreign countries, ultimately affecting the leadership structures in place. African leaders are advised to look inwards for solutions that challenge national sovereignty. Bad leadership in Africa has been traced to the corruption and greed of leaders. Therefore, there

is a need to eradicate these social vices militating against development at the grassroots level. African ideals and values need to be preached and taught in the minds of the young ones to set the pace for good leadership.

In an article, Greg Mill posited that the commonplaceness of poverty is due to the bad choices African leaders make.[43] Academics postulate the need for African leaders to adopt homegrown solutions to problems of national development. This is possible if there is homegrown leadership. The few African leaders celebrated today could make imprints because they identified with the people, those who brought them to power and thus centered their plans and programs concerning the people's welfare, channeling the path for development. With the ideals of good leadership, the African project would be a reality.

CONCLUSION

The USA-Africa Dialogue Series has touched on the grey issues challenging Africa in its entirety. With the identification of the problems, African academics have been able to discuss these issues and create solutions. Because there are unending discussions on issues or matters specific to Africa, academics are kept up-to-date. The conversations on this online platform facilitate knowledge production and homegrown solutions to identified problems. Doubtless, the Dialogue has facilitated a platform for cross-disciplinary communications among scholars of African extraction and their counterparts in the diaspora and all of the pan-African world. Indeed, it has created a platform for taking social media one step beyond its traditional tangential stance in that through it, serious intellectual erudition has always been taking place, and exchanges of deep scholarly ideas are facilitated. Even more than anything else, a quick survey of users of this platform would reveal the important fact that through this medium, communications among African intellectuals across different generations, from fresh graduate students to retired professors from various fields, are taking place.

43. Greg Mills, *Why Africa is Poor and what Africans can do about it* (South Africa: Penguin Random House, 2012).

PART B

THE BIG THEMES

4

CORRUPTION AND CITIZEN'S AGONIES

Corruption, or the misuse of power and public resources for personal gain, has been part of societies since humanity first organized into groups to share resources. The individuals responsible for public resources are also in the best position to engage in corrupt practices. "Arthashastra," a political treatise written by Kautilya around the 3rd century BC, compares the identification of corrupt practices with watching a fish drink water; neither activity is easily observed. The universal phenomenon of government corruption can occur in developed or undeveloped nations and happens in governments of all sizes. The key differentiator is the level of prevalence in a specific country's government.

Incidents of corruption reflect pervasive activity endemic to autocratic and democratic states worldwide in varying degrees. Modern African societies have endured substantial amounts of high-profile corruption within the corridors of government power and the halls of private companies. Corruption has eaten deep into the African continent, creating a few elites and oligarchs while most of the continent wallows in ongoing poverty. Corrupt practices have ended several African regimes, but their successors have neither been immune nor opposed to corruption.

Most African countries are ranked as some of the most corrupt nations in the world, as judged by Transparency International's Corruption Perception Index (CPI). Despite abundant natural resources, most sub-Saharan countries have ailing econo-

mies. Mismanagement has allowed government-enabled corruption to strangle attempts at economic development. A commonly accepted truism is that "Africa is very rich, but Africans are very poor." Lecuna has observed that the African people remain impoverished due to corrupt elites who benefit from corrupt practices.[1] Their ill-gotten gains are smuggled to the Western world and the Middle East through offshore bank accounts and luxuries purchased abroad.

Those who follow African politics see daily allegations of corruption reported by various media outlets. At different times, domestic and foreign investigations of African governments have revealed large-scale corruption among government officials and public servants. There are far-reaching implications for the alarms raised by this media coverage—it is a public crisis, and this hydra-headed monster must be urgently addressed to make any progress in the fight against corruption.

Governance in Africa plays a significant role in determining the relationship between elected officials and their constituents at the grassroots level. Leaders are primarily elected to allocate resources for public development. These amenities can provide a solid platform for citizens to improve their social standing, addressing the high unemployment rate that is endemic to many African countries. Politicians are expected to place such developmental efforts at the top of their political agenda.

However, high poverty levels in many African countries have been linked to government corruption. Entrenched interests are known to control government institutions so completely that the idea of national development has become a fantasy.[2] A lack of transparency in many governmental processes has affected citizen engagement at every level. Enormous amounts of resources are wasted on corrupt practices, locally and internationally, that could be channeled to address the economic concerns of African nations—these countries could have addressed their underdeveloped status many times over.[3]

The endemic nature of corruption in many African countries, especially at institutional levels, continues to block productive development, especially for countries that lack the mechanisms to address this issue. Most economic problems that plague African nations stem from widespread corruption at all sociopolitical and economic levels; their devastating effects are evident in national performance, day-to-day administration, and political operations. Democratic efforts in Africa are undermined by national corruption that hinders political consolidation.[4]

---

1. A. Lecuna, "Corruption and Size Decentralization," *Journal of Applied Economics* 15, no. 1 (2012): 139–168.

2. O. Ojo, "A Political Economy Approach to understanding Corruption and the Challenge of Human Development." In *Corruption and the Challenge of Human Development*, ed. Aina A. (Babcock University: Development Policy, Conflict and Strategic Studies, 2007).

3. Z. Momoh, *Faces of Corruption in Nigeria* (Jos: Global Multi-Services Ltd, 2009).

4. J.G. Lambsdorff, "The Transparency International Corruption Perceptions Index: Whose Perceptions are they anyway," *Citeseer*, 2003, htttp://www.citeseerx.ist.psu.edu/viewdoc/download?doi=10.1.1.

The gross inadequacies of successive African governments result from corrupt practices perpetuating the essence of governance, civil service, and public morality. Some have suggested that small amounts of corruption can assist individuals looking to overcome bureaucratic rigidities. However, this merely creates greater inefficiency—corrupt practices, such as bribes paid to bypass official processes, can lead to established patterns of governmental abuse.

DIMENSIONS OF CORRUPTION IN AFRICA

Corruption manifests in African countries at macro and micro levels. These practices are not limited to a specific segment of society, although the frequency and magnitude of these occurrences may be greater among specific groups.[5] Corrupt practices have been reported by civil societies and the public sector, making it difficult to determine where vice thrives the most. Although it has been overlooked by academic literature, public opinion surveys and media evidence point to large-scale corruption occurring in every sector of a country like Nigeria—it obstructs the delivery of public services and impacts citizens' daily lives. Measuring the intensity of corrupt practices in most sectors is difficult, but the absence of empirical evidence does not invalidate its existence. Instead, it conceals the full magnitude of the problem.

In the context of African behavior, internal corruption refers to practices conducted by leaders and citizens on African soil. This often manifests in the commonplace embezzlement of public funds, contract racketeering, and other activities. In 2005, members of the Malawian parliament allegedly looted US$3 million from the nation's treasury. One notable member of parliament, who doubled as a member of the Agricultural Development Committee, reportedly used his share of the proceeds to erect a luxury hotel in his hometown. In Zaire, the late Mobutu Sese Seko was one of the most corrupt African leaders; he regularly exploited his country's public resources to increase his wealth.

Corruption in African countries can also involve practices conducted by foreigners collaborating with local citizens. Their illicit and immoral acts can involve money laundering or bribery to win government contracts. Successive African governments have been implicated in various foreign deals that involved kickbacks, bribery, and outright theft of public property in connection with government projects.

Corruption can involve gross abuses of public office for private gain when officials deviate from accepted norms to satisfy personal greed.[6] A sitting Nigerian governor from the impoverished northern part of Nigeria was caught on camera receiving wads of foreign currency that he stored in the pockets of his *babanriga*. The ease with

---

370.4882&rep=rep1&type=pdf.

5. O. Osumah and I. Aghedo, "Challenges and Prospects of Anti-Corruption Crusade in Nigeria's Fourth Republic," *Ilorin Journal of Business and Social Science* 15, no. 2 (2013): 81–96.

6. Samuel Huntington, *Political Order in Changing Societies* (Connecticut: Yale University Press, 1978).

which the governor padded his outfit using bundles of foreign currency—oblivious to the fact that he was being recorded—almost suggested that his clothes were expressly made for such occasions. Although the video went viral during Nigeria's election period, the governor still retained his position.

Mabey and Johnson, a UK-based organization that operated civil engineering projects in countries that included Ghana, Angola, and Madagascar, was convicted of foreign bribery. The company paid huge amounts of money to government officials to secure contracts. Reports from South Africa suggest that BAE systems have been involved in corruption and bribery connected with shady arms deals and illegal weapons sales to warring African factions.

Nigeria's Halliburton scandal, for example, remains one of its most notable incidents of corruption; an executive of the company pleaded guilty to bribing various government functionaries between 1994 and 2007 to secure official contacts.[7] Other unconfirmed reports describe High Street banks facilitating money laundering arrangements in the UK for Nigerian politicians between 1999 and 2005. Two former Nigerian governors—one from Bayelsa, an oil-producing state, and the other from Plateau State, in the north—used UK banks to launder state funds for personal use. Nations like the United Kingdom monitor complex financial activities, and they were able to identify the misconduct of these Nigerian politicians, but not before one of them escaped by dressing like a woman to evade detection at the airport.

These incidents demonstrate the prevalent attitude among Africa's present crop of political leaders. A political adviser to General Sanni Abacha is said to have appropriated US$1.3 billion of his country's foreign reserves for personal use. Although he was dismissed for his actions, the stolen funds remained in his possession; his only punishment was the loss of future opportunities for theft.

A report by Amundsen tracked different dimensions of corruption in Nigeria and how they affect the country. In most African countries, corruption occurs for two reasons: rent-seeking, which diverts public funds through actions such as embezzlement, abuse of power, nepotism, and cronyism, or maintaining control over government offices and decisions, which allows continued access to rent-seeking opportunities. Government control is retained through practices that can include electoral corruption and judicial corruption.[8]

Nigeria's history, from colonial times, through the military era and into the present republic, includes countless incidents of officials exploiting public resources and abusing their positions. The private sector—especially the crude oil industry—has been a willing accomplice in these crimes.

---

7. Osumah and Aghedo, "Challenges and Prospects of Anti-Corruption."

8. G. Amundsen, "Good Governance in Nigeria. A Study in Political Economy and Donor Support," *Norad*, 2010, https://www.norad.no/en/toolspublications/publications/2010/good-governance-in-nigeria-a-study-in-political-economy-and-donor-support/.

Embezzlement, bribery, and kickbacks have frequently occurred, undermining the state's capacity to manage resources effectively.[9] Despite Nigeria's abundant natural resources, its leadership has been reluctant to distribute benefits fairly to all its citizens. Western investigations into corrupt practices have provided detailed information about incidents of embezzlement, with information about those involved, the magnitude of their involvement, and the total cost of their actions.[10] However, gaps in the country's legal and institutional systems regularly allow corrupt individuals to escape unpunished.

In 2012, the Global Witness organization reported that Nigeria had lost US$400 billion of public funds since the country's independence in 1960. Abacha is alleged to have embezzled billions of dollars during his five-year rule. Various Nigerian governments have had opportunities to reclaim part of Abacha's fortune after his demise. The Swiss government initially froze more than US$600 million of Abacha's deposits in various Swiss banks, based on the request of Nigeria's former President Olusegun Obasanjo. In 2011, US$140 million of those funds were returned to the Nigerian government. The UK government convicted James Ibori, a former governor of Nigeria, of laundering money siphoned from state coffers. The governor's numerous accounts held money far above his official salary.

Nigeria's oil sector regularly collaborates with the government's corrupt activities. The crude oil subsidy program, developed to ensure public access to refined crude oil products, has resulted in great losses for the government. Meanwhile, oil importers have entered into shady arrangements that seek profit at the expense of the public. Approximately US$6.8 billion was lost to oil subsidies between 2009 and 2011.[11] Government officials have been the major beneficiaries of these programs.

The Nigerian National Petroleum Company (NNPC) has allegedly given unfair subsidies to companies owned by government officials. Investigations have found that some importers fraudulently received subsidies without importing any fuel. Other corrupt practices, such as the oil bunkering perpetrated by organized crime groups in the Niger Delta region, and the government's complacency in dealing with the perpetrators, shows how the oil sector is entwined with government corruption in Nigeria.

---

9. Abel Blackman, "Raising Naija: A Nigerian Results-Based Transfer Scheme for Improved Public Goods & Services Delivery," *Havard Kennedy School*, 2014, http://www.hks.harvard.edu/var/ezp_site/storage/fckeditor/file/pdfs/degree-programs/mpaid/SYPA_AbelBlackman_2014.pdf.

10. United States Department of Justice, U.S. "Freezes more than $458 Million Stolen by Former Nigerian Dictator in Largest Kleptocracy Forfeiture Action ever Brought in the U.S.," *Justice*, 2014, http://www.justice.gov/opa/pr/us-freezes-more-458-million-stolen-former-nigerian-dictator-largest-kleptocracy-forfeiture.

11. Berne Declaration, "Traders Collude in Oil Corruption, says Swiss NGO," *Swiss Info*, 2013, http://www.swissinfo.ch/eng/traders-collude-in-oil-corruption--says-swiss-ngo/37260152.

Figure 4.1. "Snake in the Bank" by Michael Efionayi. Snake in the bank is one of the ridiculous excuses for missing national funds and embezzlement. It shows a corrupt potbellied politician who has a snake that swallows money in the belly.

The budgetary framework that distributes funds among Nigeria's different tiers of government also encourages wholesale corruption; financial oversight is haphazard and poorly enforced. State and local government heads can allocate funds without the proper safeguards to identify embezzlement, misappropriation, and corrupt practices. The awarding of state contracts is regularly done through nepotism, or the man-know-man system, ensuring that preferred contractors receive lucrative deals. Kick-

backs inevitably follow as standards are compromised, leaving citizens to bear the costs of a corrupt process. One Dutch company was reported to have paid bribes to secure a contract for performance-related services from an NNPC subsidiary, paying approximately US$200,000 to politicians through various intermediaries.[12]

Nepotism and cronyism have become a mainstay in many post-independence African societies. In places like Nigeria, political appointments are exclusively reserved for family members or cronies of the current leaders. Other positions in the civil service are populated based on quota systems rooted in ethnic sentimentality, religious bias, and political affiliations. The idea of meritocracy is dismissed, and efficient practices are discouraged.

Nigeria's development has been hindered by officials who make appointments based on connections instead of qualifications. Investigations have uncovered various recruitment scandals where positions are distributed among friends of political office holders to the detriment of the entire country. Such scandals normally involve positions at the NNPC and other institutions that are inaccessible to members of the public who lack inside connections. Favoritism for specific individuals and corporations is common in awarding government contracts.[13]

THE INSTITUTIONALIZATION OF CORRUPTION IN AFRICA

Institutionalizing corruption in a society results in wholesale changes to its value systems and behavioral norms. In African nations, the manifestations of corruption in the political arena show how they are integral to power. As a societal problem, it has become an accepted norm that contaminates every socio-political engagement. The retrospective analysis of a country like Nigeria reveals how corruption has permeated deep into its national fabric from the moment of independence.[14]

Corruption as a culture normalized in Africa can be traced to military interventions in politics, which have occurred in various African countries after independence. Military heads of state made brazen displays of embezzling state funds, and almost every person since then who has aspired to hold political office has done so with the intent to follow their example. As long as individuals seek office to access state coffers and the immunity from prosecution that accompanies those offices, true development will remain out of reach.

One can argue that corruption in Nigeria has bordered more on the institutionalization of the concept, not the politicization of it. The country's ruling class has been

12. O. Oarhe, "Tonic or Toxin? The State, Neopatrimonialism, and Anticorruption Efforts in Nigeria," *Journal of Policy Studies* 28, no. 1 (2013): 111–134.

13. World Economic Forum, "Global Competitiveness Report 2014–2015," *World Economic Forum*, 2016, https://reports.weforum.org/global-competitiveness-report-2014-2015/.

14. S. Akindele, "A critical analysis of corruption and its problems in Nigeria," *Anthropologist* 7, no. 1 (2005): 7–18.

a major proponent of corrupt activities, and the institutions established to counter corrupt practices remain weak. Whenever corrupt activities are identified, the ruling class benefits from multiple escape routes that make it almost impossible for anyone to face the consequences of their actions.[15]

Every society is vulnerable to corruption, although the specific details can vary depending on the circumstances. Generally, corruption is common in societies where strong institutional mechanisms are incapable of detecting, prosecuting, and punishing bad behavior. People are more likely to exploit opportunities for engaging in corrupt activities when they are less likely to be caught. This major factor contributes to the magnitude of corrupt practices in underdeveloped nations.

Globally, Africa is considered the most corrupt continent based on the number of corrupt practices that go unchecked. Many analysts point to this problem as the major reason most African countries have struggled with national development.[16] Corrupt practices, from high-level political graft to low-level bribes issued to police and security personnel, are widely accepted by ordinary Africans. These attitudes are closely related to the political clientelism and patrimonialism that characterize African governments, which blur the distinction between public and private assets.

Corruption is evident in the most casual African environments where rules that maintain order are subverted. Individuals who request basic government services find themselves joining long lines of other people relying on overwhelmed government officials. The immigration office at Alagbon, Lagos, in Nigeria, is a typical example: the wait time for individuals who request passports is not based on their place in line. Instead, it depends on their ability to convince immigration officers that their requests should be processed first. The most convincing arguments normally involve additional payments or other favors.

Political graft poses the greatest cost to Africa; petty bribes corrode institutions and undermine the people's trust in those in power. A 2009 poll found that citizens of East African nations paid significant bribes to access various public services, and academic researchers have identified links between graft and the ordinary costs of doing business. A former head of Nigeria's anti-graft commission has stated that improving a country's corruption index by a single point can lead to an increase of as much as four per cent in that country's GDP.

Unchecked corruption can increase social unrest. At the turn of the millennium, unrest in the Niger Delta region was driven by claims that oil extraction did not benefit local inhabitants. The largest oil revenues went directly to the government, and government officials allegedly siphoned off the remaining funds. Meanwhile, in-

---

15. J. Nwanegbo and J. Odigbo, "Governance, Corruption and Crisis of Governance in Post Independence Nigeria," *African Journal of Politics and Society Quarterly* 1, no. 1 (2015): 24–44.

16. S. Hanson, "Corruption in Sub-Saharan Africa," *Think Africa Press*, August 6, 2009, http://www.thinkafricapress.com/economy/causin.

vestigations found that some locals were connected to the oil thefts that occurred in the region. Other accusations suggest that some residents collude with the government and other entities to ensure that the region remains impoverished. Citizens who complain about corrupt practices are often found in compromising situations of their own, aiding and abetting such actions either ignorantly or otherwise.

HOW CORRUPTION NEGATIVELY IMPACTS VULNERABLE CITIZENS

Corruption is ubiquitous, and analysts believe Africa has the least effective mechanisms to address its economic implications. The Nigerian Corruption Index has identified the Nigeria Police Force as the country's most corrupt organization, which is supposed to bring corrupt individuals to justice. The fight against corruption in Nigeria is an uphill task.

African nations are the lowest ranked on the global standard of living index, so one must hope that drastic measures are taken to change the status quo. Corruption not only hinders a society's social and economic development. It also opposes good governance and tramples citizens' rights to hold officials accountable for illegal activity and the misappropriation of natural resources.

Many African citizens are in disadvantaged or vulnerable groups based on gender, peer status, social status, or disability. These individuals often rely on public goods and services because they have difficulty accessing equivalents from the private sector. In African societies, vulnerable individuals have few opportunities to participate in the meaningful public implementation of policies or programs. One example is the indigenous people who rely on natural resources—government policies concerning exploiting natural resources directly impact them. The survival of these people can depend on decisions made in their absence.

The exploitation of natural resources enabled by corrupt activity often leads to environmental degradation that can threaten public health. People who live in the Niger Delta region, especially in remote locations where oil exploration is most active, often find their water contaminated by crude oil. Most of these people are fishermen who depend on aquaculture for their livelihood, and pollution threatens their economic survival. Benefits from oil exploration, which should ordinarily accrue to such communities, are either misappropriated by local leaders or not distributed at all. Sometimes the proceeds are claimed by government personnel looking to increase their fortunes.

Corruption undermines the rights of indigenous people advocating for their communities. Attempts to speak out against environmental atrocities often draw reprisals from the government, as was the case with the late Ken Saro-Wiwa under the military regime of General Abacha. The government's complicity in environmental exploita-

tion makes it willing to ignore ecological damage in exchange for payments from the multinational corporations that extract oil.

The United Nations Development Program affirmed that corruption could reinforce gender marginalization in Africa.[17] In many African countries, women have difficulty accessing public services and resources due to gender bias—some of them experience sexual extortion and harassment while seeking assistance. Corruption in connection with land ownership affects women more often than men because of land's value as a resource. This can include women being prevented from inheriting land, appropriating their land for sale to multinational investors, and sexual extortion. These acts increase gender disparities while undermining the social standing of women to keep them in poverty.

Although there is a shortage of literature regarding the effects of land-related corruption on women, the "Women, Land and Corruption" resource book provides insight from extensive research across eight African countries. The study, undertaken by Transparency International, finds that:

- Women are more vulnerable to sexual extortion in return for land services
- Women receive less compensation from land acquired by external parties
- Women are excluded from negotiations with potential investors during land deals.[18]

As a form of corruption, bribery does not affect all individuals equally. Wealthy individuals may have no problem paying bribes for specific benefits, while society's poorest individuals are left unable to afford public services—demands for bribes inhibit access to basic amenities such as healthcare and education. Restricting resources and benefits to the highest bidder widens the gap between rich and poor, allowing the former to subvert systems for their benefit while leaving everyone else behind.

REACTIONS TO CORRUPTION

The corruption that cuts across Africa is received differently in different contexts. One of the ways that reactions to corruption can differ is based on gender. In Nigeria, male officials are more likely to be involved in corrupt practices than their female counterparts, a function of the proportion of women in the workforce. This phenomenon is evident in the country's various military and paramilitary organizations.

---

17. UNDP and UNIFEM, "Corruption, Accountability and Gender: Understanding the Connections," *UNDP*, 2010, http://www.undp.org/sites/g/files/zskgke326/files/publications/Corruption-accountability-and-gender.pdf.

18. Transparency International, "The Impact of Land Corruption on Women: Insights from Africa," *Transparency*, 2018, https://www.transparency.org/en/news/impact-of-land-corruption-on-women-insights-from-africa#.

When illegitimate acts are conducted by uniformed security personnel, their abuse of uniform is corruption in its own right.

For example, the Lagos state government introduced a Bus Rapid Transit (BRT) Scheme, which involved dedicated lanes for special buses to reduce traffic congestion. Corrupt individuals quickly exploited these lanes, and men in uniform began using BRT lanes without authorization—on one occasion, the then Lagos State Governor Babatunde Fashola personally arrested two military officers for illegally driving in a dedicated BRT lane.[19] Such incidents are common in Nigeria, where the men expected to uphold society's rules are the ones who frequently violate them.

In 2019, the internet was agog after a video showed soldiers assaulting operatives of the Lagos State Traffic Management Authority (LASTMA). The soldiers had been stopped for illegally using the dedicated BRT lane, and the ensuing argument led to a member of the LASTMA team being assaulted. Men conducted illegitimate acts in both BRT incidents, which may validate the UNODC assertion that men are more likely to be involved in corrupt practices.

Corrupt practices are not confined to the Nigerian military. The Nigeria Police Force and other uniformed agencies make their contributions. Cameras have caught LASTMA representatives demanding bribes from motorists who allegedly violated Lagos State traffic laws. In one instance, a motorist was escorted directly to an ATM to withdraw cash to pay the bribe.

The story of uniformed men collecting bribes remains the same in East Africa. In 2017, the *Huffington Post* reported that two Kenyan police officers were caught on camera collecting bribes.[20] And government institutions often take action to prevent their employees from facing legal consequences. Reuters reported that Kenya Police officers helped two of their colleagues escape serious consequences; a sting operation conducted by anti-graft operatives was interrupted by individuals from Kabete Police Station who fired warning shots. The arrested officers managed to escape with the bait money during the confusion.[21]

ELECTORAL CORRUPTION

The citizens of countries in Africa perceive elections differently than political elites. A fair electoral system ordinarily allows enfranchised individuals to benefit from increased participation and responsiveness to governmental processes—elections are normally a tool for holding political leaders accountable. Those who do not

19. Olasunkanmi Akoni and Monsur Olowoopejo, "Fashola 'Arrests' Col, Seargent on BRT Lane," *Vanguard Newspaper*, 2017.

20. Huffington Post, "Kenya: Corrupt Cops Caught in the Act (Video)," *Huff Post*, 2017, https://www.huffpost.com/entry/kenya-corrupt-cops-caught_n_342140.

21. Reuters, "Kenya Police Help Colleagues Escape Anti-graft Officers with Warning Shots," *Reuters*, 2018, https://www.reuters.com/article/us-kenya-corruption-idUSKCN1NY0MS.

serve the public interest should not receive support from the voting public. Elections can also reward effective leaders for delivering positive results.

Elections are important civic functions. Civil societies and other international bodies devote considerable resources to monitoring election outcomes. However, most African societies fail to manage elections objectively. Successive African governments have been incapable of holding transparent elections free from violence, which speaks volumes about how those processes are perceived. Rather than campaigning with ideas to convince the public, political elites merely polarize the electorate with monetary inducements. This financial manipulation is effective because impoverished voters are willing to exchange their votes for table scraps.

It is rare that an election—in any country in Africa—is not accompanied by violent protests and threats to the rule of law. Electoral trends in Ethiopia, Kenya, Ivory Coast, Uganda and elsewhere show the fragility of the process in African countries. The 2008 election crisis in Kenya challenged the integrity of the country's electoral system.

Despite the public's zeal, African elections subvert the same function they intend to perform. In comparing voters' demands with their candidates' results, one might conclude that neither the voters nor the individuals seeking office have any true plans for development. Although some might claim that elections in Africa fail because the political elites ignore the demands of their constituents, careful investigation reveals that voters may have failed to uphold their responsibilities.

The practice of vote trading, when voters readily sell their electoral power to the candidates who will pay the most, reveals the dynamics at work. Campaign discussions may appear rational and patriotic before elections, with questions about the ability to provide basic amenities to specific communities. The collective goal of national development suddenly vaporizes on election day, when voters are reluctant to uphold their civic responsibility without monetary inducement.

Africa's voting models indicate that many voters are only concerned about immediate personal gratification, not the long-term advantages of national development. In an election context, poverty seems to have blinded citizens to the point where minor monetary inducements are enough to sway most voters. Ultimately, elections go to the highest bidder, regardless of their true support among the electorates.

CORRUPT PRACTICES UNDERMINING DEVELOPMENTAL GOALS

International power dynamics do not rely on military strength alone; nations compete with other nations based on economic capabilities. Countries with thriving economies understand the regressive effects of corruption and take decisive action to fight it. Unfortunately, Africa's developing nations struggle to keep up with more powerful nations, yet they handle institutionalized corruption with kid gloves.

Figure 4.2. "Cash in the Sky" by Dr. Kazeem Ekeolu. As poor people suffer, money is flown abroad by crooked politicians.

Various African governments have unveiled ten- or twenty-year plans to achieve development goals through economic stimulus programs. Nigeria's Vision 20:2020 initiative, drafted in 2008, attempted to make Nigeria one of the world's 20 largest economies by 2020. This strategic plan should have concluded within 12 years, but the

year 2020 has come and gone. Nigeria's economic status has remained unchanged, and its minor improvements are irrelevant when considering its overall context.

Attainable development goals have two requirements: financial resources and a commitment to apply those resources effectively in pursuit of the goals. Nigeria and other African countries already have abundant mineral resources to provide financial support. Many countries allocate financial resources for their development initiatives during the project drafting stage. The sectors that would be affected by the project submit long-term plans for economic growth. However, this is where most implementation stops in Africa.

After the initial steps, citizens begin to see and hear stories about funds that have been embezzled, mismanaged, and misappropriated. Various officials are implicated in the siphoning or outright stealing of funds allocated to development projects. Their immoral and unpatriotic acts improve their lives at the nation's expense. This is a major reason why citizens of African countries abandon hope of national development, emigrating to saner climes.

Corruption's negative impact goes beyond the individuals involved in the acts or the agencies implicated. Citizens suffer as natural resource revenues are squandered, and governments impose levies on individuals and organizations to compensate for the shortfall. When corrupt officials steal public funds, it amounts to indirect theft from the public. Fela Anikulapo-Kuti said that the average Nigerian is robbed in three ways: leg, arms, and pen. Citizens can take direct action to address the first two forms of theft, but they are vulnerable to those who steal the nation's wealth through the power of the pen.

Perpetrators of corruption face few consequences apart from the erosion of trust among their country's citizens. Most corrupt officials retain large numbers of sympathizers who support their misdeeds in exchange for a cut of the proceeds. The prebendalistic nature of Nigerian politics ensures that these officials regularly win re-election, regardless of their past misdeeds. Prebendalism allows political elites to exploit divisions between groups for electoral support.

The masses who depend on the government for basic services—healthcare, education, and security—suffer the most harm from corrupt practices. They are affected by delays in infrastructure development, substandard products, and high costs. These failures deprive citizens of basic services that are their constitutional rights.

CORRUPTION'S IMPLICATIONS FOR THE NATION

Nations run by corrupt governments suffer from high levels of poverty, but the full implications of corruption occur on three distinct levels: economic, political, and social. African countries have an international reputation for suffering from high levels of corruption, and reputable multinational organizations have made strong

arguments against making Foreign Direct Investments in African economies. Africa cannot be a global competitor without such investments; it will struggle with low economic growth and ongoing brain drain. Bad leadership and poor management practices leech a nation's wealth, while the failure of developmental projects leaves public needs unfulfilled.

The world may recognize the economic potential of nations like Nigeria, but redirecting national resources to benefit a few elites creates fiscal distortions making it difficult to realize that potential. Income inequality increases while high levels of corruption remain. Corruption is generally seen as an obstacle to national progress; its effects are some of the most devastating defeats a nation can endure. Corruption is an antithesis to social development like an untreated, leprous finger threatens other body parts. The effects are so damaging that a nation's long-term prospects for development are harmed, limiting the prospect of foreign investments. Government corruption wastes a nation's resources, preventing the allocation of resources for public development.

On the political level, corruption undermines a government's ability to function or establish policies for national development. Corruption in Africa has fostered mistrust towards any individual in power; anyone aspiring to hold office is generally perceived as a parasite eager to consume state funds. Nigeria's democratic system has remained weak due to institutionalized corruption in the public sector. Brazen attempts to disenfranchise citizens have deprived African nations of many intelligent and effective citizens who might hold office.

The past decade has seen an increased awareness of the need to eradicate corruption in many African nations. Efforts to fight corruption have been encouraged by an international community pushing for transparency and good governance on the African continent. Pressure from international bodies has led to reforms seeking to limit incidents of corruption across various African institutions. Countries such as Liberia, Tanzania and Rwanda have made substantial progress in the fight against corruption. The African Union has also shown its commitment to fighting corruption through various treaties focused on ensuring the effective rule of law and the institutionalization of good governance, but the continent still has a long way to go.

In his 2009 visit to Ghana, then-President Barack Obama applauded the country's impressive record of good governance. However, countries like Nigeria, Kenya, and South Africa continue to progress at a snail's pace in the fight against corruption. Although they have had anti-graft agencies in place for many years, their investigation, prosecution, and prevention of corrupt practices have been ineffective due to the politicization of the process. The failure occurred because government executives funded anti-graft agencies, giving the latter control over the former.

One vivid example was the disbandment of South Africa's Directorate of Special Operations (DSO) in 2008. The DSO, popularly known as the Scorpions, investigated

incidents of corruption in the public sector. After less than a decade, the group was disbanded by a government using the national constitution to validate its actions.[22] International political analysts found that the disbandment was politically motivated, while the African National Congress (ANC) party claimed that the DSO was already being wielded as a political tool. Without any clear rationale, it is presumed that ANC leadership wanted the DSO disbanded after it dared to investigate the ANC president and other prominent party members. The effectiveness of the DSO in tackling organized crime has yet to be duplicated.

The head of an African anti-corruption agency normally struggles to navigate murky waters, entangled webs of conspiracies, implications, and accusations. The acting chairman of the Nigerian anti-graft agency (EFCC), Ibrahim Magu, was suspended and accused of failing to account for up to 332 recovered properties in 2018. Hundreds of millions of dollars in assets were missing, and other properties under his care had deteriorated due to poor management. Two vessels in the agency's possession were allegedly sunk at the NNS Beecroft naval base; reports revealed that the Nigerian navy had issued multiple warnings about the need to unload the contents of the seized vessels. Magu was also accused of failing to comply with regulations regarding the disposal of recovered assets.

Kenya's history shows how corruption can tip a nation toward political crises. Kenya's 2007 elections, which culminated in the incumbent President Kibaki claiming victory over Raila Odinga, erupted in violence that revealed sharp divisions along ethnic lines. Kibaki's inner circle was allegedly unwilling to give up power, and Odinga's followers were ostensibly looking to profit from government positions. Although the Prevention of Corruption Act has existed in Kenya since independence, it has been circumvented and undermined by government authorities.

Although media tabloids churn out weekly stories about corruption, the exposure does not result in legal proceedings. Their effort spent gathering information is ultimately wasted. When the head of Kenya's anti-corruption unit uncovered evidence that Anglo-Leasing and Finance Company Limited, a non-existent company, had received huge sums for government contracts, the attorney-general refused to prosecute the case.

SOCIAL MEDIA AND CORRUPTION

There have been many deliberations that point to corruption as the bane of African civilization. Countless studies have also revealed how African governments exploit state resources to keep foreign accounts and how the citizens bear the brunt. Undoubtedly, Africa is the global hub of corruption, and despite efforts to eradicate it,

---

22. I. Chipkin, "Whither the State? Corruption, Institutions and State-Building in South Africa," *Politikon, South African Journal of Political Studies* 40, 2 (2013): 211–231.

corrupt practices are still rampant. It is imperative to posit that the weak character of the African government contributes to the widespread corruption in African countries.[23] The agitation for the independence of African countries is for African governments to be in charge of the state's wealth and resources; however, they have not performed to the expected standards. An average African leader sees leadership positions as a money-making enterprise where they advance personal interests to the detriment of the citizens and the country. The framework of leadership structures in Africa has failed to alleviate the living conditions of the people and foster national development.[24]

African governments' lack of transparency and accountability poses a difficult problem in eradicating corruption. Furthermore, the institutions created to curb corruption engage in corrupt practices in the long run. Corruption is simply the air we breathe in Africa. Government and government officials see corruption as an integral part of society. There is a plethora of discourses on the effects of corruption in Africa, from the huge debt acquired by countries to the breakdown of law and order, to economic crises, to poor living conditions of the citizens, among others. African citizens view corruption as the embezzlement of public funds and economic wreckage; however, corrupt practices in African societies go beyond that.[25] What goes on in African societies is not corruption but a "corruption complex" which includes, among other things, "nepotism, abuse of power, embezzlement and various forms of misappropriation, influence-peddling, prevarication, insider trading and abuse of the public purse."[26] Using government machinery to assume the mantle of leadership is a form of corruption. The succession of government in Africa does not often reflect the popular choices of the citizens. This is because political leaders leverage law and institutions designed for their selfish ambitions to stay in power. Therefore, when there are postulations on corruption in Africa, it goes beyond the exploitation of the state's resources.

The challenge of curbing corruption in African societies is that it is no longer limited to governments. The citizens are also corrupt. The aphorism goes: "When water chokes you, what do you take to wash it down?" Citizens no longer see another alternative to resolving corruption than to join in corrupt practices.[27] This is one of the many other reasons why corruption is rampant in Nigeria. Over the years, the citizens have clamored for the need for the government to be total in its fight against

---

23. John Mukum Mbaku, *Corruption in Africa: Causes, Consequences, and Cleanups* (Maryland: Lexington Books, 2010).

24. Mbaku, *Corruption in Africa.*

25. Mbaku, *Corruption in Africa.*

26. Helge Rnning, "The Politics of Corruption and the Media in Africa," *Journal of African Media Studies* 1, no. 1 (2009): 155–171.

27. Victor E. Dike, "Corruption in Nigeria: A New Paradigm for Effective Control," *Africa Economic Analysis* 24, no. 8 (2005): 1–22.

corruption. However, since the government is the precursor of corruption, this proved a difficult approach. Therefore, the citizens have no choice but to become scavengers of the country's wreckage.[28] In Nigeria, class stratification also encourages corrupt practices. Here, *all animals are equal, but some are more equal than others.* Nigerians have resigned to the fate that there is no end in sight for corrupt practices. Since the problem of corruption is emblematic of the problem of bad governance, the only solution to eradicating this menace is for the emergence of astute, visionary leaders, which according to the current realities of the Nigerian environment, remains an illusion. There is a folk joke here that if God Himself comes from heaven to fight corrupt practices in Nigeria, it would not be long for Him to be an accomplice of what He fights against.

As much as the citizens have resigned to the fate that corruption is divine and no physical measures would solve it, they have still identified the use of social media as a viable weapon in the fight against corruption.[29] Through the use of social media platforms, the citizens are quick to protest visible corrupt practices in government which not only arouse political consciousness among the rest of the citizens but also draws the attention of international societies.[30] In Nigeria, transparency groups such as TRACKANG and SERAP use Twitter, a micro-blogging platform, to call out corrupt practices of the Nigerian government. The citizens also engage in the government's policies on social media platforms to identify possible corrupt practices. It was on Twitter, for example, that Nigerians were made aware that the Buhari-led administration purchased billion-naira worth of cars for the Nigerien government without ratifying it at the National Assembly. Similarly, it was on Twitter that discourses were made on the corrupt practices in the Buhari-led government. People can hide their real addresses on social media, unlike in the public sphere, where the government can, at will, hunt down discussants deliberating on its system of governance.

There is no doubt that social media helps in the war against corruption in Nigeria, as evident in continuous clamors for the end to this menace. Corruption is a pandemic in Nigeria, and the reality is that even anti-graft bodies are not immune from corrupt practices. [31] Using social media platforms makes citizens aware of corrupt practices, which makes them passionate about pressuring government officials to take appropriate measures.[32] To curb the menace of corruption, there is a need for effective

28. Dike, "Corruption in Nigeria."

29. Kamaldeen Arikewuyo Ahmed, Saudat Sallah Abdulbaqi and Rasaq Muhammad Adisa, "Anti-corruption Campaigns and Nigeria's Development: An Appraisal of Media Roles," *Acta Universitatis Danubius. Communicatio* 13, no. 2 (2019): 99–116.

30. Arikewuyo, Abdulbaqi and Adisa, "Anti-corruption Campaigns and Nigeria's Development."

31. Mala Mustapha, "Corruption in Nigeria: Conceptual and Empirical Notes," *Information, Society and Justice Journal* 3, no. 2 (2010): 165–175.

32. C.E. Uzochukwu, U.E. Patricia and C.A. Ukueze, "Harnessing Social Media Tools in the Fight against Corruption in Nigeria: Challenges and Prospects,"" *International Journal of Social Relevance Communication* 2, no. 11 (2014): 5–14.

communication on social media. It is difficult to determine the importance of social media discourses on Nigeria's development. Social media in Nigeria has been adopted as a public sphere where extensive deliberations are made on issues that concern nation-building. A quick perusal of random tweets or posts on social media platforms—Facebook and Twitter—conveys criticisms of the Nigerian government. Thus, when the issue of corrupt practices is the subject of discussion, it gets nationwide attention on these platforms. The use of social media has provided opportunities for Nigerians to engage in political conversations on aspects of national governance and nation-building.

The use of social media has affected how citizens communicate and react to issues of nation-building in Nigeria.[33] Conventionally, calling out corrupt practices in the country usually involves the conglomeration of people chanting solidarity songs and marching to government houses. Such acts are often seen as dare-devil as there is a high probability of violence occurring. However, social media has become a development tool in the fight against corruption. It gives a voice to the citizens to identify the traces of corruption in the country and scrutinize the policies and programs of the government to be sure they are corruption-free without the fear of intimidation and oppression. The use of social media to call out corrupt practices in Nigerian societies and castigate bad governance has given it the status of the fifth state.[34] The problem of national development in Nigeria hinges on the fact that corruption has penetrated every nook and cranny of society. Idumamge contends that corruption is associated "to our historical experience as a nation and problem of leadership, our level of development, level of citizens' orientation and awareness is tied to this experience."[35] The corruption problem has also affected other spheres of our national life, which foregrounds the need for the citizens to freely discuss the nation's problems in their quest to guide it on the pedestal of national development.

As the Nigerian government carries out routine regulations on traditional media organizations, social media has become an alternate platform for citizens to examine corrupt cases. Although there were attempts by the Nigerian government to curtail the freedom of expression on social media, they have proved abortive. On Twitter, the citizens report happenings in the nation's political systems. When serious corrupt practices are identified, online protest follows, forcing the government to look into the issues. The use of social media has achieved prominence so much that media organizations tap from the conversations on these platforms to report on the socio-political happenings in Nigerian society. Social media platforms are democratized platforms: the culture of social inclusiveness enables the citizenry to issue their takes

33. Uzochukwu, Patricia and Ukueze, "Harnessing Social Media Tools."
34. Uzochukwu, Patricia and Ukueze, "Harnessing Social Media Tools."
35. I. Idumamge, "Democratic Accountability and Public Trust in Nigeria," *Pointblank News*, 2002, http://wwwpointblanknews.com.

on the socio-political realities in society.[36] There is also the aspect of mobilizing the citizens and empowering them to make eradicating corruption more winnable. When there is a mass protest against the government's corrupt practices, there is a huge likelihood that the government would be forced to backtract from policies described as corrupt, which would not have been possible if it had been done traditionally. It can be confidently posited that social media influences thoughts on national development and largely influences how Nigerian governance goes about governance.

Scholars have posited that social media is an influential platform that makes fighting corruption less difficult.[37] Since corrupt practices thrive in an environment where the voices of the masses are silenced, social media offers an alternative voice. The relevance of social media in eradicating the menace of corruption cannot be overemphasized as it provides a new form of political participation among the citizenry. Discourses on national development are open to those with access to social media in Nigeria if they are interested. Social media platforms' networking opportunities provide greater political transparency and public inclusion.[38] According to a report, social media is used to track government's infrastructures, with results showing that the completion of infrastructures in Nigeria is hinged on public awareness on social media platforms.[39] The study concludes that public awareness of these projects on social media ensures that they are completed and gives the citizens the power to make the government accountable and transparent. The government is also left with no choice but to complete some of these projects because the possibility of losing elections exists when the citizens are made aware of uncompleted projects despite the allotted funds. The use of social media is changing the dynamics of good governance in Nigeria. The government now needs to engage the citizenry on social media platforms and update them on ongoing developments.

With the use of social media, citizens can confidently identify loopholes in governance. Corruption has become a perennial problem in Nigeria because the citizens and other concerned stakeholders often turn a blind eye to governance. But now, as soon as corrupt practices are identified, they are immediately posted on social media platforms forcing the governments to look into some of them. The citizens have become more conscious about developments in the country through related discourses on social media. Nigeria has a proliferation of corrupt practices because the leaders are not often scrutinized on policy formulation and implementation. Since the use of

---

36. Uzochukwu, Patricia and Ukueze, "Harnessing Social Media Tools."

37. Muhammad Yar Khan, Anam Javeed, Majid Jamal Khan, Shahab Ud Din, Asif Khurshid and Uzma Noor, "Political Participation through Social Media: Comparison of Pakistani and Malaysian Youth," *IEEE Access* 7 (2019): 35532–35543.

38. Yar Khan, Javeed, Khan, Din, Khurshid and Noor, "Political Participation through Social Media."

39. Tolu Olarenwaju, "Can Social Media help Anti-corruption Drives? A Nigerian Case Study," *The Conversation,* June 4, 2019, https://theconversation.com/can-social-media-help-anti-corruption-drives-a-nigerian-case-study-118190.

media enables the citizens to properly scrutinize the government, the latter does think twice before making public its plans and programs. In other words, social media has become an ombudsman's tool that had long eluded Nigerian society. This was especially so under Buhari's government, where the citizens were more vocal in calling out corrupt practices. The Buhari-led administration assumed its mandate on the promise of eradicating corruption but soon became very corrupt. The citizens often organized social media protests criticizing the corrupt practices of the administration. The government was forced to rethink its proposed policies and programs occasionally. Also, the citizens quickly called out Buhari's government's attempts to nominate a card-carrying member of the All Progressives Congress (APC), Lauretta Onochie, as an INEC Commissioner. This challenged electoral integrity and the citizens were relentless in their calls to ensure that the rubber-stamp National Assembly did not approve such a nomination.

Also, the Economic and Financial Crimes Commission (EFCC) has leveraged anonymous tips on social media platforms to handle some cases of corrupt practices. The Commission usually asks the citizens to inform it of any corrupt practices identified so that it can intervene. With the use of social media platforms, fighting corruption has been made easier. Nigerians have also adopted social media platforms to criticize political corruption, that is, government officials' abuse of power and authority. Citizens also point out cases of corruption in public institutions and private enterprises. Nigerians are confident that their voices will be heard immediately on social media platforms. Also, evidences of abuse of power by security operatives are brought to social media because there are possibilities that the accused would be brought to book. Social media assures the citizens that their voices will be heard. It has thus become imperative for the Nigerian government to sample the citizens' opinions via social media before certain policies are implemented. Aside from reporting corrupt practices, social media is also used to send security information to the appropriate quarters and has helped reduce crimes in society. When citizens regularly upload stories on corruption, it goes viral, and the government is forced to act on them.

In a way, social media has allowed citizens to have a holistic view of governance. Now that there is a certainty that the government can be forced to rethink its approaches or policies when there is a public uproar, the citizens are more concerned with administrative protocols, a practice that was unheard of before the advent of social media. Online protests on the government's corrupt practices are less expensive and timely to organize. There was a public uproar over the massive corruption in Buhari's government when reports emerged that the EFCC arrested the Accountant-General of the Federation over corrupt practices. The citizens immediately organized an online protest highlighting other forms of corruption in the Buhari-led administration, which had lost credibility by then. It takes only a smartphone and a good internet connection for the citizens to be involved in quests to end corruption and foreground the need for national development. With the reawakening of public con-

Figure 4.3. "Impunity" by Dr. Kazeem Ekeolu. A politician displaying stolen money in public.

sciousness, the citizens are showing signs of being interested in how they are governed. Aside from the President, his aides such as Abubakar Malami, the Attorney General of the Federation, Bashir Ahmed, and other top hierarchies in the Buhari-led government were condemned for corrupt practices on social media. The implication of this civic engagement on social media platforms is that the citizens, more than ever, are fully involved in nation-building.

When reports filtered into the media that the APC presidential candidate, Bola Ahmed Tinubu, has highlighted "money inducement" as one of his strategies to win elections, hell broke loose on Twitter. There were discourses on Tinubu's corrupt practices on social media platforms, with the citizens harping that there is a need to make informed choices on who emerges as the next president. Although corrupt practices have not completely been eradicated from the fabric of Nigerian society, social media has helped scrutinize government policies to make them more sensitive to corrupt practices. Since political gossip spreads like wildfire on social media, the citizenry is kept informed on national events as they occur. As public enlightenment has been identified as a weapon for eradicating corruption, social media is a tool for enhancing public enlightenment. The citizens do not shy away from engaging in discourses relating to national development. As Chimezie posits, social media can

change the gory narratives in Nigeria.[40] Also, the regular updates of social media platforms are more user-friendly; this further ensures that the citizens can use these user-friendly features and tools in their pursuit of a transparent and accountable government. As social media becomes more common with most Nigerians, dissemination of information as it pertains to the government has become more accessible.[41] Therefore, there is a need for Nigerians to continue to use social media platforms to fight corruption.

It is also imperative to highlight the problems associated with using social media to fight corruption. There are many cases of misinformation as some citizens peddle lies about corrupt practices inherent in a government. It also allows for character designation for those in leadership positions. While the sorry state of national affairs can be attributed to this, the citizens need not allow the government to hide under this excuse to control social media usage in the country. However, despite the limitations of social media and the tendency to raise false alarms occasionally, it has become an effective tool for checking and balancing government operatives as citizens are encouraged to be more proactive in their calls for good governance. A collective effort is needed to fight the country's current predicament. It is safe to assert that if this is possible, the stage is set. Our nation is the theater of operation. Social media is the tool, and the citizens are the actors.

WILL CORRUPTION EVER LEAVE AFRICA?

Given the widespread and brazen corruption in most African countries, it is questionable whether the continent will ever free itself from graft. It is wishful thinking to imagine that countries can make developmental progress while government corruption is present—corruption will always act as a barrier to development. Some African nations have successfully attempted to clean up their governments, but corruption in neighboring countries continually threatens to undo their efforts. Any realistic strategy for improvement must recognize that it involves two components: a person to make the corrupt request and a person to grant that request in exchange for money. One of these two people is often an ordinary citizen, and nobody will work toward a solution when they benefit from being part of the problem. The work of cleaning up corruption is not the exclusive responsibility of a country's leadership.

Leaders must form the tip of the spear that attacks government corruption. Nigeria's abundant natural wealth and human resources mean it should not be stuck in its present quagmire of inefficiency in the public sector, bad roads, unreliable electric

40. Chiemezie Chukwuka Ugochukwu, "Evaluation of Social Media Influence in the Fight against Corruption in Nigeria," *Nnamdi Azikiwe University Journal of Communication and Media Studies* 1, no. 1 (2020): 1–11.

41. Ugochukwu, "Evaluation of Social Media Influence."

service, and lack of clean water. These factors push the poor deeper into poverty. Effective, patriotic, and forward-thinking leaders are the key to good governance; progress in the fight against corruption will be illusory until the nation elects visionary individuals to positions of power. The body cannot function when the head is bad, and Africa needs constructive leadership to help its countries match the economic and socio-political development of their counterparts on other continents.

If citizens fulfill their responsibilities by electing visionary leaders, it will be a strong start to addressing the problems caused by corruption. However, leaders and citizens must collaborate to avoid sliding into dictatorship under the pretext of fighting corruption. It will require a well-focused, determined mindset to reduce corrupt practices to the lowest possible level, and it may be impossible to stamp out corruption completely—especially if it involves government overreach that would curtail individuals' liberties and civil rights.

5

BIAFRA AND THE ODUDUWA REPUBLIC

Restructuring and Secessionist Campaigns

INTRODUCTION

For some time now, there has been an increase in the rhetoric to restructure Nigeria, with the most intense demands from the South, around the demands for two new republics, Biafra and Oduduwa.[1] With public domains flooded with calls from various quarters, this concept continues to spring up in print and electronic media. Political leaders and even former presidents of Nigeria are a part of the conversation as well, while civil societies, religious leaders, and students have contributed their decibel of calls for restructuring. However, when we look at these demands holistically, the agitation seems to come from specific geopolitical zones in the country while others remain silent. Attempts to probe the rationale behind pleas for restructuring lead to existential conflicts of interest that continually undermine the intentions of those behind the actual movement.

Political observers often blame the pluralistic nature of Nigeria for virtually all the country's problems. The complexities in their way of life, customs and religious diversities among different ethnic groups of the country are a constant reminder that the

1. The name, Biafra, is a geographical space in the Gulf of Guinea, which the Igbo people adopted as their official break-away name during the Nigeria Civil War, 1967-1970, while for the Yoruba, Oduduwa is a historical and cultural creation. For the Yoruba people, the choice of Oduduwa has a more personal meaning. Oduduwa is believed to be the founding father of the Yoruba, a mythical figure whose origin has been traced to the Middle East.

unity of Nigeria is built on a faulty foundation. Understanding these complexities and the colonial government before granting independence to Nigeria ensured the establishment of a federal system wherein respective regions withhold a high degree of control over resources, developmental projects, and blueprints. However, current federalism has deviated from what was established before independence. On this note, there have been renewed calls for restructuring the political system in Nigeria. Worthy of note is that agitation for this movement comes now and then. It has become so ubiquitous that one begins to wonder why it has yet to be put in motion by successive governments.

The calls for restructuring have become a tool in the hands of politicians to sway people's preferences toward their agenda. Based on this, some level of skepticism accompanies these agitations. An outsider may be tempted to think that there is a nationalist agenda, yet this is far from the truth. Before the periodic elections in Nigeria, the people's awareness is suddenly awakened to the country's never-ending problems. With opposition parties jostling for attention, concepts are churned out before election day to make them look serious and determined to lift the country out of its predicament. Just like the mantra of change employed to oust the perceived misrule of the People's Democratic Party (PDP) in 2015, restructuring looked like another political agenda to change the relationship dynamic among entities that make up Nigeria. As political leaders perfect their schemes, the masses are more concerned with accountability and transparency of government dealings; the call for restructuring stands between the two. This ultimately led to whether the calls for restructuring were genuine. Or perhaps it is just another agenda to wrestle power from a government that is becoming unpopular as days go by.

The political setup of Nigeria hinges on federalism; in practice, it is a flawed system that has been a source of controversy even before independence. While "true" federalism might have worked perfectly, owing to the socio-cultural diversity that plagues the various ethnicities that makeup Nigeria, federalism practiced from the independence era is full of irregularities. This result is persistent inter-ethnic hostilities and tension that continue to widen the tolerance gap among federating entities in Nigeria. The crux of the hostilities stems from the agitation for true federalism that will allow for a more equitable distribution of opportunities. The fight for central control by ethnocentric individuals led to the Civil War, in which accusations and counter-accusations of marginalization and domination abound. While this may be true to some extent, other factors bordering on personal agenda stoked the Nigerian Civil War of 1967-1970. The ethnic schism leading to this war led to more than one million lives lost, which ended with the declaration of no victor, no vanquished. This was necessary to preserve the country's unity and reintegrate the secessionists into Nigeria through "Reconciliation, Rehabilitation and Reconstruction."[2]

---

2. Chinua Achebe, *There was a Country: A Personal History of Biafra* (London: Penguin Group, 2012).

Figure 5.1. "Biafra and the Oduduwa Republic Secession Threats" by Michael Efionayi. Shows the Nigerian map tearing apart and the unyielding threats by the Biafra agitators.

The second incident that ignited nationwide conscientious political unrest was the annulment of the freest and fairest election ever conducted in Nigeria: the 1993 presidential election that witnessed the late MKO Abiola winning the people's mandate. The annulment of the process by a military junta led to the agitation for a sovereign national conference as political elites in the southern part of Nigeria perceived the annulment as a northern agenda to hold onto power. Knowing that the military does not budge easily from civil demands, the concerted effort of various political groups tried unsuccessfully to ensure that the mandate was given to the winner of the annulled election.

With Nigeria transitioning into democratic rule in 1999, tension grew in another region in the southern part of Nigeria, the Niger Delta. This region is known as the

country's cash cow. The people of the Niger Delta complained of being marginalized despite being landlords of the fruit juice of the nation. The Obasanjo-led administration tried unsuccessfully to find an end to the use of oil installation by various Niger Delta militant groups until one of their kinsmen, Goodluck Jonathan, became the president of Nigeria before the country experienced a significant reduction in crude oil sabotage. It should be noted that the major grievance of the Niger Delta people related to marginalization in the distribution of resources in the country. This was borne out of the belief that the principle of derivation, an important component of fiscal federalism, was not fairly set up in the country. The initial derivation formula favored non-oil-producing states to the detriment of minority states producing the oil. This led to the 13% derivation principle.

Looking at this, it is safe to assume that political agitations in Nigeria do not always have a nationalistic output; rather, it is always an agenda by certain ethnocentric individuals to drive more resources and control to their regions. After the emergence of the Muhammadu Buhari-led administration, there were calls for reviews of pre-existing federal systems under the nomenclature of restructuring. This call, once again, came from sections within the South. The fact that southern ethnic groups are always involved in calls for the enactment of true federalism raises the position that northern regions have benefitted more from Nigeria's operating federal system. Foremost among the major proponents of restructuring are the Igbo people of South-Eastern Nigeria. Their constant agitation against the country's setup hinges on the unequal distribution of political appointments that they believe do not favor them. It is based on this agitation that the Biafra secession agenda was reignited.

UNDERSTANDING NIGERIA'S FEDERALISM AMIDST CALLS FOR RESTRUCTURING

One of Nigeria's major challenges today is corporate existence as one indivisible unit. It cannot be gainsaid that Nigeria's federalism is problematic. The practice of federalism exists only within the confines of the constitution and is invisible as it operates with a government at the center. It is expected that a federation should be made up of federating units with clearly defined independence from the center. There should be a significant level of autonomy in these federating units concerning resources, administration and security. Rather, what is obtainable in Nigeria is a situation where the federating units are dependent and subordinate to the central government. This is in perfect disharmony with the principle of federalism, allowing for greater independence of federating units. Perhaps, this is the reason for exemplifying Nigeria as a federation without federalism.[3] Nigeria's federal system is built on a high degree of central authority, culminating in national resources being concentrated at

3. Dele Babalola, "Nigeria: A Federation in Search of Federalism," [undated], *50 Shades of Federalism,* 2017. http://50shadesoffederalism.com/case-studies/nigeria-federation-search-federalism/.

the center rather than on the federating units. This centralization of national resources dates back to the military era. However, the return to democratic rule in 1999 has witnessed increased calls for true federalism that will usher in an era of self-determination of federating units and resource control. These give some credence to any calls for restructuring from any quarter, irrespective of whether such calls are genuine.

Bearing in mind such an imperfect practice of federalism, various ethnic elites continue to exploit the situation to drive toward their respective personal agendas. The essence of such agendas boils down to the need for control of state resources at the center and the opportunities accompanying such powers' acquisition. To solve the ongoing competition among ethnic-divergent elites, ruling parties often resort to arrangements of power rotation wherein presidential candidature is rotated between the North and the South on a pre-agreed basis. Such was the case between 1999 and 2015 when the ruling PDP ceded zoning to the North after the South's position had been hitherto used up by Olusegun Obasanjo. We should also note that revenue distribution plays a major role in the competition to acquire power at the center. Instead of outlining developmental ideals to drive the nation forward, Nigerian politicians are only interested in gaining the position that has unhindered access to oil wealth. This has increased the calls for restructuring, as there is a continual disagreement over the appropriate formula for sharing proceeds from crude oil and whether or not the federating units generating such income are treated fairly concerning the derivation formula. As if this is not enough, there is a constant jostle between the federal government and other tiers of government, as well as between oil-producing minority states and oil-extracting multinational organizations.

Changes in the derivation formulas do not reflect constituent states, and most do not have the requisite level of visible development. The increment of the derivation formula has only played into the hands of the region's political elites, who divert funds allocated to respective states into their coffers. It is difficult to prove that the 13% derivation allocated to oil-producing states in Nigeria from proceeds from crude oil sales has resulted in significant development for the states. Proceeds of the 13% derivation, as stated by the 1999 Constitution, have continually been mismanaged by the Niger Delta's political elites and other stakeholders.[4] Recently, some of these alleged Niger Delta political elites washed their dirty linen in public when Dr. Joy Nunieh, the Acting Managing Director of the Niger Delta Commission (NDDC), and the Minister of NDDC got involved in a series of altercations bordering on embezzlement and mismanagement of funds meant for the development of the region. All these were brought to light following accusations of sexual harassment and the subsequent dismissal of the Acting Managing Director. It is sad to note that the political elites of

4. P. P. Ugboma, "Environmental Degradation in Oil Producing Area of Niger Delta Region, Nigeria: The Need for Sustainable Development," *International Journal of Science and Technology* 4, no. 2 (2015): 75–85.

these marginalized regions are allegedly complicit in any problems facing their respective regions.

Continuous struggle between the elites of dominant ethnic groups over the control of federal power often leaves no chance for minority ethnic groups. Thus, the latter becomes of lesser importance in power and resource sharing. The plea for a true federal system of government is believed to be one viable means of ensuring that minority ethnic groups also lay a fair claim to resource allocation and political appointments. This was one of the major reasons for establishing the Principle of Federal Character so that all government-controlled institutions encapsulate the ethnic diversity of the country to foster national unity. The initiative sought to ensure that people from all ethnic groups are fairly represented in inclusive federal institutions, education, and security institutions.[5] Despite the brilliance of the initiative, the Federal Character Commission turned this tool over into the hands of the same ethnocentric elites whose only objective was sharing the national cake. Rather than being a platform to promote national unity, the Federal Character initiative only widened the gap among various ethnic groups in Nigeria.

The political dispensation that started in 1999 has experienced increased calls for true federalism through political restructuring. Cries of marginalization by self-perceived minorities are a continuation of the ethnocentric competition for political power, using the calls for restructuring to achieve their ends. To understand this, one needs to analyze the advocacy of the Niger Delta people for a restructuring system that ushered in a new distribution formula that hinged on derivation within the caprice of an existing resource control arrangement. Using environmental degradation and economic impoverishment as reasons for their agitations, the Niger Delta people were able to drive consciousness toward themselves as minorities. It should be noted that any group's first real attempt to secede from Nigeria was when Isaac Boro and his Niger Delta Volunteer Force declared the Niger Delta Republic in 1966, leading to a face-off with Federal Forces. This would last twelve days, culminating in the eventual arrest, trial and death sentence passed on the secessionists.[6] The Head of State, Yakubu Gowon, later repealed the sentence, who was persuaded by the public's call for clemency on the perpetrators.

Although some may choose to disagree, the eventual ascendancy of Goodluck Jonathan to the presidential seat was an indirect result of restructuring agitations of the Ijo people who dominate the Niger Delta axis. It is not a coincidence that Nigeria experienced a significant reduction in violence in this region afterward. However, violence later surged after Jonathan lost the seat to Muhammadu Buhari in 2015, with

5. Rotimi Suberu, *Federalism and Ethnic Conflict in Nigeria* (Washington, D.C.: United States Institute of Peace Press, 2001).

6. O. Awofeso, "Secessionist Movements and the National Question in Nigeria: A Revisit to the Quest for Political Restructuring," *Journal of Social Science and Humanities Research* 2, no. 7 (2017): 35-55.

the new militant group Niger Delta Avengers wreaking havoc in the region. Worthy of note is that other militant groups whose leaders had benefitted from the government went underground. The leader of one such group, Tompolo, was awarded a contract to secure the Niger Delta waterways during the administration of Goodluck Jonathan. To get the NDA militant group to stop their sabotaging exploits, the federal government acceded to certain demands, among them the relocation of the headquarters of multinational oil companies to the Niger Delta region.[7]

Looking at the South-Western geopolitical region of Nigeria, there have been agitations in the past with calls for a sovereign national conference after a prominent personality, MKO Abiola, was robbed of a mandate given to him by the people. The Southwest was the bedrock of agitations for political restructuring from his election until his demise. When it was time for a new democratic dispensation, this agitation played out positively for the region as the country's political elites picked Olusegun Obasanjo from the Southwest to lead the country. This pacifist move ensured that the Yoruba people reduced their political restructuring calls under nomenclature. Suffice it to say that calls for restructuring under any guise usually have some ethnocentric interest that drives them. Such calls often come from perceived disadvantages in a prevailing setup. Such perception, to some extent, is valid, and other federating units understand this. Hence, whenever a particular ethnic group decides to play the ethnic card in their calls for restructuring, it becomes a matter of national discussion, often leading to political elites of other ethnic groups acceding to such calls through various means. These are embarked upon to pacify the disadvantaged group as a sign of solidarity with their cause. Such moves should not be seen as patriotic to keep the country united. Rather, time has shown that such moves result from horse-trading and negotiations. This plays out along political party lines in the form of power rotation across geopolitical zones.

Perhaps, if there is an ethnic group that has been consistent in their agitations for political restructuring in Nigeria, it has to be the Igbo nation. The Nigeria Civil War was ignited in the backdrop of the Aburi Accord, which was set up to douse ethnic tension in the country. The consensus of the Aburi Accord was for Nigeria to operate a loose federation that would grant more power to the regions. However, the military head of the Nigerian Government, Colonel Yakubu Gowon, did not feel the same way. Post-Civil War, the Igbo nation felt marginalized and excluded from federal power despite holding some key positions under the Obasanjo administration. Having tried unsuccessfully in the past to secede from the larger entity called Nigeria, the Igbo nation continues to nurture the eventuality of secession if calls for restructuring do not become a reality. To show just how far they could go to achieve their agenda, two

7. Talatu Usman, "Niger Delta Leaders Present 16-point Demand to Buhari, want Oil Firms Relocated," *Premium Times*, November 1, 2016, http://www.premiumtimesng.com/news/headlines/214226-niger-delta-leaders-present-16-point-demand-buhari-want-oil-firms-relocated.html.

dominant secessionist movements sprang up to reignite the ethnic consciousness of the Igbo people: Movement for the Actualization of the Sovereign State of Biafra (MASSOB) and the Indigenous People of Biafra (IPOB). At this point, it is important to highlight the activities of these two movements for a better understanding of the agitations for restructuring amidst calls for secession.

THE BIAFRA AGITATIONS AMIDST CALLS FOR RESTRUCTURING

In the last decade, the Southeast geopolitical zone of Nigeria has witnessed increased struggles for the actualization of a sovereign state: Biafra. These agitations are perpetuated not on individual levels but by two major parallel movements, the Movement for the Actualization of the Sovereign State of Biafra (MASSOB) and the Indigenous People of Biafra (IPOB). A lesser-known Biafra group also calls itself the Zionist Movement (BZM). While these organizations operate unilaterally, their agitations have always been the same: call for an end to the perceived discrimination and marginalization against the Igbo people. It should be noted that if at all there is any form of discrimination against the Igbo people in Nigeria, it is not disconnected from ill feelings that have been generated as a result of the people's secessionist attitudes, which were brought to the fore and culminated into the Nigerian Civil War of 1967-1970.

It is apt to see that the vanquished still nurse war wounds while having their minds on the possibility of avenging or re-engaging the victor. Despite the pronouncement of "no victor, no vanquished" by the Nigerian government at the end of the Nigerian Civil War, one cannot acknowledge that as a mere pacifist agenda. There was indeed a vanquished whose people will never forget what they went through and how that is affecting them presently. Before the Nigerian Civil War, there had been a call for possible secession by the Premier of the Western Region, Michael Okpara. The proclamation was made against the backdrop of the federal elections in 1964. The decibel of the secession call was increased a year later when the Western Region also witnessed massive levels of election rigging against the NCNC. The Igbo political elites never knew that the nation was perhaps observing its antecedents and would later in the future make use of it to form opinions about them.

As the social media reports, the average Igbo person still evokes the Biafra consciousness, which borders on an identity that germinates a never-ending disdain for the entity called Nigeria. Against this backdrop, the first secessionist movement, MASSOB, was reborn immediately, and the country returned to civilian rule in 1999. Initially, the leadership of MASSOB, in its 25-page communiqué, highlighted the plan to establish a Biafra nation, albeit through a peaceful process. While this sounds good on paper, it is not always easy to implement. Around 2005, Uwazuruike, the MASSOB leader, was arrested and subsequently charged with treason. He experienced delayed

prosecution and was granted bail two years later to attend his mother's burial. His arrest was due to several violent confrontations MASSOB had against federal government security forces. This grew to an extent where southeast governors began to see people in the movement as irritants rather than true nationalists.[8] Governor Peter Obi of Anambra State gave a shoot-on-sight order against MASSOB activists he believed were only acting to disrupt his government.[9]

The posture of the other dominant ethnic groups that the Igbo perceive as discriminatory appears to have denied the latter's political positions in the country's administration. However, the cries of marginalization and discrimination against the Igbo do not align with mainstream Igbo political leadership. This is because they have also been involved in horse-trading and political power negotiations since 1999. For instance, the Obasanjo-led administration ensured that the Senate President position was ceded to the Igbo throughout the eight years. From this, it is evident that Igbo proponents of secession and their political elites speak with discordant tunes. A cursory look at the activities of the secession movements will also indicate some level of conflict among them.

The secessionist agenda of MASSOB was rife with internal conflicts as stakeholders could not agree on a particular modus operandi. Accusations of compromise of MASSOB leadership led to the creation of another secessionist movement, IPOB, in 2013, whose leadership initially operated from the United Kingdom. One of the major moves by IPOB was to revive the defunct Radio Biafra to sensitize the Igbo people and free them from the propaganda the Yoruba-dominated media have continually fed them.[10] Nnamdi Kanu, the leader of IPOB, has become a cult figure of sorts in Nigeria. He had been incarcerated and, when granted bail, secretly left the country. The Biafra Zionist Movement, founded by Benjamin Onwuka, also became a notorious group when it attacked the Enugu State Government House in a bid to fly the Biafran flag on its premises. This was followed by attempts to take over the Enugu State Broadcasting Service to announce the secession of Biafra from Nigeria.[11] As expected of every individual who attempts such an agenda, Onwuka also faced detention when he set up an interim government where he made himself interim president of the Biafran nation.

The secession agenda of the Igbo on multiple fronts show that they remain the most agitated sub-group within Nigeria. However, the fractionalization and disjoint-

---

8. Africa Masterweb News, "Court grants Biafra leader bail," *Africa Masterweb*, May 16, 2008, http://www.africamasterweb.com/AdSense/MassobCourtGrantsBiafraLeaderBail.html.

9. N. Kalu, *State Power, Autarchy and Political Conquest in Nigerian Federalism* (Boulder and New York: Lexington Books, 2007), 93.

10. Princeemeka12, "The United States of Biafra," *Facebook*, January 12, 2014, http://www.facebook.com/Princemeka12/posts/657700930940385.

11. Tony Edike, "Pro-Biafra group's to Seize Enugu Radio, TV Stations Foiled," *Vanguard Newspaper*, June 6, 2014.

ed moves by various movements show that some among them are motivated more by personal interest than in the interest of the Igbo nation. Where does restructuring come in here? For an entity to embark on the restructuring process, certain parts must be removed, changed, renovated or decommissioned. In Nigeria, restructuring is often taken to mean one of two things: a call for true federalism or secession. For those who perceive restructuring as a call for secession, the perceived marginalization in resource control and power sharing is enough rationale for the political elite to negotiate a process that will allow any ethnic group or federating unit to secede willingly. The essence of this is to prevent the persistent feeling of injustice and discontentment that the proponents of secession nudge.

While a significant number of people believe that the progress of Nigeria is non-negotiable, it is important to prepare for the possibility of a breakup if the present power-sharing formula continues to put certain groups like the Igbo nation at a disadvantage. The growing discontent among southern ethnic groups and their northern counterparts may not allow for a sustained Nigeria unless there is a concerted effort to remove ethnicity and religious intolerance and discourage the lack of government presence in a certain region. It is difficult for some Muslims to achieve a meaningful and lasting relationship with some Christians, making it quite difficult to achieve true unity in Nigeria. The other school of thought about restructuring in Nigeria is that there is a need for re-federalization through true federalism, adequate domestic structure, encouragement to set up regional systems, and devolving power of the state to spur communal growth. The argument is that there is a need to practice federalism to the letter by ensuring that the democratic structure is set up to give lesser powers to the center while the federating units or regional governments are granted strong autonomy. This would promote development based on the resources of respective federating units and leaves no room for complaints about one region leeching on the resources of another. On this note, it would be imperative to revisit the 2014 Confab Report, which highlighted the unbalanced, unjust and over-centralized structure of the federalism currently in practice in Nigeria.

THE ODUDUWA REPUBLIC AND AGITATION FOR SECESSION

The Yoruba nation, occupying the Southwestern region, remains a major force in the Nigerian political landscape. Known for their political sophistication, the Yoruba arguably have the greatest developmental strides among the major ethnic groups in the country. Not new to calls for secession like every other ethnic group, the Yoruba do not ascribe their nationalist calls to the backdrop of marginalization or discrimination like the Igbo and Niger Delta. The reason for this is that the most prosperous city in Nigeria, Lagos, falls under the geographical territory of the Yoruba, and they have continually leveraged the boisterousness of the city to achieve economic benefits

where other regions could not. Before independence, the Yoruba had achieved economic leaps with cocoa and a knack for formal education, which was made possible with their embrace of Christian missionaries.

Politically, the Yoruba have enjoyed having their representatives at the helm of political leadership in Nigeria, something the Igbo wish they could enjoy. The economic strength of the region, coupled with the strength of voting power, makes them very relevant politically. However, a sharp divide exists in the leadership of the Yoruba: political and ethnic. The political leadership of the Yoruba is hinged on the political class, which often uses the region's advantages to negotiate positions of power at the federal level. Ethnic leaders, on the other hand, are composed of individuals from all walks of life who believe in the Yoruba nationalist agenda. It is from the latter that murmurs and calls for an Oduduwa republic usually emanate. The self-determination agenda of the Yoruba nation is being perpetrated on various parallel fronts, much like what we have in Biafra. One such movement is the O'odua Nationalist Coalition (ONAC), which comprises 18 other pan-Yoruba groups. A statement issued and signed by Mrs. Aduke Fadahunsi and Michael Popoola urged the Yoruba to prepare for a sovereign nation: the Oduduwa Republic.

The catalyst for the call is the lingering socio-economic and political conflicts that seem to hinder the country's progress as one unit; this is a situation they believe has stunted its growth for more than five decades. They believed that the developmental plan laid by a foremost Yoruba political leader, the late Chief Obafemi Awolowo, would have manifested if it was not for the ripple effect of the Nigerian Civil War.[12] The group also called on people of Yoruba extraction residing in other geographical territories to begin alternative plans for a perceived and inevitable upheaval that would envelop the country in the face of a growing promotion of the Fulani oligarchy. The belief that the North and its political elites are propagating an irreversible extension of the Fulani emirates further down South might be mere speculation. However, Fulani's dominance in the Middle-Belt region of Nigeria gives credence to their fear.

An article surfaced on a popular tabloid in Nigeria, *Sahara Reporters*, titled "Against Secession: A Testament to Yoruba Leaders and Promoters of Oduduwa Republic," detailing specific incidences of agitations sponsored by ethnic leaders of the Yoruba. The article's author affirmed seeing a video clip of young and vibrant Yoruba youth carrying placards and canvassing to create the Oduduwa Republic. One major highlight that is worthy of mention is the assertion by some of the agitators that the Yoruba have suffered setbacks by being part of the entity called Nigeria. It claimed that as of 1959, the Yoruba nation already had a television house when nations like

12. O. Akoni, "Igbo Quit Notice: Pan Yoruba Group Calls for the Oodua Republic," *Vanguard Newspaper*, 2017.

France and many Western nations were yet to have a single one.[13] The main crux of the arguments for an Oduduwa Nation, the author believed, is not enough to warrant secession; rather, they should look at the possibility of restructuring. According to the article, times have changed, and issues need to be addressed within the context of the prevailing time so as not to risk failure through the secession agenda.[14] Rather than rush an attempt to move forward, the Yoruba nation should look back to know where the problem stemmed from and how it can be solved.

Just like the Igbo nation, voices for secession among the Yoruba ethnic group are not unified, nor is there any consensus on the issue. The Secretary-General of the Yoruba Council of Elders (YCE) stated that he is yet to see any monarch of the Yoruba extraction supporting the secessionist agenda. The Pan-Yoruba group, Yoruba Liberation Command (YOLICOM), claimed in 2017, during a world press conference at the International Press Centre (Ogba Lagos), that Nigeria was slowing down the region's development while also encouraging the maiming of Yoruba people for selfish interests. Press releases of the conference stated that the federal government has not been able to solve the challenges of peaceful coexistence amongst the ethnic groups in Nigeria and that a majority of political officeholders only serve themselves and not the people. The conference also inferred that the widely acclaimed restructuring agenda might not be sufficient for the region's progress in the long run.

While impressing the need for secession, Mr. Opeoluwa Akinola, the spokesman for the group, affirmed its support for IPOB's struggle for self-actualization if that will bring an end to the alleged marginalization that some regions in Nigeria have been experiencing for a long time. Also, in the course of the conference, the Aare Agbekoya of Yorubaland, Chief Kunle Oshodi, affirmed that the secessionist call was long overdue and the Agbekoya, a group that had in the past fought against the military government on the imposition of unfair taxes, is more than ready to play its part in the self-actualization of a sovereign Yoruba nation. In his words, "let me assure you that the Agbekoya is the Yoruba people's last hope, and we do fight except when necessary; we have shown this in the past."[15] It should be noted that the Agbekoya movement, while not comprising the same personnel as in the old times, believes that it still holds the mental and intellectual capacity to achieve any objective it sets out to accomplish.

The agitation for an Oduduwa nation did not stop in Nigeria, with the Yoruba World Congress (YWC) under the leadership of Professor Banji Akintoye and other affiliate Yoruba nationalist groups spearheading a global consciousness for the cre-

---

13. Moses Oludele Idowu, "Against Secession: Testament to Yoruba Leaders and Promoters of Oduduwa Republic," *SaharaReporters,* 2020, http//saharareporters.com/2020/09/18/against-secession-testament-yoruba-leaders-and-promoters-oduduwa-republic-moses-oludele.

14. Idowu, "Against Secession."

15. Jewel Ike-Obioha, "The Agitations for Oduduwa Republic by the Yoruba Liberation Command is a Cause to Worry," *Ventures*, July 31, 2017, http://www.venturesafrica.com/weekly-economic-index-inflation-reaches-30-month-high-oil-prices-fall/.

ation of the Oduduwa Republic. The reason for this call is similar to that of ONAC: the Yoruba Nation needs autonomy since the country has failed the Yoruba Nation. Incidentally, a diaspora rally was scheduled for October 1, 2020, when Nigeria marks its 60th independence as a sovereign nation. To show solidarity for such brave moves, the leader of the prescribed secession group IPOB, Nnamdi Kanu, also asked his followers to sit at home on that day to show empathy for the Yoruba self-determination rally. Speaking at one of the numerous Pan-Yoruba group meetings, a chieftain representing a Yoruba monarch affirmed that the conglomeration of Yoruba monarchs stands for peace and unity among the Yoruba people and nothing more. In his words, Professor Akintoye believes he can achieve self-determination through a peaceful process which remains a mystery to every intelligent person—understanding that Professor Akintoye, the leader of the Yoruba World Congress, wants to establish the sovereign Oduduwa Republic without consultation and further consent with Yoruba monarchs speaks volumes on the level of complexity that permeates the Yoruba agitations for secession.

Speaking further, High Chief Lekan Balogun affirmed that many Yoruba leaders believe more in achieving a restructured Nigeria rather than calls for a sovereign republic.[16] The Yoruba have sacrificed as much for the unity of Nigeria and would not feel the need for the country to disintegrate, albeit through whatever means. One thing that cannot be taken away is that none of the federating entities that make up Nigeria is wholly happy with the country's present situation. So it is justifiable for any ethnic group to be embittered and angry with the current state. Another elder statesman, Senator Femi Okurounmu, retorted that the secession agenda being led by the Yoruba World Congress is not a consensus of the Yoruba. He asserted that the number of groups feeling agitated in Nigeria is substantial, and only restructuring can end the frustrations. He believes restructuring will usher in a new dispensation where regions will be more autonomous. Following the same line, Chief Ebenezer Babatope affirmed that calls for secession are immature and go against the ideals of one of the foremost Yoruba political leaders, Obafemi Awolowo. Rather, he also believed that proper federalism should be established. Ambassador Yemi Farounbi also described calls for secession by certain Yoruba elements as an invitation to chaos. This further highlights the clear differences in opinions of various stakeholders concerning the creation of the Oduduwa Republic.

Conversely, a chieftain of the Pan-Yoruba group (Afenifere), Chief Wole Oke, differed, revealing in an interview that the abundant resources in the southwest region of Nigeria are enough to sustain the Oduduwa Republic. Going further, he highlighted the perceived Fulanization of Nigeria as a major reason for the secession agenda of the Yoruba people. The Publicity Secretary of Afenifere, Yinka Odumakin, also lent

16. Dayo Johnson, Dapo Akinrefon, Jimitota Onoyume and Ddemola Akinyemi, "Oduduwa Republic October Rally Divides Yoruba Leaders," *Vanguard Newspaper*, 2020.

his voice by saying that the self-determination agenda is growing stronger daily. However, he quickly reiterated that the only thing that can stop the impending secession is a restructuring agenda that will immediately highlight proper federation. It is evident that the clamor for a sovereign Yoruba nation is much like that of Biafra, and it is the result of the leadership of Nigeria remaining impervious to calls for social change. Therefore, calls for self-determination are indications of failed leadership. However, self-determination may not be the best solution because Nigeria as a nation is stronger than its parts.

SOCIAL MEDIA AND SECESSIONIST NARRATIVES

Ethnic discourses have become more prominent in Nigeria's political system as secessionist agendas are further advanced on social media platforms such as Facebook, Twitter, WhatsApp, Instagram, and YouTube, amongst others. Social media allows for the propagation of different beliefs and opinions;[17] thus, ethnic loyalists have capitalized on this unbridled freedom of speech and expression these platforms give to advocate for breakaway states in the country. It becomes easier for ethnic loyalists to interact with themselves and share open plans to achieve ethnic independence. Without social media, frequent interactions like this would be impossible or, if possible, would attract a violent crackdown on the actors involved. The Nigerian government often posits that it is committed to a united and indivisible country; thus, it unleashes brutal forces on ethnic actors committed to dividing the country. The truth is that Nigeria has been so polarized among ethnic groups that the need for ethnic independence has penetrated the stream of consciousness of most Nigerians. There are struggles for the dominance of ethnic groups over the other, which led to the fear of marginalization as governments in Nigeria often appeal to ethnic sentiments and reserve the majority of public offices for their fellow ethnic personalities.

Studies on Nigeria's religious, political, and ethnic activities have revealed that issues relating to ethnic, religious, and political intolerance challenge its sovereignty.[18] Furthermore, a brewing internal crisis continues to plague due to the violent crackdown of secessionists when a national dialogue would have helped alleviate ethnic fears and ensure national unity and progress. Based on the violence attached to ethnic struggles, ethnic loyalties have resisted social media platforms where awareness would be unrestricted.[19] Squires describes seeking alternative platforms to promote

---

17. T.S. Onayinka, C.E. Asogwa, B.A. Ajijola and J.A. Ige, "Influence of Biafra-related Social Media Contents on the Acceptance of IPOB Agenda in South-East Nigeria," *International Journal of Communication: An Interdisciplinary Journal of Communication* 24, no. 1 (2019): 49-61.

18. Olusola Samuel Oyetunde, "Nigeria: Power Sharing and the Resurgence of Separatist Agitation. The Prospect of a Consociational Model," *Conflict Studies Quarterly* 37 (2021): 54-74.

19. Innocent Chiluwa, "A Nation Divided against Itself: Biafra and the Conflicting Online Protest Discourses," *Discourse & Communication* 12, no. 4 (2018): 357-381.

awareness of any kind as a counter-public sphere.[20] The theory of a counter-public sphere, as Qian notes, provides underrepresented social groups with opportunities to speak out in their voice to enact and express diverse social positions and political identities.[21] Social media platforms enable widespread ethnic propaganda in the country. Under the Buhari-led government, ethnic struggles were commonplace. Although there were clamors for ethnic nationalism and independence during the previous government, they were not as audacious as the ethnic struggles under Buhari's government. There were visible signs of ethnicity under Buhari's government which did nothing concrete to allay the fears of Hausa/Fulani supremacy. In the South-east, there are the Indigenous People of Biafra (IPOB), spearheaded by Mazi Nnamdi Kanu, and agitations for the Oduduwa Republic in the Southwest led by Sunday Igboho; both leaders were held in custody for their activities under Buhari's administration. Asides from physical agitations, these organizations have a considerable online presence that disseminates information to their followers on the need to collaborate on ways to achieve their goals.

Among the various ethnic agitations employing social media as a tool for wider reach, the IPOB is a major stand-out. This is a pan-Igbo organization that has fearlessly advanced for the creation of Biafra. Biafra existed as an independent entity before its collapse during the civil war between 1967 and 1970, and ever since then, the Igbo people have been ostensibly marginalized. There has been a sort of unwritten rule for them not to assume top leadership positions, which underscores fear of Igbo dominance, known as Igbophobia. Since the end of the civil war, there has been no Igbo President in Nigeria as power is rotated between the North and the South-West. Thus, the IPOB clamored that the Nigerian government allows for recognizing Biafra as a country. The organization has a well-structured hierarchy, with chapters in other parts of the world. The top leaders were also in foreign countries, particularly domiciled in the United Kingdom, until the mysterious arrest of its top personality, Mazi Nnamdi Kanu, who shuttled between courts on accusations of treason throughout the latter years of Buhari's presidency. With the dominance of pro-Biafran agitations on social media platforms, especially on Twitter, clamors for the actualization of Biafra have taken a giant stride. On random occasions, there are Twitter trends for Biafran independence. Pro-Biafran agitators condemn the undemocratic principles of the government in ensuring that their dreams are not met. The dominance of the Biafran movement on Twitter has still not stopped the brutal forces the Nigerian government unleashes on them, but it has created awareness of an unquenchable movement. Also, social media gives Biafran agitators the platform to correct the public's misconceptions about their agitations. There had been narratives that external

20. Catherine R Squires, "Rethinking the Black Public Sphere: An Alternative Vocabulary for Multiple Public Spheres," *Communication Theory* 12, no. 4 (2002): 446-468.

21. Junxi Qian, "From Performance to Politics? Constructing Public and Counterpublic in the Singing of Red Songs," *European Journal of Cultural Studies* 17, no. 5 (2014): 602-628.

countries sponsored the movement to destabilize the country; however, the IPOB has highlighted the marginalization of the Igbo and what it sees as calculated moves to prevent an Igbo presidency as major reasons they want to break away from Nigeria.

According to Ibeanu, Orji, and Iwuamadi, the ceaseless agitation for Biafra could be based on three premises: those related to ethnic divisions, those around economic frustrations, and those related to state-society relations.[22] Their agitations are not limited to social media alone. They also perform routine attacks on the government's forces and infrastructures to convey their demands. Before his arrest, Mazi Kanu, with the Twitter account @MaziNnamdiKanu, condemned government practices that undermined the realization of Biafra.[23] The Buhari-led government promised to treat the pro-Biafran agitators "in the language they understand"—a tweet later deleted by Twitter over violating its community principles—and it did so. Researchers have noted that social media contributes to the escalation of the ethnic crisis in Nigeria and also influences the public perception of IPOB.[24]

The IPOB is not the major force involved in ethnic struggles in Nigeria. There are similar agitations for the creation of the Oduduwa Republic for the Yoruba people. Although this agitation is not as largely influential as the IPOB on Twitter, it has succeeded in influencing public awareness of the Oduduwa Republic. Unlike the IPOB, the creation of the Oduduwa Republic has not received wide support in the South West. Most of their demands became prominent on the heels of the Fulani herdsmen's incursion into farmlands in the Southwest and the brutal killings of residents. The progenitor of the Oduduwa Republic, Sunday Igboho, was shot into the limelight when he swore to end Fulani dominance in the Yoruba region in the aftermath of the massacre of residents at Igangan. Since then, conscious efforts have been geared towards realizing the Yoruba nation. The philosophy behind this agitation is the dire need of the Yoruba to be reflective and independent and wean themselves off any ethnic hegemony. The rise of ethnic nationalism has also contributed to the agitations on social media, with arguments positing that Nigeria is a colonial mistake and that achieving true national development lies in ethnic independence.

Agitations for the creation of Biafra are active on Twitter. There are handles identifying with the Biafran identity that launch verbal missiles at the Nigerian government in their quest for self-independence. Twitter is effective in Biafran struggles because trends get international recognition quickly. The IPOB identified Twitter as the platform to convey the harsh realities the southeasterners are forced to face in Nigeria due to their ethnic nationalism. Agitations for the actualization of Biafran,

---

22. Okechukwu Ibeanu, Nwachukwu Orji and C.K. Iwuamadi, *Biafra Separatism: Causes, Consequences and Remedies* (Enugu: Institute for Innovations in Development, 2016).

23. Mazi Nnamdi Kanu, "Twitter Post," *Twitter*, June 28, 2021, https://twitter.com/mazinnamdikanu.

24. Muhammad Auwal Ahmad, "Social Media and Hate Speech: Analysis of Comments on Biafra Agitations, Arewa Youths' Ultimatum and their Implications on Peaceful Coexistence in Nigeria," *Media and Communication Currents* 2, no. 1 (2018): 54-74.

notably on this platform, have included narratives that condemn the existence of Nigeria. To these agitators, Nigeria's entity is a mistake that could still be rectified if the composite parts go their way. The actors usually posit that they would give all it takes to achieve their mission. Largely domiciled on social media platforms, agitations have also been done physically, often leading to casualties for pro-Biafra activists. This further contributed to the unrest in the South East and called on the international communities to support Biafra's independence.

Before he was arrested, Mazi Nnamdi Kanu often condemned the Nigerian government for being forceful with Biafra supporters and saw it as an enemy. In one of his tweets alluding to the holy scripture, he condemns the Nigerian government as the enemy who would fall for Biafra to be realized:

> *Day 27 of our Prayers from the Book of Psalms Chapter 27, as divinely mandated.*
> Extract: Psalm 27:2 "When the wicked, even my enemies and my foes, came upon me to eat up my flesh, they stumbled and fell." Iseeee!!!"[25]

In his many statements, Biafra is an already-made goal, an ideology no amount of brutal force can destroy. He often discarded the belief in one Nigeria and criticized the government for doing all within its power to marginalize the Igbo. His Biafran organization, the IPOB, is always caught in continuous strife with the Federal forces, leading to many casualties on both sides. Kanu criticized the government for the continuous marginalization of the Igbo and the propagation of Hausa/Fulani hegemony. The IPOB enforced a compulsory sit-at-home order in the Southeastern States to pursue its independence plans. However, their realization is still far from reality. The IPOB also created an independent security force called the Eastern Security Network (ESN) to ensure the safety of the lives and properties of the Igbo. As Kanu tweeted:

> #IPOB remains the only constant obstacle on the path of the Fulani conquest of the rest of Nigeria. Now, the duty of Safeguarding Biafraland remains our sole focus & responsibility. This Is why #ESN was created to put an end to the unchecked atrocities against innocent Biafrans.[26]

Even though Kanu insisted that this security network is not to retaliate against the attacks from the nation's armed forces but to curb the growing cases of insecurity in the region,[27] there are recorded clashes of government forces with the ESN, which the

25. Mazi Nnamdi Kanu, "Twitter Post," *Twitter*, June 27, 2021, https://twitter.com/MaziNnamdiKanu/status/1409119811595014144?ref_src=twsrc%5Etfw.

26. Mazi Nnamdi Kanu, "Twitter Post," *Twitter*, June 26, 2021, https://twitter.com/MaziNnamdiKanu/status/1408756989505724419?s=20&t=4dPAfZzbCEt6aYEDzcOcng.

27. Mazi Nnamdi Kanu, "Twitter Post," *Twitter*, June 22, 2021, https://twitter.com/MaziNnamdiKanu/status/1407253500539682816?s=20&t=4dPAfZzbCEt6aYEDzcOcng.

Nigerian government tagged as a terrorist group and the military. Also, there were reports that the ESN perpetuates criminal activities in the region. This made the Federal government clamp down on civilian critics of Buhari. Kanu particularly blamed President Muhamamadu Buhari for the current predicament of Nigeria and showed a deep dislike for the latter. This hatred is based on the premise that the President was part of those who massacred the Igbo while he was a military officer during the civil war. Kanu openly condemned the President for attempting to Islamize and Fulanize Nigeria, which was expressive in his measures on Biafran activists. The same government would mysteriously arrest Kanu himself. On the heels of a report that President Buhari was dead and was replaced by a Sudanese called Jibrin, who looks much like Buhari, Kanu propagated this belief and shared pictures on Twitter "validating" this assumption.[28] Kanu also took swipes at the porous security architecture in Nigeria.[29] It is a known fact that the government was losing the war against terrorism and was so helpless that it resorted to playing by the insurgents' tactics. The government struggled to unleash brutal forces on the insurgents as the latter were often rebounded in the society and recruited into the army. Kanu condemned the level of insecurity in the country, stating that the government only knows how best to clamp down on peaceful Biafran protesters, not outright terrorists. He criticized the government for its delight in killings scores of pro-Biafran agitators when those who needed its heavy hand—the terrorists— were left untouched.

There is also Radio Biafra with the Twitter account "@radiobiafralive," which serves as the communication department of Biafra.[30] This account launches criticisms of Nigeria and tweets in support of Biafran independence. Radio Biafra is a propaganda arm of the IPOB as it tweets on the actualization of the Biafran dream. It became more prominent after the arrest of Nnamdi Kanu as it was vocal about what it described as an illegal arrest. Tweets clamored for the release of Kanu and condemnation of the evil practices of Buhari's regime. It is noteworthy that Kanu's arrest led to civil unrest in the South East, but the government quickly doused it. Tweets were calling for the release of Kanu with the hashtag #FreeNnamdiKanu and the actualization of Biafra. International communities were called upon to pressure the Nigerian government into releasing the Biafran leader.

There were also other Twitter accounts tuned in on Biafran struggles. *Biafra Times* projects the gory details of the Nigerian predicament in its quest to foreground the popular narrative that Nigeria cannot continue as one single entity.[31] It tweets in support of the Biafran goals and the true independence of the Igbo people in the face of

---

28. Mazi Nnamdi Kanu, "Twitter Post," *Twitter*, June 19, 2021, https://twitter.com/MaziNnamdiKanu/status/1406176773994385409?s=20&t=4dPAfZzbCEt6aYEDzcOcng.

29. Mazi Nnamdi Kanu, "Twitter Post," *Twitter*, June 28 2021, https://twitter.com/MaziNnamdiKanu/status/1409536871777058824?s=20&t=4dPAfZzbCEt6aYEDzcOcng.

30. Radio Biafra, "Twitter," Joined March, 2013, https://twitter.com/radiobiafralive.

31. Radio Biafra, "Twitter," Joined April 2015, https://twitter.com/thebiafratimes.

marginalization. It could be noted that this account foregrounds ethnic nationalism identity. It also propagates the Biafran identity. The Biafran identity has penetrated deep into the consciousness of the Igbo, with discourses that it had never been dead since the city ended years ago. For instance, the government arrested a popular Nollywood actor, Chiwetalu Agu, for spreading Biafran identity and ideology.[32] The IPOB also concerned itself with solving cases of human rights abuses perpetrated by the Ebube-Agu, a security network for the easterners similar to the Amotekun in the South-west and the Hisbah in the North. There is the *Biafran Herald*, a virtual platform supporting the quest for independence.[33] It also tweets on the precarious situation of the Nigerian nations and why self-governance is necessary. During the trend of #Biafraexit, an analysis of the tweets show that the Biafran dream is bolder than what is available in the public sphere. Cases of marginalization were foregrounded with tweets such as "self-determination is a fundamental human right."

Furthermore, agitations for a Yoruba nation (Oduduwa Republic) have dominated discourses on Twitter. Like the IPOB, Yoruba nation agitators highlight what they perceived as a rising Fulani hegemony as the need to break away. Undoubtedly, ethnic nationalism plays a part in these agitations. The creation of breakaway states is hinged on the premise that Nigeria is so polarized along ethnicity that it would only amount to a facade if it kept on as a single entity. There were reports that Yoruba youths had hoisted Oduduwa Republic flags in some parts of Lagos and other Yoruba states. However, one major hindrance to this realization is that prominent figures in the Southwest do not support the movement. For instance, Sunday Igboho, the main actor in creating the Oduduwa Republic, was heard in a video daring to attack the Ooni of Ife, Adeyeye Sunday Ogunwusi, for his alleged betrayal of the Yoruba.[34] Even if other prominent figures were involved in this struggle, they were in the background. Sunday Igboho, who had foregrounded the need for Nigeria to split into many countries, was arrested, and this was to minimize the impact of his agitations. Agitations for creating a Yoruba state did not come with a violent face-off with federal forces like the IPOB. However, tensions brewed when the Yoruba agitators were bent on expelling non-Yoruba in the states, particularly the Fulani herdsmen, whose gruesome attacks reignited the clamors for the Yoruba nation. Aside from the prominent figures not supporting them, the agitations were not keyed into by the majority of the middle-class. It appeared as if the agitations were limited to particular people.

---

32. *Premium Times*, "Popular Actor, Chiwetalu Agu, Arrested for Allegedly Recruiting for IPOB," *Premium Times*, October 7, 2021, https://www.premiumtimesng.com/news/top-news/488810-popular-actor-chiwetalu-agu-arrested-for-allegedly-recruiting-for-ipob.html.

33. Biafra Herald, "Twitter," Joined April 2015, https://twitter.com/BiafraHerald.

34. Olufemi Atoyebi, "Igboho attacks Tinubu, Ooni, Makinde, says they are 'Fulani Slaves,'" *The Cable*, February 3, 2021, https://www.thecable.ng/igboho-attacks-ooni-tinubu-and-makinde-says-they-are-fulani-slaves.

To drive home their demands for the Oduduwa Republic, a group known as the Yoruba Self-Determination Movement (YSDM), which comprises many other movements agitating for the Yoruba nation, had written to the president, Muhammadu Buhari, on the need for him to approve the independence of the Yoruba nation.[35] The group contends that the Yoruba have the necessary education and civilization to exist independently. It also alludes to popular narratives reiterating that the unity of Nigeria is a hoax and that parts willing to break must be allowed to do so. It posits that it intends to achieve this through national dialogue and negotiation. The YSDM foregrounds the instances of the porous security architecture that has contributed to the many narratives describing the nation as a failed state. It also highlights ethnic hegemony as one of the reasons it seeks the creation of the Yoruba nation, which is inclusive of the fact that there is a gradual erosion of the Yoruba culture and the povertization of its people. It posits:

> We Yoruba people solemnly and unalterably reject any arrangement that would subject us to continued membership of Nigeria.[36]

The group also posits that there is a widespread incursion of the "Fulani terrorists" and their allies into Yoruba farmlands to unleash venomous attacks aimed at the capitulation of the Yoruba as slaves of the Fulani. It argues that an imminent war in Nigeria is inevitable; thus, there is a need for a breakaway nation. The group harps that it wishes to carry out its self-determination struggle peacefully and counts on Buhari's government for support:

> ... Mr. President, along the lines of our peaceful approach and respect for the Government and laws of Nigeria, we reiterate our wish to engage in direct negotiation with the Federal Government of Nigeria, as the final stretch of our peaceful route towards the realization of our Yoruba nation's self-determination and the establishment of our Yoruba sovereign nation-state.[37]

Also, various agitations aim to penetrate the consciousness of the Yoruba and instill in them the need to solidify their efforts to achieve a Yoruba state. There were trends on Twitter #YourbaNationNow and #OduduwaRepublic, advancing for Oduduwa Republic. An analysis of some tweets reveals a need to "de-amalgamize" Nigeria. For instance, Oduduwa Republic tweeted that:

---

35. Dayo Johnson, Nnamdi Ojiego, Rotimi Ojomoyela and James Ogunnaike, "S/West Secession Letter to Buhari Divides Yoruba Leaders," *Vanguard Newspaper*, September 4, 2022..

36. Johnson, Ojiego, Ojomoyela and Ogunnaike, "S/West Secession Letter to Buhari."

37. Johnson, Ojiego, Ojomoyela and Ogunnaike. "S/West Secession Letter to Buhari."

> The agitation for the Yoruba self-determination isn't secession; rather, it's restoration. It isn't separation; rather, it's de-amalgamation. It isn't a call for war; rather, it's a call for peace and freedom.
>
> Fraudgeria is a crime against humanity. Support the Yoruba nation…"[38]

Unlike the Igbo, it is fair to say that the Yoruba have not been largely marginalized; they still hold on to top leadership positions. The initial thought in public discourses was that the agitations were a subtle clamor for a Yoruba president. However, a controversial Yoruba personality, Femi Fani-Kayode, contends that such agitations are not directed at the emergence of the Yoruba presidency. He posits that the clamor would not end even with a Bola Ahmed Tinubu presidency. As he tweeted:

> The agitation for the Oduduwa Republic cannot be deterred or dissuaded by a Tinubu Presidency. As a matter of fact, a Tinubu Presidency will only further strengthen the resolve of the separatists. This is because no-one is more hated by the Yoruba nationalists than Bola Ahmed Tinubu.[39]

There was also an analysis of the tweets made by Aare Kurunmi Kankafo, who describes himself thus "I am Yoruba first and last, Apostle of Yoruba tribalism, and the General Overseer of Yoruba nationalism industry."[40] He once tweeted that there is a need for collective efforts to ensure that the dreams of the Yoruba nation are realized:

> To all Yoruba politicians, if Yorubaland is taken over by non Yorubas how are you going to get your political mandate? How are you going to protect your political empire? This is why any right-thinking Yoruba politician should covertly and overtly support Yoruba nationalism.[41]

The Twitter user condemned the Owo Church attacks rumored to be perpetuated by Fulani herdsmen, which contributed to his stance that there must be Oduduwa Republic.[42] PraiseGod and Innocent contend that the Yoruba agitators adopt linguistic strategies such as code-switching to express solidarity.[43] The Yoruba agitators also trended #DivideNigeria in pursuance of the creation of the Yoruba state.

38. Yoruba Nation, "Twitter Post," *Twitter*, November 6, 2021, https://twitter.com/OdudwaRepublic.

39. Femi Fani-Kayode, Twitter Post, *Twitter*, April 7, 2021. https://twitter.com/realFFK/status/1379807300697874433?s=20&t=BoWsgikarVOan3z92oAzJw.

40. Aare Kurunmi Kakanfo, "Twitter," https://twitter.com/AareKurunmi.

41. Aare Kurunmi Kakanfo, Twitter Post, *Twitter*, August 12, 2022, https://twitter.com/AareKurunmi/status/1558150012063948806?s=20&t=8p-ISHlQeBm-Ba-dHWirAg.

42. Aare Kurunmi Kakanfo, Twitter Post, *Twitter*, August 12, 2022, https://twitter.com/AareKurunmi/status/1558141847981199362?s=20&t=8p-ISHlQeBm-Ba-dHWirAg.

43. PraiseGod Aminu, and Innocent Chiluwa, "Constructing Identity and Ideological Stance in Oduduwa Secessionist Discourse on Twitter," Paper presented at the 3rd World Conference on Social

Figure 5.2. "Secessionist Agitation and State Reaction" by Dr. Kazeem Ekeolu. The Nigerian government, the 2014 Confab to resolve secessionist claims and State Security in response to secessionists' agitations.

RESTRUCTURING AS A CHANGING IDEOLOGY IN NIGERIA

It is often said that the way people think reflects the impact of their history. There has been a high level of disunity in Nigeria right from independence in 1960 up until the present moment. Support for the government in Nigeria is hinged on "tribal" and ethno-religious sentiments, which mostly provide room for the support of mediocrity. Social relationships among the people of divergent ethnic groups in Nigeria are often characterized by mistrust, aggression, discrimination and prejudice.[44] The polarization of Nigeria is as old as the country itself, making it one of the most fragmented countries in Africa. To combat this, the various ethnic groups in Nigeria resort to horse-trading during elections to determine the country's leadership. It is common to find two or more dominant ethnic groups forming alliances to emerge victorious in elections.

However, every time national elections are around the corner, it is a strategic time to agitate for political rearrangements. The Buhari administration got into power chanting the "Change" mantra, while the ousted PDP government presented a cam-

---

Science Studies, Budapest Hungary, May 6-8, 2002.

44. S.F. Folarin and F.O. Oviasogie, "Insurgency and National Security Challenges in Nigeria: Looking Back, Looking Ahead," http://www.eprints.convenantuniversity.edu.ng/3243/1/Folarin.

paign mantra of "Transformation." While the two words seek to promote rearrangements of things, issues, and structures, the electorates never bothered to investigate how the two parties intended to make their respective campaign promises a reality. Rather, the masses, seemingly tired of the misrule of the ruling PDP, went all out to ensure that a new political party (APC) took the reins of government at the center. Now, the voices of the opposition echo one major thing: restructuring. It should be noted that the objective of any effective federal restructuring is three-pronged:

- Establishing a system that would promote collective identity accompanied by distributive politics
- Allowing for mutual tolerance among the federating units with respect to the rights of the aggrieved ethnic group
- Creating a political system that will ensure a just and equity-based arrangement between the federating units.[45]

In succinct terms, holistic attempts at restructuring are imperative for addressing the several imbalances in a multi-ethnic society like Nigeria. This may not be the case in the calls for restructuring in Nigeria. It looks more like a political strategy developed by a few political elites to wrestle power from the hands of the incumbent administration. If this is the case, it is safe to assume that calls for restructuring are perpetrated by a minority that intends to superimpose their will on the masses in general.

It may also be merely an attempt to sue for the redistribution and reallocation of the country's resources to favor groups calling for restructuring. From observations, one can easily deduce that calls for restructuring involve some inherent ethnic coloration. Such grievances may seem deliberate, owing to certain circumstances perceived as tendencies for domination or marginalization. The use of ethnic identity to manipulate the populace for political gains in the face of competition is not new in Nigeria due to the divergent ethnic arrangement of the country. It is also possible to misconstrue ethnic interests and agendas as nationalist ideals, forgetting that the elites may also propagate these agendas at the apex of various ethnic movements that are self-appointed. Bearing this in mind, it is apt to assume that ethnicity does not provide any form of political stability except when it serves as a manipulative tool for certain privileged individuals who intend or attempt to compete for power with their contemporaries in other ethnic groups. The position such individuals attain within societal constructs allows them to recruit their people to buy into their agendas, which are systematically framed with ethnic jingoism that is acceptable as a common interest. The structural inequality within the society makes such moves easy for perpetrators, allowing them to promote personal interest as a common interest while assuring the recruited gets a better future.[46]

---

45. Kunle Amuwo, ed., *Federalism and Political Restructuring in Nigeria* (Ibadan: Spectrum, 1998).

46. Dele Babalola, "The Efficacy of Federalism in a Multi-Ethnic State: The Nigerian Experience," *Journal of Pan African Studies* 8, no. 2 (2015): 74-92.

Without political instability, calls for restructuring do not have loud decibels. Political stability is necessary for plural states like Nigeria, depending on the elite consensus. In the absence of conflict, the elites of various ethnic societies will come together to ensure that the nation's administration is stable. As noted by Lijphart in one of his articles, the willingness of the ethnic-divergent elites to agree to a national power-sharing formula often ensures some significant levels of political stability.[47] However, the presence of the smallest form of rancor among these ethnic-divergent elites leads to political instability, giving birth to various personal agendas coated as an ethnic agenda. Little wonder, contestation for political power at the center often results in ethnoreligious conflict, a ripple effect of rivalry among competing elites of dominant ethnic groups within the nation. Nigerian politics perfectly fits this narrative. A cursory look into the alignments formed throughout the four republics will validate this assertion.

Enormous opportunities attached to holding political power at the national level motivate elites from various ethnic backgrounds to compete aggressively, each on the lookout for a smokescreen ethnic-focused agenda to sell to the kinsmen who often buy into it based on ethnic sentiments. With this, we can see why the persistent clamor for a national conference or restructuring has become a mainstay in Nigeria's political landscape. This has become a common feature used by ethnic leaders to drive personal agendas while vocalizing claims of ethnic marginalization as the rationale behind their agitations. However, there is a strong belief that the northern elite in Nigeria favors the status quo because they have been the ones who continually wield dominance over others for a long time. This may not be wholly true. During the early years of the Obasanjo-led administration, there were calls by the northern states for allocating more power to the state government. This culminated in the adoption of Sharia Law as state law in many northern states. This was read as a move to Islamize Nigeria, but such would not have been possible since the sitting president then was not a Muslim, despite granting northern states such powers. One would have expected the perceived Islamization agenda to play out when a northerner and Muslim, Umar Musa Yar' Adua, became the president after Obasanjo. However, the country experienced the waning of the Sharia Law in northern states.

RESTRUCTURING NIGERIA: THE WAY FORWARD

Restructuring denotes a change of the underlying structures of an entity to correct the defects and improve the overall performance. This may mean rearranging the parts and redefining their interrelationship to make room for more efficiency. This may take the form of political, economic, or socio-religious rearrangement. Politically, restructuring is imperative when there are noticeable flaws in the structural ar-

47. Arendt Lijphart, *Democracy in Plural Societies: A Comparative Exploration* (New Haven: Yale University Press, 1977).

rangement within the political system. In essence, it becomes imperative when the power configuration of a nation is skewed in favor of the central government to the detriment of federating units. In most pre-restructuring scenarios, the dominant federating unit always enjoys power at the center. This means the ethnic group with the highest population and numerical strength takes control of the government. However, true federalism entails that the power at the center exists at the discretion of federating units and not the other way around. When such is the case, calls for restructuring are ever-pervasive until power is devolved from the center.

The initial setup of Nigeria post-independence reflected some level of true federalism, with the three major regions (North, east and west) retaining a high level of control over their respective natural resources. The concept of resource control ensured that the three regions maintained autonomy while the center was a political mechanism to keep the three regions together. The three federating units only agreed to contribute to maintaining the central structure.[48] The emergence of political parties along ethnic lines paved the way for these three regions to adopt unique developmental projects. While the Igbo dominated the NCNC, the Yoruba nation adopted the Action Group, while the North adopted NPC. The entrenchment of ethnic politics allowed each region to develop blueprints for growth without interference from the center. This is because these three regions opened up avenues to generate revenue independently while controlling the revenue generated.

However, this was summarily terminated with the emergence of military rule in Nigeria. Crude oil exploration and commercialization necessitated this jettison of the proper federal arrangement, which would have greatly improved the eastern region. The oil boom shifted the focus of successive military governments from cash crops like cocoa to the background while resources of the minority Niger Delta sub-region became the country's cash cow and, ultimately, a major source of income. The problem created by abrogating the resource control arrangement became a catalyst for distrust and hatred along ethnic lines in Nigeria. To mitigate this, various past moves have been embarked upon to ensure that the country is restructured to ensure all federating units are not unfairly treated in the distribution of the country's resources. The proponents of restructuring believe that it is the only worthy solution to a prolonged unity among the federating units in Nigeria. Having understood the undertone of various dimensions of restructuring being propagated by various movements in Nigeria, it is clear that the country truly needs some form of restructuring to progress among the federating units. While calls for restructuring emanate from the political elites of agitated ethnic groups, it does not have to end with secession. Restructuring Nigeria for progress and unity is achievable on a wider spectrum of action both on the part of the government as well as the people. The country's unique situation

48. S. Azaiki, *Inequities in Nigerian Politics* (Lagos: Y Books, 2007).

does not allow for a singular restructuring strategy as this would be counterproductive since it would only favor some of the disadvantaged of other federating units.

In Nigeria, demands for restructuring by disadvantaged federating units are propelled by ethno-ideological and socio-economical conflicts. Depending on the pedestal side where an ethnic group finds itself, there are persistent moves of alignment by two or more ethnic groups for centrifugal positioning. This leaves opposing ethnic groups to take the profile of a balancer within the federal arrangement. Knowing that the calls for restructuring are more political than nationalist, there is a need for the government at the center to make sure that promises made to the people are kept and not politicized to favor only some. One of the major problems of the government at the center has to do with failed promises. In some situations where promises are kept, one may find that they are skewed to favor one to the detriment of the other. For instance, the Buhari administration promised monetary intervention to the poor when campaigning for the election. However, the Ministry of Humanitarian Affairs' disbursement of monetary intervention, especially during the COVID-19 lockdown, was lopsided. This is because the North has the highest number of poor people in Nigeria, and where funds are allocated to cater to the poor, they take the larger share. Restructuring should not be a mere political mantra that whets the appetite of the masses with dreams of a future utopia.

Issues relating to restructuring are constantly debated in Nigerian federal legislative chambers. The initial results of the debates led to adjustments in the revenue-sharing formula. However, this has not led to major changes because exploration rights and the sales of resources such as crude oil still reside with the federal government. This has further exacerbated the fragile nature of Nigeria as a united nation. The Niger Delta region, which has served as the cash cow of the Nigerian government, remains the least developed region, with tales of catastrophic environmental degradation of the region's ecosystem due to crude oil exploration.[49] Despite pollution being witnessed in this region, there is an inadequate effort on the part of the federal government and multinational corporations dredging oil to ensure that the region's indigenous people are adequately compensated and taken care of. The fact remains that the 13% derivation allotted to oil-producing states in the region is grossly mismanaged, leaving little or nothing for developmental purposes.

One good restructuring agenda is to improve the country's governance quality. The country's leadership has been a major challenge to true development. The systemic failure of virtually all institutions in Nigeria has made it difficult for good governance to be possible. The political elites of various federating units should focus more on good governance, reducing the poverty of their people and not pushing an agenda that reeks of personal and individual interest to divide the country. All ethnic groups must

49. Ugboma, "Environmental Degradation in Oil Producing Area."

commit to the country's unity and indivisibility for Nigeria's progress. The dividends of democracy should be spread equally, with no region or ethnic group left behind.

Corruption in the federal government corridors is huge and needs to be addressed. The systemic corruption at the first tier of government in Nigeria is worrisome. This is because the country's commonwealth is seated there. Resources should travel from the bottom up, not from top to bottom. It would have been ideal in a federal setting to see states contributing their quota to the federal government purse, not vice versa. With every state and region having some degree of autonomy, remitting to the federal purse should be the case. Suppose all regions can survive individually on the internally generated revenues (IGR) collected. In that case, states that cannot survive will have to merge with others, complement themselves, and improve their economies of scale. The fact that most federalism debates hang around restructuring points to the fact that the various dominant ethnic groups in Nigeria still believe in the concept of unity in diversity. With this, it may be concluded that the country needs to strengthen the federating structure to ensure that the union becomes more functional based on mutual benefits among federating units.

One thing that should also be understood is that no singular federating unit can match the profile Nigeria, as a conglomerate of federations, has in the event of any dissolution. Yes, the country may be experiencing bad government and leadership, but the potential of Nigeria as a nation is so great, and this would disappear in the face of dissolution. The mentality of those aspiring for positions should also be restructured; public service should not be perceived as a money-making or wealth-generating endeavor. Rather, it should be seen as a call to serve the people and ensure that the country's progress is paramount. With the country already divided along ethnic lines, the need for value reorientation becomes imperative to restore the dignity of Nigerians. Nigeria is highly polarized along ethno-religious lines, and the high level of mistrust creates a problem whose only solution is to map a pathway toward true federalism that will see all federating units become more autonomous. Rather than work assiduously to achieve this agenda, successive governments continue to play lip service to the initiative. With the northern region's persistent moves to dominate the federal arrangement for selfish gains, true federalism might not be achievable soon. There is a need to develop a nationalistic attitude and ensure equal and fair treatment by all regions of the country. Regional conflict will be removed by granting regions a high degree of autonomy, creating a pathway for peaceful coexistence and mutual acceptance.

CONCLUDING REMARKS

Nigeria is going through a difficult phase in its strive toward assuaging the anger of various ethnic groups within the nation. Peaceful coexistence among ethnic groups is laid on a weak foundation, with issues relating to fear and domination taking center stage. The perennial agitation for secession by various ethnic groups in Nigeria stems

from the flawed federal arrangement that allocates too many powers to the center while federating units are left with very little power. Secession calls may not be holistic, as we have seen in the past. Alleged marginalized regions play the secession card to get the government's attention at the center. Such calls may only get very strong if they are echoed in the backdrop of a nationalist agenda rather than a political agenda.

In essence, secession moves are more political than nationalistic. Secession agitations are a smokescreen for better government representation and a tool to experience increased attention from the central government. The moment as such has been attended to, such calls vanish into thin air, just as we have seen in the past. Secessionist agendas will only end when power allocated to the center is devolved to favor the federating units collectively. Among the more subtle calls for power devolvement from the center includes recent calls for restructuring, which is more feasible if the current government chooses to make it happen. Dousing tension created as a result of decades of misrule and mismanagement at the center will only be possible if the government assuages the anger of various ethnic groups through a simple restructuring process.

While doing this, the government needs to understand that political restructuring should not be embarked upon in a manner that will benefit only the political elites of the various regions. What is needed for the country to grow is a political restructuring project that will usher in good governance and true federalism. Among the principles that need to be of paramount importance in any restructuring are consensus orientation, accountability, transparency and government responsiveness to issues raised by the people. The aforementioned represents the core aspects of governance that can reduce the level of corruption going on at the top-tier level of government in Nigeria. Public sector corruption erodes any form of trust in government. The ripple effect is magnified by the masses' distrust of the activities of the two major governmental agencies saddled with the fight against corruption in Nigeria: the EFCC and the ICPC. The general perception that these agencies are best used for witch-hunting and political bullying has not changed. The fight against corruption, on which premise the Buhari administration got into power, is yet a mirage. And without tackling public sector corruption, there is no way the environment can be suitable for development.

The problem of Nigeria may be more than the issue of restructuring; at the least, it will put the country on the right pedestal for effective and efficient governance. Several regions within the nation have come to understand that development will be possible if they are given the autonomy to control their resources. It should also be understood that recent calls for restructuring are more serious than before. The emergence of a new crop of ethnopolitical leaders who constantly demand good governance offers some hope that past calls for restructuring embarked upon for personal gains are gradually being eroded. New calls for restructuring hammer more on good governance than resource control, which past ethnic political elites persistently clamor over to satisfy their desires.

6

FEMINISM IN A RESISTANT SOCIETY

INTRODUCTION

Nigeria, the most populous nation in Africa, is divided along various lines: by ethnicity, religious affiliation, socioeconomic status, as well as gender. While many of these divisions exist because of social processes, structural conditions, or circumstantial events, gender diversity is natural and cannot be traced to any human determinations. From time immemorial, there has been one gender superimposing its authority over the other. This dominance has been granted legitimacy through the backing of religious thought that taught that the feminine gender is inferior to its masculine counterpart. As the Abrahamic religions posit, the woman was created from the broken ribs of man.

While being subject in the past to these religious dogmas setting women behind men, the Western world has established norms that alleviate the challenge of women's unequal societal standing to men. In one such instance, Britain elected Margaret Thatcher as the first female executive in Britain in 1979 while also having the same sex as the monarchical head of state in the person of Queen Elizabeth II. While Thatcher was the first woman elected to lead a government in the United Kingdom, it might be worth noting that she was preceded by a decade or two by the popularly elected Sirimavo Bandaranaike in Ceylon/Sri Lanka, Indira Gandhi in India, and Golda Meir in Israel. Elisabeth Domitien was appointed as CAR's Prime Minister of the Bokassa dictatorship. This opened Western ideologies to granting women equal

opportunities to lead their respective countries and created a ripple effect that reached Asia, the Middle East, and Latin America.

In contrast, Islamic nations such as Saudi Arabia and Iraq continue suppressing female emancipation. Particularly in Iran, women are not given full rights as most of them are subsumed under their husbands' authority.[1] Gender discriminatory laws persist in Iran in instances of marriage, where only the husbands can determine the rights of their wives, divorce, inheritance, and women's access to justice, among a host of other discriminatory practices.[2] Leila Alikarami argues in her book titled *Women & Equality in Iran: Law, Society and Activism* that Iran struggles to implement the Convention on the Elimination of all Forms of Discrimination Against Women (CEDAW), which foregrounds gender equality, and portrays the state's resistance to give equal rights to both sexes.[3] She contends that the lack of an open-minded interpretation of Sharia, Islamic Jurisprudence, contributes to gender inequality in the country, positing that most of the government's measures towards implementing the international bills for women's rights were rejected by the Guardian Council, a body concerned with the interpretation of Islamic principles as they concern Iranian law, on the premise that it is un-Islamic.[4]

The United Nations Organization (UNO), right from its inception in 1948, had been committed to promoting gender equality. According to Article 1 of the United Nations Charter, its purposes included "to achieve international cooperation in solving international problems of an economic, social, or cultural, or humanitarian character, and in promoting and encouraging respect for human rights and fundamental freedoms for all without distinction as to race, sex, language, or religion." In 1979, the United Nations organized the Convention on the Elimination of Discrimination Against Women (CEDAW), otherwise called the international bill of rights for women, which recommended a worldwide effort to end gender-based discrimination and violence directed toward women based on gender differences. Among the behaviors included was the infliction of physical, mental, or sexual harm, as well as acts of deprivation and coercion against women across the globe, and these were categorized as internationally recognized violations of female human rights. As part of its recommendations, the UNO persuaded all participating countries to agree to work for the elimination of gender discrimination, with nations expected to establish legal sanctions, preventive measures, and civil remedies against gender discrimination. In its pursuance of gender equality, to further protect women, the United Nations organized World Conferences on Women held in China in 1995 and a Platform for Action

1. Women Living Under Muslim Laws, "Child, Early and Forced Marriage: A Multi-country Study," *A Submission to the UN Office of the High Commissioner for Human Rights* (OCHCR), 2013.

2. Women Living Under Muslim Laws, "Child, Early and Forced Marriage."

3. Leila Alikaram, *Women and Equality in Iran: Law, Society and Activism* (New York: Bloomsbury Publishing, 2019).

4. Alikaram, *Women and Equality in Iran*, 74.

Figure 6.1. "Feminism and Politics in Nigeria" by Michael Efionayi. Describes the expectations of feminism and the societal resilience that amounts to delay in acceptance into key societal positions.

that addressed the marginalization of women that prevented them from accessing societal opportunities as much as their male counterparts.[5] The conference proved a significant achievement in addressing gender equality globally. The Beijing Declaration and Platform for Action is reviewed after five years, the last being in 2020.

Even in African societies that were later inculcated in the religious thoughts of Abrahamic religions, inequalities based on gender have always been pervasive. Men and women are not granted equal access to these cultures' major ingredients of socio-economic interactions and privilege. Women experience unequal access to resources and socioeconomic conditions, especially in careers such as the military, religion, politics, and commerce; the female gender has always been under-represented. It could be argued that the gender disparity in the social climate is the effect of discrim-

5. E. E. O. Alemika and A.O. Agugua, *Gender Relations and Discrimination in Nigeria Police Force* (Ikeja: Centre for Law Enforcement Education, 2011).

ination, which is culturally bound, that portrays men as custodians of the culture and fits them into the narratives that identify them as beneficiaries of power and status.

The European Union adopted guidelines that addressed discrimination and violence against women. This aimed to combat all forms of gender discrimination while promoting equality through coordinated strategies that included promoting gender equality in decision-making, labor markets, economic independence, and strengthening women's rights worldwide to address the impunity of perpetrators of discrimination.[6]

Gender equality efforts have become more pronounced globally in modern times. Scholars and writers often discuss feminism on two distinct grounds: as a movement and as a theory. Feminism as a movement aims to reduce gender discrimination by ensuring that women possess rights in ways that are neither different nor inferior to men. Often, feminism seeks socioeconomic change that includes changing the roles of men and women within society to allow women unhindered access to the same things as men. Feminists often operate as groups, mostly of women, who position themselves as leaders in struggles to attain female gender equality.

As a theory, feminism centers on contemporary sociological analysis of the status of men and women in society, intending to use the results to boost women's standing. Feminist theorists study approaches to gender equality within a framework that often includes giving a voice to women and highlighting the roles women play in the development of any society. Feminism is the concept used to describe the variety of efforts aimed at reducing gender inequalities and promoting women's rights.[7] Feminism has shaped the perception of the female sex in Nigerian societies, as there have been campaigns to protect women and girls from sexual and domestic abuse.[8] This explains why Olufemi describes the concept as a call for justice.[9] Although there were many misconceptions about feminism, society has come to understand that it is a movement to promote female worth and emphasize equal rights.[10] Ganiat Olatokun argues that most Nigerian women do not identify themselves as feminists as they only employ the term "feminism" to advocate for women's emancipation.[11] This argument is

6. European Commission, "Strategic Engagement for Gender Equality 2016–2019," Luxembourg Publications Office of the European Union, 2016.

7. G. K. Abdullahi, "Gender Discrimination and Feminism in Nigeria," *International Journal of Economics, Commerce and Management* 3, no. 7 (2015): 7.

8. Deborah Aina-Pelemo and Jesutoye Testimony Adeboye, "Women's Right and Feminism Under the Law in Nigeria," *OAU Journal of Public Law* 1, no. 1 (2021): 158.

9. Lola Olufemi, *Feminism Interrupted: Disrupting Power* (London: Pluto Press, 2020).

10. Aina-Pelemo and Adeboye, "Women's Right and Feminism."

11. Ganiat M. Olatokun, "Nigerian Feminism: A Typology of African Feminism," *KIU Journal of Humanities* 2, no. 1 (2017): 216.

also in tandem with scholarly postulations that women's struggles should correspond to their local context and agenda.[12]

Regardless of the important roles women play in Nigeria, they have continued to be marginalized politically and socio-economically. Women are known to suffer gender discrimination in all aspects of society, such as domestic and sexual abuse, which makes it extremely difficult to advance in social status except when they are adequately supported or hiding under the shadows of men, generally their husbands or fathers. The stereotyping and trivialization of women in Nigeria are so great that their endeavors are relegated to second-class. Among the early elements complicit in developing this misogynist perception are trado-cultural and religious factors that militate against women's status and participation. Virtually all cultures in Nigeria designate the woman as a mere housekeeper, with some cultures even regarding the wife as the husband's property.[13] Perhaps this exploitation is because of the dowry paid by the husband, which some people in the same vein perceive as buying something.

In some cultures, in eastern Nigeria, a widow is bound by tradition to scrap all her hair and put through much suffering for up to a year as a mourning period for her deceased husband, but if a man loses his wife to death, nothing similar is required from him.[14] A widower may even take another wife in a few months without society raising an eyebrow. In some places, female children are not allowed to inherit from their father's possessions, as tradition holds that her share of any property should be in her husband's house.

THE EMERGENCE OF FEMINISM IN NIGERIA

Feminism has been a subject of intellectual discourse among female emancipation activists in Nigeria for quite some time, and women's liberation, which has always been the ultimate goal of feminism, has also long been part of the narrative in Nigeria. In 1914, the same year that the present territory of Nigeria was formed, Nigerian women staged a protest described by Nwando Achebe as the "Ogidi Palaver."[15] The protest was directed at the indigenous and British men, whom the protesters believed had conspired to sideline the women folk from decision-making processes.

Feminism in Nigeria focuses on the rejection of gender oppression as well as liberation from all manners of dominance by men. The oppression can come in various forms, including psychological, emotional, political, philosophical, and socio-eco-

12. Mikell Gwendolyn, ed., *African Feminism: The Politics of Survival in Sub-Saharan Africa* (Philadelphia: University of Pennsylvania Press, 1997), 4.

13. Chioma Chiazom Anagor, "African Values, Gender Inequality and Feminism: The Igbo Race," *Nigerian Journal of African Studies (NJAS)* 4, no. 1 (2022): 7.

14. Anagor, "African Values, Gender Inequality and Feminism."

15. Nwando Achebe, *The Female King of Colonial Nigeria: Ahebi Ugbabe* (Bloomington: Indiana University Press, 2011).

nomical. The subservient and condescending attitudes to women in Nigeria are evidenced in all spheres, be it the culture, traditions, and institutions. This has been explained by the degradation of women in some cultures.[16] Similarly, as argued on social media, in the Hausa culture, the female lacks access to education—likewise in the Yoruba culture too[17]— on the counts that it is of no use to them, and they are subjected to forced marriages.[18] This perception of women leads to discrimination against them, a situation that is made more worrying by religious bigotry. Mbiti noted that Africans are notoriously religious, and each people have a religious system with a set of beliefs and practices.[19] For instance, goddesses in Nigerian cultures, such as among the Yoruba and Igbo, are wives of gods and are lesser in power and authority.

Religion has greatly influenced how Africans perceive everything, and despite modernization creeping into the people's ways of doing things, the religious attachment of Nigerians continues to fan the embers of gender inequality in society. In some parts of the North, women are not allowed to sit in public buses with men due to religious indoctrination and even are mandated to mask themselves, thereby limiting their social status in the community.[20]

Women have documented struggles to correct perceived acts of discrimination as far back as the early 1900s. Amongst them was the Nwaobiala Movement of 1925, which saw women coming out to reject the imposition of colonial values and would later lead to the Women's War of 1929, where thousands of women marched to voice their agitations against economic policies directed at them. For instance, the women were asked to pay taxes. In that regard, they revolted against the colonial authorities, forming women's movements that would later play an important strategic role in the independence struggles.

Initially, feminism in Nigeria was misconstrued as anti-male acts, resulting in a negative perception of anybody and everybody promoting feminist ideologies.[21] This made society wary of feminist movements, with women activists tagged as "men haters." [22] Momentum was gained when women began to sense the gender inequalities that society promoted and subsequently made conscious attempts to secure equal

16. Anagor, "African Values, Gender Inequality and Feminism."

17. Abayomi Samuel Oyekale, "Ethnic Characterization of Gender-Inequality and Domestic Violence against Women of Reproductive Ages in Nigeria," *Studies of Tribes and Tribals* 12, no. 1 (2014): 31–41.

18. Nina Pawlak, "'Woman' and 'Man' in Hausa Language and Culture." In *Hausa Chadic Studies: In Honour of Professor Stanislaw Pilaszewicz*, eds. Nina Pawlak, Izabela Will and Ewa Siwierska (Warsawa: Elipsa, 2014).

19. J.S. Mbiti, *African Religions and Philosophy* (London: Heinemann, 1982).

20. Adejoke Adetoro, Oluwakayode Ashamu and Maikudi Lawan, "Women, Religion and Contemporary Public Transport Service in Kano Metropolis," *IFRA-Nigeria Working Papers Series* 49 (2019).

21. Mariam Marwa Abdul, Olayinka Adeleke, O. Adeyeye, A. Babalola, E. Eyo, M.T. Ibrahim and Martha Onose, "Analysis of the History, Organisations and Challenges of Feminism in Nigeria," *Nawey Nigerian Group: Academy of Management Perspectives* 18, no. 3 (2011): 136–139.

22. Abdul, Adeleke, Adeyeye, Babalola, Eyo, Ibrahim and Onose, "Analysis of the History."

opportunities for themselves and champion the promotion of women's rights. This deprivation was legitimized by the patriarchal culture prevalent in most Nigerian communities, which has continued to marginalize women in societal affairs.

This is despite Nigerian women playing an active role in the country's development from pre-colonial to post-independence times. Feminism, as it relates to Nigeria, cannot be fully understood unless the early attempts by women to be actively involved in collaborative development are evaluated.

WOMEN'S ROLES IN PRE-COLONIAL NIGERIA

Women's roles in pre-colonial Nigeria are best understood by looking at the socio-political and economic activities that they engaged in. The participation of women in the various societies that make up Nigeria was very significant, including the northern part of Nigeria, dominated by the predominantly Muslim Hausa-Fulani, who upheld the practice of *purdah* female segregation. Even in the North, research revealed that some notable women asserted their rights to public space participation by forming associations.[23] Among such women was the famous Queen Amina of Zaria, who would later become the ruler of a city-state in the male-controlled city of Zazzau. Queen Amina was a soldier who embarked on military expeditions to conquer much of the area around the River Niger and River Benue. Within Nigeria's middle-belt region, there were stories of territories founded by women, such as the Igala Kingdom, founded by a woman named Ejaunu.[24]

The kingdoms south of the River Niger and River Benue accorded relatively greater status to women, with the Yoruba people bestowing political powers to women through positions such as the *Iyalode*, who sat amongst notable chiefs in communal decision-making. That the Iyalode was the only female chief still lends credence to the authoritarian tendencies of men in society.[25] While they may have been accorded political responsibility, their opinions and submissions still had to align with the male chiefs if they were to be embraced. This greatly limited the Iyalode to a complementing influence rather than a controlling one.

THE ROLE OF COLONIALISM AND GENDER DISPARITY

With the emergence of colonial rule in Nigeria, the stage was set for excluding women from the new colonial administrations. The colonial government sought control of various Nigerian communities through religious, educational, and trading

23. Adebukola Dagunduro and Adebimpe Adenugba, "Failure to Meet up to Expectation: Examining Women's Activist Groups in the Post-colonial Period in Nigeria," *Open Cultural Studies* 4, no. 1 (2020): 24.

24. Naasin Diseye Amy, "Women Rights and Feminism in Nigeria: The Journey So Far," LL.B Project, University of Lagos, 2016, 19.

25. There were (and still are) Ìyálọ̀jà and/or Ìyáláje whose roles are also as powerful as that of Iyalode.

institutions. Colonial control of social life in the Southern part of Nigeria was operated through Christianity, which greatly altered women's roles from the late nineteenth century to the Second World War by establishing boundaries on what was morally acceptable and right. The control of economic life was made possible through laws and bureaucratic infrastructure. In the northern part of Nigeria, colonialism brought about the decline of various Islamic regimes deemed imperialistic by nature, including some institutions in the Sokoto Caliphate, which the British colonial government disbanded by sending forces under the guise of helping the Muslims in their war against the French.[26]

The emergence of the colonial government never successfully stopped the spread of Islam and the subsequent institution of the Sharia legal system in various emirates in the North. Among the various practices instituted under Sharia law was purdah, which secluded women from public spaces and government offices.[27] In this way, both Christianity and Islam played roles in limiting women's rights and their roles in Nigerian society during colonial rule, especially in limiting their political participation.

Other factors were instrumental to the institution of gender bias in colonial Nigeria. Firstly, Christianity's emphasis on monogamy and the further subjugation of women, in tandem with the doctrines that they must obey the authorities of their husbands as heads of the family as God had prescribed in the relationship of Adam and Eve, served to redefine the roles of women. Also, with the advent of Western education, there was a focus on the scholarly advancement of men to the detriment of women. There was too much emphasis on male education, as the males were expected to be integrated into the labor market more easily than their female counterparts. The British colonial government instituted new legal systems that theoretically acknowledged women's rights but treated them as legal minors in actual practice.[28] The changes significantly limited women's positions in society, leading to increased male dominance, patriarchal control, and a reduction in their fundamental human rights.

As capitalism began to take shape in the colonial economy, male-dominated businesses gained more prominence, while the colonial government gradually took over women-dominated businesses. Among them was the West African cotton industry, which had a sizeable number of women involved when it was taken over by the colonial government, thus eliminating women's ownership and trampling on their means of gaining wealth.

---

26. Mohammed S. Audu and Uzoma S. Osuala, "The British Conquest and Resistance of Sokoto Caliphate, 1897–1903: Crisis, Conflicts and Resistance," *Historical Research Letter* 22 (2015): 32.

27. L. Bergstrom, "Legacies of Colonialism and Islam for Hausa Women: An Historical Analysis, 1804 to 1960," GPID/WID Working Papers, Center for Gender in Global Context, Michigan State University, East Lansing, Michigan, 2002.

28. G. Mikell, "Introduction." In *African Feminism: The Politics of Survival in Sub-Saharan Africa*, ed. G. Mikell (Philadelphia, Pennsylvania: University of Pennsylvania Press, 1997), 1–52.

Ahebi Ugbabe, the only female warrant officer in colonial Nigeria, deserves mention when discussing feminism in Nigeria because of what she achieved during a time when women were being summarily excluded from leadership roles in Nigeria. For about thirty years, Ugbabe maintained authority over thirty-three villages known jointly as Enugu-Ezike on return from exile, leveraging her linguistic skills to build a strong political structure.[29] During her tenure, Ugbabe assumed men's roles, marrying women she assigned men to for procreation and taking responsibility for the children who took her name.[30]

Being a woman who eschewed femininity, she was at the center of various controversies, including accusations of taking away men's wives, using forced labor, and receiving bribes, as well as being perpetually unwilling to consult elders in a system where they were seen as the protectors of the culture and tradition.[31] Despite her achievements, Ugbabe was also alleged to have gone beyond the line a woman should go and performed an abomination by embarking on a ritual to bring out a sacred mask that was believed to be exclusive to men,[32] which led to her humiliation in the hands of the male-dominated elders of her clan. Not trusting that her people would give her a befitting burial, she organized her rites while still living and was buried according to the customs of male burials to show her reverence for masculinity. The exploits of Ugbabe point to the Igbo people as a community that does not consciously limit females to subservient roles, bolstered with the strongest agitations by Nigerian women during the colonial era perpetrated by women from the southeastern part of Nigeria. The relegation of women to second-class is still subconsciously ingrained in virtually all societies and ethnic groups in Nigeria, including among the Igbo.

As a result of the anti-colonial struggles in Nigeria, the Nigerian Women's Union was formed in 1947 as a resistance force. The major reason for the establishment of the feminist organization was the perceived discrimination of women in the southern region of Nigeria, a region that had hitherto experienced active female participation in public life. The colonial government had begun introducing policies limiting women's political participation, such as the adult male suffrage of 1923.[33]

During the colonial era, southern Nigeria women played active roles individually and collectively, as they formed market associations to assert their rights and maintain a significant degree of political influence in the region. In an attempt to subjugate them, the British colonial government imported the eighteenth-century model of women's status from Europe into Nigeria, further destabilizing the development of their economic, social, and political rights in Nigeria.

---

29. Achebe, *The Female King of Colonial Nigeria.*

30. Achebe, *The Female King of Colonial Nigeria,* 99.

31. Achebe, *The Female King of Colonial Nigeria,* 122.

32. Achebe, *The Female King of Colonial Nigeria,* 106.

33. David Nwogbaga, "Retrospect in Nigeria's Elections, 1923–1993." In *Democracy and Electoral Studies: A Reader*, eds. A. Itumo and J.O. Nkwede (Enugu: Kenny and Brothers, 2015), 3.

Another major resistance against colonial oppression by women in southern Nigeria was the 1948 protest by Yoruba women in Abeokuta, which was also against excessive taxation imposed by the colonial government. This and similar incidents resulted in the Federation of Nigerian Women's Societies (FNWS) in 1953, intending to emancipate the female folk in Nigeria. The activities of FNWS were more political than the tax protests, as the movement provided a platform for women to agitate for more representation and participation in Nigerian politics. As the women's movements became more influential, they became more concerned with the underrepresentation of women in politics and began to clamor for women's participation in politics through a coalition with other political parties.

There were periods when conflicts arose amongst the feminist movements of the era, as they were torn between aligning with the government and operating autonomously. In some other cases, rather than aggressive agitation against male dominance and marginalization of women, they seemed to maintain neutrality while acting within the traditional boundaries set by society.

While this was happening in the southern region of Nigeria, northern women were still restrained from political and commercial activities by the Hausa-Fulani cultural norms. Similarly, northern women had minimal commensurate resistance movements since they did not have a strong political network.

FEMINISM AND POST-COLONIAL NIGERIA

With the coming of independence, there were hopes that women's status would improve, given their active participation in the fight against the continued colonial engagement in Nigeria. Sadly, this was not the case with the emergence of military control of the corridors of power in Nigeria. As the military took over the reins of government in 1966, women's fortunes in the government dwindled seriously as there was no woman in the Nigerian military that was deemed knowledgeable enough to be involved at the zenith of the army command, and so there was no way any woman could hold any significant position in the military government. Things changed somewhat during Nigeria's return to democracy in the Second Republic from 1979 to 1983. During this era, women could participate in the electoral process, but the women in the northern region of Nigeria did not participate like their southern counterparts. Most of the women in the North were disenfranchised based on electoral requirements such as the presentation of tax receipts to vote.[34] Also, because the Hausa culture is laced with Islamic principles, the women were not at liberty to go to public places where they would mix with other sexes to vote. With the return to military rule in 1983, the improving fortunes of Nigerian women were halted with the end of democratic participation. During the Babangida regime, a feminist organization, Women

34. A. Shettima, "Engendering Nigeria's Third Republic," *African Studies Review* 38, no. 3 (1995): 61–98.

In Nigeria (WIN), was established. WIN was set up to champion women's rights. The organization recorded some achievements in ensuring the political participation of women.

From that moment until now, feminist activities have involved positive methods, as most of their activities revolving around gender equality have been assertive, conscience-igniting, and motivating. Unlike in the past, when women resorted to protests and aggressive confrontations to drive home their demands, twenty-first-century feminism in Nigeria has been non-violent and non-confrontational. This is largely hinged on the fact that there are struggles for women's emancipation and correcting the wrong notions about the female sex that dominate society and not a violent reaction to the male sex. Women in Nigeria have changed tactics from the aggressive stance of the past to the use of advocacy and lobbying to demand the emancipation and social advancement of the feminine gender.[35] This strategy has borne fruit; there has been a significant improvement in female participation in government and politics as more and more women become active in the socio-political sphere in Nigeria. Although, it is "not yet Uhuru" for them, as they still face gender-based issues in virtually all spheres of engagement.

FEMINISM IN CONTEMPORARY NIGERIA

There has been an increase in the number of feminist groups in Nigeria as the struggle to ensure equal opportunity continues to take the front stage in socio-political engagements in Nigeria. While in the past, feminist organizations were not formally organized, with many feminist activities being a matter of spontaneous, incendiary reactions. A defined feminist space began to take shape with the Women in Nigeria (WIN) formation in 1983. WIN had the agenda of establishing an ideologically feminist movement against gender discrimination in Nigeria. WIN was credited with the development of most of the self-identified feminists that are in Nigeria today.[36] While positioned as an organization existing solely for advocating social justice for women, membership was not limited to women alone as men were urged to take part on the condition that they uphold the provisions of the WIN constitution; for example, championing the rights of women and eradicating all forms of gender abuse and violence. Despite this condition in membership induction, WIN was a strong platform to act as a training ground for feminists and the feminist struggle in Nigeria. The entry requirements for potential members resulted in the induction of many people who had no clue about feminism or female gender discrimination.

35. P. Okeke, "Reconfiguring Tradition: Women's Rights and Social Status in Contemporary Nigeria," *Africa Today* 47, no. 1 (2000): 49–63.

36. Bene E. Madunagu, "The Nigerian Feminist Movement: Lessons from Women in Nigeria, WIN," *Review of African Political Economy* 35, no. 118 (2008): 672.

Figure 6.2. "Conversation on Roles in the Family and Feminism" by Dr. Kazeem Ekeolu. A couple discussing their positions in the face of growing feminist consciousness in Nigeria.

Before the establishment of WIN, the National Council of Women's Society (NWCS) had existed since 1958 as an unarmed and non-confrontational movement whose modus operandi pursued a progressive upliftment of women in Nigeria towards motherhood and development. As part of its objectives, the NWCS coordinated with international organizations to find lasting solutions to issues affecting all women in Nigeria, regardless of religion, ethnicity or socioeconomic status. The organization also continued to persuade most members to participate in Nigerian politics.

The Nigerian feminist movement organizes events for families and women, focusing on issues such as sexual abuse, economic empowerment, violence against women, the acquisition of leadership skills, and political participation. Its presence demonstrates that things are not going smoothly for the women of Nigeria, but it defies the odds imposed by stigmatization and alienation as they strive to propagate women's rights in Nigeria. These groups continue to ensure that women can enjoy their fundamental human rights as much as men in the country. Through initiatives established and promoted by the small number of women in government, coupled with assistance from the wives of governors and presidents, the government has increased awareness of women's issues.

FACTORS IMPEDING WOMEN'S EMANCIPATION

The development of feminist ideology in Nigeria has been very significant, going by the level of awareness it generates relative to what was obtainable in the past. As far back as the early nineteenth century, the efforts of women struggling against discrimination and gender-oriented violence have always been in the limelight. This was especially true during the fight for independence, as women saw this as an opportunity to make their mark in the public space. Despite these successes in correcting the misconceptions about gender equality, there are still challenges being faced by the feminist movement to liberate women from inequality and violence.

Culture plays an important role in virtually all African societies. It embodies people's ways and how they expect others to perceive them. Culture has often been invoked as a justification for the inhuman treatment of women in various societies in Nigeria, and many Nigerian communities continue to use it to explain the inequality meted out to women in Nigeria. Under the auspices of these cultures and traditions, women are persistently denied a wide range of rights while their importance in society is downplayed. This situation is made worse even as certain aspects of culture are beginning to give way because of modernization since the perceived custodians of culture continue to hold onto those traditions that expressly deal with the status of women in society. These custodians—mostly men—have continued to exhibit their chauvinistic beliefs that society exists for the benefit of men, while women are expected to submit to this dynamic without asking questions or raising protests.

Religious institutions have always been the driving force for the propagation of male dominance in Nigerian societies. Since religion has been positioned as the judge of what is morally right, feminism and women's liberation continue to suffer under its primacy. Religious dogmas are often used to suppress women, thanks to the doctrinal expositions of the Abrahamic religions that have come to replace African religions. Both religions have their share of subjugating women. These doctrines and practices make it more difficult for women to successfully implement feminist agendas to remove the barriers to their equal societal status. Many women have been religiously brainwashed to accept being second-class beings who should take male dominance as the appropriate moral code of their society. Such ingrained beliefs have made it more complex for feminists who want to reorient Nigerian women against them and other psychological barriers erected to limit female liberation, a struggle seen in most developing countries.

In education, Nigerian women have also continually been relegated to the back bench. There is a significantly lower proportion of women in Nigerian tertiary institutions as it is believed that female education is less valuable than male education since the societal expectations are that women end up in the kitchen after getting married. Among other challenges, women are also prevented from continuing their education in the event of becoming impregnated before the end of their education, as

they face a high probability of being told to withdraw from school by parents who are steeped in the belief that girls do not need education. In such cases, it becomes quite difficult for these women to continue their education after delivering their child since child-rearing is seen as the joy of womanhood. This is the primary reason for women disproportionately dropping out.

There is a gender disparity in employment opportunities. Women's chance for advancement in their jobs is low, and they are more likely to be laid off than men.[37] This has resulted in Nigerian women not having substantial access to a regular income, which continues to limit their standing in society.

In major farming settlements in Nigeria, women contribute a high percentage of the manpower, especially in food processing and marketing. They accompany their husbands to farm and take part in selling the proceeds, but if we look at the whole process from the Western construct of wealth distribution, they do not enjoy the corresponding return of their input as the husbands will always control and apportion benefits as they deem fit. In all fairness, this should be seen as an extension of the economic arrangement of the family unit. After all, in the traditional patriarchal Yoruba society, the father is expected to carry the burden of running the family's economic interests. There is, therefore, no formal distribution of the family income; instead, the central purse, consisting of the proceeds which traditionally belong to the father and his many wives and children, is centrally managed by the father.

The marginalization of women politically is also rife. Political meetings in Nigeria are held in the evenings, with men expecting their spouses to be home at night, requiring a very understanding man to allow his wife to be active politically, and this greatly limits women's involvement. Women's underrepresentation in the political system is also hinged on the assumption that electing women into public office is not productive, as they are erroneously presumed to lack the requisite raw understanding and savagery to deal with the dirty politics that are ubiquitous in Nigeria. Women do not get representation matching their numerical strength. Both in the federal and state legislative houses, they are grossly underrepresented, totaling twenty-nine.[38]

These factors greatly limit the status of women in Nigeria and are directly linked to the patriarchal worldview that presumes men's dominance of women as a birthright. Some scholars also apportion blame to the colonial government that reified this inequality with their male-centered ideologies.[39] Women are persistently trapped in a fight for survival, both within their homes and in the public space, leaving men to continue to be positioned as the custodians of society.

There are various categories of feminists existing in Nigeria. While presenting themselves as feminists, some feel compelled to uphold cultural and religious tenets

---

37. V.L. Bullough, *The Subordinate Sex* (New York: Penguin, 1974).

38. Alemika and Agugua, *Gender Relations and Discrimination.*

39. Alemika and Agugua, *Gender Relations and Discrimination.*

while they challenge the specific elements that limit women's status in society, while others feel constrained by them in general. This sharp ideological divide prevents the feminist movement from having a united front against resistance from the male-controlled Nigerian society.

THE CHALLENGES TO FEMINISM

As in most nations, the Nigerian feminist movement has its share of challenges that act as resistance to the success of its agenda. While some of these challenges are inherent within the various feminist groups, others exist outside of them. They must contend with the societal opposition to women's agenda to be less subservient to male domination, while some government policies and laws are hostile to this agenda. Many of these obstacles can be categorized as popular misconceptions about feminism, double standards faced by women, hostility on the part of the media, and a lack of recognition from the government.

Misconceptions of the Feminist Agenda

An objective, unbiased evaluation of feminist activities in Nigeria would indicate that they do not intend to disrupt the system's status quo. Rather, feminism in Nigeria aims to correct the widely held societal belief that promotes gender inequality. Most feminist groups in Nigeria believe that culture and religion are good for society and that it is not ideal to exploit cultural traditions and religions in a way that creates unfair treatment of one gender to the benefit of another.[40] In attempts to remedy the adverse effect they have on women, feminism in Nigeria has become more active, leading to them being perceived by society as mercenaries who are out to disrupt the gender balance of society.[41]

Double Standards

Some feminists in Nigeria act in a manner that reveals some level of hypocrisy and evidence of double standards. This is an internal issue within the feminist movement, as investigations show that most feminists find it easy to discuss and advocate for feminism without any issues. When these individuals find themselves outside feminist organizations, they tend to cringe at public opinion on family structure, division of labor, and other societal encumbrances. For instance, as stated severally on many social media platforms, a woman in the company of a man expects the latter to open the door for them, and the concept of "ladies first" is paramount, as women are quick to use this vocabulary to gain an advantage over men. Feminists in Nigeria have been accused of not speaking up against such exploitation of gender in favor of women,

40. Allanana Godiya Makama, "Patriarchy and Gender Inequality in Nigeria: The Way Forward." *European Scientific Journal* 9, no. 17 (2013): 119.

41. Alemika and Agugua, *Gender Relations and Discrimination.*

and this is a sensitive aspect of engagement that feminists in Nigeria need to consider to further their claim for a more balanced society.

Media Negativity Towards Feminism

Society's misconceptions about feminists and feminist movements can be attributed to media misrepresentation.[42] The Nigerian media has continually presented feminists as rebels and dissidents who intend to disrupt the balance of power to favor women.[43] The fact that feminists are centered on challenging the patriarchal ideology in the Nigerian system puts them in the same bracket as instigators of conflicts and troublemakers. Many media contents on women and their roles in society are always in tandem with widely held societal beliefs to gain audiences.[44] This has contributed to the popularization of stereotypes about women. Critics have noted that the media representation of women aims at de-personalizing them and describing them as second-rate humans.[45] Chika Asogwa gives the instance of the portrayal of women as unintelligent, wizards, prostitutes, and maids as a few of these stereotypes.[46]

Lack of Adequate Government Recognition

Most feminists and their respective organizations have constantly advocated for a more gender-balanced system, but the men control the governmental structure in most parts of Nigeria, and it is hard to institutionalize the feminist movement. The intervention of the Nigerian government in feminist priorities is still superficial, as there has yet to be a nationwide debate on the issue of gender equality. In parts of the country, women are unaware of ideologies focused on liberating them from male subjugation.

There is a need for the government to put an end to all manners of discrimination against women within public and private spaces. As a matter of urgency, the government must improve existing anti-discrimination laws while also finding new ways to promote meritocracy in various fields. The government can provide leeway for more female participation in governance and administration by making the Federal Character Commission consider gender parity as a criterion for appointing individuals into public service. In planning the developmental process needed for Nigeria, the integration of women must be included, and to that end, the government should adopt gender mainstreaming as a developmental strategy for women in Nigeria. This

---

42. Kehinde Oyesomi and Olusola Oyero, "Women's Political Invisibility in Nigeria and the Imperative of Deliberate Media Agenda." In *Women's Political Visibility and Media Access: The Case of Nigeria*, ed. Oladokun Omojola (Newcastle upon Tyne: Cambridge Scholars Publishing, 2014): 109.

43. Kehinde Oyesomi and Olusola Oyero, "Women's Political Invisibility."

44. Floribert Patrick Endong and E. Obonganwan, "Media (Mis)Representation of the Nigerian Woman as a Product of the Society," *International Journal of Gender and Women's Studies* 3, no. 1 (2015): 103.

45. Endong and Obonganwan, "Media (Mis)Representation of the Nigerian Woman," 104.

46. Chika Euphemia Asogwa, "Women Empowerment for a Holistic Development in Nigeria," *Review of European Studies* 4, no. 2 (2012): 144.

would ensure that gender is taken into cognizance by the government when major policies, interventions, and programs are undertaken. The experiences of women and men, as well as their specific interests, should be evaluated at all levels of policymaking. Gender mainstreaming is a tool that can address the root causes of gender stereotypes and other norms that promote discrimination and inequality.

Gender mainstreaming eases the removal of female inequality while protecting women's rights in a feminist-resistant society like Nigeria. It would also ensure that women get unhindered access to employment opportunities and other economic resources.

With these challenges, it is evident that resistance to feminism will continue to hold sway in Nigeria for some time and will continue to serve as an obstacle to women's societal development. No country can progress with close to half of its population suffering one form of discrimination or the other, and the gradual removal of these challenges faced by feminists will improve the capacity of women within Nigeria's social, political, and economic realms.

THE SUCCESS OF FEMINIST ACTIVITIES IN NIGERIA

Feminist activities have inspired many women to recover lost confidence in the social system in Nigeria. The movement has motivated them to strive for total liberation and socioeconomic empowerment.[47] Still, a significant number of women in Nigeria try to refrain from engaging in acts that may label them as feminists, with indications that the majority of such women make this choice due to the fear of the exclusion feminists face. A negative construction of feminism in some circles is damaging: feminism is perceived as hatred toward men, which, coupled with the belief that only frustrated and unlovable women indulge in it, limits the number of women who wish to be seen as feminists.[48]

Despite that, the post-colonial era has witnessed significant success for feminists in Nigeria. There have been general protests organized by various feminist organizations focusing on specific issues, including domestic abuse, political marginalization, sexual abuse, early child marriages, as well as misapplication of Sharia law in some northern states. To a large extent, the fusion of the Yoruba Orisa religion and the Christian catholic religion was a survival technique, not just for the devotees but also for the Orisa religion, which, in many aspects, defined the fundamental basis of life of the devotees.[49]

---

47. Maureen Nwamaka Azuike, "A Radical Feminist Approach to the Works of Zaynab Alkali," Ph.D *diss.*, University of Jos. Nigeria, 2003.

48. Azuike, "A Radical Feminist Approach."

49. Abdul, Adeleke, Adeyeye, Babalola, Eyo, Ibrahim and Onose, "Analysis of the History."

Feminists have been able to successfully bring to the mainstream gender-based abuses that women face daily in Nigeria. For instance, the Niger Delta region has witnessed women creating awareness about the destruction of their environment by multinational oil companies and agitations directed toward the continuous military occupation of their lands. The Ogoni Women Association, established in the mid-1990s during the military regime, protested issues such as rape, violence, and torture perpetrated by military personnel stationed in the region during the Abacha dictatorship.

Since the participation of Nigerian women in the 1995 Beijing Conference, there has been a more audible voice for women in the Nigerian political space. Nigerian political parties now feel more compelled to consider women when structuring political offices; some—including the All Progressives Conference (APC), the ruling party—waive or reduce party fees for women, such as the cost of aspiration tickets, to encourage their participation. Women have been encouraged to take up political posts, and there is a federal ministry fully devoted to women's issues in Nigeria, such as that of Women Affairs and Social Development, formulating and coordinating policies aimed at improving the status of women,

FEMINISM AND THE INTERNET AND SOCIAL MEDIA IN NIGERIA

Women have struggled to become adequately represented in society without most of their lives and activities subsumed under male hegemony.[50] Society has often painted women as flawed characters who need men as support systems. Although women are now breaking boundaries, dreaming dreams, and pursuing their ambitions in defiance of the already established norms still fully alive in society; women can grow on their own and do excellently well. The advent of social media has given women, or, in the general sense, the female sex, the leverage to counter-narratives or views aimed at belittling them.[51] To a large extent, this has changed public perception of gender equality. Before the era of social media, it was a difficult struggle for women to liberate themselves in a highly patriarchal society.

The emergence of the internet and social media has become a powerful platform for feminist groups to mobilize and gain the attention of a wider range of audiences. Nigerian feminists have taken to social media for the propagation of unprecedented awareness of feminism in a way that is revolutionizing the concept in the country.

Feminism, while more subdued in the past, has been riding on social media to gain acceptability and followership in the struggle against gender discrimination. Social

50. Allanana Godiya Makama, "Patriarchy and Gender Inequality."

51. Nicole Wasuna, "Hashtag Feminism: How Women and Feminists in Africa are Leveraging on Social Media to Combat Gender-based Violence," *Changing the Mainstream: Celebrating Women's Resilience*, ed. Mukabi Wanjiku Kabira, Kameri Patricia Mbote, Nkatha Kabira and Agnes Meroka, Nairobi: African Women Studies Centre, 2018).

media awareness has been employed in advocating for women's empowerment, increasing female participation in public life, and minimizing gender-directed violence.

For instance, until recently, it was taboo-like for the female gender to pursue dreams or nurse ambitions seen as exclusively reserved for the male sex, such as doctors or engineers. They were also subjected to various forms of domestic abuse and violence and were told to keep mute to save their homes.[52] Women were made to tolerate all sorts of abuses meted out by society members because of their gender. Worse still, they could not voice out. As explained above, even the mass media was ineffective in correcting these misconceptions and championing women's rights, as they also contributed to women's interiorization.[53] Oyesomi also notes that the mass media played a huge role in the widespread misconceptions about women's rights and feminism.[54] As the media was not accessible to everyone; thus, correcting these misconceptions was difficult. Asides from mass media, there were also writings thematizing the independence of women. As much as literature was generally appreciated, it still did not counter these pessimistic narratives of the female sex. Literature has attempted the need to improve the status of women in society and destroy the gender gap. This achieved little success, but the story became different with social media.

Social media has presented more opportunities to clamor for gender equality and women's rights. Feminists in Nigeria have begun to advocate for women's rights through the internet. Challenging the status quo in marriages and other relationships between men and women is a particular focus for Nigerian feminists who use social media to ignite consciousness and awareness.

In recent times, the female sex has leveraged social media to advocate for women's rights and has created public awareness of women's struggles.[55] Through public discourses on Twitter, there has been a gradual erosion of the stereotypes associated with women. Social media allows for unlimited freedom of expression and the propagation of beliefs.[56] In this regard, feminism ideology has evolved beyond theoretical conception. Feminism foregrounds gender equality, the notion that all sexes should share the same rights without necessarily being superior to the other. Using social media platforms, feminists have been able to enlighten the public on the evils of gender discrimination. Often, the female sex has been relegated; good things are attributed to the male sex, while the otherwise is for the female sex. In many instances,

---

52. Ganiat M. Olatokun, "Nigerian Feminism: A Typology of African Feminism," *KIU Journal of Humanities* 2, no. 1 (2017): 215–221.

53. Wendy Okiriguo, "Discourse Analysis of Nigerian Feminism," M.sc. Thesis, Southern Illinois University at Edwardsville, 2016.

54. Oyesomi and Oyero, "Women's Political Invisibility," 109.

55. Kehinde Oyesomi, Okorie Nelson, Omole Funke and Smith Abisola, "How Sociable are Women on Social Media? An Experiential Study on Nigerian Women," *International Journal of Research in Social Sciences* 4, no. 2 (2014): 57–72.

56. Ngozi B. Ukachi and Franca Attoh, "Trafficked Women, Patriarchy and Social Media: The Case of Benin City, Nigeria," *Covenant Journal of Communication* 7, no. 1 (2020): 108–127.

the female sex is not allowed to go to school, especially in the Northern part of the country, due to the toxic belief that they have no other lifelong ambitions than to be wives and mothers and work in the kitchen, as explained in one of the paragraphs above. However, these gory narratives concerning women are being countered by championing women's rights on social media platforms. Thus, social media has become a tool to combat gender inequality.[57] Women can freely convey their realities through social media platforms without fear of backlash. This has contributed immensely to the advancement of women's rights. The ideology that the female sex is independent now permeates the public's consciousness. It is no longer strange when women hold top leadership positions or have big goals.

There is an influx of Nigerian feminists on social media. This platform has given them what can be considered a social identity. For instance, on the Twitter platform, it is not uncommon to see tweets on women's rights activism. Women's bad experiences are shared for public knowledge and to prevent future recurrences. Giel posits that the Twitter platform has given the female sex the power to fight gender inequalities.[58] When women are abused, all it takes to create awareness or public knowledge is to tweet with a hashtag, advocating for an end to gender inequality or any other topic that concerns female folks. Scholars have postulated that the hashtag feature on Twitter makes it easier to bring the public into the know about certain issues.[59] Trending topics on Twitter are due to hashtags.

Furthermore, hashtags are also used for activism, such as feminists clamoring for women's rights which immediately falls into the trending topics. Social media has also led to the rise of cyber-feminism.[60] Cyber-feminism describes the alliance of the female sex and digital media, notably social media platforms.[61] It also foregrounds women's power in using new technologies for advocacy purposes. Cyber-feminism also includes debates about feminism to ensure gender equality.

In Nigeria, feminists are using social media for activism on anything related to women.[62] They have also been able to tune discourses to destroy the gender gap. With the help of these platforms, women have begun to break social and cultural boundaries that describe them as second-rated humans. Due to the accessibility of Twitter to many people, it has become easier for women to condemn evil practices meted on them due to the certainty that their voices would be heard. It can be argued that social

57. Wasuna, "Hashtag Feminism."

58. Katelyn Anne Giel, "Hashtag Feminism: An Analysis of Social Media as a Feminist Platform," Ph.D *diss.*, Arizona State University, 2015.

59. Giel, "Hashtag Feminism."

60. Laura M Handy, "CyberFeminism: Virtual Activism, Real Change," Ph.D *diss.*, University of Puget Sound, 2001.

61. Handy, "CyberFeminism."

62. Pamela Flores, Nancy Regina Gómez, Alana Farrah Roa and Risa Whitson, "Reviving Feminism through Social Media: From the Classroom to Online and Offline Public Spaces," *Gender and Education* 32, no. 6 (2020): 751–766.

media platforms are the go-to for the female sex in cases of gender violence. At some point, Nigerian social media was enmeshed in discourses championing women's rights. This was on the heels of an essay published by Chimamanda Ngozi Adichie titled *We Should All Be Feminists*. As Wendy notes, a Twitter campaign was launched to project the plights of women in Nigerian society with the hashtag #BeingFemaleinNigeria.[63] Many Nigerian women use this hashtag to share the harsh realities they are made to face in society. Some of the tweets included:

> #BeingFemaleInNigeria. When she gets raped, why did you dress like that? When she gets beaten by her husband, what did you do to him? #BeingFemaleInNigeria. Your husband cooked? And you opened your mouth and ate the food? What kind of woman are you? #BeingFemaleInNigeria. You can't buy property unless you are married first, if not, you won't find a good man. #BeingFemaleInNigeria is tipping the restaurant worker with YOUR money from YOUR bag but the worker thanking your male companion instead.[64]

There are identified Twitter accounts involved in the gospel of feminism and women empowerment in Nigeria. However, it is important to reiterate that these accounts are majorly involved in championing women and human rights, alleviating the conditions of the girlchild, and correcting misconceptions about gender equality. Among them is the Feminist Coalition Twitter, whose motto reads: "championing equality for women in Nigerian society."[65] An analysis of its tweets reveals that it is involved in the struggle for women's emancipation and the need for women to break social and cultural exists, that is, the need to live a life of their own as an independent entity. The Coalition also provides quality and free education to the girl child. According to a UNICEF study, close to 18.5 million children are out of school in Nigeria. [66] Its tweet reveals that it had trained some girls' children educationally and is looking forward to training more. [67] The Coalition posits that educated children are "a testament to what people can achieve when given the right opportunities" and harped that it "will continue to work to educate more girls. As always, thank you to our corporate and private donors. None of this would be possible without you."[68]

63. Wendy Okiriguo, "Discourse Analysis of Nigerian Feminism," M.Sc. Thesis, Southern Illinois University Edwardsville, 2016.

64. Okiriguo, "Discourse Analysis of Nigerian Feminism."

65. Feministcoalition, twitter handle, https://twitter.com/feminist_co.

66. Channels Television, "Nigeria has 18.5 million Children out of School," *Channels Television*, May 12, 2022, https://www.channelstv.com/2022/05/12/nigeria-has-18-5-million-children-out-of-school-unicef/.

67. Feministcoalition, Twitter Post, *Twitter*, August 11, 2022, https://twitter.com/feminist_co/status/1557694060005150721?s=20&t=cVU59ns8vLddlwlebkLkKw.

68. Feminist Coalition, "An Update on the Feminist Coalition Girls Education Program," *Feminist Coalition*, August 11, 2022, https://feministcoalition.medium.com/an-update-on-the-feminist-coalition-girls-education-program-d8db5e84dda7.

This singular act is needed to effectively break the stereotypes that the girlchildren are not worthy of education. The girls trained by this Coalition went on to win prizes in different subjects. It can be posited that the rate at which girlchildren are enrolled in schools and going all the way to the university is due to a paradigm shift in society based on the knowledge of the importance of education to all sexes; though, this cannot be solely attributed to the efforts of the Feminist Coalition. Also, in a tweet, the Coalition announced that it provided food to women across different parts of the country.[69] Women in different parts of the country are subjected to poor living conditions and are left to undertake the burden of child-rearing, sometimes with little or no support from their fathers, especially in rural areas or lower-class families. From the instances above, it is obvious that the Feminist Coalition are landlocked in the struggle for a better living for women, which some males leverage to degrade them, further foregrounding the fact that they must not be relegated to the background. This feminist group also assists women in taking jobs that society reserved exclusively for women. In a tweet, it announced there would be driving jobs for interested men, enabling them to be financially independent.[70]

Through its tweets, it was discovered that this feminist group is not only involved in the struggle for women's emancipation. As stated above, it is also concerned with issues relating to human rights. This was evident during its support for the #ENDSARS struggles. The group advocated ceaselessly for the end of police brutality and other extra-judicial killings, calling on the government to take appropriate measures. # ENDSARS struggle will forever be a dark point in the history of the nation's democracy. What started as a peaceful protest ended with the death of innocent citizens; beyond setting up a commission to investigate the incident, the government since then had not taken any measures to bring the perpetrators of such dastardly acts to book; thus, the continuous clamors to get justice for the victims remains an illusion. At the same time, Feminist Coalition involved itself with the need for woman's emancipation, ElectHer advocates for the adequate representation of women in political offices. Its Twitter biography reads: "We are bridging inequality gaps by increasing women's political representation and leadership one Africa country at a time!"[71]

In the history of the nation's political system, women have been grossly marginalized and under-represented. A careful review of the number of female legislators in the National Assembly informs that the number is not up to 30% (they are 29 in total) as the bulk of Nigerian legislators is of the male sex. In political parties, too, women are not at the forefront. The only posts exclusively reserved for them are women leaders and Head of Market Women, among a host of other posts a woman should head

69. Feministcoalition, Twitter Post, *Twitter*, December, 2021, https://twitter.com/feminist_co/status/1471754019735486464?s=20&t=wb_8HJPvh58fJ_B_xNfB3w.

70. Feministcoalition, Twitter Post, *Twitter*, March, 2021, https://twitter.com/feminist_co/status/1368924726471626755?s=20&t=wb_8HJPvh58fJ_B_xNfB3w.

71. ElectHER, Twitter handle, https://twitter.com/ElectHER_NG.

by their nomenclatures. Elect Her is "a party-agnostic organization committed to increasing women's political inclusion across Africa through Behavioral Change Communications, Community Building, Capacity Development, and increased access to Social, Human, Technological and Financial Capital."[72] Many factors contribute to the under-representation of women in politics. One of them includes the poor perception of women as not-to-good-leaders. There is the belief that women do not have the resilience to withstand the rigors and vigor that come with assuming top leadership positions. Although this belief is largely erroneous, no female governor or president has existed in the nation's history. In other countries, women are doing exceptionally well in top positions; countries such as Germany have female presidents. Also, one of the most powerful females in the world is Queen Elizabeth, England's Monarchical Head of State.

To bring this discussion homeward, the first female Director General of the World Trade Organization (WTO) is a Nigerian, Ngozi Okonjo-Iweala. ElectHer reveals in a tweet that it organizes capacity-building programs to arouse women's interest in politics.[73] Another hindrance to adequate women's representation in politics is the lack of political structure. The bulk of the political structure in the country is comprised of males and headed by the same. There is limited chance for the female sex to break in at all. This is why it becomes imperative that women become prominent forces in the nation's democratic system.

Furthermore, an unhealthy political environment largely contributes to the under-representation of women in politics. Politics, in its general sense, is viewed as a dirty game played by dirty players in Nigeria. This assumption could be valid if one considers the violence associated with politicking in the country. In such a dangerous political climate, it could be difficult for women to excel.

Also, there is the Nigerian Women Trust Fund (NWTF) with the motto, "... closing the gender gap in governance at all levels." [74] Just like Elect Her, it is also involved in the struggle for the holistic representation of women in political affairs. It organizes training for women to increase their participation in the political affairs of Nigeria. A tweet charges the women to participate in their civil rights by voting during elections.[75] This group also acts as an electoral observer, part of the wider efforts to ensure free, fair, and credible elections. Twitter accounts such as She Codes Africa[76] also aim at providing equal opportunities for women interested in coding. An analysis of its tweets aims to widen the gap between the female sex and opportunities in technology.

---

72. ElectHER, https://elect-her.org.

73. ElectHER, Twitter Post, *Twitter*, July 2022, https://twitter.com/ElectHER_NG/status/1547351415982637056?s=20&t=Rgj_byav_DnpQ-A78hJhag.

74. Nigerian Women Trust Fund, Twitter handle, https://twitter.com/womenfundng.

75. Nigerian Women Trust Fund, Twitter Post, *Twitter*, July 6, 2022, https://twitter.com/womenfundng/status/1544659458571264002?s=20&t=VaixbDJaubPZdEZXCVrRbQ.

76. She Code Africa, Twitter handle, https://twitter.com/SheCodeAfrica.

Minority Africa projected the activism of Amarachi Nickabugu with a Twitter account, "@a_nickabugu," who publicizes laws that are repressive of the women folks in a trend, #EverydayFeminism.[77] In one of her tweets, she noted that one of the Nigeria Police Force's regulations sanctions the dismissal of any unmarried female police officer who gets pregnant. As the tweet read:

> According to the Nigeria Police Regulations, an unmarried female Police Officer who becomes pregnant shall be dismissed from the Force and will not be re-enlisted unless the Inspector-General of Police so approves. #everydayfeminism.[78]

Following the tweets was a public uproar on how constituted authorities in Nigeria also sideline women. The law has been repealed. She also tweeted about the legal sanctioning of men exercising domestic abuse on women in Northern Nigeria:

> Section 55(1)(d) of the Penal Code (applicable in Northern Nigeria) makes it lawful for a man to beat his wife for the purpose of "correcting" her. #everydayfeminism. [79]

Furthermore, a group named Stand To End Rape Initiative (STER) is committed to helping rape victims so that many victims can get justice and live without stigma. In several tweets, it condemns various incidences of rape and charges society with playing a major role in eradicating it.[80] It was also at the forefront of the #StandtoEndRape, which sought to project the evils of sexual abuse.[81] The group was also at the forefront of ensuring that the law punished Baba Ijesa, a popular Yoruba actor caught on camera engaging in illicit sexual activities with a minor. After court hearings, the actor was sentenced to 16 years imprisonment.

There are a few actresses who identify with feminism. Kate Henshaw is a prominent voice in the struggle for women's emancipation. She has often countered narratives aimed at commodifying women. She condemned jungle justice meted out to a young lady allegedly caught in a pretty crime. She tweeted:

---

77. S.T.E.R. Rape, Twitter handle, https://twitter.com/search?q=%23StandtoEndRape&src=typed_query.

78. Cannonball, Twitter Post, *Twitter*, July 2020, https://twitter.com/a_nickabugu/status/1283098939923865601?s=20&t=DFXJ9lxOt8YzX5bN28Ga1Q.

79. Cannonball, Twitter Post, *Twitter*, May 2020, https://twitter.com/a_nickabugu/status/1264627564301225985?s=20&t=gT3WfUvs-BbLdLvFLstTxA.

80. S.T.E.R. initiative, Twitter Post, *Twitter*, May, 2019, https://twitter.com/StandtoEndRape/status/1124213458713624576?s=20&t=aRFMRVQP4zRawEXpH0KF7g.

81. Cannonball, Twitter Post, *Twitter*, July 2020, https://twitter.com/a_nickabugu/status/1283098939923865601?s=20&t=DFXJ9lxOt8YzX5bN28Ga1Q.

> I was forwarded this disturbing video of a young lady who allegedly stole a phone... The (sic) was she was stripped naked was heart breaking and then as if that was not enough, she was stoned with scotch bonnet peppers and one inserted into her private part. Why is it so easy to dehumanize women, knowing fully well that stripping her naked totally destroys her self-esteem ...? [82]

Another popular actress, who also is a leading figure in championing women's rights, Bimbo Akintola, contends that while she is an ardent supporter of feminism, humanism is the best way to ensure gender equality. [83]

There are many feminists in Nigeria whose social media presence has galvanized women to demystify the perception that it is a man's world. The best-known feminists on social media in Nigeria include Ada Ujaligwa, Olutimehin Adegbeye, Ozzy Etomi, Modupe Odele and Nkechi Bianze. These women are known to use their social media accounts in an outspoken and unapologetic manner to send powerfully worded messages to young women on the need to challenge the status quo, not only within the political sphere but also in all walks of social engagement.

In 2017, Ada Ujaligwa, a well-known feminist in Nigeria, examined the issue of infidelity by men and how women should respond.[84] According to her, the days of complete female subjugation and men who flagrantly cheat on their wives and expect them to endure it seem to be receding to the past because of the increasing awareness of gender equality in marriage, which has been raised regularly through social media. Ujaligwa argues that women are becoming aggressive in their response to men's infidelity despite age-old cultural norms, and women are beginning to take actions that balance infidelity out. She advises that rather than becoming emotionally traumatized because of a man's unfaithfulness, women should also seek to cheat and date other men, warning men not to "start what you cannot bear your wife to do to do to you. Think it well before deciding to have a mistress because your wife might also look out for a young man that would give you a run for your money."[85] In this way, women can fight against the cultural acceptance of male infidelity, bolstered by some traditions allowing for men to take multiple wives.

While reflecting on her formative years, Ujaligwa talks about growing up in a society that positions men as the head in various walks of life, from the family to the

---

82. Kate Henshaw, Twitter Post, *Twitter*, February 2019, https://twitter.com/HenshawKate/status/1092710787985129472?s=20&t=onBWOaW1pPLn2HzQ6IIjw.

83. Onu Stephen, "Feminism too Toxic, I Prefer Humanism—Bimbo Akintola," *Premium Times*, May 18, 2022. https://www.premiumtimesng.com/entertainment/nollywood/530894-feminism-too-toxic-i-prefer-humanism-bimbo-akintola.html.

84. Ada Ujaligwa, "The Truth Sounds like Hate to those who Hate the Truth," *Keskus*, May 22, 2017, http://keskus.ng/2017/05/22/viewpoint/98/truth-sounds-like-hate-to-those-who-hate-the-truth-by-princess-ada-ujaligwa/.

85. Ujaligwa, "The Truth Sounds like Hate."

army, business, and government. She affirmed learning to perceive male dominance as a divine right and argued that the academic world did not do enough to push into the curriculum the exploits of Nigerian women of the past who were instrumental in shaping society during their time. She mentioned women such as Olufunmilayo Ransome-Kuti, Oyinkan Abayomi, Queen Amina of Zazzau, Charlotte Obasa, Margaret Ekpo and a host of others who should have their names written in the annals of Nigerian history of the way of men like Herbert Macaulay and Tafawa Balewa.

Another feminist who is very active on social media is Nkechi Bianze. In one of her Facebook posts, she discussed her reason for dumping the Christian faith, citing the illogic of the ideology that a woman was made from a man's ribs.[86] She emphatically stated that she left Christianity because she understood that the Bible ranked men above women and that no rationale justified that biblical assertion other than the chauvinistic attitude of men. She subsequently affirmed that she would only be willing to give Christianity another chance if anyone could prove the Bible was not against gender equality.

Bianze defended feminism against blame for the increase in the number of divorces in Nigeria, rather arguing that it was the tendency for men to control and dominate women at fault and that while the women of the older generations permitted this does not mean the current generation would condone it as well. She advised men to realize that more and more women are becoming more enlightened, empowered, and educated to understand their rights in society. To cap it off on a hilarious note, she stated that a time would come when the requirement for a husband would include such a man being a feminist! Bianze outlines feminist perspectives in other articles. She has advocated for recognition of female leadership skills, suggesting that the lack of women in Nigerian executive roles, focusing on the education system, is an artificial condition, as Western countries have more meritocratic systems that allow women to rise into leadership and allow their societies to take full advantage of their skills. [87] She also outlined the social consequences of gender roles for men and women, which leaves women indoctrinated to accept themselves as inferior and forces them to rely on the men in their lives to make even crucial emergency decisions, as in the example she offers about a child who died while his mother sought to ask her husband what she was supposed to do.[88]

Nigerian feminists use the internet and social media to advocate for gender equality and women's rights and describe the goals and history of the feminist movement.

---

86. Adunni Amodeni, "Women did not come from Men's Rib—Lady Reveals why she left Christianity," *Legit*, August 29, 2018, https://www.legit.ng/1189072-women-mens-ribs-lady-reveals-left-christianity.html.

87. Nkechi Bianze, "Leadership is a Human, not Male Attribute," *Women*, November 9, 2017, http://woman.ng/2017/11/leadership-human-not-male-attribute/.

88. Nkechi Bianze, "The Consequences of Stereotyping Gender Roles," *Women* August 31, 2017, http://woman.ng/2017/08/consequences-stereotyping-gender-roles/.

In her article "Feminism in Nigeria Cannot Be Stopped," [89] popular feminist Sunny Unekwu affirmed the term "daughters of Chimamanda" as coinage for people like her who use social media for women's rights advocacy. Prominent author Chimamanda Adichie has played a significant role in Nigeria's spread of feminist ideology. While she has received criticism for focusing only on middle-class feminist issues in Nigeria, she has tackled many other issues related to feminism. She has noted that many cultural elements, such as dress, have changed over time in Nigeria and that the chauvinistic tendencies of Nigerian men must be let go, regardless of their traditional and religious justifications.[90]

Unekwu has attempted to explain to men the level and types of oppression and trauma women often go through because of their gender, promoting feminist analysis by calling to the empathy of male readers:

> Women have been groped by strange men, catcalled, called names and abused physically or sexually by men and then blamed for being a victim. As a man, to have a clue of what it is to be a woman in Nigeria, imagine having a strange woman grab your crotch on the street and tell you that you turn her on while her female counterparts laugh and jeer at you. Now, this is just a tiny bit of it. As a man, you never know the fear of walking alone at night or during the day, you do not know about the unease that comes with walking past a group of the opposite sex.[91]

To build male acceptance of feminism, she clarifies that not all Nigerian men are naturally misogynistic. Some do not feel emasculated by feminist advocacy as they understand that it is not aimed at ridding them of their power; rather, it is for the improvement of the other gender. She equated men and women to the two wings of a bird that must work in equal measures to create balance and propulsion in flight.

Feminists like Modupe Odele foray beyond discourse and activism on gender bias to political activism. As a lawyer, she rendered legal services to free persons arrested by the police during and after the #EndSARS protests in 2020. She also helped distribute funds to keep the protest going at different venues nationwide under the aegis of the *Feminists* Coalition. She had her passport seized by the Nigerian Immigration Service, along with a few others, as a show of power by the government but her standing in society helped in the quick stoppage of the harassment, highlighting the importance of elite involvement in nation-building.

---

89. Sunny Unekwu, "Feminism in Nigeria can not be Stopped," *Kalahari Review*, November 6, 2018, https://kalaharireview.com/feminism-in-nigeria-can-not-be-stopped-1cdb3e7ca2bc.

90. Lisa Allardice, "Chimamanda Ngozie Adichie— This could be the Beginning of a Revolution," *The Guardian*, April 28, 2014.

91. Allardice, "Chimamanda Ngozie Adichie."

Social media is credited for amplifying women's voices and has created public awareness of the dire need to champion women's rights. Social media platforms, especially Twitter, have been used for campaigns against sexuality, women, and child abuse.[92] Takahashi contends that social media has helped counter-narratives on degrading the female sex.[93] Women are certain that their voices are beginning to be heard due to social media. Since social media allows networking opportunities, they can leverage this to share their afflictions and get much-needed assistance.[94] This is based on the premise that social media is a tool for persuasion. Feminist discourses and trends on Twitter help produce educative and intellectual messages on gender harassment. It could be said that the plethora of narratives now commonplace in society is due to the civic learning on feminism predominant on social media platforms.

CONCLUDING REMARKS

Feminism is a movement that is relevant in all countries of the world; even advanced societies have their share of feminists fighting for gender equality. Discrimination based on gender is now globally frowned upon as every nation continues to aspire for greater gender equality in all fields of endeavor. In the case of Nigeria, there are efforts toward improving the status of women through empowerment programs.

Feminists and feminist organizations continue to emphasize the need for enlightenment about women's rights to remove the religious and cultural constraints that impede the full integration of women into the developmental process. While it will be apt to appreciate the level of agitation from feminists in Nigeria, little success has been recorded, not because of incapability but because there are opposing forces bent on suppressing them. A setback on feminism is an outrageous attempt to place demands that do not align with the customs and traditions of Nigeria.

While the laws of advanced nations provide leeway to feminism by granting women preferential status, Nigeria cannot boast of such. As is common in Nigeria, women cannot be harassed and trampled upon in advanced countries. Although many men in society always perceive feminism as a threat to their socio-political status, the question is, is it needed in a country like Nigeria? The answer is yes, as women and girls are subjected daily to abuse by men, with the older generation not spared from such

---

92. Abdulgaffar Olawale Arikewuyo, B. Özad and Saudat Salah Abdulbaqi, "Role of Social Media in Eradicating Violence among Young Nigerian Females: A Study of Nigerian Students in Eastern Mediterranean University." Paper presented at the 6th International Conference on Gender Studies: Gender, Conflict, War and Peace, Famagusta, North Cyprus, March, 2017.

93. Toshie Takahashi, "MySpace or Mixi? Japanese Engagement with SNS (Social Networking Sites) in the Global Age," *New Media & Society* 12, no. 3 (2010): 453–475.

94. Arikewuyo, Özad and Abdulbaqi, "Role of Social Media in Eradicating Violence."

inhuman treatment. Feminism is very much needed in a society that cannot protect girls from being abducted in secondary schools.

Feminism is necessary to allow everyone, irrespective of gender, to reach their full potential. For this to happen, the burden exerted through religion and the prevailing culture of patriarchy must be scrapped, while modernization should be embraced to militate against the continued discrimination against women. The gross incompatibility of culture and gender equality in Nigeria cannot be downplayed; one will have to give way to the other for progress to be achieved.

7

SEXUALITY IN THE PUBLIC DOMAIN

INTRODUCTION

Social media is a viable platform for disseminating information, including positive and negative issues. Research has posited that social media has more ways of harming users' health because of decreased parental supervision and increased provocative behavior related to bullying, sex, violence, and drinking.[1] There are further arguments that while social media may improve learning opportunities, foster communication and socialization, and increase access to health information, it can also result in cyberbullying or harassment, depression, and, most especially, sexuality.[2] Sexuality is generally referred to as any discursive activity with a sexual undertone, for instance, uploading a sexy picture on social media. Each gender wants sexual attraction, and intimate relations are connected to sexuality.[3] Social media and young people's sexual cultures are becoming increasingly entwined with the formation of the physical and symbolic forms of social media, which are ever more ubiquitous, personal, and mobile.[4]

1. Paul Best, Roger Manktelow and Brian Taylor, "Online Communication, Social Media and Adolescent Wellbeing: A Systematic Narrative Review," *Children and Youth Services Review* 41 (2014): 27–36.

2. Amy Adele Hasinoff, "Sexting as Media Production: Rethinking Social Media and Sexuality," *New Media & Society* 15, no. 4 (2013): 449–465.

3. Hasinoff, "Sexting as Media Production."

4. Megan Landry, Monique Turner, Amita Vyas and Susan Wood, "Social Media and Sexual Behavior among Adolescents: Is there a Link?" *JMIR Public Health and Surveillance* 3, no. 2 (2017): e7149.

The emerging social changes, including those surrounding sexual discourse, that accompany the expansion of information and communication technology (ICT) can re-energize people and re-orient them against the traditional practices of their society. Social media platforms such as Facebook have changed the way that sexuality and sex-oriented discussions are propagated, but public attention seems to have shifted focus away from their advantages—such as networking opportunities—and towards the adverse effects on certain strata of the population that unhindered access to them can have. This is especially true for teenagers and adolescents, who are becoming more vulnerable to exposure to sexual and illicit content on these platforms.

Social media platforms are used to promote sexually overt content. If social media were not all-inclusive platforms for both young and old, it would have been possible to overlook the topics discussed, but this is not the case as teenagers and adolescents are embracing social media. These sexual discussions are not in any way unjustified or illegitimate for adults. Rather, maturity should be a requisite for them, a scarce trait among the young.

Some countries have decided to put in place legislation to limit young people and adolescents' access to certain explicit content, partly to prevent them from coming in contact with sexually explicit discussions on social media. For instance, in the United States of America, congressional hearings were held in 2006[5] concerning sexual materials on social media platforms and their accompanying effect on school-age people. A bill sponsored by Congressman Michael Fitzpatrick (R-PA) named the Deleting Online Predators Act of 2006 (H.R. 5319) was passed with a sweeping majority, and a companion version was subsequently included in the Senate as part of the Protecting Children in the 21st Century Act.[6]

Social media is very popular among younger generations, often with troubling implications, as more than 60% of them check and make updates daily,[7] and content analysis reveals that 20% of young people around the world post sexually revealing visual content on their profiles at least once a month.[8] While much research has pointed out that sexually related content on social media platforms is increasing, the reasons for such growth have yet to be investigated, begging the question if this trend is attributable to the mass media, social media, or both.

Witnessing this preponderance of sexual materials on social media is becoming appalling. It has reached a crescendo that calls for action, especially when the younger generation has a higher stake in the activities on these platforms. The dangers of

5. Vries Lloyd, "House Misfires on Internet Safety," *CBS News*, August 1, 2006, https://www.cbsnews.com/news/house-misfires-on-internet-safety/.

6. Protecting Children in the 21st Century Act, S. 49, 110th Cong. (2007).

7. Amanda Lenhart, Kristen Purcell, Aaron Smith and Kathryn Zickuhr, *Social Media and Mobile Internet use among Teens and Young Adults* (Washington, DC: Pew Internet American Life Project, 2010).

8. S. Kapidzic and S.C. Herring, "Race, Gender, and Self-Presentation in Teen Profile Photographs," *New Media and Society* 17, (2015): 958–976.

this transition are likely to have greater adverse effects on African societies, leading to erosion of cultures. More so, we are in an age where sexual and reproductive health challenges threaten human existence generally. It is expedient that attempts are made to examine the abuse of social media platforms and the implications on teenagers and adolescents, some of which include sexual gratification and objectification.

Many studies on social media and sexuality have concentrated on the gendered aspects of self-representation, such as sexy photographs and sexual communication (sexting), examining both the acceptance of and opposition to specific gender and sexual ideas.[9] Other studies have examined the benefits and drawbacks of using social media to support sexual developmental tasks by examining individual (e.g., demographic and skill-related) and contextual.[10] The youth actively consume contents that are available on social media platforms, and there are discussions on how this information may affect their sexual attitudes and social norms at a crucial developmental stage. While the mass media and the internet can provide young people with the required information about sexual health and good relationships, several studies have indicated that the media influences teens' sexual activities both positively and negatively.

Studies have revealed a general increase in sex-related portrayals and discussions on social media platforms, including explicit sexual dialogues and demonstrations.[11] The availability of sexually explicit content has significantly risen on social media because social networking platforms allow users to share images, videos, and other content publicly and privately, which affects sexual conduct in public and private. Media portrayals uphold a constant set of sexual and relationship norms and does not always feature sexually responsible role models.[12] Thus, it is pertinent that youth are educated on the proper use of social media. Parents are also expected to be involved in their ward's patterns and choices of media use. On random occasions, Nigerian Twittersphere could be replete with discourses relating to sex, for example, the worst sex experience of users; and discussions like this trend widely. If it were to be in the public sphere offline, such discussions would have been frowned upon because a public discussion of sex is still seen as obscene. The reality is that when youth are not exposed to these conversations in private spaces, they find them available on social media platforms.

---

9. Kapidzic and Herring, "Race, Gender, and Self-Presentation."

10. Sander De Ridder, "Social Media and Young People's Sexualities: Values, Norms, and Battlegrounds," *Social Media+ Society* 3, no. 4 (2017): 1–11.

11. Olanrewaju Olugbenga Akinola and A. A. Ogunsanya, "Construction of Nuances on WhatsApp and BBM by Nigerian Students," *Journal of Humanities, Social Science and Creative Arts* 13, no. 1 (2018): 1–13.

12. Christian Okechukwu Aleke, Lois Nnenna Omaka-Amari and Nkiru Edith Obande-Ogbuinya, "Consequences of Social Media use among Adolescents in Nigeria," *International Journal of Innovative Science and Research Technology* 3, no. 4 (2018): 766–773.

UNDERSTANDING THE PREPONDERANCE OF SOCIAL MEDIA

Social media helps in the propagation of beliefs and opinions and has also increased the propensity of discussions springing up that border on immorality and illicit material, exposing people to ideas that can ultimately lead to them being abused or engage in the abuse of others. This is premised on cultivation theory, which suggests that frequent exposure to certain ideological information increases the likelihood of that information being accepted, often to the detriment of existing values and beliefs that are altered by adopting such information.

This theory clarifies how the frequency and degree of exposure to sexually-related content on social media can change values, beliefs and how accompanying issues are understood. Invariably, constant exposure to sexual discussions on social media will eventually lead to a habit or an addiction, resulting in unique effects on younger generations of social media users.[13]

Social learning theory emphasizes behavior learned through psychological and social adjustments resulting from accumulating a series of socially-motivating contents.[14] The fundamental element of the theory is the reinforcement principle, which points to how behavior is learned by observing that certain actions are applauded rather than punished. Observed behavior is learned from real-life models: parents, siblings, friends, teachers, heroes, or audio-visual media content.

As such, it is easy to understand the reason for the increase in sexual discussions on social media platforms. The social development of young people in Nigeria is focused on entertainment. They tend to model themselves according to the lives of their favorite actor, actress, celebrity, artist, musician, or otherwise popular individual they hold in high esteem. Many adopt the same moral standards as their favorite celebrity or entertainment personality, and any behavior contrary to the adopted values begins to wane. This makes them more occupied with sexual discussions, while the Nigerian cultural norm of keeping sexual discussions a private affair is gradually relegated to the sidelines.

The emergence of new information and communication technologies has ushered in a new social-molding tool that relegates family values, cultural norms, and traditional control mechanisms to lesser relevance. The dominant role social media now plays has weakened the social fabric of moral values, replacing it with self-directed permissiveness that has led the younger generation to engage in nudity, pornography, and sexual promiscuity. Parents are becoming less aware of the kinds of discussion children engage in because of the personalized nature of smartphones.

---

13. Hasinoff, "Sexting as Media Production," 449–465.
14. A. Bandura, *Social Learning Theory* (New Jersey: Prentice-Hall, 1977).

At some point, a social media platform becomes boring to a subset of its users when sexually-oriented topics are not trending,[15] one of the reasons that Facebook is experiencing decreasing popularity relative to dating sites like Tinder.[16] There is a growing perception that Facebook is a source of news rather than a platform to engage in unhindered socialization. Other platforms like Snapchat offer an enabling environment for young people who want to engage in playful and sexual communication with fellow users, characterized by spontaneity, privacy, flirtation, and intimacy.[17]

In the entertainment industry, publications are often perceived as incomplete if no images of scantily dressed females exist. The increase in sexualized visuals that populate the entertainment industry is appalling and a cause for concern because the younger generations are avid consumers of entertainment offerings. While many African homes harbor well-known reluctance to open discussions about sexuality in the household, it is difficult to stop a family member from having those conversations with their peers on social media platforms with the availability of smartphones and internet connectivity.

Posting sexual content on social media is one of the ways female actors increase their appeal to their fans and followers. An example of this is the Nollywood actress, Etinosa, who was alleged to have stripped naked on the popular MC Galaxy's Instagram Live, with the content trending online for some days.[18] As popularity is the hallmark of celebrities, many—especially female celebrities—are quick to use sexually-oriented content to drive people to their social media pages and accounts.

GLOBALIZATION AND ITS CONSEQUENCES

Globalization is built on the foundation of human activities being unified into a single concept and ideology. It is both a process and a movement that seeks to bring everything together: economies, standards, cultures, and all accompanying socialization elements.[19] Cultural globalization, as an extension, is focused on bringing the whole world into a singular moral and behavioral framework but there is no denying

15. J. Van Ouytsel, M. Walrave and K. Ponnet, "How Schools can Help their Students to Strengthen their Online Reputations," *The Clearing House: A Journal of Educational Strategies, Issues and Ideas* 87, no. 4 (2014): 180–185.

16. V. Luckerson, "Is Facebook Losing its Cool? Some Teens Think So," *Time*, March 8, 2013, http://business.time.com/2013/03/08/is-facebook-losing-its-cool-some-teens-think-so/.

17. Joseph B. Bayer, Nicole B. Ellison, Sarita Y. Schoenebeck and Emily B. Falk, "Sharing the Small Moments: Ephemeral Social Interaction on Snapchat," *Information, Communication & Society* 19, no. 7 (2016): 956–977.

18. TVC Entertainment, "Video: Actress Etinosa Strips Naked on MC Galaxy's Instagram Live," *TVC Entertainment*, March 16, 2019, https://www.tvcentertainment.tv/2019/03/16/video-actress-etinosa-strips-naked-on-mc-galaxys-instagram-live/.

19. Obasi Igwe, *Politics and Globe Dictionary* (Enugu: Keny & Brothers Enterprises, 2007).

that cultural globalization covertly seeks to favor the values of dominant civilizations to the detriment of developing societies like those in Africa. In the context of sexual discussions on social media platforms, the growing number of young African people engaging in them is based on the premise that the world is changing; hence, everybody must follow suit.

With Western cultures allowing young people to engage in sexual discussions unhindered, African youths are beginning to embrace the behavior despite the prevailing societal values of their home nations not conforming to it. Large aspects of the cultural norms of African societies are being eroded by the subconscious embrace of Western value systems in the name of globalization. The reckless sexual attitudes of individuals in the Western world championing cultural globalization have created undesirable consequences; various investigations reveal that more than a million abortions were carried out within the USA in 2011, with 33% of those receiving abortions unmarried and 12% being unmarried youths with relationship problems.[20] Africans adopting such values is sure to result in a catastrophe much greater than many African societies faced with the advent of imported religious values.

Social media is reshaping sexual norms in a very symbolic manner. It is not strange to see vulnerable younger Africans using self-guiding moral premises as strategies to encourage sexual communication on social networking sites. They gradually lose the self-discipline to handle the ubiquity of sexual content they encounter online daily. On another level, social media emergence has succeeded in breaking the taboo of what ought to be discussed within a society, and for this reason, those sexual discussions perceived as not worthy of being discussed openly in the past are on the rise. Social media platforms have provided the opportunity to air one's views without as much fear of reproach as the case has been in the past. This has changed the narrative by increasing the freedom and vulnerability of young people.

The overwhelming presence of social media has robbed individuals of certain moral principles, including self-discipline. Many are left in a dilemma—weighing the perception that sexual discussion on social media can potentially increase the spread of sexually-related diseases and the fact that people have the right and liberty to discuss whatever suits them online if they are adults. While they see sexual communication as private, they simultaneously see it as normal for individuals to post sexy pictures and look for dating partners on social media platforms.[21]

Understanding that semiotically encoded messages can be decoded in many ways is critical. For instance, a woman posting a picture of herself and her partner kissing is bound to be perceived in various ways by the audience. It becomes difficult to as-

20. David Crary, "CDC: US Abortion Rate Falls to the Lowest Level in Decades," *Associated Press*, November 23, 2016, https://apnews.com/ccf0b462a6d84f9eabef0846566d1291/cdc-us-abortion-rate-falls-lowest-level-decades.

21. Van Ouytsel, Walrave, and Ponnet, "How Schools can help their Students."

certain what message is being passed and whether it is received as acceptable as it is subject to personal judgments.

Different religious and social ideals govern us, and we cannot agree on a general standard to evaluate morality. This was brought to the fore in 2007 when the video of an actress from Muslim-dominated northern Nigeria went viral on the internet. The eight-minute video clip captured the actress and her boyfriend in acts seen as sexually immoral in the North, leading to the actress being expelled from the Hausa-language film industry.[22] Such videos have been posted online several times by practitioners in Nollywood, the Christian-dominated southern Nigeria movie industry, without any form of penalty meted out to those involved by the industry gatekeepers.

There are risks and opportunities in posting on social media, no matter how we perceive it. While sexual discussions can be used to restrain the immature from endangering themselves through unsafe sexual practices, exposure to such content can also spur someone to secretly engage in it. Such nature has been present in humans since creation, as in the Biblical story of Adam, who, despite being told not to engage in a particular line of action, ended up doing exactly that.

SOCIAL MEDIA AS A SOCIALIZATION TOOL

Media is an indispensable tool to disseminate information to a larger part of society, capable of presenting factual and fictional information with the potential to shape public opinion and effect structural change in the audience. In today's world, the media's role as an author of change is becoming more worrisome, especially in matters related to sexuality. Controversies keep increasing concerning how sexuality and sexually explicit information are exchanged in the media.[23]

The adoption of social media as a socialization medium has become a global norm, bringing people from all walks of life, irrespective of age, race, or religion, into the same community. The present world is a global village where an individual's comment can go far beyond their physical location or the borders of their country, requiring large amounts of time and money investment in technological devices to participate.

To better understand the extent to which social media can offer potentially dangerous and sexually explicit content to users, one needs to access chat rooms like those available on the social media platform 2go, hitherto one of the most attractive social media platforms for teenagers and adolescents.[24] Most chat rooms on platforms like 2go are open to anyone who wants to participate, and any discussion may crop

22. New York Times, "Sex Video Outrages Northern Nigeria," *New York Times*, August 14, 2007, https://www.nytimes.com/2007/08/14/movies/14arts-SEXVIDEOOUTR_BRF.html.

23. Richmond Tiemoko and Arit Oku-Egbas, "Monitoring Media Coverage of Sexuality: An Introduction," in *Sexuality In Media: Emerging Issues in Africa,* ed. Africa Regional Sexuality Resource Centre (Lagos: Africa Regional Sexuality Resource Centre, 2006), 6–10.

24. Tiemoko and Oku-Egbas, "Monitoring Media Coverage of Sexuality."

up. Discussions sway from one entertaining topic to another, but many youths describe chat rooms as unpleasant places full of unsavory people.[25]

The discussions in chat rooms are live, with the messages visible to all users in the chat room at that particular time. Users within a chat room can engage in multiple ongoing discussions, with conversations discussing various topics within the same chat room sometimes occurring simultaneously. It is impossible to censor the talk in such chat rooms. Hence any user can be exposed to sexually-oriented discussions without intending to. Although social media platforms monitor chats for compliance with certain rules and regulations, this does not stop members from engaging in sex-related conversations since the moderators cannot be online every time of the day. Other social media platforms allow users to use picture profiles that other members can view.

Instant messaging is another social media tool people use to interact with others online. While instant messaging is similar to chat rooms, the differentiating factor is that they are directed at specific people by someone initiating a conversation with them. It is often possible for users to message people they do not know, making it possible for users to be exposed to sex-related content unwillingly.

Blogs are spaces where people journal online on personal experiences, feelings, fictional stories, news stories, or commentaries. Many blogs also have a dedicated area where readers can comment, usually in response to specific blog posts, allowing unknown individuals to potentially offer unsolicited or unwanted content.

Social networking sites like Facebook integrate the functions of blogs, instant messaging, and chat rooms. On Facebook, users can create accounts that contain profile pictures, while communication with friends and acquaintances on the user's friend list can be done in real-time, like instant messaging and, with the capability of joining groups, Facebook offers the functionality of chat rooms. This makes it easy for users to be exposed to sexually oriented discussions, though some other social networking sites have age requirements for users. MySpace users, for example, must be fourteen years old and above, while those below sixteen have their profiles designated as private to guard their engagements. While some social networking sites have reporting protocols to report illegal or offensive uploaded content, there is no standard to determine what is sexually offensive and what is not.[26]

Another important factor of social media is that it is populated by literate individuals who enjoy modern technology and devices, which includes most young people. Despite the importance of social media platforms as predominant information transmitters indispensable to development, they can be used to expose young people to

25. J. Wolak, J. K. Mitchell and D. Finkelhor, "Online Victimization of Youth: 5 Years Later," National Center for Missing and Exploited Children Bulletin #07-06-025 (Alexandria, VA: National Center for Missing and Exploited Children, 2006).

26. Wolak, Mitchell and Finkelhor, "Online Victimization of Youth: 5 Years Later."

sexual imagery that is hostile to sustainable development. Rather than using social media for educational or entertainment purposes, young people may waste their time on frivolities like sexual discussions that are inimical to development. With mobile phones becoming the personal companions of younger generations, it is imperative to evaluate the kind of information they are most attracted to. The negative effects of unguarded access to the internet and social networking sites will likely fall more on vulnerable young people.

In present-day Nigeria, social media has quickly become a major part of the lives of every member of the household. Consciously or unconsciously, people are substituting social media activities for family bonds. Parents, who should make conscious efforts to ensure that their children's social relationships do not move to the cyber world, are also caught up in a dilemma. Left on their own, the young are exposed to sexual materials that encourage moral decadence. Social media has become a double-edged weapon, as dangerous as it is beneficial in the younger generation's hands. Young people can use these social media platforms for educational purposes; after all, many educative groups can be, and are, hosted on these platforms.

WHAT MAKES SOCIAL MEDIA TICK?

Social media has brought immense changes to socialization processes, leaving only a fraction of the elderly population out of its scope. The opportunity to make contact with friends and loved ones without recourse to distance, engage in business transactions remotely, and watch media without requiring a television has become realized thanks to social media.[27] It acts as a connecting point for friends and family, leading to the cooperative exchange of information visually or auditorily on a mass scale. Education has been made simpler, as grade school and college students can accomplish tasks and assignments more easily than their predecessors.

Social media has become a powerful tool for shaping and ordering how individuals perceive certain issues, operating through four main elements: popularity, programmability, connectivity, and communicability.[28]

The popularity of social media has led to people using it to test the acceptance or rejection of certain aspects of society. A single post containing sexual content may go viral within minutes, giving the impression that the people sharing it do so to affirm their alignment or affiliation with it. When the original poster of sexual-oriented content is a celebrity, the posted material becomes an object of popular discussion for a time. Within such periods, anyone active on social media will be overwhelmed by

27. Roberto Melotti, Jon Heron, Matthew Hickman, John Macleod, Ricardo Araya and Glyn Lewis, "Adolescent Alcohol and Tobacco use and Early Socioeconomic Position: The ALSPAC Birth Cohort," *Pediatrics* 127, no. 4 (2011): 948–55.

28. J. van Dijck and T. Poell, "Understanding Social Media Logic," *Media and Communication* 1, no. 1 (2013): 2–14.

the ubiquity of the posts to the point that they are forced to also contribute to the discussion, positively or negatively, or log out for a while. When this happens, the original celebrity poster tests its popularity and increases its visibility among fans and critics alike.

The programmability of social media platforms is their ability to steer users to particular subjects by giving them constant updates on what their peers and social class are discussing. The use of hashtags on Twitter is a prominent example of how platforms are programmed to deliver trending content to users. While a user might be reluctant to follow certain discussions on social media, if the majority of the user's followers or handles the user follows are participating, then it is almost impossible to bypass them. As much as the human mind is developed to be disciplined, too much pressure bends willpower, and, before long, the user will be forced to either follow the discussions passively without commenting or contribute their own opinion. Many social media platforms are programmed to prioritize presenting users with trending topics, irrespective of their subject.

Social media's connectivity ensures that users who share demographic characteristics can be linked and interact but are not built to compartmentalize nor differentiate users based on these characteristics, making it possible for users to be exposed to content from outside groups to which they belong. The result is that young people may become vulnerable to sexually explicit content. Connectivity also makes it difficult for users to know who has access to their accounts; although some social media platforms, such as Facebook, have features that make it possible to determine the people viewing certain content by limiting access to users selected as friends, the feature is not foolproof.

Social media makes communication much easier than physical proximity, making individuals bolder in sharing their thoughts without fear of punishment or immediate reproach. It has also allowed many younger people to use social media to establish romantic and intimate relationships, with dating platforms such as Tinder built around establishing relationships without censorship or restriction.[29] This has exposed people to sexually motivated discussions, changing the age-old tradition of limiting sex talks to private discussions and establishing a means of connecting people to engage in illicit sex talks.[30]

---

29. M.M.P. Vanden Abeele, "Mobile Lifestyles: Conceptualizing Heterogeneity in Mobile Youth Culture," *New Media & Society* 18, (2014): 908–26.

30. S.R. Sumter, L. Vandenbosch and L. Ligtenberg, "Love Me Tinder: Untangling Emerging Adults' Motivations for Using the Dating Application Tinder," *Telematics and Informatics* 34, (2017): 67–78.

SOCIAL MEDIA'S IMPACT ON MORALITY

A common moral code among many societies in Nigeria revolves around discussions related to sexuality. Sex, in the context of African societies, is a rite and an act that should be covert. So great is the reverence attached to sex that it is not an issue that is brought up for discussion often. The two dominant religions in Nigeria, Islam and Christianity, forbid and frown on premarital sex, so many societies in Nigeria discourage conversations relating to sex and sexuality as it is presumed that talking about it is tantamount to encouraging young people to engage in premarital sex.[31]

Every act of human beings, whether deliberate or not, face moral adjudication in society. While individuals may have the free will to act as they deem fit, they are still liable to have their actions evaluated or analyzed by their parents or guardians to check if it conforms with what the generality of the people believes in. Engaging in social media activities may not be subjected to such evaluations since it is an emerging tool, but this does not mean its usage cannot be examined to ascertain if it conforms to acceptable standards. While Nigerian society does not frown at social media usage, as a rule, the manner and context of how it is used in specific situations often lead to evaluations aimed at determining moral justifications. Among the forms of discussions persistently scrutinized by society are those that are sexually oriented.

The effect of this change from face-to-face to virtual communication has encouraged individuals to challenge the status quo by engaging in discussions that were hitherto rarely permitted in personal interactions. Persistent exposure to sexual conversations may increase sexual behavior, ultimately leading to moral decadence. With the myriad of sexual discussions populating various platforms, it becomes easy for adolescents and young adults to align with these discussions, leading to the growing uneasiness of parents and moralists in Nigeria. As noted earlier, social media greatly threatens the preservation of certain cultural norms and family values.[32]

There exists an air of discomfort whenever issues connected to sex are discussed in contemporary African societies. Any adult that grew up in Nigeria has had, at one point or another, the experience of watching a movie with their parents, discussing and interacting about the film, when suddenly, a sex scene crops up. The boisterity in the atmosphere immediately transforms into an awkward silence, with everyone hoping that the scene does not drag on for too long. While watching Nollywood movies are family bonding sessions in the past, the experience has changed. Before, sex was a taboo that nobody dared to discuss, making watching a film a silent abomination.[33] Among some Nigerian communities, some words must not be spoken in public, with

31. Melody Adebisi, "Why is Sexual Health Such a Taboo Topic in Africa?" *West African Careers*, 2018, http://westafricancareers.com/sexual-health-taboo-topic-africa/.

32. Adebisi, "Why is Sexual Health Such a Taboo Topic in Africa?"

33. Mell Nyoko, "Why African Parents can't Talk about Sex," *This is Africa*, February 3, 2014, https://thisisafrica.me/politics-and-society/why-african-parents-cant-talk-about-sex/.

sex-related conversations perceived as obscene since they revolve around human genitals, sexual desires, and sexual acts, but this seems to have changed with the emergence of social media.[34] Essentially, social media has become the biggest communication platform in the world, changing the mode and content of interpersonal relationships among divergent users.

There is a looming danger for the cultural heritage of Nigerian societies, as younger generations are becoming disconnected from the values their parents grew up with. Sexual discussions on social networking sites have unleashed a strong assault on family values, causing a shift away from morality. It could be argued that the advent of social media platforms is changing the dynamics of sexual talks or discussions.

The increasing prevalence of indecent dressing too can be traced to social media.[35] Using cultivation theory, it is understandable that the exposure of a large percentage of young people to sexual material on social media has contributed to the embrace of a clothing culture that promotes nudity in various degrees. The youth bulge theory proposes that whatever the youth embrace as trendy or in vogue may become an acceptable standard in society,[36] increasing the effectiveness of social networking sites as tools for promoting immorality. Even religious institutions are not left out of this trend, as many find themselves faced with an increasing level of indecent dressing among their congregations.

Evaluating how younger generations make sense of sexual discussions in the rapidly evolving social media space will lead to understanding how social media is a tool to promote immorality and social decadence in the modern world. The link exists; Moreno found out that the prominence of sexual discussions on the Facebook walls of undergraduates accurately affirmed their intention to become sexually active.[37]

In addition to sourcing answers from their peers, young people are greatly influenced by the media and entertainment industry, including television, movies, games, and song lyrics, alongside the internet and social media.[38] The particular influence of social media on sexual behavior has been clear for some time,[39] emerging as a new

34. Felix Ngunzo Kioli, Rosh Were Allan and Onkware Kennedy, "Traditional Perspectives and Control Mechanisms of Adolescent Sexual Behavior in Kenya," *International Journal of Sociology and Anthropology* 4, no. 1 (2012): 5.

35. Nkechi G. Onah and Nche George Chrıstıan, "The Moral Implication of Social Media Phenomenon in Nigeria," *Mediterranean Journal of Social Sciences* 5, no. 20 (2014): 2231–2231.

36. Joseph Omolo, "Trends of Antisocial Behaviour Among Minors in Nairobi Populous Estates: A Study of Karen and Runda Estates," *Journal of Family Studies* 13, no. 4 (2014): 165–75.

37. M. Moreno, Libby N. Brockman, Judith N. Wasserheit and Dimitri A. Christakis, "A Pilot Evaluation of Older Adolescents Sexual Reference Displays on Facebook," *Journal of Sex Research* 49, no. 4 (2012): 390–99.

38. S. Coleman and P.M. Shane, eds. *Connecting Democracy: Online Consultation and the Flow of Political Communication* (Massachusetts: MIT Press, 2011).

39. Jane D. Brown, ed. *Managing the Media Monster: The Influence of Media (From Television to Text Messages) on Teen Sexual Behavior* (Washington, DC: National Campaign to Prevent Teen and Unplanned

dimension of sexual information dissemination among all social strata, including young people. Social media gives open access to all. Thus there is the propagation of different beliefs and opinions.

VULNERABILITY OF ADOLESCENTS TO SEXUAL CONTENT ON SOCIAL MEDIA

Adolescents have numerous needs, and it is important that they become more informed and educated about their sexuality. In Nigeria, adolescents face many emotional, psychological, cultural, and social challenges.[40] Among their needs is the desire to be more independent, advance their cognitive abilities, and engage in interpersonal relationships with family and peers, leading to broader connections with others. Since many African societies frown at open discussions related to sex, girls are especially prevented from discussing or confiding in their parents regarding matters relating to sex. The female African adolescent is restrained from making decisions regarding their sexuality, even though she faces the prospect of sexual advances from older men.

The transition from childhood to adulthood presents innumerable pressures. Many young men and women experiencing it become desperate to be informed on various issues about their changing lives and sexual orientations. While they may not easily get answers to their queries from parents and siblings, they can often resort to peers to access such information.

Social media platforms have become abodes of sex-driven discussions, without reference to the prevailing culture and norms of the society of its participants. Social media is eroding the African culture of private discussions relating to sex and sexuality, shaping a new social order wherein indigenous customs are relegated to the background in favor of imported ideologies.

Sex-related discussions on social media negatively influence the young because adolescents' inquisitiveness often pushes them to try out what are exclusively adult activities, owing to the self-belief that they are mature enough to partake in such discussions. Knowing that sexual discussions are likely to ignite a dormant or yet-to-be-triggered consciousness relating to sensuality and sexuality among young people, it is important to understand that social media has become a dangerous place for the vulnerable. Even though adolescents may have the requisite discipline to close their ears and eyes to such illicit content, their susceptibility to peer pressure cannot be ruled out. Left unguarded with an uncontrollable sea of sexually oriented contents, the tendency for the nation to experience breakdown in values and family units is high.

Pregnancy, 2008).

40. Emmanuel Amoo and E. Adeyemi, "Scanty Dressing Habit and Sexual Comportment Among Adolescent Girls in Metropolitan Lagos: Implications for HIV/AIDS Incidence," *Gender and Behaviour* 18, no. 1 (2010): 2806–2824.

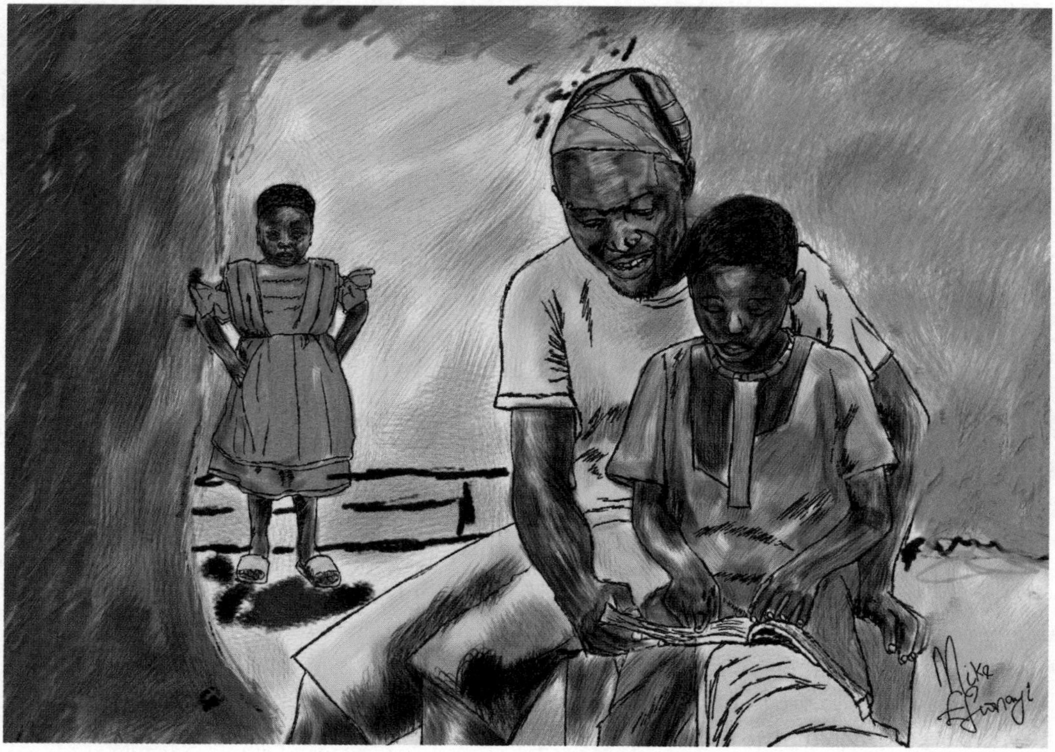

Figure 7.1. "The Neglected" by Michael Efionayi. A father educates his male child while denying the female child the right to education. It depicts discrimination and neglect on a gender basis.

The explosive growth of internet users has been traced to the increasing awareness of its potential positive impacts on its users.[41] Young people of school age are equipped with devices with internet access to aid their learning, and some tertiary institutions provide online portals for registration and e-learning, making it imperative for undergraduates to access the internet. There are presently more than 500 million cell phones within Africa alone,[42] and Nigeria, while only possessing 3.6% of the total number of cell phones in Africa in 2004, saw a dramatic increase to 24% and 33% by 2010 and 2012, respectively.

The bulk of this increment can be attributed to the 22%—48% female—of Nigerians that are adolescents, especially those below 25 years of age. As they become more attracted to the internet and social media, they get roped into casual conversations about sex that may trip them up. Does biological capability for copulation and reproduction

41. A. Lenhart, A.M. Madden and P. Hitlin, *Teens and Technology: Youth Are Leading the Transition to a Fully Wired and Mobile Nation* (Washington, DC: Pew Internet and American Life, 2005).

42. International Telecommunication Union, *The World in 2013: ICT Facts and Figures*, ICT Data and Statistics Division, Telecommunication Development Bureau (Geneva: International Telecommunication Union), 2013.

imply social maturity to act as responsible fathers and mothers? This is debatable, especially given the country's issues with child marriage on the one hand and vulnerability to sexual assault. One thing is certain, there must always be a high degree of reproductive health literacy to prevent unwanted effects of overt sexuality that social media seems to breed.

Most discussions on social media platforms are engineered and driven by young people, making any form of adult control quite difficult.[43] At times, it is glaringly obvious that young people influence what is discussed on social media more than older adults.[44] Sexual discussions on social media platforms are championed by yet-to-be-mature young adults stuck between adolescent rationalizations, an affinity for trendy issues, and an adult mindset manifested as a result of their coming of age; with little disposition to being controlled by older ones.

Every adult understands that social media platforms increase the potential for young people to come in contact, however unconsciously, with sexually-oriented discussions often featuring contributions by adults. This assertion does not come from an empirical viewpoint but cannot be disproved rationally. While some platforms like Youtube use age restrictions to censor access to sexually explicit content, circumventing such restrictions takes nothing more than the falsification of age by the young or the old, or the willful disobedience of content providers to state if their content is for mature audiences. Sadly, these social media platforms do not have any means of confirming if users truly are the age they affirm.

SOCIAL MEDIA AND SEXUAL HARASSMENT

Making sexual jokes, bragging about sexual prowess, and sharing sexually explicit graffiti are among the ways social media users harass and are harassed daily. For instance, an innocent Facebook user going through their timeline may find sexually explicit content tagged to someone on their friend list. These contents may harass their thoughts and elicit unwanted feelings relating to sex. Innocent social media users may even be exposed to sexually suggestive content exchanged between two adults when they appear on their respective timelines.

Some studies validate the assertion that indiscriminate use of social media tends to increase the incidence of sexual harassment. Dooley, Hearn and Treyvaud revealed that 43.5% of young people that accessed sexual content were exposed to

43. Teresa Swist, Philippa Collin, Jane McCormack and Amanda Third, "Social Media and the Wellbeing of Children and Young People: A Literature Review." Prepared for the Commissioner for Children and Young People, Western Australia, 2015.

44. S. Livingstone, G. Mascheroni and E. Staksrud, *Developing a Framework for Researching Children's Online Risks and Opportunities in Europe* (London: The London School of Economics and Political Science, 2015).

sexual harassment.[45] Through sexual discussions on social media platforms, behaviors such as rape and premarital sex by minors have become increasingly common. Little wonder that abortions and the use of contraceptives are on the rise among younger generations.[46]

Sexual harassment is often used to blackmail individuals and subject them to exploitation. In this age of smartphones, people are quick to record their sexual exploits and nudity on their communication devices, and most times, the danger of such acts may not be perceived at the point of the recording. Such videos can suddenly get posted to social media and become subjects of discussion for days, causing regret to creep in for the victim from the resulting harassment. At the same time, such an individual might have felt good viewing themselves in various stages of nakedness or sharing these images with someone specific; depression sets in when evil people get hold of such videos and make them go viral. Ultimately, the blame would swing from those who intentionally uploaded the contents to the victim who made themselves observable performing such a private act.

Exposure to sexual content on social media platforms leads to more negative consequences than positive ones. Sexual discussions on social media are embarked upon without recourse to any form of censorship or disclaimer, allowing them to be encountered without warning. Sometimes, mature individuals may engage in them, forgetting that their younger siblings who appear on their friend list could be exposed to such content. If these vulnerable siblings begin to engage in sexual vices, it is difficult to pin the blame on the older siblings who unintentionally exposed them to the sex-related content. This has caused many family problems and may degenerate into lifelong animosity among family members. Engaging in sexual discussions on social media often haunts individuals in ways they never envisaged. Potential employers have been known to browse through the social media handles of potential employees, making decisions based on their online activities.[47] Sexual conversations on social media have even been known to lead to violent deaths; for example, an ex-soldier was alleged to have killed his girlfriend because of some messages he saw on her phone that suggested she was flirting with a man.[48]

This reflects how individuals can become entangled in sexual discussions on social media platforms and the consequences that could result. In the most visible cases, the intended targets of social media blackmail are celebrities. In February 2020, the Twit-

45. J.J. Dooley, L. Hearn and R. Treyvaud, *Review of Existing Australian and International Cyber-Safety Research* (Perth: Child Health Promotion Research Centre, Edith Cowan University, 2009),

46. A. Barak, "Sexual Harassment on the Internet," *Social Science Computer Review* 23, no. 1 (2005): 79–93.

47. A.G. Dempsey, Michael L. Sulkowski, Rebecca Nichols and Eric A. Storch, "Differences Between Peer Victimization in Cyber and Physical Settings and Associated Psychosocial Adjustment in Early Adolescence," *Psychology in the Schools*, 46, no. 10 (2009): 962–972.

48. Jude Owuamanam, "Ex-Soldier Kills Girlfriend Over Text Messages," *Punch*, March 15, 2016.

ter space was awash with the leaked video of a popular Nigerian actress, Maryam Booth, where she was completely naked and was aware of being recorded. Whether or not she consented to it could not be ascertained.[49]

PROMOTION OF SEXUAL CONTENT ON SOCIAL MEDIA PLATFORMS BY NIGERIAN MUSICIANS

Musicians and social media influencers also aid the consumption of sexual content in Nigeria. It could be argued that the entertainment industry in the country has enabled the prominence of sexual content available in cyberspace and social media platforms specifically. Nigerian celebrities promote sexuality through their music and videos, as well as random posts on their social media platforms. This act is common to musicians and social media influencers who seek a significant number of followers, want more viewers and subscribers, and more fans. This effect is that teenagers with their smartphones can be strongly influenced by celebrities and the social media they utilize. One could notice the rise and development of music videos because of their enormous ability to express a wide range of ideas, feelings, and emotions. This arguably has led to musicians' financial success and the popularity of the hip-hop genre. However, there is growing concern about how music affects how people perceive women in society.

Tiwa Savage is among the numerous musicians promoting sexual content with their social media platforms. Tiwa Savage once posted a picture of her nude body on Instagram.[50] The post struck a chord among her followers; some argued that she is a role model to the younger generation and should not be seen posting such pictures, while others believed that she is at liberty to post whatever she wants on her account. Tiwa Savage did not respond to the discussions. She has also been seen on numerous occasions during her music concerts clad in revealing clothes. On a particular occasion, Nigerian Twittersphere was in an uproar when her leaked sex video dominated the space.[51] Although she has no power over circumstances like a leaked video, she did not suffer a serious backlash from it. One of the disadvantages of social media is that it is difficult to regulate what comes in. Before the platforms themselves take off sex-related videos on their space, the damage would have been done already. It has been established that sexuality in music has increased in intensity and frequency as women are constantly exposed to images that dictate who they should be, how they should look, and how they should balance their lives. As a result, research has been conducted on how women are portrayed and objectified in the media. This is sexual

---

49. Makinde Azeez. "(18+) Popular Hausa Actress, Maryam Booth Naked Video Leaked on Social Media", *Naijaloaded*, February 7, 2020. https://www.naijaloaded.com.ng/entertainment/18-popular-hausa-actress-maryam-booth-naked-video-leaked-on-social-media-watch-video.

50. https://www.instagram.com/tiwasavage/?hl=en.

51. https://twitter.com/hashtag/tiwasavageleakedtape?lang=en&src=hash.

objectification, the experience of being treated as a body valued primarily for use or consumption by others.

Another Nigerian musician that promotes sexual content in his songs and social media accounts is the Soapy crooner Naira Marley, a controversial Nigerian rapper. He once said on Twitter that all he wants in life is sex, even at the expense of his eternal life. As he tweeted:

> "I want some nasty sex that there'll be no questioning I'm going to hell."[52]

In another tweet, he said he wishes to indulge in sexual relations with a mother and her daughter. As he tweeted:

> "I have d right to threesome, as long as it's consensual and legal."[53]

In his songs, there is a plethora of sexual innuendos. It could be argued that his teeming fan base were attracted by the explicit sexual content in his songs. For instance, after he sang "Puta," where he foregrounded bodily attributes of the female sex, he asked his followers to make short clips of themselves shaking their rear vigorously and post them on Instagram. Naira Marley's music videos often feature greater sexual objectification than other performers but he is not alone in posts like this. The YBNL boss, Olamide Adedeji, is also guilty of this. One of his older tracks, "Story for the gods," was banned for endorsing overt sexuality by exposing the ladies' privates and even showing some sexual harassment on screen. In 2019, after releasing the video for his single, "Pawon," Olamide, who controls a large fanbase of 9.7m and 5.7m followers on Instagram and Twitter, respectively, personally announced the "Pawon challenge," a challenge where ladies show the magnificence of their butts by twerking, through his Instagram handle. According to Olamide, the winner of the challenge goes home with a cash prize. However, not only fans joined this challenge; even celebrities like Teni Makanaki and Toyin Lawani were also seen participating.

A popular female social media influencer, Mandy Kiss, divulges details of her sexual adventures. She boasts of a large domestic and international clientele and hails herself as the President of prostitute celebrities. She stated out loud that anything could be kept in her private part as long as the client smells well, looks good, and has plenty money for her pleasure. Vulgar words are the watchword and anthem of this female celebrity who has no other content than to boast of her sexual explorations. Just like Mandy Kiss, Oba Solomoni, a controversial cleric who controls more than a hundred and fifty thousand followers on Tiktok and Instagram, is also known for

---

52. https://twitter.com/officialnairam1/status/1264540090929426433?s=20&t=s5i8e3MJ-9ndU-3wiob99gQ.

53. https://twitter.com/officialnairam1/status/1395506678196539394?s=20&t=cx3jbeE8sy7Zw-MP28qOaig.

boasting about his sexual prowess. On his Tik Tok page, Oba Solomoni Agbaye 1, there are videos where he made this claim with obscene words. Similar videos are also available on his Instagram account.[54] Oba Solomoni is the originator of the popular tune made by YK Beats, "Oma ma yi bii steering ni," translatable to "you'll be turning it like the steering wheel." In one of his videos, where he made this assertion, Oba Solomoni condemned men who do not know how to dominate a woman in bed in his usual vulgar manner. Another big name on Tik-Tok is a sixty-something-year-old woman who is nicknamed Mama Esabod, known to promote nothing but indecency. This woman once boasted on one of her Tik-Tok videos that she could be sexually available to a man of any age.[55] Mama Esabod is also known for boasting about her big pudendum, big enough to scare any man. Following the footsteps of celebrities whose daily immorality persists can cause youths grief because it may affect their sexual and social lives, now and later in life. It is, therefore, true to a reasonable extent that celebrities have contributed immensely to the decline in decency among individuals on social media.

Also, some online shows discuss sex. These are common on social media platforms as well. There is a YouTube channel called Krakstv,[56] which has a similar name on Instagram. Although its sexual content is for entertainment purposes, it does not rule out that there are sex talks. It uploads videos tagged "social experiment" where random people are asked questions about their sexual life. In one of its videos, random people were asked about the most important activity during foreplay.[57] This discussion was purely sexual, and responses were purely sexual, with the discussants saying how they prefer foreplay to be done and what their partners should do to make the foreplay more interesting. The respondents affirmed that foreplay is a prerequisite for good sex as it is insensitive to just jump to sex. In another video, people were asked if they would allow their parents to watch them have sex for 20 million naira.[58] One could argue that these questions are just to elicit humor, but there is no doubt that the undertones are pure sexual talks. Some respondents said they would not do it, while some were indifferent.

In another video, respondents were asked if they would bring their romantic partners for a one-night stand with 10 million naira as payment.[59] Responses varied between affirmation and negation, with those who did not support questioning the ra-

54. Solomoni Oba, "Instagram Page," *Instagram*, https://www.instagram.com/oba_solomonii/?hl=en.

55. Olabimpe Idowu, TikTok Post, *Tiktok*, https://www.tiktok.com/@olabimsy_tee2collection1/video/7069843190811020550?is_from_webapp=v1&item_id=7069843190811020550&lang=en.

56. KraksTV, Youtube channel, https://www.youtube.com/c/KraksHQ.

57. Kraks TV, "What's the most Important Activity during Foreplay? *Kraks Sex Talk*," June 5, 2021, https://www.youtube.com/watch?v=olB5Hvtn36M.

58. Kraks TV, "Would you Allow your Parents Watch you have S3x for 20 Million Naira?" *KraksTV Vox-Pop*, July 26, 2021, https://www.youtube.com/watch?v=FwA59256220.

59. Kraks TV, "₦10m to bring your Partner for a One-Night Stand, what will you do?" *KraksTV Voxpop*, September 20, 2021, https://www.youtube.com/watch?v=AXQj7M7Nstc.

tionality of sexual gratification and objectification of their partners because of money. In another video, the discussants were asked about the most dangerous sex style they had ever tried. Undoubtedly, these are sexual content. Also, discussants were asked what their craziest sexual experience was.[60] One of the discussants said it was during her first sex. Another said it was being caught having sex at home by her father.[61] Most of the shows hosted on Krakstv are rated 18+, but it is quite accessible to those below 18. They are not barred from viewing these kinds of shows. As much as this could be argued to be for entertainment purposes, it can be confidently posited that they are sexual content, though made consumable specifically for adults but could fall into the hands of children and teenagers.

In short video clips hosted on YouTube, the theme of sex is foregrounded. There is a content analysis of a video titled "Sex" posted on YouTube by House 21 TV.[62] The characters in the video were the popular musician, Falz, popular TV personality Toke Makinwa, and the popular comedian Bovi. The video presents the character of Abiodun and Stephanie (Falz and Toke), who scheduled a session with the therapist (Bovi) to discuss their sex life. Stephanie particularly complained that her husband does not give her enough sexual fantasies. Usually, in movies, references to sex are not very explicit, but the contrary is the case here as it involves explicit sex talk.

Contrary to widely held belief, these social media platforms do not flag off discussions on sex. What they delete on their platforms are porn-rated videos. One could argue that the video presents the realities in many marriages where the husband or the wife undermines the importance of sex in marriage based on their busy schedule; there is no doubt that the video fits into sexual content as well.

Furthermore, sex videos randomly find their way to social media platforms, especially Twitter. Sometimes, sex videos are leaked by third parties for malicious purposes like revenge porn or to cause embarrassment or disaffection for the people in such leaked videos. At other times, it stems from accidental release of such extremely private moments, such as when a used phone is sold off without properly wiping the memory. When it is leaked for malicious purposes, usually the female is the target. In two major instances, there were leaked sex videos of a Ladoke Akintola University of Technology student involved in illicit sex with an unidentified person.[63] The video was shared and trended with #Lautech.[64] The challenge with these social media platforms is the unpredictability when sex videos become available on them. There was

60. Kraks TV, "What's the most Dangerous S3x Style you have Tried?" *Kraks Sex Talk*, July 16, 2021, https://www.youtube.com/watch?v=EXZZg8x-N8c.

61. Kraks TV, "What's the most Dangerous S3x Style."

62. House 21 TV, "Episode 3—Sex," *House 21 TV*, August 21, 2020, https://www.youtube.com/watch?v=mf6KYTmT0Ik.

63. Mc_freedom, "Twitter Post," *Twitter*, Febriary 25, 2021, https://twitter.com/search?q=%23lautechleakedvideo&f=video.

64. https://twitter.com/search?q=%23lautech&src=typed_query.

also a leaked sex video on Twitter of a Babcock University student having sex with a young man allegedly in a remand home.[65] The institution waded in and rusticated the female student. Another sex video was leaked to Twitter where a lady identified as an Akwa Ibom student was engaging in sexual activities with an unidentified man.[66]

USING SOCIAL MEDIA POSITIVELY FOR SEXUAL HEALTH EDUCATION

Sexual health has become a sensitive topic around the globe, worsened by the increase in sexually transmitted infections, it has led the World Health Organization to recommend that people be more properly educated on sexual health. With the emergence and growing acceptability of social media as the most popular tool for socialization, its potential for the effective promotion of safe sexual practices cannot be underestimated. It is inadequate to talk about sexual discussions on social media platforms without pointing out the positive discussions aimed at eradicating the negative consequences of social media platforms discussed earlier.

One growing trend is using social media to promote sexual health information. Many health organizations in Australia use social media for sexual health promotions, mostly targeting young people. The pilot project was undertaken by the Burnet Institute at the University of Melbourne, using Facebook, Youtube, Twitter, Flickr, and a host of other popular social media platforms for interactive sexual health communication with individuals between 16 and 22 years of age.[67] Social media is also used to provide interpersonal skills to assist young people in exploring their values and goals while ensuring that they make responsible decisions concerning dating and other sexual activities.[68]

The sexual culture of the younger generation is becoming increasingly intertwined with social media, with their sexuality shaped by the forms of materials and discussions there.[69] These audio-visual materials form part of the socio-technological forces that re-organize social media users' sexual practices and desires through persistent circulation and distribution.[70] Some of the platforms facilitate a change in cultural

---

65. TVC Connect, Twitter Post," *Twitter*, November 20, 2019, https://twitter.com/tvcconnect/status/1197391542496968704?lang=en.

66. https://twitter.com widenewspaper/status/1528500457584226304/.

67. J. Gold, Alisa E. Pedrana, Mark A. Stoove, Shanton Chang, Steve Howard, Jason Asselin, Olivia Ilic, Colin Batrouney and Margaret E. Hellard, "Developing Health Promotion Interventions on Social Networking Sites: Recommendations from the FaceSpace Project," *Journal of Medical Internet Research* 14, no. 1 (2012): 1–11.

68. Advocates for Youth, "Sex Education Programs: Definitions & Point-by-Point Comparison," *Advocates for Youth*, http://www.advocatesforyouth.org/publications/publications-a-z/655-sex-education-programs-definitions-and-point-by-point-comparison.

69. Livingstone, Mascheroni and Staksrud, *Developing a Framework.*

70. van Dijck and Poell, "Understanding Social Media Logic."

Figure 7.2. "Gay and Stigmatization" by Dr. Kazeem Ekeolu. Two lesbians afraid of freely expressing their sexuality in public because of the strong resistance and stigmatization.

dynamics, which in turn affects the conventions of many societies in Africa and makes it difficult for individuals to resist getting entangled with sexually explicit content on social media.

Many organizations concerned with adolescent sexual health in the United States already use social media platforms to improve young people's access to sexual health information. Widgets and apps have been developed with varying features. They are being integrated into social media platforms like Facebook and MySpace. Video-sharing sites like YouTube, and other relatively unpopular ones like TeeVee, are being used by organizations to promote sexual health information among adolescents.

Teensource.org, a website run by the California Family Health Council, uses its YouTube channel to advise teens and young adults on maintaining responsible sexual lifestyles.

In Africa, some taboos make sexuality a topic that often remains unspoken and trying to talk about it can be met with very harsh criticism.[71] In the West, sexual education is expected to start from home, but African homes do not share such an ideology. Notwithstanding, the children will have to learn it elsewhere, one way or the other.

With the increased use of social media by a large proportion of people in the world, it has become imperative that social media platforms are exploited positively to prevent the incidence of sexually transmitted diseases and sexual exploitation. With close to half of the world population being active on at least one social media platform, it is a powerful tool for disseminating and exchanging information. The World Health Organization's recommendation is to increase people's education on sexual health.

CONCLUSION

The conclusions raised herein are my ideas and normative beliefs on how the danger of sexual discussions in the Nigerian social media space can be managed and minimized. Sexual discussions on social media remain an issue that will continue to generate concern from the public, especially among the older generations and others who believe in upholding older family and traditional values. Events have repeatedly shown that attempts to embrace foreign values often end with relegating and relinquishing the pre-existing values that we grow up with. Every blessed day, the battle to uphold indigenous family values is lost. The younger generations are embracing Western values, and it is just a matter of time before African cultural values are eroded because social media will always be populated by younger generations and serve as an important socialization tool for them. The alignment of the internet with peer culture has succeeded in ensuring that discussions on social media are controlled by young people, which means that the older generations will continue to find it difficult to sway discussions away from sexuality if the young are bent on discussing it. Except if there is a conscious attempt by parents to aggressively monitor and advise their children on the potential dangers of engaging in sexual discussions with peers online, there will be a gradual erosion of African moral values.

Sexuality and sexual discussions, while not entirely bad, can only be beneficial if attempts are made to direct them positively. This can only be possible if organizations and the government take bold steps to tap into the advantages and power of social

71. Adebisi, "Why is Sexual Health Such a Taboo Topic in Africa?"

media and embark on sexual health education efforts to teach the younger generations. Making use of social media for sexual health education may provide a way to ensure that online sexual discussions are engaged constructively rather than destructively. This would ensure that older Nigerians have a controlling stake in the discussions that young people engage in on social media.

8

CONVERSATIONS ON QUEER PEOPLE IN A CONSERVATIVE SOCIETY

The transition from adolescence to adulthood is always a challenging time for individuals, according to an influential school of thought, which also asserts that this is a time when their society ascribes value judgments to their behavior, and there is always a probability that they will identify with minority groups that are frowned upon in their culture. These behaviors can increase the negative attitudes they face, often leading to low self-esteem, social isolation, and sometimes depression.

A particularly scrutinized culture in Nigeria is queerness, an umbrella term for sexual or gender minorities, including gay, lesbian, and trans/non-gender-conforming individuals. Queer people in Nigeria are extremely vulnerable, as they remain targets of homophobic violence in all nooks and crannies of the country. On February 17, 2016, Akinnifesi Olumide of Ondo State was beaten to death on suspicion of being a homosexual by an angry mob alleging that he was caught in a compromising situation with another man.[1] Although the other man escaped the mob, Olumide was not as lucky. This was not the first time individuals in Nigeria faced "jungle justice" on suspicion of being gay. Sometimes, such mob actions are embarked on in the presence

1. Wale Odunsi, "TIERS Condemns Murder of Akinnifesi Olubunmi over Alleged Homosexualism," *Daily Post*, March 15, 2016, https://dailypost.ng/2016/03/15/tiers-condemns-murder-of-akinnifesi-olubunmi-over-alleged-homosexualism/.

Figure 8.1. "Caricature of Bobrisky and Naija James Brown" by Michael Efionayi. The caricature of Bobrisky and Naija James Brown, both cross-dressers, engages the public scene despite the people's reservations about it.

of security officials, who do nothing to stop such cruel acts, implicitly condoning the mobbing of such individuals. An unverified case happened in 2013 when two men were killed in the presence of security officials who did nothing to de-escalate the situation. The security operatives instead walked away from the scene on hearing that the individuals being attacked by the mob had died.[2]

Nigerians view queerness and same-sex sexual orientation as unreligious, un-cultural and alien. The incidents of communities rounding up individuals on suspicion of homosexuality and meting out humiliating punishments reached a crescendo, leading to the government's involvement. Section 36 (4) of the Nigerian criminal code states that whenever any person is charged with a criminal offense, they shall— unless the charge is withdrawn—be entitled to a fair hearing in public within a reasonable time by a formal court or tribunal,[3] but there have been reports of queer individuals being denied rights to a fair hearing even as no individual has been convicted of the murder of Akinnifesi Olumide. This situation is a potent example of Nigerians' gross averseness towards queerness.

2. Bella Naija, "Horrific: 2 Alleged Gay Nigerian Men Beaten to Death as Policemen & Passersby [sic] Watch," *BellaNaija*, February 7, 2014, http://www.bellanaija.com/2014/02/horrific-2-gay-nigerian-men-beaten-to-death-as-policemen-passersby-watch/.

3. Constitution of the Federal Republic of Nigeria, 1999, as amended (CFRN 1999, as amended).

A HISTORICAL PERSPECTIVE OF QUEER EMERGENCE IN NIGERIA

Nigeria, like many African countries, culturally perceives queer (popularly called LGBTQ+ in the Western world) orientations as taboo, often leading to anyone caught in the act or merely suspected of being gay being punished in varying degrees by the authorities or the society as a whole. Notwithstanding this, there have been documented reports by many scholars attesting to the existence of same-sex sexual activities and transgenderism in Africa long before the colonialists came to our shores.[4] While many people in government in Africa are quick to defend the promulgation of laws targeting homosexuality on the precept that it is un-African and an imported vice, the reality is that it has been with us for ages, albeit practiced in secrecy.

With the concept of human rights becoming globally acceptable, it is expected that individuals in all countries will be allowed to determine how they intend to make choices on personal issues, as much as they do not affect others directly. Still, the institution of liberal human rights is greatly limited in African countries like Nigeria. In the past, some cultures, like the Efik and Igbo cultures, considered twins evil beings that represented bad omens to families when they were born. This was not until explorers and missionaries like Mary Slessor came to Africa that such thoughts were largely laid to rest.[5] Same-sex sexual relationships are supposed to be a private matter, and it is expected that the government is not supposed to interfere in the private affairs of individuals, as they remain part of the fundamental human rights of individuals.

Same-sex sexual orientations have always been illegal in Nigeria, even before the colonial era. Traditional African societies have been observed to mete stringent punishments on individuals caught engaging in homosexuality. In some African communities, such punishment comes in rituals, payment of fines, or public shaming to make those guilty of homosexuality change their minds and renounce their taboo sexual orientation. The Abrahamic religions that dominate Africa's landscape provide no leeway for queerness. The Christian Bible forbids same-sex sexual relationships, while the Quran does not condone them. While the bulk of Nigerian Christians does not advocate death sentences for individuals caught in acts tied to homosexuality, the Muslims largely are not that tolerant, as the sharia code demands that such perpetrators be put to death through savage acts like stoning.

---

4. V. O Ayeni, "Human Rights and the Criminalisation of Same-sex Relationships in Nigeria: A Critique of the Same-sex Marriage (Prohibition) Act." In *Protecting the Human Rights of Sexual Minorities in Contemporay Africa*, ed. Sylvie Namwase and Adrian Jjuuko (Pretoria: Pretoria University Law Press, 2017), 210.

5. Elijah Obinna, "Bridging the Divide: The Legacies of Mary Slessor,'Queen'of Calabar, Nigeria," *Studies in World Christianity* 17, no. 3 (2011): 275–293.

Nigeria is neither an overtly Islamic nor Christian country, and this secularity of the country is expressed by the lack of state enforcement of religious codes on the citizens. Moral codes, that is, the way the society views the behaviors and attitudes of others, may be subjected to religious dictates, but when conflict arises over-interpreting them by the courts of law, it becomes necessary for the government to mediate through the application of the Nigerian constitution, the highest law of the land[6] that was derived from the laws of Britain after independence. While the criminal code introduced in southern Nigeria stipulated a fourteen-year jail term for homosexuals, the sentence was death in northern Nigeria if the Sharia courts heard such a case. While there had been attempts as early as 2006 to introduce a nationwide bill prohibiting same-sex marriage, it was not until 2014 that the bill could successfully get to the president's table and was signed.[7]

The enactment of the Same-Sex Marriage Prohibition Act 2013 catalyzed nationwide discriminatory practices against persons perceived as homosexual in Nigeria and extended the same punishment to individuals that knowingly assist others engaged in homosexuality. This gave Nigeria's security agencies the leeway to arrest individuals based solely on suspicion, with no investigation. To make matters worse, this law undermines business for hotels, as they often turn away men who intend to use single rooms for some time for fear of being prosecuted as accomplices to homosexual acts. Examples of such blatant abuse of power included arresting twenty-one young men organizing an all-male party in 2015.[8] They were only released after being made to make small bail payments, something that the Nigerian police persistently publicized. There has not been a single conviction in Nigeria concerning same-sex marriages. Most cases that relate to homosexuality are settled out of court, as the individuals concerned are always in fear of the negative publicity and societal disapproval that their prosecution might confer on them, irrespective of their innocence.

Queerness is not outlawed in Nigeria by the guaranteed freedom of expression included in the 1999 constitution. Given that it is often difficult to prove the sexual orientation of an individual just by their appearance and manner, it becomes a daunting task to identify and question any individual for prosecution unless in situations where they have openly stated their orientation.

Homosexuality and same-sex partnerships are beginning to gain more prominence in the Western world, with various governments embracing frameworks that endorse such acts and countries like the United States of America have established an enabling atmosphere that gives protection to queer individuals. In Nigeria and Africa,

---

6. Sec. 1 (3) CFRN 1999, as amended.

7. Felix Onuah, "Nigerian President Signs Anti-gay Bill into Law," *Reuters*, January 13, 2014. https://www.reuters.com/article/nigeria-gay-idUSL6N0KN2PP20140113.

8. MaDailyGist, "Gay Party Busted By Police in Ibadan. 21 Men With 122 Condoms Arrested," *MaDailyGist*, May 18, 2015, https://madailygist.ng/2015/gay-party-busted-by-police-in-ibadan-21-men-with-122-condoms-arrested-read-more/.

by extension, religious and cultural ideologies have established stiff opposition to queerness, with the government of Nigeria subsequently stifling queer voices in a manner criticized by human rights groups like Amnesty International.[9]

This law has been perceived as a perfect example of rash legislation that has emerged from Africa recently to fight same-sex orientations. As a gay activist and proponent, Bisi Alimi argued in the opening remark of the report *Not Dancing to Their Music* (2017) that the establishment of the Same-Sex Marriage Prohibition Act 2013 opened doors of hate and prejudice toward certain minorities with the legislation giving indirect support for homophobic jungle justice and the summary lynching of human beings who are supposed to be protected by law in Nigeria.[10] This same activist had to flee the country in 2004 when he openly declared his sexual orientation, so he has a firsthand understanding of threats faced by queer Nigerians. In his words, hiding sexual orientation from friends and families is often stressful but necessary for social and legal reasons in countries like Nigeria. In Nigeria and some other African countries, same-sex relationships are often secret, subjecting them to the horrors of isolation.

THE SOCIAL MEDIA INFLUENCE OF QUEER PEOPLE IN NIGERIA

Social media's emergence has improved the citizenry's perception of homosexuality. While identifying as gay or lesbian in the past was sure to attract condemnation and possibly assault, the increase in social networking sites has lent a helping hand to people who intend to come out of the closet. The existence of social networks has improved, to a large extent, support for gay people and campaigns against homophobic issues in Nigeria while decreasing negative views from the public.

Undoubtedly, social media, to a large extent, has helped to change the narratives about sexual minorities in Nigeria as more queer people use the platforms to make a powerful proclamation about their sexual identities.[11] The law prohibiting same-sex marriage and another proclaiming penalty to those caught in same-sex relations still stand; however, social media has given voices to persons described as LGBTQ. The fact that the narratives are changing on social media does not often translate into a welcoming attitude toward homosexuality in the public sphere, as it is still seen as

9. Kingsley Obiejesi, "Amnesty International Attacking us for Opposing Gay Rights, says DHQ," *ICIR Nigeria,* February 24, 2018, https://www.icirnigeria.org/amnesty-international-attacking-us-for-opposing-gay-rights-says-dhq/.

10. Bisi Alimi, Petra Boynton, Zuzana Struharova and Gary Wood, *"Not Dancing to their Music": The Effects of Homophobia, Biphobia and Transphobia on the Lives of LGBT People in Nigeria* (Lagos: Bisi Alimi Foundation, 2017).

11. Michael O. Ukonu, Luke I. Anorue, Ugochukwu Ololo and Habibat M. Olawoyin, "Climate of Conformism: Social Media users' Opinion on Homosexuality in Nigeria," *SAGE Open* 11, no. 3 (2021): 1–12.

largely unreligious, un-cultural, and alien to Nigerian society. Efforts by the LGBTQ community in Nigeria to ensure that society comes to terms with the knowledge that people can be homosexual have not proved effective in changing these narratives. Sexual minorities do not have freedom of expression in Nigeria as the government clamps down on them, and society negatively reacts to their identities.

With the advent of social media platforms, LGBTQ persons have enjoyed the freedom of expression and have garnered collective efforts to change public perception of homosexuality. Scholars have posited that online networking platforms such as Facebook, Twitter, and Instagram, amongst others, allow engaging in socio-political advocacy and activism.[12] This is especially true if one brings to the fore the activism of LGBTQ persons in Nigeria. These LGBTQ persons have used social media platforms to organize online protests, drawing the attention of the Nigerian public and international stakeholders to pressure the Nigerian government to recognize their rights. They have been able to arouse public consciousness on the understanding that homosexuality is an identity (that is, it is biologically possible for a person to feel sexual intimacy with the same sex) and culture. However, most of the negative attributes meted out to them, as explained in the preceding paragraphs, are largely based on religious reasons. Nigeria is home to two of the most influential religions in the world: Islam and Christianity, and both religious doctrines condemn same-sex relations. In the holy scriptures, it was recorded that Jehovah destroyed the city of Sodom and Gomorrah for similar practices queer persons are clamoring to be recognized in the country.

Coming out of the closet is a process that is largely seen as being detrimental to the person that undergoes it, but social media networks can provide security for them. Various online communities have been set up since the promulgation of the anti-gay law in Nigeria to provide a haven against homophobia and hostility towards gay socialization and interaction. This establishment of these platforms has provided immense benefits for gay writers, celebrities, and other highly visible Nigerians as it provides a meeting place devoid of the physical, social, and legal hazards the anti-gay law has imposed on gay people associating.

A good understanding of social network theory is needed to understand the level and nature of social media's impact on homosexuals in Nigeria and the process of coming out of the closet. Within the framework of this theory, it is believed that as individuals move through life, they tend to develop social networks aimed at providing support and assistance for their identities.[13] These networks are generated through affiliation, association, or collaboration.

---

12. Evan Mwangi, "Queer Agency in Kenya's Digital Media," *African Studies Review* 57, no. 2 (2014): 93–113.

13. Wenlin Liu, Anupreet Sidhu, Amanda M. Beacom and Thomas W. Valente, "Social Network Theory." In *The International Encyclopedia of Media Effects*, ed. Patrick Rossler (West Sussex: John Wiley & Sons, Inc, 2017): 1–12.

Among the major reasons for the emergence of queer social media groups are the social stigma associated with homosexuality in Nigeria. From time immemorial, there has been the perception that homosexuality is obscure and immoral in African societies. The perceived abnormality of homosexuality results in self-degradation and self-hate in gay Africans, which often shows in their social engagements. With the creation of Facebook groups such as *Men in Nigeria* and *Female in Nigeria,* queer individuals have become more vocal and active in expressing their sexual preferences. Initially, as expected, there were negative reactions against these individuals, at least gay men who publicized their sexual orientation on *The Men in Nigeria* group. As more and more queer people exploited the cyber-presence of these groups to their advantage, the antagonism began to simmer down.

Overall, there has been a significant decrease in the level of criticism and homophobia exhibited against queer individuals on social media. This has been aided by factors such as the perception that the anti-gay law was more of a political gambit than public policymaking undergone by the Jonathan administration to garner support from religious groups for his re-election. While this may not be verifiable, it indicates that the masses in Nigeria have come to ascribe specific anti-gay actions of their government as tools for selfish desire and not for the benefit of society.

Additionally, the Nigerian Twittersphere trended with #SodomandGomorrah, which contained homophobic tweets eulogizing the government for its unwavering stance on its discrimination of homosexuals in the country.[14] Despite the hostile environment in the country, LGBTQ persons are leveraging social media platforms, especially Twitter, to create awareness of their sexual identities and effect a behavioral change in the public. Twitter, a microblogging platform, has been largely adopted by LGBTQ persons to ceaselessly advocate for recognizing their sexual constructs. This has arguably recorded little success as a few Nigerian musicians and social media influencers have thrown support behind the group. Nigerian queer persons have also used Twitter to create a sort of digital community where they would be able to share pieces of information as they concern with sexual minorities to strengthen their awareness.[15] Since it has been posited that social media helps in shaping opinions, there is a growing change in dynamics as it concerns issues relating to the LGBTQ community in Nigeria.[16] This is evident in their online support on social media platforms, especially Twitter. Although, this online support has not been largely translatable to the physical setting.

Despite the seeming influence of the LGBTQ on the Nigerian Twittersphere, they have often been confronted by other Twitter users who do not believe in their sexual

---

14. https://twitter.com/hashtag/sodomandgomorah?src=hashtag_click.

15. Paul Onanuga, "Coming out and Reaching out: Linguistic Advocacy on Queer Nigerian Twitter," *Journal of African Cultural Studies* 33, no. 4 (2021): 489–504.

16. Onanuga, "Coming out and Reaching out."

identity. It is pertinent to add that sexual minorities are considered barbaric and animalistic, among other derogatory terms in Nigeria. Nigerian Twittersphere was once dominated by a heated virtual disagreement between the LGBTQ community and the Arewa Twitter users, largely comprised of Northern Muslims, and criticized the clamor for acknowledging same-sex marriage relations as purely anti-Islamic and attracting divine punishment.[17] Their arguments were largely hinged on the premise that Nigeria is a religious country and western values would not erode religious practices in the country. Also, tweets from those who identified with the LGBTQ community argued that there is freedom of love and everyone has the liberty to choose whom they want for intimacy or sexual relations. In Western countries like the United States of America, LGBTQ rights are recognized. The rainbow has been used as a symbol to showcase the support of sexual minorities worldwide. In Nigeria, however, their rights remain only recognized in cyberspace. The LGBTQ community in the country has also organized empowerment programs for its members to solidify their efforts for the government to recognize their rights.

The collective action of several human rights and advocacy groups, such as Mental Aware Nigeria, The Equality Hub, and She Writes Woman, has also reduced homophobic attitudes on social media. These groups have successfully tried to educate citizens on the right of individuals to make choices in their lives and the freedom to decide whom and which association to belong to. Not stopping there, these advocacy groups have also been active in dispelling various myths that demonize homosexuality, such as the perception that homosexuality is responsible for the spread of HIV in Nigeria. Dispelling such fallacies was made possible through education-focused media drives.

The emergence of social media has made it possible for queer people in Nigeria to offer insight into their lives by bringing their challenging stories to social media for others to identify with. In 2020, there was an increase in police harassment of queer individuals in Nigeria.[18] Most of these individuals spread their experiences through digital media, which often exhume sympathy from wide audiences who may otherwise never be exposed to these stories.

Another factor that aided the reduction of homophobia on social media is the low levels of censorship of social media activities in Nigeria. This has enabled writers, celebrities, and other professionals to churn out queer-themed films, documentaries, and literature. With the establishment of *Q-Zine*, a pan-African magazine for LGBTQ persons both locally and in the diaspora, there has been a great improvement in online interaction among the gay community in Nigeria. Social media platforms such as

---

17. Abba Jameel, "Twitter Post," *Twitter*, July 2020, https://twitter.com/search?q=%23ArewaAgainstLGBTQ&src=typed_query.

18. Alexis Akwagyiram, "A Police Raid, Viral Vidoes and the Broken Lives of Nigerian Gay Suspects," *Reuters*, February 24, 2020, https://www.reuters.com/article/us-nigeria-lgbt-widerimage-idUSKCN20I105.

this have encouraged researchers to investigate issues revolving around homosexuality stereotypes and dispel certain unverified postulations. With the springing up of gay-specific platforms, the question about queer communities in Nigeria has moved from whether or not they exist to the amount of space they occupy in social media engagements.

A look at some of the social media accounts of queer celebrities and writers in Nigeria shows they are amassing teeming online influence. For instance, the popular transwoman Idris Okuneye, known as 'Bobrisky,' has become one of the most famous people in Nigeria, with as many as 1.7 million followers on Facebook and Twitter combined. The sheer number of fan pages attributed to Bobrisky alone shows how much queerness is becoming a major attraction on social media. More than thirty Bobrisky accounts on Instagram make it quite cumbersome to ascertain which is the original account. One such Facebook account, *Okuneye Idris Bobrisky*, gets as many as five thousand likes per picture, though there are many negative comments. Bobrisky has previously stated that her gender performances are just acts. However, it is normal to hear crossdressers denying their queerness to divert talk from the legitimacy of their right to exist as queer persons.[19] However, she has addressed the public on why she became transgender, positing that she had long wished to be a woman because women are powerful persons, and most do not know how to wield the resources at their disposal.[20]

In July 2019, the most popular blogger in Nigeria, Linda Ikeji, posted the comments retrieved from the Facebook account of a Nigerian lawyer who purported to be a homosexual. This was not the first time she used her blog to compromise the privacy of perceived queer individuals, despite the homophobic attitude of many Nigerians. If she intended to degrade their sexual preferences, the comments to the post acted contrary to her wishes. Most comments spoke in favor of the lawyer, with many commenters condemning her action and demanding that she pull the post down. This is a good demonstration that perceptions about homosexuality are beginning to change, thanks to the emergence of social media.

Another social media celebrity who proudly promotes homosexuality in Nigeria is Bisi Alimi, the self-proclaimed first queer personality to declare his sexual orientation publicly. Alimi constantly uses social media to drive home his agitations for gay freedom in Nigeria. This led to his establishing a foundation—the Bisi Alimi Foundation—to advocate for gay rights and dignity in Nigeria.[21] In 2019, Bisi Alimi aggres-

19. Pink Panther, "I am not Trans, I'm Just a Cross Dresser... I am not Gay or Bisexual...' Bobrisky and Dele Momodu Engage in a Viral Interview about Sexuality and Gender Identity," *Kito Diaries*, August 1, 2020, https://kitodiaries.com/bobrisky-and-dele-momodu-engage-in-a-viral-interview-that-shows-their-ignorance-regarding-sexuality-and-gender-identity/.

20. James Ojo, "Bobrisky: Why I Decided to be a Woman," *The Cable*, September 22, 2021, https://lifestyle.thecable.ng/bobrisky-why-i-decided-to-become-a-woman/.

21. Bisi Alimi Foundation, https://www.bisialimifoundation.org.

sively promoted the first openly gay event in Nigeria on social media, despite the existence of the anti-gay law. The event, tagged "Night of Diversity 2019," was held in October and made possible in partnership with the Elton John AIDS Foundation. Although he left the shores of Nigeria in 2007 following threats that followed his public statement of his sexuality, Bisi Alimi defied all odds to come back to Nigeria to successfully organize the event. Expressing his joy at the magnitude of the event's success, he took to his Instagram page to say, "I am so emotional this morning, as I never thought this event was going to be successfully held in Nigeria in my lifetime. We organized a LGBTQ event and the crowd came out for it, both straight and homosexuals graced the event."[22] A significant number of straight people also partook in the event, indicating the growing number of people becoming sympathetic to the gay cause in Nigeria. The fact that such an event went peacefully without police harassment or disruptions from any quarters demonstrates the growing courage and boldness of queer people in Nigeria, made possible by social media activities.

While celebrities with queer personalities like Bobrisky find it easy to garner followers, other well-known promoters of queer rights, like writers, do not have such success with their social media engagements, albeit often in less open social media communities like Q-Zine that mainly serve for documentation of experiences and imaginations. Individuals such as Romeo Oriogun and Jude Dibia are among the notable writers whose works, while available on the internet, are not widely embraced due to the lack of a strong reading culture amongst Nigerians. Despite this, it is important to review some of their works to appreciate the rich content of their messages relating to homosexuality and queer freedom and how their efforts at promoting queer nature through fiction writing stir reactions from their readers.

Various Nigerian personalities have lent their support to the LGBTQ community in Nigeria. Although it has still not gotten to the grassroots level, this has proved an increasing awareness of recognizing same-sex people in Nigeria. Kiki Mordi, a former BBC journalist, tweeted in support of the LGBTQ persons.[23] She criticized the Nigerian government for its failure to recognize the rights of sexual minorities. As she tweeted:

> It's almost 2020 & same-sex marriage is still illegal in Nigeria.Like two people (of the same sex) can love themselves and want to build a family for themselves just like you & I but can't because it's illegal for them.
>
> A damn shame! We're already on the wrong side of history.[24]

---

22. Michael Bamidele, "Bisi Alimi Organises LGBT Event in Lagos," *Guardian*, October 30, 2019.

23. Grand Commander of Feminist Battalion, Twitter Post, December 26, 2019, https://twitter.com/kikimordi/status/1210272328732626944?s=20&t=OtBw2cv6ukSPC6twKbRedw.

24. Grand Commander of Feminist Battalion.

However, what she got as a response was a severe backlash from most Nigerian Twitter users, who criticized her for clamoring for the recognition of these rights. She was reminded that her fame should not be used to advance such things as LGBTQ rights.[25] This attitude portrays that the advocacy of the queer community has not largely won over the Nigerian public. Also, Nigerian musicians are not left out in the struggles to recognize sexual minorities. A popular Nigerian musician formerly signed under the YBNL record label, Temmie Ovwasa, often took to social media platforms to reiterate her sexual identity. She describes herself as a proud lesbian. In one of her social media posts, she condemned child abuse and expressed joy in being a lesbian as she would not be involved in childbearing and rearing. [26] As she put it:

> I should birth kids so that you people can traumatize them, So that I can raise them in love & send them to school to be beaten by teachers, leave them with relatives for them to be raped, I'm glad I'm a lesbian & don't have to worry about them accidentally coming! God forbid!!![27]

In one of her tweets, the Duduke crooner, Simi, also showed solidarity for the LGBTQ community. She contends that queer persons should not be discriminated against based on their sexual identities. [28]

Furthermore, social media personalities like Aisha Yesufu took a positive stance toward the LGBTQ community. In one of her tweets, she expressed approval of the liberty of individuals to love whomever they wish to love, contending that homosexuality is not alien to the Nigerian culture.[29] As she tweeted:

> You do not need anyone liking your choice of sexuality. All you need is to be given the right to practice your sexuality. Homosexuality was freely practiced in Nigeria for hundreds of years and I witnessed same sex marriages in the 80s.
>
> So, calm down, it is not a new discovery.[30]

This tweet did not come without a backlash. This is because Aisha Yesufu is from the Northern part of the country, which is predominantly Muslim and is expected to

25. Nathaniel Bivan, December 26 2019, https://twitter.com/nathanielbivan/status/1210327832347455488?s=20&t=OtBw2cv6ukSPC6twKbRedw.

26. Adekunle Fajana, "Singer, Temmie Ovwasa, never wants to have Kids, she Discloses why", *Ripples Nigeria*, August 5, 2022, https://www.ripplesnigeria.com/singer-temmie-ovwasa-never-wants-to-have-kids-she-discloses-why/.

27. Fajana, "Singer, Temmie Ovwasa, never wants to have kids."

28. Simi, "Twitter Post," *Twitter*, August 3 2020, https://twitter.com/SympLySimi/status/1290305584231743489?s=20&t=yrZgdosy-aGRDkI0swrREQ.

29. Aisha Yesufu, "Twitter Post," *Twitter*, January 11, 2021, https://twitter.com/AishaYesufu/status/1348582486943657989?s=20&t=qPCln7iuQKA7yvGUi3mHw.

30. Yesufu, "Twitter Post."

shun any activities related to homosexuality. Nigeria has been ranked in some quarters as the most homophobic country in the world, and this best summarizes the negative attitudes the society elicits toward queer persons in the country. The popular crossdresser in the Nigerian entertainment industry, Denrele Edun, also supported the rights of LGBTQ persons. He tweeted that people should be allowed to love whomsoever they want.[31] The popular actor Charly Boy also lent his voice to the community because his daughter is a lesbian. In an interview, he posited that he found it difficult to comprehend the news of his daughter's homosexuality but was left with no choice but to support her sexual identity.[32] The support from influential Nigerians has further strengthened the awareness of queer persons in Nigerian society.

Some organizations are committed to giving a platform for LGBTQ persons in Nigeria. These organizations have a teeming online presence and have helped ensure that sexual minorities fit into society like the rest of others. The Initiative for Equal Rights "@TIERsNigeria" is committed to recognizing the rights of everyone, especially those of queer persons.[33] It describes itself as an "NGO working to create a society where human rights are guaranteed regardless of status, identity, orientation, and affiliation." An analysis of its tweets shows that the organization is committed to helping the LGBTQ overcome some challenges, especially discrimination, they are subjected to in their day-to-day lives through empowerment programs. It also provides pro bono legal services for those who may have been victimized due to their sexual identity. Despite the efforts of the LGBTQ community to ensure that the Nigerian government changes its stance on homosexuality, there are incidents of brutal harassment against this set of people. Asides from the government, society still shows hatred toward homosexuals. The notion that people could be homosexual from birth has not fully penetrated the public's consciousness. Those who are homosexuals or promote homosexuality are seen as possessed by evil spirits by the religious public.

There is also a platform, No Strings NG "@NoStringsNG," which is "Nigeria's #1 advocacy and resource platform for LGBTQ+ news, information, podcast, opinions, etc."[34] This virtual platform projects the happenings within the homosexual community in Nigeria. In the mainstream media, homosexuals are not given adequate representation, with research positing that the newspapers also fuel the negative reactions that are largely meted out to LGBTQ persons. An analysis of some tweets shows that the platform offers genuine support for LGBTQ rights by amplifying their voices in the media. It also promotes gay-related matters. It serves as a sort of entertainment platform for sexual minorities. Its tweets have called for the inclusion of these people

---

31. Denrele Edun, "Twitter Post," *Twitter*, June 3, 2020, https://twitter.com/DENRELE_EDUN/status/1268198082585509888?s=20&t=k3Qx1S12tvJ35IPhpOmC1A.

32. Charly Boy, "Twitter Post," *Twitter*, November 19, 2020, https://twitter.com/AreaFada1/status/1329661397270138882?s=20&t=8kpwcRR1zux7FM4HNrtSIw.

33. The Initiative for Drug Addicts, Twitter handle, https://twitter.com/TIERsNigeria.

34. NoStringsNG, https://twitter.com/nostringsng.

into society, underscoring the need for everyone to be treated with equality and respect, irrespective of the sexual identities they choose to live with. It is also concerned with how the 2023 presidential candidates would help change the narrative as they relate to the LGBTQ community in Nigeria. There have been collective efforts by queer persons to ensure that the Nigerian government fully recognizes this community. These virtual platforms attempt to change the grim narratives associated with queer people in Nigeria. It is known that queer persons are discriminated against in jobs, among others; unidentified persons have killed some. Research has further postulated that the public perception of queer persons in the country is often discriminatory, a perception that has been previously posited is largely based on religious reasons.[35] The clamor for recognizing LGBTQ rights in Nigeria has often included the fact that homosexuality or same-sex marriage is not alien to Nigerian culture. In the Igbo culture, research has revealed instances of same-sex marriage.[36] For instance, an elite woman could marry a fellow woman even when no sexual intimacy was involved.

Twitter has continued to give LGBTQ persons the platform to fight various forms of homophobia. It has further given them the voice to fight various forms of social, cultural, or political discrimination against queer people. A popular gay activist in the country, Edafe Okporo, announces his marriage to his male partner on Twitter. He captioned it: "It's a dream come true."[37] The son of a prominent politician, Bola Okupe, also took to Instagram to announce his sexual identity to the world. He captioned the post: "I am Gay AF."[38] More people are using social media platforms to unashamedly proclaim their sexual identities, which has helped them get much-needed support from the LGBTQ community. Bisi Alimi, the first Nigerian to declare his sexual identity on television, has continued to offer physical and online support to those with sexual minorities. There is also a virtual platform called Queer Nigeria, "@lgbtqiNigeria," which supports the LGBTQ community. This platform is also concerned with how the 2023 presidential candidates would help change the narrative as they relate to the LGBTQ community in Nigeria. There have been collective efforts by queer persons to ensure that the Nigerian government fully recognizes this community. Another virtual platform, identified as Nigeria Gay "@naijaqueer," "tweets to support Nigeria Queer and LGBTQ community and to promote SDG 10 by reducing inequalities".[39] It changes the public consciousness of homosexuals and offers training programs for queer in Nigeria. It also tweets to champion queer representation in the country.

35. Kehinde Okanlawon, "Perceptions and Attitudes of Heterosexual Nigerian University Students towards Homosexuality and LGB Persons," *Journal of LGBT Youth* 17, no. 2 (2020): 149–176.

36. Nwando Achebe, *Female King of Colonial Nigeria: Ahebi Ugbabe* (Bloomington: Indiana University Press, 2011).

37. Edafe Okporo, "Twitter Post," *Twitter*, July 7, 2022, https://twitter.com/EdafeOkporo/status/1548798570563772417?s=20&t=K6evvbJ7-vuvg6B1hSOaJg.

38. Bolu Okupe, Instagram post, https://www.instagram.com/p/CKREamUs0y5/?hl=en.

39. Nigeria Gay, Twitter handle, https://twitter.com/naijaqueer.

Queer persons have also taken to Twitter to protest against a proposed bill that would punish crossdressers. A bill was sponsored in the House of Representatives to see crossdressers get 6-month imprisonment. In a hashtag #WithdrawCrossdressers-Bill, queers persons used Twitter to voice their disapproval of the proposed bill, with tweets in favor of the rights of the LGBTQ community.[40] Queer persons criticized the bigotry of the Nigerian government into leaving important issues that affect the country to channel all of its might into intimidating the LGBTQ community in the country. Inibehe Effiong, a legal practitioner based in Lagos, described the proposed cross-dressers as largely insensitive. She questioned the rationality behind regulating dress codes for gender in a democratic dispensation like Nigeria, harping that the proposed bill is "the height of legislative misadventure and redundancy."[41] Like the queer persons highlighted, the lawyer criticized the legislators for leaving out many other pressing issues in the country to regulate dress codes. Effiong contends that there is no cross-dressing epidemic in the country that would warrant the proposition of such a bill. The bill has not been passed into law. On another occasion, Nigerian queer people trended #RepealSSMPA, calling for revoking the prohibition of same-sex marriage act that had been signed into law by former President Jonathan in 2014.[42] The hashtag activism is a clamor for the Nigerian government to scrap the anti-gay law. Nigerian queers took to Twitter to lament the discrimination they have been subjected to in Nigerian society because of the legal stance on their sexual constructs. A tweet contends for the freedom of the queers.

A Twitter user tweeted the discrimination two queer persons faced during the #EndSARS struggles when their fellow protesters chased them because they did not fit in as the rest of the citizens.[43] There were also videos on Twitter where queer persons staged a physical protest in May 2022 at the Unity fountain in the capital Abuja as part of wider efforts for the government to recognize them. The activism also trended with the hashtag #QueerLiberationNow.[44] It was a daredevil approach for the community to confront the government on the dire need for the latter to recognize their rights and sanction their recognition in society. Tweets included the need for homosexuals to be part of Nigeria's sociopolitical climate. The fact that the activism was not televised reiterates the media's underrepresentation of the community. There was also hashtag activism of #QueerLivesMatter, which clamored for the rights of the LGBTQ community by projecting the harsh realities these individuals face in Nigeri-

---

40. Ifeanyi, "Twitter Post," *Twitter*, https://twitter.com/hashtag/WithdrawCrossdressersBill?src=hashtag_click.

41. Inibehe Effiong, "The Cross Dressing Bill is Dead on Arrival," *Premium Times*, April 6, 2022, https://www.premiumtimesng.com/opinion/522251-the-cross-dressing-bill-is-dead-on-arrival-by-inibehe-effiong.html.

42. https://twitter.com/hashtag/RepealSSMPA?src=hashtag_click.

43. Cannonball, "Twitter Post," *Twitter*, March 21, 2021, https://twitter.com/a_nickabugu/status/1373555199885860869?s=20&t=tOMC5V4JYxrKzeoh3dj1qw.

44. https://twitter.com/search?q=%23QueerLiberationNow&src=typed_query&f=top.

Figure 8.2. "Gay Couple Studying How to Get Babies" by Dr. Kazeem Ekeolu. It depicts two Nigerian gay men trying to learn how to have babies and the procedures to do so.

an society.[45] The trend also sought justice for those killed due to their sexual identities. Social media has greatly affected how queer persons see themselves in the Nigerian community and allowed them to be bolder about their sexual identities.

THE EMERGENCE OF QUEER-THEMED LITERATURE IN NIGERIA

The concept of queerness, covering homosexuality, bisexuality, and other minority sexual and gender identities, is a relatively new phenomenon in Nigeria and its accompanying literature, even as it has been growing for a long time around the globe. Queerness concerning African culture and literature is new.

Still, there has been an increased awareness of homosexuality in African literature, with several writers breaking from the negative cultural backdrop to a sympathetic and compassionate stance on queerness and queer people. Third-generation Nigerian writers born decades after independence have begun to delve into themes previously perceived as taboo in Nigeria. This situation has been helped by the spread of inter-

45. https://twitter.com/hashtag/QueerLivesMatter?src=hashtag_click.

national LGBTQ movements across the globe, with the internet adding impetus through the facilitation of dialogue and intellectual exchanges across the globe on the issue of same-sex sexual orientation. A 2014 Caine Prize for African Writing press release included the chairperson, Jackie Kay, communicating her impression on the increasing amount of literature on same-sex desire and gay themes coming out of Africa.

Evaluating fictional literature coming out of Nigeria, despite the country's overly draconian legislation towards homosexuality, there has been a paradigm shift of perception from the public on the issue of queerness in Nigeria, driven by respected and internationally-acclaimed figures like Wole Soyinka, Jude Dibia, and Romeo Oriogun, to mention a few. The Nigerian literary community, which had in the past embarked on criticism bordering on homophobia, has begun exploring the daily fears, pleasures, and anxieties of queer individuals and the people around them. Writers like Raymond Williams refer to queer Nigerian literature as emergent, a connotation that portrays it as a resistance to dominant discourses that had not existed before while also producing stories depicting same-sex desires positively despite the societal perceptions of them as immoral.

WOLE SOYINKA'S *THE INTERPRETERS*

Wole Soyinka's work *The Interpreters*, originally published in 1965,[46] is one of the earliest pieces of literature, at least known in the West, that depicts the perceived importation of queer ideology and its prior existence in Nigeria. The novel revolves around a character whose sexual preferences are interpreted in distinct ways by some other major characters, indicating perceptions of the Black man and homosexuality as a mix of disgust, anger, pity, outright contempt, and disregard. The gay main character, Joe Golder, tells his acquaintance, a Nigerian journalist named Sagoe:

> "Do you think I don't know of your Emirs and their little boys? You seem to be oblivious that history is my subject. Do you probably think I don't know of the exclusive coteries existing in Lagos?"[47]

The Interpreters depicts homosexuality as a Western construct and a weird, bordering on deviant behavior. Golder is an African American who brought the taboo from overseas to the shores of Africa, a deliberate attempt to put into the reader's mind that homosexuality was introduced into Nigeria and other African countries by foreigners like Golder. While it may be true that African traditions were opposed to such perceived obscenities, Golder offers a contrasting view. His conversation with Sagoe

46. Wole Soyinka, *The Interpreters* (London: Andre Deutsch, 1965).

47. Soyinka, *The Interpreters*, 199.

points to homosexuality being in existence in Africa, albeit practiced covertly among the affluent and the nobility.

Sagoe is quick to feign ignorance, affirming that Golder seems better placed to get such information. No matter how fictional it may seem, this conversation points to homosexuality in northern Nigeria, thereby disproving Sagoe's position that, unlike Nigeria, the USA is a country of perverts. Sagoe's response to Golder's assertion reveals a defeat from a person who had given up the argument but still managed to hold on to his beliefs. Throughout the novel, Sagoe continually shows more anger towards Golder, with the latter persisting in raising Golder's ire with his constant grandstanding.

The famed conversation between Golder and Sagoe reverberated in some later queer African scholarship, such as Dunton's "Wheyting Be Dat?".[48] In this critique, Joe Golder is depicted as a predatory homosexual and implicated in the death of the young Noah, who allegedly jumped to his death. Anyone who has read the novel cannot deny that Golder's overly sexual advances towards Noah resulted in the latter taking his own life. Rather than give in to Golder's strange advances, he chooses to die, which leads to Golder feeling confused and guilty simultaneously. Noah's decision affirmed the average Black man's outright contempt for same-sex sexual relationships, demonstrated by cases of individuals being lynched on suspicion of being gay before the passage of the Same Sex Marriage Prohibition Act 2013.

The response of Black men to queerness can also be inferred from the conversation between Kola, Bandele, and Egbo after the incident that led to the death of Noah. With Golder becoming hysterical after seeing the consequence of his actions, he was sedated for his mind to become momentarily peaceful. Bandele said:

> I was asleep, and I heard him knocking on the door wildly. He came in already hysterical, babbling, incoherent. Anyway I managed to gather that Noah took fright when he began the usual stuff.[49]

In this moment and throughout the literature, Bandele exhibits pity in response to Golder's overt display of his sexual preference. He perceives him as a man who had formed a habit in a more tolerant society, finding himself in an intolerant one. Such an individual would, to grandstand as a reaction, overly perform his orientation for his ego not to be neglected. Golder had no intention to cause Noah's death, hence the sympathetic response to his situation.

This sentiment towards him follows Golder's status as a westerner, relaying the African perception that queer ideology is a foreign concept. While this might seem

48. Chris Dunton, "'Wheyting be Dat?' The Treatment of Homosexuality in African Literature," *Research in African Literatures* 20, no. 3 (1989): 422–48.

49. Soyinka, *The Interpreters*, 236.

remotely true, it does not obscure the prior existence of homosexuals on the African continent before contact with the Western world. Desai emphasizes this by depicting Golder as a light-skinned African gay man that could easily pass as a white man but chose not to.[50]

The complexity of Golder's character provides indirect evidence of the existence of queer personalities within Africa, with Soyinka preferring not to directly bring the subject matter of identity into the discourse, rather focusing on the existence of queer love. This obliqueness becomes more pronounced when the people refer to Golder as an American even while he classifies himself as an African, despite his skin saying the contrary. Similarly, despite claiming: "You know, I am a misanthrope. I do not like human beings. I like to be alone, what is wrong with that?"[51] he demonstrates persistent friendliness with people throughout the novel.

The impression is that the people of Western cultures have long practiced same-sex sexual relationships with less hesitancy to communicate their orientation in many environments. This contrasts sharply with their counterparts in Nigeria and other African countries, who wisely remain in the closet to avoid facing the wrath of a society that accords them with zero tolerance.

Golder's disposition to communicate his sexual preferences illustrates a man who ignores the conscience of his immediate society and its antagonism towards all manners of aberrations, queerness inclusive. Unlike his society of origin, he troops the streets in the dark, hoping to meet willing partners but is unsuccessful. He also uses his financial resources to take students to theatres and engage them in discussions about male beauty, only to find out that virtually all of them don't care about the subject matter, nor are they inclined towards same-sex relationships. Not wanting to feel defeated, he scouts daily for prey, fearlessly asserting his homosexuality, seeing nothing wrong with it. He is not ready to accept the sad reality that Western and African cultures are different and seeks ways to satisfy his desires. This leads to him being blackmailed by his houseboy, a situation that is only curtailed with the intervention of a lawyer.

The homophobic aspect of African societies is evident in various areas of *The Interpreters*. Notable was the perplexity and anger of Egbo on confirming that Golder is gay:

> His hand, which had touched Joe Golder suddenly felt foreign to his body and he got out of the car and wiped it on grass dew. Bandele and Kola stared at him,

50. Guarav Desai, "Out in Africa," *Genders* 25 (1997): 120–143, referenced in Mark Mathuray, "Intimacies Between Men: Modernism, African Homosexualities and Masculinist Anxieties in Wole Soyinka's *The Interpreters*," *Journal of Postcolonial Writing* 50, no. 6 (2014): 635–647.

51. Soyinka, *The Interpreters*, 185.

> isolated from this hatred they had not known in Egbo, and the sudden angry spasms that seemed to overtake each emotion of his body.[52]

This reaction marks a quick reversal, as Egbo had previously given comfort to Golder after Noah's demise by bending over Golder and placing his hands on his knee:

> "What's all this? What's this stuff business? Egbo asked (ignorant of what Kola meant by the word, stuff.) Didn't you know? Bandele asked (this was supposed to be a rhetorical question). What am I supposed to know? Egbo retorted. About Joe Golder, he's queer."
>
> From vileness below human imagining, Egbo snatched his hand away, his face distorted with revulsion and a sense of the degrading contamination. He threw himself forward, at the back as at some noxious insect, and he felt his entire body crawl in disgust.[53]

This depiction shows Africans' aversion to homosexuality, seen as standing totally against the norms and values of society. It is perceived as abstract and only exists in the mind's imagination. The consciousness of homosexuality is not wholly lost but is covert and perceived as alien. As many scholars have pointed out, queerness is suppressed in Black societies in the name of societal values, with the necessity of covertness.[54]

QUEER PORTRAYAL IN JUDE DIBIA'S *WALKING WITH SHADOWS*

Sociology and anthropology scholars have asserted that African writers tend to refrain from depicting same-sex relationships until Jude Dibia's *Walking With Shadows*.[55] Since then, there has been a sharp increase in open, same-sex literature with gay themes in Africa, overriding the initial denial of their basic existence in Africa made for political and racial reasons. When *Walking with Shadows* broke new ground on queer representation in Nigeria, many critics and internet bloggers reacted negatively to varying degrees, ranging from loathing to outright rejection of homosexuality. Not a single critic came out to applaud the work of Jude Dibia without significant reservations. Onyerionwu acclaimed that *Walking with Shadows* remains a talking point in Nigerian literature due to its audacity in exploring unique themes like queerness and same-sex sexual relationships, positing that it would be difficult to find any other Nigerian novel that would successfully reach the level in terms of the critical appeal of Jude Dibia's work.

---

52. Soyinka, *The Interpreters*, 236.

53. Soyinka, *The Interpreters*, 236.

54. Sylvie Namwase and Adrian Jjuuko, eds. *Protecting the Human Rights of Sexual Minorities in Contemporary Africa* (Pretoria: Pretoria University Law Press, 2017).

55. Jude Dibia, *Walking with Shadows* (Lagos: BlackSands Books, 2005).

This highlights the level of attention ascribed to the work in Nigeria. While people like Onyerionwu praised the author for his audacity to go to such yet-to-be-tapped themes, there were a host of others, albeit among the general public, who felt it was inappropriate for a writer of African background to indulge in such topics. This view was supported by the argument that queerness goes against the traditional values in Nigerian folklore and that bringing it to the fore was an attempt to promote a perceived vice to the youth.

The work of Jude Dibia cannot hold the credit of being the first Nigerian work of literature to hold a sympathetic view of homosexuality. Before it, there was Chris Ubani's *Graceland* (2004). Still, *Walking with the Shadows* provides a compelling and pioneering account, exploring what it means to be queer and silent about it in Nigeria. It follows the story of three different queer individuals, with two (Femi and Abdul) sharing a sexual relationship and tending to ignore society's perception of their sexual preferences. On the other hand, Adrian lives a life of suppression daily due to wanting to submit to the dictates of society. Aware of the negative perception that his immediate society tends to hold against homosexuals like him, he becomes a recluse and secretive about his gayness. This leads him to relegate his sexual orientation to the background while trying as much as possible to exhibit the normal life of a heterosexual man.

The nature of Adrian's character was built as a child, discovering that he has an attachment to effeminate things while growing up. He thinks that his same-sex attraction will disappear with time, reinforced by his belief that his baptism from Ebele (his birth name) to Adrian (his baptismal name) would lead to rebirth to channel him from his past to a new life. Rather than play ball with fellow boys, he prefers to engage in girls' activities such as *ringa-ringa roses.* As Jude makes clear, Adrian had been told several times that the game was meant for girls and not boys like him, but his love for such feminine-oriented games led him to live a life of procrastination.[56] Little did he know that his predisposition to playing with girls would characterize his future sexual personality. His childhood experiences haunt Adrian as he enters adulthood, with a persistent sense of guilt resulting from the memories that had been stamped into his mind.

His brother Chika has always noticed Adrian as a loner who tended to make himself an outcast, even at a very tender age. He observed something different about his elder brother, ranging from his timidity amongst boys to his propensity to secretly peep at their father after his bath. He always thought of talking to Adrian about this but was drawn back. The totality of Chika's observations of his elder brother points to a boy fighting some demons deep within him but could not bring himself to speak about it to anyone.

---

56. Dibia, *Walking with Shadows.*

Jude Dibia painted Adrian as a boy who yearned to be loved and accepted but found nobody willing to give him this, his brothers inclusive. Even his parents, who were supposed to be his backbone, treated him differently than his siblings, and he was exposed to ridicule and bullying from his brothers. He got beaten by his father for a crime he did not commit, and the real culprit, Chika, nurtured a guilty feeling for allowing his elder brother to get punished despite being innocent. Chika saw his elder brother further go into reclusion that day, which he continues to do whenever the world seems to be against him, and as an adult considers their childhood:

> Chika asked himself. He realized that Ebele's difference as a child had been the source of major concern and fear for their family; this was the only way Chika could explain this to himself. Why else would their parents have ignored him? And his brothers had also ignored him as well. He was never there. He was invisible more or less. He was a sissy! And everyone hated a sissy. He cried easily; he was too frail and wasn't just like his brothers.[57]

This childhood experience culminated in Adrian withdrawing into his shell, leaving him with no companion except himself. Seemingly as a move to build a defense mechanism, he would imagine his father just leaving the bathroom, with water dripping from his body.

Adrian finally made his way out of Nigeria to London, an indication of the perception of Africans that the Western world provides a haven for queer individuals holed up in the hostile environment of Africa. This depiction is also seen in Chinelo Okparanta's short story "America,"[58] which details the journey of a lesbian from her society in the Niger Delta area of Nigeria to join up with her lover in America, where she believes she will be free from evil eyes. Unlike Adrian, she seems aware that America has its fair share of hostility towards queer people.

Dibia carefully shows the reader how homosexuals do not necessarily isolate themselves as they did in the past. They still live lifestyles that conform to societal norms, like being involved in a heterosexual marriage while also engaging in homosexuality, but Adrian's wife discovers his sexual preferences, which leads to the destruction of the marriage. Rather than stay in isolation after his marital crash, Adrian chooses to spend time with individuals who share his sexual orientation, Abdul and Femi. Trying to understand how they cope with pressure from gossip, Abdul answers that he has his own life to live and does not necessarily engage in overt displays of his homosexuality. But Abdul hid his sexual preference from his father because he knew that his father might not be able to live with the reality of the situation. Like Adrian, Abdul never wants anyone to get hurt because of his sexual orientation.

---

57. Dibia, *Walking with Shadows*.
58. Chinelo Okparanta, "America," *Granta* 118,February 2, 2012, http://www.granta.com/america/.

This demonstrates how many queer Nigerians have found ways of negotiating the hazards of homophobia in a hostile country like Nigeria. While some go the way of Adrian by maintaining heterosexual relationships as a smokescreen, other gays get married to lesbians to complement their sexual orientations. Dibia describes Adrian's wife, Ada, feeling bad about her husband's situation and confiding in her friend, who takes her to meet other women with similar problems. She is surprised that some of them had no reservations about the arrangement of a cover marriage, as their spouses provide for the family's basic needs. She learns that there is a growing number of influential gays and lesbians in Nigeria, with many choosing to be secretive about their orientation and thereby maintain their lifestyle. She eventually realizes that the society she lives in is changing quickly to accommodate what she believes to be fringe relationships. To further present the ubiquity of same-sex desires, Dibia provides a scene where Adrian meets a gay businessman married to a woman he met at a bar. While these characters might be fictional, they point to how queer people attempt to fit into societies despite their sexual identities.

The complexity of Jude Dibia's *Walking with Shadows* can be perceived in the development of minor characters that contradict Adrian's presupposition of the different outlook for queerness between Nigeria and the Western world and what migrant African gays can expect from the Western world. This is presented through the exploits of the character George who, despite being gay, was exposed to extreme racism in Europe, making him miss home and wish to return and never set foot in the West again, demonstrating the flaw in Adrian's perception that the Western world provides a haven for queer Africans. Dibia offered a controversial explanation regarding queerness and its emerging identity:

> I have come to learn . . . that being gay has nothing to do with the physical action of sex nor a person's sexual preference, be it with the opposite sex or same sex. Sleeping with a man or a woman will always remain the individual's choice. I am gay because it is who I am. It is the way I see the world.[59]

Hoad, cited in Green-Simms (2016), refers to this statement as incoherent interiority[60] because it became hard to discern what Adrian means by comparing queerness to music. I believe this was an attempt by Dibia to counter the perceived perverseness that Africans equate with queerness. Dibia appeals to the reader's compassion by sympathetically bringing to the fore the daily challenges of homosexuals in Nigeria, choosing to take an essentialist point of view rather than an oppositional one.

---

59. Dibia, *Walking with Shadows*, 207.

60. Lindsey Green-Simms, "The Emergent Queer: Homosexuality and Nigerian Fiction in the 21st Century," *Research in African Literatures* 47, no. 2 (2016): 151.

This novel remains one of the few works that offer a sympathetic view of same-sex sexual relationships in Nigeria, particularly as it is directed toward the African reader and not the Western audience. There were reports of various publishers in Nigeria being reluctant to be involved in the promotion of Jude Dibia's *Walking with Shadows.* During the 2013 Writers' Conference in South Africa, Dibia affirmed in an interview that his objective was to change the perception of Nigerians concerning homosexuality.[61] He told of his brother giving a copy of the novel to a colleague at work who, after reading it, confirmed that the book made him rethink his homophobic attitude.

A BRIEF COMPARISON BETWEEN WOLE SOYINKA AND JUDE DIBIA'S WORKS

A careful analysis of the contents of *The Interpreters* and *Walking with Shadows* reveals the contrasting depictions of queerness. While Wole Soyinka wrote from an unsympathetic point of view, Dibia's work exhibited a high level of sympathy for homosexuals and their challenges in Nigeria. *The Interpreters* presents homosexuality as a strange, foreign ideology to Africa, running against the culture of the people and taboo. *Walking with Shadows* conversely portrays gayness as a universal concept transcending continental borders as a purely humanistic rather than cultural identity.

Looking at the main gay characters in the two novels, we find one character who seems very proud of his queer nature and is ready to communicate it without any inhibitions in Golder, while the other, Adrian, is shy, believing that their homosexuality is not right and trying his best to suppress his queer orientation by eventually marrying a member of the opposite sex. He has to confess his past sexual desires to his wife while making her understand that he gave up his concealed sexual identity for her. It is evident that Adrian wanted to regain his wife's trust, but the effort was unsuccessful. The attitude of those around him buttresses his belief that queerness is sacrilege, a crime to the people around him that requires spiritual cleansing to remove. Unlike Golder's pride in his sexuality, Adrian wants to keep his sexual orientation as secret as possible, hoping to be cured of homosexuality through divine intervention. Not only does he conceal this aspect of himself from others, but he also tries as much as possible to push his queerness to the subconscious level since he understands that the society he finds himself in is not in sync with his innate desires. Not wanting to face the consequences, he strives for heterosexual conformity.

Golder feels no misgivings about his sexual orientation, primarily aiming to satisfy himself and not his society. This does not provide room for his queerness, although he constantly sees a false green light in his search for a gay partner. His more open sexual orientation is a vulnerability and almost lands him in serious trouble as he becomes

61. Katarina Hoije, "Nigerian Novelists Reflects on Anti-Gay Law," *VOA*, August 15, 2015, https://www.voanews.com/a/nigerian-novelist-reflects-on-anti-gay-law/2917666.html.

the victim of a blackmail attempt by his houseboy. Golder accepts the reality of his identity and continues to seek ways to pleasure himself, seeing nothing wrong with his sexual desires. Never for a moment does he fear the consequences of his sexual preference because he is bent on self-gratification. This leads to reckless abandonment, culminating in his advances at Noah, who dies trying to repel him. This avoidable consequence shocks him, and for the first time, he feels the negative ramifications of his sexuality. It is difficult to feel sympathy for someone like Golder, who aggressively tries to satisfy his sexual urges to the detriment of another person's life. On the other hand, it is easy to be sympathetic to Adrian's plight; despite concluding that queerness is part of nature, something he can do very little about, he tries to fool himself into thinking he can kill this urge and become 'normal,' like other heterosexuals.

ROMEO ORIOGUN'S POETIC QUEERNESS

With poets in Africa dishing out the same old, overused themes of love, life, and death, the emergence of a unique and courageous voice full of strength, power, and passion will stand out. This is the case with Olusegun Romeo Oriogun, who uses poetry to offer a voice for the LGBTQ community. In his poem "burnt men," Oriogun showcases his refusal to accede that queerness is evil; rather, it is a path that reveals enlightenment taking over the world. The poem's opening lines confront the hostile attitude often disguised as a societal good. He conveys the message that he is the defender of everything queer, those who are persistently sentenced to isolation and death by society:

> a preacher said gay men are dead men.
> i wake up to the smell of burnt men
> in my veins
> i swear my tongue burns
> every time I say the word love,
> I do not know when men began to burn men
> for saying the word love
> but I know that a man in love
> is so close to God,
> he can hear his heartbeat [62]

The poem refers to the substantial threat faced by queer people in Africa, as they are not given any hidden or safe place. The religious institutions that are supposed to provide a haven turn their backs on them based on their doctrines about queer sexual orientations. The biblical cities Sodom and Gomorrah were said to be corrupt so-

62. Olusegun Romeo Oriogun, "Burnt Men," *Praxis Magazine*, 2016, http://www.praxismagonline.com/wp-content/uploads/2016/04/Burnt-Men-by-Oluwasegun-Romeo-Oriogun.pdf.

cieties whose height of malpractice was their indulgence in same-sex sexual relationships. With God seemingly displeased with such acts, He embarked on destroying the city. It is believed that if gays and lesbians are not punished and removed from the face of the earth, what happened to the inhabitants of Sodom and Gomorrah might revisit us all.

The poem "burnt men" challenges this line of thought, affirming that homosexuals are still encompassed within the universal love code that the world is built upon. Love remains love regardless of gender. His view is contrasted with that of the preacher who believes that gays are harbingers of destruction to the world; instead, Oriogun contends that the love displayed by homosexuals furthers God's expectation that all human beings should love themselves for a better world. The theme of this particular poem is the hostility of the religions in Nigeria towards homosexuality. Most incidents of jungle justice in Nigeria are perpetrated by burning criminal culprits. Oriogun alludes to this with the word "burnt," the likely death sentence that will be meted out to gays if they are caught in the act. It is no more simply a matter of being prosecuted through the legal system. Rather, gays must be aware of the threat from their fellow Nigerians, even if the arms of the law seem too short to catch up with them.

Oriogun raises the ante on the issue of violence meted out to the queer community in Nigeria with the opening line of another poem, "How to Survive the Fire,"[63] where he says that the first rule of survival is to run. This reminds me of the jungle justice murder of Akinnifesi Olumide discussed earlier, with his lover able to escape the killers, unlike Olumide.

> The first rule of survival is to Run,
> I tell you this to understand how memories
> are floods drowning a lonely man,
> how the sight of a man burning
> in a park stays with you;
> his voice becoming yours at night.

The memories of a fellow queer person being burnt to death through mob actions are sure to leave people like the man with Olumide with sleepless nights. He does not need to be present at the execution scene to have imagery of the torture and eventual death his intimate would be subjected to. Oriogun notes how these murders are not limited to any region or city but rather are ubiquitous across Nigeria:

> Say Lagos; say Onitsha; say Lafia;
> say cities where the only freedom

63. Olusegun Romeo Oriogun, "How to Survive the Fire," in *14: An Anthology of Queer Art/We are Flowers*, ed. Rapum Kambili, January 14, 2017, https://brittlepaper.com/wp-content/uploads/2017/01/14-AN-ANTHOLOGY-OF-QUEER-ART-WE-ARE-FLOWERS.pdf.

> for a man who loves another man is to leave.
> I tell you this to understand my silence,
> to understand why I crawled into my voice,
> I do not want to die.
> There is nowhere safe in this city of mine[64]

His poetry reveals the dilemma most queer people in Nigeria are left with: if you want to express homosexuality safely, the best choice is to leave the country in the same manner as Idibia's Adrian, though whether this will truly allow escape from homophobia is questionable.

In another gay-themed poem, "Wreckage,"[65] Oriogun takes the reader through threats towards queerness in Nigeria beyond violence, describing the substitution of lost love with another in the context of sexual erasure. For a full understanding and appreciation of this poem, it must be analyzed from two perspectives. First, it becomes important to consider the images and feelings evoked in the poem and, second, the meaning of the metaphors employed.

> I see you in abandoned ships,
> You walk through cabins that hold scented memories of lovers
> The ballroom where we danced before our clothes fell into the water
> Calls your name, and you dance to strains of memory
> This death of ships filled with flowers leave me in tears
> This place of death and life mourns in silence
> While two lovers with dead hearts
> Stare at pictures that will leave pools of tears in their bones

The opening line of "Wreckage" paints a dreadful situation. This is a sad reminder of the reality for queer individuals in Nigeria. With the promulgation of the same-sex marriage prohibition law, it becomes the safest choice for gays to either think twice, abandon their perceived illicit orientation, or face the music. "Walking through the cabins that hold scented memories of lovers" is a coded attempt to bring to the reader's mind—far more apparent if the reader is gay—that all of what remains of queer romanticism in the face of public persecution is the memories of the past.

Oriogun can communicate the dangerous memories that queer attitudes bring to mind in the modern world. For anybody conversant with the story of Sodom and Gomorrah and their eventual demise, the memory of massive destruction brought on their inhabitants for the gross immorality (homosexuality inclusive) being practiced serves as a threat. An average Christian's thoughts automatically switch to the Sodom

---

64. Oriogun, "How to Survive the Fire."
65. Oriogun, "Wreckage," *Burnt Men*: 2.

and Gomorrah story when considering same-sex sexual relationships, which lend the name for the legalistic pejorative 'sodomy.'

The only means of survival for queer people implied by the poem is for them to persevere by inhibiting their inner yearnings and orientations. The poem describes the likely consequence of same-sex relationships in Nigeria, with both the anti-gay laws in place and the government implicitly providing a guillotine for the masses to take the law into their own hands. "Ships filled with flowers" is probably a euphemism for the gay community seemingly being killed by the public and government authorities. Oriogun ends "Wreckage" on a sympathetic note as he immerses the reader into the sad reality of the vulnerability of all queer individuals in Nigeria and the world beyond. The gloomy days are just starting for homosexuals in Nigeria despite various people's emerging awareness and sympathetic position.

Oriogun focuses on the nature of queer identities in Nigeria in "freedom."[66] It explores individuals caught in hostile enclaves due to being what they are. He starts with "birds will find a home anywhere," an attempt to equate the challenges of queer individuals to that of the air's fowls whose homes are naturally arboreal. The uniqueness of birds as flying creatures sets them apart from all other arboreal animals, with the freedom to find a home anywhere.

> birds will find home anywhere
> it is the secret of life
> to call somewhere strange home
> to walk into houses and make a nest out of nothing

Queer people, much like birds, as one commentator said, will call wherever they can be comfortable and safe, no matter how strange or whether or not they belong, their home. A bird will never make a nest in a house fraught with danger.

> some call the road home
> they will look for love in tree branches
> they will talk deep into the night
> waiting for a voice to rise from dusty lanes
> they will learn that love comes from homes within the heart

Just as birds chirp through the night deep within tree branches, homosexual people are prone to spend time in their own company, as they understand the consequences of exposure. As Oriogun captures, there is the tendency for gay individuals to express their orientation secretly, in perpetual fear of being caught, just as birds "wait for a voice to rise from the dusty lanes."

66. Oriogun, "Freedom," *Burnt Men*: 9.

I've learnt that people die before they live
burying themselves deep within their souls,
I've learnt that love starts with a small o
that wraps itself around the tongue
before it travels round the world,
I've learnt to shape my mouth into a roof
and make a home out of my bones.

As a parting shot, the poet still draws up sympathy for queerness, pointing out that those who feel oppressed due to their sexual orientation often face depression. This suffering can be likened to death deep inside the soul. For this to be alleviated, the poet offers a hopeful example: "I have learnt to shape my mouth into a roof and make a home out of my bones." They are advised to try to refrain from discussing their sexual orientation as much as possible but should hold onto it deep within themselves.

In "theory of dark rooms,"[67] Oriogun tries to bring to the fore the secret challenges of queer Nigerians. He does not necessarily have to be gay to understand what they go through behind the curtains; however, being one allows him to portray homosexuals' day-to-day realities. Loneliness permeates the daily lives of queer people in Africa, as they must not be found displaying their sexual preferences in public or risk humiliation, rejection, and possibly punishment that can often include their health or even lives. The average African queer person only enjoys life openly in the company of equals. This is often short-lived because they will have to depart from time to time to mingle with heterosexual-oriented individuals who cannot comprehend their sexual choices.

there are many reasons for dark rooms.
1. we were born to sadness.
2. the world covered our skin with dead faces.
3. our aloneness is a being that speaks to walls.
4. no one listened to the songs in our blood.
5. the songs we heard drowned in rivers of days.
6. we are waiting for someone.
7. love should come to desolate cities.
8. our stories are filled with lonely windows.
9. we have learnt to live in our world.

"Dark rooms," as used in the poem, is an abstract term for the challenges and uncertainties that spring up from being gay. As clearly noted by the poet, there are many reasons for such uncertainty, ranging from a habit that makes individuals retreat to

67. Oriogun, "Theory of Dark Rooms," *Burnt Men*: 17.

their shells in reaction to pain to inner yearnings that cannot be communicated for fear of rejection. No one is ever ready to understand with a queer person the reason for their orientation.

> we sit by windows, waiting for a voice,
> for a familiar footstep, for a face
> that will bring an end to the sky
> that holds broken stories over our heads.

The voice constantly being waited on seems to be that of growing sympathy for queer Africans. While celebrities like Bisi Alimi have become familiar faces for the gay community in Nigeria, writers and poets have tried to bring their issues to the public's glare while subtly educating the people about the harmlessness of queerness. Expectations are beginning to change as Nigeria contends with new gender identities because of figures like Bobrisky, who may just be at the frontier of the emancipation of queerness in Nigeria. Her birthday bash and the fact that there was little the government could do to pin her down with charges related to homosexuality despite the furor that followed is a good indication of the emerging empathy towards queerness in Africa.

Romeo Oriogun has continually brought to the fore the challenges faced by queer people in Nigeria through his poems and aggressive activism. In an interview, he confirmed the dangers of being queer in Nigeria, as the society tries to force individuals to conform to what it perceives as normal behavior.[68] His work is believed to be drawn from his personal experiences and a series of studies that he has carried out concerning homosexuality in Nigeria. His poems have appeared in globally acclaimed papers such as the Prairie Schooner and Connotation Press, and his manuscript, "My Body is No Miracle,"[69] was nominated for the Sillerman First Book Prize for African Poets. These achievements have positioned him as a poet to be reckoned with, and his sympathetic position concerning queer Nigerians makes him stand out as a true change agent.

CHIMAMANDA ADICHIE'S VOICE ON QUEERNESS

When the same-sex marriage prohibition law was enacted in 2014, the internationally acclaimed African writer Chimamanda Adichie was one of the first to speak out against it. According to her, it was an undemocratic representation of injustice at its worst. While granting an interview for Scoop magazine, Adichie talked about a

68. Oriogun, "Theory of Dark Rooms," 17.

69. Geosi Gyasi, "Interview with 2017 Brunel International African Poetry Prize Shortlisted Poet, Romeo Oriogun," *GeosiReads*, April 23, 2017,. https://geosireads.wordpress.com/2017/04/23/interview-with-2017-brunel-international-african-poetry-prize-shortlisted-poet-romeo-oriogun/.

classmate known to act effeminate when growing up. Despite not being confirmed as queer, he faced constant torture from the society where he lived, leading to him almost being thrown from the balcony of a second-floor building. People like Sochukwuma, the classmate Adichie talked about, are constantly harassed, not for being gay but for being who they are. The law was silent to protect them as nobody has successfully been prosecuted for the extrajudicial killing of people perceived to be queer in Nigeria.

Adichie did not just speak sympathetically in favor of gays in Nigeria after promulgating the anti-gay law. Her first attempt at presenting a queer ideology was her short story collection, *The Thing Around Your Neck.*[70] In "On Monday Last Week,"[71] Adichie tells the story of a female immigrant, Kamara, who, after moving to the USA to join her husband, met with Tracy, an African American artist. Kamara was babysitting for Tracy when the latter took an interest in her, coercing her to pose nude for modeling purposes. This ignites a dormant nature in Kamara as she fantasizes about having a sexual affair with another woman. Kamara communicates her desires to her friend Chinwe, who perceives it as foolishness to be attracted to the same sex. Not feeling discouraged, she waits endlessly for Tracy to push her invitation further.

While she was rationalizing that Tracy was stylishly passing an invitation to her, it was later affirmed not to be so because Tracy also extended the modeling offer to her son's French tutor, showing that she was just being businesslike. Adichie establishes how the inner cravings of individuals can be exhibited. However, her conceptualization neither stigmatizes homosexuality nor attempts to disprove its existence. She paints same-sex sexual attraction as a choice an individual should be allowed to make without prejudice.

"Jumping Monkey Hill"[72] takes a political dimension, with Adichie emphasizing how homosexuality is being silenced. She posits that too much emphasizing and re-emphasizing the issue of queerness is a challenge to its existence. The story revolves around a young writer of Nigerian origin who goes on a writer's retreat in South Africa. At the retreat, a lesbian writer from another African country tells how her lover was killed for being queer. While the convener of the retreat—not an African—tells her that African societies do not frown against homosexuality, the writer who told the story quickly reminded them that she was an African from Senegal. The convener continues to dismiss her story, subsequently silencing her.

What follows is an outburst of silence. The story was clear in its message: no one should present homosexuality as an un-African ideology, as most of the other writers

---

70. Chimamanda Adichie, *The Thing Around Your Neck* (New York: Alfred A. Knopf, 2009).

71. Chimamanda Adichie, "On Monday Last Week." In the Collection, *The Thing Around Your Neck*, 74–94.

72. Chimamanda Adichie, "Jumping Monkey Hill." In the Collection, *The Thing Around Your Neck*, 95–114.

silently amuse themselves with the convener's attempt to ridicule the young Senegalese writer, much the same way Sagoe does in *The Interpreters*. The story works because the homosexual theme initially looks like just a subplot, but as the reader immerses themselves into the story, it is easy to see that the storyline is focused on the silence as persistently used to depict the failure of people to speak out against sexism. Ujunwa, the protagonist, was not gay and could speak to the people's conscience on the flaws of keeping silent in the face of the perceived dehumanization of people simply because of their sexual orientation.

"The Shivering"[73] presents a gay character who kept details of his orientation secret until circumstances made him spill it out to a third party in detail. The gay character, Chinedu, meets with Ukamaka, who lost her ex-boyfriend to a plane crash in Nigeria, in the United States. They strike up a friendship, leading to Ukamaka confiding in Chinedu on the challenges she went through in her relationship with someone who seemed not to love her as she did him. This eventually causes Chinedu to open up about his past gay relationship with Abidemi, who chose to marry a woman. Although Abidemi intended to continue the relationship with Chinedu, the latter felt betrayed. This reveals how far people go in Nigeria to hide their homosexual preferences, building up smokescreen relationships to mask their innate desires. The story shows how difficult it is for gay people to openly tell their stories without feeling guilty. While it was easy for Ukamaka to tell her own story of the betrayal of love, Chinedu could not do so because of the need not to expose that he was gay.

In all, these three stories present homosexuality as not being different from heterosexual relationships, except for the dangers faced. Adichie, through her stories, has been able to challenge the perception that heterosexuality is the only normal sexual desire worthy of a human being. She has depicted heterosexuality as a problem, as many who engage in it still nurse or carry out homosexual desires, albeit secretly.

CONCLUDING REMARKS

Several social media platforms are emerging to promote homosexuality and queer literature in Nigeria while offering queer individuals the opportunity to interact openly. Amongst them is Q-Zine, an online platform for queer African youths. Established in 2011, almost the same time the anti-gay law was introduced in Nigeria, Q-Zine made it a duty to provide a legitimate outlet for queer Africans to promote the richness of queer life in African society. Most writers who contribute to the journal may not outrightly identify as queer, but they risk being ascribed as such, especially since their literature is presented in a manner that shows sympathy for queerness in Nigeria.

73. Chimamanda Adichie, "The Shivering." In the Collection, *The Thing Around Your Neck*: 142–66.

Also, in 2011, some weeks after the introduction of the anti-gay legislation in Nigeria, another online community of Nigerian writers, *NigeriansTalk.org*, began presenting their stances on gay issues in Nigeria. The initial exposition was written by one of the editors, Kola Tubosun, who stated that the law had impeded writers from talking more openly about what the government treats as a criminal orientation. This ignited a consciousness among the writers' community to deliver to the platform their fictional and true-life experiences of queerness in Nigeria. Among the first set of stories sent in was Dibia's "Witness,"[74] a story about a gay HIV patient who, with his doctor, was beaten by a mob on suspicion of being involved in a gay relationship right before the police.

Some of the writers—Wole Soyinka, Jude Dibia, Romeo Oriogun, and Chimamanda Adichie—whose works were chosen for this chapter are popular within the literary and reading society in Nigeria, but a significant number of the populace, for economic or other reasons, are yet to have access to their works. This is owing to the lack of an effective reading culture in Nigeria, coupled with the fact that gay literature is yet to be fully accepted by those that develop a likeness for reading. The coming of the internet has managed to bridge the gap a little, as queer literature, as well as queer writers, are beginning to have cross-cultural audiences.

Although some of the literature in this piece presents some of the political undertones concerning queer orientations, they only provide the tip of the challenges faced by homosexuals in Nigeria. With the existence of Q-Zine and other platforms like *NigeriansTalk*, more and more challenges are brought to the fore through fictional stories and true-life experiences.

---

74. Jude Dibia, "Witness," *Nigeria Talk*, January 31, 2014, https://nigerianstalk.org/2014/01/31/witness/.

9

SOCIAL MEDIA AND YOUTH PARTICIPATION

INTRODUCTION

The emergence of social media, aided by the internet, has established a new *modus operandi* in various spheres of human engagement. The dramatic transformation of human interactions and communications with social media has paved the way for improved non-physical interactions and made it possible for individuals to influence one another on a new level entirely. The increased capacity of information and communication technologies to impact interpersonal relations has led to the rise in the adoption and embrace of social networking sites, leading to a paradigm shift in public perception of political processes.

Most social media platforms are built to ensure that individuals sharing personal relationships are interconnected, a situation that raises the bar concerning their interactions. This has led to a decentralization of peer interactions on a scale wherein it becomes easy for anybody and everybody to voice out and participate in a series of communal endeavors that affect the totality of the populace. More and more people, who hitherto were not comfortable with giving their opinions on various societal issues, have suddenly found an avenue that bequeaths them some reasonable degrees of comfortability and security concerning airing their views on particular matters.[1]

1. Amedie Jacob, "The Impact of Social Media on Society," *Advanced Writing: Pop Culture Intersections* 2 (2015): 1–19.

Figure 9.1. "Social Media and Youth Participation" by Michael Efionayi. It depicts the youth and the variety of social media platforms they engage in.

The interactional and communication changes brought about by the internet have led to the establishment of pseudo-groups and online associations that promote and discuss shared interests in virtually all areas of socialization, such as sports, entertainment, marriage, and politics. While political participation in the past has been limited to physical communications, social media has allowed everyone to participate in politics in a more dynamic environment. In recent times, politics has become a mainstream subject of discussion on various social networking sites such as Facebook and Twitter, with these two popular social media platforms widely believed to have the

potential to consciously spur people to political participation.[2] Political engagements have moved from mere physical interactions to quasi-physical engagements.

Political participation in the past depended on partisan membership and other demographics as well as psychological factors. However, social media has changed the *status quo*, with ICT improving its quota in the relevant and important political participation and engagement avenues. The US elections that brought in Barrack Obama revealed the importance of social media as a tool for political participation. The impact of social media usage on the outcome of the US presidential election of 2011 opened the eyes of social media users to the extent to which it can be used to impact the result of elections.

The motivation to participate in the electoral process has always generated divergent views. While some schools of thought believe it should be made mandatory, others believe it should remain a matter of self-determination and predisposition. The obvious point that cannot be argued is that ensuring democracy thrives is essential. Information is a major factor that can motivate people to engage in political participation. Many people, especially the younger generation, lack the motivation to participate without the requisite information.

With social media becoming an integral part of the everyday lives of individuals, there has been an increase in online participation of certain demographic distribution within society, that is, the youths. Social media is positioned as a game-changer in modern political landscapes due to the capability to increase political participation among the youth, who represent the largest users.[3] The reason for this is quite logical: the social media space is populated by the younger generation, ensuring they are provided with a tool to interact and socialize. The youths represent an age bracket that is believed to be the most active in physical communal activities and social media engagements. Suffice it to say that political participation has moved from the days when individuals had to stand on street corners to whisper political matters in a bid to maintain a level of security consciousness, to be replaced by social media engagements that assure members of a relatively higher level of anonymity and security. In the past, political participation, while not the exclusivity of the aged and adults, has always witnessed a significantly low number of youths showing interest in the process.

2. Stefan Stieglitz and Linh Dang-Xuan, "Social Media and Political Communication: A Social Media Analytics Framework," *Social Network Analysis and Mining* 3 (2012): 1277–1291.

3. E. D. Aronson, "Cyber-Politics: How New Media has Revolutionized Electoral Politics in the United States," *Colgate Academic Review*9, no. 7 (2012): 148–194.

SOCIAL MEDIA AND POLITICAL PARTICIPATION

The major driving point of any democratic arrangement is not complete without the active participation of the citizenry in the political process. This process does not infer voting alone; rather, the political process comprises all activities combined to ensure that the people are involved in governance in one way or the other. The political process will certainly include political campaigns, interactive sessions with political aspirants, freedom of choice, and freedom of expression, as well as various other ingredients that combine to actualize democratic engagement. This means that democracy can only thrive when known and unknown barriers do not hinder political participation. The utmost principle of any democratic government depends on its citizens' political participation level.[4]

Political participation describes the activities that include individuals making decisions relating to their interests, demands and alignment with a political ideology. It outlines the various mechanisms through which people express their opinions and views while exercising their influence within the political process.[5] In other words, we may perceive political participation as citizens' engagements on issues that border on socio-political discussions, which are believed to be yardsticks for choosing leaders to govern the country. The commonality of political participation is what differentiates democracy from authoritarian regimes. Also important is that political participation may be perceived from varying dimensions. Political participation may be necessitated by external factors that ultimately lead to individuals' participation in events and activities that determine the selection of political representatives. Such participation may also be in the form of electing political office holders locally or nationally. The political participation of a vast number of individuals is influenced in one way or the other through peer pressure and the bandwagon of public opinion. The people's perception of a political cause may result from a series of short bursts of information or interactions which, after a time, becomes an assertion propagated across platforms.

Conventionally, the participation of citizens in the political process is made possible by interacting and communicating with political candidates or outright criticisms against them. There is the fundamental belief that an involved citizenry is central to governance. Citizens are expected to be constantly involved in debates, discussions and arguments, all of which largely indicate active political engagement. This does not mean that all citizens must exercise such rights. Voluntary participation is a norm, as they may choose to either participate in the political process or abstain.

---

4. Odoemelam Adibe and Adim Chibuwe, "Social Media, Electioneering and Sustenance of Democracy in Africa: A SWOT Analysis," A Paper Presented at the African Media and Democracy Conference (AMDC), Accra, Ghana, 2011.

5. Arthur Chatora, "Encouraging Political Participation in Africa: The Potentials of Social Media Platforms," Institute for Security Studies. Situation Report, 2012.

The reasons for reluctance to participate in the populace's political process can result from one or more factors that ultimately present the political process as non-transparent. In developing countries like the majority of African nations, citizens have developed a mentality that the political process is more of a smokescreen as the process is often marred with various irregularities. These had led to a loss of confidence in the political process. The younger generations hold this mindset the most, as they are born and grew up to witness years of large-scale rigging, ballot-snatching, electoral violence, and other unimpressive events accompanying elections in countries like Nigeria. It paints a scenario that voting is a wasteful and dangerous endeavor since the results would, in the end, be manipulated to favor whomever the government of the day intends.

However, with the emergence of the internet, there has been a new perception of the electoral process. The emergence of social media drives today's political landscape. By providing a platform for individuals to share political information and air their opinion on political issues, social media has become an information medium that allows for the spread of information at a speed that conventional media could not. The assertion that social media enhances political participation, especially among youths who form the majority of social media users, cannot be downgraded. It helps shape political interactions by segmenting the audience through coverage and exposure. With social media engagements, there exists a high degree of access to shared opinions and media selectivity through information reposting. This invariably elevates the users from mere information consumers to micropublishers, becoming active agents in the political processes.[6]

With this, individuals sharing the same social media platform often unintentionally come across information. This has resulted in an increased number of young men and women in the political process. With the voting age being 18 years across various countries, the political perception of teenagers and young adults is driven by public opinion, which is often promoted through discussions on social networking sites. Ordinarily, young adults may not nurture any thought toward a certain political ideology. However, constant exposure to political discussion among the slightly older generations on social media gives them some level of information regarding the political happenings around the country.

With more youths getting to the age of political enfranchisement, there is a constant jostle among the political class as each political candidate seeks to ensure that they sway the newly enfranchised young adults to their side of the political divide. However, they are often met with a brick wall, as the youths, due to their naivety of the political terrain, do not feel motivated to be involved in the political process. With the coming of the various social networking sites, there has been a shift from seeming

6. J.M. Jacka and P.R. Scott, *Auditing Social Media: A Governance and Risk Guide* (New York: John Wiley and Sons Incorporated, 2011).

reluctance to an increasing need to be involved. This is consistent with the proposition of Anderson et al. that Information and Communication Technologies (ICT) seem to provide a renewed hope for political change.[7] Political change is inevitable because of the drive to see that the political process brings forth leaders who will change the governance status quo. In Nigeria, for instance, participation in the electoral process has recently been understood as a fundamental key to ensuring that people play active roles in appointing the country's leadership. Such participation paves the way for citizens of voting age to exercise their franchise to determine who governs them.

Suffice it to say that the emergence of social media has suddenly passed a reasonable degree of political power to the people. In other words, it is safe to say that social media has become an empowering agent for an otherwise disenfranchised population. Established authorities are now being proactively challenged in an impossible-to-escape manner. Information gathering through social media has resulted in people consuming media content as they want and not as the media producers schedule it. Accessing political information is no more limited by time and place, a given when consuming information from traditional media. Fortunately, social media usage as political dissemination and information-gathering tool is relatively cheap.

YOUTH PARTICIPATION IN POLITICS BEFORE AND AFTER THE EMERGENCE OF SOCIAL MEDIA

Before the advent of social media, participation in Nigerian politics included a limited mix of activities that may include joining political parties or groups, engaging in face-to-face interactions, embarking on question-and-answer and media talk shows with political aspirants, and getting involved in political campaigns. However, the emergence of the internet and social media has offered a more dynamic approach to political participation, with the most basic such as contributing to political discussions online as well as participating in social media-driven protests, petitions, and volunteering, all in a bid to be involved in the political process.[8]

Political communication scholars have argued about the declining political participation of youths since the beginning of the 21st century. This phenomenon is not unique to Africa alone but prevalent across the globe. Despite the numerical strength of the youths in Nigeria, the apathy towards political participation has always been an issue of concern amongst politicians and political analysts who believe that youth participation in politics will not only benefit them but will also improve the political

7. Anderson Unwuchola, Toyin Adinlewa and Kenneth Udeh, "An Appraisal of the Role of ICT as a Tool for Participatory Democracy in Nigeria," *MCC* 1, no. 1 (2017): 69–87.

8. Gary Tang and Francis L. Lee, "Facebook Use and Political Participation: The Impact of Exposure to Shared Political Information, Connections with Public Political Actors, and Network Structural Heterogeneity," *Social Science Computer Review* 31, no. 6 (2013): 763–773.

system of the country. As noted by some scholars, youth participation is important as it offers insight into their participation in the future.[9]

Even though the youth in Nigeria is endowed with strength numerically, their carefree and lackadaisical attitude toward politics and other civic responsibilities has led to them not influencing political issues to their potential. Before the advent of social media, Nigerian youths refrained from political participation on the conception that it was not mandatory and that their involvement had little impact on the overall outcomes. A reasonable proportion had, over the years, become disoriented and disappointed with the intrigues that follow representative government and the large-scale electoral rigging that often creates the impression that participation in the electoral process is a waste of time.

The youth's dispassionate attitude has created a vacuum and allowed politicians and political leaders to exploit the situation to their advantage. The political class in Nigeria never wished for the contrary, as they know that youth participation in politics would spell doom for themselves, especially when such youths decide to vie for elected positions. Rather than encourage the youths to take an active part in the political process, the political elites and elders in the Nigerian political system perpetually discourage youth participation by making use of thugs to silence the potential vibrancy among the small number of youths who are active in the political sphere. The discouragement accompanying such actions is one of the major reasons for offline youth political participation in Nigeria.

However, there has been a steady increase in youth participation in Nigerian politics since the emergence of social media platforms. Political interaction and communications on various social media platforms have resulted in the resurgence of the hitherto lost morale of Nigerian youths to engage in their civic responsibilities. The reason for this is simple; social media has provided a secure, easy-to-use, and non-physical platform wherein youths can develop extensive networks for engaging and discussing politics and governance issues.

Social media platforms like Facebook and Twitter offer Nigerian youths an avenue to express themselves without fear or favor while accessing political information and interacting with their peers on political matters.[10] The advantage of this is that it has changed the apathetic stance of Nigerian youths relating to civic responsibilities as they remain the least active demographic strata that, despite being enfranchised, do not feel the impulse to be actively involved.

---

9. G. Vissers, S.M. Hooghe, D. Stolle and V. Maheo, "The Impact of Mobilization Media on Off-line and Online Participation: Are Mobilization Effects Medium-specific?" *Social Science Computer Review* 30, no. 2 (2012): 152–169.

10. Temitayo Odeyemi and Oludare Mosunmola, "Stakeholders, ICTs platforms and the 2015 general elections in Nigeria," Presented at the National Conference on the 2015 General Elections in Nigeria: The Real Issues. held at The Electoral Institute, Independent National Electoral Commission, Abuja, Nigeria, July 27 and 28, 2015.

Figure 9.2. "Tiktok Influencer Video" by Dr. Kazeem Ekeolu. Shows most of the expected content on Tiktok and other social media platforms that engage the youth.

With mobile devices on the increase, youths who in the past never felt compunction about being actively involved in politics have seen themselves engaging in political interactions on social media platforms, owing to the high interchange of political information on social media platforms. Much of this political information is rendered as user-generated content aimed at educating, informing, influencing or impacting the readers to use it as a reference for their respective political participation.[11] By

11. R.D. Putnam, *Bowling Alone: The Collapse and Revival of the American Community* (New York, US: Simon & Schuster: 2000).

2011, the Nigerian political system began to experience the benefits of information and communication technologies, with several political aspirants and parties using social media to enlighten and sway the public to their side. This perhaps was necessitated by the fact that the political stakeholders saw the growing influence of social media on public opinion.

As an addendum to this conversation, it is safe to presume that the internet can develop a society within a society wherein individuals meet and interact in a non-physical manner. Such interactions may also follow real-time discussions among individuals spread across more than one geo-location, thereby invalidating the barrier of space in communication. Irrespective of group, race or educational background, social media communications are established to reach all and sundry without discrimination or sentiments. Amongst other things, the internet has significantly enhanced the political mobilization of Nigerian youths with the power of social media.

THEORETICAL PERSPECTIVE OF SOCIAL MEDIA AND POLITICS: AGENDA SETTING THEORY

To better understand social media's impact on politics, it is important to briefly discuss the agenda-setting theory. The agenda-setting for politics is the process of using the media (both mass and social) to publicize and assign relative importance to certain political issues. In essence, the agenda-setting theory perfectly describes the effect of social media on politics, as the former can influence people's perceptions of the latter.

The media has always been a strategic tool for political processes such as campaigns, electioneering and vote-influencing. Some scholars in the past affirmed that the mass media remains one of the major influencers of political perceptions and voting behavior.[12] Studies of electoral processes worldwide validate the premise that political entities use the media to manifest the effects of agenda-setting theory. By understanding the immense influence that the media has on the audience, stakeholders in the political process churn out content on these media, creating a lasting impression on the audience. However, this has changed with the emergence of social media. The question to be asked is: to what extent do social media platforms influence people's perceptions and political engagement? While scholars like Hindman posit that social media has done little to broaden political engagement, Panagapoulos states that modern technology has continued to impact political processes, especially when adapted successfully. In countries around the world, social media has become a tool not only for online fundraising and disseminating political information but also for

12. Rudiger Schmitt-Beck and Christian Mackenrodt, "Social Networks and Mass Media as Mobilizers and Ddemobilizers: A Study of Turnout at a German Local Election," *Electoral Studies* no. 29 (2010): 392–404.

strengthening and optimizing democracy. With social media platforms, influencing people's perception of what should be acceptable and worthy becomes easy.

The agenda-setting theory also underpins that social media determines what political issue must be discussed at any time.[13] By bringing it into the discussion, it is safe to presume that agenda-setting theory explains the functions and roles of social media in driving the public's perception toward a predefined path concerning the political process of a particular time. It also delineates the influence social media has on shaping the public perception and notions towards specific political issues, which are believed to be of paramount importance at such times. Against this backdrop, it becomes easy to understand why political leaders and stakeholders adopt social media platforms such as Twitter and Facebook to promote certain agendas in building political campaigns. The essence is to drive the audience, as the general public, towards their personal opinions and agenda. All around the world, social media is enhancing political participation in a new dimension, and the major beneficiaries are the youths, who are known as the largest social strata that make the most use of social media platforms for a variety of usages.

THEORETICAL PERSPECTIVE OF YOUTH AND POLITICS: USES AND GRATIFICATION THEORY

Having looked at the theoretical perspective underpinning social media and politics, it is equally important to discuss the theoretical perspective that provides an impetus for youth participation in politics. The theory that comes to mind is the uses and gratification theory which explains the rationale for certain individuals using particular media based on the gratification expected. It is more concerned with what individuals do with particular media rather than what such media does to individuals. Also, the theory provides a humanistic approach to media use and its effects on the users. The uses and gratification theory explains how certain conceptualizations confer power on the users. This, however, can be discussed from two distinct viewpoints: the youth and the political class.

Nigerian youths, having been characterized as showing lackadaisical attitudes towards political processes in the past, have suddenly experienced a spike in their political participation with the emergence of social media. While they often felt insecure in the past, voicing out their reservations and opinions on politically-oriented discussions, the emergence of social media has improved their lots, providing them with the platform to discuss political issues with some level of safety that could not be guaranteed in the past.

---

13. B. Folarin, *Theories of Mass Communication: An Introductory Text* (Ibadan: Stirling-Horden Publishers, 1998), 31.

On the other hand, the political class is spurred to use social media owing to its immense benefits to them as gratification. By underpinning the uses and gratification theory to the political class in Nigeria, it is safe to assert that Nigerian politicians and their pool of supporters make use of social media platforms like Facebook and Twitter to reach across to targeted strata of electorates that they could not reach out through the traditional media. Suffice it to say that the youths who have suddenly found selves participating in politics represent potential targets of such social media engagements by politicians and their supporters.

One major thrust of the uses and gratification theory is that the users of a particular media have needs, and in satisfying these needs, they are ultimately exposed to some other stimuli that allow them to fulfill specific gratification.[14] In essence, youths, the highest social media users, intentionally use social media platforms to partake in activities and events they are not initially disposed to. They can use social media to suit their purposes, including political participation.[15]

SOCIAL MEDIA IMPACT ON MODERN ELECTIONS

In the last decade and a half, the potency and adoption of social media for political campaigns have increased the need for more studies on the subject matter. There has been a shift in the political landscape, as social media has raised the bar of political campaigns in Nigeria as well as in other countries across the globe. Over the past years, many changes have been observed in the political landscape of various countries. Political campaigns in the past took place in front of crowds gathered in a town hall and through convention media like radio stations, TV stations and billboards. This has gradually changed as social media allows the political class to reach a much younger generation of eligible voters yet to be aligned with any political platform.[16] There is no better place to engage these teeming youths than the social media platforms where they are known to form the majority of users. Against this backdrop, it becomes imperative for any politician willing to garner their support to extend his or her political activities to the social media space where interactions with the youths are better achieved. Although the prevalence of the older generation is also beginning to grow on social networking sites, it remains a space for youths and the younger generations. The popularity of social networking sites among the youth provides an enabling environment for political aspirants to promote themselves and interact with

14. G. Adeyanju and M. Haruna, "Uses of SMS in Campaigns: An Assessment of the 2011 General Elections and Post-election Violence in Northern Nigeria," 2012.

15. A.O. Akinwunmi, "New Media, Political Campaigns and Violence in Nigeria." Paper presented at the ACCE, Covenant University, Ota, September 2011, 3.

16. Jacob Maslow, "How Social Media is Influencing Elections," *The Times of Israel*, 2019, https://blogs.timesofisrael.com/how-is-social-media-influencing-elections/.

the electorates.[17] A reasonable number of political aspirants are driven to open social media accounts like Snapchat, Facebook and Twitter to interact with their followers and the electorate. It provides an effective avenue for eliciting a response from the electorate regarding their aspirations and other campaign issues. Social media engagements also allow the political class to reveal other sides of themselves to the electorate

The 2008 Presidential Election in the US

In 2008, the eventual winner of the US presidential election, Barrack Obama, evidently made use of Facebook to endear himself to particular groups of electorates, especially young people. Through social media platforms, Obama built relationships with a larger supporter base, culminating in his success in the election. This seemingly insignificant tactic of social media adoption for election purposes was the first clear indication of a shift from conventional media campaigns. A close look at some figures relating to the social media followership of Obama and his competitor, McCain, sheds more light on the strategic influence of social media on the election. In the build-up to the election, Obama had more than 2,000,000 American supporters on Facebook while McCain had a little over 600,000; on Twitter, Obama had more than 112,000 supporters tweeting in favor of him while McCain could only manage 4,600. Lastly, the Barack Obama channel had 115,000 subscribers, while the John McCain channel had only 28,000 subscribers.[18]

Although the traditional media still plays a significant role in the campaign processes in the form of debates and politically-motivated press conferences, the interactional and information-sharing attribute of the various social media platforms has enhanced participatory communication among the populace. Social media platforms have enabled political aspirants to capture targeted voters through e-campaign strategies like online dialogues, personalized messages and responsive discussions.[19] Through social media engagements, the political system in Nigeria is reaching more youths in a manner that the conventional mass media could not, with communications between aspirants and the youths taking a more direct approach. Online engagement is not limited to political aspirants alone but also to political parties that have realized that social media is a rich source of political following if it is used right. By keeping regular contact and giving updates, individuals initially unmotivated by the political process may become attached.

---

17. Jessica Vitak, Paul Zube, Andrew Smock, Caleb Carr, Nicole Ellison and Cliff Lampe, "Poking" People to Participate: Facebook and Political Participation in the 2008 Election." Paper presented at the annual conference of the International Communication Association, Chicago 2009, 9.

18. Soumitra Dutta and Matthew Fraser, "Obama and the 'Facebook Effect,'" *Media Post*, November 17, 2008, http://www.mediapost.com/publications/article/94861.

19. Karen Ross and Tobias Bürger, "Face to Face (Book) Social Media, Political Campaigning and the Unbearable Lightness of being there," *Political Science* 66 (2014): 46–62.

Today, there are enough shreds of evidence that support the fact that the inherent features of social media platforms make it possible to use them for several forms of political participation, such as engaging in online political discussions or playing the role of influencers by dropping notes and comments on political events as they arise. Harfoush noted that Obama's online campaign reaped immense benefits as the politician could reach new supporters and promote wider participation.[20] His successor, President Donald Trump's greatest asset was the extensive use of social media to reach the masses to win the 2016 presidential election.[21] These are enough proof that advanced countries of the world have come to understand the effectiveness of social media usage for political purposes, which is fast becoming a game changer in politics. Social media political campaigns promote disclosure and interactivity between the political class and the electorates.

The 2014 Mauritius General Elections and India's General Elections

Mauritius takes a top position in the democratic league of African countries. It is a country with an impressive democratic history worthy of emulation by any African country. The country is reputed to have a political system that upholds political rights while also giving civil liberties organizations and the media a free hand to operate.[22] In 2014, Mauritius witnessed an election with all the political parties using social media to impress the electorate. The most aggressive use of social media in the election came from the opposition parties, Alliance Lepep and other smaller parties.[23] The reason for this was not far-fetched; the opposition realized that the traditional media had become compromised, becoming a tool for the incumbent government. There was a need to exploit other media to disseminate information, and the fact that social media is freely accessible and a cheaper option made sense.

In an attempt to discredit the incumbent government, which had formed a powerful alliance with another party, the Alliance Lepep made use of Facebook to upload short videos to demonstrate the unholy relationship between the two. Although the 2014 general elections brought little constructive ideological exchange, the infusion of social media into the campaign strategies ensured that all parties had an equal footing and reached the electorates. The Alliance Lepep was successful as it wrestled power from the alliance formed by the incumbent, with the former winning 43 seats

---

20. Rahof Harfoush, *Yes, We Did! An Inside Look at how Social Media Built the Obama Brand* (New York: New Riders, 2009), 14.

21. Alfred Ng, "Donald Trump's Social Media would Doom him in a Job Interview," *cnet*, 2016, https://www.cnet.com/news/donald-trump-twitter-social-media-job-interview-tweets/.

22. Freedom House Report, "Freedom in the World," *Freedom House*, 2016, https://freedomhouse.org/sites/default/files/FH_FITW_Report_2016.pdf.

23. Roukaya Kasenally and Dooshweena Awatar, "Social Media, Elections and Political Engagements: The 2014 General Elections in Mauritius," *Journal of African Elections* 16, no. 2 (2015): 47–70.

while the latter ended up with only 13 seats. This, perhaps, is one of the major eye-openers to the strategic importance of social media in political campaigns.

In the same year, on another continent, there was the longest campaign ever recorded in India's electoral process history. The 2014 general elections in India have many unique characteristics. Among these was the use of social media to reach out to the electorates. Incidentally, the Bharatiya Janata Party (BJP) became the first party since 1984 to win an absolute majority in the country's parliament. This was possible due to the party's successful use of social media campaigns.[24] The Prime Ministerial candidate of the party, Narendra Modi, used an aggressive social media strategy throughout the campaign by ensuring that he was always online to interact and answer questions on social media from the electorates. By the end of the election, she had won the seat and gathered more than 16 million likes on his Facebook page, becoming the 6th most followed political leader on Twitter in the world.

As we have briefly identified the impact of social media on elections in advanced democracies like the USA, it is imperative to also look into the Nigerian political system. This is important for the understanding of social media and its influence on politics in the Nigerian context. Although social media has been a strong influence in the US political process for more than a decade now, it was not until the 2015 general elections before Nigeria got a taste of how impactful social media could be on elections. It is worth noting that before that, in 2011, a test run of the power of social media on the Nigerian electoral process was embarked upon. Political discourse took a whole new dimension, with the focus shifting from conventional media to social media. This resulted in overcoming a shortage of political information that has always been a feature of prior elections.

The participatory nature of Facebook became a tool of political aspirants for disseminating political information as well as campaigns and propaganda, all in a bid to sway social media users to their sides. To validate this assertion, an investigation was carried out by the Department of International Development (DFID). The result indicated that Twitter influenced and mobilized individuals to vote for particular candidates during the election.[25] This is the first time political aspirants massively utilize social media as a recruitment ground for political influencers and supporters/sympathizers. The social media space became an avenue to encourage people to vote and

24. Kalyani Chadha and Pallavi Guha, "The Bharatiya Janata Party's Online Campaign and Citizen Involvement in India's 2014 Election," *International Journal of Communication* 10 (2016): 4389–4406.

25. Jamie Bartlett, Alex Krasodomski-Jones, Nengak Daniel, Ali Fisher and Sasha Jesperson, "Social media for election communication and monitoring in Nigeria," A report prepared for the Department for International Development (DFID), 2015, https://www.demos.co.uk/wp-content/uploads/2015/11/Social-Media-in-Nigerian-Election.pdf.

follow up on the results to prevent the electoral norm of manipulation and rigging that pervades the Nigerian political system.[26]

However, the politicians were not alone in this journey. Several other groups, like non-governmental organizations and civil associations, also began using social media to influence voters' decisions. Although, the difference between them was that while the politicians were exploiting the social media space for personal agenda, the civil groups were believed to be utilizing it for charitable purposes. The general belief was that civil societies utilized social media to champion a conscientious political process that was not hinged on blind followership or sentimentalism. Several Twitter hashtags kept trending for weeks, including #GMB15 and #FeBuhari, which were used by the opposition to counter hashtags like #MeetGej and #WhyiwillvoteGEJ that the incumbent PDP government used. In the build-up to the election, the two most popular parties in Nigeria (PDP and APC) kept using social media platforms for accusations and counter-accusations relating to fraudulent activities each other.

The civil societies, on the other hand, played the role of civic rights advocates by churning out their hashtags #VoteNotFight, #NigeriaDecides and #iPledgeToVote, amongst others. The essence was to increase the awareness of the need to ensure that as many people as possible are influenced into participating in the elections. It cannot be ascertained whether it was a means of catalyzing the youths that populate the social media space to participate. But the relationship remains that youths are the largest population on social media platforms, and politicians and civil rights groups saw the need to use social media to improve political participation in Nigeria. Suffice it to say that a scholar concluded that the role of social media was deployed to shape opinions and increase the political awareness of Nigerian youths during the 2015 general elections.[27]

The 2015 general elections in Nigeria extended the battle intensities to social media on Election Day proper. Throughout the voting period, there were constant updates from both verifiable and unverifiable quarters on incidences of underage voting in the north, vote-buying in the south and nationwide arrests of individuals caught in the act of political thuggery and ballot snatching. The collation of results was another hilarious episode as virtually every social media user turned to unofficial INEC, doling out results, confirmed and unconfirmed. In the twinkle of an eye, social media had become a watchdog of the electoral process in Nigeria. Media houses and civil rights groups also used various social media handles to inform the public about results across the country.

26. Olanrewaju Abdus-Samad Temitope and Rahayu Ahmad, "The Role of Social Media During the 2015 Voting Process in the Nigeria Election," *Research Journal of Applied Sciences* 12 (2017): 281–287.

27. Fatima Ijeoma Emetumah, "Social Media as a Factor for Increased Frontiers of Democracy in Nigeria's 2015 Presidential Election," *British Journal of Education, Society & Behavioural Science* 17 (2016): 1–9.

It should also be noted that many Nigerian youths were involved in the electioneering process as the Nigerian government had recruited its ad-hoc staff from the National Youths Service Corps (NYSC). This perhaps ensured that many youths had first-hand information on election results in virtually every political ward in the country even before INEC announced the official results. As votes were counted and collated, results surfaced on social media platforms even before INEC officially announced them. Whether official or not, such results were quickly shared on various social networking sites. As observed, this added credence to the electoral process, although there were reports of little discrepancies in some areas. In this regard, the 2015 general election in Nigeria was said to have been decided and directed by social media due to its impact on the electoral process.[28]

The 2015 general elections in Nigeria revealed how much of an impact social media can wield on the electoral process. Everyone saw a unique reason to use social media to drive a particular political agenda, from political aspirants to civil rights groups and the electorates.

What remained unclear was if social media contributed to the success of the eventual winners of the elections. While scholars like Emetumah asserted that social media contributed to the success of APC in the presidential elections, others believed that social media's influence on the choice of the eventual winners was negligible.[29]

SOCIAL MEDIA AND PROPAGANDA

Most studies on the role of social media in politics have focused on identifying the positive impact of the former on the latter. Focus has always been on how the social media space is used to promote political participation, election campaigns and politically-motivated interactive sessions and interviews.[30] However, social media use for political propaganda has not generated much interest among academicians and scholars.[31] This area perhaps is important if we are to understand the full role of social media in politics in Nigeria. While research has focused on the positive impacts of social media on the political participation of youths in a system, scholars like Olabamiji and Udende have called for more research on the negative impact of social media on the political process in Nigeria.

---

28. U. E. Udoka, "Social Media and Political Effects: A Case Study of the 2015 Nigeria's Presidential Election," *International Journal of Social Science and Humanities Research* 3, no. 2 (2016): 134–141.

29. E.S. Asemah, "Use of Social Media in the 2015 Presidential Election in Nigeria," *Mass Communicator: International Journal of Communication Studies* 11 (2017): 4–11.

30. Bente Kalsnes, "The Social Media Paradox Explained: Comparing Political Parties' Facebook Strategy Versus Practice," *Social Media+ Society* 2, no. 2 (2016): 205–217.

31. Daniel Kreiss, "Seizing the Moment: The Presidential Campaigns' use of Twitter during the 2012 Electoral Cycle," *New Media and Society* 18, no. 8 (2014): 1473–1490.

That social media has suddenly become an effective tool to drive a political agenda is not news. Broadcasting of political opinions has moved away from conventional interviews and talk shows on the traditional media to participatory and interactive sessions with electorates on social media networks. And the two major sets of individuals that adopt the social media space for political purposes are the political candidates and their supporters/followers who fall amongst the larger electorates.

The use of social media for political purposes is diverse and sometimes very specific. While political candidates may use it for campaigns, political advertisements and interactional purposes, the possibility of promoting propaganda lies somewhere between these. This is because it is always difficult to ascertain certain information shared on social media platforms, especially when conventional media do not disclose such information. The freedom of speech attributed to social media creates an avenue to exploit it for covert means which may not be clear to the audience or other social media users.

In today's political battle rings, there is a persistent need for political parties and candidates to churn out information relating to ideological values, ethical arguments, and proposals of blueprints to tackle societal problems as well as political policies and goals. This is called political communication and is the process of negotiating messages relating to the objectives and rationale for political change or ideological embrace. The strategic importance of political communication fundamentally allows for including particular elements in information constantly disseminated to the public. Going by its strategic importance to political campaigns, the social media space has become a new tool for communicating and disseminating political information.

Comparing information dissemination on social media and traditional media reveals that the inherent flaws of social media usage for political purposes are higher than in the latter. Information spread through social media is mostly unregulated and unverified, and there are no measures put in place to scrutinize comments. This makes it possible for misinformation and misrepresentation to be spread by people for selfish motives. The prevalence of misinformation on social media falls under the propagandist ideology of selling what is not to the people to curry favor from them. Such favors might be in the form of promising what is impossible to achieve or tarnishing opponents' images with untrue propositions and assertions.

The propagation of false information on social media may be intentional or unintentional. However, spreading such information (either misinformation or disinformation) often leads to detrimental consequences for the intended target.

The strength of social media as an influencing platform serves to the advantage of political candidates and political parties to voice their selfish thoughts by sending out cheap propaganda with little effort. The 2015 general elections in Nigeria had their fair share of social media propaganda. Before the election, the two dominant political

parties, PDP and APC, embarked on accusations and counter-accusations while spreading false information on various social media platforms through their social media followers. Social media, rather than being a tool for championing political ideologies, became a tool for propagating unreliable information. Amongst other things, social media also became an avenue to mar the political profiles of individuals and parties, not to talk of hate messages and videos of the political class.

There were reports of various dysfunctions on the social media pages of many political aspirants in Nigeria during the 2015 general elections. Acts such as deliberate distortion of information relating to opponents, use of vulgar and abusive language and misrepresentation of facts relating to performance were freely engaged to influence the electorate.[32] With this, it is safe to affirm that social media abhors fundamental flaws which politicians, for personal gains, may exploit. Intimidating, maligning and discrediting political opponents through misleading information is the major bane of the political use of social media space. So bad was the build-up to the 2015 general elections in Nigeria that it was difficult to ascertain which social media information was true and which was not.

The aggressive use of propaganda before the 2015 general elections in Nigeria also resulted in the propagation of propaganda in the form of manifestos with unrealistic targets. The major opposition party, APC, embarked on promises which may ordinarily sound impressive to the ignorant but overly impossible to the well-informed. A vivid example of such was the proposition that there would be a ban on government officials traveling abroad for medical treatment. When the APC campaign team propagated this promise, it sounded possible to the followers. Non-partisan electorates also praised this move, believing it would curb unnecessary waste of funds for treatment abroad. It was believed that his administration would usher in a new, improved health sector that would cater to every Nigerian, irrespective of social status. Three years into his government, the president himself, Muhammadu Buhari, had traveled to the United Kingdom five times to treat various undisclosed illnesses.[33] To make it worse, after sustaining injuries from a power bike crash in the state's capital, the president's son was flown in an air ambulance to the United Kingdom for treatment. He was also flown back in a chartered aircraft, triggering a public outcry.

The change mantra, the backbone of the 2015 APC manifesto, also included the promise of ensuring that the state of origin is replaced with the state of residence in the documentation of citizens across the country. The rationale behind this was to put an end to the incessant discrimination meted on citizens by virtue of their origins. In an attempt to sway the electorate, the opposition APC pledged to initiate policies that will

---

32. Oberiri Destiny Apuke and Ivo Nkasire Apollos, "Public Perception of the Role of Facebook usage in Political Campaigns in Nigeria," *Informing Science: International Journal of Community Development & Management Studies* 1 (2017): 85–102.

33. Mayowa Tijani, "Behold the 62 Failed 2015 Election Campaign Promises of Muhammadu Buhari and APC," *TheCable*, 2019, https://www.thecable.ng/promoted-behold-the-62-failed-2015-election-campaign-promises-of-muhammadu-buhari-and-apc.

ensure that citizens become free to live and work in any part of the country by removing the state of origin, ethnicity and religious affiliations from the official documentation. Social media was agog with applause by the opposition supporters who believed that the messiah was truly around the corner. The opposition got two terms of eight years, and there was no initiative to that effect. Discrimination continues to reign even as Professor Ghali-Ibrahim affirmed that the federal government is yet to achieve the campaign promise of ending ethnic discrimination.[34] From the preceding, it is glaring that propaganda remains a key component of the Nigerian political process.

SOCIAL MEDIA AND DEMOCRATIZATION IN NIGERIA

There is no doubt that social media is changing the dynamics of Nigerian politics.[35] It has helped shape political engagements and ultimately aroused youth's interest in politics.[36] Political discourses hosted on social media platforms have facilitated political awareness and awakened national consciousness among the citizenry. The easy accessibility of social media platforms has made the youth concerned with their nation's political system. Most Nigerians who have access to social media are the youth who are now becoming more concerned about the state of the nation's affairs. With social media platforms, the youth actively engage in policies and programs of the government as well as criticize their failings. Even as the notion of youth being the leaders of tomorrow seems to be an illusion, they are taking the gauntlet, challenging the ineptitude of the leaders and putting in efforts, the larger chunk being online on social media platforms, to ensure a good leadership structure in the country.

Nigerian youth have leveraged social media platforms, especially Twitter, Facebook, and WhatsApp, to create virtual communities where deliberations concerning the nation's affairs are held, thus promoting civic engagement. It has been an age-long position that the youth are the drivers of the nation's progress; this seems to be happening if there is a consideration of how the youth have stretched political engagements on social media. Although there is still a disparity between youth political engagements on social media and physical participation in politics, social media has facilitated increasing political awareness cannot be denied. Asides from the youth, political leaders are now in terms with the knowledge that social media is a veritable tool for electioneering.[37] Thus they also have adopted these platforms to engage the

34. Ismail Mudashir and Fidelis Mac-Leva, "APC Manifesto: Questions over Buhari's Campaign Promises," *Daily Trust*, May 29, 2020.

35. Jamie Hitchen, Jonathan Fisher, Idayat Hassan and Nic Cheeseman, "Whatsapp and Nigeria's 2019 Elections: Mobilising the People, Protecting the Vote," *Africa Portal*, July 1, 2019, www.africaportal.org/publications/whatsapp-and-nigerias-2019-elections-mobilising-people-protecting-vote/.

36. Ajayi I. Ajayi and Samson A. Adesote, "The Social Media and Consolidation of Democracy in Nigeria: Uses, Potentials and Challenges," *African Journal of Sustainable Development* 6, no. 1 (2016): 93–112.

37. Adebiyi Rasheed Ademola, Ajetunmobi Umar Olansile and Olawale Jelilat Opeyemi, "Connected but not Engaged: A Tale of Two Governorship Candidates' Social Media Mobilization in a Gubernatorial Contest in Oyo State, Southwest Nigeria." *Interactions: Society and New Modernities* 38 (2020): 78–105.

cyber-citizenry on the agenda they have for the nation, as well as to disseminate information on what they have been able to achieve. In this regard, it can be posited that social media is helping in the consolidation of democracy in Nigeria. Undoubtedly, the nation's democracy is on a very shaky foundation. The fact that social media has further enhanced transparency and accountability on the part of the government cannot be ruled out.[38] In cases where there is a public uproar on the government's failings, the issues are mostly addressed on social media platforms first-hand.

Among all other social media platforms, Nigerian youth have mostly identified with Twitter, a microblogging platform, for political mobilization and participation.[39] Thus, political engagements and discourses are mostly hosted on Twitter. Scholars have posited that the predominance of political or civic engagements on Twitter is because the platform helps to shape public opinions better and influence collective action compared to other social media platforms.[40] The hashtag feature on Twitter helps collate discussions on a particular subject, making it easier for national and international engagements, which sums up the postulation that the platform has helped shape the landscape of political communication in Nigeria. Social media are also used for information purposes, especially concerning political issues in the country.[41] When the award-winning journalist David Hundeyin tweeted that the Buhari-led government had purchased cars for the Niger government, public attention was aroused. As he tweeted:

> I'm going to put this on Twitter because @WestAfricaWeek is a long-read platform that doesn't do breaking news, and this needs to be out there...
>
> Why is @MBuhari's government purchasing vehicles for a foreign government? Is this an extension of the same nonsensical decision-making that saw it prioritize a railway to Maradi?[42]

First off, before the tweet, it was not public knowledge that the Nigerian government had set aside close to 1.145 billion naira to purchase cars that would help the Nigerien government in its counter-terrorism measures. After the tweet, there were concerns about the president's affiliations with Niger. The same government had approved a

38. Ademola, Olansile and Opeyemi, "Connected but not Engaged: A Tale of Two Governorship."

39. Tunde Opeibi, "The Twittersphere as Political Engagement Space: A Study of Social Media usage in Election Campaigns in Nigeria," *Digital Studies/Le champ numérique* 9, no. 1 (2019): 1–32.

40. Michele Zappavigna, ed., *Discourse of Twitter and Social Media: How we use Language to Create Affiliation on the Web* (New York: Continuum, 2012).

41. Omobolanle Seri Fasola, Omobolanle Seri and Adekunle Emmanuel Oyadeyi, "Influence of Social Media on Youth Participation in Politics in Nigeria: A Case of the 2015/2019 General Elections." *Journal of Social Sciences and Public Policy* 13, no. 2 (2021): 1–20.

42. https://twitter.com/DavidHundeyin/status/1554575730650013697?s=20&t=Op_XwknzVcD2ha4kKHyKxw.

railway construction from Kano to the same country, while the nation begs for infrastructural development in other areas. The tweet and the engagements that trailed it forced the government to inform the public why it decided to purchase cars for another country when it struggles with counter-terrorism efforts at home. If there were no social media platforms, the news would not have filtered out as well as it did. As there is an increasing awareness of national governance, social media further helps the youth to speak against the anomalies in governance. Also, the friendly appeal of social media platforms, which is not usually the same as the public sphere, has enabled the youth to be citizen journalists who become watchdogs of the government's actions and inactions. Kperogi posits that social media has given the citizens a sort of Big Brother role that keeps them updated on national governance.[43]

Research has also revealed that social media facilitates a sort of e-government that describes the use of information and communication technologies to improve proper governance.[44] These platforms also allow for massive communication and public discourses on bad governance in Nigeria. Most of the discussions of the failings of President Buhari's government are done on Twitter, sometimes with the hashtag #Buhari[45], where the citizens often make a comparison of the current regime with the previous government; analyze the promises made by Buhari with the current realities, among a host of others. Thus, the youth bring the current leadership crisis to the fore while concomitantly stimulating the public interest in the indispensability of good governance. The #GetYourPVC trend reiterated the increasing political awareness among the citizenry on Nigerian Twittersphere.[46] The youth seemed to have realized that calling out corrupt practices or any other related vices is not enough to steer the nation's affairs to the right destination, that the bulk efforts of ensuring good governance and national development lie in getting the choice of leadership right. Thus #GetYourPVC became a reminder for the youth and the citizenry to obtain their Permanent Voters Card (PVC), a prerequisite for electing good leaders. This hashtag arguably caused a large turnout of PVC registration and collection. According to the Independent National Electoral Commission (INEC) figures on Nigerians that have obtained PVCs, there was a 14.64% increase (96.3 million total registered voters) compared to the previous figures in 2019 (84.00-million total registered voters).[47] It

43. Farooq A Kperogi, "Networked Social Journalism: Media, Citizen Participation and Democracy in Nigeria." In *Participatory Politics and Citizen Journalism in a Networked Africa*, ed. edited by Bruce Mutsvairo (London: Palgrave Macmillan, 2016), 19–33.

44. A.K. Abdulkareem, Abdullateef Ameen and Ajadi Abdulrasaq Ishola, "A Review of e-government as a Tool for Building Citizens Trust in the Nigerian Government," *Sahel Analyst: Journal of Management Sciences* 13, no. 2 (2016): 10.

45. https://twitter.com/search?q=%23Buhari&src=typeahead_click&f=top.

46. https://twitter.com/search?q=%23GetyourPVC&src=typed_query.

47. Denis Amata, "2023 Election: Completed PVC Registration Across Nigeria in 5 Charts," *Dataphyte*, August 3, 2022, https://www.dataphyte.com/latest-reports/elections/2023-election-completed-pvc-registration-across-nigeria-in-5-charts/.

can thus be confidently posited that social media is a tool for political mobilization and participation. As Dauda and Simon further contend, new media platforms such as social media platforms "are formidable forces of democracy" as they help to bridge the information gap between the rulers and the ruled, thus extending the frontiers of political interaction.[48]

Since the advent of social media, there has been a paradigm shift in the political behaviors of the youth in Nigeria.[49] Initially, the youth were seen as passive in the nation's politics and governance. However, with their active engagement on social media platforms, they are now at the forefront of the struggle for good governance. Nigerian youth have leveraged social media to promote democratic tenets that are largely absent in the nation's system of governance, which has proved effective in restructuring the leadership structure in the country as the leaders are becoming more responsive to the citizens. The government also engages with the citizenry on social media. It is imperative to note that candidates have realized the importance of the youth's support in pursuing political offices. It can be established that Nigerian youth has now become a formidable structure as Nigerian politicians cannot afford to relegate them as they had done in the past. A statistic from the electoral commission shows that the youth are the most registered voters totaling over 50% of other categories of voters. It can be thus posited that the task of getting the right leadership in 2023 was on youths.

The three major presidential candidates, Asiwaju Bola Tinubu, Atiku Abubakar and Peter Obi, constantly struggle to seek the youth's validation. Because a chunk of the Nigerian youth is available on social media, these three candidates are putting more effort into trying to win them over. For instance, during the International Youth Day celebration, the three candidates tweeted about how the youths are an integral part of every government and how they represent the future and the ideas of the Nigerian dreams. An assessment of the current political landscape predicts that the next president of Nigeria will come from the candidates above. These candidates have leveraged Twitter to enhance electoral credibility and garner political support. Among the three candidates, Peter Obi is the one that actively engages with the youth on this platform the most, fuelling sarcastic narratives that he only has an online structure that does not win elections in Nigeria. On the need for Nigerians to elect good leaders, Obi tweeted:

---

48. Dauda Ishaya Suntai and Tordue Simon Targema, "New Media and Democracy in Nigeria: An Appraisal of the Opportunities and Threats in the Terrain," *Brazilian journal of african studies* 2, no. 4 (2017): 198–209.

49. Mande Ande Mande, Lambe Kayode Mustapha, Bahiyah Omar, Maryam Lasisi Mustapha, and Ismail Sheikh Yusuf Ahmed, "Social Media Content Preferences and Political Participation among Nigerian Youths," *Romanian Journal of Communication and Public Relations* 24, no. 1 (2022): 7–23.

> Dear Nigerian Youths, as you listen to the aspirants of the ruling party jostle for their party's ticket, think and ask if they can offer tomorrow what they could not provide in 7 years; and if you are doing better than you were seven years ago.—PO #getyourpvc.[50]

The youth are passionate that Nigeria must not get it wrong in 2023, or it could be a final straw that would break the nation into smithereens. A careful observation of the Nigerian nation reveals myriad predicaments that have hindered its growth and development. It is imperative to note that under the Buhari-led government, the youth were in a hostile environment, especially when one brings to the fore the massacre of youthful protesters in Lekki over police reforms, #EndSARS. The year 2023, according to the youth, would be a game-changer, as evident in their increased political awareness, participation, and proper scrutiny of the presidential candidates.

Nigerian Twittersphere trended with the hashtag #VoteWisely.[51] This was to remind the populace that choosing another bad leader would be too much to bear, especially as a majority of Nigerians posited that it was a costly mistake voting out former President Goodluck Jonathan for current president Muhammadu Buhari. If there were to be a comparison between the administration of these two governments, surely Nigerians would prefer that of Goodluck Jonathan. The hashtag also awakened national consciousness on the importance of good leadership and how good leadership equals good governance. Tweets under this trend highlighted the need for Nigerians to actively engage the candidates to get it right.[52] As scholars have posited, good governance is the bedrock of national development; without it, a nation cannot grow.[53] Many commentaries have posited that the problem with Nigeria is the problem of bad governance. Save for the early years after independence. The country has struggled to elect good leaders and enjoy the dividends of democracy. In Nigeria, the dividends of democracy are the economic crisis and economic hardship the country and its citizens suffer from. Through the stimulation of the public interest in politics with #VoteWisely, there is becoming a change in the public perception as regards electioneering. Elections are no longer an avenue for political leaders to buy votes and voters, according to the narratives on Twittersphere. Although, these narratives are yet to take full effect in physical settings as there are still many instances of vote-buying.

Also, the Twitter space was trended with #WeCantContinueLikethis.[54] This hashtag highlighted the citizenry's frustrations with the current regime. And in truism, Nige-

50. https://twitter.com/PeterObi/status/1534286179985772544?s=20&t=9UAa6f525Z29H_1FLTeBMA.
51. https://twitter.com/search?q=%23Votewisely&src=typed_query.
52. https://twitter.com/julietkego/status/1561356042415611904?s=20&t=guEoVHqVP_1QMtiMq_BOgQ.
53. A. Chepkirui, "Principles of Good Governance," *IDOSR Journal of Arts and Humanities* 6, no. 1 (2021): 47.
54. https://twitter.com/hashtag/WeCantContinueLikeThis?src=hashtag_click.

ria cannot continue like this. It seems the nation is on auto-pilot. The prices of goods and services soar unexpectedly, and the citizens are not guaranteed adequate security. If anything, this hashtag activism foregrounds that, more than ever, the public is concerned about national growth and development. A popular presidential candidate and activist, Omoyele Sowore, criticized the current regime's inept leadership and administrative misadventure using the hashtag #WeCantContinueLikethis. Sowore was arrested for leading a protest tagged #RevolutionNow, under the allegations that he attempted to topple Buhari's governance. As he tweeted:

> To get a used car you've to go to Benin Rep, to buy gasoline in bulk you have to go to Niger Rep, to get a good education you have to go to Ghana & now to travel outside Nigeria you'd need to go to Togo. Nigeria has fallen. The giant that failed Africa. #WeCantContinueLikeThis.[55]

Nigerian Twitter users also vent their disapproval of how the country is currently run.[56]

Nigerian youth also trended #EnoughisEnough, which reiterated that there must be collaborative efforts from Nigerians in all spheres of life to ensure that the country does not face another leadership crisis like the situation they are currently experiencing. With social media, Nigerian youths are making their voices heard. Through constant communication and interaction, Nigerian youth have built a digital network that would effectively transform the nation's political history. Furthermore, the hashtag #2023Elections contextualize the fact that the youths have identified that year as the year all must be given politically to ensure that the nation is redeemed, as tweets highlighted the need for the citizenry to curb the menace of political apathy and participate in the general elections.[57] The youth have also taken online activism to the local area. A group of Nigerian musicians and entertainers, including Folarin Falana, popularly called Falz, Teniola, and Debo Adedayo, known as Mr. Macaroni, were part of a free concert organized for the youth as part of the wider efforts to arouse their political consciousness.[58] It was a free concert with PVC as the gate pass. Nigerian youth are also using Twitter for political campaigns. Tweets like #PeterObiFor2023, #Atiku, and #BATSHE dominated Nigerian Twitterspace in 2022. There were also trends with the hashtag #WeAreTheSolution which seemed to foreground that the

---

55. https://twitter.com/YeleSowore/status/1560580839972319232?s=20&t=0pgWDKC5chsikq-uzSDEZA.

56. https://twitter.com/AdejumoKabir2/status/1560893384356761601?s=20&t=0pgWDKC5chsikq-uzSDEZA.

57. https://twitter.com/hashtag/2023Elections?src=hashtag_click.

58. The Will. "2Baba, Falz, others to hold Free Concert in Lagos, Make PVC Compulsory Entry Ticket," *The Will*, June 10, 2022. https://thewillnigeria.com/news/2baba-falz-others-to-hold-free-concert-in-lagos-make-pvc-compulsory-entry-ticket/.

citizens' right choice of leadership would solve the nation's myriad of problems.[59] Tweets included the need for a leader with a developmental ideology to steer the nation's affairs.[60] There was also #RevolutionNow, with tweets reiterating the dire need for the citizenry to take an active part in governance and continue their collective efforts for a better Nigeria. There was also a trend with the hashtag #Enikure,[61] with tweets that condemned the Buhari-led government's administrative failures and Nigerian leaders' general intellectual impotence. The trend mainly had tweets by the Lagos-based lawyer and author of Do Not Die in Their War, Dele Farotimi, who often tweeted on Nigeria's leadership crisis under President Buhari. He often condemned Buhari's ethnoreligious bigotry[62] and inspires Nigerians to get it right at the general elections.

A coterie of Nigerian youths who are musicians, and media influencers, among others, have used their social media accounts to criticize the nation's political affairs. Rinu Oduala, the prominent #EndSARS activist, often criticized bad governance and corruption practices in the Buhari-led government. As she tweeted:

> "Bad governance no dey look tribe."
> When Nigerian soldiers went to the Lekki Toll Gate, they didn't ask protesters which tribe they came from.
> They just started shooting."
> #RinuSpaces #2023Elections"[63]

She also catalyzed the citizenry to elect astute and visionary leaders come 2023. Also, Debo Adedayo (Mr. Macaroni) called Nigerians to put in collective efforts, unite in the face of adversities, and not allow themselves to become pawns for corrupt political leaders.[64] In another tweet, he criticizes the corrupt practices among Nigerian politicians, alluding to reports where termites were reported to have eaten billions of naira. Mr. Macaroni questioned the rationality behind singing praises of politicians when they commission one or two projects they are bound to do as the government.[65] Another prominent EndSARS activist, Aisha Yesufu, tweeted that the citizenry should be involved in governance. As she tweeted:

---

59. https://twitter.com/hashtag/WeAreTheSolution?src=hashtag_click.

60. https://twitter.com/aaclagosyouths/status/1559213163928764417?s=20&t=nFdFOjz7oWIJO-qQOtfoacQ.

61. https://twitter.com/hashtag/Enikure?src=hashtag_click.

62. https://twitter.com/DeleFarotimi/status/1561225072085458945?s=20&t=Y80Gk1DqN4Ed-pY-9J43lag.

63. https://twitter.com/SavvyRinu/status/1543312382130360320?s=20&t=xyXLHJMEVOMR4i-o2DH4IUQ.

64. https://twitter.com/mrmacaronii/status/1523951346675822592?s=20&t=PVcNtPSdK0pn4ZSl-HX4yEw.

65. https://twitter.com/mrmacaronii/status/1560539849353994241?s=20&t=RIGFlIt-YIF0lJlzrM-wc1A.

"If those who give us bad governance do not give up, we also have no business giving up!
The fight for a great Nigeria is on!
#GetYourPVC
#1For5PVC"[66]

The masses have largely been rendered passive in the nation's governance, and it seemed they were content with it. Yesufu's tweets underscore that the people are part and parcel of governance and must continue their struggle for a greater Nigeria.

THE WAY FORWARD FOR CREDIBLE ELECTIONS

Political participation has taken a new dimension in Nigeria with the advent of social media. The mass following of elections and political processes in Nigeria has taken another turn, going by how social media platforms were used for various purposes, albeit formally and informally. The plethora of political engagements on social media platforms has ignited the consciousness of Nigerian society's reluctant but important political strata: the youths. To them, everything about Nigeria elections is bad because electoral mandates have turned into purchased commodities, hence not reflecting the true position of things.

People can now sit in the comfort of their homes and be actively engaged in the political process. Several years before the advent of social media platforms, the average Nigerian youth perceived political participation as a waste of time and effort, owing to the large-scale electoral malpractices that seemed to have enveloped the political process in Nigeria. In truth, such a stance is blameless when we look holistically at the level of misconduct exhibited in the political sphere by the various incumbent governments and their political opponents.

A most astounding improvement that has been evident since the emergence of social media is the improvement of freedom of speech. Social networking sites have accorded citizens the much-sought platform for expressing their thoughts. Criticism of political officeholders and the government has risen due to reduced fear of harassment or arrest. In the past, politicians and political candidates have been misled by their sycophant followers. Praise singers are wont to perpetually engage in acts that paint false pictures of mass acceptance of political candidates and government policies at the grass-root level. However, social media has opened up the avenue to confirm the popularity of various government policies. A vivid example was the nationwide condemnation of the federal government-sponsored rural grazing reserve project. So loud was the agitation against the initiative was so loud that the federal government was left with no option but to suspend it.

66. https://twitter.com/AishaYesufu/status/1495716150793183233?s=20&t=bV9wSctSqB3eNAaOURMoSw.

Also, social media can serve as an effective tool for combating the spate of electoral violence that permeates the political landscape of Nigeria. The perpetrators of electoral vices such as ballot snatching and physical harassment of voters will automatically be restrained from their practices, knowing fully well that such acts can be recorded and posted on social media platforms for all to see. This can serve as a deterrent for such practices that politicians recruit to cause mayhem during elections.

On the part of political candidates, social media has raised the bar of communal engagements. The political class is becoming more aware that social media is beginning to change how the electorates respond to political issues in the build-up to elections and after. For any aspirant intending to take up elected office in Nigeria, there is a need to carefully put plans in place to use social networking sites for interactional purposes if such wants to enjoy the inherent benefits of social media. Nigerian politicians can emulate their counterparts in the western world, who have seen the strategic importance of social media communication as an effective tool for shaping their images in the eyes of the electorates.

Rather than being reactionary, politicians can proactively integrate social media into their campaign practices to target the youths, whose numerical strength is enough to sway voters. Going forward, Nigerian politicians need to harness the avalanche of social media platforms provided by internet technology to market their ideologies and manifestos to gain more support from the electorates, especially the youths. It is not enough to merely gather followers on social media; rather, there should be plans to inform them of the policies and programs they should expect. Political engagements on social media that are established to inform electorates on expected policies and programs will automatically serve as references that can be revisited in the future. This will curb the incidences of empty promises that have become Nigerian politicians' bane.

As a developing nation, political leaders must use social media engagements as a cost-cutting technique for seeking public opinion on governmental and political issues. This would ensure that the will and opinion of the masses are crucial to any policies that the government intends to undertake. In the 2015 election, social media worked effectively for Muhammadu Buhari, as social media platforms were agog with live situation reporting from the citizens. Much of the information shared on social media would have been subjected to filtration if they were left in the hands of the traditional media.

Social media lends credence to participatory democracy by granting some degree of transparency and accuracy to the political process. In countries like Nigeria, where political participation is reluctant, social media has abhorred the capability of measuring public opinion. In essence, the role of social media as a tool for driving political participation, especially among the youth, cannot be underestimated. The world is embracing digitalization, with technology becoming an important determinant of

how we interact and interrelate. Nigeria, as a nation, cannot afford to be left behind. The need to embrace technology is paramount for effective and qualitative political participation. Countries like the USA have already developed online voting platforms. While this may seem expensive, it lends more credibility to the electoral process and will go a long way to reduce electoral malpractices, ensuring freer and fairer elections in the future.

However, it is equally ideal to consider the political class's negative use of social media. In Nigeria's 2015 and 2019 general elections, the political propaganda instituted in party campaigns was huge. Bearing this in mind, there is a need to put in place measures to discourage politicians and their supporters from using social media to propagate dysfunctional messages before and during elections. The legislative assembly should include, in the electoral reforms currently being debated, severe punishment for the indiscriminate use of social media for disseminating propaganda and misinforming the public. There should be a means of monitoring and regulating the various social media platforms to minimize the inherent weaknesses while also maximizing the intrinsic values of information and communication technology in the electoral process. To achieve this, the various laws regulating media engagement should be reviewed to address the technicalities of the new media technologies.

Lastly, political parties in Nigeria have turned social media into effective weapons to attack and undermine the images of political opponents. A cursory look at the 2015 and 2019 elections will point at gross character assassinations by the two major parties, PDP and APC. There were allegations and counter-allegations by supporters of both parties, which resulted in the spread of false information on social media. For democracy to thrive in Nigeria, political parties need to operate within ethical boundaries; rather than engaging in electoral warfare. Political parties should be encouraged to promote their ideologies without the need to degrade or maim the profiles of alleged opponents in the name of electioneering. The political use of social media should be precipitated on the doctrine of truth and honesty, as these will enable the electorates to have an undiluted perspective of political issues. It is only through this that Nigerians can get efficient people into government.

On the part of the government, there is a need to find means of mobilizing support for policies and projects before executing or implementing them. The government must ensure constant communication through social media on planned projects and initiatives, especially when the benefits of such initiatives are not fully understood. This would assist in quelling any tension such initiatives may generate. Beyond politics and governance, individuals, non-governmental organizations, civil societies and other bodies that want to pursue any genuine agenda involving the youths can exploit the immense benefits of social media platforms as mobilization grounds for such causes. Just like the Arab Spring swept across the Arab countries, genuine political causes can always be kick-started from social networking sites.

10

SORO-SOKE

#ENDSARS and Youth Resistance

The #ENDSARS hashtag was a massive campaign, initially launched around 2017 by human rights defenders and social activists. Segun Awosanya's (popularly known as Segalink) Twitter handle is prominent among these leaders. The #ENDSARS campaign was initiated to draw attention to the gross human rights violations perpetually committed by a special arm of the Nigeria Police Force, tasked with fighting violent crimes like kidnapping and armed robberies in Nigeria.

The online campaign against the activities of the police officers drafted into the SARS unit started with a petition by the convener of the movement, Segun Awosanya, which was initially signed by more than ten thousand Nigerians, and subsequently submitted to the National assembly. The petition, which sought to scrap the police unit, was embarked upon on the backdrop of a video footage showing the extrajudicial killing of a man. Within 12 hours of signing the online petition, the #ENDSARS hashtag became a trending topic on Twitter, with more than 400,000 tweets on the first day alone. From this time onwards, the #ENDSARS hashtag became a recurring topic anytime the unlawful activities of police officers are being discussed on social media.

The widespread documentation of extrajudicial killings, torture and wanton extortions by police officers drafted to this special unit culminated in a protest of unprecedented magnitude on the shores of Nigeria. Citizens of the country marched out in

great numbers calling for the proscription of the special unit and bringing to justice officers that, in the past, have been confirmed to perpetrate such acts. With videos of police brutality and extortion constantly circulated as pieces of evidence against the police unit, the Nigeria Police Force, after initial denials of the involvement of their personnel, finally admitted to their complicity with a promise of real reforms.

While the initial campaigns against police brutality in Nigeria have always stayed on social media, keen observers will understand that it was just a matter of time before the campaign spilled over to the streets if nothing was done to limit the excesses of the SARS operatives. Several isolated cases of police brutality in several parts of the country, especially in the south, led to a mass protest in October 2020, with young Nigerians turning out across various states to agitate for the scrapping of the dreaded SARS police unit. During the campaign, various shreds of evidence and accusations were presented to show the atrocities police officers committed without recourse to justice or established protocols. The campaign also went a step further to expose the depth of the rot within the police system, Segun Awosanya revealed that the Nigeria Police Force operates a non-recognizable code of conduct or operational responsibilities. Further stressing his assertions, he affirmed that the SARS unit had become a consortium of corrupt police officers who perceived themselves as self-styled judges and executioners with little or no respect for the fundamental human rights of citizens, especially young people.

A BRIEF HISTORY OF SARS

The Special Anti-Robbery Squad (SARS) was established in 1992 when there was a high prevalence of armed robberies in the southwestern region of Nigeria. Amongst such notorious armed robbers was Shina Rambo, whose terror reign shook the nooks and crannies of Lagos and its environs before the formation of the SARS. The SARS was mandated to operate like a faceless arm, performing undercover and violent confrontations with armed robbers in the southwest. The need for the unit spread to other states across Nigeria as time passed, with little done about its structure and codes of conduct.

There have been recurring fears amidst reports of police brutality since the turn of the millennium. The Nigerian movie industry, Nollywood, provided its fair share of police brutality through several movie productions, indicating the travails many citizens go through in the hands of corrupt and trigger-happy police officers who can kill for the flimsiest of excuses. However, we should not forget that the SARS had initially played its roles effectively in combating violent crimes across Nigeria at the early formation of the unit.

According to CSP Simeon Danladi, the police officer that was instrumental in setting up the SARS police unit, the special unit, one of the 14 crime and investigations divisions in the Nigeria Police Force, has deviated from its initial mandate.

Looking at the deviation over the years, it is safe to assume that the SARS unit has transformed from an effective crime-fighting unit to one that wears the robe of impunity with pride. The matter is made worse by the fact that the personnel drafted into the unit act like state officials who, by their duties, are immune to justice, irrespective of the criminality they perpetrate in the course of discharging their duties.

Rather than continue to fight crimes for which they were established, the SARS has become somewhat of a terrorist cell, inflicting unimaginable terror on the citizens they have sworn to protect. The several stories about SARS officers' impunity are a microcosm of the Nigeria Police Force that has continued to deteriorate over the years. Since the days of the military regime, the impunity of Nigeria's police personnel has been unimpressive, with several instances of the Nigerian government using the police to quell any demonstration or agitation against it. For instance, in April 1978, the police force killed several armless Nigerian undergraduates for having the temerity to query the policies of the Olusegun Obasanjo military regime. Also, in 1981, an award-winning athlete, Dele Udoh, was gunned down over an argument with a police officer.

The "Kill and Go" label as a tag for the Nigeria Police Force has turned the security apparatus into a shameless brand. In Nigeria, trying to become a police officer already creates an impression of a corruptible mind. Despite their special designation, SARS officers do not spare anyone in their reign of impunity. To become their victim, you only need to drive a good car, wear a sporty look, speak like a foreigner and hold an expensive smartphone. And when they do not find anyone fitting into this description, they can go as far as prying into people's bags in random stops and searches. In this case, just about anything becomes an object of suspicion.

Instead of embarking on legitimate acts to curb armed robbery and violent crimes in Nigeria, the SARS unit appears to be part and parcel of the crimes within the country. The motivating factor for a significant proportion of the personnel drafted into the unit was access to illegal money since they believed belonging to the unit gave them additional powers to use firearms without recourse to ammunition audit.

THE #ENDSARS PROTESTS IN RETROSPECT

The #ENDSARS protest was a campaign against the police over an issue that had dragged on for a considerable period before the protests. To understand the importance of such protests, one must understand the history of police brutality in Nigeria. From the colonial period, the creation of the Nigeria Police Force was to promote the agenda of the colonialists.[1] The resistance against colonial rule in several communities reinforced the need for a legitimate armed agency that would use force to sup-

1. Human Rights Watch, ""Rest in Pieces": Police Torture and Deaths in Custody in Nigeria," *Human Rights Watch*, July 27, 2005, https://www.hrw.org:https://www.hrw.org/report/2005/07/27/rest-pieces/police-torture-and-deaths-custody-nigeria.

Figure 10.1. "Sorosoke EndSARS" by Michael Efionayi. A depiction of Aisha Yesufu and other #EndSARS protesters.

press the people's resistance. First created for the Colony of Lagos in 1861, the use of violence by the newly created security force instantly established a disconnection between itself and the people. This foundational disconnect between the protectors and the protected resulted in a perception that the former had already failed in its responsibilities towards the latter. "Police is your friend" is a cliché in Nigerian parlance used to describe the relationship between the security outfits and the citizenry; the police are not your friend. This local parlance is an ironic rendition seen in police stations and posts, indicating that the Nigeria Police Force is the citizens' friend. The reason for the people twisting such terminology is not unconnected with the fact that the Nigeria Police Force has persistently harassed and assaulted the people; hence there is low level of trust for the men in black uniform. This perhaps explains why the notorious police unit known as SARS never had a good reputation amongst the people. The abuse of power by law enforcement agencies in Nigeria is not limited to the police force alone; however, the ever-constant contact between the police force and the civilian populace always puts the two on a coalition course.

The local and international media have long described the relationship between law enforcement agencies and the citizens they are mandated to protect as one built on the bedrock of extortions, brutality and unlawful arrests.[2] Incidences of police officers mounting checkpoints for the sole purpose of extorting money from motorists are rife in many cities across Nigeria. Unfortunately, the helpless motorists do not have the wherewithal to discountenance such corrupt practices since non-conformity is accompanied by threats to kill such motorists. In the local terminology, it is normal to hear an armed police officer say, "I will shoot you, and nothing will happen." The concluding part of the statement forewarns the potential victim that in the case of an actual shooting, the police officer might not have to face any consequence. This is not a new practice.

The SARS unit has a long reputation for unlawful arrests, harassment, extortion, and invasion of people's privacy without recourse to fundamental human rights. It might not have become a public outcry if the dreaded unit had not taken their abuse of citizens' rights further by engaging in random extrajudicial killings. Kelechi Madu, Canada's first Black Justice Minister and Solicitor for the government of Alberta, narrated how some officers of the SARS unit killed his cousin, Christiantus Nwabueze, sometime in 2013.[3] In his narrative, he affirmed sending a petition to the country's National Assembly for a probe to be set up for the case. Unfortunately, the Nigeria Police Force did everything possible to ensure that the investigation never yielded any positives. While this is not the only documented complaint against the officers of SARS in Nigeria, it speaks volumes. There are several gory narratives of the painful experiences of many individuals in the hands of this dreaded unit. Despite the constant complaints of the people, the Nigerian government simply turned a deaf ear, doing next to nothing to get the situation to change.

From its inception, the #ENDSARS campaign has been gathering increasing attention. With over a thousand tweets on Twitter detailing the daily incidences of SARS brutality in cities across Nigeria, the traditional media was compelled to follow suit in reporting such atrocities. Perhaps, this validates the assertion that social media can only drive public opinion when the object of attention is successfully transferred and received by the traditional media.[4] Local traditional media in Nigeria were obliged to follow up on the initial Twitter reports of SARS brutality. For instance, a report by Business Day Newspaper detailed the launching of the Twitter #ENDSARS campaign. This was also followed up by international media, such as the BBC, detailing the horrifying acts of police brutality found in videos posted on Twitter.

2. Amnesty International, "Nigeria: Special Police Squad 'Get Rich' Torturing Detainees and Demanding Bribes in Exchange for Freedom," *Amnesty International*, September 21, 2016, https://www.amnesty.org/en/latest/news/2016/09/nigeriaspecial-police-squad-get-rich-torturing-detainees/.

3. Sodiq Oyeleke, "Changing SARS Name not Significant Reform, Alberta, Justice Minister, Kaycee Madu," *The Punch*, October 18, 2020.

4. E. Gidengil, *Canadian Democracy from the Ground Up: Perceptions and Performance* (Vancouver: UBC Press, 2014).

October 2020 will, for a long time, linger in the memories of Nigerians for two major reasons, one being that Nigeria celebrated 60 years of independence from colonial rule. Little did anyone imagine that a few days after the independence celebrations, the nation would witness nationwide demonstrations that would shake the major cities across the country. The last straw was a video circulated on social media, which pointed at yet another extrajudicial killing by men of the SARS unit. As with most modern protests, the demonstration started from the social media space, with several individuals and celebrities calling for the disbandment of the SARS unit. The #ENDSARS hashtag, which had become a mainstay on Twitter, began trending again. Suffice it to say that this was not the first time calls had been made on social media for the disbandment of the SARS police unit. Every time such a call was made, the government only played lip service by promising to find a lasting solution to the problem.

However, this time, the protest was not going to end on social media, as various individuals began to recount their ordeals in the hands of these trigger-happy officers. Just as we have seen in the past, online activisms through hashtags are strategic to offline activism as the former creates the needed awareness to engage in the latter. Online activism creates awareness and an avenue to demand solutions from the appropriate quarters and set an agenda for the public. As noted by Olson, online and offline activisms are symbiotic as each strengthens and grows the other.[5] This played out perfectly during the #ENDSARS protests.

In response to these ordeals and pent-up anger against an unresponsive government, the youths took to the streets in large swaths, blocking major highways and interlink roads, thereby halting economic activities in Lagos, Abuja and other major cities across the country. The demonstrations intensify from the early days of October. What started as a three-day protest to call for the disbandment of SARS would eventually last for fourteen days. On the first day of the protest (October 7), large swaths of youths embarked on a march towards the Police Force Headquarters with placards carrying various messages such as "Protect, not exploit," Nigerian Police, stop killing us."[6]

As days passed, the protests spread across the country, with national and international celebrities lending their voices to the situation and expressing support for the protesters. To assuage the tempers of the protesters, the President Buhari-led administration finally yielded on October 11 by announcing the disbandment of the SARS unit. This was not enough, as many activists deemed the government response as a temporary solution that did not adequately tackle the past misconducts of the police officers in the SARS unit.

---

5. C. Olson, "#BringBackOurGirls: Digital Communities Supporting Real-world Change and Influencing Mainstream Media Agendas," *Feminist Media Studies* 16, no. 5 (2016): 772-787.

6. Nairametrics, "#ENDSARS: A Day by Day Timeline of the Protest that has brought Nigeria to its Knees," *Nairametrics*, 2020, https://nairametrics.com/2020/10/25/endsars-protest-a-timeline-of-all-the-major-events-from-october-3rd/.

The protesters, true to their intent, introduced another dimension by raising the bar of their demands to include broader improvements in governance. From #ENDSARS, the protesters' agitation metamorphosed into #EndPoliceBrutality and ultimately to #EndBadGovernance. Perhaps, the change in the demand of the protesters gave impetus for continuous protests days after the federal government announced the disbandment of the SARS unit. Despite affirming the absence of leadership, the protesters came up with a five-point demand for the government to look into; if there is any possibility of peacefully ending the protest. These included:

- Ensuring that all victims of police brutality and their families are compensated and the perpetrators brought to book;
- Setting up with immediate effect, an independent body that will investigate the several complaints of the victims with a view of prosecuting the perpetrators;
- Wholesale psychological re-evaluation of all police officers drafted to the SARS unit before assigning them to other units;
- Immediate increment of the salary structure of the police force to reduce their extortion; and
- The unconditional release of all protesters that have been arrested across Nigeria.

The government, not knowing how to effectively end the protests, used the usual tactics of force to quell them. On October 20, 2020, the epicenter of the Lagos #ENDSARS protests (Lekki Toll Gate) witnessed the appearance of soldiers, allegedly from Dodan barracks, disrupting the peaceful protests through the use of live fire. This resulted in the killing of several protesters while hundreds experienced various degrees of injuries. This violent crackdown was globally condemned, but as with many other repressible acts from dictatorial and insincere governments, the deed had been done.

It should also be noted that the #ENDSARS campaign was initially downplayed as a mere political gimmick and not a social agitation. However, the reality dawned on the government as the movement grew rapidly, eventually getting so big that it forced the government's hands into disbanding the SARS unit of the Nigeria Police Force. It also warranted the government to examine the atrocities concerning the protesters' demands.

The #ENDSARS protests did also have their bad sides. While one set of vibrant young Nigerians who truly wanted change marched out to let the government understand the reality on the ground, another set of young Nigerians perceived the protests as the perfect avenue to embark on dangerous and ill-motivated missions. The widescale destruction of public properties and looting of selected private properties was unprecedented. In Lagos, shops belonging to private citizens were vandalized and looted, especially those that were unfortunate to have proximity to the famous Shoprite malls. It may also be said that specific properties belonging to known and

prominent politicians were targeted. Although the two groups of young Nigerians were operating on parallel grounds, it would be sheer hypocrisy to shy away from reality; they share a common disdain for those in power.

While young, vibrant, educated Nigerians were strategically making their grievances known to the government in respect of police brutality, their semi-educated and destructive contemporaries indulged in sabotaging acts that, if not checked, may lead the country to a total breakdown of law and order. If the government had been playing the diplomatic card with the brave youths involved in the #ENDSARS Protests, the same would not work with the other group embarking on anarchy. To this end, it became imperative that the government find an emergency solution to the problem at hand. Nevertheless, the major highlight of the destruction points to one fact; the people, having languished in poverty and hardships for too long, were ready to burn the country to the ground if need be.

Realizing that it could no longer use the diplomatic card to treat the #ENDSARS Protests and the accompanying imbroglio, the government missed the step as expected. To quell the ongoing destruction, curfews were imposed in several states and cities where the #ENDSARS Protests had the strongest holds, and the state security apparatuses were called in once again to secure lives and properties. While it was imperative to get the saboteurs off the dangerous mission, the peaceful #ENDSARS protesters should have read the writings on the wall and returned to their shells, perhaps to re-strategize and come up with a counter-plan. However, the leaderless structure of the protesters resulted in total hatred of the imposed curfew, an indication of a group daring the government.

Prominent members of the protests, Aisha Yesufu and Falz the Bahd Guy, initially used their respective social media handles to persuade the #ENDSARS protesters to obey the curfew imposition and move away from their various protest points across the country. On October 19, 2020, the Abuja end of the protests met with army formations that successfully took them off the streets. The curfew in Lagos was announced the next day, with instructions for all and sundry to be off the streets by 4 pm. This was to curtail the continuous sabotage of government properties and looting of private properties. The peaceful protesters that gathered at the Lekki Toll Gate were not going to have any of this, defying all odds to continue the protests until late evening.

THE LEGITIMACY OF THE # ENDSARS' PROTESTS

Nigeria is a signatory to several international human rights treaties that discourage torture and brutality by state security apparatus. The prohibition of torture under international law was first recognized in 1948 under Article 5 of the Universal Declaration of Human Rights (UDH). Subsequent regional and international human rights laws were framed from this particular document. A cursory look at the Nigerian constitution, while prohibiting the use of torture, did not explicitly criminalize it.

According to Section 34 (1) of the Nigerian Constitution, every individual is entitled to respect for the dignity of his person, and no person shall be subjected to torture or inhuman or degrading treatment.

While there have been attempts in the past by Nigerian governments to set up preventive mechanisms against torture and police brutality, such mechanisms have suffered neglect and lacked the resources to effectively carry out their objectives. For instance, the National Committee Against Torture (NCAT), set up in 2009, has continually complained about the government not allocating the requisite resources stated in the agency's yearly operational budgets. The first attempt to criminalize torture and inhuman treatment by security apparatus was made by President Buhari, who, in 2017, signed into law the Nigerian Anti-Torture Act, which provides penalties for violations. However, this has not stopped officers of the Nigeria Police Force, as well as SARS, from embarking on actions that violate citizens' fundamental human rights. Juxtaposing the Nigeria Police Force Order 237 (which guides the use of firearms by the police) with the United Nations Basic Principles on the use of firearms by law enforcement agents, one can conclude that the Nigerian constitution is a far cry from granting the citizens internationally accepted standards of human rights.

The Anti-Torture Bill sought to prohibit and criminalize incidences of torture by all law enforcement agents. According to the Bill, **any person who tortures another, as defined in Section 4 of this Act, is guilty of an offense and is liable on conviction to imprisonment for a term not exceeding twenty-five years.** The import of this law was that any act of torture by security agents becomes a crime punishable by law. However, the law's signage has not stopped the gross use of torture by SARS officers in several of their outposts, with no officer being charged for crimes bordering on torture. To enable the easy implementation of the law, the federal government made arrangements for training and education of the personnel in SARS on the need to abide by the law. The safeguards against falling into the crime were not enough motivation for the overly-corrupt SARS officers to act with some level of sanity.

The notoriety of SARS officers' wanton torture, arrest and summary execution of suspects reached a crescendo between 2014 and 2016 when the international human rights organizations decided to embark on extensive investigations on the subject matter. The result of the report, published in September 2016, affirmed that the Nigeria Police Force has a unit that was supposed to combat violent crimes. Rather than discharge their duties, this unit had been systematically torturing detainees in its custody on the pretense of extracting confessional statements from them.[7] Following the reports of several human rights violations, it became imperative to ascertain specific locations where such atrocities are committed. This led to the digging up of a place that was later tagged the headquarters of human rights violations in Nigeria. This place is located deep within the southeastern state of Anambra in Nigeria.

7. Udoru Orizu, "Gory Tales from Awkuzu SARS in Anambra," *Thisday*, October 20, 2020.

When one begins to highlight the eyewitness accounts of the notorious SARS outpost in Oyi Local Government Area of Anambra State, it becomes imperative to ascertain if truly the government educated the so-called SARS officers on the Anti-Torture Law. Referred to as Awkuzu SARS, individuals who had contact with the outpost-turned-torture-center never had good stories to tell. With a five-level cell structure, the SARS outpost was designed to inflict varying degrees of physical, emotional and psychological trauma on detainees, depending on the gravity of the offense hung on the suspect's head. While reporters are often called in to be treated to the parade of suspects with allegations of kidnappings, armed robberies, and internet fraud, some journalists reported that subsequent interviews of some of these suspects often rubbished the claims of their oppressors.

Coming out alive from Akwuzu is a very low probability. There are times when people arrested for trumped charges are summarily executed before the victim's family has the chance to secure his or her bail.[8] Other reports claim that the cells of Awkuzu SARS often become so congested that the officers intermittently kill some innocent detainees rather than release them. Reports of decomposing bodies of up to 35 people were found floating on the Ezu River along the boundaries between Anambra and Enugu states. Awkuzu SARS is not far from this river. It took a series of investigations that lasted several years before it was proven beyond doubt that the bodies found floating on the river were dumped there by SARS officers from the Awkuzu unit.

Among the notable cases of gross misconduct by SARS Akwuzu was the case of Miracle Onwe, a young man who was accused of laptop theft and subsequently detained in the notorious detention center. According to the victim's report, the unit's commander directed the officers to hang him upside down with ropes and hit him with all manner of iron till he became unconscious. He would later gain consciousness inside an interrogation hall.[9] After being denied food for close to forty days, surviving on water smuggled into his cell by other inmates, he was taken to court and subsequently charged with armed robbery; the case was later thrown out of court for lack of evidence. Miracle told Amnesty International that up to eight of his fellow detainees died of starvation during his incarceration. What made the situation worse was that Miracle wrote the then Inspector General of Police, seeking an investigation of his illegal detainment and assault; he never got any reasonable response from the IGP.

One would have expected that the passage of the Anti-Torture Bill into Law would force the hands of these torture merchants, but that was not the case. The case of Sunday Bang, some months after the president signed the Anti-Torture Bill into law, perhaps opened the people's eyes to the vanity of expecting any reorientation from these dreaded Police units. The young Sunday was a robbery suspect because he vis-

8. Vincent Ujumadu, "Awkuzu SARS: Nigeria's Most Dreaded Specialized Police Unit," *Vanguard Newspaper*, October 17, 2020.

9. Amnesty International Interview, 2017.

ited his girlfriend's home a few hours before the robbery. Detained for five weeks without access to his legal counsel, he was beaten with hardwood on his hands and legs until blood loss left him unconscious.[10] Today, the young man, an amateur boxer, could not follow his dream of professional boxing again. Pieces of evidence suggested that his hands were specifically targeted for torture. Eventually, the main robbers were apprehended. However, the SARS criminals refused to release the innocent man, fearing that his physical appearance would lead to charges being pressed against them for illegal torture and harassment.

THE FEMINIST ANGLE OF THE #ENDSARS PROTESTS

If there is one thing that stands out in the #ENDSARS protests, it has to be the strategic involvement of women. In a patriarchal nation like Nigeria, the assumption is that women should be excluded from violent or aggressive political engagements. While in the past, the likes of Queen Amina of Zaria, Moremi, and Madam Efunroye Tinubu etched their names in the annals of history, many other women could not claim the mantle of leadership. Although Nigerian women have been involved in gender equality agitations for quite some time, one would never have believed that they would be the major heroes of the #ENDSARS protests. While the nation's history often downplays the contributions of female activists as mere appendages of their male counterparts, it should be noted that women have been actively involved in agitations dating back to colonial times. For instance, the late Olufunmilayo Ransome-Kuti successfully participated in and led demonstrations against the colonial government, despite not being given the requisite permits for such engagements. All these withered after independence, with little seen in active feminine participation in social change movements and reforms.

The Nigerian women were suddenly brought to the fore once again on the backdrop of the #ENDSARS protests. Perhaps a distinctive character of the #ENDSARS protests is that prominent young women rose to steer and sustain an agitation against police brutality in Nigeria. Noteworthy is the fact that most high-profile SARS harassment was meted out on young Nigerians, including cases of sexual assault against women.

When the #ENDSARS protests began in October 2020, there was a general conception that the movement was devoid of organized leadership or central authority coordinating the affairs. This may be far from the truth. While it may be difficult to attribute leadership to the protests, one cannot fail to admit that the funds that kept the movement going for days came from somewhere. The protesters must thank a non-governmental organization called "The Feminist Coalition." A cursory look at the group's official website will impress on the reader a group of young Nigerian fem-

10. Amnesty International Interview, 2018.

inists whose mission is to champion equality for women in Nigerian society, focusing on education, financial freedom, and representation in public office.[11] It is rather innovative seeing a group of feminists coming together to advocate for not only gender equality but also good governance. Consisting of 14 women from varying backgrounds, the Feminist Coalition became the unofficial voice of the #ENDSARS Protests, raising close to $40,000 to support the protests across Nigeria.

When Feyikemi Abudu and her co-host, Jola Ayeye, were speaking about their frustrations with the conduct of SARS officers in one of their podcasts in 2017, little did these two know that they would be much involved three years later to serve as support system providers for a greater wave of agitation against SARS officers. Both based in Lagos, they became a core part of the #ENDSARS protests by disseminating information through their respective social media handles and being part of a network of fundraisers and disbursers for protesters across Lagos. Being part of the Feminist Coalition group, they represent an increasing hope for gender equality in Nigeria.

As protesters filed on the roads, depending solely on selves, rejecting donations from various political interest groups and assisting one another with needs, they could not resist the mouth-watering mutual aids in the form of donations that the Feminist Coalition sought to make available for the protesters across Nigeria. Sourcing finances from crowd-funding and international bodies, the Feminist Coalition was able to stand as the bedrock of the #ENDSARS Protests during and after the Lekki Shooting debacle. As Rinu Oduala (a notable female social reformer) noted, the #ENDSARS Protests would not have succeeded for long without the assistance coming from the Feminist Coalition.[12] Rinu Oduala, in addition to being part of the protests, would raise up to $10,500 to support protest logistics during the struggle. Not only did the group provide logistics and other strategic aids to the #ENDSARS movement, but they also provided medical help for the injured protesters while assisting with the legal process of ensuring the release of the protesters who had been arrested in the course of the demonstrations.

With several social reform groups like Sowore's RevolutionNow trying endlessly to play an active role in the #ENDSARS protests, only the Feminist Coalition was lucky enough to get the undiluted alliance with the youths who had hitherto stood on the fact that they did not want the protests to have any known leadership. Perhaps, this was borne out of the fact that it would be difficult for the government to eventually clamp down on anyone in the aftermath of the struggle. Also, there was some disdain for existing social reform groups, as the protesting youths believed such organizations might end up taking unnecessary glory, which may lead to exploiting such for per-

---

11. Feminist Coalition official website.

12. Shayera Dark, "Female Leadership in Nigeria's ENDSARS Movement helped it Grow, Then Gave it Staying Power," *Quartz Africa*, November 3, 2020, https://qz.com/africa/1925923/female-leadership-in-nigerias-endsars-protests-was-vital/.

sonal motives. As one of the protesters noted, "Nobody should be allowed to ride on the #ENDSARS Protests for political gains."[13]

The level of transparency displayed by the Feminist Coalition is worth applauding. Giving a day-by-day analysis of funds collected and disbursed, the group was able to once again underpin the manner of leadership that Nigerians should embrace. At a time when the government had quelled the protests, the Feminist Coalition made use of the social handles and official website to communicate to all parties that they had ceased sourcing for funds, and what was left of the unspent monies were channeled at medical and legal interventions for those involved in the protests. Consoling every Nigerian who had lost any loved one during the struggle, the group admonished the youths to withdraw to their shells and stay alive for future engagements, adding that what was paramount was the welfare and safety of the Nigerian Youth.[14]

One woman that will forever be remembered whenever the #ENDSARS protests come up for discussion is Aisha Yesufu. Coming from an ethnic group with the least tolerance for women's political activism, Aisha Yesufu carved a name for herself as a co-organizer of the famous Bring Back Our Girls movement that agitated for the safe return of the Chibok schoolgirls that Boko Haram terrorists abducted in 2014. Attired in a flowing hijab, Aisha Yesufu's picture became a de facto symbol of the #ENDSARS protests. On October 10, 2020, she defied all odds to lead the #ENDSARS protests in Abuja without caring about police harassment. In one of her narratives, she spoke of her boldness and refusal to cower in the face of police presence, holding her fist up in an environment where law enforcement agents were shooting to disperse the protesting crowd. Her famous pose in hijab with her fist raised high has been tagged the "Nigerian Statue of Liberty" and will forever remain in the hearts of Nigerians involved in the #ENDSARS struggles. In her interview with BBC, Aisha Yesufu affirmed her role in the #ENDSARS protests and further spoke about her motivations for being active.[15] One could easily understand that she was compelled to make a difference for the country's youths.

Another female Nigerian whose exploits during the #ENDSARS protests are worth mentioning is Catherine Udeh, popular known as DJ Switch. Being a celebrity, she not only risked her career as one of the many females on the frontline of the protests but also risked her life to make sure that a perspective that would hitherto have been suppressed came to the fore; the incident of the Lekki Toll Gate shooting. Despite the majority of the celebrities withdrawing from the Lekki Toll Gate end of the Lagos #ENDSARS protests when the curfew was announced, the youthful DJ Switch re-

---

13. Innocent Etteng, "#ENDSARS: Inside Nigeria's Fight to End Police Brutality," *Yes Magazine*, October 29, 2020, https://www.yesmagazine.org/social-justice/2020/10/29/nigeria-end-sars-protests/.

14. Morenike Taire and Ebunoluwa Sessou, "Feminist Coalition Directs Youths to Stay Home," *Vanguard Newspaper*, 2020.

15. "Aisha Yesufu: ENDSARS is a Fight for the Next generations of Nigerian," *British Broadcasting Corporation*, 2020, https://www.bbc.com/news/av/world-africa-54577611.

mained on the ground and was credited with a live-streamed video of the army shooting that fateful evening. Many Nigerians owe her an appreciation for her courage to ensure that people had a glimpse of the shooting as it unfolded.

With the increased agitation for gender equality in Nigeria for some time now, it is not difficult to understand the reasons for women's unequaled participation in the #ENDSARS struggle. Many have been primed to engage in agitations so much that it has become second nature. Talking about her involvement in the #ENDSARS protests, Oluwaseun Ayodeji Osowobi, a female rights activist whose organization, "Stand To End Rape," seeks mental support for victims of gender-based violence, affirmed that nobody, irrespective of gender, is safe from police brutality in Nigeria. She spoke further of women who had lost their children to police brutality, those who had been raped and sexually harassed by law enforcement agents, and those who had died due to such experiences. To her, rising against police brutality is a responsibility that every woman should be motivated to join. As Abudu noted in one of her interviews, the need for women to be at the top at every level of society becomes more important, especially in an inherently patriarchal country. Through their active involvement in coordinating the #ENDSARS protests, Nigerian women are willing to lead the country when the need arises. The success of their respective involvement perhaps indicates that they would not fail the country when such leadership tasks are placed on their part.

EXPLAINING THE #ENDSARS PROTESTS

As pointed out earlier, the #ENDSARS protests represent pent-up anger over several problems that have compounded the woes of Nigerians for a long time. The government's gross failure to implement adequate development and growth through governance has turned every government official into a lawbreaker and a potentially corrupt individual. The absence of prompt and effective investigations into several cases of torture and harassment by law enforcement agents in Nigeria has resulted in a climate where impunity reigns supreme. Before the #ENDSARS protests, no instance of punishment was meted out on erring police officers and the SARS personnel.

The Nigeria Police Force has continued to show a lack of zeal to regulate and monitor the conduct of its officers while on duty. While receiving hundreds of petitions affirming the gross misconduct of police personnel in discharging their duties, the Nigeria Police Force never sees it obligatory to investigate claims of such misconduct until it gets beyond salvage. Even though the Police Force has an internal review mechanism that recommends punitive actions against any erring police personnel in the face of professional misconduct, the partiality and bias often introduced into such processes ensure nothing substantial is ever witnessed. To ensure an effective response to citizens' complaints, the Complaint Response Unit (CRU) was initiated in 2015. The CRU's failure to prosecute erring police officers gives the impression of a paper tiger. Amnesty International reportedly met with the CRU, requesting informa-

Figure 10.2. "End Police Brutality" by Dr. Kazeem Ekeolu. Aisha Yesufu and other EndSARS protesters are protesting against police brutality in Nigeria.

tion on the number of complaints successfully handled. Nothing meaningful was produced, validating that the CRU was only established as a Public Relations gimmick.[16] The various moves by the Nigeria Police Force to institute control mechanisms over the conduct of its officers have so far ended in null, with nothing as evidence to show that there are effective mechanisms to deal with erring officers.

The absence of an effective mechanism to ensure justice for victims of human rights violations by law enforcement agents in Nigeria is one catalyst to the #ENDSARS Protests. In 2016, a coalition of human rights organizations raised a petition against a particular SARS officer named James Nwafor, stationed in the dreaded Awkuzu, concerning gross human rights violations.[17] All attempts to get the IGP to investigate the petition amounted to nothing, with Amnesty International later reporting that no SARS officer was brought to account for the petition. The SARS officer was subsequently transferred to another unit in a show of power. This act is evidently against the principles of International laws since it is expected that governments are saddled with the responsibility of giving justice to the people whose human rights have been violated. When eventually there seems to be a possibility of seeking redress in the law courts, victims are faced with a judicial system that drags such complaints with snail-like speed. In some cases, police officers and their cohorts may threaten to silence individuals who intend to get justice for the violation of their rights.

Several reports of SARS officers torturing innocent people to force them to implicate themselves and own up to crimes they did not commit is another factor that may have triggered the #ENDSARS protests. There was the sad case of John Eze, an undergraduate who was arrested along with his friends on the grounds of their engagement in a campus fraternity. Their detainment in Anambra was followed by days of being subjected to all manners of torture. According to the victim, the torture resulted from their reluctance to admit to charges they knew nothing about.[18] Unfortunately, the victim had to admit to something he was innocent of, and the officers subsequently communicated this to his parents, demanding hefty sums to secure his bail. When an agreement could not be reached, John's case was transferred to court on the grounds of belonging to an unlawful association. The court eventually granted bail to John, with the prosecuting police officer later telling John that he would have shot him in the leg if he knew John was going to get a good lawyer to secure his bail.

---

16. Amnesty International Interview Abuja, 2018.

17. Okey Nwanguma, "A Call for Prompt, Impartial and Exhaustive Investigation of CSP James Nwafor of Special Anti-Robbery Squad (SARS) Awkuzu, Anambra State," *Sahara Reporters*, January 18, 2015, https://saharareporters.com/2015/01/18/noprin-calls-igp-investigate-activities-csp-james-nwafor-and-check-impunity-special-anti.

18. Amnesty International, "Nigeria: Time to End Impunity, Torture and other Violations by Special Anti-robbery Squad (SARS)," *Amnesty International*, June 26, 2020, https://www.amnesty.org/en/documents/afr44/9505/2020/en/.

Against the backdrop of the #ENDSARS agitations, some quarters believed that #ReformSARS should have been the agitation. While such a perspective may sound rational, the government's antecedent of failed reform promises nullified such a standpoint. In the past, the Nigerian government had planned and communicated its readiness to reform SARS, with no movement of such ever coming to light. In 2008, a Presidential Committee was set up to recommend ways to reform the Nigeria Police Force despite the step was taken in 2006 and the recommendation was yet to be implemented. The reason is not far-fetched, there was a change in administration in 2007, and the administration had no trust in the recommendations set out by the committee of the past administration.

To calm the nerves of #ENDSARS agitators in 2018, the Buhari-led administration called for a total overhaul of the SARS unit based on accusations of human rights violations by members of the unit. Human Rights offices were set up in Police commands, while the federal government mandated the state-controlled Human Rights Commission to institute a panel to investigate reported cases of unlawful detention, extortion, and inhuman treatment of innocent citizens. From the complaints received, the panel recommended the dismissal of 37 SARS officers and further prosecution of 24 others. As reported by Amnesty International in May 2020, the recommendation has yet to be adopted. In succinct terms, it becomes arduous to convince anyone that SARS reform was viable for ending the constant incidences of police brutality in Nigeria.

IMPLICATIONS OF THE #ENDSARS PROTESTS

It is evident that a new social contract is currently being drawn in Nigeria. Nigerians are on the path of establishing a new understanding of how public servants are expected to relate to the people. The #ENDSARS protests represent Nigerians' most significant attempt to rise against instances of police forces acting with impunity over the citizens they swore to protect. The protest is unprecedented, going by the standards of organized demonstrations in Nigeria. Like other agitations, the government used the superior force of the law enforcement apparatus to suppress the participants. The pattern of exploiting state security agencies to quell agitations in Nigeria is an inheritance from the British colonialists. When one remembers the Aba Women's War of 1929 and the Enugu Colliery Strike of 1949, the trend of government deploying quasi-military forces to subjugate citizens becomes evident. However, the present crop of Nigerian youths do not harbor any memories of military rule and its accompanying brutality. Unlike the older generation, they do not have their psyche etched to fear men in uniform.

The #ENDSARS protests changed the status quo by creating a powerful movement driven by young, vibrant Nigerians who embarked on a two-week agitation that shook the government to its roots. Nigeria's youth involvement in protests dates back

to colonial times; the independence agitation also started as a youth protest. Unlike in the past, the young, vibrant protesters that took the stage of the #ENDSARS protests allegedly trooped into the streets with no identifiable leadership structure to coordinate and manage the situation. This may not be true, owing to the level of organization and the open-source funding embarked upon by NGOs like the Feminist Coalition.

Noteworthy is the fact that the #ENDSARS protests presented a once-in-a-lifetime opportunity for the youths to force the leadership into addressing critical issues affecting the people. The various state governments are beginning to understand the importance of developing a good relationship with those they govern. The #ENDSARS protests became an avenue for young Nigerians to voice their resentment of the persistently failed leadership that has handicapped the nation's progress for decades. This may be in accordance with a former president, Olusegun Obasanjo's statement that the country is sitting on a keg of gunpowder concerning the younger generations.[19] While the leaders thought the protest was another attempt at mischief by the younger generation, they had a change in perception as the protests dragged on for days continuously. To this end, the success of the protests can be ascertained by the eventual disbandment of the SARs Unit, as well as the setting up of panels to investigate the atrocities of law enforcement agents before and during the protests. The implication is that Nigerian youths have shown the determination and confidence needed to bring about the desired change. Coming at a time when the #BLACKLIVES MATTER protests in the USA are still fresh in memory, the #ENDSARS protests have only served as further evidence of the impunity of police brutality upon perceived marginalized communities.

The level of cohesion, from financing the movement through crowd-funding to the provision of medical and legal services in the aftermath of the protests, is a pointer to the fact that the country can get better only when those saddled with the responsibilities of administration are not motivated by personal gain. To get the vibrant protesters off the streets, the government embarked on a series of actions, with states such as Lagos, Edo, Oyo, Delta and others setting up judicial commissions to look into the atrocities of SARS. The states also set up emergency support funds as compensation for victims of police brutality. Suffice it to say that this was a rare occasion when the Nigerian government succumbed to the people's demands. As part of attempts to assuage the tempers of the protesters, the Minister of Justice, Abubakar Malami, set up a committee headed by the Executive Secretary of the National Human Rights Commission, Tony Ojukwu, who summarily recommended the dismissal of 35 SARS personnel who had been fingered in various forms of misconduct, including extrajudicial killings.

---

19. Biola Kay, "#ENDSARS will never be Forgotten in the Nigerian History," *Brumpost*, 2020, https://www.brumpost.com/endsars-will-never-be-forgotten-in-the-nigerian-history/.

One symbolic meaning to the deployment of the military to unarmed protesters in Lekki is that the country's democracy is yet to understand the true principles of its existence. While the country's leadership prides itself on being civilian, the military instinct remains. The Buhari government was willing to take actions bordering on totalitarianism. The refusal of the president to address the citizens' concerns as at when due points to the ineffectual leadership that the country was enveloped in. As many believed, his silence on the issue indicates an unconcerned, unsympathetic leader's body language.

In all these, there is growing optimism that Nigerian youths are beginning to wield their powers, showcasing the capacity to stage agitations that will compel the country's leadership to accede to their demands. While the demonstration might have been over, the success gained with the bravery of the protesters is a step in the right direction for Nigeria and Africa at large. The protests have reignited a new level of political consciousness among the youths who had hitherto displayed a non-committal mindset to politics and governance in Nigeria. The nationwide disillusionment and disorientation concerning the state of the economy have suddenly become the major talking points among the citizens.

Given the relevance of Nigeria in Africa, the #ENDSARS protests are bound to command continental attention. It is more than likely that social activists and reformists in other African countries will borrow a leaf from the Nigeria model to develop their agitations. While the protests may seem over, the supporters will concentrate more on observing how the government treats their demands. They have shown the spirits of warriors who have chosen to live to fight another day. They have simply designed a template for future social agitations to hold the government more accountable and responsible to the people. The fact that young men and women could come together to make the government jittery indicates the dawn of a new era where those managing the system will have to ensure that the system works for all and not a few privileged individuals. The #ENDSARS protests changed the political space: it has opened the people's minds to the fact that they can achieve a lot whenever they come together to fight for a common goal. This is one of the key ingredients for people ready to move to the next level.

WHAT DO WE EXPECT TO SEE IN THE FUTURE?

Expecting anything different from what has been obtainable in the past from the Nigeria Police Force is a mirage. Established against the backdrop of colonial administration, the Nigeria Police Force, from inception, has acted as a tool for suppression, domination, and humiliation. These antecedents make it an aberration to expect something different. Times without number, panels and committees have been set up to reform the Nigeria Police Force. This has been constantly complemented by civil society groups and the international community drawing attention to the gross hu-

man rights abuses by the police force. The failure of the country's leadership to find a permanent solution to the impunity of police officers indicates a never-ending problem. The establishment of another police unit to take over the responsibilities of SARS may look good on paper; however, without wholesale reorientation of the police officers, it will only amount to putting old wine in a new bottle.

One clear thing about the #ENDSARS campaign is that it expressed the youth's prowess. The protest was not limited to agitations against police brutality alone; rather, it was the result of pent-up angst against a country whose leadership has continually mismanaged its affairs. It is an agitation against using power to allow the free reign of impunity not just by security agencies alone but by the Nigerian government. While the younger generation had waited patiently for the older ones to set the pace for a total revamp of the public sector, they have grown weary and are now showing signs of taking the bulls by the horns.

The #ENDSARS protest has produced a new and emerging set of heroes and liberators. Social reformers like Omoyele Sowore and his supporters acted as a spark to ignite the fire, while the likes of Aisha Yesufu, Segun Awosanya, Folarin Falana (Falz), Debo Adedayo (Mr. Macaroni), Catherine Udeh (DJ Switch), Rinu Oduala and a host of others have stood up to be counted in the list of emerging heroes of a new Nigerian nation. The youths are now leading themselves rather than waiting to be led by the older generation, who have led them in the wrong direction for a long time.

There is a need to reform the Nigeria Police Force and other law enforcement agencies. Eradicating the rot in the Nigerian system does not stop at the law enforcement agencies' doorstep; rather, there is a need for mass reorientation in all MDAs. Getting the right people at the helm of affairs is sacrosanct if any improvement is to be experienced.

It is noteworthy that the #ENDSARS protests are unequaled when we look at the size, duration, and international publicity they gathered. Beginning early in October, the protests received the support of international celebrities worldwide, including artists such as Drake, Trey Songs, Diddy and many others.[20] Nairametrics also reported that female celebrities like Beyonce, Rihanna and Nicki Minaj also used their social media handles to lend a voice to the #ENDSARS protests.

Despite operating from the shadows, the brains behind the protests should be applauded for the swift way they organized and ensured that the protesters lacked virtually nothing on the various battlefronts. Worthy of note was the prosthetic leg given to one female protester who initially had one of her legs amputated. The manner of effective organization and management evidenced by the activities of the fundraisers

20. Karla Rodriguez, Drake, "Burna Boy, Diddy and more stars Show Support for Nigeria's #ENDSARS Movement," *Revolt TV*, October 11, 2020, https://www.revolt.tv/2020/10/11/21511426/celebrities-show-support-for-endsars-movement-in-nigeria.

and other strategists is a microcosm of the expectation of the people from the Nigerian government.

The #ENDSARS protests of October 2020 will go down in the annals of Nigeria's history as a time when the youths rose to challenge the excesses of government agencies without fear of intimidation, imprisonment or harassment. The protests indicate a shift from the old mindset of fearfully succumbing to the whims of the government to a fearless agitation that was only suppressed by the power of the gun. It will be on record as one of those rare moments when Nigerians rose beyond ethnic bigotry and ethnic sentiments to collectively speak out against the barriers to national development: bad governance, oppressive reign of impunity by government officials, injustice, and police brutality.

At the surface level, the #EndSARS protest seems like a revolution against police brutality that transcended into a societal menace; but on a closer look, it becomes obvious that it also encompassed a form of political revolution/resistance embarked on by the youth against their leaders. By and large, the youths are absent in the governance structure, and those in power have no real plans for them. As the rate of unemployment increases, the youths are left loitering in the streets to pursue employment opportunities. The EndSARS movement thus helped to jolt the youth back into political consciousness. It further emboldened them to advocate for what is right, which are the policies and programs that would empower them and place them on the pedestal of development. It could be argued that the sociopolitical climate limits the youth from excelling. How can the youths represent the dreams and aspirations of the Nigerian project when there are no measures to achieve this?

The EndSARS movement has ultimately enlightened the youth on the dire need for political participation. The youth are at the forefront of political struggles and national development. It could be argued that the system had relegated them for too long, and they seem to have taken up the challenge to advance good governance. In saner climes, the youth represents the symbol or agents of change, and any serious government aiming at holistic national development would consider them in their plans. The Nigerian government arguably does not have plans for the majority of the masses, not to talk of the youth who have been said many times to be the future leaders. President Buhari had first irked the youths when he described them as lazy. This arguably showed that the government does not see the youths as change agents. Also, political leaders have capitalized on the desperation of the youths in their quest for excellence to employ them as thugs during election periods.

Youth activism is still ongoing. The dream for a better Nigeria still lives in the hearts of the youths as they have leveraged social media platforms to pursue their quest for excellence. The youths are now becoming more daring in condemning bad governance. The aftermath of the #EndSARS protest did not seem to slow them down. They have often posited that the memories of the Lekki Massacre would forever push them in the quest for a better Nigeria. On Twitter, Facebook, Instagram

and a host of other social media platforms, the youths are rebellious against the government, as evident in their online activism. They now seem to be more politically conscious. The United Nations Youth Strategy (2030) stipulates that the youth have the resilience to inspire political changes and development in their respective nations. This seems to be happening in Nigeria. Nigerian youths created a wall between themselves and the Buhari government. On numerous occasions, Mr. Macaroni, Falz, amongst a host of other prominent youths rejected any participation or collaboration with the government as many among them hoped that a different set of leaders will emerge in 2023.

The political awareness that characterizes youth activism is drawn from personal experiences, notably the #EndSARS protest. And as the government continues to deny the massacre and blame the youth as perpetrators of violence, the latter continues to preserve the memories of those who lost their lives. Hashtags like #WeWillNotForget had dominated the Nigerian Twittersphere, and tweets acknowledging those who lost their lives in the quest for good governance. The hashtag also reminded the youth of the dire need to participate in governance and elect good leaders at the general elections. Undoubtedly, October 2020 would forever be the darkest point in the history of the nation's democracy when the Nigerian government fired live bullets at its citizens. Aisha Yesufu tweeted:

> May the souls of all those that were killed during #EndSars continue to rest in peace. May God give their families, friends and loved ones the fortitude to bear the loss.
> #AfterTheTearsWhatNext.
> #EndSARSMemorial #NigeriaMustWorkInOurLifetime.[21]

This hashtag activism served as a wake-up call for most youth to see to the emergence of leaders passionate about youth development and not one that limits their growth. For instance, Mr. Macaroni urged the youths to consider the events of October 2020 before choosing leaders. As he tweeted:

> Dear Nigerian Youth, when that time comes to cast your vote, remember the pain and sadness from October 2020, remember the lack of an enabling environment for you to succeed as a citizen of Nigeria. By then, No one will need to tell you who to vote for!!!
> VOTE WISELY![22]

---

21. https://twitter.com/AishaYesufu/status/1455132454348591107?s=20&t=b618bWU6BwQHhRkwlKBddg.

22. https://twitter.com/mrmacaronii/status/1559122852338700289?s=20&t=B_VfNfrXXQUf1sDxahoeg.

The Nigerian Twittersphere has also been trended with #EndSARSMemorial, highlighting the events at the Toll Gate and preserving the memories of the dead. When trends like this dominate Twitter, posts are laced with political undertones. As stated earlier, the events of 2020 affected the youths' psyche regarding their nation's political development. Tweets under this hashtag also criticized the government for the plan it placed on Twitter.[23]

As a result of the hostile environment, most youths are keyed into the plans of leaving Nigeria and starting afresh in foreign countries. Rinu Oduala, one of the prominent #EndSARS activists, left the country for elsewhere, perhaps as a safety measure. Also, the convener of the #EndSARS movement, Segun Awosanya (Segalink), left the country. There are no official estimates of youths who have left the country. It seemed to have reached the point where the youths thought the only solution was to leave Nigeria. We cannot talk about national development without bringing the youths into the central focus. Those who are staying back to agitate for good governance deserve to be credited. The best form of change the country can experience is good leadership; the weapon of change is voting for the right candidates.

There were also trends like #NigeriaMustWorkInOurLifetime, reiterating youthful enthusiasm for the country to improve. Under the hashtag, former Minister of Education, Oby Ezekwesili, catalyzed the youth to be united and collected in checkmating what she described as "political monopolists." According to her tweet:

> "The day Africa'sAfrica's Women and Youth discover their leverage and collectively say, "Enough!" it will be Checkmate! to our Political Monopolists.
> Question is, "will they ever overcome the Collective Action Dilemma?"
> That's the real obstacle.[24]

Twitter has given the platform for youth resistance as they have leveraged it to call out bad leadership, among other challenges the nation faces. Twitter has become a platform where the youth cultivate political knowledge, which is effective for national development. It has also given them the power to drive the nation to change and seek social justice, especially for those killed in cold blood on October 2020. The government has not taken responsibility for the gruesome murders. Despite the White Paper released by the Lagos State Judicial Panel of Inquiry for EndSARS victims that stated explicitly that there was a massacre, the government has only shifted the blame.

Furthermore, the youths are determined to pursue their dreams for a greater Nigeria. The EndSARS movement has reignited the need for political participation. Nigerian youths now see the need to be involved in governance and wield power to

---

23. https://twitter.com/akintollgate/status/1457749125383049219?s=20&t=b618bWU6BwQHhRkwlKBddg.

24. https://twitter.com/obyezeks/status/1499053405544800259?s=20&t=Dt5bLDiOOl_ZC7A0e9Sx8g.

control political narratives. Despite the numerous challenges, they have managed to forge ahead. Many commentaries have posited that it takes youthful afflatus to drive the nation to progress. Often the youths have been charged to take the gauntlet, and now they seem to have keyed into this narrative. The youths call out government inadequacies on social media platforms and defy their anti-populist policies.

The youths no longer resign their fates to the hope that something good will come. The first step in the restructuring of Nigeria is in the area of leadership. The country seems to have been cursed with bad leadership. The government has not largely represented the people's wishes, and it does not seem easy to survive in an environment where the governors do not put the masses at the center of their policies. When the youths trend a hashtag criticizing bad governance, the government believes they have been sponsored by the opposition party to bring down the country. If the government were self-reflective, they would have known that the citizenry had coped with them for too long without enjoying the dividends of democracy. The youth have remained largely politically aware and are the ones to shoulder the burden of national development. And to achieve this, they need to be at the forefront of political struggles and be relentless in their clamors for good governance.

PART C

PROMINENT FIGURES

11

PIUS ADESANMI

The Pursuit of Knowledge

INTRODUCTION

Pius Adesanmi was one of the very first Nigerian scholars to discover and maximize the use of social media. The world that Adesanmi created was an interconnected space, all thanks to social media.[1] Through social media, as Adesanmi did, human beings have now fully understood the need to uphold common ties and shared affinity, which international organizations have struggled to foster. One of the huge importance of social media is the networking opportunities and cultural ties created, considering the diversities and complexities of this ever-evolving world.[2] As social media began to dominate the Nigerian digital space, it fulfilled, as expectedly, the recognition of Nigerians' oneness. Social media created an avenue for Nigerians to communicate frequently, share jokes, dialogue on important societal or national issues, understand one another better, and the likes. It could be argued that social media is a unifying factor in Nigerian politics.[3] However, this does not mean that the dominance or heavy reliance on social media

1. Simeon Edosomwan, Sitalaskshmi Kalangot Prakasan, Doriane Kouame, Jonelle Watson and Tom Seymour, "The History of Social Media and its Impact on Business," *Journal of Applied Management and Entrepreneurship* 16, no. 3 (2011): 79.
2. Brian D. Loader and Dan Mercea, *Social Media and Democracy* (London: Routledge, 2012), 275.
3. Ifeoma Vivian Dunu and Chinwe Elizabeth Uzochukwu, "Social Media: An Effective Tool for Social Mobilization in Nigeria," *Journal of Humanities and Social Science* 20, no. 4, (2015): 10–21.

does not bring along its disadvantages.[4] Adesanmi was a preeminent symbol of what social media represented to Nigeria.

As social media becomes a platform for important discourses rather than entertainment, citizens and academic scholars engage social media for elaborate discussions, especially on Nigerian politics. After all, the political system is the basic structure in which the framework of a nation stands.[5] Social media platforms, most especially Mark Zuckerberg-owned Facebook, give ample room for the uncontrolled flow of communication on issues of national importance, which would not have been effective in the public sphere.[6] Social media thus became an important channel for commenting on the affairs of the nations. Discourses on social media also achieved wider deliberations and consultations.

Adebola Adesanmi, university professor, writer, poet, and critic, was among the numerous academics who identified social media as a veritable tool for critiquing the nation's affairs. He effectively employed social media platforms such as Facebook and Twitter to comment on the state of national affairs and how it continued to crumble despite the widespread optimism that projected it as the African superpower after independence. For Adesanmi, perhaps the most efficient way to get the citizens and other stakeholders concerned about the progress of their fatherland was by engaging them on a common platform that does not enhance the class stratification mostly associated with the Nigerian public sphere. Both Facebook and Twitter accommodate the old and the young, the rich and the poor, and all genders;[7] thus, Adesanmi effectively used his teeming influence as a social media paladin to capture the attention of his fellow Nigerian citizens on the political, social, economic, and even spiritual happenings of the nation.

This chapter explores the literary presence of the master satirist, Adesanmi, on social media platforms, how he was able to unify citizens' discussions on the realities within their milieu, and how this attempted to shape the dynamics of the nation's political system. Adesanmi, known for his ideological translucence and unfearful and unabashed acerbic but witty remarks on Nigeria's politics, achieved a role model status among the younger generation who employ social media as a tool for opposing the government's divide-and-rule policies.

It is agreeable that the Nigerian intellectual circle is full of thousands of scholars and commentators whose nimble works and thoughts are worthy of being examined. But Adesanmi fits into the trajectory of the context of this book with the peculiarities

4. Adil Jamil Zaru, "Effect of Social Media on Society," *International Journal of New Technology and Research* 2 (2016): 39–44.

5. G. Shabbir Cheema, *Building Democratic Institutions: Governance Reform in Developing Countries* (Connecticut: Kumarian Press, 2005).

6. Clay Shirky, "The Political Power of Social Media: Technology, the Public Sphere and Political Change," *Foreign Affairs* 90, no. 1 (2011): 28–41.

7. Shirky, "The Political Power of Social Media," 28–41.

Figure 11.1. "Pius Adesanmi's Naija No Dey Carry Last" by Michael Efionayi. One of Pius Adesanmi's popular books and a depiction of his discussion.

of the niches it plugs into. Adesanmi had clear-cut convictions about the benefits of social media and utilized it to its loftiest reach of possibilities and benefits. If a conversation was made around social media and its interrelatedness with Nigerian society and issues raised within it, Adesanmi's dexterous thoughts and insights could not be missed as they were pertinent to this phenomenon.

Adesanmi's views and convictions were expressed in an analytical approach, carefully putting issues into perspective, criticizing with necessary details, and making recommendations with contemporary peculiarities in mind. He made his acerbic positions objectively, passing them across with the instrumentalities of scholarly orientations and social media dynamics. His ideas about Nigeria and expectations of Africa as a continent provided arrays of useful materials and ideas for understanding.

He successfully expressed them, making thousands of his followers on Facebook and Twitter inclined to anticipate them. He held physical and social media audiences at the horn, commanding attention and creating positive impressions. Hence, his place as a prominent figure who interacted with major themes in Nigeria vis-à-vis the peculiarities of social media drew interest and, as such, needs to be discussed.

Adesanmi's interactions and opinions showed his dynamic inclinations across all reasonable social issues. He was always ready to pass his take on matters that cut across politics, social values, economics, security, and other sectors that affect the Nigerian state. His diversity of opinion and special attention to Nigeria and Africa and how they relate to global issues also fostered the selection of his views as worthy ecclesiastics.

BIOGRAPHY

If Adesanmi had a say in selecting the country of his birth, he would have chosen Nigeria for many obvious reasons. Nigeria, to Adesanmi, represents a country that has failed to explore its full potential. It is now known as "a crippled giant,"[8] to borrow Eghosa Osaghae's phrase, that needs urgent reforms and revolutions. He once said he was in an "abusive relationship" with Nigeria. He put it squarely in an interview:

> I am in an abusive relationship with Nigeria. No experience can reduce my commitment to Nigeria, no matter how horrific. Nigeria is that nasty, abusive, beastly husband who is physically violent, beats and hurts you but you remain in that relationship and people wonder why.[9]

Born to the Adesanmi family on February 27, 1972, in the small community of Isanlu in the Yagba Local Government Area of Kogi State, Nigeria,[10] Adesanmi created an impression of himself as a precocious child while growing up. In the early stages of his life, he showed that he was to explore the world of letters, leaving an indelible milestone in the industry of books as soon as he set his feet in it. Becoming a literary maverick is a deliberate process: Adesanmi took his time to sail through the ocean of books, consuming all sorts of books—fiction, non-fiction, and historical books—which proved instrumental in his expertise in the art and craft of writing as

8. Eghosa E. Osaghae, *Crippled Giant: Nigeria Since Independence* (Bloomington: Indiana University Press, 1998).

9. Pius Adesanmi, "Exclusive: Pius Adesanmi's Last Interview—Near Death Experience, Abusive Relationship, Buhari's Cluelessness," *Premium Times*, March 19, 2019, https://www.premiumtimesng.com/news/headlines/320882-exclusive-pius-adesanmis-last-interview-near-death-accident-abusive-relationship-buharis-cluelessness.html.

10. Pius Adesanmi, "Professor Pius Adesanmi: Award-Winning Writer, Activist and Academician," *Konnect Africa*, 2013, http://www.konnectafrica.net/professor-pius-adesanmi-award-winning-writer-activist-and-academician/.

well as honed his style. Adesanmi had his secondary education at Titcombe College, Egbe, Kogi State.[11] The school provided a fertile ground for Adesanmi's future literary harvests.[12] After his secondary school education, he proceeded to the University of Ilorin, Kwara State, where he graduated summa cum laude in French in 1992.[13] Perhaps due to its growing influence as the acclaimed hub of cultural and literary creativity, Adesanmi bagged a Master's degree in French at the University of Ibadan in 1998.[14] It could be said that Adesanmi's fruitful relationship with literary bigwigs such as Niyi Osundare and Femi Osofisan during his study at the University of Ibadan was instrumental in defining his literary career. Also, his symbiotic interactions with emerging poets of the late 1990s, such as Remi Raji-Oyelade and others, helped give Adesanmi's literary career a strong footing.[15]

For an uncanny man like Adesanmi, a little learning is dangerous; to assuage his relentless thirst for knowledge, he pursued a Ph.D. in French Studies from the University of British Columbia, Canada, and graduated in 2002.[16] Adesanmi's uncanny thoughts were evident in his literary and research works as he perfected a style not similar to many, which perhaps accounted for the meteoric rise in his literary and academic career. Adesanmi would later take up a teaching position as an Assistant Professor of Comparative Studies at the University of Pennsylvania, United States of America, between 2002 and 2005.[17] He was awarded a US green card within these years.

Furthermore, his brilliant pedagogical skills and excellent research output played key factors. The ebullient African scholar left the University of Pennsylvania to take up another teaching position as a Literature and African Studies professor at the University of Ottawa, Canada, from 2006 until his tragic death in 2019.[18] Due to his scholarly output, Adesanmi was a Fellow of the French Institute for Research in Africa (IFRA) between 1993 and 1997 and a fellow of the French Institute of South Africa (IFAS) between 1998 and 2000.[19] His research interests mainly cut across African literature and studies, and he wrote and spoke extensively on the dire need for Africa

11. Pius Adesanmi, "Someone once Advised me to Try and be like Reno Omokri so I can make it Instead of making Noise all the Time," *Jarushub*, March 30, 2013, https://www.jarushub.com/somebody-once-advised-me-to-try-and-be-like-reno-omokri-so-i-can-also-make-it-instead-of-making-noise-all-the-time-pius-adesanmi/.

12. Adesanmi, "Someone Once Advised me."

13. A. Ibrahim, "Pius Adesanmi for ANA Convention," *Daily Trust*, October 7, 2012..

14. Ibrahim, "Pius Adesanmi for ANA Convention."

15. Adesanmi, "Someone Once Advised me."

16. Adesanmi, "Someone Once Advised me."

17. Ibrahim, "Pius Adesanmi for ANA Convention."

18. BBC, "Ethiopian Airlines: The Victims of 'a Global Tragedy,'" *BBC News*, April 4, 2019, https://www.bbc.com/news/world-africa-47522028.

19. Ibrahim, "Pius Adesanmi for ANA Convention."

to reconnect with its roots and recognize its potential to be acknowledged as a super force by the Western world.[20]

Adesanmi was a widely traveled scholar and served as visiting lecturer to universities in Europe, Africa, and North America. He was a household name in leading newspapers in Nigeria, where he wrote articles with political undertones.[21] For many of his followers, the way he criticized the socio-political realities in the country was in a simple but not simplistic language, without fear or favor. He wrote critical essays in peer-reviewed journals, contributed literary reviews, and edited books. Adesanmi's overall excellence in literary creativity was evident in bagging the Association of Nigerian Authors' Prize in 2001 for his poetry collection *The Wayfarer and Other Poems*.[22] He also won the inaugural Penguin Prize for African Writing in the non-fiction category for his 2010 book, *You're Not a Country, Africa*![23] He was also an awardee of the Canadian Bureau of International Education Leadership Award in 2017[24] and published books such as *The Wayfarer and Other Poems* in 2001; *You're Not a Country, Africa*! published in 2010; *Naija No Dey Carry Last: Thoughts Of a Nation in Progress*, a collection of satirical essays on Nigeria published in 2015; and *Who Owns the Problem? Africa and the Struggle for Agency* published posthumously in 2020.

A married man, Adesanmi often talked about his family on his social media, especially his mother, Ma Adesanmi, and 'Tise, his daughter.[25] He was an example of a scholar who does not hide under the canopy of intense academic exercise as an excuse to neglect his family. He probably believed that a great scholar is also a great family man. Despite his fruitful career outside Nigeria, Adesanmi never abandoned the roots that gave life to him. Africa was an endearment to him, and he lived for the continent. His concerns revolved around how the continent could wake from its great slumber and take the reins. He believed Africans could only develop Africa, and this notion should be a uniform national pledge for everyone.

A distinguished man of many parts, Adesanmi was a university professor, social and political commentator, literary critic, author, poet, satirist, columnist, pan-Af-

---

20. The Review of Pius Adesanmi's Curriculum Vitae.

21. Pius Adesanmi wrote extensive opinion and satirical articles in major Nigerian newspapers such as *Sahara Reporters* and *Premium Times*.

22. African Writing Online, "50 African Writers; A Special AW Profile," *African Writing Online*, [undated] http://www.african-writing.com/aug/profiles2.htm.

23. Tracey, "The Winners of the Penguin Prizes for African Writing," *Penguin Books Live*, September 6, 2010, http://penguin.bookslive.co.za/blog/2010/09/06/the-winners-of-the-penguin-prizes-for-african-writing/.

24. T. Adebayo, "Premium Times Columnist Pius Adesanmi Wins Prestigious Canadian Award", *Premium Times*, September 14, 2017, https://www.premiumtimesng.com/news/more-news/243299-premium-times-columnist-pius-adesanmi-win-prestigious-canadian-award.html.

25. J. Nasiru, "Obituary: In our Heart Lies Pius Adesanmi, the Prophet who Foretold his Death," *TheCable*, March 12, 2019, https://www.thecable.ng/obituary-in-our-hearts-lie-pius-adesanmi-the-prophet-who-foretold-his-death.

ricanist, and teacher. He was a worthy mentor to younger people who looked up to him as a demi-god, but he was not. Like everyone else, he was a mere mortal and, as the popular lingo goes, "a pencil in the hands of the creator." Adesanmi's humble lifestyle appealed to many; little wonder he had huge followership on Facebook and Twitter—amounting to over forty thousand each before his unfortunate exit in 2019.[26] His humorous, deft language was evident in how he passed his message across. Adesanmi was an ingenious scholar and undoubtedly one of African literature's crèmes de la crème.

LITERARY WRITINGS

Adesanmi was a towering figure in the field of African literature. He published extensively in learned journals and had four books to his credit: a poetry collection (*The Wayfarer and Other Poems* (2001)), a collection of satirical essays (*Naija No Dey Carry Last* (2015)), a non-fictional work (*You're Not a Country, Africa!* (2011)), and a collection of critical essays (*Who Owns the Problem? Africa and the Struggle for Agency* (2020)). Adesanmi's works enjoyed critical reviews from scholars in academia, and he was known to have effectively employed satire as a veritable channel of communication to pass commentaries on the social ills of his dear homeland.

As a master of wits and words, Adesanmi adeptly employed satire to deliver hot takes on Nigeria's system of government. This validates why his satirical pieces carry political messages to the rulers and the ruled. Satire provides a veiled reference in attacking social ills, but not veiled enough for the readers to misconstrue the target audience. In African countries where speaking against tyranny carries capital punishment, where speaking against government inadequacies attracts the enemies-of-the-state tag, and where criticizing failed political demagogues comes with severing ties to one's motherland, satire has been adopted to attack these ills. In the world of literature, satire is a slippery term that cannot be pinpointed to a single definition; however, in *A Glossary of Literary Terms,* M. H. Abrams defines satire as "the literary art of diminishing or derogating a subject by making it ridiculous and evoking toward it attitudes of amusement, contempt, scorn, or indignation."[27] Put simply, satire is the literary act of revealing societal ills in coded or private language with the aim that exposed follies can be corrected.[28]

In his collection of satirical essays, *Naija No Dey Carry Last,*[29] Adesanmi embarked on scathing remarks on the crumbling state of affairs and offered formidable insights

---

26. Sources were analysis of Pius Adesanmi's Facebook and Twitter profiles.

27. Meyer Howard Abrams and Geoffrey Harpham, *A Glossary of Literary Terms* (Boston: Cengage Learning, 2014), 309.

28. Conal Condren, "Satire and Definition," *Humor* 25, no. 4, (2012): 379.

29. Pius Adesanmi, *Naija No Dey, Carry Last!: Thoughts on a Nation in Progress* (Lagos: Origami Books, 2015).

into the complexities and diversities that have characterized Nigeria's political system.[30] The book's title carries a political metaphor, "Naija no dey carry last." In proper English, "Nigeria does not take the rear position," as if to say Nigeria is the primus inter pares. However, the reality is that Nigeria occupies the rear position in terms of executing citizens-centered policies and maintaining a world-class infrastructure and security architecture, to name a few. Through irony mocking the giant of Africa, Adesanmi held no bar in casting light on the ills of an ailing nation that, despite all treatment, has remained in the Intensive Care Unit.

Besides revealing political messages, reading these satirical essays shows the master satirist's everlasting love for Nigeria. By publishing a book that, in one way or another, touches on the gray issues affecting the nation, Adesanmi proved himself to be a committed literary author who, despite the good quality of life he was enjoying abroad, could not ignore the common ache of his nation, unlike some other diaspora academics who, after leaving the country and amassing relative popularity, forget their homeland and fraternize with the foreign countries. In these satirical collections, Adesanmi unraveled a clairvoyant perspective of the happenings in his country.[31] He dwelled excessively on Nigeria's political conditions to ensure that the readers would come to terms with the harsh realities of their nation. Through humor and a panoramic use of language, Adesanmi effectively reflected and refracted Nigeria's deplorable conditions and how these conditions have always made the country's ship sink slowly.

By projecting these realities, the author believed that the masses would remember the conditions that collapsed the once-booming state of affairs and work in unison to salvage a dying nation. To reconstruct the ugly present, the masses must be reminded of the beautiful past. The themes in *Naija No Dey Carry Last* portray a failure of leadership among all other shenanigans in Nigeria, thus lending credence to Achebe's age-long dictum that the problem of Nigeria "is simply and squarely a failure of leadership."[32] In this regard, Adesanmi satirizes the activities, policies, and programs of former presidents, including Umaru Musa Yar'Adua and Goodluck Ebele Jonathan. He illuminates how institutions in the nation's political system suffer annihilation from savior-tagged political leaders. The three arms of government were not excused from the satirist's acerbic remarks, joining the ranks of Wole Soyinka, who had adopted satire for disseminating political messages. *Naija No Dey Carry Last* is replete with ironies and humor and conveys the evils of corruption, nepotism, deplorable national infrastructures, and other issues of national importance to the public for them to take action.

---

30. Udo Okoronkwo-Chukwu, "Naija No Dey Carry Last: Pius Adesanmi and the Complexity of A Nation in Progress," *European Journal of English Language and Literature Studies* 4, no. 7, (2016), 43–44.
31. Okoronkwo-Chukwu, "Naija No Dey Carry Last."
32. Chinua Achebe, *The Trouble with Nigeria* (London: Heinemann, 1984).

Away from his satirical masterpiece, Adesanmi also used poetry to draw the masses' attention to the political quagmire that Nigeria faces as a nation. In *Wayfarer and Other Poems*,[33] Adesanmi launches lyrical missiles on the oppressive nature of our national leaders, which was more prominent during the days of the military kleptomaniacs. The poetry collection dwells on writers, poets, and journalists who were forced into exile and suffered the unconducive environment and governance system of their native land. The poet employs powerful renditions and literary imagination to resist the military oppression of the 1990s. Generally, the nation was on a wrong course, and the military government was at its plundering best during these periods, with massive killings of citizens, bloody coups and counter-coups, depletion of the nation's resources, and heavy borrowings from foreign organizations only to be used for imprudent spending.[34]

During these military periods, the nation experienced what could be regarded as the freest and fairest elections, which the late Chief Moshood Abiola won in 1993; however, rather than for democracy and the wishes of the people to prevail, military high-handedness dominated.[35] Due to his unwavering commitment despite the shambles Nigeria was becoming, Adesanmi evokes powerful images of the disillusionment and postcolonial failure the country had degenerated into. In "University of Ibadan," the poet not only brought to the fore the creative consciousness that dominated the poetry club but also metaphorically lamented how the literary world is effectively monitored by the security operatives—under the "radar of the SSS."[36] The government of the day reserves brutal punishment for poets responding to their society; they prefer poets responding to poets as if the country's travails should be summarily dismissed or termed as a form of entertainment. The poet also passed commentaries on how the harsh political climate eventually forced these artists into exile, with Europe accommodating this influx and thus becoming a hub of the free flow of knowledge.

In *Who Owns the Problem? Africa's Struggle for Agency*,[37] Adesanmi raises cogent concerns on the slumbering state of Africa. He argues that Africa, as a community of nations, lost its prestige the moment it discarded its cultural heritage. How has Africa become a mere on-looker in global affairs?[38] The answer is not far-fetched from the neglect of African roots and traditional beliefs. Some proverbs affirm this: "The dog forgets the pathway to home when it ignores the hunter's home-calling whistles;" and

33. Pius Adesanmi, *The Wayfarer and Other Poems* (Mosman: Oracle Books, 2001).

34. Max Siollun, *Soldiers of Fortune: Nigerian Politics Under Buhari and Babangida (1983–1993)* (Abuja: Cassava Republic Press, 2013).

35. Siollun, *Soldiers of Fortune*.

36. James Yeku, "Revisiting Pius Adesanmi's The Wayfarer and Other Poems," *James Yeku*, January 11, 2020, https://jamesyeku.com/2020/01/11/revisiting-pius-adesanmis-the-wayfarer-and-other-poems/.

37. Pius Adesanmi, *Who Owns the Problem?: Africa and the Struggle for Agency* (Michigan: Michigan State University Press, 2020).

38. Adesanmi, *Who Owns the Problem?*

"The river that abandons its source becomes a mere dry land in a matter of time." Despite pessimistic western narratives, Africa is a self-reliant world that other continents need as a pillar system. The collection of African values, norms, arts and artifacts, literature, folklore, etc., define it as a hub of knowledge. However, the inferiorization of our belief systems has rendered the African value systems impotent, a dormant volcano.

In this collection of essays, Adesanmi bemoaned the evil effects of civilization, as many other Nigerian writers had done before him. The great Achebe, regarded as the father of African literature, used his writings to rebel against the dominance of western culture and tradition. In his magnum opus, *Things Fall Apart*,[39] Achebe brought to the fore the dangers of the commodification of the African value systems and the associated disaster. Adesanmi does something literary similar in *Who Owns the Problem? Africa's Struggle for Agency*, exposing how weak African institutions have continued to contribute to the perennial problems of poverty, bad governance, and grotesque leadership.

The book further queries pan-Africanists on their silence as Africa transcends into a mere asterisk in the international polity, asking valid questions on how Africa can rise to the complex challenges of this digital age. In this book, Adesanmi shares the belief that Africa can rediscover itself as soon as it reconnects with its roots; he argues that a romance with the foundational knowledge is pivotal for the re-emergence of Africa as a world superpower. The author further contends that Africa should rediscover its complex indigenous music system. This proved a genuine call because western music is also a tool that enhances the neglect of Africanism. Rediscovering Africa's performative modes through the unification of diverse African oral traditions is a potent tool to promote Africanism and break Africa off the yokes of western intimidation and oppression. The book underscores the author's love for Africa; it is a clarion call for Africans to remember their identities and recognize their complexities to create a unique world of their own that all and sundry would respect.

In his non-fiction, *You're not a Country, Africa!*,[40] Adesanmi employs Menippean satire to offer formidable insights into the complexities and diversities of the African continent. Menippean satire is a form of literary art that mocks and attacks the mental attitudes of a group of people and interrogates the philosophical and intellectual reasoning of persons, institutions, and countries. As Olusola Ogunbayo puts it: "This form of satire resembles the innuendoes and moral inclinations of some Nigerian folktales."[41] Baldick defines it as a "form of intellectually humorous work characterized by miscellaneous contents, displays of curious erudition, and comical discus-

---

39. Chinua Achebe, *Things Fall Apart* (London: Heinemann, 2021).

40. Pius Adesanmi, *You're Not a Country, Africa* (Cape Town: Penguin Random House South Africa, 2012).

41. Olusola Ogunbayo, "Menippean Satire in Postcolonial African Literature: A Reading of Pius Adesanmi's You're Not a Country, Africa," *Nokoko* 9 (2021): 71.

Figure 11.2. "The Scholar" by Dr. Kazeem Ekeolu. A scholar at work.

sions on philosophical topics."[42] Through this collection of essays, Adesanmi unravels his love for Africa vis-à-vis portraying the abundance of (regrettably) unfulfilled potentials inherent in the continent and concomitantly using satire to illuminate Africa's disparities while questioning the effectiveness of African value systems with the

42. Chris Baldick, *The Concise Oxford Dictionary of Literary Terms* (Oxford: Oxford University Press, 1996).

aim that the readers (Africans) would begin to trail the pathways of progress and prosperity.[43]

Additionally, in this collection of essays, Adesanmi launches unrestrained criticisms of the intellectual impotence that has come to be identified with Africa, thus transforming Africa into a cesspool of backwardness. The author adopts Yoruba philosophical conventions to attack the socio-political realities of the African continent. Adesanmi believes that if Africa is serious about getting back on track, then leading questions that underscore the problems bedeviling Africa as a nation must be asked. One who asks does not go astray: asking the right questions foregrounds the problems, which makes creating solutions for them easier. Adesanmi argues that a giant stride towards rediscovering Africa as a superb cultural heritage is for Africans to reconnect with their roots.

Also, Adesanmi admonishes in these essays that Africans generally should never close their ears to the beautiful memories of African traditions and values systems as these are important for the overall civilization and progress of the continent. Upholding tradition is very important, for with it comes the progress and prosperity of one's nation. This is why we can understand Adesanmi's unrelenting call for rediscovering and for Africans to be proud of their heritage. The author did not fail to launch severe criticisms of the western world for its myopic yet continuously pessimistic narratives of the African continent. To the western countries, Africa is not an existing place; it is a dark continent, and what is expected of a dark continent if not the emergence of dark, unintelligent, and uninspiring people?

There is a plethora of popular literature on Africans rejecting the parochial views of the western world on Africa, which has amassed considerable success. This explains why the great Kenyan writer, Ngũgĩ Wa Thiong'o, argues that writing in the colonialist's language, the English language, does not spell well for the continent. He argues that African writers should write in their indigenous languages.[44] Similarly, Adesanmi criticizes the denigration of Africans by the western world based on "color." In his eulogy for Africa's music, Adesanmi condemns westerners who visibly appreciate the melody of African music but hate to acknowledge the artists. He questions the mentality behind liking the content and disliking the container concerning the westerner's comments on African music and expresses his fervid displeasure on how race has continually polarized the world; another of the author's foregrounding points is why Africa must learn to live on its own and in its way.[45]

Adesanmi also faults the "satanification" of African religion with the dominance of imported religions, especially Christianity. It can be confidently posited that the pro-

43. Ogunbayo, "Menippean Satire in Postcolonial African Literature," 74.

44. Ngũgĩ Wa Thiong'o, "The Language of African Literature." In *Colonial Discourse and Post-Colonial Theory*, eds. Patrick Williams and Laura Chrisman (London: Routledge, 2015), 435–455.

45. Ogunbayo, "Menippean Satire in Postcolonial African Literature," 74.

liferation of Islam and Christianity and the universal spiritual correctness associated with them provoked a sort of radical departure from African traditional religion. The adherents of these religions usually postulate in defense of their faith that it encompasses the best ideas and spiritual philosophy apparent in their lifestyles. Nigeria is one of the most religious countries in the world, but the country has not been able to use this to end corruption. The leaders usually campaign under the canopy of religion to attract a kind of savior-complex mentality but quickly transform into religiously-empty leaders as soon as they hold the most-coveted political posts. For instance, in "Why I Will Not Emulate Jesus," Adesanmi questions the intention of sharing in the beliefs of these faiths when its adherents are the worst leaders. He asks rhetorically: "...why am I asked to emulate Jesus or Mohammed by rulers whose lifestyle and (mis) handling of our affairs are diametrically opposed to the prescriptions of both deities?"[46] With irony and humor, he attacks the lifestyle of extravagant and bombastic lifestyles of influential Christian leaders in Nigeria, such as Pastors Chris Oyakhilome, Chris Okotie, Enoch Adeboye, and David Oyedepo. Adesanmi's allusion to these names begs the reasoning behind religious ideologies in this country. One of the richest pastors in the world is a Nigerian;[47] however, Jesus Christ, whom the Christians follow, lived a poor, humble lifestyle in his mission on earth. It is paradoxical enough to imagine that wealthy religious leaders and their institutions have not contributed significantly to ameliorating the nation's affairs placed in this wreckage by their brothers and sisters in faith.

PIUS ADESANMI: THE ONLINE ACTIVIST

The introduction of digital technology has done more good than harm.[48] As the world slips into the digital era, it has become imperative to hone digital skills to properly navigate our day-to-day activities. The introduction of digital technology gave birth to social media and social media platforms, which have effectively changed conversations.[49] In Nigeria, social media have been significant in shaping political narratives. The citizens have adopted these platforms, especially Facebook and Twitter, to deliberate on national discourses. For instance, the best way to analyze the citizens' views on the policies of the government in power is to check through social media for related discussions. Rather than for Nigerians to run to the traditional press to project poor governance, they can do so effectively on social media.

---

46. Adesanmi, *You're Not a Country, Africa.*

47. A. Kamasi, "Top 15 Richest Pastors in the World and their Net Worth," *Pulse*, October 21, 2020, https://www.pulse.com.gh/filla/top-15-richest-pastors-in-the-world-and-their-net-worth/lwj95ky.

48. Michael Fitzgerald, Nina Kruschwitz, Didier Bonnet and Michael Welch, "Embracing Digital Technology: A New Strategic Imperative," *MIT Sloan Management Review* 55, no. 2 (2014): 4.

49. Mary Chayko, "Techno-Social Life: The Internet, Digital Technology, and Social Connectedness," *Sociology Compass* 8, no. 7 (2014): 980.

Nigeria has its share of bad leaders; therefore, the citizens will also voice their displeasure using social media, and the results have been great. Nigerians now use social media to launch criticisms against unconducive government policies. Social media can accommodate digital, online, or social media activism. Social media activism, otherwise known as digital/online/cyber activism, occurs mostly when social media users organize political protests or demonstrations on social media platforms intending to effect political and social change.[50] Mary Joyce pontificates that digital activism involves all manner of activism "that use digital network infrastructure."[51] Nigerians are now becoming social media activists, reducing the intimidation and oppression of physical activism. When a political officer holder falters, such a person is "dragged"[52] on social media, almost to the point of resignation from the position held. Nigerians also use social media platforms to instill political consciousness in their minds. By calling out bad governance and speaking against the ills associated with poor policies, Nigerians, through social media platforms, have reawakened their political consciousness.

It is a known fact that Adesanmi was an established social media warrior who spoke and wrote, without fear or prejudice, against hilarities that are associated with Nigerian governance. Unsurprisingly, his followership on social media platforms—Facebook and Twitter—can be pinpointed to his truthful takes on national affairs. Adesanmi's style of online activism had a different approach: he used his writings to disseminate cogent pieces of information that queried the questionable policies of the government. He believed that when the citizens are educated about the political affairs of their nation, it would effectively inform their decision-making.

Adesanmi was not interested in leveraging his great online presence to catalyze the frustrated masses to topple the government, nor was he interested in holding political posts through his ceaseless calls to national consciousness. His major focus was to see his country rekindle the effective political leadership that started from independence. The pan-Africanist scholar employed opinion articles and satirical pieces for his effective online activism. These literary pieces of information enabled the citizens to be aware of the national happenings; after all, for effective transformation of the state of affairs, the citizens must be aware of what needs to be changed. For without the necessary information, change cannot occur.

---

50. Marcos Sivitanides and Vivek Shah, "The Era of Digital Activism, *Conference for Information Systems Applied Research* 4, no. 1842 (2011).

51. Mary C. Joyce, *Digital Activism Decoded: The New Mechanics of Change* (New York: International Debate Education Association, 2010).

52. This is a Nigerian social media parlance describing the netizen often acerbic attacks on erring personalities. It may take the form of abuses, curses on the accused or graphics satirizing these personalities.

In an essay titled "ASUU: A Personal Voyage Around A Strike," Adesanmi criticized the nation's political class for its dilly-dally on educational matters.[53] In saner climes, education is a priority, with students and teachers enjoying certain privileges. But in Nigeria, education has often been relegated just like other important national matters. The lack of effective educational policies, argued Adesanmi, is key to the sub-standard educational sector, which almost cost his life. The author was involved in a fatal accident in Nigeria and would have lost his life due to poor health institutions, which is the direct result of poor educational institutions. Adesanmi criticized the Nigerian government for negatively transforming educational matters into political propaganda, such that almost every successive government campaign includes prioritizing the nation's educational affairs. He lamented that the abnormality in the state of education in Nigeria reflects the poor political leadership the country continuously suffers from, harping that the cultivation of teaching excellence in the nation is restrained by poor digital skills and poor pedagogical approaches.

Like other educational stakeholders, Adesanmi reminded the citizens that the government must take charge of the crumbling state of educational affairs if it is enthusiastic about developing "a powerful weapon to develop the world." Education's importance for a nation's survival cannot be over-emphasized. As the Yoruba aphorism posits, "ọmọ tí a kò tọ́, á gbé ilé tí a bá kọ́ tà," meaning a child who is not properly educated will discard the values of a household's tradition. Education is key to building patriotic citizens who would transmogrify Nigeria's poor political leadership culture.

In "It Will Get Worse Before It Gets Better," Adesanmi satirized the nation's leaders' political ideologies, which often clamored that the citizens need to make certain sacrifices for the peace and progress of their fatherland, what he called the "democracy of sacrifice."[54] Nigeria's political demagogues are known to sugar-coat the masses into believing that whatever hardship they are experiencing is a mere prerequisite for the comfort to follow; however, this comfort and a better standard of living never come. Adesanmi criticized this political ideology, believing that the citizens have experienced enough hardship and should not be made to suffer more hardships because of a soon-to-come Utopia.

An analysis of the state of Nigerian affairs projects that the citizens are in the lowest cadre of living and often have their hopes subsumed in the political agenda (read propaganda) of contesting political leaders. Adesanmi pinpointed the failure of Nigeria's political leadership to a romance with mediocrity. It is not surprising for political leaders to offer a mediocre justification for their system of governance. Mediocrity is associated with the political class in Nigeria. An investment in knowledge is the bed-

53. Pius Adesanmi, "ASUU: A Personal Voyage around a Strike," *Sahara Reporters*, November 29, 2018, https://saharareporters.com/2018/11/29/asuu-personal-voyage-around-strike-pius-adesanmi.

54. Pius Adesanmi, "It will get Worse before it gets Better," *Sahara Reporters*, May 14, 2016, https://saharareporters.com/2016/05/14/it-will-get-worse-it-gets-better-pius-adesanmi.

rock for the progress of every nation, but the reverse has often been the case for Nigeria. Here, mediocrity is beatified as intellectualism. Adesanmi supported the nation in reconnecting with good values system, which would ultimately form a pool of endless knowledge. He succeeded in inspiring the readers, who are the citizens, to be voracious in their thirst for knowledge, as this would be key to unlocking the county's unfulfilled potential.

Similarly, in "Shit & The Sum(mary) Of A Presidency," Adesanmi was critical of President Muhammadu Buhari-led government, especially in the spate of unchecked attacks. The third year of Buhari's government witnessed audacious insurgent attacks.[55] However, rather than the government taking charge and improving the security architecture, it resorted to blame games. Adesanmi criticized the lack of sensitivity on the part of the government, which took comfort in issuing long-winding statements on national security rather than providing a viable solution. Many citizens had thought President Buhari, a retired Major General, would handle the security situation differently, but the reverse was the case. The government often took no measures until attacks happened. Adesanmi criticized the Nigerian government for such silly approaches to security matters. From his location in Ottawa, he constantly charged the Nigerian government to take the protection of the lives and properties of its citizens seriously. He projected the insecurity predicament to the masses, who eventually cried out against the seeming helplessness of the government. Thus, Adesanmi became the voice of the masses and the government's watchdog.

In a satirical piece, "An Excellent Case for Buhari's Second Term," Adesanmi was critical of the rationality of Nigerians' choice of leaders while also lamenting the deplorable culture of the country's political leaders.[56] Nigerians are known to fully support leaders who promise them heaven on earth without questioning their campaign promises, and then they are quick to lament and organize pseudo-protests when such a leader fails. Asides from their erroneous choice of leadership, Nigerian citizens are also involved in illogical addiction to the government in power even when it becomes obvious they have nothing to offer. In this piece, Adesanmi, through irony and humor, projected the faulty thinking abilities of those who clamored for President Buhari's second term. The citizens had removed the so-called puppet president, Goodluck Jonathan, with the belief that the retired Major General would bring the Nigeria of their dreams. But Buhari failed—perhaps worse than his predecessor—yet Nigeria still wanted him for another tenure. The author was critical of these bad choices, prefigurating the disaster associated with their bad choices of leaders.

55. Pius Adesanmi, "Shit & the Sum(mary) of a Presidency," *Sahara Reporters*, February 5, 2018, https://saharareporters.com/2018/02/05/shit-summary-presidency-pius-adesanmi.

56. Pius Adesanmi, "An Excellent Case for Buhari's Second Term," *Premium Times*, April 10, 2018, https://opinion.premiumtimesng.com/2018/04/10/an-excellent-case-for-buharis-second-term-by-pius-adesanmi/.

Adesanmi once launched the KickOut Siddon Look Movement to arouse political consciousness in the minds of Nigerians. The political movement was hosted in the digital space and was borne out of the dire need of the citizens to not only be fully aware of their nation's affairs but also be part of the structure of the government. Put simply, the people are the government, and the government is the people. Adesanmi believed that ensuring the forward trajectory of the nation's affairs enables the masses' consciousness of their fatherland's political happenings. When the masses are adequately conscientious, they would not be easily taken by the sweet words of political leaders who believe in electoral rigging to stay long in power. With the movement, Adesanmi's vision was crystal clear: sensitizing the citizens who would elect good leaders with brilliant political ideologies would eventually rekindle the once-admired culture of political leadership in the country.

As he described it, KickOut Siddon Look Movement "is a grassroots political movement that will combine all kinds of strategies to conscientize our people. We certainly aren't going to limit things to social media. Our ultimate aim—we are ambitious—is to have cells in every local government area of Nigeria."[57] The movement was a composition of patriotic Nigerians who devoted their time and resources to restructuring political narratives in the country. The movement enjoyed remarkable success. One major importance of online/digital activism is that it allows the freedom for people to build effective relationships that will oppose political structures and ultimately facilitate the emergence of better political leaders. Social media did not only foster networking opportunities for Adesanmi, but he also leveraged his huge followership to revive the spirit of national and political consciousness in the minds of the citizens to effect social and political change in the nation's history.

THE MANY LEGACIES OF PIUS ADESANMI

Adesanmi was a household name in the African literary space, not just for his excellent academic outputs but also for his support to other emerging African literati. He contributed concrete scholarships to African literature and was known for encouraging others and giving the upcoming ones a chance to explore and create an identity for themselves.[58] A particular attribute of Adesanmi that endeared many to him was his humility and simplicity. Not many scholars of his reputation are known to combine brilliancy with humility.

As stated earlier, Adesanmi was a literary bigwig and had won numerous awards. As a pan-Africanist scholar, he contributed extensive research on African literature that other African scholars had supported. His admonitions for the Africa-must-develop-Africa approach facilitated inward thinking on the development of Africa by

57. Adesanmi, "Someone Once Advised me."

58. Temitope B. Oriola and W. Andy Knight, "In Memoriam—Professor Pius Adesanmi (1972–2019)," *African Security* 12, no. 1, (2019): 1–2.

Africans. Unfortunately, discussions centered on the development of Africa usually come from international countries and organizations. Africa had relegated its affairs to the hands of those who contributed pessimistic narratives on its existence. Thus, it is unsurprising that he issued acerbic statements about Africa's political class, especially Nigeria.

For Adesanmi, narratives on Africa must be propagated by Africans. We must not leave our body of knowledge to the fate of western criticisms. Adesanmi put in great efforts to build an Institute of African Studies at Carleton University, where he could share his passion for African literature among his students. In Emma Bider's exaltation of Adesanmi's ingenuity in African literature, the author noted the latter's unique teaching approaches, especially in portraying positive visual images of African literature.[59] Bider notes that while Adesanmi was interpreting J. P. Clark's "Abiku," he took off his shirt and showed the class the scars on his body being an *abiku* himself: such was his passion for African literature. The bitter truth is that despite great writers emerging from Africa, not many African scholars have made it a duty to research African writers. African literature is a committed literary art.[60] It responds to society; thus, African writers should respond to society in their writings.

Adesanmi's career centered on Africa. He lived and died for Africa, a reason he is remembered today. He trailed the path of Uhuru Kenyatta, Nelson Mandela, Wole Soyinka, Chinua Achebe, and the likes who have ceaselessly admonished that Africa must develop itself, saying that "Africa for Africa," and have clamored for Africa to go back to its roots. An analysis of Africa in the modern world depicts that it shares one of the most unfavorable statistics in the world: African countries are on the list of the most terrorized countries in the world; the most poverty-stricken countries; countries with the worst press freedom; countries with the worst governance; countries with shaky democracy, and countries with the number of out-of-school children, to mention a few of these gory statistics.

One cannot observe Africa's sorry state of affairs and posit that all is well. This underscores Adesanmi's huge concern for the development of Africa, as reflected in his writing and numerous speeches[61] on the need for Africa to take charge of its life. Adesanmi believed that the inferiorization of African arts is because Africans have lost their history. It is a bitter reality that the great continent does not boast of a for-

---

59. Emma Bider, "The Privilege of Editing #WhoOwnsTheProblem: Remembering Pius Adesanmi," *Nokoko* 9 (2021): 135.

60. Femi Ojo-Ade, "Of Culture, Commitment, and Construction: Reflections on African Literature," *Transition* 53 (1991): 4–24.

61. Pius Adesanmi, "Dowry: Managing Africa's Many Lovers," Keynote Lecture Delivered at the Annual Conference of the African Studies Course Union, University of Toronto, 2013, 15.

midable unity and a sense of purpose. Adesanmi spoke against the disillusionment of Africa and the danger of thinking all is well when it is not.[62]

Many African scholars have written extensively on the disillusionment of post-independent Africa. If one could posit that Africa was exploited and massively undeveloped by the colonialists, have African leaders not done more plundering than the colonialists? Therefore, the problem of Africa is also Africans! Through oral and written forms, Adesanmi criticized African leaders who have shown little concern for the development of their countries. He postulated that African leaders must embrace African values to ensure the continent's development, and he believed that the continent would undergo social and political change. At every opportunity, Adesanmi devoted his time and resources to the continuous development of African literature and Africa in general.[63] He showed fervid displeasure on the mediocrity associated with Africa's political leadership; from Nigeria to other African countries, he satirizes the failure of leadership, simultaneously putting the leaders on their toes.

Adesanmi's commentaries on Africa have helped catalyze the youths burning with passion for Pan-Africanism.[64] Africa's future is bright when the youth share African ideas and values, and Adesanmi led by example. As a towering figure in African literature, his cultural commentaries on Africa developed into a reservoir of knowledge for other scholars to tap from. He called out against the stereotypes associated with Africa and warned against the summary dismissal of the African continent as a heterogeneous community.[65] Also, he contributed extensively to the codification of African arts, along with other African scholars. His teachings have distorted the poor image of Africa formed in Western students' minds. To many, Africa is another small and relatively unknown "country" globally, where animals cohabit with humans in tails parading their environment unclad. Adesanmi's giant strides in academia were influential in correcting these misconceptions. He countered these unfortunate narratives of Africa brilliantly in *You're Not A Country, Africa!* where he took a swipe at the colonialist mentality of Africa and questioned the Europeans' soi-disant ideologies and intellectualism. Adesanmi repeatedly called for the unification of African intellectuals, whom he believed were the continent's foundation of knowledge.[66]

Away from his innumerable contributions to African literature, Adesanmi created a lasting impression on young people because of his peculiar lifestyle. He was not known to be bombastic or excessively overbearing due to his prominence. If anything,

---

62. Blair Rutherford, "Incorporeal Words: The Tragic Passing of Pius Adesanmi," *Nokoko* 7 (2019): iix–xiii.

63. Samuel Ojo Oloruntoba, "Pius Adesanmi: A Paradigm Shift in Pan African Humanity," *Nokoko* 9 (2021): 54–69.

64. Oloruntoba, "Pius Adesanmi: A Paradigm Shift," 54–69.

65. Pius Adesanmi, "From Post-Global to Post-Truth: African Literature beyond Commonsense," *Cambridge Journal of Postcolonial Literary Inquiry* 4, no. 2 (2017): 271–279.

66. Oloruntoba, "Pius Adesanmi: A Paradigm Shift," 54–69.

Adesanmi devoted his energy, material, and immaterial resources to the growth of young African intellectuals. This is why he referred young African scholars for scholarships and courses on African studies. He was a source of inspiration to many writers who found it difficult to hone their writing craft and a source of encouragement to young African students who have contemplated furthering their studies. The pan-Africanist scholar gave the manuscript of *Who Owns Africa?: Africa Struggle for Agency* to a graduate student who had not yet matured as an editor for proofreading, and on numerous occasions, he sought advice from those younger than him.[67] A major trait that endears the young to the elder is the latter's ability to believe in the prospects of the former. Adesanmi created a symbiotic relationship with his mentees and did not claim to be Mr. Know-it-all despite his uncanny thinking abilities. He never wrote any of his mentees, friends, or acquaintances off; his humorous lifestyle was straightforward enough for others to follow. He disproved mediocrity in all forms and encouraged his booming supporters to embrace the same. Adesanmi believed that half-learning is similar to ignorance and should be shunned by everyone.

Adesanmi's students often noted his unique approach to their development. He was not known as the professor who took pride in belittling his students during intellectual conversations. He engaged in fruitful discussions with his younger peers and employed vivid illustrations to lead them to the best perspective. Adesanmi's office was always open for students to come in and seek clarifications and even for further debates.[68] His friendly and accommodating personality made this very effective. Adesanmi was a teacher of teachers. He inculcated in his students the importance of language and how language can be made flexible to effect political and social change. He also catalyzed his peers to be passionate about the development of Africa, harping that Africa cannot afford to be neglected, or else its body of knowledge and the heroic pasts of its forefathers will become fragments of distant memories. He instilled African consciousness and patriotism in the minds of his supporters. His mentees have followed his lead in using their creative expertise to clamor aggressively for the redefinition of Africa. Adesanmi was proud of his African heritage and interlinked with many others in applying African experiences. To many of his peers, Adesanmi was a man who did not violate his dictates.

With his rampant influence, Adesanmi led younger peers towards adopting African humanity, that is, the spirit of Ubuntu.[69] He believed in humanity and encouraged others to do the same. Every part of him portrayed African ideals, which were infectious to those associated with him.[70] Despite being a widely-traveled scholar, he nev-

67. Bider, "The Privilege of Editing."

68. Bider, "The Privilege of Editing."

69. Oloruntoba, "Pius Adesanmi: A Paradigm Shift," 54–69.

70. Justin Villamil and Yossie Olaleye, "In Pius Adesanmi's Speech and Writing, there is Hope for a Pan-African Future," *Africa at LSE*, February 25, 2016, www.blogs.lse.ac.uk/africaatlse/2016/02/25/in-pius-adesanmis-speech-and-writing-there-is-hope-for-a-pan-african-future/.

er discarded his African roots, thus passing a genuine message to those who identify with his ideologies that solidifying their (African) identity is paramount. His contemporary, Chuma Nwokolo, once said of him as one who committed his entire life to the "service of humanity."[71] Most of his mentees have identified with his notion of being committed to humanity.

By criticizing the government's questionable policies, Adesanmi created political correctness in the minds of his readers and aroused political consciousness in the minds of his numerous followers, which ultimately informed their decision on the kind of governance they wanted. Either with opinion articles or satires, he was quick to call out bad governance and the oppression of the masses. He queried the mental attitudes of the Nigerian leaders when they went out of bounds, and he was very much committed to the Nigerian project.

To paraphrase Nelson Mandela, the world will only respect Africa as soon as Nigeria takes charge. If Nigeria had effectively harnessed its resources, it would have become a powerful nation, showcasing African superiority. Unfortunately, Nigeria is a country of would-have-been and could-have-become. It still sinks into the cesspool of directionlessness, mainly due to failed political leadership. The country's shenanigans do not escape Adesanmi's ceaseless but overtly patriotic criticisms, serving as a watchdog for Nigeria's cycle of selfish leaders.

Nigeria is riddled with the ineffectiveness of the government, and it gradually slips into an era of nothingness. Like Adesanmi, many social and political commentators have shown concerns about the urgent need for restructuring. Nigeria's continued existence must be protected at all costs. In his constant reflections on the Nigerian state of affairs, Adesanmi was vociferous about the government's slow approach to important discourses. It is ironic for a Nigerian to profess his patriotism for the country in empty words. Adesanmi effectively combined words with actions in projecting the sorry state of affairs and creating a national consciousness in the minds of the citizens. He would be forever remembered as the social critic who, despite his strong linkages with the top echelon of the Nigerian government, did not fail to criticize their shortcomings and bad policies.

DEATH

In African philosophy, death bears the tag of an unexpected guest and is often treated with fear and respect, but death is only seen as a welcoming visitor for the aged. So, when the news of Adesanmi's death started flying around on March 10, 2019, it was unbelievable.[72] This was a man in his prime! However, the news was true:

71. Chuma Nwokolo, "An Epitaph for Pius Adesanmi," *Nwokolo,* March 11, 2019, https://nwokolo.com/y/an-epitaph-for-pius-adesanmi/.

72. Oriola and Knight, "In Memoriam."

the great African scholar had lost his life in an air crash on his way to Nairobi. Even when the veracity of his death was confirmed, many were still in doubt and had hoped he was not in the crashed flight. By night, the literary world was mourning—Adesanmi was gone. This Abiku will no longer return with many more scars. Adesanmi carried his dreams of a better Africa to the grave. He lived and died for Africa, and his legacy lives on. His contributions to African literature and his lifelong commitment to African values cannot be erased as long as this world exists. He was a household name in the book industry and the world of social media and will be forever remembered for his enthusiasm for extolling anything African.

In his lifetime, Adesanmi proved that he was a man who lived according to his principles that were deeply rooted in Africanism. An astute scholar, Adesanmi was intellectually flexible, and this intellectual flexibility is obtained in his many inputs in African literature. Described as a brother and confidant, Adesanmi effectively catalyzed young peers and influenced their passion for African literature. His unique pedagogical approaches will forever dwell in the minds of those fortunate enough to listen to the wits of this literary genius within the four walls of the classroom. Adesanmi effectively adopted the Socratic teaching method as he was often involved in intellectual deliberations with his students. Many of his students are now emerging voices in African literature.

In his tribute to Adesanmi, Professor of History Moses Ochonu described him as a scholar who would not come to terms with mediocrity.[73] Ochonu stated that Adesanmi often expressed his disavowal of anything mediocre and frowned at those who embraced it. Ochonu further described him as one who detested racial inequality, which is evident in his passion for humanity. Adesanmi was seen as an African gentleman. In my tribute to him, I described his huge influence and how he could have used it in Africa's transformation. He "connected thousands of people with the bigger ambition of the application of modernity."[74]

Adesanmi lived a worthy life of repute and was a role model to many emerging voices in African literature. In the compilation of tributes in Adesanmi's honor, he was described as an incredible asset to Africa. Many of his close associates blamed death for taking such a generous scholar in his prime. If death could have avoided anyone, it could have been Adesanmi. Of all the articles and literary writing devoted to his memory, they all pointed out one fact: Adesanmi was a good man. This brings to the fore the popular African proverb that a good name is better than riches. In his lifetime, he did not claim to be what he was not and, despite his intimidating person-

---

73. Moses Ochonu, "Pius Adesanmi: A Tribute and a Debt," *Premium Times*, March 23, 2019, https://opinion.premiumtimesng.com/2019/03/22/pius-adesanmi-a-tribute-and-a-debt-by-moses-e-ochonu/.

74. Toyin Falola, "Pius Adesanmi: The Man who Leaves and Lives," *Yoruba Studies Review* 3, no. 2 (2019): 1–7.

ality, lived a humble life. His unfortunate exit will remain in the memories of those who identified with his ideologies.

One thing we can learn from Adesanmi is his patriotism for Africa and how he countered pessimistic narratives about the continent. Despite the luxury he enjoyed as a scholar in foreign universities, he did not forget about the termagant problems of his origin. Adesanmi lived all his life fighting for the development of Africa. He identified poor political leadership as the key factor dragging the continent backward. His satirical pieces and opinion articles mostly bear the common theme of criticizing the grotesque political leaders the continent has been doomed to have. Politics was Adesanmi's core interest, and he used his literary writings to reignite the political consciousness of Africans, especially Nigerians. For this and many more reasons, his legacy lives on.

CONCLUSION

With the mention of Adesanmi, Africa comes to mind because he devoted his life and time to Africa—to the point of death. He was on African duty before the ill-fated airline crash that took his life. Africa meant many things to Adesanmi, especially as a world power of knowledge. In his lifetime, he fought with many writings and speech characters who summarily dismissed Africa as the "dark continent." He countered racist ideologies on Africa and, at every opportunity, projected the beauties, values, and ideologies of Africa. According to him, no one can help in the development of Africa except Africans themselves; this is why he often underscored the primacy of reconnecting to African values and philosophy. He often clamored for the re-embrace of African cultural heritage, which would be consequential to the growth and civilization of Africa.

Adesanmi had a fine personality and admirable art of careful analyses of societal issues, evidenced in his life, publications, and social media posts. He represented a link between two worlds, one of which is the noble academic sphere and the contemporary general inclinations of social media that fast redefine society's conditionality. He pitched himself in several intellectual discussions examining African and Nigerian themes and proffering recommended approaches to solve social vices and situations. His representation of the two spheres was attributed to the deserved respect that followed his positions on social issues. This further justifies the cause for studying his pearls of wisdom and sets the admired perspectives afoot.

Adesanmi was a projection of the disappointment and sentiments of Nigerian citizens. He could plug himself into the themes of people's discussions and reactions and further presented those positions within logical reasoning and examination. He was a character in the plot of the public's languish but played his role from a more constructive and intellectual perspective. He was the public in their right senses, projecting facts and suggesting recommendations. However, like millions of citizens who

have projected their dissatisfactions and commentaries about the state of things, he represented the spectator who propelled himself as an embodiment of enlightenment but distinguished by his understanding.

While alive, he called himself a teacher, not only to students within his academic influence and teaching but also to the members of the public to whom he lent his wealth of knowledge and understanding. The life he led and his brilliance would make one agree more with how he described himself. While representing the projection of the public views on the despicable state of the country, he served as a guard for charting the direction of the public sentiments and conversation with the intent to collect their focus on the right direction.

As evident from the above discussions, Adesanmi dedicated his time to criticizing national and continental issues, but it was crystal clear that he never had a foreclosed mind on hope for a better Nigeria and an admired continent. He was a figure of hope between the rains of criticism that continually fell from the clouds of social media and society in general. When he discussed important issues, he did not do that with the finality of prophesized doom but with blisters of hope contingent on the right approaches and good leadership. He became an applicable subject in this matter, especially because of his ability to commute the tenets of Pan-Africanism into contemporary systems and conditions.[75] As a link between academic ethicalities and contemporary phenomena, he propelled his Africanist convictions and hopes for development in the construction of his scholarship and opinions academically and within social media shenanigans.

Adesanmi was a household name in the field of African literature. He wrote in-depth research on African literature and gave speeches on the field. As a pan-Africanist scholar, he believed in the spirit of humanity and Ubuntu, the African philosophy of togetherness and unity. Africa, to Adesanmi, represented an important part and pillar system of the world, not a mere appendage that could be discarded at will. He criticized Africa's political leadership in his lifetime, often using Nigeria as a paradigm. He amassed huge social media followership and employed his teeming online presence to drive home his points. He was a great family man; his death left a space in the heart of his loved ones and his name, memories, and legacies are imprinted in the book industry. Social media, the source of his intellectual attainment, has doubled as the source of retaining his legacy.

75. Oloruntoba, "Pius Adesanmi: A Paradigm," 54–69.

12

AYO OLUKOTUN

Inside the Boundless Dimensions of Nigeria

In his award-winning weekly column for *Punch* newspaper, Ayo Olukotun reflects on the various dimensions of the nature of institutions in Nigeria, including security, funding of education, economy, healthcare, and governance. The weekly essay is posted on the USA-Africa Dialogue, and it gets fed into other social media platforms. Thus, Olukotun deploys both traditional and digital media to attain a large audience.

Olukotun is a noted Professor of Political Science at Olabisi Onabanjo University, Ogun State, Nigeria, a member of the Governing Council of the Courier and Logistics Institute, and has had many other impressive experiences in the academy and public service. Olukotun focuses on the interconnected, diverse relationships between the dimensions of Nigeria's political, social, and economic sectors. He dissects and challenges Nigeria's current, past, and future happenings in his weekly columns. This chapter will analyze many of Olukotun's columns and explore his thoughts on Nigeria's experiences and troubles.

Subjecting Olukotun's views to scholarly analyses and discussion might lead to difficult conclusions because of the trends and volume of his scholarly exploits. One thing that stands out is how he handles political issues and examines emerging policies. As a respectable political scientist, his opinions expose his act of making Nigeria his lab and carrying out tests and research on the political scenes of the nation. He is

Figure 12.1. "The Opium of Ayo Olokotun's Diversity" by Michael Efionayi. Depicts the injecting of the diversified messages of Ayo Olukotun that fit almost into all dimensions of Nigerian society and his adaptation to social media dynamics.

a political watchman who stands guard at the brewing of new government policies or the emergence of political matters. He also follows the process of their operations to logically criticize their progression.[1] As a columnist, his opinions and analysis attract a wide readership following his perspicacity and nicety on how best a political decision would have been made. His approach has allowed his opinions to be respected by the public, providing a reasonable justification for this chapter.

Another relevance of Olukotun is his compatibility with the underlying focus of this book on social media and its major thematic preoccupations. Olukotun, inten-

1. Samuel Sunday Idowu, Jide Ibietan and Ayo Olukotun, "Privatization of Power Sector in Nigeria: An Evaluation of Ibadan and Ikeja Electricity Distribution Companies Performance (2005–2018)," *International Journal of Public Administration* 43, no. 16 (2020): 1413–1420.

tionally or coincidentally, has provided a journey of the Nigerian media from its history to its contemporary operations. His work provides the opportunity to trace the transition of the media and the dynamics that social media has brought in contemporary times.[2] He has recounted how the media has struggled with existing political systems and the battle for democracy. In his examination, he has also discussed the instrumentality of the media, especially for political themes and politically related actions.[3] His research and publications suggest that there is a link between the media—social media included—and society,[4] as both of them affect each other, and the government's disposition to freedom determines the operation of the media.

Aside from his clever thoughts on the media, its transition and operation with society and government, he believes that if social media and the norms it introduced are well harnessed, it could be a pathway to ensuring citizens' engagement, development of democracy and continuous empowerment.[5] He also believes in the tendency of social media to create momentum and pressure that may backfire on government and its failures to meet general expectations.[6]

BAD GOVERNANCE IN NIGERIA

Olukotun explores the problem of bad governance in Nigeria as this predicament has continued to undermine the nation's development. There have been many interventions on the issue of bad governance in the country from concerned stakeholders passionate about the country's progress. Bad governance stems from bad leaders that assume the mandate of leadership and appear unconcerned as the country battles for survival. An analysis of the nation's development shows a country that struggles to move with the pace of other African countries like South Africa and Mauritius. Olukotun examines this theme of bad governance so the readers (citizens) can reflect on the state of affairs and become conscious of their decisions concerning national development.

A careful analysis of some of Olukotun's articles about governance in Nigeria between 2015 and 2023 foreshadows what every objective writer and political analyst has posited in the past. That is, the Buhari administration came into power riding the

2. Ayo Olukotun, "The Transition and the Media," *African Journal of Political Science / Revue Africaine de Science Politique* 5, no. 2 (2000): 31–44.

3. Ayo Olukotun, "Traditional Protest Media and Anti-Military Struggle in Nigeria 1988–1999," *African Affairs* 101, no. 403 (2002): 193–211. See also Ayo Olukoyun, "Media Accountability and Democracy in Nigeria, 1999–2003," *African Studies Review* 47, no. 3 (2004): 69–90.

4. Ayo Olukotun, "Repressive State and Resurgent Media under Nigeria's Military Dictatorship, 1988–98," Nordiska Africa Institute Vol. 126, (2004).

5. Ayo Olukotun, "Social Media and Pathways to Inclusive Development," *The Punch, 26th February 2016, Retrieved on August 12, 2022 through https://punchng.com/social-media-and-pathways-to-inclusive-development/.*

6. Olukotun, "Social Media and Pathways to Inclusive Development."

waves of a campaign of calumny against the past administration, promising the citizens both what was within their ambits and what was not. While some political apologists unsuccessfully tried to paint the Buhari administration as a blessing to Nigeria, various assessments contained in reports provided by authoritative bodies such as the African Development Bank described Nigeria as a country characterized by worsening economic indices such as a high unemployment rate, an increasing poverty rate, and high debt service obligations. In other words, Nigeria seemed like a nation bedeviled by crises of utmost proportions. These unfavorable economic outlooks are coupled with the naira's low purchasing power and capital flight.

The initial conditions not only reflect the economic challenges faced across the nation but also indicate a major problem of governance in Nigeria—its high cost. In the article "Reducing the Cost of Governance in Nigeria: The Ayes Have it," Olukotun investigates the prospect of mitigating this existential problem.[7] According to the article, every government official or department knows very well that the cost of governance in Nigeria is very high, yet a lack of audacity to implement policies to reduce expenses remains an obstacle. Providing an example, Olukotun references the Steve Orosanye Panel, set up by the Goodluck Jonathan administration, which was aimed at reducing governance costs in Nigeria through mooted ideas such as merging ministries and decommissioning redundant ones. As expected of unserious leadership, the wherewithal to implement the panel's recommendations became non-existent. Like several reports in the past, the panel's recommendations never saw the light of day, despite the financial resources allocated to achieve its set objectives.

In 2018, Nigeria's Transparency International corruption rating was a mere 27/100, indicating that Nigeria is a highly corrupt country. Nigeria was also ranked 144th out of 180 countries in general progress, indicating an extremely low position relative to other countries. In the column, "Needless Controversy over TI Rating," Olukotun grips at the notion that the low TI scores are not Nigeria's only trouble.[8] Concerning these scores, Olukotun posits that Nigeria must improve how it handles bad news about itself. Olukotun states, even before officials studied the details of the 2017 survey, that a public statement was issued by the presidential spokesperson querying the methodology of TI, denouncing findings, and speculating that Buhari's opponents influenced TI.[9] Olukotun calls Nigeria a country of bad losers, stating that its people tend to drum up conspiracy theories as a response whenever Nigeria loses. This assessment raises the question, if Nigeria's response to shortcomings is adopting a defensive manner rather than seeking ways to unite and improve, how will Nigeria move forward? Olukotun suggests that Nigeria must "outgrow the mentality of applauding

7. Ayo Olukotun, "Reducing the Cost of Governance: The Ayes have it," *The Punch*, October 11, 2019. *Retrieved on August 12, 2022 through https://punchng.com/reducing-the-cost-of-governance-the-ayes-have-it/.*

8. Ayo Olukotun, "Needless Controversy over TI Rating," *The Punch*, March 1, 2018. Retrieved on August 12, 2022 through https://punchng.com/needless-controversy-over-ti-rating/.

9. Olukotun, "Needless Controversy over TI Rating."

organizations that endorse us/rank us favorably while berating those who score us poorly."[10]

Furthermore, Nigeria is not asking, "why is our TI rating low?" Instead, as Olukotun states, Nigeria rains invectives on the electoral commission and blames the low rating on outside conspiracists. In his column, Olukotun investigates the challenges Nigeria faces and offers potential reforms; one such issue is a lack of funding for Nigerian soldiers. In his column, "Defense Sector Spending: Have We Come Full Circle?" Olukotun states that the funds meant for Nigerian soldiers to procure arms are not, in fact, properly disbursed.[11] He suggests that these funds are stolen, diverted, or inefficiently administered, as Nigeria's defense ability is less than sub-par. This assertion aligns with claims and observations of corruption and how it fuels other problems concerning Nigerian citizens' and soldiers' safety and security. The main issue that Olukotun shines a light on is that Nigerian soldiers are poorly equipped and are thus fighting their way to death.[12]

Misdirected allocation of funds and high expenses permeate all governmental agencies in Nigeria, including the arms of government. The practice of bicameral legislature is very expensive, especially for developing nations like Nigeria. In commenting on this topic, Olukotun references notable legislators who have spoken against funds wastage within the federal legislative chambers. Specifically, his article referenced the exploit of a former governor, Peter Obi. Obi offered to be the lone designated participant at the conference to cut down the bogus amount budgeted for a conference, as opposed to the estimated budget allotted for 30 people.[13] The inability of successive governments to find a lasting solution to the high cost of governance, despite acknowledging the gravity of the problem, reveals the systemic weakness of the government institution to act effectively:

> Have you noticed that Italy, a European country beset by soaring debts, has recently reduced the size of its parliament? It was done in a fit of self-discipline and an effort to save the country from looming bankruptcy, by the parliamentarians themselves. The Lower House was reduced from 650 to 400 while the Senate was reduced in numbers from 315 to 200, saving thereby 1,000,000 Euros, in one year and 10,000,000 Euros in ten years.[14]

---

10. Olukotun, "Needless Controversy over TI Rating."

11. Ayo Olukotun, "Defence Sector Spending: Have we Come Full Circle?" *The Punch*, December 27, 2018, Retrieved on August 12, 2022 through https://punchng.com/defence-sector-spending-have-we-come-full-circle/.

12. Olukotun, "Defence Sector Spending: Have we Come Full Circle?"

13. Ayo Olukotun, "Reducing Cost of Governance in Nigeria," *Opinion Nigeria*, October 12, 2019, Retrieved on August 12, 2022 through http://www.opinionnigeria.com/reducing-the-cost-of-governance-in-nigeria-the-ayes-have-it-by-ayo-olukotun/.

14. Olukotun, "Reducing Cost of Governance in Nigeria."

Nations with efficient government institutions do not find it difficult to implement policies to improve their countries. This is the huge gap between government institutions in African countries and the western world. The failure to acknowledge that government exists to ensure communal development and progress remains the major factor that pushes African nations regressively.

In one of his articles, Olukotun affirms that the template to assess the Buhari administration's performance was delivered six years earlier when promises were being churned out during the electoral campaigns of 2015. As Olukotun states, empty promises have been part of Nigeria's political history for some time. For example, in the 2014/2015 election, Buhari and the All Progressives Congress (APC) promised to demolish Boko Haram and the Islamic State in West Africa in their first three months of power. Additionally, the APC stated that the party would create 3 million jobs annually and stop exporting refined petroleum products. During the same campaign, there were also promises that one free meal would be provided each day for public primary school students. Only a few of these were fulfilled. According to Olukotun, "... in our terrain, promises are made almost in jest, and with the unwritten assumption that they are meant to be broken. This is an unfortunate development that is bound to wash over into the way in which citizens perceive politicians and what they say."[15]

The Buhari administration's many promises included tackling insecurity, improving the economy, and reducing corruption. Six years later, Olukotun interjects that the enthusiasms of the earlier years appeared to have waned, with public thefts appearing to soar. Among the corruption centers noted by Olukotun, the Nigerian Pension Commission, the Niger Delta Development Commission, and the Nigerian Ports Authority have been the most familiar targets of corrupt practices. Since 2019, these three government agencies have been involved in cases of alleged looting of public funds. Unfortunately, the perpetrators are being handled delicately and, in some cases, have become a theatre to entertain the public. Such offenders and offenses are passed from one administration to another without adequately addressing the problem(s). At the end of it all, what we have in Nigeria are political administrations that do not have the wherewithal or sustained momentum to tackle corruption and its ill effects on society.

To further highlight the level of decadent governance and false promise in Nigeria, in "Buhari's Medical Leave and Resident Doctors' Strike," Olukotun focuses on one of the campaign promises of Buhari[16] —his administration would ensure that public servants do not embark on foreign trips abroad for medical leaves and interventions. Such a campaign promise could only mean his administration would ensure the

15. Olukotun, "Reducing Cost of Governance in Nigeria."

16. Ayo Olukotun, "Buhari's Medical Leave and Resident Doctors' Strike," *The Punch,* April 2, 2021. Retrieved on August 12, 2022 through https://punchng.com/buharis-medical-leave-and-resident-doctors-strike/.

health sector is funded effectively to ensure efficacy and growth. The poor conditions of service provided within the Nigerian health sector have always been the cause for repeated strikes by health workers, and the trend was no different, probably worse, under the Buhari regime. When the COVID-19 pandemic was taking its toll on health workers, the resident doctors in Nigeria, among other things, demanded an upward adjustment of their hazard allowance and the pandemic-inducement allowance. Meanwhile, the president of the country deemed it fit to travel abroad for what is tagged a "routine medical checkup," a conviviality to sugarcoat the persistent waste of state resources on the personal problems of the leader. According to Olukotun:

> The two issues have expectedly generated spirited conversation, not just on the status of healthcare in the country but also on the insistence of top political leaders to enjoy, at taxpayers' expense, the luxury of medical tourism.[17]

While medical tourism is of no consequence under the assumption that an individual is expending their hard-earned resources on frivolous foreign medical trips, Buhari was a public official. In such a position, not only are financial benefits more than adequate, but the position granted him access to public funds under his discretion. The famed Aso Rock Clinic is captured as a standalone item with its annual budgetary allocations. If the institution is not deemed fit to provide quality medical care for the president, it can be understood that not only is the character of the officials contestable, but the quality and efficacy of healthcare funding in the country are poor. The president regressed on his promise to end medical tourism. Instead, he was part of public officials who frequently traveled abroad for medical care, illogically utilized national resources, and called into question his and others' faith in the Nigerian health sector and its staff. In discussing the liberties and loopholes utilized by government officials, Olukotun calls into question the belief in Nigerian nationalism and the limits of corruption. Olukotun further states:

> It was hoped that COVID-19 would have taught the important lesson that it is extremely risky to depend on the medical infrastructure built by other countries for the day may come when such infrastructure is not accessible.[18]

The above conversation raises stark questions regarding the status and efficacy of the Nigerian healthcare system, whereas medical trips abroad are perceived as the only way to access quality healthcare. Where does this leave ordinary citizens with no resources to embark on foreign trips for medical intervention? As the nation's healthcare sector is in abject disarray, Olukotun believes that medical tourism will continue to be a mainstay that serves the exclusive set of individuals at the corridors of power

17. Olukotun, "Buhari's Medical Leave and Resident Doctors' Strike."
18. Olukotun, "Buhari's Medical Leave and Resident Doctors' Strike."

in Nigeria. To make matters worse, medical practitioners leave the country in droves, as their services are needed elsewhere where they are valued. The huge brain drain resulting from the continuous flight of professional personnel may well spell doom for any policies aimed at developing the human resources of Nigeria in the foreseeable future.

A cursory look at many of the points raised by Olukotun paints a picture of a dysfunctional governance system that is a ground for other nations to exploit to their advantage. As noted by Olukotun, the British Council projected that many countries would continue to benefit from the Nigerian government's inadequacies since the country's leadership has failed to focus on the issues that count most. While the nation's health sector remains in disarray, it is estimated that Britain derives close to GBP1 billion from the political class in Nigeria persistently seeking assistance outside the country's shores. The Nigerian political class appears to turn a deaf ear to issues concerning the nation; they seem disconnected from the reality of the country's troubled existence, fixating their attention on what to steal from the nation's treasury. Inadvertently, it may take several years before these anomalies can be corrected despite these problems being entrenched in the minds of every citizen, the electorate inclusive.

Olukotun does not fail to address the policies of the Buhari administration, which could provide the necessary impetus to solve some of the country's existing problems. While the energy sector has experienced significant improvement in the last six years, new projects aimed at improving power generation cannot be discounted. In the article titled "Weak Scorecard and failing Social Contract," Olukotun notes:

> A careful examination of the factsheet by government spokespersons reveals that it conflates the initiation or flag-off of new projects with groundbreaking achievements. To give an example, listed in the 'blessings' for which Nigerians should be thankful is the Solar Power Naija initiated in April 2021 and is projected, if it succeeds, to provide five million households with off grid power. For Nigerians, who are putting up with the woes of rising cost of electricity and virtually stagnant distribution of power, the project must be regarded tongue-in-cheek as a marvelous blessing indeed. So much for publicists and their whitewashing antics...[19]

As rightly noted by the columnist, the objective of any truthful assessment of governance is the consideration of how effective the policies of an administration are and how workable they are towards building a society that will improve the condition of the people. Using this model, one is tempted to affirm that government assessment should be done to evaluate specific governments and ascertain how their projects lift

19. Ayo Olukotun, "Weak Scorecard and failing Social Contract," *The Punch*, June 4, 2021, Retrieved on August 12, 2022 through https://punchng.com/weak-scorecard-and-failing-social-contract/.

the citizens from their respective problems. This is the social contract between the government and the governed; any imbalances witnessed will act as a vitiating element towards the social contract. In other words, the focal point of government administration is to improve the lives of the governed. This is the reason politics and governance are mutually inclusive. As Olukotun points out below, discussing one without referencing the other will provide unbalanced arguments:

> Buhari correctly identified insecurity as a pivotal governance problem at the beginning of his tenure. He went on to pursue the agenda vigorously to the point where the government spokesperson could say that Boko Haram had been "technically defeated." Obviously, the gains of those earlier years have been reversed to the point where Boko Haram is seizing communities very close to the seat of government.[20]

Despite the recession and the devastating COVID-19 pandemic, the progress made by the Buhari administration concerning infrastructure cannot be disregarded. As noted by Olukotun, some of these infrastructural projects were initiated by the immediate past administration. However, claiming credit for completion should be expected since governance is a continuum. More laudable is the fact that new infrastructural projects were initiated:

> The rail route between Kaduna and Abuja became very busy recently when bandits turned the road travel into a nightmare as they occupied several parts of the road. Although the raging insecurity tends to loom larger than any possible achievements, the management of COVID-19 fallouts by the Presidential Task Force and the health ministry may have helped somewhat in minimizing thus far the lurking danger of widespread outbreak.[21]

Olukotun applauds the Buhari-led administration's efforts to ensure that attention was paid to education. In an attempt to improve the infrastructure of some of these educational institutions, the Buhari administration provided solar and gas power to some federal universities as well as teaching hospitals. He also highlighted various areas of neglect, especially in the tertiary education sector, which has persistently fallen in global ratings.

In the article titled "Diminishing Governance amidst Escalating Insecurity," Olukotun provides the report of a Singapore-based NGO that ranked nations based on

---

20. Ayo Olukotun, "Diminishing Governance amidst Escalating Insecurity," *The Punch*, April 30, 2021. Retrieved on August 12, 2022 through https://punchng.com/diminishing-governance-amidst-escalating-insecurity/.

21. Olukotun, "Diminishing Governance amidst Escalating Insecurity."

their governments' capabilities and the outcome of government policies.[22] Unfortunately, Nigeria was ranked 101 out of 104 countries.[23] This report further verified the level of decadence governance has reached in Nigeria. Chief among the indices used for this ranking are leadership and foresight, strong institutions, the country's attractiveness to the market, and global influence and reputation. Olukotun envisions Nigeria bouncing back to become a developmental hub in Africa. The journey towards this achievement has yet to be embarked upon; hence one can only pray and hope that the country's leadership will shift its focus from personal interest to national interest.

In his article titled "Anguished Nation left Stranded by its Leaders," Olukotun criticizes poor governance in Nigeria, which has prevented the county from moving forward.[24] Nigeria is at the point it is because the leaders are not driving her to progress. Despite the abundance of natural endowment, the local economy is not thriving since the country heavily relies on importation. Even though the country is one of the oil-producing states, it has no local refineries; thus, it refines crude oil in other countries and then pays a huge sum of money for fuel importation. Anyone passionate about Nigeria's development cannot afford to be oblivious to the challenge of bad leadership. In this essay, he queried the government's alienation of the citizens. In saner climes, the state and the people are in unity. The reality is different in Nigeria. Put simply, Nigeria's state and people are always in contention. The government shows its lack of concern for the welfare of the citizens. As Olukotun argues, class stratification enables the government to be removed from the hardship the citizens face. In Nigeria, government houses are well-built structures with abundant luxuries compared to the dilapidated settlements of the masses who voted the government into power.

Furthermore, Olukotun laments the endless fuel scarcity in the country. Hardly a year passes in Nigeria without long queues to purchase Premium Motor Spirit, locally known as petrol, at filling stations. As he put it: "…Nigerians are spending precious and quality time in fuel queues, scavenging for the increasingly scarce PMS priced out of the reach of many even when Buhari says that subsidy is not being removed."[25] It begs the question of why Nigeria does not have a functional refinery. Why would it refine crude oil overseas and pay money to import? The problem of fuel scarcity, as Olukotun points out, conveys the type of leadership Nigeria operates. Asides from the scarcity of fuel in Nigeria, fuel prices are never stable. When there is an increase, the prices are often difficult to return to normal. When the citizens express displeasure with the spike in fuel prices, the Nigerian government is often quick to point out other oil-producing countries like Saudi Arabia, where fuel prices are higher than Nigeria's. Reactions often included the dichotomy in the govern-

22. Olukotun, "Diminishing Governance amidst Escalating Insecurity."

23. Olukotun, "Diminishing Governance amidst Escalating Insecurity."

24. Ayo Olukotun, "Anguished Nation left Stranded by its Leaders," *The Punch*, 24 June 2022. Retrieved on August 12, 2022 through https://punchng.com/anguished-nation-left-stranded-by-its-leaders/.

25. Olukotun. "Anguished Nation left Stranded by its Leaders."

ment's comparison with Saudi Arabia, which has a more balanced economy than Nigeria and whose citizens get better minimum wages than their Nigerian counterparts. The Nigerian government has tactically left the solution to fuel scarcity to private individuals. Africa's richest man, Aliko Dangote, has begun to build a private refinery which, on completion, would help resolve the predicament of fuel importation and fuel prices in the country. Olukotun also harbors hope that the completion of the Dangote Refinery, as it is known, "will cushion the perennial breakdown in the fuel supply chain."

The columnist does not spare the government's failure to provide adequate electricity. Preceding and succeeding governments in Nigeria had always promised 24/7 electricity, but this has not been the case. The megawatts of electricity the nation generates are insufficient for a country with this huge population. Businesses and business owners suffer from the government's ineptitude in providing maximum electricity, which is also why the local economy is not thriving. The state of electricity in Nigeria is embarrassing for the status it occupies in Africa and the world in general. Despite a change in ownership of the Power Holding Company of Nigeria (PHCN), the problem persists. As Olukotun points out: "In spite of repeated promises, the electric power situation has gone from bad to worse, attended by serial breakdowns of the National Power Grid in the face of upward cascades in the unit price of electricity. Only recently, the Nigeria Labour Congress put it aptly when it said that Nigerians are paying for megawatts of darkness."[26] Thus, the Nigerian government must look into the problem of inadequate electricity and find a long-lasting solution.

In Nigeria, many people always express their desire to run for political office. They often leverage their little fame and borrow from Martin Luther King's quotes to contest political posts. It is not strange that twenty people may want to run for political office. However, many of them lack the intellectual capacity to perform in such offices—they know this, but they still contest anyway. Olukotun criticizes the trend in an article titled "Jamboree of Presidential Aspirants, Shortage of Turnaround Ideas."[27] He identified the lack of politically vibrant leaders as the cause of the crack in the nation's democratic system. Good governance remains elusive in Nigeria despite being a democratic dispensation. In an interview with *The Conversation*, Olukotun further notes how vote-buying contributes to the proliferation of bad governance in Nigeria, thus widening the cracks in its democracy.[28] Sadly, those who occupy leadership positions in Nigeria financially induce the voters the most. Voters no longer choose leaders

---

26. Olukotun. "Anguished Nation left Stranded by its Leaders."

27. Ayo Olukotun, "Jamboree of Presidential Aspirants, Shortage of Turnaround Ideas," *The Punch*, January 28, 2022, Retrieved on August 12, 2022 through https://punchng.com/jamboree-of-presidential-aspirants-shortage-of-turnaround-ideas/.

28. Ayo Olukotun, "Money is Breaking Democracy in Nigeria," *The Conversation*, 12 June 2022, Retrieved on August 12, 2022 through https://theconversation.com/money-is-breaking-democracy-in-nigeria-184595.

based on integrity or meritocracy; they vote for political leaders who give the most money. The fact that most of these voters are of the low class does not help, as they see elections as a money-making business to fend for themselves. Leadership positions in Nigeria in recent times seem to be for the highest bidders. This explains why political leaders exploit state resources to recoup their investments.

INSECURITY IN NIGERIA

In most of Ayo Olukotun's writing on the commonplace of insecurity in Nigeria, he often pointed out an already-known fact: Nigeria is in the firm grips of evil machinations—Boko Haram, bandits, and a host of other militant formations. An overview of Nigeria's security structure reveals the armed forces' ineffectiveness and inefficiency. Security is a very important aspect of any country aiming at growth and development. With adequate security, foreign investors would be comfortable doing business in such a country. It is well-known that the problem of insecurity in Nigeria has scared off foreign investors; thus, the country has relied on importation since most of the government-owned industries are dysfunctional. Nigerian citizens live in abject fear of those commonly described as "unknown gunmen." Hardly a day passes in the country without reports of militancy. The country's security architecture is so porous that even the Very Important Persons (VIPs) are not immune from the calamity of insecurity. It would be expected that Nigeria's Armed Force, one of the strongest in Africa, under the command of President Muhammadu Buhari, would change the gory narrative, but this was not the case. The victims of insecurity in the country include the security operatives—what a shame!

Ayo Olukotun brings to the fore the issues surrounding insecurity in the country. Like many other concerned stakeholders, he criticizes the ineptitude and silence of the Nigerian government in the wake of the security crisis. Whenever there is a militancy case, the Nigerian government expresses shock, ending there. There are usually no stringent measures the government carries out to forestall further attacks. The Nigerian government does posit that the insurgents are "technically defeated." Asides from the ambiguity of this term, there is a need for further assessment. If the insurgents are "technically defeated," why are they still active and, in most cases, show their technical supremacy over the military forces? Olukotun points out how the Nigerian government's politicking of security challenges could prove a fatal blow to the country's continued existence.

Despite reports from international organizations on infiltrating deadly terrorist groups into Nigeria due to porous insecurity, the government has not felt the need to take charge—other than its little preparations. The end is in sight for a nation that undergoes an internal struggle with insurgents and is on the losing side. This is not to be pessimistic because Nigerians are often away from reality. National development is often in tandem with adequate security. Olukotun, in his articles or interventions,

Figure 12.2. "Ayo Olukotun, The Don" by Dr. Kazeem Ekeolu. Ayo Olukotun is within the bounds of Nigeria, and the book signifies his commitment to the Nigerian cause.

calls on the government to do something worthwhile to curb insecurity. There is no safe place in Nigeria. The country sits atop a barrel of gunpowder—a calamity is waiting. The issue of insecurity contributes to the endless discourses of the citizens who suffer from severe hardships. A Nigerian from the South-west cannot afford to journey to the North-west by road. If there is an attempt to make such a trip, it is almost certain that such a voyager would not return home.

Several of Olukotun's articles pinpoint the insecurity that has befallen the country, especially in the last five years. Before this, religious extremism-fueled terrorism was the major issue encapsulated whenever there were discussions of national insecurity in Nigeria. However, this has taken a new dimension; while there is a significant reduction in terrorism activity in the country, the rise in banditry and kidnappings seems to compensate. A lack of concentration deepens Nigeria's new spate of insecurity as it knows no socio-economic divide. A cursory look at the activities of terrorists in Nigeria will reveal a preponderance of terrorist activities in places domiciled by the economically less privileged. Kidnapping and armed banditry, on the other hand, do not distinguish between the rich and the poor.

In the column "Lame Response to Unending Security Jitters," Olukotun brings up a point made by Abdulaziz Yari, the governor of Zamfara.[29] By then, bandits had terrorized the Nigerian state of Zamfara for over a year, and Yari believed these bandits were better equipped than Nigeria's own defense military. Yari states: "they (the bandits) are in control of the kind of weapons that the (army) command in Zamfara does not have. In one armory alone, they have over five hundred AK 47s, we saw them." In response to Yari's comments, Olukotun again draws on the country's structure and considers its institutions' efficacy in determining whether Nigeria has given enough to support its security infrastructure amid hardships.[30]

This security issue does not end here, as the Nigerian army is not the only military defense that needs better funding. Olukotun also brings up the challenges Nigeria faces in the maritime sector. Armed pirates are a real issue in Nigeria, and the Nigerian navy does not have the supplies or platform to effectively run and protect Nigeria's waterways. In his column, Olukotun clearly states that Nigeria has been robbed of over 15 billion dollars in the last 15 years. This loss results from the gross markup of arms procurement contracts, the award of phantom defense contracts, and the enactment of rackets calculated to divert funds meant to shore up defense capability.[31]

Olukotun furthers the notion of inept security funding by referencing the Kajuru crisis in the Kaduna state, in which gunmen killed nearly 70 people in two attacks.[32] He states that this situation has brought the insecure situation of Nigerian lives and property to the frontline, along with the necessity of reforms. According to a report by the International Rescue Committee (IRC), Nigeria is one of the 10 countries with the biggest risk of humanitarian emergency for the year 2019. Thus, Olukotun states it will be fascinating to figure out how the government and various security institutions will handle this issue. Olukotun believes that the deterioration of security in Nigeria is due to the "divorce between policy science and the actual work of security organizations."

29. Ayo Olukotun, "Lame Response to Unending Security Jitters," *The Punch*, March 21, 2019. Retrieved on August 12, 2022 through https://punchng.com/lame-response-to-unending-security-jitters/.

30. Olukotun, "Lame Response to Unending Security Jitters."

31. Olukotun, "Lame Response to Unending Security Jitters."

32. Olukotun, "Lame Response to Unending Security Jitters."

Additionally, the author has noticed a shift from governance to politics and political competition. What is being observed is a resounding lack of public officials and agencies involved in the issues plaguing the people and the nation. Rather, politicians have resorted to surface-fixing policies and recycling campaign promises and hopes for a future that is impossible to achieve without the dedication of serious time and effort.

Olukotun did note that the Federal Executive Council approved a budget of 8.5 billion naira to aid Nigerian states that have been overrun by security conflicts, including Adamawa, Benue, Bornu, Taraba, Yobe, and Zamfara. However, Kaduna, a conflict location, was not mentioned on the list. Olukotun questions whether or not it is more consequential to proactively act to prevent humanitarian catastrophes or if the government should administer remedies after the harm has already been done. Overall, Olukotun highlights that security infrastructure is currently in awful condition, and there seems to be little action to be taken to fix this issue. He states that Nigeria no longer sees this security issue as only a police action problem but rather one of a federal proportion. The writer further opines that the security contingents are related to high unemployment and poverty. "Communities, long excluded from the orbit of governance and abandoned by an incompetent state, will sooner than later breed monsters that are hard to slay. That means, a holistic response must see crime as a social, rather than a law and order problem."[33]

In the article "The Siege to Kaduna and an Emir's Travails," Olukotun references the gradual increment in raids and kidnappings in Kaduna State, one of the bedrocks of the Northern oligarchs.[34] Kaduna state and its environs have become a fertile ground for the lucrative kidnapping business enveloping the country. In Olukotun's words:

> For the better part of this year [2021], Kaduna State has witnessed spectacular raids on schools, institutions of tertiary education as well as prominent individuals, the latest of which is the Emir of Kajuru, who, along with his throne and family members was captured and forcibly moved to a kidnappers' den. The 85-year-old emir was released a day or two later, but the bandits cruelly held on to his dependants demanding a ransom of N200 million as price for securing their release. Grievously but characteristically, there was no police presence throughout the duration of the nocturnal seizure of Kajuru, notwithstanding the fact that it warehouses a local government secretariat and is a mere half-an-hour drive from the Kaduna metropolis which boasts established police and military presence.[35]

---

33. Olukotun, "Lame Response to Unending Security Jitters."

34. Ayo Olukotun, "The Siege to Kaduna and an Emir's Travails," *The Punch,* July 16, 2021. Retrieved on August 12, 2022 through https://punchng.com/the-siege-to-kaduna-and-an-emirs-travails/.

35. Olukotun, "The Siege to Kaduna and an Emir's Travails."

Further discussing the issue of insecurity in Nigeria, Olukotun affirms that the level of insecurity in Nigeria acts as a barrier to socio-economic growth and political stability. He also asserts that it hurts the country's survival and prospects for future elections. Looking at the Emir's abduction, it becomes easy to understand that insecurity in Nigeria is on a pedestal that leaves no room for any form of perceived immunity. According to Olukotun, the state's security apparatus cannot avert worst-case scenarios and consequences. This pointer is that the Nigerian security forces are grossly underequipped to encountering hostile criminal forces.

The absence of effective government institutions in the agrarian communities that make up the northern part of Nigeria makes it easy for the banditry to thrive therein. This has resulted in a large population of helpless rural dwellers acting in the nation's food basket capacity. As the writer retorted, the depth of insecurity of lives and property in Nigeria has produced a climate of uncertainty and a bleak future for the country. Within this, politicians are busy scheming from one electioneering period to another, unconcerned about how to tackle the impending doom facing the country. The political game of seeking power is played without the expected purpose of moving the nation forward; rather, it is based on accessing the national cake.

The various dimensions of insecurity constitute a great problem for the country due to its negative effect on the productivity levels of other sectors like manufacturing, agriculture, trade, foreign investment, and the safety of the citizens.[36] Kidnappings and banditry are the new normal in several northern states, with whole communities finding no other solution than to relocate in droves. In the southern part of Nigeria, insecurity in the region has been blamed on northerners disguising themselves as herdsmen to inflict mayhem on unsuspecting communities. From observations, one can deduce that the increased agitation for secession by southern elements is heavily influenced by the threatening presence of Fulani herdsmen in several places. Olukotun further validates this:

> The recent alert by some Yoruba groups and leaders of a possible invasion by killer herdsmen of their territory can only compound an already desperate situation. The economy as mentioned at the outset touches a raw nerve as it connects with livelihood, lifespan, and virtually every area of governance. Performance ranges from dismal to mediocre as policy continues to go back and forth like a yo-yo.[37]

From the several points noted by Olukotun, it is evident that the strides of the Buhari administration were very few, further leading to a weak scorecard when it comes to an objective assessment of governance. Though most sectors need substantial devel-

36. Olukotun, "The Siege to Kaduna and an Emir's Travails."
37. Olukotun, "The Siege to Kaduna and an Emir's Travails."

opment and change, it is only when elections are around the corner that governance issues become paramount in the minds of the electorates. While citizens are swayed by false claims by those running for office, Olukotun's analysis of the Buhari administration indicates it was arduous for Buhari to improve his scorecard based on his campaign promises. He probably will not be remembered as the leader that took Nigeria out of the dilemma of bad governance.

Providing hope, Olukotun posits that "all is not lost," as the presidency has decided to seek the option of contracting foreign mercenaries to fight the various armed insurrections being mounted by dissidents from the northern part of Nigeria. Although it is expected that a state of emergency may be declared if the situation becomes unbearable, the capacity of Nigeria's armed forces to engage dissidents should be strengthened through worthwhile expenditure.

The problem of insecurity in Nigeria is further compounded by what Olukotun describes as the failure of the government to take security reports seriously. In his article, "Insecurity: A nation sleepwalking in utter peril," he condemns the Kuje Prison attack.[38] If the Nigerian government were a serious one, it would have ended the "madness" of insurgent attacks after the Kuje Prison attacks. The terrorists were reported to have operated unhindered during this dastardly act. The security operatives at this prison admitted they were neither tactically nor militarily matchable against the terrorists. The terrorists operated with such freedom that reports from reliable quarters posited they had enough time to give Islamic lectures after the operations.[39] Despite the security intelligence that there was an imminent attack, the Nigerian government—like it usually does—failed to act in time! After the attacks, there were similarly no substantial efforts from the government to improve security. Olukotun, in this article, criticizes the government's wishy-washy measures on the issue of security which often gives credence to reports that the Buhari-led government was in cahoots with militants. The level of terrorism in Nigeria has bothered concerned stakeholders about the sovereignty of the country because a nation that reduces recurring issues of insecurity to press statements and divine intervention is close to becoming a failed state, if not one already.

Through his illumination of the state of security in Nigeria, Olukotun informs the citizens that there is a proverbial fire on the mountain. It is now left to whether the citizens should "run" or for the government to take charge. If the government's body language is to be considered, the former seems the most viable solution. Security experts have cautioned about the government's soft approach to terrorism, yet it has not changed tactics. The paradox here is that despite the nation's porous security ar-

---

38. Ayo Olukotun, "Insecurity: a nation sleepwalking in utter peril," *The Punch*, 29 July 2022, Retrieved on August 12, 2022 through https://punchng.com/insecurity-a-nation-sleepwalking-in-utter-peril/.

39. Sade Owoyemi, "The Insider: Boko Haram Gave 15-Min Quranic Lecture to Kuje Inmates Before Setting Them Free," *FIJ*, 6 July 2022, Retrieved on August 12, 2022 through https://fij.ng/article/the-insider-boko-haram-gave-15-min-quranic-lecture-to-kuje-inmates-before-setting-them-free/.

chitecture, it would be the first to send military assistance to other African countries battling to counter insurgents. In a thematically-similar article titled "Abuja-Kaduna rail: NRC's astonishing misplacement of priorities," Olukotun further beams light on the ills of insecurity.[40] He wrote the articles in the aftermath of the terrorist attack on the Abuja-Kaduna train service.

This development further brought pain to the hearts of ailing citizens and established the nation's security operatives as mere charlatans. Terrorists have taken over virtually all spaces in Nigeria's climate. The Abuja-Kaduna rail attack is one of many other attestations. Passengers were abducted after the terrorists seized control of the Abuja-Kaduna railway. Most passengers have not regained freedom (when writing in September 2022), with the militants demanding a huge sum of money before anyone can be released. Olukotun criticizes the government for not taking any urgent steps as if to say that it holds no importance to the lives and properties of the citizen. There were reports that the Nigerian government left the abducted passengers to their fates, with families of the abductees lamenting the government's negligence.[41] Olukotun queries the approach of the Nigerian Railway Corporation (NRC) and the government in general on securing these victims. In the aftermath of the attacks, President Buhari directed the NRC to set up a control room to forestall future attacks, but the directive did not produce the anticipated changes. Olukotun thus criticizes the problem of communication within the Nigerian government. As he puts it, "One of the mysteries of the current regime concerns how regularly instructions, ultimatums, and even warnings from the president are flouted."[42] Olukotun also criticizes the Transport Minister, Rotimi Amaechi, for leaving out security designs in the nation's railway restructuring.

The silence of the political class characterizes Nigeria's problem of insecurity. Olukotun examines this in an article titled "Insecurity: Political class terrifying silence."[43] By "silence," Olukotun means the lack of collective efforts by the political class to end insecurity. He alludes to the ordeals of a retired university professor, Duro Adegboye, in the den of kidnappers and the failure of the political class to come to the rescue to further foreground the issue of insecurity. The militants have become so audacious that they seem concerned with the electoral process in the country. He criticizes the

---

40. Ayo Olukotun, "Abuja-Kaduna rail: NRC's astonishing misplacement of priorities", *The Punch*, 20 May 2022. Retrieved on August 12, 2022 through https://punchng.com/abuja-kaduna-rail-nrcs-astonishing-misplacement-of-priorities/.

41. Nasir Ayitogo, "Kaduna Train Attack: Kidnapped Victim's Relatives Protest in Abuja," *Premium Times*, 25 July 2022. Retrieved on August 12, 2022 through https://www.premiumtimesng.com/news/top-news/544833-kaduna-train-attack-kidnapped-victims-relatives-protest-in-abuja.html.

42. Ayo Olukotun, "Abuja-Kaduna rail: NRC's Astonishing Misplacement of Priorities," *The Punch*, 20 May 2022. Retrieved on August 12, 2022 through https://punchng.com/abuja-kaduna-rail-nrcs-astonishing-misplacement-of-priorities/.

43. Ayo Olukotun, "Insecurity: Political Class Terrifying Silence," *The Punch*, 1 July 2022. Retrieved on August 12, 2022 through https://punchng.com/insecurity-political-class-terrifying-silence/.

political class for their silence in the aftermath of insecurity. He contends: "Let us ask the question, amidst all these occurrences, when was the last time a notable politician or member of the political class addressed a press conference drawing attention to tragic occurrences, escalating toll of deaths and rising number of terrorists of different descriptions maintaining governance by forcibly occupying parts of Nigerian territory?"[44] The silence of the political elites translates that they are impervious to the citizen's welfare. Despite their silence, the issue of insecurity has degenerated so badly that the political elites are not safe from attacks. The Presidential guards were attacked by terrorists,[45] fueling reports of an imminent attack at the seat of power, the Presidential Villa, nicknamed Aso Rock. When the terrorists can be so daring as to list the president as their next target, the reality is clear for all to see. Olukotun references the United States of America's rescue operation for its kidnapped citizen in Nigeria to illustrate not only the damning level of insecurity in the country but also as a sort of didactic pathway for the Nigerian government to take a new leaf on how it can care for its citizens.

In "Will Insecurity Jinx 2023 Elections," Olukotun raises cogent issues on insecurity and elections.[46] He fears the security crisis may affect the transition of government in 2023. His fears are valid. If the terrorists continue to possess territories in Nigeria, then it would not be pessimistic to suggest that this would take a toll on the general elections. The Nigerian citizens harbor Olukotun's fears too. This show how damning Nigeria's security crisis is. The terrorists have been said to form an internal government in Nigeria where Nigerians are forced to pay taxes and from where they launch coordinated attacks. There are predictions that the terrorists may disrupt the electoral process, ultimately increasing political apathy in the country. Olukotun laments the growing trend of terrorism that the mere mention of imminent terrorist attacks is enough to send the top echelons of Nigeria's political class into palpitations and last-minute efforts to stem the tide. He argues: "True, for now, the terrorists have not announced a political agenda, being more interested in the lure of easy cash from ransom, but who says they may not develop one and begin to attack the infrastructure of elections or persons in the wake of performing their civic duty of voting."[47] At any rate, and as this columnist consistently argues, it is strange, if not tragic, that it is the terrorists that are steps ahead of law enforcement and not the other way round." [48]

---

44. Olukotun, "Insecurity: Political Class Terrifying Silence."

45. Adebayo Taiwo-Hassan, "Exclusive: Inside Details of how the Nigerian Presidential Guards Fell into Terrorist Ambush," *Premium Times*, 3 August 2022, Retrieved on August 12, 2022 through https://www.premiumtimesng.com/news/headlines/546381-exclusive-inside-details-of-how-nigerian-presidential-guards-fell-into-terrorist-ambush.html.

46. Ayo Olukotun, "Will Insecurity Jinx 2023 Elections," *The Punch*, April 15, 2022, Retrieved on August 12, 2022 through https://punchng.com/will-insecurity-jinx-2023-elections/.

47. Ayo Olukotun, "Will Insecurity Jinx 2023 Elections."

48. Ayo Olukotun, "Will Insecurity Jinx 2023 Elections."

EDUCATIONAL DECADENCE IN NIGERIA

One of the major expectations from any functional and effective government is to ensure that it nurtures the learning culture of the citizens. This is reinforced by public, private, and international initiatives, as education is regarded as one of the United Nation's Sustainable Developmental Goals. Governments worldwide perceive the education sector as the bedrock of development and advancement, hence the zeal to establish elaborate policies to ensure that education is provided to the citizenry. Olukotun affirms in "How We Dropped the Ball on Quality Education in Nigeria" that the Nigerian government is yet to make any meaningful progress in achieving impressive education standards. As rightly noted by the columnist, the drop in the quality of education is traceable to the absence of educational policies that will ensure the maintenance of a particular standard.

Along with the political and defense sectors, another necessary institutional reform Olukotun mentions in his columns is the education system in Nigeria. In his column, "Falana and the Search for an Effective TETFUND," Olukotun discusses TETFUND or The Tertiary Education Trust Fund. TETFUND, an acronym for Tertiary Education Trust Fund, was established by the Federal Government of Nigeria in 2011. It was formed to disburse, manage, and monitor the education tax to Nigerian tertiary institutions owned by the government. Olukotun posits that TETFUND is not only problematic in its usage but is rarely put to its intended task. Olukotun has positioned TETFUND as a reason why Nigeria does not have proper education. "TETFUND is a fruit of the many struggles by the Academic Staff Union of universities to address the issues of perennial underfunding in Nigerian Universities. The pity, however, is that while TETFUND projects, especially in the areas of physical infrastructure, are in evidence across tertiary institutions owned by the government, only a fraction, and a tiny one at that of the huge funds amassed under the Act has been disbursed."[49]

Olukotun questions if the government faces a lack of awareness about the deteriorating state of the education system or simply a lack of interest. There are frequent closures of universities because of strikes, an alarmingly high rate of students dropping out of school, and a very low number of students enrolling in private tertiary universities. Olukotun knows that the government has done little to figure out a way to fund the universities. There has been no benchmarking progress made to help reform Nigerian education.[50]

The government must focus on the issue of decaying educational standards, as Olukotun states that quality education will not just appear. In his column, "The Elusive Search for Quality Education," he highlights that good education needs a society

49. Ayo Olukotun, "Falana and the Search for an Effective Tetfund," *The Punch*, March 21, 2019. Retrieved on August 12, 2022 through https://punchng.com/falana-and-the-search-for-an-effective-tetfund/.

50. Olukotun, "Falana and the Search for an Effective TETFUND."

where mediocrity and unethical shortcuts are not the standards. The standard must be "a function of quality instruction, taken by capable and motivated teachers in a pleasant learning environment."[51] To obtain and provide quality education, Nigeria must reform the training of educators and reinvent the educational landscape. Education must prioritize continuous assessment and lifelong learning. Currently, Nigerian students are crowded into unsanitary and far-from-perfect buildings for their education. Olukotun recognizes this fact and states that "In sum, a gamut of reforms is required to revitalize the current comatose status of our educational system as well as revive a semblance of the kind of quality education which once defined them and gave them a niche on the world map. It will be nice if such issues begin to preoccupy our politicians currently engaged in all-out-fight for the 2015 elections."[52]

In his writings, Olukotun explores not only the poor quality of education available in Nigeria but also the lack of diversity in educational programs. In his column "Dearth of Nigerian CEOs in Nigeria-Based Multinationals," Olukotun highlights the need for business education. The former deputy Governor of the Central Bank, Dr. Obed Mailafia, had argued that Nigeria has specifically downgraded business and management education in the educational sector. Dr. Mailafia highlights that no premium business school matches the scale of Harvard Business School or likely any standard business school in the United States.[53]

While Nigeria's universities do offer training and degrees in management, the government has continued to fail to fund the universities. Much like the lack of proper funding in the defense sector, the lack of world-class education stems from the lack of good funding. One of the results of the lack of funding and emphasis on business and management education has been a lower investment in the business sector. The poor management programs have caused Nigerians to lack proper education to teach them how to run and maintain a business. Olukotun states, "the voice of Africa's giant, once commanding and compelling in continental affairs, is increasingly dwindling to a barely audible squeak."[54] There is a lack of Nigerian representation in positions like CEO, President, or other chief management opportunities. Wale Babalakin, a Nigerian businessman, lawyer, and philanthropist, has commented that "the advent of indigenous CEOs in foreign companies on our soil is virtually over, punctuated, of course, by a few honorable exceptions."[55] In agreement with Babalakin's observation, Olukotun refers to the story of a man from Kenya who was redeployed from a nearby African country to be the chief executive of a big company in Nigeria in his writings.

51. Ayo Olukotun, "The Elusive Search for Quality Education," *The Punch*, November 26, 2013.

52. Olukotun, "The Elusive Search for Quality Education."

53. Ayo Olukotun, "Dearth of Nigerian CEO's in Nigeria-Based Multinationals," *The Punch*, November 13, 2018. Retrieved on August 12, 2022 through https://punchng.com/dearth-of-indigenous-ceos-in-nigeria-based-multinationals/.

54. Olukotun, "Dearth of Nigerian CEO's in Nigeria-Based Multinationals."

55. Olukotun, "Dearth of Nigerian CEO's in Nigeria-Based Multinationals."

Olukotun feels that this situation, which is by no means an isolated incident, tugs at the Nigerian sense of self-worth. While it reaffirms a sense of the capability of Africans, it remains that Nigerians are equally capable and should be CEOs or managing big businesses with better access to education.

The burden of substandard education is reflected in virtually all areas of endeavor. Employers in various sectors of the Nigerian economy complain about the deluge of unemployable graduates coupled with diminishing jobs.[56] One cannot fail to acknowledge the fact that the term "unemployable graduate" was coined in Nigeria to characterize a graduate whose intellectual capacity does not level up with the certificate being brandished. The expectation from such individuals falls below reality; performing basic tasks such as writing memos or articulating positions is taken for granted or relegated to the background. This situation has reached a crescendo wherein teachers cannot effectively articulate their positions to the students. Olukotun noted that not long ago, even the Governor of Kaduna State, Mallam El-Rufai, witnessed a high proportion of state school teachers finding it difficult to exhibit the requisite competencies needed to teach students in school.

The Nigerian government has continually failed to maintain standards in the education sector, including higher and tertiary institutions. In the past, public universities in Nigeria prided themselves on maintaining impressive standards. In the last two decades, however, there has been a gradual erosion of standards in Nigeria's public universities, with private universities becoming more influential and attractive to those that can afford them. Olukotun heaped the major blame on the government as it has persistently refused to effectively fund public universities, resulting in, and inciting incessant strikes that lead to disruptions in the academic activities of the institutions. Citing Falola's excerpts at the convocation lecture of Adekunle Ajasin University held in 2017, Olukotun retorted that the inadequacy of the university curricula of Nigerian universities is evident in the lack of necessary interdisciplinary coverage that will make them more relevant to the present-day.

> Yoked to a colonial model which it once replicated but now merely parodies, it faces multiple challenges of chronic underfunding, endemic or structured disorder, over centralization, provincialism in an unflattering sense, disconnect from shop floor realities of the workplace and as Professor Toyin Falola, quoted in the opening paragraph argued, it lacks topicality.[57]

---

56. Ayo Olukotun, "How We Dropped the Ball on Quality Education in Nigeria," *Opinion Nigeria,* November 2, 2019. Retrieved on August 12, 2022 through http://www.opinionnigeria.com/how-we-dropped-the-ball-on-quality-education-in-nigeria-by-ayo-olukotun/.

57. Ayo Olukotun, "Tweaking University Education for Youth Empowerment," *People's Daily,* October 15, 2019. Retrieved on August 12, 2022 through https://peoplesdailyng.com/tweaking-university-education-for-youth-empowerment-2/.

Attempts by the Nigerian government to cushion the effect of unemployment through various programs like YOUWIN, SURE-P, and N-Power are merely attempts to solve the surface problems of youth unemployment in Nigeria. The looming disaster, as Olukotun notes in many of his articles, can only be averted by the government's honest effort toward overhauling the education system to give room for maintainable and sustainable standards. Much like the outside world, the university system has been taken over by lecturers who now play dirty politics to gain control of the system for personal payments. Further quoting Falola in the article, Olukotun affirms that "a considerable number of Nigerian universities are not managed by intellectual minds but by ethnic and religious bigots or by profit driven entrepreneurs."[58] The comments and observations of these scholars, along with the difficulties faced by students and graduates, suggest a need to overhaul the reward and incentive system in the administration of educational institutions for the education sector to experience excellence and increased productivity.

While the public universities in Nigeria are being consigned to obsolesce, their counterparts in the private sector are beginning to fill the vacuum through the provision of standard learning environments that enhance the productivity of both the students and the lecturers. Although it may be argued that the fees charged by the latter are not modest, it is just a matter of time before Nigeria becomes a place brewing with a large pool of private tertiary institutions. The only hope is that the standards produced by private universities do not mirror that of public universities. In the article "Licensing 20 Private Universities is a Blunder," Olukotun notes that there is already a glut of undercapitalized, undersubscribed, and poorly clad universities where the student population is less than 10% of the total population of the people on the campus.[59] Private universities should be established for education and development; these empty ventures attest to continuously developing problems that merge with the government and private sectors. The key to establishing a desirable educational sector is to establish sound educational policies wherein the private universities will act as a subset of such policy implementation. Establishing private universities to make money will only add to the mediocre perception of tertiary institutions.

Olukotun also laments the sorry state of the Nigerian tertiary education system vis a vis the perennial "ASUU strike" in an article titled "Persisting ASUU Strike and Governance Crisis."[60] He criticizes the government for taking the tertiary education system with levity. After admission into federal universities, the students remain unsure when they will complete their studies—even when four, five, or six years are

58. Olukotun, "Tweaking University Education for Youth Empowerment."

59. Ayo Olukotun, "Licensing 20 Private Universities is a Blunder," *The Punch*, April 16, 2021, Retrieved on August 12, 2022 through https://punchng.com/licensing-20-private-universities-is-a-blunder/.

60. Ayo Olukotun, "Persisting ASUU Strike and Governance Crisis," *The Punch*, 22 April 2022, Retrieved on August 12, 2022 through https://punchng.com/column-persisting-asuu-strike-and-governance-crisis/.

stipulated. The reason for this pessimism is the cyclical industrial strike action carried out by the Academic Staff Union of Universities (ASUU), who are continually in a rift with the Nigerian government over a host of issues ranging from unpaid salaries to poor state of universities, etc. When this strike occurs, the Nigerian government does not often respond quickly; thus, the strike action is prolonged. Federal university students are forced to go home and keep themselves updated on the precarious situation. There is a joke among these university students that ASUU "strikes" better than thunder! Olukotun berates the political class for lying idle in the state of the "virtual collapse of education." The sad truth is that the children of Nigeria's political elites are not in public-owned varsities in Nigeria. They are all scattered in top-tier varsities worldwide—which best summarizes the government's lackadaisical attitude to the education sector.

FLAWED POLITICAL PROCESS IN NIGERIA

In February 2019, Nigeria held general elections to elect the President, Vice President, the House of Representatives, and Senate. The elections were meant to be held on the 16th of February; however, the Independent Electoral Commission postponed the voting by one week. The INEC cited logistical challenges in promptly getting the electoral materials to polling stations as the reason for the postponement. In response to the postponed elections, Olukotun states: "Though there are precedents for the decision in Nigeria's political history of bizarre twists and turns, it was traumatizing for the electorate, damaging to our international image and will, in all probability, result in voter fatigue and diminished turn out tomorrow."[61]

In a column written before the postponement was made public, Olukotun describes the scene in Nigeria: "So, as polling day, Saturday, 16th February, draws closer, concerned citizens are holding peace rallies, and walks around the country to emphasize to the political class that peace is indivisible, that they owe the nation the duty to comport themselves in a civil and orderly manner."[62] Olukotun notes that the country seemed to be in disarray. Towards the end of his column, Olukotun reminds readers that there is life after the elections, and Nigerians must confront that reality. He states that whoever wins the elections must begin working towards creating better infrastructure and a better Nigeria immediately.

In the spirit of rebuilding the nation, Olukotun directly addresses civil society institutions within his articles. In his column "Our Election, Our Destiny," Olukotun reflects on the pressing need for the improvement of civil society. The first step to bettering civil society lies within voting numbers. In 2015, only 44 percent of regis-

61. Ayo Olukotun, "Finally, the Election holds?" *The Punch*, February 21, 2019. Retrieved on August 12, 2022 through https://punchng.com/finally-the-election-holds/.

62. Ayo Olukotun, "The Election and Beyond," *The Punch*, February 14, 2019, Retrieved on August 12, 2022 through https://punchng.com/the-election-and-beyond/.

tered voters voted in the Presidential election. This 44 percent translates to 16 percent of the country's population.[63] How can an election be true, valid, and serious if only 16 percent of the country's voice is heard? Olukotun highlights that the voters in Nigeria "represent a cardinal segment of the process in that their apathy or non-compliance with the rules can undo the elections, or at least diminish them."[64] He states that it is the civic responsibility of eligible voters to show up and defend their votes in future elections.

Voters must also be educated on the political climate to defend their votes. Olukotun touches on the notion that democracy is not genuine unless voters are aware and conscious about whom they vote for. Voters must educate themselves before they vote.[65] Olukotun states that every possible effort should make voting easy, credible, and transparent. Olukotun recalls the election in 2011, in which there was an allegation that the People's Democratic Party had manipulated the results of northern Nigeria's votes. Buhari's supporters then went on a rampage and killing spree, in which over 1,000 Nigerians were killed. In response to the violent elections in 2011, Olukotun states: "Nigerians should be smarter than those party hawks shouting themselves hoarse, creating sensational ripples, threatening our peace and telling us that the election is an all-time contest between good and evil, hell and heaven. Knowing that the elections, whichever way they go, will not determine much should create a sober mood and a reflective one concerning how a country so blessed got into this downswing of leadership demolition."[66] However, Nigeria must ensure that the voting structure is credible and reliable.

The idea of rigging elections is a topic that Olukotun highlights in multiple columns. In "The Election and Beyond," Olukotun remembers a conversation he once had with a senior colleague. Olukotun asked the colleague why politicians in advanced democracies have never considered rigging elections as an option. The colleague responds: "I think it is their sense of history, the fear that when the history books are written, it will be mentioned that it is so and so that brought an end to British, French or American democracy, as the case may be."[67] Olukotun remarks on the other possible reasons advanced democracies such as the United States have and likely will never unfairly represent the votes of its people. He states that, unlike Nigeria, advanced democracies have a vigilant civil society that watches over the state. In addition, advanced democracies have electoral institutions that have built a culture of respect and virtue.

In "Eurasia's Troubling Projections on the 2019 Elections," Olukotun quips that all elections, aside from those of 2015, have been accompanied by "sensational irregular-

63. Olukotun, "The Election and Beyond."
64. Olukotun, "The Election and Beyond."
65. Olukotun, "The Election and Beyond."
66. Olukotun, "The Election and Beyond."
67. Olukotun, "The Election and Beyond."

ities and malfeasance."[68] Olukotun states that the issue of rigging elections is due to the "tribe of elections forgers, which has totally replaced politicians of an earlier generation with a commitment to genuinely serve the people." Before the election results were revealed, according to the Eurasia Group, the world's largest political-risk consultancy, a second term for Buhari would cause Nigeria to continue to muddle through the next four years with a small amount of progress on policy. However, the Eurasia Group predicted that if Atiku Abubakar wins the elections, "there is likely to be a return to the kind of rent-seeking habits witnessed under the Peoples' Democratic Party in earlier regimes, thus outweighing his keener intellect and vigor in comparison to Buhari." Before Buhari was re-elected, Olukotun emphasized that the elected President of Nigeria addressed the state of national unity. He cited that Nigeria is currently more ethnically and religiously divided than it had ever been since the civil war. According to Olukotun, Buhari must keep his promise to adhere to his inclusive mandate to "extend the frontier of our federalism and nationalism." He calls for the recasting and reconstitution of the flagship program and expresses that Buhari must reform the administration's flagship program to have a looser interpretation. Buhari also must focus on the pressing issue of poverty, as Olukotun writes that economic and political life have been neglected in Nigeria's past.

However, Olukotun knows that the government is not the only body in Nigeria capable of making change. In his column "Governance Takeaways from the Upheaval in France," Olukotun alludes to the situation of Emmanuel Macron, the President of France. Despite Macron's elected status, the Yellow Vests Protest, a movement of the French public for economic justice, exercised sovereignty by insisting that Macron should step down because of the government's failure. Olukotun states that if the Nigerian democracy grew beyond electoralism, perhaps the Nigerian people could learn that they can make a change, not just the elected party or political billionaires. Olukotun highlights that democratic elections are only a starting point in building a successful nation. He uses the example of the French Yellow Vests Protest to show that the general public can make a change outside of the polls. Olukotun asks: "How beneficial will it be if Nigerian leaders will learn to face issues, acknowledge their mistakes and blind spots, apologize for them, and show that the people ought to be the driving force of a worthy democratic project."[69] In "Straw Debates and Politics as Escapism," Olukotun highlights that for Nigeria to improve, the public must organize social movements that challenge the current governance, and political structures, much like the French public did.

---

68. Ayo Olukotun, "Eurasia's Troubling Projections on the 2019 Elections," *The Punch*, January 17, 2019, Retrieved on August 12, 2022 through https://punchng.com/eurasias-troubling-projections-on-the-2019-elections/.

69. Ayo Olukotun, "Governance Takeaways from the upheaval in France," *The Punch*, December 12, 2019, Retrieved on August 12, 2022 through https://punchng.com/governance-takeaways-from-the-upheaval-in-france/.

One major problem with Nigerian leaders is that they tend to make empty promises. In "We Need Conversations, Not Sweet-Nothings," Olukotun stresses that the 2019 election season held many likely unfulfillable promises. The top contenders were Buhari, who represented the All Progressives Congress, and Alhaji Abubakar Atiku of the People's Democratic Party. One of the empty promises that Buhari's party made was a fanfare called "Next Level." This included promises that would ensure and promote the development of economic, social, and political sectors. Meanwhile, Buhari promised to create jobs for 1 million graduates and create a public-private sector system to help 10 million Nigerians. Additionally, under the Anchor borrowers' scheme, Buhari said he would create several million jobs, which would speed up the job creation process for 1 million farmers, another 1.5 million jobs for the livestock transformation project, and several other millions of jobs related to agriculture and manufacturing.[70]

Atiku Abubakar, former vice-president of Nigeria and 2019 presidential candidate, came up with a promise dubbed the "Atiku Plan," assuring the electorate that this plan would solve Nigeria's long-term and short-term complaints. The plan was essentially 45 promises that involved noticeable transportation improvement through restructuring and creating more jobs in the field of industrial development. The Atiku Plan also called for a dramatic increase in power generation, as it promised that by 2025, manufacturing would soar from its current fraction of 9% of GDP to 30% of GDP.[71]

HEALTHCARE EDUCATION/ISSUES EXAMINED BY OLUKOTUN

Education regarding healthcare is another key issue in Nigeria. Olukotun mentions how there is a strong disconnect between Nigeria and the rest of the world in terms of medical research and scholarship. The World Health Organization (WHO) considers Nigeria's healthcare system to be one of the weakest in the world. Olukotun states that "... health is one of the worst funded and poorly managed social service in the country's annual budgets. The 2013 budget, for instance, earmarked a paltry 5.7 percent of the budget to health, and this is the highest allocation the sector has received in the last couple of years."[72]

With a foundation of questionable funding and extravagant governance, as discussed above, in Nigeria, it is common for political elites to travel to established nations for treatment. For example, Nigeria's former president, Muhammadu Buhari, visited London several times for his healthcare needs. Nigeria's inadequate funding

70. Ayo Olukotun, "Election: We Need Conversations, Not Sweet Nothings," *The Punch*, January 3, 2019. Retrieved on August 12, 2022 through https://punchng.com/elections-we-need-conversations-not-sweet-nothings/.

71. Olukotun, "Election: We Need Conversations, Not Sweet Nothings."

72. Ayo Olukotun, "Our Growing Medical Tourism to India," *The Punch*, July 26, 2013.

for its healthcare sector, poor planning and development, and the recurrence of workers' strikes cripple vital institutions like the health sector. Thus, eliminating any incentive for wealthy individuals to invest in native infrastructure.

In his column "Our Growing Medical Tourism to India," Olukotun highlights Nigeria's health relations with India. Olukotun states that India has become the country of choice for Nigerians who can afford to pay their way elsewhere for healthcare.[73] The Indian government supports its healthcare system by allowing hospital proprietors easy access to funds and providing hospital security to care for the hospital infrastructure. However, as Olukotun explains, the Nigerian government deals with its health sector differently. In Nigeria, while the public health sectors are desolate and unsteady, the private health institutions are run on their own, just as any other Nigerian business. Citizens run the private health sectors but with no government support. "It is estimated that Nigeria loses over N30 billion annually to foreign medical treatment necessitated by the failure to pay attention to Nigeria's health needs."[74]

Another interesting point that Olukotun mentions is that in India, many doctors go elsewhere to study and then return to India to set up their practice. However, Nigerian healthcare providers who earn their credentials or begin practicing in the United States or elsewhere are reluctant to return to Nigeria to practice medicine because of the lack of government support and poor infrastructure. Olukotun contends that this fact alludes to the demand for Nigeria to focus on creating quality healthcare. Specifically, Nigeria must focus on private sector participation, healthcare research, and healthcare education and training. Olukotun explains that Nigeria must prioritize healthcare in national funding and create a place for doctors willing to practice in Nigeria.[75]

REFLECTIONS

Throughout his many columns for *Punch* newspaper, Olukotun offers insightful, unique, and profound ideas and opinions about Nigeria. A careful review of Olukotun's intervention reveals the ailment Nigeria faces through the perspectives of security funding, education, economy, health care, and elections. His columns reflect the political state of Nigeria and how this affects its position in global affairs. Olukotun's suggested reforms, improvements, and suggestions showcase his profound knowledge and passion for Nigeria and Africa.

The summary of Nigeria's myriad of problems can be pinpointed as bad governance. The current state of governance is another and perhaps the most vital issue Nigeria faces. Political scientist, Professor Adigun Agbaje, described Nigeria's current

73. Olukotun, "Our Growing Medical Tourism to India."
74. Olukotun, "Our Growing Medical Tourism to India."
75. Olukotun, "Our Growing Medical Tourism to India."

political malaise as "electoralism." This refers to the idea that democratic elections are held routinely. However, it is understood that elections will not change the general public's lives.[76] That being established, Olukotun highlights that Nigeria's political leaders' acceptance of the idea of voter sovereignty, even though all who participate and exist under the system know that they do not decide much, is a comforting illusion for Nigeria.

Nigeria's general political sphere is based on the idea that Nigeria has a low government standard. Olukotun states that Nigerians tend to speculate that all unending woes result from bad governance and institutions. Therefore, whenever an event in Nigeria is considered "groundbreaking" or innovative, the general public does not ask questions and considers the event great. For example, in Buhari's 2018 Democracy Day Broadcast, the president brought up his idea of making progress in the tertiary education sector. Buhari stated that: "Over the last three years, Government has approved the establishment of one new federal polytechnic, granted licenses for the establishment of four state and fourteen private owned universities as well as twelve private polytechnics."[77] The fact that Buhari labeled granting licenses for private, and state-owned universities as an "achievement" does not seem quite right, as, in Nigeria, government and private owners do not pay salaries regularly. This is an example of using false statements to sway voters and create a false sense of accomplishment on the government's behalf.

Another example of false achievements lies in the sphere of road construction. In his column, "Will 2019 Reverse the Crisis of Underperformance?", Olukotun states that every pool of government officials in Nigeria has attempted to begin a road expansion and rehabilitation project. The reasoning is that the government awards this road rehabilitation project at an excessively high cost, thus causing an inevitable and associated payback. These projects are not completed by the government that started them because the prices of completing them escalate. Thus, the next elected government completes the projects and is considered to have achieved something great, even though their completion in "road construction is little more than the competition of abandoned projects by a successor government."[78] Olukotun calls this a chronic underperformance and states that this practice is so regular and has become so common in Nigerian democracy that federal and state governments expect to be congratulated. Olukotun suggests that the Nigerian public must increase its "buy-in" to the democratic project to solve this problem. He says it is not enough to complain or issue a press release when something troubling occurs. He warns that "democracy is too

76. Ayo Olukotun, "Democracy Day and Anxieties About 2019," *The Punch*, May 24, 2018, Retrieved on August 12, 2022 through https://punchng.com/democracy-day-and-anxieties-about-2019/.

77. Ayo Olukotun, "Will 2019 Reverse the Crisis of Underperformance?" *The Punch*, May 31, 2018. Retrieved on August 12, 2022 through https://punchng.com/will-2019-reverse-the-crisis-of-underperformance/.

78. Olukotun, "Will 2019 Reverse the Crisis of Underperformance?"

important to be left to these politicians." In his column, "Straw Debates and Politics as Escapism," Olukotun states that many of Nigeria's problems do not arise from wrong policies; rather, they stem from the failure to continue implementation.[79]

Along with false achievements, Olukotun warns that how Nigeria handles democracy must be reformed. Olukotun argues that elections are supposed to be about "national renewal and a reimagining of the social contract." However, Olukotun doubts that the politicians realize this, as they tend to carry on with their lives as "Nigeria bleeds."[80] In other countries, Electoral Commissions are driven anonymously to ensure electoral integrity. However, in Nigeria, Electoral Commissions are driven differently. According to Olukotun, they are publicity driven and "road-shows oriented." The 2019 election showcased these features, as the death toll was close to 30 Nigerians, several of whom were killed for simply showing up and exercising their civil rights/duties.

The fair implementation of elections also remains a challenge to democracy within countries under the hands of corrupt politicians and agencies. For example, the role of the Independent Electoral Commission (INEC) is to oversee the elections in Nigeria and make sure they remain free, fair, and credible. However, the INEC has been at the center of many controversies. In the 2019 presidential elections, the INEC was accused of cases of ballot paper unavailability, shortage of smart card readers, and canceling valid votes. Olukotun states that to redeem its image, the INEC must overcome the drama and controversy.[81]

Security agencies also play a vital role as institutions that spearhead Nigerian elections. The role of security agencies is to maintain law and order. Additionally, they must keep impartiality in mind to ensure the success of elections. Olukotun reflects this importance, as the political society tends to work out of self-interest rather than the larger good. Thus, it is vital that for elections to run smoothly, people must step into a neutral and unbiased space that politicians cannot. If the security agencies are biased and clear about which party they want to emerge victorious while punishing the other party, Olukotun states that the security agencies will be doing Nigeria a great disservice.[82] Olukotun suggests that the solutions to the problems facing Nigerians, as discussed above, as well as others, stem from the government. He proposes that the Nigerian government create rewards for companies employing Nigerians in high executive positions. Additionally, the government should create short- and medium-term policies to help Nigerian businesses and industries rise in global development.

79. Ayo Olukotun, "Political Scientists and the Debate on Political Restructuring," *The Punch*, April 25, 2019, Retrieved on August 12, 2022 through https://punchng.com/political-scientists-and-the-debate-on-political-restructuring/.

80. Olukotun, "Lame Response to Unending Security Jitters," *The Punch*, March 21, 2019.

81. Ayo Olukotun, "Our Election, Our Destiny," *The Punch*, February 7, 2019. Retrieved on August 12, 2022 through https://punchng.com/our-election-our-destiny/.

82. Olukotun, "Our Election, Our Destiny."

Olukotun also harps on the need for the country to have good leaders who would drive the nation's overall progress and prosperity. Since the country's problem is leadership, it is pertinent to note that there is a need to emerge good and visionary leaders. The lack of visionary leaders in Nigeria makes Olukotun explore the need to end this menace in an article titled "Who is Nigeria's Desmond Tutu?"[83] Desmond Tutu was a South African Archbishop who used his religious influence to advance the principle of peace and prosperity and was instrumental in ending apartheid and other forms of racism in the country. By invoking the name Tutu as a grounding metonymy, Olukotun reinstates the need for Nigeria to have leaders who can leave indelible imprints in the history and development of the country. The sad fact is that Nigeria seems to be afflicted with leaders who are merely interested in the tussle of power and authority than in leaving everlasting legacies. Olukotun further alludes to the fact that a step towards the emergence of great, Tutu-like leaders in Nigeria will be evidenced by the true independence of the Electoral Commission. In the same mechanism, he calls for spiritual leaders in the country to embrace Tutu's ideals in speaking against the ills of bad governance. Olukotun charges the citizens to continue in their quest for good leadership.

To gain public attention, it is easy to queue at the back of many scholars that correctly wail about the problems of Nigeria without critical examination of other possibilities of problems and sources that the government does not make itself and does not constitute society alone. The social phenomena must be viewed from the points of citizens and the government, with their contributory roles put under reasonable lenses of criticism. Olukotun represents that bridge of reasonability that makes one think beyond obvious facts and sentiments but connects the dots to make sense of social issues. He represents an objective thinker who ascribes society's fault to it when due, takes time to appreciate the unsung good things the Nigerian government is doing but criticizes when needed.

His opinions are more or less like a living documentary of the media history and explanation of how the media interacts with the people and government, exploiting forms of hostility and instrumentalities that the two have employed in responding to it. Hence, his relevance to this piece cannot be underestimated as it serves as an accurate prominent figure for its purpose of discussion.

Olukotun's fierce and fearless writing style is a breath of fresh air. The medley of thoughts in his columns provides a highly grounded yet vast, inexhaustible, relevant conversation pool. With assorted musing on the nation's (in)security, education funding (or lack thereof), the ailing economy, epileptic healthcare, and abysmal governance, Olukotun constantly hits the bull's eye of Nigeria's social disability and dysfunctionality. Delving into society's ills by criticizing the nation's political apparatus,

83. Ayo Olukotun, "Who is Nigeria's Desmond Tutu?" *The Punch* 31 December 2021, Retrieved on August 12, 2022 through https://punchng.com/who-is-nigerias-desmond-tutu/.

in particular, is like daring to step on the deified ground that even angels dread to tread. Yet, that is exactly what Olukotun has done to date, and he has done so with poise and without apologies. For example, his perspective on the surging and endemic weight of corruption has always defied the rule of conventional wisdom, which warns that you do not tell Nigerian politicians that corruption is wrong.

Olukotun has done this in more ways than one. But even more importantly, Olukotun successfully integrates popular journalistic writing with serious academic scripting, a feat attainable by a few in the world of journalism, a reminder of legendary journalists like George Will of the *Washington Post*. We can only hope that his unique style of telling the truth becomes a prototype that aspiring writers may strive to emulate.

13

AYO OLUKOTUN

The Pulse of the Nation

INTRODUCTION

Nigeria presents itself to the world in fascinating contrasts and as a study in unrealized expectations and beckoning greatness frustrated by adversity and self-inflicted wounds.[1]

Professor Ayo Olukotun has undoubtedly established himself as a formidable voice to be reckoned with in his unflinching reflection and refraction of the nation's sociopolitical and cultural realities. In a calm yet invasive manner, he highlights the abnormalities, the so-called "adversity and self-inflicted wounds," plaguing our society against a standard dim fit of a progressive one, which we aspire to become. He confers upon himself the selfless duty to carefully examine the "fascinating contrasts" that bedevil our society. His musings are charged with commonplace and contemporary realities with no overt interest in a particular issue but in every issue that borders across the development of the nation, from the deplorable state of the healthcare system, political inefficiency, and economic issues to the increasingly degrading standard of education and level of security in the country.

In whatsoever issue he dabbles in, he does not show sentiment. He says it as it is; hence, his musings are apt with no evasive turn at daring truths. First, he identifies an

1. Ayo Olukotun, "PDP's Self Destructive Quarrels and Growing Irrelevance," *The Punch*, September 1, 2016.

issue, a societal menace; he analyzes it and then proffers feasible and intellectually driven solutions. And when he has been accused of excessive analysis of issues other than straightforward attack, he opines that he leaves his "postulations open for the purpose of empirical testing, in order to confirm, modify, or refute them,"[2] which further proves him as an objective-minded writer. In the dreariest of issues, the conclusions to his reflections are steeped in an uncommon disposition of optimism. Take, for instance, his reflections on the performance of the Lagos State Governor Ambode in his first two years in office, yet Olukotun didn't fail to offer his rebuttal when he started veering off the path that earned him his good remark in previous commentaries, starting with the inappropriate dismissal of the Chaplain due to an issue that ensued between the latter and the Governor's wife.[3] His opinions are objective civil political discourse not marred with partisanship nor clouded with personal sentiments.

In anticipation of the February 2019 presidential election, he asks, "why is there so much apprehension and foreboding when the presidential race is mainly between two politicians of northern extraction who belong to the same religion?"[4] In his usual subtle manner of criticism, through the above expression, he expresses the level of disunity to which the nation has been relegated by ethnicity and religion, which rather than "becoming a bulwark for the anti-corruption crusade, it reflects and refracts underlying and preexisting tension," and by those he referred to as "political gladiators" that has turned the affairs of the nation into warfare, those "who acts out of cynical self-interest, not caring for the larger good"[5] and hence are not to be (entirely) trusted with the affairs of the nation, especially as regards electioneering. He warns about the stasis of this abnormality; according to him, as far as public offices remain "an arena of obscene wealth"[6] acquisition, things would remain the same. Through his writings, he has marked himself distinct as a progressive-thinking fellow with the ultimate consciousness and zeal to drive our society toward collective development.

In his musings, where he painstakingly reflects on the menace plundering our society, he never fails to express his concern for the general welfare of the masses, and of the society itself, those who bear the brunt of weak and inefficient governance of the affairs of the nation has unfortunately been committed to continuously; in his words, the increasingly "declining quality of lives" as experienced in the nation is "occasioned by erratic and poor service delivery in virtually every department of social and economic endeavours."[7] In one of such instance, while introspecting about the future of the nation in "What will Nigeria Look Like in 2023?" bearing in mind

2. Ayo Olukotun, "Is Excellence Possible in Nigeria? A Postscript," *The Punch,* July 6, 2017. See also Ayo Olukotun, "A Farewell to Civil Political Discourse?" *The Punch*, April 28, 2016.

3. Ayo Olukotun, "Ambode: Off Keynote in a Melodious Verse," *The Punch,* June 1, 2017.

4. Ayo Olukotun, "The Election and Beyond," *The Punch,* February 14, 2019.

5. Ayo Olukotun, "Our Election, Our Destiny," *The Punch,* February 7, 2019.

6. Ayo Olukotun, "Whatever Happened to the Culture of Resignation?" *The Punch,* October 24, 2018.

7. Ayo Olukotun, "What will Nigeria Look Like in 2023?" *The Punch*, February 1, 2019.

the possible division of the nation based on the increasing tension of the ethnoreligious and political crises in the nation, he expresses thus: "unfortunately, it is doubtful, whether the forthcoming elections, will be about the issues that count. Political rhetoric has found a way of evading or avoiding major governance issues that relate to those factors that make life longer, more livable and more enjoyed."[8]

His musings are inquisitive, marked with sarcastic interrogations and rhetorical questions, which he suggests answers to and expresses his wary despair. These are evident in the titles. In other instances, he plunges into extensive metaphorical illustrations, diversions if you like or what he calls 'short take' to foreground his subject, an attempt he describes as "a technique for breaking and for lightening the boredom of reading grey matters, which tends to put off the wider reading public."[9] But in contrast, these diversions are themselves topical issues that are worthy of an elaborate rumination as the subjects of the discourse in which they are embedded. Thus, his commentaries are laced with multiple subjects of discussion, which are seamlessly interwoven to highlight a common issue the writer aims to draw the readers' attention to. In one of such instances, he compared the civility and diplomacy with which the French Prime Minister doused the agitations of the protesting citizens over valid concerns to the crudeness and lack of tact often displayed by Nigerian political leaders within the premises of the same concerns, even more awful. In his usual manner of subtle ridicule, he states, "Nigerian politicians usually come back from France to regale us with the narratives of the splendid beauty of Paris, and the aesthetics of its major cities. We search in vain for what lessons they bring home about governance."[10]

Olukotun fits in appropriately as the nation's pulse first because of his ability to engage the nation from a diversified stand extending the tentacles of his discussions, sensitization, analyses, and criticism to almost all parts of the society. This makes him present the nation to us as it is, exposing its strides and caprices in his engagements. He provides a clear thought on politics and governance, as well as what should be expected in a reasonable democratic state like Nigeria and run those ideas along with political occurrences in the nation. Being in academics has given him the impetus to address the nation's dwindling educational standards. His discussions extend to other specific discussion areas like health, security, power, and the like. Such diversity provides the citizens with information on how the nation fares, making his views worthy of discussion.

Secondly, Olukotun wears the gird of experience and embeds himself into research that widens the horizon of his analytical school, which helps him follow the nation's

8. Ayo Olukotun, "Olaniyi Ashimi, the Fatal Cost of Governance Decay," *The Punch*, December 19, 2018.

9. Ayo Olukotun, "2019: Harvest of Aspirants, Shortage of Policy Ideas." *The Punch*, September 6, 2018.

10. Ayo Olukotun, "Governance Takeaways from the Upheaval in France," *The Punch*, December 12, 2018.

Figure 13.1. "Abela" by Michael Efionayi. Ayo Olukotun burning out like a candle to provide light and clarity.

developmental steps, warns against underdevelopment, and recommends steps against developmental reversal. He is like the nation's "Chi," or guiding angel warning and directing its leadership in its entirety. In his appraisal of Professor Banji Oyeyinka's positions, he has stated that the nation needs to stop its journey to perdition by revitalizing its developmental strategies. Oyeyinka noted that Nigeria has fallen from being the major exporter of about 43 percent of global palm oil production to less than 2 percent.

He has also linked Nigeria's underdevelopment to different factors, including insecurity, which he believes is travailing over the government's readiness, and other causes.[11] This view of his has been substantiated by certain developments in the nation, including the incident at Kuje Prisons which was claimed to have been forewarned, and he regarded the attitudes of the government and authorities as "sleepwalking."[12] From a logical conclusion and the right observation of Olukotun, a nation that is not proactive on security challenges is on the verge of adapting it as a culture.[13] Olukotun continues to monitor these developmental movements and the clogs that

11. Ayo Olukotun, "Insecurity: The Opportunity Cost of Dilly-Dallying," *The Punch,* August 5, 2022.
12. Ayo Olukotun, "Insecurity: A Nation Sleepwalking in Utter Peril," *The Punch,* July 29, 2022.
13. Ayo Olukotun, "Insecurity: Political Class Terrifying Silence," *The Punch,* July 1, 2022.

militate against their progressive wheels; this positions him as one to monitor the analyses of national steps and policies.

POLITICS AND GOVERNANCE

> Leadership, that vital ingredient that drives nations and people to achievement beyond their dreams, has been Nigeria's soft underbelly for decades. Over recycled, jaded politicians bereft of new ideas, exhausted army generals feigning democratic credentials and skilful manipulators of compromised electoral processes, straddle a disappearing unlucky nation.[14]

His untiring voice never ceases to chastise the menace of politics and governance, which are the most comprehensive way of ensuring the nation's development. Highlighting the aspiring political leaders' ineptitude, he comments, "Even the most lucid of them are spending time telling us how evil their opponents are, instead of setting out a map of the Promised Land to which they will presumably lead us if they win the election."[15] Of the many follies he charges at in Nigerian politics, the lack of fundamental ideological standings in our political system is most foregrounded in his writings.

On the inefficacy of the political system operated in the country, he expresses the need for "clear governance ideas that will jumpstart sustainable development and reset the political arena"[16] and not the political competitions among numerous parties "whose names one does not remember...barren of party identity and policy discussion,"[17] even when the jostle for power is just between two political parties which are devoid of significance and replete with the same set of political members who hop between the parties based on self-gratifying reasons. The lack of these substantial ideologies in the formation of political parties and their policy is accountable for the deplorable system of governance and development in the country—"a linkage between the repetitive maladies the nation experience, and the nature of our politics, which is almost totally bereft of policy debate."[18]

Restructuring the nation's political community would create the necessary channel to "transfer some of the edifying indigenous cultural values into the national political realm"[19] to develop the nation based on existing pan-African political ideologies and true democratic policies. Further, on the need for an enhanced political system with clear ideological policies, his comment on the coalition of political parties[20] at differ-

14. Ayo Olukotun, "Buhari and the Second Term Controversy," *The Punch,* November 23, 2017.
15. Ayo Olukotun, "National Degree Exams for Undergraduates?" *The Punch,* January 24, 2019.
16. Ayo Olukotun, "Ambode: A Postscript," *The Punch,* October 11, 2018.
17. Ayo Olukotun, "2019: Harvest of Aspirants, Shortage of Policy Ideas." *The Punch,* September 6, 2018.
18. Olukotun, "2019: Harvest of Aspirants."
19. Ayo Olukotun, "Falola and Olubadan's 90th Birthday Lecture," *The Punch,* August 23, 2018.
20. Ayo Olukotun, "Much Ado about the Coalition of Opposition Parties," *The Punch,* July 12, 2018.

ent election periods in the country for the sole objective of un-sitting a ruling party/leader highlights the inherent weakness in the ideological foundation of these political parties that merely jostle for the acquisition of political power, and not the development of the nation, in his words: "Evidently, there was ideologically speaking no platform, no minimal threshold of agreed principles which bound the loose coalition,"[21] and which stirs the same reason for the continuous decamping from a political party to another.

The political system, as it is, "has boxed itself into a corner of false choices in which there is little to choose among a riot of jaded political aspirants and expired office holders,"[22] which leaves him with the doubt and impression that the 2019 general election "will provide noticeable departures from the saga of underachievement and low score governance."[23] It is on this note that he suggests the need for the constitution to be amended to allow independent candidatures to vie for political posts outside the premises of political parties, and the need to look into other minor political parties was also highlighted to break the yoke of governance by the incompetent dominant political parties as well to widen the choices from which the people can elect. This helps to understand his agitations during the internal strife encountered by the major oppositional party, PDP, in the wake of the governance transition to their rival party; the extinction of this strong oppositional party, in his view, is a threat to the democratic consolidation of the nation for "If the country will eventually transit from the current wilderness of deferred greatness to the world stage however, it must get among other things its democratic governance right, by alternating power smoothly between its major parties in free and fair elections."[24] Likewise, the presence of a strong and "effective opposition representing itself morally and ideologically"[25] to hold the current dispensation accountable for its inadequacies and flaws, as well as to offer alternative views to the affairs of the nation.

In line with the reformation of "Not too Young to Run" in the Nigerian political clime, the columnist offers his view as to how the young can get themselves in the political affairs of the nation, not by aiming for the highest posts as was witnessed in the last presidential election but by towing the line of Justin Trudeau and Emmanuel Macron who leveraged on their fathers' political affluence and as an apprentice of Trudeau respectively "Fundamentally, the prospects of youths making landmark political change are functions of factors such as their intellectual capital, as this relates to ideological conviction, moral stamina, preparation for office, and the power of

21. Ayo Olukotun, "APC and Tinubu's Uphill Assignment." *The Punch,* February 15, 2018.

22. Ayo Olukotun, "Will 2019 Reverse the Crisis of Underperformance?" *The Punch,* May 31, 2018.

23. Olukotun, "Will 2019 Reverse the Crisis."

24. Ayo Olukotun, "PDP's Self Destructive Quarrels and Growing Irrelevance," *The Punch,* September 1, 2016.

25. Ayo Olukotun, "PDP: An Opposition Absent from Duty," *The Punch,* May 5, 2016.

institutions to act as checks on their tendencies for impetuous interventions."[26] His point is that if there would be a comprehensive reformation of the Nigerian political system, it ought to start from the grassroots, and there is the need for leadership experience in steering the affairs of the nation, which can only be acquired as a sort of apprenticeship "at the feet of the established, even if they end up overthrowing all they stood for."[27]

He has been particularly critical of the clandestine gimmick of the Buhari government's anti-corruption policy and stance, what he refers to as a "theatre of elite fracture"[28] and "an anti-corruption programme targeted mainly at the opposition will result in a reformed public service."[29] In another musing, he projects that "the war against corruption, which by the way is far from being won, cannot be a substitute for emphatic governance reforms powered by an agenda of state building which pays close attention to the challenges, short term and medium term, posed by the galloping insecurity."[30] Among his admonishments in "Beyond the Presidential and National Assembly Elections"[31] when the Buhari-led government was re-elected is the need to widen the scope of programs to be accomplished by the administration to include the eradication of poverty, provision of jobs, standard education and healthcare, and the insurance of lives and property across the plains of the nation, especially the regions affected by terrorism. Still very relevant to the governance of this nation is his admonishment to the Buhari-led administration in the middle of its first-year tenure:

> Buhari should begin to create a fresh narrative of governmental vigour and policy focus, in place of the current drift. He can best do this by keeping his house in order, beginning from the presidency and the cabinet which sometimes resemble, in their discordance, houses of commotion. He should rejig his cabinet, in order to prioritize policy delivery, and in the same breath should not shy away from taking fundamental decisions that can lift the country out of the current doldrums.[32]

Delving into the alarming indignant refusal of the political and administrative leaders to resign despite the numerous and glaring allegations of corruption leveled against them. In his usual comparative mode, he draws a contrast between these leaders and their foreign counterparts that have thrown in as little as on the ground of ideological

---

26. Ayo Olukotun, "Macron and Nigerian Youths' Leadership Bid," *The Punch*, May 11, 2017.
27. Olukotun, "Macron and Nigerian Youths' Leadership."
28. Ayo Olukotun, "Elite Conflicts and the Anti Corruption Policy," *The Punch*, May 18, 2017.
29. Ayo Olukotun, "Will Pay Rise End Predatory Policing?" *The Punch*, November 29, 2018.
30. Ayo Olukotun, "Rising Insecurity: A Nation's Soft Underbelly," *The Punch*, April 10, 2018.
31. Ayo Olukotun, "Beyond the Presidential and National Assembly Elections," *The Punch*, February 28, 2019.
32. Ayo Olukotun, "Buhari: The Renewed Debate on Underperformance," *The Punch*, October 18, 2017.

differences; according to him, "All of these will be less baffling if the administration had not openly committed itself to an anti-corruption crusade."[33] The current dispensation of political and administrative leaders' rejection of objective criticism, which can help drive the nation towards development, is well-expressed by the columnist at different times.[34]

Likewise, he highlights the partisan views of the government publicists, those who have tarnished their image as reputable media persons by (blindly) defending the follies of those in government, even when such flaws are too evident to be overlooked. As he succinctly put it, "it is crying shame that government publicists continue to be invited to government on terms which suggest that they would trade off their reputation or integrity for political spoils, with the understanding that they would defend their principals, right or wrong, and at any and every cost. Hence government information departments have become the graveyard of many reputations because of an approach to the job which majors on propaganda and hero worship, as opposed to democratic discourse."[35]

He gave his contemptuous remark on the performance of the Buhari administration and its failure to drive Nigeria toward tangible development. On this note, he suggests Buhari's re-election for a second tenure was not worth thinking about,[36] coupled with the numerous serious health challenges that threaten the administration of his government and the country at large. His concern not only aligns with that of every sane citizen of the country but also indicates the rise of an unaccountable crop of leaders by patting their authoritarian nature and their usual 'politricks,' highlighting their lack of remorse as a stampede on the intelligence and rights of the people. On the undemocratic style of governance of the Buhari-led administration, yet reelected, he calls our attention to the impending danger, not only of the unruly style of governance but also for its indisposition towards objective criticism by all and sundry, including the elder statesmen, which shows "The current distemper in which even our elder statesmen feel compelled to take up political cudgels to the failure of civic organizations and collective platforms."[37]

33. Olukotun, "Whatever Happened to the Culture of Resignation?" *The Punch,* October 24, 2018.

34. In "A Farewell to Civil Political Discourse?" he laments the mannerism at which constructive criticism and civil political discourse that could gear the nations towards a collective development are marred by abusive reactions from those with opposing views. On a personal note, he gave instances of two impolite personal messages, "which represent a sample from a raucous chorus of dissenters and naysayers," replete with scoff and scorn that he received as a response to his assessment of the President Muhammadu Buhari administration. This shows an unhealthy trend of dwindling quality public conversation, which is a necessity to sustain the health of our national democracy. Ayo Olukotun, "A Farewell to Civil Political Discourse?" *The Punch*, April 29, 2016.

35. Ayo Olukotun, "Garba Shehu and the Discourse of Settlement," *The Punch,* October 4, 2017.

36. Olukotun, "Buhari and the Second Term Controversy."

37. Ayo Olukotun, "Elder Statesmen and Controversial Interventions," *The Punch,* April 5, 2018.

On the legacy of Awolowo's principle of regional governance and excellence, the writer beckons on all true political and governance reformers to "all who genuinely believe in it to rally round the agenda of a restructured Nigeria where the energies of the constituent parts can be unleashed."[38] The need to restructure the nation's system of governance, or perhaps to put, the need to realign it within the premises of true federalism on which the nation was established, is increasingly becoming expedient, and the failure to do so by past and present administrations has been largely responsible for the nation's underdevelopment, weak and ineffective governance. As succinctly expressed by the writer, "it should be obvious that a nation so hopelessly divided such as Nigeria is today, cannot make much progress regarding our many governance woes without revisiting the terms of our unity in diversity,"[39] which is federalism. Also, on the opulent system of governance practiced in Nigeria, he clamors for the reformation of the system, economic-wise, to reduce the burden of "servicing office holders at the centre, the two legislative houses"[40] on the nation's economy and to drastically put in check the enticement that pulls politicians into governance by way of reducing their salary and other corrupt means of embezzling the public funds to make such positions available to those who truly want to develop the nation.

A part consequence of the lack of strong and visionary governance in the country, as expressed by the writer, is the continuous partisan abandonment of the project by political leaders in government, which has not only led to the ruins that are evident in such projects but also accounts for the lack of social facilities that are pertinent to the welfare of the people and the development of the society. It also results in the duplicity of the same projects by different governments and the non-accountability and wastage of public funds appropriated to such projects. In his usual suggestive manner, he remarks that "Sanctions should be meted out to those guilty of concluding to cheating the public in one or another. In addition, government machinery should be streamlined, especially in hard times like these, to reduce duplication of projects by different arms of the government, often embarking on them in an overlapping manner."[41]

The writer, on several occasions, has called for proactive measures in the governance of the nation in all sectors, "which reacts to disasters rather than anticipate them"[42] and "a strategy of strengthening law enforcement and other institutions, to the point where it is easier to detect corruption before it happens should be embarked upon."[43] Drawing from instances in the advanced nations that have braced themselves

38. Ayo Olukotun, "Awolowo Dosunmu: A Political Dynasty at the Crossroad," *The Punch*, February 22, 2018.

39. Ayo Olukotun, "June 12 and the Quest for True Federalism," *The Punch*, June 15, 2016.

40. Ayo Olukotun, "Beyond Survival: Remapping Nigeria for Greatness," *The Punch*, September 28, 2017.

41. Ayo Olukotun, "Abandoned Projects and State Decay," *The Punch*, October 6, 2016.

42. Ayo Olukotun, "IPOB and the National Question," *The Punch*, September 14, 2017.

43. Ayo Olukotun, "Anti Corruption: The Suspension of Buhari's Top Aides," *The Punch*, April 20, 2017.

against an odd or a challenge, rather than the aftermath's actions that do little to douse the consequences of an event, it is better "to understand." An example of such a proactive measure on the nation's economy is the sustenance of the excess crude oil revenue account[44] established by former President Olusegun Obasanjo to cater to the unmitigated economic challenge in the nation. But the current dispensation of "Politicians prefer to blame their opponents and to exonerate their parties for culpability for the country's lot." Just the same way that the current administration has frowned on all criticism and objections which are not in their favor, especially by other international-ranking bodies on education, health, governance transparency, security, poverty, corruption, etc.[45] Thence, the writer calls for "Tender words and decisive ameliorative actions must replace the current tendency to rehash old discredited scripts or blame critics or past leaders for political failure."[46]

EDUCATION AND LITERACY

As a worthy academic and intellectual, it is only logical that he often weighs in on the educational state of the country, especially as regards its weak policy and regulations, which are inheritances of the military regime, the deteriorating state of facilities and broadened scope due to inadequate funding, unstable calendar due to consistent teachers' strike, all of which have contributed to the waning value of education in the country. The latter has one of the dominant reasons he gave for the unsuitability of the unified national exam for all final-year undergraduates in Nigeria as proposed by Chief Afe Babalola, which in his view, "will drive the [educational] system in the direction of uniformity, rigidity, and over-centralization."[47] He, however, agrees with an assertion made by Chief Afe Babalola, on another occasion, on the dwindling standard of education in the country as a result of both the limited power of teaching personnel and the incompetency of some of the available ones, what he aptly describes as "a double whammy, in which a dire shortage of academics is compounded by the lack of attention to good and effective teaching."[48]

Similarly, he laments the wretched state of the government-owned research institutes in the country due to insufficient funding by the government, whose "politicians can easily raise billions of naira to fund a presidential or gubernatorial campaign, but funding research is beyond their ken."[49] These research institutes are formulated to provide advice to the government in respective sectors on the implementation of

44. Ayo Olukotun, "Beyond Survival: Remapping Nigeria for Greatness," *The Punch*, September 28, 2017.

45. Ayo Olukotun, "Needless Controversy over TI Rating," *The Punch*, March 1, 2018.

46. Ayo Olukotun, "A Tale of Two Protests," *The Punch*, February 16, 2017.

47. Ayo Olukotun, "National Degree Exams for Undergraduates?" *The Punch*, January 24, 2019.

48. Olukotun, "2019: Harvest of Aspirants."

49. Ayo Olukotun, "Researcher's Strike and a Disappearing Research Culture," *The Punch*, March 15, 2018.

policies that are crucial to national planning; hence, in his view, "If primary national institutions such as the NNPC lack vital data about the industry in which they operate in [due to poor funding, lack of infrastructure and the failure of the government to abide by agreed policies and regulations], how can they plan for the future?"[50] Reflecting on the contribution and reward of maintaining world-class research institutes to national and global development, he gave the example of Canada's intervention in eradicating Ebola, even though the country was not affected, in 2014 through the Zmapp drug discovered in the National Microbiology Laboratory at Winnipeg. The degradation that has befallen the nation's educational and research institutes indicates how far the country is from active and serious development.

Also, he has given his unrestrained voice to the need to restructure the nation's educational policies and regulations that are "yoked to a colonial model which it once replicated but now parodies"[51] to truly achieve the millennium and world-class educational goal of quality education. As it should be, true education should be geared towards the enhancement of society by equipping people with the necessary skills, methodologies and tools to solve their immediate societal challenges, and not just some redundant theoretical ideology that has no place and value in the development of the nation. It is in line with this view, in reflection of a convocation lecture I gave at Adekunle Ajasin University on December 7, 2017, that he succinctly expresses that "universities must be wooed away from splendid isolation from the rest of the society to becoming crucial players in the social and economic concerns of their immediate surroundings."[52]

Further, he denounces the proliferation of privately-owned tertiary institutions as no effective solution to the country's dwindling standard of quality education. He argues for the consolidation of the already existing institutions other than increasing the number of universities with no unique dimension or contribution to the nation's educational system or general development, indicating that "90% of the existing private universities do not fill their student quota, while the number of private universities put together only have 7% of the student population in our universities,"[53] which flaws the proposed objective that backs the creation of such universities to attend to the growing number of Nigerian youths in need of higher education due to excessive fee charges and limited academic curriculum. In his words, "You cannot build quality by multiplying poorly conceived institutions several of them, at the borderline of decency."[54] As he points out, the consolidation of the existing educational institutions should begin at the basic levels up to the higher ones and not just be limited to the

50. Olukotun, "Researcher's Strike."
51. Ayo Olukotun, "Tweaking University Education to Empower Youth," *The Punch*, December 7, 2017.
52. Olukotun, "Tweaking University Education."
53. Ayo Olukotun, "Private University Licenses and Policy Vacuum," *The Punch*, December 21, 2017.
54. Olukotun, "Private University Licenses."

tertiary ones. However, in his rebuttal of the proliferation of the establishments of private higher institutions, he does acknowledge the contribution a handful are making to the educational system of the country and believes that the government-owned tertiary institutions have a couple of things to learn from their private counterpart to drive the educational standard towards the deserved level, among which are the stability of academic calendar, prompt decision making and policy implementation, good managerial culture as well as the "interesting practice whereby lecturers in private universities are expected to submit at the beginning of each semester instructional materials replete with courses outlines, summaries of lecture notes," which would help to ensure that a standard quality of education is imparted to the students and to account for the performance and "the extent to which lecturers are updating and keeping abreast of developments in their disciplines."[55]

Perhaps, the Nigerian leaders fail to understand that the consequences of a terrible education system are not limited to just the decay in infrastructure. It cuts across all nodes of society and impedes the development of the same, "nations can be destroyed by substandard education, which ensures that doctors are half baked, engineers are ill-trained, and accountants do not measure up to the billings of their profession"[56] whose ripple effect is the increased rate of unemployment, the larger of whom would involve themselves in terrorism, robbery and (cyber)fraud; and the lack of professionals to attend to the needs and challenges bedeviling the society thereby further retrogressing the society; a substantial decrease in the economic buoyancy and standard of living of the people. Similarly, he decries the dying culture of reading in the nation, which is a result of a mix of the lack of facilities, as in the dilapidating public and national libraries, poor educational standards as well as the indifference of the people to the culture of reading, which consequently leads to the divergence of political power from intellect.[57]

Without a stable and efficient educational system, the country would keep gyring in its fortuitous cycle of underdevelopment that would worsen with time and as other societies develop. A typical example of the comprehensive decadence of our educational system was unearthed in Kaduna in 2017 when the Primary School Teachers failed the same examination they are supposed to teach their pupils.[58] According to the writer, "we do not even have accurate data concerning the extent of educational decay at primary and secondary school levels. Proffering solutions to problems that have not been accurately diagnosed is the equivalent of a journey without maps."[59] A

55. Ayo Olukotun, "What our Public Universities can Learn from Private Ones," *The Punch*, June 22, 2016.

56. Ayo Olukotun, "A Nation's Unending Search for Quality Education," *The Punch*, November 16, 2018.

57. Ayo Olukotun, "Comatose Libraries and a Disappearing Nation," *The Punch*, October 20, 2016.

58. Ayo Olukotun, "Kaduna's Teacher and the Dilemma of Reform," *The Punch*, November 8, 2017.

59. Olukotun, "A Nation's Unending Search."

rather radical solution he provided to the notion of true nationalism is that the wards of our political leaders should be made mandatory to have their wards educated in the country up to their first degree; in his exact words, he contemplates "how can the system be healed if all the doctors who should cure it go to all lengths to ensure that their wards do not partake of it?"[60] The aim of this, undoubtedly, is to bring to notice the havoc that has been wrecked on our educational system and perhaps create the necessary impetus to effect change.

Propagating the moral and national character of persistence in the face of difficulties, the writer cites the example of a young lady, Elizabeth Odefuwa, who purportedly wrote the UTME seven times before gaining admission into the tertiary institution to study her chosen course and finished with a first class. The writer highlights three things; 1) the inefficacy of our educational system as it is flawed as a true tool of imparting knowledge and how it has also denied many others (many of whom would have given up) access to higher education;[61] 2) the moral teaching of the value of persistence against adversity; 3), the metaphorical comparison between the state of the nation and the experience of the lady, that despite the tumultuous hardship that plagues the country, there is a glorious future ahead. However, on the literal level, he laments that "Of course, it would be nice if Nigerian leaders could focus on building a society where it will be much easy to achieve one's dream. But successive governments have turned the country into a graveyard of aborted dreams and failed destinies."[62]

HEALTH

In a sympathetic reflection, he decries the direful condition of the health sector in Nigeria and how lives have been "rudely terminated because of all too familiar stories of medical negligence and decay."[63] Nigerian health care is rated as one of the poorest by the World Health Organization, and the country is known for its high infant mortality rate, making it one of the deadliest places to be born and live in the world.

It is painful that the provided facilities are inadequate and not of the modern standard, but what is more painful is the deplorable state of the available facilities, the sloppiness and incompetence of the healthcare workers, whom he did not fail to accost in his compassionate dash for the untimely death of Ashimi and others who have been the unfortunate victims of the appalling state of the country's health sector that is on the "verge of graduating into undertakers, whereby unlucky patients are sent to

60. Ayo Olukotun, "Okogie and Nigeria's Unending Search for Leadership," *The Punch,* July 21, 2017.

61. In his short take in "June 12 and the Quest for True Federalism," he addressed the inefficiency of the Joint Admission Matriculation Board examination in being a reliable tool of accessing the students' knowledge, much reason for the need of the Post UTME exam by the public universities to cross-check the "sometimes erratic scores form the Joint Admission Matriculation Board" examination obtained by the students. Ayo Olukotun, "June 12 and the Quest for True Federalism," *The Punch,* June 17, 2016.

62. Ayo Olukotun, "Odefuwa: A Handbook for Surviving Adversity," *The Punch,* March 30, 2017.

63. Olukotun, "Olaniyi Ashimi."

their graves."[64] The unavailability of oxygen or fuel to transport a severely injured person is evidence and the height of the decadence that has struck the nation's health system. Needless to say is the negligence of the political leaders toward the dwindling state of their followers' welfare because they have "enough resources to escape the medical bedlam at home, by jetting abroad now and then for treatment, or because they don't "give a damn" about the fact that too many Nigerians are dying from governance decay."[65] Aside from their negligence, their lack of confidence to subject themselves to treatment by our local medical professionals and facilities reflects their insensitivity and failure as leaders in the nation's affairs.

The deplorable state of the country's health sector is likewise responsible for the increasing migration of Nigerian-trained medical professionals to European and American countries[66] where their services are needed, cherished, and well-rewarded. In its own right, this brain drain of medical experts does more to plunge the country into worse health maladies by further offsetting the doctor-people ratio. From another perspective, he highlights the ironic downturn of this event whereby the medical experts obtained their training, tuition-free from primary to tertiary, in Nigeria but have been forcefully pushed to seek a greener pasture outside the environment that provided them their education, just as the political leaders seek their medical treatments outside the country. The provision of cutting-edge medical equipment and facilities, the facilitation of a conducive working environment and policy, and the allocation of funds sufficient enough to sustain the smooth running and continuous development of the nation's health sector are among the solution proffered by the writer. In his usual expression of optimism that the country can be revived, he compared the present state of Nigeria to that of India but whose collective action has revitalized the nation's development, especially in the provision of world standard health care.

To revive the nation's health sector from its present state of comatose; first, there is the need to beef up the yearly budgetary allocation to health to be at par, at least, with the 15% recommended by several health international organizations, which would see to the provision of the necessary modern medical equipment and facilities to enhance our health care services and to provide the health care workers with the impetus and environment to operate efficiently, "after all, meaningful reform ought to proceed from improved funding."[67] Second, there is the need to attend to the low availability of competent human resources in the health sector, which has incredibly offset the recommended WHO ratio of Doctors to patients from 1:600 to 1: 4000. The availability of efficient working space and environment would help to reduce the

64. Ayo Olukotun, "Hospitals as Undertakers? Saving a Dying Healthy Sector," *The Punch*, September 21, 2017.

65. Olukotun, "Olaniyi Ashimi."

66. Ayo Olukotun, "Health Sector Brain Drain: Rising Cost of Inaction," *The Punch*, April 26, 2018.

67. Olukotun, "Hospitals as Undertakers?"

brain-drain of medical professionals the nation is experiencing at the moment by retaining them to contribute to the improvement of the nation's healthcare system.

SECURITY

Kidnapping, robbery, terrorism and the herdsmen killing in the middle belt are central security issues he accords to leadership negligence and weak governance whose security policies and regulations are not firm and efficient enough to ensure the safety of the people and to eradicate the security menace holding the nation at ransom. While he rightly identifies the rise in insecurity as a global predicament, giving instances of increasing criminal acts in America and Britain as valid examples, he states certain factors have only made it worse in "Nigeria by an upward cascade in violent crime, the surge in youth unemployment, delicate interethnic relations, ineffective public administration and the palpable underdeveloped security architecture being overwhelmed by increasingly audacious criminal gangs brandishing sophisticated weapons."[68]

The excessive deployment of security personnel to guard corporate organizations, political leaders and the rich, as well as "low skills, poor training facilities, weak morale and deficiencies in logistics, response to emergencies and weaponry,"[69] are among the factors he identified for the poor performance of the police force in ensuring safety in the country. Likewise, the shortage of funds for the police force for better equipment and smooth operation has resulted in the resolve of the institution to resort to public funding and donations from the rich people in the society who might as well be criminals as well as charging both complainants and suspects to carry out a criminal investigation. In his view, the fight against corruption is incomprehensive and ineffective without first reforming the police force, "an undermanned, underequipped and obviously corrupt institution," to ensure the lives and properties of the people the government has sworn to serve.[70]

While expressing his view on the increment in the salary of the police force, which is purportedly to assuage the overwhelming burden to ensure safety in our communities by the security persons, he rightly pinpoints the flaws inherent in the security system of the country, which should have been given more priority as a means to salvage the burden of maintaining credibility and ensuring internal security. The lack of substantial weaponry, supporting infrastructure, inefficient skills, inadequate police-to-citizen ratio and the deplorable standard of living of the security officers are among the issues he highlighted as causes of the weak level of security in the state, and

68. Olukotun, "Rising Insecurity."
69. Olukotun, "Rising Insecurity."
70. Ayo Olukotun, "Fighting Corruption without Rebuilding the Police," *The Punch*, February 17, 2016.

not the salary, which of course is necessary but does not "translate into an efficient and effective force."[71]

Numerous suggestions have been offered on police reform, at different intervals, from the government of President Olusegun Obasanjo to Goodluck Jonathan but none of the recommendations in the reports on how to restructure the police force were ever adopted nor implemented. Accordingly, he opines that "the goal of any such reform should be to come up with a capable and well-resourced police force that is citizen friendly, decentralized vertically and horizontally and is willing to emphasize intelligence, crime prevention, 'beat' specialization and community policing."[72]

POWER

Like the deplorable level of many social amenities and facilities in the nation, he bemoans the disappointing state of power supply in the country, what he referred to as "the preeminent symbol of governmental incompetence in Nigeria."[73] The erratic power supply, abrupt power shortage, irregular power supply and distribution to arbitrary billing are among the abnormalities plaguing the stability of electricity in the country. The ripple effect of this electricity menace is unending. The cost of escaping the consequences of this unstable power supply has its consequences, perhaps worse. The use of power generating sets by those with the means to power it has been opted for as the alternative to the erratic power supply, which contributes immensely to the pollution of the environment, noise and air depletion, which affects the general welfare of the people.

In indicating other downsides, he expresses that "One can only imagine other associated costs of blackouts such as the snuffing out of struggling businesses unable to cope with the escalating overhead bills, the wiping out of the narrow leeway for families who can no longer balance their budgets and the rise in criminal gangs which employ the cover of darkness to carry out reprehensible acts."[74] Despite the numerous suggestions on how the nation's electricity supply can be stabilized and enhanced, among which are diversifying energy sources, attracting investment in power generation and actively regulating activities of the distributing companies foregrounded by the columnist, the country is still stuck in darkness, year after year with no clear indication of a turnaround anytime soon.

In "Consumer Woes in Austere Times,"[75] from the dire shortage of water supply and electricity, the lack of an effective security system to the irregularity of the services provided by private institutions, which does not match international standards

71. Olukotun, "Will Pay Rise End?"
72. Olukotun, "Fighting Corruption without Rebuilding."
73. Ayo Olukotun, "Any Hope for Overcoming the Electricity Jinx?" *The Punch,* June 21, 2018.
74. Olukotun, "Any Hope for Overcoming?"
75. Ayo Olukotun, "Consumer Woes in Austere Times," *The Punch,* June 21, 2016.

Figure 13.2. "The Pulse of the Nation" by Dr. Kazeem Ekeolu. This is a caricature of Nigeria with the insight of Ayo Olukotun with a Pulse Oximeter.

and practice, Olukotun laments the helplessness of the citizens to enjoy the basic amenities and services they are entitled to, even those paid for. Not only should these basic services and amenities be made available, but the providers must be enforced by the government and various civil society institutions to respect and protect the consumers' fundamental rights.

ECONOMY AND RELIGION

He lends his voice to the worsening state of the nation's economy, what he refers to as "the loss of economic vibrancy and de-industrialization suffered by the country."[76] The lack of investment in the business sector, shortage of indigenous entrepreneurship, the failure to harness the nation's human resources, and inadequate funding of education, among others, are some of the reasons he identified well as a cause of the crumbling economy. Also, he asserts the poor relationship between the state, industrial and business sectors, and the academy as a significant cause of the economy's degradation. While lamenting the "Dearth of Nigerian CEOs in Nigeria-Based Multinationals," he holds the government at the jugular for its negligence in bringing its political weight to bear by creating rewards for companies that "engage in the mentorship and consequent appointment of Nigerian CEOs"[77] in multinational establishments located in the country.

Expressing his view on the interconnection existing between the church and state and how both, especially the former, have tremendously failed to uphold the integrity and duties that align them to the people as safe abodes; the writer decries not only the inability of the church and other religious bodies to condemn the abnormalities plaguing our societies but also how they have been immensely plunged into the filth they ought to cleanse. Rather than offer salvation and assistance to the people, the religious bodies, in their multitudes, have become safe havens for political gladiators and other perpetrators of evil. A consequence of such an evil intricate relationship between the state (political leaders) and the religious bodies is the lack of integrity, honesty, spirituality, and a host of other virtues that the latter should be known for, the leaders who have repressed themselves to the biddings of the state thereby reducing their power and autonomy.[78]

CONCLUSION

> ...liberating Nigeria from this dimension[s] of backwardness will be the equivalent of a second independence.[79]

His musings decimate feasible and intellectual solutions for the collective advancement of our society. Nevertheless, his commentaries are not only steeped in highlighting the weaknesses inherent in our society and preferring solutions as a true socialist realist, but they are ended with optimism that reflects an imminent better

---

76. Ayo Olukotun, "Dearth of Nigerian CEOs in Nigeria-Based Multinationals," *The Punch*, November 13, 2018.
77. Olukotun, "Dearth of Nigerian CEOs."
78. Ayo Olukotun, "Corruption: Osinbajo's Indictment of our Churches," *The Punch*, June 22, 2017. See also Olukotun, "Ambode: Off Keynote."
79. Olukotun, "Any Hope for Overcoming?"

society. Overall, he is particularly clear-minded and expressive in his view on the need for intellectual polity and strength in the collective advancement of the nation, which, perhaps, is the most important involvement in the proper governance of Nigeria. In his words: "A capable state doesn't not come into existence by mouthing slogans but by the conscious programme of reformist elite taking the necessary steps to build one"[80] and "More important is the need for a political elite, armed with the correct political vision and script of transforming security institutions, as part of a wider state building project."[81]

In "Where is President Buhari's think tank,"[82] he foretells the flaws and inadequacies of the Buhari-led administration due to the lack of intellectual resources to admonish the government on various policies "that only a policy think tank can provide," a forte which is distant to the interests of our political class of elite whose consumption of policies excellence he describes as "shallow, fragmentary, and irregular." To drive his point home, he contrasts the current dispensation of political leaders to the likes of Chief Obafemi Awolowo, "who maintained and drew from the wisdom of a court of intellectuals and thinkers while sitting among them as one of the tribe."[83] He is particular about the tangible contribution scholars can make to political science in steering the nation's affairs in the right direction. In his view, "Political scientists as philosophers have a duty not only to theorize and build elegant models but to rule, administer and make policies at the highest levels of government,"[84] sighting the example of Prof. Attahiru Jega's, a political scientist, immense effort as the chairman of INEC in conducting the fairest election in the democratic history of the nation.

In his rumination, he remarks that "How different Nigerian history would have been if we had a political class which can sustain a think-tank and the decency of responsible intellectual dissent" and suggests that "politicians who lack the gravitas to hold their own in the battle of governance prescriptions cannot and should not be allowed to lead Nigeria out of its current wilderness of wasted opportunities."[85]

Further expounding on the "stinging rebuke" made by Bill Gates, which has been a major issue on the front burner of Prof. Olukotun's musing on the reclining condition of the nation as a result of government policies that "If Nigeria is to move out of its current arrested grove and fulfill its potential as an economic tiger playing on the world stage, then it must embrace a capable and developmental state bound by a social contract with the people, who as at now magically come into reckoning only when their votes are needed to sustain or recycle non-performing elites and admin-

80. Olukotun, "Will Pay Rise End?"
81. Olukotun, "Will Pay Rise End?"
82. Ayo Olukotun, "Where is President Buhari's Think Tank?" *The Punch*, January 8, 2016.
83. Olukotun, "Where is President Buhari's Think Tank?"
84. Ayo Olukotun, "Interrogating a Shallow Democracy," *The Punch*, March 23, 2017.
85. Ayo Olukotun, "Awolowo Dosunmu: A Political Dynasty at the Crossroad," *The Punch*, February 22, 2018.

istrations."[86] Alongside the call for a vibrant contribution of intellectuals in the political domain, he continuously enjoins the larger populace, those he refers to as the "precious asset"[87] to get involved in politics and governance till we all achieve our desired Nigeria because "Democracy is too important to be left to these politicians."[88] The drastic drop in the number of voters during the last presidential and national election, which is the lowest in the history of Nigerian electoral practice, compared to the 2019 general election is a manifestation of the people's indifference towards politics and the governance of the nation, a rather unhealthy attitude towards democracy.

Contrasting the performance of the Buhari-led administration against the intentions and promises as advanced in their manifestoes during the electoral process, Olukotun points out the fact that "the newspapers are filled daily with cries of anguish and frustrations by Nigerians who are tormented by ever-dwindling power, runaway mark-up in the price of essential services, continuous decay of transportation infrastructure as well as the sorry plight of tertiary and basic education;"[89] an indication that the country has been plunging into a state of a misnomer since the inception of the administration, a deplorable state which has since gotten worse over the years. With the implementation of the "Buharimeter" at the inception of the administration to ensure governmental accountability, the writer highlights the increasing need for the larger populace to hold the government accountable for their performance following their proposed plans, especially their failure "to make any appreciable dent on important governance problems"[90] that are vital to the growth of the society.

These collective energies, from the civil society, intellectuals, elder statesmen and every other person, are needed to drive the desired political change into manifestation. In his usual prognostic manner, he envisages a future whose people "will ponder how a civil society with an eminent cast of characters and internationally acclaimed actors, end up ever so often with a dysfunctional government, populated by mediocrities, crooks, and more than a fair share of legislators who have reduced governance to jestful, low grade entertainment."[91] The revitalization of the country, the writer admits,[92] can only be made possible by the presence of active and efficient governance, which can harness the resources of the country to ensure its for-so-long delayed development and advancement, placing Nigeria in its rightful place among other developed nations in the world. Like the rhetoric of change advanced by the Buhari administration,[93] which the citizens became indifferent to, a change in the bedeviling

86. Ayo Olukotun, "Bill Gate's Refreshingly Blunt Charge to our Leaders," *The Punch*, March 29, 2018.
87. Olukotun, "Okogie and Nigeria's Unending Search."
88. Olukotun, "Will 2019 Reverse the Crisis?"
89. Ayo Olukotun, "Buharimeter: A Wake up Call," *The Punch*, July 14, 2016.
90. Olukotun, "Buharimeter."
91. Olukotun, "Okogie and Nigeria's Unending Search."
92. Olukotun, "Is Excellence Possible in Nigeria?"
93. Ayo Olukotun, "The Raging Debate on the Change Mantra," *The Punch*, September 15, 2016.

realities of the nation through good governance is the only gateway to the comprehensive reformation of the country.

Olukotun represents one of the logical and informed stalwart voices that help the public form reasonable and logical opinions about governmental activities, policies, and other political development in the country. His importance in the discussions and conversations about the nation's state stems from his ability to reflect on social and political refractions and vices that have ambushed the nation on its journey to development. He is a critic but what makes him a pulse of the nation is his ability to not just sit in the critic's armchair alone but provide possible and sustainable solutions to the Nigerian problems through recommendations spelled out in many of his opinion posts and publications.

Olukotun believes that it is impossible to separate politics from development and thus explains his predisposition to political developments in Nigeria. Hence, he often calls for transforming the nation's polity and responsible officeholders. After this is achieved, efforts can be made toward ideological and sustainable development. As a believer in Pan-African principles, he is convinced that Nigerian and African politics should be injected with doses of indigenous cultural values that create channels for internal solutions. He never resists making his opinions known about the performance of the Buhari administration, stressing his failures to champion sustainable development and provide a good standard of living.

14

ABIMBOLA ADELAKUN

Remaking Society

INTRODUCTION

It is not easy to rationalize why certain public figures feed their followers with mind-blowing thoughts on diverse areas of life. For some of these public opinion influencers, the need to constantly churn out personal opinions of issues around the polity may often be misconstrued and misunderstood. However, as one becomes endeared to particular people's works, one begins to understand the vibes in their messages. The issues such individuals tend to dwell on and how they relay their messages lead to their respective followers/audience entering into their world to understand where they are coming from and the direction of their thoughts.

Abimbola Adelakun, an author and a columnist, is one such individual. She may not present herself as a public figure, nor would she accept that she is a public opinion influencer. But, in reality, these are the least of what she can be described for anyone that follows her columns and her academic and literary credentials. I am one of her ardent followers, which comes naturally when one looks at it from an academic point of view. Our paths met through our respective academic engagements. I would later find out that her interests center around what I also love to read and write about, African culture, religious creativity, and Nigerian politics. She served as part of the judges for the inaugural edition of The Toyin Falola Prize, a project established by young people to motivate young African writers to reach deep into the core

of African history and cultures, reaffirming and remaking the histories in more creative manners.

Abimbola Adelakun held Nigeria like a theatre wherein different fascinating dramas and literature engage the spectators but with a rather boring impression and feelings close to nightmares. What other purpose would a person visit a theatre if not to be buried in the ecstasy of its entertaining messages, touches of life and offering of clearance for imagination? But for Adelakun, she sat as a judge, analyzing and a spectator trying to understand the various dramas displayed. She holds every instance of occurrence in the country, like one analysis of a piece of literature and passes her opinions and convictions with endearing bluntness. She does not cover her positions with shy cloaks of inconclusiveness but pitches her tents when necessary.

As a blunt and committed writer, she has been able to make relevant positions from the standpoint of a critical mind touching on several problems that face the country. She has been able to do this with consistent resolutions and alertness to pass a view on immediate and arising social issues but with dexterous care for details and facts. With such consistency and courage to pass critical messages, Adelakun appeals to me as a social critic whose positions must be understood. If you ask, why Abimbola Adelakun? I can only refer to her resoluteness and critical opinions evident in her publications and how they convincingly touch on social issues.

As stated in other chapters, there might be many like Adelakun whose scholarship might attract interest and command an audience. However, Adelakun's interest in contemporary African culture, and its manifestations, in addition to how they interact with societal norms and historical convictions, exhibits her uniqueness. If this work must rightly connect with contemporary society and emerging cultures, Adelakun is the relevant scholar who answers questions about those phenomena. Hence, she spells out brewed opinions on religion, gender, culture, politics and heritage in columns and weekly publications with a sense of newness from the previous. She analyses and lives in the contemporary, explaining my interest in her scholarship.

The scholarship quests of Adelakun into the threads that hold the society together and contemporary issues do not stop at those affecting African and Nigerian society. But she extended her research and opinion tentacles to issues affecting Africans in the diaspora, understudying their activities, progress and social conditions they face; one such inquiry was done in partnership with me.[1] She has dedicated time to addressing controversial issues like #BlackLivesMatter, among other worrisome developments.

Aside from this, the underlying purport of this piece centers on contemporary developments and issues with roots in the dynamics of social media. Adelakun, in

1. Abimbola Adelakun and Toyin Falola, eds., *Art, Creativity, and Politics in Africa and the Diaspora* (Berlin: Springer, 2018).

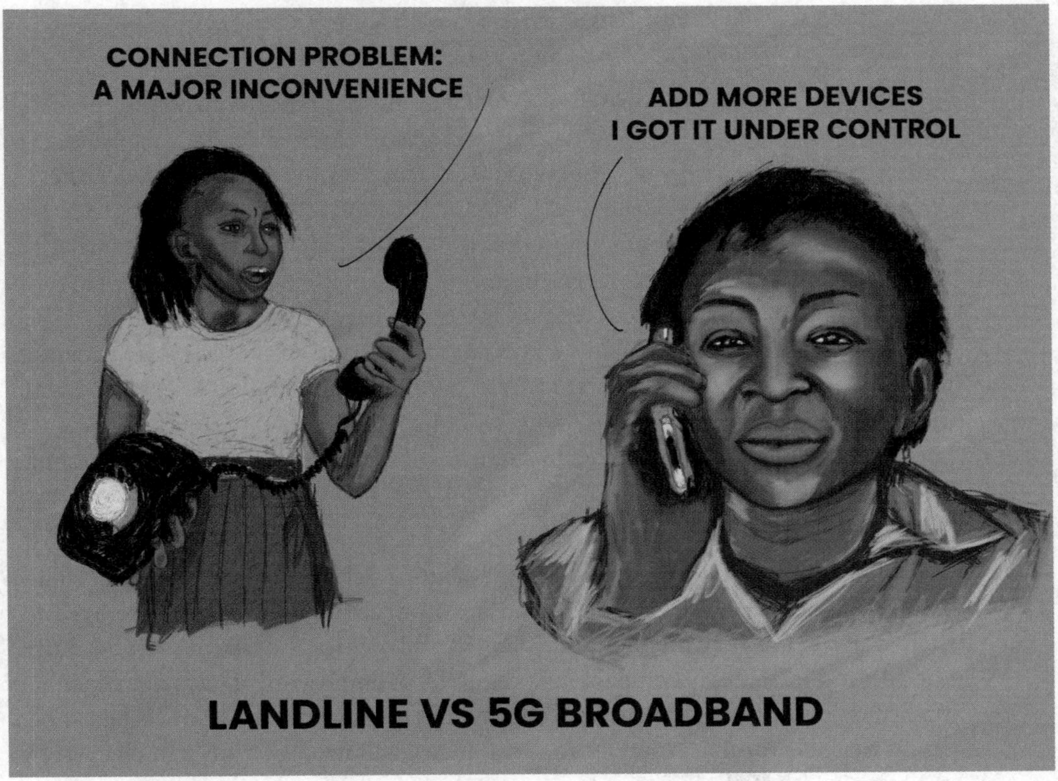

Figure 14.1. "Abimbola Adelakun" by Michael Efionayi. Abimbola Adelakun, having a dispassionate discussion.

conjunction with others, has put the new media, social media, and novel means of communication under examination lens and their impacts on society and how they have paved new paths for social phenomena.[2] Another way she has interacted with social media and contemporary themes is by understudying and analyzing its interaction with subjects of feminism and its representation on some of the platforms.[3]

This chapter represents an attempt to unearth and uncover some of the contemporary issues that recur in Adelakun's numerous articles and literature, in addition to her newspaper columns which feed the social media networks. The richness of her weekly columns makes it quite easy to lay hands on her thoughts on various burning issues that continue to shape the minds of her readers and followers.

2. Ayobami Ojebode, Dimeji Togunde and Abimbola Adelakun, "Secrecy, Security and Social Exchange: New Media and Cross-Generational Dating in Nigeria," *International Journal of Sociology of the Family* 37, no. 2 (2011): 307–327.

3. Abimbola Adelakun, "Feminism, Social Media, and Misbegotten Debates," *Proud Flesh: New Afrikan Journal of Culture, Politics and Consciousness* 21 (2020).

THE PATRIARCHAL THEME CONVEYED IN ADELAKUN'S LITERARY WORKS

Adelakun's *Under the Brown Rusted Roof* may give the perception of a book written to mirror one of the most notable ancient cities in Nigeria, Ibadan.[4] However, the book's central theme reveals the patriarchal nature inherent in African societies. While this may not represent the reality of the situation in totality, it points to certain culturally shared beliefs about how individuals are expected to be within society. The establishment of gender stereotypes in the book fits perfectly into the systemic functional linguistic theory that focuses on the transitivity of systems within social settings. The dynamics of polygamy, a popular family concept in Africa, are accompanied by the intrigues and politics that play out between the father as the head of the family and the women (co-wives) who jostle for the remaining leadership roles that are left vacant. One may be forced to allude to leadership roles being shared amongst the women in a polygamous setting in the order of first come, first served; validating such becomes a daunting task.

In her book, *Under the Brown Rusted Roofs*, Adelakun presents certain Yoruba family practices. Among these is the patriarchal structure upheld in the average African family. Set in Ibadan, one of the oldest Yoruba cities, Adelakun's work captured the political intrigues accompanying patriarchy and polygamy. The major characters in the book, Alhaji Arigbabuwo and Baba N'sale, demonstrated the typical patriarchal ideals that the Yoruba society is known for. Arigbabuwo, the patriarch character in the book, is denoted as a man who, despite the emergence of formal education, never felt inclined to go to school, ultimately believing that he does not need to be formally educated to become who he wanted to become. This, he minced no word to communicate with his father. To him, the fame he had succeeded in getting across the many 'agboles' within his community is enough to propel him to success in any endeavor he chooses. Ultimately, he became a prosperous merchant after he and his brother, Kareem Elelubo, inherited their mother's *elubo* business, which nurtured the two to prosperity.

The age-old belief among Africans that the male reserves some social exclusivity is perfectly rendered. The egotistical feeling of being better than the female folk leads to the feeling of being ascribed more societal value than women. The chauvinistic theme is seen several times in this fictional piece as two central male characters persistently exhibit it in their dealings with the female characters. Alake, one of Baba N'sale's numerous wives, suffered the pains of male chauvinism. Being the newest among the wives when she married, she was constantly reminded of her role as the youngest wife, responsible for most household chores without any additional rewards. Despite this, she has to satisfy the egotistic urge of the alpha male. She would later find a

4. Abimbola Adelakun, *Under the Brown Rusted Roofs* (Ibadan: Kraftgriots, 2008).

solution to this by feigning sickness many times and getting pregnant to get some reprieve from household chores.

A glaring exhibition of male chauvinism is brought to play with Arigbabuwo's practice of engaging in sexual acts with his women based on a roster that determines whom he spends the night with. He has sex partially clothed while mandating his wives to be completely naked before such sexual sports. Arigbabuwo followed that line of thought because of a story his father told him about the ridicule that was meted out on a certain Alaafin of Oyo due to going fully naked while having sex with one of his wives.

Another minor male character that highlights the phallocentric theme in *Under the Brown Rusted Roofs* is Rafiu (Arigbabuwo's eldest son), who is noted as enjoying the proverbial sweetness of honey but always ready to curse out the mere sighting of the bees.[5] He can not control his craving, which leads to him shouldering a responsibility he is unprepared for. He is always excited to engage in sexual intercourse with his lover, Mulika, but would go haywire when the result of the intercourse comes out—pregnancy. At that point, he remembers that his lover has a disfigured leg and is not suitable to be his wife. Rafiu also exhibited the superiority complex of the African male folk as he is prone to go violent whenever he feels Mulika irritated him, even though the woman labors through thick and thin to bear his child.

In religion and gender, Adelakun continued her narrative centering on the patriarchal system inherent in the African system, discussing the theatrical representation of a notable matriarch in the Yoruba folklore. In most African oral history, commercial and economic successes have always been an attribute of men, the reason being that the man is, by culture, expected to be the economic driver of the family. It is a patriarchal society, leaving just a little relevance for women. Financial and economic activities are perceived as the exclusivity of the man. Efunsetan Aniwura was one of the rare women in history that contested such a narrative as she embarked on doing what society believed was reserved for men, involvement in trade and business.[6]

Efunsetan rose to become a very successful trader and attained the highest socio-political status reserved for women, becoming the Iyalode of Ibadan in the era of the famous Aare Latoosa.[7] Suffice it to say that this position often raises the occupier to a chieftain within the monarchical structure. In essence, a woman conferred with the title of Iyalode becomes a member of the council of chiefs. In most cases, she is the only female allowed by tradition to be in the council, and she remains the leader of

5. Adelakun, *Under the Brown Rusted Roofs.*

6. Amon Simba, Ebere Ume Kalu, Vincent Onodugo, Chinwe R. Okoyeuzu and Oyedele Martins Ogundana, "Women Entrepreneurs in Nigeria." In *Women Entrepreneurs in Sub-Saharan Africa*, eds. Marina Dabić, Léo-Paul Dana, Dina Modestus Nziku and Veland Ramadani (Cham, Switzerland: Springer, 2022).

7. Olawale F. Idowu and Sunday A. Ogunode, "Gender and the Politics of Exclusion in Pre-Colonial Ibadan: The Case of Iyalode Efunsetan Aniwura," *The Journal of Traditions & Beliefs* 2, no. 1 (2016): 21.

the women folk within such a society. Of course, such ambitiousness was expected to come at a price, as there is little or no mention of her husband in oral history. However, this does not translate to not having one, as there was a brief mention of a child that she was alleged to eventually lose.

Some African men are wired to immediately portray a woman that wields power as irrational and evil. These may stem from egocentrism or sheer chauvinistic tendencies, but it remains a fact that cannot be disputed easily. The ambition to constantly limit the powers of the feminine folks in African society has been entrenched in the prehistoric culture and traditions that we all met. This, according to Adelakun, was evident in the most notable theatrical rendition of the Efunsetan character by the late Ishola Ogunsola in the 1970s and 1980s, a version of Akinwumi Isola's storyline. Adelakun progressed in her evaluation, affirming that the playwright, Ishola Ogunsola presented Efunsetan as a malevolent witch whose economic and political power was the result of her supernatural power, and this allowed her to perpetrate evil.[8]

The tendency for African males to despise the dominance of the feminine gender is carried out unconsciously by ensuring that every powerful woman is ultimately subjugated. If there are no other means to do this, male violence becomes the only option. This assertion is also evident if we go by Adelakun's words that Efunsetan became a victim of male violence both in life and after death. Perhaps, we should look at this from two perspectives; in life and after death.

In life, the sad end of Efunsetan Aniwura came from her fallout with another notable chief and warlord, Aare Latoosa, the reason being Aniwura's opinion that the latter was constantly engaging in pointless wars.[9] To this end, she had to withdraw her support from Latoosa's military adventures. While this may seem rational from a neutral point of view, it represented abhorrence from the warlord's perspective, who mobilized the remaining all-male council-in-chiefs to depose her as the Iyalode. The monarchical structure is arranged so that the occupier of a position holds it for a lifetime. The occupier's death is the only rational reason to search for another occupier. And in any situation whereby an occupier is removed based on any wrongdoing, such occupier may be adjudged to have died, not physically but socially. Such a deposed leader may be partially excommunicated or avoided by society.

In death, the portrayal of Efunsetan, especially by the theatrics of the late Ishola Ogunsola, represents a deliberate attempt to present her as evil and anti-maternal. This can be equated to character assassination ipso facto. The play went a long way to impress upon the people that Efunsetan was, in fact, a cruel woman. Such character representation may not be true if we go by other scholarly research about Efunsetan that does not agree with Ishola's damaging theatric rendition of Efunsetan. As Ad-

8. Abimbola Adelakun, "The Ghosts of Performance Past: Theatre, Gender, Religion and Cultural Memory," *Religion and Gender* 7, no. 2 (2017): 147–164.

9. Adelakun, "The Ghosts of Performance Past."

Figure 14.2. "A Clearing Bulldozer" by Dr. Kazeem Ekeolu. A Bulldozer clearing rubbish depicts Adelakun's desire that society's problems be cleared out.

elakun pointed out in "The Ghosts of Performance Past: Theatre, Gender, Religion and Cultural Memory," the stage play of Efunsetan Aniwura by the late Ishola Ogunsola succeeded in denigrating the female legend, leading to a not-so-true perception formed by the people about her character. So appalling was the characterization of Efunsetan Aniwura that the woman that played the role, Iyabode Ogunsola, was noted to have affirmed how her interpretation of the Efunsetan character affected her real life; with a significant number of people not able to delineate her actual character from that of the character she played. Ogunleye also further stated another noteworthy assertion that should not go unnoted. At a time when Efunsetan Aniwura's edifice was to be erected in Ibadan, Ishola Ogunsola's portrayal of the legend had left a strong print on the people so much that objections were raised, as many people opined that immortalizing Efunsetan is nothing but a celebration of an evil mind.[10] The vast amount of literature on Efunsetan Aniwura is not enough to change the perception people ingested from the theatrical rendition of the late Ishola Ogunshola. Today, the

10. Foluke Ogunleye, "A Male-Centric Modification of History; Efunsetan Aniwura Revisited," *History in Africa* 31 (2004): 303–318.

very spot where the portrait of Efunsetan Aniwura used to stand in the center of Ibadan is empty.

THE THEME OF POLYGAMY IN ADELAKUN'S LITERARY WORKS

Polygamy has been ingrained in African societies from time immemorial. We must quickly add that polygyny is predominantly practiced in much of Africa, where a man can legally marry two or more women. This is opposed to the other aspect of polygamy, known as polyandry, where a woman could legally be married to two or more men. Due to the agrarian culture that the African societies were built upon, there was a need for large family structures that resulted in a workforce. The bigger the farmland, the more workforce was needed to till it. Perhaps, this explains the reason for the continent being one that still finds it difficult to let go of the polygamist mindset. The concept of polygamy was reinforced with the advent of Islam, a religion that supports polygamy as an ideal marriage concept. The tendency for a man to be polygamous is common among men who believe they are financially capable of being responsible for more wives. It starts with the want to satisfy sexual desires outside the man's immediate family circle. By keeping a mistress, the foundation for a polygamous home is unconsciously being laid. When pregnancy eventually sets in, there is little left for the legitimate wife to do other than accept her fate and live with the reality of the situation. Although polygamy was validated as a means of limiting the sexual promiscuity of men in a patriarchal society, it is always counterproductive, as we would see subsequently.

In *Under the Brown Rusted Roofs*, Adelakun exposes the reader to the prevalence of polygamy within the Yoruba marriage tradition.[11] The focal point of attraction is perfectly balanced between the pros and cons of polygamy that is presented to the reader to reflect the inherent inadequacies of certain Yoruba cultural practices and the likely consequences. This is brought to the fore by the major character in the book, Alhaji Arigbabuwo and subsequently followed up by minor characters such as Baba N'sale. Being the pack's alpha male, Arigbabuwo does not shy away from lashing out violently at any lesser member of the pack to reinstate and reassert his authority over them. His two wives (Afusa and Sikira) knew enough to perpetrate any dastardly attitude in his presence. However, his financial capability allowed him to operate as a good father and husband. He is not one to display acts of stinginess towards any of his family, children, and wives. The same cannot be said for the other polygamous patriarch, Baba N'Sale, who happened to be a bosom friend of Arigbabuwo. Baba N'sale maintained a harem of eight wives, with five leaving him for greener pastures. Although he is portrayed as a miser, he tries as much as possible not to extend this unholy attitude to his children.

---

11. Adelakun, *Under the Brown Rusted Roofs.*

Polygamy, as exhibited in *Under the Brown Rusted Roofs,* is a system that may seem to excite the man, but the women feel its side effect. The generally held notion by African men of the times past that polygamy is the test of the financial buoyancy of a man is put on display by Adelakun. The number of women a man marries reflects his financial ability. However, this may not be wholly true when we relate it to Arigbabuwo, the richer of the two polygamists but had fewer wives than Baba N'sale.

The greatest side effect of polygamy remains the potentiality of experiencing neglect by not only the women but the egotistical men. While Baba N'sale was generous to take the persistent loss of his wives to other wealthier men, Arigbabuwo was not. Having his ego deflated when Sikira eventually left him for another wealthier man, he hesitantly went ahead to marry another wife (Moriyeba) on the advice of his friend, Baba N'sale, to stroke his ego and pass the message that he has more than enough to cater for more women, making the proverb, "Olówó gbà'yàwó ọ̀lẹ̀" (The rich snatches away the wife of the lazy man) nullified. Baba N'sale, on his part, while being bedridden in the hospital, continues to boast that he was as strong as a young man and to show that he would marry another wife when he eventually leaves the hospital. This was coming at a time when the hordes of children were wallowing in perpetual penury under his brown rusted roof.

Under the Brown Rusted Roofs may have initially designated polygamy as a luxurious agenda for the men with the financial capability; however, this is not a holy writ, as the reader would later see.[12] Bringing the discourse to reality, Adelakun, in one of her publications, "Emir Sanusi's regulation of Polygamy," observes that it becomes evident that polygamy is becoming more of a societal problem as a significant number of men take more wives than they can cater for. The deposed monarch affirmed his determination to propose a law that would "regulate the practice of polygamy and other social ills in his territory."[13] It doesn't take a wordsmith to understand the level of ideality that the contraption of polygamy and social ills connotes. It is easy to read sentimental meaning into the opinion of Sanusi by affirming that he also married four wives. But Adelakun was quick to point out that Sanusi's proposition is commendable as it seeks to curtail the exploitation of religious laws for unshackling the lustful urges of men who may not be financially capable of such adventures.[14] This statement connotes an attempt to close the loophole created by religious indoctrination and ensure that measures are implemented to discourage incessant abuse of religious dogmas.

While the agrarian societies supported polygamy based on the reality of the time, Adelakun noted that the era of mechanized farming should have eroded the polygamist mindset from the minds of its proponents. Rather than establish an enviable

12. Adelakun, *Under the Brown Rusted Roofs.*

13. Abimbola Adelakun, "Emir Sanusi's Regulation of Polygamy," *Punch*, February 23, 2017, https://www.opinionnigeria.com/emir-sanusis-regulation-of-polygamy-by-abimbola-adelakun/.

14. Adelakun, "Emir Sanusi's Regulation."

workforce, polygamy has only led to an increase in children that could not be effectively catered for, as is evident in northern Nigeria, where polygamy is rife. A legislator of northern extraction, Ado-Doguwa also alluded to the dangers of polygamy when he ridiculed himself by bringing his four wives to the federal legislative chambers, telling those who cared to listen that his polygamous mindset was a symbol of power. Adelakun noted in the article "Between Polygamy and Irresponsibility" that the legislator was quick to share a mind-blowing secret: his father was a polygamist who left behind over 80 children, many of whom the legislator had to take responsibility for.[15]

Ado-Doguwa succeeded, albeit unintentionally, in supporting the belief that many northern polygamists were not economically capable of catering to their innate desires. With no meaningful wealth to train children, polygamists end up being individuals whose major impact is contributing their quota to the population explosion, as Adelakun rightly noted in the article. While wanting to respect cultural and religious sentimentalities, it is equally important to note the impacts such exuberances leave on society. The northern regions of Nigeria are known for low contributions to the economic growth and development of the country. Rather, the region is immersed in activities that persistently drag the country down. The large pools of resources harvested from the southern region of Nigeria are transferred to the north to solve problems they created for themselves. That is why it is important to always discourage indulgence in certain practices, which may be backed by religion and culture but have been noted as negatively impacting society's overall well-being. The agrarian age is gone, which has somewhat limited the advantages polygamy bequeaths to families.

Adelakun also noted that Sanusi may have made a valid point in his proposition, but the inherent contradictions reveal another problem. How do we juxtapose the fact that a major critic of polygamy is also a polygamist, an unrepentant one? The BBC reported that the deposed Emir of Kano, Sanusi Lamido Sanusi suggested polygamy was responsible for many poor people in the north, a situation that rippled to the rise of Islamic militancy in Muslim-dominated North-eastern Nigeria.[16] This may not be unconnected with the Royal Society Scientific Journal report that alluded to the assertion that polygamous societies are prone to incidences that support theft, war and gender-related violence. Many offspring from polygamous marriages begets an abundance of uneducated children. It should be noted that challenging a practice that has been ingrained into the culture of the people will be an uphill task, especially now that Sanusi has been deposed as Emir and no longer wields any form of authority over the people anymore. Furthermore, the rationale for men who have the wherewithal to engage in polygamous practice is no more tenable since it has been established that

---

15. Abimbola Adelakun, "Ado-Doguwa: Between Polygamy and Irresponsibility," *Punch,* February 13, 2020.

16. BBC, "Why Does a Nigerian Muslim Leader want to Restrict Polygamy?" *BBC News,* February 22, 2017, https://www.bbc.com/news/world-africa-39038459.

the majority of the wealthy individuals like Doguwa and Sanusi exist solely on government funds; hence they too may not be economically capable of engaging in polygamous practices if we leave out the state funds.[17]

POLITICAL VIOLENCE IN NIGERIA FROM ADELAKUN'S PERSPECTIVE

Violence is not resident in any singular location around the world. In Nigeria, however, it is a lifestyle, a culture that is practiced with impunity and outright disdain for authority.[18] And while discussing violence, it is important to denote its typology. While various forms exist, some kinds of violence are prevalent in certain parts of the world. Political violence is a form that Africans still have to contend with, even in this modern age. *Under the Brown Rusted Roofs* presents the reader with the manner of violence that was ever-present during the various military rules in Nigeria.

From overtaking legitimate governments under the feign of trying to maintain a peaceful and corruption-free country to subjecting civilians to varying degrees of humiliation to stamp their authority, military juntas in Nigeria have institutionalized political violence in Nigeria. Adelakun referenced this with the Iya-Loja being lashed violently beyond recognition by soldiers meant to protect unarmed citizens. Mulika, Rafiu's wife, also had her fair share of political violence as she was subjected to political brutality when she was met in the company of other women who wanted to fetch water.

However, we may excuse the military government's use of violence by its war-like mindset. What becomes inexcusable is civilian rulers, supposed to uphold the tenets of democracy, also use violence to achieve their political aspirations. Adelakun perfectly captured this through the character, Alhaji Kudeti, who believes that politics is a do-or-die affair and victory can only be achieved through a bloodbath. In one part of the text, the politician could be heard rhetorically asking the Chairman of his political party: "Do you think the other party will strip babies to their backs and watch us win the election just like that?"[19]

The case of some other minor characters also lends credence to the institutionalization of political violence. Chief Olatunbosun and his political opponent, Eruobodo, engaged in a strong political rivalry that led to the former's demise. The political scene in Nigeria has also witnessed the assassinations of political opponents before an election, a vivid example being the case of the late Engineer Funsho Williams who had publicly vowed to wrestle control of the wealthiest state in Nigeria, Lagos, from the hands of the ruling party, Alliance for Democracy. Although his campaign man-

---

17. Adelakun, "Ado-Doguwa."
18. Abimbola Adelakun, "Impunity: Nigeria's First Violence," *Punch*, March 23, 2017.
19. Adelakun, *Under the Brown Rusted Roofs*, 209.

ager and one of his intra-party competitors were arrested, no substantive investigation was carried out.

With such insinuations, as noted, one begins to wonder if the democracy in existence in Nigeria is the same one that is being practiced in western countries. The disposition to perceive elections as a battle may have been borne out of desperation, not from the zeal to render servitude to the citizenry; rather, it is based on the mindset of selfish will to take power and exploit it for personal gains. The journey to attain political positions in Nigeria becomes not a race where the competitors see one another as contemporaries, instead pitching them against themselves as enemies would.

ADELAKUN'S THOUGHT ON GENDER-BASED VIOLENCE

Gender-targeted violence in Nigeria can be said to be aided by the patriarchal culture inherent in various ethnic cultures in Nigeria. And in trying to give an excuse, it is ubiquitous to find labels that are, at best nauseating to the ears of the intelligent. Noting the spate of sexual harassment of women in Nigeria, Adelakun referred to a federal lawmaker from Borno state, Ahmed Jaha, saying that women who wanted to avoid the possibility of being raped should learn to dress decently, alluding that men get easily turned on by indecency.[20] This may sound logical if the survey carried out in 2019 by the UK-based media house, *The Independent* is anything to go by.[21] This supported another earlier survey conducted in the USA, where many respondents affirmed that sexual harassment on campuses happens because the victim unintentionally asked for it. Adelakun noted that most of the men in the survey affirmed that a woman's clothing could be a catalyst for unwarranted sexual harassment. It would have made quite a lot of sense if such a comment originated from women. However, the disposition to shift the blame of wrongdoing from the perpetrator to the victim does not validate or legitimize the act.

The above scenarios point to one eventuality: gender-targeted violence should not be attributed to the victim's acts but the perpetrator's motives and intentions. Cruelty towards the female gender did not start today, but it continues to exist unabated due to the religious and cultural super-imposition of the male gender on its female counterpart. Positing that sexual harassment such as rape happens majorly on the precept of indecent dressing may not be right if we probe further into rape cases like the one that led to the death of Vera Omozuwa, who was subjected to rape while studying inside a church. Would it be appropriate to say that her killers seemingly singled her out for dressing and trailed her to the church to perpetuate their dastardly acts? While the answer to this question may vary, it would be perfect for supporting the writer's opinion that 'rapists do not see clothes; they see a potential victim.' Based on this sa-

---

20. Abimbola Adelakun, "Rape: Men are Truly not Wood," *Punch*, June 11, 2020.
21. Adelakun, "Rape: Men are Truly not Wood."

lient fact, it will also be illogical to point at indecent dressing as the cause of several rape cases around the country. Abimbola Adelakun listed some rape cases that rendered the notion of indecent dressing as causality and a fallacy of illicit generalization when offered as logical argument: infant rape committed by a 38-year-old man, gang-rape by four men on a 12-year-old girl, a young man raping his mother, a 70-year-old woman raped by a 25-year-old man, to mention a few.

In the article "Men are not Wood," Adelakun was able to drive home one salient point; every act perpetrated by a man went through some form of rationality or thought process. Such thoughts may be influenced by a perceived superiority over the feminine gender or the tendency to subdue a physically weaker gender for self-seeking pleasure. This proffers to the male a predatory, albeit domineering mindset towards the female. Predators may not necessarily be fatalists in their actions, but they desire to act on the vulnerabilities of their prey. This assertion represents a sad reality that men in a patriarchal society must come to terms with.

With this, it becomes evident that nowhere is deemed a sanctuary when trying to rationalize the occurrences and incidences of gender-targeted violence. Adelakun supports the realization of this sad fact in the Uwa case; there are neither sacred places nor sanctuaries for anyone.[22] Nigerians live in a society that has no respect for divinity. Killings in religious houses and worship centers did not start with Uwa, and they may not end with it. The security structure within the country does not give room for adequate investigations to reveal the perpetrators of heinous crimes. This automatically leads to criminals going away with various degrees of criminalities.

The situations beg to wonder if Nigeria will ever be able to put in place a system that will uphold justice as far as gender-targeted violence is concerned. According to a report by Mrs. Pauline Tallen in 2019, more than two million women and girls in Nigeria get sexually molested every year.[23] This may not be far from the truth if we go by the report that also affirmed that 3 out of 10 Nigerians confirmed to know at least one person that has been raped in the past. However, there is a high possibility that the figure increases or victims are getting bolder in reporting the cases. I will opt for the latter owing to the number of past cases of sexual violence that victims have reported in recent times. Although such claims may not be easily confirmed, the sheer alacrity of alluding to being sexually molested by people in the past pins the onus on the accused to defend such allegations.

22. Abimbola Adelakun, "Raped in the Church," *Punch*, June 4, 2020.

23. NexTier SPD, "Sexual Violence: Why the Rise?" *NexTier SPD*, June 9, 2020, https://nextierspd.com/sexual-violence-why-the-rise/.

ADELAKUN'S PERSPECTIVE ON AFRICAN PENTECOSTALISM

Pentecostalism may not have originated from Africa; however, the continent is home to the world's largest Pentecostal churches today. The growth of Pentecostalism in Africa can be connected to the development of local initiatives that were not passive towards the new religion permeating the continent. While some African churches gained autonomy from the missionaries that brought the religion, some other dissident Christians embarked on moves to establish churches modeled according to their respective inhibitions. Locals' acceptability of such dissident churches paved the way for more individuals to become self-styled religious leaders with unique Christian worship doctrines.

So great is the numerical strength of Pentecostal churches in Africa, and Adelakun confirmed this when she stated in her doctoral thesis that 44 percent of the world is in Africa.[24] That Africa is home to the largest denominations of Pentecostal churches is not coincidental. This is not unconnected with important doctrines that are the bedrock of Pentecostalism: healing, deliverance and miracle. In many Pentecostal churches, these events are planned carefully during services or at crusades, and the objective is to rid individuals of negative forces and evil machinations that are believed to be responsible for such individuals' perennial problems.

Adelakun, in the thesis, referenced instances of these, one example being a testimony by a Pentecostal brother whose search for the cure to a particular sickness took him across three different continents, albeit unsuccessfully. The hearing eventually took place in the famous Pentecostal church in Nigeria, Winners Chapel, not before subjecting himself to self-humiliating gestures like rolling on the floor of the church auditorium, seeking divine intervention. In some particular Pentecostal denominations, deliverances and healing may go violent, leading to the person being held firmly to the ground and compelled to free themself for the evacuation of the malignant powers within such bodies.

One major reason for the proliferation of Pentecostal movements in Nigeria can be ascribed to various socio-economic problems faced by a high proportion of the polity; they promise the possibilities of turning around the everyday problems individuals face. The Pentecostal movement embarks on promises of improved living standards for its followers through deliverances and spiritual cleansing. In some cases, Pentecostal denominations' spiritual leaders may use semantics to confuse the minds of vulnerable followers. For instance, phrases such as "being rich in Christ" may allude to individuals suffering from poverty due to their being socio-economically handicapped but needing reassurance that they are spiritually blessed. Such a phrase may also be used to stroke the ego of followers into believing that spiritual

---

24. Abimbola Adelakun, "Godmentality: Pentecostalism as Performance in Nigeria," PhD *diss.*, The University of Texas at Austin, 2017.

riches are a precept to material riches as followers are encouraged to seek the kingdom of God first, and all other things will automatically fall into place.

As Adelakun would further note, rolling on the floor is a concept that she termed "The Widow Morality," an act that not only indicated humility and modesty but a staged performance that is supposed to impress God and ensure that the prayers and supplications are answered:

> The Widow Morality is a recreation of the Nietzschean concept of the slave-master morality conjoined with a parable from the Bible. The parable, the Widow and the Judge were one of Jesus' teachings to his followers. He was showing them the kind of behavior that can prompt their receiving answers from God and analysis is a re-reading of the text to not only pry out the dynamics of the God-man relationship in intercessory prayer but also to maintain the theological content of the interaction in a way Nietzsche's master-slave morality does not capture.[25]

Pentecostalism is built on the backdrop of spiritual consciousness and the expectation of the physical manifestation of divine powers. Such manifestations may often be perceived as illogical and irrational by an outsider, but believers will always be quick to counter with faith conjectures like 'with God, all things are possible.' Also, it is said in the Holy Bible that a believer whose faith is as tiny as a mustard seed may cause a physically grounded mountain to shift location. Such conjectures do not always give room for further rationalizing the belief in the physical manifestation of divine powers. African Christians embrace Pentecostalism due to the myriads of socio-economic problems they face.[26]

In "Pentecostal Panoptimism and the Phantasm of the Ultimate Power," Adelakun alluded to a certain Pentecostal denomination founded in Nigeria that focuses on violent prayers as a means of breaking from the yoke of perceived principalities and evil forces.[27] To support the assertion that Pentecostalism in Africa is a product of the mixture of local spiritual indoctrination and imported Christian lore, Adelakun made remarks on the repeated chants of words; die, perish, fire etc., to invoke the manifestation of heavenly beings.[28] This perhaps explains the interface between the incantation culture of African Traditional Religions and Pentecostalism:

---

25. Adelakun, "Godmentality," 74.

26. Cedric Mayrargue, "The Paradoxes of Pentecostalism in Sub-Saharan Africa," *Sub-Saharan African Program,* 2008.

27. Abimbola Adelakun, "Pentecostal Panopticism and the Phantasm of "The Ultimate Power"," In *Pentecostalism and Politics in Africa,* eds. Adeshina Afolayan, Olajumoke Yacob-Haliso and Toyin Falola (Cham, Switzerland: Palgrave Macmillan, 2018), 101–118.

28. Adelakun, "Pentecostal Panopticism."

> Every evil monitoring gadget, remote control devices and every witchcraft coven assigned against my life and destiny be destroyed by the Holy Ghost fire, in the name of Jesus .... Every spiritual screen and radar, spiritual mirror, spiritual tape, spiritual camera, spiritual satellite and all spiritual properties that Satan has set to monitor me, break into pieces, in the name of Jesus.[29]

The tendency to physically invoke spiritual beings to fight physical and real-life battles is strong in Africa. In fact, the warped belief may sometimes be taken too far as solutions to economic woes that befall many of our countries. To shed more light on this, Adelakun asserted that the yearning of Pentecostals is validated, fashioning the Bible to become a weapon of warfare that every Christian should wield when faced with any challenge, physical ones inclusive.[30] Quite a number of Pentecostals go as far as rejecting western medications, subsequently heaving their potential healing on prayers that are rendered in chants and invocations.

To add to the impurity of imported Christian faith into Africa, Pentecostal movement founders added various African traditional religious concepts such as visions, ecstatic dances, divine revelations, spiritual cleansing, demon exorcism and others to establish unique pseudo-denominations within the Pentecostal sphere. In the case of the Aladura churches, whose worship modes have imprints of Yoruba religions,[31] the disposition to engage in rituals mimics traditional worship but on a different religious pedestal. The use of animals for spiritual cleansing may be ascribed to the Old Testament of the Bible; the New Testament was alleged to have replaced that with the bloodshed on the Cross of Calvary. However, the Aladura Churches are still known to engage in rites that involve propitiations of the higher power through animal sacrifice and using certain spiritual materials like the candle and incense burning to engage in spiritual cleansing.

The success attributed to Pentecostal worship often comes from testimonies that sometimes defeat any sense of rationality or logic. While some may tend towards being hilarious, to say the least, others are outrightly unbelievable. For example, Adelakun noted that testimony time becomes when adherents independently submit themselves on the altar to give narratives of how God had acted on their behalf.[32] The major point of note in testimonies is the victorious element accompanying them. An individual suddenly faced with a difficult task may find himself or herself wriggling out of such without understanding how such became possible. Many testimonies are spun to raise the congregation's consciousness of the powers of divine interventions. In one of such testimonies described by Adelakun, a woman narrated how she gave birth to a "deaf and dumb" girl. After searching for a solution for thirteen years, she contacted the

29. Adelakun, "Pentecostal Panopticism," 101.
30. Adelakun, "The Ghosts of Performance Past."
31. Adelakun, "The Ghosts of Performance Past."
32. Adelakun, "Godmentality."

General Overseer of Mountain of Fire and Miracles, Daniel Olukoya. Her contact with the man of God led to her receiving anointing oil which she subsequently used on the child. A child who had never spoken or heard a word since birth started to speak and communicate effortlessly with people. After rendering such extra stories, the congregation normally shouts praise to the Almighty God that made the impossible possible. While one may not challenge the empirical evidence inherent in the experience of the believer, one stoops to be cautious of the tendency to immortalize the commonplace occurrence, becoming sublime when it is a natural or scientific process.

For a believer in the faith to rationalize that such miracles are mere fables automatically makes such a believer an unbeliever or a doubting Thomas. Such interesting renditions show how impossibilities are presented as possible, not by the church leadership but by individuals who want to appear God-favored or God-graced. However, the seeming impossibilities made possible through miracles and healing are the major essence of belief in Pentecostalism. The vagrant display of falsity in the name of testimonies is sometimes embarked upon on the premise that the Almighty God becomes obliged to protect such individuals who try to portray the omnipotence of God as a manifestation that can be experienced. By ascribing the possibility of impossibilities to God, the devil and his minions are shamed and refrained from stealing people's victories.[33] Closely looking at components of African Traditional Religions, it becomes easy to understand the reason for the wholesale embrace of Pentecostalism in Nigeria.

ADELAKUN ON COMPLEX SOCIO-POLITICAL ISSUES

Abimbola Adelakun dwells on the myriad of problems bedeviling Nigeria's socio-political system from the lenses of religious violence, leadership struggles, and societal decadence. A careful analysis of Nigeria's socio-political climate reveals that it suffers from the proliferation of the above conditions, and there is a need for this plethora of issues to be brought to the fore so that necessary actions can be taken to steer the nation to sanity. The challenge with Nigeria is the failure to wriggle herself out of her current predicament. Discourses on the country's predicament are often reduced to a coterie of individuals who are passionate about developing their country. Even when there are similar discourses on the precarious situation the nation faces in the public sphere, there is still a need for constant communication on the state of affairs so that the narratives could be much better. Through her articles on Nigeria's socio-political climate, Adelakun has become a relentless critic of these issues and aims to ensure there are necessary interventions from appropriate quarters.

Adelakun, like other Nigerian essayists passionate about Nigeria's project, examines political issues as they affect the nation. It is a fact that the nation's political system is in the hands of a few individuals who are more concerned about amassing

33. Adelakun, "Godmentality."

political influence than driving the nation to progress. With the failure of the nation's political system, it would be delusional to posit that the country can regain its past glory and continue in that development. The challenge with Nigeria's political system, as it is generally posited, is that of bad leaders. Those who wield political class in the country are aristocratic oligarchs who see the seats of power as opportunities to consolidate their teeming influence. Nigerians are concerned about the challenges of leadership, and even when they are resolute that the lightening of bad leadership or governance would not strike twice, they are usually left with no better choices. During the electoral process, the citizens are forced to choose between the bad and the worse; the good is never an option here because they often do not make it to the final candidacy and do not have what is termed as "political structure," that is, loads of money and other machinery that win elections in Nigeria. The nation's political process is so flawed that the common belief citizens harbor on this narrative change is divine or spiritual intervention.

Adelakun is well-known for her no-holds-barred criticisms of the nation's political leaders. Unlike some columnists, who indirectly refer to their subject matters, Adelakun does not criticize her subject matters in veiled references. In her article titled, "Tinubu Presidency: Affliction must not Rise a Second Time," Adelakun cautions Nigeria's populace against the emergence of the Lagos godfather, Asiwaju Bola Tinubu as the president after the failed leadership of Buhari and the All Progressives Congress (APC) in general.[34] In this essay, Adelakun beams light on Tinubu's obsession with the presidency and warns of the calamity to follow if he assumes the mantle of leadership. Bola Tinubu had never hidden his desire to take over from Buhari, even when both appeared similar in political ideologies and would not bring the change the country needed. Tinubu gets praised by his ardent followers as a visionary leader who single-handedly transformed Lagos state from an untidy city to a megacity. Adelakun watered down these descriptions. According to Adelakun, the blunt truth is that if Lagos were to be used as a parameter for Tinubu's success, Nigeria would further plunge down the pedestal of progress. Nigeria is riddled with many challenges that another leadership mistake could prove fatal. There is a saying that Nigeria—both as a country and as a people—is resilient and can withstand anything. This postulation would prove impotence in the wake of another leadership crisis. Adelakun argues that no matter how much rebranding Tinubu's followers would do for him, it would not bring the change the country so much craves or deserves. As she put it: "Nigeria urgently needs a turning point. Everybody—including even some of Tinubu's close associates—knows he does not represent the future. Some things should be left where they were buried, and that includes Tinubu's presidential dreams."[35] Aside from the fact that Tinubu's claim for excellence is highly contestable, no one really knows the

34. Abimbola Adelakun, "Tinubu Presidency: Affliction must not Rise a Second Time," *The Punch*, January 13, 2022.

35. Adelakun, "Tinubu Presidency."

man as his "identity is shrouded in incredulous falsehoods." Despite being praised as a political hunter, Tinubu's choice of leadership is often a calamity and here is the "democrat" attributed a savior-complex mentality.

In another article titled "Tinubu vs. Atiku: Two Desperados Running against Nigeria," Adelakun laments that Nigeria's top leadership position is between Bola Tinubu and Atiku Abubakar, who is more interested in fulfilling their dreams and ambitions than in exhibiting good governance.[36] Atiku Abubakar has had his eyes on the presidency since 1993. It has thus become obvious that his obsession cannot be particularly tied to his willingness to serve; rather, it is more of fulfilling a childhood dream. Adelakun notes the desperation among the duos for the presidency and how fatal it would be for the nation's political history, especially as the race, realistically speaking, is limited between the two. Both are very old and know that this is their final push for the presidency; thus, they would stop at nothing to translate their ambitions into reality. However, if any of them gains, Nigeria ultimately loses—thus, the endless list of problems recycles. Adelakun further criticizes the fact that Nigeria's choice of leadership is limited to two political parties—the Peoples Democratic Party (PDP) and the All Progressives Party (APC). Although Nigeria operates a multi-party system, in theory, it is from these two parties that political leaders are recycled. According to Adelakun, "It is somehow tempting to lament how our presidential choices have been largely bracketed between these two lackluster candidates, but that was in the offing all along. The poor choices of Atiku and Tinubu did not creep in on us; we zombie-walked into their emergence over time...."[37]

It is not overstated to posit that the dominance of the two political parties in Nigeria results from the absence of a stronger political party, which political analysts call the "third force." The absence of a third force is mainly because Nigerian politicians are opportunists who only wish to identify with power and authority and continue to scavenge from the country's wreck. This situation worsens because anyone who desires to contest political offices only does so to enjoy their fair share of exploiting the state's wealth and resources. Although, the Labour Party (LP) has been seen as the potential third force that can liberate the country from the shackles of the PDP and APC. The fact that the LP's presidential candidate for 2023 is Peter Obi, a former governor of Anambra state, and also taking cognizance of his fanatic supporters who are passionate about the nation's progress, there may be credence in this narrative. Adelakun examines the need for candidacy outside PDP and APC in an article titled "Funke Akindele might be Good for Lagos politics."[38] The popular and well-accomplished actress is a deputy governorship candidate of the PDP in Lagos state. Lagos state is a well-known stronghold of the APC, which has reigned for close to 23 years,

36. Abimbola Adelakun, "Tinubu vs Atiku: Two Desperados Running against Nigeria," *The Punch*, June 9, 2022.

37. Adelakun, "Tinubu vs Atiku."

38. Abimbola Adelakun, "Funke Akindele might be Good for Lagos Politics," *The Punch*, July 21, 2022.

yet the city has not experienced so great a transformation that it would be ranked as one of the best 30 cities in the world. Adelakun believes that Funke Akindele's candidacy and possible emergence can be a boon for Lagos, thus eradicating godfatherism. According to Adelakun, "... I still view her (Funke Akindele's) candidature as savvy. She is accomplished and can hold her own. Compared to the APC counterparts, she is not the one whom one godfather would run a derisive eye over and say, "Without me, eleyi will not be occupying this position today." [39]

However, if the previous elections in Nigeria are to be referenced, the possibility of a third force taking over Nigeria's leadership structure might remain an illusion. This perhaps contributes to the common sarcasm among Nigerians about the nation's flawed political process that the right candidates do not win elections in the country. In this article, Adelakun contends that Funke Akindele (a metaphor for "third force") could liberate Lagos state (a metaphor for Nigeria). She posits: "If Akindele can hire a team of experts in politics, economics, and culture to prepare her for electioneering, her candidature might be the boost Lagos politics needs. The state politics, now entirely ceded to the APC political machinery and machination, has entered a state of ennui."[40]

Adelakun also touched on the perennial problem of insecurity that worsened under the Buhari-led government. In an article titled "Bandits will eventually get to Buhari,"[41] Adelakun projects the damning situation of insecurity in the country. This essay was written on the heels of an attack by the Presidential Brigade Guards. For the terrorists to unleash terror on an elite force that protects the president shows that the problem of insecurity is out of hand. Before this incident, there was an attack on the presidential security guards on their way to the president's hometown Daura in Katsina state. There were also reports that the president himself was not safe from abduction by the bandits. The level of terrorism grew exponentially under Buhari's watch, even though his campaign promises included ending the insurgency. So, terrible was the level of insecurity under Buhari that the political class was also affected. As each day passed, the level of insurgency increased. It got so bad that the nation's armed forces often had to bribe insurgents to retrieve stolen weapons. Adelakun criticizes Buhari's leadership style regarding insecurity. His government was not iron-handed in its many approaches to quench the fire of insurgency.

A president is the most protected person in any country, but in a situation where the security architecture is so weakened as not to guarantee maximum security of the former, it interprets that the country is in the firm grip of militants. As Adelakun posits, "No president in Nigerian history has been as much of a disaster as Buhari. His government has been entirely underwhelming; the man is so lazy that there is no point

39. Adelakun, "Funke Akindele might be Good."
40. Adelakun, "Funke Akindele might be Good."
41. Abimbola Adelakun, "Bandits will Eventually get to Buhari," *The Punch*, August 4, 2022.

in his rudderless leadership that he decides to take charge of affairs. If there is something almost everyone will agree with now, it is that Buhari's leadership abilities were grossly exaggerated and that the man never had even the slightest interest in redirecting Nigeria away from failure towards prosperity."[42] Also, in an article titled "Banditry and Atiku's 90% voters", Adelakun laments the commonplace of banditry in the northern region, which now spreads to every part of the country.[43] As she contends, the problem of banditry shows that the nation is dysfunctional. Media reports on the insurgency carried out by the bandits reveal that the country as a whole is not safe from imminent attacks. During media interviews, the bandits have often said that the nation's leadership failure is to be blamed for their militancy, although this does not justify their actions. The country has lost the battle against terrorism which is evident from reports that the government often has to reach compromises with criminal warlords—rather than unleashing terror on them. Discourses in the public sphere often included the possibility that the "political leaders" who might be sponsoring terrorism in the country are closer to the president and the nation's armed forces.

There is a great need for the government to change this gory narrative of insecurity in Nigeria. The spate of militant attacks has proven that security is not the top agenda of the Nigerian government. The promise of adequate security tops the campaigns of every presidential candidate in Nigeria, yet on getting to the office, they never find a permanent solution to the crisis. Adelakun identifies the perennial problem of insecurity to bad leadership and challenges the political class to salvage Nigeria from recurring dastardly attacks. This includes the need to reform the nation's security apparatus and pool resources together with collective action in the war against terrorism. Adelakun further charges the presidential candidates to think of concrete approaches to improve security in the country. But first, they must be good leaders, as this would end the security crisis that has now woven the fabric of Nigerian society and the other challenges the country faces.

Adelakun, in her essays, also examines the problem of religious violence in the country. Discussions on religion usually take a sensitive approach in Nigerian politics to avoid sparking controversies that could incite religious violence. Even though many Nigerians would posit that humanity—the need for humans to co-exist in peace and harmony—is the greatest religion, reality has shown that it only takes an alleged blasphemy of either Islam or Christianity to spark off religious tensions in the country. In her article titled "Arresting Deborah's killers is the easy part," Adelakun criticizes the fact that religious issues continue to affect the nation's political system.[44] It is a well-known fact that political leaders also appeal to religious sentiments to get to the seat of power. She further laments that most of these self-acclaimed religious

42. Adelakun, "Bandits will Eventually get to Buhari."
43. Abimbola Adelakun, "Banditry and Atiku's 90% Voters," *The Punch*, July 28, 2022.
44. Abimbola Adelakun, "Arresting Deborah's Killers is the Easy Part," *The Punch*, May 19, 2022.

crusaders often are not punished for their criminal actions. Nigeria is so polarized along religious lines that it would be assumed that the Northern part of the country operates an independent legal system superior to the Nigerian Constitution. This assumption is valid, considering that most Northerners, mainly Muslims, are often quick to perpetuate gruesome murders in the name of fighting for God. Worse still, they do go unpunished. Adelakun examines the issue of blasphemy, especially as it applies to Islam. Most victims of religious violence, such as Deborah Samuel, are accused of blasphemy. It then becomes imperative to question whether God, whom these criminals fight for in the name of religion, is so powerless as to need them to perpetuate evil activities.

Adelakun criticizes the use of religious violence as "a weapon of social cohesion," highlighting the need for the collective efforts of the tiers of government to put an end to this menace, harping that "What Nigeria needs are people who believe in the country well enough to fight for its redemption. We need a leadership class that believes in protecting the principles of democratic freedom with the same passion those religious fundamentalists exercised when they killed Deborah. They must stand up to these fanatics and remind them that Nigeria's democracy guarantees us freedom. . . ."[45] She further foregrounds the dire need for religious harmony in an article titled "Yoruba Muslims vs. Yoruba Christians."[46] Over the years, the relationship among the Yoruba has been riddled with religious insecurities as both the Christians and the Muslims in the Southwestern part of the country pursue religious dominance at every opportunity. Adelakun, in this essay, identifies the reason for religious tensions among these people of the same tribe as the fear of religious domination. The situation has gone worse than it has crept into the job appointment process—each religious faithful only wants to appoint those from their religion at the expense of meritocracy. When Christians and Muslims attain political powers, they tend to build a structure with people from their religion. The fear of the domination of one religion over the other contributes to the outburst on the Muslim-Muslim ticket of the APC for the 2023 general elections. The Christians believe that the re-emergence of APC at the top leadership position would challenge their religious practices even when it is obvious the same religion's ticket was a political calculation. If it were to be another way around, Muslims would similarly feel marginalized. Religion has eaten deep into the nation's political system that religious differences are considered before certain appointments can be made and for candidates to contest at the polls.

The plethora of social vices in the country is due to societal decadence resulting from a failing education system. In secondary schools especially, the students are becoming wild, and the teachers have been unable to curb this menace. When there were reports that secondary students at Chrisland secondary school in Lagos state

45. Adelakun, "Arresting Deborah's Killers."

46. Abimbola Adelakun. "Yoruba Muslims vs Yoruba Christians," *The Punch*, November 11, 2021.

indulged in illicit sex, the shock it sent to the public was enormous. There were postulations that if teenagers could be exposed to mundane practices, it would show how morally bankrupt the society is because the experiences these teenagers got were commonplace. Adelakun dwells on this theme in her essay.

In an article titled "It should never take more than one disaster," Adelakun portrays the failing education system in Nigeria vis-a-vis the death of a 12-year-old student, Sylvester Oromoni, from bullying in school.[47] She laments that the educational system seems to fail in the quest to produce future leaders. The death of Sylvester Oromoni sparked widespread outrage and made concerned stakeholders question the legitimacy of the nation's educational institutions. This unfortunate scenario also contributed to the calls for educational reforms in secondary schools, especially so students would no longer become victims of unfortunate incidents. Bullying has become a menace in secondary schools in Nigeria, and Adelakun contends that parents contribute to this menace. When there are reports of bullying, parents erroneously believe their children need such experience to be stronger and tougher in their quest for success when such acts contribute to the trauma of psychological disorder among the affected students and should be frowned upon. Adelakun admonished the government to rethink reforms in secondary school education.

ADELAKUN'S THOUGHTS ON CORRUPTION

Any critic of the Nigerian government can never be far from the truth when such criticism is directed at the corrupt practices ingrained in the corridors of power and in virtually all public domains whose control and management fall within the caprices of the government. Attempts at highlighting the defects of the Nigerian state can never be complete if no mention is made of the high-level corrupt practices that go on in the public sector of the economy. It is herculean to choose just one government-run institution in Nigeria that can be absolved of corruption. Even the so-called anti-graft agencies, the Economic and Financial Crimes Commission (EFCC) and its counterpart, the Independent Corrupt Practices Commission (ICPC), have their share of irregularities.

The Buhari administration, controlled by the APC-led government, took over power against the backdrop of tackling the hydra-headed monster called corruption. As with many other campaign promises, this may have been quite easy to mouth; the major problem is ensuring that such promises were implemented and executed. In the article "The Real Trouble with Magu," Adelakun quoted the EFCC Acting Chairman, Ibrahim Magu, to affirm that corruption is the worst societal ill that pervades any nation.[48] However, Adelakun noted the unintelligence of the man, saddled with head-

47. Abimbola Adelakun. "It should never take more than one Disaster," *The Punch*, December 9, 2021.
48. Abimbola Adelakun, "The Real Trouble with Magu," *The Punch*, March 5, 2020.

ing the anti-graft agency, when he suggested, in the presence of the President, that the deadly coronavirus was caused by corruption. The import of this is that Magu comes to the average discerning mind as mediocre at best and does not have a professional idea of what the agency he heads was established for.

The global perception of Nigeria as a "fantastically corrupt country" cannot be overstated. And while Buhari's government positioned itself as the progenitor of a new corruption-free Nigeria, there was little to be felt of the administration's fight against corruption. As Adelakun opined in "Nigeria is Fantastically Corrupt, what's New?" if truly there is a portrait of a new Nigeria in the making, the Buhari administration did not in any way pass off such signals to the world. The several cases of corruption in various government agencies in Nigeria reveal the level of hypocrisy and sentimentalism of the leadership in the fight against corruption. The grand-scale deception of the Buhari administration and his purported fight against corruption leads to only one conclusion: the country is yet to see the kind of leaders that will truly uphold a patriotic fight against corruption. The widespread perception of President Muhammadu Buhari as an incorruptible individual holds water to only some levels, and it is a notion that was promoted by a conglomerate of highly corrupt politicians that banded together to put him in power. However, Adelakun retorted that promoting the idea of a president being better than the people he leads is wrong and absurd.[49]

To indicate the level at which corruption permeated the corridor of power in Nigeria, Adelakun noted the sad incident of Vice President Yemi Osinbajo being implicated alongside Magu, the EFCC chairman, in a 4-billion-naira slush fund racketeering. This was not the first time the second-in-command of the country's leadership would be implicated in shady deals that border on corruption. In saner environments, it would have been expected of him to resign and subsequently clear his name from the mess. That may represent asking for too much since democratic leaders in third-world nations like Nigeria are yet to reach such sophisticated levels of human engagement. As expected, Adelakun, in her article "Osinbajo: Beyond the Nostrum," retorted that rather than recuse himself of the corrupt charges, VP Osinbajo was quick to play the 'legal' card, a proven method of silencing media reportage of such issues. The vice president's legal counsel swung into action, coercing the Inspector General of Police to investigate the allegations and raise criminal charges against the media bloggers that disseminated such purported 'false' allegations.[50]

Adelakun raised a valid question in the article: in the event of the police investigation yielding positives and validating the accusation, what next? Political leaders in Nigeria, especially those in power, are known to be protected by the government. Either through humungous immunity clauses or the backdoor policy of sweeping

49. Abimbola Adelakun, "Nigeria is Fantastically Corrupt, What's Next?" *Opinion Nigeria*, May 12, 2016, https://www.opinionnigeria.com/nigeria-is-fantastically-corrupt-what-s-new-by-abimbola-adelakun/.

50. Abimbola Adelakun, "Osinbajo: Beyond the Nostrum," *The Punch*, July 16, 2020.

cases under the carpet, successive governments in Nigeria have always indicated reluctance to prosecute fellow allies in government. For a government that was elected on the premise of an ability to fight corruption, someone who was as highly regarded as VP Osinbajo was, being involved in such a mess was a terrible signal. To conclude the narrative, Adelakun noted that the government could not continue to employ state power to silence its traducers. Perhaps this vividly represents what the erstwhile National Chairman of the APC quoted saying, "join our party, and all your sins will be forgiven."[51] This statement establishes a definite conjecture; in attempting to lure members to its fold, the ruling APC-led government is ever-ready to waive just about any crimes or corrupt practices that such 'cross-carpeters' may have been engaged in in the past.

Although the semantics involved in the message may be confusing, some noteworthy events lend credence to this assertion. For instance, Orji Uzor Kalu, a former Abia state governor who had been jailed for his involvement in corruption while in office, was suddenly freed by the Nigerian Supreme Court just some months into his jail term.[52] This was done to confer some level of legitimacy on his release, to the amazement of the EFCC that collated pieces of evidence against him. The charges against him were committed while he was a member of the PDP, the previous ruling party. Despite being one of the most notable figures in the party, Kalu defected to join the APC in 2016, a year after the party successfully wrestled control of the government from the hands of the PDP. This singular act may have been his saving grace from the indictment. His defection to the APC had elicited criticism from PDP members and political opponents who said it was an attempt to cover up his corruption trial and a desperate move to revitalize his waning political influence.[53] Perhaps his defection embodies the conjectures of Adams Oshiomole, who have suddenly taken the position of God to forgive the sins of any politician from the opposition that turns a new leave by showing interest in allying with the ruling APC.

To lay bare the large-scale corrupt practices that play out in the corridors of power, Adelakun conformed to the thoughts of like minds that corruption is a game in Nigeria.[54] At a time, we heard that a snake swallowed billions of naira kept in one of the government agencies in Nigeria. To wriggle out of corruption allegations, political elites in Nigeria have perfected various methods to elicit sympathy from certain quarters of the populace. Adelakun further mentions individuals like Mohammed Bello,

---

51. Sahara Reporters, "Join APC and all your Sins will be Forgiven," *Sahara Reporters*, January 18, 2019. http://saharareporters.com/2019/01/18/join-apc-and-all-your-sins-will-be-forgiven-oshiomhole-declares.

52. Iwok Iniobong and Godfrey Ofurun, "Why Orji Kalu's Freedon Riles EFCC," *Business Day*, May 10, 2020, https://businessday.ng/politics/article/why-orji-kalus-freedom-riles-efcc/.

53. Iniobong and Ofurun, "Why Orji Kalu's Freedon Riles EFCC."

54. Abimbola Adelakun, "How Anti-Corruption became a Game," *Opinion Nigeria*, January 28, 2016, https://www.opinionnigeria.com/how-anti-corruption-became-a-game-by-abimbola-adelakun/.

who appeared in court in a wheelchair in a bid to court sympathy. Before this, numerous political figures were revealing varying degrees of illnesses to arm-twist the government to refrain from prosecuting them.

The EFCC, which is supposed to work independently, has been turned into a weapon for harassing the opposition both within and outside the reins of the ruling party. This did not start with the Buhari administration, but it was more pronounced therein. Corruption among the political elites, like the government, is a continuum in Nigeria for the foreseeable future. To borrow a leaf from Adelakun's "Black Lives Matter," corruption in Nigeria was built on corruption and will, for a long time, continue to reproduce corruption in different colors and shades.[55] If the leadership of anti-graft agencies like the EFCC can be accused of being also involved in corrupt practices, then it begs the question; where and how will the fight against corruption be successfully fought and won? Yes, Ibrahim Magu's appointment as the Acting Chairman was terminated based on allegations of corruption, but no one is hopeful that his replacement will do wonders.

ADELAKUN ON THE SCOURGE OF RELIGIOUS TERRORISM

Every region except for the South-Western region of Nigeria seems to have specific problems. While the Niger Delta in the past had been plagued with sabotage in the form of oil installation bombings, the south-east, their closest neighbors, play host to violent agitations to support the secessionist mindset that has always been on the minds of their leaders from the time of the first and only civil war that ravaged the country decades ago.

The northern region, which comprises the north-east, north-west and north-central, had in the past also played host to religious extremism that often led to targeted attacks by the Muslims who represent the majority against the minority Christians who are mostly southerners that migrated north for various reasons. This is not to say that the north does not have its portion of Christians, albeit in very small measure. Under the military government of Buhari in the early 80s, the Maitatsine religious riots that enveloped northern Nigeria were successfully quelled by military power. There was relative peace until 2009 when a new and more deadly form of religious extremism reared its ugly head with the Boko Haram Uprising. Suffice it to say that the Niger Delta sabotage of the country's crude oil installations became child's play compared to what the Islamic fundamentalist that founded the Boko Haram movement presented to the Nigerian government. While both insurrections witnessed the use of bombs for destruction, the latter's disposition to make humans rather than

55. Abimbola Adelakun, "Black Lives Matter! Nigerian Lives Matter!: Language and Why Performance Matters," *Genealogy* 3, no. 2 (2019): 19.

installations targets of its offensive ensured that it remains the greatest uprising against the Nigerian state since its return to democracy in 1999.

The Boko Haram uprising represents an attempt by extremists to impose certain ideologies on a secular society like Nigeria. While it is possible to trace the roots of such blatant grandstanding to the Maitatsine riots of the 1980s, the allowance of state-imposed sharia law in many states in the north may have contributed to its growth. An article by Abimbola Adelakun in 2012 detailed the dilemma of the man who defeated the Maitatsine extremists in 1985—General Muhammadu Buhari. Comparing the precarious situation of the former military man to the challenges faced by Jesus concerning the question of paying taxes, Adelakun brought to the fore the irony of a society governed by a multi-dimensional perception of situations. While being chosen by faceless terrorists to act as a mediator between the government and itself would have spelled doom for the man who would later become the nation's president three years later. Adelakun rightly opined that accepting such a gesture may have connoted two distinct thoughts; either that he was a sponsor of the group or an apologist to the movement. Either way, it represents a lose-lose situation. However, rejecting such a gesture also came with its demerits, as some of his detractors were quick to affirm that he was not willing to be a worthy tool to ensure that the ruling PDP government became successful in the fight against terrorism.

Adelakun also opined that the Niger Delta struggle might have been built on a reasonable foundation of marginalization. The Boko Haram insurgency represents a conflict that is neither legitimate nor reasonable. While negotiations with the terrorist organization may have seemed ideal, the fact that the fundamentalists operate on a multi-lateral splinter cell leadership structure makes it difficult to ascertain the authenticity of their demands. To conclude the article, Adelakun asserted that there is no basis for negotiating with the Boko Haram insurgents; they had embarked on wholesale killings across villages in the country's north-eastern region; hence they should be made to answer for their crimes.

Fast-forward to eight years later, and a bill was purportedly sponsored by a serving senator, Ibrahim Gaidam representing Yobe East senatorial district (one of the major states ravaged by Boko haram insurgency) to re-integrate captured Boko Haram terrorists back into the society.[56] Such bills sound funny, as it was expected for the government to provide funds to educate and re-integrate killers and murderers who have continued destabilizing a region that should have been agitating for socio-economic improvement. Analysts quickly equated the gesture to a similar reintegration program developed for Niger Delta Militants. However, the sheer idiosyncrasies of Gaidam were exposed when he affirmed in a press conference that his objective was to ensure that Boko Haram members are allowed to enter mainstream politics while also

56. Abimbola Adelakun, "Gaidam and the Spirit of Northern Entitlement," *The Punch*, February 27, 2020.

being allowed full rights as normal citizens in the country.[57] Perhaps the senator failed to understand that the ideal correctional centers for morally decadent individuals, such as religious extremists, are the prisons where they are already holed up. For an elected representative from a region ravaged by religious terrorism to persuade the government to grant such criminals rehabilitation reeks of bigotry.

As further highlighted by Adelakun, Gaidam's position on what should be done for terrorists represents the attitude of entitlement that northern politicians continue to display. He is not alone in this assertion, as President Muhammadu Buhari also voiced something similar in 2018 when he suggested rehabilitation and reintegration for repentant Boko Haram members. What they forget is this; unlike the Niger Delta militants who were motivated by socio-economic marginalization, the Boko Haram movement is motivated by a global campaign to impose religious ideologies on conquered regions worldwide. It does not matter whether Muslims or Christians dominate such regions.

The tendency for northerners to persistently perceive themselves as upholding the divine right to the immeasurable appropriation of resources for problems they brought upon themselves continues to grow. If not, it becomes difficult to understand why they suggest rehabilitation instead of imprisonment for Islamic fundamentalists. It would have amounted to sheer indulgence to use state funds to rehabilitate individuals whose leadership continues to cause mayhem and deaths to the people without any hopes of repentance. One of the campaign promises of the Buhari administration was to ensure that the Boko Haram insurgency was brought to an end. Unfortunately, the administration had to make do with platitudes like "technically defeated." As noted by Adelakun in her article "The Truth of Boko Haram," the publicity that accompanies incidents of Boko Haram members capturing Christian leaders and executing them based on the reluctance of the government to accede to their demands continues to embolden the terrorist organization.[58]

It happened at a time when the administration embarked on vain attempts to let the world know that Boko Haram had indeed been defeated. Also, 17 soldiers were ambushed and killed around the time. In contrast, many others were captured by the Boko Haram insurgents. All the military hierarchy of the country could do was deny such reports. This is not new also; many Nigerians have developed the attitude of never trusting the reports from the government on such issues due to the falsehoods that are churned out to water down the magnitude of the situation. In the Yobe and Borno states of Nigeria, the security of lives cannot be guaranteed anymore as they continue to experience Boko Haram activities; the convoy of the governor of one of the two states was attacked while five aid workers were recently kidnapped and killed by the terrorist organization. All these are coming at a time when the first spiritual

57. Adelakun, "Gaidam and the Spirit of Northern Entitlement."
58. Abimbola Adelakun, "What is the Truth of Boko Haram?" *The Punch,* January 23, 2020.

leader of the sect was killed and four years after the Buhari administration affirmed that the terrorist organization had been technically defeated.

The country's leadership projected that they were doing their best to ensure the security of the lives and property of the people. However, the masses were powerless in responding to their game as the Buhari administration succeeded in allocating billions to a newly chartered North-East Development Commission (NEDC) to cater to the ruins resulting from the Boko Haram insurgency in the region. Not seeming enough, the Ministry of Humanitarian Affairs, Disaster Management and Social Development were also established to manage the fallouts of the Boko Haram crisis.[59] To the keen observer, the creation of two distinct government parastatal to tackle the same problem means one of two things: either the administration's leadership is not informed, or there is a covert attempt to waste the country's funds on a grand scale. It is likely to be a combination of the two. First, the suggestion by Buhari that the World Bank should concentrate development efforts on the north-eastern region of Nigeria at the expense of other regions is lame. Secondly, re-integrating captured terrorists who have been indoctrinated into the ideologies of Islamic fundamentalism may look good on paper but can pose serious dangers to the citizenry. Adelakun retorted that the ruling APC government seems to have accepted defeat through President Buhari's body language, which reveals that of an individual who has given up hope and subsequently realized that his promise to defeat the insurgency might not be achievable in the short term.

CONCLUSION

In a nutshell, Adelakun's inexorable writings represent a body of work that proffers a meeting point between facts and fiction. She epitomizes intellectual versatility at its best. Through her work, historical and cultural truths are revealed in literary creativity. Yet, she provides fearless journalistic penmanship that confronts political anomalies without mincing words, even in a nation that suffers a drought of truth. She addresses issues of gender inequities from the vantage point of womanism rather than from the critical reactionary style of feminism, bringing organic flavor to an otherwise contentious theme. Adelakun and her works have boldly scripted our world on the sands of time for these and many other reasons. We honor her brilliance with this writing with the aspirations that her work may continue to baffle our intellectual curiosities and tickle our instinctive fancies.

Adelakun represents a mirror of our society, reaching down to all the possible necks of the woods that constitute scholarly appreciation. One of the fascinating ways she has expressed this diversity is her inquiry into a matter like dating in tertiary institutions and other sublime social issues that might ordinarily not intrigue many

59. Adelakun, "What is the Truth of Boko Haram?"

researchers.[60] So, she does not only mirror the obvious societal issues that attract general commentaries and reactions but others that touch the core of society. She has successfully directed herself to link the effect of religion on society, drawing from the attributes of extremism, the possible misuse of Pentecostalism and excessive adoration of spiritualism. While these positions are appreciated, she scholarly approached them from the angle of intellectual rigor, common sense and logicality.

60. Ayobami Ojebode, Dimeji Togunde and Abimbola Adelakun, "Beyond Money and Gifts: Social Capital as Motivation for Cross-generational Dating among Tertiary School Female Students in South West Nigeria," *Journal of Social Sciences* 5, no. 4 (2010): 169–182.

15

BAMIDELE ADEMOLA-OLATEJU

Narrating the Nation

When describing an individual, many things come to the fore—her traits, attitudes, dispositions, outputs and many more. Summing up these is not always easy, as it is difficult to fully capture another person's characteristics. Such is the case of the subject of this work.

Many people will describe Bamidele Ademola-Olateju in different ways. But one thing no one can take away from her is the activism that seems to dot all aspects of her person—her talks and soliloquies especially. Perhaps more than anything, she is preoccupied with issues centering around the masses, the oppressed, and the helpless citizens. This makes it rational to follow her and observe the mindset with which she torchlights various events that continue to shape Nigeria. Ademola-Olateju does not allow her ethnoreligious affiliations to sentimentalize her renditions. She is typically objective on issues, going out of her way to restore the dignity of the oppressed, with whom she hardly has any prior relationships. This is why some of her followers call her the general overseer; they can see she is always ready to lend her voice to the cause of the masses when circumstances demand it.

Bamidele Ademola-Olateju can easily be described as one of the most popular columnists for *Premium Times*. Her constant exploration and analysis of the Nigerian situation position her as an Amazon in Nigeria's social media space. When investigating her writings, it is said that she often spends hours driving into the nooks and

crannies of Lagos, even venturing into places dreaded by the elites. She would casually let anyone realize the need to understand the conscience of the people she enthusiastically fights for. These people come from a social class different from the elites, and she needs to be with them, feel their pains, and understand their positions before speaking out for them. It is necessary to recognize how the lower class perceives the entity called Nigeria if one wants to truly take up advocacy against it.

Essentially, Ademola-Olateju does not confine herself to the Southwest; she proudly promotes the ideal Nigeria, which she believes has been handicapped by leadership without clear visions and followership based on ethnic sentimentalism, which often leads to hostility against perceived opposition voices. How did Nigeria get to this unfortunate position? This is one of the questions that often drive Ademola-Olateju to traverse the length and breadth of Nigeria, looking for answers and the factors responsible for this decadence.

Another thing worth noting in her engagements is her disposition toward the youth, mostly under thirty years, which she thoughtfully describes as the orphaned generation. Theirs represents a generation largely uneducated on the sanctity of values, morals, and ethics and the danger of misplaced priorities. Even though every generation should have its fair share of role models, this generation seems to be blessed with questionable role models, as most youths celebrate criminals and highly corrupt individuals. Public perception of criminality has shifted greatly among young people, unlike the older generations that enjoyed the grace of exemplary role models. Perhaps Ademola-Olateju focuses on this generation primarily because of their lackadaisical and lackluster attitude to issues that border on the national consciousness. Though faced with autocratic military regimes and decrees meant to silence all oppositions and dissent, the older generations never stopped criticizing the governments, fighting tooth and nail against anti-people policies. Ademola-Olateju is disturbed by the young generation's inexplicable apathy to things that matter to them and their nation.

This does not mean that she is determined to denigrate the younger generation. Some might describe her thoughts about the younger generation as overly harsh. Yet, people like her need to stand up to the task if we expect a positive change from the present situation. Documented thoughts of people like Tai Solarin and his book titled *Towards Nigeria's Moral Governance* are left on the shelves of libraries, while the youth are glued to time-wasting and value-reducing activities on the social media space.[1] However, as Ademola-Olateju often admits, a reasonable percentage of this young generation is making the country proud, even though the leadership of Nigeria has offered them nothing to facilitate their personal development and nurture their potential.

---

1. Tai Solarin, *Towards Nigeria's Moral Governance* (Ikenne: Mayflower School, 1959).

Ademola-Olateju's fixation on the younger generation is hinged on her belief that they are strategic to the future of Nigeria. With the country going downhill, they represent the only hope for mapping a new direction. And social media offers them the resources needed to be more enlightened about happenings worldwide. Role models abound in the Western world if Nigeria does not offer them.

In a system where the males are supposed to be more politically inclined, Ademola-Olateju's grasp of political matters sets a message that forms some of the major themes of this book. She represents the image of an adept political analyst, from whose book many should take a leaf. She takes time to understand events unfolding from an informed vantage point and gives attention to political details, conscientiously drawing people's attention to national issues. Seeing such representation, it is only reasonable for one to be moved by her political taste and analyses.

More so, she presents an opportunity to experiment with a feminist theme discussed in the Nigerian context in previous chapters. This is because she is not only gender-conscious of the mainstream discussions but also an active member of society who provides inspiration and reference points for further feminist discussions.

Many scholars and columnists who air their views on the nation's state often do that from the armchairs of observations without political commitments to the nation. It is easy to criticize from the sidelines without knowing the intricacies of particular policies like a politician would do. To find Ademola-Olateju in the political oceans, charting her way into the Ondo State policy formation process as the Commissioner for Information, is intriguing, making her more fascinating to study. It is, however, unbelievable that despite her political leanings, she has maintained the sanity of a critic and analyst as she still dissects political matters from an observer's perspective but with the touch of a participant. The choice of Ademola-Olateju provides an option to see things from a politician's standpoint and tap into active political minds.

Ademola-Olateju is predisposed to utilizing social media to put forth her opinions and sensitize the public. She is a social media influencer with more than 45,000 Facebook followers while improving her audience on other social media platforms. While the excesses attributed to social media are understandable, Ademola-Olateju exhibits sanity and employs social media's functionalities to educate her audience. This makes her a perfect fit for a discussion with an underlying social media impression.

THE FRAY OF ELECTIONEERING IN NIGERIA

As obtainable in many other nations, elections in Nigeria are often centered around two major political parties, who share the largest stakes in executive and legislative seats, leaving the other numerous minority parties scrambling for the crumbs. Personality and profiles are often insufficient to sway voters to a particular candidate. The potential to win elective positions in Nigeria depends largely on political party affiliations, while personality only plays a minor part. By and large, any individual who

aspires to an elective post would have to be on one of the two major political party platforms to be perceived as a serious contender. Sometimes, aspirants need not bother themselves with personal profiles; they only have to be involved with the ruling political party. The publicity and popularity of the political party determine the aspirants' chances of winning.

The emerging trend in electioneering in Nigeria has left so much to be desired by the electorates. Nigeria's political blocs, which did not seem to have any campaign promises in the past, have shifted the gear. The new device for winning elections is to canvass the electorates with vain promises that they know are impossible given the country's resources. The Nigerian electorates always seem to know the winner of any election, even before it starts. As earlier stated, what guarantees electoral victory is membership in one of the two dominant parties. Any aspirant that intends to change the status quo surely has a serious hurdle to scale.

This does not mean the electorates cannot make their votes count. Ademola-Olateju noted during the Osun elections that voting alone is not enough; making it count is vital, as the Osun electorates showed.[2] The main lesson from the Osun elections is voting and subsequently waiting to ensure that the votes are protected from saboteurs. Ademola-Olateju further affirmed that established checks and balances could only appreciate true democracy. This, she believes, is the missing link in Nigerian politics. The struggle to uphold true democracy can only thrive by ensuring that all government institutions strictly adhere to democratic tenets.

The incumbent governments in Nigeria often use voter suppression tactics to dissuade opposition sympathizers from performing their civic responsibilities. Some incumbent presidents have in the past intimidated the electorates with state security agencies. Ademola-Olateju reminds her teeming readers of Jonathan Goodluck's attempt to use the election to perpetuate oppression and dictatorial tendencies in Nigeria's democracy. He almost mocked democracy by persistently using the power of incumbency to manipulate state machinery to do his bidding. Ultimately, he was forced to relinquish powers after a strong amalgam was formed to oust him. Of course, this amalgam was greatly successful due to the input of political juggernauts like Tinubu, Saraki and others.

Judging Goodluck Jonathan's tendencies for undemocratic practices would have been justified if the succeeding government had not modified his antecedents to their advantage. For instance, prebendalism characterized the 2019 Kogi Elections; the APC-led federal government unabashedly utilized state resources to get the incum-

---

2. Bamidele Ademola-Olateju, "Osun Elections Shows you can make your Vote Count," *Premium Times,* August 12, 2014, https://opinion.premiumtimesng.com/2014/08/12/osun-elections-shows-you-can-make-your-vote-count-by-bamidele-ademola-olateju/.

Figure 15.1. "Bamidele Ademola-Olateju Narrating the Nation" by Michael Efionayi. Depiction of Bamidele Ademola-Olateju teaching about the nation.

bent governor back to the state house.[3] As Ademola-Olateju notes in the article, "Prebendalism: Are Vote Buying and Voter Intimidation Here to Stay?," the APC-led federal government was aware of the odds against the incumbent, Yahaya Bello, winning, owing to the bad records in his first term.[4] This forced the party into providing funds and human resources in the form of federal security agents to manipulate the electoral process. The financial resources provided for the governor would have improved his record if such was provided when the Kogi State Government could not pay the civil servants. All tenets of democracy were flagrantly degraded with reports of ballot snatching in opposition strongholds, and once again, all hope of making the people's votes count was smothered.

Gradually, this practice is getting institutionalized, and it remains to be seen if future governments will not follow such paths. The absence of a level playing field in Nigerian elections has made it difficult to witness what can be objectively termed free and fair elections. The noticeable trend indicates a persistent decline in ideal politicking. Ademola-Olateju notes, 'The desire to win elections as if elections are ends in

3. Bamidele Ademola-Olateju, "Prebendalism: Are Vote Buying and Voter Intimidation here to Stay?" *Premium Times*, November 19, 2019, https://opinion.premiumtimesng.com/2019/11/19/prebendalism-are-vote-buying-and-voter-intimidation-here-to-stay-by-bamidele-ademola-olateju/.

4. Ademola-Olateju, "Prebendalism."

themselves is derivative of the 'end justifies the means' culture taking root in the country.' [5] It is so clear that Nigeria's commitment to democracy is paper-thin. In the end, the corrupt politicians continue to win elections in Nigeria while democratic ideals are lost. The poor electorates are becoming more dependent on cash stipends before they exercise their civic responsibilities. The effect is the scarcity of credible and dependable candidates that could drive the nation progressively. Rather than rising and demanding adequate reforms to ensure improved democratic ideals, the poor electorates are driven by sentiment and cash disbursements that come only in elections. Ademola-Olateju notes that "a great Nigeria cannot emerge from this prebendal state unless we effect changes in our political institutions and culture."[6]

In her article titled "Sowore Does Not Have To Win," written before the 2019 general elections in Nigeria, Ademola-Olateju points out that Sowore as a presidential candidate, knows full well that he stands just an atom's chance of winning the election owing to the kind of party politics that holds sway in Nigeria.[7] It is generally accepted that politics and elections are a game of numbers. Sowore, no matter his popularity, cannot get the sympathy of voters due to various factors. The minority that voted for him represents a tiny percentage of the enlightened and educated youths who understand true change. In a country where politics is played along ethnic and religious lines, it becomes an arduous task for revolutionaries like Sowore to gain the mandate of the masses.

Someone of his stature would not want to join the array of corrupt politicians that populate the major political parties in Nigeria. However, Ademola-Olateju believed that those things should not stop Sowore from contesting, if not for anything but to disrupt the political space. She adds that challenging the status quo is a scarce concept in Nigeria. People like Sowore must continue to rise to the challenge for the nation to progress. Nigerians cannot afford to leave everything as it is. She believed that anyone who wants to achieve something meaningful must be willing to disrupt the state of things. Leaders who changed the world did so due to their willingness to challenge the powers and political systems of their time. Of course, this would always come with its risks. Indeed, Sowore's exploits in Nigeria's political landscape will surely open Nigeria's politics to youths hungry for a real change, not the phony change brandished by the fading generations of politicians. Ademola-Olateju noted that 2019 would herald the discovery of the hitherto unknown.[8]

Despite having brilliant and revolutionary ideas that can turn the country's fortune around for good, the fact that Sowore is an activist is sure to serve to his disadvantage. This is because the Nigerian polity is yet to fully align with revolutionary conscious-

5. Ademola-Olateju, "Prebendalism."

6. Ademola-Olateju, "Prebendalism."

7. Bamidele Ademola-Olateju, "Sowore does not have to Win," *Sahara Reporters,* April 8, 2018, https://saharareporters.com/2018/04/08/sowore-does-not-have-win-bamidele-ademola-olateju.

8. Ademola-Olateju, "Sowore does not have to Win."

ness to understand the position of such activisms. Since the electioneering process in the present Nigerian political landscape is hinged on expending large sums of money on promotions, campaigns and inducements, brilliant but 'no-so-rich' aspirants like Sowore stand no chance. Nigeria is not ready for candidates like Sowore due to the stranglehold of the various political cabals on the masses. Nobody has done something meaningful in the world without disrupting the status quo ante, challenging the powers that be, and competing against the prevailing processes. This will surely come with accompanying risks and associated costs.

In a move to perfectly describe what Sowore is doing to the Nigerian youth, Ademola-Olateju states that 'motivating' is an understatement, coining the term "motivacting." This word, I believe, is used in the context of appealing to the people's consciousness to act as true agents of change. Such a bold step is commendable in the least. Nigeria is deeply in need of a disruptive mindset to change its political processes.[9] If anything looks more like true change, then Sowore's exploits in Nigeria's political space are a change from the pre-existing.[10]

Shortly after the election of Buhari in 2015, Ademola-Olateju wrote an article detailing her observations about the government. While not feeling surprised by the turn of events, she points out that she had developed some optimism that Buhari would at least rein in the contending power structures and perennial power hijackers who continue to penetrate the governmental structures for personal enrichment. But she admits to making an error in developing such optimism as she later found out that he was no different from other oligarchs that populate the Nigerian political landscape; though she was somewhat objective by emphatically stating that Buhari was still a level above many others, owing to his honesty. However, the same myopic perspective on governance Buhari exhibited continues to plague successive governments.

In her article '2023: Nigeria's Make or Break Presidential Election,'[11] Ademola-Olateju analyses the leading presidential candidates for the 2023 Presidential Election, their possibilities and the definite expected change in political norms. She predicts that the 2023 election will be very competitive; therefore, the winner might not be able to pull more than 37% of the total vote, against the usual experience since 1999. Nigerian presidential election candidacy since 1999 has been dominated by two candidatures belonging to two political parties. This does not mean that no other candidates or parties have been fielding their interests in every election, but their candidates did not garner the needed political impetus and support like the two leading parties. She notes that four leading candidates—Atiku Abubakar, Bola Tinubu, Peter Obi and Rabiu Kwankwaso—broke the norms of political aspirations, with each

9. Ademola-Olateju, "Sowore does not have to Win."

10. Ademola-Olateju, "Sowore does not have to Win."

11. Bamidele Ademola-Olateju, "2023: Nigeria's Make or Break Presidential Election," *Premium Times*, August 9, 2022, https://www.premiumtimesng.com/opinion/547851-2023-nigerias-make-or-break-presidential-election-by-bamidele-ademola-olateju.html.

having a stronghold and potential to win the political race.[12] She predicted that a possible outcome of this reality is that the winner might not be able to control the National Assembly because it might be impossible to retain the majority, as has been the case since Nigeria reverted to democracy in 1999.

Ademola-Olateju's prediction concerning the possible outcome of the 2023 elections was that Peter Obi might be the primary candidate Tinubu would have to contend with as he could gain 25% of the votes needed from the Southeast and Southwest regions and Benue State. She then submits that Tinubu could amass 55% to 60% of votes from the Southwest. She also analyses the political possibilities in the Northern states and provides insights into what each candidate may expect from the Northern political behaviors. She concludes that though she does not expect Peter Obi to be victorious at the poll, she cannot dismiss the fact that a massive pull of reasonable millions of votes would send a statement about the evolution of the Nigerian democracy.[13]

GODFATHERISM IN NIGERIAN POLITICS

Godfatherism has varying connotations depending on the relationship existing within such context. In the Catholic Church tradition, a godfather is someone chosen by a young man in the process of being baptized or getting married. It does not have to be his relative; it can be any congregation member. The position is a counseling capacity to guide the young man into responsible living. This is quite different from the concept of godfatherism in politics. Political godfathers are rich men who contribute immensely to political campaigns to promote their preferred candidates. The candidates often become indebted to the godfathers in exchange for such favors.

Godfatherism is an area of Nigerian politics that seems to be out of the control of the electorates. It has been entrenched in our politics, even before independence. The late Chief Obafemi Awolowo was a political godfather in Southwestern Nigeria, as was the late Sir Ahmadu Bello in the North. The godsons of these two prominent politicians would later metamorphose into Afenifere and the Kaduna mafia, respectively. However, godfatherism should not be perceived as a wholly African concept. Early thinkers such as Plato and Tacitus talked extensively about the concentration of state power in the hands of very few people. Contemporary thinkers like Karl Marx also devoted some thoughts to the elite class' use and misuse of political power. Thus, from time immemorial, the residence of political power in a few hegemons has always been an issue of discussion.

Talking about godfatherism in Nigeria, Dr. Jibrin Ibrahim, in a BBC interview, described political godfathers as men who retain the power to determine who gets nominated and who subsequently wins an election in a particular state. They build an

12. Ademola-Olateju, "2023: Nigeria's Make or Break Presidential Election."
13. Ademola-Olateju, "2023: Nigeria's Make or Break Presidential Election."

array of loyalists around themselves, using them to manipulate the rest of the electorates. This arrangement is perfected with monetary incentives.

Till today, political godfathers still dictate the events in Nigerian politics. The founding fathers of the popular political parties in Nigeria are godfathers in their own right. They take the kingmakers' position, albeit covertly, deciding who gets particular roles and portfolios. Ademola-Olateju noted this when she affirmed that Tinubu should take credit for Buhari's ascension to power in 2015. While some might disagree, Ademola-Olateju raises some serious posers that validate her affirmation. One, Buhari would not have survived the primaries.[14] He had no money to prosecute such a mission in a political realm where delegates are won through financial inducements. Atiku, who was the main contender, would have swept him off his feet with his abundance of wealth but for Tinubu, who craftily swayed the game to favor Buhari. Despite the gambit by the incumbent, Goodluck Jonathan, to stiff the opposition by postponing the elections to starve the All Progressives Congress (APC), its ranks could not be weakened.

Everyone, even Buhari's close associates, was surprised. Ademola-Olateju calls the famed Tinubu the bell cow of Nigerian politics. He is the *Baba Isale* (patron of the underworld) of Southwestern politics. His consent to a candidate's aspiration is enough to guarantee the coveted political seat for such a candidate. His methodology for human management is close to a mafia-styled structure, and he remains at the top. He always knows how to manipulate the structures of any political party he belongs to support his cause. This he has engaged perfectly owing to the population advantage of Lagos, the state he once ruled as a governor and has been controlling by proxy afterward.

If anyone has portrayed a political godfather accurately in Nigeria, it is Tinubu. Ademola-Olateju asserts that he remains the only politician in Nigeria with a pipeline of excellence through which both competent and unknown politicians gain prominence to lead.[15] He may be ruthless, displaying traits of a mafia don, but he has succeeded in developing a large pool of politicians who are now leaders by their rights. Kayode Fayemi, despite his political sagacity, once had a problem laying claim to his mandate; Tinubu bailed him out. Tinubu did the same for other governors like Abiola Ajimobi and Ibikunle Amosun. Numerous others not included here have benefited immensely from Tinubu's position as a political godfather. After Awolowo, only Tinubu solidified his position as a father figure to aspiring politicians in the Southwest. His forward-thinking capacity can also be seen in how he got delegates to hand

14. Bamidele Ademola-Olateju, "Tinubu—The Political Huckster and Ambitions," *Adeyemi Juwon*, January 16, 2018, http://adeyemijuwon.com.ng/2018/01/16/tinubu-political-huckster-ambitions-bamidele-ademola-olateju/.

15. Ademola-Olateju, "Tinubu—The Political Huckster."

him the party ticket for the 2023 presidential elections by calling in previous favors and reassuring others.

So strong is Tinubu's status as a political godfather that he single-handedly handpicked President Muhammadu Buhari's running mate. However, this was not without its drama and internal bickering.[16] While other powerbrokers like Saraki and some of Tinubu's political mentees wanted Rotimi Amaechi to take the position, Tinubu believed he had earned the right to pick the slot. This he successfully did with the picking of Professor Yemi Osinbajo, another of his long-term protégés.

Some of his political mentees have sometimes stood against him to wrestle control of state machinery from him. During the 2015 election strategizing, Tinubu allegedly exercised the right to handpick the governor of Lagos, but one of his stooges, Babatunde Raji Fashola, thought otherwise. In the end, the *Jagaban,* as he is fondly called, came out tops. Ademola-Olateju also pointed out that Tinubu fought one of the greatest political battles of his life—minus the 2023 elections—in the bid to make Ambode the Governor of Lagos after Fashola's exit in 2015.[17] Ambode almost lost the election but for Tinubu's sagacity. Feeling betrayed by his one-time stooges, he fought back, trying unsuccessfully to stop him from being appointed as a minister in Buhari's government.

Sensing his continued posture as the be-all and end-all of Southwestern Nigeria's political clime, the coalition against him grew. Strangely, those camping against him were those he single-handedly brought to the political limelight. Two distinct proverbs are apt for this narrative. The first warns never to bite the fingers that feed you, while the other advises that when a child is mature enough to have his hoe, they should not be deprived of it.[18]

However, Tinubu knows better than to allow any of his political sons to establish parallel political bases. He would always let them understand that he wields the overall power that determines where the political wave is headed; this is probably because he needed the show of strength for his presidential bid. Neither Fashola nor Ambode was allowed to build their political bases. The latter was further humiliated by being denied the party ticket for re-election. It would be safe to suggest that Ademola-Olateju strongly reveres the godfather status of the mighty *Jagaban*. Like or hate him, Tinubu is Southwest politic's *capo di tutti capi*. He has maintained his stronghold on the polity due to the high poverty level in the nation. Ademola-Olateju notes that aspirants only need to share meager sums like a thousand naira to sway voters toward themselves. The psyche of the masses has been greatly twisted by poverty, which is what godfathers like Tinubu bank on to perpetuate their political dominance in the

16. Ademola-Olateju, "Tinubu—The Political Huckster."
17. Ademola-Olateju, "Tinubu—The Political Huckster."
18. Ademola-Olateju, "Tinubu—The Political Huckster."

state. He is a master strategist and political huckster in the mold of the Chicago dons of old.[19]

He has, over the years, solidified his godfather status by taking control of the most populous state and commercial nerve of Nigeria, Lagos. In one of her articles, Ademola-Olateju highlights his alleged imposition of candidates on the party faithful. While the imposition of candidates did not start with Asiwaju, he does this without respect for anybody. His demeanor and body language are of the overlord who cares, not whose ox is gored. Suffice it to say that someone like Sowore would have stood a better chance of winning elections in Nigeria if he had surrendered to the whims of political godfathers like Tinubu. This will, however, be counterproductive to everything and anything that revolutionaries like him intend to bring into governance.

In all these, Ademola-Olateju affirms that Tinubu need not be concerned with building himself anymore. He has reached the status of a political godfather, which undoubtedly makes him an overlord in his domain. His decisions persistently create enemies as he seeks to remodel himself. Several of his stooges banded together to fight him from issue to issue. Even Vice-President Osinbajo sought to wrestle the 2023 presidential tickets from him as his tenure drew close. Ademola-Olateju is afraid the continuous imbroglio will likely not end well for the Southwestern people, as it may be counterproductive to the region's cause. To her, these mentees have not acquired power potent enough to seek independence from Asiwaju.[20] They tried to romance the Northern oligarchs to usurp their godfather's powers, but Tinubu had courted them well; they stood with him in his bid to be President. Also, they should learn from Asiwaju's situation; if Buhari and the Northern cabal could try to discard him pre-2023, they too can be discarded in the future. A Yoruba adage says you cannot investigate your father's death without wielding a sword. They may be technocrats by their own standards, but politics is a different ball game altogether. Tinubu remains a political godfather and has continued to show those who care to know that his stake in Nigerian politics cannot be disputed.

ADEMOLA-OLATEJU: GOOD GOVERNANCE AND NATION-BUILDING

Governance in Nigeria is a topic that evokes divergent opinions and emotions among people. While sentiments might be exhibited by loyalists of various governments, past and present, objective evaluation of issues cannot be suppressed as long as individuals like Ademola-Olateju populate the world. Still, no one can refute that the Nigerian government and, by extension, the public sector are characterized by a

19. Ademola-Olateju, "Tinubu—The Political Huckster."

20. Bamidele Ademola-Olateju, "Kleptocracy: What are Treasury Looters Really Thinking," *Premium Times*, August 15, 2017, http://opinion.premiumtimesng.com/2017/08/15/kleptocracy-what-are-treasury-looters-really-thinking-by-bamidele-ademola-olateju/.

high degree of inefficiency and kleptocracy. Unlike the private sector, auditing is persistently sidelined in the public sector; the situation worsens because the country continues to generate so much from crude oil. Corruption is quite celebrated by Nigerians holding trust positions.[21] Siphoning public funds for personal uses has become endemic to Nigeria. All these occur because successive governments fail to implement adequate measures to promote effective internal and external audits. Despite the continual increase in the global price of crude oil, a significant proportion of Nigeria's oil revenue goes to private pockets. In the article, Ademola-Olateju adds that it is more shameful that those in public offices in Nigeria are wont to steal funds in measures they would never need in a lifetime.

Transparency and accountability should be one of the government's core responsibilities to the citizenry. This is needed to assure the populace that the people's interest is paramount to the government, and individuals found in compromising acts should be made to face the wrath of the law. Sadly, this only happens when the government intends to witch-hunt particular individuals. While it is remotely possible to finance the nation's budget from internally generated funds, Nigerian leaders make matters worse by stealing. Public officers launder these stolen funds in Western economies, enriching such countries to the detriment of their home countries.

With rises in the price of crude oil globally, Nigeria, a stakeholder in OPEC, still finds it hard to profit from the situation. Those saddled with ensuring that an average Nigerian enjoys the proceeds through people-oriented measures would rather impose more hardship on the poor. As Ademola-Olateju notes in her article titled 'We Cannot Profit from the Rise in Oil Prices,' Nigeria has continued to live beyond its means.[22] Despite raking in billions from oil sales, the country's leadership still borrows money to finance programs yet pads budgets annually. The author's claim that no one wants to lend money to Nigeria again is hyperbolic; Nigeria would continue to find willing lenders to push the nation deeper and deeper into debt.

The sympathizers of the present government will always finger the past government for the inadequacies of the present government, while the sympathizers of the past government pass the buck to the preceding one. The blame game continues until the blame is finally dumped on colonialism. In her book, *For the Love of Country*, Ademola-Olateju embarks on an exciting and educative political analysis. Her criticisms reveal the concerns of a patriotic mind. She evaluates various government departments in Nigeria while focusing more on the pursuit of accountability expected of Nigerian leaders, not leaving out the responsibilities of the youths and other social

---

21. Bamidele Ademola-Olateju, "The Siege of Kleptocrats and Kakistocrats," *Premium Times*, February 11, 2020, https://opinion.premiumtimesng.com/2020/02/11/the-siege-of-kleptocrats-and-kakistocrats-by-bamidele-ademola-olateju/.

22. Bamidele Ademola-Olateju, "[Bamidele Upfront] Falling Oil Prices is Nigeria's Destiny," *Premium Times*, May 28, 2013, https://www.premiumtimesng.com/opinion/136506-bamidele-upfront-falling-oil-prices-is-nigerias-destiny-by-bamidele-ademola-olateju.html.

strata of the nation. Stressing that various governments in Nigeria have been subpar in quality leadership delivery, she demands, among others, equity and justice.[23] In her unique analytical way, she predicts the events that would likely shape Nigeria's economic development in the future.

Nigeria has always been blessed with an array of female activists, from the colonial era when the likes of Mrs. Olufunmilayo Ransome-Kuti founded the Nigerian Women's Union to agitate for women's equality in the social and political landscape. However, Nigeria has not experienced the sight of a female personality that combines politics with activism. Mrs. Ademola-Olateju is a rare breed in this mold. Her social media engagements always focus on issues that she believes are inhibiting the country's progress. She often highlights various self-inflicted inadequacies and errors that continually position Nigeria as a country whose potentials are not fully realized due to poor leadership. Ademola-Olateju's collection of essays in *For the Love of Country* affirms her position as a colossus out to change the narrative of regular lamentations about issues of governance in Nigeria. The book reveals a feminine character blessed with creative originality and high intellect. She spends time examining the persistent problems that have handicapped development in Nigeria. One of them is the epileptic power supply that continues to limit the potential of virtually all the country's economic sectors. She does not only examine the problem but also offers her views on the possible solutions and the way forward for Nigeria.

It becomes so easy to be moved to action by just reading *For the Love of Country*. You would quickly understand why she is described as one of her generation's most influential female activists. She has constantly refused to be silenced by fear or distort the truth about the state of things. One of her most visible thoughts is her strong conviction that Nigeria's return to true federalism will lead to prosperity and self-reliance on a level that will put the country on par with other emerging economies.

Sometimes, her conjectures elicit controversy among her followers and audience. For instance, in part one of *For the Love of Country*, she discusses the level of perversion that pastors and other religious leaders engage in to milk their followers.[24] She affirms that the love of money has swayed the clergy away from Christ. Some are even enmeshed in Nigeria's dirty politics characterized by bigotry and sentimentalism. Rather than frame issues around morals, Nigerian religious leaders seem to be more concerned with the prosperity gospel, all in the name of Christ. The situation becomes more ironic when we consider the church universities whose average congregation finds it hard to enroll their children due to the exorbitant tuition fees. The early missionaries that built schools never monetized them like the present-day churches. As Ademola-Olateju objectively points out, all these reveal the loss of com-

---

23. Bamidele Ademola-Olateju, *For the Love of Country* (California: CreateSpace Independent Publishing Platform, 2016).

24. Ademola-Olateju, *For the Love of Country*.

passion for the faithful and the subsequent embracement of greed by church owners in Nigeria.

This unfortunate situation keeps enriching the rich while the poor become poorer. Ademola-Olateju opines in *For the Love of Country* that religious platforms have failed to provide the necessary moral codes to move the country forward.[25] She also believes that education is not overly encouraged because the more educated a person is, the lesser such individuals believe in miracles. To solve this, she warns that religious platforms must focus on how followers can acquire skills through subsidized education.[26]

While evaluating the underclass status of the Nigerian youth, Ademola-Olateju notes that they could redress their precarious situation by using the power of votes to alter the cause of events and take their destinies into their hands. She believes this is imperative if the youth want to experience qualitative leadership. She is quick to rebuke the Nigerian youth as she considers their involvement in fraudulent deals and money-making activities. But the blame will remotely fall on the government that fails to invest effectively in education. While the Nigerian youth can be perceived as vibrant, energetic and dynamic, successive governments continue to cannibalize them through deliberate acts of deprivation. This leaves the nation with many disoriented, miseducated and shallow-thinking youths who take pride in indulging in exaggerated material acquisitions.

There is a shortage of role models in Nigeria. Ademola-Olateju notes that the average Nigerian youth now perceives education as a waste of time. This can be blamed on the antiquated education system in Nigeria. Rote learning remains the mode of teaching at a time when other nations are developing their education sectors with state-of-the-art technologies to facilitate learning. The notable consequences of a poor educational system are underdevelopment and armed insurrection.

Ademola-Olateju highlights the qualities the youth should seek when electing their leaders—integrity, empathy, vision and courage. She affirms that Nigeria lacks political leaders with such traits as every elected or potential public officeholder seems to be more mindful of personal economic development than national development. The present crop of Nigeria's political leaders does not share the agonies of the masses. Like their predecessors, they are largely concerned with what they can gain from leading the country, not what the masses can benefit from their leadership. They remain very insensitive to the plight of the masses. Rather than embark on projects geared toward improving the masses, they amass wealth by depriving the citizens of their basic amenities and infrastructure rights.

---

25. Ademola-Olateju, *For the Love of Country*.
26. Bamidele Ademola-Olateju, "The Abuse of Faith by Pastors," *Premium Times*, July 23, 2019, https://opinion.premiumtimesng.com/2019/07/23/the-abuse-of-faith-by-pastors-by-bamidele-ademola-olateju/.

Greed is a celebrated vice among the ruling elites since it provides benefits without measures for them all. To justify their iniquity, they extend peanuts and crumbs to their grassroots supporters, who continue to sing their praises while becoming more impoverished.

The theme of nation-building is central to Ademola-Olateju's essays. She identifies the many challenges that have stunted the nation's progress. While exploring this theme, Ademola-Olateju calls on stakeholders to intensify their patriotic calls and efforts for national development. She does not only point accusing fingers at political leaders who contribute to the country's ruins but also suggests ways the country can overcome this nightmare. As she foregrounds in her essays, nation-building is a collective effort, not a task for the government alone. The government would require the people's support to wriggle the country out of its predicament. Typically, the Nigerian government and its people are always at war. This ultimately affects national development.

Apart from the theme of nation-building, Ademola-Olateju also examines the indicators that have continued to plunge the country into crises. Before the calls for nation-building can be productive, there is a need to identify the nation's prevailing problems. Although Nigeria's problems are hydra-headed, Ademola-Olateju limits the causative factors to bad governance. Bad governance is a common topic among most Nigerian political columnists. Only their approaches to this topic are different; their points of view are usually the same. In her essays, Ademola-Olateju examines the country's perennial problem of bad governance and its implication for national development. There is no gainsaying that the key to unlocking the untapped national potential is good governance. Successive Nigerian governments have struggled to provide good governance, and the citizens are tired of the untold hardships bad governance has brought the country. Indeed, a change in leadership structure in Nigeria to one that identifies with the people's needs would result in a definite change in the country's situation.

Sadly, the Nigerian system of government makes good governance almost impossible. The presidential system of government gives room for misuse of power as it gives no real power to the state governments, which often depend on the federal government for development. Many political analysts have clamored for true federalism adopted in the early years of independence, granting the states autonomy and allowing them to develop independently. In the article "Federalism Means Eating What You Kill," Ademola-Olateju examines the country's dire need to revert to federalism.[27] Federalism underscores the notion that the federal/central government should not be solely concerned with the nation's development, as in the case of the presidential system of government. Ademola-Olateju contends that Nigeria's inde-

27. Bamidele Ademola-Olateju, "Federalism Means Eating what you Kill," *Premium Times,* September 7, 2021, https://www.premiumtimesng.com/opinion/483578-federalism-means-eating-what-you-kill.html.

pendence started with federalism and achieved remarkable results. She posits that federalism succeeded in independence because the founding fathers—Chief Obafemi Awolowo, Dr. Nnamdi Azikiwe, and Sir Ahmadu Bello—recognized the need for each region (North, East, and South) to be concerned with their development according to their political, economic and cultural peculiarities. In that system, each region constantly struggled to be the best developed. For example, the free education policy initiated in the Western region by the late Chief Obafemi Awolowo challenged other regions to implement similar programs.

Nigeria was doing well with federalism until military intervention abolished it, paving the way for a unitary system of government in which the central government concerned itself with the development of all the states in the country. In her argument for the re-establishment of a federal system of government in Nigeria, Ademola-Olateju alludes to the Governor of Rivers State, Nyesom Wike's legal win over the federal government on the legal tussle to allow the state governments to receive value-added tax (VAT) 'for consumption carried out within its jurisdiction.' She contends that

> Time has run out! We can't continue on the same disastrous trajectory. We need to face the inconvenient truths and advance the greater good for everyone, regardless of ethnicity, religion and other dividers. The shortsighted unitary system has bitten us all; it enabled laziness, dependency, and allowed the power elite and their cronies to gather our nuts and shell it for themselves and their families. Across the geopolitical zones, overarching poverty has become a constant and it is now feeding agitations and annoyances across Nigeria under different guises.[28]

In this article, she foregrounds the re-adoption of the 1963 Republican constitution, which would bring back federalism, which she sees as the key to Nigeria's development.

Ademola-Olateju also criticizes Nigeria's pandering to an autocratic state, as evident in the Buhari-led government's subtle approaches to regulating the citizens' freedom of expression. To Nigerians, Buhari's administration failed, and no amount of rebranding or propaganda can change this narrative. Instead of advancing the country, his tenure reversed its fortunes; thus, the citizens, at every opportunity, were rebellious to his government. Most of their actions against the government occur on social media platforms such as Twitter and Facebook. The citizens' cyber-activism sent shock waves to the corridors of power and amassed international recognition that the Nigerian government was forced to regulate social media activities under the guise that they constitute a national threat. In her article, "Eavesdropping, Censorship and the Voyeuristic State," Ademola-Olateju is critical of the Nigerian government's

28. Ademola-Olateju, "Federalism Means Eating what you Kill."

stifling of the citizens' fundamental human rights, particularly the freedom of expression.[29] She berates the National Assembly's moves to introduce bills to monitor communications systems in all parts of the country, similar to "the kind the Saudis used to monitor Jamal Khashoggi's messages." It asks why the Nigerian government would ever consider such action. Despite the various challenges and increasing threats to the country's continued existence calling for the government's attention and actions, the administration focused on regulating communication and telecommunication in the country. What a shame! It appears that the Buhari-led administration saw the citizens as the top enemy of the state.

When Buhari took over power, the country moved from one crisis to another, undermining its sovereignty without effective measures to counter them. Ademola-Olateju contends that the Nigerian government's proposal to intercept the communications system is to invade the citizens' privacy and mute their voices which remain vocal in the event of bad governance. She laments, "It is a shame that a government that cannot protect us from terrorism, banditry, armed robbery, is seeking to prevent us from talking about and showcasing their ineptitude to the world."[30] She knocks the Nigerian government for not concerning itself with developing adequate welfare programs for the masses but rather focusing on attempting to remove the people from governance through draconian laws. In a thematically-similar article titled 'Digital Authoritarianism and the Echoes of Decree 4', Ademola-Olateju criticizes the infamous Twitter ban by the Buhari-led government.[31] Nigerians identify with Twitter, the micro-blogging platform, among other social media platforms, for cyber-activism. They often lament bad leadership on Twitter.

Nigerians' cyber-activism was prominent on Twitter during the #EndSARS Movement, where they protested against extra-judicial killings. The movement came on the heels of the spate of killings of many youths, notably by the infamous Special Anti-Robbery Squad (SARS), under the guise that they were all *yahoo boys*, a local lingo for internet fraudsters. The Nigerian government saw no need to curb these senseless killings of innocent youths until the citizens decided to stand up and speak up. The movement caught the attention of international communities who pressured the Nigerian government to do the needful. But the movement was quenched with military force, recording casualties that could be regarded as the greatest massacre since the nation's re-adoption of democracy in 1999.

---

29. Bamidele Ademola-Olateju, "Eavesdropping, Censorship and the Voyeuristic State," *Premium Times*, July 13, 2021, https://www.premiumtimesng.com/opinion/473323-eavesdropping-censorship-and-the-voyeuristic-state-by-bamidele-ademola-olateju.html.

30. Ademola-Olateju, "Eavesdropping, Censorship and the Voyeuristic State."

31. Bamidele Ademola-Olateju, "Digital Authoritarianism and the Echoes of Decree 4," *Premium Times*, June 8, 2021, https://www.premiumtimesng.com/opinion/466420-digital-authoritarianism-and-the-echoes-of-decree-4-by-bamidele-ademola-olateju.html.

In the article, Ademola-Olateju criticizes the autocratic style of President Muhammadu Buhari in a democratic dispensation. She further reminisces on Decree 4, which Buhari enacted during his regime as a military head of state. According to her, Decree 4 was "the most repressive press law ever enacted in Nigeria." The signs were visible from the start: President Buhari did not believe in freedom of expression, which is why many of his regulations looked to revert the country to an autocratic state. Ademola-Olateju blames the National Assembly for being mere onlookers as the nation reverted to the dark days of military dictatorship. Under their watch, the Nigerian government conveniently formulates and executes plans that undermine democratic principles. The government posited that the Twitter ban was needed to limit security threats. However, the same government did not see the rising level of insurgency in the country as a threat to national security. President Buhari would be remembered for one thing: he leaves issues of utmost importance for unimportant issues, thus jeopardizing national development. Ademola-Olateju calls for international sanctions on countries like Nigeria that implement digital authoritarianism:

> It is not too late for the United States and other liberal democracies to tighten export controls on technologies that advance digital authoritarianism. The world is heading down a slippery slope if the free world is not united at sanctioning digital authoritarianism and companies that supply them with equipment. The time is ripe for the United Nations to develop a digital governance charter.[32]

She also examines the challenge of ethnonationalism and how it undermines national development. The problem of ethnicity has riddled the nation's political system. Most Nigerians are mostly patriotic to their ethnic groups and not to Nigeria as a nation. Marginalization cases, especially under President Buhari's leadership, exacerbated the problem of ethnic identities and loyalties. However, this challenge could be traced to the nation's independence. Within the first decade of independence, the fears of ethnic dominance and marginalization provoked a civil war, and since then, it has become difficult for governance to cut across all sections or regions in the country. At independence, political leaders identified with ethnic interests as they found it hard to pursue issues of genuine national interests. Likewise, President Muhammadu Buhari's system of governance was more sympathetic to the Hausa-Fulani group than to the generality of Nigerians. Contrary to his campaign mantra, the President did nothing to show Nigerians that he truly belongs to nobody.

The Indigenous People of Biafra (IPOB) are constantly facing the armed forces in the Southeast over secessionist struggles. Arguably, the Igbo claim to be the most marginalized group in Nigeria, as there is a sort of resentment or fear for an Igbo to

32. Ademola-Olateju, "Digital Authoritarianism."

assume leadership. The political class has hitherto not seen the need to curb the rising issue of ethnonationalism. In an article titled "Ethnonationalism as a Rational Response to What Nigeria is," Ademola-Olateju examines the rise of ethnonationalism and concludes that the menace has eaten deep into the Nigerian system so much that the citizens do not identify themselves as Nigerians at first.[33] She further states that ethnonationalism is prevalent in modern Nigerian society due to the fear of marginalization prominent, for example, in the Buhari-led government.

Also, there are agitations from the Southwestern part of the country to break away from Nigeria. The Yoruba people were not known for secessionist struggles until under the leadership of President Buhari. Before he was incarcerated, Sunday Igboho was the prominent figure in the agitation for the "Oduduwa Republic"—a breakaway nation for the Yoruba people. He identified the gruesome killings of the Yoruba people by the Fulani herdsmen that went rampant without the federal government's interventions as the ground for his ethnic-nationalist struggles. Ademola-Olateju decries the government's continued failure to take appropriate measures to curb ethnonationalism. When the generality of the citizens is sold on the idea that their ethnic interests come first, there can be no national development. She argues that delaying efforts to make Nigeria a united entity is dangerous as ethnic differences could bring another disaster akin to the Civil War. She stresses that the country needs a leadership that would douse ethnic interests and catalyzes all the citizens toward exhibiting Nigerian nationalism—a trait that almost died under Buhari's regime. She puts it thus:

> Nigeria needs leadership. Both the leaders and the led must believe that politics is a variable sum game, there must be a reckoning and acceptance that respect for rights of one people does not supercede the rights of others.[34]

Ademola-Olateju did not leave out the menace of bad leadership in Nigeria. In an article titled "Even the Finest Wine can Turn to Vinegar," she calls for collective efforts toward resolving the country's leadership crisis.[35] She declares that relying on divine intervention to solve the challenge of bad leadership in the country is a waste of effort, as Nigerians must be conscious of their choices during electioneering. Since the return to democracy in 1999, Nigeria has not particularly had young leaders, forcing one to think that the country operates gerontocracy in place of democracy. Perhaps

---

33. Bamidele Ademola-Olateju, "Ethnonationalism as a Rational Response to what Nigeria is," *Premium Times*, June 1, 2021, https://www.premiumtimesng.com/opinion/465026-ethnonationalism-as-a-rational-response-to-what-nigeria-is-by-bamidele-ademola-olateju.html.

34. Ademola-Olateju, "Ethnonationalism as a Rational Response."

35. Bamidele Ademola-Olateju, "Even the Finest Wine can Turn to Vinegar," *Premium Times*, May 8, 2021, https://www.premiumtimesng.com/opinion/462215-even-the-finest-wines-can-turn-to-vinegar-by-bamidele-ademola-olateju.html.

the root of bad leadership in the country is the influx of gerontocrats in leadership positions. The youth have been marginalized in governance.

Referencing the regimes of late President Musa Yar'Adua and President Muhammadu Buhari, Ademola-Olateju emphasizes the need to consider "physical health and mental agility" while making leadership choices. It seems paradoxical that Atiku Abubakar or Bola Tinubu—both with deteriorating health challenges—got the tickets from Nigeria's biggest political parties and popular support. She further charges Nigerians to "reject any presidential candidate that is too old, frail, and out of touch with a changing world," as we cannot allow the selfish ambitions of the gerontocrats to undermine our national development. She notes that Nigeria's crises are "intergenerational" and would need astute leadership to resolve them—not leaders that would be battling severe health challenges in power. According to her, "...The crises we face need the input and ideas of the generations they will most affect. Achieving these will require encouraging selfless youth leadership."[36] Apparently, her advice was ignored.

Moreover, Ademola-Olateju questions the intellectual sagacity of Nigerian leaders in "The Evil Geniuses in Nigeria's Political Arena."[37] In this essay, she criticizes the anti-people policies and programs that characterized the Buhari-led administration. She describes the country's leadership structure as 'evil geniuses', many of whom are not interested in deploying their insights and skills to improve the country. We must understand that the issue of bad leadership in Nigeria is not due to a shortage of qualified leaders; the problem is that these leaders do not see the need to be visionary. They would rather advance their interests and vendettas than be concerned about the progress of their nation.

Most of the policies and programs these 'evil geniuses' implement only bring new problems. Ademola-Olateju rightly reasons Nigerian leaders do not identify with long-term plans: "...our rulers disdain work. They are power drunk and are always in for quick fixes." In another article titled "The Economic Consequences of Having Luddites in Charge," she examines the problem of bad leadership and its overall consequence on the nation's economic growth and development.[38] Nigeria suffers from economic crises because its leaders are not genuinely disposed to economic development. Economic development to them means "personal development"—converting the state's wealth for personal use. The columnist charges the masses to fight the leaders into identifying with the tenets of democracy, which would stir the necessary innovations and inventions for the country. She states that the government, for instance,

36. Ademola-Olateju, "Even the Finest Wine."

37. Bamidele Ademola-Olateju, "The Evil Geniuses in Nigeria's Political Arena," *Premium Times*, May 18, 2021, https://www.premiumtimesng.com/opinion/462215-even-the-finest-wines-can-turn-to-vinegar-by-bamidele-ademola-olateju.html.

38. Bamidele Ademola-Olateju, "The Economic Consequences of having Luddites in Charge," *Premium Times*, June 22, 2021, https://www.premiumtimesng.com/opinion/469272-the-economic-consequences-of-having-luddites-in-charge-by-bamidele-ademola-olateju.html.

needs to make deliberate investments in the country to forestall the mass exodus of youth seeking greener pastures.

Ademola-Olateju, in an article titled "Yoruba Youths: Endangered and in Need of Repositioning," laments the disorientation among the Yoruba youth as evident in their criminal activities.[39] Cultism is a rampant social vice among the Yoruba youth, leading to a breakdown of law and order. Many Yoruba youths are also involved in internet fraud, known in the local parlance as *yahoo-yahoo*. She warns that this menace will go out of hand if appropriate measures are not taken. Ademola-Olateju attributes the prevalence of youth's disorientation to the destruction of the rural agrarian economy and the explosion in the urban population. There is an urgent need for public enlightenment to reorientate these youth. According to her, civic reorientation and the interventions of religious organizations and the mass media would effectively preach traditional values to the youth. She further suggests that the government should establish apprenticeship and orientation programs to curb societal decadence and produce better citizens.

Furthermore, in an article titled "Nigeria: Taking a Stand for Freedom and Liberty," Ademola-Olateju charges the populace to make conscious efforts for the development of Nigeria.[40] She declares that Nigerians possess the power to restructure their dear motherland, charging everyone to be conscious of the socio-political crises confronting the nation to create solutions needed to place Nigeria on the pedestal of success. Ademola-Olateju shares the pains of countless Nigerians experiencing hardships, harping that the people must be relentless in their stance to eradicate the plague of bad governance. She encourages Nigerians thus: "We must be ready to reconstruct any sense of shared purpose that we may have enjoyed to this point. To purge the evil from this land and to rid all antecedents that fed it, our best is what we have to do by every legal, constitutional, and moral means. . . ." National development will remain an illusion if the people remain mute in the face of intimidation and oppression. She urges them to rise to the challenge so the country can, like a phoenix, rise from its ruins. She declares: "The sin of silence and inaction by the righteous, allows the wicked to rule. Take a stand! For freedom and liberty." Ademola-Olateju's many interventions in the state of affairs in Nigeria reveal the country's many predicaments and how it can get right on track. By maintaining that the people should be at the forefront of national development, she emphasizes the need for unity between the state and the people. The government should not be left alone in governance; the people should also be active in the democratic process. With this, there can be hope for the country.

---

39. Bamidele Ademola-Olateju, "Yoruba Youths: Endangered and in Need of Repositioning," *Premium Times*, August 7, 2022, https://www.premiumtimesng.com/opinion/547378-yoruba-youths-endangered-and-in-need-of-repositioning-by-bamidele-ademola-olateju.html.

40. Bamidele Ademola-Olateju, "Nigeria: Taking a Stand for Freedom and Liberty," *Premium Times*, September 14, 2021, https://www.premiumtimesng.com/opinion/484761-nigeria-taking-a-stand-for-freedom-and-liberty-by-bamidele-ademola-olateju.html.

EDUCATION AND ITS INHERENT DEFICIENCIES IN NIGERIA

Investment in education is key for any nation that aspires to progressive development. Failure in this area still affects most African countries—even countries like Nigeria, which enjoy global patronage of their crude oil, budget inadequately for education. In "Education in Nigeria: The Missteps, the Gaps," Ademola-Olateju recalls that in the mid-1970s, when the oil boom began, a significant proportion of Nigeria's budget was spent on education, leading to a rise in enrollments and appreciation for Western formal education.[41] However, toward the late 1970s, things started to take a downturn. Through the then Colonel Ahmadu Ali (Education Minister), General Olusegun Obasanjo slashed university funding senselessly in a decision akin to beheading as a cure for headaches.[42] This culminated in the Ali Must Go crisis, and from thence, Nigeria started to experience brain-drain, as people who wanted quality education felt the handicapped funding of the education sector would never produce quality service for them.

This trend of poor funding was perpetuated by successive governments, resulting in a sharp decline in quality education. The increased funding these governments seemed to put in place was not commensurate with population growth and its attendant increase in prospective students. The budget planners refused to understand that commensurate allocation was needed for the sustainable development of the education sector. Ademola-Olateju aptly states in the article that the short-sightedness of the successive governments and their inability to plan effectively for onward maintenance created huge gaps in the education sector. No identifiable upgrades were planned for the established educational institutions. While personnel in other sectors of the economy enjoyed a significant increase in remuneration, teachers were not afforded such. Under the military rule that Nigeria had spent a significant amount of its existence as a nation, defense ate up a greater proportion of annual budgets. The emergence of civilian rule has done little to help the situation. Even though there were attempts to increase the education budgets, embezzlement of such funds was already a given.

Ademola-Olateju has also described Nigeria as an infrastructural wasteland.[43] With most of the country's infrastructure lying in decay, what should one expect from the education sector? All the infrastructure that would rationally be expected to enhance quality education is never considered pivotal to the nation's development. Ademola-Olateju could not have said it any better when she affirms that the neglect of education by the Nigerian government is systemic, with the rot in one education

41. Bamidele Ademola-Olateju, "Education in Nigeria: The Missteps, the Gaps," *Sahara Reporters*, April 8, 2013, https://saharareporters.com/2013/04/08/education-nigeria-missteps-gaps-part-one-bamidele-ademola-olateju.

42. Ademola-Olateju, "Education in Nigeria."

43. Ademola-Olateju, "Education in Nigeria."

segment feeding on another. Classrooms are overpopulated, laboratories are not adequately equipped, and students are forced to share apparatuses in laughable ways. More laughable is that, in present-day Nigeria, there are still schools where pupils sit down under trees to take classes. Justin W. van Fleet, in his research for the Brookings Institution, described our education woes aptly: "If you want a glimpse into Africa's education crisis there is no better vantage point than the town of Bodinga, located in the impoverished Savannah region of Sokoto state in north-western Nigeria."[44] With no study books, the pupils are taken through rote learning; as a result, most children can hardly read and write at the appropriate time. It must also be noted that Sokoto state holds the record for the world's biggest gender gaps in education.

The poor maintenance culture of the political officeholders is laid bare in the education sector. Dilapidated buildings and the non-availability of basic equipment in the schools point to the total neglect of the infrastructure that was hitherto installed with tax-payers' funds. Ademola-Olateju told a sad story relating to the poor maintenance culture in Nigeria. On a journey back to her secondary school, she saw a school that had gone from grace to grass. With the science laboratory looking more like a shrine and pipe-borne water no longer running in the faucets, the school, as she described it, is a ghost of its former self. Physical activities such as sports have been degraded, with the school inter-house sports only limited to track events. Ademola-Olateju explains that this is a far cry from what was available during her time—hockey, badminton, etc. It summarizes the gross decadence in infrastructure in the erstwhile well-equipped schools. She notes that though the decline of educational infrastructure started during her time, no one had envisaged it would degenerate into such a hopeless state without any measures to redeem the situation. The gap between the quality of outputs of secondary schools in cities like Lagos and their counterparts in villages like Omu-Aran is so wide that one wonders if the two are administered using the same curriculum. As Ademola-Olateju rightly asks, should society expect equal performance outcomes from students who are not provided with education essentials? How are they expected to fare when they find themselves among their better-equipped contemporaries?

Ademola-Olateju persistently refers to Nigeria as a nation held hostage by a few greedy men and individuals whose only objective is to loot the nation's commonwealth. Their desperation to enrich themselves has decimated the various sectors of the economy, especially the education system. Rather than improving the public schools that populate the country, these elites are contented with establishing private schools for their fellow rich or, in most cases, sending their wards overseas for the quality education they have failed to provide.

This situation has made access to quality education a luxury for the masses. The tradition of providing scholarships for gifted students no more caters to the poor

44. Ademola-Olateju, "Education in Nigeria."

because many of the organizations providing the scholarships favor private schools that children of the affluent mostly populate.

Despite all these setbacks, Nigeria still provides students who excel remarkably in international examinations and competitions, some of whom are disadvantaged children who struggle to pass through dilapidated classrooms and poor infrastructure.

THE POLITICS OF RELIGIOSITY IN NIGERIA

There is an overarching belief that religion is a social phenomenon that impacts the other aspects of socialization within any society. Religion has taken hold of people's thought processes so much that every action is believed to have supernatural inputs. The effect of this mindset is a nation whose citizens persistently put their hope not in the knowledge and brilliance of its leaders but in supernatural and divine intervention. An over-ascription of physical events to the supernatural devalues the volition and intention of human beings. While most ethnic groups in Nigeria had their unique religions in the past, most have been relegated to the background in favor of foreign religions brought either by incursions or colonialism. Embracing these religions is not the issue; the problem is that Nigerians have substituted logical thought for religious submission. One of the most celebrated elected representatives in Nigeria and a serving minister, Mr. Babatunde Raji Fashola, corroborated this assertion when he stated in an interfaith conference that the Nigerian system is best described as one where people tend to pray hard rather than work hard.[45] He stated that this mindset is detrimental to the country if we ever want to experience development. In the daily lives of an average Nigerian, too much is left in the hands of God. Anything done is attributed to the Almighty. A child passes an examination, and the parents give glory to God. Someone successfully built a house, and God is given the glory.

In Ademola-Olateju's words, Nigeria is a nation populated with incredulously ignorant individuals whose primitive acquiescence to gods and the supernatural has not given way to superior modern thought processes and scientific facts despite their consumption of modern products.[46] This is sad. It is so easy to hear people invoke the name of God at intervals to project a sense of self-righteousness and self-submission to God. Even the man who acquires money illegally would ascribe his success to God. Moral aberrations are condoned, with a large percentage of the populace ensconced in religious buildings for the sole objective of urging the Almighty creator to take up human responsibilities. This is worrisome because it comes from a country that prides itself as the giant of Africa, with a relatively high number of educated people.

---

45. Sunday Eno-Abasi, Chris Irekamba and Abdulganiyu Alabi, "Nigeria: Religiosity, Faith and the Missing Link," *The Guardian,* December 15, 2019.

46. Bamidele Ademola-Olateju, "[Bamidele Upfront]: Nigeria and we its 170 Million Stupid People," *Premium Times,* October 22, 2013, https://www.premiumtimesng.com/opinion/147023-bamidele-upfront-nigeria-170million-stupid-people-bamidele-ademola--olateju.html.

The government and the multitude of political appointees, having understood this mindset, exploit it to give the citizenry a false sense of hope. Complain about Nigeria's inadequate health care facilities, and you will hear the next respondent say, "Disease will not be our portion, in Jesus' name." How else should a nation that expects God to do for them what their leaders ought to do be described other than being foolish? Substituting inane stupidity for sophisticated religiosity is the norm in Nigeria, and it becomes more offensive when this is pointed out. Calling on God for problems created by the country's leadership is tantamount to burdening Him with self-inflicted injuries.

Religion has a significant influence on the political choices of Nigerian electorates. Whether a particular aspirant or candidate possesses any meaningful manifesto does not matter. Nigerians are largely disposed to consider the religious leaning of political office candidates to determine their choices. This bigoted stance is often preached or supported by the large population of spiritual and religious leaders that dot the country's religious landscape. Ademola-Olateju could not be far from the truth when, in her article "The Nigerian Clergy, Politics and Violation of Moral Philosophy," she notes that rather than framing issues around philosophical ideals, the clergy in Nigeria are preoccupied with inciting their followers with political statements.[47] They get so involved in politics that it begs whether they have no stake in politics. This only stands to prove the fact that political interference has corrupted many religious leaders in Nigeria.

The church leadership in Nigeria is no more concerned with providing the spiritual nourishment needed to mold good Christians. The present crop of Christian religious leaders has so much to learn from past religious leaders, such as Desmond Tutu, who confronted the apartheid government of South Africa. Ademola-Olateju rightly points out that pastors are expected to lead the congregation in speaking out against issues that adversely affect the people.[48] During electioneering and political campaigns, there is a need for serious circumspection by religious leaders. Their opinions are sacrosanct; hence, they need to guide the flock in the direction that will usher in true change and development.

Still, on this subject, Ademola-Olateju also brings to attention the unholy race for material possession among church leaders. Religion seems to have substituted dogmatism for rationality in a country with many poor people. Real-life decisions are often made under spiritual influence. The people have ascribed unwarranted relevance to religion that they hardly make real-life decisions logically. Some clergy even dissuade their followers from using scientifically certified medical drugs for various

47. Bamidele Ademola-Olateju, "The Nigerian Clergy, Politics and Violation of Moral Philosophy," *Premium Times,* January 27, 2015, https://opinion.premiumtimesng.com/2015/01/27/nigerian-clergy-politics-violation-moral-philosophy-bamidele-ademola--olateju/.

48. Ademola-Olateju, "The Nigerian Clergy."

ailments. Instead, they are made to believe that the power of God cures all sicknesses and diseases.

The trappings of designer suits, bulletproof luxury cars, private jets and the general gratification of material possessions have pushed our pastors into compromising religious zeal to curry favor from moneyed men, robbing their congregants and seeking government patronage.[49] But the narrative is changing, as there is a growing tendency for Nigerians to rub mud in the faces of these alleged men of God. Some Christians are already coming to terms with the biblical oratory that discourages the magnification of the acts of men of God.

When we need to elect intelligent and selfless leaders to political offices, we suddenly become sentimental by voting along religious lines. Afterward, we put our hopes on God to do what the elected leader ought to do. Would it not be better to elect God as the president if the citizens truly believe that only God can solve the myriads of problems holding the country down? Do I need to pay for the services of a medical doctor who tells me to put my hope in the Lord to be healed of physical ailments?

The mantra of work and prayer has been somewhat changed to prayer and hope. Only in countries like Nigeria would you find people starting a meeting with prayers, telling lies throughout the meeting, and ending it with prayers. Nigeria is a crowd in a bumbling concert, living in the hope of landing on the island of tranquility, designed, worked and delivered from heaven without human sweat.[50]

The concept of faith has been abused in Nigeria. Self-styled pastors indulge in degrading acts that make one question if the Holy Spirit truly leads them. Their obscene and ostentatious lifestyles only serve to warn that the body of Christ is in serious and urgent need of accountability and responsibility.[51] The followers, already silenced by biblical verses that elevate these men of God beyond reproach, can only watch the theatrics. In Nigeria, challenging the church to be accountable is perceived as an affront against the Almighty, thereby promoting the vain belief that religious leaders are infallible in discharging their duties and responsibilities. This allows for actions bordering on criminality to go unpunished as much as men of God perpetrate such. It would not be out of place to declare that religion has failed the country greatly. In the article "Abuse of Faith by Pastors," Bamidele opines that dismissing the immoralities perpetrated by pastors and other church leaders in the Nigerian religious landscape is morally reprehensible.[52]

Politically, the government is quick to spend endlessly on annual pilgrimages for political officeholders and their respective stalwarts while finding it hard to sponsor the nation's pool of science graduates abroad for more knowledge. Perhaps this same

---

49. Ademola-Olateju, "The Nigerian Clergy."
50. Ademola-Olateju, "The Nigerian Clergy."
51. Ademola-Olateju, "The Abuse of Faith by Pastors."
52. Ademola-Olateju, "The Abuse of Faith by Pastors."

mindset makes political officeholders in Nigeria prioritize building churches and mosques rather than building standard and well-equipped schools or granting scholarships to reputable institutions.[53]

The outcome of all these is a nation holed up with the past in a rapidly changing world. The Abrahamic religion practiced by most Nigerians is imbued with gross malfeasance. It has produced a people that harp on miracles and magic instead of looking to take charge of their lives and taking control of situations. The main beneficiaries of this skewed mindset are the religious entrepreneurs that falsely position themselves as men of God. These individuals continue to prosper to the detriment of the followers who consistently donate their tokens as tithes and offerings. Gradually, tokens become mounds of cash that allow religious leaders to live in luxury. They exploit the ignorance of the poor and unsuspecting followers to enrich themselves while giving the people a false hope of heavenly prosperity. In "Religion as a Tool for Impoverishing Nigerians," Ademola-Olateju remarks that, in Africa, the most impoverished people are often told their reward is in heaven and that they should be thankful for being alive.[54] On the contrary, the other Abrahamic religion is trying hard to promote intergenerational poverty through fundamentalism and insurgency. As Ademola-Olateju says, there is an urgent need for a renaissance in the people's mindset, from thinking less of an unsure afterlife to making the best of life.

CONCLUSION

Ademola-Olateju is a political activist and columnist who knows her onions and has the right political inclinations that have added flesh to all her assertions and positions on political issues in Nigeria. She is not the contemporary and conventional critic that sits in their high chairs of criticism and stays off the political waters. She puts her legs into the waters to face the waves in the Nigerian political cloud. She represents a link between partisan and observatory political participation and has become an interesting and prominent figure to draw from. Her transition from a spectator to a gladiator pushes her ahead in the fulcrum of political analyses.

She is not just a critic or a politician who links with the people but also a social media influencer changing the face of modern media. She represents a link between the old media and the new media, giving people access to her activities with the papers alongside getting the right impressions. Her activities on social media have been moving toward public sensitization, political discussions, analyzing global issues, and avenues for public discussions. Ademola-Olateju stays relevant in the major political discourses in the country.

53. Bamidele Ademola-Olateju, "Religion as a Tool for Impoverishing Nigerians," *Premium Times*, November 3, 2015, https://opinion.premiumtimesng.com/2015/11/03/religion-as-a-tool-for-impoverishing-nigerians-bamidele-ademola-olateju/.

54. Ademola-Olateju, "Religion as a Tool."

16

GLORIA EMEAGWALI

Conversations on Africa

INTRODUCTION

Being an academic historian, it is simply rational that I engage in discussions with colleagues. The latter comes in many forms: peers, contemporaries, academic equals, and others. Such discussions do not necessarily have to take the form of historical issues. However, when I can engage colleagues with whom I share the same discipline and specialization, I ensure my antenna is activated to catch the signals churned out. This becomes important for me to understand why such a colleague entertains particular opinions at particular times. One such is Dr. Gloria Emeagwali, a respected professor of history at Central Connecticut State University.

Not only a historian by career, but Professor Emeagwali has also distinguished herself as a proven public speaker, reviewer, researcher, social activist, and video-documentary producer. Aside from writing numerous articles and journals, she has also authored and co-authored several publications. Being a historian, her extensive investigations regarding Africa's past heritage and culture often come to the fore whenever issues bordering on the present and future predicaments of the continent are up for discussion. I always evaluate and analyze her thoughts and opinions when we are part of a discussion group. This I do not to counter her arguments but to ascertain their rationale.

Emeagwali's more prominent research focuses on African history. However, she currently focuses more on the historical context of African indigenous technology and how it impacts the continent's economic growth. These have not gone unnoticed as her website has gained the recognition of the United Nations Economic, Scientific and Cultural Organization (UNESCO) as among the foremost authoritative websites on African affairs. In the subsequent section, I will discuss Emeagwali's thoughts on some African issues, which I have amassed through personal interaction, group discussion, and readings of some of her journals and articles.

Considering Emeagwali as a right fit for discussion and exploration of her scholarship in this chapter is not a hard decision to make, despite the ocean of scholars whose pieces and brilliance are also worthy of being discussed. She has a proven ability to connect several ends and ideologies to fit into concepts and pave a path to join multi-lineal ideologies in explaining present issues. Choosing her became even more appropriate due to the diversity of the themes discussed in previous chapters and her ability to penetrate them with admirable insights.

Society has been evolving and will keep evolving, bringing dynamics and perspectives unfathomed in past times. This process of change inherent in society and inexcusable splits societal phenomena into segments, producing new cultures and embracing cultural diffusion from different areas. This creates a new perspective different from initially relatable and orthodox ones and, as such, institutes novel norms and systems around which society must evolve. While these phenomena and developments are unstoppable, Emeagwali is immersed in the wild pool of those changes to fish connective lines to social and continental issues. Doing this with utmost ideological details, she has produced literature encouraging the urge to study.

One of Emeagwali's ways of linking one age to another is her inquiries into the evolvement of technology and science and her appreciation of them in the contemporary era. However, what interests me in making her ideas a subject of study does not stop at such attributes but also an exploration of African indigenous technology and science with an encouraging analysis that would rightly convince one that the African nation has never been a continent without history, and the concepts of technology and science are not strange on the African soil, but the continent has been remarkable in discovery and advancement of technology in their way. She further plugged herself into similar themes, such as medicine, that gained its root in the past African society before the full-blown processes of globalization. She raised questions on other thematic subjects with historical relevance and contemporary appreciation. With such endeavours, one cannot but further appreciate her scholarship and provide discussions that open windows to their understanding.

In the internet age and the injections of the dynamics of social media into societal realities, one needs to incline oneself with ideas that fit into the new dynamics. Emeagwali has been able to establish her academic relevance in the middle of all this, and one of the ways she did this was by creating her website that creates an avenue for

Figure 16.1. "Gloria Emeagwali, Pan-Africanism" by Michael Efionayi. A team worker.

disseminating history and understanding of contemporary Africa. With these strides of hers, the trajectories of this chapter are made easy to touch on important themes in society.

As part of the themes discussed in previous chapters, the issue of identification, feminism, sexuality and the place of women was discussed to interact with the contemporary social situations and the way the people, especially in Africa and Nigeria, see the themes. These themes are fundamental to the continued peaceful existence of

society, public opinions and sentiments. They are points of discourse that cannot be excused. If one looks for a brilliant mind with convictions that properly commune with these themes, Emeagwali and positions are the square pegs in the square hole that provide a basis for the desired areas of engagement. As such, interlocutions around her and her positions are appropriate for this chapter.

EMEAGWALI ON AFRICAN FEMALE CIRCUMCISION

The concept of female circumcision is rife in Africa and is a practice that is embarked upon in line with the dictates of several African societies. It is a practice that emphasizes group rather than individual needs. The networks of mutually interrelated and interdependent groups in African societies accord more priority to communal sentiments rather than self-induced rationalizations of various practices. Female circumcision is predominantly practised in Africa's Nile, Sahara, Horn and Sahel regions, with Nigeria claiming an estimated 25% of female circumcision prevalence globally. Among the most notable societies that practice it in Africa are the Fulani people, the Maasai people, and the Kikuyu people, both of which are in East Africa. The first recorded practice of female circumcision in Africa can be traced to 4000 years back in ancient Egypt. UNICEF claims that the subjection of girls to female genital mutilation in Nigeria is a legendary practice and is done through the unhealthy traditional process of inflicting girls with genital pains without their consent.[1] This is perpetrated majorly in the southern parts of the country. This borders on the violation of girls' fundamental human rights through forced belief in cultural norms that have existed for generations.

For many societies in Africa, the reasons for female circumcision range from being a cultural practice to religious obligations, as well as norms. There are various reasons for the condemnation of such practice, among them being the possibility of medical complications and painful experiences coupled with the fact that it is harmful and denies girls future sexual satisfaction. There is also the belief that the most difficult yet joyous times of a woman's life include the day of circumcision, the day of marriage, and childbirth.[2] Circumcision of females is also done in three distinct forms; clitoridectomy, excision and infibulation.[3] The justifications for circumcision are solely based on superstitions perceived as preservatives for purification and chastity.[4] In the editorial titled "Female Circumcision in Africa," Emeagwali gave an insight into the world of female circumcision by highlighting the increasing incidences of victims narrating their respective experiences associated with female genital mutilation, a

1. Tony Hodges, "Children's and Women's Rights in Nigeria: A Wake-up Call: Situation Assessment and Analysis, 2001," *National Planning Commission*, 2001.

2. Melvin Konner, "Mutilated in the Name of Tradition," *New York Times*, April 15 1990.

3. A.A. Anzaku, A.G. Angbalaga and A. C. Achetu, "Implication of Female Genital Mutilation in Nigeria as Portal for Infectious Diseases," *Journal of Bacteriology and Infectious Disease* 2, no. 1 (2018): 28–30.

4. J.A. Verzin, "Sequelae of Female Circumcision," *Tropical Doctor* 5, no. 4 (1975): 163–169.

practice that may be perfectly construed as violence against the female folk.[5] The editorial gives the reader an insight into the analyses of three African women as they treat the explosive issue of female circumcision. Each stage is perceived as a transition from one stage to another.

Female circumcision goes by another less impressive nomenclature used whenever people who do not feel at ease with the concept discuss it. Such names may be perceived by the preconception of giving a dog a bad name to hang it. However, one cannot but understand that that is what it is. Female Genital Mutilation is used to describe female circumcision by critics of the practice. In one of my numerous conversations with some academic colleagues, the issue of female circumcision cropped up. Kenneth Harrow made us understand that female circumcision is not exclusive to African societies alone. He referenced the first clitoridectomy performed in the West as far back as 1858 in England. In his explanation, Harrow made it known that a certain Isaac Baker Brown, who published his successes in treating female masturbators through genital operation, was heavily criticized and subsequently expelled from the London Obstetrical Society. Cornelius Hamelberg also contributed his thought, detailing the events that led to banning female circumcision in places like Sweden, where pockets of closely-knit migrant communities still engage in the practice.

Another interlocutor, John Mbaku, retorted that he was not concerned with whether or not Europeans once practised acts that shared close similarities with female circumcision. He says, "What concerns me is what is happening to girls in Africa—this is my main and only concern." Mbaku would go on to affirm that it was not fair to compare male circumcision with female circumcision since the former is not embarked upon on the backdrop of fears about the child being promiscuous if not circumcised. Mbaku concluded that female circumcision is horrible and barbaric and should not be encouraged in the modern world. Emeagwali also followed Mbaku's line of thought, expatiating further that no female should be made to experience such inhuman practice based on a wrongheaded notion of predisposition to promiscuity.[6] However, she failed to subscribe to the denigration of the practice by calling it female genital mutilation. She opined that calling the practice by such nomenclatures only reveals the double standards people exhibit in the face of social phenomena. In Afolayan's memoir, *Fate of Our Mothers*, a recollection of his childhood experience and village life, he expressed his witness of the goriness of female circumcision and resolved never to allow such an ordeal to be done to his female children.[7]

Emeagwali further introduced another perspective to the discourse by detailing certain possibilities and eventualities regarding the practice. From her point of view,

5. Gloria Emeagwali, "Female Circumcision in Africa," *Africa Update* 3, no. 2 (1996).

6. Gloria Emeagwali, "Tireless Campaigner against FGM Dies in London, 207," *USA-Africa Dialogue Series*, 2014, https://groups.google.com/g/usaafricadialogue/c/h9cPezE0qVc/m/RAYJDUubAx0J.

7. Michael Oladejo Afoláyan, *Fate of Our Mothers: The Collected Memories of an African Village Boy* (Austin: Pan-African University Press, 2015).

she believed that establishing regulations to halt the practice would only lead to the perpetrators moving the practice underground. In other words, attempts to criminalize it would be counterproductive. Another female in the conversation delivered some impressive thoughts on the practice. Rather than upholding the belief that female circumcision is a culture, she referred to it as a societal tradition that may have outlived its implications. She also pointed out that in her early years of growing up, she witnessed women circumcised still engaging in promiscuous acts. In essence, she perceived that female circumcision is a practice that will eventually be wiped away as more and more people reject any affinity for it. Her argument is hinged on Darwin's evolution theory, which teaches that all things are subject to change whether there are conscious efforts to ensure the change.

From the discussions, I could piece together Emeagwali's position on the issue of female circumcision. First, it should not be encouraged anymore, and no child should be subjected to the practice based on promiscuity. In the editorial 'Female Circumcision in Nigeria,' Emeagwali referenced another scholar, Ifeyinwa Iweriebor, who posited that the practitioners of female circumcision in Nigeria do not engage in the practice to deliberately harm the children. Rather, such practices are based on noble reasons that align with cultures and rites of passage. Speaking further on this, Emeagwali noted that the day chosen for female circumcision for any woman connotes a day of accomplishment and recognition, despite the expectations of fear and pain.[8]

Also, she feels uncomfortable with the practice's bad tag. Rather than refer to it as female genital mutilation, Emeagwali referred to it as genital cutting, which does not sound too condescending or denigrating. In the end, one thing remains clear. None of the participants in the discussion wholly supports the practice of female circumcision. Kenneth Harrow, who happened to be the only American in the dialogue, affirmed that he was not supporting the practice.[9] Rather, he believed that Africans at home should be the ones agitating against the eradication of such practices and not international bodies. International bodies against the practice are simply a case of crying more than the bereaved. Harrow believes Africans should exert inner resolve to end the practice and not subject themselves to pressures from outsiders.

EMEAGWALI'S THOUGHTS ON WOMEN AS DEVELOPMENT AGENCY

It is a well-known fact that African countries experience the highest rate of developmental challenges among the continents in the world. The absence of decent jobs to cater to the growing population of countries like Nigeria presents serious problems for the people. The female population bears the larger burden of this challenge owing

---

8. Emeagwali, "Female Circumcision in Africa."

9. Kenneth W. Harrow, ed., *African Cinema Postcolonial and Feminist Readings* (Trenton: Africa World Press, 1999).

to the age-old custom that tends to suppress women's economic capabilities. Yet, African women have been constantly referred to as a powerful untapped economic force that can improve the continent's developmental challenges if proper planning is established. The gender biases targeted at women in economic and legal frameworks often limit African countries' human, social and financial capital. The corporate environment also does not afford women equal opportunities, leading to most women switching to the informal sector for economic engagements. Despite their attempts to be active in the informal sector, the interconnections of certain socio-cultural norms do not encourage African women's involvement in businesses, leading to a significant proportion of female entrepreneurs lacking access to support networks. Their negotiating power within the community is greatly limited, thereby increasing the level of poverty among women when compared to men.

Emeagwali argued in one of her articles that women in third-world countries, like in many African countries, are the proverbial hewers of wood and drawers of water and are severely hit by the continual deterioration in the level of amenities for which lending organizations are largely responsible, owing to their onerous conditionality. However, there is a need for African countries to look inwards and find means of improving women's economic standing by ascertaining specific sectors where the expertise of the women will be of much benefit. To achieve this objective, African countries must carry out structural and systemic changes that will embark on more gender-inclusiveness by incorporating more women into mainstream economic development planning. The main drivers of job creation in Africa are small and medium-scale enterprises, and women take are believed to take up to one-third of the registered SMEs in Africa. This assertion is also reinforced in another article wherein Emeagwali retorted that African societies have always experienced vibrant informal sectors, which she referred to as the second economy.[10] Among the sectors in the vibrant informal sectors, textile manufacturing, food processing, and metallurgy take up a significant portion of technical and specialized engagements. The skills are often passed on from one generation to another, leading to the persistent existence of a second economy that is rich in expertise. Emeagwali may be apt to assert that the survival of the informal sector in various African countries is a testament to the resilience and growth potential that the environment provides for the people.

Various African governments facilitate women-owned SMEs to cushion the gender gap in the SME sector. However, such efforts seem insufficient as women continue to face challenges that have a ripple effect on the continent's development. Ordinarily, women's impact on the community's development may seem negligible. However, when one looks at the redundancy created by locking out women from

---

10. Gloria Emeagwali, "African Indigenous Knowledge Systems and the Legacy of Africa." In *Indigenous Knowledge Systems and Development in Africa*, eds. Samuel Ojo Oloruntoba, Adeshina Afolayan and Olajumoke Yacob-Haliso (Cham, Switzerland: Palgrave Macmillan, 2020), 37–55.

income-generating activities, a clear picture begins to emerge. A nuclear family in a conventional African setting depends on the man as the head of the family. Provision of livelihood is heaped on such individuals while the woman is saddled with maintaining the home. A cursory look at the woman's responsibilities will reveal a significant portion of time wasted on idleness. Such times, if invested in income-generating activities by the woman, will go a long way to upping the ante and improving the economic standing of the woman and, by extension, the family.

One such sector on which Emeagwali exerts inner resolve is the food and agro-processing industry. Emeagwali noted that African civilization is associated with a specific methodology in preparing and consuming food in manners that reflect some level of uniformity across the continent.[11] In Nigeria, cassava production has a historical context. Cassava is the most dominant staple food in most Nigerian communities. In Africa, indigenous fermented foods are mostly derived from cassava tubers, cereal legumes, milk and other local products.[12] With improved technology, changes can occur in Garri (cassava flakes) processing, giving women a central role in developing such a sector. The agricultural expertise of African countries would have improved greatly if the continent had not been neglected technologically. Among the various problems affecting African countries, Emeagwali identified the high rate of obsolescence of contemporary technology.[13]

However, it is important to understand that cassava was not indigenous to Africa like oil palms, millets, and cereals. As Emeagwali rightly affirmed, cassava was introduced to Nigeria through the Portuguese during the 16th century during the era of trade along the shores of the Atlantic Ocean, in the region that now comprises what is known as Southwestern and Southeastern Nigeria. In the article "Technology Transfer: Explaining the Japanese Success Story," Emeagwali stated that innovations in the agrarian sector through the diffusion of new technologies greatly increased the income level of Japan as a nation.[14] To harness the dividend of human capital, it is important for African nations to fully include women across various socio-economic boards. Such transformations at the systems level can yield more development through gen-

11. Gloria Emeagwali, "History of Science in Non-West Traditions: Africa." In *An Introduction to the History of Science in Non-Western Traditions*, eds. Douglas Allchin and Robert DeKosky (Seattle: History of Science Society, Seattle, 1999).

12. Gloria Emeagwali, "Intersections between Africa's Indigenous Knowledge Systems and History." In *African Indigenous Knowledge and the Disciplines*, eds., Gloria Emeagwali and George J. Sefa Dei (Rotterdam: SensePublishers, 2014), 1–17.

13. Gloria Emeagwali, "Eurocentrism of Science and Technology and the History." In *African Indigenous Science and Knowledge System: Triumph and Tribulations: Essays in Honour of Professor Gloria Thomas-Emeagwali*, eds. Olayemi Akinwumi, Okpeh Ochayi Okpeh, C. B. N. Ogbogbo and Adoyi Onoja (Abuja: Roots Books & Journals Limited, 2007).

14. Gloria Emeagwali, "Technology Transfer: Explaining the Japanese Success Story," *Journal of Contemporary Asia* 21, no. 4 (1991): 504–512.

der-inclusive government facilitation of SME growth. The development of African countries will never reach its full potential without promoting women to the status of full economic citizens through inclusion in growth processes and policies.

COLONIZATION AND AFRICA'S DEVELOPMENT

Historians frequently face the reoccurrence of questions to understand the causes of underdevelopment in once-flourishing societies that have become known in international relations as third-world countries, wherein most African countries fall. The consensus of development thoughts in Africa revolves around colonialism and the colonial era. However, biased opinions are used to either support or argue against the positive impacts of colonial rule in Africa. For large swaths of the 20th century, most African countries found themselves under the colonial control of European Nations during a time that is now referred to as the European Scramble for Africa. This colonial period, as recorded by early historians, affirmed the developmental strides that African societies experienced as incentives for colonial domination. However, this may not be overly true if we go by the arguments put forth by academicians like Emegwali and writers such as Ewout Frankema.

Emeagwali noted that various African societies had developed scientific processes to solve problems as far back as the third century BC. While many such processes may be attributed to Egypt, it does not infer that Egypt held exclusivity. The major thing that worked to Egypt's advantage was record-keeping and documentation, which many other African societies, especially the Sub-Saharan region, never fully exploited. Emeagwali opined that using hieroglyphics in Africa predates Sumerian and Mesopotamia writings. And the Egyptian propensity for record-keeping also inspired Hebrew and Arabic scripts.[15] Emeagwali, in the article, provided a conjecture to support some of the arguments raised. The earliest known description of the brain was from the recorded documents of the Egyptians. Perhaps there was no documentation of such scientific feats; such feats would not have been ascribed to them. Emeagwali also noted that various African societies applied scientific knowledge to chemical processes; this culminated in the cloth-dying process, leather tanning, and distillation of various liquids, especially beer and fermented beverages.

The Christian religious thoughts and a formalized educational process were purported to accompany colonialists to Africa, and the Christian missionaries executed these under the supervision of the various colonial administrations. However, Emeagwali's article, "History of Science in Non-Western Traditions: Africa," affirmed the existence of formalized education arrangements in Egypt. To further confirm her position, the article referenced that the majority of what resulted in the advancement

15. Emeagwali, "Eurocentrism of Science and Technology."

of Greek Sciences was derived from Egypt, a feat made possible through the Greek conquest of Egypt circa 332 BCE.[16]

To erase these, the colonial conquest of Africa ensured that the undocumented socio-cultural aspects of various African societies were either deliberately refabricated or suppressed. This fact was magnified in Emeagwali's article, "Eurocentrism and the History of Sciences and Technology," where she affirmed that the strategy of selective omission of information was used to suppress significant inventions carried out by non-Europeans.[17] By so doing, many imbalances were established. The denial of African history and cultures undertaken with the sole objective of establishing and imposing western norms, cultures and religious doctrines was perfectly carried out with the introduction of innovations and technologies used to hoodwink African leaders to relegate their own cultures and norms to a lesser position. Before the coming of colonialists, internal state formation processes established a blueprint for development in various African societies. While early civilizations dating back thousands of years ago documented technological feats of northern Africa; the regions of Egypt, Aksum and Nubia, Sub-Saharan Africa, during the initial contact with Europeans, were also reputed to have achieved technological feats such as the irrigation terraces of Gwoza, as well as the earthworks of Benin in West Africa.[18] Southern Africa has its fair share of technological feats in the form of sculptured temples and walled enclosures as evidence of indigenous technological developments.

These processes were disrupted with the entrance of colonial administration, bringing about an administration that gave room for political instability and corruption. Colonialism was hinged on the extraction of resources from Africa to Europe. Private side extractions were established to ensure that raw materials were constantly sought by engaging African farmers and businessmen in trades for export. The public side of the extraction was hinged on the construction of rails and roads to ease the carriage of goods from place to place until such goods eventually got transported to Europe. By evaluating these two strategies holistically, one is tempted to agree with the school of thought that posits that all developments embarked upon by colonial regimes in Africa were done for selfish purposes. What the colonial rulers sought to achieve was not development, in essence. Rather, they only wanted to satisfy their inordinate ambitions of benefiting by extracting resources from African societies for their own countries.

As Emeagwali noted in the article "Colonialism," the colonial administration is best described as a process of exploitation focused on establishing a capitalist relationship for the socio-cultural and economic aggrandizement of the colonizers to the

16. Emeagwali, "History of Science in Non-Western Culture."
17. Emeagwali, "Eurocentrism of Science."
18. Emeagwali, "Eurocentrism of Science."

detriment of the colonized.[19] This was done by covert and psychological means using superior military and diplomatic strategies. One needs to understand that before the coming of colonialism, African societies had their forms of technology. Emeagwali further supported this assertion in the article "History of Science in Non-Western Traditions," affirming that many parts of Africa, especially the city-state, empires and kingdoms, developed their science and technological feats uniquely.[20] The development of such indigenous technology was greatly hindered to a large extent by colonial domination which shifted the focus of African economies to cash crop cultivation, thereby destabilizing the existing processes that would have encouraged technological growth in African societies.[21] Cloth-weaving, brass works and the erection of edifices had been severally embarked upon before the vast societies of Africa had contact with Europeans. Emeagwali also noted that the advancements in farming in West Africa were so great that captives taken as slaves to the New World led to enormous strides in the society's agronomical exploits. The supply of African slaves to American plantations reached an all-time high during the late 18th century and paved the way for expanding land-intensive tropical agronomy.[22]

Colonialism led to the dumping of foreign textiles and iron products to facilitate European exports into African societies. Similarly, they could hoodwink Africans into believing their indigenous cultures, religions, and norms were inferior. The Europeans also manipulated Africans into believing they needed to change their dressing mode and other socio-cultural concepts. Therefore, African nations' manufacturing capabilities were deliberately undermined by establishing laws and regulations to suppress the continent's technological development. Among the most affected were metallurgists who were involved in iron fabrications for the modelling of farm implements.[23] The blacksmiths were not alone in the maladministration brought by the colonialists; African medical practitioners who had been serving their people for ages were confronted with regulations that greatly hindered their practice. Emeagwali added that the vast array of medicinal plants and herbs used to treat various allergies and diseases were exported to European laboratories and brought back as imported drugs. They became substitutes for ingesting the same herbs in more potent forms.

The result of this is that African businessmen opt for commodity export. With the establishment of regulations that discouraged local distillations, the only option for farmers was to export such plants to be used as raw materials for European-manufactured drugs. The European Scramble for Africa broadened the African continent's position as a source of raw materials like copper, cotton and rubber, as well as cash

19. Gloria Emeagwali, "Colonialism." In *African Indigenous Science and Knowledge System: Triumph and Tribulations.*

20. Emeagwali, "History of Science in Non-Western Culture."

21. Emeagwali, "Colonialism."

22. Herbert S. Klein, *The Atlantic Slave Trade* (Cambridge: Cambridge University Press, 2010).

23. Emeagwali, "Colonialism."

crops like cocoa and tobacco. Not limiting the negative impacts to this alone, Africa became a source of support for the well-being of Europeans and Americans as the continent provided cheap labor, raw materials and markets, playing a key role in building the Atlantic system that was an important factor of development in both Europe and America.

Colonialism may be gone, but the scars are yet to heal in many African societies. Imperialism has taken over, and the development of African countries is largely dependent on relations with the western world. While countries like China have suddenly entered the fray to limit the intensity of African dependence on the western world, the Asian Powerhouse does not seem to have anything contrary to what the western world wants from Africa; exploitation for personal benefits.

EMEAGWALI'S POSITION ON AFRICAN SCIENCE AND KNOWLEDGE SYSTEMS

Africa is purported to have the oldest record of technological achievements in world history. Shreds of evidence of stone tools and magnificent edifications that dotted various African societies would not have been possible without the existence of scientific knowledge systems. Various aspects of medieval and contemporary Africa point to building constructions in varying dimensions, conceptualizations, decorative principles and typologies, revealing a continent home to the earliest thinkers and problem solvers who made use of calculations and estimations to arrive at enviable feats.[24] Such advanced civilizations should not be attributed to the northern African enclaves alone. The impressive feats incorporated into buildings included permanent scaffolding done in the Malian region. Emeagwali mentioned that derelict ruins of walled cities in the northern part of present-day Nigeria complement those found in Ethiopia and Zimbabwe, all signifying the existence of craftsmen in Africa from a long time past.

Modern discussions relating to scientific knowledge and systems have shifted focus away from Africa to other more developed continents. Little attention is given to the study of African knowledge systems despite the notable contributions of the continent to developments in Mathematics, Metallurgy and Astronomy, to mention a few. Perhaps, there is a need to answer one pertinent question; Is Africa's Science and Knowledge systems different from modern science? Maurice Richter affirmed that science includes all activities whose roots are traceable to several ancient cultures.[25] This presupposition validates the claim that Africa had distinct forms of science and scientific knowledge, irrespective of the level of crudeness about modern science. As Emeagwali rightly noted, the solar calendar used worldwide evolved from the ancient

24. Emeagwali, "History of Science in Non-Western Culture."

25. Maurice N. Richter, *Science as a Cultural Process* (London: Frederick Muller Limited, 1973).

Egyptian calendar of twelve months, in concordance with the rising of Sirius from the horizon with the Sun. In other words, any assertion that leans on the premise that science is alien to African societies before contact with Europeans does not hold water. This, in conjunction with the works of other African scholars such as Christian Emedolu and Jonathan Chimakonam, seems to draw support to the premise that there are countless numbers of contributions by African civilization toward science within the continent beyond.

In one of my unending dialectics with Emeagwali, the issue of African agriculture cropped up. The genesis of the discussion stemmed from an article written by Wengrow and associates, which sought to deny the existence of African agriculture on the precept that other civilizations outside Africa also practised agriculture. The authors claimed that animals such as goats were introduced to Africa from Asia. However, such false notions are the kinds of assertions one would automatically expect Emeagwali to counter logically. And this she did perfectly by affirming that every continent has a unique topography, environment and ecological factors that ensure independent agricultural experiences. Emeagwali further proved her assertion right by referencing the existence of the Ethiopian Ibex, an African mountain goat that exists only in Africa. The limitation of the Walla ibex to Africa alone renders the thoughts of Wengrow et al. void. Her observations remain valid as the authors erroneously failed to tag Africa as the bedrock of humanity, a point Biko also supported in the discussion.[26]

Emeagwali's "African Indigenous Knowledge Systems: Implications for the Curriculum" indicates the possibility of returning to the fore the seemingly lost glory of Africa's contribution to global scientific knowledge systems. According to Emeagwali, the article was developed to explore the multiple linkages between the African indigenous knowledge systems and the accompanying curriculum related to teaching strategies, objectives and instructional resources contained therein.[27]

To understand the necessity of what Emeagwali sought from the article, it is important to understand the core nature of science, which is described as an organized and systematic procedure of gathering knowledge about the phenomenon to condense such knowledge into principles and laws.[28] The values and potentialities of scientific inquiry depend on acknowledging local practices within a particular environment to evaluate and analyze systematic indigenous knowledge and its methodologies. The direction of Emeagwali's description of the African scientific knowledge

---

26. David Wengrow, Michael Dee, Sarah Foster, Alice Stevenson and Christopher Bronk Ramsey, "Cultural Convergence in the Neolithic of the Nile Valley: a Prehistoric Perspective on Egypt's Place in Africa," *Antiquity* 88, no. 339 (2014): 95–111.

27. Gloria Emeagwali, "African Indigenous Knowledge Systems (AIK): Implications for the Curriculum." In *Ghana in Africa and the World: Essays in Honor of Adu Boahen*, ed. Toyin Falola (New Jersey: Africa World Press, 2003).

28. Edward Wilson, *Consilience: The Unity of Knowledge* (New York: Vintage, 1998).

system is like that of Alozie, who posited that African science is developed based on the African man's observations and investigations of his environment to achieve a higher level of understanding of the environment to aid in manipulating and controlling nature's forces to his advantage.[29] This is embarked upon to escape the uncertainties that characterize the natural phenomena in the environment. This description also complicates the earlier question concerning the differences between African and modern science. Perhaps she was right in yet another discussion wherein she pointed out that many European and western researchers are simply suffering from Egyptophobia, a form of intellectual paralysis resulting from fear and loathing, which Emeagwali presumed to encourage the abdication of research responsibilities into ancient African developmental models. Such a syndrome, as she noted, is driven by an excessive ambition to massage the egos of the forces that uphold Eurocentric propaganda.[30]

The description put forth by Alozie also applies to modern scientific inquiry. This further leads to another query; is African science referred to as such simply because it was developed by an African or because it only applies to the African continent alone? As dissimilar as it may seem, Emeagwali identified the intersection between European science (modern science) and African science by describing the two as parallel desires to negotiate nature through sequential processes that hinge on the formulation of hypotheses, engagement in experimental procedures, all done to propound a theory or predict occurrences.[31] Any scientific knowledge is established on the grounds of intuition, conjectures or observed outcomes; however, there must be some form of regularity that is devoid of conclusions based on trial by error.

Many aspects of African science and knowledge systems have been categorized under the umbrella of esoteric concepts and, as such, are devoid of objective theorizations. However, it is a great injustice to follow this line of thought since the essence of scientific inquiry is to investigate the unknown with the intent of providing appropriate rationality for such observations. As it may be labelled, African science has existed for thousands of years and served as a basis for modern science. Emeagwali argued that the extensive collections of Marcel Griaule had deepened the understanding of Malian cosmological myths related to the structure of matter and the physical world.[32] The field of mathematics is not left out, with ancient Egyptians having incorporated mathematical concepts such as square roots and quadratic equations into their mathematical processes before the arrival of Greek geometrical concepts.

Rather than appreciate all these glaring feats, Emeagwali noted that Europeans engaged in an assessment of double standards, in which many of the technological

29. Princewill Alozie, "History and Philosophy of Science in Ancient Africa." In *History and Philosophy of Science*, 2nd ed., ed. Alozie Princewill (Calabar: Clear Lines Publications, 2001), 2–32.

30. Gloria Emeagwali, "Definition of Egyptophobia," *USA-Africa Dialogue Series*, 2014, https://groups.google.com/g/usaafricadialogue/c/AIk6ZTgqiZk/m/3fg2v3wOBAAJ.

31. Emeagwali, "African Indigenous Knowledge Systems."

32. Emeagwali, "History of Science in Non-Western Culture."

feats of African societies were being classified as artistic designations that are only fit for art museums. These levels of appreciation may seem edifying on the surface, but in reality, nothing is edifying about them. What should be appreciated, according to Emeagwali, is the technicality of the various scientific creations. It would have been apt if the Europeans categorized African scientific feats under two broad compositions; traditional and modern. Following this line of engagement makes it easier to compare western science and the categorizations individually. Perhaps, this will provide the needed leverage to ascertain the loophole and the strong points of the two classifications of African science. The delineating factor is that African traditional science (encapsulating ancient discoveries by ancient African civilizations) is quite different from modern African science, which is also dissimilar to western scientific methodology. Emeagwali claims that modern science is associated with scientific discoveries from the 17th century, whether of European origins or Africa. However, the feats achieved by modern scientists may not have been possible if ancient scientific knowledge had been isolated. She noted this fact when she affirmed that modern mathematical concepts without the Hindu-Arabic numeral system that was used for solving complex equations.

Emeagwali put forth an approach that points to the systematic nature of African indigenous knowledge that was achieved through several methodical transitions that have been witnessed. This is like the exposition of Chimakonam that explained the five methodical captures of African science: trial and error, inter-science, intro-science, semi-science and causal science.[33] This provides a paradigm shift in African experimental science consolidated systematically. In essence, the categorizations above are enough evidence to relish the inherent esoteric attributes that permeate the culture of various African societies.

Emeagwali, in "African Indigenous Knowledge Systems: Implication for the Curriculum," affirmed that conceptual issues relating to the identity of African indigenous knowledge systems remain an underlying challenge faced by African knowledge repositories. The theoretical and methodological issues relating to African science can be resolved by developing a structured framework within a predefined curriculum. The need to include African indigenous knowledge systems is beyond what is described above alone. Some rationales and strategies have been used by western science to distort the achievements of African science through a process of disinformation. However, Emeagwali pointed out that the recognition and subsequent appreciation of African knowledge systems remain a healing source for the several distortions and trivializations inflicted by Eurocentric rationality.

33. Jonathan Chimakonam, "Towards a Theory of African Science: Methods and Justification," *IOSR Journal of Pharmacy and Biological Sciences* 3, no 1 (2012): 33–41.

Emeagwali wrote extensively on the African indigenous knowledge system (AIK) and its various applications.[34] A plethora of Western narratives erroneously notes that the African continent did not have an established system before the advent of colonialism. The repertoire of the African knowledge system had been described as informal by Western scholars. Emeagwali challenges many Eurocentric criticisms of the inferiorization of African indigenous knowledge systems. She contends that there are various historical and scientific contributions made by Africans, which are often discarded by the westerners who constantly argued—though erroneously—that the bedrock of civilization was based on their knowledge system. Emeagwali posits that the various innovations and inventions from the African indigenous knowledge may have occurred outside the precincts of modern scientific knowledge but should be belittled. She further argues that Western science should consider that innovations do not take place solely in laboratories, as constant interaction with one's environment leads to a breakthrough in innovations and inventions.[35]

As Emeagwali posited, the African indigenous knowledge system comprised various epistemologies and value systems developed by African societies according to studies of their environments and a mix of different cultures. This knowledge system was developed based on trial and error and empirical practices relating to the African worldview. The respect for ancestral wisdom formed the basis of the African knowledge system. Studies have argued for the need for the African knowledge system to be anti-colonial and anti-racist in efforts to counter "western epistemological hegemonic systems and its beliefs in all ramifications."[36] Scholars further argue that there is a need to study and codify the African knowledge system, which offers different perspectives in understanding different aspects of the world, past and present, and is also important for post-colonialism.[37]

The African knowledge system is based on environmentalism, methodological pluralism, communitarianism, and reciprocity.[38] Environmentalism underpins the "indigenous cosmologies and theological systems" replete in the African knowledge system. This includes the recognition of African gods and goddesses and practices peculiar to different African cultures. Methodological pluralism refers to the pragmatic aspect of the knowledge system and how it has varied over the years. Communitarianism and reciprocity refer to the shared identity among Africans, which influenced the development of mutually benefiting programs and the advancement of

---

34. Gloria Emeagwali and Edward Shizha, "Interconnecting History, African Indigenous Knowledge Systems and Science." In *African Indigenous Knowledge and the Sciences: Journeys into the Past and Present*, eds. Gloria Emeagwali and Edward Shizha (Berlin: Springer, 2016), 1–11.

35. Emeagwali and Shizha, "Interconnecting History."

36. George J Dei and Jill Vickers, "Anti-Racism Education: Theory & Practice," *Journal of Canadian Studies* 32, no. 2 (1997): 175.

37. George J Dei, Budd L. Hall and Dorothy Goldin Rosenberg, *Indigenous Knowledges in Global Contexts: Multiple Readings of Our World* (Toronto: University of Toronto Press).

38. Emeagwali, "African Indigenous Knowledge Systems," 37–55.

"socialistic modes of existence." The indigenous African societies were built on the principles of communitarianism which highlights the need for the members of the societies to work together to achieve collective progress. The principle of individualism was never an ideology of the African societies where the knowledge system originated, as Africans emphasized the need for networking and interconnectedness. This perhaps explains the reason why African cultures are not necessarily distinct. Emeagwali points out technologies birthed by the African knowledge system; this includes the development of iron-making industries in Tanzania, which "contributed to the technological heritage of humanity." This technology, as noted by scholars such as Okafor, was used in the treatment and production of fuel, foregrounding the cultural importance of African iron metallurgy.[39] Emeagwali argues that preserving African science and technology, which were disrupted by slavery and colonialism, would have fast-tracked technological advancement in African countries. She also noted that the dominance of western science hindered the development of African technologies.

Emeagwali countered the narrative eulogizing colonialism for developing the modern educational system in Africa that produced men such as Bishop Ajayi Crowther and Chief Obafemi Awolowo, among many others. Emeagwali argued about the fate of the missionaries who brought western education to Africa if there were no lands to plunder, resources to steal, or slaves to export under the guise of fulfilling Biblical injunctions. She contends that the western education system was built "on centuries of knowledge transfer from Africa and Asia." According to Emeagwali:

> The Western educational establishment on which these missionaries relied was constructed on centuries of knowledge transfer, from Africa and Asia, including the very paper on which they wrote their treatizes and epistles—granted that Egyptian paper was plant-based whilst the Chinese prototype was based on cellulose pulp. The two in sequence facilitated the documentation central to the kind of system they introduced. The oldest known printed book is not the Bible of Gutenberg but Buddhism's Diamond Sutra.[40]

She also noted:

> West Africa's history, and the historical process, did not begin with the missionaries. Thousands of years before them, around 9500 BCE people in the region called Mali would have launched ceramic manufacture. Three thousand years

39. Edwin Eme Okafor. "Twenty-Five Centuries of Bloomery Iron Smelting in Nigeria," In *The Origins of Metallurgy in Africa: New Lights on its Antiquity. West and Central Africa*, ed. Hamady Bocoum (Paris: UNESCO Publishing, 2004), 43–54.

40. Gloria Emeagwali, "Barewa (Modified)," *USA-Africa Dialogue Series*, May 27, 2021, https://groups.google.com/g/usaafricadialogue/c/DIx776QPa_8.

> later around 6000 BCE, the Dufuna boat would have been created—paving the way for local navigation. Around 3000 BCE, the people of Nigeria (and Cameroon) would have invented raffia cloth, and now we know that iron metallurgy would go back as early as 2300 BCE, not only in Northern Nigeria but also in Central Africa.... The human spirit is indomitable—especially when unhindered by debilitating psychological obstructions.[41]

Emeagwali foregrounded the importance of the African knowledge system and how its adoption would contribute to the development of African countries. However, the influx of western civilization to the African continent has relegated the indigenous knowledge system to the backyard; there is a great need to re-identify with African values systems for the continent's overall civilization.

All the disciplines that come together to form what is referred to as African science and knowledge systems should not follow the connotation or interpretation given to them by the western world. African scholars like Emeagwali should see African studies as a part of a wider project that is embarked upon to transform the knowledge systems in the continent. African indigenous knowledge systems, as Emeagwali called it, should not be just for the contribution of accumulated knowledge about Africa; rather, the indigenous knowledge systems should seek the development of Africa-based tradition of research and inquiries which are carried out directly or indirectly by Africans. Western scientific scholars may, after seeing such, be forced to contribute to the problem-solving processes through research implementations. It is important for modern scientific knowledge to also spring up from Africa and not be perceived as the exclusivity of the societies outside the continent alone.

EMEAGWALI ON AFRICAN TRADITIONAL MEDICINE

In a similar vein to the issue of the African knowledge system, Emeagwali also threw her voice behind the relegation and delineation of the existing African traditional medicine system for the acceptance and embrace of Western medicine that accompanied colonialism to the shores of Africa. African traditional medicine is perhaps the oldest and most assorted of all therapeutic systems in the world. Being considered the cradle of mankind, coupled with a rich biological and cultural diversity, Africa is home to varying forms of traditional medicine and healing practices. The thousand years' African approach to treating diseases and curative methodologies has become an issue ascribed to unorthodoxy based on the assertion that the methodologies lack scientific proof and empirical evaluation. In the past, large aspects of African traditional medicine were termed primitive compared to conventional western medicine. However, this notion has been relegated to scientific investigations focused

41. Emeagwali, "Barewa (Modified)."

on a better understanding of the therapeutic activities encapsulated in African traditional medicine.

Emeagwali noted that African traditional medicine consists of the whole body of knowledge about treating diseases and explaining illnesses and sicknesses. In truth, the African traditional medicine system encapsulated practices that have their roots grounded in the culture and religious beliefs of the various African societies. This should not be perceived as strange or obtuse since every society has its culture and beliefs serving as the root for various practices from medicine to the way of life and entertainment. The arrival of what is perceived as conventional medicine today is better understood when we factor in the rationale for African societies to substitute whole aspects of their culture and norms for western-imported ideologies. However, Emeagwali stated that African traditional medicine, like other aspects of African cultural beliefs, remains relevant outside the continent. This stems from the popular belief that African traditional medicine is more effective than western (conventional) medicine in treating specific ailments.[42] This cannot be ignored in the face of various reports that point to the increasing global adoption of complementary or alternative medicine.

Occasioned by varying degrees of successes and failures, Emeagwali noted that African traditional medicine refused to be static over time, with the core areas of its practices and acceptability evident in various parts of Africa and beyond. Regarding the methodology adopted, Emeagwali indicated that the diagnosis process follows a particular methodology that includes physical observation of the patient, with close attention placed on specific body parts. Wide consultations with the family members follow this to ascertain if there is any history of similar cases within the family. Worthy of note is the fact that Emeagwali pointed out instances whereby the patient's urine is observed while body temperature is taken. However, the part that seems strange and not synchronized with conventional medicine is divination (sand gazing and water gazing) to ascertain the root cause of ailments and sicknesses. Although Emeagwali noted that this depends on the illness's nature, it sets the stage for adopting methods that include infusions, elixirs, and enemas.[43] This varies from one African society to another, with slight modifications to the inherent similarities in the diagnosis processes. In other words, African traditional medicine provides a holistic health care system organized into three levels; divination, herbalism and spiritualism.[44] The reason is not far-fetched; the causes of sicknesses and ailments are perceived as having both natural and supernatural causes. Perhaps, this explains why Emeagwali noted that the success of African traditional medical interventions often

---

42. Gloria Emeagwali, and George J. Sefa Dei, *African Indigenous Knowledge and the Disciplines* (Berlin: Springer, 2014).

43. Emeagwali et al, *African Indigenous Knowledge and the Disciplines.*

44. Ezekwesili-Ofili Josephine Ozioma and Okaka Antoinette Nwamaka Chinwe, "Herbal Medicines in African Traditional Medicine," *Herbal Medicine 10* (2019): 191–214.

integrates both the physical and the metaphysical. For instance, she mentioned the widely held assumption among African traditional healers that supposes that leaves, roots and barks should be gathered at midday, midnight and late evening, respectively, if their potency is to be effectively maintained.[45] To validate this, she explained that practitioners believe plants emit radiations and energy patterns that are only understood and detectable by psychics. Certain aspects of African traditional medicine specialize in providing communication channels with ancestral spirits as a support system for effective medical intervention.

Providing more information on the methodology of curative medicine in African societies, Emeagwali presented a wide range of techniques, such as heat therapy, hydrotherapy and orthopaedics, with particular African societies noted for a large pool of specialists in specialized healing processes. The article provided, for instance, the Funtua people in northern Nigeria, who are noted to specialize in bone-setting and other orthopaedic care. An important dissimilarity between African traditional medicine and conventional medicine involves the process of amputation, which is less practised in the former. Vaccination and quarantine are also present in African traditional medicine, with countries like Ethiopia laying claim to medical processes such as hot baths, hot cloth treatment and inhalation of essential oils to treat specific ailments.[46]

The surgical procedures contained in African traditional medicine, as cited by Emeagwali, include incisions, scarifications and circumcisions, while other processes include the removal of tonsils, ear lobe perforations, etc. Like the cesarean section, African societies possess childbirth interventions that take the form of dissection of the abdominal walls to get the fetus out of the womb. This points to the advancement of African traditional medicine and its similarities with the same conventional medicine adopted as a substitute.

EMEAGWALI'S THOUGHTS ON ISLAM IN NIGERIA

Nigeria is home to the sixth-largest Muslim community in the whole world. With Islam being the most embraced religion in Nigeria, albeit to a slight degree, the various aspects of Islamic religious norms and practices are always subject to discussion among scholars and researchers. Owing to this fact, it becomes understandable to witness scholars like Emeagwali penning her thoughts on the Islamic religion. This is not to say that she is a Muslim, nor is she one to denigrate a religion that she does not practice. I could deduce this in one of our engagements where she pointed out the flaws of an essay by Tola Adeniyi titled "Islam and Religious Imperialism." While Emeagwali was quick to note that the author seemed to have ignored the equally disconcerting connection between Christianity and religious imperialism, she be-

45. Gloria Emeagwali and Edward Shizha, eds., *African Indigenous Knowledge.*
46. R. Pankhurst, *The Medical History of Ethiopia* (Trenton: Red Sea Press, 1990).

lieved that a holistic attempt to discuss religious imperialism through Islam alone would only amount to a lopsided narrative that would be perceived as placing one religion on a holier than thou pedestal over others.[47]

The massive spread of Islam in Nigeria can be partly attributed to the Usman Dan Fodio conquest of the Hausa states. However, this does not mean that he brought Islam to Nigeria, as the Borno Empire had already adopted Islam before the rise of Usman Dan Fodio. This explains the assertion by Emeagwali in her article "Islam and gender in Nigeria" that there is a great density of Muslims in the northern parts of Nigeria, with the western part having an almost balanced number of Islamic and Christian worshippers.[48] The result of this balance is a society that tends more toward secularism, with no clear-cut religious practice evident within the society. These situations even lead to a belief by some northern Muslims that their contemporaries in the west are not full Muslims. The region with a sparse distribution of Muslims in the eastern region of Nigeria did not have any recorded history of contact with Islamic scholars in their history.

One major aspect of Islamic practice that Emeagwali put forth in her article concerns the issue of marriage, wherein Islamic injunctions support the concept of polygamy. It should also be noted that polygamy, although supported by Islam, is not new to many societies in Nigeria either. The western region of Nigeria, initially known to compose of the Yoruba people, has adopted polygamy as a culture for a very long time. This may be partially responsible for the region's quick embrace of Islam. The challenge posed by Emeagwali concerning the Islamic practice of polygamy hinges on the Quranic injunction that states that all wives should be loved equally in a polygamous arrangement. This, as Emeagwali noted, is in sharp contrast to the pre-existing norm that encouraged discrimination and favoritism among wives betrothed to one man. Suffice it to say that the polygamous arrangement in existence before the emergence of Islam in Nigeria factors in a hierarchical structure of wives, depending on their respective ages and the time they are married. This was done to delegate responsibilities within the home since the culture obliges the junior wives to perform more house chores than the senior wives.

Another important highlight of the Islamic practice in Nigeria centers on inheritance and how it should be managed. Emeagwali retorted that the pre-Islamic practice of many societies in Nigeria allowed for usufruct land rights by women irrespective of their social status. With the introduction of Islam into various Nigerian societies, especially the north, new inheritance patterns were introduced. These patterns paved the way for women's entitlements to the shares of properties of deceased

47. Gloria Emeagwali, Excerpts from https://groups.google.com/g/usaafricadialogue/c/7-izuVV1P_w/m/ilC9WviWBQAJ.

48. Gloria Emeagwali, "Islam and Gender: The Nigerian Case." In *Muslim Women's Choices: Religious Belief and Social Reality,* eds. Camillia Fawzi El-Solh and Judy Mabro (Rhode Island: Berg, 1994).

male kin. The Islamic injunction of Maliki, wherein daughters can get up to 50% of the inheritance left by their fathers, is incomparable with the societal customs where inheritance is strictly patrilineal or a situation that only favors the eldest male descendant of the deceased, as is common among the Tiv and Gwari people. There are fringes of societies in Nigeria whose customs allow females to hold inheritances if there are no male heirs to the deceased. As Emeagwali noted, the introduction of Islam in Nigeria changed the pre-existing patterns of inheritance to favor the womenfolk. The perceptible dominance of the patriarchal system in Nigeria may be a myopic view, as Emeagwali brought forward points to prove that patriarchal power in Nigeria has been exaggerated for quite some time. In her words, "However, it may be that the power of patriarchy in the formation of existing perceptions of the societal organization has been overestimated and that researchers have generally failed to discern underlying matriarchal tendencies and other indications of female power." In essence, the introduction of Islam in Nigeria did not just reduce patriarchal dominance; it also rejuvenated a matriarchal system that had been submerged with the latter's spread.

A distinguishing practice between the Northern Nigerian Muslims and their counterpart in the south has been highlighted by Emeagwali in several of her articles on the practice of child marriage. According to the article, a survey undertaken in Zaria, Kaduna, indicated that 90% of Muslim women are married off to suitors before they reach fifteen. This trend, while not discouraged in Islam, is hardly practised in the southern part of Nigeria, where the consensus is that liberal Islam is the norm. However, what constitutes liberal Islam may also be taken to mean the followers do not practice the whole Islamic injunctions to the letter. Conversely, historians and scholars have pointed out that child marriage is not a religious concept per se; rather, it is a cultural norm among the identities in the Middle East, the home of Arabs. Some religious manuscripts, termed "Apocryphal," seemed to rationalize this argument with stories that explicitly state that the Virgin Mary, who birthed Jesus, was also within the age age-range of thirteen to fifteen when she was conceived of the Holy Spirit.[49] While this remains invalidated by any part of the bible, the onus of such assertion supports the premise that early marriage is more of a race culture in the Middle East and not an Islamic dogma.

As Emeagwali discussed it, the practice of purdah in Nigeria exists on three planes: voluntary seclusion, partial seclusion, and total seclusion. The determinant of which form of seclusion a married woman will embrace is based on certain factors like social status and education level. Emeagwali implicitly affirmed that purdah is evolving from total seclusion to milder forms as more Muslim women embrace formal education. This shows that the practice of total purdah was popular at a time when a reasonable proportion of Muslim women did not take to formal education or formal

49. Philip J. King and Lawrence E. Stager, *Life in Biblical Israel* (Louisville: Westminster John Knox Press, 2001).

employment. They are married off; to serve in the capacity of housewives, who are not expected to participate in any form of economic activity save for childbearing and home-caring. However, not all sections of Muslims uphold this practice. Emeagwali attributed the growth of the Tijaniyya movement as a catalyst for the reduction in the embrace of purdah among Muslims in Nigeria. Unlike its counterpart, the Quadriyya, the Tijaniyya offers some degree of liberty to women, allowing them to take up leadership roles while limiting the female gender to specific societal roles. Some other factors that influence the practice of purdah, according to Emeagwali, may include class origin and proximity or urbanized communities. So to say, many Muslim women are abandoning the practice of purdah, even in the northern part of Nigeria, where it was rampant in times past. Muslim women are now inclined to mix freely with men while also becoming involved in economic activities to cushion the difficulties and dependence on men for sustenance.[50] The elite Muslims seem not to embrace the concept of purdah since their outward approach to living encourages them to be in the company of their wives in social engagements. Emeagwali's article further noted that they are also dropping the practice for various reasons; paramount is the engagement in economic activities to reduce dependence on their respective husbands.

Islamic injunctions relating to divorce are an area that is not given enough discussion owing to the topic's sensitivity. However, Emeagwali captured some specific elements that are worth noting. Among these is that Muslim men in Nigeria do not feel obligated to state any reason for embarking on divorce; the women do not enjoy such benefits. For Muslim women, seeking a divorce may only be possible if there is evidence that the husband has not been performing his duties as the head of the house. Such duties may revolve around providing for the family's economic needs or failure to perform his manly roles as the husband. Other pre-emptions that may legitimize divorce claims originating from Muslim women in Nigeria may include instances of wrongful accusations of adultery by the husband, a change of religion by the husband, as well as total disillusionment with the marriage since some Muslim women are betrothed at an age when they are too immature to understand the concept of marriage. Despite all these valid premises to legitimize the call for divorce by Muslim women, Emeagwali still found out in her research that northern Muslim women hardly engage in such practices. This may not be unconnected with their strong inclination to remain subservient to their respective husbands as religion dictates. This is not the case with Muslim women in southern Nigeria, where Emeagwali noted increased incidences of Muslim women filing for divorce in places like Ilorin.[51] The social stigmatization of divorced women is no more.

To conclude this section, Emeagwali opined that the emergence of Islam in Nigeria brought as much as it took away. It may be argued that certain negative ingredients

---

50. Emeagwali, "Islam and Gender."
51. Emeagwali, "Islam and Gender."

accompanied the adoption of Islam in several Nigerian societies. We cannot rule out the positivity too. The introduction of female seclusion through the practice of purdah has resulted in the loss of independence by a significant population of women. The patriarchal orientation supported by the various Quranic injunctions placed men at a greater advantage over women, with the latter expected to be subservient to the former. However, the major gain of the women concerning Islamic injunctions comes in the area of inheritance, wherein they are placed on a footing that seems to be better than what was applicable in the pre-Islamic era.

EMEAGWALI'S PERSPECTIVE ON THE GENERALIZATION OF FULANI PASTORALISTS AS TERRORISTS

For some years, there have been constant accusations that Fulani pastoralists engage in criminal activities in many parts of Nigeria. While contributing to the economy as the major distributors of livestock to virtually all corners of the country, the continuous altercations these nomads have with farmers, especially in the southern parts of Nigeria, continue to present serious security challenges to the entire polity. Although the leadership of the pastoralists has always come out to debunk claims of their members being involved in violent confrontations that often lead to death, there is no denying their involvement in certain violent confrontations. While discussing the incidences of mass atrocities committed in Nigeria, Jibrin Ibrahim, in one of his editorial columns, retorted that the violence between Fulani pastoralists and farmers has been on for more than five decades under the backdrop of the ending of the burti system of cattle movement which ensured that Fulani pastoralists move their herds without destroying crops. This led to uncontrolled cattle grazing that ultimately led to the destruction of cultivated plants.

The level of violence perpetrated by criminal elements within the Fulani pastoralists group is felt across the country. From the invasion of farmlands in major farming settlements in Nigeria to random and targeted kidnapping of individuals along with the interstate networks across the country, the scourge of Fulani herdsmen remains a security threat to Nigeria. Many of these nomads move about in the cattle company, armed with varying degrees of weapons. Some are even known to arm themselves with sophisticated weapons, the kinds found in the hands of the country's security forces. Many a time, the attacks by these elements are coordinated in such a way as to catch their targets unaware. They operate at times when their potential victims are at their most vulnerable points, such as midnights. The manner of killing does not only target men but is often extended to defenceless and helpless women and children.

While Emeagwali quickly interjected by appreciating the analysis done by Jibrin, she laid bare a caveat that has always been in some people's minds: the possibility of the criminal elements among the Fulani pastoralists linking up with the dreaded Boko haram insurgents that have continued to invoke mayhem on the country. The

pointer raised here is very important if we look at the similarities of the personnel involved in the two parallel engagements. They are drawn from the multitudes of northerners who have deep knowledge of the uninhabited terrains of the country. Bearing this in mind, it becomes easy for the strategists of the dreaded sect to recruit from these strata to exploit their knowledge for their violent ambitions. Emeagwali's interjection may seem like setting a soft landing for the Fulani pastoralists' apologists, but one cannot simply cast aspersions based on random thoughts or musings from some quarters.

Within the discourse context, aspects of the article tend to position the Fulani pastoralists as victims forced to reciprocate the ills meted on them by the leaderships of communities where they have clashed with farmers. While responding to Michael O. Afolayan's response indicating innocent ignorance of the violence perpetrated by Fulani herdsmen across Nigeria, I laid bare what I felt was the truth from my perspective. The Fulani herdsmen, in my opinion, have perfected the act of liaising with certain intellectual media personalities that tend to present the former as victims rather than designate them as the bloodthirsty figures they are. Surprisingly, Emeagwali's conviction did not tow the same line. She seemed not to accept the ethnic profiling that presents Fulani herdsmen as a group of bloodthirsty and violent men. Her rationalization is worth magnifying; she sought certain clarifications which I believe are valid. Do we ascribe the violent nature of Fulani pastoralists to genetic factors, or is it a factor linked to sociological, psychological or militant reactions to a problem created because of environmental stress?[52] Perhaps, we may also trace it to economic issues resulting from the expansionary moves to cater to the ever-increasing cattle.

Going further, Emeagwali noted that the Fulani pastoralists' expertise in animal husbandry accords them a high level of relevance, and these are parts of the feats that should be appreciated rather than trying to criminalize the totality of their activities because of the actions of a few corrupt and criminally-minded ones. Anyone conversant with Nigeria's agricultural sector cannot downplay the importance of farming to the economy. On this note, Emeagwali also affirmed that it is equally important to vigorously protect the rights and livelihood of the farmers. In essence, Emeagwali pointed out the Fulani pastoralists' and farmers' complementary importance and interdependence. She opined that this could be strengthened with relevant regulations and policies and a continuous dialogue between the two. However, one factor that Emeagwali failed to consider is that the problems between the Fulani pastoralists and the farmers are always ignited by the former.

Most farmers in Nigeria do not barricade their farmlands, making it easy for wandering cattle herds to stray into such farms and embark on the mass destruction of crops. Then farmers of host communities try to resist the destructive activities of the

52. Gloria Emeagwali, "Excerpts from the Discussion, Mass Atrocities in Nigeria," *USA-Africa Dialogue Series*, 2019, https://groups.google.com/g/usaafricadialogue/c/OM24q-SSywc/m/TtAt3UpQBQAJ.

Fulani pastoralists, and the marauders become violent, leading to attacks against the hosts. It is worth noting that these actions are often carried out with the aid of foreign Fulani mercenaries from neighboring countries like Niger, Chad, and Mali. What manner of response does one expect from a farmer who reaches his farmland to witness the destruction of his livelihood by seeming straying herds of cattle? The pastoralist, on their part, is made up of uneducated nomads who do not seem to rationalize the negative effects of their actions. To them, every lush green plant is food for their cattle, not minding whether such plants are the exclusive economic properties of others. Such an unfortunate situation needs an unsentimental view before it can be efficiently tackled.

One other aspect that I believe Emeagwali did not also look at is that the movement of cattle within the forests and jungles has given room for kidnappers and terrorists to perpetrate their evil acts. In essence, the Fulani pastoralist culture has become a tool used by bandits and criminals from the same Fulani extraction to commit heinous crimes against farmers and society. Eyewitness accounts of kidnappings on various interstate roads in Nigeria point to the complicity or involvement of shabbily dressed and vicious-looking individuals who share very close similarities with the Fulani herdsmen. During Muhammadu Buhari's administration, the federal government did not help matters too when, at a time of high-level complaints against the criminal activities of the herdsmen, it sought to introduce a grazing scheme that involved partitioning lands from all states for herdsmen to graze their cattle.

Also, Emeagwali failed to note that the demonization of the name Fulani or Fulani herdsmen was made possible by the actions of the Fulani themselves. Rather than come out to talk against the criminal activities, of which accusing fingers are pointed at the Fulani pastoralists, we see ethnic bigotry and a case of hubris among the members of a particular group. The dominant attitude among the Fulani is characterized by active support, justification, and a subtext acquiescence of the criminal activities of certain elements on the backdrop of the latter sharing ethnic affinity with the former. I do not want to think these points are lost on Emeagwali either. There is an urgent need for the federal government to summon the political will to find a permanent resolution to the clashes between Fulani herdsmen and their hosts in various communities to prevent further escalation that may inadvertently lead to the loss of lives and properties.

The implication of the criminalization of the activities of Fulani pastoralists is a ticking time bomb. Many believe the country's leadership is not taking enough measures to ensure criminal activities are brought to book. To make matters worse, the security agencies expected to tackle this situation are often overwhelmed by the sophisticated weapons that several arrested Fulani herdsmen are caught with. Sometimes, they catch some of them in possession of military fatigues, which they use to disguise as highway security personnel to perpetrate their evil acts. Such acts make it difficult to distinguish between authentic highway security personnel and potential

kidnappers and criminals. The destruction of people's farmlands and the kidnapping and invasion of communities by suspected marauders who seem not to be distinguishable from Fulani herdsmen continue to pitch communities and ethnic groups against the Fulani people. And it does not get better when we factor in the fact that the country's president is of Fulani extraction. Whether Emeagwali's assertion is right remains to be seen, but evidence suggests that Fulani herdsmen are complicit in a lot of communal violence and kidnappings in Nigeria. While regions such as the southwest have developed security initiatives in the form of state police to tackle the never-ending menace of Fulani pastoralists, other regions are yet to have any worthwhile projects in place to tackle this, meaning that the end is not yet in sight.

EMEAGWALI: THE CHALLENGE OF AFRICAN DEVELOPMENT

Many scholars have written extensively on the challenge of African development and proffering solutions needed for the continent to move forward. Emeagwali traced the challenge of African development to African countries' lack of financial independence. Most African countries do not have the total say on economic development within their territories as they often identify with the plans and programs mapped out by foreign countries and institutions such as the World Bank and the International Monetary Fund (IMF). The implication of implementing these policies is that they do not bring much-needed development to these African countries. Some of these plans, on implementation, further deteriorate the current economic crises. The interventions of these world institutions in developing African countries often seem detached from the realities. Studies have shown that home-grown solutions are needed to drive African countries. The reality is that world interventions come with harsh economic conditions, described as prerequisites for economic development.

In an essay titled "The Neo-Liberal Agenda and the IMF/World Bank Structural Adjustment Programs with Reference to Africa," Emeagwali examines the economic austerities that come with implementing IMF/ World Bank's policies for economic development in African countries.[53] She contends that African countries were being coerced to implement Structural Adjustments Programs (SAPs) to save their economies from ruin. However, the results of these programs hinder growth and national development and place African citizens under severe hardships. Implementing some of these economic reforms requires African governments to devalue their national currencies, deregulate prices, and auction infrastructures to protect their economies.[54] Emeagwali argues that these reforms contribute to increased unemployment and poverty in African countries. In the essay, the historian questions the motives

53. Gloria Emeagwali, "The Neo-Liberal Agenda and the IMF/World Bank Structural Adjustment Programs with Reference to Africa," *Critical Perspectives on Neoliberal Globalization, Development and Education in Africa and Asia*, ed. Dip Kapoor (Netherland: Brill, 2011), 1–13.

54. Emeagwali, "The Neo-Liberal Agenda."

behind these economic reforms in Africa initiated by world interventions. In the long run, she notes that these economic reforms reduce the autonomy of African countries as the task of strengthening African economies is left in the hands of foreign investors. Emeagwali was not the only historian wary of the World Bank/IMF economic reforms on African countries; Perkins posits that these institutions sometimes deliberately contribute to the indebtedness of African countries, especially those under dictatorship.[55] Perkins also postulates that world economic institutions often encourage third-world countries to take loans to salvage their economic crisis, further contributing to a spike in debt revenues.

Emeagwali foregrounds instances where international economic reforms have ruined African economies. During the economic crisis in Somalia, the IMF forced the government to devalue its currencies, among other harsh economic measures, to wriggle out of its predicament. In the long run, however, these reforms spelled more economic calamity in Somalia.[56] There was an immediate spike in the process of goods and services after the Somali currency was devalued; there was similarly an increase in unemployment and urban population. The Somali economy was not salvaged despite these reforms. A similar scenario also played out in South Africa, where the lending practices of the IMF became questionable. The IMF lent the South African government two billion dollars during the apartheid regime; however, most of the proposed economic reforms included the retention of the apartheid-era financial organizations and the privatization of South African public enterprises.[57] There were also arguments on how SAP contributed to Nigeria's economic ruin. In the early 1980s, Nigeria suffered the worst economic conditions caused by corruption and poor economic planning of Shehu Shagari's government. On hijacking power, the Buhari and Idiagbon-led administration tried to salvage the economy by implementing creative policies that would not tally with the IMF reforms. However, with the coming to power of Ibrahim Babangida, economic reforms in the country looked like the IMF policies. Despite the widespread criticisms that Nigeria should not adopt the IMF economic policies, the Babangida-led administration did the exact opposite. Economic analysts have posited that adopting the IMF policies for economic reforms in Nigeria caused the rapid deterioration of the nation's economy, especially as sectors such as education, health, and social services were grossly affected by these reforms.

A plethora of popular literature criticizes the economic effects of the World Bank and IMF interventions in ailing economies. In his book, *Globalization and its Discontents*, Joseph Stiglitz argued that these financial organizations often contribute to the continuous economic crisis in the countries they are supposedly rescuing from the

55. John Perkins, *Confessions of an Economic Hitman* (Berrett: Koehler Publishers, 2004).
56. Emeagwali, "The Neo-Liberal Agenda."
57. Emeagwali, "The Neo-Liberal Agenda."

wreckage.[58] Using Ethiopia as a case study where IMF reforms dealt a severe blow to economies, he posits that the IMF wanted Ethiopia to break its largest bank and allow Western competitors in its markets as part of the economic reforms.[59] Even when some African countries are aware that the economic reforms recommended by these financial institutions would not ultimately transform their economies, they are usually left with no better options. It could be argued that the World Bank and IMF sometimes capitalize on the desperations of African countries to save their crumbling economies from implementing their economic reforms. Aside from this, some African countries that are quick to adopt these economic reforms without adequate scrutiny do so with the misconception that the outside world has the best solutions to their problems. Despite the many postulations that African countries should be conscious of proposed economic reforms by these financial organizations, this has still not stopped African governments from taking loans and implementing these reforms.

The solutions to economic crises in African countries do not lie in interventions from the World Bank or IMF. African governments need to think about local policies that would drive their economies to progress. There is a need for the adoption of home-grown approaches toward salvaging economies. This lies in the development of local economies. This issue is that African countries rely heavily on Western countries, which is perhaps the reason the latter thinks it can confidently assess African problems. African countries must come to terms with the fact that they must be deliberate about economic growth and development. No one understands the problems of Africa rather than Africans. Thus, in mapping out plans and programs to foster economic development, African governments need to be conscious of the welfare of the people. In this regard, Emeagwali called for a focus on local economies as this is a necessary pathway for progress.[60] She posited that development programs in Africa should consider the citizens' overall welfare. Put differently, the citizens should be the focus of development plans in African countries. Emeagwali posited that African countries need to get on the pathway of development which should be evident in providing such things as clean water, health, education, and the building of local technologies.

Aside from the need for economic development, Emeagwali also identified the leadership crisis in Africa as a major setback for development. She cites the ongoing internal strife in Ethiopia as an example.[61] Ethiopia is witnessing civil unrest that has

58. Joseph Stiglitz and Robert M. Pike, "Globalization and its Discontents," *Canadian Journal of Sociology* 29, no. 2 (2004): 321.

59. Stiglitz and Pike, "Globalization and its Discontents."

60. Gloria Emeagwali, "Supports the Call for Local Technologies," *Liberal Arts Instructional Technology Services*, The University of Texas, https://www.laits.utexas.edu/africa/ads/91.html.

61. Gloria Emeagwali, "Ethiopia on the Brink as Crisis Threatens 'Peace and Stability' of Region—but what has Fueled the Conflict and Criticism of Biden's Response?" *The Conversation*, November 18, 2021, https://theconversation.com/ethiopia-on-the-brink-as-crisis-threatens-peace-and-stability-of-region-but-what-has-fueled-the-conflict-and-criticism-of-bidens-response-171785.

continued to challenge its national development and existence.[62] The crisis in Ethiopia's Tigray region worsens daily—with many deaths and loss of properties, thus, contributing to the country's instability and the Horn of Africa. Despite concerns from international communities to end the humanitarian disaster, the situation has not been much different. The war in the Tigray region resulted from a clash between forces loyal to the Tigray People's Liberation Army (TPLF) and the forces loyal to the Ethiopian army. The Ethiopian army employed brutal force to suppress the rebellion in the region, with the United Nations Human Rights positing that both sides were guilty of war crimes. The Ethiopian government has employed different approaches to capitulate the Tigray region, leading to a severe humanitarian crisis that the world struggles to contend with. As a result of the civil war, famine broke out in the Tigray region, and many lives were lost.

Emeagwali argued that the fighting in the Tigray region is particularly intense as there are concerns about rape cases and starvation among thousands of people.[63] She posited that the cause of the war was the age-long strife between the TPLF-controlled forces and the Ethiopian army. Despite the emergence of President Abiy Ahmed, who won the Nobel Prize for Peace, many efforts have not been made to douse the tensions and political resentment among the Tigray people. The Tigrayans had controlled much of the Ethiopian government in the past and ruled largely by ethnicity; thus, one could understand why they were in continuous strife with the central government after they lost their grip on power and authority. Emeagwali noted that the conflict in Ethiopia would affect the security architecture and economic conditions of countries like Sudan, Kenya, and Eritrea. The influx of refugees from Ethiopia to these countries would also escalate their economic crises. Aside from this, the fact that the Ethiopian government expends all its resources quenching secessionist struggles and the agenda of the Tigrayans could cause the penetration of deadly terrorist groups like Al-Shabab into Ethiopian territories, which the government would find difficult to contain. There were also fears that the internal strife could lead to an all-out civil war, a precarious situation similar to that of Nigeria in its early years of independence, where millions of lives and properties were lost. A civil war in Ethiopia would provoke the division of the countries into various political entities, which would be catastrophic. Emeagwali argued that even though there is a possibility of a civil war in Ethiopia, the African Union (AU) and particularly other African states can force both warring parties to promote peace.[64] The Ethiopian government has implemented harsh measures against the rebellious Tigrayans. Emeagwali argued that a huge step toward resolving the crisis is the need for the Tigrayans to accept the leadership of

62. Daniel Merino, Gemma Ware and Godfred Boafo, "Tigray: The Devastating Toll of Ethiopia's Vicious Year of War—Podcast," *The Conversation*, November 4, 2021, https://theconversation.com/tigray-the-devastating-toll-of-ethiopias-vicious-year-of-war-podcast-171138.

63. Emeagwali, "Ethiopia on the Brink."

64. Emeagwali, "Ethiopia on the Brink."

Figure 16.2. "Africa before or behind us?" Dr. Kazeem Ekeolu. Conversation between two people on whether Africa should be put before or behind us.

Prime Minister Abiy and the Ethiopian government to rethink its stance on the description of the Tigrayan forces as a terrorist organization.

It could be observed that the cause of leadership problems in Africa can be pinpointed as the fear of ethnic dominance. African countries comprised different ethnic groups. Tensions begin to rise when the government in power shows any form of sympathy to an ethnic group over others. This immediately fuels the crisis, and when the issues continue to escalate, it is not long before internal strife occurs. Most African governments, on assuming power begin to identify with ethnic groups, which mostly have the majority of people and often relegate others. Plans and programs usually take the format of ethnicity rather than considering the welfare of all the citizens. The problem with leadership structures in most African countries is that they often neglect that ethnic affiliation is disastrous for national development; thus, the need to represent the totality of the people in governance.

A similar scenario plays out in Nigeria, the most populated African country. There are cases of secessionist agenda because of the perceived ethnic affiliation of the current regime. This is not to say that there were no cases of ethnicity in the previous government before this. It became rampant under President Buhari's administration. The Indigenous People of Biafra (IPOB), led by Mazi Nnamdi Kanu, continued to attack government infrastructures in the country's southeastern part. The Nigerian government, in turn, has often responded with brutal force as instability slowly gathers in the region. The Igbo people still advanced the creation of Biafra, which led to the country's civil war. The failure of the Nigerian government to keep the marauding Fulani herdsmen in check has also contributed to the rising problem of ethnicity in Nigeria. The southwestern part of the country is involved in the struggle to form a break-away state. Ethnic tensions are rising, which are further complicated by the brutal responses from the central government when a nationwide dialogue would have been affected. There are predictions based on the valid assumption that if tensions like this are not finally resolved, another civil war is very likely. The Nigerian government has been charged with making conscious efforts to solve the problem of ethnicities as they affect national development.

CONCLUSION

As this chapter shows, the body of literature generated in Emeagwali's writings on many issues relating to Africa and the pan-African world is worth intellectual attention and serious scholarly recognition. Her focus on issues that touch on challenges, pains and potentials of Africa and the African Diaspora will always generate a loud conversation and cheerlead positive energies in safeguarding the future of the African social and intellectual dialogues.

As a leading female figure, Emeagwali's engagement with social matters and discussions of different phenomena of society exhibit her representation of a versatile scholar who would fit well into many areas of discussion and contextualize things in line with major epochs and themes. Thus, she represents the right adaptation to the previous themes of this book and a prestigious source of engagement.

She remains an exception to the general trend of the public and opinions, being particularly critical and unsentimental in most of her approaches to public matters by providing reasonable and enlightening caveats worthy of changing the trajectories of public opinions. One of the ways she has exhibited this attribute was her refusal to join the general attitude of ethnic profiling that easily tags the Fulani as possible terrorists. Her interjections and insistence on other possibilities in this kind of theme and other thematic preoccupations make her represent the experienced and professional scholars careful not to fall into public opinion pits.

No matter how one tries to be open-minded, especially with matters concerning female rights and themes around them, although it might not be the case in many

instances, there are tendencies to man-explain many of these positions either ignorantly or based on unconscious cultural orientations that might not adequately address the issues dispassionately enough. However, Emeagwali represents a critical interlocutor on women and gender rights in society. She depicts an astute thinker who approaches sensitive issues with the certainty of knowledge born from understanding and meticulous research.

The ability of Emeagwali to connect with African indigenous epistemology and attributes posits her as a Pan-African-minded individual who exhibits the desired Africanist touch among African scholars. She did not just structure the ideas that formulate her positions but created pieces of evidence to substantiate the claims of other Pan-Africanists to foster anti-ethnocentric discussions aimed at redefining the African image and proving that it had never been a place of deprivation without culture, science, history or civilization. As a result, she expects the development of the continent and the utilization of its resources. I hope that her courageous efforts in triggering these conversations on the development of the continent of Africa will continue unchained and unabated.

17

FAROOQ KPEROGI

Two Nigerian Presidents

INTRODUCTION

Criticism, political participation, and public opinions are true tests of democratic parties and practices anywhere in the world. They project the extent to which any country would be ready to allow the expression of fundamental rights accruable to their citizens with the public's interest in mind. On this basis, individuals like Dr. Farooq Kperogi, a social critic, have risen with sharpened scalpels of articulation to dissect social and political issues that touch the existence of the entire citizenry. Nigerian problems are too enormous not to expect such a reaction from the society, so much so that it has almost converted all citizens to critics. Unexplained increases in the cost of living, high unemployment rates, insecurity, corruption, and a load of other social and political issues forming a congress of problems have steered up complaints and public reactions.

The political load-downs from the administration of President Goodluck Ebele Jonathan to the presidency of General Muhammadu Buhari in 2015 have been engaging but increasing momentum from year to year with new developments worthy of pushing critics to put pen on paper. President Goodluck Jonathan's administration and his supposed unpreparedness faced administrative issues, made policies people found unfriendly, and ran the country despite the waves of pressure that emanated from all angles. The top of this criticism was the "Occupy Nigeria" protest in January 2012 after the removal of fuel subsidies and a hike in pump prices. Although the

Figure 17.1. "A Digital Rebel" by Michael Efionayi. Farooq Kperogi and Nigerian Presidential Candidates

government submitted to the pressure of 2012, the momentum continued until his tenure ended.

The "Change Mantra" from the All Progressives Congress, a coalition of some opposing parties, utilized the built momentum from Jonathan's administration as trajectories of their campaign. People bought the mission statement of President Buhari and Pastor Osinbajo, hoping to see a new Nigeria. When the anticipated "Change" administration started, one would have expected it to be close to the yearnings of Nigerians and probably lead to a reduction in the level of criticism. However, it seems things have gotten worse despite routine criticisms.

Kperogi has put himself up as a chronicler in documenting the activities and failures of individual presidents. This is because he has been able to pass opinions and analyses on almost every major political incident that has entered the public domain in the past twelve years. This has made him important in the face of Nigerian political development, and his contributions to political conversations command weight and respect in this regard. To properly appreciate political discussions and developments as well as reactions that follow specific actions of both governments, Kperogi's lens is important to see through many complexities.

Despite the meltdowns that followed President Jonathan's administration, the nation had only been climbing the hills of criticism, attracting more critics than the

previous administration. Kperogi can be seen as a reflection of the citizens' dissatisfaction and the expression of their grievances through a more analytic perspective. The careful examination of political issues positions the peoples' interests and voices in a more articulated way.

The relationship between Kperogi and the public is more evaluative from the social media angle. Kperogi has about 143,000 followers on both Facebook and Twitter. Through these mediums, he has been able to engage people's minds and create avenues for public conversations. His role underscores the influence of social media on the Nigerian political space and the dynamics they bring. One could see the social media development of Kperogi's criticism from the Jonathan administration to Buhari's tenure. Realizing the materiality of social media, he has joined other advocates against tyrannic policies in the disguise of censoring social media usage.[1]

THE EFFECTS OF WEB 2.0 AND SOCIAL MEDIA IN NIGERIA

The mid-2000s brought fame to a new trend in the internet world and the World Wide Web ecosystem. This new form of the World Wide Web and internet services was called Web 2.0 by Darci DiNucci in 1999.[2] The advent of Web 2.0 is more of a conscious discovery of a change in trends, innovations, and inventions than an upgrade or a switch to a newer version of the World Wide Web and the internet. Thus, Web 2.0 was more about how inventions and innovations in the technology space were prioritizing interactive media. Before Web 2.0, the internet and the World Wide Web were rife with an asynchronous communication model where the receiver could not react to messages immediately or communicate with the sender in real time. Interfaces and communication platforms focus on sending information without necessarily prioritizing feedback.

The advent of Web 2.0—with its interactive feature—significantly shifted how humans communicated and interacted. Social media platforms such as Facebook, Twitter, Instagram, WhatsApp, and the recent sensation, TikTok, are all part of Web 2.0. While some of these platforms arrived earlier than others, one noticeable thing is that some of them, such as Facebook, have stayed relevant for decades because their decision-makers understand the fundamental rule of relevance—anticipating, actively seeking out, and satisfying user needs. Social media platforms have largely evolved to focus on making interactions quick, real, synchronous, and real-time. Today, social media platforms have become an integral part of our lives, so much so that they now moderate political discourses and ads, and two of the most popular platforms—Facebook and Twitter—were powerful enough to ban the then President of the United

1. Farooq Kperogi, *Digital Dissidence and Social Media Censorship in Africa* (Oxfordshire: Taylor & Francis, 2022).

2. Cristina Aced Toledano, "Web 2.0: The Origin of the Word that has Changed the way we Understand Public Relations," Barcelona International Conference, July 2–3, 2013.

States, Donald Trump, at the height of the Covid-19 socio-politico-health crisis, with Twitter banning him permanently from the platform.[3]

Social media platforms were an instant hit in Nigeria for several reasons. It must be noted that before Web 2.0, Nigeria had become quite famous due to some citizens' fraudulent use of the email platform. As with other technological innovations, social media platforms received wide acceptance and use in Nigeria, which they continue to enjoy today. Nigeria has the most time on social media of all African countries, only second to the Philippines in the world![4] And if those were not jaw-dropping statistics, consider that in gauging the acceptance and use of social media based on the number of users per country, Nigeria still ranks as Africa's first and the world's 8th.[5] Therefore, it is not surprising that Nigeria has drawn the attention of the CEOs and founders of some of the biggest social media platforms, from Facebook's Mark Zuckerberg to Twitter's former CEO, Jack Dorsey. They recognize the potential weight of Nigeria in the social media world.

The popularity, acceptance, and use of social media platforms in Nigeria gave rise to concerns, especially in the quarters of the institution that once held the sole rights to public information—the Press. Social media platforms held more than the promise of networking and reaching friends and family members in real time. They were also a means of sharing and exchanging information, and gradually, people began to share and exchange non-personal information via these platformsnews stories, opinions, pictorial news stories, video coverage of events and happenings, and the list goes on. With time, social media platforms became a means of sharing and exchanging information and having discourses, and the attention gradually shifted from the traditional media—national dailies and radio and TV stations.

While these platforms did not fully lose the attention they had from people, it was obvious that social media platforms were becoming the go-to platforms for discussions—like the cafés of the French renaissance period. Change, or what some people call adaptability, is the only constant thing. Thus, media houses, press organizations, and journalistic outfits learned to metamorphose, shift shape, and conform to the new reality brought upon humanity by the advent of social media platforms.

---

3. Twitter, "Permanent Suspension of @realDonaldTrump," *Twitter*, January 8, 2021, https://blog.twitter.com/en_us/topics/company/2020/suspension.

4. Victor Oluwole, "Nigerians Spend the most Time on Social Media in Africa, Global Report Finds," *Business Insider*, May 22, 2021, https://africa.businessinsider.com/local/lifestyle/nigerians-spend-the-most-time-on-social-media-in-africa-global-report-finds/037h2hm#:~:text=The%20Social%20Flagship%20Report%20April,3%3A32)%20and%20Ghana.

5. Statista Research Department, "Social Network users in Leading Markets 2026," *Statista,* April 28, 2022, https://www.statista.com/statistics/278341/number-of-social-network-users-in-selected-countries/#:~:text=China%20is%20the%20biggest%20social,million%20current%20social%20media%20users.

THE RISE IN SOCIAL COMMENTARY AND NICHE CREATION ON SOCIAL MEDIA PLATFORMS

At the heart of one of the most significant changes that social media platforms had on the world was a dynamic shift in the style and method of social commentary. Before Web 2.0, interactive media and social media platforms, social commentaries, and engagements were never without the involvement of the Fourth Estate. It was either that people had to send in their comments to newspapers, call in on the radio and TV shows, or become newspaper columnists, if they had the resources, to make their thoughts and comments known. However, social media platforms changed that reality, making social commentary on what should be largely in the hands of the people.

Also, the aims of social media platforms are not uniform; the plan and design differ even in the use and engagement strategy. Nonetheless, these platforms have become important to all aspects of our lives. The Nigerian living in Ibadan can access the uproar in the United States in real-time. The Puerto Rican can access information on the Russo-Ukrainian war without leaving the comfort of their room.

Meta and Twitter, among other big-tech companies, committed huge resources to ensure that social media platforms are sources of verifiable and real-time news, especially from the COVID-19 pandemic era in 2020. Thus, while it is true that these social media platforms are still rife with unverified, false, and misleading news, media houses, government agencies and organizations, and journalistic outfits have come to recognize them as an integral and influential part of the workings of countries and their citizens. This is evident in how some governments have attempted to clamp down on the use of social media platforms, as in the case of the infamous seven-month Twitter ban by the Nigerian government.[6] There was also the round of questioning that Meta CEO Mark Zuckerberg went through at the United States Congress and Senate on the safety of the Facebook platform for its users.[7]

Social commentators, critics, and political analysts have learned to flow with the tide and blend with the times. Their audience has evolved from solely relying on traditional media to prioritizing new (social) media and supplementing it with traditional media. Media houses have also started registering their footprints, tracing their readers to where they are—social media platforms. This does not mean that traditional media have gone extinct. The sale of newspapers continued massively and continues till today. Radio and TV stations still have active listeners, watchers, and ardent followers. Most content consumers have switched to easier-to-consume and stand-

6. Nimi Princewill and Stephanie Busari, "Nigeria Bans Twitter after Company Deletes President Buhari's Tweet," *CNN*, June 5, 2021, https://edition.cnn.com/2021/06/04/africa/nigeria-suspends-twitter-operations-intl/index.html.

7. The New York Times, "Mark Zuckerberg Testimony: Senators Question Facebook's Commitment to Privacy," *The New York Times*, April 10, 2018, https://www.nytimes.com/2018/04/10/us/politics/mark-zuckerberg-testimony.html.

alone content pieces on social media platforms. Yes, it is social media platforms that have made this shift possible. They have not only made it possible, but they have also made it sustainable. This chapter will focus on the digital presence and social commentary of Kperogi on Facebook

Facebook's evolution is a big contributor to the individualized social commentary economy. When Facebook provided users with the ability to create content on walls, the creator economy on the platform boomed. Soon, followership was not restricted to companies or celebrities alone. Individual creators could amass followers based on the strength and the value of the content they pushed out. People started to take the platform seriously, with varying forms of content—entertainment, op-eds, weekly columns, factsheets, and political commentary, among others. Thus, relatable value became the single most important ingredient for gaining followers, so much so that individual creators began to amass followers and engagement, which recognized companies and corporate entities still struggle to do to date.

Social media platforms turned content creation and social commentary into easily accessible niches for the content consumer and the content creator. Content on social media platforms is reader-focused and reader-centered. There is a content avalanche where creators quickly recognize that they are not the only content suppliers; thus, the reader is king. In this vein, content creators and social commentators on social media have learned to prioritize readers and their needs in the content creation process. The focus is now more on trying to tailor content toward reader behaviors.

A 2014 Reuters Institute for the Study of Journalism report noticed a change in content consumption patterns influenced by social media and smartphones.[8] One of the most interesting discoveries in this report that somehow predicted the future is that individual journalists became an important consideration for why people would follow and consume news from some brands.[9] Reader behaviors on social media, such as wanting to read in one's comfort and in real-time without having to wait on the newspaper vendor or going out to get newspapers or radio and TV intervals, wanting to read in larger, well-spaced fonts, as against the tiny and fused fonts used by newspapers, among other things—have largely contributed to the new dynamic in news consumption and sourcing. These consumer behaviors led to the migration of journalists and media houses to social media platforms, including microblogging platforms like Twitter. The Facebook and Twitter feeds are rife with news from individuals and media houses. As a collaboration, media houses allow their staffers to front their brand to kick back brand loyalty and follow their company.

---

8. Nick Newman and David Levy, eds. "Reuters Institute Digital News Report, 2014: Tracking the Future of News," *Reuters Institute*, https://reutersinstitute.politics.ox.ac.uk/sites/default/files/research/files/Reuters%2520Institute%2520Digital%2520News%2520Report%25202014.pdf.

9. Newman and Levy, "Reuters Institute Digital News Report."

Figure 17.2. "Obasanjo and Buhari Dragging Nigeria" by Dr. Kazeem Ekeolu. A struggle between two ex-presidents, Obasanjo and Buhari.

Another thing of note is how these social media platforms have differing usage. Twitter is a microblogging platform where short, punchy, breaking, or sensational news trend quickly. Additionally, individuals could give in-depth analysis via Twitter threads and Twitter spaces. However, Twitter is not the go-to platform for in-depth analysis and discourses. When it comes to that, Facebook is the favorite platform for some reasons. Firstly, Facebook favors long-form content. Secondly, it makes it quick-

er and easier for followers to locate content by their most-engaged creators. Thirdly, it drives the highest traffic to websites of all social media platforms.[10] As a result, long-form content creators can extract valuable excerpts and share them on Facebook while directing their followership base and target audience to read the full piece on their website.

The reality this brought for individual creators is that they do not need to seek acceptance as columnists in newspapers or with major media houses before they can significantly grow their followership base or become a force to be reckoned with in social and political discourses. This gave prominence to online columns and news stories, the category of social commentary to which Kperogi belongs.

A LOOK INTO THE CHARACTERISTICS OF SOCIAL COMMENTARY BY SOCIAL MEDIA USERS

How have the likes of Kperogi gained authority and maintained influence on social media platforms, doing what they would have done solely on the pages of a newspaper or at a radio station ten or fifteen years ago? Social commentary on social media did not start during the earliest years of the creation of social media platforms. People's initial use of social media did not tend toward political or social commentary. The platforms were strictly used to engage and relate interactively. Thus, socio-political commentators and critics like Kperogi had a robust journalistic careers before migrating to Facebook. He was a one-time newspaper columnist at *The Daily Trust* and is currently a columnist at *The Nigerian Tribune* and *The People's Gazette*.

Kperogi's socio-political commentary did not start yesterday; neither did it start the day he joined social media. However, a deep dive into Facebook archives will reveal the pattern of Kperogi's Facebook use in his earliest days on the platform. Kperogi has no Facebook footprint before 2009. So, it is safe to say that he either joined the platform in 2009 or was a passive user and observer before 2009. In 2009, specifically on December 10, 2009, Kperogi's wall had what could be termed his earliest attempt at socio-political commentary on social media. It is a simple, one-line post sharing a link to his weekly column in *The People's Daily*—a piece that has been lost to the contingencies of *The People's Daily* transitioning to a new website.[11]

Kperogi's earliest use of social media platforms for socio-political commentary is an apt representation of how social media platforms were used years ago for content sharing. Individuals and brands focused on directing readers to an external link. As seen from Kperogi's December 10, 2009 post, such a strategy called for little engagement in reactions and comments. That means social commentators and critics had

10. Kyle Byers, "What 3.25 Billion Website Visits Tell us about the Internet's Top Traffic Sources," *Growth Badger*, April 5, 2020, https://growthbadger.com/traffic-study/.

11. The People's Daily, http://www.peoplesdailyng.com. The previous website was http://www.peoplesdaily-online.com.

poor insights into reader behaviors and how to tailor their subsequent content to match the readers' yearnings.

In 2009, a Facebook group named "Farooq Kperogi Fan Club" was created by M. D. Aminu; however, Kperogi's relationship with the group was only noticed in 2011 when he started to share his weekly column with the group. This greatly impacted Kperogi's Facebook presence as it gave him direct access to people who were so interested in his writings that they willingly joined a Facebook group to read, discuss, and comment on his weekly column. By 2022, that Facebook group had close to 23,000 members. In 2010, Kperogi launched his blog—Notes from Atlanta, and the frequency of his Facebook posts increased significantly. However, a detour was seen that year, toward 2013, as Kperogi's blog posts focus on English grammar and communication.

By 2015, the consumption behaviors of Facebook users had changed, and social commentators and critics knew well to adapt to the change. Facebook had started favoring long-form thought pieces, which were not lost on Kperogi. His content was beginning to generate significant engagements at this point, and so did his followership base grow. Today, Kperogi is not only a Professor of Journalism and Emerging Media in theory but also one in practice, looking at how he has successfully built his brand on Facebook and Twitter, with over 122,000 followers on Facebook[12] and over 94,000 on Twitter.[13]

People follow social commentators and critics on social media for various reasons. One is that these social commentators and critics guarantee the people a continual supply of valuable socio-political content. The content helps people stay abreast of socio-political trends in the country. Some people solely rely on the content of these socio-political commentators and critics, while others only supplement their ardent followership of news stories and national trends with analysis by social critics and commentators. This is similar to how people ardently follow news stories and trends as announced by radio and TV stations and yet, listen to special radio or TV shows dedicated to analyzing recent happenings in the country. While there is a similarity between why people follow social commentators and critics; and why others ardently follow socio-political radio programs, TV shows, and newspaper columns, there is a disparity between the practices of social commentary on social media and social commentary in traditional media. Facebook allows users to create posts of up to 63,206 characters.[14] That is between 8000 to 15,000 words. Although Facebook is amply generous with the liberty given to users to create long-form content, Facebook posts are often bite-sized and highly optimized to attract and retain readers—hardly numbering up to 10 paragraphs.

---

12. Facebook, "Farooq Kperogi," *Facebook*, https://web.facebook.com/farooqkperogi.
13. Twitter, "Farooq Kperogi," *Twitter*, https://twitter.com/farooqkperogi.
14. Jacqueline Zote, "How Long should Social Posts be? Try this Socia Media Character Counter," *Sprout Social*, August 25, 2021, https://sproutsocial.com/insights/social-media-character-counter/.

Furthermore, social commentary on social media allows for real-time comments and analysis. Readers can reply to posts, sewing another long thread of arguments and counter-arguments in the comment section on social media platforms. This makes it easier to engage commentators. Commentators fond of replying to their readers or giving them attention are rewarded with more followers, shares, retweets, and likes, among many other reactions.

Facebook, for one, is a social media platform that allows readers to express their reactions to posts, not only through comments but by choice of reaction buttons. In February 2016, Facebook made it possible for users to react to posts using a like, love, wow, sad, angry, or care button (the care button was introduced at the height of the Covid-19 pandemic in 2020).[15] The power of these Facebook reactions is that one can easily gauge the level of reception meted out to one's post based on the reactions. And while the reactions might be somewhat skewed disproportionately, effective use of the sad, angry, or caring reaction will quickly tell how readers feel toward a post without necessarily visiting the comment section to read views. The ability to gauge public perception through Facebook reactions also helps social commentators and critics understand how their message has been received, what their next post should be on, what the people think of current happenings, and what angle they should approach the current happenings.

Another good thing that emanates from social media for social commentary is that the social commentator can quickly tell the reception level of their writing style and format, thus knowing when to tweak their style and format to meet audience needs. A case in point is Kperogi, who evolved in his use of the Facebook platform for social commentary from mere sharing a link with users, to creating short-form pieces, to creating long-form pieces. In the evolution process, Kperogi found that his audience engaged in his antagonistic analysis of happenings more than in his other content pieces, and he has focused on that ever since, amassing a large following in the process. It is called defining your brand. He has defined his brand in that form and created a brand perception in the audience's minds so that when people think of expository antagonistic pieces, the name that comes to mind is Kperogi.

Like Kperogi, another Nigerian social commentator and critic who uses Facebook to share socio-political views is Lasisi Olagunju, an Editor at *The Nigerian Tribune* whose "Monday Lines" column generates significant traction and engagement on Facebook.[16] Olagunju also uses the platform-focused content-sharing method that does not involve directing readers to an external link. Social commentary by analysts and commentators using social media has some distinct characteristics, especially in style and format. While it is true that each analyst and commentator has a language

15. Yasmeen Abutaleb and Arathy S. Nair, "'Wow': Facebook Launches 'Reactions' Worldwide," *Reuters*, February 24, 2016, https://www.reuters.com/article/us-facebook-reactions-idUSKCN0VX1L7.

16. Facebook, "Lasisi Olagunju," *Facebook*, https://web.facebook.com/lasisi.olagunju.

choice and use that defines their brand and distinguishes them from others, it sometimes also contributes to why such analysts and commentators have a large following.

AN OVERVIEW OF FAROOQ KPEROGI'S INFLUENCE ON SOCIAL MEDIA

Kperogi is a Nigerian socio-political commentator who has successfully built his followership base on the two most-used social media platforms for socio-political discussions—Facebook and Twitter. As noted earlier, he has over 300,000 followers on both platforms, and Kperogi is not a mainstream journalist, as it were. Aside from being a Professor of Journalism and Emerging Media, his only journalism career is being a columnist at media and news houses. Kperogi's story is worthy of study because he is one of the social media's most influential Nigerian socio-political commentators. His Facebook posts and tweets generate engagements in their thousands—reactions, comments, shares, and retweets. He is also one of the most followed journalism and media-related individuals on the two social media platforms, especially in journalism.

Influence is not necessarily full acceptance or absence of dissenting voices or antagonists. Kperogi's social media encounters aptly prove this. He is a social commentator and critic with positive and negative reactions to his posts. An interesting dynamic in the reactions to his posts, which we will consider extensively in another sub-chapter, is how there is a shift in the type of reaction that readers give to Kperogi's posts based on whether or not the post gorges their bias. This inherently shows how human bias forms the larger part of the basis for human reactions.

FAROOQ KPEROGI ON GOODLUCK JONATHAN

Kperogi's earliest writing centers on former president Goodluck Ebele Jonathan surfaced on April 16, 2010, when Jonathan was Nigeria's Acting President.[17] The piece, "Dr. Goodluck Jonathan, that was Embarrassing!" was Kperogi's political commentary on then Acting President Goodluck Jonathan's journey to the United States for the Nuclear Summit of April 2010. Kperogi's piece on this event—and his subsequent pieces on Goodluck Jonathan and his tenure—beam the headlights on the dynamics of the Musa Yar'Adua administration and how Jonathan, who was previously a behind-the-scenes actor in the administration, suddenly came to the limelight and had responsibilities thrust on him due to Yar'Adua's ailing health and the need for a prolonged medical trip. Clichéd as it may seem, the first impression, as they say, truly matters, and in the case of Kperogi and his views on Goodluck Jonathan, the first

17. Farooq A. Kperogi, "Dr. Goodluck Jonathan, that was Embarrassing!" *Notes from Atlanta,* April 16, 2010, https://www.farooqkperogi.com/2010/04/dr-goodluck-jonathan-that-was.html.

impression, spoken of without mincing words in his first piece on the former president, truly mattered.

Kperogi's criticism of Goodluck Jonathan's first outing as Nigeria's Acting President was his lack of coherence, composure and ignorance of Nigeria's foreign policy. There was also Jonathan's oversimplification of the situation in Nigeria, which demonstrated his lack of clarity on the current happenings in the country—a case of the Acting President living in his crafted Utopian Nigeria, devoid of reality. In the piece, Kperogi laments the ill-preparation of the Acting President for the Nuclear Summit.

This piece is an apt representation of the dynamics of power in Nigeria compared to other countries. Nigeria (with a Hofstede's score of 80) is a country with a high power distance compared to Western countries such as the United States (with a Hofstede's score of 40), the United Kingdom (with a Hofstede's score of 35), and Canada (with a Hofstede's score of 39).[18] The interpretation of a high power distance is that power is significantly skewed in all sectors of the Nigerian state and even at all stages, so much so that the President does not see the Vice-President as his co-pilot but as a subordinate, often a ceremonial one. Thus, if there is no health or other reason for the President or Governor to be away from the office, the average Vice-President or Deputy Governor in any Nigerian government would be almost unknown to the people, with little to no roles to perform in that government. That was the case with Goodluck Jonathan until he was suddenly trusted with the mandate to lead the country, no thanks to Musa Yar'Adua's ill health.

At this period, Kperogi had not started to tap into the real-time interactive power of Web 2.0. Thus, his routine was to publish his column in newspapers and on news websites online, receive comments and reactions via email, and respond to such comments and reactions in a subsequent column—the traditional columnist. In later publications, dated April 24, 2010,[19] and May 16, 2010,[20] Kperogi battles a barrage of criticisms and comments for his first-ever piece on Goodluck Jonathan, to which the social commentator was prepared and to which he replied. Those three pieces point to some undeniable truths: Kperogi's criticism of Jonathan, especially for his cluelessness about the most mundane news stories and details that the everyday Nigerian knows is not poor journalistic action. It was needed. However, some would question the tone of voice, especially how harsh it was.

There is also the grossly incredulous accommodation of political gaffes and must-not-happens by the populace, an accommodation glaringly fueled by bias. Thus,

---

18. Hofstede Insights, "Country Comparison: Canada, Nigeria, the United Kingdom, and the United States," *Hofstede Insights*, June 21, 2021, https://www.hofstede-insights.com/country-comparison/canada,nigeria,the-uk,the-usa/.

19. Farooq A. Kperogi, "Jonathan's Embarrassing U.S. Visit: A Response to Critics," *Notes from Atlanta*, April 24, 2010, https://www.farooqkperogi.com/2010/04/jonathans-embarrassing-us-visit.html.

20. Farooq A. Kperogi, "Re: Dr. Goodluck Jonathan, that was Embarrassing!" *Notes from Atlanta*, May 16, 2010, https://www.farooqkperogi.com/2010/05/re-dr-goodluck-jonathan-that-was.html.

staunch supporters of the then Acting President, Goodluck Jonathan, soaked in religious and ethnic bias, never reconciled the truthfulness of Kperogi's outcry with the reality. And Kperogi aptly captures that in the statement below:

> Jonathan's problem during his visit here wasn't merely one of avoidably appalling grammar and unmentionable protocol blunders; it was also one of a disturbing deficiency of substance in his speeches and interviews. That anybody would excuse, tolerate, and even celebrate this presidential mediocrity is disturbing, to say the least. I only hope we will democratise this new-found toleration for presidential mediocrity and extend it to every subsequent occupant of Aso Rock irrespective of geographic and ethnic origins.[21]

Over the years, as we would soon see by extrapolating Kperogi's consistent sociopolitical commentaries, the average Nigerian, educated or not, reacts based on their fundamental bias. The difference is that while the supposedly educated might take longer to burst uncontrollably, first masking their reactions in carefully picked words, the uneducated quickly demonstrate how far gone they are in their loss of reason to bias. But soon enough, if you engage the supposedly educated for long enough, their bias comes to the surface, towering even above their education, logic, and reasoning.

It is surprising that many people, as evidenced in the emails Kperogi published, echo his summation, whether they positively agree with him or not. So, it is not a matter of these people not seeing the same things Kperogi lamented about in any piece; they verbally attacked him about it. In this case, they saw it but did not attach as much value as Kperogi did to political gaffes such as that. Or, they attach as much value but do not care as they have biased support and unquestioned loyalty for the then Acting President. This mentality, one where people know what is right or wrong but deliberately choose to jeopardize reasoning or truthfulness, sacrificing them on the altar of bias, is one of the strongest forces against Nigeria's unification, progress, and development as a state. Thus, people are content to have an incompetent, clueless, dissociated president so long as they have no personal issues with him or are direct or indirect beneficiaries of his government. Sharing the same ethnic roots or religious affiliations with the said leader may also be a reason to have closed eyes to gross incompetence.

Kperogi's criticism of the Goodluck Jonathan government did not wane, even as Jonathan was sworn in as Nigeria's President on May 6, 2010, following the demise of former President Umaru Musa Yar'Adua.[22] If anything, the criticisms became stronger and more consistent, positioning Kperogi as one of the most vocal critics of the Jonathan government. Kperogi wrote on the most important problems that bedeviled the

---

21. Kperogi, "Jonathan's Embarrassing U.S. Visit."
22. David Smith, "Goodluck Jonathan Sworn in as Nigerian President," *The Guardian*, May 6, 2010.

Goodluck Jonathan administration, and the most mundane things were not left out. One such mundane thing is the show of shame that became of Nigeria's then-First Lady, Patience Jonathan. Mrs. Patience Jonathan became increasingly popular for her unscrupulous and disgracing comments regarding national issues. As the United States media made sport by constantly airing issues of President Trump's media gaffes, having utmost fun and never running out of content, the Nigerian media made sport of Patience Jonathan. It was a terrible and unprecedented era! It was the first time a First Lady would be so out in the people's faces.

On that, Kperogi wrote his "Patience Jonathan's Peculiar Grammar,"[23] dated March 19, 2021. Patience Jonathan was one of the strongest forces during Goodluck Jonathan's election campaign, which led to his victory against arch-rival, Muhammadu Buhari of the then Congress for Progressive Change (CPC).[24] However, her active involvement came at a heavy price for the Nigerian government and citizens, as she constantly committed inexcusable grammatical blunders that made the country the butt of jokes within and outside the Nigerian territory. This was also an opportunity for staunch Jonathan critics like Kperogi to ax down the then President and First Lady, which he did in his articles. It is beyond surprising that there was no system in place to help the then-First Lady coherently communicate or that she merely did not consider her office important enough to merit some efforts on her part to coherently communicate with the public. And if that were the case, why did she continually have outings, far more than the average First Lady is known to have?

On serious and significant issues that bedeviled the Nigerian state during the governance of Goodluck Ebele Jonathan, Kperogi was equally vocal. From the killings in Jos to the fuel scarcity and subsidy removal that rocked Goodluck Jonathan's tenure, Kperogi waxed more influential. One proof of his becoming brazen and influential in his approach to his commentaries and criticisms was the October 22, 2011 piece titled, "Fuel Subsidy Removal: Time to "Occupy" Nigeria.[25] This piece, one of the most powerful Kperogi has ever written, played its part in the Occupy Nigeria protest of January 2012, a nationwide protest against the removal of fuel subsidies, with reported deaths.[26]

The Occupy Nigeria protest happened about three months after Kperogi's piece. In this piece, Kperogi alludes to the worldwide Occupy protest as a means of raising the Nigerian populace's consciousness to see the need for what he believed must be done. In the United States and some other countries, numbering up to 100, the people were

23. Farooq A. Kperogi, "Patience Jonathan's Peculiar Grammar, *Notes from Atlanta*, March 19, 2011, https://www.farooqkperogi.com/2011/03/patience-jonathans-peculiar-grammar.html.

24. Reuters, "Table-Nigerian Presidential Election Results," *Reuters*, April 18, 2011. https://www.reuters.com/article/nigeria-elections-results-idAFLDE73G05B20110418.

25. Farooq A. Kperogi, "Fuel Subsidy Removal: Time to "Occupy" Nigeria!" *Notes from Atlanta*, October 22, 2011, https://www.farooqkperogi.com/2011/10/fuel-subsidy-removal-time-to-occupy.html.

26. *Vanguard*, "12 Killed as Subsidy Protests Turn Bloody," *Vanguard Newspaper*, January 10, 2012.

speaking up to power, challenging elitist agendas, and revolting against the marginalization of the grassroots.

In his Occupy Nigeria piece, Kperogi laments the dilly-dallying of Nigerian governments, from Sani Abacha down to Olusegun Obasanjo and Goodluck Jonathan. Each of these presidents promised the final removal of the fuel subsidy, also painting reasons why the subsidy had to be removed; and how a hike in the fuel process was necessary to help stabilize the economy, remove the crushing weight of the subsidy on Nigerians' fuel consumption from the government's shoulders, and deregulate the petroleum sector. Each promised a final removal, yet, their successor would still find something to scrape and a reason to hike fuel prices. It is as if the Nigerian fuel subsidy is palm wine in a gourd, and no matter how one president poured, there would still be dregs and drops for the succeeding president to pour. Kperogi analyzed the trends by successive Nigerian governments and the blatant lies they told, so much so that his prediction was surefire as if he were an anointed prophet. In the piece's ninth paragraph, he says:

> The government is about to push the masses of Nigerians to a *cul-de-sac*. When that happens, the masses would be faced with only two options: fight back fiercely and doggedly or submit to incremental but sure death. If it is true that self-preservation is the first law of nature, I expect a sustained, single-minded, and uncompromising battle in the coming months. The time may have finally come when the fault-lines of ethnicity and religion that have historically divided Nigerians will no longer matter.[27]

And true to his words, three months later, Nigeria experienced a social-media-masterminded and nationwide protest.

In what came to be termed overwhelming applause and lauding of Kperogi's piece on occupying Nigeria are several replies supporting his call for the protest, as can be seen in his subsequent column titled, "Re: Fuel Subsidy Removal: Time to "Occupy" Nigeria."[28] Seeing the level of reception of the piece, Kperogi deployed an important journalistic skill by reinforcing his initial piece on the fuel subsidy with yet another piece. The new piece, dated November 5, 2011, "Biggest Scandal in "Oil Subsidy Removal" Fraud."[29] In the piece, Kperogi extensively brings to the fore the inanities of fuel extraction, processing, exportation, and petroleum importation in Nigeria, notably the shady deal the Goodluck Jonathan-led administration had with Trafigura, a

27. Kperogi, "Fuel Subsidy Removal."

28. Farooq A. Kperogi, "Re: Fuel Subsidy Removal: Time to "Occupy" Nigeria!" *Notes from Atlanta*, October, 22, 2011, https://www.farooqkperogi.com/2011/10/re-fuel-subsidy-removal-time-to-occupy.html.

29. Farooq A. Kperogi, "Biggest Scandal in Oil "Subsidy Removal Fraud," *Notes from Atlanta*, November 5, 2011, https://www.farooqkperogi.com/2011/11/biggest-scandal-in-oil-subsidy-removal.html.

petroleum-processing company notorious for selling badly processed and toxic petroleum products to third-world countries.[30]

These revelations further sparked the populace's anger at the planned removal of the petrol subsidy, culminating in the January 2 – 14 Occupy Nigeria protest, which was eventually cut short after the Nigeria Labor Congress and the Trade Union joined forces with the protesters. The fuel subsidy removal was just one of the incidents that sealed Kperogi's belief in Goodluck Jonathan's tenure as a failed government. Another phenomenon that took a large chunk of Kperogi's critique of the Jonathan administration was the handling of the Boko Haram cases, which was a pertinent and pressing issue on the lips of every Nigerian at that time.

Kperogi extensively wrote on the Boko Haram menace in Nigeria. His views on the Boko Haram menace are diverse, looking into different polarities of the situations that emanated, including misrepresentation of the terrorist group, how biases surfaced to define how people differently saw the Boko Haram group, a generalization that rounded off all Northern Muslims as the Boko Haram sect, common among Southern Christians; the politicization of the Boko Haram group's menace by the people in government, among other bias-based summations.[31] The horrendous Boko Haram group's despicable acts penetrated the Nigerian country and released fear and suspicion into the populace that profiling was at its highest. This profiling was so commonplace and widely believed that so long as a perpetrator had the remotest similarities with the preconceived notions of the Boko Haram group and its members, such an act was tagged as one perpetrated by the Boko Haram group. This gave the group undue notoriety and fueled the nation's dread of the group.

Nigerians had many counts against the Goodluck Jonathan administration, and the chief of them was how he handled the mitigation of the Boko Haram sect's menace; whether or not the media gave undue attention to the group is not the issue. The issue at hand is that the Goodluck Jonathan government was largely clueless about what to do to stop the group, a cluelessness they had a hard time hiding from the populace. It was this glaring cluelessness that several journalists, columnists, and media houses capitalized on to fan the embers of Boko Haram-related news and events. That is not to say that Kperogi did not lament and condemn the mindless killings orchestrated in the country, some of which the Boko Haram group claimed responsibility for.

His May 5, 2012 piece titled, "Somalization of Nigeria and Imperative of Privatized Governance,"[32] is a well of emotions that showcases not only great condemnation of

---

30. Afrol News, "Dangerous Gasoline Offloaded in Nigeria, Ghana," *Afrol News*, June 24, 2011, http://www.afrol.com/articles/29529.

31. Farooq A. Kperogi, "Boko Haram as an Empty Signifier," *Notes from Atlanta*, January 7, 2012, https://www.farooqkperogi.com/2012/01/boko-haram-as-empty-signifier.html.

32. Farooq A. Kperogi, "Somalization of Nigeria and Imperative of Privatized Governance," *Notes from Atlanta*, May 5, 2012, https://www.farooqkperogi.com/2012/05/somaliazation-of-nigeria-and-imperative.html.

the acts of the Boko Haram group and how the Goodluck Jonathan government was reacting to the incessant killings but also an empathetic note on the ordeals that families of the abruptly murdered Nigerians have been made to go through. However, it was not all criticism of the Jonathan administration from Kperogi. A few times, Kperogi lauded some actions by the Jonathan government, notably the declaration of a state of emergency in Borno, Yobe, and Adamawa. This was a Jonathan move he wholeheartedly lauded in his May 25, 2013 article, "The Malcolm Xian Logic in Jonathan's Praiseworthy Boko Haram Offensive."[33]

As the 2015 general elections drew nigh, Kperogi's writings on the happenings in the country intensified. From writing on the revelations of corruption to the ludicrously forceful hegemony of Boko Haram in the Northern part of the country to the Nigerian Army's distasteful and condemnable wiping out of hundreds of residents of the Bana community for their inability to produce the names of the Boko Haram assailants that killed some soldiers.

Kperogi's output confirmed the cliché, "may your ink never run dry." And while he did not explicitly declare support for Buhari in his writings, he showed that he was fully against a Goodluck Jonathan re-election. Kperogi's Facebook post, dated December 6, 2016, reads in part: "I used to say that it was impossible for any Nigerian president to be worse than Jonathan. That was how much I despised him. So, in May 2015, I started out investing enormous hopes in Buhari to transform Nigeria and to build enduring institutions. . . ."[34]

The next sub-topic in this chapter will show how true Kperogi's judgment of Muhammadu Buhari was and what Kperogi's thoughts and writings on the Muhammadu Buhari administration ended up becoming.

FAROOQ KPEROGI ON MUHAMMADU BUHARI

The presidential election that brought Muhammadu Buhari to power was held on March 28, 2015, after a postponement from the initially set date of February 14, 2015.[35] In the months leading up to this election, there were varying beliefs, fears, reactions, and actions based on these beliefs and fears. For one, the Goodluck Jonathan camp knew that several counts against it would make it difficult to win the election, from the reckless corruption of his cabinet members and appointees to the

33. Farooq A. Kperogi, "The Malcolm Xian Logic in Jonathan's Praiseworthy Boko Haram Offensive," *Notes from Atlanta*, May 25, 2013, https://www.farooqkperogi.com/2013/05/the-malcolm-xian-logic-in-jonathans.html.

34. Farooq Kperogi's Facebook Post in Farooq Kperogu Fan Club, December 6, 2016, https://www.facebook.com/farooqkperogi.

35. Julia Payne, "Nigeria Postpones Feb. 14 Presidential Election to March 28: INEC," *Reuters*, February 8, 2015, https://www.reuters.com/article/us-nigeria-election-idUSKBN0LB0TL20150208.

disgrace brought about by the Boko Haram group to Dame Patience Jonathan's embarrassment of the government, but to mention a few.

There was also the unification of the Action Congress of Nigeria (ACN), the Congress for Progressive Change (CPC), the All Nigeria People's Party (ANPP), some disgruntled members of the All Progressives Grand Alliance (APGA), and a faction of the People's Democratic called the New PDP.[36] This unification birthed the All Progressives Congress (APC) in February 2013 and was approved by the Independent National Electoral Commission (INEC) in July 2013. The newly formed party, having Muhammadu Buhari and Yemi Osinbajo as its candidates for the prime seats in Aso Rock, posed the greatest threat to the re-election of incumbent Goodluck Jonathan. The party made good on its threat, receiving the mandate delivered to it by the Nigerian people in a first-of-its-kind defeat of an incumbent president since the country returned to a democratic system of governance in 1999.

Buhari and Osinbajo prepared primly and properly with the best Public Relations stunt Nigeria has ever witnessed during any of its elections. There was a psychological study of the needs of the Nigerian people, which led to the adoption of the slogan "change" and the presentation of Muhammadu Buhari, down to his training and past rule during the military era, as the no-nonsense messiah who would bring change to Nigeria, deliver it from the corruption that has deeply infested the national fabric, and rescue it from the clueless claws that have made citizens tremble at the mention of Boko Haram. He had his military training and rank as a general for the latter and the stories of his military rule as proof for the former.

The nation was going through heightened emotions, which also seeped into the tip of journalists' pens. In what can be termed as his first-ever piece on Muhammadu Buhari, which came months before the president's election to power in March 2015, Kperogi's opening statement shows implied approval of Buhari's emergence as the next president—not true for any other reason but the fact that he considered Goodluck Jonathan as the worst president to ever lead the country and believed that anyone, apart from Goodluck Jonathan, should get the people's mandate, come March 2015.[37] Kperogi's wish was granted, and he was so delighted that he called Buhari's emergence his best birthday gift.

The emergence of Muhammadu Buhari as Nigeria's President led to a string of reactions from Kperogi that could be described as initially cautious, then hopeful, then dejectedly bitter, and angry. Buhari won the election against an incumbent. Kperogi's year-long dream had come to pass. Yet, his first column after Buhari's emergence is an exemplary piece warning Buhari of what he should expect. When a coun-

36. All Progressives Congress, "About APC," *All Progressive Congress Official Website*, https://officialapc.ng/about-us/.

37. Farooq A. Kperogi, "Between Obama's "Birthers" and Buhari's "WASCers," *Notes from Atlanta*, January 24, 2015, https://www.farooqkperogi.com/2015/01/between-obamas-birthers-and-buharis.html.

try has degenerated to such low levels as it was during the Goodluck Jonathan administration, rebuilding takes time, and the people, expecting results from the Man for Change, might be too impatient. That was a piece of good advice from Kperogi to the then President-elect, filled with respect and a genuine wish to see the retired general's administration succeed. The cautionary message extended further to show one of the most admirable traits of Kperogi—his loyalty lies with the people, what he deems beneficial to the people, and what is in the people's interests. Thus, he quickly warned Buhari that should his government tow the path laid by his predecessor; there would be unending backlash from critics like him.[38]

Buhari's emergence brought high hopes for Kperogi, who believed that the retired general and principled man would outperform his predecessor and lead Nigeria toward a path of true change. This, he explicitly expresses in his May 16, 2015 article titled, *Six Reasons Why Incoming Buhari Government Fills Me with Hope.*[39] In the piece, Kperogi is realistic enough to concede that the Buhari-led administration would not be perfect. However, he extolled some early acts of the then President-elect that served as pointers to what Kperogi termed a promising tenure. Among those acts are Buhari's playing the principled-and no-nonsense-retired-general script.

Reading that piece by Kperogi in 2022 and knowing that those things indeed happened about years ago, it is almost impossible to reconcile the Buhari that Kperogi describes in that piece and the actions credited to him with the Buhari who was quiet on major national issues, dissociated himself from how the government is being run, earning the reputation of being utterly clueless. The President took Nigerians through something worse than hell—if hell were the Goodluck Jonathan administration—so much so that what was a mediocre administration is what Nigerians now ruefully look back on and hope for. And yes, they hope for the Jonathan era, when things were abysmally poor, but compared to the Buhari administrations, "better."

Kperogi's hopes in the Buhari administration were sustained for long, allowing Buhari more benefit of the doubt than he gave Goodluck Jonathan. Remember that Kperogi lashed out at Goodluck Jonathan for his abysmal representation of Nigeria at his first-ever public outing as the then Acting President, naming political gaffes, cluelessness, and grammatical inaccuracies as some of the sins of the former president. It is also worthy of note that this display severely impacted Kperogi's perception of Goodluck Jonathan, shaped his thoughts on the former president's competence and also contributed to his contrarian critique of the deeds of the Jonathan administration, which is justifiable in fairness to the social commentator, vis-à-vis the actions and gross inaction of the Jonathan-led government.

---

38. Kperogi, "Between Obama's 'Birthers.'"

39. Farooq A. Kperogi, "Six Reasons why Incoming Buhari Government fills me with Hope," *Notes from Atlanta*, May 16, 2015, https://www.farooqkperogi.com/2015/05/6-reasons-why-incoming-buhari.html.

However, Muhammadu Buhari likewise made a blunder when he referred to the then-German Chancellor, Angela Merkel, as President Michelle, not of Germany, but West Germany. Kperogi excuses Buhari's gaffe in his June 20, 2015 piece, "Criticizing Buhari Over "President Michelle of West Germany" Gaffe is Ignorant."[40] The piece excuses Buhari's first official gaffe for old age and points out similar scenarios with some former world leaders like the United States' Ronald Reagan. Perhaps, Goodluck Jonathan did not enjoy any leniency from the socio-political commentator because his gaffe could not have been excused for old age or any other thing, and the gaffes were more than one.

To err is human; to dash raised hopes is likewise human. For all it was worth, Kperogi, who represented millions of Nigerians in this case, truly believed that Buhari would bring change to Nigeria. That belief was snuffed out of the hopefuls within one year of Buhari's administration as the president. Kperogi captures this in his September 21, 2016, post on Facebook:

> We elected Buhari because we believed he would not only practice but would institutionalise good governance, transparency, accountability, "change," and all that good stuff, after the unexampled blight and venality we experienced in our immediate past. Why shouldn't we? He is a 70-something-year-old man with a reputation for bluntness and asceticism who is getting a second chance to rule Nigeria. We thought because of his age, experience, and personal moral philosophy he would be obsessed with legacy building and actively getting rid of the old, ineffectual ways that got us to where we are. But what have we seen so far? A continuation, and in some cases a doubling down, of the corruption, cronyism, elite insensitivity, etc. of the past...[41]

The scales fell off. The president was tired of playing according to the script that brought him to power. And for once, the people were made to see the real faces behind the masks of change that the All Progressives Congress (APC) leaders wore. Contrarian and harsh pieces came in succession from Kperogi. At this time, the significant pieces he had written during the Jonathan administration, which not only generated traffic and went viral, but also sparked some actions, notably forming part of what sprung up the Occupy Nigeria protest, brought an enormous increase to Kperogi's influence on social media. His posts were shared; he gained followers in the thousands, and his content pieces went viral.

---

40. Farooq A. Kperogi, "Criticizing Buhari over "President Michelle of West Germany" Gaffe is Ignorant," *Notes from Atlant*, June 20, 2015, https://www.farooqkperogi.com/2015/06/criticizing-buhari-over-president.html.

41. Farooq A. Kperogi, "Farooq Kperogi on the Buhari Government's Continuation of the Corruption of the Jonathan Government," *Facebook*, September 21, 2016, https://www.facebook.com/47904265/posts/pfbid02WqGdYcQ7zoqRVLJ88bnJyvh92xq8JEMRoEWehcgF3fWEnUgisSsU85Ey5iHxQ7gyl/?app=fbl.

Leveraging this, Kperogi made it a habit to attack Buhari's government, not only to attack but to call for change. After all, if the people were promised change but never saw the similitude of positive change, it behooves the Fourth Estate to ensure that the said change comes to the people—even if it were in trickles. One of Kperogi's earliest pieces calling for change during Buhari's first administration is his critique of Fowler's falsification of academic degrees.[42] Kperogi laments the ineptitude of the Buhari-led government. Things were so bad that, according to Kperogi, the best thing to mitigate the crisis was for Buhari to cease making any moves and leave in 2019. Kperogi's wish was not granted this time around. In a December 6, 2016 post, he says:

> ... Now with the unceasing rash of counter-intuitive, mutually contradictory, insanely irrational, and thoughtless policy prescriptions from this government, the very foundation of the country is tanking before our very eyes, and I just hope Buhari never does anything again till 2019 when his tenure will expire—and with it the torment he is inflicting on Nigeria. A stagnant, do-nothing Buhari is now better for the country than this madness we're witnessing! Nigeria is fast sinking to the nadir of despair and ruination.[43]

Such was the proportion of the Buhari-led government's ineptitude early in the administration. An ineptitude that degenerated into gross violation of human rights, daylight, and brazen corruption, to mention a few, lasting till 2023.

The Buhari administration is perhaps Kperogi's most productive period as a social commentator. Such is always the case when the people in power are grossly incompetent, brazenly corrupt, evilly fascist, dissociative, and clueless. To highlight about 100 powerful pieces or more that Kperogi wrote within this period would require pages upon pages. In the early days of Buhari's first tenure, he rocked the country with another fuel price hike. Kperogi wrote three pieces of content to spur the people to react against the unjust hike in fuel prices. In his May 14, 2016 piece, he calls for another Occupy Nigeria protest.[44] However, this call was more about trying to show why it is unacceptable for Nigerians to accept the fuel price hike tied to deregulation and subsidy removal than truly calling for a protest. In the piece, Kperogi does not fail to recognize the factors that would make another protest less appealing to the people, as compared to the success achieved by his 2012 piece.

---

42. Farooq A. Kperogi, "On Fowler's Fake Doctorate and Integrity Deficit," *Notes from Atlanta*, August 29, 2015, https://www.farooqkperogi.com/2015/08/on-fowlers-fake-doctorate-and-integrity.html.

43. Farooq A. Kperogi, "Farooq Kperogi on the Ineptitude of the Buhari Government," *Facebook*, December 6, 2016, https://www.facebook.com/47904265/posts/pfbid035fnWGwDqqKiGG8AGceBJkFRZ132tSR3sPP5MfoAJdCKgYhJ22WLKsHTKwPu6xe4ml/?app=fbl.

44. Farooq A. Kperogi, "Petrol Price Hike: Time to Occupy Nigeria Again," *Notes from Atlanta* (Blog), May 14, 2016, https://www.farooqkperogi.com/2016/05/petrol-price-hike-time-to-occupy.html.

Yet, Kperogi followed this May 14 piece with two other pieces, the one on May 15, 2016,[45] and the final on May 21, 2016.[46] He wrote three pieces within a week! There was no protest against the planned fuel price hike of 2016. However, there were widespread comments from the people who directly suffered from this hike. As Kperogi opines, it is grossly unjust that the Nigerian people were made to buy fuel at exorbitant prices, higher than what was obtainable in the United States, especially at a time when the United States minimum wage was over ten times that of Nigeria. In the end, this piece can be named as one of those positively changing pieces Kperogi wrote, as the planned petrol price hike of 2017 never saw the light of day.

One can disagree with Kperogi on some of his writings. It is no new thing to disagree with his approach and tone. However, one undeniable thing is that Kperogi is a brilliant mind, and he shows it again in his apt capturing of the traumatic scar that the Buhari government wrought on Nigerians with the word "change." Kperogi touched on this topic before it gained popularity during Buhari's second term.

In his September 25, 2016 piece, "Transformation of "Change" from God Term to Devil Term in Nigeria," Kperogi shows how the maladministration of the Buhari government has robbed the word change of its universally appealing and positive connotation, especially in the minds of Nigerians. Today, a mention of the word change in Nigeria does not bring positive memories at all, and writers now have to deploy the marker "positive" when talking about change to help it retain its pure form. This marker deployment has become a subconscious move (you might find that I have used it in this piece, too), and that is the extent to which the Buhari government scarred the Nigerian people. Kperogi opines in the piece:

> "Change has now come to be associated with lies, deceit, hypocrisy, double standards, endless whining and blame-shifting by people in government, descent from bad to worse in living conditions, incompetence in high places, unpreparedness, astonishing elite insensitivity, economic and social bondage, pauperisation, reverse Robin Hoodism (which I once defined as robbing of the poor to enrich the rich), personalisation of power, extreme nepotism and provincialism, facile and arrogant disavowal of promises made during campaigns, etc.
>
> These are all attributes of the current "change" administration embodies in colossal measure, which will certainly cause the "change" slogan to become irretrievably damaged in Nigeria's linguistic, rhetorical, and political landscape."[47]

---

45. Farooq A. Kperogi, "Fuel Price Hike: The Language and Grammatical Illogic of a Regulated Deregulation," *Notes from Atlanta,* May 15, 2016, https://www.farooqkperogi.com/2016/05/fuel-price-hike-language-and.html.

46. Farooq A. Kperogi, "Unraveling of the Monumental Fraud in Petro Price Hike," *Notes from Atlanta,* May 21, 2016, https://www.farooqkperogi.com/2016/05/unraveling-of-monumental-fraud-in-petro.html.

47. Farooq A. Kperogi, "Transformation of "Change" from God Term to Devil Term in Nigeria," *Notes from Atlanta,* September 25, 2016, https://www.farooqkperogi.com/2016/09/transformation-of-change-from-god-term.html.

In October 2018, as the 2019 presidential election drew nearer, one could see the same pattern Kperogi took in 2015 that ultimately resulted in victory for Buhari. In the same way, he considered Buhari the less favorable deep blue sea and Jonathan, the unfavorable devil; he considered Atiku Abubakar a no-no for the Nigerian presidency but still a hesitantly better option to Buhari. He makes this known in his piece, "Atiku's Emergence and End of the Road for Buhari."[48] Kperogi confessed during the Jonathan administration that Goodluck Jonathan was the worst president Nigeria had ever had and has had to confess, yet again, that the abysmal Goodluck Jonathan administration bests the Muhammadu Buhari administration. His case against Buhari, which is frankly any true and unbiased Nigerian's case against Buhari, goes beyond administrative incompetence. Buhari demonstrated that beyond incompetence and cluelessness, he is also a nepotistic leader with fascist tendencies.

However, Kperogi's written campaigns against Buhari's re-election did not result in a favorable outcome as they did against Goodluck Jonathan. In 2019, Buhari, who had previously indicated an interest in just one term of office, won his re-election bid; and so started another spate of horrendous and dissociative governance, which continued until 2023. As the months rolled into years, the Buhari administration's deeds made available more stories to critique for Kperogi—from the nepotism that saw Buhari appoint several family members to government, setting the record as the Nigerian Head of State with the highest number of his family members in government,[49] to his expository on how Buhari is a corruption enabler.[50]

It is one of the biggest ironies since the independence of Nigeria and the return of democratic rule in 1999 that the man who rode to power on the wings of fairness and a proposed anti-corruption campaign is the same man under whose watch corruption has been the most daring and commonplace. All you need to do to receive the presidential immunity that allows you to engage in corrupt practices without a backlash is membership in the All Progressives Congress.

---

48. Farooq A. Kperogi, "Atiku's Emergence and End of the Road for Buhari," *Notes from Atlanta*, October 13, 2018, https://www.farooqkperogi.com/2018/10/atikus-emergence-and-end-of-road-for.html.

49. Farooq A. Kperogi, "Government of Buhari's Family, by his Family, and for his Family," *Notes from Atlanta*, November 23, 2019, https://www.farooqkperogi.com/2019/11/government-of-buharis-family-by-his.html.

50. Farooq A. Kperogi, "Corruption is Thriving not in Spite of Buhari but because of him," *Notes from Atlanta*, November 23, 2019, https://www.farooqkperogi.com/2020/07/corruption-is-thriving-not-in-spite-of.html.

THROUGH THE EYE OF FAROOQ KPEROGI: PARALLELS AND CONTRASTS BETWEEN THE JONATHAN AND BUHARI ADMINISTRATIONS

Few journalists, social commentators, and critics have been as consistent as Kperogi in his written contributions to Nigeria's socio-political landscape. Taking into account Kperogi's socio-political output for the past 12 years—which cover the Goodluck Jonathan administration and a good part of the Muhammadu Buhari administrations—the pattern tells that Kperogi's writings come from a place greater than his personal needs or benefits, which ultimately eliminate political bias from the list of his drive for his writings.

Although his approach and the consistency of his writings might make it difficult to believe, Kperogi has no personal vendetta against whoever is in power, and the contrarian stand is not one he has taken for sport. It is easy for blind loyalists and apologists to immediately pass Kperogi's style and consistency for either a need to get noticed by the one in government, bias, or pure hatred. However, the pattern that has presented itself, which you must have also noticed while reading the previous pages of this chapter, is that Kperogi holds no loyalty to any elected or appointed political official. That principle forms the basis of his socio-political commentary, so much so that he could praise a political official at the start of their administration and have high hopes for them. This was the case with Buhari and Kperogi's proclaimed friend, Pantami.

What patterns can we point to in the administrations of Buhari and Jonathan, based on what has been obtainable in their governments and how Kperogi has spoken about both political leaders? Goodluck Jonathan's administration can be likened to a cancerous parasite that ate deep into the fragile system of the Nigerian state entity. If fate did not bring death upon Umaru Musa Yar'Adua, Goodluck Jonathan would never have nursed the idea of becoming the nation's president. From the outset, Jonathan is not someone cut out for the role, and, like Namadi Sambo, his running mate and vice, Jonathan would have retired to other things after the expiration of the expected eight years Yar Adua would have spent in government.

However, things happened as they did, and Goodluck Jonathan became the chosen man until the end of Yar'Adua's tenure a year later. Although Goodluck Jonathan showed tendencies right from his first day in office as the Acting President, the people gave him the benefit of the doubt, and being someone portrayed via the powerful Everyman Archetype that the larger percentage of the Nigerian population can relate to and which those at the corridors of power believed they could easily manipulate and control, Jonathan won his proper first bid in 2011. What followed after is nothing to write home about. Jonathan's government was rife with incompetence, a lackadaisical attitude that allowed cabinet members and appointed officials to rampage corrosively through the nation's coffers, pilfering and laundering. As if that were not

enough, there was selective denial, in that the Nigerian state trembled at the mention of the Boko Haram sect. Their words became law, and Jonathan clearly showed that he was a clueless man leading a clueless government that had no way of performing its most important duty of securing citizens' lives and property. They rather offered amnesty to the sect, which the group downright rejected.[51]

Goodluck Jonathan's government rode Nigerians through seven hells so hard that they would readily have embraced Olusegun Obasanjo's third term or resurrection of Umaru Musa Yar'Adua. It is said that when you experience hell, you begin to fantasize about the deep blue sea as paradise. And that was the case with Nigerians in 2015. Some bad reputation preceded Muhammadu Buhari when the 2015 general elections drew near. However, the people were fully fed up with a Goodluck Jonathan administration—they could not imagine going through what they went through at the hands of Jonathan for yet another four years—that they began to have selective amnesia as to the bad reputation preceding Buhari, and fully bought into the way the All Progressives Congress packaged him. This was perhaps the biggest con in the history of Nigeria. Even Kperogi fell for the Buhari scam out of his hatred for a Jonathan re-election.

Laying the deeds of the Buhari government side-by-side with those of the Goodluck Jonathan administration, the only reasonable conclusion one can arrive at is that there is an undisclosed competition to outperform the latter negatively. That could be the only plausible explanation for how a government that the people banked on to save them and bring about change has done nothing close to that. There has been no standard measurement, but anyone who has been to Nigeria during the two administrations can tell that for every absurdity, ridiculousness, gross misconduct, corruption, and disregard for citizens, among other political crimes that the Jonathan administration committed, the Buhari administration committed at least threefold. Things were that bad during this administration.

All the problems that befell Nigeria during Goodluck Jonathan's administration have not been rolled away. They have rather been made worse. And it is only due to a worse ordeal at the hands of Muhammadu Buhari that could make Goodluck Jonathan brazen enough to *nicodemously* accept the APC nomination form bought for him in hopes that he could return to power.[52] As ludicrous as it sounded that the Jonathan government would rather offer amnesty to terrorists it was meant to clamp down on, it is even more appalling that the Buhari government fully planned to put an amnesty in place for "repentant" terrorists and has pardoned over 1000 of them.[53] For every act

51. BBC, "Nigeria's Boko Haram Rejects Jonathan's Amnesty Idea," *BBC News*, April 11, 2013, https://www.bbc.com/news/world-africa-22105476.

52. News Agency of Nigeria, "Jonathan Joins APC in Bayelsa, Finally Accepts Presidential Nomination Forms from Fulani Group," *Peoples Gazette*, May 11, 2022, https://gazettengr.com/just-in-jonathan-joins-apc-in-bayelsa-finally-accepts-presidential-nomination-forms-from-fulani-group/.

53. Sahara Reporters, "Revealed: How Buhari's Government Pardoned Over 1, 000 Boko Haram Fighters Despite Ruling out Amnesty in 2015," *Sahara Reporters*, May 5, 2021, https://saharareporters.

of cluelessness, fuel subsidy removal, kidnapping, and terrorism during the Jonathan government, the Buhari government matched and surpassed them. During Buhari's administration, killing and kidnapping became a monthly affair. The kidnapping of the Chibok girls fundamentally changed Nigeria and even shook the world.

We cannot, for whatever reasons, extol the Goodluck Jonathan administration. In comparing the Jonathan and Buhari administrations, what we can say is that the former was bad, very much so. However, the latter is much worse than the former, which is very bad. Yet, these quantifiers still do not aptly represent how unacceptable and unimaginable the administrations of these two supposed leaders have been in Nigeria.

GAUGING THE IMPACTS OF SOCIAL MEDIA COMMENTARY ON NIGERIAN GOVERNANCE: CONVERSATIONS SPARKED BY FAROOQ KPEROGI'S POSTS

Looking at how things have played out in Nigeria's ecosystem for the past 12 years, the valid conclusion is that social media commentary—of which we have had Kperogi as a case study—has been very much impactful on governance in Nigeria. Kperogi's 2011 piece largely sparked conversations that led to the Occupy Nigeria protest of January 2012. The same Kperogi is now a socio-political influencer on Twitter and Facebook, whose Nigerian-related comments get thousands of reactions, millions of views, hundreds of engagements, comments, shares, and retweets.

Perhaps, the strongest influence Kperogi's posts have on Nigeria's ecosystem is via retweets and shares. Kperogi has hundreds of thousands of followers on both Twitter and Facebook, as mentioned earlier. Thus, there is little possibility that Kperogi's posts would be seen by people who do not follow him on both platforms. However, for each publication, there are shares on Facebook and retweets on Twitter, which mean that people who follow Kperogi—who also have hundreds, thousands, tens of thousands, and hundreds of thousands in followership strength—give their followers the ability to see Kperogi's posts, even if those followers of his followers do not directly follow him. Thus, with his followership strength of close to over 140,000, Kperogi has the potential to get his socio-political commentary—as shared on social media—to millions of people.

Kperogi understands this. He most likely follows the analytics and insights via his social media publishing tools. He knows the leverage social media gives him, leverage he would not have been able to rightly quantify if it were traditional media. He could readily check how much traffic his website, "Notes From Atlanta," generates monthly. He understands the brand he has created for himself, what his mission is, how it is much bigger than himself, and its potential to truly disrupt things in the camp of the

---

com/2021/05/05/revealed-how-buhari%E2%80%99s-government-pardoned-over-1-000-boko-haram-fighters-despite-ruling.

ineptitude and nation-hating drivers of the Nigerian entity. And for this, he is willing to sacrifice friendships, ax down harshly on anyone, and analyze issues—always devoid of political bias—as he deems right.

CONCLUSION

In rounding off this chapter, we have to come to terms with and begin to consciously study and invest in the potential of social media as a driver for positive change in governments in different parts of the world. Social media offers ripple effects. Look beyond Kperogi and his hundreds of thousands of followers to Debo Adedayo, who has millions of followers, to the ones who have tens of thousands of followers, and Bisi Olagunju, with thousands of followers. What if these individuals uniformly pumped out content and socio-political criticisms at Kperogi's pace and consistency? True, these other two people mentioned above are doing so already. But what if other people like them joined, and their followers shared and retweeted, getting the word to the nooks and crannies of the internet?

A relatable instance of this was the process that brought about the #EndSARS protest of 2020. The protest started as an online movement against police brutality in Nigeria. Social media influencers and celebrities tweeted through public sentiments and caused nationwide engagement online. It only took one of them to intimate people of his plan to carry out a protest which brought out thousands of Nigerian youths. Without giving underserving credit to social media and its dynamics, one cannot dispute the fact that with the likes of Kperogi and his consistency in the activities and policies of the government, social media could be a major factor in creating a new trajectory.

Consider how important social media has become in the life and existence of Nigerians—whose country is social media's biggest gold mine in Africa. We must consider how the two biggest protests have rocked the country within the last ten years and how they were orchestrated on social media. Only then could we truly come to terms with how powerful social media has become as a tool that shapes governance worldwide. And as peculiar as Nigeria's case is, it is not an exception.

18

FAROOQ KPEROGI

The 2023 Elections

President Muhammadu Buhari's days in office are over. Whether the people were satisfied or displeased with his policies and results or approach to leadership ceased to be of much concern on May 29, 2023, when he vacated office. All the same, Buhari could pass as one of the most criticized presidents since Nigeria's return to democracy in 1999. Farooq Kperogi and a legion of critics were always on the watch to spit fire at every incidence in the country, hitting the President with no reservation.[1] As Wole Soyinka perceptively said, "The greatest threat to freedom is the absence of criticism;" hence, the President must have acclimatized to the tenets of democracy—criticism, an attribute not well expressed during his military junta as Head of State in 1983.[2]

However, the heat and waves of criticism against the perceived ineptitude of his government started waning, and attention was directed toward analyzing those who sought to take the baton from Buhari through the 2023 election. One may be unsure whether it was a distraction or redirection of criticism, but one thing is crystal clear, Buhari was no longer the sole target of public criticism. The major presidential can-

1. Farooq Kperogi, ed., *Digital Dissidence and Social Media Censorship in Africa* (Oxfordshire, Taylor & Francis, 2022).

2. Chidiebere J. Onwutuebe, "Military Culture and Political Leadership in Nigeria's Democracy," *African Identities* (2022): 1–21.

Figure 18.1. "Emilokan! Let People Decide" by Michael Efionayi. Atiku and Tinubu, both candidates in the 2023 elections.

didates of the 2023 General Elections momentarily usurped the people's attention. They perhaps attracted more attention than the political events of the 2015 General Elections with the promise of bringing a new face to government. As the 2023 elections approached, the Nigerian political critic army seemed to renew its weapons and update its strategies to acknowledge the upcoming change of baton. Unsurprisingly, Kperogi's opinions became what many Nigerians anticipated as he painstakingly addressed Nigeria's political developments and surgically analyzed unfolding issues relating to the elections. With such brilliant contributions and increasing public coverage, Kperogi and his opinions about the 2023 elections became necessary to discuss.

One phenomenon identifiable with the 2023 elections is the widespread social media usage by the political gladiators, the critics, and the citizenry. Although one cannot assert that most of the Nigerian population or voters are active users of these platforms, it is obvious that they are fast becoming another battlefield for the elections. Social media engagement thickened among Nigerians, as some described themselves as "Obidient" in solidarity with Peter Obi. Some others proclaimed themselves "Atikulated" in support of former Vice President Atiku Abubakar, while the "BATified" signified support for Bola Ahmed Tinubu.[3] The political environment on

3. Akeem Lasisi, "What Word Formation is Involved in BATified, Atikulated and Obi-dient?" *The Punch,* June 21, 2022.

social media grew with political trends rising from one event to the other, followed by criticism, buzzwords, bashing, insults and personal views. As noted in the last chapter, in this noisy market called social media, Kperogi pitched his tent, contributing meaningfully to intellectual engagements. He has risen to an influencer's status with more than 117,000 followers on Twitter, 140,000 followers on Facebook and more on other platforms. Hence, he is a foremost discourse driver on social media and a major commentator capable of charting trajectories for political and national discussions. All these make him an interesting figure whose views are material.

If political participation is paramount to the survival of democracy in Nigeria and the success of elections, it must be encouraged among the people. Kperogi was one of those engaging the society to ensure increased participation in the 2023 elections. Kperogi's "Notes from Atlanta" serves as political updates with annotated analyses and criticism to enlighten the public in general. Aside from "Notes from Atlanta," Kperogi invested his time in engaging the public in columns, publications, and social media posts. He, therefore, becomes critical to the 2023 electoral discourse.

Nigeria, as a so-called democratically governed entity, has gone through different phases of electoral wonderments, the bulk of which is worrisome. The conundrum is that the entity has witnessed stagnancy and progress in its electoral processes. On the one hand, the claim that Nigeria's electoral and electioneering processes have developed is true, as electoral violence has left the level of a widespread calamity to being witnessed only in some parts of the country.

Today, voters are not as scared of going to the polls as they were 10 or 20 years ago. They can also see that elections are becoming fairer and can no longer be easily manipulated. This is made possible by the Electoral Act 2022, which legitimized the electronic transmission of results, thus allowing the citizens to follow the results tally live. It also considers the number of accredited voters to determine over-voting and result declaration under duress as a factor for annulling election results at the tribunal.[4]

Legalizing these measures by the Independent National Electoral Commission has renewed the electorate's faith in the country's electoral process—even if some electoral malpractices remain in the system, as was evident in the 2022 elections in Edo, Anambra, and Osun States. Elections in those states were swung according to the electorate's choice, leading Ademola Adeleke to defeat an incumbent governor in Osun State. In Edo State, Governor Godwin Obaseki won re-election against all odds. His erstwhile godfather, Adams Oshiomole, who helped him win the first term, was against his re-election, a move that led Obaseki to defect to the Peoples Democratic Party (PDP). There were no reported cases of electoral violence, marginalization of voters, or voter intimidation in all these cases. Still, voter turnout was poor, as less

4. Festus Ogun, "Key Provisions of Electoral Act, 2022," *TheCable*, April 19, 2022, https://www.thecable.ng/review-key-provisions-of-electoral-act-2022.

than 50% of the registered voters voted in the most recent of these elections, the Osun State election of July 2022.[5]

From a different perspective, electoral processes in Nigeria cannot be said to have witnessed significant changes. One, there is an endless recycling of the same set of politicians. Political parties witness multiple-member shuffling, where rich and influential politicians can afford to defect to other parties multiple times for personal interest. The minimum votes required to elect leaders during the embryonic years of Nigeria's independence still stand as the benchmark for political leadership over 60 years later.

Also, Nigeria's voter behavior has remained the same since the 1964/1965 elections. Nigerian voters are known to vote across two major divisive lines—ethnic and religious. This manifested at the 1964 elections where the Northern Peoples Congress, the National Congress of Nigeria and the Cameroons, and the Action Group contested, the last two being for the Eastern and Western parts of the country, respectively. Today, Nigerian voters are still divided along ethnic and religious lines, evident in the "it's time for the South to rule" outcry and the now popularized phrase "emi lokan," loosely translated as "it is my turn!" made by the All Progressives Congress' flagbearer, Ahmed Tinubu.[6]

Unsurprisingly, there were widespread arguments, discourses, and outcries over the choice of Ahmed Bola Tinubu's running mate, Kashim Shettima, seeing as both candidates for the ruling party's presidential slot at the coming polls are Muslims. In subsequent parts of this chapter, we will look into Kperogi's commentaries at the height of ethnic and religious struggles over candidacy among the ruling party members.

About a year before the swearing-in of the next set of Nigeria's political leaders, the election frenzy raged across the country. Essentially, the rave is central to the president's office, as gubernatorial elections usually generate little to no heat until probably a few weeks or months before the election day. This recurring phenomenon in Nigeria's electioneering processes mocks the fact that Nigeria is a federation of one central government, 36 states, and 744 local governments.

Nigerians approach elections as if the presidential seat is the only important political position for significant positive changes in the multi-ethnic, socio-political, and geographical entity. Perhaps it is. The current political structure of the country and its constitution make political offices in other tiers of government somewhat irrelevant. This indifference to state and local governments' political issues or discourses is largely tied to the financial dependency of state governments on the federal government.[7]

---

5. Dennis Amata, "#Osundecides: Only 42.16% of Registered Voters Voted in the Osun Governorship Election," *Data Phyte,* July 18, 2022. https://www.dataphyte.com/latest-reports/elections/osundecides-only-42-16-of-registered-voters-voted-in-the-osun-governorship-election/.

6. Alade Rotimi-John, "Emi L'okan Entitlement Bogey as Metaphor," *The Guardian,* June 20, 2022.

7. Lawrence O. Akinboyo and Martins O. Apinran "States' Fiscal Dependency and Implications on Monetary Management in Nigeria, *CBN Bullion* 42, no. 4, (2018): 12–27.

A well-functioning Nigeria requires both a functional federal government and equally functional state and local governments, but only a few Nigerians deem state and local governments as equally important to overall good governance and national stability because the local governments leech on and are fully dependent on the state governments the same way state governments are largely dependent on the federal government.

As earlier indicated, this chapter critically examines and brings to light Farooq Kperogi's extensive commentaries on the 2023 elections through four main sub-points, namely:

i. Flagbearer selection style and campaign patterns in Nigerian elections: 2023 through Kperogi's lens;
ii. Examining Kperogi's commentaries on the role of religion in Nigerian elections;
iii. Examining Kperogi's commentaries on the role of ethnicity in Nigerian elections; and
iv. Voter education in Nigeria: the role of the emerging and new media.

There is no denying the media's role in determining the direction of electioneering affairs. This does not happen in Nigeria alone, as Cambridge Analytica leveraged data from Facebook to push their media narrative to targeted voters during the United States 2016 electioneering process, which is said to have significantly influenced the voters.[8]

FLAGBEARER SELECTION STYLE AND CAMPAIGN PATTERNS IN NIGERIAN ELECTIONS: 2023 THROUGH KPEROGI'S LENS

As obtainable in several other democracies worldwide, Nigeria's electioneering activities for every election year start at the party level. Nigeria operates a multi-party system. However, only two of its parties have succeeded on a large scale since its return to democracy in 1999. Furthermore, the success of one of those parties, the All Progressives Congress (APC), is largely hinged on the coalition of the three biggest opposition parties pre-2015.[9]

Thus, although Nigeria is a multi-party system, it essentially experiences a two-party system at the federal level. Another peculiarity of the Nigerian political space is the unilateral ideology that binds its parties, thus paving the way for serial defection

---

8. Ted Johnson, "D.C. Attorney General Sues Facebook over Data Misuse in 2016 Election," *Variety*, December 19, 2018, https://variety.com/2018/politics/news/d-c-attorney-general-sues-facebook-over-data-misuse-in-2016-election-1203093256/.

9. All Progressives Congress, "About APC," *Official APC*, November 11, 2020, https://officialapc.ng/about-us/.

from one political party to the other. This is not possible in some democracies like the United States and the United Kingdom that the country's democracy is modeled after. Unlike Nigeria, these countries have ideology-based political parties; these ideologies form the basis for everything the parties practice, from their stance on immigration to abortion, and gun ownership, among other issues.

Party flagbearer selection is as political in Nigeria as the national elections themselves. In 2022, political parties announced their flagbearers for positions at the federal and state levels in preparation for the 2023 elections. This process was not without its inanities and shenanigans, some of which were well documented and critiqued by social commentators and journalists, including Kperogi. These party shenanigans at the level of party primaries eventually birthed a strong third force in the coming elections—Peter Obi, then of the Peoples Democratic Party but now the flagbearer of the Labor Party.

In discussing the flagbearer selection and campaign patterns, our focus will be on the ruling party, the leading opposition party, and the newly strengthened third force. One of the popular features of flagbearer selection common to Nigeria's dominant political parties—the All Progressives Congress (APC) and the Peoples Democratic Party (PDP)—is the outrageous cost of nomination and aspirant forms. Tracing this from when the All Progressives Congress was formed in 2013, in preparations for the 2015 elections, the least amount any of these two parties has had for the presidential nomination form is 12 million naira, as fixed by the Peoples Democratic Party for the 2019 elections.[10] The All Progressives Congress has recorded the highest amount of money pegged for a single form—100 million naira for the 2023 elections' presidential aspirants.[11]

The outrageous prices of nomination and expression of interest forms in these political parties is a mystery that defies all logical explanations, especially as Nigeria is a country where fuel needs to be subsidized, and over 82 million Nigerians live on less than $1 per day.[12] The question is, what gave birth to the staggering disparity in the financial strength of the average Nigerian and the political class that wields such financial power that aspirants who have no assurance of winning their party primaries could release hundreds of millions of naira without batting an eyelid?

The answer to that question is not difficult to discover. Politics in Nigeria is a very lucrative business with a huge return on investment. The widespread and deep-root-

---

10. Nasir Ayitogo, "2019: PDP Commences Sale of Nomination Forms" *Premium Times*, August 28, 2018, https://www.premiumtimesng.com/news/top-news/281577-2019-pdp-commences-sale-of-nomination-forms.html.

11. Bakare Majeed, " 2023: APC Fixes Presidential Forms for N100 Million, Adopts Indirect Primaries," *Premium Times*, April 20, 2022, https://www.premiumtimesng.com/news/headlines/524823-updated-2023-apc-fixes-presidential-forms-for-n100-million-adopts-indirect-primaries.html.

12. Mayowa Tijani, "Did you know Nigeria's Poverty Line is Less than a Dollar a Day?" *TheCable*, June 17, 2021, https://www.thecable.ng/did-you-know-nigerias-poverty-line-is-less-than-a-dollar-a-day.

ed corruption in the country ensures that every political officeholder gets multiple folds of whatever they spend on the electioneering process. Thus, people with questionable wealth could very well venture into politics to cover traces of their ill-gotten wealth and laundered money.

On April 30, 2022, in an article titled, "Only These Kinds of People Will Buy Nomination Forms for N100m,"[13] Kperogi rightly identified four kinds of people who would readily buy the APC presidential forms for such an amount. He names them: the overly bullish political investors, rich drug addicts, mentally deranged people with ill-gotten wealth, and political gamblers. He further notes that only someone from this group would buy a nomination form for that price without so much as little assurance of clinching the ticket.

While it is true that Kperogi might have aimed to score non-personal insulting points against the brash aspirants, there is no denying his right to such claims, especially in the face of the events that preceded the primary elections across the major parties in Nigeria. The months that led to the presidential primaries were not approached with the same intensity by the political parties. For instance, the All Progressives Congress was lax about its primaries, so much so that there were speculations that the party would not be formidable at the polls. Aspirants were buying forms; however, the party was largely undecided on the type of primaries it would employ—whether to raise a consensus candidate like it did at the last two polls or conduct direct primaries to determine the flagbearer.

APC's laxity preparatory to its presidential primaries was glaring compared to the intensity displayed by the other parties. First, they postponed the election from May 29 and 30 to June 6 to 8. Apart from this, some actions and inactions of party stakeholders, party executive council members, and even aspirants showed they were ill-prepared for any serious primaries. There were also mixed expectations. Some were confident that the President would support his Vice, Yemi Osinbajo, as the party's anointed candidate. There were also speculations that Ahmed Lawan, the Senate President, would emerge as the consensus candidate. Others believed that the party would have its direct primaries.

Eventually, between June 6 and 8, the APC held its presidential primaries, where 13 qualified candidates made a mockery of a democratic election. It was a national show of shame devoid of respect for the electorate and the nation. Candidates stepped up to the podium only to step down and concede their ambition to Bola Ahmed Tinubu, who later emerged as the flagbearer. Tinubu won the election by 1,271 votes in an election with about 2,000 voting delegates.[14]

13. Farooq Kperogi, "Only these Kinds of People will Buy Nomination Forms for N100m," *Notes from Atlanta*, April 30, 2022, https://www.farooqkperogi.com/2022/04/only-these-kinds-of-people-will-buy.html.

14. David Royal, "Tinubu Defeats Osinbajo, Amaechi, Wins APC Presidential Primary," *Vanguard Newspaper,* June 8, 2022.

In a June 21, 2022 article titled "Two Signs APC Still Not Ready to Govern After Buhari," Kperogi gives his thoughts on what everyone identified as APC's ill-preparedness and lackadaisical attitude toward the 2023 electoral processes.[15] The article narrates instances in the past few months that confirm this view. These instances include a haphazard presidential primaries election, the unexplained postponement, and the engagement of a placeholder running mate for the eventual flagbearer. In comparison to the Peoples Democratic Party, these events put the All Progressives Congress in a bad light.

Before this piece, Kperogi had written extensively on what the presidency or potential presidency of Tinubu, Saraki, Wike, Ahmed Lawan, and Osinbajo could mean for Nigeria. These articles can be seen as attempts to warn the public against falling for the same political shenanigans that these aspirants usually play to win unsuspecting citizens over and rule the country. Talking about the pre-primaries period, there is hardly any Nigerian columnist and social commentator who was as vocal as Kperogi in writing about the political players across all parties. Compared to the All Progressives Congress, the Peoples Democratic Party had a similarly crass presidential primary election that saw Aminu Tambuwal step down for Atiku Abubakar, thus forging a Northern alliance in the party, despite the clamor for a Southern flagbearer.

Before this, one of the party's promising candidates and Atiku's running mate at the 2019 polls, Peter Obi, had left the party, seeing the moves to pander the party to Atiku. If Atiku Abubakar had not emerged as the party's flagbearer, it would have fallen on the Governor of Rivers State, Nyesome Wike, a man whose aspirations hold no weight beyond his unrelenting quest to be given power and the opportunity to deal with the ruling All Progressives Congress. The primary elections of the two major parties portray some features that have come to be known with the presidential primaries and pre-election activities in Nigeria.

First on the list is reckless and unchecked spending. Besides paying exorbitant fees for nomination and expression of interest forms, political aspirants are notorious for financial and power contests at the presidential primaries. This also takes place in smaller parties, as seen in what one of the Action Democratic Congress' aspirants, Kingsley Moghalu, wrote in his resignation letter.[16] Presidential primaries in Nigeria are a case of the highest bidder where money is recklessly thrown around, so much so that the Economic and Financial Crimes Commission sends troops to primary elections to curtail the spending of ill-gotten and stolen wealth. But the presence of the Commission's troops has little to no effect. To put the recklessness of the spending into perspective, a news report had it that a PDP's presidential primaries' delegate,

15. Farooq Kperogi, "Two Signs APC Still Not Ready to Govern after Buhari," *Notes from Atlanta,* June 21, 2022. https://www.farooqkperogi.com/2022/06/two-signs-apc-still-not-ready-to-govern.html.

16. Samson Adenekan, "Days after Losing Presidential Bid, Moghalu Resigns from ADC," *Premium Times,* June 14, 2022, https://www.premiumtimesng.com/news/top-news/536891-days-after-losing-presidential-bid-moghalu-resigns-from-adc.html.

Tanko Sabo, donated 12 million naira to his constituency members after returning from the primaries.[17] The unscrupulous vote buying at the presidential primaries is not new in Nigeria. It's known to everyone that Tanko Sabo won the delegate slot by promising to give some of his earnings from the primaries to his constituents.

Another characteristic of presidential primaries in Nigeria is the emergence of aggrieved parties. Often, people feel they should have emerged as their party flagbearers but end up losing their bid. The aggrieved parties can be further divided into two groups: those who later defect to another party and those who choose to stay in the party. After the PDP's presidential primaries, some of the aggrieved parties that emerged were Peter Obi and Nyesom Wike. Peter Obi defected before the party's primaries and eventually emerged as the Labor Party's flagbearer. Wike remains that unpredictable aggrieved party member.

EXAMINING KPEROGI'S COMMENTARIES ON THE ROLE OF RELIGION IN NIGERIAN ELECTIONS

Politics is a social phenomenon that is largely hinged on interests. Political stakeholders, the electorate, aspirants, political parties—all these groups of people have various interests for which they actively participate in politics. Thus, a fraction of political outcomes portrays how well different groups of people can align their interests to reach a common ground. Or in another case, it shows how powerfully a group can push its interests to the fore to emerge the most formidable, thus winning by popularity.

This implies that factional interests are not alien even to developed democracies. However, the nature of the factional interests distinguishes such countries from underdeveloped democracies like Nigeria. In Nigeria, interests are so personal and diverse, and this utter lack of national consciousness and identity alienates the concept of mutual agreements, concessions, and compromises in the Nigerian political space. One factor impeding Nigeria's development is that its people are too self-centered to set aside differences, grievances, and personal interests for the common good. Indeed, the common good is a concept that does not exist within the Nigerian spatial entity.

Religion is another factor that makes Nigerians rate personal interests above communal ones. Nigeria is a spatial and social entity of strongly religious people. According to statistics, about 9 in 10 Nigerians identify as being religious.[18] Islam and Christianity are the most popular religions in the country. Religion plays an integral role in the daily life of the average Nigerian. Frequently, Nigerians only advocate against the

---

17. Kayode Oyero, "PDP Delegate Donates N12M Received from Aspirants to Kaduna Constituents," *The Punch*, June 2, 2022.

18. O.S. Nag, "Most Religious Countries in the World," *World Atlas*, January 11, 2018, https://www.worldatlas.com/articles/most-religious-countries-in-the-world.html.

religionization of the country or for equal religious representation to favor personal religion. Thus, there is content if the supposedly marginalized are not theirs.

To further put into perspective how religious the country is, we must first acknowledge that the Nigerian constitution does not explicitly recognize the country as a secular entity. Although the constitution states that the government shall not adopt any religion as the state religion, it does not excuse the influence of religion on the government or government decisions. Another phenomenon that lends credence to how religious Nigeria is as a spatial, political and social entity is that 12 of its 36 states practice sharia law.[19]

In Nigeria, religion does not only influence the government; it is also a tool the government and aspiring political officeholders leverage to win the people to their side. A Nigerian politician who knows how to weave religious narratives and wield religious sentiments would readily win Nigerians over, even if he lacks concrete plans for the country's development. In other words, religion forms a big part of the political processes in Nigeria. Nigerians weigh their political options on religious considerations. That is why terms such as Southern Muslims and Northern Christians are common within the Nigerian political space. These terms betray Nigerians' religious bias when deciding essential matters such as national development and selecting the right leaders. For many Nigerians, sharing the same religion with a political aspirant is a sufficient reason to vote for them. No matter how competent the opponent(s) may be, having someone representing their religious interests in the government is enough for them.

But political antecedents have shown that religious and ethnic affinities do not necessarily translate to better treatment for the people. For example, the kidnappings, killings, terrorism, insurgency, and insecurity in Muslim-populated Northern Nigeria worsened under President Muhammadu Buhari, although he is a Muslim and a former military general—two factors that one would deem qualifying enough to represent the people's interests when they voted him to power. In a March 5, 2022 article titled "Tinubu, Dogara, and the Prison and Poison of Religious Politics," Kperogi brings to the fore the pervasive sentiments in relation to religious beliefs and politics in Nigeria. His opening paragraph is as shown below:

> The two most disadvantaged groups in Nigeria's representational politics are Northern Christians and Southern Muslims. In Nigeria's internal geopolitics, these two groups are structurally invisible, politically subjugated, and told to be content with their political and symbolic marginality.[20]

---

19. Human Rights Watch, "Political Shari'a"? Human Rights and Islamic Law in Northern Nigeria," *Human Rights Watch*, September 21, 2004, https://www.hrw.org/report/2004/09/21/political-sharia/human-rights-and-islamic-law-northern-nigeria#:~:text=Acknowledgements111,I.,a%20(Islamic%20law)%20courts.

20. Farooq Kperogi, "Tinubu, Dogara and the Prison and Poison of Religious Politics," *Notes from Atlanta*, March 5, 2022, https://www.farooqkperogi.com/2022/03/tinubu-dogara-and-prison-and-poison-of.html.

Kperogi further analyzes how ethnoreligious considerations influence the choice of running mates among presidential flagbearers in Nigeria. Politicians believe in the polarization of Nigerian voters, viz: the Southern and the Northern voters; the Christian and Muslim voters. Thus, if a Southern Muslim wants to contest as president, such a candidate thinks their best chances of winning lie in picking a polarized politician as their running mate—a Northern Christian.

Kperogi's piece sheds light on Tinubu's plans to deploy this same strategy that has been the trump card of the Nigerian political space since the beginning of the fourth republic—from the Southern Christian Obasanjo and his Northern Muslim Vice, Atiku, to a Northern Muslim Yar'Adua and his Southern Christian Vice, Jonathan, to a Southern Christian Jonathan and his Northern Muslim Vice, Sambo, to a Northern Muslim Buhari and his Southern Christian Vice, Osinbajo.

However, the peculiarity of a Southern Muslim Tinubu and a Northern Christian Dogara is that they belong to two politically marginalized groups. To curry the favor of the North and gain the Northern votes in an election is to have either a Northern Muslim presidential candidate or a Northern Muslim running mate. Having a Northern Christian candidate will not win any candidate enough votes in a predominantly Muslim Northern Nigeria. In Kperogi's view, Tinubu abandoned his initial plan of fielding Yakubu Dogara as his running mate. In certain terms, Kperogi claims that the influential Northern class had informed Tinubu that he would not get their support if he chose Dogara.[21]

Subsequently, Tinubu, upon emerging as the All Progressives Congress' flagbearer for the 2023 presidential election, selected Kashim Shettima, a Northern Muslim, as his running mate. Although the Tinubu Campaign Group sought to douse the consequent waves of reactions, claiming that competence was the only factor considered in selecting a running mate, Tinubu's choice of Kashim Shettima is but a political game of where and who he believes would help him achieve his ambition of becoming Nigeria's next president.

The North is considered Nigeria's highest-voting region and a hardly divided political side, in that Northern votes are resoundingly given to whomever sentiments, interests, and the Northern elite have selected. A candidate anointed and accepted by the Northern elite is guaranteed a more resounding success in the North than in the fairly divided South, where no aspirant is guaranteed unanimous support.

Against political antecedents that favor the polarization of flagbearers' selection across Nigeria's major parties, Tinubu made a choice he believed would favor his cause. This brazen choice has sparked widespread controversies in the country. Political analysts and social commentators have waded into the ensuing debates and postulations. While some declare that Tinubu's choice of a running mate disregards the

21. Kperogi, "Tinubu, Dogara and the Prison."

Christian section of the electorates and that not even his ambition is worth such a disregard, others reason that he selected a candidate that offers him the surest guarantee of being Muhammadu Buhari's successor.

In his piece titled "Osun's Christian-Christian Ticket, APC's Muslim-Muslim Ticket, and Religion in Yorubaland,"[22] Kperogi aptly captures the religious bias of Nigerians when there is no polarized selection of flagbearers. He notes that, in Tinubu's case, the bulk of the people outraged by his choice will be Christians, not necessarily because they are ardent believers in fairness, but because the unfairness is not in their favor.

Another incident that shows the depth of religious influence on electoral decisions among Nigerian voters is the APC's convocation of some supposed members of the Christian Association of Nigeria at the unveiling of Kashim Shettima as Tinubu's running mate. The gathering of these supposed bishops shows that Tinubu or his campaign team are not as brazen in their choice of a non-polarized running mate as much as they seem.

In his article titled "The Tinubu-Shettima Fake Bishops Saga,"[23] Kperogi heavily criticizes the crassness of the All Progressives Congress' abysmal strategy to forcefully create an acceptance for their choice where none is existent. In paying fake bishops to endorse Shettima, the party drew more polarizing attention to Tinubu's unexpected choice of a running mate. Through that singular act, they have validated the outcries against the Muslim-Muslim ticket, and Tinubu's team must be prepared to face the consequences of its unpopular choice. The desperate move to openly endorse Shettima as Tinubu's running mate has not only revealed that APC cares for the validation of the Christian community more than they would explicitly state but also exposed their unbridled disregard for the beliefs and concerns of the Christians, as the "bishops" were shabbily dressed in off-putting regalia.

Ahead of the All Progressives Congress' presidential primaries, Kperogi published opinion essays and exposés on some political aspirants who tended to leverage their religion and appeal to religious feelings in their campaigns. Among the aspirants in that category, Kperogi singled out the Vice President, Prof. Yemi Osinbajo, a pastor at The Redeemed Christian Church of God, one of Nigeria's largest churches. He had earlier criticized Yemi Osinbajo in the company of Buhari and Tinubu, and rightly so, seeing as one was the most influential in bringing upon Nigeria a Buhari-led government and the other is the Vice President of a man who will go down in history as one of the worst presidents the country has ever had.

---

22. Farooq Kperogi "Osun's Christian-Christian Ticket, APC's Muslim-Muslim Ticket, and Religion in Yorubaland," *Notes from Atlanta,* July 18, 2022, https://www.farooqkperogi.com/2022/07/osuns-christian-christian-ticket-apcs.html.

23. Farooq Kperogi, "The Tinubu-Shettima Fake Bishops Saga," *Notes from Atlanta,* July 20, 2022, https://www.farooqkperogi.com/2022/07/the-tinubu-shettima-fake-bishops-saga.html.

However, Kperogi launched targeted criticism of Osinbajo with his March 10, 2022 piece titled "RCCG's Dangerous Foray into Politics for Osinbajo."[24] In this piece, Kperogi addresses the memo The Redeemed Christian Church of God issued in February 2022 regarding the church's creation of the Office of the Directorate of Politics and Governance. He probes further into the memo and the purpose of such a directorate in the church, especially alluding to a prophecy by the church's General Overseer, Pastor Enoch Adeboye, that Nigeria would have a democratically elected president from within the church in his lifetime. The creation of such a directorate in the church further proves that the concepts of "politicization of religion" and "religionization of politics" have taken root in the Nigerian spatial entity. In response to the church's memo, Bola Ahmed Tinubu also admonished Muslims to create political departments.[25]

In a perhaps stronger and more widely shared piece titled "10 Reasons Osinbajo Will Ignite a Religious Civil War,"[26] Kperogi argues, in clear terms, that Yemi Osinbajo emerging as the All Progressives Congress' flagbearer could mean an easy victory for him but a national disaster for Nigerians, especially those who are not of his religious faith. In calling on Nigerians to be wary of an Osinbajo presidency due to his tendency to be a religious zealot, Kperogi's piece brings to the fore the unmistakable role religion plays in Nigerian politics and among the electorate as a tool that can be wielded or used to call the citizens to order.

EXAMINING KPEROGI'S COMMENTARIES ON THE ROLE OF ETHNICITY IN NIGERIAN ELECTIONS

Nigeria is a country that consists of deeply ethnocentric people. While the love for one's ethnicity is not a bad thing in itself and should even be encouraged, in Nigeria's case, the people's ethnocentricity is at the expense of collective cohesion, which should foster national development, progress, and unity.

Another peculiar thing about ethnicity in Nigeria is that although Nigeria is a multi-ethnic country boasting up to 250 ethnic groups,[27] ethnopolitical discourses, arrangements, and arguments are often between the three major ethnic groups: Igbo, Yoruba, and Hausa-Fulani. People from any of these three ethnic groups are quick to advocate against their group's marginalization or support the need for them to pro-

---

24. Farooq Kperogi, "RCCG's Dangerous Foray into Politics for Osinbajo," *Note from Atlanta*, March 10, 2022, https://www.farooqkperogi.com/2022/03/rccgs-dangerous-foray-into-politics-for.html.

25. Sunday Ochogwu, "2023: Tinubu asks Muslims to Create Political Departments like Redeemed Church," *Daily Post*, March 20, 2022, https://dailypost.ng/2022/03/20/2023-tinubu-asks-muslims-to-create-political-departments-like-redeemed-church/.

26. Farooq Kperogi, "10 Reasons Osinbajo will Ignite a Religious Civil War," *Notes from Atlanta*, March 21, 2022, https://www.farooqkperogi.com/2022/03/10-reasons-osinbajo-will-ignite.html.

27. Ajato Gandonu, "Nigeria's 250 Ethnic Groups: Realities and Assumptions." In *Perspectives on Ethnicity*, ed. Regina E. Holloman and Serghei A. Arutiunov (Berlin: De Gruyter Mouton, 2011), 243–280.

Figure 18.2. "Nigerian Election" by Dr. Kazeem Ekeolu. National Youth Service Corps conducting elections.

duce the nation's next president. They insensitively disregard the gross marginalization of other ethnic groups like the Ijo, Tiv, Idoma, and Kanuri, among others. Such is the oversimplification of ethnicity in Nigeria that people across the country consider others as either Igbo, Yoruba, or Hausa-Fulani, which extends to the discourses about federalism, federal characters, and the election of the country's president.

Ethnicity is one of the two strongest factors affecting Nigerian elections, the other being religion. Some scholars and political analysts view these two factors as interwoven and thus posit the ethnoreligious concept. However, ethnicity and religion as factors in Nigerian elections must be distinctly considered because Southern Nigeria does not overwhelmingly practice one religion compared to Northern Nigeria. Ethnicity is an integral part of the day-to-day operations in the nooks and crannies of the socio-political entity called Nigeria. Ethnic bigotry, nepotism, ethnicity-fueled favoritism, ethnic dissonance, ethnic superiority and ethnic marginalization are some of its effects in Nigeria. The average Nigerian is only concerned about their ethnic group and largely disconnected from the realities of other ethnic groups.

Like religion, ethnic consciousness causes polarization in flagbearer selection across all political parties in the country. A study of the choice of running mates across different political parties shows that flagbearers select their running mates

based on how well they can buy into the sympathy and consideration of ethnic groups in Nigeria. Many political aspirants are prone to playing the ethnic card. They are quick to forget that Nigeria's constitution makes it impossible for any politician to emerge as the president without having the goodwill of the Nigerian people across different ethnic groups—and not people from his ethnic group alone—seeing as the country does not practice a simple-majority system. To emerge as Nigeria's president, aspirants have to sail through the hurdles of winning the highest number of votes and having at least 25% of the votes in two-thirds of the 36 states. Thus, it is counter-productive for a presidential aspirant in Nigeria to lay the foundation of his political ambition on the ethnic bias, disregard for other ethnic groups, or the elevation of their ethnic group above others.

Bola Tinubu of the All Progressives Congress and Atiku Abubakar of the Peoples Democratic Party have exhibited this behavior. Tinubu clung to his ethnic group earlier in his presidential bid before he was assured of being his party flagbearer. In an utter display of ethnocentricism and self-centeredness, he fought that the party's presidency has to be zoned to the South West and that the Yoruba have no better person than him.[28] In a not-so-similar act, Atiku Abubakar granted Channels TV an interview, where he openly undermined voter education and voter consciousness in the North. He was quick to cede to claims about the North to support his narrative, saying that an outrageous 90% of Northern voters are "not tuned to social media" and are thus deaf to the campaigns of other aspirants.[29]

Supporters of the leading political parties and candidates also wield the weapon of ethnicity. They deploy ethnicity to promote their candidates and weave false narratives against the opposition. For instance, Bola Tinubu and Atiku Abubakar's supporters have clamored against the leading candidate in the third force, Peter Obi. This clamor stems from Obi's ethnic roots, one which has seen APC and PDP's supporters suggest that Obi need not contest since there have been repeated agitations from his tribe to secede from Nigeria. The forces behind this narrative have failed to consider some things. One, no proof links Peter Obi directly or indirectly to the secessionists. Two, there has also been secessionist agitation among the Yoruba people, recently reinforced by the leadership of Sunday Igboho. Yet, it would be grossly unfair to pin this on Bola Tinubu or to consider him unfit to contest for the presidency because of the Yoruba nation's agitators.

Ethnicity and religion cannot be removed from the political narratives of Nigerian elections. Kperogi tried to project what could happen along ethnic and religious lines during the 2023 elections, putting both Tinubu and Peter Obi into consideration.[30] He

---

28. Gbemiga Ogunleye, "Tinubu goes for the Broke," *The Punch*, June 6, 2022.

29. Farooq Kperogi, "Atiku's Interview and Unfair Tinubu Muslim-Muslim," *Notes from Atlanta*, July 23, 2022, https://www.farooqkperogi.com/2022/07/atikus-interview-and-unfair-tinubu.html .

30. Farooq Kperogi, "Tinubu and Obi will either Affirm or Destroy these Two Theories in 2023," *Nigerian Tribune*, August 13, 2022.

noted that Obafemi Awolowo and MKO Abiola, alongside other politicians from recent elections, have enjoyed the ethnic advantage in the past. However, he predicted that the 2023 election might make a difference, especially between the candidacy of Tinubu and Obi in the southern part of Nigeria and especially the South West.[31] He also noted that the possibility of religious factors strengthening Obi's stance, especially among Christians in the South West, might be another twist to the drama.[32] He suggested that Peter Obi's social media popularity could translate to voting, given its instrumentality in Buhari's 2015 election and a reasonable increase in voters' registrations driven by social media movements.[33]

VOTER EDUCATION IN NIGERIA: THE ROLE OF THE EMERGING AND NEW MEDIA

Voter education, voter consciousness, and voter turnout are three inter-related concepts in Nigerian elections, and the 2023 elections were not any different, especially as the gubernatorial elections of 2021 and 2022 have valuable insights that served to predict the possible happenings at the 2023 polls. Voter education is an ever-recurring concept in the Nigerian political space because while the people seem informed, some of their actions betray any form of political education. Vote buying, disenfranchisement, and voter manipulation are some things that Nigerian politicians bank upon during the polls. That is one reason political parties disburse huge sums of money for "grassroots mobilization."

This grassroots mobilization is nothing but the provision of foodstuff and paltry sums of money for massive vote buying. Political parties often contest to win over more electorate members with their largesse. Vote buying in Nigeria is an act that swings both ways—it takes two to tango. It involves the active participation of the electorate and the political parties. Several members of the electorate across local government areas consider the election year a time to make money off political candidates—this mindset is shared by the educated and the uneducated. Vote-buying is as old as Nigeria's independence. According to research, even the 1993 election, touted to be Nigeria's freest and fairest, witnessed vote-buying at a sum between 120 million naira and 1 billion naira.[34]

Thus, Nigerian political officeholders know that election or re-election is not based on antecedents, promise, competence, or performance but on how well they can satisfy the ephemeral cravings of the electorate during the election. A federal represen-

31. Kperogi, "Tinubu and Obi."
32. Kperogi, "Tinubu and Obi."
33. Kperogi, "Tinubu and Obi."
34. Evelyn Okakwu, "Nigeria's 'Freest' Election Witnessed Vote-Buying 'Worth N120m to N1bn'—Group," *Premium Times,* April 16, 2019 https://www.premiumtimesng.com/news/more-news/325718-nigerias-freest-election-witnessed-vote-buying-worth-n120m-to-n1bn-group.html.

tative can then stay away from his constituency and constituents for three of their four years in office, returning during the fourth year to curry his people's favors, spend money, and get re-elected. This pattern is so common in Nigeria that people hardly find it absurd for a political officeholder or an aspirant to assuredly declare that they would "deliver" their constituency, polling unit or local government, in which case "deliver" means they would win their constituency for their party.

In his June 21, 2022 article titled "PVCs as Poverty Verification Cards,"[35] Kperogi expounds on how rife vote-buying is during Nigerian elections, stating that voter's card has become Poverty Verification Card, through which voters can comfortably trade their future for immediate financial gratification. He notes that the pitiable show that was the gubernatorial election in Ekiti State is a premonition to what may happen at the 2023 presidential election, seeing as Nigeria is the poverty capital of the world, where millions are despondently poor.

The situation of the Nigerian electorate is such that the voters, although having adequate voter education and knowing the consequences of vote-buying, still go ahead to trade their votes for paltry sums or foodstuff from the political parties. This is a grave situation for the country because the electorate has come to expect aspirants to offer them something for their votes, so much so that any aspirant that decides against such a heinous act is considered unserious about winning the election. As a result, some aspirants choose to invest in pleasing the electorate's demands on election day. They win the election and then abandon their constituency and constituents while garnering returns in multiple folds on the investment they made at the polls. Sadly, the electorate hardly cares about this malleable phenomenon. Nigeria is a parody where the electorate hardly holds its leaders accountable.

Despite this, presidential elections in Nigeria still face low voter turnout. At any stage of Nigeria's democracy, it has never witnessed a voter turnout of 50% or higher of its registered voters. That is to say, millions of Nigerians register for the permanent voter's card but end up not exercising their franchise at the elections. One would think that as the country ages and the people become more politically conscious, voter turnout percentage would improve, but such is not the case. Things seem worse, as the Independent National Electoral Commission (INEC) puts voter turnout between 30% and 35% in the country.[36]

It would not be out of place to say Nigeria practices faux democracy, seeing as the electoral decisions in the country are made by a lesser percentage of the country's eligible voters. Thus, whoever emerges as the president is not necessarily the choice

35. Farooq Kperogi, "PVCs as 'Poverty Verification Cards,'" *Notes from Atlanta*, June 2, 2022, https://www.farooqkperogi.com/2022/06/pvcs-as-poverty-verification-cards.html.

36. Premium Times, "Voter Turnout in Nigerian Elections around 35%—INEC," *Premium Times*, February 9, 2021, https://www.premiumtimesng.com/news/more-news/441649-voter-turnout-in-nigerian-elections-around-35-inec.html.

of the people but the choice of the few people who vote. Such is the conundrum of elections in the country. Among other reasons, Nigerians register for the permanent voter's card because it is a means of registration and a good and free alternative to other means of registration and identification like a driver's license or passport.

Some people register and end up not collecting their voter's card due to the fear of electoral violence, migration from their local registration point, etc. Indeed, relocation from one ward to another within the same town or city or even to another local government area or state should not be strong enough to disenfranchise people. But many other things keep the people out of the polls. Apart from being discouraged by the stressful processes involved in registering for the permanent voter's card in Nigeria, there is an ingrained distrust in the election regulatory body, Independent National Electoral Commission. Nigeria has a history of election rigging from one government to the other. As a result, some Nigerians, from one generation to the other, have lost trust in the system, as they have been forced to believe that people's votes are useless. Consequently, millions of eligible Nigerians do not have voter cards and have never considered voting at the polls.

Nonetheless, we cannot but acknowledge the role the new media has been playing in educating voters, raising voter consciousness and awareness, and combating low voter turnout. Solving the problem of low voter turnout in Nigeria and massively educating the voters is an endeavor that needs strategic implementation. Although the contributions of the new media have their downsides, such as the widespread fake news and cyberbullying, new media achieved a lot for the 2023 elections.

It has, for instance, shown that organic support for a political candidate is possible in Nigeria. Since defecting to the Labor Party, Obi has enjoyed massive support online, which has further spurred other candidates to strengthen their online presence and engage Obi's supporters online. Social media has also served to debunk the lies peddled by different political parties. The benefit to our democracy is that now, more than ever, voters are informed, and the choice of a wrong leader can no longer be attributed to ignorance.

The role that social commentators like Kperogi have played and continue to play in voter education and raising voter consciousness and awareness cannot be undermined. Social commentators, with their large following on social media platforms, help voters form informed opinions of the political candidates, thus exposing the lies that the campaign teams of these candidates might have crafted to deceive them.

Kperogi consistently writes about aspirants and the political issues surrounding them to get the electorate adequately informed and duly warned about them. The relentlessness of his writing efforts is one of his strengths, as opinions, if not constantly revisited, are quick to die. Kperogi has also taken over social media to assume the role of a watchman that blows the whistle on every political development in the country, thereby constantly invoking important political discourses among the people. In

one of his Twitter posts, he stated that Nyesom Wike's "inconsolably infantile temper tantrums" have justified whatever wisdom made Atiku Abubakar decide against him as his running mate in the 2023 presidential election.[37] Wike was one of the presidential candidates in the PDP primaries and the major candidate from Southern Nigeria. After losing the primaries, he was put forward as Atiku's running mate, but the latter picked Ifeanyi Okowa against general expectations. Since then, Wike has been in different controversial discussions and reactions, showing his disappointment with the development.

In another post, Kperogi criticized the controversial clergymen's appearance at the APC's unveiling of Shettima as Tinubu's running mate in the 2023 presidential election. The APC had been alleged to have placed fake clergymen on display at the unveiling, indirectly stating the support of the Christian folks for their candidacy. Before this incident, the leadership of the Christian Association of Nigeria had rejected the controversial Muslim-Muslim ticket.[38] However, Tinubu and the APC have unsurprisingly refuted such claims, stating that the bishops were unknown but not close to being fake.[39] This rebuttal seemed not enough to convince the public, including Kperogi, as it reacted with further criticism. Kperogi regarded it as "sophomoric and tragicomical self-own."[40]

CONCLUSION

We have examined the history of presidential elections in Nigeria, and also, through the study of Kperogi's writings, we have traced patterns that came to play in the months leading to the 2023 presidential polls in Nigeria. The country is a faux multi-party system, as the Nigerian political dream is to emerge as a flagbearer of the Peoples Democratic Party or the All Progressives Congress. Furthermore, there is a thin or non-existent line between the ideologies of political parties in Nigeria, such that defecting from one party to the other is rampant. In Nigeria, what matters most is the aspirant's personal interests, and they would go to any length to achieve those interests, including defecting from their party to their supposed opposition party. If

37. Farooq Kperogi, "Wike's Continuing, Inconsolably Infantile Temper Tantrums Weeks after Losing the PDP Presidential Primary help to Dramatize the Wisdom in Atiku's Decision to Pass him over for the Position of Running Mate. Wike Lacks the Temperaments and Maturity to be President or Vice President," *Twitter,* August 12, 2022, https://twitter.com/farooqkperogi/status/1558110878465236994?s=20&t=V0P_y4iQf_jXkGe6XudnaA.

38. Luminous Jannamike, "2023: We'll Reject Muslim-Muslim Ticket—CAN," *Vanguard Newspaper*, July 19, 2022.

39. Omeiza Ajayi, "I didn't Hire Fake Christian Clerics for Shettima's Unveiling—Tinubu," *Vanguard Newspaper*, July 21, 2022.

40. Farooq Kperogi, "The Tinubu-Shettima Fake Bishops Saga. The fake Bishops Misadventure at Tinubu's Unveiling of Shettima as his Running Mate is such a Sophomoric and Tragicomical Self-own. It both Needlessly Aggrandized the Lack of Religious Pluralism in the APC Presidential Ticket it was Supposed," *Twitter,* July 20, 2022.

Figure 18.3. "Awaiting 2023," Dr. Kazeem Ekeolu

Nigerian politicians can fluidly defect from one party to the other, it will be illogical to claim that these parties have distinct political ideologies that influence their decisions and modus operandi.

Nigeria has a long way to go in all aspects of its electoral processes. The change needed is a systemic one that would be far-reaching, touching aspirants, political parties, the election regulatory body, the electorate, and the election officials. Nigeria needs to address these issues head-on from all angles. Solving these issues one-by-one will make little or no difference because if one is attended to and the others are not, they will continue to fester and probably render the first one ineffective.

As future elections draw close, political writings and commentaries are expected to intensify. Kperogi will, without doubt, continue to write about the Nigerian political space and the handwriting on the wall as it concerns elections. He represents a watchman observing and criticizing the political developments and testing the waves as they

roll toward the election. He has also portrayed himself as an advocate of media freedom and checked social media censorship. Kperogi does not believe in sacrificing the people's freedom of expression for mere political control and unfounded policies.[41]

In a heavily polarized country like Nigeria, the role of socio-political commentators cannot be overemphasized. If such commentators have achieved a status like Kperogi's—one that shows that their motivation does not lie in the financial benefits they could gain from aspirants or the government—they should be encouraged and motivated to write consistently. Nonetheless, there is the need to have writings that would not further aggravate the polarity of the country.

41. Kperogi, *Digital Dissidence.*

19

MOSES OCHONU

The Nigerian Nation, the University System, and the Corrupt Country

INTRODUCTION

Today's Nigerian situation is not without precedent. Bad decisions and degrading developments may have facilitated recent problems, but these issues have been building momentum for many years. Every nation reflects its history, and Nigeria has cultivated political and social antecedents that have grown to choke society. Either the country's foundations have not been sturdy enough, or successive governments and citizens have worked to destroy society instead of strengthening it.

The genesis of Nigeria's problems can be connected to history and past decisions. Historian Moses Ochonu has linked the Nigerian past and present, charting a course that the nation can follow to improve its future. Ochonu carries a torch—one lit by insights from the past—that he uses to illuminate the path to a brighter Nigerian future.[1] As a historian, Nigeria's past has taught him what a path to perdition looks like. He has warned the Nigerian public to avoid these paths, but it remains to be seen whether they will listen.

Ochonu's importance comes from his understanding of Nigerian corruption, its context, and its interactions with key components of Nigerian society. Corruption

1. Toyin Falola, "Professor Moses Ochonu: A Historical March into the Future," *Premium Times*, September 6, 2017, https://opinion.premiumtimesng.com/2017/09/06/professor-moses-ochonu-a-historical-march-into-the-future-by-toyin-falola/.

was a national characteristic even before the British colonizers transferred the mantle of leadership to Nigeria, and it has remained an identifiable part of the country's history. Corruption is one of the major threats to Nigeria's future, and Ochonu has traced its influence throughout history. His work identifies corruption in various institutions, its effects, and the individuals who enable it.

Nigeria is endowed with abundant natural resources, especially crude oil, and those resources have caused problems for the country's development since the oil boom in the early 1970s. Nigeria's human capital, while exceptional, has difficulty competing in international markets. Ochonu has repeatedly pointed out the corruption that has eaten deep into every sphere of Nigerian socio-political engagement, and its effects have made it difficult for the country to make political or economic advances. Political actors have contributed to Nigeria's decadence, with various governments pursuing destructive goals. The present generation may wish to blame post-colonial political leaders, but even before independence, the leadership of Nigeria's component regions enabled the entrenchment of corruption.

Political leadership, as a term, is not limited to various governments and their representatives. The totality of the political class, comprised of elites and the bourgeoisie, gradually attained the influence necessary to pressure successive governments while avoiding scrutiny during agitations for proper political representation. Military and civilian governments have held the reins of governance in Nigeria, and each one has institutionalized the corruption encouraged by political leadership before independence.

Political corruption has ravaged Nigeria so thoroughly that formerly cherished values have disappeared along with the rest of the country's potential. Paradoxically, the world's eighth-largest producer of crude oil has more than 40% of its population living below the poverty line. This situation exists due to massive political graft and wanton mismanagement of crude oil proceeds.[2] The political class participates in governance not to develop the nation but to pursue their own goals and amass personal wealth at the expense of the people.

No country in the world has seen steady growth and development in every aspect of society, but selfless political leadership makes the difference between progress and stagnation. Chinua Achebe has noted that bad leadership is the root cause of Nigeria's problems:

> Nothing is basically wrong with Nigeria with respect to land, climate, and water or the air we breathe. The major problem of Nigeria is the reluctance and inabil-

2. World Bank, "Deep Structural Reforms Guided by Evidence are Urgently Needed to Lift Millions of Nigerians out of Poverty," *The World Bank*, March 22, 2022.

ity of the leadership to rise to respond to a personal example, which is the hallmark of great leaders.[3]

Many issues affect Nigeria, including the absence of basic amenities and the lack of adequate research and development, but increasing corruption from successive governments has been the primary factor hindering growth and development in the country. It affects every aspect of the Nigerian government, with graft at the highest levels enabling corruption in the lower cadres, seen as police extortion, port congestion, ghost workers, election irregularities, and civil service redundancies.

Ochonu has noted that incidents of corruption are endemic to many nations and every religious faith. Corrupt practices existed in ancient civilizations in Egypt, Rome, and Greece, and they have been passed from generation to generation.[4] A major differentiating factor between the corruption of the past and present is the all-encompassing level at which it is practiced. The epidemic of corruption throughout Nigeria's political landscape has defied all known remedies. Corruption in Nigeria is akin to what Aristotle described as "taking more water to free yourself from the chokehold of water."[5]

These legacies have been left by the practices and economic structure of Nigeria's colonial exploitation. The British colonial administration forayed into present-day Nigeria and came into contact with various distinct kingdoms and clans from the South up to the North. In the Middle Belt, a hybrid of Northern and Southern cultures, the British colonial government attempted to establish political uniformity; they schemed to implement a caliphate-like political structure more suitable for their selfish objectives. Ochonu has pointed out a flaw in this plan: British indirect rule was only possible through the Hausa Caliphate because the Northern part of Nigeria had previously developed a centralized political authority.[6] Such an authority did not exist in the various communities and clans that made up the Middle Belt region.

To ensure the success of their misapplied tactics, the British colonial administration embarked on a series of campaigns to divide and rule local groups, making national unity in Nigeria difficult. The vast Middle Belt region contains the River Niger and River Benue, which the Royal Niger Company needed for trade purposes. This made the region quite important to the British colonial government. The European governance required in the Middle Belt was starkly incompatible with the Hausa Caliphate structure, but Lord Lugard used propaganda to disguise its shortcomings. He believed

---

3. Chinua Achebe, *The Trouble with Nigeria* (Oxford: Heinemann Educational Publishers, 1984).

4. Seymour Martin Lipset and Gabriel Salman Lenz, "Corruption, Culture, and Markets." In *Culture Matters*, eds. Lawrence E. Harrison and Samuel P. Huntington. New York: Basic, 2000), 112.

5. J. L. Creed and A.E. Wardman, trans. *The Philosophy of Aristotle* (New York: New American Library, 1963).

6. Moses Ochonu, "Colonialism within Colonialism: The Hausa-Caliphate Imaginary and the British Colonial Administration of the Nigerian Middle Belt," *African Studies Quarterly* 10, no. 2 (2008): 95–127.

the indirect rule system would impose a centralized civil authority that maintained law and order in tribal communities. Despite the success of indirect rule in Northern Nigeria, the British colonial government faced an ongoing series of problems.

Early footholds for political corruption were found in the forceful entrenchment of indirect rule. The colonial administration implemented these policies in some regions of Nigeria for their selfish motives, not for local development. Ochonu has noted that the contradictory British commitments to a functional, cultural homogeneity catalyzed an administrative crisis. It ultimately led to conflict and ethnic suspicion in the Middle Belt.[7]

The British introduction of indirect rule caused untold havoc in the Middle Belt and allowed Northern Fulani nomads to infiltrate a once-impregnable fortress, creating problems that persisted in the region. The Tiv people, who comprise most Middle Belt inhabitants, had successfully defended themselves against Fulani incursions before the advent of colonialism. The Islamic caliphate of the North had been locked in a stalemate with communities in the Middle Belt, halting its expansionary efforts. As Ochonu has argued, precolonial tensions created deep resentment and fear among Middle Belt residents, leaving them suspicious of anything and everything that came from the North.[8]

Colonialists opened the Middle Belt to the Northern caliphs. Successors of the early nineteenth-century jihadist leaders exploited the opportunity presented by the British colonialist actions. Ochonu has pointed out that some among them saw the entire Middle Belt region as a part of the Zazzau Emirate, including the Niger-Benue confluence. A Fulani allegedly stated that he would give England's monarch a place on the coast in the confluence—which God had bestowed on them—to build a town that would affirm their supremacy over the Middle Belt. This was an ongoing concern for the region's indigenous inhabitants. The British perception of the Northern emirate was shaped by an initial report from Lord Lugard, who claimed that the Islamic political institution of the Hausa-Fulani held sway over the entire Northern region, including its coastal areas. This approach relegated the Tiv, Igala, and other coastal groups to minority status.

POST-COLONIAL CORRUPTION

The British government planned to perpetuate its imperialistic rule by shifting power to Northern Nigeria. The region's precolonial system of government seemed more appealing to colonial administrators than the system in the rest of Nigeria. Ochonu noted that the British approach to Nigeria was similar to their strategy in

7. Ochonu, "Colonialism Within Colonialism."
8. Ochonu, "Colonialism Within Colonialism."

Figure 19.1. "Moses Ochonu, Nigeria and the Corrupt Country" by Michael Efionayi. Moses Ochonu, a corruption ranking and logo of Toyin Falola Interview.

Asia, giving covert support to the North by granting it significant administrative power over other regions in Nigeria.

The British withdrawal from Nigeria left a set of political leaders that had received British training to handle the reins of government. Before its departure, the colonial government reported that public servants in Nigeria and other African countries were taking a personal financial interest in their government work—the government openly acknowledged that the political class was exploiting national resources for personal enrichment. The first Nigerian republic after independence, led by Nnamdi Azikiwe and Abubakar Tafawa Balewa, was marked by corrupt practices. Public officials competed to loot government funds, and they displayed their ill-gotten wealth both wantonly and recklessly.

Nigeria's corruption between 1960 and 1963 left every citizen doubting whether a single good man existed among those who held public office. After colonial withdrawal, the mindset of this first set of public officials focused on amassing wealth and living extravagantly is easily explained. Ochonu rhetorically asked how Africans were expected to react to the structures and opportunities that the colonial authorities had left behind.[9] The overt greed of those who inherited control from the colonial administrators invited the first military intervention in Nigerian politics, occurring less than

9. Moses Ochonu, "African Colonial Economies: Land, Labor, and Livelihoods," *History Compass* 11, no. 2, 2013: 91–103.

six years after the British departure. In most African nations, military takeovers of civilian governments occur as attempts to address corruption and limited development progress. This does not always solve the problem, as coups can be led by individuals who engage in even more corrupt practices that show the deposed political class as mere novices.

In Nigeria, the military junta of Major-General Johnson Aguiyi-Ironsi ousted the first republican government and set up an inquiry to investigate past involvement in various corrupt practices. The public was initially enthusiastic about seeing an end to the civilian government's widespread corruption, but a counter-coup brought in a new junta under the leadership of Yakubu Gowon. The Gowon administration freed every politician detained due to corruption charges, suggesting that the military was no different from civilian regimes.

Gowon was a regular focus of discussions concerning his inexplicable wealth. In 1974, his name regularly appeared in Nigerian daily publications alongside other public officials accused of siphoning off the proceeds of rapidly increasing crude oil sales. His administration was toppled by yet another junta, which appointed a new military head of state. The new leader, General Murtala Muhammed, publicly declared the extent of his assets and insisted on greater transparency for the finances of public officials. His regime instituted a series of financial probes that exposed the misdeeds of previous military governors, summarily dismissing them from the armed forces.

Under the Murtala Muhammed-led military government, the Belgore Commission of Inquiry investigated contract irregularities within the Ministry of Defense to expose self-dealing. His efforts to clean up Nigeria's government were cut short after six months when he was assassinated in office. Murtala Muhammed's Chief of Staff, Obasanjo, successfully returned power to a civilian government, culminating in the establishment of the Second Republic.

The oil boom made Nigeria a financial success overnight, and there were more than enough opportunities for public officers to steal. A sum of $16 billion in oil revenue was allegedly lost to corruption between 1979 and 1983, and that figure does not account for the deliberate mismanagement of funds that had been concealed through acts of sabotage damaging various national buildings. Shagari, the democratically elected president that succeeded the Murtala junta, was a weak leader who could not administer the country effectively. Various members of his cabinet were involved in the graft that stole billions of naira, with elected public officials conducting mass looting of public funds.

Ochonu has observed that political corruption is represented in the Hausa moral discourse as *fashi da mukami*, a term that describes robbery through political influence.[10] Shagari allowed his northern friends, most notably Umaru Dikko, to engage

10. Moses Ochonu, "Corruption and Political Culture in Africa: History, Meaning, and the Problem of Naming," *The Law and Development Review* 4, no. 3 (2011): 27–58.

in *fashi da mukami* without being held accountable. Eventually, General Buhari—an individual from the North who remains perceived as one of Nigeria's few leaders with integrity—took action to remove the corrupt Shagari government. This was positioned as another attempt to rescue Nigeria from corruption.

Buhari aimed to restore discipline and integrity to public office, showing little respect for human rights while arresting and jailing governors and commissioners. Critics attacked the extreme measures used in his fight against corruption, and those who stood to benefit from ongoing graft were intent on fighting back. General Ibrahim Babangida deposed Buhari on the pretext of Buhari's lack of respect for human rights. Ochonu has described corruption as a willful departure from a moral system, and although Buhari's government had no financial scandals, its disrespect for human rights can be described as the oppressive actions of corrupted minds.

The Babangida government's ideology was the polar opposite of the Buhari administration. Buhari was determined to eradicate corruption through various heavy-handed policies, like the institutionalization of the War Against Indiscipline Brigade, but Babangida was determined to institutionalize corruption. Under Babangida's regime, public officials and civil servants engaged in unprecedented corruption. Babangida sanctioned corruption in various government parastatals across Nigeria while pardoning corrupt officials who had previously been convicted by the Murtala and Buhari governments. Not only were they released, but Babangida also returned the assets that the previous governments had seized.[11]

Babangida's most egregious act of corruption was his cancellation of Nigeria's most free and fair election. He used flimsy pretexts to justify his actions, and the public outcry that followed the annulment created serious problems for his government. Babangida was ultimately compelled to transfer power to an interim national government after eight years in office. The interim government lasted less than a hundred days before another military junta seized control from civilians once again.

Under Nigeria's military administration, General Abacha introduced a unique form of corruption perpetrated by him and his cronies. Ochonu has stated that their venality surpassed that of other notorious African leaders, such as Mobutu Sese Seko.[12] Today, Nigeria's government still receives calls from Western governments demanding a return of assets stolen by Abacha. It is estimated that Abacha and his family stole more than $4 billion from the Nigerian public between 1993 and his death in 1998.[13]

General Abacha was replaced by Abdulsami Abubakar, who was committed to restoring democracy in Nigeria. Abubakar's brief tenure gave few opportunities to

11. Alex Gboyega, *Corruption and Democratization in Nigeria* (Ibadan: Agba Areo, 1996).
12. Gboyega, *Corruption and Democratization.*
13. Chris W. Ogbondah, "Political Repression in Nigeria, 1993–1998: A Critical Examination of One Aspect of the Perils of Military Dictatorship," *Africa Spectrum* 35, no. 2 (2000): 231–242.

evaluate his government, but the democratically elected leaders serving from 1999 until today bear some responsibility for the ongoing, monumental levels of corruption in Nigeria.

The People's Democratic Party (PDP) government, led by Obasanjo, took systematic steps to limit corruption by establishing two anti-graft institutions: the Economic and Financial Crime Commission (EFCC) and the Independent and Corrupt Practices Commission (ICPC). The ICPC addressed domestic concerns over bribery, graft, and abuse of public office, and the EFCC was established as a response to pressure from the international community—Nigeria's government was compelled to show that it was participating in the global fight against money laundering. The ICPC limits its investigations to public officials, and the EFCC can investigate private citizens who appear to be living beyond their means. Although these efforts have been moderately successful, securing more than 100 convictions in 2014 and 2,220 convictions in 2021,[14] they regularly face political interference that limits their ability to prosecute high-profile politicians.

Corruption in Nigeria has turned crude oil, one of the country's greatest assets, into a curse for the nation. Nigerian citizens and the world expected the oil boom to bring substantial public development. However, crude oil revenue has divided the country further, and the standard of living continues to decline while public institutions collapse.

The ongoing battle against Nigerian corruption continues, and some initially believed that the Buhari administration substantially reduced corrupt practices. On the other hand, political leadership has been complicit in selectively convicting public officials. The national chairman of Nigeria's All Progressives Congress (APC) allegedly claimed, "If you join our party, your sins are forgiven." This was regarding a senator the EFCC had investigated; those investigations were halted after the senator left the PDP to join the APC. The Buhari government successfully convicted three former governors—Jolly Nyame, Joshua Dariye, and Orji Uzor Kalu—sentencing them to twenty-eight years, fourteen years, and twelve years, respectively. However, Orji Uzor Kalu's conviction was overturned by the Supreme Court, and unfortunately, the optimism of reducing corruption was misplaced.

Nigerian corruption takes various forms, existing in varying aspects of public life. Major decision-makers who formulate the nation's laws commit political corruption at the highest level of government. Corrupt practices at this level are mostly unchecked, involving multiple actors and making it difficult to indict any one person for such practices. If venerated political leaders such as Obafemi Awolowo have been allegedly implicated in corruption for personal enrichment, then it shows just how

14. *Vanguard Nigeria*, January 6, 2022.

Figure 19.2. "Corruption in Academia" by Dr. Kazeem Ekeolu. A student offering a bribe to a professor who rejected it, a reflection of how a societal problem affects the nation.

decadent Nigeria's political leaders have been and how widespread the problem remains.

Political corruption affects decision-making processes, allowing various individuals to manipulate outcomes and distort good governance. Although Nigerians have demanded a reduction in the allowances paid to government legislators, these individuals have found little reason to address the public's concerns. Politics in Nigeria is perceived as a money-making endeavor, and political aspirants are ready to dole out campaign funds as an investment that pays off in access to taxpayer money after attaining office.

Another prevalent form of corruption occurs within the sphere of public administration. Widespread corruption in schools, hospitals, police stations, and licensing offices is regularly encountered by Nigerian citizens. Individual misdeeds may occur on a small scale, but their mere existence points to a flawed system. Prominent announcements in police stations assert that bail is free, but Nigerians know that any relative or acquaintance caught in a police net will need to pay a bribe to be released, even when they are innocent.

Personal relationships are often necessary to obtain police services in Nigeria, and even then, there may be an expectation of money changing hands. An anecdote from Ochonu detailed how Mobutu Sese Seko gave a speech in Kinshasa that endorsed bureaucratic corruption in post-colonial Zaire.[15] This validation of bureaucratic corruption was followed by instances of political leaders enjoining civil servants and public officials to engage in theft as long as it was conducted properly. Civil servants are told they can steal a little, but not so much that they become rich overnight.

Ochonu is a popular commentator on Nigerian affairs. Despite his location in the Diaspora, his observations about Nigeria's political system remain grounded in reality. His essays describe problems that have permeated the country and hindered its development. He often contextualizes Nigeria's predicaments by identifying corruption and failed political leadership. These in-depth discussions of the complex issues that have jammed the gears of national development also identify possible solutions.

Ochonu's criticism of the Nigerian government and its inherent corruption has served as a wake-up call for citizens to unite and oppose bad governance. Many commentaries have identified how Nigeria's failed political leadership undermines its democracy and threatens its continued existence. Although Nigeria returned to democracy in 1999, its economic and socio-political challenges have remained the same, lurching from one problem to another. Ochonu has been a strong voice calling for restructuring a national political system that has been a failure from any perspective.

Democracy has not brought much-needed development to Nigeria. Although democracy is widely regarded as the best form of government, it has been unable to deliver public improvements in Nigeria because of bad governance enabled by bad leadership. Leaders often fail to consider the welfare of the people who voted them into office. Ochonu regularly criticizes such bad leaders and bad governance.

For Nigerians, leadership positions are an opportunity to reap excessive rewards and avoid the daily hardships faced by constituents. Ochonu argues that Nigeria has not received the much-anticipated dividends of democracy because government officials are more interested in appearing popular than in running the state.[16] Nigerian leaders exploit public office for private gain, building dubious political structures that cement their grip on the reins of power. Ochonu asserts that the failure of democracy in Nigeria, caused by failed political leadership, contributes to the absence of real governance and the proliferation of corruption. According to Ochonu, the primary focus of Nigeria's political leadership is an obsession with displays of power.[17] The actions of Nigerian leaders show that they would rather use their authority to intim-

15. Ochonu, "Corruption and Political Culture."

16. Moses Ochonu, "Democracy and the Performance of Power: Observations from Nigeria," *Ufahamu: A Journal of African Studies* 31 (2005): 1–2.

17. Ochonu, "Democracy and the Performance."

idate the masses instead of governing effectively. Political leaders regularly trample upon the citizens' rights.

Ochonu has also criticized how political leaders exercise their power.[18] Politicians focus on amassing popularity and recouping their political investments in their early years in power. They only execute projects toward the end of their tenures to convince the public that maintaining their administration would be a continuity of good governance. When these politicians are re-elected, they completely abandon the projects. It has become an unwritten rule in Nigeria's political system that government officials do not perform their expected duties after re-election. This behavior has led some to push for a constitutional amendment limiting politicians to a single term in office.

Ochonu posits that the political behavior of Nigeria's political class borders on megalomania—it is an obsession with the exercise of power, and "elected officials have immersed themselves so deeply in the thrills of domination that they are no longer capable of imagining themselves outside the confines of governance."[19] Nigerian leaders have normalized the personalization of governmental authority, which makes it difficult for smooth transitions between administrations and further erodes the quality of political leadership in the country.

During elections, Nigerians witness a phenomenon described as seasonal corruption. In a country that prides itself as a model democracy for other African nations, hardly an election goes by without evidence of vote-buying, intimidation tactics, and security forces used to influence electoral outcomes. In a Lagos hotel, an individual was caught with ballot papers on the eve of an election and taken to a police station. An elected official rushed to the station and had the criminal released, which shows the magnitude of corruption in Nigeria. Beyond the institutionalized corruption in Nigeria, other corrupt practices include:

- Favoritism, where resources are distributed based on political alignment.
- Nepotism, where public officials give patronage positions to friends and family.
- Embezzlement, when elected officials steal public assets, is the primary way wealth is created among Nigeria's political class.

Flagrant displays of wealth among Nigeria's political class show how deeply corruption is entrenched. After assuming public office, most elected and appointed officials in Nigeria accumulate riches through shady deals and corrupt practices. Many enter office with only a modest income but most rapidly show a dramatic increase in prosperity. There is little doubt as to the source of their success. The citizens are motivated, but they have limited opportunities for economic success without political

18. Ochonu, "Democracy and the Performance."
19. Ochonu, "Democracy and the Performance."

connections. Some states in Nigeria owe their civil servants up to six months' salary, yet their elected officials showcase their vast wealth and opulent lifestyles on social media. We expect civil servants to be productive and honest, but they have children to raise and bills to pay. These public officials have no option but to engage in bureaucratic corruption.

Charles Chukwuemeka has argued that Nigeria's political leadership results from the country's quasi-democracy.[20] Despite its governmental transition in 1999, Nigeria remains influenced by military leaders, which explains the autocracy within its democracy. Chukwuemeka has argued that military leaders are often rebranded as democrats to participate in elections, but they find it difficult to represent democratic ideals and principles after attaining office. Most of Nigeria's leaders after 1999 have been former military officials—this includes former president Olusegun Obasanjo and President Muhammadu Buhari—and the country has spent less time under the administration of civilian presidents like Musa Yar'dua and Goodluck Jonathan.

Some arguments have also suggested that Nigeria's democracy is a quasi-military government.[21] Chukwuemeka has highlighted instances of dictatorship during Obasanjo's regime, which included the Odi military massacre in November 1999. A similar scenario played out under the Buhari-led administration 21 years later, described as the Lekki Massacre. Democracy faces exceptional struggles in a complex territory like Nigeria when the military remains politically active. Former military officials announce their ambitions for public office after they retire, but a leopard cannot change its spots.

Ochonu is a vehement critic of the Buhari-led administration. His honest, acerbic remarks challenge its weak leadership. Under Buhari's administration, Nigeria moved out of the frying pan and into the fire. Buhari's predecessor was bullied out of office by Nigerians who were fed up with ineffective governance, and they had hoped that Buhari would rescue the nation. However, Buhari is no different regarding bad management and corruption.

In an article titled "Nigeria: The shattering of Buhari's Mythology," Ochonu criticized the government for abandoning its electoral promises and appearing clueless during a national disaster,[22] noting that Buhari was greeted with optimism and expectations for change. However, Nigeria's situation deteriorated during his tenure; an honest assessment of Buhari's leadership would conclude that he had failed. Under Buhari, a former military ruler, security threats increased, the economy suffered, and

20. Charles Chukwuemeka Nweke, "Democracy, Leadership and Nation Building in Nigeria," *Ogirisi: A New Journal of African Studies* 11 (2015): 154–167.

21. Nweke, "Democracy, Leadership and Nation Building."

22. Moses Ochonu, "Nigeria: The Shattering of Buhari's Mythology," *African Arguments*, August 4, 2016, https://africanarguments.org/2016/08/nigeria-the-shattering-of-the-buhari-mythology/v.

ongoing problems with power generation kept shutting down the country's electrical grid. The administration was in charge of a failed state where little was functional.

Ochonu's point was that faith in Buhari's government was misplaced after seeing the extent of his unpreparedness and broken promises. Citizens had made yet another mistake in their choice of candidate, and Buhari himself recognized it while his government blamed their predecessors. Debts increased under Buhari, and citizens suffered from various economic hardships. Imprudent government spending had plunged the nation into an economic crisis, and Buhari's public statements were detached from Nigeria's reality.

Buhari tried to list his government's accomplishments when none was found. He once described the militants as "technically defeated," but the country's weak security architecture left citizens bracing for daily insurgent activity. Citizens were driven out of their homes by security threats while the Nigerian government remained clueless; it donated cars to address insecurity. Even the Buhari government's focus on the security situation in the Niger Delta region was questionable, considering that the rest of the country was burning. Buhari's failed leadership suggested that calamity would follow if Nigeria elects a similar candidate in 2023.

Ochonu criticized the corrupt practices that infest Nigeria's democratic system, especially under Buhari's watch.[23] Corruption is the bane of national development, and Buhari came into power promising to eradicate corruption. Only a few years into his tenure, his government became irredeemably corrupt, and the practices continued while Nigeria's economy suffered. Citizens learned that every Nigerian government promises to address corrupt practices, but few take effective action. Despite the reports of corrupt practices in Buhari's administration, the president made no credible effort to eradicate them.

The effort to rid Nigerian society of corruption requires the involvement of the entire country, not just its elected officials. Ochonu recounted how Nigeria plunged into an economic crisis during the early years of Buhari's administration, leading to severe hardship for the public.[24] They were asked to make sacrifices to cleanse the country of corruption, but they could not bear additional suffering. Instead, they clamored for a return to the corruption that had at least improved their living conditions, comparing the past administration with Buhari's regime. The slogan "Bring Back Corruption" has replaced the idea of good governance. It is not a specific request for corruption but a catchphrase used to demand improved living conditions.

---

23. Ochonu, "Nigeria: The Shattering of Buhari's Mythology."

24. Moses E. Ochonu. "Bring Back Corruption: A Critique of Neoliberal Anti-Corruption Rhetoric," *The News*, September 8, 2016.

EFFECTS OF CORRUPTION ON THE NATION

Public corruption has had a major impact on Nigeria's socio-political and economic development, stalling the country's economic growth and leaving little in the budget for important functions like education. In the 2020 budget passed by the National Assembly, ₦34 billion was authorized for education, and ₦37 billion was earmarked for the renovation of the National Assembly Complex, which had only cost ₦9 billion to build.[25] These details were overlooked in the enthusiasm over the budget's speedy passage, hailed as the first time in Nigeria's history that a budget was approved before the beginning of the fiscal year.

Nigeria's government officials regularly manipulate government spending for their gain. The APC government had promised to establish intervention programs to feed primary school children, but the implementation favored a specific ethnic group. In 2019, the Swiss government returned $300 million to Nigeria as part of its promise to restore looted funds, and the federal government declared that it would distribute the proceeds to benefit low-income families.[26] The beneficiaries all came from the same ethnic group, which has the highest proportion of poor people in Nigeria.

The corrupt practices of Nigeria's political class are linked with their idea that running for office is a business venture. Aspirants take out loans from financial institutions to fund their campaigns, expecting their new office to provide the funds necessary for repayment. The return on investment comes from embezzlement and corrupt practices.

Rampant corruption has also prevented Nigeria from accessing foreign aid. Donors are reluctant to give funds that will be stolen, and the International Monetary Fund has withdrawn developmental support in some corrupt nations. The World Bank is also unwilling to loan money to nations with overtly corrupt governments.

Corruption has destabilized Nigeria's progress because various military interventions, which topple democratic governments under the pretext of fighting corruption, often become more corrupt than the civilian governments they replaced. Nigerian corruption has affected the quality of service delivered by public enterprises and undermined the efforts of private companies. Davis Peck, the Bishop of Guilford, stated that British investors are often reluctant to invest in Nigeria because of bribery, delays in payment, and an absolute refusal to pay for services already rendered. These practices have trapped Nigeria in the abyss of poverty. Individuals who have spent long periods in the country claim it is impossible to avoid corruption in Nigeria. Moral

25. Queen Esther Iroanusi, "Buhari Approves N37 Billion for National Assembly Renovation," *Premium Times,* December 16, 2019, https://www.premiumtimesng.com/news/top-news/368458-buhari-approves-n37-billion-for-national-assembly-renovation.html.

26. BBC "'Abacha Loot' to be given to Poor Nigerians," *News*, June 29, 2018. www.bbc.com/news/world-africa-44654931.

issues have gone unresolved while the government has been unable to establish proper mechanisms to assist businesses and individuals.

Corruption has also affected social relationships between Nigeria's ethnic groups, exacerbating existing integration challenges. Yoruba people in the southwest saw the cancellation of the 1993 election as a gross abuse of power by Northern oligarchs. When a reconciliation and correction panel was set up years later, Northern politicians were reluctant to testify about atrocities committed by Northern military dictators—like Ibrahim Babangida and Buhari—because of the ethnic ties they shared with the perpetrators. Abacha showered the political class with public funds, winning admirers who declared that he was the only leader capable of delivering progress for the country.

The consequences of corruption are too many, and they should be controlled. The corruption plague has thoroughly infected Nigeria's political landscape and must be treated with every available medicine. The problem cannot be solved overnight, but it is still solvable. Proper implementation is the key to success. The Buhari administration, which came to power promising to fight corruption, did little to address the problem. Many public officials have been involved in corruption cases, including Abdullahi Ganduje, a state governor from the APC. Ganduje was caught on video collecting bribes from contract consultants, and the federal government has done nothing to prosecute the governor; judicial proceedings have been halted due to a narrow interpretation of the immunity clause claiming to protect executive officers from prosecution while in office.[27]

Panels dedicated to stopping corruption have only been partially successful. They cannot be more effective until they are supported by a public shift in opinion that embraces a better value system—one where citizens are not encouraged to grab anything that comes their way by any means possible. Nigeria's youth have grown discouraged by the lack of available jobs after they complete their tertiary education. Instead, they participate in get-rich-quick schemes and pursue illegitimate opportunities to generate income.

To win the war against corruption, government decisions should adhere to strict ethical standards. The key lies not only in clearly making laws but also in rigorously upholding them. Without new ethical standards, the structures to fight graft would be merely another source of illicit funds for corrupt officials. Efficient checks and balances are needed, along with greater separation of powers within different branches of government. Those entrusted with the tools to fight corruption must understand the need to act with integrity, ensuring their goals are attainable. With adequate ethical standards, it becomes simple to limit the activity of officials seeking personal gain and to impose stringent penalties against those who violate the rules.

---

27. Emeka Nwachukwu and Murtala Adewale, "Nigerians Seek Ganduje's Resignation over Fresh 'Bribery Video,'" *The Guardian*, November 1, 2018.

The government should establish permanent structures for tackling corruption rather than temporary panels or ad-hoc committees investigating corrupt individuals. Citizens should also resist bribing public officials because corruption is only possible when opportunities are presented. Nigerians cannot experience true development until the public mindset has embraced ethical value systems. The media also plays a role in this fight, educating the public about their rights and exposing political misdeeds. Taming corruption is only possible when words are linked with actions. Good governance, transparency, and accountability are indispensable in society's successful battle against the monster of corruption.

THREATS TO DEMOCRACY

Nigeria is an amalgam that includes many ethnicities, but its socio-political landscape has been dominated by Northern groups that compose the Hausa-Fulani hegemony. The term "Hausa" denotes a people, a language, and a physical landscape—the savanna area of Nigeria that was homogenized by the jihadist conquest of Usman Dan Fodio. This conquest imposed a centralized political authority on various northern states, fusing them into a single unit that spoke a common language.

Ochonu has noted that Hausa is not merely a language; it has become synonymous with socialization and unites a constellation of economic, cultural, and socio-political connotations. Hausa's role as a lingua franca in Northern Nigeria reveals how it has been intertwined with trade and Islamic practices for centuries.[28] Ethnic groups in Nigeria can be majorities or minorities, and religion can be a distinct aspect of some ethnic groups. Northern Nigeria is perceived to be dominated by Muslims, Christians largely occupy the Southeast and Coastal South, and the southwest region is considered to be more balanced, with Muslims having a very slight numerical advantage.

Nigeria's majority ethnic groups are the Hausa, Igbo, and Yoruba, and the country's minority groups are too numerous to be counted. These smaller populations are categorized as linguistically and historically distinct due to their historical evolutions within larger ethnic groups. They have long played subordinate roles in Nigeria's socio-political stage. The Fulani are not a minority group, despite their numerical minority in Northern Nigeria. The jihad of Usman Dan Fodio attempted to purge pre-Islamic Hausa practices from the North, replacing them with norms and values that were considered purely Islamic. This process established the Sokoto Caliphate, which subsequently dominated various minority non-Muslim groups within its territory.

The Fulani central authority used violence to rule over Northern Nigeria's many groups. The British aided this domination by providing resources and support.[29]

---

28. E. J. Arnett, *The Rise of the Sokoto Fulani: Being a Paraphrase and in Some Parts a Translation of the Infaku'l Maisuri of Sultan Mohammed Bello* (London: School of Oriental and African Studies, 1922).

29. Moses Ochonu, *Colonialism by Proxy: Hausa Imperial Agents and Middle Belt Consciousness in Nigeria* (Indiana: Indiana University Press, 2013).

Northern Muslims remain wary of Christian minority groups, which can be seen in the violent conflict that followed the successful election of Patrick Yakowa, a Christian, as the Governor of Kaduna state. The conflict was one of the most violent incidents in Nigeria that did not involve military forces.[30] Northern Nigeria's non-Muslim minority ethnic groups have regularly resisted Hausa-Fulani dominance; one example is the resistance against implementing the Sharia law in Kaduna State.

In his article "Why Liberal Democracy is a Threat in Nigeria,"[31] Ochonu made startling remarks about the waste of resources that accompanies Nigerian electioneering. In 2015, Nigeria had a population of 190 million and spent $625 million conducting elections. Ochonu noted that India, which had 1.2 billion people, spent $600 million. Nigeria is often listed among the most impoverished nations in the world, and yet various Nigerian governments have wasted monumental amounts of resources to conduct elections—close to a billion dollars is spent on elections on a quadrennial basis. Despite this spending, there is no guarantee that elections are free, fair, or legitimate. Every election since 1999 has been followed by violence and death that place additional strains on the political system.

Ochonu has argued that Nigeria's flawed electoral process affects the stability of democracy.[32] Electoral violence makes it difficult for the people to manifest their will, and autocratic tendencies prevent the development of democratic principles. Ochonu has argued that adopting liberal democracy does not reflect "homegrown political struggles. Nor did it emanate from the deliberative and ideological disputations of Nigeria's vibrant public sphere."[33] He has also criticized Nigerian political leaders for failing to comprehend the nuances of liberal democracy before adopting it.

Ochonu has asserted that liberal democracy is maintained by accountability and transparency, which are absent from Nigeria's political system. He has also highlighted the costs of liberal democracy, which can be seen in huge sums spent on elections that fail to reflect the will of the public and the additional expenses involved with running a bi-cameral legislature. In Ochonu's view, Nigerian democracy needs an overhaul. The country must work toward "the African political culture of consensus," adopting a new, homegrown system of governance.

Violent, election-related deaths are perpetrated by two distinct groups identified by Ochonu: political thugs and security agencies, especially the military.[34] Every ruling government in Nigeria has deployed soldiers to polling places, allegedly to maintain peace, although this is a flagrant violation of the Nigerian Electoral Act. At every

---

30. S.K. Bello, "Political and Electoral Violence in Nigeria: Mapping, Evolution and Patterns," *IFRA Nigeria Working Papers* 49, University of Ibadan, 2015.

31. Moses Ochonu, "Why Liberal Democracy is a Threat in Nigeria," *Logos: A Journal of Modern Society and Culture* 18, no. 1 (2019).

32. Ochonu, "Why Liberal Democracy is a Threat in Nigeria."

33. Ochonu, "Why Liberal Democracy is a Threat in Nigeria."

34. Ochonu, "Why Liberal Democracy is a Threat in Nigeria."

election, the presence of armed men in uniform is a potent reminder of the incumbent government's efforts to maintain its hold on the polity. Elections in Nigeria are often followed by such severe unrest that individuals migrate to regions that are considered safe because they are under the control of their kinsmen. Citizens have lost faith in any incumbent government's ability to organize free and fair elections.

Additional problems are created by elected officials who are driven to keep themselves in power for as long as constitutionally possible. Immediately after attaining office, politicians begin scheming to claim another term. Ochonu described Buhari as an example of a paradox: democratic pretenders who constantly undermine Nigeria's democratic process. Buhari promised to introduce market-oriented policies for Nigeria's economy, but they never materialized. Ochonu has also argued that Buhari failed in his promise to combat corruption—the president targeted corruption among his opposition while overlooking the corrupt politicians in his party. Like every government in Nigeria, his administration thumbed its nose at the electorate, believing that it could win a second term through electoral manipulation and silencing its opposition.

Nigerians believed that democracy was a political system that could deliver much-needed developmental strides for their country, but the events from 1999 to the present have continued to leave most Nigerians disappointed. Ochonu has pointed out that the alleged link between democracy and improved living standards has not become a reality in Nigeria, even after more than two decades of uninterrupted democratic governance. Nigeria's political class has perfected the art of corruption by subverting legal processes originally established to promote transparency and accountability.

In their eagerness to legitimize corrupt practices, Nigerian legislators regularly enact laws that enable the theft of public funds. Ruling elites have exploited democratic processes to mismanage the country for their benefit. Nigeria's elected officials are some of the highest-paid public servants in the world, and their country's economy remains in shambles. A close analysis of Nigeria's annual budgets reveals that more than half of the country's revenue is paid to elected officials. Democracy has become costly, and a reasonable portion of Nigerians have begun to doubt that it is an improvement over military rule.

Ochonu has openly stated that democracy has failed in Nigeria and Africa, tracking a major shift in public opinion from 1999 to the present. Some Nigerians remain hopeful that their democratic system will improve over time, expecting the country to eventually develop mature democratic processes. These arguments insist that the freedom enjoyed under democratic governance is worthwhile, even in situations where democratically elected leaders rig elections and steal public funds. The Buhari administration's human rights records challenged these assertions—the extrajudicial killings of Shiite Muslims in 2015 and the ongoing detention of Shiite leader El-Zakzaky raise valid questions about the freedom of Nigeria's citizens.

Nigeria's democratic leadership has also repressed professional media outlets. In early 2019, the Buhari government invaded the Daily Trust newspaper's premises in a manner reminiscent of Nigeria's military misrule.[35] As the free press is trampled, it becomes harder to defend democracy in Nigeria. The news media was muzzled, and journalists were subject to surveillance and intimidation, caging the Nigerian press under an authoritarian leadership that pretended to be democratic. Ochonu points out that removing Onnoghen Walter, the former Chief Justice of the Federation, established prima facie evidence of the Buhari administration's threats to human rights.

The failure of the Nigerian democratic system, and the restriction of human rights under successive democratic governments, have threatened the country's stability and developmental progress. However, these setbacks do not make a case for authoritarian leadership. Ochonu has emphasized that dictatorship cannot solve the problems brought by democratic failure, no matter how benevolent it may be. Rotational democracy has frequently been discussed as an alternative to Nigeria's hegemonic democracy, even though another school of thought suggests that rotational democracy itself opposes the tenets of true democracy. The rotational presidency model should not be completely dismissed in a country that has already imposed plans to promote equal representation, such as the federal character principle in most Nigerian institutions. Ochonu has argued that Nigeria can only turn democracy into an asset by retaining the principles of liberal democracy in a democratic system that is creative enough to suit the country's socio-political and cultural realities.[36]

Democracy exists so that members of society can experience equal participation and representation in governance. In Nigeria, democracy has failed to achieve the first goal, and its citizens have not worked hard enough to achieve the second. Nigerians have reduced their democratic activity to a quadrennial endeavor, believing their input is only valid during the election. This perception is flawed; electoral democracy is an ongoing process to refine and reinforce socio-political dynamics. Nigeria's democracy must be reorganized to support a broader public involvement in governance. In proposing a solution to Nigeria's unending democratic and political problems, Ochonu has said:

> if the top vote-getter gets the office of president; the next top vote-getter gets the office vice president, etc. On the legislative side, if the top vote-getter gets the federal legislative seat for a constituency, the next top two or three vote-getters get the state assembly seats, and the next top three vote-getters get the local government legislative seats, etc.[37]

35. Ochonu, "Why Liberal Democracy is a Threat in Nigeria."
36. Ochonu, "Why Liberal Democracy is a Threat in Nigeria."
37. Ochonu, "Why Liberal Democracy is a Threat in Nigeria."

Ochonu's suggestion describes a democratic process that would produce big and small winners. A proportional allocation of elected positions would mitigate the negative effects of winner-take-all systems by producing a multi-tiered series of victories. Aspirants would be encouraged to run in elections because they were more likely to become part of the administration even if they did not win outright.

Ochonu's blueprint for the survival of democracy in Nigeria deserves careful attention. However, the suggestion for proportional allocation of elected positions may sound good on paper but may not enable the necessary developments in real life. It isn't easy to find examples of elected Nigerian officials working together for a common goal; envisioning multiple aspirants collaborating under disparate levels of authority seems unlikely.

UNIVERSITY EDUCATION ISSUES IN NIGERIA

Ochonu is an ardent critic of the rot in Nigeria's university system, and he has demanded an intervention to address the crisis. He not only condemns the failures that have hindered the growth and development of Nigerian universities, but he has also offered suggestions for improvement. Although many of his approaches to improving the Nigerian university system are described as detached from reality, the truth is that they provide outside-the-box thinking to forge new paths forward.

A careful analysis of Nigerian universities reveals an ongoing decline. University education has been accused of failing to produce useful knowledge for Nigerian society. Part of the problem stems from the anti-intellectualism of government officials who show little commitment to the education sector.[38] University education is a public good that requires state investment, but Nigeria's government has wavered in this commitment, especially regarding research and development. Problems began in the mid-1970s for Nigeria and many other developing economies, reflecting "a much wider socio-economic and political crisis."[39] Graduates from Nigeria's federal universities lag behind their foreign counterparts; the best universities in the country are privately run institutions that continue to invest in research and development.

Ochonu has pointed out that Nigeria and other nations have important roles in supporting education that encourages national socio-economic and political development. These efforts require effective tertiary institutions. The World Bank has affirmed that higher education is fundamental to establishing a sound economy and developing skilled human capital.[40] Nigeria's national policy on education should articulate how this can be achieved. The Federal Ministry of Education, which has outlined the core

---

38. Jimi O Adesina, "Global Trends in Higher Education Reform: What Lessons for Nigeria?" *Journal of Higher Education in Africa/Revue de l'enseignement supérieur en Afrique* 4, no. 1 (2006): 1–23.

39. Adesina, "Global Trends in Higher Education Reform."

40. World Bank, *World Development Report 1998/1999: Knowledge for Development* (New York: Oxford University Press, 1999).

aims of tertiary education in Nigeria, has explained that education contributes to national development through manpower training, the development of intellectual capabilities, and the promotion of scholarship and community service.[41]

Effective tertiary education can sharpen the skills of a nation's citizens while transforming its society and economy to improve national competitiveness. Nigeria's higher education system should vigorously emphasize qualified teaching, research, and development work and provide services to communities through extramural activities. Nigeria's population is increasing, and tertiary institutions should be able to accommodate a larger number of students seeking degrees. However, the potential of Nigerian institutions has always been hindered by problems related to efficiency, quality, and finance. The number of private universities in Nigeria tackling the inadequacies of the tertiary education system has increased sharply.

When we consider tertiary institutions and their importance for national development, the funds allocated to these citadels of learning are more than mere expenses. These are long-term investments that will be beneficial for the entire nation. The benefits are seen in various aspects of society related to lower crime rates, less brain drain, and other cascading benefits. Sadly, the immense benefits of an efficient tertiary education system have been thwarted by problems with corruption. Institutionalized graft has inhibited educational goals, which has impaired the nation's development as a whole.

The management of Nigeria's tertiary institutions can be assessed from two perspectives: internal and external. Internal management of each institution is charted by its organogram—goal setting, policy formulation, and other administrative functions are performed by a governing council that consists of the institution's top echelon of leadership. External management is conducted by Nigeria's National Universities Commission (NUC), which coordinates the activities of every university in Nigeria. There is also the Academic Staff Union of Universities (ASUU), which is a level of quasi-external management. The ASUU operates as a liaison between the internal and external levels of management, providing input on internal management while communicating with external management.

In a 2019 article, Ochonu attacked the ASUU as a growing problem for Nigerian universities.[42] He asserted that the organization had tried the same strategy for several years without seeing different results. In the past, the organization had made progress in the struggle for a more efficient and effective university system, but its activi-

41. Federal Ministry of Education, *National Policy on Education*, 4th ed. (Lagos: National Education Research and Development Council, 2004).

42. Moses Ochonu, "Buhari is not the Problem of Nigerian University, ASUU is," *People's Daily*, November 29, 2019, https://peoplesdailyng.com/buhari-is-not-the-problem-of-nigerian-university-asuu-is/.

ties in the past decade suggest an organization struggling unsuccessfully to reinvent itself.[43]

ASUU's singular weapon for achieving its mission and pressing demands has always been labor strikes. The recent strike was accompanied by propaganda that attacked the federal government's planned introduction of school fees, but it was motivated by the non-implementation of the revised 2009 FG-ASUU agreement. This agreement was renegotiated in 2013 after a prolonged strike.[44] Lecturers have introduced a profit motive that has gradually eroded the age-old concept of academia as a place for ideas. Academic careers are not the highest-paying jobs in Nigeria, but these lecturers are not poorly paid.[45]

Ochonu has criticized concerned stakeholders for neglecting Nigeria's educational system. Multiple discourses among academics have lamented how Nigeria's university system is comatose. These deliberations cite the fact that the university system's design is incongruous with Nigerian society, which threatens its ongoing viability and foregrounds the need for urgent restructuring. The challenge is not specifically limited to inadequate funding or a lack of commitment from government agencies; Ochonu highlights the cyclical strike actions of the Academic Staff Union of Universities (ASUU) and their confrontations with the federal government, which often leads to the shutdown of federal universities. Knowledge production is paused during these confrontations, and students feel the brunt of the impact.

Ochonu has criticized ASUU for its orthodox approach to reforming the university system. His concern is that the government never addresses ASUU's demands, and breakdowns in negotiations extend the duration of strike actions. Ochonu has also suggested that inadequate funding and the lack of commitment from the government are not the major causes of deterioration in the university system. Instead, he has pointed to internal factors, such as corrupt academic practices perpetuated by university lecturers, which have largely been unaddressed.[46] Ochonu has described ASUU as the proverbial lantern illuminating the flaws of another while failing to recognize its shortcomings. He suggests that ASUU should look inwards and engage in self-reflection. When there are allegations of unethical conduct in federal universities, the union often turns a blind eye; the organization is quick to defend even its most guilty members and blames the government for neglecting the university system.

Recurring strikes have become counterproductive for the ASUU because no matter how legitimate their grievances may be, the students and their parents feel most of the impact. This has led to ASUU being criticized as a bunch of selfish, money-

43. Ochonu, "Buhari is not the Problem."

44. Ochonu, "Buhari is not the Problem."

45. Ochonu, "Buhari is not the Problem."

46. Moses Ochonu, "The Problem of ASUU and way Forward," *Notes from Atlanta*, 16 January 2021, https://www.farooqkperogi.com/2021/01/problem-of-asuu-and-way-froward.html#.YAJ0iFnE_M4.twitter.

grabbing individuals who do not care about how their actions affect other stakeholders. Strike actions have become so frequent in Nigeria's tertiary education system that it is difficult for graduate students to complete their studies within a predictable time frame. Private universities do not suffer these problems but charge exceptionally high fees. Many stakeholders in the university system had previously supported strike actions as valid tools for making demands, but their ongoing application has eroded the public's sympathy. Ochonu has pointed out that a professional body, like ASUU, should know when to fight and compromise to be effective—the group must develop other methods.

Nigeria's government has played its role in continuing the tertiary education strikes and has mastered a strategy to exploit ASUU leadership. The government puts forward dubious agreements, and the quasi-external ASUU fails to understand that most of these agreements are unrealistic; the agreements have been engineered by a government that does not prioritize the nation's interests. They are little more than choreographed rituals intended to save face and issue bribes through the ASUU in the form of paid backlogs of allowances.[47] It is how the government buys additional time to continue its operations without public pressure, expecting to repeat the process indefinitely. Agreements between the federal government and ASUU have become a periodic effort to show the latter's attempts at asserting its importance, demonstrating its power by shutting down activities in Nigeria's most prestigious educational institutions.

Although university education should be viewed as a tool for national development, Nigeria has reversed this perspective. ASUU may see itself as the custodian of the country's university system, but it has lost public support due to its perennial strike actions. Public opinion sees the union as a body of troublemakers who waste students' futures to pursue futile goals. It is difficult to challenge this assertion because strike actions have not brought much-needed improvements to Nigerian universities.

The Nigerian government appears to have beaten the union at its own game, which explains the feeble responses to union demands. Ochonu has criticized the union for its lack of accountability and its failure to uphold ethical standards among its members, writing that most Nigerians "consider lecturers to be self-absorbed, tone-deaf, insensitive, and navel-gazing operatives who are incapable of seeing how they have become part of the problem" affecting university education in the country.[48]

Ochonu has pointed out that the ASUU has been absent from discourse that addresses the "problems of poor and non-existent teaching; rampant sexual harassment; poor supervision and mentorship; corruption and ethical violations; plagiarism; a

47. Ochonu, "The Problem of ASUU."
48. Ochonu, "The Problem of ASUU."

flawed academic staff recruitment process," and other issues.[49] He has gone so far as to describe it as an identity crisis for ASUU that must be resolved—in addressing the failings of its members and winning back public support, ASUU would make giant strides toward repairing the rot in the university system. Ochonu also recommends student evaluations to ensure discipline among the lecturers and a Students' Bill of Rights to meet student needs and protect the public from corrupt practices.

However, Ochonu has also recognized ASUU victories that have brought some reforms to the university system, such as developing TETFUND to sponsor infrastructure and other projects.[50] He remains disappointed that the union has not leveraged its victories for continued improvements in teaching and research, stating that internal factors "such as corruption, absence of commitment on the part of many lecturers, poor ethics, laziness, bad academic job recruitment practices, careerist resistance to rigorous academic publishing requirements and scrutiny, and the absence of proper academic accountability metrics are major problems that need to be addressed" to salvage Nigeria's university system.[51]

Ochonu sees the current university funding model as unsustainable, declaring that sole reliance on the government for funding will not work. The painful truth is that Nigeria's government does not have the funds to support forty-nine federal universities. This means that other funding models should be explored, involving increased autonomy for federal universities, higher tuition fees, partial privatization, and other options. According to Ochonu:

> You must charge higher tuition and provide financial aid offsets on a need-based determination to keep access open to brilliant but financially incapable students. You have to partially privatize, at the very least, a reform that would raise higher revenue, institute strict financial controls, and pay better wages while demanding quality performance and better learning outcomes.[52]

One example is how Kwara State University—with little support from the Kwara State Government—developed a sustainable model for funding and administration. Collective efforts are needed to restore the spirit of scholarship and academic inquiry in Nigeria's university education system. Several factors threaten Nigeria's tertiary institutions, including:

- Funding: Inadequate funding is the most critical challenge facing Nigeria's tertiary institutions, and it has always interfered with the education sector's

49. Moses Ochonu, "For the Record: My Three Recent Facebook Reflections on the Current ASUU-FG Faceoff and my Proposals for a Holistic, Sustainable Solutions," *USA Africa Dialogue*, February 19, 2022, https://groups.google.com/g/usaafricadialogue/c/cr0u8DXZLhc
50. Ochonu, "For the Record."
51. Ochonu, "For the Record."
52. Ochonu, "For the Record."

development. Funding difficulties have prevented institutions from building lecture halls, acquiring materials to develop student curricula, and equipping laboratories to meet global standards.[53] Although the ASUU-FGN Re-Negotiation Committee has previously affirmed that Nigeria's educational development requires improved capability for both applied and theoretical knowledge, the Nigerian government has not granted the funding to improve that capability.

- Policy Implementation: Underperforming students struggle with poor education delivery in Nigeria's tertiary institutions. Knowledgeable individuals have drafted policies, but implementing those policies has become an arduous task—implementation challenges include a lack of government support and the mismanagement of funds. Lecturers are less concerned with teaching effectively and more interested in personal research that can improve their status, ignoring the needs of their students.
- Resource Scarcity: Nigerian universities can be improved with high-quality human and material resources. Higher education requires adequate teaching staff; they are the central support of the tertiary education system. A solution must go beyond placing a premium on infrastructure and improving lecturers' salaries and allowances; additional staff and learning materials are necessary. Successful institutions are more than physical structures—what occurs within such buildings determines their quality. Many Nigerian universities have many courses that fail to be accredited due to a lack of individuals capable of teaching them.
- Frequent Strikes: The ASUU's periodic closure of universities through strike actions affects the productivity of lecturers and strains undergraduate resources. Many such strikes have focused on improving conditions for university staff. Private universities, which are rarely affected by strikes, charge exorbitant fees that only Nigeria's super-rich can afford. Frequent strikes leave the students unable to fully understand their coursework because their learning schedule has been compressed into a shorter academic calendar. This lowers standards of quality and undermines the products of the university system.

CONCLUSION

Moses Ochonu has outlined the interplay between the state of Nigeria, its history, ongoing corruption, and how these dynamics have affected every sector and institution in the country. He is a scholar and a critic with extensive knowledge of history, an active political consciousness, and an urgent desire for societal transformation. The roots of modern Nigerian society trace back to the precolonial era, with precolo-

53. R. Asiyai, "Trade Union Disputes and their Perceived Impacts on the University System in Nigeria," Ph.D *diss.*, Delta State University, Abraka, Nigeria, 2005.

nial influences that coexist with contemporary forces. Some of the problems faced by Nigeria's present-day society can be tracked through history to the current moment. Ochonu's opinions and approach have vindicated this assertion in his exploration of Nigerian issues.

Ochonu's publications and opinions are a chronicle of Nigeria's history of corruption. Nigeria's post-colonial era included democratic systems and military rule, and it is impossible to say which was the norm—history seems to have recorded more time under military regimes than under democratic administrations. Despite this ambiguousness, Ochonu has diagnosed each era of corrupt practices and outlined their effects on society.

Ochonu's positions often find the reasons for failed political leadership existing within institutional failures. Despite residing in the Diaspora, he has intimated himself with Nigeria's political and social events, following the news as it unfolds and viewing it from an analytic angle. He is the representation of an average Nigerian who believes that the government has failed to promote the welfare of its citizens; instead, the government is obsessed with demonstrating its power.

Ochonu's contributions are contentious, but they are consistently honest. His beautifully acerbic comments challenge the motives behind government decisions, policies, and actions. He has been particularly disappointed by Nigerian citizens who have enthusiastically expelled governments from office, hoping for change, only to find that they have repeated a painful cycle of suffering and underdevelopment, especially under the Buhari-led administrations. In his articles and publications, his opinions on the Buhari administration identify other public figures who should share the blame.

Ochonu has grave concerns about the Nigerian educational system, which continues to fall behind global standards. In 2020, students of Nigeria's federal universities endured an indefinite strike for nine months. A similar incident occurred in 2022 when students suffered under a strike that lasted eight months and showed little hope of finding a lasting solution. Ochonu has used his voice to speak on behalf of these students, identifying problems within Nigerian universities that are internal and external. The internal problems include unfavorable policies, corruption, and inefficiency, while the external problems are government ineptitude and broader societal challenges.

20

ANTHONY AKINOLA

The Treatise of a Detribalized Writer

INTRODUCTION

Public analysts worldwide are often accused of taking sides in political issues. The propensity for an individual to be biased in evaluating a political issue may be perceived as human nature. However, a thorough analysis devoid of bias or sentiment is necessary for someone who persistently seeks to present issues matter-of-factly. This is the mindset of a core nationalist.

Akinola[1] was born into a well-connected political family. His father, Chief Josiah Akinola, was a National Council of Nigerian Citizens (NCNC) member. Following independence and in coalition with the Northern People's Congress (NPC), they formed the first Federal Government. Therefore, Akinola's exposure to the dynamics of politics in the Nigerian system came at an early age. His knack for expository political issues and governance in Nigeria reflected this. Those who knew him will tell anyone who chooses to listen that Akinola was one of the most detribalized Nigerians. He consistently advocated for the indivisibility of Nigeria based on his conviction that the unity of Nigeria provides the black race with a loud standing in the global world.

In times like this, when the unity of Nigeria is attacked by the fear of secession, to compare the state of the nation and the thickness of the texture of the country's unity

1. Anthony Akinola died in 2021.

to those before the Civil War of 1967 and not see that the factors that led to the war are regaining strength in contemporary Nigeria due to the increased rate in the agitations, and obvious diversification would be dangerous oblivion. We can agree that the Nigerian Civil War ended a long time ago, but the ghost of the war continues to haunt the nation even today. The war ended, but the nation could not assuage the Biafran ideology. The claims that the southeastern parts of the nation, comprising the Igbo, are marginalized in the social and political arrangement of the country have created sentiments that steer up reactions and confrontations. The Movement for the Actualization of the Sovereign State of Biafra (MASSOB) was one of the agitation groups from 1999 that created constant public demands for the free state of Biafra; other bodies like the Biafran Zionist Movement (BZM) established in 2010, and Indigenous People of Biafra (IPOB) led by Nnamdi Kanu have increased their activities.[2] This has caused political and social tensions in the southeast, with attacks and sit-at-home orders forming parallel orders against those of the legitimate institutions of the states.

The threats to national unity caused by the Biafra agitation for secession have attracted different governmental actions, including the arrest of Nnamdi Kanu of IPOB. However, secession is no more adding pressure from one end but has included agitations from the southwest demanding the creation of the Yoruba Nation and disengagement from the nation amalgamated in 1914. Sunday Igboho-led Yoruba Nation agitations were premised on the recent attacks and kidnappings rocking the boats of Yoruba states. An example of this was the herdsmen's attacks on the farms and people in the southwest.[3] The herdsmen are mostly Fulani nomads that seek greener pastures by intrudingly entering the farms of the indigenes. These occurrences, including ethnic blame attributions on several banditries, kidnappings, and terror attacks in the country, have spiked up agitations that affect the core of Nigerian unity.

Aside from the ethnic differences from the angle of secession, ethnicity has been very predominant in the formation of people's decisions, their actions, and the discharge of public duties. In a nation with over 200 ethnic groups scattered across the country and a high Power Distance Index, it is impossible not to expect ethnic sentiments and confrontations in almost all sectors of society. Drawing from this and other divisional factors which should have portrayed strength in diversity, the issue of ethnic conflicts and tension must always be discussed in contemporary conversations, and if such conversations must follow the right trajectories, Akinola, with his load of contributions and publications on matters affecting the unity of Nigeria and how they manifest in different ways in the society cannot go without mention.

---

2. Hussain Taofik Oyewo, "Threat of Secession: The Biafran Story," *Conflict Trends* 2019, no. 3 (2019): 47–55.

3. Bolaji Omitola, Solomon Adedire, Olawale Olufemi Akinrinde, Olumide Omodunbi, and Mary Magdalene Sackflame, "The Triangle of Terror: Boko Haram, Fulani Herdsmen, Bandits and Organized Insecurity in Nigeria," *Studia Securitatis* 15, no. 1 (2021): 21–33.

Figure 20.1. "Anthony Akinola At Work" by Dr. Kazeem Ekeolu

With over 500 essays published in national and international magazines and newspapers, Akinola's extensive write-ups provide a rich compendium from which one can understand the intrigues and dynamics of the Nigerian political system in the modern era. Akinola has addressed critical issues like secession, the influence of eth-

nicity on elections, as well as rotational presidency in line with social events.[4] Getting all his works together under specific headings is difficult for anyone. However, I have spent some time picking up some of his articles to establish his positions on political issues.

These positions were borne out of years of experience and research dedicated to critical examinations of political development in the country. He has made appreciable contributions to political issues and has become one of the nation's reputable political analysts—a role he has been playing for about forty years. Aside from his takes on the Nigerian character of diversity, he has appraised the role of corruption in politics,[5] political systems,[6] questions of democracies,[7] and opinions of military regimes.[8] Hence, picking some of his articles and commentary on the nation's unity, diversity and ethnicity come from his conviction about the quality of his wealth of knowledge.

SECESSION AGITATIONS

In the article "Short-Sighted Separatist Agitators," Akinola referred to the perceived intelligentsia that believed the disintegration of Nigeria was an eventuality rather than a possibility. Those who wish to see Nigeria disintegrate or collapse would be happy at the spate of insecurity that seems to envelope various parts of the country. The undertone of the message quickly pointed to the same Western world that brought together several ethnic groups to form the nation called Nigeria. As Akinola rightly noted, when one begins to imagine the level of doomsday prophecies constantly churned out by the Western media concerning Nigeria, then it becomes easy to understand why the author affirmed that "they have always believed themselves to be members of the superior race, while the nations they subjected to the colonial rule are vastly inferior."

To lay further credence to his perspective, Akinola retorted that in the event of another civil war like the one Nigeria witnessed between 1967 and 1970, it should not come as a surprise to see the so-called Western powers embark on another partitioning of Nigeria, albeit into smaller groups; this would only ensure that the potentials

4. Anthony Akinola, "The Concept of a Rotational Presidency in Nigeria," *The Round Table* 85, no. 337 (1996): 13–24.

5. Anthony Akinola, "A History of Corruption," *Niger Delta Congress*, July 21, 2008, http://www.nigerdeltacongress.com/articles/a history of corruption.htm.

6. Anthony Akinola, "Manufacturing the Two-Party System in Nigeria," *Journal of Commonwealth & Comparative Politics* 28, no. 3 (1990): 309–327. See also Anthony Akinola, *Party Coalitions in Nigeria: History, Trends and Prospects* (Lagos: Safari Books Ltd., 2014).

7. Anthony Akinola, *Democracy in Nigeria: Thoughts and Selected Commentaries* (Morrisville: Lulu Press, Inc., 2015).

8. Anthony Akinola, "Review of The Abacha Regime and the June 12 Crisis," *The Journal of Modern African Studies* 33, no. 4 (1995): 710–711.

for the country to be great are reduced to the barest minimum. While Nigeria was still perceived as a burden of the British during the Nigerian Civil War, no Western nation gave it thought that the young African nation possessed all the potential to be great. This possibly was why the Western powers ensured that the country remained one.[9] Akinola further inferred what has always been said concerning the amalgamation of the country into one entity; this singular act of the perceived wise Western powers is the foundational problem of Nigeria. According to Akinola, it would have been justified if the various ethnic groups forced into this union were allowed to determine whether or not they intended to be part of the larger entity that came to be called Nigeria. The then visionary leaders of various ethnic minorities and majorities should have decided independently to be part of establishing a massive nation with the size and population needed to truly attain greatness. A similar blueprint was used in the development of the United States of America, which expanded from thirteen states at independence to fifty in recent times.

Taking a cue from history, Akinola decried the high level of misinformed youths in the Nigerian political space. In "Posterity Will Not Forgive Another Civil War," Akinola harped on the demerits of ethnic sentimentality and bigotry. According to Akinola, these two ills are the foundation of the persistent animosity among Nigeria's three dominant ethnic groups. The author referenced the early days of politicking when ethnic sentimentalities were not the deciding factors for accommodating or embracing political leadership. The days of celebrating astute political leaders have been substituted with blind followership based on ethnic alignments. These have resulted in a renewed sense of ethnic-oriented ideological warfare that pitches the major ethnic groups against one another. The major catalyst that fueled the Nigerian Civil War is being brandished again. The Nigerians in the diaspora seem comfortable adding more fuel to an already-tensed situation through their actions and inactions to ensure the doomsday prediction of Nigeria's collapse comes to fruition.[10] Given the negativity that accompanies discussions that center on the remote causes of the Nigerian Civil War, Akinola reflected on the lopsided arrangement bequeathed to Nigeria at the point of independence, with the North having a slight advantage over the South:

> Suffice it to say that the creation of Nigeria was designed, first and foremost, to serve the interests of the colonial masters. The federation bequeathed to Nigerians at independence was lopsided, with political power skewing heavily in favour of the North to the detriment of the then southern regions, Eastern and Western. The colonial approach to education and religion could hardly be described as an effort directed at promoting unity in a nation of different languages and cultures.[11]

9. Anthony Akinola, "Short-Sighted Separatist Agitators," *The Guardian*, April 1, 2021.
10. Anthony Akinola, "Posterity will not Forgive another Civil War," *The Guardian*, January 24, 2020.
11. Akinola, "Posterity will not Forgive."

He provided a major perspective toward understanding the events that led to the Nigerian Civil War, as he ascribed it to the South attempting to upstage a structure perceived as retrogressive to the progress of the key political actors from the region.[12] Whether this is true or not, one only needs to ponder on the agitation of the Northern political elite, who successfully agitated for 50% of the seats at the Federal House of Assembly at the 1950 Constitutional Conference. However, it would not have been possible for the North to achieve this without the help of a portion of the South that shares ethnic differences with the other dominant Southern majority ethnic groups. Akinola further stated:

> ...the South continued to challenge what had constituted northern primacy in politics resulting in a succession of crises. The census crisis of 1962–3 and the contentious federal election of 1964 saw an otherwise divided South singing in unison. It would be naive to assume that the feelings of ethnic politicians did not influence the thinking of soldiers, no matter what was their pretensions to patriotism and non-partisanship, and this was what came into force on January 15, 1966, when a bloody coup attempt terminated our teething experiment at democratic politics.[13]

This laid the foundation for a sequence of conflicts that finally led to the separatist agenda pursued by Lt. Col. Odumegwu Ojukwu, the Eastern Region's then-military governor. Another salient fact brought forward was that the secessionist plan was thought out; crude oil deposits had been discovered in the Southeastern region of Nigeria, bequeathing to the region a commodity with great value. Invariably, the Aburi Accord was undertaken, with the street-smart Ojukwu pushing for a federal arrangement that would favor the Eastern Region economically. In the face of this all, as Akinola noted, the major powers were only interested in the oil and not in finding a fairground for the belligerents. As it was in the past, so is it presently; the major powers are competing furiously for spheres of influence, and any notion of secession would only help them partition the great country into smaller nations that can be exploited in isolation.

As Akinola rightly pointed out, no region in present-day Nigeria could have achieved what it did, were it not for the oil wealth generated in the last fifty years from the Niger Delta region.[14] He noted that the fragile unity of Nigeria seems to only experience stress during periods of extreme tension. The author resisted the general belief that the 1914 Amalgamation was a mistake, preferring to uphold the notion that such narratives are only put forth by political opportunists who want to profit from its collapse. To bolster his assertion, Akinola emphatically stressed that power-

12. Akinola, "Posterity will not Forgive."
13. Akinola, "Posterity will not Forgive."
14. Anthony Akinola, "Beyond Sixty Years of Independence," *The Guardian*, September 28, 2020.

ful nations result from amalgams, Britain and the USA being leading examples. China, despite its size, still feels the need to harness small portions like Hong Kong and Taiwan to be stronger. The article concluded with strong wordings that underscore the patriotic nature of the author:

> With leadership that can drive forward the values of unity, it might not be long before we appreciate the importance of our potentials in an ever-competitive world. Nigeria can be one of the great nations of the world.[15]

One notable observation from the article "Short-Sighted Separatist Agitators" is the author's conviction that politicians sponsor secession agitations in Nigeria. While accusations bordering on perceived marginalization may sound genuine, Akinola affirmed that this is an excuse often blown out of proportion. The exaggerated issue of marginalization was made worse by President Muhammadu Buhari's docile attitude to issues that seem to convey ethnic undertones. For instance, the rampant outcry regarding the atrocities by Fulani herdsmen across the country witnessed little response from the President, who, incidentally, happens to be from the Fulani group. In other words, calls for secession from alleged proscribed groups like the Nnamdi Kanu-led Indigenous People of Biafra (IPOB) may sound justifiable if one looks at the body language of the sitting president on the spate of killings allegedly perpetrated by Fulani herdsmen and bandits across the country. This is not to relegate the sinister motives of several stakeholders involved in secession agitations in Nigeria. Chief among these is the politicking that aims to ensure that Nigeria returns to the system of regional government where the central government is less powerful. According to Akinola, the attempted secession of Biafra (which culminated in the Nigerian Civil War) resulted in the division of Nigeria into 12 states.[16] However, the states' creation triggered hatred before the Biafra secession and the Nigerian Civil War. Akinola also has this to say:

> ... the issue of state creation had predated independence in 1960 and had been contested violently by the minority ethnic nationalities, especially those of the Eastern and Northern Regions of the Nigerian federation. In recent years, even among the assumed homogeneous Yoruba group, the need to curtail the hostile rivalry between the Ooni of Ife and the Alaafin of Oyo, petty as it might seem in the eyes of many, was one argument advanced as a justification for splitting old Oyo State into two: Oyo and Osun States. Ekiti people insisted on a state of their own, even though they were the dominant grouping in the old Ondo State. The Ijebus have not given up on having a state of their own carved out of Ogun Stata.[17]

15. Akinola, "Beyond Sixty Years of Independence."
16. Akinola, "Beyond Sixty Years of Independence."
17. Akinola, "Beyond Sixty Years of Independence."

The above presents a strong conviction of the affinity among the several homogenous and heterogenous communities within the Nigerian space. In other words, secessionist plans and calls for true federalism hinge on power play among various blocs; true federalism is only possible when regions remain autonomous federating units.

As the case has been from inception, Akinola highlighted the major problem of Nigeria as bad leadership. Borrowing a leaf from Chinua Achebe's "The Trouble with Nigeria," the author had this to say:

> Our nation has had a great misfortune with a string of post-independence purposeless leaders, more ethnic than national in their orientations. The military ones have been ordinary in the art of managing a plural society. The immediate reminder that the civil war of 1967–70 had not concluded matters came in April 1990 when an attempted coup challenged the very essence of our nation, with the coup leaders announcing a temporary expulsion of some key states of the north from the Nigerian federation.[18]

However, Akinola patriotically raised some positives; chief among them is the uninterrupted civil rule since 1999 and the conviction of a large proportion of the populace that military rule in Nigeria has become a buried issue. To provide more facts about the brittle unity of Nigeria, Akinola noted that the country had produced four presidents since the emergence of the fourth republic in 1999, two each coming from the North and the South. He also opined that the Nigerian system had witnessed reduced hegemony, unlike in the past. The balance of power between the North and the South has led to a situation where no region has outright superiority over the other. But this might be Akinola's entitled opinion since the way political appointments are shared still show some element of favoritism for the North, though this is subject to cross-analysis and deep evaluations. Providing solutions to the challenge of bad leadership that the country seems not to know how to wriggle out of, Akinola suggested that administrations should ensure that political appointments are more balanced, and true democrats should rise and take the mantle rather than allow opportunistic politicians to hold sway in the political process. His reason for this is not far-fetched; those that brought the country to its knees are opportunistic politicians who are only driven to seek elective power for selfish motives.

In conclusion, one can only assume that Akinola's patriotic side precedes his objective assessment of Nigeria's problem. He declared that it would be improper for true Nigerians to put the nations on a pedestal that would result in another civil war. He also provided a worthy option—the possibility of having a collective voice that will focus on identifying how true federalism can be achieved, albeit peaceful and

18. Akinola, "Posterity will not Forgive."

non-violent.[19] Another noteworthy fact is that the agitation for true federalism should not be based on sectional greed or political arrogance; rather, it should indicate a true path toward national development. As the author holistically pointed out, agitating for a break-up of Nigeria should not be an option if the country's full potential must be realized in the future.

ROTATIONAL PRESIDENCY: IDEAL OR NOT?

Anthony Akinola was always quick to discuss the concept of a rotational presidency in Nigeria. While this concept is not enshrined in the country's constitution, it has become a political tool used by political parties to promote long-lasting unity among its ethnically-diverse members. The persistent feuds in the Nigerian political space hinge on the acceptance or rejection of political leadership based on ethnic sentimentalism. The Northerner is never fully convinced that a president from the Southern extraction will prioritize the interest of the North in the course of governance and vice-versa. Without a doubt, this was the rationale behind the adoption of the rotational presidency by political parties in Nigeria. The sixteen years of rule by the People's Democratic Party witnessed the adoption of a rotational presidency when it was agreed that the presidential candidate to contest the 2007 general election should come from the North. On this arrangement, Akinola had this to say:

> The People's Democratic Party (PDP) arrangement to rotate the presidency between the South and North is an acknowledgement of the existence of a most disturbing national problem and an effort to provide a practical solution to it. The PDP approach would appear to have reasonably stabilized Nigerian democracy in the last 20 years, and the fear of 'ethnic hegemony' would not appear as pronounced as it once was. However, we do not have a 'rotational presidency' yet. The principle is yet to be accommodated in the national constitution where its 'nitty-gritty' can be spelt out.[20]

From the above, it is evident that the author also perceived the rotational presidency as a concept that ensures the reduction of ethnic-motivated political feuds. The agreements of rotational presidency in political parties are not holy writ. They are often entered into in a gentlemanly manner, with nothing written down to the effect, making such agreements fairly easy to breach. Akinola also provided a soft validation when he claimed that the ruling party, PDP, lost the 2015 election because the North felt cheated of their political right within the party. While the PDP successfully zoned the presidency to the North in the 2007 general elections, the death of President Umaru Musa Yar'Adua two years later resulted in a Southerner (Goodluck Jonathan)

19. Akinola, "Posterity will not Forgive."
20. Anthony Akinola, "Formalizing Rotational Presidency," *The Guardian*, June 30, 2019.

ascending the presidency. After spending six years, the Northern power bloc in the party felt it was just fair for PDP to work towards a northern presidency. However, the then-president, Goodluck Jonathan, was eyeing possible re-election. The clash of motives provided enough condiment to ensure that PDP lost the election, paving the way for the emergence of a new political party at the center.

Criticisms of the concept of rotational presidency make a valid argument that the concept does not give room for the emergence of the best candidate. This may be right if one understands the intricacies of political zoning offices in specific regions. However, the complexities of the Nigerian political space make it suitable to adopt power rotation. To lay this argument to rest, Akinola stated thus:

> There are 'best candidates' in every region of the Nigerian federation, seeking an opportunity to bring their leadership qualities to bear on all of us. A nation can design a democratic structure that accommodates its realities. There is no universal structure of democracy; what is universal about democracy are the basic principles that govern it.

This is based on the fact that the then-president was from the South. With the emergence of the All Progressives Congress as the ruling party, there were talks of an initial agreement that the eight years administration of Buhari would be accompanied by the subsequent projection of a presidential candidate from the South. In view of this, it becomes expedient to ascertain Akinola's position on the concept of the rotational presidency.

In another context, Akinola retorted that critics wrongly compare the American democratic system with what is available in Nigeria, forgetting that what is applicable in one society may not be appropriate in another. According to the writer, "Nigerians who make uninformed comparisons between their nation and America, the fact the north of the latter had produced more presidents than its south, need to be told that American regions are not divided along cultural or ethnic lines."[21]

Americans may choose to vote based on competence since the society is structured in a way that ensures no state can feel marginalized or dominated by another. This is because the American system confers equal representation on states without reference to unequal size and population. The Electoral College protects smaller states from the overbearing power of bigger ones. So, it is inappropriate to compare the complexities of the American political system with Nigeria's.

> A constitutional or political arrangement must accommodate the emotions and sentiments of those it is designed to serve if its usefulness is to survive the test

---

21. Anthony Akinola, "The Fallacy of So-Called Competence over Zoning," *The Guardian*, August 6, 2020.

of time. One has said it before, and one is repeating it here, that the success of the American constitution is the acknowledgment by America's founding fathers that the problem of cleavage can only be resolved by addressing it.[22]

Concerning Nigeria, any political analyst will observe that the major ethnic groups are in perpetual rivalry and competition for the ultimate political prize—control of the center. Owing to this, there are bound to be reservations from the less advantaged ethnic groupings during election periods. The stable political terrain witnessed since 1999 can be attributed to the zoning agreement the ruling political parties entered into. PDP toed the line until the agreement was circumstantially degraded in the 2015 general elections. With APC coming to power in 2015, there have been calls for the party to zone the presidency ticket to the South, and such calls sound legitimate, despite not being in the constitution. This understanding will always inform preoccupation with the destination of the presidency in 2023 and beyond.[23] While some elements in the party have been observed to voice out their reservations about the expected zoning, the emergence of various movements supporting a Southern presidential candidate in the next general elections is a pointer to the unspoken rule that the party understands the implications of reneging on the gentlemanly agreement made during the 2015 general elections.

In the article "The Fallacy of So-Called Competence over Zoning," Akinola raised the argument for a rotational presidency further by churning out thought-provoking insights on why zoning seems more appropriate for Nigeria's political terrain. The argument that zoning discourages the choice of competent leadership is preposterous, as Akinola revealed to his audience. Arguments around regional advantage drive the claim to prioritize competence over zoning. In a country like Nigeria, political arguments will always uncover the ethnic sentiment that resides with the people, no matter how anyone tries to cover it. Akinola stated in a section of the article that his position as a Nigerian patriot does not afford him the luxury of engaging in ethnic profiling. Going a few lines further in the same paragraph, he stated thus, "If one must be brutally honest, it is in the comparatively more educated south, not the north, that an argument of so-called competence should be rending the air."[24]

The subtle attempt to remind the reader that one ethnic group is more educated than others within the Nigerian political space resonates with the earlier proposition that ethnic sentimentalism cannot be eroded from the Nigerian mindset. While the writer's affirmation sounds holistic and true to some extent, harping on it to make a validation sounds like an ethnic slur, and such propositions, if care is not taken, may be perceived in a bad light. Coming back to the issue of competence, Akinola assert-

22. Akinola, "The Fallacy of So-Called Competence."

23. Anthony Akinola, "Rotational Presidency is Central to Nigeria's Future," *The Punch*, September 27, 2019.

24. Akinola, "The Fallacy of So-Called Competence."

ed that competence comes with proven performance on the job and cannot be evaluated in isolation. Even if competence is to be prioritized during the election of political leaders, Akinola stated that the Nigerian populace does not have a significant proportion of voters that can be objective enough to vote based on competence without exhibiting noticeable levels of ethnic or religious bias. This makes the argument of competence over zoning fundamentally flawed in the case of Nigeria. Perhaps, the comment below will throw more light on the logical argument put forth by Akinola: "Were the next two or three presidents to come from a regional grouping, there will not be a few who will be moaning and groaning about a hegemonic situation."[25]

A close look at the aforestated reveals the logical reason the rotational presidency remains the most viable option for the progress of Nigeria's political system. From the 1960s to recent times, leadership tussles in Nigeria have been built on ethnic suspicions; the Nigerian polity takes sides with their ethnic kinsmen in power when people from other ethnic groups express reservations.

The dynamics of the Nigerian socio-political system best accommodate the rotational presidency as the appropriate leadership structure.[26] There is no universal structure for the practice of democracy; hence, nations tend to modify it to suit the peculiarities of their surroundings. According to the author, the fact that the two dominant political platforms in Nigeria stay true to the tenet of rotational presidency suggests the conviction of the ethnically-diverse political elites that political zoning provides the best option for the progress of the nation. Akinola was a staunch proponent of the rotational presidency; he stuck to the belief that the rotational presidency remains the appropriate leadership structure for Nigeria.

However, the cunning ones do not stay true to one proposition; they say one thing today and another tomorrow. Akinola further noted that the reaffirmation of President Buhari to remain steadfast toward the actualization of true federalism is a pointer to the fact that the rotational presidency is one vital tool for enhancing the principle of federalism. Its enshrinement in Nigeria's constitution is another issue, but it would not be out of place to actively promote the adoption of a rotational presidency. Akinola saw it as a subject ripe for debate in the National Assembly. The constitutional debate of 2014 proposed such, too, with emphasis placed on a single-tenure arrangement to reduce the impatience that accompanies politicians' aspirations, as revealed by the thoughts of Governor Nasir El-Rufai of Kaduna State, who proposed that his party, APC, should jettison the zoning arrangement.[27] According to the writer, the single-tenure arrangement would provide a huge solution to the persistent issue of the destination of the presidency.

25. Akinola, "The Fallacy of So-Called Competence."
26. Akinola, "The Fallacy of So-Called Competence."
27. Akinola, "Rotational Presidency is Central."

In "Revisiting Jonathan's Single-Term Proposal," Akinola argued that the single-term concept is the result of an informed opinion that has been recommended to various governments as far back as the military regime of Ibrahim Babangida. In Akinola's words, "the proposal by President Goodluck Jonathan calls for thorough debate, and its relevance and desirability are being echoed in the run-up to the 2019 elections."[28] While the political environment of America allows for the effective adoption and practice of the two-term presidency arrangement, the Nigerian political space is not fit for such an arrangement. To counter the argument that a single-term presidency will give room for non-performance, Akinola argued that the political party machinery of the ruling party would not sleep by while a single-term president messes up the party's prospects in future elections.[29]

GOVERNANCE IN NIGERIA

One recurring theme associated with governance in Nigeria is the wastage of the country's commonwealth in the name of governance. At various points, accusations have been put forth on the gross expense of governance in Nigeria. A political representation that, ordinarily, should be a vocation has been turned into a lucrative career in Nigeria. Most political aspirants are not moved by what they can offer society but by what they can get perks from representing the people. Governance has become an attractive means of accumulating wealth rather than a barrier to service delivery. The primary motive for most political aspirants is money; hence, this has increased the cost of administration and governance. Tragically, political officeholders go home with millions every month while the country finds it difficult to pay minimum wage to the millions of masses. While ordinary citizens find it difficult to get their pensions paid when due, the political space is awash with former governors-turned-ministers collecting pensions (as former governors) and salaries (as ministers). Probably in reaction to this public outcry, the Lagos State Governor, Babajide Sanwo-Olu, embarked on the move to halt the implementation of the pension law that accords benefits to past governors and their deputies.

Several legislators have also voiced their reservations about this, although the people's perception toward such vociferations by the scheme's beneficiaries can be likened to a thief advising his victim on securing his property. Legislators like Ben Murray Bruce upheld this notion during his time in the Senate. The incumbent Speaker of the House of Representatives, Femi Gbajabiamila, also commented on reducing governance costs in Nigeria. However, I chose to dissect Akinola's view on the subject matter. This is because he is one of the few writers who have been hammering on this for a long time. As far back as the mid-1980s, Akinola had been raising posers toward reducing governance costs through calls for reducing the number of Senate seats ac-

28. Anthony Akinola, "Revisiting Jonathan's Single-Term Proposal," *The Guardian*, November 1, 2018.
29. Akinola, "Revisiting Jonathan's Single-Term Proposal."

crued to each state in Nigeria. His alleged memorandum to the military government led by Ibrahim Babangida eventually came through, as the Nigerian Senate was reduced from five to three per state. While his input toward the achievement may be perceived as an exaggeration, the fact that he raised a memorandum to that effect and his recommendation eventually saw the light of day reflects his deep thoughts on how progress can be achieved concerning governance in Nigeria. For an individual to make recommendations to a military administration that adopted them speaks volumes of his ingenuity in proffering solutions to governmental problems.

The call for reducing the cost of governance is not limited to legislators. Akinola alluded to the Governor of Ekiti State, Kayode Fayemi's concerns about the disturbing increase in the cost of governance in Nigeria. When those elected into government increase the decibel toward reducing governance costs in the country, one begins to understand how deep-rooted the problem is. The cut below from Akinola's "Still on Reducing the Cost of Governance" provides some insights:

> Kayode Fayemi, Governor of Ekiti State, recently joined the crowd of agitators by calling for a unicameral legislature. He would like the Senate to be scrapped. Even before him, former Governor Rochas Okorocha of Imo State, now a senator, had called for the number of senators per state to be reduced to one. It is gratifying to note that these political elites share the common concern of ordinary Nigerians, even when one may not agree with their suggestions.[30]

The fact that a significant number of political officeholders accept that the cost of governance be reduced should, however, not be perceived as political advancement. Akinola rightly noted that most of these public servants only pay lip service to the problem; they do so not with all sincerity but to appear thoughtful and generous in the eyes of the masses.

The proper thing to do is to embark on policies to water down the several means through which governance costs are bloated. Cutting down the cost of governance has always been the clamor from a wide range of groups—youths, civil societies, and political officeholders. The Oronsaye Committee, established by the Goodluck Jonathan administration, was charged with a similar mandate. The recommendation contained in the committee's report led to the approval of the scrapping, merging and conversion of various government agencies. While it may sound illogical to scrap or merge existing agencies, it is noteworthy that the Revenue Mobilisation Allocation and Fiscal Commission (RMAFC) reported that several MDAs in Nigeria have similar and overlapping functions and responsibilities. This makes it imperative to merge some and scrap others to reduce duplication of responsibilities and curtail waste.

---

30. Anthony Akinola, "Still on Reducing the Cost of Governance," *The Guardian*, October 17, 2019.

Such moves are expedient, especially when the government faces dwindling revenue from natural resources. As Akinola noted, "the need for a reduction in the number of ministers and advisers at every level of governance cannot be overemphasized."[31] However, the obstacles to the implementation of such ideas are huge. For instance, it is an open secret that ministers are picked from each state of the federation. Reducing the number of ministers will lead to some states being overlooked for ministerial slots; this presents another rationale for complaints bordering on marginalization from the affected states. To circumvent this, Akinola presented another perspective:

> It is enough that we respect geographical spread, especially since our nation has been demarcated into six geo-political zones. Nigerians would need to be educated about this, not least because they are the very ones who complain if a member of their clan has not been nominated as minister. They even quarrel over the portfolios of political appointees.[32]

In other words, the reduction in governance cost is one area that needs to be undertaken holistically to forestall another series of murmurs and grumbles from disadvantaged regions and ethnic groups. This is probably why another political officeholder, the Sokoto State Governor, Aminu Tambuwal, cautioned that reduction in the cost of governance must be done methodically and strategically to avoid the adverse effect on the nation's economy.[33] In light of this, the consensus is that the high cost of governance deprives the nation of the necessary resources to embark on developmental initiatives. Akinola further raised the bar by asserting that "the disturbing cost of governance in Nigeria is more of the result of our corruption and prodigal culture than anything else."[34] The greed of the political elite is evidenced in the perception of a great number of citizens that the senators' huge salaries and other emoluments form a major part of the wasteful venture associated with governance. Akinola also followed such a line of thought:

> The salaries and emoluments of elected officials should, and must, be decided by an independent body if that is not already the case. Moreover, these elected officials have their defined responsibilities. Senators, for instance, are lawmakers. It is laughable when they claim it is also part of their responsibility to execute projects in their communities. That responsibility belongs to state and local governments and should not allow senators to defraud the public.[35]

---

31. Akinola, "Still on Reducing the Cost of Governance."
32. Akinola, "Still on Reducing the Cost of Governance."
33. Editorials, "Reducing Cost of Governance," *Thisday*, January 7, 2020.
34. Akinola, "Still on Reducing the Cost of Governance."
35. Akinola, "Still on Reducing the Cost of Governance."

The greed of Nigerian senators is further emphasized in Akinola's article "Restructuring the Senate," where he ascribed the present problems to the authors of the Nigerian constitution, who were more concerned with establishing political structure than highlighting the fundamental principles guiding the establishment of the political structures. The leadership of the Senate is perceived as a position to garner more juice rather than to act in the capacity of a leader as the position demands. The intrigues and acrimony accompanying the election of the senate president in Nigeria magnify the bloated ego of the aspirants. This makes it quite easy to remove any elected senate president based on disagreements on the house floor.[36] Given such circumstances, Nigeria has witnessed the impeachment of a sizable number of senate presidents, and as Akinola noted, some had been forced to resign their position. In the face of such problems, Akinola prescribed adopting the American legislative system where the vice president acts in the capacity of the senate president. This would curb the frequent impeachment and removal of senate presidents. The major benefit of this is that the Senate will be structured to assert the principle for which the position was established and not merely another position available for senators to scheme on its occupation. Akinola submitted this:

> While major political parties can continue to have their principal officers—majority leader and minority leader, for instance—as well as constitute essential committees, the fact remains that the election of the president among members results in unhealthy competition and divisions as well as constitutes a cult of leadership that could be detrimental to relations between members and, possibly, the executive arm of government.[37]

While meditating on this, it is also important to consider ways of reducing the legislature's funding. Akinola regards the allocation of billions of naira to constituency projects as corruption and recommends it should be scrapped. While these projects may look ideal, they create an avenue for legislators to embezzle funds. The reason for this is not far-fetched; infrastructural projects and implementation fall under the auspices of the executive arm of the government, not under the legislature. Besides, the details of some of the constituency projects are shrouded in secrecy; most times, the constituents do not have access to information regarding what their respective representatives collected and what was expended.

For instance, the *Guardian* newspaper reported the recovery of items worth more than 117 million naira, believed to be owned by the Senator representing Enugu North Senatorial District by the Independent and Corrupt Practices Commission

---

36. Anthony Akinola, "Restructuring the Senate," *The Guardian*, May 2, 2019.
37. Akinola, "Restructuring the Senate."

(ICPC) through its Constituency Projects Tracking Initiative.[38] Another report by Premium Times stated that "Nigerian federal lawmakers, in connivance with executing agencies, have perfected fraudulent means of pocketing billions of naira under the guise of constituency projects."[39] One such way is vague capacity-building and empowerment projects. *The News Nigeria* reported an instance of a Benue State legislator empowering his constituents with ropes. Such occurrences validate the outcry that "the so-called constituency project allowances that gulp billions of naira—often diverted into private pockets—would need to be removed."[40]

When aspirants gunning for legislative positions begin to make promises that focus on facilitating infrastructural developments, one begins to assume whether such aspirants have an idea of what legislative representation entails. To make matters worse, the constituents they intend to represent have little idea what is expected from them. Invariably, the promises become the bait to lure ignorant citizens into voting them into positions. Reacting to this, Akinola stated that it is imperative to educate the people on the duties of specific political positions; lawmakers are elected, and their duties center on making laws, not the execution of projects. Going by this, Akinola opined that the federal government should consciously implement policies to reduce governance costs. To cap it all, he declared thus:

> Educating them is part of the essence of democracy. Appropriate and integrative as the presidential system of government could be for our multi-ethnic and multi-religious society, it is the corruption as well as the greed and wasteful spending of elected politicians that create apprehension in the minds of ordinary Nigerians.[41]

ELECTIONS IN NIGERIA

Discussions on politics and electioneering are hard to overlook for anyone who chooses to focus on governance in Nigeria. This is hinged on the interrelationship and interdependence of the three concepts: governance, politics and elections. The political terrain in Nigeria is populated with hilarious scenarios, projections and eventualities that it is often so easy to ascertain where the balance is shifting toward. The failure of incumbent administrations to organize free and fair elections devoid of corrupt practices and irregularities makes it all the more predictable. Akinola discussed some comedic scenes that have become a mainstay in the Nigerian political

---

38. Sunday Eno-Abasi, "Constituency Projects: Still a Long way to getting Value for Money," *The Guardian*, April 5, 2020.

39. Editorial, "How NASS Members Corner Billions via Constituency Projects-ICPC," *Daily Asset*, December 16, 2019. shttps://dailyasset.ng/how-nass-members-corner-billions-via-constituency-projects-icpc/.

40. Akinola, "Restructuring the Senate."

41. Akinola, "Restructuring the Senate."

system. In one of his write-ups, he noted that Nigeria is a rare nation where switching between political parties is a norm. It is possible to witness a politician move from party A to party B, only to return to party A when events do not seem to work in his favor. Atiku Abubakar, Aminu Tambuwal, Bukola Saraki and Femi Fani-Kayode are popular politicians that fit the narrative. The rise in organized political defections in Nigeria has reached an alarming level, further portraying the nation's democracy as held by a few. Most turncoats involved in these defections often blame the absence of internal democracy for their actions; however, this is not always the case.

Akinola stated, "while this phenomenon is an isolated case in the settled democratic nations of the world, the scale of its occurrence in our nation is baffling."[42] This viewpoint is worthy of note, especially when discussing the potential pitfalls of Africa's version of democracy. The selfish interests of politicians are laid bare by the incessant traversing between political parties, albeit in a pre-planned manner that indicates nothing but a show of greed and discontentment. If such defections are investigated, the reasons provided are mostly devoid of rationality or logic. Only in Nigeria would one witness more than twenty federal legislators defecting *en masse* from one party to another in a wanton display of perceived might.[43] Akinola reviewed one major factor underlying such defections—what is the constitution's position concerning an elected officeholder defecting from one political party to another? Such scenarios may be strange to the originators of Western democracy; it is a core feature of politics and elections in Nigeria. As Akinola rightly affirmed, such insensibilities can only make sense when the defecting political officeholder subjects himself to another election to ascertain whether his constituents actually voted based on his personality or perhaps he rode on the popularity of a political party to win the position. Such procedures will go a long way to express the minds of the majority of voters.

Nigeria's political parties lack clear-cut ideologies, making it easy for politicians to hobnob between parties unhindered. In other words, the defections we see are not driven by ideological differences; rather, they result from self-centered calculations of potential gains from the political process. The spate of inter-party migration is so huge that John Oyegun, the then National Chairman of the All Progressives Congress, was reported to have stated that PDP members should stay in their party, further adding that the spate of defections is not good for the political development of the country. The intermittent migration of key politicians between various political parties has unique implications; such moves are often borne out of the need to showcase political might, and it does not portray the beauty of the democratic process. The politicians' inability to achieve their inordinate ambitions in a particular party often results in premeditated defections. Akinola provided a perfect instance:

42. Anthony Akinola, "Migrating Politicians and 2019 Elections," *The Guardian*, August 27, 2018.
43. Akinola, "Migrating Politicians."

Goodluck Jonathan's failure to win the 2015 presidential election can hardly be explained outside the departure of key politicians from his Peoples Democratic Party in 2013. That departure from the PDP to the All Progressives Congress included five serving governors, several elected senators, and the House of Representatives members.[44]

In essence, defection has become a strong tool to test political might. Internal squabbles for dominance by several power blocs within the party result in disagreements. On close observation, the disagreements may result from rifts due to regional differences or wholesale rejection of the ambition of specific political aspirants. Akinola pointed out that Goodluck Jonathan's loss in the 2015 election resulted from the animosity of the Northern power bloc toward his ambition. With the Northern bloc perceiving that the zoning arrangement had been usurped, his ascendancy into the position after the demise of Yar'Adua did not go down well with them. The feeling of being cheated by this and the determination of Jonathan to seek re-election at all costs led to the departure of key politicians from the PDP. This move, as expected, isolated the unpopular incumbent President. The lack of a strong grassroots structure culminated in the ousting of President Jonathan. Perhaps the situation would have been different if the people had accepted him in the same manner as Benue State Governor Samuel Ortom.

The most vital element of any effective political system is the opportunity to vote for government policies and philosophies. On this basis, political parties with divergent ideologies and philosophies are formed, as it provides the people with a choice. Unfortunately, the Nigerian political system does not provide clear choices for the masses. It is difficult to outline any clear-cut ideological differences between the two most popular political parties, especially when politicians indiscriminately move from one party to another. To make it more cumbersome, Nigerian voters are not accustomed to the technicalities that sway elections. Such technicalities as televised debates are protocols within the Nigerian political space. While televised debates do not automatically produce a better candidate, it presents voters with the opportunity of having foreknowledge of the policies a particular candidate intends to pursue if given the mandate. Akinola provided more insight into this:

> The essence of televised political debates would be appreciated in a society, such as America or Great Britain, where prospective voters can see it as an opportunity to evaluate the policies, preparedness and demeanour of those who seek to govern them. It must, however, also be warned that a great leader may not be the best of debaters.[45]

---

44. Akinola, "Migrating Politicians."

45. Anthony Akinola, "History, Essence and Limits of Televised Debates" *The Guardian*, November 12, 2019.

Undecided voters in the American electoral system use the opportunity provided by televised debates to determine whom to vote for in the election. This is borne out of the need to understand the ideological differences between the debating candidates without being partial.

In "The Incumbency Factor in Presidential Election," Akinola provided another strong ingredient of partisan politics. Incumbency factor in the election, while not being given, presents a significant advantage for one candidate. In Akinola's words:

> We talk of the 'incumbency factor' in an election in which one of the competitors is the occupant of the position being contested. Otherwise, an incumbent not involved in an election is referred to as an 'open seat' election. The presidential elections of 2003, 2011 and 2015 have played out the incumbency factor. Olusegun Obasanjo sought re-election in 2003, while Goodluck Jonathan did the same in 2015. Jonathan succeeded Yar-Adua, who died in office in 2010 and was, therefore, an incumbent President when he contested and won an election of his own in 2011.[46]

As explained by Akinola, the power of incumbency represents the advantages accrued to a sitting elected officeholder over his challengers. In most cases, the incumbency factor is enjoyed based on other factors such as visible achievements, popularity, control of state machinery, experience, or access to state funds. In some cases, the incumbency factor is exploited negatively, especially in African democratic settings where elected public officeholders use state apparatus to subjugate opposition. Akinola opined that using security agents to intimidate the supporters of the opposition during election campaigns and voting hours forms the greatest negativity attached to the use of incumbency power. This is closely followed by the use of state resources to bribe voters and potential opponents to silence them; the incumbency factor's positives and negatives make it difficult for newcomers to defeat sitting elected officeholders. However, this does not contradict the fact that incumbents have lost African elections. As pointed out by the writer, an incumbent must have performed extremely badly for him or her to be defeated, and that is where the anti-incumbency factor comes into play.[47] Referencing the famous defeat of Jimmy Carter in the 1980 US election, Akinola disclosed how events could quickly turn against the incumbent, leading to a negative public perception of the administration.

While it remains true that incumbency factors confer more advantages on the beneficiary, voters' apathy may work against such candidates, especially when the public perception of the administration is not appreciable. For instance, Akinola noted that the Iranian Hostage Crisis was enough to dent the image of Carter's adminis-

46. Anthony Akinola, "The Incumbency Factor in Presidential Elections," *The Guardian*, June 13, 2018.
47. Akinola, "The Incumbency Factor."

tration because he could not deal with the situation effectively. Similarly, Jonathan's administration's perceived inefficiency in the face of the Boko Haram uprising was enough to dent his public image. However, this does not mean Jonathan lost entirely due to this; other factors also contributed to his loss. Akinola added that religion and ethnic sentimentalism are potent factors in Nigerian politics that can make or mar a political candidate.[48] The competitive nature of politics puts the incumbent in the spotlight; in other words, a leader's actions or inactions are placed under the microscope to determine the administration's credibility. Akinola provided some examples:

> There are those who have said that the declaration of June 12 as Democracy Day was politically-motivated, geared towards getting votes for the re-election of Buhari in 2019. One may ask, what does a politician ever do that is not geared towards securing support? Those who have consistently advocated what Buhari has now put into effect would, all things being equal, want to reward him in a future election. To quite a number of others, that declaration has not changed anything. When Ronald Reagan signed the birthday of Martin Luther King, Jr. as a holiday into law in 1983, after many years of campaigning for it, many states showed a lukewarm attitude to the development. It was not until the year 2000 that all the 50 states of the American federation upheld and marked the birthday of the great civil rights campaigner as a public holiday.[49]

Unfortunately, the opposition always has something to complain about to stand a chance against the incumbent. However, the sharp contrast between the American and Nigerian systems is bare. Akinola affirmed that the opinion poll is a strong determinant of electoral success in the former's system; this factor has little or no value in the latter. Providing evidence to this effect, Akinola argued that Jimmy Carter may have achieved electoral success in his re-election bid if the Iranian Hostage Crisis had changed positively at the last minute. In democratic settings like Nigeria, opinion polls are determined by what the political elite dish out to their teeming supporters. For instance, the National Leader of APC, Bola Tinubu, only needs to communicate his preferred candidacy for his supporters to follow suit without any personal investigation. The belief that a political leader's opinion is divine remains one of Nigeria's major banes of political development.

Akinola's views concerning elections in Nigeria are not all doom and gloom. The writer could still pick up some positives, going by the contents of the article titled "Some Positive Takes from a Chaotic Election." As the writer observed, the political process of Nigeria is getting more mature, at the least. The reduction in the occurrence of ballot snatching, election rigging and vote-buying is one positive highlighted by the writer. While many may not share this opinion, the fact that there are reduced

48. Akinola, "The Incumbency Factor."
49. Akinola, "The Incumbency Factor."

complaints from the opposition lends credence to his opinions. One aspect of the article should catch any avid reader's attention:

> One positive I take from our collective crudity is that the will of the majority prevailed in quite a number of the states. For instance, I had been plotting within myself how I would celebrate the electoral victory of Adebayo Adelabu, grandson of Adegoke Adelabu' Penkelemesi until I spoke with a few people from Oyo State. I had thought the legendary and passionate support Ibadan people gave Adegoke Adelabu would rub off on the grandson, who was a gubernatorial candidate on the platform of the All Progressives Congress. However, I was warned that Adebayo might not win the election. According to those I spoke with, the election would be an opportunity to punish the 'arrogance' and 'intransigence' of the incumbent governor, Abiola Ajimobi, who also lost his bid to be elected Senator.[50]

The above conjoins two salient points discussed earlier. One is that the actions or inactions of the incumbent can lead to voters' apathy, a fact that is captured in Akinola's exposition that the people of Oyo State, in an attempt to punish the incumbent governor, decided against voting for the governor's party, even though the candidate with the party ticket was one that ordinarily should get the support of the people, owing to his grandfather's status in the society. The second is that the days of blindly following political leaders are fading away. Adegoke Adelabu was a notable Ibadan politician who was respected and highly honored. However, this was not enough reason for the Ibadan people to vote for his grandson. Indeed, these are positive takes, as the article's name indicates.

The future of elections in Nigeria is sunny if Akinola's notes are anything to go by. One more factor that may shift the balance is for the youths to be more involved. As accurately pointed out by the writer, the youths should look beyond social media activism and become more involved in partisan politics if they are truly ready to change the narrative. The advocacy of youths borders on forming an exclusive youth party that can defeat the existing political parties to pave the way for the younger generation to assume political authority in Nigeria. However, Akinola noted that democracy is not so simplistic to allow for such. He affirmed that democracy is like an organization where those who seek to get to the top do so by climbing the ladder.[51] In reality, youth participation in politics is not strange in Nigeria; the vast numbers of politicians pre-independence and a short while after independence were young, vibrant and dynamic men and women. Akinola provided some worthy examples for the doubting reader, one of whom was Matthew Mbu, who became a federal minister at 23 between 1953 and 1954. While this trend was allegedly truncated by the advent of

50. Anthony Akinola, "Some Positive takes from a Chaotic Election," *The Guardian*, April 11, 2019.
51. Anthony Akinola, "How Military Coup Stalled Youth Participation," *The Guardian*, May 10, 2018.

military rule in Nigeria, Akinola affirmed that the Nigerian youths could make a grand re-entry into the political process and grow in it, as is the case in established democratic nations.[52] The first step has been achieved, which is agitation for lowering the bar of entry into elected offices so that youths can make their entries into governmental positions very early. The next stage is for the youths to infiltrate the dominant political parties to make their impacts felt; this is the only possible means of arm-twisting the old politicians whose experience in politics may not be easily defeated by simply forming a parallel political party to upstage the existing ones that already have a strong grassroots structure.

CONCLUSION

Nigeria boils of ethnic pressures and agitations of secession that have been holding the unity of the nation to ransom. Understandably, the nation passes through a phase that is felt by individuals, making life practically difficult for many of them. When others use these unfolding events to prophesy the doomsday of Nigerian unity, Akinola refuses to join the bandwagon and provides a different stance that passes the message of hope and warns of the dangers of secession. In "Short-Sighted Separatist Agitators," he warned against the quick assumption of an inevitable division and how this would not serve the Nigerian interest.

By doing this, Akinola did not just put the minds of critics and those that appreciate his thoughts in limbo, but he followed up his positions with some convictions he believed, when observed, would strengthen Nigerian unity. One of these observations was his belief in a rotational presidency, not just at the party level but recognized by the nation. Ordinarily, one would easily subscribe to the arguments of placing merit over ethnicity. However, Akinola has shown how what seems like a commonsensical decision might be nonsense in Nigeria. He has stated that all parts of the nation are capable of providing the best candidates that are needed. This positions him as a sage with radically different thoughts from general perspectives. Therefore, seeing the details and analyses of his positions, it would not be out of place to posit that he represents rare wisdom in society.

In all of these, there is one attribute one can easily deduce from his opinions and conviction: Akinola is a chip off the old block of the Nigerian nationalists that foregrounded the unity of the nation. Akinola is a nationalist who would not desist from warning us of the consequences of further attacking the nation's unity. Hence, looking at him as a detribalized sage and scholar is a worthy and insightful effort. Breaking through the stiff barrier of resistance mounted against true nationalism in Nigeria is a feat that could be attained only when the way of thinking of the country's average citizens starts to resemble Akinola's nationalist points of view.

52. Akinola, "How Military Coup Stalled Youth Participation."

21

VICTOR ASEMOTA

Technology and Societal Development

Human beings may not have experienced any biological changes throughout history, but the society wherein they live is prone to continuous changes due to development. This continuous development is a product of harnessed knowledge and information that ultimately results in technological advancement and effects on societal value systems. The world is in an era where people's existence is divided between physical and virtual reality. Many human activities are already being relegated to the virtual world due to technological advancements in various fields.

The last two decades have witnessed a revolution in computation and communication among individuals within the global society. The technological advancement experienced within the period mentioned above has led to increased information and communication technology use. These advancements have also presented opportunities and challenges to society in diverse measures. The wide-ranging effects of technological innovations across the domains of society have led technology analysts like Victor Asemota to pen a compendium of thoughts based on his experiences regarding technology within and outside his field of endeavor. From policymakers in government to the private sector, technological advancement has resulted in the emergence of alternatives that seek to improve the status quo. Peer-to-peer interactions have been enhanced, with distance no longer a barrier to communication. In the labor sector, computerized control systems have resulted in more effec-

tive coordination of operations. Technology has led to the availability of choices. However, it should be noted that the choices present long-lasting consequences, and there is a need to analyze Asemota's thoughts to understand the socio-economic impacts of technology.

The most significant technological advancements have been made possible due to the emergence of the internet. With it, information and communication have become more encompassing. Commerce has suddenly become very easy, while other economic and social activities have been greatly altered to ensure seamless individual interactions. Various private sectors like retail trading, finance, and banking in Nigeria are beginning to experience significant improvements. The Nigerian public sector has also experienced its fair share of improved efficiency, albeit with some reluctance in accepting the change that accompanies technology adoption.

It is impossible to discuss contemporary developments and issues about the nation through the lenses of notable contemporary individuals without discussing technology, the hallmark of modern society. Technology has attracted and determined the projection of different sectors of society, determining their efficiencies and operations. In a similar manner that politics and social issues are often talked about, technology and technological development have created a niche that has erupted in conversations everywhere in the world. One of those that have advanced these conversations is Asemota. Although Nigerian society is quite shilly-shallying on the adoption and applicability of technological solutions in many aspects of society, the country is progressing. Asemota has become one of the propellers of public consciousness on the need to adjust reasonably to the realities of technology and accept the benefits it offers. His positions in some of his publications and columns have distinguished him enough to be discussed.

Asemota is not new to the Nigerian tech world. Having founded his tech startup, SwiftaCorp, more than 20 years ago, he is one of the pioneers of African Software and Technology services providers, operating in more than 14 African countries. He has also been instrumental in the fintech sector by co-founding Mobile Financial Services Accelerator (MFISA), a fintech company that has successfully powered several payment platforms in Africa. Asemota's core belief rests on harnessing the knowledge of African professionals around the globe to ensure that Africa has as much stake in the area of technological inventions as much as their global counterparts.

Victor Asemota drives the consciousness of the Nigerian public toward twenty-first-century realities, especially the increasing predominance of fintech. Fintech is a contemporary reality that has come to stay even in Nigeria. It is fast defining Nigerian citizens' financial and commercial operations, reducing the influence of the conventional banking and finance system. As a co-founder of the Mobile Financial Services Accelerator (MFISA), as well as his consistent expressions on the country's progress, development, and underperformance in an adaptation of fintech, he has been able to

Figure 21.1. "Victor Asemota, Fintech and New Technology" by Michael Efionayi. Depiction of Victor Asemota and his fascination with new technology and fintech.

project himself to the fore of conversations in the country. His understanding and participation in fintech-related activities and other technological realities have made his views interesting to understand and gain insight into technological advancement in Nigeria and Africa.

Asemota is one of the few that believe that although African society needs technological advancement and AI actualization, applying a similar approach as used in any country in Africa might not fit into the needs and necessities of the African society. He believes that AI actualization and localization in Africa must be done to adapt and reflect the "African Context" if Africa must be a global powerhouse of advanced technology. He had retorted the need to factor the African context into Machine Language and constructions of AI if technology would be locally relevant and yield solutions for the benefit of the continent and the world.[1] Examining the peculiarities of

1. Victor Osaretin Asemota, "'Ghana is the Future of Africa': Why Google Built an AI Lab in Accra," *CNN*, July 15, 2018. https://edition.cnn.com/2018/07/14/africa/google-ghana-ai/index.html.

African conditions, he had taught the public, through the opinions of Dr. Omoju Miller, that innovative approaches to Africa must be similar to those used in the Chinese societies, which have brought about brilliant and globally relevant technologies.[2] This opinion and many others he had started in his publication and articles have presented him as someone who understands the continent's technological needs and approaches to realizing them.

The relevance of Asemota in technological discussions in Nigerian and African society can also be drawn from his social media engagements and conversations. Asemota has over 250,000 followers on Twitter and engages in technological and social issues. Social media has allowed him to diversify his contribution to the Nigerian situation from technological development to political issues and consciousness.[3] With such influence in the technology world and his ability to relate them to social issues, it is crystal clear that his views, contributions, and activities have become important to discuss.

INFORMATION AND COMMUNICATION TECHNOLOGY HUB DEVELOPMENT IN NIGERIA

Nigeria may not be among the most enviable technological hubs in the world; no African country is considered as such. ICT developments are not Nigeria's strong niche, as many African nations operate more of a consumer society rather than a manufacturing enclave. It is pardonable if the situation is analyzed from a government-induced human capital development perspective. It is not like one does not have the wherewithal to compare among the rest in ICT development, but the government has never been supportive of the moves by the private sector; no encouragement is accorded to young and ambitious technological hands to operate in their best elements. However, this has not stopped them from taking strides that have resulted in some achievements in ICT-hub development. One such hub is the famous Lagos Computer Village in Ikeja, known simply as Otigba.

One may wonder why it has to be Lagos. As Asemota affirmed in his article 'Nigeria's Technology Sector: A Coming of Age?' Lagos remains the most favorable location for tech advancement due to its resources and infrastructural advantage over any other place in Nigeria.[4] Since enterprise technology was Nigeria's first wave of technologies, it made sense that the state with the largest pool of enterprises automatical-

2. Asemota, "'Ghana is the Future of Africa.'"

3. Victor Osaretin Asemota, "I think we keep making the mistake of not realizing what Nigeria really is and comparing it with what it is not. Nigeria is NOT a Nation. It is an amalgamation of communities. The diversity and complexity are not advantages when politics is involved. They become liabilities," *Twitter*, August 18, 2022, https://twitter.com/asemota/status/1560276293891260418?s=20&t=Soejv4873YfNduF-Ad92bQ.

4. Victor Osaretin Asemota, "Nigeria's Technology Sector: A Coming of Age?" *The Guardian*, September 23, 2016.

ly became the beneficiary. Also, the advent of consumer technology such as mobile phones and home-use personal computer systems needs a state with a large consumer population to thrive; Lagos trumps other states in Nigeria. The existence of markets for particular products determines the success or failure of enterprises in such an industry. It does not matter how efficiently such organizations are run or their financial buoyancy; they are likely to fail if the market does not exist for their respective products and services. It does not matter how good the product or service is. Due to its population, Lagos is virtually a perfect market for all consumer products, from groceries to tech devices and software.

The focus of the mainstream ICT market in the state's capital is not unconnected with its being central and easily accessible, as against Surulere, which served as the technology hub for enterprise solutions technology before the advent of consumer technology.[5] Computer Village is located strategically at the heart of the state's capital, Ikeja. It is so popular that Sarah Lacy, founder of San Francisco-based tech blog 'Pando' referred to it as Nigeria's equivalent of BestBuy Supermarket, a famous technology market in the US.[6] Asemota, in the article, 'Otigba: The Experiment that Grew into a Tech market,' upped the ante, describing the Ikeja Computer Village as Nigeria's own Silicon Valley.[7] The comparisons may be a little awkward if efforts are expended detailing what operates in Silicon Valley and Ikeja Computer Village. The author was quick to offer further explanations by emphatically stating that while the former is populated with software developers, the itinerary of the people in the latter is best described as tech entrepreneurs who engage in the business of technology hardware and support services. This feat did not come easy; it took foresight and determination on the part of a few ambitious individuals to project the impending ICT boom that was about to be experienced in Nigeria, and they had to back up their foresight with ICT investment decisions that would ensure that they tap into the prospects.

The story of Otigba is enough for anyone to understand how ambitious Nigerians can be if provided with the necessary implements to forge competition. As Asemota noted, what operates in Ikeja Computer Village is more than competition among tech experts but a systemic arrangement that fosters collaboration and cooperation. Business activities in the tech environment involve individuals from diverse backgrounds, helping one another and synergizing efforts to give satisfaction to consumers while ensuring that each individual along the chain gets compensated for being in the chain. With such collaborations, one would not be surprised that individuals of varying age groups are littered around the area, getting involved in the complex business arrangements in Otigba. Owing to the high level of unemployment the country faces, Ikeja

5. Asemota, "Nigeria's Technology Sector."

6. Victor Osaretin Asemota, "Otigba: The Experiment that Grew into a Tech Market," *The Guardian*, March 15, 2017.

7. Asemota, "Otigba: The Experiment that Grew."

Computer Village has become an ICT hub that offers "hustling" opportunities for anyone who can be patient enough to understand the market dynamics. Without being a shop owner, one can make a living by knowing one's way around and being able to imprint on prospective tech buyers to depend on him for any task. Sometimes, all it takes is a proper understanding of where prospective buyers can buy what; this is enough for one to position oneself as the perceived owner of tech shops. By taking the buyer to the seller under the disguise that you either own the shop or your relative owns it, there is an attributable interest from the profit made by the actual seller on the such buyer.

The Nigerian ICT industry is not limited to tech hardware; a growing number of software development experts do not operate out of the famed Computer Village but from another part of the Lagos metropolis; Yaba. As Asemota stated, despite little encouragement from the government, these sets of experts have been able to kick off the software tech revolution with support from international ICT giants like Google, MainOne and Microsoft.[8] Schemes like Microsoft's BizSpark startup, which are developed to assist in providing free cloud infrastructure, have benefited Nigeria immensely. While other states may not boast of the presence of tech hardware environments like Computer Village, new ICT initiatives are springing up across the country. Other cities such as Abuja, Kaduna, and Port Harcourt are changing rapidly. Tech entrepreneurs are looking beyond Lagos to ensure Nigeria's ICT industry's development. Asemota further mentioned nHub, an ICT hub located in Jos and founded by David Daser, while another company SpringPort Group, founded by Nigerians in the diaspora, confirmed raising more than $1 billion from various US investors to develop a technology village in Ife, another notable ancient city in the southwestern region of Nigeria.[9]

Asemota may not be a tech entrepreneur, but he continually improved many young, dynamic and ambitious individuals in the industry, showcasing their dreams, aspirations, and activities. However, he does not limit his propositions to positivity attached to technology industries alone but also to the possible dangers. In 'Otigba: the Experiment that Grew into a Tech Market,' he raised a poser on the impending dangers of the likely implosion of the market.[10] Highlighting the challenges that may result from the market growing beyond its present location, he consistently brings issues worth ruminating on to the fore. With the government constantly evaluating the possibility of relocating the Computer Village elsewhere, Asemota's thoughts should be applauded. As he retorted in the final parts of the article, nothing else may kill the Computer Village except a hostile government.

8. Asemota, "Nigeria's Technology Sector."
9. Asemota, "Nigeria's Technology Sector."
10. Asemota, "Otigba: The Experiment that Grew."

GROWING TECH START-UPS IN AFRICA

African countries are the least developed regarding tech startup and innovation culture. Technology and its advancement have never been a strong point in Africa. The lack of research opportunities has resulted in brain drain, as African-born individuals do not believe they can achieve their potential if they do not move to societies that afford citizens the requisite implements for improvement. Asemota's entry into the technology development world coincided with the time the founders of Google brainstormed on expanding into the African market.[11] While the founders of Google were able to witness their project become a reality, Asemota and his crew saw the death of theirs in 2000, only for them to resurrect it four years later, when Google had already gone public with an IPO that raised $1.67 billion. The difference between these two sets of founders, as Asemota noted in the article, was neither a lack of ideas nor their respective proximity to the famed Silicon Valley, which provides tech start-ups with many resources that aid their growth. Rather, Asemota alluded to the success of Google's founders to how they started and not where they started from. In his opinion, tech companies with strong foundations will always have a greater opportunity for growth and success because of other exogenous factors that work to their advantage. While people may think that most of the factors are extrinsic and linked to the surrounding ecosystems, they miss out on the most important intrinsic factors, such as the make-up of the team that determines the foundation of companies.[12]

However, the rise in the number of technology hubs across the continent shows signs of improvement in recent times. The rise in computer engineering talents across Africa has positioned it as the fastest-growing environment for developers globally. The past two years have witnessed an increase in the number of technology hubs by 50%, with many of these hubs playing crucial roles in the incubation of several businesses as well as fueling technological innovations within the continent.[13] The Forbes report further validated this, which affirmed that African tech start-ups experienced the best year in 2019, with more than 300 tech companies receiving funding of $461.6 million.[14] A significant proportion of grants and startup funds to African tech companies follow a definite pattern; 90% of the funding goes to individuals who have established strong connections within the right circles due to their sojourn out of Africa.[15] Shedding more light on the discourse, Asemota opined that this trend is because

11. Victor Osaretin Asemota, "Start-up Ventures 101," *The Guardian*, April 17, 2019.

12. Asemota, "Start-up Ventures 101."

13. Yomi Kazeem, "The Biggest Trends in African Tech Start-ups," *Quartz Africa*, December 31, 2019, https://qz.com/africa/1777241/the-biggest-trends-in-african-tech-start-ups-and-innovation-2019/.

14. Toby Shapshak, "African Tech Start-ups have Record Investment Year in 2019," *Forbes: Enterprise Tech*, January 20, 2020, https://www.forbes.com/sites/tobyshapshak/2020/01/20/african-tech-start-ups-have-record-investment-year-in-2019/#4585436032f9.

15. Victor Osaretin Asemota, "Why African Entrepreneurs need to Think Bigger," *The Guardian*, July 19, 2017.

many foreign-schooled African tech startup founders understood the market better than their locally-schooled counterparts.

The tech industry favors organizations that solve particular problems and provide technology consumers with what they want. As Asemota noted in the article, the technology market does not reward organizations for solving problems. Rather, technology investors are on the constant lookout for innovations that offer scalable solutions. Serving a customer successfully takes beyond just solving their problems; you must also ensure that your product helps them achieve their desired outcome.[16] For tech start-ups to stand a better chance in the industry, Asemota advised that African startup companies should offer scalable solutions, not just solve problems. Perhaps this was the mindset of the creators of the MAZA health startup in Ghana.

Asemota detailed in "Design and Thinking Financial Services Innovation" operations and attributes of the MAZA model, which sought to provide tricycles to riders for business purposes. However, one key aspect of the model was that every beneficiary of the arrangement has to dedicate some portion of their business operations to serve the pregnant people who may require transport services within the community the riders are operating. Pregnant women are meant to pay a subscription fee to enjoy the transportation service. However, providing this solution did not meet the recipients of the model. Most poor pregnant women want transportation from their homes to their final destination and a holistic model that would provide them with a platform that makes the payment for services seamless and flexible. The creators of MAZA Health Transport did not consider the desire for a more flexible payment method. Many of these women had no money in banks that could be used to fast-track the subscription process. Others do not have the cash to pay for the services since their wealth is tied to their produce on farmlands with which they engage in barter trades among themselves. Mobile devices given to some rural women for the initiative were transferred to the husbands, whom Asemota referred to as early adopters of mobile payment systems. Hence, there is an expectation for the acceptance of capital or materials in place of currency to effect subscription to the platform.

At the end of it all, a wonderful fintech initiative was brought to an abrupt end due to little quirks relating to service payment.[17] The failure to implement adequate measures in the planning process was counterproductive. The subset of individuals that would have employed or utilized the fintech initiative could not because they are not accustomed to the payment methods lined out. The fintech did not want simple solutions but rather solutions that were scalable and convenient for them. However, it has

16. Victor Osaretin Asemota, "Designing African Tech Start-ups for Trust," *The Guardian*, August 8, 2018.

17. Victor Osaretin Asemota, "Design Thinking and Financial Services Innovation," *The Guardian*, July 11, 2018.

not been able to develop models that would fit certain people's specific demands and orientations.

This mindset parallels the one employed by a South African-based tech company, Carry1st, founded by a Sierra Leonean Cordel Robbin-Coker and Lucy Pary. Focusing its efforts on gaming, the tech company raked in close to a million downloads of its first game, Carry1st Trivia, in South Africa, Nigeria, and Kenya. This feat was enough for the company to win the Best News and Entertainment Solution at the 2019 Apps Africa Innovation Awards.

What served to Carry1st's advantage was their collaboration with individuals who understand the need to synergize efforts to innovate and achieve. Start-ups in Nigeria are yet to fully grasp the idea of collaboration and how it improves their respective lots. In "Corporate Collaboration as Growth and Exit Opportunity," Asemota referenced a Nigerian founder, Olayinka, who, while facing struggles to build a unique digital commerce startup that brings together traders and buyers, got a partnership offer from a bank.[18] The bank intended to buy his innovations. Rather than see the whole deal as an exit strategy, Olayinka made it known that he was not ready to sell, preferring to render the tech service as an outsider. While the option seemed the best logically, Asemota quickly affirmed that he and Olayinka eventually realized they got it wrong. In further assertions, Asemota retorted that tech start-ups should understand that exits, arranged as acquisitions, drive the tech industry in places like the USA. Solving the customers' problems of an acquirer is the easiest way to become an acquisition target. This is the only way to be relevant in the tech market, as the industry does not only reward problem-solving, but also tech startup investors are more concerned with innovations that provide scalable solutions. If a product provides problem-solving and scalable solutions, it is more likely to be relevant to the tech market.

However, African tech start-ups are yet to understand this dynamism, owing to the low trust in many African countries' corporate environments. Conversely, the level of distrust between established companies and start-ups in Africa exists due to perceived disruptions of the status quo. While tech start-ups uphold the belief that they can change the status quo with technology, established companies believe that such an occurrence may put them at a disadvantage. What both parties fail to understand, as Asemota connoted, is that they need each other now more than ever.[19] Instead of looking at the whole arrangement from the perspective of disruptions, it would be ideal to see it as optimizations that would improve service delivery while also laying a foundation for technological development. Asemota further acclaimed that build-

18. Victor Osaretin Asemota, "Corporate Collaboration as Growth and Exit Opportunity," *The Guardian*, August 29, 2018.

19. Asemota, "Corporate Collaboration as Growth."

ing trust is a precursor of innovative ecosystems.[20] As Asemota noted in 'Start-up Ventures 101', successful ecosystems are built by teams that maintain strong partnerships, which is evident in many successful companies such as Larry and Sergey of Google; Bill Gates and Paul Allen; Steve Jobs and Steve Wozniak; Paul Graham and Jessica Livingston, to mention a few.

The trust issues do not end among partnerships. Tech start-ups in Nigeria often fail to make some necessary moves, making it difficult to garner the level of trust potential customers need to key into their products. Asemota affirmed in "Designing African Tech Start-ups for Trust" that tech entrepreneurs often make the mistake of not doing enough in advertising. In some countries in the global south, like Nigeria, where advance fee fraud is rampant, it is always difficult to distinguish what is fraudulent and what is not, especially if such products are relatively unknown. Many tech start-ups fail simply because they do not indulge in the requisite level of publicity. However, depending solely on publicity does not lead to success. Many tech start-ups have engaged in advertising without putting in place mechanisms to ensure the products are available to consumers, thereby losing their trust and confidence.

The potential for overlapping interests provides great advantages for tech partnerships, and most tech start-ups need the inputs of existing organizations more than the latter needs the former. For instance, banks and telecommunication companies already have customers that need digital solutions to myriad digital challenges. So, it is ideal for fintech start-ups to undergo acquisition, as means of partnerships do not exist within a particular ecosystem alone. In 2019, Co-creation HUB (CcHUB), one of Nigeria's pioneer innovation hubs, successfully acquired iHUB, another leading tech hub in Kenya.

The founder of Flutterwave, a tech startup, also contributed to the issue of partnership when he mentioned that building a known brand as an African startup takes more than a decade, and the best way to mitigate this is by engaging in partnerships as a core business strategy. Despite the challenges, tech start-ups continue to mature rapidly across the continent as local talent becomes more ubiquitous. South Africa is the most fertile ground for tech start-ups in Africa. Also, Nigeria and Kenya remain the leading markets for funding, while Egypt recently displaced South Africa from the third spot for tech startup investments in Africa.[21]

While attempting to catch up with the rest of the world technologically, the African technology sector seemed to have skipped certain steps, as Asemota opined in 'Start-up Ventures 101'. Although the environment may inevitably fuel the needed technological growth in Africa, very little is being done to ensure that businesses survive or

---

20. Asemota, "Corporate Collaboration as Growth."

21. Tom Jackson, "How Egypt Established itself as an African Tech Hub to be Reckoned with in 2019," *Disrupt Africa,* February 4, 2020, https://disrupt-africa.com/2020/02/how-egypt-established-itself-as-an-african-tech-hub-to-be-reckoned-with-in-2019/.

thrive within the environment. The lack of adequate basic infrastructure, such as energy, automatically limits the potential of many tech start-ups and grounded tech companies. Building a sustainable ecosystem without putting in place the requisite infrastructure that will propel growth in such ecosystems will not reduce the mortality rates of start-ups. The availability of funds is not enough to ensure relative success compared to other countries. There should be a focus shift from growth to understanding the importance of improving infrastructure and the fundamentals of the tech market in Africa. Rapid growth will be counterproductive if there is a lack of awareness of market insights and a solid collaboration between tech start-ups and more established companies.

TECHNOLOGY AS A MECHANISM TO FIGHT CORRUPTION

The Nigerian public sector is riddled with corruption; this fact cannot be ignored. Successive governments have failed to develop adequate mechanisms to fight public sector corruption. Even the Buhari administration, whose major electoral promise was to tackle corruption in the public sector, did not have any clear-cut policy to end the destructive practice. So, how can a nation immersed in wide-scale corruption in the public sector embark on wholesale problem-solving? Affirming that corruption in Nigeria is a societal mindset is a plausible assertion. From individuals to the private sector and, ultimately, the public sector, there is this perception that goals can only be achieved by engaging in one form of a corrupt practice or the other. The conception of such ideas, consciously or unconsciously, has turned the public sector into an environment with no moral balance needed for extolling sound virtues. The Nigerian public sector is populated with institutions with high levels of inefficiency due to the lackadaisical attitude of those empowered to make such institutions work.

However, the rapid spread of digitalization and ICT in Africa has opened the door to revolutionizing public service delivery concerning the menace of corruption. Detection and prevention of corruption have been made possible with the emergence of various technologies employed to ensure individuals deliver public sector goods in line with regulation. Before the emergence of the internet, the majority of the corrupt in the public sector is rarely recognized by the citizens. Cover-ups are perfectly perpetrated to ensure that the knowledge of such practices is limited to the government corridors alone. However, the technological revolution changed the dynamics of reporting to accommodate the online dissemination of information to reach a wider and more informed audience who populate the internet. Over the years, the rapid development of ICT came with the promise that it could reduce corruption in government-controlled institutions.

During the early 2000s, recordkeeping was bitten by the Y2K bug, leading to a switch from paper documentation to electronic. This process was sure to expose the high corruption level in various government parastatals. Nevertheless, the move was

necessary to ease the rigors of certain documentation processes. One such was recalled in Asemota's "Tackling Public Sector Corruption Starts and Ends with Technology," where he alluded to a Finance Commissioner who needed to physically sign up to ten thousand payment warrants every month.[22] Such processes may be exposed to fraud as people will find means of exploiting the manual method of validating accounts payable due to the sheer number of documents to be signed; hence the commissioner needed a revamped and fraud-proof system.

Asemota affirmed another salient fact while detailing his experience of being chosen as one of the tech experts to implement custom-built solutions for a government parastatal. The documentation given to him explicitly stated the public sector processes for implementing the newly built ERP systems solutions. According to Asemota, "This manual sped up our implementation process, and the client was surprised at the results. It revealed things they did not want to be exposed and we were promptly kicked out with payments still outstanding to us". This explains one sad reality; the government-controlled public sector is rife with shady arrangements and deals that have been kept from the public for a long time; hence the government is reluctant to put in place mechanisms that may expose such practices. As Asemota noted, anyone who witnesses corruption during their first experience with a government-controlled establishment may feel like giving up on the public sector.

The two scenarios painted by Asemota logically point to one thing; the rigorous processes are not the problem, but rather the people are. The objective of introducing technology as a replacement for manual processes is best described as a change necessitated by the need for optimizations. Asemota's experiences in the public sector upheld the claim that the outcomes of technological changes are often at variance with the motivations of those who benefit from inefficiencies in the public sector. With technology being all about change, the people who have participated in corrupt activities may eventually be exposed to new technologies; thus, they will aggressively refuse such change, no matter how beneficial it would be for operations. Asemota communicated this in the previously mentioned article by stating emphatically that 60% of ERP implementations during that time had been unable to achieve their objectives because the people sabotaged the efforts.[23]

Fast forward to more than a decade later, the Nigerian public sector has widely adopted technological change, with many government-owned institutions experiencing vast improvements in their operations due to outsourcing technology. For instance, Asemota referenced the introduction of the Single Treasury Account (TSA) and BVN as technological platforms introduced to curb the menace of corrupt practices. While such technological change can be applauded, it may not be enough to

22. Victor Osaretin Asemota, "Tackling Public Sector Corruption Starts and Ends with Technology," *The Guardian*, April 18, 2018.

23. Asemota, "Tackling Public Sector Corruption."

stop the people whose mindsets have been greatly corroded by corruption. As Asemota noted, no amount of change management or arrests will stop corruption if the government is not constantly proactive and checking for loopholes that may be exploited. Of paramount importance to this is the practice of transparency to combat the opacity prevalent in most government-controlled institutions. While technology is not introduced expressly to stop corruption, its adoption opens up the operations, documentation, and processes that are somewhat impossible to hide. The implementation of BVN has checked many incidences of corrupt practices. However, there is still more that can be achieved if, as Asemota ascribed, the government embarks on outsourcing the technology-driven processes of most of its institutions. This will go a long way to offer transparency and permanency since cloud storage systems cannot be easily tampered with or manipulated the way paper documentation can.

The digital revolution is gradually changing the rules of the corruption game.[24] Technological advances continue to aid the fight against corruption worldwide, prompting both the government and the private sector to improve their levels of transparency while offering the citizens the opportunity to demand more accountability. If care is not taken, countries like Nigeria may not enjoy the full potential of technology adoption in the fight against corruption. As processes are being changed, the people that benefit from the opaque systems initially in place are also evolving, looking for new ways to mask their corrupt practices.

TECHNOLOGY AS A TOOL FOR EFFECTIVE ELECTIONEERING IN NIGERIA

Technology impacts many social engagements, and discussing any subject matter without referencing technology becomes daunting. The introduction of technology into the electoral process provides the possibility of experiencing elections that are free from irregularities. Under the Military regime of Ibrahim Badamosi Babangida, Nigeria witnessed the freest and fairest election ever. It was not a matter of the military being more adept at conducting elections; but rather, it was the preponderance of a nation whose people, seemingly exhausted with the nuances of the dictatorial regime, felt obligated to ensure that the chance for the civilian rule was not jeopardized by electoral bickering that often leads to invalidation of elections.

However, the advent of the fourth republic, which started in 1999, has resulted in claims and counter-claims of electoral malpractices during every election in Nigeria. Unlike 1993, when the opposition accepted its defeat by a stronger and more popular candidate, elections post-1999 have always witnessed rigging, ballot-snatching, maiming, intimidation, and violence. These are some of the numerous challenges that

24. Carlos Santiso, "Integrity Tech: Three ways Governments can use Technology to Disrupt Corruption," *apolitical*, February 26, 2019, https://apolitical.co/en/solution_article/integrity-tech-disrupt-corruption.

lead to the self- disenfranchisement by voters in Nigeria.[25] The wanton destruction of lives and properties during elections in Nigeria should give any sane individual course to rationalize whether or not there is any hope for future free and fair elections in the country. While many citizens are quick to get hold of their voter's cards before elections, a larger proportion chooses not to exercise their civic right of voting owing to one or more malpractices. However, the emergence of technology in the electoral space is changing this narrative. The internet revolution, having raised the bar of electioneering in Nigeria, is a useful tool that can change how elections are conducted in Nigeria.

People quickly say that elections are not won on social media, a cliché that Asemota opined is spurred from misunderstanding. Going further, he retorted in his article 'The Future of Election is Digital' that "election is not conducted on social media, and nobody wins elections on social media because they all currently lose to apathy."[26] Truly, elections may not be won on social media, but the platforms accord a great opportunity to sway an unresponsive political subset, the youths, who, according to the data of the National Electoral Commission, make up 51% of registered voters in Nigeria in 2019.[27] As Asemota noted, a large proportion of the electorates in Nigeria are becoming politically active in the electoral process. The analogous model of organizing political campaigns and engaging the electorates may have worked in the past, owing to the non-existence of digitalization. However, the digitalization of campaign processes does not mean an end to offline campaign activities. Asemota believes that digital channels for electoral propagation are crucial to promoting awareness about candidates and encouraging feedback mechanisms through online engagements. Digital channels exist to improve electoral campaign efficiency, ensuring that the political game is not solely limited to offline grass-root organizations.

Looking at the 2015 and 2019 elections, it is glaring that technological advancements are beginning to impact elections in Nigeria. Perhaps, Asemota affirmed this in his article "Can Technology help to Win Nigerian Elections," when he asserted that technology is becoming a significant influence in Nigerian elections and would continue to be in future elections. The introduction of Smart card readers saw a significant reduction in incidences of multiple voting. As mentioned earlier, the electoral processes of the years also witnessed unprecedented usage of social media for electoral campaigns and fundraising in Nigeria. Asemota furthered his assertion by detailing

---

25. Michael Bratton, "Vote Buying and Violence in Nigerian Election Campaigns," *Electoral Studies* 27, no. 4 (2008): 621–632.

26. Victor Osaretin Asemota, "The Future of Election Campaign is Digital," *The Guardian*, March 6, 2019.

27. Olu Awofeso and Paul A. Irabor, "Youth Unemployment and Electoral Violence in Nigeria: A Case of the 2019 General Elections," *Elections and Electoral Violence in Nigeria*, eds. Kelechi John Mary Ani and Victor Ojakorotu (Singapore: Palgrave Macmillan, 2022), 35–49.

how in 2015, President Buhari's campaign organization raised campaign funds through the sales of scratch cards to their followers and the electorates.[28]

Not only were they able to raise funds, but they also ensured that they were granted access to the mobile phone numbers of those that loaded such cards, serving as a means to further open up lines of communications with them. As Asemota noted, this innovative use of ICT in election campaigns was very effective, making coordinating communication with the electorate easier. The diffusion of technology across Africa is a huge blessing due to the opportunity accorded to millions of people to interrelate with one another with minimal capital investment. This is reminiscent of the Obama electoral campaign, where messages are sent to random and targeted people, soliciting donations and contributions, thereby giving the electorates a sense of belonging in the whole procedure. It becomes easier to understand Asemota's perspectives when we factor in the successes of Barack Obama's use of social media to canvass for funds as well as followership, not to mention the sheer number of volunteers recruited online for the sole objective of embarking on door-to-door campaigns on behalf of the candidate.[29]

Voter apathy among Nigerians has been a major factor in the past because they could not change the status quo concerning the country's leadership. With the coming of social media, communication backed by technology is already changing the game by helping to ignite the consciousness of the politically dormant youths who, due to the perception that elections are corrupt, scarcely participated in the past.

Not a politician himself, Asemota also brought attention to his involvement in the election of his friend, who contested for the Chairmanship of Ikeja Local Government in Lagos, Nigeria. Individuals of Asemota's caliber are not always actively involved in campaigns to usher individuals into elected positions. When such does happen, one can be sure it is from a strictly personal relationship. While alluding that digital advertising was not enough to give the electoral mandate to his friend, Asemota claimed that 'we could have also gathered as much data as possible about the actual voters and their preferences through mobile channels to have a productive ground game.'[30]

Further stating the importance of technology to elections in Nigeria, Asemota pointed to the level of online engagement of the 2015 and 2019 presidential elections in Nigeria and how it opened up some degree of transparency that was not characteristic of prior elections before 2015. In his words, future trends favor 'ownership' cre-

28. Victor Osaretin Asemota, "Can Technology help to Win Nigerian Election?" *The Guardian*, January 24, 2018.

29. Asemota, "Can Technology help?"

30. Asemota, "Can Technology help?"

ated through technology rather than bribery with 'stomach infrastructure.'[31] Noting that it was the promise of transparency that endeared the minds of the people to the ruling political party, it is apt to posit that technology would have aided the propagation of the transparency agenda if the Buhari administration had actualized the dream of reforming the electoral laws to uphold electronic voting in a bid to discourage and eliminate the malpractices that Nigerian elections have been known for.

The tendency for technology to greatly reduce instances of electoral malpractices such as result sheet mutilation, ballot stuffing, multiple voting, and alteration of results cannot be overstated. Although the Independent Electoral Commission (INEC) has tried several approaches to improve the conduct and management of elections in Nigeria, they have yet to effectively use sophisticated technologies to ensure credible elections. The Automatic Fingerprint Identification System (AFIS), which was introduced in the 2015 election, was marked with inefficiencies as there were countless complaints of the technological devices being unable to fulfill their task. At the end of it all, most polling booths still used the paper ballot, thereby rendering the purchase of the technologies a waste. The concept of e-voting is yet to fully take shape in Nigeria, despite huge funds being spent in the past to ensure its realization. Transparency and accountability remain part of the problems that will continue to mar Nigerian electoral processes if technology is not adopted. The 2019 presidential election witnessed accusations and counter-accusations regarding the purported non-usage of the INEC server, which had been commissioned for use.

As it stands, technology offers many advantages to Nigeria's electoral processes. However, one should not forget that it has its cons as well. The wrong use of social media to sway voters was perfectly utilized in the 2015 election, with political parties engaging in smear campaigns to gain the upper hand. Fake news and the propagation of unrealistic election promises through social media do not indicate good signals for future elections.

HOW TECH START-UPS ARE IMPROVING BANKING SERVICES IN NIGERIA

Fintech products and services worldwide have succeeded by taking an innovative approach that puts people first. Previous banking services may have wasted unnecessary time as individuals intending to carry out basic financial transactions needed to take a detour and get into banking halls to achieve this. However, fintech has improved this experience significantly, and banks are suddenly not the go-to places for basic transactions. Hence, tech start-ups in Africa have been contributing to the drive to make sure that the banking experiences of bank customers are improved. One area

31. Victor Osaretin Asemota, "The Future of Election Campaign is Digital," *The Guardian*, March 6, 2019.

that has improved this experience significantly is the design of fintech apps. The relationship between fintech providers and banks is mutually dependent as they both need each other to survive in a rapidly changing world.

Asemota noted in 'Banking Technology and the Unhappily Banked' that there is a rapidly growing chasm between fintech companies and banks. Despite fintech companies such as Interswitch and Systemspecs having continually assisted banks in developing platforms for coordinating payment transactions among customers, bank customers seem to be discontent with services. In the past, the migration was from old generations to newer ones. The so-called newer generations have suddenly grown old, too, with a new generation of financial services providers powered by technology.[32] Before the advent of fintech and their respective innovations, performing basic financial transactions like depositing and withdrawing personal funds meant going to the bank to spend long hours in queues. Bank customers feel dissatisfied with the number of hours spent trying to carry out simple transactions due to the sheer number of people waiting to carry out the same transaction. The digital age brought about a change, with the bank regulator in Nigeria encouraging the concept of electronic banking. The so-called new-generation banks, seeing an opportunity to lay claim to a bigger market share, were the first to tap into electronic banking. As a result, new-generation banks, such as Zenith Bank and Guaranty Trust bank, can boast a larger customer base than old-generation banks like the Union Bank of Africa.

The latest technological trend has made it easy for financial services companies to set up substitutes for conventional banks. Recently, fintech companies are beginning to look beyond after successfully taking the role of financial intermediaries between the clients of various banks. The likely migration away from conventional banks may be further spurred by the experiences of bank deposit customers who seem to be experiencing losses, hence not enjoying any significant advantage of keeping money in commercial banks. Asemota rightly acclaimed such when he assumed that people would likely remain unbanked due to the friction and lack of advantage in utilizing banking services in Nigeria.[33] Asemota further mentioned some business owners that have been forced to rely only on cash transactions due to losses they incur as a result of bank charges. The financial services regulators in the country seem to be doing little to alleviate these challenges. Asemota noted that if the banking sector shared the same level of compliance with the regulation as in the Nigerian telecommunication sector, many of the financial institutions would have faced severe penalties due to the non-ending complaints of customers and customer service issues.

Comparing the competition among banks with the competition in the telecommunication sector, the financial services sector in Nigeria operates like a loosely related

32. Victor Osaretin Asemota, "Bank Technology and the Unhappily Banked," *The Guardian*, June 20, 2018.

33. Asemota, "Bank Technology."

singular unit. The service charges are almost identical, with no clear product differentiation. The absence of competition results from competitors providing perfectly homogenous products and services with near-identical costs. However, fintech is changing the narratives with the emergence of challenger banks, especially in Nigeria, as recognized by Asemota. Challenger banks are new retail banks different from conventional banks but provide fintech services and features that make banking more convenient for clients.[34] If the conventional banks in Nigeria are not perfectly equipped to serve the vast numbers of customers in the country, banks that are adequately capitalized will inevitably control the market and banking culture.

The unhappiness of bank customers seems to have taken a new dimension that Asemota alluded to. Banking halls are experiencing a new wave; they are no longer processing simple transactions since fintech has provided better platforms. Rather, the banking halls are populated with customers coming for various complaints that need to be sorted out. The emergent problem of customer service-related issues has resulted in untold hardships on the customers' end. A financial settlement transaction between two banks through third-party fintech platforms like Flutterwave may take up to seventy-two hours to be sorted. Within this period, the customer is held in limbo, unable to complete the transaction nor access his or her funds hooked somewhere between the three parties involved in the transactions. This increasing air of despair, Asemota noted, only pushes the customer to seek alternatives elsewhere in the form of consumer credits and others.[35] Iyin Aboyeji affirmed that what people want is to be able to operate digital banking services as seamlessly as their various social media accounts.[36]

The global competitive landscape has necessitated an adequately regulated financial sector that will improve the many bank deposit customers and their ever-constant service issues. There is an increased need for developing a robust regulatory structure for the fintech sector in Nigeria. The two major regulators, the Central Bank of Nigeria and the National Communications Commission (NCC) should be able to provide oversight functions of the country's several segments of the fintech sector, despite ambiguities in the current laws governing their activities. Nigeria's fintech and digital banking industry can only achieve global standards through concurrent evaluations of the activities and quality of services offered to customers, most of whom are perpetually unhappy with the customer-care services presently offered.

---

34. Ifedapo Adeleye, Franklin Ngwu, Nkemdilim Iheanachor, Ebes Esho, Chijioke Oji, Theresa Onaji-Benson and Chris Ogbechie, "Banking on Africa: Can Emerging Pan-African Banks Outcompete their Global Rivals?" *Africa's Competitiveness in the Global Economy*, eds. Ifedapo Adeleye and Mark Esposito (Cham, Switzerland: Palgrave Macmillan, 2018), 113–136.

35. Asemota, "Bank Technology."

36. Alexander Onukwue, "Nigerian Banks want Fintech Collaborations, but for Specific and Unique Needs," *Tech Cabal*, July 22, 2020, https://techcabal.com/2020/07/22/banks-fintech-collaboration/.

Fintech companies and banks in Nigeria are engaged in collaborations that replicate frontend-backend dynamism. Abubakar Suleiman, CEO of Sterling Bank, asserted in his interviews that his company is looking for specific problem-solving tech to deliver solutions to the urban poor without making them worse through service charges. This is coming, despite the company's collaboration with Social Lender, a fintech company that uses social media public data as an index for lending funds to individuals. The innovative design by Social Lender gives more credence to Asemota's assertion that design thinking has become a standard of successful technology products because such innovations put people first.[37] Understandably, fintech start-ups need profitability to survive; however, survival can only be certain if people see the huge benefits of adopting such technology. Making sure that the product offers users increased efficiency for particular issues will automatically attract them to its consumption.

When a technological platform offers a cost-effective environment for a particular service, it is possible for the consumers of the service to adapt and embrace it. In the case of financial transactions, however, this may not be overly true, as a significant proportion of deposit customers in countries like Nigeria may feel insecure putting their funds in financial institutions that are not physically accessible. In essence, the future of fintech and banks rests on developing a relationship that depends largely on meeting the common needs of the aforementioned customers within a mutually beneficial arrangement.

Some fintech companies, having metamorphosed into digital banks, have begun partnerships with conventional banks in Nigeria. Breaking away from convention to embrace digital banks like Kuda may not appeal to those opposed to the dynamism of change. However, it might not take long before digital banks like Kuda merge conventional banks' operational practices with theirs. Kuda has already established partnerships with commercial banks (Zenith bank, Guaranty trust bank, Access bank) to use their physical platforms (banking halls and automated teller machines) for its basic banking services, over-the-counter deposits, and withdrawals from ATMs. Piggyvest, another fintech start-up, has a partnership arrangement with Providus bank to create direct deposit account numbers for its fintech users.

ASEMOTA: TIPS FOR START-UP SUCCESS IN AFRICA

Asemota also shared insightful insights on how start-ups can thrive in Africa. His vast experience in the technology sector and numerous engagements in commerce and economics rank him as the numero uno of African business. He corrected the widely-held beliefs that the goal of every startup is to create wealth or make profits, positing that when start-ups are fixated on money-making, they tend not to achieve

37. Asemota, "Design Thinking."

significant success.[38] Undoubtedly, the goal of every business is to make money; Asemota, however, contends that African start-ups need to resist the thought of making profits at the initial stage. He posited that small businesses tend to create value that solves real societal problems when they are not profit-oriented. Solutions to these problems would enable the business to generate real future profits. This, according to him, is why not-for-profit businesses are accruing more benefits.

The investor guru also catalyzed businesses to develop an original model of thinking.[39] The emphasis on originality in business enterprises cannot be overstated, as it gives leverage over the completion and an opportunity to stand out and dominate the market ecosystem. He posited that as a founder cum investor, he finds original ideas exciting. As he puts it: "originality interests me a lot."[40] He further posited that thinking differently would caution investors from not making costly mistakes, harping that they had made a mistake from lack of originality in thinking. He contends that most start-ups fail because the investors or founders do not have domain knowledge or knowledge of the market ecosystem and "had no business doing what they were doing," which ultimately translates to failure in the long run. He argued that originality should be foregrounded in the business ideology of investors and founders. Asemota's postulations on the notion of originality summarize why some businesses boom while others struggle to thrive. A business enterprise cannot afford to keep doing the same thing and expect different results. In a market system characterized by fierce competition, start-ups that cannot afford to shape up would be phased out. A key to building a strong business experience as Asemota foregrounds innovative methodologies. The context seems true if one evaluates the success of top companies in Nigeria, Africa, and other parts of the world.

Asemota also warned investors to take into consideration the market fragmentation in Africa.[41] He posits that the African market is young and fragmented; thus, investors must understand the dynamics of African markets before launching a product or service. Investors, therefore, need to take into cognizance the various factors that influence the market ecosystem in Africa as this would enable them to identify the strengths and weaknesses of the market ecosystem, which would prove handy in their business-oriented ventures. Investors need to assess their business environment and target audience. Asemota explains that start-ups must take a different approach to the African market ecosystem. One popular ideology regarding doing business or creating value is that big ideas succeed quickly. Contrary to this popular expression, he contends that simple ideas succeed in Africa. As he put it: "The simple things

38. Game Thinking TV, "4 Key Insights for Start-ups Success in Africa, with Victor Asemota," *Game Thinking TV*, May 5, 2022. https://www.youtube.com/watch?v=5x0ND9Z3ef4.

39. Game Thinking TV, "4 Key Insights for Start-ups."

40. Game Thinking TV, "4 Key Insights for Start-ups."

41. Game Thinking TV, "4 Key Insights for Start-ups."

(ideas) are the most successful in Africa." Thus, what is needed is for investors to identify what others see as a little problem, then build on it.

Asemota cited the problem of savings in Nigeria.[42] Most Nigerians, especially the lower and middle classes, find it hard to save. The simple reason is that they spend largely on their basic needs, while others contend with impulsive buying. Even when they keep money in banks, there are no definite, effective saving models. Asemota posited that he had told some Nigerian banks to develop an effective saving model for their customers. However, PiggyVest came to solve Nigeria's spending and saving problem. Their Piggybank Wallet has been helping Nigerians to save money.[43] In 2021, the Nigerian-based online savings helped Nigerians save 585 million dollars.[44] The financial app also helps to teach Nigerians financial discipline. With features like "Withdrawal days," users could withdraw their money without any charges but would pay a penalty fee of 2.5% when they take out money outside the Withdrawal days, ultimately teaching the users financial prudence. Another feature called "Automated Saving" enables the users to save automatically, and they do not worry about their funds as the saving app is built on a high-security system that fends off fraud attacks. There is also a feature, "Quick Save," which allows users to save manually. Many Nigerians have credited the saving app for instilling the principle of financial responsibility among users.[45] As its co-founder, Joshua Chibueze, posited of the saving app, "PiggyVest is a place where you keep your money that is your own money."[46]

Simple ideas like solving spending problems allow PiggyVest to thrive in the Nigerian Market. Asemota reiterated that start-ups must build the simplest solution for the simplest problems. Put differently, start-ups need to think from a narrow perspective. From a narrow perspective, it interprets that they should check for the simplest problems consumers face and build a business mechanism to address them. Who would think that Nigerians save their money elsewhere than banks? The best idea is to think out of the box, argued Asemota: this helps a business enterprise keep topping charts.

---

42. Game Thinking TV, "4 Key Insights for Start-ups."

43. PiggyVest, "How the Piggybank Wallet is helping Millions of Nigerians Save," *PiggyVest blog*, April 22, 2022, https://blog.piggyvest.com/save/how-the-piggybank-wallet-is-helping-millions-of-nigerians-save/.

44. Digital Times, "How PiggyVesthelped Nigerians Save $585 million in 2021," *Digital Times*, January 5, 2022, https://www.digitaltimes.africa/how-piggyvest-helped-nigerians-save-585-million-in-2021/#.

45. PiggyVest, "How the Piggybank Wallet is helping."

46. Ruth Okwumbu-Imafiadon, "We wanted to help users pay themselves first—Piggyvest," *Nairametrics*, October 3, 2020, https://nairametrics.com/2020/10/03/we-wanted-to-help-users-pay-themselves-first-piggyvest/.

HOW NIGERIANS CAN COPE WITH THE CHANGING SITUATION OF WORK

Around the world, technological innovations are improving the concept of work. Every young adult or older individual needs to engage in one form of work. Work is a part of life that we cannot just do without. Asemota affirmed in "The Technology Freelancer Problem" that technology has become the most accessible means of making things happen.[47] Whether paid jobs, freelancing, or fraudulent engagements, technology has improved how people work. Learning code writing and programming on mobile phones is now possible, a feat that would not have been possible without technological advances. The good thing for Africans is that the internet has made it easier to have access to materials without recourse to location. Unlike three decades ago, when it was expected for any Nigerian to travel overseas to improve education and knowledge, technology has provided the opportunity to learn in the comfort of the home if equipped with the right equipment.

Individuals working within the realm of freelancing are the largest beneficiaries of technology. Some aspects of work in corporate environments are not routine but occur often. Such tasks, for most organizations, run into high overheads. To avoid such unnecessary costs, many organizations hire freelancers. Asemota posited that many organizations avoid bloated overhead costs by giving out aspects of their work to parties outside the company's perimeter. Freelancers have become the new consultants, as corporations rely on them to get aspects of work done. Despite the ramped employment of freelancers, Asemota suggested that companies that employ the services of freelancers should not expect anything innovative. This is because freelancers have realized that their services are sought after because they are a cost-effective solution; hence they reciprocate with equal efforts.

Freelance working arrangements offer organizations the potential to experience better outputs from freelancers. For example, many people, such as Editi Effiong, whom Asemota claimed generates the best innovative ideas while under the shower, have improved the outputs of organizations. Although this may sound awkward, the ease of working in a comfortable environment can improve individuals' outputs. Alluding to this assertion, Asemota affirmed that the methodology of Effiong, while not easily subjected to scientific testing, may prove to be effective as the subject continues to propose great ideas that have led to winning projects.[48] In furtherance of this conception, Asemota noted that creativity starts from comfortability at home, and because he works from home, he strives to create an environment that offers optimal productivity. Decision fatigue is much reduced when working from home; this is one of the many advantages of freelance working.

---

47. Victor Osaretin Asemota, "The Technology of Freelancer Problem," *The Guardian*, February 7, 2018.

48. Victor Osaretin Asemota, "Innovation Starts from Home," *The Guardian*, January 10, 2018.

Another recurring theme that is gaining prominence in the global labor industry is remote work. The capability to work from outside the confines of a corporate office has recently become a mainstream operation. The rise of this concept cannot be discussed without mentioning technology and how technological developments continue to make remote work easier. While industries and businesses were slow to adopt the concept of remote work, unforeseen problems have necessitated its adoption. For instance, the recent global pandemic almost crippled the operations and survival of many organizations, with the lucky ones being those that had already developed a blueprint that incorporates remote working. Some organizations never evaluated the potential benefits of remote work until the emergence of the coronavirus pandemic.

While discussing his personal experience with remote work, Asemota referred to Paul Onwuanibe's famous TEDs Euston talk, where the latter affirmed that many African businesses would be better off adopting the next century's business model, which gave very little room for the concept of employees converging in one space to work.[49] Of course, this was before the pandemic, forcing many businesses to re-strategize and evaluate the possibilities of adopting a remote work blueprint. One needs to observe the itinerary of employees in traffic-prone cities like Lagos to understand how beneficial a remote working system would be to overall productivity and output. Individuals, in a bid to make sure they are not caught in the daily traffic caused by the early morning rush, leave their homes in the darkness of the morning and may not get back till late at night.

The stress of such an everyday routine is sure to affect the productivity of such individuals because they find it difficult to have quality rest. Checking the engagements of these individuals, one may find out that their work engagements are strictly limited to a computer system and the availability of the internet. As Asemota noted, some of these organizations, especially the ones with a sizable use of the internet and computer system, do not need physical offices.[50] Technological advancement has resulted in a paradigm shift, with companies like Automatic (the company that built Word Press) having over 600 employees working from wherever they like. Such overall modifications to operations will not only increase productivity but also reduce the overheads of organizations.

Remote working does not automatically mean that employees must stay in bed or at home all day. Understandably, some organizations dread the possibility of employees not showing determination and attention when confined to their homes. In the article 'The Era of Remote Work,' Asemota retorted that the next century's business model is the provision of shared co-working spaces provided by third parties. Companies such as WeWork are among the most prominent companies that offer organi-

49. Victor Osaretin Asemota, "The Era of Remote Work," *The Guardian*, November 1, 2017.
50. Asemota, "The Era of Remote Work."

zations the possibility of sharing workspaces. To significantly reduce their overheads, organizations are embracing the concept of remote working by renting workspaces in locations that offer proximity to new markets and employee residences. Some stress factors have been mitigated by eliminating the daily commuting of employees and allowing them to work in environments that offer them comfort.

Workstations are becoming ubiquitous in cities like Lagos. Rather than opening new offices in various locations for expansionary purposes, organizations may opt for convenient co-working spaces provided by third parties. This removes the hassle and burden of huge overheads associated with building or renting office spaces. Remote working offers new perspectives about work positions to many employees. Some may see it as a reward for their excellence, while others may perceive it as a move focused on assessing the level of discipline they, as employees, have to work without physical supervision.

Further detailing his experiences regarding remote working, Asemota referenced how he could kick off operations in several African countries, where he and his teams had to make do with the clients' physical locations as temporary offices. Describing the 24/7/365 Mesh Support model he developed, Asemota built a dedicated team of engineers working in the client's location and supervisory teams moving around to ensure that the engineers carry out their responsibilities in conformity with their job details. The need for a central coordination location was satisfied with coffee shops, hotels, bars and restaurants.[51] All these happened as a result of the company not being able to afford to rent physical spaces nor being able to pay for co-working environments. Managing and coordinating the remote teams was made possible through mobile application software like G-Suite. The need to meet with his colleagues daily was non-existent; those who were supposed to collaborate did so remotely except when physical contacts were necessary.

Among Asemota conclusions on remote work is that many African-owned organizations have yet to fully grasp the benefits and importance of working remotely. They are still holed up in a model that will become obsolete shortly. The COVID-19 lockdown did prove him right, as some start-ups like BizNuture have found that remote work suits them better. Although some of these organizations may not be blamed, the prevalence of fraudulent engagements in Nigeria makes it quite risky to deal with an organization with no physical location. According to him, this initially prompted the model of employees being sent to the client's physical location to work while supervision and coordination are done remotely. It is a business model that, when planned properly, will benefit many large multinational companies rendering services. Asemota quickly noted the challenges his organization faced by adopting a remote working model. The organization lost a lot of business opportunities because

51. Asemota, "The Era of Remote Work."

Figure 21.2. "Artificial Intelligence and Security" by Dr. Kazeem Ekeolu. A projection of the development of technology to address the nation's problems.

some clients could not fathom why a company would not have a physical location. While he had previously rented office spaces in locations that offered a short commute, he soon found that the overheads were unnecessary, leading to the office being shut down.

As Asemota rightly opined in the article, technological advances have provided necessary communication outlets that render physical offices unnecessary, thus limiting the need for technology workers to commute daily.[52] Organizations are beginning to understand the vanity of having an office full of employees whose performances may be impeded by the stress encountered due to daily commuting. What matters most to an employee is not the physical presence but optimal productivity. The flexibility of remote working for employees is immense. They are not subjected to strict schedules, making it easier to multitask between work and personal engagements. This may not be permissible in a physical office space, and management will always frown at such practices. However, it should be understood that productivity is not about being physically present. Rather it should be based on completing what is required effectively. A common misconception is that workers engaged in remote work, in reality, do not work. While it is possible that an employee expected to work remotely ends up not working as expected, many organizations that embrace remote work have means of measuring the key performance indicators (KPI) for employees. The same indicators may be used to assess remote workers without leaving any aspect untouched.

Billionaires have been produced from business models that encourage remote working, and Nigeria tech entrepreneurs, as well as service-oriented businesses, can tap from a business model that is sure to deliver the next century's billionaires. Telecommuting and remote work arrangements are not a perfect substitute for physical office space models; they offer complementary advantages, especially for organizations with operations cutting across a wide geographical location. The need to situate administrative offices in every locality can be greatly reduced by developing a business model that will place more emphasis on employee efficiency, resulting from convenient working arrangements, in comparison to the current status quo where employees undergo stress to get to work, only to experience a reduction in performance due to the pressures of commuting.

CONCLUDING REMARKS

Various works by Asemota regarding technological advancement and development indicate that the ongoing technological revolution presents enormous social and economic advantages to Nigeria as a nation. Tech entrepreneurship is very crucial for the technological development of Nigeria, and the onus falls on tech start-ups to continue improving on what is on the ground despite the unfavorable environment that they are operating. Countries like Nigeria and Egypt generate almost 38% of their GDP from micro-entrepreneurs, and this can be improved upon if more tech start-ups continue to spring up.

---

52. Asemota, "The Era of Remote Work."

Technological advancements create a dependence on technology, eventually making it easier to accomplish many tasks. As these advancements continue, mankind's dependency on technology will only expand. Looking through Asemota's contributions and positions, one would realize and understand this development more and see further the necessities of technology in African societies. He, therefore, represents an embodiment of a conscious reminder of the need for society to adjust to these technological needs and the need to make technological innovations fit into the African context.

Despite this, there are accompanying risks and dangers attached to technological advancement that need to be addressed. Dependence on technology may hurt people in the eventuality of failure. As Murphy's Law dictates, anything that can go wrong will surely go wrong. This means that technology can also malfunction, leading to a temporary collapse. In the case of such eventualities, what solutions have been established to limit the burden of such failures? The question represents other ways tech start-ups can exploit to give people what they want and not simply provide solutions. This is only possible by embarking on continuous social scientific investigations to manage the inherent risks of technology adoption. Such investigations will be valuable for social policy and technology design because the array of choices being made now may be difficult to modify in the future.

22

JIBRIN IBRAHIM

Nigerian Politics

INTRODUCTION

Dr. Jibrin Ibrahim is a professor of political science who served as the Director of the Centre for Democracy & Development (CDD), a regional research, advocacy and training non-governmental organization for West Africa. Within the CDD, he also participated in research for the Election Analysis Centre in a role that gave him particular insight into the election process within Nigeria. Furthermore, he was previously the Nigeria Country Director of Global Rights.[1] Dr. Ibrahim has over 30 years of experience in civic engagement. He once served on the Electoral Reform Committee established by late President Umaru Yar' Adua. Previously, he was the National Convenor of the Citizen's Forum for Constitutional Reform, a coalition of 90 non-governmental organizations seeking to reform the 1999 Nigerian Constitution. Understanding his opinions on the election process is one of the best ways to comprehend his views on Nigerian politics, and by analyzing Dr. Ibrahim's perspective on the 2019 general election process, we can better develop a view of his take on Nigerian politics.

Ibrahim maintains a weekly column in *Daily Trust*, which is recirculated on other platforms. The weekly pieces are rich and invite widespread comments. They are impressive resources to create a profile of his thoughts and mindset going into the dem-

1. Jibrin Ibrahim, "Prof Jibrin Ibrahim," *Centre for Democracy and Development*, September 18, 2022, http://www.cddwestafrica.org/?team=henry-smith-2-2-4-2-2-2-2.

ocratic process beginning in January 2018. He has proven to be material to discussions on the political state of Nigeria and issues surrounding it because of his interests and involvement in some of the political developments as stated above. However, his participation in the National Conference organized by former President Goodluck Jonathan in finding solutions to many problems of the nation can also not be underestimated. These made him and his thoughts worthy lenses to understand the country's political atmosphere. With about 34,000 followers on Twitter and Facebook, Ibrahim's contributions have been positioned to fit into the social media theme and sources of information that shape Nigerian political conversations on social media.

I will first explore Ibrahim's article, "2018 and the Return of Politics," by analyzing a trend analysis he published in 2017 on presidential action or inaction projections.[2] He argued within the original projection that the keyword for 2017 that defined the political and economic dynamics remained the same in 2018.[3] Ibrahim stated that in 2016, the President refused to and was incapable of making political appointments and that in 2017, All Progressives Congress (APC) barons could not restrain themselves from struggling for power as politicians do. They did so with gusto, given their fury at winning power in 2015 and "President Buhari's decision to block a significant slice of the APC political class from access to power."[4] Ibrahim questioned President Buhari for asking governors and stakeholders to submit a list of candidates for appointments.[5]

According to Ibrahim, President Buhari hates politics and distrusts politicians, and he could change these things about himself. As President Buhari was preparing to announce his candidacy for a second term, Ibrahim did not believe he was returning to a life he enjoyed. Party primaries were scheduled for late 2018 in preparation for the presidential election on February 16, 2019. Ibrahim observed notable resentment within the APC in 2017 about the President's political inertia, but there was limited action, except for Atiku Abubakar, who returned to the Peoples Democratic Party (PDP). Ibrahim believed the struggle for a presidential nomination in the party primaries would be bloody and that, with the party's governors in control, Atiku may have struggled to covet the ticket.[6] Moving into the start of the election, Ibrahim posed many questions: What happened to the political coalition to bring Buhari to power? To what extent does Buhari maintain fanatical support "in his core northern base? Does Tinubu still control the South West political machine, and would he be prepared to deploy it to get Buhari re-elected if he does? Does Tinubu have a Plan B?"[7]

2. Jibrin Ibrahim, "2018 and the Return of Politics," *Daily Trust*, January 5, 2018,

3. Ibrahim, "2018 and the Return of Politics."

4. Ibrahim, "2018 and the Return of Politics," *Premium Times*, January 5, 2018, https://opinion.premiumtimesng.com/2018/01/05/2018-and-the-return-of-politics-by-jibrin-ibrahim/.

5. Ibrahim, "2018 and the Return of Politics."

6. Ibrahim, "2018 and the Return of Politics."

7. Jibrin Ibrahim, "The Third Force," *Daily Trust*, February 9, 2018.

Figure 22.1. "Jibrin Ibrahim and Discussion on Nigerian Politics" by Michael Efionayi. Jibrin Ibrahim at a news conference.

Ibrahim argued that the most important question early in the election was whether Nigerian constituents would vote for the PDP, knowing how the party ruled and ruined the country. He believed that Nigeria was in a state of crisis and that the economic crisis accelerated the social decomposition of society and increased anarchic responses by the youth engaged "in self-help projects based on kidnapping, cattle rustling, and rural banditry."[8] The violence was accompanied by the Boko Haram calamity and the revival of militancy in the Niger Delta, which created a massive security challenge. The Nigerian military and police forces were unable to adequately address these concerns. Ibrahim noted that Nigerians engaged in the election process hinged on President Buhari's promises to improve security.

8. Ibrahim, "2018 and the Return of Politics."

Ibrahim closed the article by noting that the average Nigerian voter is in an agonizing decision-making dilemma. The Buhari administration did not sufficiently deliver on its promise of improved security, the creation of more jobs, or a successful war against corruption. They would, therefore, have great difficulty on the campaign trail for re-election. The PDP would not find it easier to campaign, as memories of sixteen years of bad governance remained strong. Nigerian elections have been binary, and people may be forced, according to Ibrahim, to decide on the principles of the least terrible option rather than a choice they believe in.

JIBRIN IBRAHIM, GOVERNANCES, POLITICS AND THE STATE OF THE NATION

The political journey of Nigeria has been a rough road zigzagging from positivity to negativity and drenched with historical heritage, ethnicity, and societal backgrounds right before the colonial period to the contemporary political interactions in the country. To speak of the nation's state is to show how the nation has fared so far, comparing the characteristics of the past to the present. If the past suggests the future, then there is a high possibility that the key to contemporary issues that form today's state of the nation might be found in the past. Ibrahim also subscribed to the fact that the foundational characteristics of the country might not have changed as much, as some of the present political characteristics can be traced to historical developments of the country.

In "Nigeria and the Legacy of the Military,"[9] Ibrahim retorted on Fola Fagbule and Feyi Fawehinmi's brilliance in the masterpiece they wrote, *Formation: The Making of Nigeria From Jihad to Amalgamation*,[10] which chronicles the political development of the country from Usman Dan Fodio's Jihad to the 1914 amalgamation, touching on the core values of some of the political entities that existed in the country. In concluding his thought on the strength of these entities and the dented intentions of the colonialists, Ibrahim described Lugard thus, "...the murderer was a repeat offender with the Inemo massacre of 1914, having 60 people killed and the 1918 Adubi incident, during which he organized the killing of over 600 Egba protesters.[11] He further stated that the country's political character had not changed so much before the colonial period, during colonialism, and during the post-colonial era. Capturing this, he noted, "The Nigerian state has consistently resorted to violence and military force to

9. Jibrin Ibrahim, "The Making of Nigeria: From Jihad to Amalgamation," *Premium Times*, September 3, 2021, https://www.premiumtimesng.com/opinion/482783-the-making-of-nigeria-from-jihad-to-amalgamation-by-jibrin-ibrahim.html.

10. Fola Fagbule and Feyi Fawehinmi, *Formation: The Making of Nigeria from Jihad to Amalgamation* (Abuja and London: Cassava Republic, 2021), 357.

11. Ibrahim, "The Making of Nigeria."

address political differences. This is still the situation today. Clearly, the time has come for us to learn to negotiate to resolve our differences."[12]

These attitudes, along with other characteristics of the Nigerian political atmosphere, were concreted by the authoritarian rule during military rule, continuing the high centralization of power and increasing Nigeria's power distance by a great proportion. In "Nigeria and the Legacy of the Military,"[13] Ibrahim analyzed Max Siollun's account[14] of the Nigerian military regime and the concentration of an authoritative ruling system. Tracing the country's problems from history gives one the right understanding of the genesis of the Nigerian problem and how best to approach them. The nation is like a trembling cup heated by many troubles. There is almost a problem worthy of conversation in every angle of society, from education, security, and bad leaders, among others, contributing to the reduction in the nation's standard of living.

If elements of dysfunctional political practices stain the country's political orientation in the past, what has become of the democracy the nation practices now? Nigeria returned to democratic tracks in 1999 and has had six general elections and four democratically elected presidents. However, one cannot say that Nigerian democracy is rightly practiced or its tenets upheld. Professor Stephen Adebanji Akintoye noted that the Nigerian President is the most powerful government official in the world, with large unchecked powers and discretions.[15] Whether his claims are factually true might not be easy to state, but the country's Power Distance Index (PDI) is estimated at 80%, according to the Hofstede Cultural Dimension index, and it is obvious how the political class and elite take advantage of it.[16] It is universally understood that a high PDI score in any society indicates that the society has accepted unfair and unequal hierarchical distribution of power and individuals have accepted their places in the system. Also, several occasions have shown how authorities have exercised powers and governed the country despite being in a democratic era. Violence during elections, trampling of fundamental rights, and the denial of the dividends of democracy are a few of the many sours of Nigerian democracy.[17]

Several of Ibrahim's publications have shown his admission to the discouraging state of Nigerian democracy. One of the most interesting was his analysis of the movie "King of Boys," which depicts Nigerian and Lagos' political scenes, atrocities, and

12. Ibrahim, "The Making of Nigeria."

13. Jibrin Ibrahim, "Nigeria and the Legacy of the Military," *Premium Times*, September 10, 2013, https://www.premiumtimesng.com/opinion/144406-nigeria-legacy-military-jibrin-ibrahim.html.

14. Max Siollun, *Soldiers of Fortune: Nigerian Politics under Buhari and Babangida (1983-1993)* (Abuja: Cassava Republic Press, 2013).

15. Stephen Adebanji Akintoye, "Nigeria's President is the Most Powerful Official of any Country in the World - Prof. Akintoye," *Channels Television*, September 25, 2017, https://youtu.be/Uk3MpBpqhvA.

16. Hofstede Insights, "What about Nigeria," *Country Comparison Nigeria*, 2022, August 23, 2022, https://www.hofstede-insights.com/country-comparison/nigeria/.

17. Parvathi Vasudevan, "Democracy in Nigeria," *Economic and Political Weekly* 46, no. 20 (2011): 26–27.

behaviors.[18] In "Nigeria, Democratic Politics and the "King of Boys," a criticism of the movie and an Independence Day message, Ibrahim did not deny the tensions that question the democratic practices in the nation but was particular about Kemi Adetiba's position, whom he believed posited that there might not be a way to salvage Nigeria's democracy.[19] Reacting to Adetiba's stance, Ibrahim wrote:

> No, Kemi Adetiba, this message is wrong. Yes, we have a lot of criminals as actors in Nigeria's political arena but not all politicians are the pawns of criminals… Maybe the problem with the film is the way it captures Nigeria's zeitgeist—the spirit of the time. There appears to be a double reality in Nigerian politics, with a surface layer in which candidates emerge, contest in elections, win and are sworn into power, with a holy text in one hand and the Constitution in the other. Then there is a second, not so hidden layer of cabals, criminal enterprise and armed thugs, one which directs the affairs of state in the interests of the godfathers and against the interests of the people. The subliminal message is one of a disempowered citizenry. The Nigerian voter therefore has very little agency in the struggle for democracy.[20]

Ibrahim's position is understandable. One cannot throw the baby with the bath water, and one cannot throw away the honest efforts of society and the government, as well as the activities that have shown that democracy is still evident in the country. Hence, one cannot conclude that the nation would not transform to the point of practicing the true democracy the citizens desire. In one article, he charged the government to create a workable strategy to revitalize Nigerian democracy;[21] in another, he believed that Nigerians must be politically active to put the government in check and take the nation back from cabals. He captured this thus:

> There would be a future for Nigerian democracy under two conditions. First, Nigerians must stop voting for candidates on the basis of sentiments. If we all decide to vote on the CAPACITY TO PERFORM, we will begin to have elected officials who have come to serve the people, rather than the normal self-serving scenario. Secondly, Nigerians must massively register as members of political

---

18. Kemi Adetiba (Director), *King of Boys (Film)*, Lagos, Kemi Adetiba Visuals, October 20, 2018: 169 minutes.

19. Jibrin Ibrahim, "Nigeria, Democratic Politics and the "King of Boys"," *Premium Times*, October 1, 2021, https://www.premiumtimesng.com/opinion/487609-nigeria-democratic-politics-and-the-king-of-boys-by-jibrin-ibrahim.html.

20. Ibrahim, "Nigeria, Democratic Politics."

21. Jibrin Ibrahim, "Building National Consensus on Consolidating Democracy," *Premium Times*, February 18, 2022, https://www.premiumtimesng.com/opinion/512230-building-national-consensus-on-consolidating-democracy-by-jibrin-ibrahim.html.

parties and insist on choosing candidates themselves in the primaries. Citizens must OVERTHROW the godfathers and takeover the parties.[22]

While the nation must hope that democratic practices will gain normalcy as Ibrahim wishes, one cannot ignore how corruption is not only denying the country the dividend of democracy but is also putting a rope around the nation's neck, choking national resources and wealth out into the pockets of selfish individuals. Although it is easy to ascribe corrupt practices to political officeholders, citizens and civil servants also have corruption and bribery running through their bloodstreams.

In 2014, Ibrahim lamented the level of corruption in the state and how it had affected the economy. To him, the corrupt practices of the Nigerian political and official classes are beyond mere corruption but pure insanity. The Chairman of Virgin Group explained that the primary reason they withdrew Virgin Airlines from the Nigerian aviation industry was the choking corrupt attitudes and bribery mentality of the politicians and regulatory agencies who saw government as a platform to accrue benefits and favors to themselves.[23] He also retorted how the Malaysian Gardens project in Abuja was affected by the unnecessary demands of the Nigerian politicians for 80% of accruable lands, forcing the Malaysian government out of the arrangement. From the Nigerian National Petroleum Corporation (NNPC) non-remittance of about $49.8 billion, or whatever figure it was adjusted to, to the missing $50 billion under the watch of the Central Bank of Nigeria, there was nothing else Ibrahim could use to describe this distasteful culture other than insanity.[24] This description is accurate because there is no way to describe the commitment to ruining the nation other than absolute madness.

No one says that the countries making landmark influences internationally and locally are free from corrupt practices, but if those practices had been at the detriment of the nation's progress, there would have been more countries in a similar state as Nigeria today. Sadly, only a handful of countries worldwide come close to the corruption witnessed in Nigeria. Before the 2015 elections, the Buhari change mantra gave the impression that corrupt practices would be curbed and the nation would be raised from its knees of destitution. Nigerians did not figure out that these promises of a comfortable and corrupt-free government were much ado about nothing, as the administration was unable to show significant progress until the end of its tenure.

---

22. Jibrin Ibrahim, "Democratizing Nigerian Democracy," *Premium Times*, June 25, 2021, https://www.premiumtimesng.com/opinion/469872-democratising-nigerian-democracy-by-jibrin-ibrahim.html.

23. Ibrahim, "Democratizing Nigerian Democracy."

24. Jibrin Ibrahim, "From Corruption to Ruling Class Insanity," *Premium Times*, February 17, 2014, https://www.premiumtimesng.com/opinion/155273-corruption-ruling-class-insanity-jibrin-ibrahim.html.

The anti-corruption campaign, one of the foci of Buhari's campaign, increased Nigerians' expectations and made him a specimen for Ibrahim's analyses. President Buhari had claimed that the fuel subsidy was of no essence and was only a means to finance and encourage corruption in the country. Unfortunately, throughout his tenure, the President did not end the supposed waste of funds but got the approval of the National Assembly to service it with N4 trillion.[25] The presidency and those in its service and appointment faced different corruption charges, like the Secretary to Government of the Federation, Babachir Lawal, who was rumored and alleged to have contracted money worth about N200 million for revitalizing those affected by the Boko Haram insurgency. To the people's surprise, the Buhari-led government defended the Secretary with a claim that he was not properly indicted. Another recent accusation was the N80 Billion embezzlement by Ahmed Idris, the Accountant General of the federation. The Socio-Economic Rights and Accountability Project (SERAP) also reported that in 2019, about N323.5 billion could not be accounted for by federal MDAs. In 2016, the late Abba Kyari, the former Chief of Staff, was linked to a ₦500 million bribe by MTN Nigeria Communications to persuade the government to reconsider the $5 billion fine awarded to the company.[26] The government dismissed this claim and another 29 million naira bribe claim in 2018 as baseless.[27] Regardless of the authenticity of these reports, it seems the country, under the administration of President Buhari, was thrown into the deep sea of corruption with no lifelines to rescue it. These allegations and many others made Ibrahim conclude thus:

> At the end of Buhari's tenure, it would be fascinating to curate the tales of corruption around the Central Bank of Nigeria, which for now is composed of rumours and speculations. Those who voted for Buhari thinking they were installing an anti-corruption czar are now the most bitterly disappointed citizens. Their shock is likely to grow as the legacy of corruption unfolds.[28]

One of the most frustrating incidences of Nigerian corruption and bribery is that the politicians are not ashamed of it and do not mind what is at stake.[29]

Corruption is one way the Nigerian government at all levels fails its citizens, but in considering the various breakdowns in different sectors, one would realize that almost half of the citizens are in the carnivals of anguish, dancing to constant tones of

---

25. Ibrahim, "From Corruption to Ruling Class Insanity."

26. Kingsley Omonobi, "N500m MTN Bribery Allegation: Presidency Orders Probe of Abba Kyari," *Vanguard*, October 21, 2016.

27. Premium Times, "Presidency Speaks on Corruption Allegations against Buhari's Chief of Staff," *Premium Times*, September 8, 2018, https://www.premiumtimesng.com/news/top-news/282922-presidency-speaks-on-corruption-allegations-against-buharis-chief-of-staff.html.

28. Jibrin Ibrahim, "Corruption and the Buhari Legacy," *Premium Times*, May 20, 2022, https://www.premiumtimesng.com/opinion/531216-corruption-and-the-buhari-legacy-by-jibrin-ibrahim.html.

29. Ibrahim, "Corruption and the Buhari Legacy."

poverty and insecurity, among other social problems. As Ibrahim put it, "Nigeria is on the edge,"[30] and one cannot blame citizens that try to escape it.

With the rate of corruption and the inability of the Buhari-led administration to resolve basic issues affecting the country, it is easy to conclude that he left the country much worse than he met it. Ibrahim reiterated this fact when he realized that he had been singing the same songs of lamentation and was tired of the fact that those issues he addressed only got worse. He expressed his frustration thus:

> Sometimes one is forced to repeat himself over and over again simply because that is what the facts dictate. I cannot remember how many times I have prefaced my articles with the phrase that Nigeria has never had it so bad. For the umpteenth time therefore, I have never seen Nigeria in such dire straits.[31]

Insecurity is the main threat to the nation's peace, with average citizens not knowing what will befall them the next day. The economy dwindles downward, rendering the prices of basic commodities unaffordable and casting the curse of poverty on citizens. Religious and ethnic diversity, which should have been virtues that speed up the country's development, has proven to be more the muse of problems than they are for development. The Nigerian leaders' approach and mindset make the future "bleak," as Ibrahim had noted.[32]

Has Nigeria and the government been doing anything that might change the state of the nation? Yes. Have the efforts of the government been effective and appropriate? No. The government has made notable efforts toward making life easier for the citizens. One such project is revitalizing and reforming the Nigerian railway, making interstate and city journeys more comfortable.[33] Another innovative idea was the 774,000 job opportunities meant to cover the 774 local governments in the country.[34] The problems with these projects were their ineffectiveness, unsustainability, corruption, and implementation problems. On the railway project, Duluidas Nigeria Limited and other aggrieved companies accused the Ministry of Transformation of illegally contracting the project worth N91.7 billion to the Chinese company, China Civil Engineering Construction Company (CCECC).[35] They believed that the contract was

30. Ibrahim, "Corruption and the Buhari Legacy."

31. Jibrin Ibrahim, "Nigeria on the Edge," *Premium Times*, August 5, 2022, https://www.premiumtimesng.com/opinion/547029-nigeria-on-the-edge-by-jibrin-ibrahim.html.

32. Ibrahim, "Nigeria on the Edge."

33. NAN, "NRC Begins Lagos-Abeokuta-Ibadan Rail Services," *The Guardian*, December 7, 2020, https://guardian.ng/news/nrc-begins-lagos-abeokuta-ibadan-rail-services/.

34. Premium Times, "Federal Govt Releases Details of Programme to Employ 774,000 Nigerians," *Premium Times*, May 28, 2020, https://www.premiumtimesng.com/news/headlines/395041-just-in-programme-to-employ-774000-nigerians-starts-october-minister-announces.html.

35. Ameh Ochojila, "Amaechi, Malami Sued over Alleged Illegal Award of N91.7b Rail Contract to Chinese," *The Guardian*, February 4, 2022.

denied them not for a good reason but for favoritism. Other criticisms following the projects are relative costliness[36] and insecurity, especially the March 28, 2022, terrorist attack on the Abuja-Kaduna rail.[37] On job employment, Mr. Quadri Olaleye, the President of the Trade Union Congress (TUC), described the scheme as a "scam" with little to no evidence of employment.[38]

Ibrahim has taken the time to examine the projects supposedly carried out by the Buhari-led administration and exposed how many were "scams," as Mr. Quadri Olaleye of the TUC had summed the 774,000-employment opportunity. In "Alternative Facts and the Buhari Legacy," Ibrahim put the president's assertions on a reality scale, stating that the proclaimed achievements were "alternative facts" showing the opposite of reality.[39] He expressed this thus:

> My sense is that a real distance has developed between the president and reality, and the interstices in-between have been packed full by narrators of alternative facts. The sad reality might therefore be that the president believes he has been the greatest positive force in the history of Nigeria.[40]

Ibrahim referred to the reports of Stears Business on the state of the nation from the assumption of office by President Buhari. It was noted that as of June 2022, the nation's GDP had reduced to 1% from the 6.5% before the president assumed office. The inflation level increased to 15.5%, causing commodities and other factors to increase. The living standard in 2023 was also projected to be similar to 1980. With these facts, Ibrahim was surprised that the president concluded that his administration had positive impacts when the nation's state swung toward the negative index during his tenure. He also argued that despite his claims, the president had not fulfilled his campaign promises, including 40,000 MW of electricity supply and 3 million employments.[41]

Ibrahim also faulted the Rice Paddy Pyramids displayed by the Central Bank of Nigeria (CBN) and the federal government, which was supposed to imply that Nigeria has started producing more of its rice as "Photo OP." The CBN governor stated that

---

36. Geoff Iyatse, Femi Adekoya, Benjamin Alade and Joke Falaju, "Lagos-Ibadan Rail Service in Costly, Unfriendly Takeoff," *The Guardian,* December 11, 2020.

37. Noah Banjo, "85 Days After, Buhari Orders Immediate Rescue of Abuja-Kaduna Train Attack Victims," *The Guardian,* June 21, 2022.

38. Gloria Nwafor, "TUC Flays FG over 774,000 Jobs' Scheme," *The Guardian,* October 12, 2021,

39. Jibrin Ibrahim, "Alternative Facts and the Buhari Legacy," *Premium Times,* June 24, 2022, https://www.premiumtimesng.com/opinion/538883-alternative-facts-and-the-buhari-legacy-by-jibrin-ibrahim.html.

40. Ibrahim, "Alternative Facts and the Buhari Legacy."

41. Ibrahim, "Alternative Facts and the Buhari Legacy."

rice importation from Thailand had been reduced by 99.83%.[42] One may assume that this means that local production has had a proportional increase, but Ibrahim quickly clarified that the importation of rice from the Benin Republic had increased drastically too.[43] Speaking of many Nigerians, Ibrahim believed that the government had lost respect for its citizens since they could publicly misstate facts and reality. He expressed this embarrassment as follows:

> What is annoying to us, Nigerian citizens, is that government views and treats the policy arena uniquely as a space for propaganda and information manipulation, rather than a genuine conversation space on action steps to address national problems. That is why the focus is on optics rather than facts. I do wish that our governments try to treat us with more respect. It's sad that they do not know we are adults who know what they are doing and have the power as citizens and voters to place or remove them from power; or do we?[44]

Ibrahim argues that the government and the country have lost their thinking caps when reeling out policies that get lost in ineffectiveness. He concludes that the country has developed a culture of failed public policies, which he traced from Obasanjo's establishment of the Institute for Peace and Conflict Resolution (IPCR) in 2000, whose reports have not been given adequate attention. He cited two of some of the controversial policies of the government.[45] First was the 2021 Twitter ban in Nigeria for months, which was bypassed with the use of VPN access by many Twitter users.[46] The second was the Central Bank of Nigeria's ban on cryptocurrency transactions, which affected direct bank recognition of the transaction.[47] This policy became ineffective as the traders started using available peer-to-peer trading policies to boycott the complications.[48] He stated that the nation had lost touch with the need to carefully process policies and ensure their effectiveness. This attitude affects other positive policies as they become ineffective or inapplicable in certain situations.

Ibrahim summed up the country's problems into three dimensions, especially as they emanate from the problems above.[49] The first dimension includes those affecting

42. Jibrin Ibrahim, "Lack of Respect: How Our Politicians Speak to Us," *Premium Times,* January 21, 2022, https://www.premiumtimesng.com/opinion/507020-lack-of-respect-how-our-politicians-speak-to-us-by-jibrin-ibrahim.html.
43. Ibrahim, "Lack of Respect."
44. Ibrahim, "Lack of Respect."
45. Ibrahim, "Lack of Respect."
46. Ibrahim, "Lack of Respect."
47. Ibrahim, "Lack of Respect."
48. Ibrahim, "Lack of Respect."
49. Jibrin Ibrahim, "Nigeria: The Urgency of Stopping the Drift Towards Anarchy," *Premium Times,* April 9, 2021, https://www.premiumtimesng.com/opinion/454025-nigeria-the-urgency-of-stopping-the-drift-towards-anarchy-by-jibrin-ibrahim.html.

the nation's political economy, especially caused by corruption and bad leadership.[50] The second is termed "crisis of citizenship," which includes insecurity, ethnic tension, and other issues affecting the citizenry. The third dimension is those affecting the democratic desires and aspirations of the citizens, made impossible by the current political culture in the country.[51] According to Ibrahim, the country is living on the edge of this trilogy of problems, and if no action is taken, the process toward anarchy will one day be completed. This is not a prophecy; it is an objective reality, and recent occurrences substantiate this trajectory. On April 9, 2021, Ibrahim propelled this substantiation by stating the country's current situation, which shows the nation's road to anarchy.[52] On April 5, 2021, the Imo State Correctional facility was attacked, and gunmen released 1,844 inmates. This set of people moved to Police Headquarters in the state to also set about 600 suspects held free.[53] Also, on June 5, 2022, ISWAP attacked Kuje Custodial Holding and released over 800 inmates, including terrorists and deadly criminals.[54]

On April 3, 2021, the Governor of Zamfara, Bello Matawalle, stated that about 30,000 gunmen and bandits raked in about N970 million from captives from 2011 to 2019.[55] Although the number of bandits and terrorists across the country is not handy, thousands of people have either died or been kidnapped by these unscrupulous individuals, and millions have been displaced. The Chairman of the National Peace Committee, General Abdulsalami Abubakar, also noted that there are about 6 million deadly weapons across the country in the wrong hands, making guns and deadly weapons far from being luxuries.[56] It also seems that the ticking bomb of anarchy showed the country a demo during the mayhem after the #EndSARS protests, with about 250 police stations set on fire and 22 police officers murdered.[57] Is Nigeria in a state of anarchy? If the answer is negative, with the obvious attacks on law and order, the nation seems close to it.

In many of his opinion posts and contributions, Ibrahim addressed the alarming security state of the country. One must state emphatically that the Nigerian security

50. Ibrahim, "Nigeria: The Urgency of Stopping."

51. Ibrahim, "Nigeria: The Urgency of Stopping."

52. Ibrahim, "Nigeria: The Urgency of Stopping."

53. Charles Ogugbuaja, Collins Osuji, Lawrence Njoku and John Akubo, "1,844 Inmates Roam Free After Imo Prison Break," *The Guardian*, April 6, 2021.

54. Samson Adenekan, "Profiles of 'VIP' Inmates in Kuje Prison before Attack," *Premium Times*, July 13, 2022, https://www.premiumtimesng.com/news/headlines/542323-profiles-of-vip-inmates-in-kuje-prison-before-attack.html#:~:text=Despite%20early%20warnings%2C%20the%20Kuje,over%2060%20Boko%20Haram%20terrorists.

55. Ibrahim, "Nigeria: The Urgency of Stopping."

56. Premium Times, "Six Million Weapons in Circulation in Nigeria – Abdulsalami Abubakar," *Premium Times*, April 8, 2021, https://www.premiumtimesng.com/news/top-news/453878-six-million-weapons-in-circulation-in-nigeria-abdulsalami-abubakar.html.

57. ThisDay News, "#EndSARS: Death Toll Now 73 with 205 Police Stations Burnt," *ThisDay*, October 31, 2020.

Figure 22.2. "Jibrin Ibrahim and Nigerian Political Party System" by Dr. Kazeem Ekeolu. Depicts Jibrin's scholarship on political parties.

problem did not start with Buhari's administration but was inherited from past governments. In 2014, the Jonathan administration admitted this reality, accepting that the condition was more like the country was at war.[58] At this time, the North East was chiefly the concentration of terrorist attacks and other problems.[59] This does not mean that other parts of the country were not affected by the incidences, but there were more serious occurrences when he published the essay than in the past. Ibrahim believed those problems affected peace in the country and continued to "shrink civic space."[60] Despite Buhari's martial background and campaign promises, the security situation got worse, and Ibrahim believed the President probably did not know that his house was burning. Ibrahim sarcastically had to remind the President of the troubling developments in the country, part of which was the threat of kidnapping the president.[61]

Threatening to kidnap a sitting President showed how much these marauders had taken the government for a joke and called the bluff of all the promised commitments to end the issue. The issue of kidnapping did not start during Buhari's tenure, and the lackadaisical attitudes of each successive administration are not unfamiliar, as the Jonathan administration was initially passive in addressing the Chibok Girls' kidnap issue.[62] Kidnapping gained strength under Buhari's dispensation as criminals built a business around it, causing mayhem to unsuspecting victims.[63]

During President Buhari's tenure, it became hard to distinguish banditry from established terrorism. The bandits upped their game, increasing their presence on highways, killing, kidnapping, and causing terror.[64] Ibrahim concludes that the government was confused about the best way to approach these issues and lacked any productive strategy.[65] More so, he that the government had a contributory responsibility to the state of security in the country and the confidence through which bandits

58. Jibrin Ibrahim, "As the War Intensifies," *Premium Times*, March 2, 2014, https://www.premiumtimesng.com/opinion/156057-as-the-war-intensifies-by-jibrin-ibrahim.html.

59. Ibrahim, "As the War Intensifies."

60. Jibrin Ibrahim, "Nigeria's Shrinking Civic Space," *Premium Times*, May 7, 2021, https://www.premiumtimesng.com/opinion/459981-nigerias-shrinking-civic-space-by-jibrin-ibrahim.html.

61. Jibrin Ibrahim, "Things I wish my President Knows," *Premium Times*, July 29, 2022, https://www.premiumtimesng.com/opinion/545649-things-i-wish-my-president-knows-by-jibrin-ibrahim.html.

62. Jibrin Ibrahim, "Chibok Girls and the Reluctant President," *Premium Times,* June 1, 2014, https://www.premiumtimesng.com/opinion/161812-chibok-girls-reluctant-president-jibrin-ibrahim.html.

63. Jibrin Ibrahim, "Kidnapping for Ransom: Can Nigeria Survive the "Third Wave"?" *Premium Time,* August 6, 2021, https://www.premiumtimesng.com/opinion/477805-kidnapping-for-ransom-can-nigeria-survive-the-third-wave-by-jibrin-ibrahim.html.

64. Jibrin Ibrahim, "As Bandits/Terrorists Tighten the Noose around Our Necks," *Premium Times,* April 1, 2022, https://www.premiumtimesng.com/opinion/521247-as-bandits-terrorists-tighten-the-noose-around-our-necks-by-jibrin-ibrahim.html.

65. Ibrahim, "As Bandits/Terrorists Tighten the Noose."

act. He expressed this thus, "The worsening problems of insecurity in Nigeria can be clearly attributed to the criminal liability of government and its security agencies."[66]

Looking at these hurdles and other problems affecting the country, what is the country's expected future following this trajectory? Although subsequent chapters would discuss these possible projections, Ibrahim gave insights into what should be expected. He believed that if Nigeria had a favorable future, the government must wake up from its slumber, stop abdicating responsibility to the citizens, and prioritize good governance. He stated this when he said:

> My hope and prayer for 2022 is the beginning of the task of reconstructing the Nigerian state. We cannot allow our political community to continue to crumble and suffer the outcome of state collapse. Rebuilding the state must take the form of a new approach based on good governance, in which there is the effective, transparent and accountable use of public resources to provide public goods for citizens. If those who exercise state power cannot use it to improve the lives and livelihoods of citizens, then they would have to be replaced. Our state must also recover the capacity to have the monopoly of the use of legitimate violence in society. The armed forces and the police, in particular, must be rebuilt. As the state recovers, our traditional and religious institutions, as well as civil society, have a huge role in playing their part in rebuilding the state. But then, as I argue above, our governing class has abdicated its role in running the state. Who then will start the process of rebuilding the state? That is the question for 2022.[67]

Ibrahim asked what would come out of Nigerian situations, and he did not disagree that if this path of destitution is followed, there might be an inevitable doomsday. However, he believed that one must think differently and individuals must take the responsibility of taking the task seriously.[68] He believed there was a need for national discussions and political strategy to keep the country apart. On this, he wrote:

> By returning to our foundational principles of democracy and federalism, those who have decided they must opt out of the nation can begin to reflect on the possibility of one more attempt at nation-building. It will not be easy and it will take time. My message is that for us to get on the trajectory of state and nation-

---

66. Ibrahim, "As Bandits/Terrorists Tighten the Noose."

67. Jibrin Ibrahim, "The State in Question as 2021 Draws to a Close," *Premium Times*, December 31, 2021, https://www.premiumtimesng.com/opinion/503294-the-state-in-question-as-2021-draws-to-a-close-by-jibrin-ibrahim.html.

68. Jibrin Ibrahim, "Building Social Cohesion: Its Ineluctable, the Nigerians are Emerging," *Premium Times*, https://www.premiumtimesng.com/opinion/481520-building-social-cohesion-its-ineluctable-the-nigerians-are-emerging-by-jibrin-ibrahim.html.

> building, we need political assurances that Nigeria is worth fighting for and that can only flow out of a successful national dialogue.[69]

JIBRIN IBRAHIM AND ACADEMIC STAFF UNION OF UNIVERSITIES (ASUU) STRIKES

Taking the state of the nation from the perspective of education, one cannot argue against the obvious deplorable state of the Nigerian educational system. Of all the ways the educational system has failed, the incessant strike actions of academic and non-academic unions in tertiary institutions have gained intensive discussion. The Academic Staff Union of Universities' industrial action has been a major concern for the progress of the Nigerian university systems. The Union announces strike actions almost every year, indefinitely putting the nation and the students in confusion, causing delays and loss of opportunities. Different opinions have been relayed on whom to be held accountable for these incessant strikes to determine whether ASUU and their demands have been out of place and inappropriately articulated or whether the federal government has been lackadaisical about them.

Ibrahim's position on the ASUU strike is clear. He accepts that the federal government has been irresponsible and hypocritical in handling the ASUU crisis. He states, "The fact of the matter is that the Nigerian Government is irresponsible and never fully implements deals it signs."[70] His position was drawn from his years of active participation in the Union's activities when he was the ASUU Secretary in 1982 in his early years at Ahmadu Bello University. From his experience, the problem has never been about getting the government to sign agreements on the demands of ASUU; getting them to implement the agreements has always been arduous. These attitudes have been reoccurring from one government to the other, creating a cycle that leads to subsequent strikes. Nine years after he made this position, he has been able to maintain it in his column post addressing the 2022 strike, where he stated again that:

> ASUU is right that government promises but never delivers, so they should be held accountable for what they have promised. The fact of the matter, however, is that the Nigerian government is irresponsible and signs deals it has no intention of complying with, which affects all stakeholders within and outside the education sector. The struggle for a responsive and accountable government is a much larger one and goes far beyond the ASUU struggle.[71]

---

69. Ibrahim, "The State in Question."

70. Jibrin Ibrahim, "Conversation with My ASUU Comrades: Let's Get Real," *Premium Times*, October 14, 2013, https://www.premiumtimesng.com/opinion/146584-conversation-asuu-comrades-lets-get-real-jibrin-ibrahim.html.

71. Jibrin Ibrahim, "Options on the Titanic ASUU/Government Battle," *Premium Times*, February 25, 2022, https://www.premiumtimesng.com/opinion/513780-options-on-the-titanic-asuu-government-battle-by-jibrin-ibrahim.html.

Ibrahim's prophecy and analysis in his 2013 article[72] seem right, seeing that the same cycle process continued to date and needed to state the same position in 2022.[73] If the nation continues on this path, one should not expect a favorable future, as education is the root of national development.

However, what made Ibrahim's contribution unique was not his retort to the ineptitudes of the federal government but his engagement of the Union, a need to change their approach to making their demands. In 2013, he believed that the conventional approach of ASUU would keep failing to get the desired results, and he recommended this: "ASUU must start a conversation about a profound change in tactics. More minimalist and attainable targets must be set and advocacy must be broadened to address the National Assembly and other institutions."[74]

While Ibrahim sees ASUU's struggles as valid, he thinks that the recurring strikes for about forty years must be looked at from a different angle. He posited that ASUU must see that the problem it faces and the government's attitude is not only faced by them but affects other sectors too. In light of this, he argues that the present demands of the Union might not consider the government's failures to be committed to anything and the nation's current state.[75] He advised that "ASUU must go into introspection and learn what every trade unionist knows the gains in the struggle are never total; they are always incremental."[76]

The struggle between ASUU is the tale of two fighting elephants, with the suffering students as victims. The ineffective funding and low standards of Nigerian institutions are not the only problems, but also the continuous faceoff between ASUU and the government has denied students access to education. The alternatives are expensive and can only be afforded through scholarships or buoyant financiers.[77] These alternatives are to either study abroad or attend private universities not affected by the ASUU strike. Ibrahim saw this as a challenge, seeing that they only serve 10% of the country's total student population. These private institutions are not open to all students because of their exorbitant fees and serve as a distraction to public universities by poaching their lecturers who decide to double the shifts. Ibrahim captured this well when he noted that:

> The original argument for the establishment of private universities was to create more access for students but the reality today is that the private sector has not substantially increased access. In addition, private universities have not really

72. Ibrahim, "Conversation with My ASUU Comrades."
73. Ibrahim, "Options on the Titanic ASUU/Government Battle."
74. Ibrahim, "Conversation with My ASUU Comrades."
75. Ibrahim, "Options on the Titanic ASUU/Government Battle."
76. Ibrahim, "Options on the Titanic ASUU/Government Battle."
77. Jibrin Ibrahim, "Memory and the IBB Legacy," *Premium Times,* August 13, 2021, https://www.premiumtimesng.com/opinion/479009-memory-and-the-ibb-legacy-by-jibrin-ibrahim.html.

recruited and trained their own faculty, they poach from the public sector for staff and are dependent on moonlighting.[78]

Undoubtedly, the future of every nation largely depends on its people, and if such a future must not be gloomy as current situations suggest, the country must understand the necessity of investing in education. If many people, including Ibrahim, can disagree with ASUU's approaches, the nation cannot deny that their constant request for the revitalization of the educational sector is out of place, as that would be an assurance for future development.

JIBRIN IBRAHIM AND THE 2023 GENERAL ELECTIONS

Ibrahim, by virtue of his experience and discipline, understands the political makeup of the country, as well as electoral paraphernalia. Analyzing his take on Nigerian electoral processes and politics from the operations of party systems in Nigeria would give one foundational idea into the subject matter. Ibrahim has dedicated his time to explaining the functionalities and cultures of the political parties in Nigeria on different occasions. In "Turmoil or Sanity in the Party System," he noted that the party system in Nigeria, which he believed was single-party dominant in 1999, developed into a two-party dominant.[79] The political incident that created the possible breaking away of the People's Democratic Movement from the People'sPDP in 2013 was becoming a development challenging the strong structure of two-party domination;[80] however, this was sustained up till the 2019 election.

The APC and the People'sPDP have been the two dominant political parties in the country. The character of these parties is that they do not have basic or concrete distinguishing ideologies that set them aside. This made it easy for politicians to move or cross-carpet at convenient times. Since the establishment of the APC, it has positioned itself as an alternative to the PDP, carrying almost the same character as the PDP, trying to poach notable members of the party.[81] Seeing the redistribution of members and mandates and the continuous swapping by major political figures like

78. Jibrin Ibrahim, "The Private University as Enterprise: Limits of Academic Capitalism," *Premium Times*, January 14, 2022, https://www.premiumtimesng.com/opinion/505768-the-private-university-as-enterprise-limits-of-academic-capitalism-by-jibrin-ibrahim.html.

79. Jibrin Ibrahim, "Turmoil or Sanity in the Party System," *Premium Times*, September 2, 2013,https://www.premiumtimesng.com/opinion/143977-turmoil-sanity-party-system-jibrin-ibrahim.html.

80. Ibrahim, "Turmoil or Sanity."

81. Jibrin Ibrahim, "APC and the Challenge of Improving Political Parties," *Premium Times*, November 4, 2013, https://www.premiumtimesng.com/opinion/147752-apc-challenge-improving-political-parties-jibrin-ibrahim.html.

Atiku Abubakar, one cannot but conclude that the two parties are not far from each other in identity and ideology. [82]

As usual, the forthcoming 2023 general elections have been drawing attention from every corner, with different critics raising issues to be addressed. As Ibrahim has always done, he has also given notable attention to the forthcoming elections, addressing issues as they arise and develop.[83] He reiterated the culture of lies that politicians in the country practice to convince the people. He, therefore, tried to point Nigerians to the untruthfulness of many of the presidential hopefuls, participants in respective party primaries and other active players in Nigerian politics.[84] Atiku Abubakar and Femi Fani-Kayode are political sojourners who change parties as political developments require. Atiku was quoted to have once stated that the PDP, from which he sought candidacy in the 2019 and 2023 elections, was "beyond redemption" and that he would never have a reason to rejoin the party, especially during the turbulence that hit the party during the Jonathan administration. Femi Fani-Kayode had also sworn to die rather than join APC, where he serves as an appointee now.[85] Bello Mohammad Matawalle, Peter Obi, Rotimi Amaechi, Godswill Akpabio, and Tony Momoh are examples of those who have sworn never to join a party but later became active members of the same party.[86] This further shows Nigerian politicians' lack of ideological conviction and the predominance of lies in the political circle. Ibrahim asserts that the audacity to tell lies is substantiated by the citizens' expectation of them to do the same and have some dishonest features as part of the prerequisite for an average Nigerian politician.[87]

The first major threshold every presidential candidate must cross is to ensure that he or she secures the party's nomination as the candidate. To do this, the candidates must be able to win their respective party primaries. As expected, the APC and PDP's primaries have gained national attention. However, it should be noted that the Nigerian public space is fast remolding the predominance of the two parties and their candidates, as Peter Obi, under the Labour Party, has been able to make himself a third option and a strong one for that matter. The organization of party primaries has always been about those with the financial capacity, connections, and names to pull off other contestants before clinching the ticket. These realities, among other reasons,

82. Jibrin Ibrahim, "Differentiating APC from the PDP," *Premium Times,* December 22, 2013, https://www.premiumtimesng.com/opinion/151899-differentiating-apc-pdp-jibrin-ibrahim.html.

83. Jibrin Ibrahim, "The Looming Vacancy in Aso Rock," *Premium Times*, May 6, 2022, https://www.premiumtimesng.com/opinion/527985-the-looming-vacancy-in-aso-rock-by-jibrin-ibrahim.html.

84. Jibrin Ibrahim, "Civics and the Words and Deeds of a Nigerian Politician," *Premium Times*, March 18, 2022, https://www.premiumtimesng.com/opinion/517986-civics-and-the-words-and-deeds-of-a-nigerian-politician-by-jibrin-ibrahim.html.

85. Ibrahim, "Civics and the Words."

86. Ibrahim, "Civics and the Words."

87. Ibrahim, "Civics and the Words."

had made Peter Obi declare leaving the PDP a few days before the primaries and later got the presidential candidacy under the Labour Party.

Transactional politics have been a thing in the Nigerian political space, and Ibrahim discusses this in his article, "Party Primaries and the Limits of Transactional Politics."[88] In this article, Ibrahim started with Peter Obi's exit from PDP with the fear that candidates would be expected to buy about 4000 delegates with around $20,000 each, which was summed up to about $80 million.[89] Adam Namadi, a candidate for the Kaduna House of Assembly, had requested a refund of about N76 million he gave to party delegates.[90] This attitude is not limited to the PDP but also characterized the APC party primaries, as Rotimi Amaechi lamented.[91] What played out at the respective primaries is a microcosm of what happens at general elections. An example of this was the rumored vote-buying attempts at the 2022 Osun and Ekiti State elections.[92] While decrying this political state of things, especially among the parties, Ibrahim shows that the parties must change this culture, depend on popular and sellable candidates, and educate the voters.[93]

Another development that has risen from the brouhaha of the processes that led to the 2023 elections is the power shift from the north to the south and the religious combination ticket. After Buhari's administration, many Nigerians believed that the next president would be from the southern part of the country, as the president from the north would have spent eight years in office. Ibrahim noted that zoning and regionalism as a political arrangement for the presidential seat have been predominant since the 1993 general election. Since 1999, political elites have switched the presidential seat from south to north to ensure balance. Hence, Ibrahim insists that, preventing the presidency from being shifted to the south is mischievous. He highlights the shift and the propriety of allowing power shift to the south thus:

> What is on the agenda today is that the North agreed to power shift to the South in 1999, to address the strong feelings provoked by the power elongation antics of Generals Babangida and Abacha, and the result was the emergence of Gen-

88. Jibrin Ibrahim, "Party Primaries and the Limits of Transactional Politics," *Premium Times*, May 27, 2022, https://www.premiumtimesng.com/opinion/532736-party-primaries-and-the-limits-of-transactional-politics-by-jibrin-ibrahim.html.

89. Ibrahim, "Party Primaries and the Limits."

90. Ibrahim, "Party Primaries and the Limits."

91. Bakare Majeed, 2023: Delegates Bribed to Vote at APC Presidential Primary, Amaechi Alleges," *Premium Times*, July 25, 2022, https://www.premiumtimesng.com/news/headlines/544781-2023-delegates-bribed-to-vote-at-apc-presidential-primary-amaechi-alleges.html.

92. Biodun Busari, "Osun Election: Hope for Nigeria, Voters Rejecting Money Left, Right – Davido," *Vanguard*, July 16, 2022.

93. Jibrin Ibrahim, "To Fix Nigerian Politics, Parties Must Embrace the Popularity Principle," *Premium Times*, April 2, 2021, https://www.premiumtimesng.com/opinion/452845-to-fix-nigerian-politics-parties-must-embrace-the-popularity-principle-by-jibrin-ibrahim.html.

eral Obasanjo as president on the platform of the Peoples' Democratic Party (PDP), which accepted the principle of power shift. Obasanjo, however, precipitated a crisis with his third term bid, which put a spanner in the works. Thankfully, he did not succeed and was stopped by the struggle of Nigerians and power shift to the North happened with the emergence of Yar'Adua, who died before his tenure ended. Then President Jonathan emerged in a context of uncertainty over the continuation of the arrangement when he contested the following general election. The victory of President Buhari for a second term means this time, the North would have its full eight-year term. In this context, opposing power shift to the South can only be described as dangerous political mischief.

Similar in intensity to the issue of the ethno-regional shift of power was the religious pairing of the presidential and vice-presidential candidates. Since 1999, the President and Vice-President have always been from two different religions, one a Christian and the other a Muslim. However, this convention has been attacked by recent political developments. The fuse was created by the APC's resolve to pick Bola Ahmed Tinubu, a Muslim, and Shettima, a Muslim, as presidential and vice-presidential candidates.[94] Ibrahim stated that on one side, some Nigerians believe that since the incumbent president is a Muslim, the presidential ticket should be left to a Christian. Conversely, the two candidates being Muslims, did not appeal to many of the Nigerian population.[95] Ibrahim noted that the fear and theories of many Muslims opposing this pairing is the alleged Islamization of the nation, evidenced by the increase in the number of Muslims in political and strategic offices.[96]

The drama summing up the road to the 2023 elections has been scintillating, almost forming comic relief for the daily tragedies of many Nigerians. However, the mantle of leadership must be passed in 2023, and another person would be allowed to save the nation from crumbling. Seeing the needs of the people, Ibrahim has drawn up recommendations to save the nation politically and criteria any intending leader must fulfill.[97]

He pleads that the Nigerian expectation of bad flaws from the political class must stop, and the citizens must not indulge "lack of integrity and competence" from any-

---

94. Oxford Analytica, "Tinubu's Vice-Presidential Pick may Divide Nigerians," *Emerald Expert Briefings*, July 11, 2022, https://www.emerald.com/insight/content/doi/10.1108/OXAN-ES271390/full/html

95. Jibrin Ibrahim, "The Muslim-Muslim Ticket and Religious Mobilisation in Nigeria," *Premium Times*, July 15, 2022, https://www.premiumtimesng.com/opinion/542736-the-muslim-muslim-ticket-and-religious-mobilisation-in-nigeria-by-jibrin-ibrahim.html.

96. Ibrahim, "The Muslim-Muslim Ticket."

97. Jibrin Ibrahim, "Developing Criteria for Good Leadership Selection in Nigeria," *Premium Times*, March 25, 2022, https://www.premiumtimesng.com/opinion/519531-developing-criteria-for-good-leadership-selection-in-nigeria-by-jibrin-ibrahim.html.

one.[98] This attitude has encouraged politicians to act as they deem fit and become lackadaisical about the nation's state and the citizens' interests. In addition, he argues that political parties must be able to practice party democracy first before there can be an assurance of its practice in the country at large.[99] To achieve this, he warns they must be ready to allow ordinary party members to take control of the party and limit the influence of godfathers in determining the party's affairs. He stressed that a candidate should only qualify for a position if they have a realistic vision, integrity, respect, and knowledge of the tenets of democracy.[100]

KANO, INEC AND THE 2019 ELECTIONS

In February 2018, a local scandal in the Kano government occurred when videos were circulated of boys thumb-printing multiple ballot papers. Ibrahim labels this entry "Kano, INEC, and the 2019 Elections." It led to genuine alarm over the implications of such behaviors for elections the following year. INEC was blamed across the country, and the body responded by saying it had nothing to do with the election, which they argued was organized by the body constitutionally empowered to do so, the State Independent Electoral Commission.

Ibrahim points out that the State Independent Electoral Commissions are not independent of state governors, and they deny citizens the right to elect chairs and councilors at the local government level, imposing lists that governors drew up. He argues for a constitutional alteration allowing INEC to take over the conduct of local government elections.[101]

For the first time since the return of democracy in 1999, INEC adhered to the provisions of the Electoral Act by conducting Continuous Voter Registration (CVR). In April 2017, INEC established voter registration on a continuous, year-round basis as provided by law. Initially, turnout for the registration was low until religious organizations urged their members to register. Ibrahim notes that this was a good indication that Nigerians were beginning to accept that both the voters' list and the elections improved in integrity and credibility. He believed that the response and focus of the Kano scandal should have been to protect the integrity and credibility of the voters' roll.

In same February 2018, the National Assembly concluded the process of rescheduling the elections. Changes introduced to the sequence of the elections disturbed Ibrahim greatly because of the implications for the independence of INEC. According to Paragraph 15 (1) of the Third Schedule of the 1999 Constitution, INEC has the power "to organize, undertake and supervise all elections to the offices of the Presi-

---

98. Ibrahim, "Developing Criteria for Good Leadership."
99. Ibrahim, "Developing Criteria for Good Leadership."
100. Ibrahim, "Developing Criteria for Good Leadership."
101. Jibrin Ibrahim, "Kano, INEC and the 2019 Elections," *Daily Trust*, February 16, 2018.

dent and Vice-President, the Governor and Deputy Governor of a State, and the membership of the Senate, the House of Representatives, and the House of Assembly of each State of the Federation." In previous cycles, State and National Assembly elections were held before governorship and presidential elections; INEC has already determined the dates and sequence for the 2019 elections. Ibrahim argues that there was no purpose in isolating the former or putting them ahead of the latter. He thought it would have been more logical to group federal elections on one day, have state-level elections on another, or group legislative elections on one day and those into executive positions on another.[102] Ibrahim notes that the main problem with the new schedule is that organizing three elections instead of the customary two would pose a huge financial burden on national resources, especially when the country was emerging from an economic recession. He ends the write-up by noting that laws are serious instruments and should not be made in selfish interest without consideration of national interest.

One year later, when the elections were upon Nigeria, Ibrahim titled his column "2019 and the Search for National Renewal." He begins by arguing that the main concern for 2019 is the struggle to re-establish rural peace. He notes that rural banditry had become the country's defining characteristic and that ordinary people were the targets of banditry, arson, kidnapping and mass murder. This also affected the elite as they had no additional security to move through the world. He posits that there were extreme consequences for decades of misrule as Nigerians fought back against the irresponsible ruling classes. Ibrahim concludes that the key issue for 2019 was whether the Nigerian State could begin to reverse banditry, gangsterism and mass atrocities by millions of young people whom the government failed to educate or provide jobs.[103] He thought that over time, Nigeria transferred its social vices into the political terrain, fervently insisting that godfathers run Nigerian politics. Political leaders emerged to contest votes from Nigerians because they bribed their way through the primaries, and some even killed their opponents to ensure an absence of formidable competition. Ibrahim admits it is no longer possible for a good and honest person to be a politician because the first criterion in Nigerian politics is that one must have stolen massive amounts of money from the citizens. He thinks any country unwilling to allow a good person access to a political office could never "hope to progress. The result is that every election produces a class of political officeholders who are worse than[104] their predecessors. Ibrahim is convinced that the worst in society has mastered the art of reproducing themselves while the good ones look on and pray.[105]

Regarding the election, Ibrahim writes that the campaign strategy of the ruling APC was to paint the PDP opposition candidate, Atiku Abubakar, as a corrupt indi-

102. Ibrahim, "Kano, INEC and the 2019 Elections."
103. Jibrin Ibrahim, "2019 and the Search for National Renewal," *Daily Trust*, January 4, 2019.
104. Ibrahim, "2019 and the Search."
105. Ibrahim, "2019 and the Search."

vidual who would loot the national treasury dry if voted into office. The PDP response was to assert that President Buhari, his family, and cohorts had also succumbed to corruption, and Abubakar was not worse than what Buhari was accused of. The campaign's language was "he is corrupt" and "he, too, is corrupt." Ibrahim notes this language as pathetic. He reprimands politicians and asserts that all contestants must have an equal share of slander in mass media, but regulatory authorities did not enforce this notion.[106]

Ibrahim sees that money has become the lifeblood of Nigerian politics, and virtually all politicians play the money game. Politicians pay huge amounts to all stakeholders, including all groups influencing politics, such as security officials and INEC staff. They also extend money to grassroots political organizations. Having spoken to some gubernatorial candidates that contested this maneuver, Ibrahim was informed that the money allegedly went to party executives at the ward and local government levels, including the chair and exco, women and youth. However, these politicians were unsure whether the funds reached their intended recipients.[107] The story of the primaries was that the money spent on "structures" did not matter. Regardless of whether the grassroots organizations received the money, party barons made subsequent decisions to cancel the primaries, impose "consensus" candidates, or declare whomever they wanted as the candidate. Ibrahim suggests that the reality of Nigerian politics is never expressed in the formal narrative of the national discourse. The democratic process spelled out in the Constitution is not operational. To rebuild Nigeria, he thinks that a serious analysis of its condition is required and that the resolution for the 2019 election should be focused on liberating Nigerian politics and society from the minority of crooks that dominate society and impose their unfavorable values on national life.

With the 2019 elections just one week away, Ibrahim wrote his next column, "The 2019 Elections: A Call for Caution and Hope," where he argues that election stakeholders, himself included, needed to caution themselves about extremely reckless statements that could lead to uninformed opinions.[108] He contemplates that in 2015, there was a qualitative leap forward on the scale that the outcome was universally praised, not only "because it led to an alternation of power from the incumbent to the opposition party, but mainly because the result reflected the choice made"[109] by voters. He encouraged Nigeria to continue moving up the integrity scale with the 2019 general elections. This meant that Nigerians must ensure that their words and utterances would lead toward credible results rather than spreading fear and hatred, which could transform the elections into chaos and violence.

106. Ibrahim, "2019 and the Search."
107. Ibrahim, "2019 and the Search."
108. Jibrin Ibrahim, "The 2019 Elections: A Call for Caution and Hope," *Daily Trust*, February 8, 2019.
109. Ibrahim, "The 2019 Elections."

Ibrahim explores examples of parties utilizing language to spur violence in the elections. He believed both the PDP and the Coalition of United Political Parties (CUPP) have made reckless "and unsubstantiated allegations about the intention of the Federal Government and the Election Management Body to massively rig the elections."[110] He asserts that such statements were a disservice to election integrity because they started sowing doubts in the mind of voters, which could lead to violence if people believed the allegations to be true.[111] The government's irresponsibility is something he focuses on frequently throughout his writing.

Even though the two leading candidates had the same identity profile, which "reduced the identity stakes and tension of the electoral campaign,"[112] ethnoreligious tensions persist, according to Ibrahim. Massacres associated with the farmer-herder crisis over the few previous years created a great deal of antipathy along the divide between cattle-rearing Fulani-Muslim and Christian-Farmer, even though the dynamics of the conflicts were not forged along religious lines. Many Christians who voted believed President Buhari did not work hard enough to protect them. Ibrahim is of the view that these dynamics pushed many in the Muslim community to rally behind President Buhari. Essentially, identity division played a significant role in the elections.

Having been a student of Nigerian politics for quite some time, Ibrahim was aware of the country's history of abuse of incumbency powers that affected electoral outcomes. However, he notes that measures such as the electoral register, the permanent voter's card and the card reader create transparency and curb electoral fraud. The most important development has been the increased vigilance of the Nigerian voter. They were not going to allow anyone to change electoral outcomes, so there was no need, Ibrahim thinks, to unnecessarily heat the political system.[113] He notes that his favorite part of this particular election was the search for evidence on who was leading. Both the PDP and APC were engaged in photo editing and analyses to convince voters that their candidate's rallies were attracting more crowds than the other. This is considered fine as long as voters make the ultimate choice. According to him, what is most important is the return of civility in Nigerian campaign discourse.

More so than the actual political candidates, Ibrahim impresses upon the importance of the 2019 general election as, by far, the largest in Nigeria's political history. There were 73 presidential candidates and 1,008 people seeking to be state governors. Over 23,000 candidates were competing for seats in total. Nigeria has been searching for new politicians for a long time, and they appeared in great numbers. He hoped that the variety of options would create opportunities for new parties to make inroads

110. Ibrahim, "The 2019 Elections."
111. Ibrahim, "The 2019 Elections."
112. Ibrahim, "The 2019 Elections."
113. Ibrahim, "The 2019 Elections."

into office that year and in the coming years. Ibrahim says that the greatest challenge facing Nigerian democracy remains the absence of a real and functional party system.[114] In February 2019, there were 91 registered political parties in the country. Only two of them had any real power and member participation. With 23,000 new politicians in the arena, he believed that the 2019 election was an opportunity to focus on the winner and how Nigerians could significantly improve their political system afterward. He signed off his post, noting that he would observe and report on the elections from the Election Analysis Centre (EAC) established by the Centre for Democracy and Development (CDD).

The day before the election, Ibrahim wrote "Analysing the 2019 General Election." As someone who worked within the Election Analysis Centre, he had an interesting insight into the hectic nature of elections and data analysis. Some of the trends that the Election Analysis Centre compiled were explored within this column. His focus was primarily on the implications of the anti-corruption war on "electoral politics, particularly for party political and campaign financing, electoral adjudication,"[115] and the "excessive" political embeddedness of the judiciary.[116]

Ibrahim argues that one of the most notable positive takeaways of the 2019 general election was the large number of contestants that entered the political fray: 23,316 people running for just over 1500 constituency positions. Many of the candidates were young and were inspired by the "not too young to run" law and movement. Though many of them were slated to fail in this election, he thinks that their presence signals that the future of Nigeria is bright. Many Nigerians noted this election as the last time they would vote for older candidates represented by leading presidential contenders, Atiku Abubakar and Muhammadu Buhari.

Ibrahim explains that the Independent National Electoral Commission (INEC) was subjected to a litany of negative attacks, many of which were unfair and against their will and preparedness to organize free, fair, and credible elections. He ponders that Nigerians need to consider the fact that there was a considerable investment by INEC in technology solutions and administrative systems that significantly improved the integrity of the elections. It would be impossible to return to the Maurice Iwu days when an INEC Chairman could "sit in Abuja and announce fictitious election results."[117]

In his forum column, Ibrahim discussed how the Analysis Centre prepared extensive documentation on trends in Nigeria's electoral history and politics since 1999. It provided insight into themes such as identity and electoral politics, registration of

---

114. Ibrahim, "The 2019 Elections."

115. Jibrin Ibrahim, Analyzing the 2019 General Elections, *News Diary*, February 22, 2019, https://newsdiaryonline.com/analysing-the-2019-general-elections-by-jibrin-ibrahim/.

116. Ibrahim, "Analyzing the 2019 General Elections."

117. Ibrahim, "Analyzing the 2019 General Elections."

political parties, voter registration, voter turnout, voter literacy, battleground and swing states, and electoral security and electoral violence. Focusing on the work of the EAC was a great way to draw attention to the impact of registered political parties en masse "on the electoral process. If not on the dominance of the two leading parties," attention was paid to the complication and increased size of the actual ballots that complicated the voting and counting process and increased the number of spoiled ballots.

On the day prior to the election, like an election referee, Ibrahim wrote a column titled "Is INEC Ready for Tomorrow's Elections?" His answer to the question was no. He believed that INEC was not properly ready, although it should have been. He found it particularly unfortunate that they covered up their lack of preparation and deceived Nigerians, nay, the world, when they claimed to be ready when they were not. They also angered all stakeholders by refusing to postpone until five hours before the elections.[118] Ibrahim believed that since the INEC was aware of the realities of conducting such an extensive national deployment of human resources and materials, they should have been better equipped rather than doling out excuses after failing to perform as expected. Within 16 months, INEC registered over 14 million Nigerians as new voters and made their cards available for collection. They recruited and trained roughly 1 million young and inexperienced people to serve as ad hoc staff. In addition, INEC had to print 421.7 million ballots for six scheduled elections as well as 13.6 million leaves of result forms for the presidential election alone. The logistics were notably overwhelming, with 91 political parties and 23,316 candidates for whom votes were cast in 119,973 polling units.[119]

Given the delay and rescheduled election, many people took to questioning INEC. Some of the questions that Ibrahim thought should be raised are: Have they addressed concerns that certain sensitive materials deployed in various parts of the country ahead of the new dates are fully secured? Have materials sent to the wrong states been retrieved and rerouted correctly? Has INEC taken advantage of the extra time provided by the postponement of the elections to rapidly and robustly address all project and logistical management and public communication weaknesses that were made apparent?

The election delay affected many Nigerians, particularly businesses and voters who traveled hundreds of miles to polling units. Some, unaware of the postponement, even turned up in the morning to vote. It was unclear whether those who traveled to cast their ballot were willing to repeat the journey. Ibrahim states in his column the importance of noting that some voters did not believe the elections were postponed due to logistical challenges. There was speculation of a plot to rig the

118. Jibrin Ibrahim, "Is INEC Ready for Tomorrow's Elections?" *Daily Trust,* February 22, 2019.
119. Ibrahim, "Is INEC Ready."

elections. The process of confidence building in the electoral process must, therefore, continue.[120]

Ibrahim asserts that it is important to continue challenging the proliferation of dangerous hate speech in circulation. There was also a considerable amount of growing violence in some states by political leaders who fueled the tension. The PDP presidential candidate, Abubakar Atiku, accused the Buhari administration of disenfranchising voters to ensure low voter turnout. Senator Godswill Akpabio accused the INEC officials of colluding with Akwa Ibom State Governor Udom Emmanuel to manipulate the elections. President Muhammadu Buhari, on his part, said INEC's "incompetence" was unacceptable. But nothing brought more furor than his comment at the emergency meeting of the APC: anybody who tries to snatch ballot boxes or encourage thugs to cause a disturbance would do so "at the expense of his life." The PDP quickly condemned his statement as a "direct call for jungle justice." Ibrahim believed that political leaders at that time should have desisted from further tormenting the political system.

Ibrahim also suggests that the rise of insecurity in the country was impacting the deployment of officials for observer groups and INEC. Outside Boko Haram, armed banditry, especially in Zamfara State, could have affected voting. The crisis gradually became a sizable problem across the north-western zone of Nigeria. He viewed the election as a pivotal step in democratic consolidation and one in which all measures must be taken to get it right.

On the day of the election, Ibrahim wrote "The Presidential Election and its Aftermath" in his weekly column. Muhammadu Buhari of the APC won with 15,191,847 votes and his formidable opponent, Atiku Abubakar, came in second with 11,262,978. With this considerable gap, some might assume that the question of victory is settled in favor of Buhari. However, Ibrahim concludes that nothing could be that simple.[121] The leading opposition, Abubakar, described the election essentially as a farce: "On Election Day, we saw the implementation of grand theft of the people's will. I am not one for hyperbole, so I will just let the facts speak for themselves. The 'facts' he cited included the following: In Akwa Ibom, for instance, the results showed a statistical impossibility of a 62% drop in voter numbers from the 2015 elections, even where voter registration and PVC collection rates were much higher. This pattern was repeated in strongholds of the People's Democratic Party, including in Delta, Rivers, Abia and Benue states."[122] Abubakar rejected the results based on "the electoral fraud perpetrated by the Buhari administration this past Saturday" and decided to go to court to combat the results.[123]

---

120. Ibrahim, "Is INEC Ready."
121. Jibrin Ibrahim, "The Presidential Election and its Aftermath," *Daily Trust*, March 1, 2019.
122. Ibrahim, "The Presidential Election."
123. Ibrahim, "The Presidential Election."

Ibrahim did not believe that there was substantial evidence of fraud, as Abubakar claimed. He arrived at this conclusion because YIAGA AFRICA conducted a parallel vote count using the PVT methodology, which was the gold standard in the citizen observation approach. ICT also came to a clear conclusion using a random statistical sample of 1,515 polling units in every local government area and state. Their findings on the presidential elections were as follows: "All Progressives Congress, APC, should receive between 50.0 percent and 55.8 percent of the votes. The People's Democratic Party, PDP, should receive between 41.2 percent and 47.0 percent of the votes. These figures are consistent with the official results as announced by INEC. For both APC and PDP, the official results fall within the PVT estimated ranges."

To Ibrahim, there should be no argument about the electoral outcome since result sheets were handed over to party agents in virtually all 176,993 polling units and stations and 8,809 wards, 774 local governments, 36 States, and FCT collation centers in Nigeria. This was, according to Ibrahim, enough information for the justice system to establish the truth of the figures issued by the Electoral Commission.[124] In the period leading up to the elections, there was widespread fear that security agencies would be used as agents of voter suppression. Ibrahim notes that this did not occur on a large scale and was just the fear fueled by the media. Adequate security personnel was generally deployed for duty in most polling units, and they did their job fairly well. There were cases of illegal use of security agents, and once again, establishing the scale was key in determining the credibility of the elections.

Given the trouble with voter security in many polling locations, Ibrahim demonstrates that the general elections provided a further illustration of the anti-democratic culture of the country's mainstream political class through their engagement in various forms of political brigandage and their do-or-die attitude toward the elections. In places like Imo and Rivers States, incumbents abused their powers to determine the outcome of the elections. If ordinary citizens were the winners of these elections, the underlying zero-sum attitude and approach of the country's mainstream political class left much to be desired.

Ibrahim's greatest concern about the election, evident in the map of voters in the presidential elections, is ethnoreligious bias in the geographical distribution of the votes. In the period leading up to and during the elections, there were excessively high levels of ethnoreligious mobilization and the use of hate speech. He thinks this is a matter of concern, and Nigeria should be much more proactive in addressing issues around inclusiveness.[125] His final assessment is that the voting process and its management generally went well despite the hitches outlined above, which explains his assertion that the results appear to reflect how most Nigerians voted. Ibrahim commends the determination of the nation to exercise their franchise despite the odds

124. Ibrahim, "The Presidential Election."
125. Ibrahim, "The Presidential Election."

militating against their ability to do so and hopes that problems identified on election day will be addressed adequately and urgently.

With the general elections behind him, Ibrahim explored the election of Nigeria's governors and members of the State Houses of Assembly by reflecting upon the past elections in his column "Completing the 2019 Electoral Process."[126] While many commentators argued that the elections were marked by excessive violence, given the number of people killed, Ibrahim notes that the issue should be addressed in relative terms. The country was living within its "normal" condition of violence with an active insurgency in the North East, rural banditry and farmer-herder clashes in about 18 States, widespread kidnapping for ransom, violent agitations for Biafran secession, and the ongoing militancy in the Niger Delta. He accepts that the 2019 election was technically a slight decline in Nigerian society's "normal" level of violence.[127]

Ibrahim suggests that the importance of the governor and state assembly elections stems from the fact that governors are in the most strategic position since they often have a direct bearing on good governance and improved or worsening security. The State Houses of Assembly were historically incapable of out-maneuvering governors. This leads to the greatest challenge to good governance, as a relatively high percentage of them are corrupt, irresponsible in their mandate, and are often virtually absent from their respective States. His hope for the government was that citizens closely monitored and assessed the performance of their governors and were ready to sanction ruinous governors in the elections.[128]

Due to precedence, Ibrahim holds that there is a strong possibility that some governors would be tempted to use vast resources to affect electoral outcomes. In the previous election cycle, some sitting governors in Gombe and Oyo States lost their senatorial bids, and in the case of Imo State, the governor was alleged to have forced the returning officer to declare him elected under duress. As Nigerian governors consider any challenge to their desires as unacceptable behavior requiring punishment, security agencies must do their due diligence to ensure that governors, too, abide by the law.

Following concerns about the conduct of security agencies, specifically allegations of misconduct among soldiers in the presidential and National Assembly elections, Ibrahim shares his opinion: All security agents must act accordingly within the rules of engagement and the code of conduct while maintaining respect for fundamental human rights when carrying out their assigned roles. The Chief of Army Staff, Lt. Gen. Tukur Buratai, disclosed that the governors of Bayelsa, Oyo and Ogun States had lodged a formal complaint against some soldiers with the Army Head-

126. Jibrin Ibrahim, "Completing the 2019 Electoral Process," *Daily Trust*, March 8, 2019.
127. Ibrahim, "Completing the 2019 Electoral Process."
128. Ibrahim, "Completing the 2019 Electoral Process."

quarters. There were also numerous reports of violence and unprofessional army activity in Rivers State.

Ibrahim notes that civil servants must not take any unlawful orders from any politician, no matter how high up in the chain of command, if it jeopardizes the integrity of the elections. The elections have become notably divisive, and Nigerians are split right down the middle along ethnic, zonal, and religious lines; therefore, they must not create an even deeper crisis of confidence in their nationhood. Ibrahim accepts that the significant circulation of fake news and hate speech left a clear mark on this election, which put many communities within Nigeria on edge. Nigerians must not allow politicians to push them toward the brink of chaos for selfish purposes. For this reason, it is impractical to suggest that armed security personnel should be eliminated from security provisioning during the elections. There are too many armed political thugs, criminal gangs, and ethnic militia in circulation; their activities must be checked. He also thinks citizens have a key role to play by insisting that elections be conducted in conformity with established rules.

Alongside the Working Group on Peacebuilding and Governance in Nigeria, Ibrahim appealed to all institutions and citizens to conduct themselves peacefully and with integrity to ensure that the outcomes of the elections are legitimate and accepted by the people. All stakeholders—INEC, the political parties and their supporters, and Nigeria's security forces—must abide by the law and establish best practices.

According to Ibrahim, INEC must continue providing a level playing field for all candidates, parties, and voters to uphold the sanctity of the electoral process and its outcome. This must include improved competence and transparency and frequent, clear, and robust communication with Nigerians on all aspects of the Commission's work. It is Ibrahim's opinion that Nigeria must stop the brigandage culture and do-or-die politics. Candidates for the elections, party officials, and supporters must avoid behavior and actions that would undermine the credibility of the electoral process or lead to a breach of peace. Security institutions must uphold the principles of professionalism and respect for human rights at all times in discharging their duties. They must also ensure absolute impartiality and avoid any action that could cast doubt.

In conclusion, Ibrahim, having participated heavily in civil society organizations for the past 25 years, is of the view that Nigeria can provide a more solid footing to build political harmony and stability. The 2019 elections were very divisive due to the extremely negative campaigns employed. However, it is precisely for this reason that organizing the final round of elections in a manner that is fair, credible, and violence-free is the first step toward national reconciliation.

CONCLUSION

Political development in Nigeria has always been an interesting subject of discussion but needs to be addressed from the vantage point of knowledge and critical analysis. While many people can raise Nigerian political issues even at newspaper vendor stands, Ibrahim represents a figure of manual and trajectory that first reminds the people of preceding developments that put those events in context and analytically explain political issues. Hence, the average Nigerian can discuss those developments based on Ibrahim's insightful analysis.

As a political scientist and a nationalist, Ibrahim understands the indicators that Nigeria has left developmental tracks and has taken directions to possible self-destruction with unfavorable public policies and destructive political occurrences. Corruption, poor living conditions, and unrepentant bad leaders are the troubles Nigerians have fallen on. Ibrahim has been able to engage with these factors and influence the citizens and general polity to provide reasonable recommended solutions.

23

IMAGINATIONS OF THE FUTURE OF NIGERIA

Nations are defined by the existence and interactions of the pseudo-societies they contain, and each has unique cultures, norms, and ideals. The intricacies of the relationships between these groups are often inseparable from the larger events that impact the nation as a whole. Philosophical concepts can divide societies along specific lines—including religion, language, history, traditional norms, and other culture-specific delineations—but there are also more practical forces at work, such as political or economic leadership, administrative development, and national identities. The conflicts that arise from the interchange between these forces can provide insights into the future of modern societies or nation-states.

A country's leadership is formalized and institutionalized in its current government, which makes it difficult to discuss national leadership without considering the elements of governance. Individuals who administer the affairs of a nation receive their mandates through elections and are expected to provide physical, political, and economic stability. When societies exhibit an unacceptable level of instability, voters hold their governing bodies responsible. Non-state actors, such as NGOs and other private entities, may initiate plans to complement the efforts of the state machinery, but their efforts will amount to naught if the State cannot ensure the availability of effective platforms for promoting progress.

Nigeria's citizens have long endured flawed systems that continually bedevil their country, and none of the elements complicit in the degeneration of Nigeria's fortunes can be discussed in isolation. This chapter examines the country's prospects by examining several factors and allowing for an improved understanding of the complex nature of the country's problems.

Nigeria's limiting factors are interrelated, and evaluating them must involve a multi-pronged approach to expose the deepest core of the interactions that threaten the country. Every Nigerian must recognize that without targeted efforts, the enormous potential of an entire nation may be squandered. Nigeria has been dubbed the giant of Africa, and its abundant mineral resources are sufficiently complemented by its human resources to develop it into a global superpower. This chapter will assess the factors that threaten this future and determine what lies ahead.

LEADERSHIP FAILURE

Every society depends on effective leadership for growth and success. National leadership involves several tasks that range from governing individuals, managing social groups, and influencing people to follow or establish norms and opinions. Effective leadership is a dominant component in any nation-state that works with other internal factors to drive society in a specific direction.

A nation's progress is determined by its institutions' success in transitioning from a particular state of existence to a more desirable one. Leadership is like beauty—hard to define but instantly recognizable.[1] One can suggest that leadership and beauty are determined relative to their observers; one party may identify policies as good leadership even if another party dismisses them as failures. The salient point is that the benefits people derive from government policies affect their perceptions of the policies' effectiveness and impacts. Leadership is subjective, but universal standards differentiate good leadership from bad leadership. In Nigeria, bad leadership is easily identifiable as unmerited political appointments and incompetent people serving in political positions.

Political appointments in Nigeria are deeply rooted in the concept of vested interests, and people can buy their way into offices through various illegitimate means. Some individuals see leadership roles as birthrights or inheritances to be abused for personal gain.[2] When such practices are widespread, they cultivate a national pool of ineptitude comprised of individuals seeking to recover the costs incurred while acquiring their positions. Nigeria's political landscape is characterized by an unhealthy rivalry that prevents an objective discussion of national issues. Nigeria has suffered

1. Warren G. Bennis and Joan Goldsmith, *Learning to Lead: A Workbook on Becoming a Leader* (New York: Basic Books), 2003.

2. Chinenye Ochulor, "Failure of Leadership in Nigeria," *American Journal of Social and Management Sciences* 2, no. 3 (2011): 265–271.

under misrule from independence to the present moment, largely due to a lack of training for political leaders and people who aspire to elected offices. Leadership training does not automatically bestow leadership capabilities, but it gives aspiring officeholders a shared understanding of effective representative leadership. Without this knowledge, leading people through representative government is impossible, and the nation is exposed to uncertainty.

Nigeria's public administration is built on a foundation of irregularity and corrupt practices institutionalized from the country's earliest existence as a sovereign entity. Similar ailments have afflicted virtually every nation in Africa, but countries such as Ghana, Rwanda, and South Africa have made strides in nation-building. This suggests that the lack of advancement stems from problems unique to Nigeria. Most of Africa's British-colonized countries have made substantial national progress, and Nigeria has abundant natural resources and a large population—the most populous black nation in the world. Lagos, its former capital city, is also the most populated city in Africa. Developing countries such as Malaysia, Singapore, and Indonesia, previously on par with it, have become powerful economic engines over the last four decades. Nigeria's outcomes show a clear discrepancy.

Nigeria has suffered from relentless economic crises caused by financial corruption in the corridors of power. Self-serving leaders encourage the creation of a permanently impoverished class of people, and members of marginalized groups constantly seek to improve their status by institutionalizing corruption in every aspect of socio-political and economic engagement. Political prebendalism prevents these groups from implementing effective developmental policies, and specific ethnic and cultural interests seek benefits from having their members attain political influence.

The emphasis on ethnic boundaries is a major leadership challenge in Nigeria; ethnic sentimentalism and ethnic divisiveness are entrenched forces.[3] Nigeria's political history is written with an ethnic pen that has recorded distrustful accusations and counter-accusations between factions that developed into the Nigerian Civil War. The war left scars on Nigeria's society, history, policy, and economy that have yet to be properly addressed and healed. There was an attempt to mend relationships with a mantra of "no victor, no vanquished," but many are unwilling to question the assumptions they learned during the conflict. These generational biases persist today, more than fifty years after the end of the Nigerian Civil War, and ethnicity remains a powerfully divisive force.

Over the past two decades of democratic rule, the failure of Nigeria's political leadership has also been enabled by an absence of political parties with clear ideologies. According to Dr. Kayode Fayemi, former Governor of Ekiti State, the Nigerian political space is not made up of political parties but political platforms that propel people

---

3. Jacob Omede and Andrew Abdul Omede, "Terrorism and Insecurity in Nigeria: Moral, Values and Religious Education as Panaceas," *Journal of Education and Practice* 6, no. 11 (2015): 120–126.

into elected office.[4] This explains why Nigeria's political elites regularly move from one political party to another, seeking leverage to gain political positions. Such a scenario played out in the gubernatorial election of Edo State, where the incumbent governor defected to the opposition party when his original party was unwilling to nominate him for a second term. This type of political jockeying undermines Nigeria's political system[5] and leads to individuals attaining offices based on their political connections.

Nigerian voters must pay attention to the government's actions and inactions to prevent poor governance from enveloping the country. The country's sovereignty belongs to its people, who should be the source of political power. Unfortunately, many Nigerians are complicit in the country's leadership failures, either through actively supporting corrupt practices or by remaining silent when they should make their voices heard.

STATE OF INSECURITY

Security is essential for the growth and development of any nation. Peaceful nations foster economic growth by being attractive destinations for foreign investors. Nations also benefit from domestic investors who can make decisions without concern about security threats.[6] No nation is fully immune to security concerns, but a country's institutions can be judged by their ability to manage turbulent situations.

Nigeria currently faces several security challenges that impair its developmental capabilities. Violent extremism has disrupted Nigeria for over a decade, and increasing numbers of banditry and kidnappings in the North show that the country does not enjoy peace and tranquility.[7] The secessionist movement revived in South-Eastern Nigeria is an ongoing threat whose atrocities are worsening daily. Clashes between farmers and Fulani herdsmen continue unabated, with an increasing number of alleged kidnappings. President Muhammadu Buhari's affirmation of Nigeria's state of emergency is linked with the widely circulated threats from the Boko Haram insurrection in the North-Eastern region. Nigeria's conflicts, therefore, are complicated and multidimensional.

The Boko Haram insurgency is the preeminent security challenge. After it retreated from the urban settlements it held before 2015, the terrorist organization changed

4. Leke Baiyewu, "Nigeria Lacks Proper Parties Yet, Says Fayemi," *The Punch,* April 2, 2021,

5. Ayọkunle Olumuyiwa Ọmọbọwale and Akinpẹlu Ọlanrewaju Olutayọ, "Political Clientelism and Rural Development in South-Western Nigeria," *Africa: Journal of the International African Institute* 80, no. 3 (2010): 453–472.

6. P. Loungaui and A. Razin, "How Beneficial is Foreign Direct Investment for Developing Countries?" *Finance and Development* 38, no. 1 (2001): 6–9.

7. Bonaventure Ikechukwu Ozoigbo, "Insecurity in Nigeria: Genesis, Consequences and Panacea," *European Journal of Social Sciences Studies* 4, no. 4 (2019): 270–281.

Figure 23.1. "Imagination of the Future of Nigeria" by Michael Efionayi. A picture of Nigeria and its presidents since 1999, asking what lies ahead after the 62nd Independence Anniversary.

tactics to focus on rural settlements along the borders shared by Nigeria, Cameroon, and Chad. Its leaders concealed themselves in the Sambisa forest and mounted daring attacks on villages and towns along North-Eastern Nigeria's national borders. The Nigerian troops' withdrawal from major North-Eastern military bases effectively cut off Borno State from the rest of the country and gave the insurrectionists an advantage, which allowed it to easily overrun minor outposts and mock the Nigerian military with pictures of the weaponry they seized during each attack.

Renewed Boko Haram hostilities are heightening threat levels in Northern Nigeria, especially in the northeast.[8] The presidency had announced the terrorist organization's technical defeat some years ago, but an unwillingness to follow through on efforts made at the time has led to sporadic resurgences. The government made covert

8. Nkechi O. Anyadike and O. Nkechi, "Boko Haram and National Security Challenges in Nigeria: Causes and Solutions," *Journal of Economics and Sustainable Development* 4, no. 5 (2013): 12–23.

arrests and detained unnamed Nigerians who had financed terrorism, but these accomplishments were not widely recognized because the government did not publicize the names of the individuals involved.[9] The militant Islamist group now rarely launches attacks outside the North-Eastern region, but recent news reports state that Boko Haram insurgents have hoisted flags in Niger State, which borders the Federal Capital Territory. As noted earlier, Governor Abubakar Bello of Niger State has confirmed the reports and warned that the presence of insurgents in his State threatens the national capital, Abuja, a mere 150 kilometers away.[10]

Criminal gangs wreak havoc in the North-West region, embarking on wide-scale kidnappings and maiming. In acts reminiscent of the 2014 Chibok schoolgirls' kidnappings, these armed bandits exploit the volatility of the Northern region to embark on mass kidnappings that hold secondary school students for ransom.[11] The criminals were initially encouraged by the discovery of gold in Zamfara, but they have gone from fighting for control of gold mines to organizing kidnappings that demand ransoms from the government. The government insists that it does not pay ransom to release kidnap victims, but widespread distrust leads some citizens to question the fate of the victims.[12]

Numerous historical and religious accounts inspired the practice of using violence for political objectives. The biblical story of Moses exemplifies an experience of loss and difficulty by a people. The tale is familiar to many faiths and cultural backgrounds and makes it easier to understand the justifications for violence in Nigeria's South-Eastern region. Nnamdi Kanu led the Indigenous People of Biafra (IPOB) activities and established the Eastern Security Network (ESN). After the wanton killing of Nigeria's security forces in various South-Eastern states, IPOB's transition from aggressive verbal campaigns to armed conflict with security agencies in some acclaimed Biafran states became clear. This poses a direct threat to the security of the region and the nation.[13] The group began with an underground radio presence in the South-East, but it has grown bolder since the ESN was established toward the end of 2020.

The ESN was allegedly formed to address the atrocities of Fulani herdsmen. It was an outgrowth of the *Amotekun* formation, which sought to ensure security in the South-Western region against marauding Fulani herdsmen. The herdsmen became aggressive enough to require the creation of regional security forces that could drive

---

9. Ademola Olonilua, "FG Uncovers 96 Terrorist Sponsors, Arrests 45 Suspects," *Daily Trust*, February 3, 2022.

10. Louis Achi, "As Terrorists Take Battle to the Seat of Power," *Thisday*, July 31, 2022.

11. Jacob Zenn, "Boko Haram and the Kidnapping of the Chibok Schoolgirls," *CTC Sentinel* 7, no. 5 (2014): 1–8.

12. Olajumoke Ayandele, "Confronting Nigeria's Kaduna Crisis," *Africa Center*, February 2, 2021, http://www.africacenter.org/spotlight/confronting-nigerias-kaduna-crisis/.

13. Taofeek Olanrewaju Alabi and Adewale Kazeem Ayeloja, "Hate Speech and Security Challenges: A Pragmatic Study of Nnamdi Kanu's Speeches in the South-Eastern Nigeria," *International Journal of English Research* 5, no. 4 (2019): 1–9.

them out of the forests, where they planned kidnappings, highway robberies, raids on villagers, and the destruction of farms. The establishment of *Amotekun* and ESN has limited the frequency of criminal herdsmen activity, although it involved sacking entire Fulani settlements in some parts of Oyo, South-Western Nigeria. These efforts were led by Sunday Adeyemo, better known as Sunday Igboho, a self-proclaimed activist who launched one of the most daring individual crusades in Southern Nigeria.

The ESN is pursuing similar goals, although its creation accompanied a rise in armed face-offs with security agencies in the Northeast and the Orlu skirmish between the ESN and Nigerian Security Forces. It has inflamed tensions in the region; recent attacks by gunmen on police stations and other security outposts have plunged the region into a crisis reminiscent of the 1967 Civil War. Ongoing skirmishes between the ESN and Nigeria's security forces may, if not stopped, eventually turn into a full-scale armed conflict.

FAILURE OF THE NIGERIAN STATE

The failure of Nigeria's leadership can be traced to a flawed political system that requires urgent attention. Understanding the root causes of the problem can provide insights into how Nigeria can develop and occupy its rightful position on the global stage. To see the desired developments, however, Nigerians must actively chart a new course to reclaim their country from failed leadership. Although the limited number of opportunities for empowerment remains an ongoing challenge, citizens must be prepared to claim them the moment they are available.

There have been frequent reports of corrupt practices among government employees and public officeholders since Nigeria's return to democracy in 1999. Despite Nigeria's massive economic potential, its development has been, at best, uneven, and political conflicts have stalled the growth of many regions. Like other nations suffering from developmental deficits, Nigeria also experiences loss of territorial control, the illegitimate use of force to suppress citizens' opinions, and many government institutions that cannot justify their continued existence.[14] These problems are further compounded by a lack of responsibility among public officeholders.

The Nigerian State has a huge potential for success, but its inherent challenges are just as enormous. The country's multi-ethnic dynamics present a major barrier to national development. And its decline began when Nigeria's leaders started to exploit ethnic and religious sentimentalism to acquire and retain power immediately after the departure of the British colonialists.

Nigeria's political space is built on ethnic, regional, community and religious ties. The country's entrenched culture of political patronage encourages leaders to reward

14. Fund for Peace and Foreign Policy, "The Failed States Index 2007," July/August 2007, http://www.foreignpolicy.com/story/cms.php?story_id=3865.

their supporters so that they can win elections.[15] Nigeria was initially divided into three major regions during the early stages of its sovereign existence, but Nigeria's governance has always involved two regions making temporary partnerships to the detriment of the excluded third. No single region holds enough of a majority to control the central government, but they all jockey for advantage in a zero-sum game.

When any region is slighted by the other two, it accuses the government of corruption and mismanagement.[16] On this basis, the justification given for Nigeria's first military coup was a claim to rein in the excesses of the civilian government at the time. Because of the ethnic sentiment that followed that first coup, there was a series of military counter-coups, followed by the Civil War of 1967. The issue is worse now, more than four decades later, as ethnic and religious sentiments in national politics continue to pit Nigeria against itself, even as its financial reserves are depleted by global declines in the price of crude oil.

The ethnic framing of national issues in the country has sometimes escalated into physical conflicts. The Igbo who occupy the South-Eastern region mounted an uprising in the 1960s, and their present-day agitation for secession is a point of contention among the totality of the Igbo community. Secessionist agitations complicate the matter from the Yoruba people who occupy Nigeria's South-Western region. Religion and ethnicity have become weapons used by the political class to mobilize their kin for legitimacy to power but paradoxically to divide the public and block national progress. People who should be working together to fight for their rights are told that they should perceive each other as enemies. This is an old, familiar strategy that the political class has always applied, and the cycle can only end when the public abandons ethnic and religious disputes to embrace peaceful coexistence.

Nigeria's most violent conflicts have been between Northern and Southern residents. The increasing number of kidnappings in Southern Nigeria is blamed on Fulani dissidents from the North. These nomadic people, who travel the breadth of West Africa from the Futa Jalon Highlands to Cameroun, are perceived as threats by their host communities in Southern Nigeria. Persistent conflicts between North and South have inflamed ethnic nationalism and regionalist sentiment in Southern Nigeria.

Religion also divides the country, with Muslims dominating the North and Christians holding the South. The concept of religious pluralism embraces the divergence and diversity of faiths existing within a given society,[17] and its absence has prevented

---

15. Daniel Jordan Smith, *A Culture of Corruption: Everyday Deception and Popular Discontent in Nigeria* (Princeton: Princeton University Press, 2007).

16. Chris Kwaja, "Nigeria's Pernicious Drivers of Ethno-Religious Conflict," *Africa Center for Strategic Studies,* July 31, 2011, https://africacenter.org/publication/nigerias-pernicious-drivers-of-ethno-religious-conflict/#:~:text=Ever%20since%2C%20local%20elections%20and,are%20the%20real%20root%20causes.

17. Christian O. Ele, "Religious Pluralism and Sustainable Development in Nigeria," *African Research Review* 13, no. 1 (2019): 26–37.

Nigerians' unity. The alleged "Islamisation agenda" of the Nigerian State is decried by the National Christian Elders Forum (NCEF), which includes Theophilus Danjuma, a former Nigerian minister of defense. An NCEF publication alleges that the Federal Government's Islamization agenda was bent on destroying democracy while supporting *jihad* in the form of the Boko Haram uprising and clashes between Fulani herdsmen and Southern farmers. Political *jihad* claims threaten democratic tenets to entrench *Sharia* ideology in national legislation.

Since independence, most of Nigeria's heads of state have come from the North, and Nigeria is a member of the Organization of Islamic Countries (OIC) despite its official status as a secular State. Given these facts, the constant demands for secession by the South are understandable. Not only do Muslims wield outsized influence over national institutions, but the Muslim-dominated North is also known for acts of religious intolerance. Remarks from political leaders have fueled allegations of Nigeria's looming Islamization. The first Northern premier, Ahmadu Bello, was committed to ensuring that Nigeria and other African nations became Islamic. This desire has, rightly or otherwise, been attributed also to every other political leader from the North. Bello, the Sardauna of Sokoto, affirmed:

> I have earlier spoken of conversion of non-Muslims to Islam. I would like to say that this is only a beginning as there are other areas we have not yet tapped. I hope when we claim Nigeria, we will go further afield in Africa.[18]

Though he died more than fifty years ago and ideological divisions among his supporters have weakened them, the perception of an Islamization agenda has, nevertheless, driven endless ethnoreligious conflicts between Northern and Southern Nigeria.

Residents of Southern Nigeria are skeptical about the Fulani's claim of being mere herdsmen engaged in animal husbandry. They believe, on the contrary, that the Fulani are covert Islamic missionaries who intend to occupy spaces in Southern Nigeria to further the Islamic agenda. Policy conflicts, such as the Grazing Reserve Bill, are evidence of the Federal Government's support for Fulani nomads in all of Nigeria's 36 states. The Bill has provisions that seem to encourage Northern Fulani migration into Southern lands, and Catholic Bishops in Lagos condemned it. They stated:

> . . . we reject the proposed move by the Federal Government to establish Cattle Colonies across the various states of the Federation as a way of finding a lasting solution to the herdsmen/farmers clashes.[19]

---

18. Christian O. Ele, "Islamization of Nigeria: Implications for Sustainable Peace," *International Journal of Social Sciences and English Literature* 2 (2018): 13–19.

19. Chijioke Jannah, "Catholic Bishops Speak on Proposed Cattle Colonies," *Daily Post*, February 4, 2018, https://dailypost.ng/2018/02/04/catholic-bishops-speak-proposed-cattle-colonies/.

Figure 23.2. "Happy Citizens in Harmony" by Dr. Kazeem Ekeolu. Four citizens are in cooperation and smile, no matter the background; projects future unity.

Abimbola Adelakun has suggested that both religions want to see their religious culture become dominant.[20] While highlighting some of the actions former President Goodluck Ebele Jonathan took, Adelakun presented an objective view that shows parties on both sides of the religious divide engaging in similar political strategies and launching equally unfounded accusations.

No genuine effort to unite Nigeria would be recognized in the current political environment, as ethnic and religious values can hardly align with socio-economic

20. Abimbola Adelakun, "Fighting Islamization of Nigeria," *Punch*, September 28, 2017.

initiatives that foster unity within the country. Many people will, unfortunately, continue to be adversely affected by the nation's history of corruption and division. As long as religious and political leaders continue to encourage animosity between polarized regions, peace cannot realistically be expected to reign.[21] Any momentary peace may merely be an interlude during which warring parties redraw their plans for resuming conflicts.

Scores of interrelated problems have had distinct effects on Nigeria's development—one can discuss them for days without running out of materials. The fundamental fact is that their origins and potency are linked, and citizens bear the brunt of these challenges. Nigerians are plagued by security concerns, ineffective leadership, economic adversity, and inadequate infrastructure. Even if Nigeria is not yet viewed as a failed State, it is teetering dangerously close to being one. Failed nations must pay a heavy price, and much of it is already being borne by Nigeria's current citizens. Poverty and low living standards reflect the simultaneous existence of these challenges.

Forty percent of Nigeria's citizens—almost half of the country's population—live below the poverty line, and the national unemployment rate was 33% as of January 2022.[22] The entire continent of Africa struggles with poverty, but Nigeria's internal dynamics are worsening its effects. The government periodically initiates policies and programs to alleviate poverty.[23] A few of them are the National Poverty Eradication Programme, Better Life for Rural Women, the National Directorate of Employment, and River Basin Development Authorities.[24] However, these efforts are always undermined by government dysfunction and public corruption.[25]

Small businesses cannot thrive where infrastructure and basic amenities are missing, and their absence lower standards of living. Nigeria's economic performance and public investments have left its citizens struggling to survive. The country's deplorable living standards have led to other problems, like security concerns, that contribute to and deepen the cycle of poverty. Nigeria has fallen far short of its citizens' developmental dreams at its independence.

Social media allow citizens to publicize their concerns, spread information quickly, and pressure the government to make meaningful changes. Social commentators

---

21. Oluwakemi Okenyodo, "Governance, Accountability, and Security in Nigeria," *Africa Center for Strategic Studies,* June 21, 2016, https://africacenter.org/publication/governance-accountability-security-nigeria-html/.

22. Anthony Otaru, "40% of Nigerian Population Live below Poverty Line," *The Guardian,* January 27, 2022.

23. Segun Oshewolo, "Galloping Poverty in Nigeria: An Appraisal of Government Interventionist Policies," *Journal of Sustainable Development in Africa* 12, no. 6 (2010): 264–274.

24. Victoria Voelwoen Danaan, "Analysing Poverty in Nigeria through Theoretical Lenses," *Journal of Sustainable Development* 11, no. 1 (2018): 20–31.

25. Ali Madina Dankumo, Suryati Ishak, Yasmin Bani, and Hanny Zurina Hamza, "The Relationship between Public Expenditure, Corruption and Poverty in Nigeria," *Journal Ekonomi dan Studi Pembangunan* 11, no. 1 (2019): 76–89.

like Pius Adesanmi (now late), Farooq Kperogi, and others have called for increased governmental accountability.[26] The wide reach of social media has enabled people from different regions to identify several areas where the government needs to improve. Despite criticism, however, there have been no tangible changes.

The high cost of living, low quality of life, and continuing public criticism show how present-day Nigeria has failed its citizens. The lagging educational system is one of the greatest threats to Nigeria's future access to human resources. Many Nigerians who find opportunities abroad are leaving to improve their lives. That is contemporary Nigeria's reality, and public sentiments continue to prove it. Despite these challenges, however, Nigeria can attain its great potential once it begins to take steps to realize it.

THE FUTURE OF DEMOCRACY

Democracy hinges on free and fair elections, judicial independence, freedom of the press, and active public interest groups that help shape government policies. The weak implementation of democratic values in Nigeria has led to haphazard developments. The country supposedly practices fiscal federalism, but this is on paper, and its principles are non-existent; elective representation is seen as a gateway to the accumulation of wealth and riches. This prevailing political arrangement allows the central government to profit from Nigeria's resources while excluding the individual regions that produced them. This arrangement has led to public agitation for political restructuring, but which political typology will work best for Nigeria remains a mystery.

Some have noted that Nigeria inherited a haphazard political arrangement from the British colonial government, but this does not explain the country's current democratic dysfunction. Nigerians currently suffer from the idea that political office is a career path where success is measured by the volume of wealth that a person acquires. Candidates for office do not thus aspire to serve the public; they seek to improve their socio-economic status through high salaries and allowances permitted by the federal constitution. Leaders of political parties also rig local elections to deprive the country of political representatives who should have gotten to offices through free and fair elections.

Democracy is currently not working well for Nigeria because people do not trust their leaders. The absence of effective mechanisms for public input into government policies has contributed to some of the endless strikes at many government institutions. Though democracy should provide an enabling environment for citizens and their elected representatives to thrive economically, Nigeria's democracy has transformed into a system that enriches leaders at the people's and the nation's expense.

---

26. Pius Adesanmi, "Before it is too Late for Her," *Sahara Reporters*, June 1, 2018, https://saharareporters.com/2018/06/01/it-too-late-her-pius-adesanmi.

This has made victims of people who voted these leaders into office while also punishing impoverished individuals and pushed to the margins of society by government policies. True democracy protects the people's right to demand government accountability, but Nigeria's version fails to protect the people's right to decent living standards.

Although some civic organizations that should check the excesses of government are complicit in having some underhand arrangements with Nigeria's leadership, many others are sidelined or hindered from carrying out their duties. As Kofi Annan has noted, developing nations will never experience prosperity without good governance and responsible regulations.[27] Put differently, a nation's economic progress is determined by its embrace of democratic principles, and transparency and accountability from government officials are ingrained in these principles. Regrettably, not only do Nigeria's leaders claim power without adequate democratic processes, but they also fail to uphold democratic principles while in office.

Without the necessary mechanisms to ensure accountability and transparency in Nigeria's democratic system, political leaders enter into social contracts and deliberately renege on their agreements with citizens. The abuse of personal power enables corrupt practices among Nigeria's political leaders. Consequently, there is little regard for the needs of the constituents who are deprived of basic amenities while leaders pursue personal goals and primitive acquisitions of wealth. Guseh and Oritsejafor have affirmed that the relative economic successes in South Africa and Ghana depended on political freedom and transparency in governance.[28]

In a governmental context, public morality influences the conduct of private individuals tasked with exerting influence over state machinery. When public morality and politics are intertwined, they can create a system that encourages responsibility while ensuring the citizens' rights to life, liberty, and the pursuit of happiness. The absence of public morality encourages corrupt practices like fraud, embezzlement, and nepotism, which neglect the public interest to satisfy private desires. These entrench an official lawlessness system in security agencies like the army and the police. Nigeria's political corruption is a crisis strangulating the democratic processes capable of delivering the desired development to Nigeria.

Implementing appropriate sectoral reforms is the only way to guarantee Nigeria's development and economic growth. For instance, true fiscal federalism would ensure that every region has a degree of independence and self-sufficiency. Substantial regional autonomy under new fiscal arrangements should inspire new policies influenc-

27. S. Adejumobi, "Democracy, Good Governance and Constitutionalism in Africa." In *Governance: Nigeria and the World*, ed., Sylvester Odion-Akhaine (Ikeja: Centre for Constitutionalism and Demilitarisation, 2004).

28. J.S. Guseh and E. Oritsejafor, "Democracy and Economic Growth in Africa: The Cases of Ghana and South Africa," *Journal of Third World Studies* 22, no. 2 (2005): 121–137.

ing each region's socio-economic development.[29] Nigeria could distribute its wealth in ways that would benefit the various regions. There is also a need to redefine Nigeria's political landscape to mandate new ideologies that put the people at the forefront of political representation. Political corruption begets high poverty levels, a lack of trust in leadership, ethnic rivalries, income inequality, social disorder, and underdevelopment.[30] Political corruption is linked with social immorality, and Nigeria must devise a system that disincentivizes these vices. The country's current institutional deficits encourage social injustice and civil strife while negatively impacting societal development.

A society consists of the culture and the norms shared by all its members. Because change is inevitable, these beliefs evolve. In Nigeria, change can allow Nigerian citizens to succeed if their rights—especially their right to free expression—are protected. The contemporary ideology of human rights can be adapted to suit Nigeria's circumstances. In light of the changing nature of culture and social orientations, Nigeria adopted a new concept of justice and ways of treating individuals after interacting with the rest of the world. Globalization has also greatly influenced the further adjustment of these values.

Nigeria's future must include the systematic protection of human rights beyond written legislation.[31] Nigeria's government and its officials may face some uncomfortable criticism; democracy, however, thrives on the citizens' right to free expression. Other rights, especially respect for human dignity, must also be upheld. Government parastatals, police, security forces, and other agencies must respect the citizens' fundamental rights.

Many organizations and progressive movements in Nigeria advocate the cause of human rights, gender equality, and gender mainstreaming.[32] And while these organizations and relevant laws and policies are gradually providing opportunities and advancing toward equal representation, the cultural gap that still discriminates against women must be addressed.[33] The Nigeria of the future should protect women's rights and provide a level playing field for both men and women.

Evidence of inequality abounds all across present-day Nigeria. In several professions, especially in unorganized labor, women are neither respected nor compensated

---

29. F.N.O. Mimiko, "Political and Constitutional Reforms," *Nigeria's Reform Programme: Issues and Challenges,* eds. H. Saliu, Amali, B. and R. Olawepo, (Ibadan: Vantage Publishers, 2007), 303–316.

30. O.O. Adegboyega, "The Dearth of Public Morality in Nigeria," *International Journal of Arts and Culture in Society* 4, no. 3 (2007): 63–67.

31. Sunny Nwachukwu, Austin Aghamelo and Nwaneri Stanley, "An Account of Human Right Violations in Nigeria (Pre-British, British And Post Independence)," *European Scientific Journal* 10, no. 10 (2014): 230–239.

32. Kelly Brian Ovie Ejumudo, "Gender Equality and Women Empowerment in Nigeria: The Desirability and Inevitability of a Pragmatic Approach," *Developing Country Studies* 3, no. 4 (2013): 59–66.

33. Ejumudo, "Gender Equality and Women," 59–66.

equally to their male counterparts. Some corporations' attempts to address this shortfall have failed due to personal biases perpetuating discrimination against women. The issue of inequality is worsened by some traditional practices and cultural norms which restrict women's rights in society. Female genital mutilation (FGM) is a particularly grisly example that remains in practice in several parts of Nigerian society despite the enactment of laws in some states to put a stop to it.[34] Other issues, such as the lack of access to education, justice, and protection, limit women's opportunities.[35] Without respect for the rights of women and the institutionalization of gender mainstreaming, Nigeria is unlikely to attain the great potential it has the capacity for.

ECONOMIC STATURE

Nigeria's economic situation is best described as "a paradox of plenty," a term applied to wasteful societies blessed with abundant mineral resources. It is also called "the Dutch disease" This paradox occurs when large amounts of mineral resources, such as crude oil, inhibit a nation's economic growth. A nation blessed with such resources is naturally expected to possess great wealth. However, the presence of such resources has, in many places, ironically, caused economic stagnation—where the exploitation of those resources is the sole source of wealth generation.

Rather than harness the revenues realized from the sales of the country's natural resources, Nigeria's corrupt leadership diverts these revenues for their personal use. Before crude oil was discovered in Nigeria, each region engaged in various economic activities, maintaining a trade balance. The South-Western region, for instance, produced cocoa, a major cash crop, and exported it globally. The North also had a booming economy, evidenced by the groundnut pyramids and other food crops. However, the discovery of crude oil and the nationalization of mineral resources led to a change in the government's priorities. National investment focused on oil reserves instead of business growth, and the proceeds from the resources were not used to provide basic amenities.[36] Instead, the revenue streams lined the pockets of federal leaders and oil company executives.

Nigeria's resource curse comes from its over-reliance on a single commodity. This endures due to the absence of a strong process or system to ensure government revenue collection and allocation transparency. Rather than provide amenities such as electricity, roads, and housing, it has created a well-fed political class living amidst

34. Kelechukwu Godslove Egbulonu and Ifesinachi Sandra Eleonu, "Gender Inequality and Economic Growth in Nigeria (1990–2016)," *International Journal of Gender and Women Studies* 6, no. 1 (2018): 159–167.

35. Okpeh Okpeh, *Mainstreaming Gender in the African Development Process: A Critic of NEPAD and the Women Question* (Nigeria: BSU Press, 2005)

36. B.O. Iganiga, "Evaluation of the Nigerian Financial Sector Reforms using Behavioural Models," *Journal of Economics* 1, no. 2 (2010): 65–75.

poverty-stricken citizens, which has led to economic inequality and a massive gap between political leaders and average citizens. The inequality is even more pronounced in the Northern region, which has produced several national leaders, though its education system lags far behind its peers.[37]

Nigeria's stakeholders are aware of its capacity for growth. During military rule, government initiatives focused on Nigeria's economic development to ease its competition in the global marketplace. These birthed "Vision 2000," drafted under the military regime of Ibrahim Badamosi Babangida, and "Vision 20:2020," conceived by President Olusegun Obasanjo in 2006. The country's leadership knows that economic development is possible. The more recent plans were drafted to place Nigeria among the top 20 economies by 2020 through sustained regional and global leadership. Though it was an admirable objective, the country's leadership neglected to effectively apply its resources and thus failed to meet the goal.

Civil strife and instability also hinder economic development. In addition to the threat posed by Boko Haram, illegal miners and bandits have become more active in search of gold. As of March 2020, more than 210,000 people were internally displaced due to banditry in Northern Nigeria; most displaced people had to relocate to communities along the border between Nigeria and the Niger Republic.

Nigeria's economy may continue to experience major setbacks despite indicators that would otherwise suggest good economic health. Socio-political volatility and ineffective policies remain major drawbacks.[38] The country's dependence solely on revenue from oil, a single commodity, led to its failure to diversify its economy and develop other industries. Positive economic indicators point to the capacity for growth and development, but poor governance continues to hinder the implementation of sustainable economic policies. Nigeria has potential, but it must be accompanied by a determination to harness that potential for sustainable long-term growth.

Despite Nigeria's many setbacks, global economic analysts still regard it as the largest economy in Africa. A report by Goldman Sachs identified Nigeria as one of the 11 countries that could become economic leaders in the future. These results were based on projections for GDP growth, and the report concluded that Nigeria has the potential to become one of the world's 20 largest economies by 2025.[39] However, a few factors may prevent this outcome and limit Nigeria's ability to deliver economic growth—crude oil's declining global demand, for instance, is one of them. It is another reason the country's leadership needs to make conscious efforts at socio-economic

---

37. A.H. Ekpo and O.J. Umoh, "An Overview of the Nigerian Economic Growth and Development," *Daily Newspaper*, July 14, 2012.

38. M.I. Obadan and S.E. Edo, "Nigeria's Economic Governance Structures and Growth Performance in Perspective," *The Nigerian Journal of Economic and Social Studies* 50, no. 1 (2008): 99–118.

39. B. Alonaizi and Yousr Gadhoum, "The Next 11: Emerging Investment Market," 1st International Conference on Advanced Research (ICAR-2017), Bahrain, Manama, 2017, 53–62.

reform to change Nigeria's trajectory. The extent of the reform's success will determine whether Nigeria becomes a global leader.

Many Nigerians already envision their escape from their current predicament. Nigerians can, however, build a realistic and attainable Nigeria instead of a utopian fantasy. And although the country's current economic situation and societal dynamics need major reforms, Nigeria is blessed with human and material resources that have captured the world's attention and can turn the tide through effective leadership.

Several recommendations can be made to improve Nigeria's economy, including solutions to the impending problems of drought, local production shortfalls, and hostile conditions for local businesses. Nigeria's commercial landscape must allow local businesses and industries to thrive. Activities must shift away from an economy of consumers to support an economy of producers. In 2021, Nigeria's international agricultural trade, valued at about N3.24 trillion, included about N2.23 trillion of imports that vastly exceeded the number of exports.[40] Nigeria's heavy dependency on imported products negatively impacts many sectors of its economy. In 2020, 70% of the medications used in Nigeria were imported, and only 30% were locally produced in Nigeria.[41]

THE ROLE OF CITIZENS IN THE IMAGINED FUTURE

A society is a reflection of its citizens. The quality of interactions among a society's residents also suggests its status.[42] Government policies and actions play a big role in shaping a society's development—it is, after all, a core government role to steer society. Because government is a continuum, it is the bridge between the past, present, and future of societies which directs their journey into the future. The actions of a government thus determine the success of society and its vision for the country.

Societies' success, however, also greatly depends on citizens who simultaneously create and mirror the values of their countries. A country's aspirations can equally be gleaned from interactions among its citizens. And since citizens define their society, they are fundamental to determining its identity and vision. The citizens' vision is, after all, their nation's vision.

Identifying who determines a society's status often creates a dichotomy between the citizens and leaders. Leaders directly influence societies through the blueprints they develop for their society's progress.[43] But leaders are, themselves, citizens first. In

---

40. Nike Popoola, "Food Imports Exceed Exports by ₦2.23tn in 12 Months," *Punch,* April 4, 2022.

41. Editorial, "Nigeria's Huge Import-dependency Syndrome," *The Guardian,* October 4, 2020.

42. Sarah Yerkes and Marwan Muasher, eds. *Decentralization in Tunisia: Empowering Towns, Engaging People* (Washington, DC: Carnegie Endowment for International Peace, 2018), 21–24.

43. Li Ji, Ping Ping Fu, Irene Chow and T.K. Peng, "Societal Development and the Change of Leadership Style in Oriental Chinese Societies," *Journal of Developing Societies* 18, no. 1 (2002): 46–63.

a democratic society, they are elected and supported by the citizens. A society's leaders are thus reflections of its citizens.

Citizens' involvement in nation-building often determines the progress of a nation. The character of these citizens, who are also the country's resources, reflects their nation's image. Therefore, citizens' capacity must be developed and harnessed for nation-building in Nigeria's projected and imagined future. The first step toward an envisioned Nigeria is developing its education to empower citizens with the requisite knowledge to compete with their counterparts from other nations. This will provide the citizens with opportunities for engagement and prevent the loss of talent through brain drain.

Government alone cannot drive a society's change and development; the government and its citizens make up the fibers required to weave the fabric of society. The Nigerian State has long been plagued with bad leadership and corrupt individuals, but Nigerian citizens must also improve their developmental efforts. The hope and aspirations for a better Nigeria depend on the imaginations of the citizens. This is a fact the citizens must recognize and work toward.

Political participation is essential in a democratic government, and the citizens' participation is essential for Nigeria's political atmosphere to be cleansed of corruption and bad leadership.[44] Nigeria is a democracy and is expected to remain one (or any form of improvement over dictatorship) in the future. In an ideal democracy, representation and leadership are people-centered, and leadership should not be part of the people's problems. High rates of corruption cripple the government's efficiency, and flawed electioneering processes enable corruption.[45] And though political participation might not be the sole solution for Nigeria's leadership issues, it is essential for holding the government accountable.

Political participation is unbalanced in Nigeria.[46] The most noteworthy form of political participation among Nigerians occurs through public discussions and criticism.[47] Nigerians are conscious of their unfavorable political circumstances and make their voices heard through tools like social media. Individuals like Farooq Kperogi, Pius Adesanmi, and other brilliant minds continually analyze society's conditions and

44. Geraint Parry and George Moyser, "More Participation, More Democracy?" In *Democracy: A Reader*, eds. Ricardo Blaug and John Schwarzmantel (West Sussex: Columbia University Press, 2016), 386–390.

45. Onodugo Ifeanyi Chris, "Leadership Challenges and Nigerian Development," *International Journal of Scientific Research in Science and Technology* 1, no. 5 (2015): 2395–6011.

46. Sylvia Uchenna Agu, Vincent Onyekwelu Sunday Okeke, and Adeline N. Idike, "Voters Apathy and Revival of Genuine Political Participation in Nigeria," *Mediterranean Journal of Social Sciences* 4, no. 3 (2013): 439–439.

47. Innocent Chiluwa, "On Political Participation: Discursive Pragmatics and Social Interaction in Nolitics," *Studies in Literature and Language* 2, no. 2 (2011): 80–92.

the government's activities.[48] Citizens also engage in criticism and protests to express their concerns.[49] All these demonstrate a political consciousness capable of persuading the government to meet the citizens' aspirations.

Electoral participation in Nigeria has declined dramatically since the restoration of democratic government in 1999. This has serious implications. For example, the 2003 presidential election saw a 69% general participation rate, whereas the 2019 presidential election saw only a 35% participation rate.[50] In 1999, the total number of voters was about 30 million, and the total number in 2019 was around 28 million.[51] There were more than 119 million Nigerian residents in 1999,[52] and the population has increased to more than 211 million.[53] Though the population has increased by 90% since 1999, and the number of registered voters has increased by over 26 million voters (approximately 45%) from 57,938,945[54] in the February 1999 election to 84,004.084[55] as of the 2019 presidential election, the number of voter turnout in the 2019 presidential election was about 2 million lower than the 1999 election.

Ironically, citizens complain about the government while refusing to perform their civic duty of participating in the electoral process. This lack of involvement may prevent Nigeria from meeting Goldman Sachs' forecast for economic strength in 2025.[56] Despite this, one can be optimistic about Nigeria's future and Nigerians' vision for it. Citizens must become more politically active by consciously exercising their voting rights. A higher voter turnout means a more representative government and more citizens that will hold politicians accountable. Voting is the first step toward actualizing the citizens' dream of a better Nigeria. The citizens must understand that criticism without electoral participation is counterproductive.

Nigeria's political problems will be difficult to resolve, but citizens can be more than just tools for reformation or facilitators of revolution. An imagined future for Nigeria is only possible if citizens exhibit the core ideas of positive citizenship and promote peaceful coexistence. Civil societies must embark on greater sensitization

---

48. Udo Okoronkwo-Chukwu, "Naija No Dey Carry Last: Pius Adesanmi and the Complexity of a Nation in Progress," *European Journal of English Language and Literature Studies* 4, no. 7 (2016): 40–47.

49. Solomon Ibrahim Hari, "The Evolution of Social Protest in Nigeria: The Role of Social Media in the "#OccupyNigeria" Protest," *International Journal of Humanities and Social Science Invention* 3, no. 9 (2014): 33–39.

50. Olusanya E. Olubusoye, Olalekan J. Akintande and Eric A. Vance, "Transforming Evidence to Action: The Case of Election Participation in Nigeria," *Chance* 34, no. 3 (2021): 13–23.

51. Olubusoye, Akintande and Vance, "Transforming Evidence to Action," 13–23.

52. United Nations Population Division, "Population, Total-Nigeria," *The World Bank*, 2022, https://data.worldbank.org/indicator/SP.POP.TOTL?locations=NG

53. United Nations Population Division, "Population, Total-Nigeria."

54. *Vanguard*, "Presidential Elections 1999–2011 in Figures," April 23, 2011.

55. Independent National Electoral Commission, "Report of the 2019 General Election," *INEC Nigeria*, 2020, 112, https://www.inecnigeria.org/wp-content/uploads/2020/11/REPORT-OF-THE-2019-GENERAL-ELECTION.pdf

56. Alonaizi and Gadhoum, "The Next 11," 53–62.

efforts to foster development. Resourceful citizens are more likely to initiate constructive innovations and inventions than the government.

CONCLUDING REMARKS

The social contract between Nigerians and the government desperately needs to be restored. Observable trends suggest a likely decline: constant in-fighting and ethnic conflicts continue despite attempts at reform. The increased polarizing politics between the North and the South have deepened grievances to unprecedented levels, threatening the safety of democracy and its participants. The fight against federal corruption also remains a formidable obstacle because leaders are reluctant to identify and condemn the sources of bad behavior.

Worsening insecurity makes it easy to predict a grim future for Nigeria. Regional and ethnocultural conflicts dominate every interaction and prevent meaningful development. It remains to be seen how the current administration will address the armed conflicts disrupting Nigeria's fragile peace. The presidency has exhibited little concern for pressing issues, leading some to question its motives, compassion, humanity, investment, and competence. Nigeria's leadership must identify a new structure to provide enduring peace and meaningful socio-economic development.

Government action is necessary for a favorable Nigerian future, but citizens must also be ready to uphold the values of democracy. Democracy is for the people, and they must be involved if they want to protect it. Citizens must proactively address issues that affect their country by participating in elections and fostering development. Good citizenship gives hope that Nigeria can move toward a better future by surmounting its security problems and other challenges it currently experiences.

24

SPECTATORS AND GLADIATORS

The Impact of Social Media

INTRODUCTION

The world has subscribed to different forms of governments emanating from their historical experience, social constructs, and cultural diffusions over time, and they kept adjusting to discover how best society should be governed. In Nigeria, democracy is a system gradually growing with the people. Although there were periods of military interference, the country has had a rough run with a democratic system since 1999. In this sense, whether or not democracy is properly practiced is not the question, but the country has been practicing it steadily since 1999.[1]

Hence, the systems and how the citizens interpret the concept of governance are predicated on the democratic instinct that the country believes to be in existence. No matter how democracy is defined, the basic ideology behind it is the inclusiveness of the generality of the citizens in the political and social prowess of governance and taking into cognizance the aggregate position of the people.[2] This outlines one cogent factor of democracy: political participation. Political participation is a major pillar upon which the tenets of democracy are built, and it is a *sine qua non* of the political

1. Adeyinka Theresa Ajayi and E. Oladipo Ojo, "Democracy in Nigeria: Practice, Problems and Prospects," *Journal of Developing Country Studies* 4, no. 22 (2014): 107-125.
2. Iris Marion Young, *Inclusion and Democracy* (Oxford: Oxford University Press, 2002).

process.[3] In Nigeria, political participation has served as the medium to evaluate, participate in, and influence political processes in the country. Right from the period the ideology of democracy was developed and properly adopted globally, political participation has been a parameter to measure democracy and the government's commitment to democratic processes.

Verba and Nie elucidate the instrumentality of political participation by stating, "Where few take part in decisions, there is little democracy; the more participation there is in decisions, the more democracy there is."[4] However, we are aware of the level and dynamics of political participation in which some scholars have been able to build certain levels of stratification around them. This is because the austerity of political position is not always within reach of an average citizen; thus, a small percent of the society successfully climbs to such a level of influence. This informed the inciting ideology behind the stratification of society based on their levels of participation. The ideas of stratification have a deep root in Marxist theories of political and social stratifications that have developed other theories of political participation in line with an elitist approach. Some influential political scholars who followed the elitist approach to explaining such subject matter are Mosca[5] and Pareto,[6] who premise political participation on the actions and the nature of political elites in the society.

Clearer views on political participation continued to emanate, one of which was Robinson's attempt to classify participation into three strata that are quite interrelated but also largely dissimilar. The first of the three strata are the "spectators" that see politics and elections as "mass spectacles," the second is what Robinson understood as "Citizens" who are concerned about voting in elections, and the third strata are the "Partisans" who are concerned about seeking election and the election of their candidate or whosoever they support into a political seat in the society. Milbrath provides a more insightful opinion and model on the stratification of political participation and participators. He emphasized the presence of three stratifications of the hierarchical ladder of political participation. They include spectators, transitional, and gladiators, and people who belong to these categories can exhibit attributes or activities that would automatically classify them as belonging to all. Milbrath's stratification model is in line with Robinson's understanding of political participation but captures a progressive hierarchical development of citizens, amounting to a shift from one point to another.

---

3. Séverine Deneulin, "Democracy and Political Participation." In *An Introduction to the Human Development and Capability Approach*, ed. S. Deneulin (London: Routledge, 2009), 207-213.

4. Norman H. Nie, *Participation in America: Political Democracy and Social Equality* (New York: Harper & Row, 1972).

5. Gaetano Mosca, *The Ruling Class*, trans. Hannah D. Kahn (New York: McGraw-Hill, 1939).

6. Vilfredo Pareto, *The Mind and Society*, trans., A. Bongiorno (New York: Harcourt, Brace, and Co., 1935).

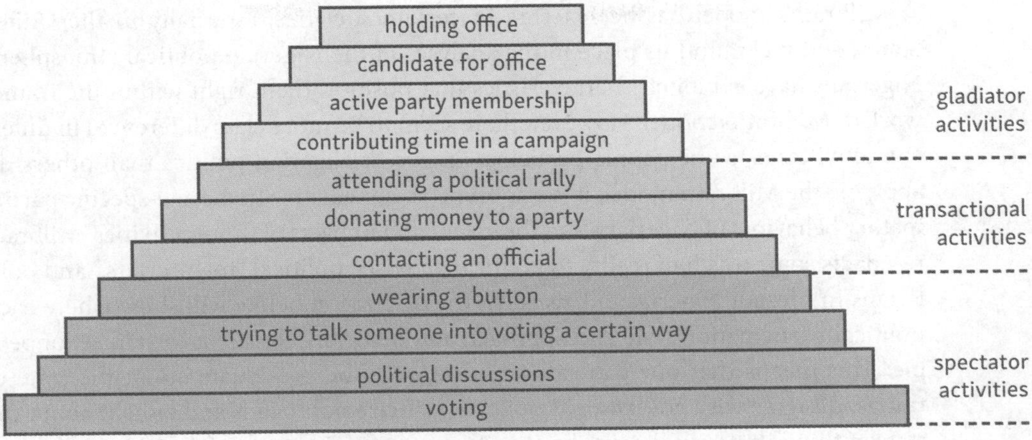

Fig 1: Hierarchical Representation of Milbrath's Model in terms of the activities of each stratum[11]

Milbrath's model of political participation is based on people's political involvement and how they respond to political stimuli in their respective societies. Hence, the three-strata model is built to further capture approaches and examples of the activities of the people that fall under each stratum. Milbrath further outlines relative activities ascribable to each stratum to ascertain the scope he has created.[7] Gladiators are the major decision-makers of society who are office holders, individuals who contest political positions, members of political parties, and those dedicated to political campaigns.[8] The transitions are between the gladiators and the spectators, as they have a link to the two sets of people. They attend and participate in a political rally organized by a party or candidates to garner support and educate the people. The transitional also donates money to candidates or political parties and has access to government officials to persuade or interact with them.[9] The spectators form a larger set of people as almost everyone in the society, especially in Nigeria, carries out the primary activities of a spectator. The first thing most spectators do is to create and participate in political discussions and engage in conversations about the societal situation. In addition, the spectators hold beliefs on politics and persuade people to share in them or to vote for a preferred individual or candidate. They outline characteristics they believe a voter should examine before making any decision in the political process, and lastly, they are the average voters in society.[10]

---

7. Lester Milbrath, *Political Participation* (Chicago: Rand McNally College Publishing Company, 1965).
8. Salad Mohamud Ali, "Decentralization and Political Participation in Wadajir District, Mogadishu, Somalia," Ph.D *diss.*, Kampala International University, 2015.
9. Ali, "Decentralization and Political Participation."
10. Ali, "Decentralization and Political Participation."
11. Milbrath, *Political Participation*, 1965, 18. See also Ali, "Decentralization and Political Participation."

Milbrath's model has been tested in certain societies, especially in the United States, and it can find its place in the analyses of the Nigerian political atmosphere. Nigerians have exhibited characteristics that position them right within the framework of Milbrath's model. However, there seem to be more class differences in different activities as some people participate more in Nigerian politics than others. In applying the Milbrath model, it is important to be sensitive to the age-specific participatory behaviors of Nigerians and the extent and impacts of those activities. Milbrath re-enacts some touch of reality to political activists, political "town-criers," and politicians in present Nigeria, and, as such, the discussion below will show where each political participation style and approach automatically classify a certain set of people. This means that one can exhibit knowledge, be passionate about the state of things, disagree with government policies, criticize politicians and lament about the state of things but would never be classified to get to the arena of decision-making as gladiators. This means that being politically conscious does not necessarily amount to being politically active; they are different ball games.

Without mincing words, the political participation stratification by Milbrath is not out of context in the Nigerian situation; it has given a clearer perspective on political analysis.[12] Indisputably, the internet and social media have been game changers in every social sector and have redefined the Nigerian political scenes. Societal construction, political behaviors, and cultural subscriptions are now largely predicated on the instrumentality of social media.[13] Hence, the presence of social media in contemporary political discussion will be discussed and examined vis-à-vis Milbrath's positions on political participation, all within the Nigerian context. It is pertinent to redefine the roles of the spectators, the transitional, and the gladiators to see how social media has created role exodus within the same political ladder. Examples will be drawn from the works and positions of reputable social media users, especially those discussed in the previous chapters, to substantially elucidate the subject matter.

ROLES AND POSITIONS OF NIGERIAN SPECTATORS

At the bottom of the pyramid of political participation in the Milbrath model are the Spectators who also have their level of involvement, one more involved than the other.[14] At the very base are non-partisan individuals who do not care about the country's political state; they do not vote nor know much about the developments and incidents that happen in the country. They are probably engrossed in surviving the

---

12. Ayo Awopeju, "2011 Presidential Election and the Political Participation in Nigeria," *Canadian Social Science* 8, no. 2 (2012): 96-103.

13. Robin Effing, Jos Van Hillegersberg and Theo Huibers, "Social Media and Political Participation: Are Facebook, Twitter and Youtube Democratizing our Political Systems?" In *Electronic Participation. ePart 2011. Lecture Notes in Computer Science*, eds. Efthimios Tambouris, Ann Macintosh and Hans de Bruijn (Switzerland: Springer, Berlin, Heidelberg, 2011), 25-35.

14. Milbrath, *Political Participation.*

Figure 24.1. "Physical and Social Media Onlookers" by Michael Efionayi. Depiction of someone needing help with social media engagement of the seen and onlookers.

day and fighting against poverty. However, in Nigeria, spectators who do not want to discuss the nation's state are rare; they wait at bus stops, and newspaper vendors stand to analyze political events and interpret them based on their world views. They are the average market women and men who come out to vote–and a sizeable number of them would do so if there is enough financial remuneration. The Nigerian spectators are also averagely educated citizens who are literate and understand, to a certain level, the basic duties of a government. Hence, they project what the government should do and when it is possible to do it.

The role of the spectators has received new dynamics of attention in recent years with the growth of general subscriptions to social media platforms.[15] Social media has become the new conversation point that allows more people to express their opinions about the country's problems.[16] Agger and Ostrom's stratification of political partici-

15. Nnanyelugo Okoro and Kenneth Adibe Nwafor, "Social Media and Political Participation in Nigeria during the 2011 General Elections: The Lapses and the Lessons," *Global Journal of Arts Humanities and Social Sciences* 1, no. 3 (2013): 29-46.

16. Abdulmutallib Ado Abubakar, "Political Participation and Discourse in Social Media during the 2011 Presidential Electioneering," *The Nigerian Journal of Communication* 10, no. 1 (2012): 96-116.

pants explains how to analyze most Nigerian political spectators.[17] They give five classes of participants, four of which capture the roles of modern Nigerian citizens on social media. The first set is the non-participants who do not bother themselves about what goes on in the country as long as they can do their business and work without interference. This set of people is part of the spectators that Milbrath tried to explain in his model. While I must state that many Nigerians belong to this category, the country's current situation has moved people away from this to complainants and talkers.

The second set is the "workers" who fall under the category of gladiators. They get involved actively in public issues and are careless about the cheers and boos of the spectators. They are the leading politicians in the country. They bring the fight, and the spectators cheer or boo them for their ideas, results, and failures. However, they top the hierarchy of political power and participation and have access to matters that can affect the lives of Nigerians in general. No matter how politically conscious or knowledgeable a person is, he or she cannot be categorized as politically active. Hence, mere tweets or Facebook posts about political matters do not guarantee that those issues will change; at most, they are reactions of a spectator telling the gladiators what to do.

The third category of Agger and Ostrom's strata are the "listeners" who follow the country's political developments and partake in conversations about policies but fall under the spectators' category. Another tier of this model is the "talkers."[18] They form most of today's social media influencers and activists who always talk about the nation's state at every point. They spread political information, whether true or false, among the people but cannot change any of those issues. The last stratum is the "advisers," who advise the public and the politicians on how best to handle issues and provide general recommendations on ideas that can move the nation forward.[19] The advisers are well-informed and include people like Dr. Reuben Abati, who understands the rudiment of political leadership and has an analytical approach to providing recommendations on finding solutions to Nigerian problems.[20]

One of Nigeria's prolific figures who have been able to harness the opportunities of social media to address national issues and create consciousness was the late Pius Adesanmi. Like other popular notable writers, Adesanmi employed literature to picture the country's situations through satirical representations. One of his popular satirical works, *Naija No Dey Carry Last*, addresses the country's problems and re-

---

17. Robert E. Agger and Vincent Ostrom, "The Political Structure of a Small Community," *Public Opinion Quarterly* 20, no. 1 (1956): 81-89.

18. Agger and Ostrom, "The Political Structure," 81-89.

19. Agger and Ostrom, "The Political Structure," 91-89.

20. Emma Bider, "The Privilege of Editing #WhoOwnsTheProblem: Remembering Pius Adesanmi," *Nokoko* 9 (2021): 135-138.

enacts national memory.[21] Like the wise older man in conventional African tales and folklore, Adesanmi was a prophet, lamenting the Nigerian situation and warning against the worst expectations that could further befall the country. Adesanmi's *Naija No Dey Carry Last* raised concerns against the administrations of former Presidents Umaru Musa Yar'Adua and Goodluck Jonathan and certain actions detrimental to the potential progress of the nation, especially between 2008 and 2014.[22] Adesanmi criticized the government's "negative civilization," such as Yar'Adua's decision to build one million latrines across the country on World Water and Sanitation Day.[23] Aside from this, he further criticized the reversed development in the nation, dwelling on the decline in the health sector that make Nigerian politicians seek healthcare outside the country.[24] Adesanmi's words of wisdom could also be gathered from his various papers and articles on the nation's state.

While Pius Adesanmi's scholarly contributions will always be appreciated within the Nigerian political criticism circle, his use of social media to show his positions about political events, activities and politicians added to the continuous spotlight on him. Social media helped Adesanmi to be a teacher to many Nigerians without limitations. His comments, tweets, and posts are still on his page as a reminder of his resolutions and convictions about the country. One of his many criticisms was his allegation that a former Governor of Ogun State did not pay many months' arrears to workers and should not be sent to the senate but rather to the zoo.[25] More of his opinions are based on the state of the nation, the inactions of the government and a message that the government can do better.[26]

Another example of a notable spectator in Nigeria is Ayo Olukotun, who has been very proactive in analyzing governmental decisions and tyranny in the face of supposed democracy. He gave a vivid angle to the examination of the media and authoritarian government's censorship. Ayo Olukotun positioned a link from 1993 to the present day, always providing necessary criticism of the nation's state.[27] Recently, he wrote on the state of insecurity in the nation as regards the Kuje Prison attack, noting the carelessness of the government despite reported warnings and reports that suggested the possibilities of the event in time past.[28] Olukotun's scholarship on freedom

---

21. Pius Adesanmi, *Naija No Dey Carry Last: Thoughts on a Nation in Progress* (Lagos: Origami Books, 2015).

22. Udo Okoronkwo-Chukwu, "Naija No Dey Carry Last: Pius Adesanmi and the Complexity of a Nation in Progress," *European Journal of English Language and Literature Studies* 4, no. 7 (2016): 40-47.

23. Adesanmi, *Naija No Dey Carry Last*.

24. Okoronkwo-Chukwu, "Naija No Dey Carry Last," 40-47.

25. Pius Adesanmi, "Tweet," *Twitter*, March 3, 2019, https://Twitter.Com/Pius_Adesanmi/Status/1102221667781160961?S=20&T=Skkogjsudlc0dojqpkjdza.

26. Pius Adesanmi, "Reflections on Darkness," *Nigerian Tribune*, February 24, 2019.

27. Ayo Olukotun, "Authoritarian State, Crisis of Democratization and the Underground Media in Nigeria," *African Affairs* 101, no. 404 (2002): 317-342.

28. Ayo Olukotun, "Insecurity: A Nation Sleepwalking in Utter Peril," *The Punch*, July 27, 2022.

of the press and the media, especially from the military dictatorship era to the present day, is notable and commendable.[29]

Abimbola Adelakun can be added to the list of Nigerians who have raised their necks for remarkable identification among the spectators through scholarship. She has also been able to critically address societal issues and analyze incidences and political commentaries to create a critical analytic window into matters.[30] Adelakun has also written in columns and papers about religious practices, media, and the country's general state.[31]

If we would talk about the dynamics that social media has brought to the country's political culture, we must also talk about someone like Farooq Kperogi, who has established himself in journalism and has given brilliant thoughts on emerging media. Farooq Kperogi has never relented in publishing his opinions on political matters and analyzing the political occurrences in Nigeria. As time rolled towards the 2023 election, he expressed his opinions about some of the candidates on paper, ranging from Tinubu[32] and Obi[33] to Atiku. He believes in the citizens' duty to hold the government accountable and constantly seek good governance.[34] This is seen in his readiness to address emerging issues within the political arena and teach the people what they must do in the coming elections and what should be expected.[35] A scholar like this does not bury his head within the academic responsibilities of a teacher but employs his dexterity in analyzing the country's major issues.[36]

Kperogi understands the dynamics of social media and how much it could be employed in dissidence. His position on using social media as a form of criticizing the government's policies in a democratic state such as Nigeria is clear, and he holds a strong position against the government's censorship of social media and other

29. Ayo Olukotun, "Traditional Protest Media and Anti-Military Struggle in Nigeria 1988–1999," *African Affairs* 101, no. 403 (2002): 193-211; Ayo Olukotun, *Repressive State and Resurgent Media under Nigeria's Military Dictatorship, 1988-98* (Sweden: Nordic Africa Institute, 2004); Ayo Olukotun and Sharon Adetutu Omotoso, eds. *Political Communication in Africa* (Cham, Switzerland: Springer International Publishing, 2017); Ayo Olukotun, "Governance and the Media in an Emergent Democracy: A Study of the Role, Record and Changing Profile of the Nigerian Media 1999-2017," An Inaugural Lecture of the Oba (Dr.) Kayode Adetona, CFR, Professorial Chair in Governance, Olabisi Onabanjo University, Ago-Iwoye, May 10, 2017.

30. Abimbola Adelakun, "Banditry and Atiku's '90% Voters," *The Punch,* July 28, 2022.

31. Abimbola Adelakun, "The Spirit Names the Child: Pentecostal Names and Trans-Ethics." In *The Palgrave Handbook of African Social Ethics*, eds. Nimi Wariboko and Toyin Falola (New York: Springer International Publishing, 2020), 543-567.

32. Farooq Kperogi, "Tinubu would be Sunday Igboho if he's Denied APC Ticket," *Nigerian Tribune,* June 4, 2022.

33. Farooq Kperogi, "Why Peter Obi may become President in 2023 by Default," *Nigerian Tribune,* July 16, 2022.

34. Farooq Kperogi, "My Ideal Nigerian President in 2023," *Nigerian Tribune,* March 26, 2022.

35. Kperogi, "My Ideal Nigerian President in 2023."

36. Farooq Kperogi, "With Upcoming Toxic Fuel Price Hike, it's a Sad New Year," *Nigerian Tribune,* January 1, 2022.

media. Kperogi expresses this in his book *Digital Dissidence and Social Media Censorship in Africa.*[37] He references the dictatorial approach of many African countries towards the freedom of the people to express themselves and the inconvenience that many governments feel about the free usage of social media. He states that countries like Nigeria, Zimbabwe, Kenya, Morocco, Zambia, Equatorial Guinea, and Botswana spy on the phone activities of their citizens and thereby censor the data and information being disseminated.[38] His reaction to President Buhari's ban on Twitter in Nigeria shows the typical African government's intolerance for the use of social media in the country.

As a social media user, Kperogi traced the history of social media in Nigeria and its impact on the nation. The different uses of social media were also explained in the context of an emerging approach that assures some protection and privacy. However, what Kperogi did was investigate certain ways the African leaders have attempted to sabotage the freedom of expression in the name of controlling the use of social media.[39] Kperogi and many reasonable scholars believe this action is authoritarian, especially when it is intended to shield the government from criticism from the masses.

Starting from Kperogi back to Pius Adesanmi, it is obvious that these scholars understand the Nigerian situation and have been able to herald the social inquiries into the causes and effects of political actions. The right scholars and social influencers in Nigeria have been able to ridicule the pathetic state of the country and the cluelessness of our leaders in finding a long-lasting solution to those problems. However, as long as these breeds of scholars do not belong to the apex of the Milbrath pyramid of political participators, they are, at best, spectators and transitionals who do not take action on those issues they complain about.[40] Like Agger and Ostrom's five strata, they largely constitute the talkers, listeners, and advisers.[41]

The spectators loudly cheer and boo at every stimulus caused by the gladiators. While the gladiators engage themselves in the arena, the spectators watch and shout, but in no circumstance do they generally participate in the fight of the gladiators. This explains the contradictions of the role of the spectators and the gladiators; hence, as far as none of the scholars and opinion makers participate actively in the governance process of the country either through running for positions, holding positions or actively engaging in a campaign and party as seen in the case of Bamidele Ademola-Olateju who later became a commissioner, Sowore who is an activist turned presidential contestant and others. They are spectators, and no matter the shouts, they will always be spectators.

---

37. Farooq Kperogi, ed., *Digital Dissidence and Social Media Censorship in Africa* (Oxfordshire: Taylor & Francis, 2022).
38. Kperogi, *Digital Dissidence and Social Media.*
39. Kperogi, *Digital Dissidence and Social Media.*
40. Milbrath, *Political Participation.*
41. Agger and Ostrom, "The Political Structure." 81-89.

Aside from these scholars, social media has increased the number of spectators to a certain extent, causing a shift of influence on the spectators.[42] Social media has become a veritable tool to harness more youth consciousness in the country's political situation, though not necessarily amounting to definite and active participation. It exposes them to information and different analyses of political incidents. Although much of the information available is not always verifiable truth, social media form a conversation point for people. It has brought a new perspective to civic activism in Nigeria and helped create more voices that call for accountability from the government every day. With the youth's disposition to social media, voting on these platforms might amount to more electoral participation than the conventional election, but the peculiarity of social media and the country would not allow it. This shows how social media has become a necessity for Nigerian democracy and makes us understand why Kperogi and others would never support the government's censorship of these platforms.

Aside from being an instrument of political participation, social media has a different side to handling its usefulness. It has become a necessary political instrument that even gladiators use to propagate their agenda and canvass the support of the people despite being the platforms from which they take the greatest criticism. Politicians have been able to take the gladiators' fight to the supposed spectators' stands. Social media has become a marketplace where one sells commodities, accommodating both the gladiator and the spectators. With its effect and necessity, an itching question is whether or not it has been able to lift the spectators' faces and make them as more participatory as the gladiators. It is important to remember that most of the strata on classifying the extent of political participation have been based on the general influence of individuals on governmental issues. Still, social media has made citizens that are non-partisan or do not have political affiliations more conscious of the gladiators' decision-making process. With their reactions, they are fast becoming relevant stakeholders. Hence, would we not make the mistake of sticking by Milbrath's three-stratum model of Gladiators, Transitional and Spectators? Or is social media a fog or deceptive façade that makes the spectators look like they are becoming as influential as the gladiators?

I have spoken about the scholarship of some important persons and how social media has added to their relevance, drawing them into direct contact with politicians and information about politicians, including making them important in the country's decision-making process. It is convincing enough to say that the role of many of the political critics in the country who write in columns, make online posts, and give critical analyses of issues in papers and scholarly works has not made them go beyond spectatorship. Considering the social media dynamics that have amplified the spec-

42. Rodney Ciboh, "An Exploratory Study of Older Adults⊠ Social Media use and Social Capital in Nigeria," *Athens Journal of Mass Media and Communications* 3, no. 2 (2017): 149-165.

Figure 24.2. "Electoral Violence and Social Media" by Dr. Kazeem Ekeolu. Ballot snatching and citizen social media spectatorship.

tators' roles is reasonable. Truly, social media tend to be accessible to everyone and increase the possibility of a high range of communication across the country. With consistency, it is agreeable that such communicators become more influential in the political space. This explains the spread of several political movements in the country and civic dissidence and how, despite the amplification of the cheers and boos of the spectators, with or without social media, their voices only become louder; it does not promote them to the role of a gladiator, especially in the case of Nigeria. The fact that even the gladiators have taken their fights to the spectators' stand does not mean the spectators are now part of the fighters.

SOCIAL MEDIA AND NATIONAL CONSCIOUSNESS

The strings that tie all levels of political participation in every society is the attention given to political and national issues. However, the level of that attention and actions that back them up define where they should be placed.[43] It is important to also know that what constitutes the stimuli that breed attention does not end at the external factors but personal interests and convictions. However, the Nigerian situation

43. Jan W. van Deth, "What is Political Participation?" *The International Encyclopedia of Political Communication* 49, no. 3 (2016): 349-367.

does not need one to develop personal reasons to be conscious of national and political issues, as these issues often affect or potentially affect everyone. From time immemorial, momentums have been built to allow citizens to develop these attentions, and, in Nigeria, they define the current national interactions.[44] The attention inherent in political participation is no other thing but national consciousness that determines how the citizens interact with their societies.

As political participation is to every democracy, so is national and political consciousness to political participation. What breeds participation are information and knowledge, and what breeds information and knowledge is consciousness about a particular subject matter, such as national issues and concerns. National and political consciousness has been the foundation for different political changes and revolutions in Nigeria and other countries. Social and political events, as well as government policies and performance, have been primary inciters of political and national consciousness, especially in Nigerian history. The use of the media to educate Nigerians, leading to active nationalism, constant criticism, opposition to the military government, and citizens' continuous criticism of the democratic government have accounted for certain shifts in the country's political construction and structures. In certain instances, the public might not need the government to be the source of the stimuli that account for needed consciousness. When notorious issues like economic and security matters keep affecting the citizens, they are expected to be automatically conscious of their political environment as they hope for a change and solution.

From a global vantage point, we could say that the situation in Sri Lanka demonstrates the increase in the people's political consciousness and reactions to issues.[45] This is because decisions and national issues affected them personally, and there was no need for the government to force their consciousness. Sri Lankans suffered from issues similar to those that Nigerians are presently facing. They were hit by inflation above 50 percent. The citizens could not access healthcare, basic needs, and power supply.[46] This incident kept developing momentum that later became unbearable for the citizens and led to a national protest that was taken to the heart of the capital, resulting in an invasion of the government house and the disappearance of the Prime Minister.[47] A similar pattern happened in Nigeria in 2020 when the #EndSARS protest gained global attention.[48]

---

44. Michael Watts, "On Peasant Diffidence: Non-Revolt, Resistance, and Hidden Forms of Political Consciousness in Northern Nigeria, 1900-1945." In *Global Crises and Social Movements: Global Crises and Social Movements*, ed. Edmund Burke (Boulder: Lynne Rienner, 2019), 117-144.

45. Deepak Joseph, "An Overview of Sri Lankan Economic Crisis 2022 and how it Affects India," *International Journal of Recent Advances in Multidisciplinary Topics* 3, no. 4 (2022): 58-59.

46. Ayeshea Perera, "Sri Lanka: Why is the Country in an Economic Crisis?" *BBC News*, July 16, 2022, https://www.bbc.com/news/world-61028138

47. Perera, "Sri Lanka."

48. Usman A. Ojedokun, Yetunde O. Ogunleye, and Adeyinka A. Aderinto, "Mass Mobilization for Police Accountability: The Case of Nigeria's #EndSARS Protest," *Policing: A Journal of Policy and Practice* 15,

No matter how they come, national and political consciousness generate political participation in varying degrees. The sources of this consciousness are numerous, and in the contemporary period, one might not be able to state a single source of national consciousness. Events in society and the media have always been remarkable forces that have increased people's consciousness about their society. It happened in the colonial and military eras, and it is happening now. In the contemporary period, social media have proven to be the major driver of national and political consciousness and has given people the platform to be talkers, listeners, advisers, critics or analysts, even in the convenience of their rooms.[49] The total number of social media subscribers was about 53.15 million in 2022, with a projection of about 103.27 million active users.[50] With such an increasing number of users, the influence of social media on the consciousness of Nigerians in a population of more than 200 million cannot be underestimated.[51]

The influence of social media on political participation in Nigeria, through the creation of national and political consciousness, has come in many ways.[52] It creates an avenue for conversations and sharing of political information.[53] These conversations are often raised among the spectators, influential individuals and media bodies that use the platforms to engage people on political matters. The newspaper companies, television, and radio stations have converted their structures to include social media engagement, thereby raising important topics.[54] In addition, the gladiators use social media to engage them to support and garner social mobilization through several platforms.[55] Certain political campaigns, both by the spectators and gladiators, have been called to mobilize people to participate in national and political matters.[56] Issues of insecurity, kidnapping, terrorism, and elections are of national concern and

no. 3 (2021): 1894-1903.

49. Agger and Ostrom, "The Political Structure," 81-89.

50. Lars Kamer, "Nigeria: Number of Social Media Users 2017-2026," *Statista,* July 21, 2022, https://www.statista.com/statistics/972907/number-of-social-network-users-in-nigeria/

51. Ayuba Y. Keziah, and Panshak Yohanna, "Nigerian Statistical Data and their Trustworthiness," *World Economics* 23, no. 1 (2022): 27-38.

52. Effing, van Hillegersberg and Huibers, "Social Media and Political Participation," 23-35.

53. Kenneth A. Nwafor, Chinedu C. Odoemelam, A. Orji-Egwu, Simon U. Nwankwo and Samuel Nweze, "Social Media and Political Participation in Africa: Issues, Challenges and Prospects." In *Communication and the New Media in Nigeria: Social Engagement, Political Development and Public Discourse,* ed. D. Wilson (Uyo: ACCE, 2013), 64-84.

54. Abdulhameed Kayode Agboola, "The Influence of New Media on Conventional Media in Nigeria," *Academic Research International* 5, no. 4 (2014): 105.

55. Xénia Farkas, and Márton Bene, "Images, Politicians, and Social Media: Patterns and Effects of Politicians' Image-based Political Communication Strategies on Social Media," *The International Journal of Press/Politics* 26, no. 1 (2021): 119-142.

56. Sebastian Stier, Arnim Bleier, Haiko Lietz and Markus Strohmaier, "Election Campaigning on Social Media: Politicians, Audiences, and the Mediation of Political Communication on Facebook and Twitter," *Political Communication* 35, no. 1 (2018): 50-74.

remain major points of discussion on different platforms.[57] The use of social media as a tool for political awareness became prominent in the periods preceding the 2011 elections. It gained more attention in the 2015 elections, and its influence on the electorates has continued to increase till contemporary times.[58]

Information brings consciousness, and social media have proven to be the source of an abundance of needed information.[59] With a tweet or Facebook post, people get first-hand and live information about matters happening in every part of the country. Government failures and performance are also often communicated across the board, and as a result, people get to form their conclusions from the array of facts and information on social media.[60] This has had an indirect link to the mobilization of people to register as voters to combat low youth turnout during elections.[61]

It may be too far-reaching, particularly in the case of Nigeria, to say that individual participation in social media conversations and reactions to issues are merely activities of spectators with nothing to do to change the polity and that those activities, regardless of the amplification provided by social media, equate the commitment and influence of such people with gladiators. Of course, Pius Adesanmi's outcries about the nation's state, Aisha Yesufu's constant lamentations about injustices and travails of Nigerians, Rinu Oduala's daily criticism, and other posts of lamentations from notable users of social media platforms have increased political and national consciousness of the people.[62] Since talking, listening, and voting are the characteristics of the spectators, without definite political action and involvement, they are only just listening and talking, with their awareness of the sanctity of the election increasing proportionately.[63] History has taught that in many instances where such consciousness keeps increasing to a certain stage, some spectators might stop being spectators; as a matter of necessity, they tend to get more involved in powers of change in a way that breeds transformation.[64] In this instance, such a person may decide to be an active politician,

---

57. Tim Highfield, "National and State–Level Politics on Social Media: Twitter, Australian Political Discussions, and the Online Commentariat," *International Journal of Electronic Governance* 6, no. 4 (2013): 342-360.

58. Z.K. Dagona, Haruna Karick and F.M. Abubakar, "Youth Participation in Social Media and Political Attitudes in Nigeria," *Journal of Sociology, Psychology and Anthropology in Practice* 5, no. 1 (2013): 1-7.

59. Christian Fuchs and Marisol Sandoval, eds. *Critique, Social Media and the Information Society* (New York: Routledge, 2014).

60. Temple Uwalaka and Jerry Watkins, "Social Media as the Fifth Estate in Nigeria: An Analysis of the 2012 Occupy Nigeria Protest," *African Journalism Studies* 39, no. 4 (2018): 22-41.

61. Oberiri Destiny Apuke and E.A. Tunca, "Understanding the Implications of Social Media Usage in the Electoral Processes and Campaigns in Nigeria," *Global Media Journal* 16, no. 31 (2018): 1-8.

62. Boluwatife Solomon Ajibola and Temitayo Isaac Odeyemi, "The Legislature as Target and Mediator of Ensuing Outcomes during Social Emergencies: Revisiting Nigeria's #Endsars Protest," *The Theory and Practice of Legislation* (2022): 1-30.

63. Agger and Ostrom, "The Political Structure," 81-89.

64. Tsegyu Santas and John Dogara Ogoshi, "An Appraisal of Mass Media Role in Consolidating Democracy in Nigeria," *African Research Review* 10, no. 1 (2016): 73-86.

a party member, or run for political posts. The messages of political and national consciousness agents on social media truly have greater effects on the citizens, but they remain spectators and transitional at best.

When the spectators get conscious and become important to the blocks of power in the country or ready to kick start a transformative revolution, can they be considered gladiators at that point? The thread of political participation that classified some as gladiators, transitional, and spectators is the influence of society's political environment and how much they can change the course of politics in society. Truly, social media have been effectively employed to instigate massive mobilization for voter registration in Nigeria, as many citizens believe they should not be left behind in deciding the rightful leaders in the next elections. Carnivals and sensitizations from social media have encouraged more voter registration, especially with the likes of Debo Adedayo (Mr. Macaroni), Folarin Falana (Falz), and other celebrities encouraging potential voters to troop out in large numbers. However, where the total number of general voters changes compared to other years and where there is a change of power according to these mobilizations, the mobilizers will remain spectators, except they have direct access to the seats of power.

Truly, social media have created a consciousness that has forced the federal government to change its position on certain issues by reversing prior decisions or making new ones. This is because the political and national consciousness from social media and other sources spread with the speed of light, and questions and agitations from every quarter sometimes choke the government to renege on unfavorable policies. The rate of national and political consciousness that spreads from social media has also developed a new sense of youth resistance to policies and politicians alike, and the country's condition has helped its development.

In 2020, the country experienced one of the biggest modes of youth resistance in history when the youth protested massively against police brutality and other issues. The #EndSARS movement was a result of a momentum built from years of police brutality, and with the positions of social media overlords like Segun Awosanya (Segalink) and other influencers and celebrities, the movement received a boost.[65] The movement changed government policies, forced the government to disband the Special Anti-Robbery Squad (SARS), set up panels, and make new policies to address the citizens' questions.[66] The involvement and participation of Nigerian citizens and especially notable social media influencers and celebrities, may look more than a just-talk-listen-and-complain approach, but it is not participatory enough to make them gladiators from their armchairs.

65. Raphael Abumchukwu Ekwunife, A.O. Ononiwu, Rosemary Effiong Akpan and H.T. Sunday, "EndSARS Protest and Centralized Police System in Nigeria," *Global Encyclopaedia of Public Administration, Public Policy, and Governance*, ed. Ali Farazmand (Switzerland: Springer Nature, 2021).

66. Ojedokun, Ogunleye and Aderinto, "Mass Mobilization for Police Accountability."

If the situation is presented in another political clime outside Nigeria, one could say that there is a steady flow of positive consequences to back the promotion of spectators to gladiators. However, this has not been substantiated by proven facts. The government tends to choose whether the outcries of these individuals should be considered. For instance, when the government banned the use of Twitter in Nigeria for about seven months, the public, especially the youth, criticized the Nigerian government, boycotted the ban, and demanded the lifting of the ban no matter the reasons given by the government. The government refused to listen to these demands until it reached an agreement with the company itself. Without necessarily taking a position on the justifiability of such a ban, it only shows that the power of influence still rests on the shoulders of the politicians and gladiators. Where they wish, they can make any spectator a hero for listening to demands and where they want, they can resolve to make them talk for long. This means that no matter how much the critics and writers, including those mentioned above, call out and influence the public to mount pressure on the government, they are still spectators as the final decisions remain in the coven of the gladiators.

SPECTATORS, CHANGE AND TRANSFORMATION

For a society to be on the right track, it is expected to be on the path of development in all ramifications. Such a society's economic, social, cultural, and infrastructural sectors are expected to take an admired shape to positively affect the general citizens. The welfare of the citizens is the greatest duty of every government, and where these developments do not take place, it is difficult for the citizens to feel like they are living in a good society. Hence, every government is measured by the rate of development that has occurred and how best society's standard of living of the society has increased. The examination, reactions, comments, analyses and appraisal of the performance or failures of the government form a larger part of what constitutes political participation. What the people do about the developmental state and the situation of the government point to their position on the political participation ladder.

The government has to ensure positive change and transformation capable of increasing the standard of living. In Nigeria, the level of infrastructural availability across all areas of the country is not enough to alleviate the people's condition of living of the people. Currently, Nigeria has been borrowing to build more infrastructures, and according to President Muhammadu Buhari, Nigeria needs about $1.5 trillion to reduce the gap of lack of infrastructural development across the country for ten years, a figure that seems to beam no hope.[67] The World Bank Poverty Assessment of Nigeria

---

67. Johnbosco Agbakwuru, "Nigeria Needs $1.5trn in 10-yrs to Bridge Infrastructure Gap—Buhari," *Vanguard Nigeria*, November 2, 2021,

states that in every ten Nigerians, four live below the poverty line. This places Nigeria among the countries with the highest number of poor people globally.[68]

Insecurity, unemployment, educational challenges, and many other problems have plagued Nigeria for so long that many citizens have become part-time activists. Hence, it is expected that the reactions of Nigerian citizens would increase their consciousness, as well as their level of political participation. This explains why individuals have been quite involved in discussions on national situations as they seek solutions and criticize the government for failure to provide needed amenities and development. Farooq Kperogi is a social media personality who has refused to be silent about the nation's plight, blaming the situation on the government and the political blocks. Kperogi examined the recent performance of the Nigerian government's excess crude oil account as of 2015, which is currently left with $376,655.[69] He also lamented that despite spending about $2 billion on security, Nigeria has never been in such an insecure state since the 1967-1970 Civil War.

Through his blog and other platforms, Kperogi always makes opinions on developments in the country and how much the Nigerian government has failed in its duties with an unmatched rate of criticism and protest.[70] The dynamics of social media have contributed to the accessibility of the general public to Kperogi's opinions and raised points of conversation for other spectators. If the level of political participation and Kperogi's consciousness were weighed, he is only one of the few articulate spectators who boo the gladiators. Without an active role in Nigerian politics, the good intentions surrounding his criticisms and articulations make him more of a spectator than a gladiator.

Another remarkable spectator in the Nigerian political space is Jibrin Ibrahim. Ibrahim provides brilliant analyses of the Nigerian situation and recommendations for development. He is a believer in democracy and is always ready to state his opinions on the democratic progress and state of the nation vis-à-vis the contemporary conditions of the country. He has written papers to question Nigerian corruption issues and proffer possible solutions and approaches.[71] He has also made his positions known on the security state of the nation, as well as the practices of democracy and

---

68. The World Bank, "Deep Structural Reforms Guided by Evidence are Urgently Needed to Lift Millions of Nigerians Out of Poverty," *The World Bank,* March 22, 2022, https://www.worldbank.org/en/news/press-release/2022/03/21/afw-deep-structural-reforms-guided-by-evidence-are-urgently-needed-to-lift-millions-of-nigerians-out-of-poverty#:~:text=According%20to%20the%20report%2C%20which,below%20the%20national%20poverty%20line

69. Farooq Kperogi, "These Last Months of Buhari are like a Badly Written Horror Movie," *Notes from Atlanta,* July 30, 2022, https://www.farooqkperogi.com/2022/07/these-last-months-of-buhari-are-like.html.

70. Farooq Kperogi, "Buhari is World's most Successful Mass Hypnotist," *Notes from Atlanta,* July 24, 2022, https://www.farooqkperogi.com/2022/07/buhari-is-worlds-most-successful-mass.html.

71. Pallavi Roy, Kelechi Iwuamadi and Jibrin Ibrahim, *Breaking the Cycle of Corruption in Nigeria's Electricity Sector: A Political Settlements Analysis* (London: SOAS-ACE, 2020).

how the nation fared under military rule.[72] As a believer in democracy, he is among the many Nigerians who always anticipate favorable democratic practices and governance. Like many other columnists, Ibrahim has been dutiful in his role as a spectator through both mass media and social media to make his opinions known.[73]

As an African historian who understands the colonial and post-colonial experience of Nigerian and Africa in general, Moses Ochonu became one of the well-informed Nigerian spectators who could juxtapose the Nigerian situations to other experiences and standards and then put those contemporary experiences in papers to make his positions and opinions about them known.[74] Ochonu has lamented Nigeria's corruption rate from a more critical and analytic approach and holds the Buhari government responsible.[75] His position about the university system, the impacts of the incessant ASUU strike and corruption in the Nigerian educational system have been well articulated, critiqued, and criticized.[76] If Ochonu is a spectator, he is a remarkable one who has discharged his duties passionately and done so remarkably well.

The likes of Pius Adesanmi, Moses Ochonu, Farooq Kperogi, Jibrin Ibrahim, and other academics are not the only ones who understand the state of the nation and can analyze it through a critical lens as social media have provided more opportunities for active spectators who would provide information on the state of the nation, start conversations, and state their opinions about the issues. Many of these people have called for change and transformational development in the country to ensure that the citizens have access to the dividends of democracy. The spectators have garnered reasonable support and those who are disposed to follow their leaders, making them relevant forces in national and political consciousness. The nation's situation has not changed positively, which further increases the tempo of reactions of the people. There are demonstrations by the so-called spectators calling for immediate change in the nation's state.

The question of change and transformation that has preoccupied most of the Nigerian population has emerged in calls for revolutions and other concerning issues. There are emerging issues of secession and accompanying agitations. The Biafra-separationist agenda that caused the Nigerian Civil War in 1967 did not stop in 1970 when it was "officially" stopped; the ideology still lingers. In contemporary times,

---

72. Jibrin Ibrahim and Saleh Bala, *Civilian-led Governance and Security in Nigeria after Boko Haram* (Washington, DC: United States Institute of Peace, 2018).

73. Jibrin Ibrahim, "Things I wish my President knows," *Premium Times,* July 29, 2022, https://www.premiumtimesng.com/opinion/545649-things-i-wish-my-president-knows-by-jibrin-ibrahim.html.

74. Moses E. Ochonu, *Emirs in London: Subaltern Travel and Nigeria's Modernity* (Bloomington: Indiana University Press, 2022). See also, Moses Ochonu, "Colonial Itineraries: Muhammadu Dikko's Metropolitan Adventures," *The Journal of African History* 61, no. 2 (2020): 179-200.

75. Moses E. Ochonu, "Buhari: Corruption Enabler and Defender," *Sahara Reporters,* November 2, 2017, https://saharareporters.com/2017/11/02/buhari-corruption-enabler-and-defender-moses-e-ochonu.

76. Moses. E. Ochonu, "ASUU is a Problem of the Nigerian University System," *Sahara Reporters,* November 6, 2018, https://saharareporters.com/2018/11/06/asuu-problem-nigerian-university-system-moses-e-ochonu.

pro-Biafra separationists have expressed themselves through public engagements, protests, and other mediums, requesting separation and the creation of Biafra as a distinct sovereign state outside Nigeria.[77] Nnamdi Kanu and other pro-Biafra separationists believe that the Igbo have been marginalized and therefore have no rightful place in the Nigerian political structures in a way that would benefit them.[78] Some of these separationists have resorted to violence, reeling out sit-at-home orders and disrupting the Nigerian structures. Nnamdi Kanu and other separationists have moved beyond mere spectators as they have used their consciousness to call for a political separation in a way that is different from what a mere spectator would do.[79]

Similar agitation has emerged in the Southwest, with people like Chief Sunday Adeyemo (Sunday Igboho) demanding the Yoruba Nation that is free from the unnecessary shackles of Nigerian unity. Sunday Igboho declared the Yoruba Nation on March 17, 2020, asking the Yoruba people to be committed to the separationist agenda and how necessary it is to depart from the country.[80] Although Sunday Igboho and others who called for Yoruba secession faced different reactions, his call was born out of the people's travail and how insecurity has turned Nigerians into prey to be hunted by predatory bandits and terrorists.[81]

The call for independent Biafra and Yoruba Nation has become another national concern. If the country and the government perform their duties as and when due, these calls might be unnecessary, as what has brought about these consciousnesses is the state of the nation. As a spectator, Anthony Akinola examined this situation and emphasized the importance of co-existence despite the challenges of diversity to national unity.[82] As Akinola would agree, separationist agitations would always be a threat to the peaceful co-existence of the country and a form of pressure on the government. With the effect of social media and other factors, separationist agitations have raised political questions that put the current administration in more administrative and election troubles.[83]

The Nigerian spectators do not stop talking, listening, and criticizing the government as their forms of political participation. They have been able to make transformative contributions to society without the influence of the government. Nigerians

77. Ayo Osisanwo and Osas Iyoha, "We are not Terrorist, we are Freedom Fighters': Discourse Represen tation of the Pro-Biafra Protest in Selected Nigerian Newspapers," *Discourse & Society* 31, no. 6 (2020): 631-647.

78. Osisanwo and Iyoha, "We are Not Terrorist."

79. Osisanwo and Iyoha, "We are Not Terrorist."

80. Ehizojie Precious Okudaye, Adeline Nkwam-Uwaoma and Blessing Ajirioghene Omoevah, "Textual Analysis of Netizens' Reaction to Sunday Igboho's Declaration of a Yoruba Nation," *Sau Journal of Management and Social Sciences* 4, no. 1 (2022): 28-38.

81. Okudaye Nkwam-Uwaoma and Omoevah, "Textual Analysis of Netizens' Reaction."

82. Anthony Akinola, "Peaceful Coexistence Remains a Dream," *The Guardian*, February 11, 2021.

83. Oxford Analytica, "Separatists Threaten Nigeria Ruling Party's Chances," *Emerald Insight*, September 17, 2021, https://www.emerald.com/insight/content/doi/10.1108/OXAN-DB264189/full/html.

have been offering sponsorship to other citizens, providing healthcare services, taking the role of policing and investigation in certain instances, and extending their hands to carry out the government's duties. Nigerians have started taking the change and transformation duty into their hands, raising sensitization and encouraging developments, especially among the youth. But as these contributions do not include political processes, they do not stand a chance to raise the status of a spectator.

Truly, the basic feature distinguishing a gladiator from a spectator is the ability and power to cause or critically influence change. It is primarily premised on the ability to control and decide the nation's fate and influence those in power to do so through political means. Although spectators might be conscious that they could influence the decisions of those in power, make revolutionary moves, and cause transformation by themselves, their roles are limited to spectatorship. One would not qualify as a gladiator without direct political participation, political control or active partisanship.

SPECTATORS AS NEW NATIONAL STAKEHOLDERS

Milbrath's position categorized citizens' political participation with their activities which is defined according to their level of influence. The gladiators are those in power who seek to secure political seats and belong to political parties. This class includes all political office holders in Nigeria, former office holders, contestants in the 2023 elections, and party members who are close to influencing the state of the country. These gladiators, who might not involve themselves in the critical analyses as others do, are the ones who have the power to transform the country, and when they choose not to, the citizens stand to suffer from their ineptitude. The transitional includes elite business owners and moguls who determine the country's economic situation. They are politicians who do not hold political offices but have the power to directly and heavily influence the decisions of the political officeholders. Gladiators must take the blame. One should not attribute any blame for misgovernance to spectators like Olukotun, Kperogi, Ibrahim or Ochonu.

The evaluation of the spectators from the vantage point of the Milbrath model explains the spectators' roles in voting, influencing voting decisions, and discussing political matters. If we are to judge the participatory level of the likes of Pius Adesanmi, Moses Ochonu, Farooq Kperogi, Ayo Olukotun, Abimbola Adelakun, and others based on what they write and say about the Nigerian government and the situation, without active and direct participation in the Nigerian political processes, they are spectators who do not know where the blades cut, but only throw cheers and boos.

One should not be unaware that the country's current status has raised the level of involvement of the spectators, and their indirect impact on power is becoming highly convincing to those in authority. That is, convincing to those who care to read. Many do not bother to read. The activities of the spectators in contemporary periods have formed pressures that force the government to do certain things. For instance,

the Dapo Abiodun administration in Ogun State attracted nationwide criticism based on alleged underperformance. In July 2022, a picture of students in Iwopin from St. Kizito High School emerged on social media, where students were writing exams without chairs or tables.[84] This picture caused negative reactions from different quarters, the governor was called out, and notable political columnists made their positions known. The issue got sustained attention and widespread engagement on social media; therefore, the governor trended for a while. Shortly after this public outcry, the government succumbed to their demands, directing officials to provide facilities immediately at the school.[85]

The presence of social media and other actors has unquestionably produced new dynamics. People today have millions of followers, many of whom may be influenced and convinced to act in a certain way. This can be seen in the way the social media and social media influencers influenced the trends of the 2020 #EndSARS protest to become a national activity.[86] Also, the government has had reasons to change its decisions on various occasions. However, the balance of political power has not shifted to the spectators, despite new stakeholders being raised among them. These stakeholders are still spectators and cannot be called gladiators as they do not have enough political power to directly impact economic and political transformations.

CONCLUSION

Nigerians have proven to be ready for political criticisms and analyses of the Nigerian situation because the country's challenges have always left enough subjects to discuss. However, the development of certain consciousness among Nigerian citizens has pushed them to become more active as spectators. Some non-partisan citizens have facilitated youth resistance to change the government's decisions and caused the restructuring of certain governmental parastatals. Some have launched campaigns capable of changing the face of the polity. With the level of influence these new stakeholders are exhibiting with the help of social media, their involvement could ultimately impact the Nigerian situation.

This level of participation is encouraging and is evidence of potential hope for the transformation of Nigeria as a country. However, the tendency to complain about things without taking action, raising pressure without follow-up, and criticizing without commitment reduces these active citizens to spectators. As a result, this activeness must translate into greater political control, particularly in raising the number of informed voters.

---

84. Tola Adenubi, "After Tribune Report, Ogun Govt Supplies Desks, Chairs to School," *Nigerian Tribune,* July 19, 2022.

85. Adenubi, "After Tribune Report."

86. Omowale Adelabu, "The Role of Social Media Influencers on the Rise of Youth Activism During the EndSars Campaign," *Escae Journal of Management and Security Studies (EJMSS)* 1, no 1 (2021): 51-66.

25

SOCIAL MEDIA

Dissidence and Critique

INTRODUCTION

Thousands of critics, scholars, columnists, bloggers, and writers have contributed to understanding Nigeria's democratic structures, practices, and problems. Their innovative and enlightening ideas have suggested a broad range of new democratic trajectories—one cannot discuss the entirety of their views, but a few notable individuals have been particularly brilliant examples of precise and resourceful minds. Their personalities and proximity to important themes have made their perspectives especially relevant.

The thematic preoccupations and the contributions of such prominent figures offer a valuable understanding of Nigeria, its politics, and its democratic cultures. Although a discussion of Nigeria that uses the perspectives of these individuals may allow global society to view Nigeria from new angles, such a discussion might also be misconstrued as a propagandist's effort to elevate these individuals to achieve undeserved status. This chapter intends to align the figures with worthy, insightful, and reasonable thoughts, enabling them to prevail over baseless speculations.

The virtue of scholarship lies not in ignoring realistic arguments but in subjecting them to verification and dispassionate inquiries. Despite the previous chapters' efforts to present relevant positions on major themes, one must act as a devil's advocate to critique specific positions and compare contrasting thoughts, identifying which positions can withstand tests of conviction and challenges to their context and state-

Figure 25.1. "TF at a Zoom Meeting" by Michael Efionayi. A depiction of Toyin Falola having a conversation on a Zoom meeting.

ments. These thought-provoking positions have been carefully outlined and discussed, but they should be balanced against the facts presented by opposing voices.

SOCIAL MEDIA AND ITS CONTRADICTIONS

The advent of social media has transformed Nigeria's political space, but it has also created new challenges. As a technology, it has encouraged participatory democracy and kept the government on its toes, encouraging responsibility and transparency. However, social media users have also undermined democracy and democratization by encouraging the proliferation of ethnic demands and rivalries. Separatist agitations have been introduced into public discussions, and many citizens believe that the best outcome for Nigeria would be a dissolution into separate nations: the North for Northerners, the West for the Yoruba, and the East for the Igbo. New nations have been created on the internet with their flags, anthems, and currencies.

These tribalizing narratives are largely presented through secessionist discourse on social media platforms. Such discussions have further widened the chasm between ethnicities and the nation while blocking alternative visions to promote collective growth and development. Many citizens believe Nigeria can no longer function as a single entity, largely due to repeated popular narratives. It raises the question of how

the country has survived for so many years without a return to civil war. Pan-Africanists like me are worried, wondering if the dream of creating a united continent can ever be realized.

Where is the idea that Nigerians are their brother's keepers, and what has happened to the belief that unity and collective efforts would transform our nation? Today's agitations for Biafra and the possibility of demands for the Oduduwa Republic tomorrow suggest that we have all resigned ourselves to the idea that the country cannot thrive as a single entity. The predominance of divisive ethnic discourse on social media platforms has dampened the resolve of many Nigerians committed to the struggle for one Nigeria. We must learn from history.

Nigerians must decide whether their country's myriad problems are sufficient reasons for disbanding it. They must consider whether ethnic nationalism should replace the national consciousness. We must ask whether we have surrendered to pessimistic narratives and believe that nothing good can come from a unified nation. What has happened to our Nigerian spirit—has it been subsumed by social media platforms that favor ethnic nationalism?

Secessionist agitators claim that peaceful national dialogue could hasten the dissolution of Nigeria, and citizens are further exposed to ethnic narratives through social media. However, few discussions have constructively addressed what will happen after disintegration. If everyone agrees that the present country is beyond redemption, has anyone thought about the fate of Nigerians after things are allowed to fall apart? It is unclear whether those at the forefront of ethnic struggles have thought about developmental plans for their newly independent nations. Some agitations are merely pursued to advance the nebulous goal of self-determination.

Every visible indicator suggests that Nigeria is deteriorating, but the challenges of national development would not disappear within breakaway states. Sudan and South Sudan are immediate examples: will the two countries mend their differences or widen them further? Will the countries that split up abandon their old animosities? The Russia–Ukraine war suggests that they may not. The division of Nigeria will not change the behavior of leaders who contribute to the country's rot when the failure of Nigerian leadership cuts across the country's three major regions. When we act, we must consider what the future holds; taking action for its own sake is pointless.

The first transformation that Nigeria should experience is that of its leadership. It will require holistic efforts from all of Nigeria—from every Nigerian who remains deeply committed to the Nigerian project—to achieve an effective leadership structure for the nation. A united citizenry will allow the country to thrive, liberating it from the shackles of aristocratic oligarchs who call themselves national leaders and statesmen.

The fact is that Nigerian politicians often fail to engage in self-reflection; this is why we are ready to accept the premise that ethnonationalism is a valid solution. Ethnic

narratives have dominated social media and the public sphere despite concerned stakeholders' ongoing efforts to keep Nigeria united. Discussions about national development are laced with ethnic consciousness. Some Nigerians claim President Buhari promoted ethnonationalism, accusing him of being a Fulani apologist bent on converting the country to Islam.

Have former presidents, such as Olusegun Obasanjo and Goodluck Jonathan, advocated for every region of Nigeria? Our leaders reinforce ethnic dynamics when they are in office. If the 2023 elections resulted in an Igbo President, it might quench the Biafran agitations because the fact that an Igbo has not led Nigeria is a major grievance driving the wider struggle to achieve a Biafra nation. A Yoruba president who emerged victorious at the polls might silence the agitations for the Oduduwa Republic. But these examples show that Nigeria's fundamental problem is that of ethnic groups exerting dominance over one another. No group wishes to exist as second-class citizens.

Discussions on social media suggested that Buhari would encourage the dominance of the Fulani ethnic group. Was this the case throughout his tenure? Did Fulani herdsmen cause insurgency in the north of the country? Was that part of the country protected against the security concerns and other problems that consume the nation? Nigerians seem eager to accept narratives that circulate through social media to confirm existing biases.

Social media has increased the speed at which fake news circulates. We can argue that social media platforms have helped awaken national consciousness, but we often overlook that fake news has become a national epidemic. A country where citizens are not responsible enough to verify the news they engage with rapidly becomes polarized. Journalists are actively fighting this epidemic, but ongoing challenges remain.

Social media narratives generate much fake news, and research has indicated that some influencers spread fake news to attract more followers, regardless of the harm they cause.[1] Even those who call themselves media scholars can propagate fake news. It is difficult to accept that social media, with its negative sides, could be a useful tool for restoring democracy to Nigeria—fake news spreads rapidly and causes substantial harm. In a country where hostilities are ready to ignite between identities, classes, and religions, the spread of fake news is a powerful incendiary.

Despite warnings that Nigerian social media users should not accept all narratives uncritically, they readily identify with news stories manufactured on social media platforms, preferring them over conventional media platforms. Sensational news and half-truths are consumed daily, and a ready example is the aftermath of the Owo

1. Kelvin Inobemhe, Felix Ugber, I.L. Ojo and Tsegyu Santas, "New Media and the Proliferation of Fake News in Nigeria," *Nasarawa Journal of Multimedia and Communication Studies* 2, no. 2 (2020): 155–169.

Church Attack, which gave rise to a narrative claiming that Fulani herdsmen orchestrated the gruesome murder.

Some online news outlets repeated the false herdsmen narrative, and urgent intervention was necessary to present the truth and restore calm—Ondo State was in danger of being thrown into disarray by rumors that might have served as a springboard for another ethnic war. The ISWAP, it was claimed, perpetrated the attack, and its actions underscore the fact that Nigeria's security challenges are larger than mere ethnic animosity. If we are to keep blaming the Nigerian government for maintaining its authority by leveraging ethnic politics, then we should also acknowledge the role of individuals who disseminate harmful fake news. Nigerians must not rush to accept specific narratives that fit their preferred biases.

Action must be taken to address the misinformation that dominates political discourse on social media. The uncontrolled flow of communication and the free exchange of ideas should not be polluted with fake information. Online activism remains a valid use for social media and encourages political participation. Social media has made the Nigerian government more accountable and transparent. When citizens call out corrupt practices on public platforms, the government will address them, even if it does not address the culture of corruption that has thoroughly permeated Nigeria's political circles.

Social media has assisted with Nigeria's political development, but online activism only transforms the online narratives of Nigeria. Although these activists are catalysts, we cannot fully rely on them to complete the metamorphosis of the nation's political system. Nigerians may need to stage other protests, leading to another denied massacre. Also, they must emphasize political development at the grassroots level.

Nigeria's leadership and its management of resources are so thoroughly corrupt that they will not be fixed overnight. To change the nation's political culture, there must be a deliberate series of intentional developments or little leaps. The question is whether Nigeria's youth, who are at the center of this struggle, are willing to take it one step at a time. Their activity on social media platforms, especially Twitter, suggests that we may have given social media more credit than it deserves. A nation's transformation does not occur solely through social media.

Political discourse on social media can catalyze national development, but more efforts are needed at the local level. Political leaders who want to enact real change cannot rely only on an army of online followers. When political transformation occurs on social media, how does it affect the citizens who do not use social media? Nigeria's 2023 election preparation got Twitter flooded with hashtags like #VoteWisely, and # WeCan'tContinueLikeThis. Not every Nigerian is sold on political transformation; many believe they must eat their share amidst the ruins. As the 2023 election day draws closer, it will not be surprising to see young people who had mounted

campaigns to expel the old leadership turn around and support the people they accused of driving the country to failure.

When writers like Bamidele Ademola-Olateju, Ayo Olukotun, Abimbola Adelakun, Farooq Kperogi, and Anthony Akinola examine how ethnicity has continued to undermine Nigeria's collective growth and development, they often assert that the government is responsible. There is no doubt that ethnicity is a major problem, but the challenge of ethnonationalism that has permeated the country's consciousness may not be the government's fault alone. When Nigerians complain that other groups are attempting to perpetuate ethnic dominance, some only attempt to put their group in power.

There has been a proliferation of secessionist struggles in Nigeria. The Yoruba are agitating for a breakaway state, and so are the Igbo. Both groups fear a Fulani hegemony and the Islamization of Nigeria. After seven years under a Northern leader, this has not happened. If an Igbo President emerges, will the I.P.O.B. arguments continue? The same question can be asked of a Yoruba president. Every group fears ethnic marginalization, which is not solely the government's fault. Ordinary citizens must examine their contributions.

Nigerians frequently mount protests because their own group does not benefit; they are not arguing for a holistic government. At the grassroots level, many citizens have been convinced that each region should go its own way. Popular narratives assert that our founding fathers were not committed to Nigerian nationalism, and they have exacerbated the problem of ethnonationalism. But there has been little discussion of citizenship within the breakaway states. Do Southeast people think that crude oil is the only requirement for self-sufficiency? Do Yoruba agitators believe that brilliant minds are the only component of a nation's prosperity? Discussions of ethnicity often ignore the fact that citizens bear some responsibility.

The government cannot use ethnic politics to maintain power when its citizens are united behind a Nigerian consciousness. The lizards will not play hide and seek if there are no cracks in the wall. Citizens who continue to view their interests from an ethnic perspective will continue to be exploited by their government. The National Youth Service Scheme no longer reflects its original purpose; many members fled the states they were posted to because of ethnic animosity. South-westerners have become strangers in the East. When we talk about ethnicity, we must ask how it has become so prominent at the grassroots level, asking how citizens became convinced that Nigeria must dissolve to prosper.

We cannot solely blame the government, and we should not look for solutions that solely rely on the government. The contest among Nigeria's three presidential candidates shows the predominance of ethnic politics—putting aside the merits of individual candidates, it remains clear that support for the three of them has been drawn along ethnic lines. When ethnicity comes into play, it is difficult to remain free from

bias. The current thinking is that specific individuals deserve the presidency because they are from specific sections of the country: does this sound like a meritocracy? The country needs an astute, visionary president who can improve the fate of every Nigerian. When writers suggest that the government must address ethnic rivalries, their suggestions are inadequate. Citizens have a major role to play in eradicating this menace and must be included in the struggle.

Some have suggested that national development and an end to ethnic rivalry can be found in adopting true federalism, but these ideas ignore an important point. Federalism would mean that each region or state is autonomous and responsible for its development, which is a framework that encourages ethnic loyalties. In the early years of Nigeria's independence, the competition between the three regions was closer to struggles for ethnic supremacy than efforts for collective national growth and development. And that was when ethnic tensions were less intense than they are today.

Federalism itself cannot bring about automatic solutions. Now that most Nigerians are ethnically conscious, attempts at federalism would strengthen ethnonationalism. What would be the consequences? If it brings security and development, all is well and good. However, there will be lingering issues. The central government cannot assume responsibility for the development of every state, and it should not be the only justification for federalism. State governments demand state police, but they want those forces to be funded by the federal government. The states must look for resources to fund their police forces. In the face of these demands, the federal government should give the state governors the right to exercise power and authority as the Chief Security Officers of their states.

If the regional security outfits, such as the Hisbah in the North, Ebubeagu in the East, and Amotekun in the West, were lenses from which we should view federalism, how could we harness a Nigerian consciousness? The federal system was dismantled by Aguiyi–Ironsi because it bred ethnic affiliations, although that failed to solve the problem. Discourses on adopting federalism must include conscious attempts to recognize how it would affect the Nigerian consciousness. Restructuring must bring peace and development.

Writers like Moses Ochonu, Ayo Olukotun, Jibrin Ibrahim, Abimbola Adelakun, and Bamidele Ademola-Olateju have discussed how ongoing corruption has convinced citizens that there are no true dividends of democracy. These narratives present the government as the sole perpetrator of corruption, and bad leadership begins at the top. Although these arguments are valid, they do not address the full extent of Nigeria's corruption. Not only is the government corrupt, the citizens willingly enable corruption. It is a problem perpetuated by the state and the people; corruption could not thrive without active participation from both groups. However, these discussions focus on leadership positions and ignore corruption at the grassroots level.

As the government exploits the state's wealth, the citizens scavenge what they can from the wreckage. In a system known in pidgin as "chop-make-I-chop" politics,

those who aim for political offices have only done so to participate in corrupt practices. There is no longer a mandate to serve the public interest; politicians scramble to enrich themselves. The eradication of corruption should not be limited to the government alone—it will require holistic measures that address every tier of government.

Nigeria's corruption did not begin on a grandiose scale and must be removed locally and nationally. When government initiatives attempt to end corrupt practices, they fail to eradicate the problem. The narrative is that corruption has eaten deep into the fabric of Nigerian society, suggesting that it is beyond the government's reach. Reports of citizens siphoning funds are additional corruption instances, and no strong institution possesses the will and capability to fight corruption in Nigeria. The E.F.C.C., I.C.P.C., and other agencies are hardly immune from corruption.

When writers explore the issue of bad governance, they focus solely on the government, ignoring their enablers in public. People assert that Nigerian leaders nurture a culture of lies, making promises they cannot keep. Extensive discussions about the challenge of bad leadership have highlighted political lies as a fundamental problem. This exonerates the people who willingly believe such transparent falsehoods. The government does not elect itself. When governments fail, the citizens declare that they will do better during the next election. The next election repeats its mistakes, which leads to renewed pledges to vote even more responsibly. Each mistake is blamed on the government, and the Nigerian citizenry refuses to accept that they could be enabling bad governance.

When candidates are rebranded and presented to the public, the citizens do not subject them to much scrutiny. Voters focus on dismissing an incumbent government that has lost popular support, paying little attention to the replacements. Citizens reserve every right to scrutinize candidates and assess their records, but this is difficult and burdensome in a country where we do not know the value of history. Nigerian citizens support short-term plans over long-term solutions. That is no way to elect effective leaders; the country's problems cannot be resolved quickly.

If Nigeria has not supported effective leadership, its citizens should admit their responsibility. They have the exclusive power to elect people who can represent their interests, and their decisions must be based on meritocratic principles. However, meritocracy is often sacrificed at the altar of ethnic politics and religious conflict. Discussions about Nigeria's leadership structure are often derailed by citizens who contend that a specific "tribe" deserves to rule. Has Nigeria equated "tribalism" with meritocracy? If groups are the current measure of success, we must look beyond ethnic loyalties to solve the challenge that undermines the entire nation's growth and development.

Nigerians keep falling into the same avoidable trap. The nation is excited about its next general election, and even in the early stages of the contest, we see decisions being made due to ethnicity and religion. Meritocracy is absent from current electoral discussions. Anger, especially among the youth, is focused on removing a govern-

ment that has incapacitated the public, but there is no search for a permanent solution to the nation's ongoing leadership problem. Many Nigerians believe that the solution to bad governance merely involves the selection of leaders who are not from any major political parties.

Writers have identified the need for a third force in Nigeria's political structure, which would be a radical departure from A.P.C. and P.D.P. But will this genuinely solve Nigeria's governance problems? It seems unlikely that a nation's political structure will be immediately transformed due to the presence of a third party. Politicians have a history of crossing the carpet to retain power, and the emergence of a third force would offer new opportunities for selfish bureaucrats.

Grassroots revitalization is required because long-term leadership problems will not be solved by the emergence of a third political party. Nigerian politicians change color like chameleons to stay in power. A third force cannot enact much change when Nigeria's worst political actors can easily join its ranks. Politicians like Dino Melaye and Femi Fani-Kayode are not interested in joining a new force to reshape Nigeria's political structure as the question they will pose is: where is power located to make money?

Moses Ochonu has described the challenge of university education in Nigeria and tertiary education by extension. As a scholar in the Diaspora, Ochonu was captivated by the rich knowledge he currently accuses the Nigerian university system of losing. There seems to be a lack of new knowledge produced by universities; Nigerian graduates lag behind their foreign counterparts. Ochonu's passionate suggestions may ameliorate the falling standards of Nigeria's university system, but he has recommended that universities charge higher fees. This would make a university education unattainable for poor students unless there is a scholarship or loan system.

What happens to students who attend polytechnic schools in a society where even university graduates struggle to get jobs? Student loans can help support students seeking university education, but there are questions about how these loans would be repaid. In a country with rising unemployment rates, these students will struggle to find jobs that allow them to pay off their loans. Realistic repayment plans must accompany any proposal to offer student loans—it is not guaranteed that the government, or any agency making loans, would automatically reduce Nigeria's unemployment rate.

Beyond universities, we must consider whether polytechnics are free from the rot that has corrupted Nigeria's tertiary education system. There must be deliberations considering technical education and its relevance in the country's tertiary education system. By focusing solely on university education, we have ignored the plight of other tertiary institutions.

Scholars have largely blamed the Academic Staff Union of Universities (A.S.U.U.) for its incessant industrial strikes that have applied orthodox thinking and yielded

little results. The Union allegedly ignores reports of lecturers involved in academic corruption, which supports broader arguments asserting that corruption has become institutionalized in the university system. But university lecturers are not employees of A.S.U.U. Even if the union has looked the other way, the government can take measures to prevent corrupt practices. If A.S.U.U. is ineffective, what about the government that provides funding for universities? Government action must be part of any solution to remove corruption from the nation's educational system.

SOCIAL MEDIA: EXAGGERATED INFLUENCE AND DANGERS

Social media has introduced a radical change to Nigerian society. It has become a major component of Nigerian societies, and the influence of social media, social constructions, new culture, and social themes are part of any discussion about public development. Social media has introduced new influences to Nigerian society, and it is important to study its dynamics. However, despite its widespread adoption by the public, society has largely used social media for regressive activities. The negativity has become too obvious to ignore. Despite its ability to drive major changes and the involvement of prominent figures who have used it to address Nigeria's situation, we must resist the allure of destructive behavior.

Social media is vulnerable to falsehoods and unverifiable information, making it easy for propagandists to exploit. Issues are either blown out of proportion or taken out of context to shape public sentiment for destructive ends. The ease of creating social media accounts has made it simple to distribute lies and misinformation to confuse society. Computer programs run automated accounts to flood social media spaces with disinformation and push specific agendas.[2]

Algorithmic accounts and deliberate propagandists have manipulated pictures and video evidence to make persuasive arguments that are distorted and used out of context for malicious reasons. Studies of the 2016 United States Election exposed about 19 million false accounts designed to influence election results with impressions of acceptability and popularity.[3] Even without this interference, users propagate information to support their own biases, creating echo chambers that are strengthened by their engagement with sympathetic social media feeds.[4]

Social media spaces are especially vulnerable to misdirection when the public is already suspicious of the government. Nigerians have used social media to criticize the government and vent their concerns about policies, bills, and initiatives, which have created fertile ground for unverified anti-government posts to flourish. The Ni-

2. Kai Shu and Huan Liu, *Detecting Fake News on Social Media* (Switzerland: Springer Nature, 2022).

3. Shu and Liu, *Detecting Fake News*.

4. Matteo Cinelli, Gianmarco De Francisci Morales, Alessandro Galeazzi, Walter Quattrociocchi, and Michele Starnini, "The Echo Chamber Effect on Social Media," *Proceedings of the National Academy of Sciences* 118, no. 9 (2021): 1-8.

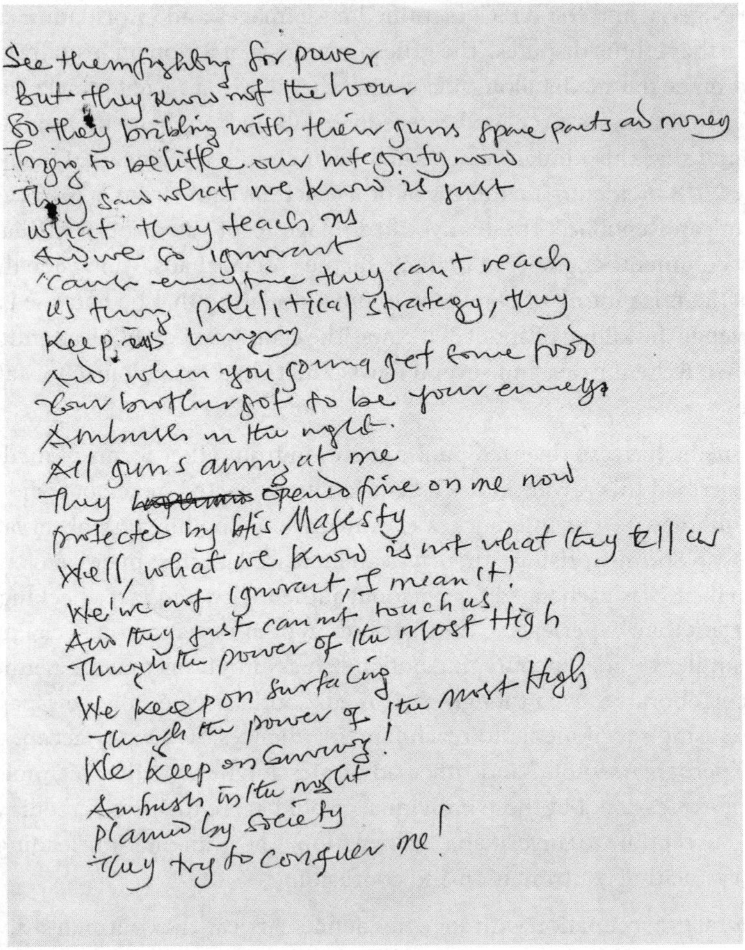
See them fighting for power
But they know not the hour
So they bribing with their guns spare parts and money
Trying to belittle our integrity now
They say what we know is just
what they teach us
And we so ignorant
'Cause everytime they can't reach
us they using political strategy, they
Keep us hungry
And when you gonna get some food
Your brother got to be your enemy
Ambush in the night
All guns aiming at me
They opened fire on me now
protected by His Majesty
Well, what we know is not what they tell us
We're not ignorant, I mean it!
And they just cannot touch us
Through the power of the Most High
We keep on surfacing
Through the power of the Most High
We keep on surviving!
Ambush in the night
Planned by society
They try to conquer me!

Figure 25.2. "Ambush in the Night" by Bob Marley. Lyrics of "Ambush in the Night" by Bob Marley.

gerian government's continuous hostility, such as its 2021 ban on Twitter, and the consistent activities of social media influencers, have made people more willing to accept misinformation.

Public sentiments criticize the government's position and actions, but that does not mean that every anti-government message is credible. During the 2020 #EndSARS protests, the atmosphere was especially tense due to public grievances about police brutality and other forms of governmental excess. This encouraged several videos and images to be taken out of context. The result was a series of disagreements over the veracity of online information, which involved the Nigerian army, the public, the government, news agencies, and international authorities.

The speed at which information circulates on social media has allowed fake news to increase societal tensions. In 2018, several attacks and inter-communal crises oc-

curred in Nigeria, and the B.B.C. identified false images and information capable of inciting further ethnic disputes. The gruesome image of a woman brutally killed was published on social media alongside claims that it was a recent attack. Pictures of around six victims were circulated, allegedly resulting from herdsmen's attacks.[5] The B.B.C. found that the woman's image had been circulating since 2011, seven years before the 2018 incident. The images of other victims came from a 2015 accident in the Dominican Republic.[6] These unverified images captivated social media, accompanied by comments engineered to incite further social chaos. Alongside these incidents was the misquoting of Danladi Circoma, declaring that he had used some attacks to avenge the killing of about 300 cows. The claim gained online attention before it was shown to be untrue, and several news outlets had to apologize for taking it at face value.

Social media has also diverted public attention from other forms of media. Kperogi has described this revolution as a demotic turn enacted by people who have decided to embrace it.[7] His inference was drawn from Chouliaraki's observation that after the Arab Spring uprisings, there was an increased interest in citizen journalism. Professionalism was exchanged for personal authenticity, and fact-checking became less important than experience.[8] The distribution of information on social media has followed similar trends, encouraging outlandish assumptions that are neither verifiable nor corroborated, even though most media outlets, especially newspaper companies, are using social media to reach larger audiences.[9] One may accept the positions of Kperogi, Asemota, and other advocates for new media, technology, and freedom of expression, but these individuals would agree that social media and new media are susceptible to unverifiable information. They can offer misleading and inflammatory, inciting confrontation and confusion.

Its cultural preoccupation with societies defines Africa. The continent's diversity of customs and societal practices make it different from other parts of the world. This diversity has supported the concepts of pan-Africanism, Afrocentrism, and the Africanization of institutions and societies. Despite its other developmental contributions, social media has been a force that neutralizes those ideas and modifies them to suit the ideologies of globalization. A global village is appealing but should not be attained at the expense of the cultural identities that define people. The globalizing processes of colonialism and the trans-Atlantic slave trade were direct attacks on

5. BBC News, "Fake News and Nigeria's Herder Crisis," *BBC*, June 29, 2018, https://www.bbc.com/news/world-africa-44655148.

6. BBC News, "Fake News and Nigeria's Herder Crisis."

7. Farooq Kperogi, "Social Media and the Demotic Turn in Africa's Media Ecology," *History Compass* 20, no. 2 (2022): e12711.

8. L. Chouliaraki, "Digital Witnessing in War Journalism: The Case of Post-Arab Spring Conflicts," *Popular Communication: The International Journal of Media and Culture* 13, no. 2 (2015):105–119.

9. Ignatius Obi Edogor, Alice Aladi Jonah and Lucky Idowu Ojo, "Influence of Social Media on Youths' usage of Traditional Mass Media in Nigeria," *New Media and Mass Communication* 31, no. 1 (2014): 55-61.

African cultural orientations, but without them, the ideas of pan-Africanism may not have been such an integral part of Africa's post-colonial struggles. Those corrosive forces may have stopped working to erode cultural identities, but social media has become another force capable of erasing the continent's identity and cultures.

Cultural boundaries often define questions of identity, sexuality, and social status. No matter how attractively Western civilization may redefine these themes, it cannot orient them within an African cultural context. These sensitive issues are widely discussed through social media, but the technology has done little to provide an African orientation. Without considering the merits of specific identities, sexualities, or roles, we must discuss how societies adapt to these ideas in the contemporary world. Social media propagates new ideologies so aggressively that it does not allow African societies to synchronize with these foreign concepts more gradually and does not readily present an approach for Africanizing them. Social media has little regard for existing attitudes or cultural integration.

It is easy to attack the Nigerian government's approach to social media, but the motivations behind its approach must be considered. Social media often creates conflict between the right to free expression and other human rights. People also find it difficult to resolve conflicts between freedom of expression and social order while protecting the right to coexist peacefully. Sections 39 and 45 of the 1999 Constitution states:

> 39 (1) Every person shall be entitled to freedom of expression, including freedom to hold opinions and to receive and impart ideas and information without interference.
> 45 (1) Nothing in sections 37, 38, 39, 40 and 41 of this Constitution shall invalidate any law that is reasonably justifiable in a democratic society
> (a) in the interest of defense, public safety, public order, public morality or public health; or
> (b) for the purpose of protecting the rights and freedom of other persons.[10]

Everyone enjoys the right to freedom of expression, but the government must ensure that such rights do not infringe on the rights of other individuals.

Symbolic, verbal, or written attacks that undermine the rights of others must be regulated. However, social media makes it difficult to enact such regulation, leaving it to the discretion of individual platform owners. This makes it easier to disparage others based on religion, politics, race, ethnicity, or gender. The government must be able to moderate expressions that encourage division, incite violence, assist terrorism, or enable other malicious consequences, but it must do so without abusing the rights of individuals.

10. Constitution of the Federal Republic of Nigeria, 1999. C23 L.F.N. 2004

Although people should be allowed to publicly challenge despotic regulations and unwarranted government censorship, even Kperogi and others would agree that the scope of digital dissent and resistance must be seen not only from the euphoria of a "reverse panoptic gaze"[11] but also from a view that respects the rights of others. Kperogi has indirectly suggested the solution in the following excerpt:

> "Hate speech" bills are being enacted in many countries on the continent even though the bills, such as in Nigeria, are fundamentally rooted in, and nurtured by, crass and deep-seated ignorance of the very meaning of "hate speech."[12]

Instead of abandoning the provisions of hate speech regulation or other reasonable regulatory instruments, energy should be directed toward controlling governmental excess in implementing those bills.

Kperogi has observed that social media has created a reverse panoptic gaze that allows society to access and criticize the government's activities and policies. It serves as a platform for unrestricted, public discussions about Nigeria's need for good governance.[13] Social media has been an effective instrument for correcting the prebendal tendencies of Nigerian government officials, giving some hope that it can return Nigerian democracy to its written tenets.[14] It has expanded the scope of governance and opened the polity to the idea of wider citizen participation, heralding the idea of netizenship.[15] Social media offers a chance to redefine contemporary politics, but will it be effective in Nigeria? Social media's effectiveness at sensitizing and mobilizing people towards specific goals should be acknowledged; it is one of its greatest attributes and has been used to consolidate Nigerian democratic practices.[16]

The #OccupyNigeria protest of 2012 was one of the earliest large-scale social media interventions in Nigerian politics. Public protests opposed increasing fuel prices and decreasing living standards, turning Facebook, Twitter, blog posts, and BlackBerry messages into additional venues for their activity. President Jonathan's administration eventually succumbed to these online and in-person protests. It was a democratic statement about the development of Nigerian democracy, but it also demonstrated the effectiveness of these tools for politicians and propagandists. They now use social

---

11. Farooq A. Kperogi, *Digital Dissidence and Social Media Censorship in Africa* (Oxfordshire: Taylor & Francis, 2022).

12. Kperogi, *Digital Dissidence and Social Media*, 11.

13. Kperogi, *Digital Dissidence and Social Media*, 11.

14. Richard Joseph, *Democracy and Prebendal Politics in Nigeria* (Cambridge: Cambridge University Press, 2014).

15. Akeem Amodu, "Prebendalism and Netizenship: Critical Notes on Good Governance and the Social Media in Nigeria," *International Journal of Research in Social Sciences* 7, no. 12 (2017): 1-11.

16. Adegboyega I. Ajayi and Samson A. Adesote, "The Social Media and Consolidation of Democracy in Nigeria: Uses, Potentials and Challenges," *African Journal of Sustainable Development* 6, no. 1 (2016): 93-112.

media to distribute political materials, which was seen in the 2019 elections. Social media's role in broader social issues can be seen in the 2020 #EndSARS protests, which started on social media.

These tools are remarkable and instrumental for the successful practice of democracy, but they are far too vulnerable to political manipulation. Although many are enthusiastic about the potential of social media, it also has the potential to be destructive. The spread of misinformation can easily overwhelm public opinion, mobilizing citizens to pursue goals that are deliberate attempts to harm Nigerian democracy. Issues relating to secessionism and other delicate subjects can quickly become divisive if the public wields the strength of social media without the wisdom of restraint.

Social media has become a major instrument for political propaganda. Although it allows individuals to demand good governance, these criticisms can also be manipulated for political gain. The #OccupyNigeria protest in 2012 attracted prominent opposition members eager to exploit the situation to their advantage. The amplifying effects of bots and trolls have the potential to drown out honest political criticism.

Social media platforms are increasingly used for organized crime and terrorism worldwide, and Nigeria is no exception. Malicious actors have created websites and dedicated servers that use social media to coordinate their operations.[17] Cybercrime, recruitment, financing, and operational planning are carried out online. The Kenya Westgate Mall attack of 2013, which lasted from September 21 to September 24, made a mockery of global security forces; Al-Shabaab held Kenya's security for ransom in the mall.[18] The incident drew local and international attention, and Twitter became a major venue for communication. Governments, local and international media outlets, the public, and terrorists used Twitter to share information and gather intelligence. Within four days of the attack, Al-Shabaab published 258 tweets to claim credit and coordinate their actions.[19]

To date, social media has not had a direct connection with the activities of Boko Haram, the major terrorist group that militates against peaceful co-existence in Nigeria. This may be due to their aversion to Western civilization and the higher level of illiteracy in northern Nigeria.[20] However, secessionists have gained support on such platforms and created groups to influence public sentiment. The spread of misinfor-

---

17. I. Nsudu and E.C. Onwe, "Social Media and Security Challenges in Nigeria: The Way Forward," *World Applied Sciences Journal* 35, no. 6 (2017): 993-999.

18. Rachel Sullivan, "Live-Tweeting Terror: A Rhetorical Analysis of @HSMPress_Twitter Updates during the 2013 Nairobi Hostage Crisis," *Critical Studies on Terrorism* 7, no. 3 (2014): 422-433.

19. Tomer Simon, Avishay Goldberg, Limor Aharonson-Daniel, Dmitry Leykin and Bruria Adini, "Twitter in the Cross Fire—the use of Social Media in the Westgate Mall Terror Attack in Kenya," *PloS ONE* 9, no. 8 (2014): 1-11.

20. Joseph Olukayode Akinbi, "Examining the Boko Haram Insurgency in Northern Nigeria and the Quest for a Permanent Resolution of the Crisis," *Global Journal of Arts, Humanities and Social Sciences* 3, no. 8 (2015): 32-45.

mation to incite violence and encourage ethnic profiling, coupled with the exposure of sensitive information, are ways in which social media can compromise Nigeria's security.

Another question is whether social media's influence is exaggerated in Nigeria's democratic and political discourse. The 2019 elections were preceded by widespread agitation against the Buhari government, largely through social media. It was assumed that he would lose the elections based on this activity, but the online opinions did not translate into offline action. A study of social media sentiments around the 2019 election shows that Buhari had more critics than supporters, which would have reduced his chances of winning if the decision had been up to these platforms. However, Nigeria's electoral process did not reflect similar sentiments.[21]

Social media agitation for the primary candidacy of A.P.C. and P.D.P. nominees never matched the reality of internal party election results.[22] Agitations for zoning changes, especially among P.D.P., and opposition to the A.P.C. Muslim–Muslim ticket on social media may not necessarily translate into results at the polls.[23] Policy dissidence, political agitation, and social media trends seldom affect the outcome of Nigeria's political system because the system relies on physical processes. After Atiku Abubakar, the P.D.P. presidential candidate noted that 90% of Northerners are not active social media users, he faced heavy backlash in the media.[24] This criticism is understandable, but Atiku's representation might not be far from the truth, especially considering the illiteracy and technological apathy in the North.

In other parts of Nigeria, many older citizens are not active on social media platforms. This is linked to regional access to technology and the overall use of social media. Out of about 210 million people, only 32.9 million Nigerians were active users of any social media platform as of January 2022. This is less than 20% of the general public, which raises questions about the overall influence of social media.[25] Kperogi has explained the emerging dynamics of social media in politics and social structures:

---

21. Oladapo Oyebode and Rita Orji, "Social Media and Sentiment Analysis: the Nigeria Presidential Election 2019," Paper read at the 2019 IEEE 10th Annual Information Technology, Electronics and Mobile Communication Conference (IEMCON), Vancouver, British Columbia, Canada, 2019, 0140-0146.

22. Nene V. Ugorji, "Party Primary Elections and Democratic Development in Nigeria: PDP and APC in Focus," *African Journal of Social and Behavioral Sciences* 12, no. 1 (2022): 158-172.

23. Kelvin Inobemhe, Galadima Audu Bala, Onakpa Mohammed Shaibu, Kingsley Inalegwu Onah and Tsegyu Santas, "Assessing the Pros and Cons of Political Communication and the Politics of Power Rotation in Nigeria," *Thoughts on Political Communication in Nigeria*, eds. Ezekiel S. Asemah, Daniel O. Ekhareafo and Tsegyu Santas (Enugu: GO University Press, 2022), 271.

24. Idowu Abdullahi, "Backlash Trails Atiku's Northern Social Media Users' Claim," *The Punch*, July 22, 2022.

25. Doris Dokua Sasu, "Total Number of Active Social Media Users in Nigeria from 2017 to 2022 (in Millions)," *Statista*, August 17, 2022, https://www.statista.com/statistics/1176096/number-of-social-media-users-nigeria/#:~:text=Number%20of%20active%20social%20media%20users%20in%20Nigeria%20 2017%2D2022&text=As%20of%20January%202022%2C%20Nigeria,social%20media%20platforms%20 in%20Nigeria.

> In the last decade, social media platforms, particularly Facebook, Twitter, WhatsApp, and Instagram, have emerged as the most consequential spaces for sociality, civic engagement, public opinion formation and accretion, critical democratic citizenship, citizen and traditional journalism, social movements, identity assertion, and dissidence against oppressive governments across Africa. The inexorably progressive intensification of Internet penetration in the continent will ensure that this will be an abiding feature of the continent's media ecology for the foreseeable future.[26]

Society is adapting to the introduction of social media, and its dynamics affect democratic and political structures. However, social media has not yet substantially affected Nigeria's political issues.

UNCELEBRATED VICTORIES OF THE NIGERIAN GOVERNMENT

The Nigerian government has always been criticized for ineptitude, anti-people policies, undemocratic activity, ineffective actions, high costs of living, and many other failures. Every government's duties are the welfare of its citizens and the development of its country; it holds territory in trust for its people, and the people expect it to be managed well. The public failings of the Nigerian government have prevented it from enjoying positive public sentiment. Bad leadership, corruption, and favoritism have become the country's Achilles heel and defining characteristics.

Public outcry is necessary for countries with high costs of living, dreadful security problems, unemployment, dysfunction, educational crises, high rates of illiteracy, and insufficient infrastructure. Democratic societies must react to governmental decisions, and positive and negative reactions should be expected. The question is whether negative comments and criticism are all that is possible with the Nigerian government. Have its officials been so ineffective that no major accomplishments can be identified?

The claims and complaints of many critics—apart from falsifications and deliberate attempts at misinformation—are true. Nigeria's contemporary situation is one where the government has failed at almost every responsibility, and there is an urgent need for decisive action. Complaints about these issues indicate that the Nigerian government has done little or nothing. Regardless of the reason, Nigerian scholars, critics, and prominent figures have readily crucified the government for failing to meet the public's expectations. In one of his articles, the late Pius Adesanmi described the Buhari government:

26. Kperogi, "Social Media and the Demotic Turn," 3.

> Part of Buhari's tragedy is his moral and ethical emptiness. If you look at the last three years, there is no positive symbolic thing that he ever did that was not coerced. Look at how long it took him to reluctantly fire the corrupt grass cutter – his friend who is still cavorting with him. Buhari must be dragged kicking and screaming to do the right thing and that is why Nigeria has literally collapsed on his head.[27]

In 2018, Adesanmi assessed the Buhari administration's handling of Nigerian security as having "…ranged from callous insouciance to depraved, snail speed lip service…."[28] Adesanmi was one of many writers who believe the Nigerian government has been less than effective.

Abimbola Adelakun, in her article on the 2020 #EndSARS protest, stated:

> It is bad enough that Nigeria faces myriad woes of insecurity and deepening poverty, but it is even far worse that we lack a government invested enough in social development to offer anything other than occasional cosmetic changes.[29]

In another assessment of the Buhari administration's performance, which she titled, "#Twitterban: Nigerian Leaders do not Believe in Nigeria," Adelakun described Nigeria's situation as a "very dark phase."

Jibrin Ibrahim agreed with the broader opinion of the Buhari government, stating that the presidency and the government seemed tired, ultimately suggesting that Buhari was anticipating his retirement to Daura.[30] The opinions of other critics, including the prominent figures discussed above, openly expressed displeasure at the state of Nigeria and asked what the government would do about it. Farooq Kperogi and others did not limit this leadership crisis to Buhari alone, suggesting that the blame should be shared with previous administrations.

Despite these opinions and factual criticisms of the Buhari government, or previous governments, these administrations have used their voices to announce their successes. As the government officials announced, the president and various governments deployed the Nigerian Army and other security operatives to address armed threats, and these forces have faced life-threatening situations. In 2019, the Buhari administration launched a National Security Strategy similar to 2014, creating a blue-

---

27. Pius Adesanmi, "An Excellent Case for Buhari's Second Term," *Premium Times*, April 10, 2018.

28. Pius Adesanmi, "Shit and the Sum(mary) of a Presidency," *Premium Times*, February 6, 2018, https://opinion.premiumtimesng.com/2018/02/06/shit-and-the-summary-of-a-presidency-by-pius-adesanmi/.

29. Abimbola Adelakun, "#EndSARS, and a Government's Perennial Failure," *The Punch*, October 21, 2021.

30. Jibrin Ibrahim, "Nigeria on the Edge," *Premium Times*, August 5, 2022, https://www.premiumtimesng.com/opinion/547029-nigeria-on-the-edge-by-jibrin-ibrahim.html.

print to salvage Nigeria's deteriorating security situation. This strategy intended to create a rescue mission that could lift the country out of its security quagmire, officials claimed, protect its sovereignty, and provide peaceful living conditions while ensuring territorial integrity and the ability to control future security threats.[31]

On May 11, 2021, the Buhari administration informed the nation that the presidency had designed and approved new security measures to address security issues in the Southeastern and Southern parts of the nation.[32] The details of these measures were never disclosed, but the announcement confirmed the president's support. On July 9, 2022, the president called a security meeting to discuss the prevalent, unrelenting attacks on citizens. These meetings, strategies, and measures signaled the administration's interest in appearing ready to make efforts and tackle pressing issues, regardless of their actual outcome.

Buhari used public celebrations to highlight some of his achievements in office. At the Democracy Day celebration on June 12, 2020, Buhari recounted his security accomplishments, stating:

> All the Local Governments that were taken over by the Boko Haram insurgents in Borno, Yobe and Adamawa have long been recovered and are now occupied by indigenes of these areas who were hitherto forced to seek a living in areas far from their ancestral homes.
>
> The total collapse of the economies of these areas, which constituted a threat to our food security, has also been reversed with the gradual recovery of farming and other economic activities.[33]

These farming activities were discussed in the following year's address. At the 2021 Democracy Day celebration, President Buhari listed some of the commendable steps that his administration had made for agricultural development. One such achievement was the Anchor Borrowers Programme, which reduced Nigeria's food import expenses from US$2.23 billion in 2014 to less than US$600 million by the end of 2018. He stated that the cost of rice imports had decreased from US$1 billion to US$18.5 million.[34] These savings were achieved by producing consumable products locally and achieving self-reliance through agricultural production. President Buhari also

31. Mukhtar Ya'u Madobi, "A Deep Look at Nigeria's Security Challenges," *Nigerian Tribune*, January 21, 2022.

32. Nasir Ayitogo, "Buhari Approves New Security Measures for South-East, South-South," *Premium Times*, May 11, 2021, https://www.premiumtimesng.com/news/headlines/460906-buhari-approves-new-security-measures-for-south-east-south-south-official.html.

33. Muhammadu Buhari, "Text of President Muhammadu Buhari's 2020 Democracy Day Address," *The Guardian*, 12 June, 2020.

34. Buhari, "Text of President Muhammadu."

launched other initiatives to benefit small and medium businesses, facilitating their growth across the country.[35]

In addition to revitalizing Nigeria's agricultural sector, the president declared that steps had been taken toward a stronger economy. A CBN-BOI N200 billion facility allegedly strengthened 60 industries and created 890,000 job opportunities across the country. Ginneries' utilization of Nigerian textiles increased to around 90%, up from 30% after a CBN N50 Billion intervention.[36] The presidency claimed that progress had been made in shifting away from an oil-based economy, with the sector contributing to about 90% of G.D.P. in the first quarter of 2021. By the end of 2020, N324 billion had allegedly been disbursed to about 136,000 micro, small, and medium enterprises, which was expected to affect the country's economic performance.[37] But how have the government's economic interventions affected individual citizens?

The government insisted that it made some progress with the development of infrastructure, although many parts of Nigeria still need infrastructure investment to support growth for businesses and individuals. On March 24, 2022, Minister of Works and Housing, Babatunde Fashola, claimed that the Second Niger Bridge was already 91% complete and expected to open in the near future.[38] The Minister added:

> The Lagos-Ibadan expressway will be delivered this year, subject to how we navigate the pricing issues. Second Niger Bridge also this year, while the main carriageway of Abuja-Kaduna-Zaria-Kano expressway is scheduled for completion by the second quarter of 2023 before the president leaves office at the end of his tenure.[39]

The President also announced a ₦15 trillion capital structure to accelerate Nigerian infrastructural development under Infraco Plc.

Railway projects were some of the government's most noticeable infrastructure successes. The Lagos–Ibadan tracks, the completion of the Itakpe–Warri standard gauge, and other newly built stations have unquestionably improved Nigeria's railway operations. New tracks completed by the Buhari administration include the 168-kilometer Abuja–Kaduna line, the 157-kilometer Lagos–Ibadan line, the 327-kilometer Warri-Ajaokuta line, and the 44.7-kilometer line in Abuja. Several other developments, including the Port Harcourt-Maiduguri line, the connection between Lagos

---

35. Buhari, "Text of President Muhammadu."
36. Buhari, "Text of President Muhammadu."
37. Buhari, "Text of President Muhammadu."
38. Press Release, "2nd Niger Bridge 91% Completed – Fashola," *Premium Times*, March 24, 2022, https://www.premiumtimesng.com/news/top-news/519443-2nd-niger-bridge-91-completed-fashola.html.
39. Press Release, "2nd Niger Bridge."

and Calabar, and the Onitsha links, have been uncelebrated efforts to revitalize the Nigerian transportation system under the supervision of Rotimi Amaechi.[40]

The Buhari administration claimed to have created 774,000 jobs across all 774 local government areas, which is noteworthy, despite the criticism it has drawn.[41] The government's N-Power project, originally designed to employ 500,000 Nigerians, later increased to accommodate 1 million people to rescue 100 million Nigerians from poverty through job creation.[42] Many of the government's announcements and activities, along with speeches delivered by the president at public celebrations, described current and future projects for the Nigerian government.

Despite these efforts, Nigeria's reality does not reflect the success of these projects, schemes, interventions, facilities, and construction projects. It is easy to fault the government for this lack of progress, largely because of corruption, ineffectiveness, party politics, favoritism, and other factors. The government has become like the Yoruba fowl whose feathers hide its sweat. Either the government has miscalculated the extent of Nigeria's needs, or it has made an inadequate effort, or it has encountered problems with implementing its plans. Nigeria's challenges persist, and critics denounce the government's inability to provide solutions. As Jibrin Ibrahim has stated, Nigeria remains on edge.[43]

RESTRUCTURING AND SECESSIONIST CAMPAIGNS

When peace, convenience, and development are absent, unity is far from certain. When they are missing, discord, hostility, and fear act like ulcers that eat through the fibers holding society together. A house divided against itself cannot stand; at best, it can remain standing for only a short period. Nigerian unity has been the elephant in the room that Nigeria's government has refused to address, despite ongoing events. The nation can do much more together than split apart. Unfortunately, greed, hostility, and bad governance have made it easier to identify the nation's differences instead of its common values.

Nigeria's troubles are not a recent development. Tekena Tamuno asserted that these problems dated back to 1914 and the country's amalgamation.[44] Ahmadu Bello, the Sardauna in the 1950s, had chronicled the Northern elites' intentions to withdraw

---

40. Ibrahim Hassan, "Nigeria and the Railway Revolution: A Ray of Opportunities Under President Muhammadu Buhari," *TheCable*, January 25, 2022, https://www.thecable.ng/nigeria-railway-revolution-opportunities-under-muhammadu-buhari.

41. Muideen Olaniyi, "774,000 Jobs Now an Annual Scheme, Says FG," *Daily Trust*, Jun 25, 2021, https://dailytrust.com/774000-jobs-now-an-annual-scheme-fg.

42. Victoria Ojeme, "FG Increases Number of N-power Beneficiaries from 500,000 to 1m, to Lift 100m out of Poverty," *Vanguard Nigeria*, May 21, 2021.

43. Ibrahim, "Nigeria on the Edge."

44. Tekena N. Tamuno, "Separatist Agitations in Nigeria since 1914," *The Journal of Modern African Studies* 8, no. 4 (1970): 563-584.

from Lugard's unpopular 1914 amalgamation. Tamuno believed that the North's economic requirements and reliance on Southern seaports were the major reasons why this plan was discouraged.[45] Tensions re-emerged in the 1950s after constitutional developments encouraged factional interests that sought to drive the North and the South apart.[46] Their ongoing momentum encouraged the 1953 Kano riot, which had secessionist goals. Secession remained at the center of national discussions in 1954, especially at the resumed constitutional conference, where the Action Group demanded to include a "right of secession" in Nigeria's constitution. Their effort was rejected, chiefly by the N.C.N.C. Tamuno recounts Nnamdi Azikiwe's opposition:

> (1) Secession from a federation is incompatible with federalism.
> (2) Secession from a federation is an illegal act.
> (3) Secession from a federation is an invitation to anarchy.
> (4) Secession from the Nigerian Federation between now and 1956 would be suicidal.[47]

Tensions continued to build in the post-independence era, erupting in an outright war from 1967 to 1970. The destructive fight for the secession of Biafra claimed many lives, yet the conditions that led to this conflict were less extreme than Nigeria's current situation. There were no terrorist attacks, poverty was not a national epidemic, and the economy was not as stagnant. Contemporary fights for Biafra and the recent agitations for the Yoruba nation are built on emotional foundations that can readily gain supporters in the current turmoil. Nnamdi Azikiwe might have taken a different position if he had faced the nation's current predicaments.

Dismissing the demands for Biafra and Yoruba nations would be an act of ignorance; their claims must be honestly considered even to those who believe in one Nigeria. A "right to secession" may not have been too extreme to request in the Buhari environment. The grievances of Biafran secessionists are driven by the Southeastern region's exclusion from Nigeria's political, social, and economic decisions.[48] A major concern in the Southeastern agitations is that no Igbo has served as Nigeria's Head of State or President since the 6-month regime of Aguiyi Ironsi. Out of 18 Nigerian administrations, only two leaders were from the Southeast—one was ceremonial, and the other was short-lived.[49] These sentiments were aggravated by president Buhari's administrative decisions, which further marginalized the Southeast. There are nine deputy inspector-general roles in the Nigerian police, and someone from the South-

---

45. Tamuno, "Separatist Agitations in Nigeria."
46. Tamuno, "Separatist Agitations in Nigeria."
47. Tamuno, "Separatist Agitations in Nigeria."
48. Hussain Taofik Oyewo, "Threat of Secession: The Biafran Story," *Conflict Trends* 2019, no. 3 (2019): 47-55.
49. Oyewo, "Threat of Secession," 47-55.

east holds only one; none are of Igbo descent.[50] Only 4 out of the 37 current Commissioners of Police in Nigeria are Igbo.[51] Similar under-representation can be found in Nigeria's ministries, departments, agencies, and other governmental parastatals.

Nigeria's federal government allocates resources and funds through state and local government areas. The Southeast has 5 states and 94 local governments, which makes it the region with the least number of states and local governments.[52] This reduces its influence on developmental allocations and strategies. There have also been allegations that the Igbo are deliberately excluded from the federal government's developmental strategies. The Buhari administration has made steps towards completing some infrastructure projects, but secessionists readily point to the abandoned effort to dredge the Niger River and the construction of the second Niger Bridge, along with the lack of upgrades to ports in Port Harcourt and Bonny Opobo, which would have given access to Aba, Nnewi, and Onitsha, opening up the area to commercial transactions.[53]

Indigenes of the Southeast have also claimed that the Nigerian government has engaged in human rights abuses and attacks on their citizens, which led Obasanjo's administration to create the Human Rights Violations Investigations Commission of Nigeria.[54] Claims of social repression in Nigeria's contemporary history have gained strength, even under the tenures of Musa Yar' Adua and Goodluck Jonathan, which sums up state antagonism in the East and Biafra-related issues.[55]

The current insecurity, poverty, unemployment, and social breakdowns have emboldened secessionists, encouraging many of them to cause mayhem and compromise the nation's peace. The Yoruba claim that they feel like second-class citizens in their country. Herdsmen and bandit attacks have incited Southwestern agitations, and almost every state in the region faces hostility from attacks on schools, farms, villages, and other important areas.[56] It is still unknown how the herdsmen acquired their weapons and transported them to the South to cause mayhem.[57] The Igangan attack, perpetrated by Fulani herdsmen in Oyo state, was a bloody conflict in 2021. On June 5, 2022, Ondo witnessed one of the most dreadful attacks; about 40 worship-

50. The Nigerian Police, "Contact of Senior Officers," *Nigeria Police Force*, https://www.npf.gov.ng/info/contacts_mgt.php.

51. The Nigerian Police, "Contact of Senior Officers."

52. Oyewo, "Threat of Secession," 47-55.

53. Oyewo, "Threat of Secession," 47-55.

54. Ngozi Ojiakor and Alex Amaechi Ugwuja, "The Igbo in Nigeria: Human Rights Abuses and the Question of Restitution, 1967-2002," *Kenneth Dike Journal of African Studies* 1, no. 1 (2020): 97-123.

55. Olalekan Adigun, "Repression of the Neo-Biafra Movement–measures, Responses, and Consequences," *Journal of Social Science Studies* 5, no. 2 (2018): 132-158.

56. Punch Editorial, "Before Criminals Overrun the South-West," *The Punch*, January 19, 2022.

57. Kunle Akinrinade, "No Respite as Southwest Communities Groan under Herdsmen Attacks," *The Nation*, Oct 2, 2021.

pers were massacred in cold blood during their Sunday service at St. Francis Catholic Church.[58]

Citizens claim that the Buhari administration has done little to address these issues. Meanwhile, individuals like Nnamdi Kanu, Sunday Igboho, and others are making allegations against the Federal Government and convincing supporters to reconsider secession based on emotional sentiments. Anthony Akinola stated that these agitations had led some Hausa youth to issue notices and warnings to Yoruba and Igbo alike. Several attacks on non-Hausa-Fulani citizens have been reported in the North.[59] Based on past and current events, who could dismiss an individual's concerns as unfounded? Anthony Akinola does not support secessionists. The Nigerian problem is not about the 1914 amalgamation; it stems from leadership problems that the entire nation has been unable to resolve. Akinola describes secessionists as "short-sighted," believing that they are misguided. He offers his approach to Nigeria's problems:

> Nigeria has the potential to be great; the component units are a lot more interdependent than many can imagine or would want to admit. There are challenges we must collectively and patriotically seek to resolve. Boko Haram insurgency, kidnapping, herdsmen nuisance, ritual murders, robbery and corruption, are major problems that transcend ethnic and religious boundaries. They are problems that can only be resolved by the collective will of Nigerians and a leadership that is both purposeful and patriotic. The possible disintegration of Nigeria cannot be a peaceful one. The separatists could end up being worse off than they were if they did not succeed in their otherwise suicidal mission.[60]

A barefoot man who flees a burning house is less concerned about exposed nails or inadequate footwear. The frustrated indigenes of Southeastern states, who have felt Nigeria's problems directly, would not describe their demands for secession as short-sighted. Those who experienced the Igangan attacks may follow the same logic. The long-term consequences of these actions may be less of a priority than more pressing concerns. The nation must not dismiss these agitations as mere hostility—their root causes must be considered.

---

58. Nasir Ayitogo, "Updated: DHQ Clarifies Statement on Owo Church Attack, says Four Suspects Arrested," *Premium Times*, August 10, 2022, https://www.premiumtimesng.com/news/headlines/548009-dhq-clarifies-statement-on-owo-church-attack-says-only-one-mastermind-arrested.html.

59. Anthony Akinola, "Short-Sighted Separatist Agitators," *The Punch*, March 29, 2021.

60. Akinola, "Short-Sighted Separatist Agitators."

REVISITING #ENDSARS: EXCESSES, CHAOS AND LIES

The history of social dissent in Nigeria has continued unfolding in recent times—the highlights include the #OccupyNigeria protests of 2012 and the #EndSARS protests of 2020. If there is any lesson to be learned, public deprivation leads to a high likelihood of public uprising, with citizens willing to battle their government. The protest's positive impact on the *volksgeist* cannot be underestimated. However, while the people count their blessings, it is possible that those blessings were acquired at too great a cost.

The Covid-19 lockdowns had a tremendous economic impact globally and in Nigeria. When the restrictions appeared to be easing after months of closed businesses, Nigerians anticipated a swift recovery. However, the nation imposed new restrictions that set off days of turmoil, and peaceful nationwide protests turned violent. Excessively brutal members of the Nigeria Police Force had pushed the youths to the point of resistance, which cost the nation much.

The Lagos Chamber of Commerce and Industry reported that about N700 billion in economic value was lost due to the #EndSARS protests.[61] There was also a decline in the purchase of non-essential goods. Nigeria's vandalized public property and infrastructure was estimated to cost about 1 trillion Naira to repair.[62] Private businesses and warehouses were looted along with public property, including police stations, bus terminals, and government facilities across the nation. Prisons were invaded, and police officers were harmed or killed. Hell was let loose on the nation, and innocent citizens suffered in the chaos and anarchy.

Some protesters had been chanting songs of solidarity, but the children of despair were ready to take advantage of the occasion—a protest against police brutality resulted in further brutality unleashed on police and innocents alike.[63] Protests that decried Nigeria's economic situation ended up dragging the country's economy several steps backward. These consequences might have been unintended, but they quickly became painful lessons for the entire country, menacing the citizens themselves. The fault does not belong to those who launched their protests with good intentions. However, the marauders might have done less damage if the protests had been more carefully coordinated.

Such protests thrive on the rapid circulation of information that sensitizes and incites people to demonstrate, which is readily done through social media. This became a vulnerability as people amplified misinformation and false evidence to direct

---

61. Ijeoma Brigid Ochi and Kingsley Chinonso Mark, "Effect of the ENDSARS Protest on the Nigerian Economy," *Global Journal of Arts, Humanities and Social Sciences* 9, no. 3 (2021): 1-15.

62. Ochi and Mark, "Effect of the ENDSARS Protest."

63. Taofeeq Adebayo Olaigbe, "Youths' Perception and Contributing Factors Towards Jungle Justice during Endsars Protests in Nigeria," *African Journal for the Psychological Studies of Social Issues* 24, no. 1 (2021): 1-10.

anger toward the government and specific politicians. In many cases, destructive propaganda was assisted by patterns of behavior weaponized to mislead the public. Nigeria's political elites had a history of engaging in questionable activities that made them easy targets.

Mohammed Adamu, the Inspector General of Police in 2020, stated that physical protests were incited by fake news generated in Ugheli, Delta State.[64] This explanation has been refuted by protesters who claim that the government tries to downplay the justifications for the protest. Different narratives have surfaced to explain the triggers for physical protests in Nigeria's major population centers.

Adamu explained that a state-financed joint security outfit, Operation Delta Safe, tried to stop a suspicious vehicle. One of the suspects, Joshua Ambrose, sustained injuries jumping from a moving police van after being apprehended. This incident involving police and other security operatives was recorded and published on the internet with misleading captions declaring that the police had shot and killed someone. The Inspector General of Police believed this information encouraged more people to join the protests.[65] Regardless of whether this event was the primary driver of protests, it is unarguably the first set of fake information related to it.

The #EndSARS protests created a profitable environment for the merchants of fake news, and they easily fooled credible media institutions. Protesters and the government disagree about the number of civilians killed during the protests, but both figures are unacceptably large. Unfortunately, the distribution of easily discredited fake news has provided the Federal Government with justification for its actions.

The #EndSARS violence on October 20, 2020, described as the "Lekki Massacre," involved many protesters who were rounded up at the Lekki Tollgate by the Nigerian Army. The government claimed that their forces were shooting in the air, while the protesters claimed that shots were fired at the people, and the incident generated heated controversy.

Yemi Alade, a Nigerian musician, posted a picture of a woman wrapped in a blood-stained Nigerian flag; the accompanying text implied that the woman had died during the October 20 shooting. The Nigeria Christian Corpers Fellowship later denounced this allegation, stating that the image was from a drama they had staged at the Independence Day celebration in Akwa Ibom. I. K. Osakioduwa, a radio presenter, dispelled a rumor that a woman named Lucia had been killed at the Lekki Tollgate incident. He explained that Lucia had died in an accident the day before the incident. Similar stories involving unrelated images and videos emerged around the protest as the subject of many claims and counter-claims. CNN and Amnesty International

64. Kehinde Abdulsalam, "How Fake News from Delta Triggered #ENDSARS Protests," *Daily Trust*, November 3, 2020.

65. Abdulsalam, "How Fake News from Delta."

were also involved in the information wars waged over the government's actions. Amnesty International published a statement on its website:

> Amnesty International has been monitoring developments across Nigeria since the #EndSars protest began on 8 October 2020. At least 56 people have died across the country since the protest began, with about 38 killed on Tuesday alone. Victims include protesters and thugs who were allegedly hired by the authorities to confront the protesters. In many cases the security forces had used excessive force in an attempt to control or stop the protests.[66]

CNN corroborated these claims with eyewitness interviews.[67] However, the Nigerian government refused to accept these facts, denying the existence of the Lekki Massacre. Lai Mohammed, the Minister for Information, Culture, and Tourism, stated:

> At earlier press conferences, I had called the reported massacre at the toll gate the first massacre in the world without blood or bodies.
> One year later, and despite ample opportunities for the families of those allegedly killed and those alleging a massacre to present evidence, there has been none: No bodies, no families, no convincing evidence, nothing. Where are the families of those who were reportedly killed at the toll gate? Did they show up at the Judicial Panel of Inquiry? If not, why? The champions of a massacre at the Lekki Toll Gate, including Amnesty International and CNN, have continued to shamelessly hold on to their unproven stand.[68]

The lies, exaggerations, and refutations continued to be exchanged between the public and the Nigerian government. However, a Judicial Panel of Inquiry established by the Lagos State government issued disturbing findings in a 309-page report.[69] The panel found that 11 people were killed at the Lekki incident, and 4 missing individuals were presumed dead.[70] The report also stated that 96 bodies were presented by Professor John Obafunwa, Lagos State University Teaching Hospital's forensic pathologist.[71] It found 48 casualties, 24 injuries sustained from gunshots, and another 15

---

66. Press Release, "Nigeria: Killing of #EndSARS Protesters by the Military must be Investigated," *Amnesty International*, October 21, 2020, https://www.amnesty.org/en/latest/press-release/2020/10/killing-of-endsars-protesters-by-the-military-must-be-investigated/.

67. Eoin McSweeney, Stephanie Busari, Katie Polglase, Bethlehem Feleke and Tim Lister, "Prison Set on Fire in Nigeria as Protest Death Toll Rises to at Least 56," *CNN*, October 22, 2020, https://edition.cnn.com/2020/10/22/africa/nigeria-protests-56-dead-jail-fire-intl/index.html.

68. Grace Obike, "Govt, Amnesty Disagree on 'Lekki Massacre'," *The Nation*, October 21, 2021.

69. Thisday, "In Damning Report, Lagos #EndSARS Panel Says 11 Killed at Lekki Tollgate," *Thisday*, 16 November, 2021.

70. *Thisday*, "In Damning Report."

71. Gboyega Akinsanmi and Segun James, "#EndSARS: 99 Dead Bodies Deposited at LASUTH, Obafunwa Reveals," *Thisday*, June 6, 2021.

individuals assaulted by the Nigerian Police.[72] The report stated that police forces continued their mayhem after the army withdrew.[73]

Activities at the Lekki Tollgate on October 20, 2020, may have resulted in the deaths of 2, as claimed by Babajide Sanwo-Olu, the governor of Lagos State;[74] the deaths of 38, as claimed by Amnesty International; or the deaths of 11, as the Judicial Panel reported, but everyone agreed that the incident involved death, gunfire, injuries, facts, and lies. Some of the claims were false, whether the government issued them, the protesters, or other institutions, and some of the facts were misrepresented in public venues.

Civil demonstration is a public right that should be exercised lawfully. The Lekki showdown was unnecessary; there were no reports of hostility from the unarmed protesters. Ordering heavily armed soldiers to attack civilians is disgraceful and disheartening. Such incidents cast doubt on whether Nigeria practices democracy, pseudo-democracy, or mere pretense.

WEIGHING THE CONTRIBUTIONS OF SOME PROMINENT FIGURES

Scholars and intellectuals have articulated their positions from analytic and factual angles, leaving little room to challenge their contributions. This further asserts their relevance for discussion and examination. However, some issues are discussed without considering important factors, options, and ideas.

Bad leadership has been identified as the primary source of Nigeria's problems. Many scholars believe that the Buhari government was unprepared for the mantle of leadership that it assumed in 2019. Pius Adesanmi was an outspoken critic of the president, challenging campaign comments that had been made about the Jonathan administration. Adesanmi published a message on Twitter:

> If Prez Buhari truly had integrity, he would have resigned the moment Dapchi happened on his watch, given all the noise he made when Chibok happened on his predecessor's watch. You had the precedence of Chibok. You should have been prepared. You were not. You dropped the ball.[75]

---

72. *Thisday*, "In Damning Report."
73. *Thisday*, "In Damning Report."
74. Ifeoluwa Adediran, "#EndSARS: Sanwo-Olu Confirms Two Deaths from Lekki Shooting," *Premium Times*, October 22, 2020, https://www.premiumtimesng.com/news/headlines/422446-endsars-sanwo-olu-confirms-two-deaths-from-lekki-shooting.html.
75. Pius Adesanmi, "If Prez Buhari truly had integrity, he would have resigned the moment Dapchi happened on his watch, given all the noise he made when Chibok happened on his predecessor's watch. You had the precedence of Chibok. You should have been prepared. You were not. You dropped the ball," *Tweet*, February 26, 2018, https://twitter.com/pius_adesanmi/status/968102522551332864?s=20&t=g8WRoufPu2IkXl7Vxs8Iog.

Adesanmi is a passionate Nigerian who took President Buhari's ineptitude personally—he detested how the country's affairs had been managed. Despite the 2015 hope, Adesanmi never wanted Buhari to happen to Nigeria again.[76]

Ayo Olukotun disagreed with several of Adesanmi's opinions. Olukotun had written about the struggles faced by different Nigerians, including an article titled "Rising Citizen's Woes and Governance Apathy."[77] Olukotun's concerns have included the president's body language and the danger of not changing in character.[78]

Abimbola Adelakun is another critic who has publicly examined the errors of Buhari's administration and how the government mismanaged Nigeria. She marvels at the president's alleged ignorance of his official duties, stating:

> No president in Nigerian history has been as much of a disaster as Buhari. His government has been entirely underwhelming; the man himself is so fundamentally lazy that there is no point in his rudderless leadership that he decided to take charge of affairs. If there is something almost everyone will agree with now, it is that Buhari's leadership abilities were grossly exaggerated and that the man never had even the slightest interest in redirecting Nigeria away from failure towards prosperity.[79]

Farooq Kperogi, Moses Ochonu and Jibrin Ibrahim hold similar sentiments on various issues and have published contributions that follow the same trajectory. Kperogi referred to the president as the "World's Most Successful Mass Hypnotist,"[80] casting doubt on his ability in several published works.[81] Ochonu has also questioned President Buhari's abilities and claims about fighting corruption. Ochonu wrote:

> Buhari's problem is not just parochialism and nepotism, which are now bywords for his administration. Perhaps his biggest character flaw is unqualified personal loyalty to his benefactors and loyalists. Time and again, it has led him into the corruption of enabling and defending graft.[82]

---

76. Adesanmi, "An Excellent Case."
77. Ayo Olukotun, "Rising Citizen's Woes and Governance Apathy," *The Punch*, March 18, 2022.
78. Ayo Olukotun, "Anguished Nation Left Stranded by its Leaders," *The Punch*, June 24, 2022.
79. Abimbola Adelakun, "Bandits will Eventually Get to Buhari," *The Punch*, August 4, 2022.
80. Farooq A. Kperogi, "Buhari is World's Most Successful Mass Hypnotist," *Notes from Atlanta*, July 24, 2022, https://www.farooqkperogi.com/2022/07/buhari-is-worlds-most-successful-mass.html.
81. Farooq Kperogi, "Buhari not Competent to Govern any Country," *The Punch*, January 29, 2017.
82. Moses E. Ochonu, "Buhari, Corruption Enabler and Defender," *Premium Times*, November 1, 2017, https://opinion.premiumtimesng.com/2017/11/01/buhari-corruption-enabler-and-defender-by-moses-e-ochonu/.

Jibrin Ibrahim's criticism of the government is regularly published in *Premium Times*, the USA-Africa Dialogue, and other media outlets.[83]

These individuals offer a consistent interpretation of the government's effectiveness. However, it would be an exaggeration to claim that the government has accomplished nothing. The question is whether President Buhari's efforts will be enough to save the country because the current state of Nigeria can easily substantiate claims regarding the government's ineffectiveness.

Many of Nigeria's problems did not start with Buhari's administration; they can be traced farther back into the country's history. President Jonathan's administration was met with similar criticism and protests, which could suggest that the country has experienced a run of bad luck in selecting its leaders. Unfortunately, leadership problems have exacerbated other problems central to the current *volksgeist*. Even if Jonathan and Buhari had made their campaign promises sincerely, there is no guarantee that their administrations would have performed differently. A fundamental problem in Nigeria is the disposition of its citizens towards leadership and participation.

The population of Nigeria was around 119.3 million in 1999,[84] and a little more than 30 million votes were cast.[85] In 2019, the population had increased by around 90% to 201 million people.[86] However, the Independent National Electoral Commission reported that a little over 28 million votes were cast. Despite a massive population increase, the number of voters in Nigeria had decreased by more than one million.

Aside from this disastrous political apathy, elections are now plagued with vote-buying scandals. Those who sell their most precious garments should not be offended when the buyer converts them into filthy rags. The Nigerian population opened its doors to bad leadership when they should have been extra careful. Nigerians will not be ready for a better Nigeria until this problem is addressed—and if Buhari's successor turns out to be worse, the nation should not grieve.

Corruption and other social vices are innate in the Nigerian population, which has generated disrespectful leaders who take integrity for granted. Before blaming the pulpit, one must blame the pew. Nigerians have tolerated poor discipline among Nigerian politicians, downplaying and disregarding the scandals around them. Some presidential candidates have boycotted debates, public discussions, and political in-

---

83. Jibrin Ibrahim, "Alternative Facts and the Buhari Legacy," *Premium Times,* June 24, 2022, https://www.premiumtimesng.com/opinion/538883-alternative-facts-and-the-buhari-legacy-by-jibrin-ibrahim.html.

84. Data Commons, "Nigeria Overview," *Data Commons*, August 30, 2022, https://datacommons.org/place/country/NGA?utm_medium=explore&mprop=count&popt=Person&hl=en.

85. Alex Kireev, "Nigeria: Presidential Election 1999," *Electoral Geography 2.0, Mapped Politics,* https://www.electoralgeography.com/new/en/countries/n/nigeria/nigeria-presidential-election-1999.html.

86. Data Commons, "Nigeria Overview."

teractions with the public, but citizens remain willing to support their positions.[87] Although this behavior should be a red flag for the nation, citizens expect neither honesty nor deliberation from an "average Nigerian politician." Critics have raised valid points about elected officials, but ordinary citizens should also be examined.

Nigeria's university system is another source of problems exacerbated by poor leadership. The Academic Staff Union of Universities has called for continuous strikes almost every year, making regular demands that go unmet by successive governments. Students bear the burden of this inaction, compromising months of planned academic sessions and opportunities due to strikes. Jibrin Ibrahim regularly restates this concern, but he has suggested that the A.S.U.U. revisit its strategies:

> A.S.U.U. must go into introspection and learn what every trade unionist knows—the gains in the struggle are never total; they are always incremental... A.S.U.U. must start a conversation about a profound change in tactics. More minimalist and attainable targets must be set and advocacy must be broadened to address the National Assembly and other institutions. My A.S.U.U. comrades, the struggle is our life but this does not mean that we cannot get real...[88]

Jibrin made this recommendation in 2013, and the problem has persisted for 9 years.

The National Assembly is aware of the predicament facing Nigerian university students. In July, Nigeria Labour Congress protests were directed at the National Assembly, demanding an immediate end to the A.S.U.U. Strike.[89] The National Assembly has also attempted strike interventions, but things do not change.[90] Moses Ochonu has publicly expressed dissatisfaction over the A.S.U.U. strikes, including the statement in his article, "A.S.U.U. Is A Problem Of The Nigerian University System":

> A.S.U.U. Strikes have become counterproductive in several ways. The government usually waits it out until A.S.U.U. is desperate for a deal—any deal—because of financial hardship occasioned by several months of its members going unpaid, and because of pressure from parents and students, who, in recent years, have turned decisively against A.S.U.U., influencing public opinion that

87. *Premium Times*, "Presidential Debate: APC Shielding Buhari's Intellectual Laziness—PDP," *Premium Times*, January 31, 2015, https://www.premiumtimesng.com/news/top-news/175990-presidential-debate-apc-shielding-buharis-intellectual-laziness-pdp.html.

88. Jibrin Ibrahim, "Conversation with my ASUU Comrades: Let's Get Real," *Premium Times*, October 14, 2013, https://www.premiumtimesng.com/opinion/146584-conversation-asuu-comrades-lets-get-real-jibrin-ibrahim.html.

89. Ayodeji Owolabi, "Photos: NLC Takes Protest to National Assembly over ASUU Strike," *TheCable*, July 27, 2022,
https://www.thecable.ng/photos-nlc-takes-protest-to-national-assembly-over-asuu-strike.

90. Ahmed Lawan, "ASUU Strike: Senate will bring back FG/ASUU to Negotiation Table – Lawan," *National Assembly*, May 11, 2022, https://nass.gov.ng/news/item/1672.

> now sees A.S.U.U. honchos as selfish, money-grabbing activists who do not have the interest of students at heart. Whether this is fair to A.S.U.U. or not is not the point. The point, rather, is that a wise, self-reflective, and self-critical body of activists tries not to overplay its hand or lose the support of its constituency or the public. A wise trade or professional union knows when to fight and when not to, and knows when a particular method of struggle has exhausted its effectiveness and lifespan and has begun to yield diminishing returns. A.S.U.U.'s laziness prevents it from making this realization. As things stand, the government has mastered the game, playing A.S.U.U. leaders like a set of drums.[91]

Farooq Kperogi has supported some of the A.S.U.U. demands, but his enthusiasm waned after extended disagreements over the "no-work-no-pay" policy.[92] One might ask: are A.S.U.U. strikes justifiable? Many Nigerian critics and scholars support the validity of A.S.U.U. demands while denouncing the group's methods. Although many have suggested that A.S.U.U. leadership should change tactics, they have not identified specific tactics that would produce results.

The A.S.U.U. strike is a war of attrition that has asked Nigerian students to bear its costs. The idea of a strike seems archaic, but it remains the only way to bring the government to the table—how else can the Union make its demands when it cannot shame the shameless? Taking to the streets in protests would only add to the ongoing protests that have failed to sway the government. Every day, thousands of Nigerians publicly criticize the government, and although a village may become familiar with the wailing of an abused wife, it does not mean that she should be blamed for her behavior. The annual strikes coordinated by A.S.U.U. does not mean their demands are outdated. A.S.U.U. should consider whether they have alternative avenues for making their demands, but strikes may be their most effective option.

CONCLUSION

The themes affecting Nigeria have been discussed in previous chapters, and analytic contributions from reputable individuals have been examined to provide insights into contemporary Nigeria. These individuals represent the voices of the people, discussing issues that affect them daily. However, other perspectives are important to establish a balanced opinion. This chapter provides additional perspectives by challenging previously examined opinions. It does not disparage the contributions of these scholars, but it considers their opinions from narrower lenses to advance argu-

---

91. Moses. E. Ochonu, "ASUU is a Problem of the Nigerian University System," *Sahara Reporter,* November 6, 2018, https://saharareporters.com/2018/11/06/asuu-problem-nigerian-university-system-moses-e-ochonu.

92. Farooq A. Kperogi, "ASUU, Call off this Strike Now," *Notes from Atlanta,* August 20, 2022, https://www.farooqkperogi.com/2022/08/asuu-call-off-this-strike-now.html.

ments for the sake of development. Although the nation needs healing—and the leaders may be crucified for it— if the fundamentals are not addressed, the destructive cycle will continue.

This chapter made a holistic critique of social media narratives to consider how they affect national development, and it identified how false narratives on social media could further divide a polarized country. Although social media has recently assisted Nigeria's political development, it cannot be solely responsible for transforming leadership structures. Much effort will be needed that involves grassroots mobilization.

This chapter also critiqued nationalist writers' interventions in Nigerian affairs. Most of their interventions, presented from a nationalist point of view, do not fully capture the general problems, as evident in the solutions proposed. These writers largely blamed the government for Nigeria's predicament while absolving citizens of any responsibility. The solution to the country's many problems must be holistic; we cannot keep talking about national development while limiting the conversation to the government's failures. The narrative must change to include those who are most directly affected and who continue to fold their arms.

Figure 25.3. "TF on Selfie!" by Dr. Kazeem Ekeolu. Depicting the trans-generational fascination with technological gadgets and social media updates.

BIBLIOGRAPHY

Abdul, Mariam Marwa, Olayinka Adeleke, O. Adeyeye, A. Babalola, E. Eyo, M. T. Ibrahim and Martha Onose. "Analysis of the History, Organisations and Challenges of Feminism in Nigeria." *Nawey Nigerian Group: Academy of Management Perspectives* 18, no. 3 (2011): 136–139.

Abdulkareem, A., Abdullateef Ameen and Ajadi Abdulrasaq Ishola. "A Review of E-government as a Tool for Building Citizens Trust in the Nigerian Government." *Sahel Analyst: Journal of Management Sciences* 13, no. 2 (2016): 10.

Abdullahi, G. "Gender Discrimination and Feminism in Nigeria." *International Journal of Economics, Commerce and Management* 3, no. 7 (2015): 7.

Abdullahi, Idowu. "Backlash Trails Atiku's Northern Social Media Users' Claim." *The Punch*, July 22, 2022.

Abdulsalam, Kehinde. "How Fake News from Delta Triggered #ENDSARS Protests." *Daily Trust*, November 3, 2020.

Abeele, M.M.P. "Mobile Lifestyles: Conceptualizing Heterogeneity in Mobile Youth Culture." *New Media & Society* 18, no. 6 (2014): 908–926.

Abel, Laurel and Abel Blackman. "Raising Naija: A Nigerian Results-Based Transfer Scheme for Improved Public Goods & Services Delivery." *Harvard Kennedy School*, 2014. www.hks.harvard.edu/var/ezp_site/storage/fckeditor/file/pdfs/degree-programs/mpaid/SYPA_AbelBlackman_2014.pdf.

Abimbade, Oluwadara, Philip Olayoku and Danielle Herro. "Millennial Activism within Nigerian Twitterscape: From Mobilization to Social Action of #ENDSARS Protest." *Social Sciences & Humanities Open* 6, no. 1 (2022): 1–9.

Abubakar, Abdulmutallib Ado. "Political Participation and Discourse in Social Media during the 2011 Presidential Electioneering." *The Nigerian Journal of Communication* 10, no. 1 (2012): 96–116.

Abutaleb, Yasmeen and Arathy S. Nair. "'Wow': Facebook Launches 'Reactions' Worldwide." *Reuters*, February 24, 2016. www.reuters.com/article/us-facebook-reactions-idUSKCN0VX1L7.

Achebe, Chinua. *The Trouble with Nigeria.* Oxford: Heinemann Educational Publishers, 1984.

Achebe, Chinua. *There was a Country: A Personal History of Biafra.* London: Penguin Group, 2012.

Achebe, Chinua. *Things Fall Apart.* London: Heinemann, 2021.

Achebe, Nwando. *The Female King of Colonial Nigeria: Ahebi Ugbabe.* Bloomington, Indiana: Indiana University Press, 2011.

Achi, Louis. "As Terrorists Take Battle to the Seat of Power." *Thisday*, July 31, 2022.

Adebayo, T. "Premium Times Columnist Pius Adesanmi Wins Prestigious Canadian Award." *Premium Times*, September 14, 2017. www.premiumtimesng.com/news/more-news/243299-premium-times-columnist-pius-adesanmi-win-prestigious-canadian-award.html.

Adebisi, Melody. "Why is Sexual Health Such a Taboo Topic in Africa?" *West African Careers*, 2018. www.westafricancareers.com/sexual-health-taboo-topic-africa/.

Adediran, Ifeoluwa. "#EndSARS: Sanwo-Olu Confirms Two Deaths from Lekki Shooting." *Premium Times*, October 22, 2020. www.premiumtimesng.com/news/headlines/422446-endsars-sanwo-olu-confirms-two-deaths-from-lekki-shooting.html.

Adegboruwa, Ebun-Olu. "If Passed, Hate Speech Bill could Transform Nigeria into Haven for Sycophants: Adegboruwa." *The Punch*, November 20, 2019.

Adegboyega, O.O. "The Dearth of Public Morality in Nigeria." *International Journal of Arts and Culture in Society* 4, no. 3 (2007): 1–8.

Adegoke, Adeboye. *Digital Rights and Privacy in Nigeria.* Abuja: Paradigm Initiative, 2020.

Adejumobi, S. "Democracy, Good Governance and Constitutionalism in Africa." In *Governance: Nigeria and the World,* edited by Sylvester Odion-Akhaine. Ikeja: Centre for Constitutionalism and Demilitarisation, 2004.

Adelabu, Omowale. "The Role of Social Media Influencers on the Rise of Youth Activism During the EndSars Campaign." *Escae Journal of Management and Security Studies (EJMSS)* 1, no 1 (2021): 51–66.

Adelakun, Abimbola and Toyin Falola. *Art, Creativity, and Politics in Africa and the Diaspora.* Berlin: Springer, 2018.

Adelakun, Abimbola. "#EndSARS, and a Government's Perennial Failure." *The Punch*, October 21, 2021.

Adelakun, Abimbola. "Ado-Doguwa: Between Polygamy and Irresponsibility." *The Punch*, February 13, 2020.

Adelakun, Abimbola. "Arresting Deborah's Killers is the Easy Part." *The Punch*, May 19, 2022.

Adelakun, Abimbola. "Banditry and Atiku's '90% Voters." *The Punch*, July 28, 2022.

Adelakun, Abimbola. "Bandits will Eventually get to Buhari." *The Punch*, August 4. 2022.

Adelakun, Abimbola. "Black Lives Matter! Nigerian Lives Matter!: Language and Why Performance Matters." *Genealogy* 3, no. 2 (2019): 19.

Adelakun, Abimbola. "Emir Sanusi's Regulation of Polygamy." *Opinion Nigeria*, February 23, 2017. www.opinionnigeria.com/emir-sanusis-regulation-of-polygamy-by-abimbola-adelakun/.

Adelakun, Abimbola. "Feminism, Social Media, and Misbegotten Debates." *Proud Flesh: New Afrikan Journal of Culture, Politics and Consciousness* 21 (2020).

Adelakun, Abimbola. "Fighting Islamization of Nigeria." *The Punch*, September 28, 2017.

Adelakun, Abimbola. "Funke Akindele might be Good for Lagos Politics." *The Punch*, July 21, 2022.

Adelakun, Abimbola. "Gaidam and the Spirit of Northern Entitlement." *The Punch*, February 27, 2020.

Adelakun, Abimbola. "God-mentality: Pentecostalism as Performance in Nigeria." Ph.D *diss.*, The University of Texas, 2017.

Adelakun, Abimbola. "How Anti-Corruption Became a Game." *Opinion Nigeria*, January 28, 2016. www.opinionnigeria.com/how-anti-corruption-became-a-game-by-abimbola-adelakun/.

Adelakun, Abimbola. "Impunity: Nigeria's First Violence." *The Punch*, March 23, 2017.

Adelakun, Abimbola. "It should Never take More than One Disaster." *The Punch*, December 9, 2021.

Adelakun, Abimbola. "Nigeria is Fantastically Corrupt, What's Next?" *Opinion Nigeria*, May 12, 2016. www.opinionnigeria.com/nigeria-is-fantastically-corrupt-whats-new-by-abimbola-adelakun/.

Adelakun, Abimbola. "Osinbajo: Beyond the Nostrum." *The Punch*, July 16, 2020.

Adelakun, Abimbola. "Pentecostal Panopticism and the Phantasm of "The Ultimate Power." In *Pentecostalism and Politics in Africa*, edited by Adeshina Afolayan, Olajumoke Yacob-Haliso and Toyin Falola. Cham, Switzerland: Palgrave Macmillan, 2018, 101–118.

Adelakun, Abimbola. "Rape: Men are Truly not Wood." *The Punch*, June 11, 2020.

Adelakun, Abimbola. "Raped in a Church." *The Punch*, June 4, 2020.

Adelakun, Abimbola. "The Ghosts of Performance Past: Theatre, Gender, Religion and Cultural Memory." *Religion and Gender* 7, no. 2 (2017): 147–163.

Adelakun, Abimbola. "The Real Trouble with Magu." *The Punch*, March 5, 2020.

Adelakun, Abimbola. "The Spirit Names the Child: Pentecostal Names and Trans-Ethics." In *The Palgrave Handbook of African Social Ethics*, edited by Nimi Wariboko and Toyin Falola. New York: Springer International Publishing, 2020, 543–567.

Adelakun, Abimbola. "Tinubu Presidency: Affliction must not Rise a Second Time." *The Punch*, January 13, 2022.

Adelakun, Abimbola. "Tinubu vs Atiku: Two Desperados Running against Nigeria." *The Punch*, June 9, 2022.

Adelakun, Abimbola. "What is the Truth of Boko Haram?" *The Punch*, January 23, 2020.

Adelakun, Abimbola. "Yoruba Muslims vs Yoruba Christians." *The Punch*, November 11, 2021.

Adelakun, Abimbola. *Under the Brown Rusted Roofs*. Ibadan: Kraftgriots, 2008.

Adeleye, Ifedapo, Franklin Ngwu, Nkemdilim Iheanachor, Ebes Esho, Chijioke Oji, Theresa Onaji-Benson and Chris Ogbechie. "Banking on Africa: Can Emerging Pan-African Banks Outcompete their Global Rivals?" In *Africa's Competitiveness in the Global Economy*, edited by Ifedapo Adeleye and Mark Esposito. Cham, Switzerland: Palgrave Macmillan, 2018, 113–136.

Ademola, Adebiyi, Ajetunmobi Umar Olansile and Olawale Jelilat Opeyemi. "Connected but not Engaged: A Tale of Two Governorship Candidates' Social Media Mobilization in a Gubernatorial Contest in Oyo State, Southwest Nigeria." *Interactions: Society and New Modernities* 38 (2020): 78–105.

Ademola-Olateju, Bamidele. "[Bamidele Upfront] Falling Oil Prices is Nigeria's Destiny." *Premium Times,* May 28, 2013. www.premiumtimesng.com/opinion/136506-bamidele-upfront-falling-oil-prices-is-nigerias-destiny-by-bamidele-ademola-Ademola-Olateju.html.

Ademola-Olateju, Bamidele. "2023: Nigeria's Make or Break Presidential Election." *Premium Times,* August 9, 2022. www.premiumtimesng.com/opinion/547851-2023-nigerias-make-or-break-presidential-election-by-bamidele-ademola-Ademola-Olateju.html.

Ademola-Olateju, Bamidele. "Digital Authoritarianism and the Echoes of Decree 4." *Premium Times*, June 8, 2021. www.premiumtimesng.com/opinion/466420-digital-authoritarianism-and-the-echoes-of-decree-4-by-bamidele-ademola-Ademola-Olateju.html.

Ademola-Olateju, Bamidele. "Eavesdropping, Censorship and the Voyeuristic State." *Premium Times*, July 13, 2021. www.premiumtimesng.com/opinion/473323-eavesdropping-censorship-and-the-voyeuristic-state-by-bamidele-ademola-Ademola-Olateju.html.

Ademola-Olateju, Bamidele. "Education in Nigeria—The Missteps, the Gaps." *Sahara Reporters,* April 8, 2013. www.saharareporters.com/2013/04/08/education-nigeria-missteps-gaps-part-one-bamidele-ademola-Ademola-Olateju.

Ademola-Olateju, Bamidele. "Ethnonationalism as a Rational Response to what Nigeria is." *Premium Times*, June 1, 2021. www.premiumtimesng.com/opinion/465026-ethnonationalism-as-a-rational-response-to-what-nigeria-is-by-bamidele-ademola-Ademola-Olateju.html.

Ademola-Olateju, Bamidele. "Even the Finest Wine can Turn to Vinegar." *Premium Times*, May 8, 2021. www.premiumtimesng.com/opinion/462215-even-the-finest-wines-can-turn-to-vinegar-by-bamidele-ademola-Ademola-Olateju.html.

Ademola-Olateju, Bamidele. "Federalism Means Eating what You Kill." *Premium Times,* September 7, 2021. www.premiumtimesng.com/opinion/483578-federalism-means-eating-what-you-kill.html.

Ademola-Olateju, Bamidele. "Kleptocracy: What Are Treasury Looters Really Thinking?" *Premium Times,* August 15, 2017. www.opinion.premiumtimesng.com/2017/08/15/kleptocracy-what-are-treasury-looters-really-thinking-bybamidele-ademola-Ademola-Olateju/.

Ademola-Olateju, Bamidele. "Nigeria: Taking a Stand for Freedom and Liberty." *Premium Times*, September 14, 2021. www.premiumtimesng.com/opinion/484761-nigeria-taking-a-stand-for-freedom-and-liberty-by-bamidele-ademola-Ademola-Olateju.html.

Ademola-Olateju, Bamidele. "Nigerian and its 170 million Stupid People." *Premium Times,* October 22, 2013. www.premiumtimesng.com/opinion/147023-bamidele-upfront-nigeria-170million-stupid-people-bamidele-ademola-Ademola-Olateju.html.

Ademola-Olateju, Bamidele. "Osun Elections Shows you can make your Vote Count." *Premium Times,* August 12, 2014. www.opinion.premiumtimesng.com/2014/08/12/osun-elections-shows-you-can-make-your-vote-count-by-bamidele-ademola-Ademola-Olateju/.

Adémólá-Olátéjú, Bámidélé. "Prebendalism: Are Vote Buying and Voter Intimidation here to Stay?" *Premium Times*, November 19, 2019. www.opinion.premiumtimesng.com/2019/11/19/prebendalism-are-vote-buying-and-voter-intimidation-here-to-stay-by-bamidele-ademola-Ademola-Olateju/.

Ademola-Olateju, Bamidele. "Religion as a Tool for Impoverishing Nigerians." *Premium Times,* November 3, 2015. www.opinion.premiumtimesng.com/2015/11/03/religion-as-a-tool-for-impoverishing-nigerians-bamidele-ademola-Ademola-Olateju/.

Ademola-Olateju, Bamidele. "Sowore does not have to Win." *Sahara Reporters,* April 8, 2018. www.saharareporters.com/2018/04/08/sowore-does-not-have-win-bamidele-ademola-Ademola-Olateju.

Ademola-Olateju, Bamidele. "The Abuse of faith by Pastors." *Premium Times,* July 23, 2019. www.opinion.premiumtimesng.com/2019/07/23/the-abuse-of-faith-by-pastors-by-bamidele-ademola-Ademola-Olateju/.

Ademola-Olateju, Bamidele. "The Economic Consequences of having Luddites in Charge." *Premium Times*, June 22, 2021. www.premiumtimesng.com/opinion/469

272-the-economic-consequences-of-having-luddites-in-charge-by-bamidele-ademola-Ademola-Olateju.html.

Ademola-Olateju, Bamidele. "The Evil Geniuses in Nigeria's Political Arena." *Premium Times*, May 18, 2021. www.premiumtimesng.com/opinion/462215-even-the-finest-wines-can-turn-to-vinegar-by-bamidele-ademola-Ademola-Olateju.html.

Ademola-Olateju, Bamidele. "The Nigerian Clergy, Politics and Violation of Moral Philosophy." *Premium Times*, January 27, 2015. www.opinion.premiumtimesng.com/2015/01/27/nigerian-clergy-politics-violation-moral-philosophy-bamidele-ademola-Ademola-Olateju/.

Ademola-Olateju, Bamidele. "The Siege of Kleptocrats and Kakistocrats." *Premium Times*, February 11, 2020. www.opinion.premiumtimesng.com/2020/02/11/the-siege-of-kleptocrats-and-kakistocrats-by-bamidele-ademola-Ademola-Olateju/.

Ademola-Olateju, Bamidele. "Tinubu—The Political Huckster and Ambitions." *Adeyemi Juwon Blog*, January 16, 2018. www.adeyemijuwon.com.ng/2018/01/16/tinubu-political-huckster-ambitions-bamidele-ademola-Ademola-Olateju/.

Ademola-Olateju, Bamidele. "Yoruba Youths: Endangered and in Need of Repositioning." *Premium Times*, August 7, 2022. www.premiumtimesng.com/opinion/547378-yoruba-youths-endangered-and-in-need-of-repositioning-by-bamidele-ademola-Ademola-Olateju.html.

Adenekan, Samson. "Days after Losing Presidential Bid, Moghalu Resigns from ADC." *Premium Times*, June 14, 2022. www.premiumtimesng.com/news/top-news/536891-days-after-losing-presidential-bid-moghalu-resigns-from-adc.html.

Adenekan, Samson. "Profiles of 'VIP' Inmates in Kuje Prison before Attack." *Premium Times*, July 13, 2022. www.premiumtimesng.com/news/headlines/542323-profiles-of-vip-inmates-in-kuje-prison-before-attack.html#:~:text=Despite%20early%20warnings%2C%20the%20Kuje,over%2060%20Boko%20Haram%20terrorists.

Adenubi, Tola. "After Tribune Report, Ogun Govt Supplies Desks, Chairs to School." *Nigerian Tribune*, July 19, 2022.

Adesanmi, Pius. "Someone once Advised me to try and be like Reno Omokri so I can make it instead of making Noise all the Time." *Jarushub*, March 30, 2013. www.jarushub.com/somebody-once-advised-me-to-try-and-be-like-reno-omokri-so-i-can-also-make-it-instead-of-making-noise-all-the-time-pius-adesanmi/.

Adesanmi, Pius. "An Excellent Case For Buhari's Second Term," *Premium Times*, April 10, 2018.

Adesanmi, Pius. "ASUU: A Personal Voyage around A Strike." *Sahara Reporters*, November 29, 2018. www.saharareporters.com/2018/11/29/asuu-personal-voyage-around-strike-pius-adesanmi.

Adesanmi, Pius. "Before it is Too Late for Her." *Sahara Reporters*, June 1, 2018. www.saharareporters.com/2018/06/01/it-too-late-her-pius-adesanmi.

Adesanmi, Pius. "Exclusive: Pius Adesanmi's Last Interview—Near Death Experience, Abusive Relationship, Buhari's Cluelessness." *Premium Times*, March 19, 2019. www.premiumtimesng.com/news/headlines/320882-exclusive-pius-adesanmis-

last-interview-near-death-accident-abusive-relationship-buharis-cluelessness.html.

Adesanmi, Pius. "From Post-Global to Post-Truth: African Lterature beyond Commonsense." *Cambridge Journal of Postcolonial Literary Inquiry* 4, no. 2 (2017): 271–279.

Adesanmi, Pius. "It will get Worse before it gets Better." *Sahara Reporters*, May 14, 2016. www.saharareporters.com/2016/05/14/it-will-get-worse-it-gets-better-pius-adesanmi.

Adesanmi, Pius. "Professor Pius Adesanmi: Award-Winning Writer, Activist and Academician." *Konnect Africa*, 2013. www.konnectafrica.net/professor-pius-adesanmi-award-winning-writer-activist-and-academician/.

Adesanmi, Pius. "Reflections on Darkness." *Nigerian Tribune*, February 24, 2019.

Adesanmi, Pius. "Shit & the Sum(mary) of a Presidency." *Sahara Reporters*, February 5, 2018. www.saharareporters.com/2018/02/05/shit-summary-presidency-pius-adesanmi.

Adesanmi, Pius. *Naija No Dey Carry Last: Thoughts on a Nation in Progress*. Lagos, Origami Books, 2015.

Adesanmi, Pius. *Who Owns the Problem?: Africa and the Struggle for Agency*. Michigan: Michigan State University Press, 2020.

Adesanmi, Pius. *You're Not a Country, Africa*. Cape Town: Penguin Random House South Africa, 2012.

Adesanmi, Pius. *The Wayfarer and Other Poems*. Mosman: Oracle Books, 2001.

Adesina, Jimi O. "Global Trends in Higher Education Reform: What Lessons for Nigeria?" *Journal of Higher Education in Africa/Revue de l'enseignement supérieur en Afrique* 4, no. 1 (2006): 1–23.

Adetiba, Kemi. *King of Boys (Film)*. Lagos: Kemi Adetiba Visuals, October 20, 2018

Adetoro, Adejoke, Oluwakayode Ashamu and Maikudi Lawan. "Women, Religion and Contemporary Public Transport Service in Kano Metropolis." *IFRA-Nigeria Working Papers Series* 49, 2019.

Adeyanju, G. and M. Haruna. "Uses of SMS in campaigns: An assessment of the 2011 general elections and post-election violence in northern Nigeria." 2012.

Adibe, Odoemelam and Adim Chibuwe. "Social Media, Electioneering and Sustenance of Democracy in Africa: A SWOT Analysis." A Paper Presented at the African Media and Democracy Conference (AMDC), Accra, Ghana, 2011.

Adichie, Chimamanda. *The Thing Around Your Neck*. New York: Alfred A. Knopf, 2009.

Adigun, Olalekan. "Repression of the Neo-Biafra Movement–measures, Responses, and Consequences." *Journal of Social Science Studies* 5, no. 2 (2018): 132–158.

Adomi, Esharenana. "Mobile Telephony in Nigeria." *Library Hi Tech News* 22, no. 4 (2005): 18–20.

Advocates for Youth. "Sex Education Programs: Definitions & Point-by-Point Comparison." *Advocates for Youth*. www.advocatesforyouth.org/publications/publica-

tions-a-z/655-sex-education-programs-definitions-and-point-by-point-comparison.

Afoláyan, Michael Oladejo. *Fate of our Mothers: The Collected Memories of an African Village Boy*. Austin: Pan-African University Press, 2015.

African Writing Online. "50 African Writers; A Special AW Profile." *African Writing Online*, [undated] accessed August 9, 2022, http://www.african-writing.com/aug/profiles2.htm

African Writing. "50 African Writers; A Special AW Profile." *African Writing*, 2007. www.african-writing.com/aug/profiles2.htm.

Afrol News. "Dangerous Gasoline Offloaded in Nigeria, Ghana." *Afrol News*, June 24, 2011. www.afrol.com/articles/29529.

Agbakwuru, Johnbosco. "Nigeria Needs $1.5trn in 10-yrs to Bridge Infrastructure Gap—Buhari." *Vanguard Newspaper*, November 2, 2021,

Agboola, Abdulhameed Kayode. "The Influence of New Media on Conventional Media in Nigeria." *Academic Research International* 5, no. 4 (2014): 105.

Agger, Robert E., and Vincent Ostrom. "The Political Structure of a Small Community." *Public Opinion Quarterly* 20, no. 1 (1956): 81–89.

Agu, Sylvia, Vincent Onyekwelu Sunday Okeke and Adeline N. Idike. "Voters Apathy and Revival of Genuine Political Participation in Nigeria." *Mediterranean Journal of Social Sciences* 4, no. 3 (2013): 439–448.

Ahmad, Muhammad. "Social Media and Hate Speech: Analysis of Comments on Biafra Agitations, Arewa Youths' Ultimatum and their Implications on Peaceful Coexistence in Nigeria." *Media and Communication Currents* 2, no. 1 (2018): 54–74.

Aina-Pelemo, Deborah and Jesutoye Testimony Adeboye. "Women's Right and Feminism Under the Law in Nigeria." *OAU Journal of Public Law*, 1, 1 (2021): 147–164.

Ajayi, Adegboyega and Samson A. Adesote. "The Social Media and Consolidation of Democracy in Nigeria: Uses, Potentials and Challenges." *African Journal of Sustainable Development* 6, no. 1 (2016): 93–112.

Ajayi, Adeyinka Theresa and E. Oladipo Ojo. "Democracy in Nigeria: Practice, Problems and Prospects." *Journal of Developing Country Studies* 4, no. 22 (2014): 107–125.

Ajayi, Omeiza. "I didn't Hire Fake Christian Clerics for Shettima's Unveiling—Tinubu." *Vanguard Newspaper*, July 21, 2022.

Ajibola, Boluwatife Solomon and Temitayo Isaac Odeyemi. "The Legislature as Target and Mediator of Ensuing Outcomes during Social Emergencies: Revisiting Nigeria's #Endsars Protest." *The Theory and Practice of Legislation* 10, no. 2 (2022): 1–30.

Akinbi, Joseph Olukayode. "Examining the Boko Haram Insurgency in Northern Nigeria and the Quest for a Permanent Resolution of the Crisis." *Global Journal of Arts, Humanities and Social Sciences* 3, no. 8 (2015): 32–45.

Akindele, S. "A Critical Analysis of Corruption and its Problems in Nigeria." *Anthropologist* 7, no. 1 (2005): 7–18.

Akinlotan, Olasunkanmi and Abdulqudus Ogundapo. "Owo Attack: How Gunmen Attacked Owo Church, Fled—Witnesses." *Premium Times*, June 12 2022.

Akinola, Anthony. "A History of Corruption." *Niger Delta Congress*, July 21, 2008. www.nigerdeltacongress.com/articles/a_history_of_corruption.htm.

Akinola, Anthony. "Beyond Sixty Years of Independence." *The Guardian*, September 28, 2020.

Akinola, Anthony. "Formalizing Rotational Presidency." *The Guardian*, June 30, 2019.

Akinola, Anthony. "History, Essence and Limits of Televised Debates." *The Guardian*, November 12, 2019.

Akinola, Anthony. "How Military Coup Stalled Youth Participation." *The Guardian*, May 10, 2018.

Akinola, Anthony. "Manufacturing the Two-Party System in Nigeria." *Journal of Commonwealth & Comparative Politics* 28, no. 3 (1990): 309–327.

Akinola, Anthony. "Migrating Politicians and 2019 Elections." *The Guardian*, August 27, 2018.

Akinola, Anthony. "Peaceful Coexistence Remains a Dream." *The Guardian*, February 11, 2021.

Akinola, Anthony. "Posterity will not Forgive Another Civil War." *The Guardian*, January 24, 2020.

Akinola, Anthony. "Restructuring the Senate." *The Guardian*, May 2, 2019.

Akinola, Anthony. "Review of The Abacha Regime and the June 12 Crisis." *The Journal of Modern African Studies* 33, no. 4 (1995): 710–711.

Akinola, Anthony. "Revisiting Jonathan's Single-Term Proposal." *The Guardian*, November 1, 2018.

Akinola, Anthony. "Rotational Presidency is Central to Nigeria's Future." *The Punch*, September 27, 2019.

Akinola, Anthony. "Short-Sighted Separatist Agitators." *The Punch*, March 29, 2021.

Akinola, Anthony. "Some Positive takes from a Chaotic Election." *The Guardian*, April 11, 2019.

Akinola, Anthony. "Still on Reducing the Cost of Governance." *The Guardian*, October 17, 2019.

Akinola, Anthony. "The Concept of a Rotational Presidency in Nigeria." *The Round Table* 85, no. 337 (1996): 13–24.

Akinola, Anthony. "The Fallacy of So-Called Competence over Zoning." *The Guardian*, August 6, 2020.

Akinola, Anthony. "The Incumbency Factor in Presidential Elections." *The Guardian*, June 13, 2018.

Akinola, Anthony. *Democracy in Nigeria: Thoughts and Selected Commentaries*. Morrisville: Lulu Press Inc., 2015.

Akinola, Olanrewaju and A.A. Ogunsanya. "Construction of Nuances on WhatsApp and BBM by Nigerian Students." *Journal of Humanities, Social Science and Creative Arts* 13, no. 1 (2018): 1–13.

Akinrinade, Kunle. "No Respite as Southwest Communities Groan under Herdsmen Attacks." *The Nation*, Oct 2, 2021.

Akinsanmi, Gboyega and Segun James. "#EndSARS: 99 Dead Bodies Deposited at LASUTH, Obafunwa Reveals." *Thisday*, June 6, 2021.

Akintoye, Stephen Adebanji. "Nigeria's President is the Most Powerful Official of any Country in the World—Prof. Akintoye." *Channels Televisison*, September 25, 2017. www.youtu.be/Uk3MpBpqhvA.

Akinwunmi, A. "New Media, Political Campaigns and Violence in Nigeria." Paper presented at the ACCE, Covenant University, Ota. September 2011.

Akoni, O. "Igbo Quit Notice: Pan Yoruba Group Calls for the Oodua Republic." *Vanguard Newspaper,* 2017.

Akwagyiram, Alexis. "A Police Raid, Viral Videos and the Broken Lives of Nigerian Gay Suspects." *Reuters*, February 24, 2020. www.reuters.com/article/us-nigeria-lgbt-widerimage-idUSKCN20I105.

Alabi, Taofeek Olanrewaju and Adewale Kazeem Ayeloja. "Hate Speech and Security Challenges: A Pragmatic study of Nnamdi Kanu's Speeches in the South-Eastern Nigeria." *International Journal of English Research* 5, no. 4 (2019): 1–9.

Aleke, Christian, Lois Nnenna Omaka-Amari and Nkiru Edith Obande-Ogbuinya. "Consequences of Social Media use Among Adolescents in Nigeria." *International Journal of Innovative Science and Research Technology* 3, no. 4 (2018): 766–773.

Alemika, E., and A.O. Agugua. *Gender Relations and Discrimination in Nigeria Police Force*. Ikeja, Nigeria: Centre for Law Enforcement Education, 2011.

Ali, Salad Mohamud. "Decentralization and Political Participation in Wadajir District, Mogadishu, Somalia." Ph.D *diss*., Kampala International University, 2015.

Alikaram, Leila. *Women and Equality in Iran: Law, Society and Activism*. New York: Bloomsbury Publishing, 2019.

Alimi, Bisi, Petra Boynton, Zuzana Struharova and Gary Wood. *Not Dancing to their Music: The Effects of Homophobia, Biphobia and Transphobia on the Lives of LGBT People in Nigeria*. Lagos: Bisi Alimi Foundation, 2017.

All Progressives Congress. "About APC." *Official All Progressive Congress*. www.officialapc.ng/about-us/.

Allardice, Lisa. "Chimamanda Ngozie Adichie—This could be the Beginning of a Revolution." *The Guardian*, April 28, 2014.

Alonaizi, B., and Yousr Gadhoum. "The Next 11: Emerging Investment Market." 1st International Conference on Advanced Research (ICAR-2017), Bahrain, Manama, 2017, 53–62.

Alozie, Princewill. "History and Philosophy of Science in Ancient Africa." In *History and Philosophy of Science*, 2nd ed., edited by Alozie Princewill. Calabar: Clear Lines Publications, 2001, 2–32.

Amata, Denis. "#Osundecides: Only 42.16% of Registered Voters Voted in the Osun Governorship Election." *Data Phyte,* July 18, 2022. www.dataphyte.com/latest-reports/elections/osundecides-only-42-16-of-registered-voters-voted-in-the-osun-governorship-election/.

Amata, Denis. "2023 Election: Completed PVC Registration across Nigeria in 5 Charts." *Data Phyte*, August 3, 2022. www.dataphyte.com/latest-reports/elections/2023-election-completed-pvc-registration-across-nigeria-in-5-charts/.

Aminu, PraiseGod and Innocent Chiluwa. "Constructing Identity and Ideological Stance in Oduduwa Secessionist Discourse on Twitter." Paper presented at the 3rd World Conference on Social Science Studies, Budapest Hungary, May 6–8, 2002.

Amnesty International. "Nigeria: Bills on Hate Speech and Social Media are Dangerous Attacks on Freedom of Expression." *Amnesty,* December 4, 2019. www.amnesty.org/en/latest/press-release/2019/12/nigeria-bills-on-hate-speech-and-social-media-are-dangerous-attacks-on-freedom-of-expression/.

Amnesty International. "Nigeria: Special Police Squad 'Get Rich' Torturing Detainees and Demanding Bribes in Exchange for Freedom." *Amnesty International*, September 21, 2016. www.amnesty.org/en/latest/news/2016/09/nigeriaspecial-police-squad-get-rich-torturing-detainees/.

Amnesty International. "Nigeria: Time to End Impunity, Torture and other Violations by Special Anti-robbery Squad (SARS)," *Amnesty International*, June 26, 2020, https://www.amnesty.org/en/documents/afr44/9505/2020/en/

Amnesty International. "Nigeria: Time to End Impunity, Torture and other Violations by SARS." Special Report, 2020.

Amodeni, Adunni. "Women did not come from Men's Rib—Lady Reveals why she left Christianity." *Legit*, August 29, 2018. www.legit.ng/1189072-women-mens-ribs-lady-reveals-left-christianity.html.

Amodu, Akeem. "Prebendalism and Netizenship: Critical Notes on Good Governance and the Social Media in Nigeria." *International Journal of Research in Social Sciences* 7, no. 12 (2017): 1–11.

Amoo, Emmanuel and E. Adeyemi. "Scanty Dressing Habit and Sexual Comportment among Adolescent Girls in Metropolitan Lagos: Implications for HIV/AIDS Incidence." *Gender and Behaviour* 8, no. 1 (2010): 2806–2824.

Amundsen, G. "Good Governance in Nigeria. A Study in Political Economy and Donor Support." *Norad,* 2010. www.norad.no/en/toolspublications/publications/2010/good-governance-in-nigeria-a-study-in-political-economy-and-donor-support/

Amuwo, Kunle. *Federalism and Political Restructuring in Nigeria*. Ibadan: Spectrum, 1998.

Amy, Naasin. "Women Rights and Feminism in Nigeria: The Journey So Far." LL.B Project, University of Lagos, 2016.

Anagor, Chioma. "African Values, Gender Inequality and Feminism: The Igbo Race." *Nigerian Journal of African Studies (NJAS)* 4, no. 1 (2022): 7.

Anika, Chude. "The Killing of Deborah Samuel." *Guardian*, May 23 2022.

Anyadike, Nkechi O., and O. Nkechi. "Boko Haram and National Security Challenges in Nigeria: Causes and Solutions." *Journal of Economics and Sustainable Development* 4, no. 5 (2013): 12–22.

Anyira, Isaac. "Internet Services in Nigerian Private Universities: A Case Study." *Library Philosophy and Practice* 2 (2011): 1.

Anzaku, Abbas Abel, Abel Gladys Angbalaga, Ale Cecilia Achetu, Akharenegbe Pedro, Oche Daniel Idibiah and Okezue Chukwuemeka James. "Implication of Female Genital Mutilation in Nigeria as Portal for Infectious Diseases." *Journal of Bacteriology and Infectious Disease* 2, no. 1 (2018): 28–30.

Apuke Oberiri. "Exploring the Extent of Press Freedom in Nigeria." *International Journal of International Relations, Media and Mass Communication Studies* 3, no. 2 (2017): 28–31.

Apuke, Oberiri and Bahiyah Omar. "Fake News and COVID-19: Modelling the Predictors of Fake News Sharing among Social Media Users." *Telematics and Informatics* 56 (2021): 1–16.

Apuke, Oberiri and Ivo Nkasire Apollos. "Public Perception of the Role of Facebook Usage in Political Campaigns in Nigeria." *Informing Science: International Journal of Community Development & Management Studies* 1 (2017): 85–101.

Apuke, Oberiri Destiny and E.A. Tunca. "Understanding the Implications of Social Media Usage in the Electoral Processes and Campaigns in Nigeria." *Global Media Journal* 16, no. 31 (2018): 1–8.

Arikewuyo, Abdulgaffar, B. Özad and Saudat Salah Abdulbaqi. "Role of Social Media in Eradicating Violence among Young Nigerian Females: A Study of Nigerian Students in Eastern Mediterranean University." Paper present at the 6th International Conference on Gender Studies: Gender, Conflict, War and Peace, Famagusta, North Cyprus, March 2017.

Arikewuyo, Ahmed, Saudat Sallah Abdulbaqi, Rasaq Muhammad Adisa. "Anti-corruption Campaigns and Nigeria's Development: An Appraisal of Media Roles." *Acta Universitatis Danubius. Communicatio* 13, no. 2 (2019): 99–116.

Arnett, E.J. *The Rise of the Sokoto Fulani: Being a Paraphrase and in Some Parts a Translation of the Infaku'l Maisuri of Sultan Mohammed Bello*. London: School of Oriental and African Studies, 1922.

Aronson, E. "Cyber-Politics: How New Media has Revolutionized Electoral Politics in the United States." *Colgate Academic Review* 9, no. 7 (2012): 148–194.

Asemah, E.S. "Use of Social Media in the 2015 Presidential Election in Nigeria." *Mass Communicator: International Journal of Communication Studies* 11, no. 3 (2017): 4–11.

Asemota, Victor Osaretin. "'Ghana is the Future of Africa': Why Google Built an AI Lab in Accra." *CNN*, July 15, 2018.

Asemota, Victor Osaretin. "Bank Technology and the Unhappily Banked." *The Guardian: Technology*, June 20, 2018.

Asemota, Victor Osaretin. "Can Technology Help to Win Nigerian Election?" *The Guardian: Technology*, January 24, 2018.

Asemota, Victor Osaretin. "Corporate Collaboration as growth and Exit Opportunity." *The Guardian*. August 29, 2018.

Asemota, Victor Osaretin. "Design Thinking and Financial Services Innovation." *The Guardian*, July 11, 2018.

Asemota, Victor Osaretin. "Designing African Tech Start-ups for Trust." *The Guardian,* August 8, 2018.

Asemota, Victor Osaretin. "Innovation Starts from Home." *The Guardian,* January 10, 2018.

Asemota, Victor Osaretin. "Nigeria's Technology Sector: A Coming of Age?" *The Guardian,* September 23, 2016.

Asemota, Victor Osaretin. "Otigba: The Experiment that Grew into a Tech Market." *The Guardian*, March 15, 2017.

Asemota, Victor Osaretin. "Start-up Ventures 101." *The Guardian*, April 17, 2019.

Asemota, Victor Osaretin. "Tackling Public Sector Corruption Starts and Ends with Technology." *The Guardian*, April 18, 2018.

Asemota, Victor Osaretin. "The Era of Remote Work." *The Guardian*, November 1, 2017.

Asemota, Victor Osaretin. "The Future of Election Campaign is Digital." *The Guardian*, March 6, 2019.

Asemota, Victor Osaretin. "The Technology of Freelancer Problem." *The Guardian,* February 07, 2018.

Asemota, Victor Osaretin. "Why African Entrepreneurs Need to Think Bigger." *The Guardian*, July 19, 2017.

Asiyai I., and E.P. Oghuvbu. An Empirical Analysis of the Causes and Challenges of Quality in Higher Education in Nigeria in the 21st Century. *Journal of Sociology and Education in Africa* 8, no. 2 (2009): 1–13.

Asiyai, R. "Trade Union Disputes and their Perceived Impacts on the University System in Nigeria." Ph.D *diss.*, Delta State University, Abraka, Nigeria, 2005.

Asogwa, Chika. "Women Empowerment for a Holistic Development in Nigeria." *Review of European Studies* 4, no. 2 (2012): 144.

Asogwa, Fedrick O., Kennedy Kelechi Ohaleme and Ugwuanyi Romanus O. "The Impact of Telecommunication Expenditure on Economic Growth in Nigeria." *Journal of Economics and Sustainable Development* 4, no. 13 (2013): 40–44.

Asogwa, Nicholas and Christian Ezeibe. "The State, Hate Speech Regulation and Sustainable Democracy in Africa: A Study of Nigeria and Kenya." *African Identities* (2020): 2–16.

Asongu, Simplice and Nicholas M. Odhiambo. "Governance and Social Media in African Countries: An Empirical Investigation." *Telecommunications Policy* 43, no. 5 (2019): 411–425.

Asongu, Simplice, Jacinta C. Nwachukwu, Stella-Maris I. Orim and Chris Pyke. "Crime and Social Media." AGDI Working Paper, No. WP/19/003, African Governance and Development Institute (AGDI), Yaoundé, 2019.

Atoyebi, Olufemi. "Igboho Attacks Tinubu, Ooni, Makinde, says they are '"Fulani Slaves.'" *TheCable*, February 3, 2021. www.thecable.ng/igboho-attacks-ooni-tinubu-and-makinde-says-they-are-fulani-slaves

Audu Mohammed and Uzoma S. Osuala. "The British Conquest and Resistance of Sokoto Caliphate, 1897–1903: Crisis, Conflicts and Resistance." *Historical Research Letter* 22 (2015): 32.

Awofeso, O. "Secessionist Movements and the National Question in Nigeria: A Revisit to the Quest for Political Restructuring." *Journal of Social Science and Humanities Research* 2, no. 7 (2017): 35–55.

Awofeso, O., and Paul A. Irabor. "Youth Unemployment and Electoral Violence in Nigeria: A Case of the 2019 General Elections." In *Elections and Electoral Violence in Nigeria*, edited by Kelechi Johnmary Ani and Victor Ojakorotu. Singapore: Palgrave Macmillan, 2022, 35–49.

Awopeju, Ayo. "2011 Presidential Election and the Political Participation in Nigeria." *Canadian Social Science* 8, no. 2 (2012): 96–103.

Ayandele, Olajumoke. "Confronting Nigeria's Kaduna Crisis." *Africa Center*, February 2, 2021. www.africacenter.org/spotlight/confronting-nigerias-kaduna-crisis/.

Ayeni, V. "Human Rights and the Criminalization of Same-sex Relationships in Nigeria: A Critique of the Same-sex Marriage (Prohibition) Act." In *Protecting the Human Rights of Sexual Minorities in Contemporary Africa*, edited by Sylvie Namwase and Adrian Jjuuko. Pretoria: Pretoria University Law Press, 2017, 210.

Ayitogo, Nasir. "2019: PDP Commences Sale of Nomination Forms." *Premium Times*, August 28, 2018. www.premiumtimesng.com/news/top-news/281577-2019-pdp-commences-sale-of-nomination-forms.html.

Ayitogo, Nasir. "Buhari Approves New Security Measures for South-East, South-South." *Premium Times*, May 11, 2021. www.premiumtimesng.com/news/headlines/460906-buhari-approves-new-security-measures-for-south-east-south-south-official.html.

Ayitogo, Nasir. "Kaduna Train Attack: Kidnapped Victim's Relatives Protest in Abuja." *Premium Times*, July 25, 2022. www.premiumtimesng.com/news/top-news/544833-kaduna-train-attack-kidnapped-victims-relatives-protest-in-abuja.html.

Ayitogo, Nasir. "Updated: DHQ Clarifies Statement on Owo Church Attack, says Four Suspects Arrested." *Premium Times*, August 10, 2022. www.premiumtimesng.com/news/headlines/548009-dhq-clarifies-statement-on-owo-church-attack-says-only-one-mastermind-arrested.html.

Azaiki, S. *Inequities in Nigerian Politics*. Nigeria: Y Books, 2007.

Azeez, Makinde. "(18+) Popular Hausa Actress, Maryam Booth Naked Video Leaked on Social Media." *Naijaloaded*, February 7, 2020. www.naijaloaded.com.ng/entertainment/18-popular-hausa-actress-maryam-booth-naked-video-leaked-on-social-media-watch-video.

Azuike, P. "A Radical Feminist Approach to the Works of Zaynab Alkali." Ph.D *diss.*, University of Jos, Nigeria, 2003.

Babaleye, Taye, P. Ibitoye and Akpobo Emokiniovo Odorume. "Influence of Social Media on Democratic Governance in Nigeria." *International Journal of Media Journalism and Mass Communications* 69, no. 1 (2020): 13–20.

Babalola, Dele. "Nigeria: A Federation in Search of Federalism." *50 Shades of Federalism*, 2017. www.50shadesoffederalism.com/case-studies/nigeria-federation-search-federalism/

Babalola, Dele. "The Efficacy of Federalism in a Multi-Ethnic State: The Nigerian Experience." *Journal of Pan African Studies* 8, no. 2 (2015): 74–92.

Baiyewu, Leke. "Nigeria Lacks Proper Parties yet, says Fayemi." *The Punch*, April 2, 2021.

Bakare, Kola, Micheal Avosetinyen, Tope Shola Akinyetun. "Race in a Maze: The Relentless Search for and Challenges of Leadership in Africa." *Afro Asian Journal of Social Sciences* 10, no. 10 (2019): 1–25.

Baldick, Chris. *The Concise Oxford Dictionary of Literary Terms*. Oxford: Oxford University Press, 1996.

Bamidele, Michael. "Bisi Alimi Organizes LGBT Event in Lagos." *Guardian*, October 30, 2019.

Bandura, A. *Social Learning Theory*. New Jersey: Prentice-Hall, 1977.

Banjo, Noah. "85 Days After, Buhari Orders Immediate Rescue of Abuja-Kaduna Train Attack Victims." *The Punch*, June 21, 2022.

Barak, A. "Sexual Harassment on the Internet." *Social Science Computer Review* 23, no. 1 (2005): 77–92.

Bartlett, Jamie, Alex Krasodomski-Jones, Nengak Daniel, Ali Fisher and Sasha Jesperson. "Social Media for Election Communication and Monitoring in Nigeria." A report prepared for the Department for International Development (DFID), 2015. www.demos.co.uk/wp-content/uploads/2015/11/Social-Media-in-Nigerian-Election.pdf.

Baum, Matthew and Philip BK Potter. "Media, Public Opinion and Foreign Policy in the Age of Social Media." *The Journal of Politics* 81, no. 2 (2019): 747–756.

Bayer, Joseph B., Nicole B. Ellison, Sarita Y. Schoenebeck and Emily B. Falk. "Sharing the Small Moments: Ephemeral Social Interaction on Snapchat." *Information, Communication & Society* 19, no. 7 (2016): 956–977.

BBC News. "Abacha Loot to be Given to Poor Nigerians." *BBC News*, June 29, 2018. www.bbc.com/news/world-africa-44654931.

BBC News. "End Sars Protests: Growing List of Celebrities Pledge Support for Demonstrators." *BBC News*, October 21, 2020. www.bbc.com/news/world-africa-54629449

BBC News. "Ethiopian Airlines: The Victims of 'A Global Tragedy.'" *BBC News*, April 4, 2019. www.bbc.com/news/world-africa-47522028.

BBC News. "Fake News and Nigeria's Herder Crisis." *BBC*, June 29, 2018. www.bbc.com/news/world-africa-44655148.

BBC News. "Letter from Africa: Why Nigerians Fear Social Media Sanctions." *BBC News*, November 7, 2020. www.bbc.com/news/world-africa-54840436.

BBC News. "Nigeria's Boko Haram Rejects Jonathan's Amnesty Idea." *BBC News*, April 11, 2013. www.bbc.com/news/world-africa-22105476.

BBC News. "Why does a Nigerian Muslim Leader want to Restrict Polygamy?" *BBC News,* February 22, 2017. www.bbc.com/news/world-africa-39038459.

Bella Naija. "Horrific: 2 Alleged Gay Nigerian Men Beaten to DEATH as Policemen & Passersby [sic] Watch." *BellaNaija*, February 7, 2014. www.bellanaija.com/2014/02/horrific-2-gay-nigerian-men-beaten-to-death-as-policemen-passersby-watch/.

Bello, S.K. "Political and Electoral Violence in Nigeria: Mapping, Evolution and Pattern." *IFRA Nigeria Working Papers* 49, University of Ibadan, 2015.

Bennis, Warren G., and Joan Goldsmith. *Learning to Lead: A Workbook on Becoming a Leader* New York: Basic Books, 2003.

Bergstrom, L. "Legacies of Colonialism and Islam for Hausa Women: An Historical Analysis, 1804 to 1960." GPID/WID Working Papers, Center for Gender in Global Context, Michigan State University, East Lansing, Michigan, 2002.

Bertot, J.C., P.T. Jaeger and J.M. Grimes. "Using ICTs to Create a Culture of Transparency: E-government and Social Media as Openness and Anti-Corruption Tools for Societies." *Government Information Quarterly* 27, no. 3 (2010): 264–271.

Best, Paul, Roger Manktelow and Brian Taylor. "Online Communication, Social Media and Adolescent Wellbeing: A Systematic Narrative Review." *Children and Youth Services Review* 41 (2014): 27–36.

Bhardwaj, Ajay. "Importance of Education in Human Life: A Holistic Approach." *International Journal of Science and Consciousness* 2, no. 2 (2016): 23–28

Bianze, Nkechi. "The Consequences of Stereotyping Gender Roles." *Women*, August 31, 2017. www.woman.ng/2017/08/consequences-stereotyping-gender-roles/.

Bider, Emma. "The Privilege of Editing #WhoOwnsTheProblem: Remembering Pius Adesanmi." *Nokoko* 9 (2021): 135.

Bratton, Michael. "Vote Buying and Violence in Nigerian Election Campaigns." *Electoral Studies* 27, no. 4 (2008): 621–632.

Brown, Jane D., ed. *Managing the Media Monster: The Influence of Media (From Television to Text Messages) on Teen Sexual Behavior.* Washington, DC: National Campaign to Prevent Teen and Unplanned Pregnancy, 2008.

Buhari, Muhammadu. "Text of President Muhammadu Buhari's 2020 Democracy Day Address." *The Guardian,* 12 June 2020.

Bullough, V. *The Subordinate Sex*. New York: Penguin, 1974.

Busari, Biodun. "Osun Election: Hope for Nigeria, Voters Rejecting Money Left, Right—Davido." *Vanguard*, July 16, 2022.

Byers, Kyle. "What 3.25 billion Website Visits Tell us about the Internet's Top Traffic Sources." *Growth Badger*, April 5, 2020. www.growthbadger.com/traffic-study/.

Chadha, Kalyani and Pallavi Guha. "The Bharatiya Janata Party's Online Campaign and Citizen Involvement in India's 2014 Election." *International Journal of Communication* 10 (2016): 4389–4406.

Channels Television. "Nigeria has 18.5 Million Children out of School." *Channels Television*, May 12, 2022. www.channelstv.com/2022/05/12/nigeria-has-18-5-million-children-out-of-school-unicef/.

Chatora, Arthur. "Encouraging Political Participation in Africa: The Potentials of Social Media Platforms." Institute for Security Studies. Situation Report, 2012.

Chayko, Mary. "Techno-Social Life: The Internet, Digital Technology, and Social Connectedness." *Sociology Compass* 8, no. 7 (2014): 976–991.

Cheema, G. *Building Democratic Institutions: Governance Reform in Developing Countries*. Kumarian Press, 2005.

Chepkirui, A. "Principles of Good Governance." *IDOSR Journal of Arts and Humanities* 6, no. 1 (2021): 47.

Chiluwa, Innocent. "A Nation Divided against Itself: Biafra and the Conflicting Online Protest Discourses." *Discourse & Communication* 12, no. 4 (2018): 357–381.

Chiluwa, Innocent. "On Political Participation: Discursive Pragmatics and Social Interaction in Nolitics." *Studies in Literature and Language* 2, no. 2 (2011): 80–92.

Chimakonam, Jonathan. "Towards a Theory of African Science: Methods and Justification." *IOSR Journal of Pharmacy and Biological Sciences* 3, no 1 (2012): 33–41.

Chipkin, I. "Whither the State? Corruption, Institutions and State-Building in South Africa." *Politikon, South African Journal of Political Studies* 40, no. 2 (2013): 211–231.

Chisom, Uzoka. "Hate speech and Freedom of Expression: Legal boundaries in Nigeria." *Library Research Journal* 4, no. 1 (2019): 111–118

Chomsky, Noam. *Media Control: The Spectacular Achievements of Propaganda*. New York City: Seven Stories Press, 1991.

Chouliaraki, L. "Digital Witnessing in War Journalism: The Case of Post-Arab Spring Conflicts." *Popular Communication: The International Journal of Media and Culture* 13, no. 2 (2015):105–119.

Chris, Onodugo. "Leadership Challenges and Nigerian Development." *International Journal of Scientific Research in Science and Technology* 1, no. 5 (2015): 2395–6011.

Chukwuere, Joshua Ebere and Chijioke Francis Onyebukwa. "The Impacts of Social Media on National Security: A View from the Northern and South-Eastern Region of Nigeria." *International Review of Management and Marketing* 8, no. 5 (2018): 50.

Ciboh, Rodney. "An Exploratory Study of Older Adults' Social Media use and Social Capital in Nigeria." *Athens Journal of Mass Media and Communications* 3, no. 2 (2017): 149–165.

Cinelli, Matteo, Gianmarco De Francisci Morales, Alessandro Galeazzi, Walter Quattrociocchi and Michele Starnini. "The Echo Chamber Effect on Social Media." *Proceedings of the National Academy of Sciences* 118, no. 9 (2021): 1–8.

Clement, Jessica. "Social Networks Ranked By Number of Users 2020." *Statista*, November 10, 2020. www.satista.com/statistics/272014/global-social-netwroks-ranked-by-number-of-users/.

Coleman, S., and P.M. Shane, eds. *Connecting Democracy: Online Consultation and the Flow of Political Communication*. Massachuset: MIT Press, 2011.

Collins, Harry, Robert Evans, Darrin Durant and Martin Weinel. *Experts and the Will of the People*. Cham, Switzerland: Palgrave Macmillan, 2020.

Condren, Conal. "Satire and Definition." *Humor* 25, no. 4 (2012): 375–399.

Counterpart International. "Social Media Networking: A Guide to Strengthening Civil Society through Social Media." *Counterpart International.* www.usaid.gov/sites/default/files/documents/1866/SMGuide4CSO.pdf.

Crary, David. "CDC: US Abortion Rate Falls to the Lowest Level in Decades." *Associated Press*, November 23, 2016. www.apnews.com/ccf0b462a6d84f9eabef0846566d1291/cdc-us-abortion-rate-falls-lowest-level-decades.

Creed J.L., and A.E. Wardman. *The Philosophy of Aristotle*, trans. New York: New American Library, 1963.

Dada, Samuel and Ebenezer Deji Ogunrinde. "A Stylistic Analysis of Nigeria Centre for Disease Control (NCDC) COVID-19 Sensitization Advertisements on Social Media." *Journal of African Studies and Sustainable Development* 3, no. 6 (2020): 153–176.

Dagona, Z.K., Haruna Karick and F.M. Abubakar. "Youth Participation in Social Media and Political Attitudes in Nigeria." *Journal of Sociology, Psychology and Anthropology in Practice* 5, no. 1 (2013): 1–7.

Dagunduro, Adebukola and Adebimpe Adenugba. "Failure to Meet up to Expectation: Examining Women's Activist Groups in the Post-colonial Period in Nigeria." *Open Cultural Studies* 4, no. 1 (2020): 23–35.

Danaan, Victoria Voelwoen. "Analysing Poverty in Nigeria through Theoretical Lenses." *Journal of Sustainable Development* 11, no. 1 (2018): 20–31.

Dankumo, Ali Madina, Suryati Ishak, Yasmin Bani and Hanny Zurina Hamza. "The Relationship between Public Expenditure, Corruption and Poverty in Nigeria." *Journal Ekonomi dan Studi Pembangunan* 11, no. 1 (2019): 76–89.

Dark, Shayera. "Female Leadership in Nigeria's ENDSARS Movement helped it Grow, Then Gave it Staying Power." *Quartz Africa*, November 3, 2020. www.qz.com/africa/1925923/female-leadership-in-nigerias-endsars-protests-was-vital/.

Data Commons. "Nigeria Overview." *Data Commons*, August 30, 2022. www.datacommons.org/place/country/NGA?utm_medium=explore&mprop=count&popt=Person&hl=en.

DeFleur, Melvin Lawrence and Sandra Ball-Rokeach. *Theories of Mass Communication* Vol. 5. New York: Longman, 1989.

Dei, George, Budd L. Hall and Dorothy Goldin Rosenberg. *Indigenous Knowledges in Global Contexts: Multiple Readings of Our World.* Toronto: University of Toronto Press, 2000.

Dei, George, Jand Jill Vickers. *Anti-Racism Education: Theory & Practice.* Halifax: Fernwood Publishing, 1997.

Dempsey, Allison G., Michael L. Sulkowski, Rebecca Nichols and Eric A. Storch. "Differences Between Peer Victimization in Cyber and Physical Settings and Associated Psychosocial Adjustment in Early Adolescence." *Psychology in the Schools*, 46, no. 10 (2009): 962–972.

Deneulin, Séverine. "Democracy and Political Participation." In *An Introduction to the Human Development and Capability Approach*, edited by S. Deneulin. London: Routledge, 2009, 207–213.

Desai, Guarav. "Out in Africa." *Genders* 25 (1997): 120–143.

Dibia, Jude. "Witness." *NigeriaTalk*, January 31, 2014. www.nigerianstalk.org/2014/01/31/witness/.

Dibia, Jude. *Walking with Shadows*. Nigeria: BlackSands Books, 2005.

Dijck, J., and T. Poell. "Understanding Social Media Logic." *Media and Communication* 1, no. 1 (2013): 2–14.

Dike, Victor. "Corruption in Nigeria: A New Paradigm for Effective Control." *Africa economic analysis* 24, no. 08 (2005): 1–22.

Dooley, Julian J., Donna CrossFollow, Lydia Hearn, Robyn Treyvaud. Review of Existing Australian and International Cyber-Safety Research. Perth: Child Health Promotion Research Centre, Edith Cowan University, 2009.

Dunton, Chris. "Wheyting be Dat?' The Treatment of Homosexuality in African Literature." *Research in African Literatures* 20, no. 3 (1989): 422–448.

Dunu, Ifeoma Vivian and Chinwe Elizabeth Uzochukwu. "Social Media: An Effective Tool for Social Mobilization in Nigeria." *Journal of Humanities and Social Science* 20, no. 4 (2015): 10–21.

Durojaiye, Seun. "Social Media Bill Threatens Freedom of Expression in Nigeria—Amnesty International." *International Center for Investigative Reporting (ICIR)*, March 9, 2020. www.icirnigeria.org/social-media-bill-threatens-freedom-of-expression-in-nigeria-amnesty-international/.

Dutta, Soumitra and Matthew Fraser. "Obama and the 'Facebook Effect.'" *Media Post*, 2008. www.mediapost.com/publications/article/94861.

Easterly, William and Yaw Nyarko. "Is the Brain Drain Good for Africa?" *Brookings Global Economy and Development Working Paper*, March 2008.

Edegoh, Leo O.N., and Ogonna W. Anunike. "Voters' Assessment of Social Media use for 2015 Electioneering Campaigns by the two Leading Political Parties in Nigeria." *African Research Review* 10, no. 4 (2016): 18–40

Edike, Tony. "Pro-Biafra Group's to Seize Enugu Radio, TV Stations Foiled." *Vanguard Newspaper*, June 6, 2014.

Editorial. "How NASS Members Corner Billions Via Constituency Projects-ICPC." *Daily Asset*, December 16, 2019.

Editorial. "Nigeria's Huge Import-dependency Syndrome." *The Guardian*, October 4, 2020.

Editorial. "Reducing Cost of Governance." *Thisday*, January 7, 2020.

Edogor, Ignatius Obi, Alice Aladi Jonah and Lucky Idowu Ojo. "Influence of Social Media on Youths' usage of Traditional Mass Media in Nigeria." *New Media and Mass Communication* 31, no. 1 (2014): 55–61.

Edosomwan, Simeon, Sitalaskshmi Kalangot Prakasan, Doriane Kouame, Jonelle Watson and Tom Seymour. "The History of Social Media and its Impact on Business." *Journal of Applied Management and Entrepreneurship* 16, no. 3 (2011): 79.

Effing, Robin, Jos Van Hillegersberg and Theo Huibers. "Social Media and Political Participation: Are Facebook, Twitter and Youtube Democratizing our Political Systems?" In *Electronic Participation. ePart 2011. Lecture Notes in Computer Science*, edited by Efthimios Tambouris, Ann Macintosh and Hans de Bruijn. Switzerland: Springer, Berlin, Heidelberg, 2011, 25–35.

Effiong, Inibehe. "The Cross Dressing Bill is Dead on Arrival." *Premium Times*, April 6, 2022. www.premiumtimesng.com/opinion/522251-the-cross-dressing-bill-is-dead-on-arrival-by-inibehe-effiong.html

Egbas, Jude. "Meet the Young Nigerians who just sold their Company for N76 Billion." *Pulse*, October 17, 2020. www.pulse.ng/business/paystack-for-n76-billion-ezra-olubi-shola-akinlade-sell-their-company-live-the-dream/3zj00kr.

Egbon, M. "Origins and Development of Television Broadcasting in Nigeria: An Inquiry into Television Development in a Non-industrialized Nation." Ph.D *diss.*, University of Wisconsin, Madison, 1977.

Egbulonu, Kelechukwu Godslove and Ifesinachi Sandra Eleonu. "Gender Inequality and Economic Growth in Nigeria (1990–2016)." *International Journal of Gender and Women Studies* 6, no. 1 (2018): 159–167.

Egielewa, Peter. "An Analysis of Media Coverage of the New Nigeria's Social Media Bill in Selected Nigerian Newspaper." *SAU Journal of Management and Social Sciences* 3 (2022): 151–162.

Ejumudo, Kelly Brian Ovie. "Gender Equality and Women Empowerment in Nigeria: The Desirability and Inevitability of a Pragmatic Approach." *Developing Country Studies* 3, no. 4 (2013): 59–66.

Ekdale, Brian, Melissa Tully. "Cambridge Analytica in Africa—What do we Know?" *Democracy in Africa*, January 10, 2020. www.democracyinafrica.org/cambridge-analytica-africa-know/.

Ekpo, A.H., and O.J. Umoh. "An Overview of the Nigerian Economic Growth and Development." *Daily Newspaper*, July 14, 2012.

Ekwunife, Raphael Abumchukwu, A.O. Ononiwu, Rosemary Effiong Akpan and H.T. Sunday. "EndSARS Protest and Centralized Police System in Nigeria." In *Global Encyclopaedia of Public Administration, Public Policy, and Governance*, edited by Ali Farazmand. Switzerland: Springer Nature, 2021.

Ele, Christian. "Islamization of Nigeria: Implications for Sustainable Peace." *International Journal of Social Sciences and English Literature* 2 (2018): 13–19.

Ele, Christian. "Religious Pluralism and Sustainable Development in Nigeria." *African Research Review* 13, no. 1 (2019): 26–37.

Emeagwali, Gloria and Constance Hilliard. "History of Science in Non-Western Traditions: Africa." In *An Introduction to the History of Science in Non-Western Traditions*, edited by Douglas Allchin and Robert DeKosky. Seattle: History of Science Society, Seattle, 1999.

Emeagwali, Gloria and Edward Shizha, eds. *African Indigenous Knowledge and the Sciences: Journeys into the Past and Present*. Berlin: Springer, 2016.

Emeagwali, Gloria and Edward Shizha. "Interconnecting History, African Indigenous Knowledge Systems and Science." In *African Indigenous Knowledge and the Sciences: Journeys into the Past and Present*, edited by Gloria Emeagwali and Edward Shizha. Berlin: Springer, 2016.

Emeagwali, Gloria and George J. Sefa Dei, eds. *African Indigenous Knowledge and the Disciplines*. Rotterdam: SensePublishers, 2014.

Emeagwali, Gloria. "African Indigenous Knowledge Systems (AIK): Implications for the Curriculum." In *Ghana in Africa and the World: Essays in Honor of Adu Boahen*, edited by Toyin Falola. New Jersey: AfricaWorld Press, 2003.

Emeagwali, Gloria. "African Indigenous Knowledge Systems and the Legacy of Africa." In *Indigenous Knowledge Systems and Development in Africa*, edited by Samuel Ojo Oloruntoba, Adeshina Afolayan and Olajumoke Yacob-Haliso. Cham, Switzerland: Palgrave Macmillan, 2020, 37–55.

Emeagwali, Gloria. "Barewa (Modified)." *USA-Africa Dialogue Series*, May 27, 2021. www.groups.google.com/g/usaafricadialogue/c/DIx776QPa_8.

Emeagwali, Gloria. "Colonialism." In *African Indigenous Science and Knowledge System: Triumpsh and Tribulations: Essays in Honour of Professor Gloria Thomas-Emeagwali*, edited by Olayemi Akinwumi, Okpeh Ochayi Okpeh, C.B.N. Ogbogbo and Adoyi Onoja. Abuja: Roots Books & Journals Limited, 2007.

Emeagwali, Gloria. "Definition of Egyptophobia." *USA-Africa Dialogue Series*, 2014. www.groups.google.com/g/usaafricadialogue/c/AIk6ZTgqiZk/m/3fg2v3wOBAAJ.

Emeagwali, Gloria. "Ethiopia on the Brink as Crisis Threatens 'Peace and Stability' of Region—but what has Fueled the Conflict and Criticism of Biden's Response?" *The Conversation*, November 18, 2021. www.theconversation.com/ethiopia-on-the-brink-as-crisis-threatens-peace-and-stability-of-region-but-what-has-fueled-the-conflict-and-criticism-of-bidens-response-171785

Emeagwali, Gloria. "Eurocentrism of Science and Technology and the History." In *African Indigenous Science and Knowledge System: Triumph and Tribulations: Essays in Honour of Professor Gloria Thomas-Emeagwali*, edited by Olayemi Akinwumi, Okpeh Ochayi Okpeh, C.B.N. Ogbogbo and Adoyi Onoja. Abuja: Roots Books & Journals Limited, 2007.

Emeagwali, Gloria. "Female Circumcision in Africa." *Africa Update* 3, no. 2 (1996).

Emeagwali, Gloria. "Intersections between Africa's Indigenous Knowledge Systems and History." In *African Indigenous Knowledge and the Disciplines*, edited by Gloria Emeagwali and George J. Sefa Dei. Rotterdam: SensePublishers, 2014, 1–17.

Emeagwali, Gloria. "Islam and Gender: The Nigerian Case." In *Muslim Women's Choices: Religious Belief and Social Reality,* edited by Camillia Fawzi El-Solh and Judy Mabro. Rhode Island: Berg, 1994.

Emeagwali, Gloria. "Supports the Call for Local Technologies." *Liberal Arts Instructional Technology Services*, The University of Texas. www.laits.utexas.edu/africa/ads/91.html

Emeagwali, Gloria. “Technology Transfer: Explaining the Japanese Success Story.” *Journal of Contemporary Asia* 21, no. 4 (1991): 504–512.

Emeagwali, Gloria. “The Neo-Liberal Agenda and the IMF/World Bank Structural Adjustment Programs with Reference to Africa.” In *Critical Perspectives on Neoliberal Globalization, Development and Education in Africa and Asia*, edited by Dip Kapoor. Netherland: Brill, 2011, 1–13.

Emeagwali, Gloria. “Tireless Campaigner against FGM Dies in London.” *USA-Africa Dialogue Series*, 2014. www.groups.google.com/g/usaafricadialogue/c/h9c-PezE0qVc/m/RAYJDUubAx0J.

Emeagwali, Gloria. Excerpts from the Discussion: Mass Atrocities in Nigeria. *USA-Africa Dialogue Series*, 2019. www.groups.google.com/g/usaafricadialogue/c/OM24q-SSywc/m/TtAt3UpQBQAJ.

Emetumah, Fatima. “Social Media as a Factor for Increased Frontiers of Democracy in Nigeria’s 2015 Presidential Election.” *British Journal of Education, Society & Behavioural Science* 17, no. 4 (2016): 1–9.

Enberg, Jasmine. “Q2 2019 Social Trends.” *eMarketer*, July 23, 2019. www.emarketer.com/content/q2-2019-social-trends.

Endong, Floribert Patrick and E. Obonganwan. “Media (Mis) Representation of the Nigerian Woman as a Product of the Society.” *International Journal of Gender and Women’s Studies* 3, no. 1 (2015): 103.

Eno-Abasi, Sunday, Chris Irekamba and Abdulganiyu Alabi. “Nigeria: Religiosity, Faith and the Missing Link.” *The Guardian,* December 15, 2019.

Eno-Abasi, Sunday. “Constituency Projects: Still a Long Way to Getting Value for Money.” April 5, 2020.

Esimokha, G., K.B. Bobmanuel and O. Asaolu. “Perception of Nigerians on Hate Speech Bill (A Study of Akungba-Okoko Residents, Ondo State).” *Journals of Humanities and Social Sciences* 24, no. 11 (2019): 59–67.

Etteng, Innocent. “#ENDSARS: Inside Nigeria’s Fight to End Police Brutality.” *Yes Magazine,* October 29, 2020. www.yesmagazine.org/social-justice/2020/10/29/nigeria-end-sars-protests/.

European Commission. “Strategic Engagement for Gender Equality 2016–2019.” Luxembourg Publications Office of the European Union, 2016.

Fagbule, Fola and Feyi Fawehinmi. *Formation: The Making of Nigeria from Jihad to Amalgamation*. Abuja: Cassava Republic Press, 2021.

Failed States Index. “Fund for Peace and Foreign Policy,” July/August 2007

Fajana, Adekunle. “Singer, Temmie Ovwasa, never wants to have Kids, she Discloses why.” *Ripples Nigeria*, August 5, 2022. www.ripplesnigeria.com/singer-temmie-ovwasa-never-wants-to-have-kids-she-discloses-why/.

Falola, Toyin. “Ọ̀wọ̀: Soaring Insecurity and the Conspiracy of State Silence.” *Premium Times*, June 9, 2022. www.premiumtimesng.com/opinion/535612-owo-soaring-insecurity-and-the-conspiracy-of-state-silence-by-toyin-falola.html.\

Falola, Toyin. “Pius Adesanmi: The Man who Leaves and Lives.” *Yoruba Studies Review* 3, no. 2 (2019).

Falola, Toyin. "Professor Moses Ochonu: A Historical March into the Future." *Premium Times*, September 6, 2017. www.opinion.premiumtimesng.com/2017/09/06/professor-moses-ochonu-a-historical-march-into-the-future-by-toyin-falola/

Falola, Toyin. "Urgent Steps towards Resolving the ASUU Strike." *Premium Times*, August 31 2020. www.opinion.premiumtimesng.com/2020/08/31/urgent-practical-steps-towards-resolving-the-asuu-strike-by-toyin-falola/

Falola, Toyin. *Yoruba Gurus: Indigenous Production of Knowledge in Africa*. Trenton: Africa World Press, 1999.

Farkas, Xénia and Márton Bene. "Images, Politicians, and Social Media: Patterns and Effects of Politicians' Image-based Political Communication Strategies on Social Media." *The International Journal of Press/Politics* 26, no. 1 (2021): 119–142.

Fashina, Abiola. *Politics in Nigeria and Social Media: The Importance for Elections & Good Governance* Book 2. Washington: Amazon Digital Services LLC - Kdp, 2022.

Fasola, Omobolanle Seri and Adekunle Emmanuel Oyadeyi. "Influence of Social Media on Youth Participation in Politics in Nigeria: A Case of the 2015/2019 General Elections." *Journal of Social Sciences and Public Policy* 13, no. 2 (2021): 1–20.

Federal Ministry of Education. *National Policy on Education*, 4th ed. Lagos, National Education Research and Development Council, 2004.

Feminist Coalition. "An Update on the Feminist Coalition Girls Education Program." *Feminist Coalition,* August 11, 2022. www.feministcoalition.medium.com/an-update-on-the-feminist-coalition-girls-education-program-d8db5e84dda7.

Fenton, Natalie. "Left Out? Digital Media, Radical Politics and Social Change." *Information, Community, and Society* 19, no. 3 (2016): 346–361.

Fitzgerald, Michael, Nina Kruschwitz, Didier Bonnet and Michael Welch. "Embracing Digital Technology: A New Strategic Imperative." *MIT Sloan Management Review* 55, no. 2 (2014): 4.

Flores, Pamela, Nancy Regina Gómez, Alana Farrah Roa and Risa Whitson. "Reviving Feminism through Social Media: From the Classroom to Online and Offline Public Spaces." *Gender and Education* 32, no. 6 (2020): 751–766.

Folarin, B. *Theories of Mass Communication: An Introductory Text*. Ibadan: Stirling-Horden Publishers, 1998.

Folarin, S., and F.O. Oviasogie. "Insurgency and National Security Challenges in Nigeria: Looking Back, Looking Ahead." www.eprints.convenantuniversity.edu.ng/3243/1/Folarin.

Folorunso, Olusegun, Rebecca O. Vincent, Adebayo Felix Adekoya and Adewale Opeoluwa Ogunde. "Diffusion of Innovation in Social Networking Sites among University Students." *International Journal of Computer Science and security* 4, no. 3 (2010): 361–372.

Freedom House Report. "Freedom in the World." *Freedom House*. www.freedomhouse.org/sites/default/files/FH_FITW_Report_2016.pdf.

Fuchs, Christian and Marisol Sandoval, eds. *Critique, Social Media and the Information Society*. New York: Routledge, 2014.

Fuchs, Christian. *Social Media: A Critical Introduction*. California: Sage, 2021.

Game Thinking TV. "4 Key Insights for Start-ups Success in Africa, with Victor Asemota." *Game Thinking TV*, May 5, 2022. www.youtube.com/watch?v=5x0ND9Z3ef4.

Gandonu, Ajato. "Nigeria's 250 Ethnic Groups: Realities and Assumptions." In *Perspectives on Ethnicity*, edited by Regina E. Holloman and Serghei A. Arutiunov. Berlin: De Gruyter Mouton, 2011, 243–280.

Gboyega, Alex. *Corruption and Democratization in Nigeria*. Ibadan: Agba Areo, 1996.

Gidengil, E., and Heather Bastedo, eds. *Canadian Democracy from the Ground Up: Perceptions and Performance*. Vancouver: UBC Press, 2014.

Giel, Katelyn Anne. "Hashtag Feminism: An Analysis of Social Media as a Feminist Platform." Ph.D *diss*., Arizona State University, 2015.

Gold, J., Alisa E. Pedrana, Mark A. Stoove, Shanton Chang, Steve Howard, Jason Asselin, Olivia Ilic, Colin Batrouney and Margaret E. Hellard. "Developing Health Promotion Interventions on Social Networking Sites: Recommendations from the FaceSpace Project." *Journal of Medical Internet Research* 14, no. 1 (2012): 1–11.

Green-Simms, Lindsey. "The Emergent Queer: Homosexuality and Nigerian Fiction in the 21st Century." *Research in African Literatures* 47, no. 2 (2016): 131–161.

Guseh, J.S., and E. Oritsejafor. "Democracy and Economic Growth in Africa: The Cases of Ghana and South Africa." *Journal of Third World Studies* 22, no. 2 (2005): 121–137.

Guterres, António. "United Nations Strategy and Plan of Action on Hate Speech." *Technical Report May*, 2019, 1–5.

Gwendolyn, Mikell, ed. *African Feminism: The Politics of Survival in Sub-saharan Africa*. Philadelphia: University of Pennsylvania Press, 1997.

Gyasi, Geosi. "Interview with 2017 Brunel International African Poetry Prize Shortlisted Poet, Romeo Oriogun." *GeosiReads*, April 23, 2017. www.geosireads.wordpress.com/2017/04/23/interview-with-2017-brunel-international-african-poetry-prize-shortlisted-poet-romeo-oriogun/

Handy, Laura. "CyberFeminism: Virtual Activism, Real Change." PhD *diss*., University of Puget Sound, 2001.

Hanson, S. "Corruption in Sub- Saharan Africa." *Think Africa Press*, August 6, 2009. www.thinkafricapress.com/economy/causin...retrieved 24/01/2021.

Harfoush, Rahof. *Yes, We Did! An Inside Look at how Social Media Built the Obama Brand*. New York: New Riders, 2009.

Hari, Solomon. "The Evolution of Social Protest in Nigeria: The Role of Social Media in the "#OccupyNigeria Protest." *International Journal of Humanities and Social Science Invention* 3, no. 9 (2014): 33–39.

Harrow, Kenneth W. *African Cinema Postcolonial and Feminist Readings*. Trenton: Africa World Press, 1999.

Hartmann, Christof. "Leverage and Linkage: How Regionalism Shapes Regime Dynamics in Africa." In *Book Democratization and Competitive Authoritarianism in Africa*, edited by Mttijs Boggard and Sebastian Elischer. Wiesbaden: Springer VS, 2016, 79–98.

Hasinoff, Amy. "Sexting as Media Production: Rethinking Social Media and Sexuality." *New Media & Society*15, no. 4 (2013): 449–465.

Hassan, Ibrahim. "Nigeria and the Railway Revolution: A Ray of Opportunities Under President Muhammadu Buhari." *TheCable*, January 25, 2022. www.thecable.ng/nigeria-railway-revolution-opportunities-under-muhammadu-buhari.

Highfield, Tim. "National and State–Level Politics on Social Media: Twitter, Australian Political Discussions, and the Online Commentariat." *International Journal of Electronic Governance* 6, no. 4 (2013): 342–360.

Hitchen, Jamie, Jonathan Fisher, Idayat Hassan and Nic Cheeseman. "Whatsapp and Nigeria's 2019 Elections: Mobilising the People, Protecting the Vote." *Africa Portal*, July 1, 2019. www.africaportal.org/publications/whatsapp-and-nigerias-2019-elections-mobilising-people-protecting-vote/

Hodges, Tony. "Children's and Women's Rights in Nigeria: A Wake-up Call: Situation Assessment and Analysis, 2001." *National Planning Commission*, 2001.

Hofstede Insights. "Country Comparison: Canada, Nigeria, the United Kingdom, and the United States." *Hofstede Insights*, June 21, 2021. www.hofstede-insights.com/country-comparison/canada,nigeria,the-uk,the-usa/

Hofstede Insights. "What about Nigeria." *Country Comparison Nigeria*, 2022. www.hofstede-insights.com/country-comparison/nigeria/.

Hoije, Katarina. "Nigerian Novelists Reflects on Anti-Gay Law." *VOA*, August 15, 2015. www.voanews.com/a/nigerian-novelist-reflects-on-anti-gay-law/2917666.html.

Huffington Post. "Kenya: Corrupt Cops Caught in the Act (Video)." *Huffpost*, 2017. www.huffpost.com/entry/kenya-corrupt-cops-caught_n_342140.

Human Rights Watch. "Political Shari'a"? Human Rights and Islamic Law in Northern Nigeria." *Human Rights Watch*, September 21, 2004. www.hrw.org/report/2004/09/21/political-sharia/human-rights-and-islamic-law-northern-nigeria#:~:text=Acknowledgements111,I.,a%20(Islamic%20law)%20courts.

Human Rights Watch. "Rest in Pieces": Police Torture and Deaths in Custody in Nigeria." *Human Rights Watch*, July 27, 2005. www.hrw.org/report/2005/07/27/rest-pieces/police-torture-and-deaths-custody-nigeria.

Huntington, S. *Political Order in Changing Societies*. Connecticut: Yale University Press, 1978.

Hutchinson, Andrew. "Facebook Continues to Add Users, Posts Strong Revenue Result in Q3." *Social Media Today*, October, 29, 2020. www.socialmediatoday.com/news/facebook-continues-to-add-users-posts-strong-revenue-result-in-q3/588090/

Ibeanu, Okechukwu, Nwachukwu Orji and C.K. Iwuamadi. *Biafra Separatism: Causes, Consequences and Remedies*. Enugu: Institute for Innovations in Development, 2016.

Ibezim-Ohaeri, Victoria. "Confronting Closing Civic Spaces in Nigeria." *SUR-International Journal on Human Rights* 26 (2017): 129

Ibrahim, A. "Pius Adesanmi for ANA Convention." *Daily Trust*, October 7, 2012.

Ibrahim, Jibrin and Saleh Bala. *Civilian-led Governance and Security in Nigeria after Boko Haram*. Washington, DC: United States Institute of Peace, 2018.

Ibrahim, Jibrin. "2018 and the Return of Politics." *Daily Trust*, January 5, 2018.

Ibrahim, Jibrin. "2019 and the Search for National Renewal." *Daily Trust*, January 4, 2019.

Ibrahim, Jibrin. "Alternative Facts and the Buhari Legacy." *Premium Times,* June 24, 2022. www.premiumtimesng.com/opinion/538883-alternative-facts-and-the-buhari-legacy-by-jibrin-ibrahim.html.

Ibrahim, Jibrin. "Analysing the 2019 General Elections." *Daily Trust*, February 15, 2019.

Ibrahim, Jibrin. "APC and the Challenge of Improving Political Parties." *Premium Times*, November 4, 2013. www.premiumtimesng.com/opinion/147752-apc-challenge-improving-political-parties-jibrin-ibrahim.html.

Ibrahim, Jibrin. "As Bandits/Terrorists Tighten the Noose around Our Necks." *Premium Time,* April 1, 2022. www.premiumtimesng.com/opinion/521247-as-bandits-terrorists-tighten-the-noose-around-our-necks-by-jibrin-ibrahim.html.

Ibrahim, Jibrin. "As the War Intensifies." *Premium Times*, March 2, 2014. www.premiumtimesng.com/opinion/156057-as-the-war-intensifies-by-jibrin-ibrahim.html.

Ibrahim, Jibrin. "Building National Consensus on Consolidating Democracy." *Premium Times*, February 18, 2022. www.premiumtimesng.com/opinion/512230-building-national-consensus-on-consolidating-democracy-by-jibrin-ibrahim.html.

Ibrahim, Jibrin. "Building Social Cohesion: Its Ineluctable, the Nigerians are Emerging." *Premium Times*, August 27, 2021. www.premiumtimesng.com/opinion/481520-building-social-cohesion-its-ineluctable-the-nigerians-are-emerging-by-jibrin-ibrahim.html.

Ibrahim, Jibrin. "Chibok Girls and the Reluctant President." *Premium Time,* June 1, 2014. www.premiumtimesng.com/opinion/161812-chibok-girls-reluctant-president-jibrin-ibrahim.html.

Ibrahim, Jibrin. "Civics and the Words and Deeds of a Nigerian Politician." *Premium Times*, March 18, 2022. www.premiumtimesng.com/opinion/517986-civics-and-the-words-and-deeds-of-a-nigerian-politician-by-jibrin-ibrahim.html.

Ibrahim, Jibrin. "Completing the 2019 Electoral Process." *Daily Trust*, March 8, 2019.

Ibrahim, Jibrin. "Conversation with my ASUU Comrades: Let's Get Real." *Premium Times*, October 14, 2013. www.premiumtimesng.com/opinion/146584-conversation-asuu-comrades-lets-get-real-jibrin-ibrahim.html.

Ibrahim, Jibrin. "Corruption and the Buhari Legacy." *Premium Times*, May 20, 2022. www.premiumtimesng.com/opinion/531216-corruption-and-the-buhari-legacy-by-jibrin-ibrahim.html.

Ibrahim, Jibrin. "Democratising Nigerian Democracy." *Premium Times*, June 25, 2021. www.premiumtimesng.com/opinion/469872-democratising-nigerian-democracy-by-jibrin-ibrahim.html.

Ibrahim, Jibrin. "Developing Criteria for Good Leadership Selection in Nigeria." *Premium Times*, March 25, 2022. www.premiumtimesng.com/opinion/519531-developing-criteria-for-good-leadership-selection-in-nigeria-by-jibrin-ibrahim.html.

Ibrahim, Jibrin. "Differentiating APC from the PDP." *Premium Times,* December 22, 2013. www.premiumtimesng.com/opinion/151899-differentiating-apc-pdp-jibrin-ibrahim.html.

Ibrahim, Jibrin. "From Corruption to Ruling Class Insanity." *Premium Times,* February 17, 2014. www.premiumtimesng.com/opinion/155273-corruption-ruling-class-insanity-jibrin-ibrahim.html.

Ibrahim, Jibrin. "Is INEC Ready for Tomorrow's Elections?" *Daily Trust,* February 22, 2019.

Ibrahim, Jibrin. "Kano, INEC and the 2019 Elections." *Daily Trust,* February 16, 2018.

Ibrahim, Jibrin. "Kidnapping for Ransom: Can Nigeria Survive the "Third Wave"?" *Premium Time,* August 6, 2021. www.premiumtimesng.com/opinion/477805-kidnapping-for-ransom-can-nigeria-survive-the-third-wave-by-jibrin-ibrahim.html.

Ibrahim, Jibrin. "Lack of Respect: How Our Politicians Speak to Us." *Premium Times,* January 21, 2022. www.premiumtimesng.com/opinion/507020-lack-of-respect-how-our-politicians-speak-to-us-by-jibrin-ibrahim.html.

Ibrahim, Jibrin. "Memory and the IBB Legacy." *Premium Times,* August 13, 2021. www.premiumtimesng.com/opinion/479009-memory-and-the-ibb-legacy-by-jibrin-ibrahim.html.

Ibrahim, Jibrin. "Nigeria and the Legacy of the Military." *Premium Times,* September 10, 2013. www.premiumtimesng.com/opinion/144406-nigeria-legacy-military-jibrin-ibrahim.html.

Ibrahim, Jibrin. "Nigeria on the Edge." *Premium Times*, August 5, 2022. www.premiumtimesng.com/opinion/547029-nigeria-on-the-edge-by-jibrin-ibrahim.html.

Ibrahim, Jibrin. "Nigeria, Democratic Politics and the 'King of Boys.'" *Premium Times,* October 1, 2021. www.premiumtimesng.com/opinion/487609-nigeria-democratic-politics-and-the-king-of-boys-by-jibrin-ibrahim.html.

Ibrahim, Jibrin. "Nigeria: The Urgency of Stopping the Drift Towards Anarchy." *Premium Times*, April 9, 2021. www.premiumtimesng.com/opinion/454025-nigeria-the-urgency-of-stopping-the-drift-towards-anarchy-by-jibrin-ibrahim.html.

Ibrahim, Jibrin. "Nigeria's Shrinking Civic Space." *Premium Times*, May 7, 2021. www.premiumtimesng.com/opinion/459981-nigerias-shrinking-civic-space-by-jibrin-ibrahim.html.

Ibrahim, Jibrin. "Options on the Titanic ASUU/Government Battle." *Premium Times,* February 25, 2022. www.premiumtimesng.com/opinion/513780-options-on-the-titanic-asuu-government-battle-by-jibrin-ibrahim.html.

Ibrahim, Jibrin. "Party Primaries and the Limits of Transactional Politics." *Premium Times*, May 27, 2022. www.premiumtimesng.com/opinion/532736-party-primaries-and-the-limits-of-transactional-politics-by-jibrin-ibrahim.html.

Ibrahim, Jibrin. "The Looming Vacancy in Aso Rock." *Premium Times*, May 6, 2022. www.premiumtimesng.com/opinion/527985-the-looming-vacancy-in-aso-rock-by-jibrin-ibrahim.html.

Ibrahim, Jibrin. "The Making of Nigeria: From Jihad to Amalgamation." *Premium Times*, September 3, 2021. www.premiumtimesng.com/opinion/482783-the-making-of-nigeria-from-jihad-to-amalgamation-by-jibrin-ibrahim.html.

Ibrahim, Jibrin. "The Muslim-Muslim Ticket and Religious Mobilisation in Nigeria." *Premium Times*, July 15, 2022. www.premiumtimesng.com/opinion/542736-the-muslim-muslim-ticket-and-religious-mobilisation-in-nigeria-by-jibrin-ibrahim.html.

Ibrahim, Jibrin. "The Presidential Election and its Aftermath." *Daily Trust*, March 1, 2019.

Ibrahim, Jibrin. "The Private University as Enterprise: Limits of Academic Capitalism." *Premium Times*, January 14, 2022. www.premiumtimesng.com/opinion/505768-the-private-university-as-enterprise-limits-of-academic-capitalism-by-jibrin-ibrahim.html.

Ibrahim, Jibrin. "The State in Question as 2021 Draws to a Close." *Premium Times*, December 31, 2021. www.premiumtimesng.com/opinion/503294-the-state-in-question-as-2021-draws-to-a-close-by-jibrin-ibrahim.html.

Ibrahim, Jibrin. "Things I Wish my President Knows." *Premium Times*, July 29, 2022. www.premiumtimesng.com/opinion/545649-things-i-wish-my-president-knows-by-jibrin-ibrahim.html.

Ibrahim, Jibrin. "To Fix Nigerian Politics, Parties Must Embrace the Popularity Principle." *Premium Times*, April 2, 2021. www.premiumtimesng.com/opinion/452845-to-fix-nigerian-politics-parties-must-embrace-the-popularity-principle-by-jibrin-ibrahim.html.

Ibrahim, Jibrin. "Turmoil or Sanity in the Party System." *Premium Times*, September 2, 2013. www.premiumtimesng.com/opinion/143977-turmoil-sanity-party-system-jibrin-ibrahim.html.

Idowu, Moses. "Against Secession: Testament to Yoruba Leaders and Promoters of Oduduwa Republic." *Sahara Reporters*, September 18, 2020. www.saharareporters.com/2020/09/18/against-secession-testament-yoruba-leaders-and-promoters-oduduwa-republic-moses-oludele.

Idowu, Olawale F. and Sunday A. Ogunode. "Gender and the Politics of Exclusion in Pre-Colonial Ibadan: The Case of Iyalode Efunsetan Aniwura." *The Journal of Traditions & Beliefs* 2, no. 21 (2016): 1–8.

Idowu, Samuel, Jide Ibietan and Ayo Olukotun. "Privatization of Power Sector in Nigeria: An Evaluation of Ibadan and Ikeja Electricity Distribution Companies Performance (2005–2018)." *International Journal of Public Administration* 43, no. 16 (2020): 1413–1420.

Idumamge, I. "Democratic Accountability and Public Trust in Nigeria." *Pointblank News*, 2002. www.pointblanknews.com.

Iganiga, B.O. "Evaluation of the Nigerian Financial Sector Reforms Using Behavioral Models." *Journal of Economics* 1, no. 2 (2010): 65–75.

Igwe, Obasi. *Politics and Globe Dictionary*. Enugu, Nigeria: Keny & Brothers Enterprises, 2007.

Ike-Obioha, Jewel. "The Agitations for Oduduwa Republic by the Yoruba Liberation Command is a Cause to Worry." *Ventures Africa*, 2017. www.venturesafrica.com/an-explainer-on-the-recent-oduduwa-republic-declaration-yoruba-land/.

Ilori, Tomiwa. "A Socio-legal Analysis of Nigeria's Protection from Internet Falsehoods, Manipulations and Other Related Matters Bill." *AfricLaw*, December 5, 2019. www.africlaw.com/2019/12/05/a-socio-legal-analysis-of-nigerias-protection-from-internet-falsehoods-manipulations-and-other-related-matters-bill/

Independent National Electoral Commission. "Report of the 2019 General Election." *INEC Nigeria*, 2020. www.inecnigeria.org/wp-content/uploads/2020/11/REPORT-OF-THE-2019-GENERAL-ELECTION.pdf.

Ingham, Kenneth. *Politics in Modern Africa: The Uneven Tribal Dimension*. London: Routledge, 1990.

Iniobong, Iwok and Godfrey Ofurun. "Why Orji Kalu's Freedom Riles EFCC." *Business Day*, May 10, 2020.

Inobemhe, Kelvin. "Social Media Regulation in a Democratic Nigeria: Challenges and Implication." *Media & Communication Currents* 5, no 1 (2022): 71–88.

Inobemhe, Kelvin, Felix Ugber, I.L. Ojo and Tsegyu Santas. "New Media and the Proliferation of Fake News in Nigeria." *Nasarawa Journal of Multimedia and Communication Studies* 2, no. 2 (2020): 155–169.

Inobemhe, Kelvin, Galadima Audu Bala, Onakpa Mohammed Shaibu, Kingsley Inalegwu Onah and Tsegyu Santas. "Assessing the Pros and Cons of Political Communication and the Politics of Power Rotation in Nigeria." In *Thoughts on Political Communication in Nigeria*, edited by Ezekiel S. Asemah, Daniel O. Ekhareafo and Tsegyu Santas. Enugu: GO University Press, 2022, 271.

International Telecommunication Union. The World in 2013: ICT Facts and Figures. ICT Data and Statistics Division, Telecommunication Development Bureau. Geneva: International Telecommunication Union.

Iroanusi, Esther. "Buhari Approves N37 Billion for National Assembly Renovation." *Premium Times,* December 16, 2019. www.premiumtimesng.com/news/top-news/368458-buhari-approves-n37-billion-for-national-assembly-renovation.html

Iroanusi, Esther. "Updated: Bill to Regulate Social Media Passes Second Reading at Senate." *Premium Times*, November 20, 2019. www.premiumtimesng.com/news/headlines/364236-just-in-bill-to-regulate-social-media-passes-second-reading-at-senate.html.

Ismaila, O., and A. Jekayinfa. "Cultural Pluralism, Reconstructive Education and Nation Building in Nigeria." *International Journal of Sociology and Anthropology* 5, no. 5 (2013): 140–146.

Iyatse, Geoff, Femi Adekoya, Benjamin Alade and Joke Falaju. "Lagos-Ibadan Rail Service in Costly, Unfriendly Takeoff." *The Guardian,* December 11, 2020.

Jacka, J., and P.R. Scott. *Auditing Social Media: A Governance and Risk Guide.* New York: John Wiley and Sons Incorporated, 2011.

Jackson, Tom. "How Egypt Established itself as an African Tech Hub to be Reckoned with in 2019." *Disrupt Africa,* February 4, 2020. www.disrupt-africa.com/2020/02/how-egypt-established-itself-as-an-african-tech-hub-to-be-reckoned-with-in-2019/.

Jacob, Amedie. "The Impact of Social Media on Society." *Advanced Writing: Pop Culture Intersections* 2 (2015): 1–19.

Jannah, Chijioke. "Catholic Bishops Speak on Proposed Cattle Colonies." *Daily Post,* February 4, 2018.

Jannamike, Luminous. "2023: We'll Reject Muslim-Muslim Ticket—CAN." *Vanguard Newspaper,* July 19, 2022.

Jasanoff, Sheila. "The Vanishing Square: Civic Learning in the Internet Age." *Hastings Center Report* 51 (2021): S5-S9

Jha, Chandan Kumar and Oasis Kodila-Tedika. "Does Social Media Promote Democracy? Some Empirical Evidence." *Journal of Policy Modeling* 42, no. 2 (2020): 271–290.

Ji, Li, Ping Ping Fu, Irene Chow and T. K. Peng. "Societal Development and the Change of Leadership Style in Oriental Chinese Societies." *Journal of Developing Societies* 18, no. 1 (2002): 46–63.

Jimada, Usman. "Social Media in the Public Sphere of Accountability in Nigeria." *Global Media Journal* 17, no. 32 (2019): 178.

John, Fredrick Friday. "Tweet and Talk: Stance of Twitter Discussants on the Candidacy of Presidential Candidates that Declared for the 2023 Election." *African Journal for the Psychological Studies of Social Issues* 25, no. 2 (2022): 42–57.

Johnson, Dayo, Dapo Akinrefon, Jimitota Onoyume and Ddemola Akinyemi. "Oduduwa Republic October Rally Divides Yoruba Leaders." *Vanguard Newspaper,* September 27, 2020.

Johnson, Dayo, Nnamdi Ojiego, Rotimi Ojomoyela and James Ogunnaike. "S/West Secession Letter to Buhari Divides Yoruba Leaders." *Vanguard Newspaper*, September 4, 2022.

Johnson, Ted. "D.C. Attorney General Sues Facebook over Data Misuse in 2016 Election." *Variety*, December 19 2018. www.variety.com/2018/politics/news/d-c-attorney-general-sues-facebook-over-data-misuse-in-2016-election-1203093256/.

Joseph, Deepak. "An Overview of Sri Lankan Economic Crisis 2022 and how it Affects India." *International Journal of Recent Advances in Multidisciplinary Topics* 3, no. 4 (2022): 58–59.

Joseph, Richard. *Democracy and Prebendal Politics in Nigeria.* Cambridge: Cambridge University Press, 2014.

Joyce, Mary C. *Digital Activism Decoded: The New Mechanics of Change.* New York: International Debate Education Association, 2010.

Kalsnes, Bente. "The Social Media Paradox Explained: Comparing Political Parties' Facebook Strategy Versus Practice." *Social Media + Society* 2, no. 2 (2016): 1–11.

Kalu, N. *State Power, Autarchy and Political Conquest in Nigerian Federalism*. Boulder and New York: Lexington Books, 2007.

Kamasi, A. "Top 15 Richest Pastors in the World and their Net Worth." *Pulse Nigeria*, October 21 2020. www.pulse.com.gh/filla/top-15-richest-pastors-in-the-world-and-their-net-worth/lwj95ky.

Kamer, Lars. "Nigeria: Number of Social Media Users 2017–2026." *Statista*, July 21, 2022. www.statista.com/statistics/972907/number-of-social-network-users-in-nigeria/

Kapidzic S. and S.C. Herring. "Race, Gender, and Self-Presentation in Teen Profile Photographs." *New Media and Society* 17, no. 6 (2015): 958–976.

Kasenally, Roukaya and Dooshweena Awatar. "Social Media, Elections and Political Engagements: The 2014 General Elections in Mauritius." *Journal of African Elections* 16, no. 2 (2015): 47–70.

Kay, Biola. "#ENDSARS will never be Forgotten in the Nigerian History." *Brumpost*, 2020. www.brumpost.com/endsars-will-never-be-forgotten-in-the-nigerian-history/.

Kayode, Olujimi. "Media, Mood and Movement: Media Impact on Social Movement in Nigeria." *Academia*, 2011. www.academia.edu/4102433/Media_Mood_and_Movement_Media_Impact_on_Socia l_Movements_in_Nigeria.

Kazeem, Yomi. "The Biggest Trends in African Tech Start-ups." *Quartz Africa*, December 31, 2019. www.qz.com/africa/1777241/the-biggest-trends-in-african-tech-start-ups-and-innovation-2019/.

Kehinde Oyesomi and Olusola Oyero. "Women's Political Invisibility in Nigeria and the Imperative of Deliberate Media Agenda." In *Women's Political Visibility and Media Access: The Case of Nigeria*, edited by Oladokun Omojola. Newcastle upon Tyne: Cambridge Scholars Publishing, 2014, 109–126.

Kehinde, Okanlawon. "Perceptions and Attitudes of Heterosexual Nigerian University Students towards Homosexuality and LGB Persons." *Journal of LGBT Youth* 17, no. 2 (2020): 149–176.

Kemp, Simon. "Digital 2020: Nigeria." *Data Reportal*, February 18, 2020. www.datareportal.com/reports/digital-2020-Nigeria

Keziah, Ayuba Y., and Panshak Yohanna. "Nigerian Statistical Data and their Trustworthiness." *World Economics* 23, no. 1 (2022): 27–38.

Khan, Muhammad Naeem, Muhammad Azeem Ashraf, Donald Seinen, Kashif Ullah Khan and Rizwan Ahmed Laar. "Social Media for Knowledge Acquisition and Dissemination: The Impact of the COVID-19 Pandemic on Collaborative Learning Driven Social Media Adoption." *Frontiers in Psychology* 12 (2021): 1–13.

Khan, Muhammad, Anam Javeed, Majid Jamal Khan, Shahab Ud Din, Asif Khurshid and Uzma Noor. "Political Participation through Social Media: Comparison of Pakistani and Malaysian Youth." *IEEE Access* 7 (2019): 35532–35543.

King, Philip J., and Lawrence E. Stager. *Life in Biblical Israel*. Louisville: Westminster John Knox Press, 2001.

Kioli, Felix, Rosh Were Allan and Onkware Kennedy. "Traditional Perspectives and Control Mechanisms of Adolescent Sexual Behavior in Kenya." *International Journal of Sociology and Anthropology* 4, no. 1 (2012): 1–7.

Kireev, Alex. "Nigeria: Presidential Election 1999." *Electoral Geography*. www.electoralgeography.com/new/en/countries/n/nigeria/nigeria-presidential-election-1999.html.

Klein, Herbert S. *The Atlantic Slave Trade*. Cambridge: Cambridge University Press, 2010.

Kodila-Tedika, Oasis. "Natural Resource Governance: Does Social Media Matter?" *Mineral Economics* 34, no. 1 (2021): 127–140.

Konner, Melvin. "Mutilated in the Name of Tradition." *The New York Times*, April 15, 1990.

Kperogi, Farooq A. "10 Reasons Osinbajo will Ignite a Religious Civil War." *Notes from Atlanta,* March 21, 2022. www.farooqkperogi.com/2022/03/10-reasons-osinbajo-will-ignite.html.

Kperogi, Farooq A. "ASUU, Call off this Strike Now." *Notes from Atlanta,* August 20, 2022. www.farooqkperogi.com/2022/08/asuu-call-off-this-strike-now.html.

Kperogi, Farooq A. "Atiku's Emergence and End of the Road for Buhari." *Notes from Atlanta,* October 13, 2018. www.farooqkperogi.com/2018/10/atikus-emergence-and-end-of-road-for.html.

Kperogi, Farooq A. "Between Obama's "Birthers" and Buhari's "WASCers." *Notes from Atlanta,* January 24, 2015. www.farooqkperogi.com/2015/01/between-obamas-birthers-and-buharis.html.

Kperogi, Farooq A. "Boko Haram as an Empty Signifier." *Notes from Atlanta,* January 7, 2012. www.farooqkperogi.com/2012/01/boko-haram-as-empty-signifier.html.

Kperogi, Farooq A. "Buhari is World's Most Successful Mass Hypnotist." *Notes from Atlanta,* July 24, 2022. www.farooqkperogi.com/2022/07/buhari-is-worlds-most-successful-mass.html.

Kperogi, Farooq A. "Buhari not Competent to Govern any Country." *The Punch*, January 29, 2017.

Kperogi, Farooq A. "My Ideal Nigerian President in 2023." *Nigerian Tribune,* March 26, 2022.

Kperogi, Farooq A. *Digital Dissidence and Social Media Censorship in Africa*. New York: Routledge, 2022.

Kperogi, Farooq. "Fuel Price Hike: The Language and Grammatical Illogic of a Regulated Deregulation." *Notes from Atlanta,* May 15, 2016. www.farooqkperogi.com/2016/05/fuel-price-hike-language-and.html.

Kperogi, Farooq. "Fuel Subsidy Removal: Time to "Occupy" Nigeria!" *Notes from Atlanta,* October 22, 2011. www.farooqkperogi.com/2011/10/fuel-subsidy-removal-time-to-occupy.html.

Kperogi, Farooq. "Jonathan's Embarrassing U.S. Visit: A Response to Critics." *Notes from Atlanta*, April 24, 2010. www.farooqkperogi.com/2010/04/jonathans-embarrassing-us-visit.html.

Kperogi, Farooq. "Networked Social Journalism: Media, Citizen Participation and Democracy in Nigeria." In *Participatory Politics and Citizen Journalism in a Networked Africa: A Connected Continent*, edited by Bruce Mutsvairo. London: Palgrave Macmillan, 2016.

Kperogi, Farooq. "On the Buhari Government's Continuation of the Corruption of the Jonathan Government." *Facebook*, September 21, 2016. www.facebook.com/47904265/posts/pfbid02WqGdYcQ7zoqRVLJ88bnJyvh92xq8JEMRoEWehcgF3fWEnUgisSsU85Ey5iHxQ7gyl/?app=fbl.

Kperogi, Farooq. "On the Ineptitude of the Buhari Government." *Facebook*, December 6, 2016. www.facebook.com/47904265/posts/pfbid035fnWGwDqqKiGG8AGceB-JkFRZ132tSR3sPP5MfoAJdCKgYhJ22WLKsHTKwPu6xe4ml/?app=fbl.

Kperogi, Farooq. "Re: Fuel Subsidy Removal: Time to "Occupy" Nigeria!" *Notes from Atlanta*, October, 22, 2011. www.farooqkperogi.com/2011/10/re-fuel-subsidy-removal-time-to-occupy.html.

Kperogi, Farooq. "Six Reasons Why Incoming Buhari Government Fills Me with Hope." *Notes from Atlanta*, May 16, 2015. www.farooqkperogi.com/2015/05/6-reasons-why-incoming-buhari.html.

Kperogi, Farooq. "Somalization of Nigeria and Imperative of Privatized Governance." *Notes from Atlanta*, May 5, 2012. www.farooqkperogi.com/2012/05/somaliazation-of-nigeria-and-imperative.html.

Kperogi, Farooq. "The Malcolm Xian Logic in Jonathan's Praiseworthy Boko Haram Offensive." *Notes from Atlanta*, May 25, 2013. www.farooqkperogi.com/2013/05/the-malcolm-xian-logic-in-jonathans.html.

Kperogi, Farooq. "Transformation of "Change" from God Term to Devil Term in Nigeria." *Notes from Atlanta*, September 25, 2016. www.farooqkperogi.com/2016/09/transformation-of-change-from-god-term.html.

Kperogi, Farooq. "Two Signs APC Still Not Ready to Govern After Buhari." *Notes from Atlanta*, June 21, 2022. www.farooqkperogi.com/2022/06/two-signs-apc-still-not-ready-to-govern.html.

Kperogi, Farooq. "Unraveling of the Monumental Fraud in Petro Price Hike." *Notes from Atlanta*, May 21, 2016. www.farooqkperogi.com/2016/05/unraveling-of-monumental-fraud-in-petro.html.

Kperogi, Farooq. "Atiku's Interview and Unfair Tinubu Muslim-Muslim." *Notes from Atlanta*, July 23, 2022. www.farooqkperogi.com/2022/07/atikus-interview-and-unfair-tinubu.html .

Kperogi, Farooq. "Biggest Scandal in Oil "Subsidy Removal Fraud." *Notes from Atlanta*, November 05, 2011. www.farooqkperogi.com/2011/11/biggest-scandal-in-oil-subsidy-removal.html.

Kperogi, Farooq. "Corruption is Thriving not In spite of Buhari but Because of him." *Notes from Atlanta*, November 23, 2019. www.farooqkperogi.com/2020/07/corruption-is-thriving-not-in-spite-of.html.

Kperogi, Farooq. "Criticizing Buhari over 'President Michelle of West Germany' Gaffe is Ignorant." *Notes from Atlanta*, June 20, 2015. www.farooqkperogi.com/2015/06/criticizing-buhari-over-president.html.

Kperogi, Farooq. "Dr. Goodluck Jonathan, that was Embarrassing!" *Notes from Atlanta,* April 16, 2010. www.farooqkperogi.com/2010/04/dr-goodluck-jonathan-that-was.html.

Kperogi, Farooq. "Government of Buhari's Family, By His Family, and For His Family." *Notes from Atlanta*, November 23, 2019. www.farooqkperogi.com/2019/11/government-of-buharis-family-by-his.html.

Kperogi, Farooq. "On Fowler's Fake Doctorate and Integrity Deficit." *Notes from Atlanta*, August 29, 2015. www.farooqkperogi.com/2015/08/on-fowlers-fake-doctorate-and-integrity.html.

Kperogi, Farooq. "Only these Kinds of People will Buy Nomination Forms for N100m." *Notes from Atlanta*, April 30, 2022. www.farooqkperogi.com/2022/04/only-these-kinds-of-people-will-buy.html.

Kperogi, Farooq. "Osun's Christian-Christian Ticket, APC's Muslim-Muslim Ticket, and Religion in Yorubaland." *Notes from Atlanta,* July 18, 2022. www.farooqkperogi.com/2022/07/osuns-christian-christian-ticket-apcs.html.

Kperogi, Farooq. "Patience Jonathan's Peculiar Grammar." *Notes from Atlanta*, March 19, 2011. www.farooqkperogi.com/2011/03/patience-jonathans-peculiar-grammar.html.

Kperogi, Farooq. "Petrol Price Hike: Time to Occupy Nigeria Again." *Notes from Atlanta*, May 14, 201. www.farooqkperogi.com/2016/05/petrol-price-hike-time-to-occupy.html.

Kperogi, Farooq. "PVCs as "Poverty Verification Cards." *Notes from Atlanta*, June 2, 2022. www.farooqkperogi.com/2022/06/pvcs-as-poverty-verification-cards.html.

Kperogi, Farooq. "RCCG's Dangerous Foray into Politics for Osinbajo." *Notes from Atlanta*, March 10, 2022. www.farooqkperogi.com/2022/03/rccgs-dangerous-foray-into-politics-for.html.

Kperogi, Farooq. "Re: Dr. Goodluck Jonathan, that was Embarrassing!" *Notes from Atlanta*, May 16, 2010. www.farooqkperogi.com/2010/05/re-dr-goodluck-jonathan-that-was.html.

Kperogi, Farooq. "Social Media and the Demotic Turn in Africa's Media Ecology." *History Compass* 20, no. 2 (2022): e12711.

Kperogi, Farooq. "The Tinubu-Shettima Fake Bishops Saga." *Notes from Atlanta,* July 20, 2022. www.farooqkperogi.com/2022/07/the-tinubu-shettima-fake-bishops-saga.html.

Kperogi, Farooq. "These Last Months of Buhari are like a Badly Written Horror Movie." *Notes from Atlanta,* July 30, 2022. www.farooqkperogi.com/2022/07/these-last-months-of-buhari-are-like.html.

Kperogi, Farooq. "Tinubu and Obi Will either Affirm or Destroy these Two Theories in 2023." *Tribune,* August 13, 2022.

Kperogi, Farooq. "Tinubu would be Sunday Igboho if he's Denied APC Ticket." *Nigerian Tribune,* June 4, 2022.

Kperogi, Farooq. "Tinubu, Dogara and the Prison and Poison of Religious Politics." *Notes from Atlanta*, March 5, 2022.

Kperogi, Farooq. "Why Peter Obi may become President in 2023 by Default." *Nigerian Tribune,* July 16, 2022.

Kperogi, Farooq. "With Upcoming Toxic Fuel Price Hike, it's a Sad New Year." *Nigerian Tribune,* January 1, 2022.

Kperogi, Farooq. Facebook Post in Farooq Kperogi Fan Club, December 6, 2016. www.facebook.com/search/posts?q=farooq%20kperogi&filters=eyJycF9jcmVhdGlvbl90aW1lOjAiOiJ7XCJuYW1lXCI6XCJjcmVhdGlvbl90aW1lXCIsXCJhcmdzXCI6XCJ7XFxcInN0YXJ0X3llYXJcXFwiOlxcXCIyMDE2XFxcIixcXFwic3RhcnRfbW9udGhcXFwiOlxcXCIyMDE2LTFcXFwiLFxcXCJlbmRfeWVhclxcXCI6XFxcIjIwMTZcXFwiLFxcXCJlbmRfbW9udGhcXFwiOlxcXCIyMDE2LTEyXFxcIixcXFwic3RhcnRfZGF5XFxcIjpcXFwiMjAxNi0xLTFcXFwiLFxcXCJlbmRfZGF5XFxcIjpcXFwiMjAxNi0xMi0zMVxcXCJ9XCJ9In0%3D&_rdc=1&_rdr.

Kraks TV. "₦10m to Bring your Partner for a One-Night Stand, what will you do? *Kraks Sex Talk*, September 20, 2021. www.youtube.com/watch?v=AXQj7M7Nstc.

Kraks TV. "What's the Most Dangerous S3x Style you have Tried? *Kraks Sex Talk*, July 16, 2021. www.youtube.com/watch?v=EXZZg8x-N8c.

Kraks TV. "What's the Most Important Activity During Foreplay?" *Kraks Sex Talk*, June 5, 2021. www.youtube.com/watch?v=olB5Hvtn36M.

Kraks TV. "Would you Allow your Parents Watch you have S3x for 20 Million Naira? *Kraks Sex Talk*, July 26, 2021. www.youtube.com/watch?v=FwA59256220.

Kreiss, Daniel. "Seizing the Moment: The Presidential Campaigns' use of Twitter during the 2012 Electoral Cycle." *New Media and Society* 18, no. 8 (2014): 1473–1490.

Kwaja, Chris. "Nigeria's Pernicious Drivers of Ethno-Religious Conflict." *Africa Center for Strategic Studies.* July 31, 2011. www.africacenter.org/publication/nigerias-pernicious-drivers-of-ethno-religious-conflict/#:~:text=Ever%20since%2C%20local%20elections%20and,are%20the%20real%20root%20causes.

Lambsdorff, J. "The Transparency International Corruption Perceptions Index: Whose Perceptions are they anyway." 2003. www.citeseerx.ist.psu.edu/viewdoc/download?doi=10.1.1.370.4882&rep=rep1&type=pdf.

Landry, Megan, Monique Turner, Amita Vyas and Susan Wood. "Social Media and Sexual Behavior among Adolescents: Is there a Link?" *JMIR Public Health and Surveillance* 3, no. 2 (2017): e28.

Lasisi, Akeem. "What Word Formation is Involved in BATified, Atikulated and Obidient?" *The Punch,* June 21, 2022.

Lasode, O. *Television Broadcasting: The Nigerian Experience (1959–1992).* Ibadan: Caltop Publications (Nig.) Ltd., 1994.

Lawan, Ahmed. "ASUU Strike: Senate will bring back FG/ASUU to Negotiation Table—Lawan." *National Assembly*, May 11, 2022. www.nass.gov.ng/news/item/1672.

Lawrence, Akinboyo and Apinran M.O. States' Fiscal Dependency and Implications on Monetary Management in Nigeria. CBN Bullion, 42, no. 4 (2018): 12–27.

Lecuna, A. "Corruption and Size Decentralization." *Journal of Applied Economics* 15, no. 1 (2012): 139–168.

Lenhart, Amanda, Kristen Purcell, Aaron Smith and Kathryn Zickuhr. *Social Media and Mobile Internet use among Teens and Young Adults*. Washington, DC: Pew Internet American Life Project, 2010.

Lijphart, Arendt. *Democracy in Plural Societies: A Comparative Exploration*. New Haven: Yale University Press, 1977.

Liman, Bashiru. *The Crisis of Insecurity in Nigeria*. Abuja: Caltop Publications (Nigeria) Limited, 2021.

Lipset, Seymour and Gabriel Salman Lenz. "Corruption, Culture, and Markets." In *Culture Matters,* edited by Lawrence E. Harrison and Samuel P. Huntington. New York: Basic, 2000, 112.

Liu, Wenlin, Anupreet Sidhu, Amanda M. Beacom and Thomas W. Valente. "Social Network Theory." In *The International Encyclopedia of Media Effects*, edited by Patrick Rossler. West Sussex: John Wiley & Sons, Inc, 2017, 1–12.

Livingstone, S., G. Mascheroni and E. Staksrud. *Developing a Framework for Researching Children's Online Risks and Opportunities in Europe*. London: The London School of Economics and Political Science, 2015.

Lloyd, Vries. "House Misfires on Internet Safety." *CBS News*, August 1, 2006. www.cbsnews.com/news/house-misfires-on-internet-safety/.

Loader, Brian and Dan Mercea. *Social Media and Democracy*. London: Routledge, 2012.

Loungaui, P., and A. Razin. "How Beneficial is Foreign Direct Investment for Developing Countries?" *Finance and Development* 38, no. 1 (2001): 6–9.

Luckerson, V. "Is Facebook Losing its Cool? Some Teens Think So." *Time*, March 8, 2013. www.business.time.com/2013/03/08/is-facebook-losing-its-cool-some-teens-think-so/.

MaDailyGist. "Gay Party Busted By Police in Ibadan. 21 Men with 122 Condoms Arrested." *MaDailyGist*, May 18, 2015. www.madailygist.ng/2015/gay-party-busted-by-police-in-ibadan-21-men-with-122-condoms-arrested-read-more/

Madobi, Mukhtar Ya'u. "A Deep Look at Nigeria's Security Challenges." *Nigerian Tribune,* January 21, 2022.

Madu, Robert and Shedrack C. Moguluwa. "Will the Social Media Lenses be the Framework for Sustainable Development in Rural Nigeria?" *Journal of African Studies* 5, no. 2 (2013): 237–254.

Madunagu, Bene. "The Nigerian Feminist Movement: Lessons from Women in Nigeria, WIN." *Review of African Political Economy* 35, no. 118 (2008): 666–672.

Majeed, Bakare. "2023: Delegates Bribed to Vote at APC Presidential Primary, Amaechi Alleges." *Premium Times,* July 25, 2022. www.premiumtimesng.com/news/headlines/544781-2023-delegates-bribed-to-vote-at-apc-presidential-primary-amaechi-alleges.html.

Majeed, Bakare. "Updated: 2023: APC Fixes Presidential Forms for N100 million, Adopts Indirect Primaries." *Premium Times Nigeria*, April 20, 2022, www.premiumtimesng.com/news/headlines/524823-updated-2023-apc-fixes-presidential-forms-for-n100-million-adopts-indirect-primaries.html.

Makama, Allanana Godiya. "Patriarchy and Gender Inequality in Nigeria: The Way Forward." *European Scientific Journal* 9, no. 17 (2013): 101–110.

Makama, Godiya. "Patriarchy and Gender Inequality in Nigeria: The Way Forward." *European Scientific Journal* 9, no. 17 (2013): 101–110.

Mande, Ande, Lambe Kayode Mustapha, Bahiyah Omar, Maryam Lasisi Mustapha and Ismail Sheikh Yusuf Ahmed. "Social Media Content Preferences and Political Participation among Nigerian Youths." *Romanian Journal of Communication and Public Relations* 24, no. 1 (2022): 7–23.

Maslow, Jacob. "How Social Media is Influencing Elections." *The Times of Israel*, 2019. www.blogs.timesofisrael.com/how-is-social-media-influencing-elections/.

Mason, K. "The Status of Women: Conceptual and Methodological Issues." *Demographic Studies Sociological Forum* 1, no. 2 (1986): 298.

Masterweb news. "Court Grants Biafra Leader Bail." *Africa Master Web*, May 16, 2008. www.africamasterweb.com/AdSense/MassobCourtGrantsBiafraLeaderBail.html.

Matfess, Hilary. "More African Countries are Blocking Internet Access during Election." *Quartz Africa*, June 2016. www.qz.com/africa/696552/more-african-countries-are-blocking-internet-access-during-elections/

Mayrargue, Cedric. "The Paradoxes of Pentecostalism in Sub-Saharan Africa." *Sub-Saharan African Program*, 2008.

Mbaku, John. *Corruption in Africa: Causes, Consequences, and Cleanups*. Maryland: Lexington Books, 2010.

Mbiti, J. *African Religions and Philosophy*. London: Heinemann, 1982.

McGregor, Shannon. "Social Media as Public Opinion: How Journalists Use Social Media to Represent Public Opinion." *Journalism* 20, no. 8 (2019): 1070–1086.

McSweeney, Eoin, Stephanie Busari, Katie Polglase, Bethlehem Feleke and Tim Lister. "Prison Set on Fire in Nigeria as Protest Death Toll Rises to at Least 56." *CNN*, October 22, 2020. www.edition.cnn.com/2020/10/22/africa/nigeria-protests-56-dead-jail-fire-intl/index.html.

Melotti, Roberto, Jon Heron, Matthew Hickman, John Macleod, Ricardo Araya and Glyn Lewis. "Adolescent Alcohol and Tobacco use and Early Socioeconomic Position: The ALSPAC Birth Cohort." *Pediatrics* 127, no. 4 (2011): 948–955.

Merino, Daniel, Gemma Ware and Godfred Boafo. "Tigray: The Devastating Toll of Ethiopia's Vicious Year of War – Podcast." *The Conversation*, November 4, 2021.

www.theconversation.com/tigray-the-devastating-toll-of-ethiopias-vicious-year-of-war-podcast-171138

Meryville University. "The Evolution of Social Media: How did it begin and where could it go Next?" *Meryville University*. www.online.maryville.edu/blog/evolution-social-media/.

Meyer, Abrams and Geoffrey Harpham. *A Glossary of Literary Terms*. Boston: Cengage Learning, 2014.

Mikell, G. "Introduction." In *African Feminism: The Politics of Survival in Sub-Saharan Africa*, edited by G. Mikell. Pennsylvania: University of Pennsylvania Press, 1997.

Milbrath, Lester. *Political Participation*. Chicago: Rand McNally College Publishing Company, 1965.

Mills, Greg. *Why Africa is Poor and what Africans can do about it*. South Africa: Penguin Random House, 2012.

Mimiko, F.N.O. "Political and Constitutional Reforms." In *Nigeria's Reform Programme: Issues and Challenges*, edited by H. Saliu, Amali, B. and R. Olawepo, Ibadan: Vantage Publishers, 2007, 303–316.

Mitchell, Charlotte. "Internet Blackouts: The Rise of Government-Imposed Shutdowns." *Al Jazeera*, June 16, 2019. www.aljazeera.com/features/2019/6/16/internet-blackouts-the-rise-of-government-imposed-shutdowns

Momoh, Z. *Faces of Corruption in Nigeria*, Jos, Global Emancipation Multi-Services Ltd., 2013.

Montagne, Renee and Charlayne Hunter-Gault. "Zimbabwe's Mugabe Hangs on to Power." *NPR*, February 23, 2007. www.npr.org/templates/story/story.php?storyId=7565571.

Moreno, M., Libby N. Brockman, Judith N. Wasserheit and Dimitri A. Christakis. "A Pilot Evaluation of Older Adolescents Sexual Reference Displays on Facebook." *The Journal of Sex Research* 49, no. 4 (2012): 390–399.

Mosca, Gaetano. *The Ruling Class*, trans. Hannah D. Kahn. New York: McGraw-Hill, 1939.

Moses, John Maikomo, Tordue Simon Targema and Jesse Ishaku. "Tale of an Ill-fated Scapegoat: National Security and the Struggle for State Regulation of Social Media in Nigeria." *Journal of Digital Media & Policy* (2022): 1–19.

Mudashir, Ismail, Fidelis Mac-Leva, Zahraddeen Yakubu Shuaibu, Abbas Jimoh, John Chuks Azu, Victoria Onehi, Chris Agabi, Zakariyya Adaramola and Clement A. Oloyede. "APC Manifesto: Questions over Buhari's Campaign Promises." *Daily Trust*, May 29, 2020.

Mustapha, Mala. "Corruption in Nigeria: Conceptual and Empirical Notes." *Information, Society and Justice Journal* 3, no. 2 (2010): 165–175.

Muzan, Allswell. "Insurgency in Nigeria: Addressing the Causes as Part of the Solution." *African Human Rights Law Journal* 14, no. 1 (2014): 217–243.

Mwangi, Evan. "Queer Agency in Kenya's Digital Media." *African Studies Review* 57, no. 2 (2014): 93–113.

Nag, O.S. "Most Religious Countries in the World." *World Atlas*, January 11, 2018. www.worldatlas.com/articles/most-religious-countries-in-the-world.html.

Namwase, Sylvie and Adrian Jjuuko, eds. *Protecting the Human Rights of Sexual Minorities in Contemporary Africa*. Pretoria: Pretoria University Law Press, 2017.

NAN. "NRC Begins Lagos-Abeokuta-Ibadan Rail Services." *The Guardian*, December 7, 2020.

Nasiru, J. "Obituary: In our Heart Lies Pius Adesanmi, the Prophet who Foretold his Death." *TheCable*, March 12, 2019. www.thecable.ng/obituary-in-our-hearts-lie-pius-adesanmi-the-prophet-who-foretold-his-death.

New York Times. "Sex Video Outrages Northern Nigeria." *New York Times*, August 14, 2007. www.nytimes.com/2007/08/14/movies/14arts-SEXVIDEOOUTR_BRF.html.

Newman, Nick and David Levy, eds. "Reuters Institute Digital News Report, 2014: Tracking the Future of News." *Reuters Institute*. www.reutersinstitute.politics.ox.ac.uk/sites/default/files/research/files/Reuters%2520Institute%2520Digital%2520News%2520Report%25202014.pdf.

News Agency of Nigeria. "Jonathan Joins APC in Bayelsa, Finally Accepts Presidential Nomination Forms from Fulani Group." *Peoples Gazette*, May 11, 2022. www.gazettengr.com/just-in-jonathan-joins-apc-in-bayelsa-finally-accepts-presidential-nomination-forms-from-fulani-group/.

NexTier SPD. "Sexual Violence: Why the Rise?" *NexTier SPD*, June 9, 2020. www.nextierspd.com/sexual-violence-why-the-rise/.

Ng, Alfred. "Donald Trump's Social Media would Doom him in a Job Interview." *CNET*, 2016. www.cnet.com/news/donald-trump-twitter-social-media-job-interview-tweets/.

Nie, Norman H. *Participation in America: Political Democracy and Social Equality*. New York: Harper & Row, 1972.

Nkechi, Onah G., and Nche G. Christian. "The Moral Implication of Social Media Phenomenon in Nigeria." *Mediterranean Journal of Sciences* 5, no. 20 (2014): 22–31.

NOI Polls. "Social Media Polls Reports." *NOI Polls*, November 2019. www.noi-polls.com

Nsudu, E.C. Onwe. "Social Media and Security Challenges in Nigeria: The Way Forward." *World Applied Sciences Journal* 35, no. 6 (2017): 993–999.

Nsudu, I., and E.C. Onwe. "Social Media and Security Challenges in Nigeria: The Way Forward." *World Applied Sciences Journal* 35, no. 6 (2017): 993–999.

Nwachukwu, E., and Murtala Adewale. "Nigerians Seek Ganduje's Resignation over Fresh 'Bribery Video.'" *The Guardian*, November 1, 2018.

Nwachukwu, E., and N. Ihebuzor. "Online Ethnocentric Hate Speech and Nigerian Youth." In *New Media and African Society; Essays, Reviews and Research*, edited by Muiru Ngugi and Kate Omenugha. Nairobi: Nairobi Academic Press, 2020.

Nwachukwu, John. "Jubril of Sudan: How Aisha, Yusuf Exposed 'Cloned Buhari'—Nnamdi Kanu" *Daily Post*, December 9, 2018. www.dailypost.ng/2018/12/09/2019-election-shehu-sani-reacts-freezing-peter-obis-accounts-efcc-okupes-home/.

Nwachukwu, Sunny, Austin Aghamelo and Nwaneri Stanley. "An Account of Human Right Violations in Nigeria (Pre-British, British and Post Independence)." *European Scientific Journal* 10, no. 10 (2014): 230–239.

Nwafor, Gloria. "TUC Flays FG over 774,000 Jobs' Scheme." *The Guardian*, October 12, 2021.

Nwafor, Kenneth A., Chinedu C. Odoemelam, A. Orji-Egwu, Simon U. Nwankwo and Samuel Nweze. "Social Media and Political Participation in Africa: Issues, Challenges and Prospects." In *Communication and the New Media in Nigeria: Social Engagement, Political Development and Public Discourse*, edited by D. Wilson. Uyo: ACCE, 2013, 64–84.

Nwanegbo, J., and J. Odigbo. "Governance, Corruption and Crisis of Governance in Post-independence Nigeria." *African Journal of Politics and Society* 1, no. 1 (2015): 24–44.

Nwanguma, Okey. "A Call for Prompt, Impartial and Exhaustive Investigation of CSP James Nwafor of Special Anti-Robbery Squad (SARS) Awkuzu, Anambra State," *Sahara Reporters*, January 18, 2015. https://saharareporters.com/2015/01/18/noprin-calls-igp-investigate-activities-csp-james-nwafor-and-check-impunity-special-anti

Nweke, Charles. "Democracy, Leadership and Nation Building in Nigeria." *Ogirisi: A New Journal of African Studies* 11 (2015): 153–167.

Nwogbaga, David. "Retrospect in Nigeria's Elections, 1923–1993." In *Democracy and Electoral Studies: A Reader*, edited by A. Itumo and J.O. Nkwede. Enugu: Kenny and Brothers, 2015, 3.

Nwokolo, C. "An Epitaph for Pius Adesanmi." *Nwokolo,* March 11, 2019. www.nwokolo.com/y/an-epitaph-for-pius-adesanmi/.

Nyoko, Mell. "Why African Parents Can't Talk about Sex." *This is Africa*, February 3, 2014. www.thisisafrica.me/politics-and-society/why-african-parents-cant-talk-about-sex/.

Oarhe, O. "Tonic or Toxin? The State, Neopatrimonialism, and Anticorruption Efforts in Nigeria." *Journal of Policy Studies* 28, no. 1 (2013): 111–134.

Obadan, M.I., and S.E. Edo. "Nigeria's Economic Governance Structures and Growth Performance in Perspective." *The Nigerian Journal of Economic and Social Studies* 50, no. 1 (2008): 99–118.

Obi-Ani, Ngozika, Chinenye Anikwenze and Mathias Chukwudi Isiani. "Social Media and the Covid-19 Pandemic: Observations from Nigeria." *Cogent Arts & Humanities* 7, no. 1 (2020): 1–15.

Obiejesi, Kingsley. "Amnesty International Attacking us for Opposing Gay Rights, says DHQ." *ICIR Nigeria,* February 24, 2018. www.icirnigeria.org/amnesty-international-attacking-us-for-opposing-gay-rights-says-dhq/

Obike, Grace. "Govt, Amnesty Disagree on 'Lekki Massacre'." *The Nation,* October 21, 2021.

Obinna, Elijah. "Bridging the Divide: The Legacies of Mary Slessor, 'Queen' of Calabar, Nigeria." *Studies in World Christianity* 17, no. 3 (2011): 275–293.

Ochi, Ijeoma Brigid and Kingsley Chinonso Mark. “Effect of the ENDSARS Protest on the Nigerian Economy.” *Global Journal of Arts, Humanities and Social Sciences* 9, no. 3 (2021): 1–15.

Ochogwu, Sunday. “2023: Tinubu asks Muslims to Create Political Departments like Redeemed Church.” *Daily Post Nigeria*, March 20, 2022. www.dailypost.ng/2022/03/20/2023-tinubu-asks-muslims-to-create-political-departments-like-redeemed-church/.

Ochojila, Ameh. “Amaechi, Malami Sued over Alleged Illegal Award of N91.7b Rail Contract to Chinese.” *The Guardian*, February 4, 2022.

Ochonu, Moses E. “ASUU is a Problem of the Nigerian University System.” *Sahara Reporters*, November 6, 2018. www.saharareporters.com/2018/11/06/asuu-problem-nigerian-university-system-moses-e-ochonu.

Ochonu, Moses E. “Buhari: Corruption Enabler and Defender.” *Sahara Reporters*, November 2, 2017. www.saharareporters.com/2017/11/02/buhari-corruption-enabler-and-defender-moses-e-ochonu.

Ochonu, Moses E. “Colonial Itineraries: Muhammadu Dikko’s Metropolitan Adventures.” *The Journal of African History* 61, no. 2 (2020): 179–200.

Ochonu, Moses E. *Emirs in London: Subaltern Travel and Nigeria’s Modernity*. Bloomington: Indiana University Press, 2022.

Ochonu, Moses. “African Colonial Economies: Land, Labor, and Livelihoods.” *History Compass* 11, no. 2 (2013): 91–103.

Ochonu, Moses. “Bring Back Corruption: A Critique of Neoliberal Anti-Corruption Rhetoric.” *The News*, September 8, 2016.

Ochonu, Moses. “Buhari is not the Problem of Nigerian University, ASUU is.” *People’s Daily*, November 29, 2019. www.peoplesdailyng.com/buhari-is-not-the-problem-of-nigerian-university-asuu-is/.

Ochonu, Moses. “Colonialism within Colonialism: The Hausa-Caliphate Imaginary and the British Colonial Administration of the Nigerian Middle Belt.” *African Studies Quarterly* 10, no. 2 (2008): 95–127.

Ochonu, Moses. “Corruption and Political Culture in Africa: History, Meaning, and the Problem of Naming.” *The Law and Development* Review 4, no. 3 (2011): 27–58.

Ochonu, Moses. “Democracy and the Performance of Power: Observations from Nigeria.” *Ufahamu: A Journal of African Studies* 31, nos. 1–2 (2005): 70–89.

Ochonu, Moses. “For the Record: My Three Recent Facebook Reflections on the Current ASUU-FG Faceoff and my Proposals for a Holistic, Sustainable Solutions”, *US-Africa Dialogue*, February 19, 2022. www.groups.google.com/g/usaafricadialogue/c/cr0u8DXZLhc.

Ochonu, Moses. “Nigeria: The Shattering of Buhari’s Mythology.” *African Arguments*, August 4, 2016. www.africanarguments.org/2016/08/nigeria-the-shattering-of-the-buhari-mythology/v.

Ochonu, Moses. “Pius Adesanmi: A Tribute and a Debt.” *Premium Times*, March 23, 2019. www.opinion.premiumtimesng.com/2019/03/22/pius-adesanmi-a-tribute-and-a-debt-by-moses-e-ochonu/.

Ochonu, Moses. "The Problem of ASUU and Way Forward." *Notes from Atlanta*, January 16, 2021. www.farooqkperogi.com/2021/01/problem-of-asuu-and-way-froward.html#.YAJ0iFnE_M4.twitter.

Ochonu, Moses. "Why Liberal Democracy is a Threat in Nigeria." *Logos: A Journal of Modern Society and Culture* 18, no. 1 (2019).

Ochulor, Chinenye. "Failure of Leadership in Nigeria." *American Journal of Social and Management Sciences* 2, no. 3 (2011): 265–271.

Odeyemi, Temitayo and Oludare Mosunmola. "Stakeholders, ICTs Platforms and the 2015 General Elections in Nigeria." Presented at the National Conference on the 2015 General Elections in Nigeria: The Real Issues. held at The Electoral Institute, Independent National Electoral Commission, Abuja, Nigeria, July 27 and 28, 2015.

Odumeru, Jonathan. "Freedom of Misinformation: Balancing Fundamental Freedoms whilst Curbing Misinformation in Nigeria." *The Public Sphere: Journal of Public Policy* 10, no. 1 (2022): 89–108.

Odunsi, Wale. "TIERS Condemns Murder of Akinnifesi Olubunmi over Alleged Homosexualism." *Daily Post*, March 15, 2016. www.dailypost.ng/2016/03/15/tiers-condemns-murder-of-akinnifesi-olubunmi-over-alleged-homosexualism/.

Odutola, Koleade. "Diaspora and Imagined Nationality: USA-Africa Dialogue and Cyberframing Nigerian Nationhood." PhD *diss.*, Rutgers University-Graduate School-New Brunswick, 2010.

Ogbondah, Chris W. "Political Repression in Nigeria, 1993–1998: A Critical Examination of One Aspect of the Perils of Military Dictatorship." *Africa Spectrum* 35, no. 2 (2000): 321–242.

Ogugbuaja, Charles, Collins Osuji, Lawrence Njoku and John Akubo. "1,844 Inmates Roam Free after Imo Prison Break." *The Guardian*, April 6, 2021.

Ogun, Festus. "Key Provisions of Electoral Act, 2022." *TheCable*, April 19, 2022. www.thecable.ng/review-key-provisions-of-electoral-act-2022.

Ogunbamowojun, Elizabeth. "Fact-Check: Is Adamu Garba's Crowwe First Social Networking Platform Built In Africa As Claimed?" *Sahara Reporters*, June 21, 2021. www.saharareporters.com/2021/06/21/fact-check-adamu-garbas-crowwe-first-social-networking-platform-built-africa-claimed

Ogunbayo, Olusola. "Menippean Satire in Postcolonial African Literature: A Reading of Pius Adesanmi's You're Not a Country, Africa." *Nokoko* 9 (2021): 71.

Ogundipe, Samuel. "Police Begin Search for Kidnapped Ganduje Critic Dadiyata." *Premium Times*, August 3, 2019. www.premiumtimesng.com/news/top-news/344614-police-begin-search-for-kidnapped-ganduje-critic-dadiyata.html.

Ogunleye, Foluke. "A Male-Centric Modification of History; Efunsetan Aniwura Revisited." *History in Africa* 31, (2004): 303–318.

Ogunleye, Gbemiga. "Tinubu Goes for the Broke." *The Punch*, June 6, 2022.

Ogunode, Jacob and Abubakar Musa. "Higher education in Nigeria: Challenges and the Ways Forward." *Electronic Research Journal of Behavioural Sciences* 3 (2020): 84–98.

Ojakorotu, Victor, Ebere Florence Nnanwube and Kelechi Johnmary Ani. "An Evaluation of the Concepts of Dangerous and Hate Speeches, and Their Security Implications in the Social Media Era Nigeria." *Gender and Behaviour* 17, no. 1 (2019): 12417–12428.

Ojebode, Ayobami, Dimeji Togunde and Abimbola Adelakun. "Beyond Money and Gifts: Social Capital as Motivation for Cross-generational Dating among Tertiary School Female Students in South West Nigeria." *Journal of Social Sciences* 5, no. 4 (2010): 169–182.

Ojebode, Ayobami, Dimeji Togunde and Abimbola Adelakun. "Secrecy, Security and Social Exchange: New Media and Cross-Generational Dating in Nigeria." *International Journal of Sociology of the Family* 37, no. 2 (2011): 307–327.

Ojedokun, Usman A., Yetunde O. Ogunleye and Adeyinka A. Aderinto. "Mass Mobilization for Police Accountability: The Case of Nigeria's #EndSARS Protest." *Policing: A Journal of Policy and Practice* 15, no. 3 (2021): 1894–1903.

Ojeme, Victoria. "FG increases Number of N-power Beneficiaries from 500,000 to 1m, to Lift 100m Out of Poverty." *Vanguard Newspaper,* May 21, 2021.

Ojiakor, Ngozi and Alex Amaechi Ugwuja. "The Igbo in Nigeria: Human Rights Abuses and the Question of Restitution, 1967–2002." *Kenneth Dike Journal of African Studies* 1, no. 1 (2020): 97–123.

Ojo, James. "Bobrisky: Why I Decided to be a Woman." *TheCable*, September 22, 2021. www.lifestyle.thecable.ng/bobrisky-why-i-decided-to-become-a-woman/.

Ojo, O. "A Political Economy Approach to Understanding Corruption and the Challenge of Human Development." In *Corruption and the Challenge of Human Development*, edited by Aina A. Babcock University: Development: Policy, Conflict and Strategic Studies, 2007.

Ojo-Ade, Femi. "Of Culture, Commitment, and Construction: Reflections on African Literature." *Transition* 53 (1991): 4–24.

Okafor, Chiamakar. "Rwanda President, Paul Kagame to seek re-election in 2024." *Premium Times*, July 11, 2021. www.premiumtimesng.com/news/more-news/542040-rwanda-president-paul-kagame-to-seek-re-election-in-2024.html.

Okafor, Edwin Eme. "Twenty-Five Centuries of Bloomery Iron Smelting in Nigeria." In *The Origins of Metallurgy in Africa: New Lights on its Antiquity. West and Central Africa*, edited by Hamady Bocoum. Paris: UNESCO Publishing, 2004, 43–54.

Okakwu, Evelyn. "Nigeria's 'Freest' Election Witnessed Vote-Buying 'Worth N120m to N1bn'—Group." *Premium Times*, April 16, 2019. www.premiumtimesng.com/news/more-news/325718-nigerias-freest-election-witnessed-vote-buying-worth-n120m-to-n1bn-group.html.

Okeke, P. "Reconfiguring Tradition: Women's Rights and Social Status in Contemporary Nigeria." *Africa Today* 47, no. 1 (2000): 49–63.

Okenyodo, Oluwakemi. "Governance, Accountability, and Security in Nigeria." *Africa Center for Strategic Studies,* June 21, 2016. www.africacenter.org/publication/governance-accountability-security-nigeria-html/.

Okiriguo, Wendy. "Discourse Analysis of Nigerian Feminism." M.Sc. Thesis, Southern Illinois University at Edwardsville, 2016.

Okonjo-Iweala, Ngozi. *Fighting Corruption is Dangerous: The Story behind the Headlines.* Cambridge: MIT Press, 2018.

Okonkwo, Emeka, Afamefuna Eyisi and Nneoma G. Ololo. "Social Media Platforms and their Contributions to Tourism Development and Promotion in Nigeria." *Nsukka Journal of Humanities* 23, no .2 (2015): 103–117.

Okoro, Nnanyelugo and Kenneth Adibe Nwafor. "Social Media and Political Participation in Nigeria during the 2011 General Elections: The Lapses and the Lessons." *Global Journal of Arts Humanities and Social Sciences* 1, no. 3 (2013): 29–46.

Okoronkwo-Chukwu, Udo. "Naija No Dey Carry Last: Pius Adesanmi and the Complexity of a Nation in Progress." *European Journal of English Language and Literature Studies* 4, no. 7 (2016): 40–47.

Okparanta, Chinelo. "America." *Granta*, February 2, 2012. www.granta.com/america/.

Okpeh Okpeh. *Mainstreaming Gender in the African Development Process: A Critic of NEPAD and the Women Question.* Nigeria: BSU Press, 2005.

Okudaye, Ehizojie Precious, Adeline Nkwam-Uwaoma and Blessing Ajirioghene Omoevah. "Textual Analysis of Netizens' Reaction to Sunday Igboho's Declaration of a Yoruba Nation." *Sau Journal of Management and Social Sciences* 4, no. 1 (2022): 28–38.

Okwuchukwu, Okafor Godson, Emmanuel Ngozi and Uzuegbunam Chikezie Emmanuel. "The Media and Challenges of National Identity in Nigeria." *American Journal of Social Sciences* 2, no. 3 (2014): 49–55.

Okwumbu-Imafiadon, Ruth. "We Wanted to Help users Pay Themselves First—Piggyvest." *Nairametrics*, October 3, 2020. www.nairametrics.com/2020/10/03/we-wanted-to-help-users-pay-themselves-first-piggyvest/.

Oladapo, Oyewole and Babatunde Raphael Ojebuyi. "Nature and Outcome of Nigeria's #NoToSocialMediaBill Twitter Protest against the Frivolous Petitions Bill 2015." In *Impacts of the Media on African Socio-Economic Development*, edited by Nelson Okorie, Babatunde Raphael Ojebuyi, Abiodun Salawu. USA: IGI Global, 2017, 106–124.

Olaigbe, Taofeeq Adebayo. "Youths' Perception and Contributing Factors Towards Jungle Justice during Endsars Protests in Nigeria." *African Journal for the Psychological Studies of Social Issues* 24, no. 1 (2021): 1–10.

Olaniyi, Muideen. "774,000 Jobs Now an Annual Scheme, Says FG." *Daily Trust,* June 25, 2021.

Olaopa, Tunji. "ASUU's Unwinnable Battles: The Need to Change Tactics", *Daily Trust,* March 16, 2022.

Olarenwaju, Tolu. "Can Social Media help Anti-corruption Drives? A Nigerian Case Study." *The Conversation,* June 4, 2019. www.theconversation.com/can-social-media-help-anti-corruption-drives-a-nigerian-case-study-118190.

Olasinde, E. Akani. "An Analysis of the Influence of Social Media Sites on Nigerian Undergraduates." *International Policy Brief Series - Education & Science Journal* 4, no. 1 (2014): 53–65.

Olasunkanmi, Akoni and Monsur Olowoopejo. "Fashola 'Arrests' Col, Seargent on BRT Lane." *Vanguard Newspaper*, July 17, 2012.

Olatokun, Ganiat. "Nigerian Feminism: A Typology of African Feminism." *KIU Journal of Humanities* 2, no. 1 (2017): 216.

Olonilua, Ademola. "FG Uncovers 96 Terrorist Sponsors, Arrests 45 Suspects." *Daily Trust*, February 3, 2022.

Oloruntoba, Samuel. "Pius Adesanmi: A Paradigm Shift in Pan African Humanity." *Nokoko* 9, (2021): 54–69.

Oloyede, I. "Press Freedom: A Conceptual Analysis." *Journal of Social Sciences* 11, no. 2 (2015): 101–109.

Oloyede, Ridwan and Douglas Onah. "A Comparative Analysis between the Digital Rights and Freedom Bill and other Legislation in Nigeria." *Paradigm Initiative Report*, December 2020.

Olson, C. "#BringBackOurGirls: Digital Communities Supporting Real-world Change and Influencing Mainstream Media Agendas." *Feminist Media Studies* 16, no. 5 (2016): 772–787.

Olu, Ladele, V. Olufemi Adefela and Olu Lasekan. *History Of Nigerian Broadcasting Corporation*. Ibadan: Ibadan University Press, 1979.

Olubusoye, Olusanya E., Olalekan J. Akintande and Eric A. Vance. "Transforming Evidence to Action: The Case of Election Participation in Nigeria." *Chance* 34, no. 3 (2021): 13–23.

Olufemi, Lola. *Feminism, Interrupted: Disrupting Power*. London: Pluto Press, 2020.

Olujimi, Kayode, Olutunde Aremu and Noeem Thanny. "Media, Mood and Movement: Media Impact on Social Movement in Nigeria." *Academia*. www.academia.edu/4102433/Media_Mood_and_Movement_Media_Impact_on_Social_Movements_in_Nigeria

Olukotun, Ayo "Will Pay Rise End Predatory Policing." *The Punch*, November 29, 2018.

Olukotun, Ayo and Sharon Adetutu Omotoso, eds. *Political Communication in Africa*. Cham: Springer International Publishing, 2017.

Olukotun, Ayo. "2019: Harvest of Aspirants, Shortage of Policy Ideas." *The Punch*, September 6, 2018.

Olukotun, Ayo. "A Farewell to Civil Political Discourse?" *The Punch*, April 28, 2016.

Olukotun, Ayo. "A Nation's Unending Search for Quality Education." *The Punch*, November 16, 2018.

Olukotun, Ayo. "A Tale of Two Protests." *The Punch*, February 16, 2017.

Olukotun, Ayo. "Abandoned Projects and State Decay." *The Punch*, October 6, 2016.

Olukotun, Ayo. "Abuja-Kaduna Rail: NRC's Astonishing Misplacement of Priorities." *The Punch*, May 20, 2022.

Olukotun, Ayo. "Ambode: A Postscript." *The Punch,* October 11, 2018.

Olukotun, Ayo. "Ambode: Off Keynote in a Melodious Verse." *The Punch,* June 1, 2017.

Olukotun, Ayo. "Anguished Nation Left Stranded by its Leaders." *The Punch,* June 24, 2022.

Olukotun, Ayo. "Anti-Corruption: The Suspension of Buhari's Top Aides." *The Punch,* April 20, 2017.

Olukotun, Ayo. "Any Hope for Overcoming the Electricity Jinx?" *The Punch,* June 21, 2018.

Olukotun, Ayo. "APC and Tinubu's Uphill Assignment." *The Punch,* February 15, 2018.

Olukotun, Ayo. "Authoritarian State, Crisis of Democratization and the Underground Media in Nigeria." *African Affairs* 101, no. 404 (2002): 317–342.

Olukotun, Ayo. "Awolowo Dosunmu: A Political Dynasty at the Crossroad." *The Punch,* February 22, 2018.

Olukotun, Ayo. "Beyond Survival: Remapping Nigeria for Greatness." *The Punch,* September 28, 2017.

Olukotun, Ayo. "Beyond the Presidential and National Assembly Elections." *The Punch,* February 28, 2019.

Olukotun, Ayo. "Bill Gate's Refreshingly Blunt Charge to our Leaders." *The Punch,* March 29, 2018.

Olukotun, Ayo. "Buhari: The Renewed Debate on Underperformance." *The Punch,* October 18, 2017.

Olukotun, Ayo. "Buhari's Medical Leave and Resident Doctors' Strike." *The Punch,* April 2, 2021.

Olukotun, Ayo. "Buharimeter: A Wake Up Call." *The Punch,* July 14, 2016.

Olukotun, Ayo. "Comatose Libraries and a Disappearing Nation." *The Punch,* October 20, 2016.

Olukotun, Ayo. "Consumer Woes in Austere Times." *The Punch,* June 21, 2016.

Olukotun, Ayo. "Corruption: Osinbajo's Indictment of Our Churches." *The Punch,* June 22, 2017.

Olukotun, Ayo. "Dearth of Nigerian CEO's in Nigeria-Based Multinationals." *The Punch,* November 13, 2018.

Olukotun, Ayo. "Defence Sector Spending: Have we Come Full Circle?" *The Punch,* December 27, 2018.

Olukotun, Ayo. "Democracy Day and Anxieties About 2019." *The Punch,* May 24, 2018.

Olukotun, Ayo. "Diminishing Governance amidst Escalating Insecurity." *The Punch,* April 30, 2021.

Olukotun, Ayo. "Elder Statesmen and Controversial Interventions." *The Punch,* April 5, 2018.

Olukotun, Ayo. "Election: We Need Conversations, Not Sweet Nothings." *The Punch,* January 3, 2019.

Olukotun, Ayo. "Elite Conflicts and the Anti Corruption Policy." *The Punch,* May 18, 2017.

Olukotun, Ayo. "Eurasia's Troubling Projections on the 2019 Elections." *The Punch*, January 17, 2019.

Olukotun, Ayo. "Falana and the Search for an Effective Tetfund." *The Punch*, March 21, 2019.

Olukotun, Ayo. "Falola and Olubadan's 90th Birthday Lecture." *The Punch*, August 23, 2018.

Olukotun, Ayo. "Fighting Corruption without Rebuilding the Police." *The Punch*, February 17, 2016.

Olukotun, Ayo. "Finally, the Election holds?" *The Punch*, February 21, 2019.

Olukotun, Ayo. "Garba Shehu and the Discourse of Settlement." *The Punch*, October 4, 2017.

Olukotun, Ayo. "Governance and the Media in an Emergent Democracy: A Study of the Role, Record and Changing Profile of the Nigerian Media 1999–2017." An Inaugural Lecture of the Oba (Dr.) Kayode Adetona, CFR Professorial Chair in Governance, Olabisi Onabanjo University, Ago-Iwoye, May 10, 2017.

Olukotun, Ayo. "Governance Takeaways from the upheaval in France." *The Punch*, December 12, 2019.

Olukotun, Ayo. "Health Sector Brain Drain: Rising Cost of Inaction." *The Punch*, April 26, 2018.

Olukotun, Ayo. "Hospitals as Undertakers? Saving a Dying Healthy Sector." *The Punch*, September 21, 2017.

Olukotun, Ayo. "How we Dropped the Ball on Quality Education in Nigeria." *Opinion Nigeria*, November 2, 2019. www.opinionnigeria.com/how-we-dropped-the-ball-on-quality-education-in-nigeria-by-ayo-olukotun/.

Olukotun, Ayo. "Insecurity: A Nation Sleepwalking in Utter Peril." *The Punch*, July 29, 2022.

Olukotun, Ayo. "Insecurity: Political Class Terrifying Silence." *The Punch*, July 1, 2022.

Olukotun, Ayo. "Insecurity: The Opportunity Cost of Dilly-Dallying." *The Punch*, August 5, 2022.

Olukotun, Ayo. "Interrogating a Shallow Democracy." *The Punch*, March 23, 2017.

Olukotun, Ayo. "IPOB and the National Question." *The Punch*, September 14, 2017.

Olukotun, Ayo. "Is Excellence Possible in Nigeria? A Postscript." *The Punch*, July 6, 2017.

Olukotun, Ayo. "Jamboree of Presidential Aspirants, Shortage of Turnaround Ideas." *The Punch*, January 28, 2022.

Olukotun, Ayo. "June 12 and the Quest for True Federalism." *The Punch*, June 15, 2016.

Olukotun, Ayo. "Kaduna's Teacher and the Dilemma of Reform." *The Punch*, Nov 8, 2017.

Olukotun, Ayo. "Lame Response to Unending Security Jitters." *The Punch*, March 21, 2019.

Olukotun, Ayo. "Licensing 20 Private Universities is a Blunder." *The Punch*, April 16, 2021.

Olukotun, Ayo. "Macron and Nigerian Youths' Leadership Bid." *The Punch,* May 11, 2017.

Olukotun, Ayo. "Media Accountability and Democracy in Nigeria, 1999–2003." *African Studies Review* 47, no. 3 (2004): 69–90.

Olukotun, Ayo. "Money is Breaking Democracy in Nigeria." *The Conversation,* June 12, 2022. www.theconversation.com/money-is-breaking-democracy-in-nigeria-184595.

Olukotun, Ayo. "Much Ado about the Coalition of Opposition Parties." *The Punch,* July 12, 2018.

Olukotun, Ayo. "National Degree Exams for Undergraduates?" *The Punch,* January 24, 2019.

Olukotun, Ayo. "Needless Controversy over TI Rating." *The Punch*, March 1, 2018.

Olukotun, Ayo. "Odefuwa: A Handbook for Surviving Adversity." *The Punch,* March 30, 2017.

Olukotun, Ayo. "Okogie and Nigeria's Unending Search for Leadership." *The Punch,* July 21, 2017.

Olukotun, Ayo. "Olaniyi Ashimi, the Fatal Cost of Governance Decay." *The Punch,* December 19, 2018.

Olukotun, Ayo. "Our Election, Our Destiny." *The Punch*, February 7, 2019.

Olukotun, Ayo. "Our Growing Medical Tourism to India." *The Punch*, July 26, 2013.

Olukotun, Ayo. "PDP: An Opposition Absent from Duty." *The Punch,* May 5, 2016..

Olukotun, Ayo. "PDP's Self Destructive Quarrels and Growing Irrelevance." *The Punch,* September 1, 2016.

Olukotun, Ayo. "Persisting ASUU Strike and Governance Crisis." *The Punch*, April 22, 2022.

Olukotun, Ayo. "Political Scientists and the Debate on Political Restructuring." *The Punch*, April 25, 2019.

Olukotun, Ayo. "Private University Licenses and Policy Vacuum." *The Punch,* December 21, 2017.

Olukotun, Ayo. "Reducing the Cost of Governance: The Ayes have it." *The Punch,* October 11, 2019.

Olukotun, Ayo. "Researcher's Strike and a Disappearing Research Culture." *The Punch,* March 15, 2018.

Olukotun, Ayo. "Rising Citizen's Woes and Governance Apathy." *The Punch*, March 18, 2022.

Olukotun, Ayo. "Rising Insecurity: A Nation's Soft Underbelly." *The Punch*, April 10, 2018.

Olukotun, Ayo. "Social Media and Pathways to Inclusive Development." *The Punch,* February 26, 2016.

Olukotun, Ayo. "The Election and Beyond." *The Punch*, February 14, 2019.

Olukotun, Ayo. "The Elusive Search for Quality Education." *The Punch*, November 26, 2013.

Olukotun, Ayo. “The Raging Debate on the Change Mantra.” *The Punch,* September 15, 2016.

Olukotun, Ayo. “The Siege to Kaduna and an Emir’s Travails.” *The Punch,* July 16, 2021.

Olukotun, Ayo. “The Transition and the Media.” *African Journal of Political Science* 5, no. 2 (2000): 31–44.

Olukotun, Ayo. “Traditional Protest Media and Anti-Military Struggle in Nigeria 1988–1999.” *African Affairs* 101, no. 403 (2002): 193–211.

Olukotun, Ayo. “Tweaking University Education for Youth Empowerment.” *People’s Daily,* October 15, 2019. www.peoplesdailyng.com/tweaking-university-education-for-youth-empowerment-2/.

Olukotun, Ayo. “Weak Scorecard and Failing Social Contract.” *The Punch,* June 4, 2021.

Olukotun, Ayo. “What our Public Universities can Learn from Private Ones.” *The Punch,* June 22, 2016.

Olukotun, Ayo. “What will Nigeria Look Like in 2023?” *The Punch,* February 1, 2019.

Olukotun, Ayo. “Whatever Happened to the Culture of Resignation?” *The Punch,* October 24, 2018.

Olukotun, Ayo. “Where is President Buhari’s Think Tank?” *The Punch,* January 8, 2016.

Olukotun, Ayo. “Will 2019 Reverse the Crisis of Underperformance?” *The Punch,* May 31, 2018.

Olukotun, Ayo. “Will Insecurity Jinx 2023 Elections.” *The Punch,* April 15, 2022.

Olukotun, Ayo. *Repressive State and Resurgent Media under Nigeria’s Military Dictatorship, 1988–98.* Sweden: Nordic Africa Institute, 2004.

Olumide, Seye, Terhemba Daka and Oluwaseun Akingboye. “ISWAP behind Owo Church Attack, says FG.” *The Guardian,* June 10, 2022.

Oluwole, Victor. “Nigerians Spend the Most Time on Social Media in Africa, Global Report Finds.” *Business Insider Africa,* May 22, 2021. www.africa.businessinsider.com/local/lifestyle/nigerians-spend-the-most-time-on-social-media-in-africa-global-report-finds/037h2hm#:~:text=The%20Social%20Flagship%20Report%20April,3%3A32)%20and%20Ghana.

Omede, Jacob and Andrew Abdul Omede. “Terrorism and Insecurity in Nigeria: Moral, Values and Religious Education as Panaceas.” *Journal of Education and Practice* 6, no. 11 (2015): 120–126.

Omitola, Bolaji, Solomon Adedire, Olawale Olufemi Akinrinde, Olumide Omodunbi, and Mary Magdalene Sackflame. “The Triangle of Terror: Boko Haram, Fulani Herdsmen, Bandits and Organized Insecurity in Nigeria.” *Studia Securitatis* 15, no. 1 (2021): 21–33.

Ọmọbọwale, Ayọkunle Olumuyiwa and Akinpẹlu Ọlanrewaju Olutayọ. “Political Clientelism and Rural Development in South-Western Nigeria.” *Africa: Journal of the International African Institute* 80, no. 3 (2010): 453–472.

Omodunbi, A., P.O. Odiase, O.M. Olaniyan and A.O. Esan. "Cybercrimes in Nigeria: Analysis, Detection and Prevention." *FUOYE Journal of Engineering and Technology* 1, no.1 (2016): 37–42.

Omolo, Joseph. "Trends of Antisocial Behaviour Among Minors in Nairobi Populous Estates: A Study of Karen and Runda Estates." *Journal of Family Studies* 13, no. 4 (2014): 165–176.

Omonobi, Kingsley. "N500m MTN Bribery Allegation: Presidency Orders Probe of Abba Kyari." *Vanguard Newspaper,* October 21, 2016.

Omotayo, Funmilola and Matthew B. Folorunso. "Use of Social Media for Political Participation by Youths in Oyo State." *JeDEM-eJournal of eDemocracy and Open Government* 12, no. 1 (2020): 132–157.

Onah, Nkechi and Nche George Chrıstıan. "The Moral Implication of Social Media Phenomenon in Nigeria." *Mediterranean Journal of Social Sciences* 5, no. 20 (2014): 2231–2237.

Onanuga, Paul. "Coming Out and Reaching Out: Linguistic Advocacy on Queer Nigerian Twitter." *Journal of African Cultural Studies* 33, no. 4 (2021): 489–504.

Onayinka, T.S., C.E. Asogwa, B.A. Ajijola and J.A. Ige. "Influence of Biafra-related Social Media Contents on the Acceptance of IPOB Agenda in South-East Nigeria." *International Journal of Communication: An Interdisciplinary Journal of Communication* 24, no. 1 (2019): 49–61.

Onele, Joseph. "Social Media Bill and Madness in the Hallowed Chambers: A Call for Sanity." *SSRN Electronic Journal* (2015): 1–10.

Onuah, Felix. "Nigerian President Signs Anti-gay Bill into Law." *Reuters*, January 13, 2014. www.reuters.com/article/nigeria-gay-idUSL6N0KN2PP20140113.

Onukwue, Alexander. "Nigerian Banks want Fintech Collaborations, but for Specific and Unique Needs." *Tech Cabal,* July 22, 2020. www.techcabal.com/2020/07/22/banks-fintech-collaboration/.

Onwutuebe, Chidiebere J. "Military Culture and Political Leadership in Nigeria's Democracy." *African Identities* (2022): 1–21.

Onyejelem, Timothy E., Chinelo E. Ude-Akpeh, Ngozi E. Uduma. "The Economic Potentials of Social Media and the Nigerian Developing Society: An Appraisal." *International Journal of African and Asian Studies* 15 (2015): 108–116.

Onyekwere, Joseph. "Hate Speech Bill is Unlawful, Illegal, Unconstitutional and Undemocratic." *The Guardian,* December 3, 2019.

Onyiyechi, Ngozi J. "Taking their Destiny into their Hands: Social Media, Youth Participation and the 2015 Political Campaigns in Nigeria." *African Journalism Studies* 39, no. 1 (2018): 69–89.

Opeibi, Tunde. "The Twittersphere as Political Engagement Space: A Study of Social Media Usage in Election Campaigns in Nigeria." *Digital Studies/Le champ numérique* 9, no. 1 (2019): 1–32.

Oriogun, Olusegun. "Burnt Men." *Praxis Magazine*, 2016. www.praxismagonline.com/wp-content/uploads/2016/04/Burnt-Men-by-Oluwasegun-Romeo-Oriogun.pdf.

Oriogun, Olusegun. "How to Survive the Fire." In *14: An Anthology of Queer Art/We are Flowers*, edited by Rapum Kambili, January 14, 2017. www.brittlepaper.com/wp-content/uploads/2017/01/14-AN-ANTHOLOGY-OF-QUEER-ART-WE-ARE-FLOWERS.pdf.

Oriola, Temitope B., and W. Andy Knight. "In Memoriam—Professor Pius Adesanmi (1972–2019)." *African Security* 12, no. 1, (2019): 1–2.

Orizu, Udoru. "Gory Tales from Awkuzu SARS in Anambra." *Thisday*, October 20, 2020.

Osaghae, Eghosa. *Crippled Giant: Nigeria since Independence*. Bloomington: Indiana University Press, 1998.

Oshewolo, Segun. "Galloping Poverty in Nigeria: An Appraisal of Government Interventionist Policies." *Journal of Sustainable Development in Africa* 12, no. 6 (2010): 264–274.

Osisanwo, Ayo and Osas Iyoha. "We are not Terrorist, we are Freedom Fighters': Discourse Representation of the Pro-Biafra Protest in Selected Nigerian Newspapers." *Discourse & Society* 31, no. 6 (2020): 631–647.

Oso, Lai and Umaru Pate. *Mass Media and Society in Nigeria*. Lagos: Malthouse Publishing, 2012.

Osumah O., and I. Aghedo. "Challenges and Prospects of Anti-Corruption Crusade in Nigeria's Fourth Republic." *Ilorin Journal of Business and Social Science*15, no. 2 (2013): 81–96.

Ouytsel, J., M. Walrave and K. Ponnet. "How Schools can help their Students to Strengthen their Online Reputations." *The Clearing House: A Journal of Educational Strategies, Issues and Ideas* 87, no. 4 (2014): 180–185.

Owolabi, Ayodeji. "Photos: NLC Takes Protest to National Assembly over ASUU Strike." *TheCable*, July 27, 2022. www.thecable.ng/photos-nlc-takes-protest-to-national-assembly-over-asuu-strike.

Owoyemi, Sade. "The Insider: Boko Haram gave 15-Min Quranic Lecture to Kuje Inmates before Setting them Free." *FIJ*, July 6, 2022. www.fij.ng/article/the-insider-boko-haram-gave-15-min-quranic-lecture-to-kuje-inmates-before-setting-them-free/.

Owuamanam, Jude. "Ex-Soldier Kills Girlfriend over Text Messages." *The Punch*, March 15, 2016.

Oxford Analytica. "Separatists Threaten Nigeria Ruling Party's Chances." *Emerald Insight*, September 17, 2021. www.emerald.com/insight/content/doi/10.1108/OXAN-DB264189/full/html.

Oxford Analytica. "Tinubu's Vice-Presidential Pick May Divide Nigerians." *Emerald Expert Briefings* oxan-es, 2022.

Oyebode, Oladapo and Rita Orji. "Social Media and Sentiment Analysis: the Nigeria Presidential Election 2019." Paper read at the 2019 IEEE 10th Annual Information Technology, Electronics and Mobile Communication Conference (IEMCON), Vancouver, British Columbia, Canada, 2019.

Oyekale, Abayomi. "Ethnic Characterization of Gender-inequality and Domestic Violence against Women of Reproductive Ages in Nigeria." *Studies of Tribes and Tribals* 12, no. 1 (2014): 31–41.

Oyeleke, Sodiq. "Changing SARS Name not Significant Reform, Alberta, Justice Minister, Kaycee Madu," *The Punch*, October 18, 2020.

Oyeleke, Sodiq. "Changing SARS Name not Significant Reform, Alberta, Justice Minister, Kaycee Madu." *The Punch*, 2020.

Oyero, Kayode. "PDP Delegate Donates N12M Received from Aspirants to Kaduna Constituents." *The Punch*, June 2, 2022.

Oyesomi, Kehinde, Okorie Nelson, Omole Funke and Smith Abisola. "How Sociable are Women on Social Media? An Experiential Study on Nigerian Women." *International Journal of Research in Social Sciences* 4, no. 2 (2014): 1–16.

Oyetunde Olusola. "Nigeria: Power Sharing and the Resurgence of Separatist Agitation. The Prospect of a Consociational Model." *Conflict Studies Quarterly* 37 (2021): 54–74.

Oyewo, Hussain. "Threat of Secession: The Biafran Story." *Conflict & Resilience Monitor*, November 27, 2019. www.accord.org.za/conflict-trends/threat-of-secession/

Oyoyo, Igho. "CAN says Fake Bishops Attended Tinubu's Running Mate's Unveiling." *Leadership,* July 2022.

Ozioma, Ezekwesili-Ofili, and Okaka Antoinette Nwamaka Chinwe. "Herbal Medicines in African Traditional Medicine." In *Herbal Medicine*, edited by Philip Builders. London: IntechOpen, 2019.

Ozoigbo, Bonaventure Ikechukwu. "Insecurity in Nigeria: Genesis, Consequences and Panacea." *European Journal of Social Sciences Studies* 4, no. 4 (2019): 270–281.

Palmer, Carole, Lauren C. Teffeau and Carrie M. Pirmann. "Scholarly Information Practices in the Online Environment." *OCLC Research,* 2009. ,www.oclc.org/content/dam/research/publications/library/2009/2009-02.pdf.

Pankhurst, R. *The Medical History of Ethiopia*. Trenton: Red Sea Press, 1990.

Papacharissi, Zizi. "The Virtual Sphere: The Internet as a Public Sphere." *New Media & Society* 4, no. 1 (2002): 9–27.

Pareto, Vilfredo. *The Mind and Society*, trans. A. Bongiorno. New York: Harcourt, Brace, and Co., 1935.

Parry, Geraint and George Moyser. "More Participation, More Democracy?" In *Democracy: A Reader*, edited by Ricardo Blaug and John Schwarzmantel. West Sussex: Columbia University Press, 2016, 386–390.

Pawlak, Nina. "'Woman' and 'Man' in Hausa Language and Culture." In *Hausa Chadic Studies: In Honour of Professor Stanislaw Pilaszewicz*, edited by Nina Pawlak, Izabela Will and Ewa Siwierska. Warsawa: Elipsa, 2014.

Payne, Julia. "Nigeria Postpones Feb. 14 Presidential Election to March 28: INEC." *Reuters*, February 8, 2015. www.reuters.com/article/us-nigeria-election-idUSKBN0LB0TL20150208.

Pendry, Louise and Jessica Salvatore. "Individual and Social Benefits of Online Discussion Forums." *Computers in Human Behavior* 50 (2015): 211–220.

Perera, Ayeshea. "Sri Lanka: Why is the Country in an Economic Crisis?" *BBC*, July 16, 2022. www.bbc.com/news/world-61028138

Perkins, John. *Confessions of an Economic Hitman*, Oakland. Berrett:Koehler Publishers, 2004.

PiggyVest. "How the Piggybank Wallet is Helping Millions of Nigerians Save." *PiggyVest blog*, April 22, 2022. www.blog.piggyvest.com/save/how-the-piggybank-wallet-is-helping-millions-of-nigerians-save/.

Pink Panther. "I am not Trans, I'm Just a Cross Dresser… I am not Gay or Bisexual…" *KitoDIARIES,* August 1, 2020. www.kitodiaries.com/bobrisky-and-dele-momodu-engage-in-a-viral-interview-that-shows-their-ignorance-regarding-sexuality-and-gender-identity/

Popoola, Nike. "Food Imports Exceed Exports by N2.23tn in 12 Months." *The Punch*, April 4, 2022.

Powe, Lucas. *The Fourth Estate and the Constitution: Freedom of the Press in America.* California: University of California Press, 1992.

Powell, Jonathan, Abigail Reynolds and Mwita Chacha. "A New Coup Era for Africa?" *Conflict Trends* 4 (2021): 3–12.

Premium Times. "Federal Govt Releases Details of Programme to Employ 774,000 Nigerians." *Premium Times,* May 28, 2020. www.premiumtimesng.com/news/headlines/395041-just-in-programme-to-employ-774000-nigerians-starts-october-minister-announces.html.

Premium Times. "Popular Actor, Chiwetalu Agu, Arrested for Allegedly Recruiting for IPOB." *Premium Times,* October 7, 2021. www.premiumtimesng.com/news/top-news/488810-popular-actor-chiwetalu-agu-arrested-for-allegedly-recruiting-for-ipob.html.

Premium Times. "Presidency Speaks on Corruption Allegations against Buhari's Chief of Staff." *Premium Times,* September 8, 2018. www.premiumtimesng.com/news/top-news/282922-presidency-speaks-on-corruption-allegations-against-buharis-chief-of-staff.html.

Premium Times. "Presidential Debate: APC Shielding Buhari's Intellectual Laziness—PDP." *Premium Times,* January 31, 2015. www.premiumtimesng.com/news/top-news/175990-presidential-debate-apc-shielding-buharis-intellectual-laziness-pdp.html.

Premium Times. "Six Million Weapons in Circulation in Nigeria—Abdulsalami Abubakar." *Premium Times*, April 8, 2021. www.premiumtimesng.com/news/top-news/453878-six-million-weapons-in-circulation-in-nigeria-abdulsalami-abubakar.html.

Premium Times. "Voter Turnout in Nigerian Elections around 35% - INEC." *Premium Times Nigeria*, February 9, 2021. www.premiumtimesng.com/news/more-news/441649-voter-turnout-in-nigerian-elections-around-35-inec.html.

Press Release. "2nd Niger Bridge 91% Completed—Fashola." *Premium Times,* March 24, 2022. www.premiumtimesng.com/news/top-news/519443-2nd-niger-bridge-91-completed-fashola.html.

Press Release. "Nigeria: Killing of #EndSARS Protesters by the Military must be Investigated." *Amnesty International,* October 21, 2020. www.amnesty.org/en/latest/press-release/2020/10/killing-of-endsars-protesters-by-the-military-must-be-investigated/.

Princewill, Nimi and Stephanie Busari. "Nigeria Bans Twitter after Company Deletes President Buhari's Tweet." *CNN News,* June 5, 2021. www.edition.cnn.com/2021/06/04/africa/nigeria-suspends-twitter-operations-intl/index.html

Punch Editorial. "Before Criminals Overrun the South-West." *The Punch,* January 19, 2022.

Putnam, R.D. *Bowling Alone: The Collapse and Revival of the American Community.* New York, US: Simon & Schuster: 2000.

Qian, Junxi. "From Performance to Politics? Constructing Public and Counterpublic in the Singing of Red Songs." *European Journal of Cultural Studies* 17, no. 5 (2014): 602–628.

Raheem, Oluwafunminiyi and Mosunmola Adeojo. "'Not Your Colour, Not Your Size, Not Your Spec': Marching against Market Harassment and Molestation in Nigeria." In *African Women in Digital Spaces: Redefining Social Movements on the Continent and in the Diaspora,* edited by Msia Kibona and Wunpini Mohammed. Dar es Salaam: Mkuki na Nyota Publishers, 2022.

Reuters. "Kenya Police Help Colleagues Escape Anti-graft Officers with Warning Shots." *Reuters,* 2018. www.reuters.com/article/us-kenya-corruption-idUSKCN1NY0MS.

Richter, Maurice N. *Science as a Cultural Process.* London: Frederick Muller Limited, 1973.

Ridder, Sander. "Social Media and Young People's Sexualities: Values, Norms, and Battlegrounds." *Social Media+ Society* 3, no. 4 (2017): 1–11.

Rodriguez, Karla. Drake, Burna Boy, Diddy and more stars Show Support for Nigeria's #ENDSARS Movement. *Revolt TV,* October 11, 2020, www.revolt.tv/2020/10/11/21511426/celebrities-show-support-for-endsars-movement-in-nigeria.

Ronning, Helge. "The Politics of Corruption and the Media in Africa." *Journal of African Media Studies* 1, no. 1 (2009): 155–171.

Ross, Karen and Tobias Bürger. "Face to Face (Book) Social Media, Political Campaigning and the Unbearable Lightness of being there." *Political Science* 66, no. 1 (2014): 46–62.

Rotimi-John, Alade. "Emi L'okan Entitlement Bogey as Metaphor." *The Guardian,* June 20, 2022.

Roy, Pallavi, Kelechi Iwuamadi and Jibrin Ibrahim, *Breaking the Cycle of Corruption in Nigeria's Electricity Sector: A Political Settlements Analysis.* London: SOAS-ACE, 2020.

Royal, David. "Tinubu Defeats Osinbajo, Amaechi, Wins APC Presidential Primary." *The Vanguard Newspaper,* June 8, 2022.

Rutherford, Blair. "Incorporeal Words: The Tragic Passing of Pius Adesanmi." *Nokoko* 7 (2019): viii–xiii.

Sahara Reporters. "Join APC and all your Sins will be Forgiven." *Sahara Reporters*, January 18, 2019. www.saharareporters.com/2019/01/18/join-apc-and-all-your-sins-will-be-forgiven-oshiomhole-declares.

Sahara Reporters. "Revealed: How Buhari's Government Pardoned over 1,000 Boko Haram Fighters Despite Ruling out Amnesty in 2015." *Sahara Reporters*, May 5, 2021. www.saharareporters.com/2021/05/05/revealed-how-buhari%E2%80%99s-government-pardoned-over-1-000-boko-haram-fighters-despite-ruling.

Salawu, Bashiru and A.O. Hassan. "Ethnic Politics and its Implications for the Survival of Democracy in Nigeria." *Journal of Public Administration and Policy Research* 3, no. 2 (2011): 28–33.

Santas, Tsegyu and John Dogara Ogoshi. "An Appraisal of Mass Media Role in Consolidating Democracy in Nigeria." *African Research Review* 10, no. 1 (2016): 73–86.

Santiso, Carlos. "Integrity Tech: Three ways Governments Can use Technology to Disrupt Corruption." *aPolitical,* February 26, 2019. www.apolitical.co/en/solution_article/integrity-tech-disrupt-corruption.

Sasu, Doris Dokua. "Total Number of Active Social Media Users in Nigeria from 2017 to 2022 (in Millions)." *Statista*, August 17, 2022. www.statista.com/statistics/1176096/number-of-social-media-users-nigeria/#:~:text=Number%20of%20active%20social%20media%20users%20in%20Nigeria%202017%2D2022&text=As%20of%20January%202022%2C%20Nigeria,social%20media%20platforms%20in%20Nigeria.

Schmid, Ursula, Anna Sophie Kümpel and Diana Rieger. "How Social Media Users Perceive Different Forms of Online Hate Speech: A Qualitative Multi-Method Study." *New Media & Society* 00, no. 0 (2022): 1–19.

Schmitt-Beck, Rudiger and Christian Mackenrodt. "Social Networks and Mass Media as Mobilizers and Demobilizers: A Study of Turnout at a German Local Election." *Electoral Studies* 29 (2010): 392–404.

Shapshak, Toby. "African Tech Start-ups Have Record Investment Year in 2019." *Forbes: Enterprise Tech*, January 20, 2020. www.forbes.com/sites/tobyshapshak/2020/01/20/african-tech-start-ups-have-record-investment-year-in-2019/#4585436032f9.

Shettima, A. "Engendering Nigeria's Third Republic." *African Studies Review* 38, no. 3 (1995): 61–98.

Shirky, Clay. "The Political Power of Social Media: Technology, the Public Sphere and Political Change." *Foreign Affairs* 90, no. 1 (2011): 28–41.

Shu, Kai and Huan Liu. *Detecting Fake News on Social Media.* Switzerland: Springer Nature, 2022.

Simba, Amon, Ebere Ume Kalu, Vincent Onodugo, Chinwe R. Okoyeuzu and Oyedele Martins Ogundana. "Women Entrepreneurs in Nigeria." In *Women Entrepreneurs*

in Sub-Saharan Africa, edited by Marina Dabić, Léo-Paul Dana, Dina Modestus Nziku and Veland Ramadani. Cham, Switzerland: Springer, 2022.

Simon, Tomer, Avishay Goldberg, Limor Aharonson-Daniel, Dmitry Leykin and Bruria Adini. "Twitter in the Cross Fire—the use of Social Media in the Westgate Mall Terror Attack in Kenya." *PloS ONE* 9, no. 8 (2014): 1–11.

Siollun, Max. *Soldiers of Fortune: Nigerian Politics under Buhari and Babangida (1983–1993)*. Abuja: Cassava Republic Press, 2013.

Sivitanides, Marcos and Vivek Shah. "The Era of Digital Activism." *Conference for Information Systems Applied Research* 4, no. 1842 (2011).

Sklar, Richard. "Democracy in Africa." *African Studies Review* 26, no. 3–4 (1983): 11–24.

Smith, Daniel Jordan. *A Culture of Corruption: Everyday Deception and Popular Discontent in Nigeria*. Princeton: Princeton University Press, 2007.

Smith, David. "Goodluck Jonathan Sworn in as Nigerian President." *The Guardian*, May 6, 2010.

Solarin, Tai. *Towards Nigeria's Moral Governance*. Ikenne: Mayflower School, 1959.

Soyinka, Wole. *The Interpreters*. London: Andre Deutsch, 1965.

Squires, Catherine. "Rethinking the Black Public Sphere: An Alternative Vocabulary for Multiple Public Spheres." *Communication Theory* 12, no. 4 (2002): 446–468.

Statista Research Department. "Social Network Users in Leading Markets 2026." *Statista,* April 28, 2022. www.statista.com/statistics/278341/number-of-social-network-users-in-selected-countries/#:~:text=China%20is%20the%20biggest%20social,million%20current%20social%20media%20users.

Stephen, Onu. "Feminism too Toxic, I Prefer Humanism—Bimbo Akintola." *Premium Times*, 18 May 2022. www.premiumtimesng.com/entertainment/nollywood/530894-feminism-too-toxic-i-prefer-humanism-bimbo-akintola.html.

Stieglitz, Stefan and Linh Dang-Xuan. "Social Media and Political Communication: A Social Media Analytics Framework." *Social Network Analysis and Mining* 3 (2012): 1277–1291.

Stier, Sebastian, Arnim Bleier, Haiko Lietz and Markus Strohmaier. "Election Campaigning on Social Media: Politicians, Audiences, and the Mediation of Political Communication on Facebook and Twitter." *Political Communication* 35, no. 1 (2018): 50–74.

Stiglitz, Joseph. "Globalization and its Discontents." New York: W.W. Norton and Co., 2002.

Suberu, Rotimi. *Federalism and Ethnic Conflict in Nigeria*. Washington, D.C.: United States Institute of Peace Press, 2001.

Sulaiman, Kamaldeen. "Religious Violence in Contemporary Nigeria: Implications and Options for Peace and Stability Order." *Journal for the Study of Religion* 29, no. 1 (2016): 85–103.

Sullivan, Rachel. "Live-Tweeting Terror: A Rhetorical Analysis of @HSMPress_Twitter Updates during the 2013 Nairobi Hostage Crisis." *Critical Studies on Terrorism* 7, no. 3 (2014): 422–433.

Sumter, S. R., L. Vandenbosch and L. Ligtenberg. "Love Me Tinder: Untangling Emerging Adults' Motivations for Using the Dating Application Tinder." *Telematics and Informatics* 34, no. 1 (2017): 67–78.

Suntai, Dauda and Tordue Simon Targema. "New Media and Democracy in Nigeria: An Appraisal of the Opportunities and Threats in the Terrain." *Brazilian Journal of African Studies* 2, no. 4 (2017): 198–209.

Swist, Teresa, Philippa Collin, Jane McCormack and Amanda Third. "Social Media and the Wellbeing of Children and Young People: A Literature Review." Prepared for the Commissioner for Children and Young People, Western Australia, 2015.

Taire, Morenike and Ebunoluwa Sessou. Feminist Coalition Directs Youths to Stay Home. *Vanguard Newspaper,* 2020.

Taiwo-Hassan, Adebayo. "Exclusive: Inside Details of how the Nigerian Presidential Guards Fell into Terrorist Ambush." *Premium Times*, August 3, 2022. www.premiumtimesng.com/news/headlines/546381-exclusive-inside-details-of-how-nigerian-presidential-guards-fell-into-terrorist-ambush.html.

Takahashi, Toshie. "MySpace or Mixi? Japanese Engagement with SNS (Social Networking Sites) in the Global Age." *New Media & Society* 12, no. 3 (2010): 453–475.

Tamuno, Tekena N. "Separatist Agitations in Nigeria since 1914." *The Journal of Modern African Studies* 8, no. 4 (1970): 563–584.

Tang, Gary and Francis L. Lee. "Facebook Use and Political Participation: The Impact of Exposure to Shared Political Information, Connections with Public Political Actors, and Network Structural Heterogeneity." *Social Science Computer Review* 31, no. 6 (2013): 763–773.

Tapsoba, Sibry, Sabiou Kassoum, P. V. Houenou, B. Oni and M. Sethi. "Brain Drain and Capacity Building in Africa." ECA, IDRC, IOM, 2000.

Tebeje, Ainalem. "Brain Drain and Capacity Building in Africa." *IDRC Reports,* February 22, 2005.

Temitope, Olanrewaju and Rahayu Ahmad. "The Role of Social Media During the 2015 Voting Process in the Nigeria Election." *Research Journal of Applied Sciences* 12, no. 2 (2017): 281–287.

The New York Times. "Mark Zuckerberg Testimony: Senators Question Facebook's Commitment to Privacy." *The New York Times,* April 10, 2018. www.nytimes.com/2018/04/10/us/politics/mark-zuckerberg-testimony.html.

The Nigerian Police. "Contact of Senior Officers." *Nigeria Police Force.* www.npf.gov.ng/info/contacts_mgt.php

The Will. "2Baba, Falz, others to Hold Free Concert in Lagos, Make PVC Compulsory Entry Ticket." *The Will*, June 10, 2022. www.thewillnigeria.com/news/2baba-falz-others-to-hold-free-concert-in-lagos-make-pvc-compulsory-entry-ticket/.

The World Bank. "Deep Structural Reforms Guided by Evidence are Urgently Needed to Lift Millions of Nigerians Out of Poverty." *The World Bank,* March 22, 2022. www.worldbank.org/en/news/press-release/2022/03/21/afw-deep-structural-reforms-guided-by-evidence-are-urgently-needed-to-lift-millions-of-nigerians-out-

of-poverty#:~:text=According%20to%20the%20report%2C%20which,below%20the%20national%20poverty%20line

Thiong'o, Ngũgĩ Wa. "The Language of African Literature." In *Colonial Discourse and Post-Colonial Theory*, edited by Patrick Williams and Laura Chrisman. London, Routledge, 2015.

Thisday. "#EndSARS: Death Toll now 73 with 205 Police Stations Burnt." *Thisday,* October 31, 2020.

Thisday. "In Damning Report, Lagos #EndSARS Panel Says 11 Killed at Lekki Toll-gate." *Thisday,* 16 November, 2021.

Thomassen, Jacques ed. *Elections and Democracy: Representation and Accountability*. Oxford: Oxford University Press, 2014.

Tiemoko, Richmond, Arit Oku-Egbas. "Monitoring Media Coverage of Sexuality: An Introduction." In *Sexuality in Media: Emerging Issues in Africa,* edited by Africa Regional Sexuality Resource Centre. Lagos: Africa Regional Sexuality Resource Centre, 2006, 6–10.

Tijani, Mayowa. "Behold the 62 Failed 2015 Election Campaign Promises of Muhammadu Buhari and APC." 2019. www.thecable.ng/promoted-behold-the-62-failed-2015-election-campaign-promises-of-muhammadu-buhari-and-apc.

Tijani, Mayowa. "Did you know Nigeria's Poverty Line is Less than a Dollar a Day?" *TheCable*, June 17, 2021. www.thecable.ng/did-you-know-nigerias-poverty-line-is-less-than-a-dollar-a-day.

Toledano, Cristina Aced. "Web 2.0: The Origin of the Word that has Changed the way we Understand Public Relations." Barcelona International Conference, July 2–3, 2013.

Tracey. "The Winners of the Penguin Prizes for African Writing." *Penguin Books Live,* September 6, 2010. www.penguin.bookslive.co.za/blog/2010/09/06/the-winners-of-the-penguin-prizes-for-african-writing/.

Transparency International. "The Impact of Land Corruption on Women: Insights from Africa." *Transparency International*, 2018. www.transparency.org/en/news/impact-of-land-corruption-on-women-insights-from-africa#.

TVC Entertainment. "Video: Actress Etinosa Strips Naked on MC Galaxy's Instagram Live." *TVC Entertainment*, March 16, 2019. www.tvcentertainment.tv/2019/03/16/video-actress-etinosa-strips-naked-on-mc-galaxys-instagram-live/.

Udoka, U.E. "Social Media and Political Effects: A Case Study of the 2015 Nigeria's Presidential Election." *International Journal of Social Science and Humanities Research* 3, no. 2 (2015): 134–141.

Ugboma, P.P. "Environmental Degradation in Oil Producing Area of Niger Delta Region, Nigeria: The Need for Sustainable Development." *International Journal of Science and Technology* 4, no. 2 (2015): 75–85.

Ugochukwu, Chiemezie Chukwuka. "Evaluation of Social Media Influence in the Fight against Corruption in Nigeria." *Nnamdi Azikiwe University Journal of Communication and Media Studies* 1, no. 1 (2020): 1–11.

Ugochukwu, Chinwe E., and Uche P. Ekwugha. "New Media and Youth's Online Civic Engagement in Nigerian Politics: Potentials and Challenges." *European Scientific Journal* 10, no. 19 (2014): 203–221.

Ugorji, Nene V. "Party Primary Elections and Democratic Development in Nigeria: PDP and APC in Focus." *African Journal of Social and Behavioral Sciences* 12, no. 1 (2022): 158–172.

Ujaligwa, Ada. "The Truth Sounds like Hate to those who Hate the Truth." *Keskus*, May 22, 2017. www.keskus.ng/2017/05/22/viewpoint/98/truth-sounds-like-hate-to-those-who-hate-the-truth-by-princess-ada-ujaligwa/.

Ujumadu, Vincent. "Awkuzu SARS: Nigeria's most Dreaded Specialized Police Unit." *Vanguard Newspaper*, October 17, 2020.

Ukachi, Ngozi, Franca Attoh. "Trafficked Women, Patriarchy and Social Media: The Case of Benin City, Nigeria." *Covenant Journal of Communication* 7, no. 1 (2020): 108–127.

Ukonu, Michael, Luke I. Anorue, Ugochukwu Ololo, and Habibat M. Olawoyin. "Climate of Conformism: Social Media Users' Opinion on Homosexuality in Nigeria." *SAGE Open* 11, no. 3 (2021): 1–12.

Ukpe, William. "#ENDSARS: A Day by Day Timeline of the Protest that has brought Nigeria to its Knees." *Nairametrics*, 2020. www.nairametrics.com/2020/10/25/end-sars-protest-a-timeline-of-all-the-major-events-from-october-3rd/.

Ukpere, Wilfred and S.O.H. Benedict. Brain Drain and African Development: Any Possible Gain from the Drain?" *African Journal of Business Management* 6, no. 7 (2011): 2421–2428.

Umoru, Henry, Joseph Erunke. "NGE asks Senate to Suspend Frivolous Petitions Bill." *Vanguard Newspaper*, December 7, 2015,

UNDP and UNIFEM. "Corruption, Accountability and Gender: Understanding the Connections." *UNDP*, 2010. www.undp.org/sites/g/files/zskgke326/files/publications/Corruption-accountability-and-gender.pdf

Unekwu, Sunny. "Feminism in Nigeria cannot be Stopped." *Kalahari Review*, November 6, 2018. www.kalaharireview.com/feminism-in-nigeria-can-not-be-stopped-1cdb3e7ca2bc.

United Nations Population Division. "Population, Total-Nigeria." *The World Bank*, 2022. www.data.worldbank.org/indicator/SP.POP.TOTL?locations=NG

Unwuchola, Anderson, Toyin Adinlewa and Kenneth Udeh. "An Appraisal of the Role of ICT as a Tool for Participatory Democracy in Nigeria." *MCC* 1, no. 1 (2017): 69–87.

Usigbe, Leon. "Present Insecurity Nigeria's Greatest Threat Since Civil War—FG." *Nigerian Tribune*, September 6, 2022.

Usman, Talatu. "Niger Delta Leaders Present 16-point Demand to Buhari, Want Oil Firms Relocated." *Premium Times*, November 1, 2016. www.premiumtimesng.com/news/headlines/214226-niger-delta-leaders-present-16-point-demand-buhari-want-oil-firms-relocated.html.

Uwalaka, Temple and Jerry Watkins. "Social Media as the Fifth Estate in Nigeria: An Analysis of the 2012 Occupy Nigeria Protest." *African Journalism Studies* 39, no. 4 (2018): 22–41.

Uzochukwu, Chinwe, U.P. Ekwugha and C. A. Ukueze. "Harnessing Social Media Tools in the Fight against Corruption in Nigeria: Challenges and Prospects." *International Journal of Social Relevance Communication* 2, no. 11 (2014): 5–14.

van Deth, Jan W. "What is Political Participation?" *The International Encyclopedia of Political Communication* 49, no. 3 (2016): 349–367.

Vanguard. "12 Killed as Subsidy Protests Turn Bloody." *Vanguard Newspaper*, January 10, 2012.

Vanguard. "Presidential Elections 1999–2011 in Figures." *Vanguard Newspaper*, April 23, 2011.

Vasudevan, Parvathi. "Democracy in Nigeria." *Economic and Political Weekly* 46, no. 20 (2011).

Verzin, J.A. "Sequelae of Female Circumcision." *Tropical Doctor* 5, no. 4 (1975): 163–169.

Villamil, Justin and Yossie Olaleye. "In Pius Adesanmi's Speech and Writing, there is Hope for a Pan-African Future." *Africa at LSE*, February 25, 2016. www.blogs.lse.ac.uk/africaatlse/2016/02/25/in-pius-adesanmis-speech-and-writing-there-is-hope-for-a-pan-african-future/.

Vissers, G., S. M. Hooghe, D. Stolle and V. Maheo. "The Impact of Mobilization Media on Off-line and Online Participation: Are Mobilization Effects Medium-specific?" *Social Science Computer Review* 30, no. 2 (2012): 152–169.

Vitak, Jessica, Paul Zube, Andrew Smock, Caleb Carr, Nicole Ellison and Cliff Lampe. "Poking" People to Participate: Facebook and Political Participation in the 2008 Election. Paper presented at the annual conference of the International Communication Association, Chicago, 2009.

Wasuna, Nicole. "Hashtag Feminism: How Women and Feminists in Africa are Leveraging on Social Media to Combat Gender-based Violence." In *Changing the Mainstream: Celebrating Women's Resilience*, edited by Mukabi Wanjiku Kabira, Kameri Patricia Mbote, Nkatha Kabira and Agnes Meroka, Nairobi: African Women Studies Centre, 2018.

Watts, Michael. "On Peasant Diffidence: Non-Revolt, Resistance, and Hidden Forms of Political Consciousness in Northern Nigeria, 1900–1945." In *Global Crises and Social Movements: Global Crises and Social Movements*, edited by Edmund Burke. Boulder: Lynne Rienner, 2019, 117–144.

Wengrow, David, Michael Dee, Sarah Foster, Alice Stevenson and Christopher Bronk Ramsey. "Cultural Convergence in the Neolithic of the Nile Valley: A Prehistoric Perspective on Egypt's Place in Africa." *Antiquity* 88, no. 339 (2014): 95–111.

Westerman, David, Patric R. Spence and Brandon Van Der Heide. "Social Media as Information Source: Recency of Updates and Credibility of Information." *Journal of Computer-mediated Communication* 19, no. 2 (2014): 171–183.

Wilson, Edward. *Consilience: The Unity of Knowledge*. New York: Vintage, 1998.

Wilson, Joseph and Nuhu Gapsiso. "Social Media and the Freedom of Expression in Nigeria: Posting the Mind of a Nation." In *Perspectives on the Information Society*, edited by Jonathan Bishop. Wales: The Crocels Press Limited, 2019, 301.

Wilson, Joseph and Rahila Jibrin. "Mitigating Hate Speech in Nigeria: The Possibilities of Artificial Intelligence." *Anàlisi* 61 (2019): 17–30.

Wolak, J., J.K. Mitchell and D. Finkelhor. "Online Victimization of Youth: 5 Years Later." National Center for Missing and Exploited Children Bulletin #07-06-025. Alexandria, VA: National Center for Missing and Exploited Children, 2006.

Women Living Under Muslim Laws. "Child, Early and Forced Marriage: A Multi-country Study." *A Submission to the UN Office of the High Commissioner for Human Rights* (OCHCR), 2013.

World Bank. "Deep Structural Reforms Guided by Evidence are Urgently Needed to Lift Millions of Nigerians out of Poverty." *Press Release: New World Bank Report*, March 22, 2022.

World Bank. *World Development Report 1998/1999: Knowledge for Development*. New York: Oxford University Press, 1999.

World Economic Forum. "Global Competitiveness Report 2014–2015." *World Economic Forum,* 2016. www.reports.weforum.org/global-competitiveness-report-2014–2015/.

Yeku, J. "Revisiting Pius Adesanmi's The Wafarer and other Poems." *James Yékú,* January 11, 2020. www.jamesyeku.com/2020/01/11/revisiting-pius-adesanmis-the-wayfarer-and-other-poems/.

Yerkes Sarah and Marwan Muasher, eds. *Decentralization in Tunisia: Empowering Towns, Engaging People*. Washington, DC: Carnegie Endowment for International Peace, 2018, 21–24.

Yesufu, Aisha. "ENDSARS is a Fight for the Next Generations of Nigerian." *British Broadcasting Corporation,* 2020. www.bbc.com/news/av/world-africa-54577611.

Yilma, Kinfe. "Digital Privacy and Virtues of Multilateral Digital Constitutionalism—Preliminary Thoughts." *International Journal of Law and Information Technology* 25, no. 2 (2017): 115–138

Young, Iris Marion. *Inclusion and Democracy*. Oxford: Oxford University Press, 2002.

Zappavigna, Michele, ed. *Discourse of Twitter and Social Media: How we use Language to Create Affiliation on the Web*. New York: Continuum, 2012.

Zaru, Adil. "Effect of Social Media on Society." *International Journal of New Technology and Research (IJNTR)* 2, no. 11 (2016): 39–44.

Zenn, Jacob. "Boko Haram and the Kidnapping of the Chibok Schoolgirls." *CTC Sentinel* 7, no. 5 (2014): 1–7.

Zote, Jacqueline. "How Long should Social Posts be? Try this Socia Media Character Counter." *Sprout Social,* August 25, 2021. www.sproutsocial.com/insights/social-media-character-counter/.

INDEX

D

E